online resource centre

www.oxfordtextbooks.co.uk/orc/waelde3e/

When you visit the **Online Resource Centre** you will find a wealth of resources and bonus material to help further your study of intellectual property law, including:

For students:
- Guidance on answering discussion points
- Updates
- Web links
- Further reading
- Bonus material

! Remember to check the **Online Resource Centre** regularly for updates on recent developments and major events in law.

See the **Guide to the Online Resource Centre** on page xviii for full details.

Contemporary Intellectual Property

Law and Policy

Third Edition

Charlotte Waelde

Graeme Laurie

Abbe Brown

Smita Kheria

Jane Cornwell

OXFORD
UNIVERSITY PRESS

OXFORD
UNIVERSITY PRESS

Great Clarendon Street, Oxford, OX2 6DP,
United Kingdom

Oxford University Press is a department of the University of Oxford.
It furthers the University's objective of excellence in research, scholarship,
and education by publishing worldwide. Oxford is a registered trade mark of
Oxford University Press in the UK and in certain other countries

First edition 2008
Second edition 2011

Impression: 1

Published in the United States of America by Oxford University Press
198 Madison Avenue, New York, NY 10016, United States of America

British Library Cataloguing in Publication Data

Data available

Library of Congress Control Number: 2013940969

ISBN 978-0-19-967182-3

Printed in Great Britain by
Ashford Colour Press Ltd, Gosport, Hampshire

Acknowledgement

We are delighted to acknowledge the invaluable contribution made by Professor Hector MacQueen to this textbook over its previous two editions.

To the wonderful old times, and to an exciting future.

Preface

Time passes quickly and we have now had the privilege of preparing the third edition of *Contemporary Intellectual Property: Law and Policy*. We are in fact a new 'we'; Professor Hector MacQueen is now a Scots Law Commissioner and has moved away from this project. We, our readers, and students from Edinburgh over the years owe him a huge debt for his teaching, leadership, and friendship. We are delighted to acknowledge his contribution to this book. Charlotte Waelde, Graeme Laurie, and Abbe Brown are very pleased to welcome Smita Kheria and Jane Cornwell of the University of Edinburgh as new co-authors. Their significant expertise in teaching, researching, and practising in intellectual property make them valuable team members and we look forward to working with them in the future.

As is ever so in this stimulating field, there have been many developments since the second edition. We are also grateful to all our colleagues and readers of the book who have provided comments over the years. In response to feedback, we have created a new chapter focusing on image, personality, and publicity related concepts, and expanded the discussion of trade secrets. The ongoing legal, social, and commercial importance of these issues can be seen from consideration by the Supreme Court of the relationship between intellectual property and technical or commercial information in section 72 of the Senior Courts Act 1981 in *Phillips v Mulcaire* [2012] UKSC 28.

At the time of writing this preface, new issues continue to arise and be resolved: the EU's unitary patent package (on which we have included some comments), plain packaging of tobacco, the Leveson Inquiry, photographs of younger members of the Royal Family taken in France and the United States, the legal and social impact of Twitter, the possibility of a UK Bill of Rights, and consultations regarding Ofcom's draft Code in respect of the Digital Economy Act, to name but a few. We look forward to exploring these and other issues with you via the Online Resource Centre in due course, and hope that you continue to find this helpful. As with the second edition, we have used updated terminology in respect of courts or institutions when speaking in general terms or of new developments. We have used the older term (eg ECJ or House of Lords) when we have been speaking of specific decisions of that body—for example, *IMS Health* or *Campbell*).

Many thanks to the Schools of Law at the Universities of Edinburgh and Aberdeen for funding the excellent research support provided by Matthew Bilsland, Stefan Bauer, Evgenia Kanellopoulou, Andrew McWhirter, Philip Glover, Phoebe Li, and Cornelia Baessler. Thank you also to the OUP team for all their guidance and support, in particular Jacqueline Senior and John Carroll.

This book had its origins in the SCRIPT Centre, in its various guises at the University of Edinburgh. The generous funding of the Centre by Shepherd and Wedderburn and the Arts and Humanities Research Council may have come to an end, but the work of SCRIPT in teaching and research in the IP and technology law fields at the University of Edinburgh proceeds apace, including its exciting involvement in the AHRC-funded CREATe project.

Elsewhere, Abbe Brown is now a Senior Lecturer at the University of Aberdeen and Charlotte Waelde is Professor of Intellectual Property Law at the University of Exeter. Abbe and Charlotte are exploring the relationship between dance, disability, copyright, and human rights along with Shawn Harmon of SCRIPT and Sarah Whatley at Coventry University.

These, and other new projects, along with working on this third edition, have caused us all to pause and reflect. We are delighted to dedicate this book to the wonderful old times, and to an exciting future.

Charlotte Waelde
Graeme Laurie
Abbe Brown
Smita Kheria
Jane Cornwell
May 2013

Contents

New to this edition   xv
Walk-through guide to the educational features of this book   xvi
Guide to the Online Resource Centre   xviii
Table of cases   xix
Table of statutes   ll
Table of statutory instruments   lvii
Table of EU legislation   lix
Table of international treaties and conventions   lxiii
List of figures   lxvi
List of diagrams   lxviii
Abbreviations   lxix

Part I Introduction   1

1 Intellectual property law: an introduction   2
Introduction   2
What is intellectual property law?   3
What is intellectual property?   5
Developing intellectual property law   16
Further reading   27

Part II Copyright   29

2 Copyright 1: history, rationale, and subject matter   30
Introduction   30
History   31
Rationale of copyright   38
Subject matter   40
Author works   56
Media works   78
Further reading   82

3 Copyright 2: first ownership, moral rights, and term   84
Introduction   84
First ownership   85
Author's moral rights   98
Duration of copyright and moral rights   111
Further reading   116

4 Copyright 3: economic rights and infringement   118
Introduction   118
International background   119

Economic rights in general   121
Economic rights and primary infringements: general principles   122
Restricted acts and primary infringement: detail   128
Authorisation of infringement   156
Secondary infringement of copyright   163
Further reading   165

5   Copyright 4: exceptions, technical protection measures, and contracts   166
Introduction   166
The public domain and copyright exceptions in general   167
International background   169
Copyright exceptions in the UK   171
Other limitations on copyright   193
Technical protection measures and rights management information systems   197
Copyright exceptions, TPMs, RMIs, and contract   202
Further reading   207

6   Rights akin to copyright: database right and performers' rights   209
Introduction   209
Sui generis database right   210
Performers' rights   220
Further reading   232

7   Contemporary issues in copyright   233
Introduction   233
Context   235
Purpose of copyright   240
Specific issues   243
Further reading   259

Part III Design protection   261

8   Registered designs   263
Introduction   263
The international background to the current law   264
Development of UK and EU law   267
Designs that can be validly protected by registration   269
Complex products   298
Spare parts   301
Registration process   304
Declarations of invalidity   308
Rights given by registration, infringement, and defences   310
Interaction with other IP rights   314
Further reading   317

9   Unregistered designs   319
Introduction   319
International context   320
Historical background to UK UDR   321
UK UDR: what is a 'design'?   323

Exclusions from protection in UK UDR   329
Original and not commonplace   337
Duration   340
Rights in UK UDR   344
Assessing UK UDR   349
Interaction with copyright   350
Community UDR   355
Further reading   359

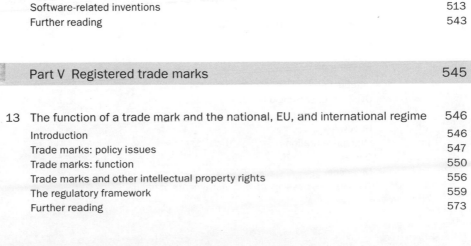

Part IV Patents   361

10 Patent regimes and the application process   363

Introduction   363
Patent regimes: past and present   364
Rationales of patent protection   368
The European dimension   371
The international dimension   376
Further reform: patent regimes in the future   386
Patent procedures   394
Further reading   403

11 Patentability and infringement   404

Introduction   404
Excluded subject matter   405
Protectable subject matter   431
Patent rights and their limits   454
Infringement proceedings   464
Revocation   477
Defences   480
Further reading   485

12 Contemporary issues in patent law   486

Introduction   486
Background   487
Biotechnological inventions   488
Software-related inventions   513
Further reading   543

Part V Registered trade marks   545

13 The function of a trade mark and the national, EU, and international regime   546

Introduction   546
Trade marks: policy issues   547
Trade marks: function   550
Trade marks and other intellectual property rights   556
The regulatory framework   559
Further reading   573

14 Definition of a trade mark and registration   575

Introduction   575
The definition of a trade mark   577
Registration: absolute grounds for refusal   588
Collective and certification trade marks   618
Relative grounds for refusal of registration   621
Use requirements   622
Further reading   629

15 Relative ground for refusing registration, infringement, and defences   630

Introduction   630
Use of a trade mark for the purposes of infringement   631
Relative grounds for refusal of registration and infringement   640
Defences to an action of infringement   673
Further reading   683

16 Contemporary issues in trade mark law   685

Introduction   685
Trade marks and domain names   685
Introduction   685
What is a domain name?   686
The registration of a domain name as a trade mark   687
Conflicts over domain names and trade marks   688
Resolution of disputes   689
*The use of trade marks on the Internet and in connection with keyword advertising
and auction sites*   697
Introduction   697
Territorial scope of protection: accessibility and disclaimers   697
Keyword advertising   702
Auction sites   706
Geographical indications   708
Introduction   708
Terminology   709
International protection   710
The EU regime   712
Further reading   723

Part VI Common law protection of intellectual property   725

17 Passing off   727

Introduction   727
Overview of passing off   728
Definitions   731
Goodwill   733
Misrepresentation   747
Damage   762
Defences   765
The Internet, passing off, and instruments of fraud   766

Unfair competition and passing off   769
Further reading   772

18 Breach of confidence   773

Introduction   773
Overview   774
Elements of action   777
Defences   790
Parties to action   792
Confidence and IP   793
Secrecy and innovation   794
IP and other information regulation   796
The impact of the HRA on breach of confidence   798
International perspectives and approaches   799
Conclusions and the future   800
Further reading   801

19 Control of information, reputation, and intellectual property   803

Scope and overview of chapter   803
How does it work in practice—some important examples   804
Personal privacy   806
Merchandising   815
Endorsement and sponsorship   823
Control of (public) image   826
Conclusions   827
Further reading   828

Part VII Intellectual property, free movement of goods, and
competition law in Europe   831

20 Free movement of goods and intellectual property rights   833

Introduction   833
Tensions between the aims of the common market and those of intellectual
property   834
Free movement of goods: case law development   837
Legitimate reasons for using a trade mark to prevent further dealing   847
International exhaustion   855
Free movement of services   864
Further reading   867

21 Intellectual property and EU competition law   868

Introduction   868
Theory of competition   869
Competition law and IP   871
Intellectual property and agreements between undertakings: Article 101 TFEU 873
Intellectual property and abuse of a dominant position: Article 102 TFEU   885
Commission v Microsoft   892
EU competition law in the UK courts: Eurodefences   897
Further reading   900

Part VIII Exploitation, enforcement, remedies, and cross-border litigation 903

22 Exploitation of intellectual property rights, enforcement, and remedies 904

    Introduction 904

    Assignment 905

    Licensing 907

    Contemporary exploitation strategies 927

    Enforcement and remedies 932

    Further reading 963

23 Intellectual property and international private law 967

    Introduction 967

    International private law 968

    Developments in the EU 974

    Contemporary developments 990

    Further reading 995

    Index 997

New to this edition

- This edition includes a new chapter, 'Control of information, reputation, and intellectual property', offering expanded coverage on such issues as commercialising reputation, personality rights, personal privacy, and publicity.
- Fully updated key case law and legislation including:
  - The Anti-Counterfeiting Trade Agreement
  - The Digital Economy Act 2010
  - *SAS Institute Inc v World Programming Ltd; FA Premier League v QC Leisure; Twentieth Century Fox v BT; Samsung v Apple; Eli Lilly v Human Genome; Diageo North America v Intercontinental Brands; Sun Microsystems v M-Tech.*

Walk-through guide to the educational features of this book

This book is full of features that are designed to help students engage with the subject matter, to acquire and refine critical and reflective skills, and to remain up-to-date with the fast-paced developments that typify intellectual property law. This guide is a step-by-step walk through these features and you should pay close attention to ensure that you get the most out of the book.

Parts

The book is divided into parts, each of which deals with a discrete area of intellectual property law. The beginning of each part contains an overview of what will be covered and an account of the key sources of law. Internet links to the actual text of these instruments are also provided.

Learning objectives

Each chapter gives an account of the learning objectives that you should be able to meet once you have worked through the chapter. For example, the first learning objective in Chapter 2 states: 'By the end of this chapter you should be able to describe and explain the development of copyright, and its rationale.' If you cannot meet the objectives, then you need to work through the chapter again!

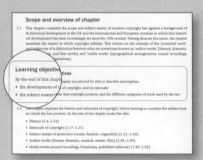

Key points

Every chapter uses key points to highlight essential features of the chapter or area of law that you need to know. These help to focus your study and serve as valuable milestones as you move through the different parts of the book.

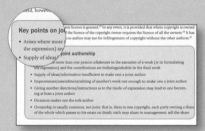

Key extracts from cases and materials

Every legal case tells a story, and we have designed the format of the book to ensure that crucial extracts and legal points are clearly communicated to the reader.

Important websites

We highlight systematically important web pages where you can check out the most up-to-date developments in your chosen area of study. Website addresses themselves will be updated on the book's Online Resource Centre www.oxfordtextbooks.co.uk/orc/waelde3e/

Questions

We ask questions throughout each chapter to help you assess your developing knowledge. These will usually be factual questions or 'reminder' questions and the answer can normally be found within the text itself.

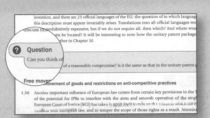

Discussion points

These points are designed to encourage you to think more widely about particular ideas and legal issues raised in a chapter. Guidance on answering discussion points will appear on the Online Resource Centre at www.oxfordtextbooks.co.uk/orc/waelde3e/

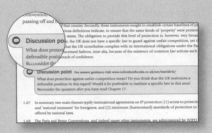

Exercises

Exercises can be used to help you with coursework and assignments that require you to undertake further research and read more widely about particular topics.

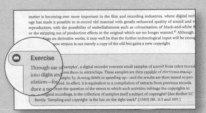

Further reading

Every chapter ends with suggestions for additional reading which are specially selected to highlight key areas of the chapter and to help you to take your learning further.

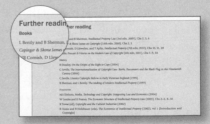

Guide to the Online Resource Centre

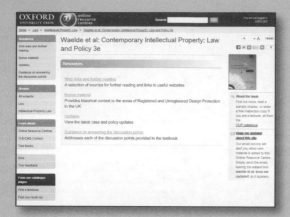

www.oxfordtextbooks.co.uk/orc/
waelde3e/

This book is accompanied by a dynamic Online Resource Centre (ORC) which is designed to enhance your learning experience and which contains the following features:

Updates

Documenting recent developments, changes in law and policy, and other information relevant to your study of intellectual property law.

Para 2.5
Add note 3a at end of fifth sentence:
3a See further Jane C Ginsburg, "'Un chose publique'?' The author's domain and the public domain in early British, French and US copyright law", (2006) 65 *Cambridge Law Journal* 636.

Paras 2.24–2.44
On the topics covered in these paragraphs (nature of a work, fixation, originality) see further Justine Pila, "An intentional view of the copyright work", (2008) 71 *Modern Law Review* 535, arguing in particular that *Walter v Lane* and *Interlego v Tyco* are wrongly decided but that *Sawkins v Hyperion* is correct. For different reasons, Nigel P Gravells, "Authorship and originality: the persistent influence of Walter v Lane" [2007] IPQ 267 also argues that *Walter v Lane* was wrongly decided and is in any event, and despite contrary judicial assertions, no longer good law.

Further reading and web links

Recently published sources for further reading will be added to the ORC, to help you in your research. New and updated web links will be provided together with links to images which can help your understanding of the law.

Articles

Authorship and ownership
J McCutcheon, 'Property in Literary Characters: Protection under Australian Copyright Law' [2007] EIPR 140.
DWK Khong, 'OrphanWorks, Abandonware and the Missing Market for Copyrighted Goods' [2007] INT.JLIT 54.

Employment and universities
T Ciro, 'Commoditising University Intellectual Property' [2007] EIPR 274.
J Hull, 'Ownership of Rights Created in Sponsored Academic Collaborations: A Note on the IDA, Statoil and Cyprotex Decisions' [2007] EIPR 6.

Phil C W Chan, "Moral rights in university students' academic works" [2007] 2 JIPLP 174.
Agustin Waisman, "Rethinking the moral right to integrity" [2008] IPQ 268

Guidance

Guidance on addressing each of the discussion points in the book will be provided in the ORC to aid your understanding of the subject-matter and help to refine your analytical skills.

Chapter 01

Para 1.38
Look at the table below. Why do each of patents, copyright and design rights ultimately expire whereas a trade mark can be protected for all time so long as it is re-registered every 10 years?

First, consider why we want IP rights to expire at all. As we say in the textbook, IP law and policy are concerned with striking a delicate balance between granting private monopoly rights and furthering certain important public interests. While the rights exist, restricted access to the subject matter of the right can be maintained. When they fall away, however, the subject matter goes into the public domain for use by any or all. Thus, on the expiry of patents valuable inventions such as pharmaceuticals can be manufactured by any company and sold at a fraction of the price. Similarly, in design law, innovative designs can be replicated and in copyright, creative works such as books, poems, films and photographs can be copied. The public interests at stake may be considerable, in the areas of health, engineering, science, architecture, fashion, and the creative industries. But what public interest is served if a trade mark becomes freely available? Or, put another way, what public interest is compromised by allowing a trade mark owner to maintain their own unique badge? Read the Part of the book that deals with trade marks and then revisit this question.

Bonus material

Two short chapters from the author team provide historical context to the areas of registered and unregistered design protection in the UK.

HISTORY OF REGISTERED DESIGN LAW IN THE UK TO 1988

8.10 Design law was invented in the UK and traces its origins back to the Calico Printers Act 1789. That Act gave two months' protection against imitation to persons producing 'any new and original pattern ... for printing linens, cottons, calicos and muslins'. At this stage, there was no need for registration, and the focus was merely on the two-dimensional and the textile industry. Fifty years later, however, inspired by a desire to improve the competitiveness of British industry in general by the adoption of better and more effective product design, the scope of the 1787 Act was extended to include patterns

Table of cases

10 Royal Berkshire Polo Club Trade Mark
[2001] RPC 32... 641
1-800 Flowers Inc v Phonenames Ltd [2000]
ETMR 369; [2000] FSR 697... 699, 977
32Red plc v WHG (International) Ltd [2012]
EWCA Civ 19; [2012] ETMR 14... 588, 590,
601, 655, 656

A Fulton Co Ltd v Grant Barnett & Co Ltd
[2001] RPC 16... 328, , 329, 330, 331, 333,
334, 338, 339, 347
A Fulton v Totes Isotoner (UK) Ltd [2004]
RPC 16... 325, 326, 339
A v B plc [2002] EWCA 337; [2003]
QB 195... 808–810, 942
A&C Black Ltd v Claude Stacey Ltd [1929] 1 Ch
177... 92
A&E Television Networks LLC v Discovery
Communications Europe Ltd [2011] EWHC
1038 (Ch)... 939
A&M Records v Napster 239 F 3d 1004
(2001)... 160
AB Volvo v Erik Veng (UK) Ltd [1988] ECR
6211... 23
Abadía Retuerta, SA v OHIM (T-237/08)
[2010] ECR II-01583... 721
ABBOTT RESPIRATORY/Dosage regime
(G02/08) [2010] EPOR 26... 443
ABC Ltd v Y [2010] EWHC 3176 (Ch); [2011]
4 All ER 113... 943
ABK v Foxwell [2002] EWHC 9, 2002 WL
499040... 784
Abraham Moon & Sons Ltd v Thornber & Ors
[2012] EWPCC 37... 43, 58
Accucard's Application (BL O/145/03)... 416
Aceites del Sur-Coosur v Koipe and OHIM
(C-498/07) [2009] ECR I-07371... 648
Actavis Group PTC EHF v Sanofi Chancery
Division [2012] EWHC 2545
(Pat)... 454
Actavis UK Ltd v Merck [2008] EWCA Civ
444... 443
Actavis UK Ltd v Novartis AG [2010] EWCA
Civ 82... 453
ACV Manufacturing NV v AIC SA [2012]
ECDR 13... 296
AD 2000 Trade Mark [1997] RPC 168... 588,
673
Adam Opel AG v Autec AG (C-48/05) [2007]
ECR I-01017... 635, 676, 677
Adept Scientific plc v BSMBionic Solutions
Management GmbH, Riemser Arzneimittel
AG [2009] EWHC 1829 (Pat)... 934

Adgistics Ltd's Application
(BLO/297/04)... 416
Adidas AG v Marca Mode CV (C-102/07)
[2008] ECR I-02439... 652
Adidas-Salomon AG and Adidas Benelux BV
v Fitnessworld (C-408/01) [2004] ETMR 10
(ECJ)... 660, 661
Adidas-Salomon AG, Adidas Italy SpA v
Gruppo Coin SpA, Oviesse [2006] ETMR
39... 660
Ad-Lib Club Ltd v Granville [1972]
RPC 673... 734
Administration des Douanes, Droits Indirects
v Rioglass SA (C-115/02) [2003] ECR
I-12705... 860
AEPI Elliniki Etaireia pros Prostasian tis
Pnevmatikis Idioktisias AE v Commission
of the European Communities (C-425/07 P)
[2009] 5 CMLR 2... 915
Aerotel Ltd v Telco Holdings Ltd & others
[2006] EWCA Civ 1371; [2007] RPC 7...
406, 407, 409, 415, 534, 538, 539
Agena Wydawnicza Technopol sp. z o.o. v
OHIM (C-54/10 P & C-55/10 P)... 601
Agencja Wydawnicza Technopol sp. z o.o. v
OHIM (C-51/10 P)... 589–592, 594, 600
Airfield NV v SABAM (C-431/09) [2012]
ECDR 3... 154
Ajit Weekly Trade Mark [2006] RPC 25... 617
Aktiebolaget Volvo v Heritage (Leicester) Ltd
[2000] FSR 253... 678
Aktiebologet Hassle v Alphapharm (2002) 212
CLR 411 (Australia)... 449
Alappat, Re 33 F 3d 1526 (Fed Cir, 1994)...
527
Alberto Severi v Regione Emilia Romagna
(C-446/07) [2009] ECR I-08041... 715
Alcon Inc v OHIM (C-192/03) [2004] ECR
I-8993; [2005] ETMR 69... 608
Alcon Inc v OHIM, Biofarma SA (C-412/05)
[2007] I-03569... 653
Alexander Fergusson & Co Ltd v Matthews
McClay & Manson Ltd 1989 SLT 795... 734
Alexander v Mackenzie (1847) 9 D 748... 140
Alfa Laval Tumba AB v Separator Spares
International Ltd [2012] EWHC 1155
(Ch)... 983
Allen & Hanburys Ltd v Generics (UK) Ltd
and Gist-Brocades NV and others and the
Comptroller-General of Patents [1986] RPC
203... 454
Allen v Bloomsbury Publishing plc [2010]
EWHC 2560 (Ch)... 134

Allen's Application (BL O/59/92)... 428

Amazon.com International Sales and Others (C-521/11)... 256

AMAZON/1-Click (T1244/07) [2011] EPOR 39... 536

Ambrosiadou v Coward [2011] EWCA Civ 409; [2011] EMLR 21... 943

American Clothing Associates SA v OHIM (C-202/08 P & C-208/08 P) [2009] ECR I-06933... 567, 617

American Cyanamid Co v Ethicon Ltd [1975] AC 396... 939, 940

AMM v HXW [2010] EWHC 2457 (QB)... 943

Amoena v Trulife, Chancery Division, unreported, 25 May 1995... 332

Amp Incorporated v Utilux Proprietary Ltd [1972] RPC 103 (HL)... 294

AMP v Persons Unknown [2011] EWHC 3454 (TCC)... 943

Anacon Corp Ltd v Environmental Research Technology Ltd [1994] FSR 659... 57, 65, 129

Anderson & Co v Lieber Code Co [1917] 2 KB 469... 58

Anheuser-Busch Inc v Budejovicky Budvar (C-96/09) [1984] FSR 413... 626, 735

Anheuser-Busch v OHIM (T-191/07) [2009] ECR II-00691... 624

Anheuser-Busch v Portugal ((App No 73049/01) (2008) 39 IIC 714... 548, 555

Annabel's (Berkeley Square) Ltd v Shock [1972] RPC 838 [1972] RPC 838... 743, 763

Ansul BV v Ajax Brandbeveiliging BV (C-40/01) [2003] ECR I-2439; [2003] RPC 40; [2005] EWCA Civ 978; [2005] ETMR 114; [2006] FSR 5; 2005 WL 1801235 (CA)... 624, 625

Anticoagulant protein/IMPERIAL (T2464/10) 25.5.2012... 504

Antiquesportfolio.com plc v Rodney Fitch & Co Ltd [2001] FSR 345... 53, 70

Anton Piller KG v Manufacturing Process Ltd [1976] Ch 55 (CA)... 936, 948

Antoni Fields v Klaus Kobec Ltd [2006] EWHC 350 (Ch)... 643

Apimed Medical Honey Ltd v Brightwake Ltd [2012] EWCA Civ 5... 444

Apis-Hristovich EOOD v Lakorda AD (C-545/07) [2009] 3 CMLR 3 (ECJ)... 217, 928

Applause Store Productions Ltd v Raphael [2008] EWHC 1781 (QB)... 808

Apple Computer Inc v Computer Edge Pty Ltd [1986] FSR 537... 60

Apple Computer Inc v Design Registry [2002] FSR 38... 270, 273

Apple Computer Inc v Microsoft Corp 709 F Supp 925, 717 F Supp 1428; 759 F Supp 1444 (1989, 1991)... 135

Application No 2323092B to register a trade mark in Class 16 by Sir Alexander Chapman Ferguson, Trade Mark Decision O/26605... 805

Apps v Weldite Products Ltd [2001] FSR 39... 792

Archive Media Publishing Ltd v MCPS (CT 116/10)... 914

Argyll v Argyll [1967] Ch 302... 778, 786

Argyllshire Weavers v Macaulay Tweeds 1965 SLT 21... 761, 762

Armin Häupl v Lidl Stiftung & Co KG (C-246/05) [2007] ECR I-04673... 624–626

Armour Pharmaceutical Co v OHIM (T-483/04) [2006] ECR II-4109... 628

Arsenal Football Club plc v Matthew Reed (C-206/01) [2001] 2 CMLR 23; [2003] Ch 454; [2003] 3 All ER (EC) 1; [2003] 3 WLR 450; [2003] RPC 144... 551, 632, 633, 747, 759, 770, 822

Arsenal Football Club plc v Reed (No 2) [2003] EWCA Civ 696; [2003] 3 All ER 865; [2003] 2 CMLR 25; [2003] ETMR 73; [2003] RPC 39... 634

Artisjus v European Commission (C-32/09) [2010] 5 CMLR 20... 917

AS Watson (Health and Beauty Continental Europe) BV and others v The Boots Company plc and others [2011] EWPCC 26... 983

Asahi Kasei Kogyo KK's Application [1991] RPC 485... 436, 493

ASG v GSA [2009] EWCA Civ 1574... 943

Ashdown v Telegraph Newspapers [2001] 4 All ER 666... 27, 182, 185, 186, 194, 196, 942

Ashizawa's Application (BL O/201/03)... 416

Ashmore v Douglas Home [1987] FSR 553... 61

Ashworth Hospital Authority v MGN Ltd [2002] UKHL 29 [2002] 1 WLR 2033 (HL)... 799

Asprey & Garrard Ltd v WRA (Guns) Ltd (t/a William R Asprey Esquire) [2002] FSR 31; [2001] EWCA Civ 1499... 675, 749

Associated Newspapers plc v Insert Media Ltd [1991] FSR 380... 748, 763

AstraZeneca AB v European Commission (T-321/05) [2010] ECR II-2805... 896

Astron Clinica Ltd and others v The Comptroller General of Patents [2008] EWHC 85 (Pat)... 408, 409, 417, 539

AT & T Knowledge Ventures' Application and another [2009] FSR 19... 417

AT Poeton (Gloucester Plating) Ltd v Horton [2001] FSR 14... 785

AT&T Corp v Excel Communications Inc 172 F 3d 1352 (Fed Cir, 1999)... 527

AT&T Knowledge Ventures LP's Patent
Application [2009] FSR 19... 540
Ate My Heart Inc v Mind Candy Ltd [2011]
EWHC 2741 (Ch)... 549, 550, 941
Athletes Foot Marketing Associates Inc v
Cobra Sports Ltd [1980] RPC 343... 740
ATT/System for generating software source
code (T204/93)... 533
Attheraces v British Horseracing Board [2005]
EWHC 1553 (Ch)... 895, 929
Attorney General v Guardian Newspapers
(No 2) [1990] 1 AC 109 Spycatcher... 8, 97,
779, 781–783, 787 806
Attorney General v Jonathan Cape Ltd [1976]
QB 752; [1975] 3 WLR 606... 783
Attorney General's Reference (No 3 of 1999),
Re [2009] UKHL 34; [2009] 3 WLR 142;
[2009] EMLR 23; [2009] HRLR 28... 812
Attorney-General v Blake [2001] 1 AC 268;
[2000] 3 WLR 625... 780
Attorney-General v Times Newspapers Ltd
[2001] 1 WLR 885... 943
Auchincloss v Agricultural & Veterinary
Supplies Ltd 1997] RPC 649; [1999]
RPC 397... 474, 481
Audi AG v OHIM (C-398/08 P) [2010] ETMR
18... 595, 599, 607
Audi AG v OHIM (T-318/09) [2011]
ECR II-03841... 605, 606
AUDI-Med Trade Mark [1998] RPC 863; [1999]
ETMR 1010... 669
August Storck KG v OHIM (C-25/05) [2006]
ECR I-05719... 595
Austin v Columbia Gramophone Co Ltd
[1917–23] MCC 398... 133
Australia Cth v Jonathan Fairfax & Sons Ltd
(180) 147 CLR 39... 781
Australian Broadcasting Corporation v Lenah
(2001) 208 CLR 199... 809
AUSTRALIAN NATIONAL UNIVERSITY/
Detection of glaucoma (T1197/02) [2007]
EPOR 9... 430
Author of a Blog v Times Newspapers Ltd
[2009] EWHC 1358 (QB); [2009] EMLR
22... 809
Autodesk Inc v Dyason and Kelly (1990) 96
ALR 57; [1992] RPC 575
(HCA)... 60, 127
Autonomy Corp Ltd v Comptroller General of
Patents, Trade Marks and Designs [2008]
EWHC 146 (Pat)... 418
Availability to the Public (G1/92) [1993]
EPOR 241... 432
Aventis v Apotex [2005] FC 1504
(Canada)... 449
Avnet Inc v Isoact Ltd [1998]
FSR 16... 643, 690

B & I Line plc v Sealink Harbours Ltd and
Sealink Stena Ltd [1992] 5 CMLR 255...
895
Baby Dan AS v Brevi Srl and Another [1999]
FSR 377 (HC)... 327, 334
Bagge v Miller [1917–23] MCC 179... 86
Baigent v Random House Group Ltd [2006]
EMLR 16; aff'd [2007] FSR 24 (CA)... 134
Bailey v Graham [2011] EWHC 2098 (Ch)...
794
Baker v Selden 101 US 99 (1879)... 41
Balmoral Trade Mark [1999] RPC 297... 645
Balston v Headline Filters Ltd (No 2) [1990]
FSR 385 (CA)... 785
Bamgboye v Reed [2002] EWHC 2922
(QB)... 222
Bang and Olufsen v OHIM (T-508/08) [2012]
ETMR 10... 613
Banghalter et Homem Christo v Sacem
(Case COMP/C2/37.219), Decision of
06.08.2002... 915
Barbara Becker v OHIM (C-51/09) [2010]
ETMR 53... 649, 818
Barclays Bank plc v RBS Advanta [1996] RPC
307... 682
Barlow Clowes Gilt Managers, Re [1992]
Ch 208; [1992] 2 WLR 36... 789
Barrymore v News Group Newspapers Ltd
[1997] FSR 600... 778
BASF v EP [1996] ETMR 51... 661
Basic Trademark SA's Trade Mark Application
[2005] RPC 25... 614
Bass v Laidlaw (1886) 13R 898... 756
Basset v Sacem (C-402/85) [1987]
ECR 1747... 864
Baumann v Fussell [1978] RPC 485
(CA)... 53, 129, 133
Bavaria NV, Bavaria Italia Srl v Bayerischer
Brauerbund eV (C-343/07) [2009] ECR
I-05491... 713, 721
Bayer AG (Meyer's) Application [1984] RPC
11... 442
Bayer Cropscience KK v Charles River
Laboratories Preclinical Services Edinburgh
Ltd [2010] CSOH 158... 947
BAYER SCHERING PHARMA AG/
Composition for contraception [2012]
EPOR 23... 426, 427
Bayer v Baird (1898) 25R 1142; (1898) 6 SLT
98... 756
BAYER/Disclaimer (T4/80) [1982] OJEPO
149... 400
BAYER/Plant growth regulating agent (G6/88)
[1990] OJEPO 114... 441
Bayerische Motoren Werke Aktiengesellschaft
v Round and Metal Ltd [2012]
ECC 28... 302, 303, 304

Bayerische Motorenwerke AG v Deenik
(C-63/97) [1999] All ER (EC) 235; [1999]
1 CMLR 1099 . . . 674, 678

Baywatch Production Co Inc v Home Video
Channel [1997] FSR 22 . . . 661

BBC Enterprises Ltd v Hi-Tech Xtravision Ltd
[1990] FSR 217 (CA) . . . 201

BBC v BSB Ltd [1992] Ch 141 . . . 175, 186

BBC v Celebrity Centre (1988) 15 IPR 333 . . .
742

BBC v HarperCollins Publishers Ltd [2010]
EWHC 2424 (Ch); [2011] EMLR 6 . . . 779,
943

BBC v Talbot [1981] FSR 228 . . . 734

BBC Worldwide v Pally Screen Printing [1998]
FSR 665 . . . 822

BBC/Colour Television Signal (T163/85)
[1990] OJEPO 379 . . . 420, 524

Beautimatic International Ltd v Mitchell
International Pharmaceuticals Ltd [1999]
ETMR 912; [2000] FSR 267 . . . 558

Beckingham v Hodgens [2002] EMLR 45;
[2003] EMLR 18 . . . 86, 88

Beecham Group's (Amoxycillin) Application
[1980] RPC 261 . . . 440

Beechwood House Publishing Ltd v Guardian
Products Ltd [2011] EWHC 22 . . . 217

Beifa Group Co Ltd v OHIM and Schwan-
Stabilo Schwanhaüßer GmbH & Co KG
(T-148/08) [2010] ETMR 42 . . . 310

Belgian Electronic Sorting Technology
(C-657/11) . . . 682

Beloff v Pressdram [1973] RPC 765 . . . 183,
184, 194, 790

Benetton Group SpA v G-Star International BV
[2008] ETMR 5 . . . 612

Bents Brewery v Hogan [1945] 2 A11 ER 570 . . .
784

BergSpechte Outdoor Reisen under
Alpinschule Edi Kobmuller GmbH v Guni
(C-278/08) [2010] RPC 19 . . . 664

Berry Birch & Noble Financial Planning Ltd
v Berwick and others 2005 WL 1991635 . . .
941

Best Buy Co Inc v Worldwide Sales
Corp Espana SL [2011] EWCA Civ 618;
[2011] Bus LR 1166; [2011] FSR 30 . . .
933

Betty's Kitchen Coronation Street Trade Mark
[2000] RPC 825 . . . 652

Bezpečnostní softwarová asociace v
Ministerstvo kultury (C-393/09) [2011]
ECDR 3 (ECJ) . . . 44, 50, 51, 60

BIBA Group v Biba Boutique [1980] RPC
143 . . . 749

Bild.T-Online.de AG & Co KG v President of
the German Patent-und Markenamt
(C-39/08) [2009] ECR I-00020 . . . 561

Bile Bean Manufacturing Co v Davidson
(1906) 8F 1181; Kinnell v Ballantine 1910
SC 246 . . . 741

Bilski v Kappos 130 S Ct 3218 (2010) . . . 528

Bilski, Re 545 F 3d 943, 88 USPQ 2d 1385
(Fed Cir, 2008) . . . 527

BIOGEN INC/Hepatitis B virus (T886/91)
[1999] EPOR 361 . . . 496

Biogen v Medeva [1997] RPC 1 . . . 371, 406,
446, 477–479, 494, 495

BioID AG v OHIM (T-91/01) (C-37/03) [2002]
ECR II-5159; [2003] ETMR 60 . . . 591, 599

Birmingham Vinegar Brewery Co v Powell
[1897] AC 710 . . . 733

Bismag Ltd v Amblins (Chemists) Ltd [1940]
Ch 667 . . . 632

Björnekulla Fruktindustrier AB v Procordia
Food AB (C-371/02) [2004] ECR I-5791;
[2005] 3 CMLR 16; [2004] ETMR 69; [2004]
RPC 45 . . . 627

Black v Murray (1870) 9 M 341 . . . 51, 54, 58

Blake v Warren [1928–35] MCC 268 . . . 74

Bloomberg LLP and Cappellini's Applications
[2007] EWHC 476 (Pat) . . . 540

Boegli-Gravures SA v Darsail-ASP Ltd [2009]
EWHC 2690 (Pat) . . . 435

Boehringer Ingelheim KG v Swingward Ltd
[2004] 3 CMLR 3 . . . 758, 848, 850, 851, 853

Boehringer Ingelheim Ltd v VetPlus Ltd [2007]
EWCA Civ 583 . . . 941

Boehringer Ingelheim Pharma GmbH & Co
KG v Munro Wholesale Medical Supplies
Ltd 2004 SC 468; [2004] ETMR 66 . . . 853,
941

Bogrich & Shape Machines Ltd's Application,
unreported, 4 November 1994 . . . 461

Bollinger v Costa Brava Wine Co Ltd [1961] 1
WLR 277 . . . 737, 761

Bonz Group v Cooke [1994] 3 NZLR 216 . . . 76

BOSCH/Electronic computer components
(T164/92) [1995] EPOR 585 . . . 522

Bosphorus Airways v Ireland (2005) 6 EHRLR
649 . . . 27

Boston Scientific BV and others v Cordis
Corporation [2000] ENPR 87 Hof (Den
Haag) . . . 980

Bovemij Verzekeringen NV v Benelux-
Merkenbureau (C-108/05) [2007] ETMR
29 . . . 604, 606

Boys v Chaplin [1969] 2 All ER 1085; [1971]
AC 356; [1969] 3 WLR 322 (HL) . . . 971, 973

Bradford & Bingley plc v Holden [2002]
EWHC 2445; [2002] WL 31962007 . . . 784,
791

Bravado Merchandising Services Ltd v
Mainstream Publishing (Edinburgh) Ltd
[1996] FSR 205 (OH) . . . 632, 642

Brestian v Try [1958] RPC 161 (CA) . . . 736

Breville Europe v Thorn EMI [1995] FSR 77... 72

Bridgeman Art Library Ltd v Corel Corp 25 F Supp 421 (1999)... 53

Brighton v Jones [2005] FSR 288... 87

Brigid Foley Ltd v Ellott [1982] RPC 433... 58, 129

Bristol Conservatories v Conservatories Custom Built [1989] RPC 455... 757

Bristol-Myers Co's Application [1969] RPC 146... 432

Bristol-Myers Squibb v Baker Norton Pharmaceuticals [2001] RPC 1... 425, 443

Bristol-Myers Squibb v Paranova (C-427/93, C-429/93 & C-436/93) [1996] ECR I-3457... 849–851

British Airways plc v Ryanair Ltd [2001] ETMR 24; [2001] FSR 32 ... 682

British Broadcasting Co v Wireless League Gazette Publishing Co [1926] Ch 433... 147

British Broadcasting Corporation v Hainey [2012] SLT 476... 191, 196

British Diabetic Association v Diabetic Society Ltd [1995] 4 All ER 812... 732

British Horseracing Board Enterprises plc v Victor Chandler (International) Ltd [2005] EWHC 1074 (Ch)... 929

British Horseracing Board v William Hill Organization Ltd (C-203/02) [2001] RPC 31; [2002] ECDR 4; [2005] RPC 13 (ECJ); [2005] RPC 35 (CA) ... 211, 212, 214, 215, 217, 219, 927–929

British Legion v British Legion Club (Street) Ltd (1931) 48 RPC 555... 740, 759

British Leyland v Armstrong Patents [1986] RPC 279; [1986] AC 577... 69, 74, 195, 322

British Medical Association v Marsh (1931) 48 RPC 565... 743, 760

British Northrop Ltd v Texteam Blackburn Ltd [1974] RPC 57... 144

British Ore Concentration Syndicate Ltd v Mineral Separation Ltd (1909) 26 RPC 124... 434

British Oxygen Co v Liquid Air Ltd [1925] Ch 383... 183

British Sky Broadcasting Group plc v Digital Satellite Warranty Cover Ltd (In Liquidation) [2012] FSR 14 (Ch D)... 211, 793

British Sky Broadcasting Group plc v Sky Home Services Ltd [2007] FSR 14... 748

British South Africa Co v Companhia de Moçambique [1893] AC 602... 970, 971, 973

British Steel plc's Patent [1992] RPC 117... 462

British Sugar v James Robertson & Sons Ltd [1997] ETMR 118... 632, 644, 650

BRITISH TECHNOLOGY / Contraceptive method (T74/93) [1995] OJEPO 712... 426

British Telecommunications v One in a Million [1999] 4 All ER 476; [1999] RPC 1... 661, 690, 692, 766–768

Brown v Mcasso Music [2005] FSR 40... 87, 149

Browne v Associated Newspapers Ltd [2007] EWHC 202 (QB)... 942, 943

BRT v SABAM (C-127/73) [1974] ECR 313... 915

Bruhn Newtech Ltd v Datanetex Ltd and Another [2012] EWPCC 17... 344-345

BRUKER/Non-invasive measurement (T385/86) [1988] EPOR 357... 430

Brüstle v Greenpeace... 509

BSH Bosch und Siemens Hausgerate GmbH v OHIM (T-310/08) (Executive Edition) [2011] ECR II-00007... 600

Buchanan v Alba Diagnostics Ltd [2004] RPC 34... 454

Budejovicky Budvar Narodni Podnik v Rudolf Ammersin GmbH (C-216/01) [2005] 1 CMLR 56; [2003] ECR I-13617; [2004] ETMR 21... 711

Budejovický Budvar, národní podnik v Rudolf Ammersin GmbH (C-478/07) [2009] ECR I-07721... 711

Budweiser Trade Marks [2000] RPC 906... 557

Built NY Inc v I-Feng Kao, OHIM Invalidity Division (ICD 0000002053) 8 May 2006... 274, 275

Bullivant, Basic Solutions Ltd v Sands [2008] EWHC 1388 (QB)... 785

Bulmer (HP) Ltd v Bollinger (J) SA [1978] RPC 79... 761, 765

Bunn v BBC [1998] 3 All ER 552; [1999] FSR 70... 789

Burberry v Cording (1909) 26 RPC 693... 743

Bureau national interprofessionnel du Cognac v Gust. Ranin Oy (C-4/10 & C-27/10) [2011] ECR I-06131... 712

Burge v Swarbrick [2007] FSR 27 ... 75, 76

Burke v Spicers Dress Design [1936] Ch 400... 75, 76

Burroughs Corporation (Perkins') Application [1974] RPC 147; [1973] FSR 439 ... 519

Burrows v Smith [2010] EWHC 22 (Ch)... 787

Byrne v Statist Co [1914] 1 KB 622... 96

C & H Engineering Ltd v F Klucznik & Sons Ltd [1992] FSR 421... 337, 347

CA Sheimer (M) Sdn Bhd's Trade Mark Application [2000] RPC 484; [2000] ETMR 1170... 666

Cabinet Office v Information Commissioner (EA/2010/0031), September 2010... 797

Cable & Wireless plc v British Telecommunications plc [1998] FSR 383... 682

Cadbury Ltd v Ulmer GmbH [1988] FSR 385... 745

Cadbury Schweppes plc v Societe des Produits Nestle SA, unreported, 14 November 2011... 606

Cadbury Schweppes Pty Ltd v Pub Squash Co Pty Ltd ... 746, 747

Cadell Davies v Stewart (1804) Mor App Literary Property No 4 June 1, 1804 FC... 778

Cala Homes (South) v Alfred McAlpine Homes East [1995] FSR 818... 86

Calvin Klein Trademark Trust v OHIM (C-254/09) [2010] ECR I-07989... 649

Campbell v Frisbee [2002] EWHC 328 (Ch); EWCA (Civ) 1375; [2002] EMLR 31... 783

Campbell v MGN Ltd [2004] 2 AC 457; [2004] UKHL 22... 774, 805, 808, 809, 811, 812, 814, 942

Campbell, Re C's Application for Judicial Review [2009] UKHL 15; [2009] 1 AC 908... 796

Campina Melkunie BV v Benelux-Merkenbureau (C-265/00) [2004] ECR I-1699; [2005] 2 CMLR 9... 598, 599

Campomar Sociedad Limitada v Nike International Ltd (2000) 46 IPR 481 (HCA)... 823

Canon Kabushiki Kaisha v Green Cartridge Co (Hong Kong) Ltd [1997] AC 728... 195, 322

Canon Kabushiki Kaisha v Metro Goldwyn Mayer Inc (C-39/97) [1998] All ER (EC) 934; [1999] 1 CMLR 77... 650, 656

CANON/Searching image data (T643/00) [2007] EPOR 1... 524

Cantor Fitzgerald v Tradition UK [2000] RPC 95... 60, 136, 516, 794

Carflow Products (UK) Ltd v Linwood Securities (Birmingham) Ltd [1996] FSR 424... 782, 793, 794

Carlsberg v Tennant Caledonian Breweries Ltd [1972] RPC 847... 742, 747

Carrick Jewellery Ltd v Ortak 1989 GWD 35–1624... 745

Cate v Devon and Exeter Constitutional Newspaper Co (1889) 40 Ch D 500... 123

Caterpillar Logistics Services v Huesca de Crean [2012] EWCA Civ 156... 789

Catnic Components Ltd v Hill and Smith Ltd [1982] RPC 183 (HL)... 470, 474, 476

CB Richard Ellis Inc v Groupement Carte Bleue [2002] RPC 31... 699

CBS Songs Ltd v Amstrad Consumer Electronics plc [1988] 1 AC 1013... 157, 159

CBS v Ames Records and Tapes [1982] Ch 91... 156, 158, 159

CC v AB [2006] EWHC 3083 (QB), 2006 WL 3485386; [2007] EMLR 11... 810

CCH Canadian Ltd v Law Society of Upper Canada [2002] 4 FC 213 (CA)... 41

CDW Graphic Design Ltd's Trade Mark Application [2003] RPC 30... 614

Celaya Emparanza y Galdos Internacional SA v Proyectos Integrales de Balizamientos SL (C-488/10) [2012] ECDR 17... 311

Cellular Clothing Co v Maxton & Murray (1899) 1 F (HL) 29... 741

Centrafarm v American Home Products [1979] FSR 189... 551

Centrafarm v Sterling & Winthrop (C-15/74) (1974) ECR 1147... 839, 845

Cephalon Inc v Orchid Europe Ltd [2010] EWHC 2945 (Pat)... 941

CFPH LLC Applications [2006] RPC 5... 538

Chaplin v Frewin [1966] Ch 71... 908

Chartered Institute of Patent Attorneys v Registrar of Trade Marks (C-307/10)... 555, 587, 643

Chelsea Man Menswear Ltd v Chelsea Girl Ltd [1987] RPC 189... 736, 763

Chill Foods (Scotland) Ltd v Cool Foods Ltd 1977 SLT 38... 751

ChipsAway International Ltd v Errol Kerr [2008] EWHC 1887 (Ch)... 925

Chiron Corp v Murex Diagnostics Ltd and others [1996] RPC 535... 453, 499

Chocoladefabriken Lindt & Sprüngli AG v Franz Hauswirth GmbH (C-529/07) [2009] ECR I-04893... 618

Chocoladefabriken Lindt & Sprüngli AG v OHIM (C-98/11 P)... 596

Chocosuisse Union des Fabricants Suisses de Chocolat v Cadbury [1999] RPC 826... 732, 738, 742, 750, 752, 754, 762

Christie v Smith's Executrix 1949 SC 572... 74

Chronopost v DHL (C-235/09) [2011] ECR I-02801... 563, 983, 984

Church of Scientology v Kaufman [1973] RPC 627; [1972] FSR 591... 791

Churchill Retired Living Ltd v Luard [2012] EWHC 1479 (Ch)... 784

CICRA v Renault [1988] ECR 6039... 888

Cinpres Gas Injection Ltd v Melea Ltd [2008] RPC 17... 460

Circ & Variete Globus Bucureşti v Uniunea Compozitorilor şi Muzicologilor din România—Asociaţia pentru Drepturi de Autor—UCMR—ADA (C-283/10) (24 November 2011)... 147, 153

CISAC Agreement, Re (COMP/C2/38.698) [2009] 4 CMLR 12 ... 879, 917

Claeryn v Klarein (1976) 7 IIC 420 ... 665

Clark v Adie (1877) 2 App Cas 315 ... 470

Clark v Associated Newspapers Ltd [1998] 1 All ER 959 ... 110, 751, 765, 821

Clarke v Bain [2008] EWHC 2636 (QB); 2008 WL 4963094 ... 976

Class International BV v Colgate-Palmolive Co and others (C-405/03) [2005] ECR I-8735 ... 860

CMI Centers for Medical Innovation v Phytopharm plc 1998 WL 1070631; [1999] FSR 235 ... 794

Coca Cola v Barr [1961] RPC 387 ... 745

Coca-Cola Co v OHIM (T-175/06) [2008] ECR II-01055 ... 651

Coca-Cola v Struthers 1968 SLT 353 ... 752

Coco v AN Clark Engineers Ltd [1968] FSR 415; [1969] RPC 41 (Ch D) ... 8, 776, 777, 778, 782, 787–790

Coditel v Cine Vog (No 1) (C-62/79) [1980] ECR 881 ... 864

Coflexip v Stolt Comex Seaway [1999] FSR 473 ... 944

Coin Controls v Suzo International [1997] 3 All ER 45 ... 984

COLLABORATIVE / Preprorennin [1990] EPOR 361 ... 478

Collaborative Research's Patent (BL O/86/94) ... 496

Collag Corp v Merck [2003] FSR 16 ... 793, 794

Commission v Council (C-176/03) [2005] ECR I-07879 ... 957

Commission v Italy (C-456/03) [2005] ECR I-5335 ... 425

Commissioner of Police of the Metropolis v Times Newspaper [2011] EWHC 2705 (QB) ... 776, 782, 799, 810

Common Services Agency v Scottish Information Commissioner [2008] UKHL 47 ... 797

Commonwealth Scientific & Industrial Research Organization's Application (BL O/248/04) ... 428

COMP/C2/38.698 [2009] 4 CMLR 12 ... 917

Companhia Muller de Bebidas v OHIM (T-472/08) [2010] ECR II-03907 ... 651

Compass-Datenbank GmbH v Republik Österreich (C-138/11) ... 931

COMPTEL/Classification method (T1784/06) [2013] EPOR 9 ... 536

Computer Associates v Altai 982 F 2d 693 (1992) ... 136

COMVIK/Two identities (T641/00) [2004] EPOR 10 ... 518

ConAgra v McCain Foods (Australia) (1992) 23 IPR 193 (Fed Ct Aus) ... 735

Conan Doyle v London Mystery Magazine Ltd (1949) 66 RPC 312 ... 822

Concrete Ltd's Application, Re (1940) 57 RPC 121 ... 271

Confetti Records v Warner Music UK Ltd [2003] EMLR 35 ... 103, 104

Conor Medsystems Inc v Angiotech Pharmaceuticals Inc and another [2007] EWCA Civ 5; [2008] RPC 28 ... 445, 449, 451, 493

Consorzio del Prosciutto di Parma v Marks & Spencer plc [1991] RPC 351 ... 732, 739

Consorzio del Prosciutto di Parma, Salumificio S Rita SpA v Asda Stores Ltd (C-108/01) [2003] 2 CMLR 21; [2003] ECR I-5121; [2004] ETMR 23 ... 708, 713, 716, 717, 718

Consorzio per la Tutela del Formaggio Gorgonzola v Käserei Champignon Hofmeister GmbH & Co KG, Eduard Bracharz GmbH (C-87/97) [1999] 1 CMLR 1203; [1999] ETMR 454 (ECJ) ... 616, 720

Consten & Grundig v EEC Commission (C-56/64) [1966] ECR 299 ... 876

Contostavlos v Mendahum [2012] EWHC 850 (QB) ... 943

Controller HMSO and Ordnance Survey v Green Amps [2007] EWHC 2755 (Ch) ... 178

Convatec Ltd v Smith & Nephew Healthcare Ltd [2011] EWHC 2039 (Pat); [2012] RPC 9 ... 469

Coogi Australia v Hysport International (1999) 157 ALR 247 ... 75

Cooper's Application 19 RPC 53 ... 419

Copad SA v Christian Dior Couture SA (C-59/08) [2009] ECR I-34210 ... 846, 855, 859

Copland v United Kingdom (App No 62617/00) (2007) 45 EHRR 37 ... 806

Copyright Licensing v University of Auckland (2002) 53 IPR 618 (NZ) ... 176

Corelli v Gray (1913) 29 TLR 570 ... 130

Corevalve Inc v Edwards Lifesciences [2009] FSR 8 ... 482

Cornelius v De Taranto (2001) 68 BMLR 62 ... 788

Corporacion Habanos SA v Mastercigars Direct Ltd [2007] EWCA Civ 176; [2007] ETMR 44 ... 857, 858

Coty Prestige Lancaster Group GmbH v Simex Trading AG (C-127/09) [2010] ETMR 41 ... 859

County Sound plc v Ocean Sound plc [1991] FSR 367 ... 747

Couture Tech Ltd v OHIM (T-232/10) [2012] ETMR 5... 615

Cowan v Millar (1895) 22R 833... 734

CPC/Flavour Concentrates (T303/86) [1989] 2 EPOR 95... 438

Cramp v Smythson [1944] AC 329... 48

Cranleigh Precision Engineering Ltd v Bryant [1965] 1 WLR 1293... 778

Crawford v Jones [2005] EWHC 2417 (Pat)... 415, 419

Cream Holdings Ltd v Banerjee [2004] UKHL 44; [2004] 3 WLR 918... 941

Creation Records Ltd v News Group Newspapers Ltd [1997] EMLR 444... 66, 74, 77, 780

Creative Technology Ltd v OHIM—José Vila Ortiz (C-314/05 P) [2006] ECR I-00086... 649

Criminal proceedings against Titus Alexander Jochen Donner (C-5/11) 21 June 2012... 144, 843, 988

Crocs Inc v Holey Soles Holdings Ltd with Partenaire Hospitalier International (OHIM Third Board of Appeal (R 9/2008-3) [2010] ECDR 11... 291

Crossley v Newsquest (Midlands South) Ltd [2008] EWHC 3054 (QB)... 780

Crosstown Music Co 1 LLC v Rive Droite Music Ltd [2010] EWCA Civ 1222... 908

Crowson Fabrics Ltd v Rider [2007] EWHC 2942 (Ch); [2008] FSR 17... 784

Crucial Music Corp (formerly Onemusic Corp) v Klondyke Management AG (formerly Point Classics AG) [2008] Bus LR 327... 979

CSC Media Group Ltd v Video Performance Ltd (CT 4/05) [2010] EWHC 2094 (Ch)... 914

Cuisenaire v Reed [1963] VR 719... 75, 129

Cuisenaire v South West Imports [1968] 1 Ex CR 493... 75

Cummins v Bond [1927] 1 Ch 167... 90

Cureton v Mark Insulations Ltd [2006] EWHC 2279 (QB)... 214

Curry v Audax [2006] ECDR 22... 921

Cybergun v OHIM (T-503/09) (AK47)... 601

CYGNUS/Device and method for sampling substances (T964/99) [2002] OJEPO 4... 430

CYGNUS/Diagnostic methods (G01/04) [2006] EPOR 15... 430, 506

Cyprotex Discovery Ltd v University of Sheffield [2004] RPC 4... 88

D & C Thompson v Kent Messenger [1975] RPC 191... 743

D Jacobson & Sons Ltd v Globe GB Ltd and another [2008] EWHC 88 (Ch)... 751

Daimler Chrysler AG v Alavi (t/a Merc) [2001] ETMR 98; [2001] RPC 42... 628, 667, 669

Danske Dagblades Forening v Newsbooster [2003] ECDR 5... 62

Dash Ltd v Philip King Tailoring Ltd 1988 GWD 7–304... 763

Davidoff & Cie SA v Gofkid (C-292/00) [2003] ECR I-389... 658–660

Day v Brownrigg (1878) 10 Ch D 294... 732

Dealertrack v Huber, No 2009-1566, -1588 (Fed Cir, 20 January 2012)... 528

Decon Laboratories Ltd v Fred Baker Scientific Ltd [2001] ETMR 46; [2001] RPC 17... 628

Dee Corporation's Application, Re [1990] RPC 159... 585

De Landtsheer Emmanuel SA v Comité Interprofessionnel du Vin de Champagne (C-381/05) [2007] I-03115... 680

Def Lepp Music v Stuart-Brown [1986] RPC 273... 971

De Garis v Neville Jeffress Pidler (1990) 18 IPR 292 (Fed Ct Aus)... 176

Delfe v Delamotte (1857) 3 K & J 581... 947

Dell Products LP's Application (BL 0/321/10)... 418

Deloitte & Touche LLP v Dickson [2005] EWHC 721 (Ch)... 799

Delves-Broughton v House of Harlot Ltd [2012] EWPCC 29... 105

De Maudsley v Palumbo [1996] FSR 447; [1996] EMLR 460... 13, 794

Derek Hughes v Neil Paxman [2006] EWCA Civ 818... 458

Designers Guild Ltd v Russell Williams (Textiles) Ltd [2001] FSR 11... 43, 124, 130, 346

Deutsche Grammophon GmbH v Metro SB Grossmarkte GmbH & Co (C-78/70) [1971] ECR 487; [1971] CMLR 631... 838, 886

Deutsche SiSi-Werke v OHIM (C-173/04 P) [2006] ECR I-551... 591, 596

Develey Holding GmbH & Co Beteiligungs KG v OHIM (C-238/06 P) [2008] ETMR 20... 566, 607

DFT v TFD [2010] EWHC 2335 (QB)... 943

DHL v Chronopost (C-235/09) [2011] ECR I-02801... 563, 983, 984

Diageo Noth America Inc v Intercontinemtal Brands (UCB) Ltd [2010] RPC 12; [2011] RPC 2... 738, 751, 762

Diagnostiko kai Therapeftiko Kentro Athinon 'Ygeia' AE v OHIM (T-7/10) [2011] ECR II-00136... 605

Diamond v Chakrabarty 447 US 303, 100 S Ct 2204 (1980)... 409, 500

Diana, Princess of Wales Trade Mark [2001] ETMR 25... 817

Dicks v Yates (1881) 18 Ch D 76... 58

Differentiated progenitor cells/ADVANCED
    CELL TECHNOLOGY (T0811/11)
    11.7.2011... 504
Directmedia Publishing GMBH v Albert-
    Ludwigs-Universitat Freiburg (C-304/07)
    [2008] ECR I-7565 (ECJ)... 216, 928
DKV v OHIM (C-104/00) [2002] ECR I-7561...
    593
DNI Holdings Ltd for the mark Sportsbetting.
    com. (R 338/2006-2)... 688
Donaldson v Beckett (1774) 2 Bro PC 129...
    32, 33
Doncaster Pharmaceuticals Group Ltd v The
    Bolton Pharmaceutical Co Ltd [2006]
    EWCA Civ 661; [2007] FSR 3... 898
Donoghue v Allied Newspapers [1938] Ch
    106... 87
Dorel Juvenile Group v OHIM (C-131/08)
    (Safety 1st)... 599
Dosage Regime/ABBOTT RESPIRATORY
    (G2/08) (2011) 42(3) IIC 257–271... 443
Douglas and others v Hello! Ltd (No 3) [2005]
    EWCA Civ 595; [2005] 3 WLR 881... 780,
    783, 807, 809, 814, 941–943
Dr August Oetker Nahrungsmittel v OHIM
    (Buonfatti/Bonfait) (T-471/09) [2011] ECR
    II-00185... 656
Dr Barnardo's Homes v Barnardo
    Amalgamated Industries (1949) 66 RPC
    103... 755, 763
Dr Reddy's Laboratories (UK) Ltd v Eli Lilly
    and Co [2008] EWHC 2345 (Pat); [2010]
    RPC 9... 440, 449, 499
Dramatico Entertainment Ltd & others v
    BSkyB & others [2012] ECDR 14 (Ch)...
    142, 154, 160, 162
Draper v Trist (1939) 56 RPC 429... 765
Dryson AB v Birger Olsson, OHIM Invalidity
    Division (ICD 0000000982), 17 March
    2006... 289
DU PONT/Appetite suppressant (T144/85)
    [1986] OJEPO 30... 427
Dualit Ltd's Trade Mark Application [1999]
    RPC 890... 588
Duck v Bates (1884) 13 QBD 843... 150
Dumez France v Hessische Landesbank
    (C-220/88) [1990] ECR I-49... 979
Dunlop Pneumatic Tyre Co v Dunlop Motor
    Co 1907 SC (HL) 15... 749, 753, 755
DUNS LICENSING ASSOCIATES/Estimating
    sales activity (T154/04) [2007] EPOR 38...
    417, 526, 535
Durferrit v OHIM—Kolene (T-224/01) [2003]
    ECR II-1589... 616
Duriron Co Inc v Hugh Jennings & Co Ltd
    [1984] FSR 1... 74
Duro Sweden AB v OHIM (T-346/07)... 598

Dyson Appliances Ltd v Hoover [2001] RPC
    26; [2002] RPC 22... 446, 449
Dyson Ltd v Qualtex (UK) Ltd [2005] RPC 19
    (HC); [2006] RPC 31 (CA)... 323, 325, 326,
    329, 330, 331, 332, 333, 334, 335-336, 339,
    341, 347
Dyson Ltd v Vax Ltd (HC) [2010] ECDR 18
    (HC); [2012] FSR 4 (CA)... 278, 284, 285,
    286, 288, 296, 311
Dyson v Registrar of Trademarks (C-321/03)
    [2007] ETMR 34... 558, 579, 611

Eastman Photographic Materials Ltd v
    Griffiths Cycle Corp (1898) 15 RPC 105...
    763
Easygroup IP Licensing Ltd v Sermbezis [2003]
    All ER (D) 25... 767
Easyjet Airline Co Ltd v Dainty (t/a
    EasyRealestate) [2002] FSR 6
    (Ch D)... 692
easyJet v Dainty [2002] FSR 111... 745, 746,
    767
Ebden v News International Ltd, unreported,
    17 May 2011... 191
eCopy Inc v OHIM (T-247/01) [2003] ETMR
    99... 604
eDate Advertising GmbH v X and Martinez v
    MGN Ltd (C-509/09 & C-161/10)... 976
Eden v Whistler DP 1900, I 497... 106
Editions Plon v France (2006) 42 EHRR 36...
    813
Edor Handelsonderneming BV v General Mills
    Fun Group, Nederlands Jurisprudentie
    1978... 655
Edwin Co Ltd v Office for Harmonisation
    in the Internal Market (Trade Marks and
    Designs) (OHIM), Elio Fiorucci [2011]
    ETMR 45... 819
Edwin v Elio Fiorucci (C-263/09) [2011] ETMR
    45... 622
EI Du Pont de Nemours (Witsiepe's)
    Application [1982] FSR 303 (HL)... 440
Eis.de GmbH v BBY Vertriebsgesellschaft mbH
    (C-91/09) [2010] ECR I-00043... 636
EISAI/Second Medical Indication (G5/83)
    [1985] OJEPO 64... 400, 425
Eisenman v Qimron (2000) 54(3) PD 817;
    [2001] ECDR 6 (Supreme Court of Israel)...
    52, 53
El Corte Inglés v OHIM Abril Sánchez and
    Ricote Saugar (BoomerangTV) (T-420/03)
    [2008] ETMR 71... 567, 652
El Corte Inglés v OHIM—Pucci (T-8/03)
    [2004] ECR II-4297... 660
Elanco Products Ltd v Mandops
    (Agrochemical Specialists) Ltd [1980] RPC
    213 (CA)... 140

Electrocoin Automatics v Coinworld [2005] ETMR 31; [2005] FSR 7; [2004] EWHC 1498 (Ch)... 661

Electrolux v Hudson [1977] RPC 312... 458

Electronic Techniques (Anglia) Ltd v Critchley Components Ltd [1997] FSR 401... 57, 65, 123, 129, 346

Eli Lilly & Co v Human Genome Sciences Inc [2011] UKSC 51; [2012] 1 All ER 1154; [2012] RPC 6... 480, 493, 497

Eli Lilly & Co's Community Trade Mark Application [2004] ETMR 4 OHIM (Second Board of Appeal)... 584

Eli Lilly and Co and another v 8PM Chemist Ltd [2008] EWCA Civ 24... 860

Elizabeth Florence Emanuel v Continental Shelf (C-259/04) [2006] ECR I-3089; [2006] ETMR 56... 616, 819

Elizabeth Jagger v John Darling and others [2005] EWHC 683 (Ch)... 942

Elle Trade Mark [1997] FSR 529; [1997] ETMR 552... 624

Elleni Holding BV v Sigla SA (R 1127/2000-3) [2005] ETMR 7... 671

El-Tawil v Comptroller General of Patents [2012] EWHC 185 (Ch)... 446

Elton John v James (1983) [1991] FSR 397... 909

Elvis Presley Enterprises Inc v Sid Shaw Elvisly Yours [1999] RPC 567... 816, 817

Elvis Presley Trade Marks [1997] RPC 543... 822

Emaco Ltd v Dyson Appliances Ltd [1999] ETMR 903... 682

EMI Electrola GmbH v Patricia Im-und Export [1989] ECR 79... 843, 846

EMI Records Ltd v CBS United Kingdom Ltd (C-51/75) [1976] ECR 811... 855

Entidad de Gestión de Derechos de los Productores Audiovisuales (EGEDA) v Magnatrading SL... 256

EPI Environmental Technologies Inc v Symphony Plastic Technologies plc [2006] EWCA Civ 3; 2006 WL 421838; [2006] 1 WLR 495... 780

Ergo Versicherungsgruppe AG v OHIM (Ergo/ Urgo) (T-220/09) [2011] ECR II-00237... 653

Ernest Turner Electrical Instruments v PRS [1943] Ch 167 (CA)... 148

Ernst August Prinz von Hannover v OHIM (T-397/09) [2011] ECR II-00159... 617

Erpo Mobelwerk GmbH v OHIM (T-138/00) [2001] ECR II-3739... 600

Erven Warnink v Townend [1979] AC 731; [1979] 3 WLR 68... 731, 737, 738, 744, 762, 763

Esprit International v OHIM (T-22/10)... 653

Essentially Biological Processes (G2/07 & G1/08) [2011] EPOR 27... 424, 501

Essex Trading Standards v Wallati Singh [2009] EWHC 520 (Admin); 2009 WL 392234... 954

Esure v Direct Line Ltd [2008] EWCA Civ 842... 651, 938

Esure/Direct Line Insurance, 13 December 2006... 669

ETK v News Group Newspapers Ltd [2011] EWCA Civ 439... 813

Eurolamb Trade Mark [1997] RPC 279... 588

Euromarket Designs Inc v Peters [2001] FSR 20 (Ch D)... 699, 977

European Ltd v Economist Newspaper Ltd [1998] FSR 283; [1998] EMLR 536; [1998] ETMR 307... 656

Evans and Evans v Focal Point Fires [2009] EWCH 2784 (Ch)... 690

Evans Medical Ltd's Patent [1998] RPC 517... 438

Evans v Hulton & Co (1924) 131 LT 534... 87

EXPANDABLE GRAFTS / Surgical device (T775/97) [2002] EPOR 24... 431

Expandable Grafts Partnership v Boston Scientific et al [1998] EIPR N-132... 980

Experience Hendrix LLC v Purple Haze Records Ltd and others [2007] FSR 31 (CA)... 221

Experience Hendrix LLC v Times Newspapers Ltd [2010] EWHC 1986 (Ch)... 946

Express Newspapers plc v Liverpool Daily Post & Echo plc [1985] FSR 306... 58, 93, 123

Express Newspapers plc v News (UK) Ltd [1990] FSR 359... 48, 52, 185

Exxon Corporation v Exxon Insurance [1982] Ch 119 (CA)... 48, 58

EXXON/Fuel Oils (T409/91) [1994] OJEPO 653... 479

FA Premier League v Panini [2003] EWCA Civ 995; [2004] FSR 1 (CA)... 191633

Fabio Perini SpA v LPC Group plc [2012] EWHC 911 (Ch)... 469

Faccenda Chicken Ltd v Fowler [1987] Ch 117; [1986] 3 WLR 288; [1986] FSR 291... 784, 789

Falco v Weller-Lindhorst (C-533/07) [2009] ECDR 14... 975

Falcon v Famous Players Film Co [1926] 2 KB 474... 157

Farmers Build Ltd v Carier Bulk Materials Handling Ltd [1999] RPC 461... 325, 326, 338, 340, 346, 766

Felix Munoz Arraisa v OHIM (Riojavina/Rioja) (C-388/10) [2011] ECR I-00042... 653

Feng Shen Technology Co Ltd v OHIM (T-227/09)... 618

Ferag AG v Muller Martini Ltd [2007] EWCA
    Civ 15 . . . 446
Ferdinand v MGN Ltd [2011] EWHC 2454
    (QB) . . . 810
Ferrero SpA v OHIM (Kinderjoghurt/Kinder)
    (C-552/09) [2011] ECR I-02063 . . . 661
Festo Corp v Shoketsu Kinzoku Kogyo
    Kabushiki Co Ltd 535 US 722 (2002) . . . 472
FIFA v Ferrero (T-444/08–T-448/08) . . . 608
Financial Times Ltd v United Kingdom (App
    No 821/03) [2010] EMLR 21; (2010) 50
    EHRR 46 . . . 810
Fine & Country Ltd v Okotoks Ltd [2012]
    EWHC 2230 (Ch) . . . 741, 749, 753
Fishburn's Application 57 RPC 245 . . . 419
Fisher v Brooker and another [2009] UKHL
    41; [2009] 1 WLR 1764; [2009] FSR 25 . . .
    88, 908
Fixtures Marketing Ltd v OPAP (C-444/02)
    [2005] ECDR 3 (ECJ) . . . 62, 63, 211–213,
    927
Fixtures Marketing Ltd v Oy Veikkaus Ab
    (C-46/02) [2004] ECR I-10365 . . . 63, 211,
    212, 927
Fixtures Marketing Ltd v Svenska Spel AB
    (C-338/02) [2005] ECDR 4 (ECJ) . . .
    211–213, 927
Flashing Badge Co Ltd v Groves [2007] FSR 36
    (HC) . . . 352, 353
Flaxcell v Freedman 1981 SLT (Notes) 131 . . .
    736
Fletcher Challenge v Fletcher Challenge Pty
    [1982] FSR 1 . . . 734
Flood v Times Newspapers Ltd [2009] EWHC
    2375 (QB); [2010] EMLR 8 . . . 810
Floris Trade Mark [2001] RPC 19 . . . 624
Flos SpA v Semeraro Casa e Famiglia SpA
    (C-168/09) [2011] ECDR 8 . . . 315, 354
Folding Attic Stairs Ltd v Loft Stairs Co Ltd
    [2009] FSR 24 . . . 432
Football Association Premier League Ltd and
    others v LCD Publishing Ltd [2007] EWHC
    3171 (Ch) . . . 899
Football Association Premier League Ltd v QC
    Leisure [2008] EWHC 1411;Murphy v Media
    Protection Services Ltd [2008] EWHC 1666
    (Admin); Football Association Premier
    League Ltd and others v QC Leisure and
    others, Murphy v Media Protection Services
    Ltd (Joined Cases C-403/08 & C-429/08)
    [2012] 1 CMLR 29 (CJ); FAPL v QC Leisure
    [2012] EWHC 108 (Ch) . . . 50, 125, 139,
    148, 153, 202, 878, 879, 899, 952174, 164,
    202, 864, 865
Football Dataco Ltd v Brittens Pools Ltd [2010]
    RPC 17 (ChD); [2011] ECDR 9 (CA) . . . 211
Football Dataco Ltd v Sportradar (C-173/11)
    [2013] FSR 4 (CJ) . . . 217, 977, 988

Football Dataco Ltd v Sportradar [2012] ECC
    26 (ChD) . . . 211, 212
Football Dataco v Yahoo (C-604/10) [2012]
    ECDR 10 . . . 51, 62, 64, 928
Football League v Littlewoods Pools [1959]
    Ch 637 . . . 61
Force India Formula One Team Ltd v 1
    Malaysia Racing Team [2010] EWCA 1051;
    [2011] ETMR 10; [2012] EWHC 616 (Ch) . . .
    776, 777, 781, 792, 825, 987
Ford Motor Co v OHIM (Ca/Ka) (T-486/07)
    [2011] ECR II 00058 . . . 653
Ford Motor's Application (T-91/99) [2000] 2
    CMLR 276 . . . 605
Forensic Telecommunications Services Ltd v
    Chief Constable of West Yorkshire Police
    [2011] EWHC 2892 (Ch) . . . 61, 64, 217, 777
Formula One Licensing BV v OHIM
    (C-196/11 P) . . . 566
Fort Dodge v Akzo [1998] FSR 222 . . . 985
Fournet v Pearson (1897) 14 TLR 82 . . . 58
Franchi v Franchi [1967] RPC 149 . . . 779
Francis Day & Hunter Ltd v Bron [1963] Ch
    587 (CA) . . . 130, 131, 133
Francis Day & Hunter Ltd v Twentieth Century
    Fox Corp Ltd [1940] AC 112 (PC) . . . 58
Francome v Mirror Group [1984] 2 All ER 408;
    [1984] 1 WLR 892 . . . 782, 790
Fraser v Evans [1969] 1 QB 349 . . . 183, 184,
    790, 792
Fraser-Woodward Ltd v BBC and another
    [2005] FSR 36 . . . 182
Frayling v Premier Upholstery Ltd and others,
    unreported, 6 November 1998 . . . 933
Freeport (C-98/06) [2007] ECR I-8319 . . . 979
Freixenet SA v OHIM (C-344/10 P &
    C-345/10) . . . 595, 607
French Connection v Sutton [2000]
    ETMR 341 . . . 743, 768
Fressoz v France (2001) 31 EHRR 2; (1999)
    5 BHRC 654 . . . 813
Frisby v British Broadcasting Corporation
    [1967] Ch 932 . . . 106
Frisdranken Industrie Winters BV v Red Bull
    Gmbh (C-119/10) . . . 631, 638
Froot Loops Trade Mark [1998] RPC 240 . . .
    588
Frosch Touristik GmbH v OHIM (C-332/09)
    [2010] ECR I-00049 . . . 588
Fruit of the Loom Inc v OHIM (T-514/10) . . .
    624
FSS Travel & Leisure Systems v Johnson [1999]
    FSR 505 (CA) . . . 781
Fujitsu's Application (BL O/121/04) [1996]
    RPC 511; [1997] RPC 608 . . . 407, 413, 416,
    514, 538
Fuller v Blackpool Winter Gardens & Pavilion
    Co Ltd [1895] 2 QB 429 . . . 66

Fundación Española para la Innovación de la Artesanía (FEIA) v Cul de Sac Espacio Creativo SL (C-32/08) [2010] RPC 13... 307

Fundacion Gala-Salvador Dali v ADAGP (C-518/08) [2010] ECDR 13... 107, 988

Future Publishing Ltd v Edge Interactive Media Inc [2011] ETMR 50... 747

Fylde Microsystems Ltd v Key Radio Systems Ltd [1998] FSR 449... 88

G v Wikimedia Foundation Inc [2009] EWHC 3148 (QB); [2010] EMLR 14... 943

Gadget Shop Ltd v Bug Com Ltd [2001] CP Rep 13 (Ch D)... 941

Gale's Application [1991] RPC 305... 407, 413, 514, 538

Galerie d'Art du Petit Champlain Inc v Théberge [2002] 2 SCR 336 (Supreme Court of Canada)... 106, 130

Galileo Brand Architecture Ltd Trade Mark Application (No 2280603) [2005] RPC 22... 641

Galileo Lebensmittel GmbH & Co KG v Commission of the European Communities (C-483/07 P) [2009] ECR I-00959... 686

Game Group plc v First Internet Technology Ltd Case 04014 ADR [2007] ETMR 78... 694

Gartside v Outram (1856) 26 LJ Ch 113... 790

Gat, Gesellschaft für Antriebstechnik mbH & Co KG v Luk Lamellen und Kupplungsbau Beteiligungs KG (C-4/03) [2006] ECR I-06509... 985

Gateway Inc v OHIM (C-57/08) [2008] ECR I-00188... 649

Gebäckpresse I ZR 126/06; [2009] GRUR 79... 357

GEC's Patent [1992] RPC 107... 463

GEMA No 1, Re [1971] CMLR D35... 915

Gemstar-TV Guide International v Virgin Media Ltd [2009] EWHC 3068 (Ch), aff'd [2011] EWCA Civ 302... 419, 540

GENENTECH ET AL/Expression in yeast (T455/91) [1995] OJEPO 684... 495

Genentech Inc's Patent [1989] RPC 147... 410, 495

GENERAL HOSPITAL/Contraceptive method (T820/92) [1995] OJEPO 113... 426

GENERAL HOSPITAL / Hair removal method (T383/03) [2005] OJEPO 159... 428

General Motors v Yplon (C-375/95) [1999] All ER (EC) 865; [1999] 3 CMLR 427... 661

General Tire and Rubber Co v Firestone Tyre and Rubber Co [1972] RPC 457... 434

Generics (UK) Ltd & others v H Lundbeck A/S [2006] EWCA Civ 1261; aff'd [2009] UKHL 12... 408, 450, 467, 479, 500

Generics (UK) Ltd (t/a Mylan) v Yeda Research & Development Co Ltd [2012] EWHC 1848 (Pat)... 478

Generics (UK) v Yeda Research and Development Co Ltd [2012] EWCA 726... 789

GENETIC SYSTEMS CORP/Synthetic antigens (G02/03) [2004] OJEPO 448... 400

George Hensher Ltd v Restawile Upholstery (Lancashire) Ltd [1976] AC 64... 48, 73–76, 351

George Outram v London Evening Newspapers (1911) 28 RPC 308... 743

GEORGETOWN UNIVERSITY/Pericardial access (T35/99) [2000] OJEPO 447... 427

Georgio Beverly Hills v OHIM (T-228/06) [2008] ECR II-00308... 648

Germany v Commission (C-465/02) [2005] ECR I-9115; [2006] ETMR 16... 713, 739

Gerolsteiner Brunnen GmbH & Co v Putsch GmbH (C-100/02) [2004] RPC 39... 674, 676

GFI Group Inc v Eaglestone [1994] FSR 535... 785

Ghazilian's Trade Mark Application [2002] ETMR 57... 614

Giacomelli Sport SpA [2000] ETMR 277... 586

Giggs v News Group Newspapers [2012] EWHC 431 (QB)... 943

Gilbert v Star Newspaper Company Ltd (1894) 11 TLR 4... 794

Gillette Co v LA-Laboratories Ltd Oy (C-228/03) [2005] All ER (EC) 940; [2005] 2 CMLR 62; [2005] ECR I-2337... 674, 677

Gimex International Groupe Import Export v Chill Bag Co Ltd and Others [2012] ECDR 25... 273, 275, 290

Glaverbel SA v British Coal Corporation [1995] RPC 255... 434

Glaverbel v OHIM (T-141/06) [2008] ETMR 37... 605, 606

Glaxo Group Ltd v Dowelhurst Ltd [2004] EWCA Civ 290; [2005] ETMR 104... 859

GlaxoSmithKline Services Unlimited v Commission of the European Communities (T-168/01) [2006] 5 CMLR 29... 846

Global Projects Management Ltd v Citigroup Inc and others [2005] EWHC 2663 (Ch)... 692

Glyn v Weston Feature Film Co [1916] 1 Ch 261... 8, 106, 194

GMG Radio Holdings v Tokyo Project Ltd [1984] RPC 293... 938

Goddin and Rennie's Application [1996] RPC 141... 461

Golden China TV Game Centre v Nintendo Co Ltd 1997 (1) SA 405 (A)... 78

Goldsmith v BCD [2011] EWHC 674 (QB); (2011) 108(14) LSG 20 ... 943

Google France Sarl v Louis Vuitton Malletier SA (C-236/08–C-238/08) [2010] RPC 19 ... 162, 548, 632, 636, 664, 705, 706, 977, 992

Gottschalk v Benson 409 US 63 (1972) ... 527

Goulbourn v OHIM—Redcats (Silk Cocoon) (T174/01) [2003] ECR II789 ... 624

Graver Tank & Manufacturing Co Inc v Linde Air Products Co 339 US 605 ... 472

Gray v News Group Newspapers Ltd [2012] EWCA Civ 48 ... 943

Gray v UVW [2010] EWHC 2367 (QB) ... 943

Great North of Scotland Railway Co v Mann (1892) 19R 1035 ... 751

Greater Glasgow Health Board's Application [1996] RPC 207 ... 459

Green Corns Ltd v Claverly Group Ltd [2005] EWHC 958 (QB); [2005] EMLR 31 ... 811

Green Lane Products Ltd v PMS International Group Ltd [2008] FSR 28 ... 276, 290, 291, 292, 307, 312

Green v Broadcasting Corp of New Zealand [1989] 2 All ER 1056 (PC) ... 48, 66

Grimme v Scott [2010] EWCA 1110 ... 468

Gromax Plasticulture Ltd v Don & Low Nonwovens Ltd [1999] RPC 367 ... 617

Gross v OHIM (T-298/10) ... 624

Grupo Promer Mon Graphic SA v Office for Harmonisation in the Internal Market (Trade Marks and Designs) (OHIM) with PepsiCo Inc (Intervener) (T-9/07) [2010] ECDR 7 ... 273, 278, 280, 281, 282, 284, 286, 307, 309, 310

GTG Sports Publications Ltd v Fitness Shop (Publications) Ltd 1983 SC 115 ... 743

Guardian Media Group plc v Associated Newspapers Ltd 2000 WL 331035 ... 941

Guild v Eskandar Ltd [2001] FSR 38 ... 339

H Lundbeck A/S v Norpharma SpA [2011] EWHC 907 (Pat) ... 433

H Young (Operations) Ltd v Medici Ltd [2003] EWHC 1589 (Ch); [2004] FSR 19 ... 642

Haberman v Jackel [1999] FSR 683 ... 450

Habib Bank Ltd v Habib Bank AG Zurich [1981] 1 WLR 1265 (CA) ... 739

Hack's Application, Re (1941) 58 RPC 91 ... 8

Hadley v Kemp [1999] EMLR 589 ... 89

Hallelujah Trade Mark [1976] RPC 605 ... 614

Hallen Co v Barbantia (UK) Ltd [1991] RPC 195 ... 446

Halliburton Energy Services Inc's Applications [2011] EWHC 2508 (Pat); [2012] RPC 129 ... 540

Halliburton Energy Services v Smith International (North Sea) Ltd [2006] RPC 2 ... 412, 438, 468, 477, 480, 538

Halliwell v Panini, unreported, 9 July 1997 (Ch D) ... 822

Handi-Craft Co v B Free World Ltd [2007] EWHC 10 (Ch) ... 449

HANKKIJA-MAATALOUS/Food additive (T1758/07) [2011] EPOR 2 ... 443

Hannover v Germany (App No 53920/00) (2005) 40 EHRR 1 ... 808–813

Harben Pumps (Scotland) Ltd v Lafferty 1989 SLT 752 ... 784

Harman Pictures NV v Osborne [1967] 1 WLR 723 ... 43, 133

Harms (Incorporated) Ltd v Martans Club Ltd [1926] Ch 870 ... 148

Harpers v Barry Henry & Co (1892) 20 R 133 ... 58

Harris' Patent [1985] RPC 19 ... 459

Harrison v Harrison [2010] ECDR 12 ... 104, 110

Harrison v Project & Design Co (Red Car) (No 1) Ltd [1978] FSR 81 ... 793

Harrison v Teton Valley [2004] EWCA Civ 1028; [2004] 1 WLR 2577; [2005] FSR 10 ... 617

Harrods Ltd v Times Newspaper Ltd [2006] EWCA Civ 294 ... 799

Harrods v Harrodian School [1996] RPC 697 ... 759, 763, 764

Harvard College v Canada (Commissioner of Patents) [2002] SCJ No 77 ... 423

HARVARD/Oncomouse [(T19/90) [1991] EPOR 525 ... 407, 422, 501

HARVARD/Transgenic animal (T315/03) [2005] EPOR 31 ... 423, 506

Hasbro Inc v 123 Nahrmittel GmbH [2011] EWHC 199 (Ch) ... 677

Havana Cigar & Tobacco Factories Ltd v Oddenino [1924] 1 Ch 179 ... 756

Hawkes & Son Ltd v Paramount Film Services [1934] Ch 593 (CA) ... 123

Hays Specialist Recruitment (Holdings) Ltd et al v Ions et al [2008] EWHC 745 (Ch) ... 784

Heidelberger Bauchemie GmbH (C-49/02) [2004] ETMR 99 ... 582, 584, 585

Henderson v Munro (1905) 7F 636 ... 757

Henderson v Radio Corporation Pty Ltd [1969] RPC 218 (High Court of New South Wales) ... 823

Henkel KGaA v OHIM (C-456/01 P) [2004] ECR I-5089; [2005] ETMR 44 ... 590, 591, 593, 595, 607

Henry Brothers (Magherafelt) Ltd v The Ministry of Defence and the Northern Ireland Office [1999] RPC 442 ... 456

Hewlett-Packard Development Co LP v Expansys UK Ltd [2005] EWHC 1495 (Ch) ... 858

Highland Distilleries Co plc v Speymalt Whisky Distributors Ltd 1985 SC 1... 742, 763

Hilti AG v Commission of the European Communities (T-30/89) [1991] ECR II-143... 872

Hines v Winnick [1947] 1 Ch 708... 820

Hinton & Higgs (UK) Ltd v Murphy 1989 SLT 450... 785

Hinton v Donaldson 1773 Mor 8307... 32

Hipp and Co v OHIM (T-221/06) [2009] ECR II-00149... 647

HITACHI/Auction method (T258/03) [2004] 12 OJEPO 575... 415, 526, 534

Hodgson v Isaac [2010] EWPCC 37... 132

Hoechst Celanese Corporation v BP Chemicals Ltd and another [1999] FSR 319... 474

HOECHST/Thio-chloroformates (T198/84) [1985] OJEPO 209... 440

Hoffmann-La Roche (102/77) [1978] ECR 1139... 551, 849, 853

Hoffmann-La Roche v DDSA [1969] FSR 410... 733

Hogan v Koala Dundee (1988) 12 IPR 508... 821

Hogan v Pacific Dunlop (1989) 12 IPR 225... 821

Holding C Vlemmix BV v Evan Hellenberg Hubar, OHIM Invalidity Division (ICD 000001303), 23 March 2006... 289

Hollinrake v Truswell [1894] 3 Ch 420... 58

Holterhoff v Freiesleben (C-2/00) [2002] All ER (EC) 665; [2002] ECR I-4187; [2002] ETMR 79; [2002] FSR 52... 636

Honda Motor Co Ltd v Neesam [2008] EWHC 338 (Ch)... 857

Hotel Cipriani SRL & others v Cipriani (Grosvenor Street) Ltd and others [2008] EWHC 3032 (Ch); [2010] EWCA Civ 110; [2010] Bus LR 1465; [2010] RPC 16... 567, 618, 674–676, 702, 735

Howard Clark v David Allan & Co Ltd 1987 SLT 271... 69, 127

HOWARD FLOREY/Relaxin (T741/91) [1995] EPOR 541... 410, 424, 494, 501

HRH Prince of Wales v Associated Newspapers Ltd (No 3) [2006] EWCA Civ 1776; [2008] Ch 57; [2007] 3 WLR 222... 97, 143, 185, 187, 195, 779, 793, 798, 812, 813

Hsiung's Patent [1992] RPC 497... 480

HTC Corp v Yozmot 33 Ltd [2010] EWHC 786 (Pat)... 435

HTC Europe Co Ltd v Apple Inc [2012] EWHC 1789 (Pat)... 419, 541

Hubbard v Vosper [1972] 2 QB 84 (CA)... 182–184, 188

European Communities (C-22/78) [1979] ECR 1869... 872

Hugo v SA Plon [2007] ECDR 9 (Cour de Cassation, France)... 106

Huston v Turner Entertainment Inc (1992) 23 IIC 702... 103

Hyde Park Residence Ltd v Yelland [2000] RPC 604 (CA)... 185, 186, 194

I v Finland (2009) 48 EHRR 31... 790

IBCOS Computer Ltd v Barclays Mercantile Highland Finance Ltd [1994] FSR 275... 136, 794

IBM/Computer Programs (T1173/97) [2000] EPOR 219... 417, 516, 519, 531, 532, 536

IBM/Computer Programs (T935/97) [1999] EPOR 301... 417, 519, 531–533

IBM/Computer related invention (T115/85) [1990] EPOR 107... 521

IBM/Database back-solving (T1149/06) [2010] EPOR 3... 526

IBM/Document abstracting and retrieving (T22/85) [1990] EPOR 98... 516, 523

IBM/Editable document form (T110/90) [1995] EPOR 185... 414, 522

IBM/Rotating displayed objects (T59/93), unreported... 522

IBM/Semantically related expressions (T52/85) [1989] EPOR 454... 523

IBM/Spell Checker (T121/85), unreported... 523

IBM/Text clarity processing (T38/86) [1990] EPOR 606... 414, 523

IBM/Text processing (T65/86) [1990] EPOR 181... 523

Icebreaker Ltd v OHIM (T-112/09) [2010] ECR II-00172... 651

ICI / Pyridine Herbicides [1986] 5 EPOR 232... 478

ICI/Cleaning plaque (T290/86) [1992] OJEPO 414... 427

i-content v OHIM (T-258/09) (Betwin) [2011] ECR II-03797... 601

Icos Decision [2002] OJEPO 293... 492, 497

IDA Ltd and others v University of Southampton and others [2006] RPC 21... 456

Ifejika v Ifejika [2012] FSR 6 (Patents County Court)... 341

IFF/Claim categories (T150/82) [1984] OJEPO 309... 400, 439

IG Farbenindustrie AG's Patents (1930) 47 RPC 289... 441

IGT's Applications [2007] EWHC 1341 (Ch)... 414

IHT International Heiztechnik v Ideal Standard (C-9/93) [1994] 3 CMLR 857;

[1994] ECR I-2789; [1995] FSR 59 . . . 698, 841, 842, 898

Il Ponte Finanziaria SpA (C-234/06 P) [2007] ECR I-07333 . . . 624

ILS Institut für Lernsysteme GmbH v OHIM (T-388/00) [2002] ECR II-04301 . . . 647

Imagination Technologies Ltd v OHIM [2008] ETMR 10 . . . 604, 691

Imagion v OHIM (T-463/08) [2011] ECR II-00206 . . . 604

Improver Corporation v Remington Consumer Products Ltd [1990] FSR 181 . . . 373, 472

IMS Health Inc v European Commission (T 104/01R) [2001] ECR II-2349 . . . 898

IMS Health v NDC Health (C-418/01) [2004] ECR I-5039 . . . 889, 895

Imutran Ltd v Uncaged Campaigns Ltd [2002] FSR 2 . . . 941

IN Newman Ltd v Richard T Adlem [2005] EWCA Civ 741 . . . 675, 749

Independent Television Publications Ltd v Time Out Ltd [1984] FSR 64 . . . 61, 182

Independiente Ltd and others v Music Trading On-Line (HK) Ltd [2003] EWHC 470 (Ch) . . . 948

Independiente Ltd v Music Trading On-line (HK) Ltd [2007] FSR 21 (Ch) . . . 144

Industrial Furnaces Ltd v Reaves [1970] RPC 605 . . . 131

Infabrics Ltd v Jaytex Ltd [1982] AC 1 . . . 143, 145

INFINEON TECHNOLOGIES/Circuit simulation I (T1227/05) [2010] EPOR 9 . . . 517

Infopaq International A/S v Danske Dagblades Forening (C-5/08) [2009] ECDR 16 . . . 44, 50, 51, 59, 125, 126, 139, 173

Infopaq International A/S v Danske Dagblades Forening (C-302/10) (Infopaq II) . . . 139, 174

Initial Services Ltd v Putterill [1967] 3 WLR 1032; [1968] 1 QB 396 . . . 790

Inlima SL's Application for a Three Dimensional Trade Mark [2000] ETMR 325 aff'd [2000] RPC 661 . . . 665

Inlima SL's Application Opposition of Adidas AG [2000] ETMR 325 . . . 663, 665, 666

Inline Logistics v UCI Logistics [2002] RPC 32 . . . 781

Innovia Films Ltd v Frito-Lay North America, Inc [2012] EWHC 790 (Pat) . . . 458

Innoweb BV v Wegener ICT Media BV (C-202/12) . . . 217

Intel Corporation Inc v CPM United Kingdom Ltd (C-252/07) [2009] ETMR 13; [2009] RPC 15 . . . 661, 663

Intel Corp Inc v Sihra [2004] ETMR 44; [2003] EWHC 17 (Ch) . . . 667

Intel Corporation v VIA Technologies Inc and Ors [2002] EWCA Civ 1905; [2003] FSR 33 . . . 897, 899

Inter Lotto (UK) Ltd v Camelot Group plc [2004] RPC 9; [2003] EWCA Civ 1132 . . . 558

Intercase Ltd v Time Computers Ltd [2004] ECDR 8 . . . 344

Interflora v Marks & Spencer (C-323/09) [2009] EWHC 1095 (Ch); [2012] EWHC 1722 (Ch) . . . 635, 664, 705, 939

Interlego AG v Tyco Industries Inc [1989] AC 217 (PC) . . . 43, 48, 53, 74, 129, 167, 334

International Flavors & Fragrances Inc (T150/82) [1984] OJEPO 309 . . . 439

International Madrid (UK) Case M706887 . . . 817

Interquell GmbH v OHIM—Provimi Ltd & SCA Nutrition Ltd (T-20/02) [2004] ECR II-01001 . . . 658

Interseroh Scrp and Metals Trading GmbH v Sonderabfall-Management-Gesellschafe Rheinland-Pfalz mbH (C-1/11) . . . 797

IPC Media Ltd v News Group Newspapers Ltd [2005] FSR 35 . . . 183, 188

IRC v Muller & Co's Margarine Ltd [1901] AC 217 . . . 733

Irvine v Talksport [2002] 2 All ER 414 . . . 759, 765, 770, 805, 825

ITS Rubber Ltd's Application [1979] RPC 318 . . . 412

ITT Promedia NV v Commission of the European Communities (T-111/96) [1998] ECR II-2937 . . . 899

ITV Broadcasting Ltd v TV Catchup Ltd (C-607/11) [2011] EWHC 2977; [2011] FSR 40 . . . 139, 151, 154, 155, 174

Ivax Pharmaceuticals UK Ltd v Akzo Nobel NV; Arrow Generics Ltd v Akzo Nobel NV [2007] RPC 3 . . . 445

J & S Davis (Holdings) Ltd v Wright Health Group [1988] RPC 403 . . . 43, 72, 76, 129

J Choo (Jersey) Ltd v Towerstone Ltd and others [2008] EWHC 346 (Ch) . . . 945

JA Diffusion SARL v Shanghai Creamode Distribution Co, Ltd (OHIM Third Board of Appeal (R 1823/2010-3) 7 November 2011 . . . 276

James Arnold & Co v Miafern Ltd [1980] RPC 397 . . . 73

Jane Austen Trade Mark [2000] RPC 879 . . . 588

Japan Tobacco Inc v OHIM (Camelo/Camel) (C-136/08) [2009] ECR I-00070 . . . 668

Jean Christian Perfumes Ltd v Thakrar [2011] EWHC 1383 (Ch) . . . 906

Jebaraj Kenneth trading as Screw You (R 495/2005-G)... 614

Jennings v Stephens [1936] Ch 469... 148

JH Coles Pty Ltd v Need [1934] AC 82... 740

JHP Ltd v BBC Worldwide Ltd and another [2008] EWHC 757; [2008] FSR 29 (Ch)... 140, 905, 908

Jian Tools v Roderick Manhattan Group Ltd [1995] FSR 924... 735

JIH v News Group Newspapers Ltd [2011] EWCA Civ 42; [2011] 2 All ER 324; [2011] EMLR 15... 943

John Haig & Co v Forth Blending Co 1954 SC 35... 744, 745, 753

John Haig & Co Ltd v John D D Haig Ltd 1957 SLT (Notes) 36... 749

John Lahiri Khan's Application (Patent Office Hearing Officer: BL O/356/06)... 415

John Richardson Computers Ltd v Flanders [1993] FSR 497... 136

John Walker & Sons Ltd v Douglas Laing & Co Ltd 1993 SLT 156... 756

John Walker & Sons v Douglas McGibbon 1972 SLT 128... 737, 756, 761

John Walker v Ost [1970] 2 All ER 106; [1970] RPC 489... 756, 761, 971

Johns-Manville Corporation's Patent [1967] RPC 479... 451

Johnson v Heat and Air Systems Ltd (1941) 58 RPC 229... 791

Johnston & Co v Orr-Ewing & Co (1882) 7 App Cas 219... 756

Jones v Ricoh UK Ltd [2010] EWHC 1743 (Ch)... 785

Jones v Tower Hamlets London Borough [2001] RPC 23... 132

Joos v Commissioner of Patents [1973] RPC 79... 427

Jose Alejandro SL v OHIM—Anheuser-Busch Inc (T-129/01) [2003] ECR II-02251... 658

Joseph Rodgers & Sons Ltd v WN Rodgers & Co (1924) 41 RPC 277... 749

Joy Music Ltd v Sunday Pictorial Newspapers [1960] 2 QB 60... 141

JS Swan v Kall Kwik [2009] CSOH 99; 2009 WL 1949468... 975

Jules Rimet Cup Ltd v Football Association [2007] EWHC 2376 (Ch)... 617

Julius Sämann Ltd v Tetrosyl Ltd [2006] EWHC 529 (Ch)... 646, 669, 670

JW Spear & Sons Ltd and Mattel Inc v Zynga [2012] EWHC 3345 (Ch)... 580

Kabushiki Kaisha Sony Computer Entertainment [2006] FSR 9; [2005] EWHC 1522 (Ch) ... 698, 858

Kabushiki Kaisha Sony Computer Entertainment v Stevens (2005) 224 CLR 193 (HCA)... 199

Kalfelis v Schröder (189/87) [1988] ECR 5565... 976, 981

Kalman and another v PCL Packaging (UK) Ltd and another [1982] FSR 406... 466

Kanal 5 Ltd v Föreningen Svedska Tonsättares Internationella Musikbyrå (STIM) UPA (C-52/07) [2008] ECR I-9275... 886

KARO STEP Trade Mark [1977] RPC 255... 69

Kastner v Rizla and another [1995] RPC 585... 474

Kavanagh Balloons Pty Ltd v Cameron Balloons Ltd [2004] RPC 5... 432

Kaye v Robertson [1991] FSR 62... 806

KCI Licensing Inc and others v Smith & Nephew plc and others [2010] EWCA Civ 1260... 468

Kean v McGivan [1982] FSR 119... 732

Kelly and another v GE Healthcare Ltd [2009] RPC 12... 463

Kennard v Lewis [1983] FSR 346... 141, 184

Kenrick & Co v Lawrence & Co (1890) 25 QBD 99... 87

Kenrick v Lawrence (1890) 25 QBD 99... 74

Keurkoop BV v Nancy Kean Gifts BV (144/81) [1983] FSR 381... 267

KGM v News Group Newspapers [2011] EWCA Civ 808... 943

Kimberly Clark v Fort Sterling [1997] FSR 877... 760

King Features Syndicate Inc v OM Kleeman Ltd [1941] AC 417... 69, 127, 355

King v The South African Weather Service [2009] FSR 6 (Supreme Court of Appeal, Republic of South Africa)... 96

Kingdom of Spain and Italian Republic v Council of the European Union (C-274/11 & C-295/11) Judgment of the Court (Grand Chamber) 16 April 2013... 374

Kingdom of the Netherlands v Council of the European Union and the European Parliament [(C-377/98) 2002] FSR 36... 497, 502, 542

Kinnell v Ballantyne 1910 SC 246... 728, 747

Kirin-Amgen Inc and others v Hoechst Marion Roussel Ltd and others [2005] 1 All ER 667; [2005] RPC 9... 370, 439, 470, 472, 475, 476, 478, 493, 499

Kirin-Amgen v Transkaryotic Therapies [2003] RPC 3 (CA)... 397, 493

Kirk v J & R Fleming [1928–35] MCC 44... 58

Kitfix Swallow Group Ltd v Great Gizmos Ltd [2007] EWHC 2668 (Ch)... 986

KK Sony Computer Entertainment and
   another v Pacific Game Technology
   (Holding) Ltd [2006] EWHC 2509 (Pat)...
   699, 858
KK Suwa Seikosha's Design Application [1982]
   RPC 166... 273
Klinische Versuche (Clinical Trials) I [1997]
   RPC 623... 482
Klinische Versuche (Clinical Trials) II [1998]
   RPC 423... 482
Knight v Beyond Properties Pty Ltd [2007] FSR
   34 (Ch)   734, 763
KOCH AND STERZEL/X-ray apparatus
   (T26/86) [1988] EPOR 72... 515, 522, 523
Koch Shipping v Richards Butler [2002] EWCA
   Civ 1280; 2002 WL 1446111
   (CA)... 788
Koinklijke KPN Nederland NV v Benelux-
   Merkenbureau (C-363/99) [2004] ECR
   I-01619... 594
Koipe Corporacion SL v OHIM (T-363/04)
   [2007] ECR II-03355... 651
Komesaroff v Mickle [1988] RPC 204... 72,
   74, 76
Koninkijke Philips Electronics NV v Princo
   Digital Disc GmbH; Koninkijke Philips
   Electronics NV v Chin-Shou Kuo [2003]
   EWHC 1598 (Ch)... 434
Koninklijke KPN Nederland NV v Benelux-
   Merkenbureau (C-363/99) [2005] 3 WLR
   649; [2005] All ER (EC) 19... 589, 591, 592,
   594, 598, 599
Koninklijke Philips Electronics NV v
   Remington Consumer Products Ltd (C-
   299/99 [2003] RPC 2; [2006] ETMR 42;
   [2006] EWCA Civ 16... 589, 610–612
KONINKLIJKE PHILIPS ELECTRONICS NV/
   Medical diagnostic imaging (T9/04) [2007]
   EPOR 10... 428
KONINKLIJKE PHILIPS ELECTRONICS/
   Picture retrieval system (T1194/97) [2000]
   OJEPO 525; [2001] EPOR 25... 420
Kraft Jacobs Suchard Ltd's Application;
   Opposition by Nestlé UK Ltd [2001] ETMR
   54... 616
Kuka Roboter GmbH (T-97/08) [2010] ECR
   II-05059... 593
Kureha Corp v OHIM (T-487/08) [2010] ECR
   II-00111... 652
Kustom Musical Amplification, Inc v OHIM
   (T-317/05) [2007] ECR II-00427... 564
Kwang Yang Motor Co, Ltd v OHIM and
   Honda Giken Kogyo Kabushiki Kaisha
   (T-10/08) [2012] ECDR 2... 300

L Woolley Jewellers Ltd v A & A Jewellery Ltd
   [2003] FSR 15... 124, 346-347

L'Oréal (UK) Ltd and Golden Ltd v Johnson
   & Johnson [2000] ETMR 691, [2000] FSR
   686... 933
L'Oréal Norge AS v Per Aarskog AS and others
   (E-9/07)... 856
L'Oreal SA v eBay International AG (C-324/09)
   [2009] EWHC 1094 (Ch); [2011] RPC 27...
   162, 699, 702, 707, 950, 988
L'Oréal SA v OHIM/Revlon (C-235/05) [2006]
   ECR I-00057... 647
L'Oreal v Bellure NV (C-487/07) [2006] EWHC
   1355 (Ch), [2007] RPC 14; [2008] RPC 9;
   2010] ETMR 47; [2010] EWCA
   Civ 535... 549, 553, 554, 636, 651,
   660, 663, 666, 671, 672, 681, 691,
   741, 746, 768
L'ORÉAL/Protection against UV (T1077/93)
   [1997] OJEPO 546... 427
La Chemise Lacoste SA v Baker Street Clothing
   Ltd (O/330/10), 9 December 2009... 656
La Marquise's Footwear Application (1947) 64
   RPC 27... 614
La Mer Technology Inc v OHIM [2008] ETMR
   9... 625
Laboratoires Goëmar SA v La Mer Technology
   Inc [2005] EWCA Civ 978; [2005] ETMR
   114; [2006] FSR 5; 2005 WL 1801235
   (CA)... 624
Ladbroke v William Hill [1964] 1 WLR 273
   (HL)... 48, 61, 122, 123
Lady Archer v Williams [2003] EWHC 1670;
   [2003] EMLR 38... 783
Lambretta Clothing Co Ltd v Teddy Smith
   (UK) Ltd [2005] RPC 6 (CA)... 324,
   327–328, 329, 339, 340, 352
Lancome Parfums et Beaute & Cie SNC v
   OHIN (C-408/08 P)... 598
Land Securities plc v Registrar of Trade Marks
   [2008] EWHC 1744 (Pat)... 587
Landor & Hawa International Ltd v Azure
   Designs Ltd [2007] FSR 9 (CA)... 295, 296,
   323, 331, 939
Lang Brothers v Goldwell 1980 SC 237... 748,
   758, 761
Lansing Linde v Kerr [1991] 1 All ER 418;
   [1991] 1 WLR 251 (CA)... 784
Laserdisken ApS v Kulturministeriet
   (C-479/04) [2006] ECR I-8089... 866
Laugh It Off Promotions CC v South African
   Breweries International (Finance) BV [2005]
   FSR 30 (Sup Ct, SA)... 672
Lauri v Renad (1892) 3 Ch 402... 91
Law Society of Upper Canada v CCH
   Canadian Ltd [2004] 1 SCR 339... 41, 123,
   158, 177, 203
Lawton v Lord David Dundas, The Times, 13
   June 1985... 42

LB (Plastics) Ltd v Swish Products Ltd [1979] RPC 537 … 130

LB Europe Ltd (t/a DuPont Liquid Packaging Systems) v Smurfit Bag In A Box SA [2008] EWHC 1231 (Ch) … 934

Le Tribunal de Premiere Instance de Nivelles, Belgium 09-1684-A (Lichôdmapwa v L'asbl Festival de Theatre de Spa) … 921

Leah v Two Worlds Publishing Ltd [1951] Ch 393 … 90

Lego Juris A/S v Mega Brands Inc (R 856/2004-G) [2007] ETMR 11 … 609

Lego Juris A/S v OHIM (T-270/06) [2009] ETMR 15 … 609

Lego Juris A/S v OHIM (C-48/09) [2010] ECR I-08403 … 558, 590, 609, 611

Lego System A/S v Lego M Lemelstrich Ltd [1983] FSR 155 … 755

Leidseplein Beheer and de Vries v Red Bull (C-65/12) … 670

LELAND STANFORD/Modified Animal [2002] EPOR 2 … 423

Leng d'Or SA v Crown Confectionery Co Ltd, OHIM Invalidity Division (ICD 000000388), 20 September 2005 … 289

Leno Merken BV v Hagelkruis Beheer BV (C-149/11) … 625

Leofelis SA and Leeside srl v Lonsdale Sports Ltd, Trade Mark Licensing Co Ltd and Sports World International Ltd [2008] EWCA Civ 640 … 907

Les Éditions Albert René v OHIM—Trucco sistemi di telecomunicazione SpA (T-311/01) … 650

Les Editions Albert René v OHIM (C-16/06) [2009] ETMR 21 … 650, 818

Leslie v Young (1894) 21 R (HL) 57 … 61

Levi Stores v Tesco Ltd [2003] RPC 18 … 866

Levi Strauss & Co v Casucci SpA (C-145/05) [2006] ECR I-03703 … 653

Levin v Farmers Supply Association of Scotland 1973 SLT (Notes) 43 … 781

Levy v Rutley (1871) LR 6 CP 523 … 86

LG Philips Co Ltd v Tatung (UK) Ltd and others [2006] EWCA Civ 1774 … 480

Libertel Groep BV v Benelux-Merkenbureau (C-104/01) [2004] Ch 83; [2004] 2 WLR 1081 … 582, 592

Lidl Belgium GmbH & Co KG v Etablissementen Franz Colruyt NV; Kingspan Group plc and another v Rockwool Ltd (C-356/04) [2011] EWHC 250 (Ch) … 682

Lidl SNC v Vierzon Distribution SA (C-159/09) [2010] ECR I-11761 … 679, 682

Lifestyle Management Ltd v Frater [2010] EWHC 3258 (TCC) … 768

Liffe Administration & Management v Pinkova [2007] RPC 30 … 459

Lilly Icos LLC and another, Pfizer Enterprises SARL and others, Merck & Co Inc and others, AstraZeneca AB and others v 8PM Chemists Ltd, Vinesh Aggarwal, RDA Kollektif Sirketi [2009] EWHC 1905 (Ch) … 939

Linde AG v Deutsches Patent- und Markenamt (C-53/01) … 591

Linde AG, Winward Industries, Rado Watch Co Ltd (C-55/01) [2003] RPC 45 … 590

Lindner Recyclingtech GmbH v Franssons Verkst ä der AB (OHIM Third Board of Appeal (R 690/2007–3) [2010] ECDR 1 … 295, 296, 300

Linoleum Manufacturing Co v Nairn (1878) 7 Ch D 834 … 744

Lion Laboratories v Evans 1985] QB 526; [1984] 3 WLR 539 … 790

Littlewoods Organisation Ltd v Harris [1978] 1 All ER 1026; [1977] 1 WLR 1472 … 785

Littlewoods Pools Application, Re (1949) 66 RPC 309 … 271

Lloyd Schuhfabrik Meyer & Co GmbH v Klijsen Handel BV (C-342/97) [1999] ECR I-3819; [1999] ETMR 690 … 656

LNS v Persons Unknown [2010] EMLR 16 … 810

Lock International plc v Beswick [1989] 1 WLR 1268; [1989] 3 All ER 373 … 785

Loendersloot (F) Internationale Expeditie v George Ballantine & Son Ltd (C-349/95) [1997] ECR I-6227 … 848, 849

London Regional Transport v Mayor of London [2001] EWCA Civ 1491, 2001 WL 825728; [2003] EMLR 4 (CA) … 777, 798, 814

Longevity Health Products v OHIM (T-190/09) [2011] ECR II-00044 … 627

Lord Advocate v Scotsman Publications Ltd 1989 SLT 705 … 776, 788

Lotus v Paperback Software 740 F Supp 37 (1990) … 135

Louis Vuitton Malletier v OHIM (T-237/10) … 605, 606

LTJ Diffusion SA v Sadas Vertbaudet SA (C-291/00) [2003] ECR 1-2799; [2003] ETMR 83; [2003] FSR 34 (ECJ) … 640, 642

Lucasfilm Ltd v Ainsworth [2009] FSR 2 (Ch D); [2009] EWCA Civ 1328 (CA); [2012] 1 AC 208 (SC) … 71, 76, 351-352, 354, 757, 972, 974, 993

Lucazeau v SACEM (C-110/88, 241/88 & 242/88) [1989] ECR 2811 … 915

Ludlow Music Inc v Robbie Williams [2001] FSR 19 … 123, 141

Lumos Skincare Ltd v Sweet Squared Ltd [2012] EWPCC 22... 733, 752

Lux Traffic Controls Ltd v Pike Signals Ltd and Faronwise Ltd [1993] RPC 107... 421, 432

Lyngstad v Anabas [1977] FSR 62... 755, 822

M+M Gesellschaft für Unternehmensberatung und Informationssysteme mbH/ OHIMMediametrie SA (T-317/01)... 658

Macallan-Glenlivet plc v Speymalt Whisky Distributors Ltd 1983 SLT 348... 763

Mackie Designs Inc v Behringer Specialised Studio Equipment (UK) Ltd [1999] RPC 717... 327

Mackie T/A 197 Aerial Photography v Askew 2009 SLT (Sh Ct) 146... 699, 976

Maclean v Moody (1858) 20 D 1154... 61

Macmillan & Co Ltd v K & J Cooper (1923) 93 LJPC 113... 48

Macmillan v Cooper (1923) 93 LJPC 113... 42

Macmillan v Suresh Chunder Deb (1890) ILR 17 Calc 951... 42, 61

Macrossan's Patent Application [2006] EWHC 705 (Ch)... 415

Madey v Duke University 307 F3d 1351 at 1362 (Fed Cir, 2002)... 482

Mag Instrument Inc v California Trading Company Norway (E-2/97) [1997] EFTA Ct Rep 129, 2008 ETMR 60... 856

Mag Instrument Inc v OHIM (C-136/02) [2004] ECR I-9165; [2005] ETMR 46... 593, 595, 607

Mail Newspapers v Express Newspapers [1987] FSR 90... 91

Makro Zelfbedieningsgroothandel e.a. v Diesel Spa (C-324/08) [2009] ECR I-10019... 840, 858

Mallory Metallurgical Products Ltd v Black Sivalls and Bryson Incorporated [1977] RPC 321... 476

Malone v Commissioner of Police of the Metropolis (No 2) [1979] 2 All ER 620; [1979] 2 WLR 700... 782, 790

MAN/Provision of product specific data (T1242/04) [2007] EPOR 45... 522

Mango Sport System Srl v Diknak (R 308/2003-1) [2005] ETMR 5... 662, 663

Mantis Surgical Ltd v Tregenza [2007] EWHC 1545 (QB)... 785

Marblehead Trading Ltd v The Stroh Brewery Co 1988 GWD 20-885... 67

Marca Mode CV v Adidas AG (C-425/98) [2000] ECR I-4861; [2000] ETMR 561... 645, 656

Marcel v Commissioner of Police of the Metropolis [1992] Ch 225; [1992] 2 WLR 50 (CA)... 789

Mardas v New York Times [2008] EWHC 3135 (QB); [2009] EMLR 8... 978

Marengo v Daily Sketch (1948) 65 RPC 242 (HL)... 820

Marinari v Lloyds Bank plc [1996] QB 217... 978

Mark Wilkinson Furniture Ltd v Woodcraft Designs (Radcliffe) Ltd [1998] FSR 63 (HC)... 329, 336, 347

Markem Corp v Zipher Ltd [2005] EWCA Civ 267; [2005] RPC 31... 793

MARKER/Beattie (T603/89) (1992) OJEPO 230... 420

Marks & Spencer v Freshfields Bruckhaus Deringer [2004] EWCA Civ 741; 2004 WL 1174253 (CA); [2005] PNLR 4; aff'g [2004] 1 WLR 2331... 789

Mars UK Ltd v Burgess Group plc [2004] EWHC 1912 (Ch)... 748

Mars UK Ltd v Teknowledge Ltd (No 1) [2000] FSR 138; The Times, 23 June 1999 (Ch D)... 194, 195, 782

Martin Luksan v Petrus van der Let (C-277/10)... 92, 256

Martin v McGuiness 2003 SLT 1424... 808

Martin v Polyplas [1969] NZLR 1046... 73

Mary Wilson Enterprises Inc's Trade Mark Application [2003] EMLR 14... 617

Mastercard International Inc v Hitachi Credit (UK) plc [2004] EWHC 1623 (Ch); [2005] ETMR 10; [2005] RPC 21... 667

Masterman's Application, Re [1991] RPC 89... 8, 298

Matratzen Concord AG v Hukla Germany SA (C-421/04) [2006] ETMR 48... 601, 602

Matratzen Concord v OHIM (C-3/03) [2004] ECR I-3657... 648, 656

Mattel Inc v MCA Records Inc 296 F 3d 894 at 905 (9th Cir, 2002)... 548

Mayne Pharma Ltd and another v Debiopharm SA and another [2006] EWHC 1123 (Pat)... 446

Mayne Pharma v Pharmacia Italia SpA [2005] EWCA Civ 137... 476

Mayo Collaborative Servs v Prometheus Labs, Inc 132 S Ct 1289 (2012)... 410, 491

Mazur Media Ltd and another v Mazur Media GmbH [2004] EWHC 1566 (Ch); [2005] 1 Lloyd's Rep 41; [2005] 1 BCLC 305; [2004] BPIR 1253... 979

McCain International v County Fair Foods [1981] RPC 69... 742

McCosh v Crow & Co (1903) 5 F 670... 110

McCulloch v May [1947] 2 All ER 845; (1948) 65 RPC 58... 754, 822, 823

McDonald and another v Graham [1994] RPC 407... 467, 481

McDonald's Hamburgers Ltd v Burger King
UK Ltd [1986] FSR 45; [1987] FSR 112...
760

McKennitt v Ash [2006] EWCA Civ 1714...
779, 808, 810, 814

Mecklermedia Corp v DC Congress GmbH
[1998] Ch 40; [1997] FSR 627... 971, 977,
988

Media Saturn Holding GmbH v OHIM
(C-92/10 P)... 600

Media Works NZ Ltd v Sky Television Network
Ltd [2007] NZHC 924... 187

Medion AG v Thomson Multimedia Sales
Germany & Austria GmbH (C-120/04)
[2006] ETMR 13... 648, 649, 652, 656

MED-PHYSICS/Treatment by surgery (G1/07)
[2010] EPOR 25 ... 428, 429, 488

Meikle v Maufe [1941] 3 All ER 144... 74, 90

Melia's Application (Patent Office Hearing
Officer: BL O/153/92)... 415

Melrose Drover Ltd v Heddle (1902) 4F
1120... 734

Memco-Med's Patent [1992] RPC 403... 462

Menashe Business Mercantile Ltd and
another v William Hill Organisation
Ltd [2003] 1 All ER 279; [2003] 1 WLR
1462... 468, 531

Mentor Corporation v Hollister Inc [1993]
RPC 7... 477

Merchandising Corp of America v Harpbond
[1983] FSR 32... 74

Merchandising Corporation of America v
Harpbond [1983] FSR 32... 68

Merck & Co Inc v Generics (UK) Ltd [2004]
RPC 31... 476

Merck & Co Inc v Stephar BV [1981] ECR
2063... 844

Merck & Co v Primecrown Ltd [1996] ECR
I-6285... 844

Merck Canada Inc v Sigma Pharmaceuticals
plc [2012] EWPCC 18... 844

Merck KGaA v Integra LifeSciences Ltd 545 US
193 (2005)... 482

Merck Sharp & Dohme Corp v Teva UK Ltd
[2011] EWCA Civ 382... 444

Mercury Communications Ltd v Mercury
Interactive (UK) Ltd [1995] FSR 850... 628

Meredith Corp v OHIM (T-524/09) [2011] ECR
II-00258... 600

Merlet v Mothercare [1986] RPC 115 (CA)...
127

Merrell Dow Pharmaceuticals Inc and another
v HN Norton & Co Ltd and others [1996]
RPC 76... 435, 437, 465

Merrill Lynch's Application [1988] RPC 1;
[1989] RPC 561... 407, 415, 514, 538

Mersey Care NHS Trust v Ackroyd (No
2) [2006] EWHC 107; [2006] EMLR 12;
[2007] EWCA Civ 101; [2008] EMLR 1;
[2007] HRLR 19... 799

Merz & Krell (C-517/99) [2001] ECR I-6959...
551

Messager v BBC [1929] AC 151... 908

Messer Group GmbH v OHIM (C-579/08)
[2020] ECR I-00002... 648

Metix v Maughan [1997] FSR 718... 72

Metro-Goldwyn-Mayer Studios Inc v Grokster
Ltd 380 F 3d 1154 (9th Cir, 2004); 545 US
913 (2005) (US Supreme Court)... 160

MGN Ltd v United Kingdom (App No
39401/04) (2011) 29 BHRC 686 (ECtHR)...
812

Microsoft Corp v Commission of European
Communities (T-201/04) [2007] ECR II-
3601... 795, 893

Microsoft Corporation v Ling and others
[2006] EWHC 1619 (Ch)... 897

Microsoft Corporation v Plato Technology Ltd
[1999] FSR 834... 944

MICROSOFT/Data Transfer (T424/03) [2006]
EPOR 40... 526, 534, 536

Midler v Ford Motor Co Inc 849 F 2d 460
(1988)... 823

Miller & Lang Ltd v Macniven & Cameron Ltd
(1908) 16 SLT 56... 74

Milliken Denmark AS v Walk Off Mats Ltd
and another [1996] FSR 292... 432

Minerva Trade Mark [2000] FSR 734... 628

Ministère Public v Tournier (C-395/87) [1989]
ECR 2521... 915, 916

MIP Metro Group Intellectual Property GmbH
& Co KG v OHIM (T-290/07) [2008] ECR
II-00315... 649

Mirage Studios v Counter-Feat Clothing [1991]
FSR 145... 755, 805

Miss World Ltd v Channel 4 [2007] ETMR 66
(Ch); [2007] EWHC 982 (Pat)... 549, 941

Miss World v James Street [1981] FSR 309...
765

Mitchell v BBC [2011] EWPCC 42... 130, 131

MMD Design & Consultancy Ltd's Patent
[1989] RPC 131... 476

MOBIL OIL III/Friction Reducing Additive
(G2/88) [1990] OJEPO 93... 441

MOBIUS/Neighbouring field (T176/84) [1986]
OJEPO 50... 445

Mölnlycke Health Care v Brightwake [2011]
EWHC 376 (Pat)... 435

Monopoly v Anti-Monopoly... 655

Monsanto Co (Brignac's) Application [1971]
RPC 153... 433

Monsanto Co v Stauffer Chemical Co and
another [1985] RPC 515... 481

Monsanto Technology LLC v Cefetra BV
(C-428/08) [2012] 3 CMLR 7; [2011] All ER
(EC) 209; [2011] FSR 6... 497

MONSANTO/Glyphosate tolerant alfalfa (T775/08) [2011] EPOR 28 ... 423, 501

Montex Holdings Ltd v Diesel SpA (C-281/05) [2006] ECR I-10881 ... 860

Montgomery v Thompson [1891] AC 217 ... 752

Moorhouse v University of New South Wales [1976] RPC 151 (HCA) ... 156–159

Morning Star Co-operative Society v Express Newspapers [1979] FSR 113 ... 753

Morrison Leahy Music Ltd v Lightbond Ltd [1993] EMLR 144 ... 104

Mosley (Max) v News Group Newspapers Ltd [2008] EWHC 1777 (QB); [2008] EMLR 20 ... 778, 810, 810, 815, 943

Mosley v United Kingdom (App No 48009/08) (2011) (53) EHRR 30; [2011] ECHR 774 ... 815, 943

Moss v Information Commissioner (EA/2011/0081), 28 February 2012 ... 797

Mothercare v Penguin Books [1988] RPC 113 ... 742, 747, 938

MS Associates v Power [1988] FSR 242 ... 135

Mulcaire v Phillips [2012] UKSC 28 ... 947

Mülhens GmbH & Co KG v OHIM (C-206/04) [2008] ETMR 69 ... 552, 645, 647, 652

Mundipharma AG v OHIM (T-256/04) [2007] ECR II-00449 ... 628

Murray v Express Newspapers plc [2007] EWHC 1908 (Ch); [2007] ECDR 20; [2007] EMLR 22; [2008] EWCA Civ 446; (2009) Ch 481 ... 810, 811

Murray v McFarquhar (1785) Mor 8309 ... 141

Mustapha El Jirari Bouzekri v OHIM (N Nickol/Nike) (T 207/09) [2011] ECR II-00324 ... 661

My Kinda Bones v Dr Peppers Stove Co [1984] FSR 289 ... 734

My Kinda Town v Soll [1983] RPC 407 ... 745

MYCOGEN/Modifying plant cells (T-694/92) [1998] EPOR 114 ... 399

Myriad v Association of Molecular Pathology ... 491

Najma Heptulla v Orient Longman Ltd [1989] FSR 598 (High Court of India) ... 89, 90

Napier v Pressdram Ltd [2009] EWCA Civ 443 ... 776

Nationsbanc Montgomery Securities LLC's Application [2000] ETMR 245 ... 687

Naturelle Trade Mark [1999] RPC 326 ... 645

Navitaire Inc v EasyJet Airline Co Ltd [2006] RPC 3 ... 42, 58, 60–62, 68, 137, 174

NEC Corp v Intel Corp 835 F 2d 1546 (1988) ... 60

Neil King's Trade Mark Application [2000] ETMR 22 ... 652

Nestlé SA's Trade Mark Application [2005] RPC 5; [2004] EWCA Civ 1008 ... 691

Network Ten Pty Ltd v TCN Channel Nine Pty Ltd (2004) 205 ALR 1 (HCA) ... 80

Neurim Pharmaceuticals v The Comptroller-General of Patents [2011] EWCA Civ 228 ... 454

Neutrogena Corporation v Golden Ltd [1996] RPC 473 ... 752

Newspaper Licensing Agency Ltd v Marks and Spencer plc [2003] 1 AC 551 ... 81, 82, 125, 142, 186

Newspaper Licensing Agency Ltd v Meltwater Holding BV [2010] EWHC 3099 (Ch); [2011] EWCA Civ 890 (CA) ... 42, 51, 59, 126

Newsweek Inc v BBC [1979] RPC 441 ... 753

NIC Instruments Ltd's Licence of Right (Design Right) Application [2005] RPC 1 (Patent Office) ... 342-343

Nichols plc v Registrar of Trade Marks (C-404/02) [2005] 1 WLR 1418; [2005] All ER (EC) 1 ... 594, 596, 597, 673, 675

Nichrotherm Electrical Co Ltd v Percy [1956] RPC 272; aff'd [1957] RPC 207 ... 778

Nieto Nuno v Fraquet (C-328/06) ... 661

Nils Svensson v Retreiver Sverige AB (C-466/12) ... 154

Nintendo Co Ltd v Playables Ltd & Another [2010] FSR 36 ... 199

Nintendo Co Ltd's Application (BL O/377/06) ... 417

NMSI Trading Ltd's Trade Mark Application (No 2449033B) [2012] RPC 7 ... 588

Noah v Shuba [1991] FSR 14 ... 95

Nokia Corporation v Her Majesty's Commissioners of Revenue & Customs [2009] EWHC 1903 (Ch); [2010] FSR 5 ... 860

Nokia Corporation v Her Majesty's Commissioners of Revenue and Customs (C-446/09 & C-495/09) [2012] ETMR 13 ... 861, 956

Nokia v Ipcom [2009] EWHC 3482 (Pat); [2011] EWCA Civ 6 ... 444

Nordmilch v OHIM (Oldenburger) (T-295/01) [2003] ECR II-4365 ... 601

Norman Kark Publications Ltd v Odhams Press Ltd [1962] 1 WLR 380 ... 734

Norowzian v Arks Ltd (No 2) [1999] FSR 79; [2000] FSR 363 ... 45, 57, 66, 67, 78, 124, 142

Northern Rock plc v The Financial Times Ltd [2007] EWHC 2677 (QB) ... 780

Norwich Pharmacal v Customs and Excise Commissioners [1974] AC 133 ... 949

Nottinghamshire Healthcare NHS Trust v News Group Newspapers Ltd [2002] EWHC 409 (Ch) ... 946, 947

Nova Productions Ltd v Mazooma Games Ltd [2006] RPC 14; [2007] RPC 25 (CA)... 43, 59, 60, 66, 68, 78, 93, 124, 516

Novartis AG v Johnson & Johnson Medical Ltd [2010] EWCA Civ 1039... 475

NOVARTIS II/ Transgenic plant (G1/98) [2000] OJEPO 111... 422, 423

Ntuli v Donald [2010] EWCA Civ 1276... 943

Numatic International Ltd v Qualtex UK Ltd [2010] RPC 25... 745, 752

Nungesser v Commission (C-258/78) [1981] ECR 45... 878

Nutrinova Nutrition Specialties & Food Ingredients GmbH v Scanchem UK Ltd (No 2) [2001] FSR 43... 944

NWL Ltd v Woods [1979] 3 All ER 614... 941

O2 Holdings Ltd v Hutchison 3G Ltd (C-533/06) [2006] EWCA Civ 1656; [2006] ETMR 55; [2008] ECR I-4231... 11, 548, 554, 593, 646, 661, 680, 681, 939

O2 Holdings Ltd's Trade Mark Application (No 2481567) [2011] RPC 22... 588

Oakley Inc v Animal Ltd [2006] RPC 9... 268

Oakley v OHIM (T-116/06) [2008] ECR II-02455... 642

Oasis Stores Ltd's Trade Mark Application [1998] RPC 631; [1999] ETMR 531... 661, 663

Oberhauser v OHIM—Petit Libero (Fifties) (T-104/01) [2002] ECR II-4359... 652

OBG Ltd v Allan, Douglas v Hello! and others [2007] UKHL 21... 805, 826

Occidental Petroleum's Application (BL O/35/84)... 427

Occlutech v AGA Medical [2011] 3 IPQ 283... 476

Och-Ziff Management Europe Ltd v Och Capital LLP [2010] EWHC 2599; [2011] ETMR 1... 624, 636, 646, 654–657, 670, 674, 752

Ocular Sciences Ltd v Aspect Vision Care Ltd (No 2) [1997] RPC 289... 322, 325, 326, 332, 337-338, 348, 781

Office Cleaning Services Ltd v Westminster Window and General Cleaning Cleaners Ltd (1946) 63 RPC 39... 742, 750

Office of Communications v Information Commissioner [2010] UKSC 2... 797

OHIM v BORCO-Marken-Import Matthiesen (C-265/09 P) [2010] ECR I-08265... 600

OHIM v Celltech R&D Ltd (C-273/05) [2007] ETMR 52... 598, 599

OHIM v Erpo Möbelwerk (C-64/02 P) [2004] ECR I-10031... 591, 599

OHIM v Shaker (C-334/05) [2007] ECR I-4529... 648, 656

OHIM v Wrigley (Doublemint) (C-191/01) [2004] ETMR 88... 590, 591, 594

Oilfield Publications Ltd v MacLachlan 1989 GWD 26-1128... 95

Omega Spielhallen GmbH (C-36/02)... 615

Omnipharm Ltd v Merial [2011] EWHC 3393 (Pat); [2013] EWCA Civ 2... 451, 780

Opinion 1/09 (Re creation of a unified patent litigation system) [2011] ECR I-1137... 373

Oracle America Inc v M-Tech Data Ltd [2012] UKSC 27; [2012] 1 WLR 2026; [2012] FSR 2... 862, 899

Orifarm and others v Merck & Co Inc [(C-400/09) 2012] 1 CMLR 10... 853

Origins Natural Resources v Origin Clothing [1995] FSR 280... 642, 646

Oscar Bronner GmbH & Co KG v Mediaprint (C-7/97) [1998] ECR I-7791... 889, 895, 898

OSCAR Trade Mark [1979] RPC 173... 622

Osteoblast-Neuronal cell transdifferentiation/ KANEKA (T1156/09) 1.6.2012... 504

O'Sullivan and another v Management Agency [1985] QB 428... 909

P Henkel v OHIM (C-144/06) [2007] ECR I-8109... 607

Padawan SL v Sociedad General de Autores y Editores de Espana (SGAE) (C-467/08) [2010] ECR I-10055... 256, 988

Pago v Tirolmilch (C-301/07) [2009] ECR I-09429... 661

Painer (Eva-Maria) v Standard Verlags GmbH (C-145/10) [2012] ECDR 6... 50, 51, 70, 191, 982

PAKI Logistics GmbH v OHIM (T-526/09) [2011] ECR II-00346... 615

Pall Corporation v Commercial Hydraulics (Bedford) Ltd [1990] FSR 329... 433

Panayiotou and others v Sony Music Entertainment [1994] EMLR 229... 909

Parfums Christian Dior and Parfums Christina Dior BV v Evora BV (C-337/95) [1998] RPC 166... 553, 678, 854

Parfums Givenchy SA v Designer Alternative Ltd [1994] RPC 243... 668

Park Court Hotel Ltd v Trans-World Hotels Ltd [1970] FSR 89)... 743

Parke, Davis v Probel (C-24/67) [1968] ECR 55... 844, 886, 887, 915

Parker-Knoll Ltd v Knoll International Ltd [1962] RPC 265 (HL)... 749

Parker v Tidball [1997] FSR 680... 334

Parks-Cramer Co v GW Thornton & Sons Ltd [1966] RPC 407 (CA)... 448

Paroc Oy AB v OHIM (T-175/08) 8 February 2011 ('insulate for life')... 600

Pasterfield v Denham [1999] FSR 168... 103, 104

Patel v Allos Therapeutics Inc 2008 WL
  2442985 (Ch)... 693
Paterson Zochonis Ltd v Merfarken Packaging
  Ltd [1983] FSR 273... 756
Peak Holding AB v Axolin-Elinor AB (C-16/03)
  [2004] ECR I-11313... 858, 859
Pearce v Ove Arup Partnership Ltd [2000] Ch
  403; [2000] 3 WLR 332; [1999] 1 All ER 769;
  [1999] FSR 525... 973, 983
Pebble Beach Co v Lombard Brands Ltd 2002
  SLT 1312... 755
Peck v United Kingdom (App No 44647/98)
  [2003] EMLR 15; (2003) 36 EHRR 41... 806
Peek & Cloppenburg KG v Cassina SpA
  (C-456/06) [2008] ECR I-2731... 840
Pegasus Security Ltd v Gilbert 1989 GWD
  26–1186... 736
Pensher Security Door Co Ltd v Sunderland
  City Council [2000] RPC 249 (CA)... 164
PENSION BENEFIT SYSTEMS/Controlling
  pension benefits systems (T931/95) [2002]
  EPOR 52... 517, 518, 525, 534
PepsiCo, Inc v Grupo Promer Mon Graphic SA
  (C-281/10 P) [2012] FSR 5... 273, 278, 280,
  281, 282
Perfetti Van Melle SpA v OHIM (C-353/09 P)
  [2011] ECR I-00012... 648
Performing Right Society v Rangers FC
  Supporters Club 1974 SC 49... 148, 149
Perry v Truefitt (1842) 6 Beav 66... 728
Perusahaan Otomobil Nasional v OHIM
  (T-581/08) [2011] ECR II-00323... 662
Peter Waterman v CBS [1993] EMLR 27... 735
Peter Williams' Application (IPO Hearing
  Officer: BL O/038/07)... 415
PETTERSSON/Queuing System (T1002/92)
  1996] EPOR 1... 525
Pfizer v Eurofood Link (UK) [2000] ETMR
  896; [2001] FSR 3... 661, 667
PFIZER/Penem (T1042/92) [1995] EPOR
  207... 440
Pharmacia Corp v Merck and Co [2002] RPC
  775... 475
Pharmon v Hoescht BV (C-19/84) [1985] ECR
  2281 ECJ... 840, 844, 847
Phildar v OHIM (T-99/06) [2009] ECR II-
  00164... 648
Philips Electronics NV v Ingman Ltd [1998]
  2 CMLR 839; [1999] FSR 112... 897
Philips Electronics NV v Remington
  Consumer Products Ltd (No 1) [1999]
  ETMR 816; [1999] RPC 809; [1998] RPC
  283... 612, 614
Philips Electronics NV v Remington
  Consumer Products Ltd (C-299/99) [2002]
  ECR I-5475; [2003] RPC 2... 294, 551, 596,
  605

PHILIPS/Public availability of an email
  transmitted via the Internet (T2/09) [2012]
  EPOR 41... 438
Phillips v Eyre (1870) LR 6 QB 1... 971
Phillips-Van Heusen Corp v OHIM (T-292/01)
  [2003] ECR II-04335... 647, 658
Phones4U Ltd v Phone4u.co.uk Ltd [2006]
  EWCA Civ 244; [2007] RPC 5... 691, 692,
  733, 751, 763, 768
Phonographic Performance (Ireland) Ltd
  v Ireland (C 162/10) [2012] ECDR 15... 230
Phonographic Performance Limited v
  Department of Trade and Industry and
  another [2004] 3 CMLR 31 (ChD)... 221
Phonographic Performance Ltd v Lion
  Breweries [1980] FSR 1 (NZ)... 150
Phonographic Performance Ltd v The Appeal
  of the British Hospitality Association and
  Other Interested Parties [2008] EWHC 2715
  (Ch); 2008 WL 4975450... 914
Pie Optiek (C- 376/11)... 686
Pioneer Electronics Capital Inc v Warner
  Music Manufacturing Europe GmbH [1997]
  RPC 757... 467
Pippig Augenoptik v Hartlauer (C-44/01)
  [2004] All ER (EC) 1156; [2004] 1 CMLR 39;
  [2003] ECR I-3095... 679
Pirtek (UK) Ltd v Joinplace Ltd [2010] EWHC
  1641 (Ch)... 925
Pitman v Hine (1884) 1 TLR 82... 45, 58
PITNEY BOWES/Undeliverable mail
  (T388/04) [2010] EPOR 13... 526
PLANT GENETIC SYSTEMS/Glutamine
  Synthetase Inhibitors (T356/93) [1995]
  EPOR 357... 407, 423, 501, 506
Plastus Kreativ AB v Minnesota Mining and
  Manufacturing Co [1995] RPC 438... 984
Plentyoffish Media Inc v Plenty More LLP
  [2011] EWHC 2568; [2012] RPC 5 (Ch)...
  735, 971
PLG Research v Ardon [1995] RPC 287... 473
Plix Products v Winstone [1985] 1 NZLR 376;
  [1986] FSR 63 ... 43, 71
Point Solutions Ltd v Focus Business Solutions
  Ltd [2006] FSR 31... 935
Pollard v Photographic Co (1889) 40 Ch D
  345... 110
Polymasc Pharmaceuticals v Charles [1999]
  FSR 711... 785
POLYMER POWDERS/Allied Colloids
  (T39/93) [1997] OJEPO 134... 495
Portakabin Ltd v Primakabin BV (C-558/08)
  [2010] RPC 19... 664
Powell v Head (1879) 12 Ch D 686... 91
Powerflex Services Pty Ltd v Data Access
  Corporation (1996) 137 ALR 498 (Fed Ct
  Aus); aff'd (1999) 202 CLR 1 (HCA)... 58

Pozzoli SPA v BDMO SA [2007] FSR 37... 447, 476

PPG INDUSTRIES/Disclaimer (G01/03) [2004] OJEPO 413... 400

PPL v British Hospitality Association [2010] EWHC 209 (Ch)... 914

PPL v Reader [2005] EWHC 416 (Ch)... 946

Practice Notice (Patents Act 1977: Patentable subject matter) (No 2) [2008] Bus LR 978... 539

Praktiker Bau- und Heimwerkermarkte AG v Deutsches Patent- und Markenamt (C-418/02) [2006] Ch 144; [2006] 2 WLR 195; [2005] ECR I-5873; [2005] ETMR 88... 585–587

Premier Brands UK Ltd v Typhoon Europe Ltd [2000] FSR 767... 628, 669, 670

Premier Luggage & Bags Ltd v Premier Co (UK) Ltd [2002] EWCA Civ 387... 675

Price Waterhouse v BCCI (In Liquidation) (No 3) [1997] 3 WLR 849; [1998] Ch 84... 789

Primark Stores Ltd v Lollypop Clothing Ltd [2001] FSR 37 (Ch D)... 641

Prince Albert v Strange (1848) 2 De G & Sm 652 (64 ER 293); aff'd (1849) 1 Mac & G 25 (41 ER 1171)... 97, 794, 806

Prince Jefri Bolkiah v KPMG [1999] 2 WLR 215; [1999] 2 AC 222 (HL)... 789

Prince plc v Prince Sports Group Inc [1998] FSR 21... 689, 933

Printers & Finishers Ltd v Holloway [1965] 1 WLR 1... 776

Pro Sieben Media AG v Carlton UK Television Ltd [1999] FSR 610 (CA)... 182

Proactive Sports Management Ltd v Rooney [2010] EWHC 1807; [2011] EWCA Civ 1444... 825, 909

ProCD v Zeidenberg 86 F 3d 1447 (7th Cir, 1996)... 203, 205

Procter & Gamble Co v OHIM (C-383/99) [2002] Ch 82; [2002] 2 WLR 485; [2002] All ER (EC) 29; [2001] ECR I-6251 ... 597, 673

Procter & Gamble Co v OHIM (T-241/05, T-262/05–T-264/05, T-346/05, T-347/05, and T-29/06–T-31/06) [2007] ECR II-01549... 595

Procter & Gamble Co v Reckitt Benckiser (UK) Ltd (CA) [2008] FSR 8 (CA)... 278, 282, 283, 288, 311

Procter & Gamble v OHIM (C-468/01–C-472/01) [2004] ECR I-5141... 591, 593, 599

Productores de Música de España v Telefónica de España SAU (C-275/06) [2008] ECR I-00271... 918

Protecting Kids the World Over (PKTWO) Ltd's Patent Application [2011] EWHC 2720 (Pat); [2012] RPC 13... 409, 540

Provident Finance Group v Hayward [1989] 3 All ER 298... 785

PRS v Bray UDC [1930] AC 377 (PC)... 157

PRS v Ciryl Theatrical Syndicate [1924] 1 KB 1... 156

PRS v Harlequin Record Shops [1979] 1 WLR 851... 148, 149

PRS v Hawthorns Hotel (Bournemouth) Ltd [1933] Ch 855... 148

PRS v Kwik-Fit Group Ltd [2008] ECDR 2... 150, 156, 164

Psytech International Ltd v OHIM (T-507/08) [2011] ECR II-00165... 594, 601, 608, 627

Purefoy Engineering Co Ltd v Sykes Boxall & Co Ltd (1955) 72 RPC 89... 130, 756

Quantel Ltd v Spaceward Microsystems Ltd [1990] RPC 83... 438

Quick [1959] GRUR 182... 665

Quick Draw LLP v Global Live Events LLP [2012] EWHC 233 (Ch)... 941

Quilty v Windsor 1999 SLT 346... 776

Quorn Hunt's Application v Opposition of Marlow Foods Ltd [2005] ETMR 11 ... 938

R Griggs Group Ltd and others v Evans and others [2005] Ch 153; [2004] EWHC 1088 (Ch); [2005] 2 WLR 513... 975, 981

R v Anne Muir, Ayr Sheriff Court http://www.law.ed.ac.uk/sln/blogentry.aspx?blogentryref=8657... 253

R v Boulter (Gary) [2008] EWCA Crim 2375; [2009] ETMR 6... 634, 954

R v Department of Health, ex p Source Infomatics (No 1) [2001] QB 424; [2000] 2 WLR 940 (CA)... 782, 788

R v Gilham [2009] EWCA Crim 2293 (CA)... 200

R v Higgs (Neil Stanley) [2008] FSR 34 (CA)... 200

R v James Rupert Isaac [2004] EWCA Crim 1082... 635

R v Johnstone [2003] UKHL 28; [2003] 1 WLR 1736; [2003] 3 All ER 884; [2003] 2 Cr App R 33; [2004] ETMR 2... 634, 953

R v Licensing Authority, ex p Smith Kline & French Laboratories Ltd (No 1) [1990] 1 AC 64... 776

R v Malik [2011] EWCA Crim 1107... 953

R v Registered Designs Appeal Tribunal, ex p Ford Motor Co [1995] 1 WLR 18 (HL)... 324

R v Rock & Overton (2010) T20097013, Gloucester Crown Court... 253

R v Secretary of State for Home Department, ex p S [2012] EWHC 955 (Admin)... 780

R (on the application of British Telecommunications Plc) v Secretary of

State for Business, Innovation and Skills [2012] 2 CMLR 23... 254

R (on the application of Ford) v Press Complaints Commission [2001] EWHC Admin 683, 2002 EMLR 5... 806

R (on the application of Northern Foods plc) v Department for Environment, Food and Rural Affairs [2005] EWHC 2971... 716

R (Veolia EA Nottinghamshire Ltd) v Nottinghamshire County Council [2010] EWCA Civ 1214... 796

Radio Rentals Ltd v Rentals Ltd (1934) 51 RPC 407... 743

Radio Taxicab (London) Ltd v Owner Drivers Radio Taxis Services [2004] RPC 19 (Ch D)... 692

Radio Telefis Eireann v EC Commission [1991] ECR II-485... 23

Rado Uhren AG's Trade Mark Application (C-55/01) [2003] ECR I-03161... 591

Raleigh International Trade Mark [2001] RPC 11... 652

Ranbaxy (UK) Ltd and another v Warner-Lambert Co [2005] EWHC 2142; [2007] RPC 4 (Pat)... 440, 453

Ratiopharm GmbH v Napp Pharmaceutical Holdings Ltd [2009] RPC 18... 480

Ravensburger v OHIM (Educa Memory Game/ Educa) (C-370/10) [2011] ECR I-00027... 653

Ravenscroft v Herbert [1980] RPC 193... 133, 134, 946

Ravil SARL v Bellon import SARL, Biraghi SpA (C-469/00) [2003] ECR I-5053; [2004] ETMR 22... 717

Raytheon Co v Comptroller General of Patents, Designs and Trade Marks [2007] EWHC 1230 (Pat)... 515

Raytheon Co's Application [1993] RPC 427... 542

RCA Corp v John Fairfax & Sons Ltd [1982] RPC 91 (NSW Supreme Court)... 156

RCA v Pollard [1983] Ch 135... 220

Really Virtual Co Ltd v UK Intellectual Property Office [2012] EWHC 1086 (Ch)... 407, 417, 541

Reckitt & Coleman Products v Borden Inc [1990] RPC 341; [1990] 1 WLR 491; 1 All ER 873... 731, 745, 752, 753

Reckitt Benckiser (Espana) SL v OHIM (T-126/03) [2005] ECR II 2861... 628

Red Dot Technologies Ltd v Apollo Fire Detectors Ltd [2007] EWHC 1166 (Ch)... 941

Red Sea Insurance v Bouygues [1995] AC 190... 971, 973

Reddaway v Banham [1896] AC 199... 742

Redrow Homes Ltd v Bett Brothers plc [1999] 1 AC 197; [1998] 1 All ER 385; [1998] FSR 345... 946

Redwood Music Ltd v Feldman & Co Ltd [1979] RPC 385... 91

Reed Executive plc and another v Reed Business Information Ltd and others [2004] ETMR 56; [2004] EWCA Civ 159... 643, 653, 702, 749, 768

Rees v Melville [1911–16] MCC 168... 133

Referral under Art. 112 (1)(a) EPC by the Technical Board of Appeal (T 992/03) (Methods for treatment by surgery) to the Enlarged Board of Appeal; Decision of the Enlarged Board of Appeal [2010] EPOR 25... 428

Regeneron Pharmaceuticals Inc v Genentech Inc [2012] EWHC 657 (Pat); [2013] EWCA Civ 93... 477, 497

Regina Glass Fibre Ltd v Werner Schuller [1972] FSR 141; [1972] RPC 229... 779

Reklos v Greece [2009] EMLR 16... 808, 811

Religious Technology Center v Lerma, 1996 WL 633131 (ED Va)... 182

Religious Technology Center v Netcom On-Line Communication Service 907 F Supp 1361 (ND Cal, 1995)... 182

Research in Motion UK Ltd v Inpro Licensing SARL [2006] RPC 20; [2007] EWCA Civ 51... 414, 506

Research in Motion UK Ltd v Visto Corporation [2008] EWCA Civ 153... 979, 985

Resolution 1165 (2005) 40 EHRR 1... 812

Response Handling v BBC [2007] CSOH 102... 941

Revlon Inc v Cripps & Lee [1980] FSR 85 (CA)... 739, 758

Rewe-Zentral AG v Bundesmonopolverwaltung fur Branntwein (120/78) [1979] ECR 649... 835

Rickless v United Artists Corp [1988] QB 40... 220

RICOH/Environmental impact information (T1147/05) [2008] EPOR 34... 527

Riemann and Co v Linco Care Ltd [2007] EWHC 3466 (Ch)... 939

RJW & SJW v The Guardian newspaper & Person or Persons Unknown (Claim no. HQ09)... 943

Roadshow Films Pty Ltd v iiNet Ltd [2012] HCA 16... 161

Robb v Green [1895] 2 QB 315... 784

Robelco v Robeco Groep (C-23/01) Robelco v Robeco Groep NV [2002] ECR I-10913... 638

Robert Allan & Partners v Scottish Ideal Homes 1972 SLT (Sh Ct)... 69

Roberton v Lewis [1976] RPC 169... 52

Robin Ray v Classic FM plc [1998] FSR 622... 42, 87

Roche Nederland BV and others v Primus and another (C-539/03) [2006] All ER (D) 186 (Jul),... 467, 980, 981

Roche Products Ltd v Kent Pharmaceuticals Ltd [2006] EWCA Civ 1775... 858

Rock Refrigeration Ltd v Jones [1997] 1 All ER 1 (CA)... 783

Rockwater v Technip France SA and another [2004] EWCA CIV 381; [2004] RPC 46... 446

Roger Bullivant Ltd v Ellis [1987] FSR 172... 776, 777, 784, 791

Rolawn Ltd v Turfmech Machinery Ltd [2008] ECDR 13... 323

Rolex Internet Auction [2005] ETMR 25... 646

Rolls Royce v Dodd [1981] FSR 517... 763

Rose Plastics GmbH v Wm Beckett & Co [1989] FSR 113... 127

Rose v Information Services Ltd [1987] FSR 254... 58

ROUSSEL-UCLAF/Thenoyl Peroxide (T36/83) [1986] OJEPO 295... 427

Rowland v Mitchell (1897) 14 RPC 37... 819

RTE and ITP v Commission (Magill) (C-241/91 P & C-242/91 P) [1995] ECR I-743... 888–890, 898

Rugby Football Union: RFU and Nike v Cotton Traders [2002] ETMR 861... 590

Ruiz Picasso and others v OHIM—DaimlerChrysler (T-185/02) [2004] ECR II-01739... 649, 653

Ruiz-Picasso and others v OHIM (C-361/04) [2006] ECR I-00643... 647, 649, 653, 818

S (A Child) (Identification: Restrictions on Publication) [2004] UKHL 47; [2005] 1 AC 593; [2004] 3 WLR 1129... 812

SA Cnl-Sucal NV v Hag GF AG (C-10/89) [1990] ECR I-3711; [1991] FSR 99... 551, 841, 847

SA Prline v SA Communication & Sales and Sarl News Invest [2002] ECDR 2 (Trib de Comm)... 62

SA Société LTJ Diffusion v SA Sadas (C-291/00) [2003] ECR I-2799; [2003] ETMR 83; [2003] FSR 34... 576

Sabaf SpA v MFI Furniture Centres Ltd and others [2004] UKHL 45; [2005] RPC 10... 449

SABAM v Netlog NV (C-360/10) [2012] 2 CMLR 18 (ECJ)... 162

Sabel BV v Puma AG (C-251/95) [1998] 1 CMLR 445... 655, 656

Sabel v Puma [1997] ECR I-6191... 645, 647, 649, 655

Saint-Gobain PAM SA v Fusion Provida Ltd and another [2005] EWCA Civ 177... 451

Salon Services (Hairdressing Supplies) Ltd v Direct Salon Services Ltd 1988 SLT 417... 740, 741, 743

Saltman Engineering Co Ltd v Campbell Engineering Co Ltd (1948) 65 RPC 203... 777

Samsung Electronics (UK) Ltd v Apple, Inc [2013] ECDR 1 (HC); [2013] ECDR 2 (CA)... 278, 284, 286, 287, 288, 296, 935, 950

Samsung Electronics Co Ltd v Apple Retail UK Ltd [2012] EWHC 2277 (Pat)... 780

Samuel Smith Old Brewery (Tadcaster) v Lee (t/a Cropton Brewery) [2012] FSR 7... 933

Samuelson v Producers Distributing Co (1931) 48 RPC 580; [1932] 1 Ch 201... 89, 820

SanDisk Corp v Koninklijke Philips Electronics NV [2007] EWHC 332 (Ch); [2007] FSR 22... 899

Sandman v Panasonic UK Ltd [1998] FSR 651... 57, 129

Sands McDougall Pty Ltd v Robinson (1917) 23 CLR 49... 52

Sandvik Aktiebolag v KR Pfiffner (UK) Ltd [2000] FSR 17... 897

Sandvik Intellectual Property AB v Kennametal UK Ltd [2011] EWHC 3311 (Pat); [2012] RPC 23... 475

SANOFI/Enantiomer (T658/91) [1996] EPOR 24... 440

SARL Céline v SA Céline (C-17/06) [1996] FSR 205... 639, 674, 675

SAS Institute Inc v World Programming Ltd (C-406/10) [2010] ECDR 15; [2012] ECDR 22 (ECJ)... 37, 51, 60, 126, 137

SAT.1 Satellitenfernsehen GmbH v OHIM (C-329/02) [2004] ECR I-8317; [2005] 1 CMLR 57; [2005] ETMR 20... 591, 593, 599, 600

Sawkins v Hyperion Records Ltd [2005] RPC 32 (CA)... 52, 53, 67, 89, 101

SBJ Stephenson v Mandy [2000] FSR 286... 776

Scandecor Developments AB v Scandecor Marketing AB [2001] UKHL 21; [2001] 2 CMLR 30; [2001] ETMR 74... 552, 627, 739, 925

Scanvaegt International A/S and another v Pelcombe Ltd and another [1998] FSR 786... 474

Scarlet Extended SA v SABAM (C-70/10) [2012] ECDR 4 (ECJ)... 162, 708, 950

Schering Chemicals Ltd v Falkman Ltd [1982] QB 1... 780

Schering's Application [1971] RPC 337 ... 426

Schlumberger Holdings Ltd v Electromagnetic Geoservices AS [2009] RPC 19 ... 445, 495

Scholes Windows Ltd v Magnet Ltd [2002] FSR 10 (CA) ... 339, 340

Schroeder Music Publishing v Macaulay [1974] 1 WLR 1308; [1974] 3 All ER 616 ... 909

Schuh Ltd v Shhh ... Ltd [2011] CSOH 123 ... 941

Schutz (UK) Ltd v Delta Containers Ltd [2011] EWHC 1712 (Ch) ... 729

Schutz (UK) Ltd v Werit UK Ltd [2011] EWCA Civ 927; [2012] FSR 2; [2013] UKSC 16; [2013] 2 All ER 177 ... 466, 906

Schweppes v Wellingtons [1984] FSR 210 ... 141

Score Draw Ltd v Alan Finch (CBD Trade Mark) [2007] EWHC 462 (Ch); [2007] FSR 20 ... 608

Scottish Milk Marketing Board v Drybroughs 1985 SLT 253 ... 755

Scottish Union & National Insurance 1909 SC 318 ... 755

Seager v Copydex Ltd (No 1) [1967] FSR 211 ... 788, 794

Sebago Inc and Ancienne Maison Dubois v GB Unic SA (C-173/98) [1999] ECR I-4103 ... 856

Second Medical Indication/EISAI (G5/83) (2011) 42(3) IIC 257–271 ... 443

Sega Enterprises Ltd v Galaxy Electronics Pty Ltd (1997) 145 ALR 21 (Fed Ct of Australia) ... 78

Selected sperm/XY (T1199/08) 3.5.2012 ... 504

Sergio Rossi SpA v OHIM (T-169/03) [2005] ECR II-00685 ... 652

Series 5 Software Ltd v Clarke [1996] 1 All ER 853; [1996], FSR 273 ... 941

SGAE v Rafael Hoteles SL (C-306/05) [2006] ECR I-11519 ... 152, 153

Shanks v Unilever plc [2011] RPC 12 ... 464

Shaw Bros v Golden Harvest [1972] RPC 559 ... 821

Shelley Films Ltd v Rex Features Ltd [1994] EMLR 134 ... 77, 780, 787

Shenzhen Taiden Industrial Co Ltd v OHIM (Trade Marks and Designs) Bosch Security Systems BV, General Court (Case T-153/08) 22 June 2010 ... 279, 280, 281, 282, 284, 286

Shetland Times v Wills [1997] FSR 604 ... 58, 80, 152

Shevill and others v Presse Alliance [1995] 2 WLR 499 ... 976, 977

Shield Mark BV v Kist (t/a Memex) (C-283/01) [2004] Ch 97; [2004] 2 WLR 1117; [2004] All ER (EC) 277 RPC ... 583

Shopalotto.com's Application [2005] EWHC 2416 (Pat); [2006] RPC 293 ... 406

SIA Schenker v Valsts iene-mumu dienests (C-93/08) [2009] ECR I-00903 ... 955

Sieckmann v Deutsches Patent- und Markenamt (C-273/00) [2003] Ch 487; [2003] 3 WLR 424 ... 581

SIEMENS / Flow measurement (T245/87) (1989) OJEPO 171 ... 426

Siemens AG v VIPA Gesellschaft für Visualislerung und Prozeßautomatisierung GmbH (C-59/05) [2006] ECR I-02147 ... 680

Siemens Schweiz AG v Thorn Security Ltd [2008] EWCA Civ 1161; [2009] Bus LR D67 ... 905

Sifam Electrical Instrument Co Ltd v Sangamo Weston Ltd [1971] 2 All ER 1074 ... 130

Silberquelle GmbH v Maselli-Strickmode GmbH (C-495/07) [2007] ECR I-00137 ... 624

Silhouette International Schmied GmbH & Co KG v Hartlauer Handelsgellschaft mbH (C-355/96) [1998] ECR I-4799 ... 22, 856, 862

Sillitoe v McGraw Hill Book Co [1983] FSR 545 ... 123, 141, 175, 179, 181–183, 188

Sinanide v La Maison Kosmeo (1928) 139 LT 365 (CA) ... 58

Slater v Wimmer [2012] EWPCC 7 (PCC) ... 91, 92

Slee and Harris's Applications [1966] RPC 194; [1966] FSR 51 ... 519

Smart Technologies ULC v OHIM (C-311/11 P) ... 591

Smart Technologies v OHIM (T-523/09) [2011] ECR II-00107 ... 600

Smith Kline & French Laboratories (Australia) v Secretary to the Department of Community Services and Health [1990] FSR 617 ... 781, 786, 789, 790, 798

Smith, Kline & French Laboratories Ltd v Evans Medical Ltd [1989] FSR 513 ... 481

Smith, Kline and French Labs Ltd v Harbottle [1980] RPC 363 ... 467

Smithkline Beecham Biologicals SA v Connaught Laboratories Inc (Disclosure of Documents) [2000] FSR 1 ... 780

Snow v Eaton Centre Ltd (1982) 70 CPR (2d) 105 (Ont) ... 103

Societa Consortile Fonografici (SCF) v Del Corso (C-135/10) [2012] ECDR 16 ... 151, 231

Societá Esplosivi Industriali SpA v Ordnance Technologies (UK) Ltd [2008] RPC 12 ... 348-349

Societe des Produits Nestle SA v Cadbury UK Ltd [2012] EWHC 2637 (Ch) ... 581, 583

Société des Produits Nestlé SA v Mars Inc (R 0506/2003-2) [2005] ETMR 37 ... 661, 662, 671

Société des Produits Nestlé SA v Mars UK Ltd (C-353/03) [2005] 3 CMLR 12; [2005] ETMR 96; [2006] FSR 2 ... 605, 607

Societe Tigest SARL v Societe Reed Expositions France [2002] ECC 29 ... 62

Society of Accountants in Edinburgh v Corporation of Accountants (1893) 20R 750 ... 743, 761

SOHEI/General purpose management system (T769/92) [1996] EPOR 253 ... 524

Solar Thomson Engineering v Barton [1977] RPC 537 ... 69, 127

Solvay SA v Honeywell Fluorine Products Europe BV, Honeywell Belgium NV and Honeywell Europe NV (C-616/10) ... 975, 985

Sony Computer Entertainment Europe Ltd v Nuplayer Ltd [2006] FSR 9; [2005] EWHC 1522 (Ch) ... 698

Sony Computer Entertainment Ltd v Electricbirdland Ltd [2005] EWHC 2296 (Ch) ... 858, 981, 982

Sony Computer Entertainment v Owen [2002] EMLR 34 ... 198, 946

Sony Music Entertainment (Germany) GmbH v Falcon Neue Medien Vertrieb GmbH (C-240/07) [2009] ECDR 13 ... 225, 843

Sony Music v Easyinternetcafé Ltd [2003] FSR 48 ... 127

Sony v Ball [2005] FSR 9 ... 200

Sony v Saray [1983] FSR 302 ... 745, 759

Sot. Lelos Kai Sia EE and others v Glaxosmith-Kline Aeve Farmadeftikon Proionton (formerly Glaxowellcome Aeve) (C-468/06–C-478/06) [2008] ECR I-7139 ... 845, 891, 895

South African Music Rights Organisation Ltd v Trust Butchers (Pty) Ltd [1978] 1 SALR 1052 ... 148, 149

South Bucks District Council and another v Porter (No 2) [2004] UKHL 33 ... 416

Souza Cruz SA v Hollywood SAS R283/1999–3 [2002] ETMR 64 ... 552, 666

Spa Monopole v OHIM [2005] ETMR 109 (CFI) ... 668

Spain v Parliament and Council (C-146/13 & C-147/13) pending ... 374

Spalding v Gamage (1915) 32 RPC 273 (HL) ... 758

Specsavers International Healthcare Ltd v Asda Stores Ltd (C-252/12) [2012] EWCA Civ 24; [2012] ETMR 17 ... 624, 637, 646, 653, 655, 662, 665, 680, 729, 747, 749, 750, 939, 944

Speechworks Ltd v Speechworks International Incorporated [2000] ETMR 982 (OH) ... 700

Speed Seal Products Ltd v Paddington [1986] 1 All ER 91; [1985] 1 WLR 1327 ... 779

Spelling Goldberg v BPC Publishing [1981] RPC 280 (CA) ... 122

Spelman v Express Newspapers [2012] EWHC 239 (QB) ... 943

Sphere Time v OHIM and Punch SAS (T-68/10) 14 June 2011 ... 280

Sportwetten GmbH Gera v OHIM/Intertops Sportwetten GmbH (T-140/02) [2006] ETMR 15 ... 615

Spraymiser Ltd & Snell v Wrightway Marketing Ltd [2000] ECDR 349 ... 339

Staeng Ltd's Patent [1996] RPC 183 ... 457, 460

Stafford-Miller's Application [1984] FSR 258 ... 426

STAIGER Trade Mark [2004] RPC 33 ... 571

Standen Engineering v Spalding & Sons [1984] FSR 554 ... 157

Stanelco Fibre Optics Ltd's Applications [2005] RPC 15 ... 456

Stannard v Reay [1967] RPC 589 ... 734

Star Industrial v Yap Kwee Kor [1976] FSR 256 (PC) ... 734

Starbucks (HK) Ltd v British Sky Broadcasting Group plc [2012] EWHC 3074 (Ch) ... 699

STATE OF ISRAEL/Tomatoes II (T1242/06) [2012] EPOR 42 ... 501

State Street Bank and Trust Co v Signature Financial Group 149 F 3d 1368 (Fed Cir, 1998) ... 527

Stephens v Avery [1988] 2 WLR 1280; [1988] 2 All ER 477; [1988] FSR 510; [1988] Ch 449 ... 778

Stephenson Jordan and Harrison v Macdonald and Evans (1952) 69 RPC 10 ... 95, 787, 791

Stichting de Thuiskopie v Opus Supplies Deutschland GmbH, Mijndert van der Lee and Hananja van der Lee (C-462/09) [2011] ECR I-05331 ... 256, 988

Stichting Natuur v College voor toelating van gewasbeschermingsmiddelen en biociden (C-266/09) ... 797

Stilton Trade Mark [1967] RPC 173 ... 620

Storck v OHIM (C-25/05 P) [2006] ECR I-5719 ... 591, 605–607

Strigl v Deutsches Patent- und Markenamt (C-90/11) ... 590, 592

Stringfellow v McCain Foods [1984] FSR 413 ... 755

Stuart v Barrett [1994] EMLR 448 ... 88

Sun Microsystems Inc v Amtec Computer Corporation Ltd [2006] EWHC 62 (Ch); [2006] FSR 35 ... 861, 898, 944

Sun Valley Foods Ltd v Vincent [2000] FSR 825... 791

Surface Technology v Young [2002] FSR 25... 786, 787

Sweeney v Macmillan Publishers Ltd [2002] RPC 35... 41

Syfait v GSK [2005] ECR I-7139... 846

Symbian Ltd's Application [2008] EWCA Civ 1066; [2009] RPC 1... 408, 413, 415, 514, 539

Syndicat international des moniteurs de ski— École de ski international (3IMS—École de ski internationale) v OHIM (T-41/10) [2011] ECR II-00126... 616, 617

Synetairismos Farmakopoion Aitolias & Akarnanias (Syfait) and others v GlaxoSmithKline plc [2005] ECR I-4609... 845

Synthon BV v SmithKline Beecham [2006] RPC 10... 434–436, 444, 478

SYSTRAN/Translating natural languages (T1177/97) [2005] EPOR 13... 523

Taittinger SA v Allbev Ltd [1993] FSR 641... 753, 761, 762, 764

Takeda Chemical Industries Ltd's SPC Applications (No 3) [2004] RPC 3... 454

Talk of the Town v Hagstrom (1991) 19 IPR 649... 73

Tate & Lyle Technology Ltd v Roquette Frères [2010] FSR 1; [2010] EWCA 1049... 411

Tate v Thomas [1921] 1 Ch 503... 87

Taverner Rutledge v Trexapalm [1977] RPC 275... 822

Technip France SA's Patent [2004] RPC 46... 476

Technograph v Mills & Rockley [1972] RPC 346... 445

Telecommunications Services Ltd v Chief Constable of West Yorkshire [2011] EWHC 2892 (Ch)... 51

TELEMECHANIQUE/Single sale (T482/89) [1992] OJEPO 646... 432

TELETRONICS/Cardiac pacing (T82/93) [1996] OJEPO 274... 431

Television New Zealand v Newsmonitor Services [1994] 2 NZLR 91 (High Ct NZ)... 176

Telsonic AG's Patent [2004] RPC 38... 476

Telstra Corporation Ltd v Australasian Performing Right Association Ltd (1997) 191 CLR 140 (HCA)... 149

Temple Island Collections Ltd v New English Teas Ltd [2012] FSR 9... 51, 70, 134

Terrapin Ltd v Builders Supply Co (Hayes) Ltd [1967] RPC 375... 788, 791

Terry v Persons Unknown [2010] 1 FCR 659... 943

Tesco Stores Ltd v Elogicom Ltd [2007] FSR 4 (Ch)... 768

Teva UK Ltd v AstraZeneca AB [2012] EWHC 655 (Pat)... 453

Teva v Gentili [2003] EWHC 5 (Pat); [2003] EWCA Civ 1545... 451

Thames Hudson Ltd v Design and Artists Copyright Society Ltd [1995] FSR 153... 953

Theakston v MGN Ltd [2002] EWHC 137 (QB); [2002] EMLR 22... 810

Thistle v Thistle Telecom Ltd 2000 SLT 262... 747

Thomas v Farr plc and Hanover Park Commercial Ltd [2007] EWCA Civ 118; [2007] ICR 932; [2007] IRLR 419... 785

Thomas v Pearce [2000] FSR 718 (CA)... 787

THOMSON / Cornea (T24/91) [1995] OJEPO 512... 426

Thomson v Dailly (1897) 24R 1173... 756

Thomson v Robertson (1888) 15R 880... 756

Threeways Pressings Ltd's Application [2012] RPC 129... 440

Tidy v Natural History Museum Trustees (1995) 37 IPR 501... 104

Tierce Ladbroke v Commission (T-504/93 P) [1997] ECR II-923... 889, 898

Tillery Valley Foods v Channel Four Television Corporation 2004 WL 1074218... 778

Tod's SpA and Tod's France SARL v Heyraud SA (C-28/04) [2005] ECR I-05781... 970

Tolley v Fry [1931] AC 333... 823

Topps Company Inc v Tom Hannah Agencies Ltd 1999 GWD 40–1957... 751

Torrington Manufacturing Co v Smith & Sons (England) Ltd [1966] RPC 285... 779

Toshiba Europe v Katun Germany (C-112/99) [2001] ECR I-7945... 680

TOSHIBA/Environmental impact estimation (T1029/06) [2010] EPOR 13... 526

Toth v Emirates & Anor [2012] EWHC 517 (Ch)... 690

Townsend's Patent Application [2004] EWHC 482 (Pat)... 418

Treadwell's Drifters Inc v RCL Ltd 1996 SLT 1048... 743, 820

Trebor Bassett Ltd v Football Association Ltd [1997] FSR 211... 633

Trimingham v Associated Newspapers Ltd [2012] EWHC 1296 (QB)... 810

Twentieth Century Fox Film Corporation & others v BT [2011] RPC 28; [2011] EWHC 2714 (Ch)... 162

Twentieth Century Fox v Newzbin [2010] ECDR 8... 154, 159, 160

Twinsectra Ltd v Yardley [2002] UKHL 12; [2002] 2 AC 164... 617

Tyburn Productions Ltd v Conan Doyle [1991] Ch 75; [1990] 1 All ER 909; [1990] 3 WLR 167; [1990] RPC 185 . . . 971, 972

UBS Wealth Management (UK) Ltd v Vestra Wealth LLP [2008] EWHC 1974 (QB); [2008] IRLR 965 . . . 791

UDV North America Inc v Brandtraders NV (C-62/08) [2009] ECR I-01279 . . . 631, 635

UK Channel Management Ltd v E! Entertainment Television Inc [2008] FSR 5 . . . 939

Ultraframe (UK) Ltd v Eurocell Building Plastics Ltd [2005] RPC 36 (CA) . . . 343

Ultraframe UK Ltd v Fielding [2004] RPC 24 . . . 458

Ultramercial v Hulu 657 F 3d 1323 (Fed Cir, 2011) . . . 528

UMG Recordings Inc and others v MP3.com Inc, 2000 WL 1262568 (SD NY) . . . 181, 193

Unilever (Davis's) Application [1983] RPC 219 . . . 426

Unilever plc v Griffin [2010] EWHC 899 (Ch) . . . 638, 824, 941

Union Carbide v BP Chemicals Ltd [1999] RPC 409 . . . 475

UNION CARBIDE/High tear strength polymers (T/396/89) [1992] EPOR 312 . . . 434

Unistraw Asset Holding Pty Ltd v Felföldi Edesseggyarto Kft (OHIM Third Board of Appeal (R 417/2009-3) [2010] ECDR 10 . . . 275, 291

United Biscuits (UK) Ltd v Asda Stores Ltd [1997] RPC 513 . . . 646, 748

United Brands Co v Commission of the European Communities (27/76) [1978] ECR 207 . . . 886

United Wire Ltd v Screen Repair Services (Scotland) Ltd [2001] RPC 24 . . . 466

Universal City Studios Inc v Corley 273 F 3d 429 (2d Cir, 2001) . . . 197

Universal City Studios Inc v Sony Corp of America 464 US 417 (1984) (US Supreme Court) . . . 157

Universal Display Corp v OHIM (T-435/11) . . . 598

Universal Music Australia Pty Ltd v Sharman License Holdings Ltd (2005) 220 ALR 1 (FCA) . . . 161

Universities UK (formerly the Committee of Vice Chancellors and Principals) v The Copyright Licensing Agency (Intervenors: Design and Artists Copyright Society) (CT 71/00, CT 72/00, CT 73/00, CT 74/00 & CT 75/01) [2002] RPC 36 . . . 914

Universities UK v Copyright Licensing Agency [2002] RPC 36 . . . 179, 188

University of London Press v University Tutorial Press [1916] 2 Ch 601 . . . 41, 47, 54, 58, 179, 181

UNIVERSITY OF UTAH/Linked breast and ovarian cancer susceptibility gene (T1213/05), unreported, September 2007 . . . 502

Upjohn (Kirkton's) Application [1976] RPC 324 . . . 426

Upjohn v Paranova (C-379/97) [1999] ECR I-6927 . . . 849, 850

US Tiffany v eBay 600 F 3d 93 at 103 (2010) . . . 707

US v Microsoft Corp 231 F Supp 2d 144 (DCC 2002) . . . 892

Valensi v British Radio Corporation [1973] RPC 337 . . . 478

Van Doren + Q GmbH v Lifestyle + Sportswear Handelsgesellschaft GmbH (C-244/00) [2003] ECR I-3051; [2003] 2 CMLR 6 . . . 861

Van Dusen v Kritz [1936] 2 KB 176 . . . 164

Van Zuylen Freres v Hag AC [1974] ECR 731 . . . 840, 841

Vedial v OHIM—France Distribution (C-106/03) [2005] ETMR 23 . . . 649, 651

Verathon Medical (Canada) Ltd v Aircraft Medical Ltd [2011] CSOH 19 . . . 470

Verein fur Konsumenteninformation v Henkel [2003] ILPr 1 ECJ (6th Chamber) . . . 976

Verein Radetzky-Orden (C-442/07) (Radetzsky) . . . 624

Vermaat and Powell v Boncrest Ltd [2001] FSR 5 . . . 76

Vermaat and Powell v Boncrest (No 2) [2002] FSR 21 . . . 164

Vestergaard Frandsen A/S v BestNet Europe Ltd [2009] EWHC 1456 (Ch); [2010] FSR 2; [2011] EWCA Civ 424 . . . 773, 780, 782, 949

VG Wort and others (C-457/11–C-460/11) . . . 256

VICOM/Computer-related invention (T208/84) [1987] OJEPO 14 . . . 411, 515, 520–522, 543

Victor Guedes Industria e Comercia SA v OHIM (C-342/09) [2010] ECR I-00134 . . . 599

Vigneux v Canadian PRS [1945] AC 108 (PC) . . . 156

Vincent v Universal Housing Co [1928–35] MCC 275 . . . 74

Vine Products v Mackenzie [1969] RPC 1 . . . 761

Virgin Atlantic Airways Ltd v Premium Aircraft Interiors Group Ltd [2009] ECDR 11 . . . 323, 325, 326, 346, 347, 471, 949

Virtual Map (Singapore) Pte Ltd v Singapore Land Authority and Anr [2009] SGCA 2... 69

Visser v Information Commissioner (EA2011/0188), 1 March 2012... 797

Visx Inc v Nidek Co Ltd and others (No 2) [1999] FSR 405... 477

VITAFRUIT [2004] ECR II-2811... 624

Vitakraft- Werke Wührmann & Sohn GmbH Co KG v OHIM (C-512/04) [2007] ECR I-00139... 649

Vlisco BV's Application [1980] RPC 509... 277

Vodafone Group plc and Vodafone Ltd v Orange Personal Communications [1997] FSR 34... 682

Volker Megel v OHIM (C-80/09) [2010] ECR I-00017... 598

Volvo v Veng (C-238/87) [1988] ECR 6211... 887, 888, 890, 898

Von Hannover v Germany (App Nos 40660/08 and 60641/08) [2012] EMLR 16... 826, 942

W v Egdell [1989] 2 WLR 689; [1989] 1 All ER 1089... 790

Wagamama Ltd v City Centre Restaurants plc [1995] FSR 713; [1996] ETMR 23... 552, 632, 655

Wagner International AG v Earlex Ltd [2012] EWHC 984 (Pat)... 435

Wainwright v Home Office [2003] UKHL 53; [2004] 2 AC 406... 806

Wainwright v United Kingdom (App No 12350/04) (2007) 44 EHRR 40... 806

Wake Forest University Health Sciences v Smith & Newphew plc [2009] EWHC 45 (Pat); [2009] FSR 11... 939

Walford v Johnston (1846) 20 D 1160... 61

Walter v Ashton [1902] 2 Ch 282... 742, 763

Walter v Lane [1900] AC 539... 52, 53

Wannabee Trade Mark, 6 November, 2000... 660

WARF/stem cells (G2/06) [2009] EPOR 15... 506, 507

Warheit and another v Olympia Tools Ltd and another [2002] EWCA Civ 1161... 474

Warner Bros v Christiansen [1988] ECR 2605... 843, 864

Warwick Film Productions v Eisinger [1969] 1 Ch 508... 94, 122

Waterford Wedgwood v Assembled Investment Ltd (C-398/07) [2009] ECR I-00075... 651, 652

Waterford Wedgwood plc v David Nagli Ltd [1998] FSR 92... 467

Waterlow Publishers v Rose, The Times, 8 December 1989 (CA)... 91, 94

Wee McGlen Trade Mark [1980] RPC 115... 758

Wellcome Foundation v Paranova (C-276/05) [2008] ECR I-10479... 852

WELLCOME/Pigs I (T116/ 85) [1989] OJEPO 13... 426

West (t/a Eastenders) v Fuller Smith & Turner [2003] EWCA Civ 48; [2003] FSR 44... 590

WEST DIRECT/Computer assisted telemarketing (T588/05) [2010] EPOR 12... 518

Westwood v Knight [2011] EWPCC 008... 729, 750, 768

WGN Continental Broadcasting Co v United Video Inc 693 F 2d 622 (7th Cir, 1982)... 78

Wham-O Manufacturing Co v Lincoln Industries Ltd [1985] RPC 127... 71, 73

Wheatley v Drillsafe Ltd [2001] RPC 7... 449, 473

Whelan Associates Inc v Jaslow Dental Laboratory Inc 797 F 2d 1222 (3rd Cir, 1986)... 135

White Horse Distillers Ltd v Gregson Associates Ltd [1984] RPC 61... 756

White v Withers LLP [2008] EWHC 2821 (QB)... 776

Wienerwald Holding AG v Kwan Wong Tan and Fong [1979] FSR 381 (Hong Kong)... 740

Wilkie v McCulloch (1823) 2 S 413... 822

Wilkinson Sword v Cripps & Lee [1982] FSR 16;... 758

William Grant & Sons Ltd v Glen Catrine Bonded Warehouse Ltd 2001 SC 901... 742, 765

William Grant & Sons Ltd v Glen Catrine Bonded Warehouse Ltd 1995 SLT 936; aff'd 2001 SC 901, 2001 SLT 1419... 756

William Grant & Sons Ltd v William Cadenhead Ltd 1985 SC 121... 742

Williamson Music Ltd v Pearson Partnership Ltd [1987] FSR 97... 123

Wilo Se v OHIM (T-282/09 & T-329/09) [2010] ECR II-00264... 593

Wilson v Broadcasting Corp of New Zealand [1990] 2 NZLR 565... 66

Wilson v Yahoo! UK Ltd [2008] EWHC 361 (Ch); [2008] ETMR 33... 704

Windsurfing Chiemsee and Wrigley v OHIM (C-191/01) [2004] 1 WLR 1728; [2004] All ER (EC) 1040; [2003] ECR I-12447; [2005] 3 CMLR 21; [2004] ETMR 9... 594, 597

Windsurfing Chiemsee Produktions- und Vertriebs GmbH v Boots-und Segelzubehor Walter Huber; Windsurfing Chiemsee Produktions und Vertriebs GmbH v Attenberger (C-108/97 & C-109/97) [2000] Ch 523; [2000] 2 WLR 205; [1999] ECR I-2779; [1999] ETMR 585... 591–593, 604, 938

Windsurfing International Inc v Tabur Marine (GB) [1985] RPC 59 . . . 443, 447–449

Windsurfing International v Commission [(C-193/83) 1986] ECR 611 . . . 876, 877, 898

Winters v Mishcon de Reya [2008] EWHC 2419 (Ch) . . . 789

Wintersteiger AG v Products 4U Sondermaschinenbau GmbH (C-523/10) . . . 977

Winward Industrie Inc's Trade Mark Application (C-54/01) [2003] ECR I-3161; [2005] 2 CMLR 44; [2003] ETMR 78; [2003] RPC 45 . . . 591

Wise Property Care Ltd v White Thomson Preservation Ltd [2008] CSIH 44 . . . 734

Wiseman v Weidenfeld & Nicolson [1985] FSR 525 . . . 87

WL Gore & Associates GmbH v Geox SpA [2008] EWHC 2311 (Pat) . . . 446

Wombles Ltd v Wombles Skips [1975] FSR 488 . . . 755, 822

Wood v Commissioner of Police of the Metropolis [2009] EWCA Civ 414; [2010] EMLR 1 . . . 811

Woodward v Hutchins [1977] 1 WLR 760; [1977] 2 All ER 751 . . . 779

Woolley v Ultimate Products Ltd [2012] EWHC 339 (Ch); [2012] EWCA Civ 1038 . . . 747, 752, 763

Wrn Ltd v Ayris [2008] EWHC 1080 (QB); [2008] IRLR 889 . . . 785

Wyeth's Application [1985] RPC 545 . . . 443

X (formerly known as Mary Bell) v SO [2003] EWHC 1101 (QB); [2003] EMLR 37 . . . 812

X (HA) v Y [1988] 2 All ER 648; [1988] RPC 379 . . . 778, 790

X v Kdg Mediatech AG (C-170/12 M) . . . 978

X v Persons Unknown [2006] EWHC 2783 (QB); [2007] EMLR 10; [2007] HRLR 4 . . . 809

Xentral LLC v OHIM (T-134/06) [2007] ECR II-05213 . . . 564

XEROX/Document summaries (T1086/07) [2012] EPOR 21 . . . 420, 523

Yeda Research and Development Co Ltd v Rhone-Poulenc Rorer International Holdings Inc and others [2008] RPC 1 . . . 457

Yell Ltd v Giboin, Zagg Ltd [2011] EWPCC 009 . . . 729, 735, 767

Yorma's AG v OHIM (Yorma's/NORMA) (T-213/09) [2011] ECR II-00019 . . . 653

Young v Robson Rhodes [1999] All ER 524 . . . 789

Zang Tumb Tuum Records Ltd v Johnson [1993] EMLR 61 . . . 910

Zero Industry Srl v OHIM (T-400/06) . . . 653

Zino Davidoff SA v A & G Imports Ltd and Levi Strauss & Co and Others v Tesco Stores Ltd and Others (C-414/99, C-415/99 and C-416/99) [2001] ECR I-08691 . . . 22, 857

Zino Davidoff SA v Bundesfinanzdirektion Südos (C-302/08) [2009] ECR I-05671 . . . 955

Zippo Trade Mark [1999] RPC 173 . . . 624

ZVS Zeitungsvertrieb Stuttgart GmbH v President of the German Patent-und Markenamt (C-43/08) [2009] ECR I-00020 . . . 561

ZYX Music GmbH v King [1997] 2 All ER 129 (CA) . . . 164

Table of statutes

Administration of Justice (Scotland)
Act 1972, s 1 ... 936

Broadcasting Act 1990, s 179(2) ... 202

Civil Jurisdiction and Judgments Act
1982 ... 974
Sch 8 ... 936
Communications Act 2003 ... 253
Companies Act 2006, s 69 ... 638
Competition Act 1998 ... 897
s 18 ... 929
Contracts (Applicable Law) Act
1990 ... 969
Copyright Act 1709 ... 31
Copyright Act 1911 ... 34, 75, 91
Copyright Act 1956 ... 35, 73
s 4(2) ... 95
s 4(3) ... 95
s 48 ... 128
s 48(1) ... 67
s 48(6) ... 150
Copyright, Designs and Patents Act
1988 ... 3, 5, 35
s 1(1) ... 44, 46
s 1(1)(b) ... 56, 67
s 1(1)(c) ... 81
s 1(2) ... 44
ss 1–8 ... 40
s 3(1) ... 40, 45, 66, 67, 515
s 3(1)(a) ... 61
s 3(1)(b) ... 59
s 3(1)(c) ... 59
s 3(3) ... 45
s 3A ... 40, 50, 64
s 3A(1) ... 61
s 3A(2) ... 46, 62
s 4(1) ... 68
s 4(1)(a) ... 74
s 4(1)(b) ... 74
s 4(2) ... 68, 71, 73, 74, 78
s 5A ... 46
s 5A(1) ... 79
s 5A(2) ... 79
s 5B ... 46
s 5B(2) ... 41, 78
s 5B(5) ... 41, 78
s 6(1) ... 80
s 6(1)(b) ... 80
s 6(1A) ... 81
s 6(2) ... 80
s 6(3) ... 92, 152

s 6(4) ... 80
s 6(6) ... 55, 81
s 8(1) ... 81
s 8(2) ... 46, 81
s 9(1) ... 85
s 9(2) ... 92
s 9(3) ... 93
s 9(4) ... 93
s 9(5) ... 94
s 10(1) ... 86
s 10(1A) ... 92
s 10(3) ... 90
s 11(1) ... 85, 90, 92
s 11(2) ... 85, 94, 95
s 12 ... 112, 113
s 12(1) ... 111
s 12(2) ... 94
s 12(8) ... 90
s 13A(2) ... 115
s 13B(6) ... 114
s 13B(9) ... 114
s 14(2) ... 81, 115
s 14(5) ... 55, 81, 115
s 15 ... 116
s 16(1) ... 121
s 16(1)(e) ... 42
s 16(2) ... 121, 156
s 16(3) ... 125
s 16(3)(a) ... 122, 133, 142, 147, 346
s 16(3)(b) ... 126
s 17(1) ... 142
s 17(2) ... 128, 138, 346
s 17(3) ... 42, 128
s 17(4) ... 78, 122, 142
s 17(5) ... 142
s 17(6) ... 120, 138, 171
s 18(1) ... 143
s 18(2) ... 143
s 18(4) ... 143
s 18A(1) ... 145
s 18A(2)(a) ... 146
s 18A(2)(b) ... 146
s 18A(3) ... 146
s 19 ... 148, 150
s 19(1) ... 147
s 19(3) ... 147
s 19(4) ... 150
s 20 ... 148, 150
s 20(1) ... 151
s 20(2) ... 151
s 20(2)(a) ... 151
s 20(2)(b) ... 151, 154

Copyright, Designs and Patents
   Act 1988 (*cont.*)
   s 21... 42, 132
   s 21(3)(a)... 155
   s 21(1)–(4)... 155
   s 21(3)(a)(i)... 138
   s 21(4)... 138
   ss 22–26... 122, 163, 164
   s 26(3)... 150
   s 28(1)... 203, 204
   s 28(4)... 180
   ss 28–76... 168
   s 28A... 139, 171, 174, 180
   s 29... 10, 142
   s 29(1)... 175
   s 29(2)... 178, 180
   s 29(3)(a)... 179
   s 29(3)(b)... 177, 179
   s 30... 11
   s 30(1)... 141, 181, 183
   s 30(1)–(3)... 175
   s 30(1A)... 184, 188
   s 30(2)... 185
   s 30(3)... 185
   ss 31A–F... 190
   s 31F(9)... 190
   s 32(1)... 188
   s 32(2)–(4)... 189
   s 32(2A)... 188
   s 32–36... 11, 188
   s 33... 189
   s 34... 189
   s 34(1)–(3)... 150, 191
   s 35... 189
   s 36... 142, 189
   s 36(3)... 204
   s 37(1)(a)... 146, 189
   ss 37–44... 189
   ss 38–42... 142
   s 40A... 146, 189
   s 44A... 190
   s 45(2)... 185, 191
   s 45(3)... 191
   ss 45–50... 191
   s 50A... 135, 171, 192, 204, 218
   s 50B... 127, 192
   s 50B(2)... 171, 175, 204
   s 50B(4)... 218
   s 50BA... 171, 192, 218
   s 50BA(2)... 175
   s 50C... 192, 204
   s 50D(2)... 171, 174, 204, 218
   s 51... 316, 324, 350–3
   s 51(1)... 350
   s 51(3)... 350, 351
   s 52... 262, 316, 321, 353–5
   s 52(4)... 354
   s 53... 316
   s 57(1)... 94

s 62... 128, 191
s 66(1)... 146
s 67... 150
s 70... 142, 193
s 71... 193
s 72(1)... 150, 164
s 72(2)... 164
s 72(3)... 150
s 73... 152
s 74... 190
s 77... 99
s 77(2)–(7)... 100, 102
s 78... 101
s 79(2)(a)... 56
s 80(1)... 103
s 80(4)(a)–(c)... 103
s 80(5)... 103
s 80(6)... 103
s 81... 105
s 82... 105
s 83... 103
s 84... 99, 110
s 85... 99
s 85(1)... 110
s 85(2)... 110
s 86... 112
s 87... 99
s 89(1)... 100
s 89(2)... 103, 110
s 90(2)... 908
s 90(3)... 95, 905
s 91(1)... 905
s 93A... 910
s 94... 99
s 96... 947
s 97(1)... 945
s 97(2)... 945
s 97A... 162
s 99... 945
s 100... 937
s 103... 99
s 103(2)... 99
s 104(2)... 85, 86, 96
s 107... 253, 953
s 107(1)... 952
s 107(1)(e)... 253
s 107(2)... 952
s 107(2A)... 253, 952
s 107(4)... 954
s 108... 945
s 109... 954
s 110... 953
s 111... 956
s 112... 956
ss 118–122... 914
s 128A... 913
s 130... 142
ss 136–141... 142
s 144(1)(a)... 914

s 144(1)(b)... 914
s 163(1)... 97
s 163(3)... 113
s 164... 114
s 164(1)... 97
s 165... 114
s 165(1)... 97
s 166... 114
s 166(1)-(5)... 97
s 166A-D... 97
s 171... 193
s 171(3)... 322
s 172(2)... 73
s 173(2)... 91
s 174... 179, 188
s 175... 144
s 175(2)... 107, 113
s 175(5)... 144
s 178... 91, 93, 183, 188
s 180(2)... 222
s 182(1)... 224
s 182(3)... 224
ss 182A-C... 223
s 182CA... 224, 230
s 182D... 230
s 183... 224
s 185(1)... 224
s 186(1)... 225
s 188(1)... 224, 225
s 191(2)-(4)... 224
s 191F-H... 230
s 191G(1)... 910
s 191J... 945
s 195... 945
s 196... 937
s 198(1A)... 953
s 198(5)... 954
s 199... 945
s 200... 954
s 204... 945
s 205C... 227
s 205D... 227
s 205E... 227
s 205F... 228
s 205G... 228
s 205I... 226
s 205J... 228
Pt III (ss 213-264)
s 213(1)... 337
s 213(2)... 323, 325
s 213(3)(a)... 330, 331
s 213(3)(b)(i)... 331-4
s 213(3)(b)(ii)... 301, 331
s 213(3)(c)... 329
s 213(4)... 337
s 213(5)... 320
s 213(6)... 323
s 214(1)... 344
s 214(2)... 324, 344

s 215(1)-(3)... 344
s 215(4)... 345
s 216(1)(a)... 340
s 216(1)(b)... 341
s 217(3)... 320
ss 217-221... 320, 321
s 221... 320
s 226(1)... 345, 348
s 226(1)(a)... 348
s 226(1)(b)... 348
s 226(2)... 346, 348
s 226(3)... 345
s 226(4)... 346
s 227... 346
s 228... 346
s 229(3)... 946
s 230... 945
s 231... 945
s 233(1)... 945
s 237... 10, 342
s 237(2)... 342
s 239... 343
s 253... 933, 934
s 255... 321
s 256... 321
s 263... 344
s 263(1)... 13, 323
s 263(3)... 345
s 296... 197
s 296(2)... 201
s 296A... 171, 192, 218
s 296B... 171, 174, 204, 218
s 296ZA... 199
s 296ZB... 200, 952
s 296ZE... 205
s 296ZE(10)... 206
s 296ZF... 200
s 296ZF(1)... 199
s 296ZF(2)... 199
s 296ZG... 201
s 297... 864
s 297A... 954
s 297B... 954
s 298... 864
s 298(1)... 201
s 298(2)... 201
s 299(1)(b)... 202
s 301... 112
Sch 1, para 11... 95
Sch 2... 225
Sch 5A, Part 1... 205
Sch 6... 112
Copyright, etc and Trade Marks (Offences and
    Enforcement) Act 2002... 560, 954
Copyright (Visually Impaired Persons)
    Act 2002... 190

Data Protection Act 1998... 253, 796
    s 2... 811

Digital Economy Act 2010... 142, 162, 248, 253
Dramatic Copyright Act 1833... 33
Dramatic and Musical and Performers'
    Protection Act 1958, s 2... 220

Engraving Copyright Act 1734... 33
Engraving Copyright Act 1766... 33
Engraving Copyright Act 1777... 33
Engraving Copyright Act 1836... 33
Enterprise Act 2002
    s 41(2)... 914
    s 55(2)... 914
    s 66(6)... 914
    s 75(2)... 914
    s 83(2)... 914
    s 138(2)... 914
    s 147(2)... 914
    s 160(2)... 914
    Sch 7... 914
Enterprise and Regulatory Reform Act 2013
    s 74... 354
    s 76... 316
    s 98... 316
    s 103(3)... 354

Fair Trading Act 1973... 919
Fine Arts Copyright Act... 33
Fraud Act 2006, s 4... 785
Freedom of Information Act 2000... 796
    s 40... 797
    s 41... 797
    s 43... 797
Freedom of Information (Scotland) Act
    2002... 796
    s 33... 797
    s 36... 797
    s 38... 797

Government of Wales Act 2006, Sch 10, para
    28... 98

Human Rights Act 1998... 27
    s 2... 813
    s 3... 196
    s 12... 773, 814
    s 12(3)... 941, 942

Law Reform (Miscellaneous Provisions)
    Act 1995... 969, 986
Law Reform (Miscellaneous Provisions)
    (Scotland) Act 1985, s 15... 776
Lectures Copyright Act 1835... 33
Legal Deposit Libraries Act 2003... 190
London Olympic Games and Paralympic
    Games Act 2006... 825

Parliament Act 1911... 114
Parliament Act 1949... 114
Patents Act 1902... 365

Patents Act 1977... 3, 365
    s 1(1)... 431
    s 1(2)... 414, 421, 431, 453, 487
    s 1(2)(b)... 411
    s 1(2)–(4)... 406
    s 1(3)... 421, 431
    s 1(4)... 421, 422
    s 1(5)... 420
    s 2... 432
    s 2(1)... 432
    s 2(2)... 432, 478
    s 2(3)... 433, 435, 478
    s 2(4)... 440
    s 2(6)... 399
    s 3... 443
    s 4... 453
    s 4(1)... 453
    s 4(2)... 399, 426
    s 4A... 406, 453
    s 4A(2)... 425
    s 4A(3)... 441, 442
    s 4A(4)... 400
    s 5(1)... 394
    s 5(2)... 394
    s 6(1)(b)... 945
    s 7(1)... 401, 456
    s 7(2)... 401
    s 7(2)(b)(c)... 456
    s 7(3)... 456
    s 7(4)... 401
    s 8... 401, 458
    s 13... 401, 456
    s 14(2)... 395
    s 14(3)... 369, 394
    s 14(5)... 396
    s 14(5)(a)... 430
    s 14(5)(c)... 395
    s 14(7)... 394, 433
    s 14(9)... 402
    s 15... 400
    s 15A... 401
    s 16(1)... 401
    s 17... 401
    s 17(5)... 409
    s 18... 401
    s 25(1)... 402
    s 27(1)... 402
    s 30... 454
    s 30(3)... 454
    s 30(4)(a)(b)... 454
    s 30(7)... 454
    s 33(1)... 455
    s 33... 906
    s 33(3)... 905
    s 36(1)... 457
    s 36(2)... 457
    s 36(3)... 454, 905
    s 36(3)(a)... 390, 457
    s 36(3)(b)... 457

s 36(6)... 905
s 37... 401
s 39... 458
s 39(1)... 459, 460
s 39(1)(a)... 459
s 40... 461
s 40(2)... 464
s 41... 461, 464
s 42(2)... 458
s 46... 455
s 46(4)... 455
s 47... 455
s 48... 10, 922
s 48(3)... 923
s 48A(1)... 923
s 48B... 923
ss 55–58... 10
ss 55–59... 456
s 56(2)... 456
s 57... 456
s 57A... 10
s 58... 454, 456
s 60... 11, 466
s 60(1)... 465, 466
s 60(1)(c)... 465, 467, 494
s 60(2)... 465
s 60(3)... 468
s 60(5)... 480
s 60(5)(a)... 313, 481
s 60(5)(b)... 313
s 60(5)(g)... 483
s 60(5)(h)... 483
s 61... 947
s 62(1)... 945
s 66(2)... 465
s 67... 454
s 67(1)... 465
s 68... 455, 906
s 69... 402, 465
s 70... 933, 934
s 72(1)... 369, 394, 477
s 72(1)(c)... 478
s 72(4A)... 390
s 74... 402
s 74A... 390
s 74B... 390
s 75(1)... 402
s 75(5)... 402
s 76(2)... 402
s 76(3)... 402
s 77... 393
s 78... 393
s 79... 433
s 89... 433
s 89A... 433
s 89B... 433
s 125... 469
s 125(1)... 404
Sch A2... 406, 421, 425, 494, 497

Patent Law Amendment Act 1852... 365
Patents Act 2004... 406
  s 1... 425
  s 2(5)... 402
  s 4... 390
  s 9... 390, 457
  s 10(3)... 464
  s 12... 933, 934
  s 13... 390
Patents and Designs Act 1907, s 93... 414
Patents and Designs Act 1919, s 93... 114
Patents, Designs and Trade Marks
    Act 1883... 365
Patents, Designs and Marks Act
    1986... 560
Performers Protection Act 1963... 220
Performers Protection Act 1972... 220
Plant Varieties Act 1997... 5
Plant Varieties and Seeds Act 1964... 5
Private International Law (Miscellaneous
    Provisions) Act 1995
  s 10... 972, 973
  s 11(1)... 972, 973
  s 12... 972
  s 13... 972, 973
Public Lending Right Act 1979... 189

Registered Designs Act 1949... 3, 267
  s 1(2)... 269, 272
  s 1(3)... 270, 298
  s 1B(1)... 274
  s 1B(3)... 277
  s 1B(4)... 277
  s 1B(5)... 289
  s 1B(6)... 290
  s 1B(8)... 299
  s 1B(8)–(9)... 273
  s 1B(9)... 299
  s 1C(1)... 293
  s 1C(3)... 297
  s 2... 277, 304
  s 2(1A)... 304
  s 2(1B)... 305
  s 3... 304
  s 3(3)... 305
  s 3A... 306
  s 3C... 306
  s 7(1)... 278, 310
  s 7(3)... 278, 311
  s 7A(1)–(3)... 313
  s 7A(2)(a)... 312
  s 7A(4)... 314
  s 7A(5)... 303, 314
  s 8(1)–(4)... 314
  s 8A... 314
  s 10... 925
  s 11... 314
  s 11ZA... 309
  s 11ZB... 308

Registered Designs Act 1949 (*cont.*)
  s 15A... 306
  s 15B... 306, 905
  s 20... 305
  s 24B... 945
  s 24C... 945
Regulation of Investigatory Powers
    Act 2000... 45, 796

Scotland Act 1998, s 92(3)... 97
Sculpture Copyright Act 1798... 33
Sculpture Copyright Act 1814... 33
Senior Courts Act 1981, s 72... 776
Statute of Anne 1709... 31, 32
Statute of Monopolies 1624... 365

Trade Marks Act 1938... 560, 585, 632,745
Trade Marks Act 1994 ... 4
  s 1... 577, 589
  s 2(2)... 728
  s 3... 558, 561, 588, 676, 677
  s 3(1)... 604
  s 3(1)(b)... 592, 593, 595, 688
  s 3(1)(b)–(d)... 608
  s 3(1)(c)... 589, 592, 594, 597
  s 3(1)(d) ... 589, 592, 594
  s 3(2)... 611
  s 3(2)(a)... 609
  s 3(2)(b)... 294, 609, 612
  s 3(2)(c)... 612
  s 3(3)... 614
  s 3(3)(b)... 616
  s 3(4)... 616
  s 3(5)... 616
  s 3(6)... 617, 622
  s 5... 588, 621, 640
  s 5(1)... 561, 641–3
  s 5(1)–(3)... 640
  s 5(2)... 561, 641, 642, 644, 652, 655, 659,
    661
  s 5(3)... 572, 658, 660
  s 5(4)... 571, 572
  s 5(5)... 622
  s 6(1)(a)... 622
  s 6(1)(b)... 571, 622
  s 6(1)(c)... 571
  s 6(2)... 571
  s 9... 562, 631
  s 9(3)... 641
  s 10 ... 588, 621, 640, 646
  s 10(1)... 558, 641–3, 690, 693, 941
  s 10(1)–(3)... 640, 698
  s 10(2)... 642, 644, 652, 655, 659, 661, 691,
    693, 941
  s 10(3)... 631, 658, 660, 667, 692, 693
  s 10(4)... 631

  s 10(5)... 632
  s 10(6)... 11, 679–82
  s 11... 673, 674
  s 11(2)... 673
  s 11(2)(a)... 674
  s 11(2)(b)... 676, 953
  s 11(2)(c)... 677
  s 12(2)... 848
  s 14... 947
  s 14(1)... 631, 641
  s 16... 945
  s 21... 933
  s 22... 555
  s 23(4)... 905
  s 24(1)... 555, 905
  s 24(2)... 906
  s 24(3)... 905
  s 25(3)... 906
  s 25(4)... 906
  s 30(1)–(5)... 631
  s 32... 556
  s 32(2)... 561
  s 32(3)... 561
  s 33(1)... 561
  s 34... 555, 556
  s 35... 561, 572
  s 35(1)... 571
  s 38... 561
  s 38(1)... 572
  s 38(2)... 572
  s 40... 562
  s 40(3)... 557
  s 44(1)... 557
  s 44(1)(c)... 556
  s 44(2)... 556
  s 46... 623, 925
  s 46(1)... 555, 626, 627
  s 46(5)... 555
  s 49... 618
  s 50... 618, 620
  s 56... 730, 735, 736
  s 56(2)... 567
  s 60... 572
  s 76... 562
  s 89... 956
  s 92... 953
  s 95... 15
  s 95(2)... 627
  s 97... 954
  s 98... 954
  s 103(2)... 641
  s 107... 631
  s 108... 561, 631
Trade Marks (Amendment) Act 1984... 560

Unfair Contract Terms Act 1977... 243

Table of statutory instruments

Artist's Resale Right Regulations 2006
(SI 2006/346)
reg 2... 107, 108
reg 3... 107, 108
reg 4... 108
reg 5... 107
reg 7... 107
reg 8... 107
reg 12... 108
reg 13... 108
reg 14... 107
reg 16... 108
reg 17... 109
Artist's Resale Right (Amendment)
Regulations 2009 (SI 2009/2792)... 107,
109
Artist's Resale Right (Amendment)
Regulations 2011 (SI 2011/2873)... 107,
109

Civil Procedure Rules 1998 (SI 1998/3132)
Pt 25... 936
PD 25A... 937
Community Design Regulations 2005
(S1 2005/2339), reg 2(5)... 934
Community Trade Mark Regulations 2006
(SI 2006/1027)... 564, 949
Company Names Adjudicator Rules 2008
(SI 2008/1738)... 638
Copyright, Designs and Patents Act 1988
(Amendment) Regulations 2010 (SI
2010/2694)... 913
Copyright (Educational Establishments)
Order 2005 (SI 2005/223)... 179
Copyright (Industrial Process and Excluded
Articles) (No 2) Order (SI 1989/1070)...
354
Copyright (Librarians and Archivists)
(Copying of Copyright Material)
Regulations 1989 (SI 1989/1212)... 189
Copyright and Related Rights Regulations
1996 (SI 1996/2967)... 221
Copyright and Related Rights Regulations
2003 (SI 2003/2498)... 171, 221
reg 24... 198
Copyright and Rights in Databases
Regulations 1997
(SI 1997/3032)... 5, 19, 61
reg 12... 215
reg 12(1)... 210, 212, 215

reg 13... 210
reg 14(1)... 213
reg 14(2)–(4A)... 214
reg 14(5)... 213
reg 15... 213
reg 16(2)... 217
reg 17... 214
reg 19... 219
reg 20... 218, 219
reg 20A... 218
reg 21... 213
reg 22... 213
reg 30... 214
Copyright and Rights in Performances
Regulations 1995 (SI 1995/3297)... 19
Copyright Rights in Performances (Moral
Rights, etc) Regulations 2006
(SI 2006/18)... 221, 225
Copyright and Rights in Performances
(Notice of Seizure) Order 1989 (SI
1989/1006)... 937
Copyright, etc and Trade Marks (Offences
and Enforcement) Act 2002
(Commencement) Order 2002
(SI 2002/2749)... 954

Design Right (Reciprocal Protection)
(No 2) Order (SI 1989/1294)... 320
Design Right (Semiconductor Topographies)
Regulations 1989 (SI 1989/1100)... 327
Duration of Copyright and Rights in
Performances Regulations 1995
(SI 1995/3297)... 19, 111, 221

Electronic Commerce (EC Directive)
Regulations 2002 (SI 2002/2013)
reg 17... 162
reg 19... 162
Environmental Information Regulations 2004
(SI 2004/3391), reg 12(5)(c)... 797
Environmental Information (Scotland)
Regulations 2004 (SI 2004/520)... 797

Intellectual Property (Enforcement, etc.)
Regulations 2006 (SI 2006/1028)... 906
reg 4(3)... 949

Legal Deposit Libraries Act 2003
(Commencement) Order 2004
(SI 2004/130)... 190

Olympics, Paralympics and London Olympics
    Association Rights (Infringement
    Proceedings) Regulations 2010
    (SI 2010/2477)... 825

Patents Regulations 2000 (SI 2000/2037)... 19,
    494
Patents Rules 2007 (SI 2007/3291)... 391
    Pt 5... 393
    r 5... 441
Patents (Fees) Rules 2007 (SI 2007/3292)... 12
Patents and Plant Variety Rights (Compulsory
    Licensing) Regulations 2002
    (SI 2002/247)... 923
Patents and Trade Marks (WTO) Regulations
    1999 (SI 1999/1899)... 922
Patents and Trade Marks (Fees) (Amendment)
    Rules 2010 (SI 2010/33)... 401

Registered Design Rules 1989
    (SI 1989/1105)... 305
    r 26... 271

Registered Designs Regulations 2001
    (SI 2001/3949)... 19, 268
Regulatory Reform (Patents) Order
    (SI 2004/2357), art 10... 905

Semi-conductor topography: Design
    Right (Semiconductor Topographies)
    Regulations 1989 (SI 1989/1100)... 5

Trade Marks Act 1994 (Commencement) Order
    1994 (SI 1994/2550)... 560
Trade Marks (Amendment) Rules 2001
    (SI 2001/2832)... 555
Trade Marks (Fees) Rules 2008 (SI 2008/1958),
    r 28... 556
Trade Marks (Proof of Use, etc) Regulations
    2004 (SI 2004/946)... 659

Unfair Terms in Consumer Contracts
    Regulations 1999 (SI 1999/2083)... 243

Table of EU legislation

Treaties and Conventions
Community Patent Convention 1975... 20
    Art 29(a)... 467
Community Patent Convention 1989
    (revised)... 20
Treaty on the Functioning of the European
    Union
    Art 34 (ex 28 EC)... 17, 21, 834, 837, 838
    Art 35... 834
    Art 36... 17, 21, 837, 838
    Art 57 (ex 50 EC)... 587
    Art 101 (ex 81 EC)... 10, 17, 22, 785, 869,
    873-885, 897-899, 915
    Art 101(1)... 879-881, 884, 885
    Art 101(2)... 879
    Art 101(3)... 879-884, 917
    Art 102 (ex 82 EC)... 10, 17, 22, 845, 869,
    885-899, 915, 916
    Art 114 (ex 95 EC)... 542
    Art 118... 18, 19, 234, 374
    Art 267 (ex 234 EC)... 845
    Art 345 (ex 295 EC)... 9, 17, 20, 21, 374,
    835, 837, 838
Treaty of Lisbon 2007... 19, 845

Regulations
Reg 17/62/EEC... 879
Reg 3842/86/EEC... 955
Reg 1768/92/EEC Supplementary Protection
    Certificate for medicinal
    products... 454
Reg 2081/92/EEC on Origin of Agricultural
    Products... 709
    Art 14(2)... 722
Reg 40/94/EC on Community trade
    mark... 19, 559, 562, 983
    Art 7(1)(c)... 600
    Art 8(1)(a)... 567
    Art 8(1)(b)... 567
    Art 8(5)... 567
    Art 9... 636
    Art 9(1)(c)... 665
    Art 15... 637
    Art 146... 955
Reg 2100/94/EC Community Plant Variety
    Rights ... 5
    Art 14(3)... 483
    Art 29... 925
Reg 1610/96/EC Supplementary Protection
    Certificate for plant protection
    products... 454

Reg 240/96/EEC on the application of
    Art 85(3) to Certain Categories of
    Technology Transfer Agreements... 22
Reg 1610/96/EC Plant Protection
    Products... 12
Reg 2790/1999/EC ... 926
Reg 44/2001/EC Brussels Regulation... 969
    Art 2... 974, 975
    Art 5... 974, 976
    Art 5(1)... 975, 976
    Art 5(3)... 976-978
    Art 6... 974
    Art 6(1)... 979-983
    Art 22... 974
    Art 22(4)... 973, 984-986
    Art 33... 990
    Art 34(1)... 990
    Art 36... 990
Reg 6/2002/EC Community Designs
    Regulation... 4, 19, 262, 267, 945
    Recital 10... 293, 296
    Recital 13... 304
    Recital 14... 273, 277, 278
    Recital 16... 355
    Recital 21... 358
    Recital 31... 315
    Recital 32... 315
    Art 3(a)... 269, 272, 273
    Art 3(b)... 270
    Art 3(c)... 298
    Art 4... 274
    Art 4(2)... 299
    Art 4(2)(a)... 300
    Art 4(2)-(3)... 273
    Art 4(3)... 299
    Art 5(1)(a)... 356
    Art 6(1)... 277
    Art 6(1)(a)... 356
    Art 6(2)... 277
    Art 7... 290
    Art 7(1)... 289
    Art 8(1)... 293, 295, 296
    Art 8(2)... 296
    Art 8(3)... 297
    Art 10(1)... 278, 310
    Art 10(2)... 278, 311
    Art 11(1)... 357
    Art 11(2)... 357
    Art 12... 308, 314
    Art 13(3)... 314
    Art 14... 306

Art 15... 307
Art 15(1)... 358
Art 15(3)... 358
Art 18... 307
Art 19(1)... 310
Art 19(2)... 358
Art 20... 313
Art 20(1)(a)... 312
Art 22... 313
Art 24... 308
Art 25... 309, 310
Art 27... 308
Art 29... 308
Art 32... 308
Art 33... 308
Art 36(2)... 307
Art 36(6)... 307
Art 45... 307
Art 47... 307
Art 51... 314
Art 52... 308
Art 67... 314
Arts 80–83... 306
Art 96(1)... 315
Art 96(2)... 315
Art 110(1)... 303, 304, 314
Reg 1/2003/EC Competition Rules
    Regulation... 880
Art 23(2)(a)... 884
Art 27(4)... 917
Reg 692/2003/EC, Art 1(1)... 718
Reg 1383/2003/EC... 955
Art 17(1)(b)... 956
Reg 1992/2003/EC, Art 5(4)... 955
Reg 772/2004/EC Technology Transfer Block
    Exemption Regulation ... 832, 926
Art 1... 881
Art 3(1)(2)... 882
Art 4(1)(2)... 882
Art 5... 883
Reg 1891/2004/EC... 955
Reg 510/2006/EC on the Protection
    of Geographical Indications and
    Designations of Origin for Agricultural
    Products and Foodstuffs... 709, 712, 718
Art 1... 713
Art 2... 713
Art 2(2)(b)... 716, 717
Art 2(3)... 714
Art 3(1)... 714
Art 3(2)... 715
Art 3(3)... 715
Art 3(4)... 721
Art 4... 715
Art 4(2)(c)... 716
Arts 5–7... 718
Art 8(1)... 719
Art 12... 720
Art 13... 719

Art 13(2)... 715
Art 14(1)... 721
Art 14(2)... 721
Reg 816/2006/EC Compulsory Licensing of
    Patents Relating to the Manufactureof
    Pharmaceutical Products for Export
    to Countries with Public Health
    Problems... 381
Reg 1901/2006/EC on medicinal products for
    paediatric use... 454
Reg 864/2007/EC Rome II ... 969, 986
Recital 26... 987
Art 4... 987
Art 6... 987
Art 8... 987
Art 8(3)... 988
Reg 593/2008/EC Rome I... 969
Art 2... 989
Art 9... 989
Reg 628/2008/EC... 719
Reg 207/2009/EC Community Trade Mark
    Regulation... 19, 562, 848
Art 1(2)... 605
Art 4... 577
Art 7... 588
Art 7(1)(b)... 591, 592
Art 7(1)(c)... 591, 592, 598, 601
Art 7(1)(e)... 608
Art 7(1)(f)... 614, 616
Art 7(1)(g)... 614
Art 7(1)(h)... 616
Art 7(1)(j)... 721
Art 7(2)... 605
Art 8 ... 588, 621, 640
Art 8(1)(a)... 641
Art 8(1)(b)... 644
Art 8(5)... 658, 661
Art 9... 588, 621, 640
Art 9(1)(a)... 641, 705
Art 9(1)(b)... 644, 705
Art 9(1)(c)... 658, 706
Art 9(2)... 631
Art 12... 597, 673
Art 13... 848
Art 14... 564
Art 15... 623
Art 16(1)... 906
Art 17(3)... 905
Art 28... 906
Art 34... 571, 572
Art 36... 564
Art 37... 564
Art 39... 564
Arts 41–43... 564
Art 45... 564
Arts 51–58... 564
Art 52... 617
Art 65... 564
Art 66... 618

Art 93(1)... 983
Art 96... 564
Art 98... 983
Art 101... 564
Art 106... 564
Art 112... 564
Reg 469/2009/EC Medicinal Products... 12, 454
Reg 566/2009/EC Protected Geographical
    Indications... 717
Reg 330/2010/EU Vertical Agreements Block
    Exemption Regulation ... 881
    Art 2... 926
    Art 2(3).., 926
    Art 4,, 926
Reg 461/2010/EU Technology Transfer Block
    Exemption Regulation... 881
Reg 1217/2010/EU Technology Transfer Block
    Exemption Regulation... 881
Reg 386/2012/EU... 956
Reg 1257/2012/EU on Patent Protection... 374
Reg 1260/2012/EU on Patent Protection
    translation arrangements... 374

Directives
Dir 84/450/EEC Misleading and Comparative
    Advertising (Amended)... 679
    Art 3a(1)... 681
Dir 87/54/EEC Legal Protection of
    Topographies of Semiconductor
    Products... 5, 15
Dir 89/104/EEC Trade Marks... 17, 559, 560
    Recital 9... 662
    Art 2... 577, 580, 581, 586
    Art 3... 582, 588
    Art 3(1)... 589
    Art 3(1)(b)... 592, 602
    Art 3(1)(c)... 591, 592, 598, 602
    Art 3(1)(g)... 819
    Art 3(3)... 580, 589
    Art 4... 588, 640
    Art 4(1)(a)... 641
    Art 4(1)(b)... 644
    Art 4(4)(a)... 658, 659
    Art 5... 588, 636, 640
    Art 5(1)... 639, 681
    Art 5(1)(a)... 641, 705
    Art 5(1)(b)... 641, 644, 659, 705
    Art 5(1)-(4)... 638
    Art 5(2)... 639, 658, 659, 665, 681, 706
    Art 5(5)... 639
    Art 6... 673
    Art 6(1)(a) .. 676
    Art 6(1)(b)... 676
Dir 91/250/EEC Software Directive... 37, 515
    Recital 7... 60
    Recitals 13-15... 60
    Art 1(3)... 49
Dir 92/100/EEC (repealed) Rental Right and
    Lending Right... 37, 145

Dir 93/83/EEC Satellite Broadcasting
    Directive... 37, 120, 221
Dir 93/98/EEC Harmonising the Term of
    Protection of Copyright and Certain
    Related Rights... 18, 19, 37, 111, 221
Dir 96/9/EC Database Directive... 37
    Recitals 1-12... 210
    Recital 17... 61, 63
    Recital 19... 64, 212
    Recital 21... 63
    Recital 28,.. 98
    Recitals 38 39... 210
    Recital 55... 214
    Art 3(1)... 50, 61
    Art 5... 120
    Art 6... 171, 188, 218
    Art 6(1)... 174
    Art 6(2)(b)... 178
    Art 6(3)... 176
    Art 7(5)... 217, 218
    Art 9... 171, 218, 219
Dir 97/55/EC Misleading and Comparative
    Advertising... 679
Dir 98/44/EC Biotechnology Directive... 19,
    406, 487
    Recital 23 .. 497
    Recital 24... 497
    Art 3(1) ... 502
    Art 3(2) ... 502
    Art 5(1)... 494, 505
    Art 5(2)... 411, 494, 504
    Art 5(3)... 497
    Art 6... 503-505
    Art 6(1)... 509
    Art 6(2)... 425, 509
    Art 6(2)(c)... 509
    Art 7... 508
Dir 98/71/EC Designs Directive ... 19, 262, 267
    Recital 7... 315
    Recital 8... 315
    Recital 11... 273
    Recital 13... 273, 277, 278
    Recital 14... 293, 296
    Recital 19... 303
    Art 1(a)... 269, 272
    Art 1(b)... 270
    Art 1(c)... 298
    Art 3(2)... 274
    Art 3(3)... 299
    Art 3(3)-(4)... 273
    Art 3(4)... 299
    Art 5(1)... 277
    Art 5(2)... 277
    Art 6... 290
    Art 6(1)... 289
    Art 7(1)... 293, 295, 296
    Art 7(2)... 296
    Art 7(3)... 297
    Art 9(1)... 278, 310

Art 9(2)... 278, 311
Art 10... 314
Art 11... 309, 310
Art 12(1)... 310
Art 13(1)(a)... 312
Art 15... 314
Art 16... 315
Art 17... 315, 354
Art 18... 303
Dir 98/84/EC Conditional Access
    Directive... 865
Dir 2000/31/EC E-Commerce
    Directive... 950
Art 12... 162
Art 13... 313
Art 14... 162
Art 14(1)... 707
Dir 2001/29/EC Information Society (InfoSoc)
    Directive... 37, 44, 170, 221, 255
Recital 4... 50
Recitals 9–11... 50
Recital 20... 50
Recital 28... 865
Recital 29... 866
Recital 33... 173
Art 2... 50, 120, 125
Art 2(a)... 126
Arts 2–4... 120
Art 4(2)... 865, 866
Art 5(1)... 174
Art 5(3)(a)... 178
Art 5(3)(b)... 190
Art 5(3)(d)... 181
Art 5(3)(h)... 191
Art 5(3)(n)... 173
Art 5(5)... 176
Art 6(4)... 205
Art 8(3)... 162, 950
Dir 2001/82/EC Veterinary Medicinal
    Products, Art 13(6)... 484
Dir 2001/83/EC Medicinal Products for
    Human Use, Art 10(5)... 484
Dir 2001/84/EC Resale Right for the Benefit of
    the Author of an Original Work
    of Art... 37, 98, 911
Recital 3... 109
Recital 17... 107, 108
Recital 19... 109
Art 8(2)... 108
Art 8(3)... 108
Dir 2003/4/EC Public Access to Environmental
    Information... 797
Dir 2003/98/EC Re-use Directive
Art 1(2)... 930
Art 2(3)... 930
Art 4... 930
Art 4(2)... 930
Art 6... 930
Art 10... 930

Art 11... 930
Dir 2004/27 Medicinal Products for Human
    Use, Art 10(6)... 484
Dir 2004/48/EC Enforcement
    Directive... 945
Arts 7–9... 948
Art 11... 162, 707, 949
Art 13... 945, 948
Dir 2005/29/EC Unfair Commercial Practices
    Directive... 679, 680
Dir 2006/114/EC Comparative Advertising
    Directive ... 679
Art 3... 681
Art 6(1)(b)... 681
Dir 2006/115/EC Rental and Lending Right
    Directive... 37, 120, 145
Dir 2006/116/EC Harmonising the Term of
    Protection of Copyright and Certain
    Related Rights... 37, 843
Art 6... 50
Dir 2008/95/EC Trade Marks
    Directive... 560
Art 2... 577, 580, 581, 586
Art 3... 582, 588
Art 3(1)... 589
Art 3(1)(b)... 592, 602, 606
Art 3(1)(c)... 591, 592, 598, 602
Art 3(1)(e)... 608, 612
Art 3(1)(f)... 614
Art 3(1)(g)... 614, 819
Art 3(2)(d)... 617
Art 3(3)... 580, 589
Art 4... 588, 621
Art 4(5)... 622
Art 5 ... 588, 621, 849
Art 5(1)(a)... 635
Art 5(3)... 631, 849
Art 7(1)... 855, 856
Art 7(2)... 848
Art 10... 564
Dir 2009/24/EC Consolidated Software
    Directive... 60
Art 1(2)... 136
Art 1(3)... 62, 64
Art 4... 120
Art 5... 171
Art 5(1)... 139, 204
Art 5(2)... 135, 218
Art 5(3)... 218
Art 5(3)(k)... 141
Art 6... 127, 171
Art 6(1)... 218
Art 7(1)(c)... 197
Art 15... 618, 620
Dir 2011/77/EU Term Directive... 19, 37,
    221, 250
Art 1(2)... 226
Art 1(2)(c)... 231
Art 2... 244

Table of international treaties and conventions

Adelphi Charter... 366, 367
Agreement on Trade-related Aspects of
    Intellectual Property Rights 1994 ... 24,
    34, 35, 39, 41, 119, 559
  Pt III, ss 2, 4, 5... 959
  Art 2... 25, 368, 570
  Art 2(1)... 570
  Art 3... 570
  Art 8(2)... 868
  Art 9... 25
  Art 9(2)... 36, 120
  Art 11... 120
  Art 13... 36, 169
  Art 14... 36
  Art 14(2)... 120
  Art 15... 570
  Art 16(1)... 570
  Art 16(2)... 660
  Art 16(3)... 660
  Art 22(1)... 709
  Art 22(2)... 711
  Art 22(4)... 711
  Art 23(1)... 711
  Art 25... 265
  Art 26... 265
  Art 26(2)... 266
  Art 26(3)... 266
  Art 27... 422, 501
  Art 27(1)... 404, 538
  Art 27(1)–(3)... 378
  Art 27(2)... 384, 389, 422
  Art 27(3)(b)... 383
  Art 31... 868
  Art 31(f)... 380
  Art 39(1)... 775
  Art 39(2)... 775
  Art 39(3)... 775, 800
  Art 40... 868
  Art 41... 960
  Art 42... 960
  Arts 42–45... 959
  Art 43... 960
  Art 48... 960
  Art 51... 960
  Art 61... 958, 960

Beijing Treaty on Audiovisal Performances
    2012 ... 26
  Art 12.3... 910
Berne Convention for the Protection of
    Literary and Artistic Works 1886... 17,
    23, 33, 38, 39, 55, 245, 367, 411, 969
  Art 2... 265
  Art 2(1)... 264
  Art 2(3)... 52
  Art 2(5)... 42, 264
  Art 2(7)... 145
  Art 5... 969
  Art 5*quinquies*... 264
  Art 5(2)... 101, 970
  Art 6*bis*... 98, 120
  Art 7... 969
  Art 7(4)... 145, 264
  Art 8... 119
  Art 9... 34, 119
  Art 9(1)... 35
  Art 9(2)... 169, 254
  Art 10... 34, 36
  Art 10*bis*... 169
  Art 11... 36, 119, 961
  Art 11*bis*... 119, 911, 961
  Art 1 *ter*... 119
  Art 12... 36, 119
  Art 13... 911
  Art 14... 119
  Art 14*ter*... 98, 109
  Art 27(2)... 98
Brussels Convention on Jurisdiction and the
    Enforcement of Judgements in Civil and
    Commercial Matters 1972... 974
  Art 16(4)... 984, 985
Budapest Treaty on the International
    Recognition of the Deposit of
    Microorganisms for the Purposes of
    Patent Procedure 1977... 26, 395

Charter of Fundamental Rights, Art 17(2)...
    27, 957
Convention on Biological Diversity 1992...
    383–384
Convention on International Exhibitions 1928
    (as amended 1951)... 441
Convention for the Protection of Performers,
    Producers of Phonograms and
    Broadcasting Organisations 1961... 16

European Convention for the Protection
    of Human Rights and Fundamental
    Freedoms 1950... 17, 26
  Art 2... 424
  Art 8... 798, 807–809, 812, 815
  Art 10... 196, 197, 775, 798, 799, 807–809,
    812, 814, 815
  Protocol 1, Art 1... 8, 548

European Patent Convention, Munich
    1973 (as amended 2000)... 26, 371,
    372, 390
  Art 14(2)... 390
  Art 52... 406, 407, 415, 420, 421, 513,
    518, 519
  Art 52(1)... 389, 405, 430
  Art 52(2)... 405, 487, 513, 514, 518, 520,
    524, 526
  Art 52(2)(c)... 533
  Art 52(3) ... 405, 513, 520, 524, 533
  Art 52(4)... 399, 425
  Arts 52–57... 517
  Art 53... 405, 406, 407, 422, 506, 507,
    518, 421, 500, 503
  Art 53(a)... 422, 424, 501, 505, 506
  Art 53(b)... 423
  Art 53(c)... 389, 400, 406, 425, 442
  Art 54... 432
  Art 54(3)... 389, 433
  Art 54(4)... 400
  Art 54(5)... 400, 442, 443
  Art 55... 432
  Art 56... 443, 542
  Art 57... 453, 497, 520
  Art 64(2)... 398, 493, 494
  Art 64(3)... 465
  Art 65... 375
  Art 69... 389, 469
  Art 69(1)... 469
  Art 82... 399
  Art 83... 477
  Art 99... 372
  Art 100... 372
  Art 102... 372
  Art 105a... 390, 402
  Art 105b(3)... 390, 480
  Art 112a... 389
  Art 112(1)(b)... 535, 536
  Art 121(1)... 390
  Art 121(3)... 390
  Art 138... 390
  Implementing Regulations
    r 23d(c)... 505
    r 27... 517
    r 29... 517
    r 43(1)... 399
    r 43(4)... 400
    r 43(5)... 398
    r 45... 398
    r 46(6)... 400
  Protocol on the Interpretation of
    Art 69... 26, 469, 470, 473, 475
    Art 2... 372, 389, 472, 473, 474,475

General Agreement on Tariffs and Trade
    1994 ... 24, 25, 378, 570

Geneva Convention for the Protection of
    Producers of Phonograms Against
    Unauthorized Duplication of their
    Phonograms 1971... 26

Hague Convention Concerning the
    International Registration of
    Industrial Designs... 17, 265
  Art 1... 990
  Art 2... 991
  Art 3... 990

International Covenant on Economic,
    Social and Cultural Rights 1966
  Art 11... 778
  Art 15(1)... 98

Lisbon Agreement for the Protection
    of Appellations of Origin and
    Their International Registration
    1958... 26
Locarno Agreement Establishing an
    International Classification for
    Industrial Designs 1968... 265
Lugano Convention on Jurisdiction
    and Enforcement of Judgements in
    Civil and Commercial Matters
    1988... 974
  Art 5(3)... 983

Madrid Agreement Concerning the
    International Registration of Marks
    1891... 17, 26, 559
  Art 1... 709
  Arts 6–7(1)... 568
Madrid Protocol 1989... 17, 560
  Art 2(1)... 568
  Art 2(2)... 568
  Art 4... 568
  Art 4bis... 568
  Art 5(1)... 568
  Art 6(1)... 568
  Art 7(1)... 568

Nice International Arrangement on the
    International Classification of Goods
    and Services... 570
  class 3... 647
  class 9... 579, 599, 650
  class 12... 649
  class 20... 601
  class 29... 651
  class 35... 585, 601, 643
  class 38... 599, 650
  class 41... 587
  class 42... 599
  class 44... 585

Paris Convention for the Protection of
   Industrial Property 1883... 23, 265,
   411, 559, 564, 969
  Art 1(2)... 367
  Art 2... 566, 567, 969
  Art 3... 368, 566
  Art 4... 368, 566, 571
  Art 4*bis*... 368
  Art 4A(1)... 265
  Art 4C... 571
  Art 4C(1)... 265
  Art 6*bis*... 566, 660, 730
  Art 6*ter*... 567
  Art 6*quinquies* ... 567
  Art 10(1)... 709
  Art 10(2)... 709
  Art 10*bis*... 567, 730
Patent Cooperation Treaty 1970 ... 17, 26
  Art 16... 376
  Art 32... 376
Patent Law Treaty 2000... 387
  Art 2... 377
  Art 5(1)... 377
  Art 5(2)... 377
  Art 21... 433

Rome Convention for the Protection of
   Performers, Producers of Phonograms
   and Broadcasting Organizations
   1961... 26, 35, 40, 55
  Art 7... 220
  Art 10... 120, 220
  Art 12... 911
  Art 13... 120, 220

Strasbourg Convention 1963 (on the Unification
   of Certain Points of Substantive Law on
   Patents for Invention)... 500
  Art 1... 373
  Art 2... 373

Singapore Treaty on the Law of Trademarks
   2006... 560
  Art 27... 569

Trademark Law Treaty 1994... 26, 559
  Art 1... 569
  Art 3... 569
  Art 5... 569
  Art 10... 569
  Art 12... 569
Treaty on Intellectual Property in Respect of
   Integrated Circuits 1989... 26

Universal Copyright Convention
   1952... 17, 26
UPOV Convention for the Protection of New
   Varieties of Plants Convention 1961...
   5, 26

Vienna Convention on the Law of Treaties,
   Art 31... 536

WIPO Copyright Treaty 1996 ... 26, 39, 41, 120
  Art 2... 36
  Art 6... 120
  Art 7... 120
  Art 8... 120
  Arts 4-8... 36
  Art 10... 169
  Arts 10-12... 36
WIPO Performances and Phonograms Treaty
   1996 ... 26, 36, 39, 120
  Art 5... 226, 229
  Art 5(1)... 228
  Art 11... 120
  Arts 12-14... 120

List of figures

8.1 Images from Community registered design no 00387584–0003   275

8.2 Images from Community registered design no 000359922–0001   276

8.3 PepsiCo Community registered design no 74463–0001   279

8.4 Grupo Promer Community registered design no 53186–0001   279

8.5 Images from Procter & Gamble Community registered
design no 000097969–0001   283

8.6 Images of the alleged infringement in *Procter & Gamble Co v Reckitt
Benckiser (UK) Ltd* [2008] FSR 8   284

8.7 Images from Dyson's UK design registration no 2,043,779   285

8.8 Images of the alleged infringement in *Dyson Ltd v Vax Ltd* [2012] FSR 4   285

10.1 Patent application for Animal Ear Protectors   396

11.1 Claimant's lintel   471

11.2 Defendant's lintel   471

13.1 *Ate My Heart Inc v Mind Candy Ltd*   550

13.2 Zoo (Reproduced with permission from Tesco Stores Limited)   552

13.3 Bass logo   557

13.4 Triangle (Reproduced with permission from SPCK Publishing and
Sheldon Press)   558

14.1 Edinburgh Law School (Reproduced with permission from University
of Edinburgh)   578

14.2 Coca-Cola bottle (Reproduced with kind permission of The Coca-Cola
Company)   578

14.3 BMW mini (Reproduced with permission from BMW (UK) Limited)   579

14.4 Purple colour (Reproduced with permission from Chemisphere Limited)   579

14.5 Dyson (Reproduced with permission from Dyson www.dyson.co.uk)   580

14.6 Musical notes (Reproduced with permission from AB Electrolux)   583

14.7 Sound waves   604

14.8 Bang & Olufsen loud speaker   613

14.9 Case T-232/10 *Couture Tech Ltd v OHIM* [2012] ETMR 5   615

14.10 Lindt bunny   619

14.11 Franz Hauswirth bunny (Reproduced with kind permission of Franz
Hauswirth GmbH)   619

14.12 Woolmark certification mark (Reproduced with the permission of The
Woolmark Company)   620

14.13 UK cartridge remanufacturers association collective mark (Reproduced
with permission from UKCRA)   621

15.1 Football Association three lions logo (Reproduced with permission
from the Football Association)   633

15.2 Arsenal Football Club logo (Reproduced with permission from Arsenal
Football Club)   634

15.3 CTM Nos 1321298 & 3418928   637

15.4   CTM Nos 449256 & 1321348   637
15.5   CTM No 5608385   637
15.6   SIR logo (Reproduced with permission from Maurer Wirtz)   647
15.7   Levi Strauss jeans   654
15.8   Casucci jeans   654
15.9   HappyDog (Reproduced with permission from HappyDog)   658
15.10 Inlima's boot-shaped bottle with three stripes   667
15.11 Alavi's Merc mark (Reproduced with permission from MERC®)   668
16.1   www.bigsave.com   688
16.2   www.bags123.com (Reproduced with permission from Boros
       Leathergoods)   688
16.3   Protected designation of origin logo   719
16.4   Protected geographical indication logo   719
19.1   Picasso mark   818
22.1   Gegal and Leneral   959

Every effort has been made to trace and contact copyright holders but this has not been possible in every case. If notified, the publisher will undertake to rectify any errors or omissions at the earliest opportunity.

List of diagrams

1.1	The cyclical pattern of intellectual property production and protection	9
1.2	Core features of the statutory intellectual property rights	14
3.1	Royalty rates table	108
3.2	Author copyright table	111
3.3	50 years table	115
5.1	Exceptions to copyright	172
6.1	Duration of database right	214
6.2	Duration of database right after substantial investment	214
6.3	Performer's rights in live performances	223
9.1	Duration of UK UDR	341
9.2	Duration of UK UDR with licences of right during last five years	342
10.1	Current internal structure of European Patent Office	372
11.1	The Improver Questions	473
15.1	Similarity and confusion	645
20.1	*Deutsche Grammophon GmbH v Metro SB Grossmarkte GmbH & Co*	838
20.2	*Centrafarm v Sterling & Winthrop*	839
20.3	*Van Zuylen Freres v Hag Ac*	841
20.4	*IHT Internationale Heiztechnik GmbH v Ideal Standard GmbH*	842
20.5	*EMI Electrola GmbH v Patricia Im- und Export*	843
20.6	*Merck & Co Inc v Stephar BV*	844
20.7	*Silhouette International Schmied GmbH & Co KG v Hartlauer Handelsgesellschaft*	856
22.1	*American Cyanamid Co v Ethicon Ltd*	940

Abbreviations

General

ACTA	Anti Counterfeiting Trade Agreement
ADNDRC	Asian Domain Name Dispute Resolution
aff'd	affirmed
APIG	All Party Parliamentary Internet Group
BAILII	British and Irish Legal Information Institute
BECS	British Equity Collecting Society
CBD	Convention on Biological Diversity
CC	Creative Commons
ccTLD	Country code Top Level Domain
CD	compact disc
CDPA 1988	Copyright, Designs and Patents Act 1988
CDR	Community Design Regulation
CFI	Court of First Instance
CIPIH	Commission on Intellectual Property Rights, Innovation and Public Health
CJEU	Court of Justice of the European Union
CLA	Copyright Licensing Authority
Cm	Command Number
CPC	Community Patent Convention
CSS	Content scramble system
CT	Copyright Tribunal
CTM	Community Trade Mark
CTMR	Community Trade Mark Regulation
DACS	Design and Artists' Copyright Society
DD EU	Directive on Legal Protection of Designs
DO	Designation of Origin
DRM	Digital rights management
DSB	Dispute Settlement Body (WTO)
DSU	Dispute Settlement Understanding (WTO)
DVD	digital versatile disk
EBA	Enlarged Board of Appeal (EPO)
EC	European Community
ECHR	European Convention on Human Rights
ECJ	European Court of Justice (now Court of Justice of the European Union)
ECtHR	European Court of Human Rights
EEA	European Economic Area
EEC	European Economic Community
EGE	European Group on Ethics in Science and New Technologies
EPC	European Patent Convention

EPO	European Patent Office
EPO	Erythropoietin
eRes	eResolution
ESTs	Expressed Sequence Tags
FACT	Federation Against Copyright Theft
FAST	Federation Against Software Theft
GATT	General Agreement on Tariffs and Trade
GI	Geographical Indication
gTLD	Generic top level domain
GUI	Graphical user interface
HCA	High Court of Australia
HRA 1998	Human Rights Act 1998
ICANN	Internet Corporation for Assigned Names and Numbers
IDN	Internationalised Domain Name
IFPI	International Federation of Phonographic Industry
IGC	Intergovernmental Committee on Intellectual Property and Genetic Resources, Traditional Knowledge and Folklore
IGWG	Intergovernmental Working Group
InfoSoc Directive	Copyright in the Information Society Directive
IP	Intellectual property
IPL	International Private Law
IPRs	intellectual property rights
ISP	Internet Service Provider
LDCs	Least Developed Countries
MCPS	Mechanical Copyright Protection Society
MMC	Monopoly and Mergers Commission
MR	Master of the Rolls
NAF	National Arbitration Forum
NZCA	New Zealand Court of Appeal
OD	Opposition Division (EPO)
OECD	Organisation for Economic Co-operation and Development
OFT	Office of Fair Trading
OHIM	Office for Harmonization in the Internal Market
OPSI	Office of Public Sector Information
OUP	Oxford University Press
P2P	peer-to-peer
PCC	Patent County Court
PCT	Patent Cooperation Treaty
PDO	Protected Designations of Origin
PGI	Protected Geographical Indication
PPL	Phonographic Performance Limited
PRS	Performing Right Society
R&D	research and development
RDA 1949	Registered Designs Act 1949
rev'd	reversed
RMI	Rights management information system
SABIP	Strategic Advisory Board for Intellectual Property Policy

SI	Statutory Instrument
SNPs	Single Nucleotide Polymorphisms
SPC	Supplementary Protection Certificate
STM	science, technical, and medical
TFEU	Treaty on the Functioning of the European Union
TLD	top level domain
TLT	Trade Mark Law Treaty
TM	trade mark
TMA 1994	Trade Marks Act 1994
TPM	Technical Protection Measure
TRIPS (Agreement on)	Trade-Related Aspects of Intellectual Property Rights
TSG	Traditional Specialty Guaranteed
TTBE	Technology Transfer Block Exemption
TTBER	Technology Transfer Block Exemption Regulation
UCITA	Uniform Computer Information Transaction Act (USA)
UDR	Unregistered Design Right
UDRP (ICANN)	Uniform Domain Name Dispute Resolution Policy
UK–IPO	United Kingdom Intellectual Property Office
UPCA	Unified Patent Court Agreement
UPOV	International Union for the Protection of New Varieties of Plants
USC	United States Code
USPTO	US Patent and Trademark Office
VBER	Vertical Agreement Block Exemption Regulation
V-C	Vice-Chancellor
WCT	WIPO Copyright Treaty
WHO	World Health Organization
WIPO	World Intellectual Property Organization
WPPT	WIPO Performances and Phonograms Treaty 1996
WTO	World Trade Organization

Law reports, journals etc

AC	Law Reports, Third Series, Appeal Cases
AIPLA QJ	American Intellectual Property Law Association Quarterly Journal
All ER	All England Law Reports
ALR	Adelaide Law Review
ALR	Aden Law Reports
ALR	Argus Law Reports (Aust)
ALR	Australian Law Reports
App Cas	Appeal Cases
BCLC	Butterworths Company Law Cases
Beav	Beavan
BPIR	Bankruptcy and Personal Insolvency Reports
Bro PC	Brown's Chancery Reports

Bus LR	Business Law Review
Ch	Law Reports, Third Series, Chancery Division
Ch D	Law Reports, Second Series, Chancery Division
CIPAJ	Chartered Institute of Patent Agents Journal
CLJ	Cambridge Law Journal
CLR	Canada Law Reports
CLR	Common Law Reports
CLR	Commonwealth Law Reports (Aust)
CLSR	Computer Law and Security Report
CML Rev	Common Market Law Review
CMLR	Common Market Law Reports
COM	European Commission Document
CP Rep	Civil Procedure Reports
CPR	Canadian Patent Reporter
Cr App Rep	Criminal Appeal Reports
Crim LR	Criminal Law Review
CSIH	Court of Session (Inner House)
CSOH	Court of Session (Outer House)
CTLR	Computer and Telecommunications Law Review
D	Session Cases, 2nd Series [Dunlop] (Sc)
De G & Sm	De Gex and Smale's Chancery Reports
EBL Rev	European Business Law Review
ECC	European Commercial Cases
ECDR	European Copyright and Design Reports
ECL&P	E-Commerce Law & Policy
ECLR	European Competition Law Review
ECR	European Court Reports
EHRLR	European Human Rights Law Review
EHRR	European Human Rights Reports
EIPR	European Intellectual Property Review
EL Rev	European Law Review
EMLR	Entertainment and Media Law Reports
EntLR	Entertainment Law Review
EPOR	European Patent Office Reports
ER	English Reports
ETMR	European Trade Mark Reports
EWCA	Crim Media neutral citation from the Court of Appeal (Criminal Division)
EWHC	Media neutral citation from the High Court
EWPCC	Media neutral citation from the Patent County Court Ex Exchequer Reports
Ex CR	Exchequer Court Reports
F	Session Cases, 5th Series [Fraser] (Sc)
F 2d	Federal Reporter, Second Series (USA)
F 3d	Federal Reporter, Third Series (USA)
F Supp	Federal Supplement (USA)
FC	Federal Court

FCA	Federal Court of Australia
FILJ	Fordham International Law Journal
FSR	Fleet Street Reports
GRUR	Gewerblicher Rechtsschutz und Urheberrecht
GWD	Green's Weekly Digest (Sc)
Harv LR	Harvard Law Review
HC	House of Commons
HL	Law Reports, First Series, English and Irish Appeals
HL	House of Lords
HMSO	Her Majesty's Stationery Office
HR	House of Representatives (USA)
IIC	International Review of Industrial Property and Copyright Law
IJL & IT	International Journal of Law and Information Technology
ILR	International Law Reports
Int TLR	International Trade Law and Regulation
IPQ	Intellectual Property Quarterly
IPR	Intellectual Property Reports
JBL	Journal of Business Law
JCLE	Journal of Competition Law and Economics
JIEL	Journal of International Economic Law
JILT	Journal of Information, Law and Technology
JIPLP	Journal of Intellectual Property Law & Practice
JML	Journal of Media Law
JR	Juridical Review
K & J	Kay & Johnson's Vice Chancellor's Reports
KB	Law Reports, Third Series, King's Bench
LJPC	Law Journal Reports, Privy Council
LMCLQ	Lloyd's Maritime and Commercial Law Quarterly
LQR	Law Quarterly Review
LR (QB)	Law Reports, Queens Bench
LSG	Law Society Gazette
LT	Law Times Reports
M	Session Cases, 3rd Series [Macpherson] (Sc)
Mac & G	Macnaghten and Gordon's Chancery Reports
MCC	Macgillivray's Copyright Cases
Med LR	Medical Law Reports
MLR	Modern Law Review
Mor	Morison's Dictionary of Decisions of the Court of Session
NZLR	New Zealand Law Reports
OJ	Official Journal of the European Communities
OJEPO	Official Journal of the European Patent Office
OJLS	Oxford Journal of Legal Studies
PC	Privy Council
PD	Law Reports, Second Series, Probate Division
QB	Queen's Bench
QBD	Law Reports, Second Series, Queen's Bench Division
R	Session Cases, 4th Series [Rettie] (Sc)

RPC	Reports of Patent Design and Trade Mark Cases
S	Senate
S	Session Cases [Shaw] (Sc)
S Ct	Supreme Court Reporter (USA)
SALR	South African Law Reports
SC	Session Cases (Sc)
SCLR	Scottish Civil Law Reports
SCR	Supreme Court Reports, Canada
SEC	(European) Commission Staff Working Document
SGCA	Singapore Court of Appeal
SLT	Scots Law Times
TLR	Times Law Reports
TMR	Trade Mark Reports
TW	Trademark World
UKHL	Media neutral citation from the House of Lords
US	United States Supreme Court Reports
USPQ	United States Patent Quarterly
VR	Victorian Reports (Aust)
WIPR	World Intellectual Property Reports
WL	Westlaw
WLR	Weekly Law Reports
WN	Weekly Notes

Part I

Introduction

1

Intellectual property law: an introduction

Introduction

Scope and overview of chapter

1.1 This chapter is an introduction to the discipline of intellectual property (IP) law. You will examine the nature of IP as well as the aims and content of IP law. A brief overview will be given of the main rights and actions which make up IP law, together with an analysis of the various themes which underpin this area of law. The importance of the European and international dimensions to IP law will be emphasised, although throughout the starting point for discussion will be the jurisdictions of the UK. Here we lay the groundwork for the rest of this book, and you should use this chapter as a platform for further in-depth study.

1.2 ### Learning objectives

By the end of this chapter you should be able to:

- define IP and the broad church that is IP law;
- articulate the aims and objectives of IP law and place it in its wider commercial setting;
- give a brief account of the range and type of intellectual property rights (IPRs) which exist;
- appreciate the relationships between different levels of IP law, that is, (a) national, (b) European and (c) international and
- understand the various influences on the formation, justifications for and development of IP law, as well as the tensions that arise when the law seeks to protect IP.

1.3 The rest of the chapter looks like this:

- What is intellectual property law? (1.4–1.17)
- What is intellectual property? (1.18–1.45)
- Developing intellectual property law (1.46–1.73)

Exercise

Before reading this chapter, ask yourself, what is 'intellectual property'? Do you think that it should receive legal protection? What form should that legal protection take? Try to justify your responses and then compare your views with what we say later.

What is intellectual property law?

1.4   This is a book about the law that protects IP. Let us begin, then, with a very brief overview of the various elements of this area of law, which at first will seem disconnected. We will then go on to explore the themes that tie these elements together, and to consider the influences that shape and form modern IP law.

1.5   IP law comprises a wide range of forms of protection for IP. It encompasses statutory and common law arrangements and has aspects which are shaped by international, European and national considerations. Under the umbrella of IP, a significant number of IPRs exist; each is tailored to protect a particular example of IP.

The statutory rights

1.6   There are four principal forms of IP, and in the UK these are protected by statute. They are as follows.

Patents: Patents Act 1977

1.7   Patent law protects *inventions*, which can be described as technical solutions to technical problems. An invention can be a product or a process. An invention is the paradigmatic example of 'industrial property'—a concept which we will explore in detail later. The Intellectual Property Office (UK–IPO) in Newport, Gwent is responsible for the grant of patents in the UK.[1] The European Patent Office in Munich is responsible for the grant of 'European' patents.[2] There is no such thing as a world patent.[3] Patents require to be registered.

Copyright: Copyright, Designs and Patents Act 1988

1.8   Copyright law is designed to protect aesthetic and artistic creations such as literary, musical, dramatic and artistic works, known as *original works*, together with *derivative works* such as films, sound recordings, cable programmes, broadcasts and the typographical arrangement of a published work (ie the way the material is laid out). Copyright was expanded considerably throughout the course of the 20th century to protect new and emerging forms of IP such as computer software and databases. Copyright protection arises on the creation of a protectable work. There is no need to register the right (cf patents).

Designs: Registered Designs Act 1949 and Copyright, Designs and Patents Act 1988

1.9   Design law protects the way a product or article 'looks'. In the UK, designs can either be protected by registration or automatically, through unregistered design protection, on the creation of a design

---

[1] http://www.ipo.gov.uk/pro-home.htm.   [2] http://www.european-patent-office.org/.
[3] Other important patent offices are the US Patent and Trademark Office http://www.uspto.gov/ and the Japanese Patent Office http://www.jpo.go.jp/.

document or an article embodying the design. The two forms of protection are not mutually exclusive. There is potential for overlap between copyright protection for artistic works and design protection, although in the UK this is a complex interaction. The UK–IPO is responsible for the grant of UK registered designs and for maintaining the Design Register. Unregistered and registered Community design rights have also been available since 2002 and 2003 respectively, governed by Regulation 6/2002/EC on Community designs. Oversight of this system and the registration process is handled by the Office for Harmonisation in the Internal Market (OHIM) in Alicante, Spain.[4]

Trade marks: Trade Marks Act 1994

1.10   Trade marks operate to distinguish the goods and services of one enterprise from those of another. They exist as badges of origin and help the consumer to avoid confusion between goods or services of variable quality. Trade marks can assist greatly in bolstering protection for goods already protected by another form of IP law. For example, patent-protected drugs will invariably carry their own trade mark, for example 'Viagra' is the trade mark for the drug sildenafil citrate, the patent on which expired in 2013. The advantage of trade marks on patented products is, however, that the trade mark can continue long after the patent has expired, for example 'Valium' . Trade mark protection is awarded by registration. In the UK, this is handled by the Trade Mark Registry, once again, at the UK–IPO in Newport. A Community trade mark is also available, awarded by the OHIM.

Common law actions

1.11   Beyond these statutory rights a number of common law actions are also considered to make up the body of IP law in the UK. We examine these in full depth in Chapters 17, 18, and 19. For now, it is only important that you understand the ambit of the two main actions.

Passing off

1.12   Passing off protects the reputation or 'goodwill' of traders in respect of their product 'get-up', name or trading style. The action becomes relevant when traders copy a rival's 'get-up' and when this leads to, or is likely to lead to, public confusion between the competing products. There is much scope for overlap between trade mark protection and passing off. Often both actions are brought in the same dispute.

Breach of confidence

1.13   The common law action of breach of confidence is often included in the definition of IP law. The action can provides ancillary support in the protection of the interests of IP producers, especially when information about IP that is going to eventually be registered must be kept out of the public domain prior to registration, for example patents and registered designs. Registrable IPRs do require full public disclosure in the course of the application process. By its protection of trade secrets, breach of confidence also provides an alternative means of protecting valuable knowledge if a decision is made (to try to) keep it permanently outside the public domain.

Sui generis rights

1.14   In more recent years a series of new IPRs has been introduced, usually because of the success of arguments that existing forms of protection are inadequate to accommodate emerging technologies, and/

---

[4] http://oami.europa.eu/ows/rw/pages/index.en.do.

or because political agendas have desired a novel and unique form of protection. Some key examples include the following:

Semi-conductor topography: Design Right (Semiconductor Topographies) Regulations 1989 (SI 1989/1100)

1.15   Semi-conductor topography concerns the layout of computer circuit boards. The UK originally created a 'topography right' in 1989 to comply with a European Directive.[5] Since then topographies have been protected as a special form of unregistered design right. The move to protect this form of IP came after pressure was brought to bear by the United States which threatened to exclude foreign nationals from protection under its law if equivalent provisions did not exist in their own countries.

Plant breeders' rights: Plant Varieties and Seeds Act 1964 and Plant Varieties Act 1997

1.16   New varieties of plants and seeds can be protected by a right of protection under UK legislation which complies with a European Community Regulation from 1994.[6] Moreover, protection of the rights in question is required by the International Union for the Protection of New Varieties of Plants (UPOV) Convention of 1961, as amended in 1991.[7]

Database rights: Copyright and Rights in Databases Regulations 1997 (SI 1997/3032), now incorporated into Copyright, Designs, Patents Act 1988

1.17   Compilations of data can receive protection in Europe as a *database* in two separate ways. First, if the structure of the compilation is original, then the structure is protected by copyright. If it is not original, then secondly, the underlying material can be protected if sufficient investment has been made in its compilation. 'Investment' is broadly defined and includes investment of both time and money. This material is protected by a 'database right' which entitles the 'maker' of the database to prevent another from extracting the whole or a significant part of the database without permission. This is a *sui generis* form of protection which is not required under international obligations. It will therefore only be accorded to foreign nationals whose country accords similar degrees of protection. Copyright protection in the contents of the database is not precluded by the existence of the new right.

 Question

What could possibly unite the disparate areas of protection which have been considered so far? Can you see any common themes that might link them together?

What is intellectual property?

1.18   In this section we will attempt to make sense of this seemingly disparate collection of legal rights. Let us begin by asking, what really is 'intellectual property'?

---

[5] Council Directive 87/54/EEC of 16 December 1986 on the legal protection of topographies of semiconductor products.
[6] Council Regulation (EC) No 2100/94 of 27 July 1994 on Community plant variety rights (as amended).
[7] UPOV Convention for the Protection of New Varieties of Plants 1961, 1991.

1.19   IP is frequently referred to as 'the novel products of human intellectual endeavour'. Yet, the use of the term 'property' to describe intellectual products implies the existence of rights and, perhaps more importantly, remedies in respect of the property and any unwarranted interference with it. A property paradigm, in turn, implies a system of control to be exercised by the right holder, that is, control of the subject matter of his property right. What makes a book *your* book in legal terms is the fact that no one can take, use or otherwise interfere with your property without your permission. At this level, IP protection operates in a similar fashion to that afforded to other forms of property. IP is concerned with identifying and controlling permissible and impermissible dealings with intellectual products, usually by reference to the consent of the right holder, at least in the first instance. However, in many other respects an analogy with tangible property rights—that is, property rights over physical entities— does not help us to understand what we mean by *intellectual* property. For example, your book will not stop being your book at midnight tonight, yet in most cases IPRs eventually expire, leaving the subject matter without an owner and so free to be used or exploited by anyone. Similarly, no one can require you to lend your book to others so that they might benefit from it, whereas with certain forms of IP compulsory licences can be granted to third parties to exploit the property in question. Finally, for all forms of IP to exist, stringent criteria must be met, with these varying with the kind of IP protection that is sought. This is not true of other forms of property which assume the quality of *property* by sheer dint of their existence.

1.20   In order to understand how and why IP is treated in this way we must first appreciate that at the broadest level of abstraction IP is concerned with protection of information. Adele's songs, Margaret Atwood's latest poem, the website that supports this textbook, Jean Paul Gaultier's designer labels, OUP's elec- tronic databases of authors, the chemical formulae for new cancer drugs, and the shape of Volvic's new- est mineral water bottle, are all protectable as IP; but equally they are all simply classes of information. Thus, unlike many forms of property, IPRs protect intangibles. This gives rise to considerable problems over the control of the property and its protection. For example, unlike tangible property, interference with IP can occur without exhaustion of the property itself. If I borrow your book you are automatically precluded from using it, but if I copy your process for refining sugar this in no way precludes you from using the process for your own ends, or indeed, from passing it to others. This makes protection and exploitation potentially problematic. It is largely for this reason that rights and remedies are not avail- able for intellectual products in the abstract. Protectable IP does not exist, therefore, in unspecific and ill-defined ideas alone. Such ideas must be reduced to some tangible embodiment before rights and remedies will accrue.[8]

1.21   But this does not explain why IPRs expire, nor why the scope of these rights can be limited in certain circumstances. To understand these features of IP protection we must ask:

 Question

Which interests are furthered, or compromised, by the protection of IP? Revisit your thoughts after you have considered the rest of this chapter.

A wide range of arguments can be put forward to justify IP. These will now be explored—and as will be seen, they are not necessarily consistent with each other.

---

[8] A possible variation on this occurs with the protection of confidential information, which need not be in written form to be protected, but must nevertheless be sufficiently identifiable to merit protection. See Chapter 18.

Moral interests

1.22   A wise and now long-dead Scottish lawyer once wrote: 'Of all things, the produce of a man's intellectual labour is most peculiarly distinguishable as his own'.[9] This neatly sums up the moral argument as to why IP is protected. Intellectual products are produced by the efforts of people who have contributed from within themselves to the creation of the new entity, and so it is thought that IP reflects a moral connection between the property and its creator. Thus, in theory at least, to protect the property is also to protect certain crucial personal interests. Such interests can be compromised, for example when control is relinquished to a third party and the property is subjected to some form of derogatory treatment. And, while a creator might happily renounce his economic stake in his property, for example by selling it, this does not mean that his moral interests are also abandoned. This sort of reasoning is directly reflected in the law of copyright, as we discuss in Chapter 3.

1.23   Another common moral reason to protect IP is because it would be unjust for others to benefit from a creator's time, labour and expenditure if it were possible simply to copy new intellectual products without fear of reprisal. The standard example is the experience of the pharmaceutical company. It is estimated that it costs upwards of $800 million to bring a new drug to market.[10] Most of this is spent in research and development and in gaining regulatory approval for the drug's safety and efficacy. However, once a drug is available it is incredibly easy to copy at a tiny fraction of this original cost. Would it be fair if rival companies were allowed to do so? Moreover, in that situation would any company go to the bother and expense of being the first to develop and market a new drug? These arguments focus, of course, on the investor or employers in respect of the innovation, rather than the individual innovator. It can also be argued that IP can lead to inefficient work to avoid existing rights, and can slow down the future innovation of others. Further, it could be said, at least in some sectors (software being a notable example) that there would be innovation without IP, and that even in pharmaceuticals there are other means, such as prizes, which would support innovation without the need for IP. This brings us to the all important issue of social interests which can be met, and hindered, by IP.

Social interests

1.24   Considerable social benefit can arise from IP. Indeed, it is precisely this argument that is advanced by pharmaceutical companies: 'give us protection for our drugs and we will have an incentive to produce them: deprive us of that protection and the incentive is gone'. This may be true, but it is also important to appreciate that social interests can be significantly compromised if IP is protected too strongly. For example, if too much market control is given to a creator then a paradigm may be established which will interfere with healthy competition which will operate to the detriment of competitors and consumers alike. Similarly, an inventor might choose to suppress a significant technological development or refuse to license it to third parties, thereby compromising social interests which could benefit from access to the technology. Indeed, these arguments help to explain why limits are placed on IPRs, and we explore them further below.

1.25   In addition, the granting of IPRs over certain novel creations can give rise to social consternation about the morality of certain acts of creation and the legal protection of them. This has been most notable in recent years in the context of the patentability of the products of the biotechnology industry. Patents

[9] Bell, *Commentaries*, I, 103.

[10] CP Adams and VV Branter, 'Estimating the cost of new drug development: is it really $802 million?' (2006) 25(2) Health Affairs 420, compare M Herper, 'The truly staggering cost of inventing new drugs' (10 February 2012) http://www.forbes.com/sites/matthewherper/2012/02/10/the-truly-staggering-cost-of-inventing-new-drugs/.

have been granted for the creation of genetically engineered human gene fragments and the development of transgenic animals which contain genetic material from foreign species, including humans. Many voices have been raised in Europe in objection to this as a fundamentally immoral practice. We explore this debate and its outcome in Chapter 12. It should be noted, however, that questions of morality in the granting of IPRs potentially impinge on all of the statutory forms of IP.[11] This is because IPRs are granted at the behest of the state. The courts are also most unwilling to treat iniquitous information as 'confidential' for the purposes of the common law.[12]

Economic interests

1.26   The economic interests of the producer of IP *and* his competitors *and* his customers will be affected when that property is exploited in the marketplace. The degree to which this occurs depends on the rights and remedies which are accorded to the property in question. It is here that we find one of the most serious areas of tension in IP protection. When IP is introduced into a market (as part of a product or through a licence to another person to make a product), it can have profound effects on the market's overall economic balance, as well as on the economic well-being of the whole geographical area in which it is exploited. There is, therefore, considerable room for dispute between the legitimate boundaries of IP protection and the encouragement of a free market economy. Indeed, this is most acutely felt within the confines of the European Union, where the commitment of member states to a single market in which goods can circulate freely between states is threatened by the exercise of IPRs, which, by their nature, potentially erect barriers to such free trade. We discuss this later in further detail.

1.27   Considering all of these interests, it should be clear that what is required is a balance that seeks to ensure that no one interest or group of interests dominates, while at the same time ensuring a fair and just degree of protection for any IP that has been produced. It is the overarching role and aim of IP law to achieve such a balance.

Policies and tensions in intellectual property

1.28   Consistent with the range of justifications for IP, the ongoing protection of IP is also driven by a number of important, and at times competing, policies. The outcome of any tussle between these policies ultimately shapes the nature and scope of IPRs and determines the future direction of IP law. Let us consider in more depth the various interests and policies at stake.

The protection of private interests through property rights

1.29   Property rights generally support and promote private interests, paramount among which is the interest of the owner to enjoy his property. Thus, these rights usually include exclusive control of the property and the right to exclude others from unauthorised use. Only in rare circumstances are the private rights of an owner curtailed to further a public interest, for example through the compulsory acquisition of land. The enjoyment of one's property is guaranteed as a matter of individual human rights,[13] and it

---

[11] See, eg, *Glyn v Weston Feature Films* [1916] 1 Ch 261 (copyright); *Re Masterman's Application* [1991] RPC 89 (registered designs); *Re Hack's Application* (1941) 58 RPC 91 (trade marks).

[12] See *Coco v AN Clark (Engineers) Ltd* [1969] RPC 41, and *Attorney General v Guardian Newspapers (No 2)* [1990] 1 AC 109.

[13] European Convention for the Protection of Human Rights and Fundamental Freedoms, 1950, Protocol 1, Art 1: 'Every natural person is entitled to the peaceful enjoyment of his possessions. No one shall be deprived of his possessions except in the public interest and subject to the conditions provided for by law and by the general principles of international law'.

is a fundamental tenet of EU law that national systems of property law should not be influenced by European measures.[14]

Reconciling public and private interests

1.30 The mere existence of IP can, however, significantly influence a number of public interests, as we have seen previously. All forms of IP contribute something new to the sum total of human knowledge, and this can occur across every conceivable realm of human experience; from the development of new pharmaceuticals to treat cancer and AIDS, to the design of more comfortable office chairs; from the creation of beautiful (and not so beautiful) works of art, literature, music or dance, to the introduction of distinctive packaging to assist consumers in distinguishing between the ever-burgeoning range of soft drinks on offer; from the splicing of genetic material to create a new strain of rose, to the improvement in processing times of computer board circuitry. All of these innovations can be the subject of IPRs, and their introduction to the public realm can surely only enrich the human condition.

1.31 It should be self-evident, then, that innovations such as these are to be encouraged, and the so-called *reward theory* of IP (see Diagram 1.1) seeks to promote this by engendering a cyclical pattern of social interaction whereby those who innovate are rewarded by the grant of property rights, which in turn act as an incentive to others to innovate, who are rewarded in their turn, and so on.

Diagram 1.1 The cyclical pattern of intellectual property production and protection

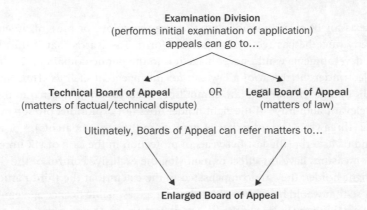

1.32 This model only serves its purpose, however, if the intellectual products find their way into the public domain, and it is one of the paradoxes of the IP regime that it seeks to promote public interests by granting private rights which—as we have seen previously—under a classic property model imply exclusive control over the subject matter. The public interest can, therefore, be jeopardised if private rights are exercised in a way that means that the property in question is not used or exploited in a public setting.

1.33 A further paradox arises from the particular type of property right that is granted. This is an exclusive right of control of what use can be made of, say, new technologies. The IP holder can exclude others from a variety of activities; for example, direct copying of their property by rivals or importation of samples of the property from a country where the price is lower, thereby stopping the importer from undercutting their prices. The potential for adverse influence from the exercise of IPRs can therefore extend across a

---

[14] Art 345 TFEU states: 'The Treaties shall in no way prejudice the rules in Member States governing the system of property ownership'.

number of public interests. Not only might various technological, scientific, artistic or consumer ends be thwarted, but overzealous use of these rights can lead to a distortion in competition, which in turn impacts on wider economic interests, including those of the individual consumer who might have to pay higher prices to obtain new products, and those of competitors who must find another way to compete.

1.34   This is not to say that the existence of exclusive rights necessarily leads to these outcomes. Indeed, economists and others argue endlessly about whether exclusive rights hinder or promote competition, in that the rights can also serve as an incentive to others to engage in their own innovation and go on to obtain their own exclusive rights. What can be said with certainty, however, is that some exercise of power can have adverse outcomes. We see this most obviously in the context of Articles 101 and 102 of the Treaty on the Functioning of the European Union (TFEU), which respectively prohibit practices amounting to anti-competitive agreements (cartels) or abuses of a dominant market position, where these are likely to affect trade between member states. Each of these prohibitions has a potential direct bearing on the ways in which IP owners can exercise their rights, and the relationship between IP and competition has been receiving increasing attention from courts, regulators and academics. We revisit these provisions later, as well as in more detail in Chapter 21.

1.35   In other contexts the matter distils, once again, into a question of striking a balance between the potentially competing public and private interests. It is in this respect that IPRs differ most significantly from traditional property rights. Consider, for example, the following features that are found in the domain of IPRs.

- In some contexts an IP owner cannot simply refuse to exploit, or prevent others from exploiting, his property once he has received protection for it. The fear is that if this were so, certain technological developments would never make it into the public domain and further innovation would be stifled under the threat of a law suit for infringement of IPRs. Thus, in the context of patents and UK unregistered design law, compulsory licences can be granted to third parties who apply to the relevant authority[15] if the right holder does not exploit his property within a certain period of time (three years from the date of grant as in the case of patents),[16] or when the IPR is nearing the end of its term (the last five years of protection in the case of UK unregistered design right).[17] These measures have the effect of removing the exclusive control of the IPR subject matter from the right holder; they are compensated to the extent that the third parties' entitlements are akin to those that would have been granted under a reasonable licence agreement, with a 'just' licence fee to be paid to the owner of the IP. A variation on this theme is the right of a government department to engage in otherwise infringing acts in relation to a patented invention without the consent of the proprietor 'for services of the Crown'.[18] Here too compensation is payable to the IP owner (or an exclusive licensee) for 'any loss resulting from his not being awarded a contract to supply the patented product or … to perform the patented process or supply a thing made by means of the patented process'.[19]

- In other contexts, an IP owner may not be able to prevent certain uses of his property by others when these uses serve another valuable public interest. For example, copyright is not infringed when a third party engages in 'permitted acts' with respect to the work. These acts include copying done for the purposes of research or private study,[20] dealings with the work for the purposes of criticism,

---

[15] This is the UK–IPO Office in the UK.   [16] Patents Act 1977, s 48.   [17] Copyright, Designs and Patents Act 1988, s 237.

[18] Patents Act 1977, ss 55–58.   [19] Patents Act 1977, s 57A.   [20] Copyright, Designs and Patents Act 1988, s 29.

review or news reporting[21] and things done for the purposes of instruction, examination or education.[22] The permitted acts in copyright law are considered to be fair dealings with the work, in that
they serve independent and worthwhile interests without unduly compromising the individual (economic) interests of the copyright holder. However, the question of what is 'fair' is a matter of endless
dispute, as we discuss in Chapter 5. Similarly, a trade mark owner cannot prevent the use of its trade
mark by a rival who simply engages in comparative advertising, that is, compares its goods or services with those of the trade mark owner, if this is done in an accurate and honest manner.[23] This latter practice is thought to encourage competition by raising consumer awareness about the range and
quality of products available on the market. This is discussed in Chapter 15.

- In all cases, as has been noted for intellectual products to qualify for protection, they must satisfy
certain predetermined criteria in order to assume the quality of *property*. The stringency of the qualification criteria for each IP right will be seen to be aligned to the strength and length of the exclusive
right that might ultimately be granted or obtained.

1.36   The balance which the law strikes between all these competing interests and ideas is endlessly controversial, with the result that proposals for reform, and actual reforms, are continuously occurring. In
the UK, the Government ordered a review of the IP system in December 2005, headed by Mr Andrew
Gowers. The review was published in December 2006 and made recommendations under seven headings: Balance, Coherence, Flexibility, Award, Use, Enforcement and Governance.[24] Another review of IP
and Growth was undertaken by Ian Hargreaves and published in 2011.[25] Many of these reports' conclusions, recommendations and steps which were subsequently taken, as well as ongoing consultations,
will be discussed later in this book.[26]

 Exercise

Compare and contrast the following forms of IP.

1.37   *Patents* protect inventions which must display *novelty*, that is, the invention must never previously have
been made available to the public by any means anywhere in the world. This is the strictest requirement
of its kind in IP law. However, if it and the other patentability criteria are met, the reward is the strongest type of IP right available. This is the right for the holder to prevent every unauthorised use of his
invention in the marketplace. Thus, rivals cannot make and sell illicit copies of the protected invention,
nor import any such copies, nor indeed sell the invention in a kit form without fear of an infringement
action.[27] There is no requirement of 'copying'—the patent owner has the power to control any use of the
invention, howsoever that arises. Thus, even if Abraham has no idea that Jacob already holds a patent for
a vacuum cleaner that employs cyclone technology, and even when there is no suggestion whatsoever of
any copying, Abraham can nevertheless be prevented from entering the public arena with his independently created version of the machine if it effectively embodies the kernel of Jacob's invention.

---

[21] Copyright, Designs and Patents Act 1988, s 30.   [22] Copyright, Designs and Patents Act 1988, ss 32–36.
[23] Trade Marks Act 1994, s 10(6), although note decision of the Court of Appeal in *O2 Holdings Ltd v Hutchison 3G Ltd* [2006] EWCA
Civ 1656, [2006] ETMR 55 regarding this provision.
[24] Gowers Review of Intellectual Property, available at http://webarchive.nationalarchives.gov.uk/+/http://www.hm-treasury.gov.
uk/d/pbr06_gowers_report_755.pdf.
[25] http://www.ipo.gov.uk/ipreview.htm.   [26] http://www.ipo.gov.uk/ipreview.htm.   [27] Patents Act 1977, s 60.

1.38   *Copyright* protects works that demonstrate *originality*. Here, originality simply means that there must be some evidence of independent skill or intellectual endeavour on the part of the creator, and that the work is not simply copied from an existing work. Thus, if we take our class on an outing to Princes Street Gardens in Edinburgh and every member of the class sketches Edinburgh Castle, each and every sketch will attract copyright protection from the moment that it is created. It does not matter that the subject is the same because the drawings themselves are original works deserving legal protection. Moreover, if half of the class also takes a photograph of the castle, each photograph will also be protected by copyright. The originality requirement is met by the simple act of holding the camera at a certain angle and the independent exercise of judgement by each person as to when they release the shutter. In the realm of copyright, it does not matter that millions of photographs have already been taken of Edinburgh Castle: *originality* does not mean *novelty* in the same sense we find in patent law. There is a good reason why different terminology is used because the threshold to qualify for protection is set at a very different level. Furthermore, none of the people who have previously photographed or sketched the castle can prevent our students from doing so. The right received in copyright law is, as the name suggests, merely a right to prevent unauthorised copying or interference with one's own work. It is not a right to control all use of the underlying subject matter. As we explain in Chapter 2, copyright relates to the particular *expression* that the IP creator gives to their work. This is just as well, for were it otherwise copyright monopolies could significantly hinder the production of works in the fields of literature and the arts. Human beings are not very imaginative creatures. We always explore the same basic themes through our stories: birth, death, love, betrayal, revenge, hate, reconciliation and salvation. Copyright does not prevent anyone writing about these subjects, it merely protects the ways in which particular stories are told.

 Question

What do 'novelty', 'individual character' and 'originality' mean in the context of design law? How, if at all, do these concepts dovetail with the previous definitions? What is the threshold criterion in trade mark law?

1.39   We can see, then, that the rights conferred by a copyright are much weaker than those conferred by a patent. Not only does this affect the nature and scope of the private rights of the property owner, but it also means that each of these IPRs will have a very different impact on the public sphere where it is exercised. Differential time limits are employed to minimise these effects. For example, a patent will initially only be granted for four years, although it can be renewed in successive years on the payment of a steadily increasing renewal fee,[28] up to a maximum of 20 years.[29] Compare this with copyright protection which, in the context of original works, lasts for the life of the author plus 70 years after their death. The compromise that is achieved balances, on the one hand, short and strong protection with, on the other, longer and weaker protection. In all cases when an IP right expires, however, the property enters the public sphere unconditionally, where it is free to be used by anyone.

[28] Patents (Fees) Rules 2007 (SI 2007/3292).
[29] A notable exception to this is the Supplementary Protection Certificate (SPC). These certificates can be granted in respect of 'medical products' and 'plant protection products' to extend legal protection for a further five years at the end of the initial 20-year period of patent protection. The market lead-in time for such products is often prolonged because of the requirement to subject them to regulatory and safety controls in the public interest. This results in a net reduction in the effectiveness of any patent that is granted, and an SPC is a means to redress this imbalance in favour of the intellectual property producer. Both forms of SPC operate under European Regulations (Regulation 469/2009 (medicinal products) 1992 OJ L182/1; Regulation 1610/96 (plant protection products) 1996 OJ L198/30).

1.40   Registration of IP is a common, although not universal, feature of protection regimes. Patents, trade marks and some design rights must be registered. In contrast, copyright protection arises whenever a work which satisfies the qualification criteria is created and UK unregistered design right exists whenever a design document is produced,[30] or an article is made to the design. Registration serves a number of functions, including identification of the subject matter to be protected, and a means to test whether the putative property is indeed 'new' (since a search of the relevant register can be carried out to determine if a similar or identical piece of property is already protected). Registers are public documents and provide a single point of reference for third parties to consider the current state of play in a particular field of innovation.

> **Discussion point** For answer guidance visit www.oxfordtextbooks.co.uk/orc/waelde3e/
>
> Look at Diagram 1.2. Why do each of patents, copyright and design rights ultimately expire whereas a trade mark can be protected for all time as long as it is re-registered every ten years?

1.41   When a right must be registered it is important to bear in mind that, as has been noted, the qualification criteria can be fairly stringent, and can call for no prior disclosure of the creation. The classic example of this is patent law, which requires that an invention must never have been made available to the public prior to the filing of an application for patent protection. This is also broadly true in the realm of registered design law.

What protection do intellectual products receive prior to registration?

1.42   Here, as noted, the importance of common law protection through the action of breach of confidence can become important. As we discuss in Chapter 18, the law of confidence protects confidential information, that is, information which is not part of the public domain. The action provides a remedy against those who disclose confidential information into that domain or are likely to do so. Thus, the threat of an action of breach of confidence can assist considerably in protecting the interests of IP producers in the period between the initial conception of their idea for a new creation and the time when they file for registration.

1.43   However, in order to receive any protection at all, you must be able to express your idea with a sufficient degree of specificity to make it realisable as a final product.[31] This does not necessarily mean that you should write it down, although you would be wise to do so, but it does require that you can give sufficient substance to the information for which you wish to claim protection. Above all, you must keep the information secret and only disclose it to those persons upon whom you can impose a duty of confidence.

> **Question**
>
> If you write your idea down you will receive a form of IP protection in addition to what may be pursued using breach of confidence. Which protection will this be? How far will this protection extend?

---

[30] Defined in Copyright, Designs and Patents Act 1988, s 263(1).   [31] *De Maudsley v Palumbo and Others* [1996] FSR 447.

Diagram 1.2 Core features of the statutory intellectual property rights

	Qualification criterion	Length of protection period	Strength of monopoly
Patents	Novelty	20 years max	Absolute monopoly
Copyright	Originality	Life of the author + 70 years for original works	Monopoly only over the expression of one's own creation
Registered designs	Novelty and with individual character	25 years max (five 5-year renewal periods)	Monopoly over use of design as it is applied to articles for which protection has been sought and granted
UK unregistered designs	Originality and not commonplace in the design field	15 years max (more limited if design exploited)	Monopoly against copying of design
Trade marks	Capacity to distinguish goods or services of right holder from those of another trader	10-year periods in perpetuity (with re-registration)	Monopoly over use of mark in respect of goods or services for which it is registered
	+ No conflict with 'earlier trade mark'	Loss of right if no use for 5 consecutive years	If mark has a reputation right holder can prevent use on 'dissimilar' goods

Summary of common themes

1.44   A series of common themes and elements run through many, and sometimes all, forms of IP protection.

- **Qualification for protection:** *newness*

All forms of IP must be 'new' in order to receive the protection of the law. However, the degree to which a creation must be new varies with each form of IP right.

- **Procedure for protection:** *registration*

Many of the statutory IPRs require registration. This assists in the identification of the property to be protected and administration of the rights to be granted.

- **Form of protection:** *control*

IP owners can control how their property is used and exploited by others. Different rights are conferred by the different IPRs. Note, however, that a common feature is that they only give a negative right of exclusion from the marketplace. That is, there is no positive entitlement to privilege or success in the market and so no real monopoly. The right is a public right to be exercised against those who would compete with the IP holder in a public forum. IP constraints rarely reach into the private sphere. Thus, as will be seen in Chapter 11, a patent is not infringed by acts done privately and for purposes which are not commercial.

- **Duration of protection:** *time limits*

One feature of the need to strike a balance in the provision of IP protection can be seen in the imposition of time limits on the duration of many IPRs. Often, this is inversely related to the strength of the right which is offered.

- **Implementation of protection:** *remedies*

The remedies which are available for infringement of IPRs are, in the main, uniform. These are:

Injunction (interdict) An action requiring a third party to desist unlawful conduct, or to prevent him engaging therein. For example, an injunction might be granted to prevent a trader from selling infringing copies of your latest CD.

Delivery up But what is to stop the rogue trader from selling his 10,000 infringing copies anyway? This remedy ensures that the infringer must hand over all infringing copies for destruction.

Damages or **Account of profits** *Damages* will be assessed by the court to reflect what, in its opinion, you have lost as a result of an infringer's activities. An *account of profits* requires that the infringer's profits made from his illegal activities be handed over to you. Note that these two remedies are mutually exclusive, that is, you must opt for one or the other—you cannot ask for both.

Summary of common expressions and notices

1.45 Here are some common expressions and notices that you will find attached to works that claim IP protection.

- **Notices of protection**

Patent pending This term is used once a patent has been applied for but before it is granted. Inventors attach this to their inventions to put rivals on notice that an application is being considered. The novelty of an invention is tested by reference to what was publicly available prior to a patent application being filed. In this period an invention must not appear in the public domain—if it does, protection will never be granted. Once an application is filed, however, marketing of the invention can go ahead without any risk of prejudice to the patent application.

© Copyright protection arises automatically whenever a qualifying work is created. However, in order to gain international recognition and reciprocity of that protection under the Universal Copyright Convention (1971), this symbol should appear on the work, together with the name of the author and the date when the work was first made publicly available.

® This symbol indicates that a trade mark is registered. Only formally registered marks are entitled to appear with this symbol. It is an offence falsely to represent that a mark is a registered trade mark.[32]

TM Intellectual property producers sometimes attach this symbol to signs, names or logos in an attempt to infer that these are trade marks. Often this happens when trade mark protection has been refused, or is unlikely to be granted, or the producer does not want to go to the time and expense of registering his mark. In Europe, this symbol has no legal effect whatsoever.

Ⓓ This notice may appear on registered designs which seek recognition under the Hague Agreement Concerning the International Registration of Industrial

---

[32] Trade Marks Act 1994, s 95.

Designs (1960). Under the 1960 agreement, the encircled D is to be accompanied by the year of the deposit, the name of the depositor and the number of the international deposit.

Ⓟ   This symbol puts others on notice that rights of producers of phonograms or performers are being claimed under the Convention for the Protection of Performers, Producers of Phonograms and Broadcasting Organisations (1961). As previously, name and date must also appear.

T   This is a similar system to those previously, this time in respect of topography rights under the EC Directive 87/54 of 16 December 1986. Where the legislation of member states provides that semiconductor products manufactured using protected topographies may carry an indication, this should be in one of the following forms: Ⓣ, T, 'T', [T], or T*.

Developing intellectual property law

1.46   IP law is more in demand now than it has ever been. Businesses are increasingly seeing IP as important for their survival, and as a consequence increased pressure has been brought to bear on IP law to provide adequate protection for new and emerging technologies. Two forms of development have been possible.[33]

- *Accretion* occurs when an existing right is extended to protect a new entity, for example the extension of copyright protection to computer software and databases.

- *Emulation* occurs when a new right is created to protect a new entity. This occurred with the advent of semiconductor topography protection and is also a device that has been used to protect the content of databases.

A paradox in development?

1.47   At the time of writing, IPRs remain creatures of national territorial effect only, with a few notable exceptions. National IP laws have been, however, under supranational influences for centuries, and indeed the drivers of modern IP development come almost exclusively from the international sphere. IP law is truly an international subject, and one cannot acquire a true understanding of the discipline by looking only at national rights.

The Map of Intellectual Property Law

National law

MOST IPRs ARE CREATURES
OF TERRITORIAL EFFECT ONLY

---

[33] See WR Cornish, 'The international relations of intellectual property' (1993) 52 CLJ 46.

European law influences on IP law

(a) Programme of harmonisation and approximation of laws
(b) EU-wide IPRs
(Community trade marks and designs)
(c) Treaty on the Functioning of the European Union
Free movement of goods and services
(Arts 345, 34 and 36)
Anti-restrictive and monopolistic practices
(Arts 101 and 102)

**International agreements,
conventions, protocols etc**

Common features:

(1) Access to protection and 'national treatment' for foreigners
(2) Minimum (harmonised) standards of protection to be offered by national laws

National law

1.48   You will see later that many international instruments and European initiatives now shape and direct IP law. Despite this, there are very few IPRs which have an effect beyond the particular country jurisdiction in which they are granted. For the IPRs that must be registered, this means that IP producers must register their rights in each jurisdiction where they seek protection. This cumbersome process is eased in some cases by international agreements that permit one application to be lodged and then considered for a number of specified countries. For example, the Patent Cooperation Treaty (1970) provides such a mechanism for patents, the Madrid Agreement Concerning the International Registration of Marks (1891) and the Madrid Protocol (1989) offer an equivalent system for trade marks and the Hague Agreement Concerning the Deposit of Industrial Designs (1925) allows for the deposit of a single design application which will be recognised throughout all countries that are signatories to the agreement. In each case, however, it is national rights which are obtained ultimately, and infringement and enforcement procedures can only be invoked in the domestic courts of individual states.

1.49   In the context of copyright, signatory countries to the Berne Convention for the Protection of Literary and Artistic Works (1886) and the Universal Copyright Convention (1952) guarantee mutual recognition of copyright to nationals of fellow signatory states.

 Exercise

To which of the previously mentioned international agreements is the UK a signatory? (Hint: each of these measures is administered by the World Intellectual Property Organization (WIPO) based in Geneva.)

A tension between legislative onslaught and judicial reticence

1.50   One outcome of this rather curious mix of national and international dimensions to IP law is that we can see the discipline being pulled in different directions depending on who is holding the reins at any given time. For example, there is a very significant push to maintain international legislative initiatives designed to extend IP protection in the economic interests of IP producers. At the same time, it will be seen throughout this book that domestic courts, especially in the UK, are often seeking to restrict the scope and influence of IPRs through the interpretations that they give to IP legislation, as regards both itself and in relation to other principles such as competition and human rights. This affects IP law in a number of different ways. For one thing, it means that there may be considerable disharmony between different countries in terms of the actual rights that IP holders enjoy. Thus, even if the substantive legal provisions are the same, as they have been agreed internationally and incorporated into the letter of domestic law, the effect given to those provisions through interpretation by the national courts can result in fairly wide variations in practice.

 Exercise

Consider whether this is an accurate statement of a phenomenon in modern IP law as you read through this book. Why might the courts approach IP questions in a manner which is different from that taken by policymakers? What are the wider implications of this disparity of approach? Which faction is likely to win out in the end? Will this be the right result?

The European dimension

1.51   It is precisely because IPRs have traditionally only been effective in individual states that the European Union has taken such an interest in this area of law. Primarily, this is because of the prospect that the exercise of IPRs within the European single market will have the effect of partitioning that market and thereby thwart one of the fundamental guiding principles of the Union, namely, that goods should be allowed to circulate freely within the single market. A moment's reflection should reveal how this can happen. If A has a patent only in France, the invention will only be protected in that country. They cannot, therefore, prevent the making or use of the invention elsewhere in the Union, nor can they control what happens to versions of the invention which they have produced once they leave French soil. However, the French patent should, in principle at least, allow them to prevent any imports into France, both of infringing goods that they have not authorised, and also of products comprising the invention which they might have sold elsewhere. While the first of these rights is thought to be permissible, the second has been severely curtailed in the name of protection of the single market. Other problems can arise when IPRs are protected unevenly within the single market's territory. For example, if copyright is protected for the life of the author plus 50 years in the UK (as used to be so), but subsists for the life of the author plus 70 years in Germany, material will fall out of copyright in the former earlier than the latter allowing it to be copied by anyone and to circulate freely except in Germany where it retains an additional 20 years of protection. Once again, this can lead to a division of the single market along private property lines.[34]

1.52   The Union has launched a three-pronged offensive on IPRs as a result of these concerns in an attempt to minimise their adverse effects.

Harmonisation and approximation of laws

1.53   The Union has been engaged in a robust programme of harmonisation (also sometimes 'approximation') of certain crucial areas of IP law for over three decades. There is more potential for such action since the Lisbon Treaty came into effect in 2009. Article 118 TFEU provides for the promulgation of

---

[34] The term of copyright protection was made uniform by Council Directive 93/98/EEC of 29 October 1993 harmonising the term of protection of copyright and certain related rights. The term of protection is now life of the author plus 70 years for original works.

'measures for the creation of European intellectual property rights to provide uniform protection of intellectual property rights throughout the Union and for the setting up of centralised Union-wide authorisation, coordination and supervision arrangements'.[35] Harmonisation has several advantages beyond ensuring that each member state applies the same legal provisions to IP protection. Perhaps most importantly, it brings the interpretation of IP law within the rubric of the Court of Justice of the European Union, and this is one way of addressing the potential for residual unevenness around the Union in the way in which IPRs are given effect by domestic courts.

1.54   Already a number of projects have been completed or are in progress. Other (wider) European initiatives also exist. Here are some key and more recent examples:

- *Patent law harmonisation* (European Patent Convention (1973 and 2000)), establishing the European Patent Office in Munich, Germany (1978). UK law was brought into line via the Patents Act 1977.[36]

- *Trade mark approximation* (UK law) Trade Marks Act 1994.[37] Establishment of the Community trade mark, administered by the OHIM, in Alicante, Spain.[38]

- Harmonisation of the *period of duration of rights in copyright* (now life of the author plus 70 years for original works, following the German model). See Duration of Copyright and Rights in Performances Regulations 1995 (SI 1995/3297).[39]

- Harmonisation of the *legal protection of databases*, now embodied in the UK under the Copyright and Rights in Databases Regulations 1997 (SI 1997/3032), as incorporated into the Copyright, Designs and Patents Act 1988.[40]

- Harmonisation of *legal protection of biotechnological inventions*. Parliament and Council Directive of July 1998, incorporated into domestic UK law in the Patents Regulations 2000 (SI 2000/2037).[41]

- Harmonisation of *design law*. The UK complied through amending the Registered Designs Act 1949 by the Registered Designs Regulations 2001 (SI 2001/3949).[42] Establishment of Community registered and unregistered design rights, administered through the OHIM.[43]

- The European Commission has adopted a proposal on a Directive for extended term protection for musical performers from 50 years to 95 years. Despite a controversial public consultation in which many stakeholders argued against such a move, the proposal led to Directive 2011/77/EU, adopted on 12 September 2011, which extends the term of protection for sound recordings from 50 years to 70 years.

- In parallel, a Green Paper was published in 2008 on copyright in the knowledge economy exploring the role of copyright in encouraging dissemination of knowledge in society and generating economic

---

[35] Treaty of Lisbon 2007/C OJ 306 17 December 2007, Art 84 inserts new Art 97A into Treaty on European Union, which became Art 118. For discussion as to the possible impact of this, see W Kingston, 'Intellectual property in the Lisbon Treaty' (2008) 30(11) EIPR 439–443.

[36] Note the European Patent Convention (EPC) is not an EU document. There are currently 38 signatories to the EPC, including the 28 member states of the EU (as at early 2013—see lists at http://www.epo.org/about-us/organisation/member-states.html).

[37] Council Directive 89/104/EEC of 21 December 1988 to approximate the laws of the member states relating to trade marks. Version 2008/95/CE consolidated version previously First Council Directive 89/104/EEC of 21 December 1988.

[38] Council Regulation (EC) No 40/94 of 20 December 1993 on the Community trade mark and see Council Regulation (EC) No 207/2009 of 26 February 2009 on the Community trade mark (codified version).

[39] Council Directive 93/98/EEC of 29 October 1993 harmonising the term of protection of copyright and certain related rights, which was replaced by Directive 2006/116/E, a consolidated version, which has now been amended by Directive 2011/77/EU.

[40] Directive 96/9/EC of the European Parliament and of the Council of 11 March 1996 on the legal protection of databases.

[41] Directive 98/44/EC of the European Parliament and of the Council of 6 July 1998 on the legal protection of biotechnological inventions.

[42] Directive 98/71/EC of the European Parliament and of the Council of 13 October 1998 on the legal protection of designs.

[43] Council Regulation (EC) No 6/2002 of 12 December 2001 on Community designs.

impact across sectors such as the arts, science, education and research, and there was a Green Paper in 2011 on online distribution of audio visual works.

Web link

The text of these initiatives, and more information on them, can be found at the following website: **http://ec.europa.eu/internal_market/copyright/index_en.htm.**

EU rights

1.55   You should note from the previous list that in two instances the European Union (formerly Community) has instituted Union-wide IPRs, which have been mentioned earlier in this chapter. The first of these was the Community trade mark, established by means of a Council Regulation in 1996.[44] It is administered through the OHIM.[45] The Council subsequently adopted the Community Design Regulation, which introduced both registered and unregistered design rights with effect throughout the Union, and which is also administered by the OHIM.[46] Neither of these measures supplants the existing frameworks for domestic protection.

 Discussion point   For answer guidance visit www.oxfordtextbooks.co.uk/orc/waelde3e/

How is it possible for the Union (and formerly the Community) to legislate on property matters when Article 345 TFEU states: 'This Treaty shall in no way prejudice the rules in Member States governing the system of property ownership'? Will the existence of a single right render national rights redundant?

1.56   Union-wide rights are the best means to resolve the tension between territorial IPRs and the aims of the single market for reasons which should be self-evident. There can be no partitioning of the market if only a unitary right can subsist throughout its territory. Moreover, the creation of new legal provisions means that mechanisms can be incorporated *ab initio* to prevent some particular uses of the IPRs which have been discussed earlier in this chapter. We explore the details and the functioning of the EU IPRs in Chapters 8, 9 and 13.

1.57   These European successes have not been easy to bring about. Often there is difficulty in getting consensus on the terms of protection, the languages to be used for registration purposes and the scope of the eventual rights to be granted. In particular, disputes about the extent of protection of spare parts held up the Community Design Regulation for a number of years. Longer still in the making has been the EU patent (formerly called the Community patent) which has been on the cards since the mid-1970s, but sufficient agreement has never been reached to bring an international instrument into force.[47] This emerged as a viable option with a proposal for a Council Regulation in 2000[48] although there was little progress until 2007 when the Commission adopted a Communication on 'Enhancing the patent

---

[44] See note 38.   [45] See note 4.   [46] See http://oami.europa.eu/ows/rw/pages/index.en.do.
[47] Convention for the European Patent for the Common Market (Community Patent Convention) (Luxembourg, 1975, revised 1989).
[48] Commission Proposal for a Council Regulation on the Community Patent, COM(00) 412 final.

system'. This became a draft Agreement to establish a unified patent litigation system, but this was found by the Court of Justice of the European Union to be beyond the legislative capacities set out in the EU Treaties. The Commission quickly turned to a proposal for unitary patent courts, which led in late 2012 to the European Parliament approving a unitary package patent, which addresses both the application and enforcement process.[49] The same problems have re-emerged over time, including the very thorny issue of language: if patent law requires that an inventor describe in intricate detail the workings of his invention, and there are 23 official languages of the EU, the question of in which language or languages this description must appear invariably arises. Translations into all official languages would make pat enting prohibitively expensive, but if we do not require all, then which? And where would any central court or courts be located? It will be interesting to note how the unitary patent package develops. We discuss this further in Chapter 10.

? Question

Can you think of a reasonable compromise? Is it the same as that in the unitary patent package?

Free movement of goods and restrictions on anti-competitive practices

1.58   Another important influence of European law comes from certain key provisions in the TFEU. Because of the potential for IPRs to interfere with the aims and smooth operation of the single market, the European Court of Justice (ECJ) has taken it upon itself to rule on the extent to which the exercise of IPRs conflicts with European law, and to temper the scope of those rights as a result. Attention has focused on the interpretation of what are now Articles 34, 36 and 345 TFEU. Article 345 specifically reserves property law matters to the member states, including IP laws, but the Court has interpreted this to mean that only the *existence* of such rights enjoy unfettered national protection. The *exercise* of those rights may be curtailed if it represents an unjustified interference with free trading practices. Articles 34 and 36 operate to prohibit unjustified restrictions upon what can be imported and exported between member states. And, while Article 36 allows restrictions upon imports if they are justified to protect 'industrial or commercial property', it will not do so if the restriction which is imposed amounts to 'arbitrary discrimination' or 'disguised restriction' on trade which is otherwise legitimate.

1.59   A common example of how the Court has taken all of these interpretations and applied them to the exercise of IPRs is found in the context of parallel imports. While it is acceptable for an IP right holder to exercise their right within a particular member state, they will be deemed to have 'exhausted' their right if they permit export to one or more member states, or exercise the right there itself or allow the right to be exercised with their (free) consent. If, then, a third party who has legitimate possession of protected goods in member state X wishes to re-import the goods into the IP right holder's country (undoubtedly at a lower price than they are being sold by the right holder), the latter cannot prevent the former from doing so, as it would represent an unfair fetter on free trade. The right holder is said to have *exhausted* their rights in this regard, and can no longer impose any restrictions on the free circulation of those goods within the single market. Thus, in one sense the scope of the IP right is modified, in that 'the right to first market' now forms part of the right but also operates as a limitation on it. In all other

[49] See details on European Parliament News, 'Parliament approved unitary patent rules' (11 December 2012) http://www. europarl.europa.eu/news/en/pressroom/content/20121210IPR04506/html/Parliament-approves-EU-unitary-patent-rules; European Commission webpage http://ec.europa.eu/internal_market/indprop/patent/index_en.htm; discussion via IPKat, eg, http://ipkitten. blogspot.co.uk/2012/12/european-council-endorses-unitary.html.

senses, however, IPRs operate normally. Note, too, that these restrictions only apply when the intellectual products have been first marketed by the right holder themselves or with their 'consent', and this has led in turn to debate about the legal meaning of consent, requiring further rulings by the ECJ.[50] This is considered in more detail in Chapter 20.

International exhaustion

1.60   All of this is done in the name of protecting the integrity of the single market, that is, in regulating what happens *within* that market. But what is the position of the right holder who wants to exercise his rights to prevent goods entering the single market from outside its borders? Well, the ECJ has ruled that the principle of 'international exhaustion' does not apply to IPRs protected within the European Economic Area (EEA) (the European Union plus the members of the European Free Trade Association, namely Iceland, Liechtenstein and Norway). Thus, when S, the manufacturer of designer sunglasses, sold his previous year's stock to a trader in Bulgaria—at that time outside the EU—he was nonetheless able to use his trade mark right in respect of the sunglasses (*Silhouette*) to prevent an Austrian retailer from buying the glasses cheaply and importing them back into the EEA to compete with the right holder.[51] This has been a very controversial decision, not least because it is seen to favour the interests of manufacturers and IP holders over the interests of European consumers, by keeping lower cost, quality products out of the European marketplace. Further, neither the product nor the mark are being held out as anything other than that which they are, namely, the goods and mark of the IP holder. Thus, in strict terms, has the trade mark right not served its function, which is to act as a mark of quality and a badge of origin, albeit that there is conduct which is covered by the exclusive rights conferred on the national trade mark owner? Again, we explore this, and other, controversial issues in this realm in Chapter 20.

Anti-competitive practices

1.61   Articles 101 and 102 TFEU operate to ensure that free trade is not compromised by unacceptable, restrictive or monopolistic practices. Article 101 prohibits, inter alia, the establishment and operation of cartels between enterprises which have as their object or effect the distortion or prevention of competition in the single market. Article 102 concerns the abuse of a dominant position within a particular market by any particular commercial enterprise, to the extent that it affects trade *between* member states. The Article offers examples of how such an abuse might be affected; namely: (a) directly or indirectly imposing unfair purchase or selling prices or other unfair trading conditions; (b) limiting production, markets or technical development to the prejudice of consumers; (c) applying dissimilar conditions to equivalent transactions with other trading parties, thereby placing them at a competitive disadvantage; (d) making the conclusion of contracts subject to acceptance by the other parties of supplementary obligations which, by their nature or according to commercial usage, have no connection with the subject of the contracts. Any agreements which contravene Article 101 or 102 are void.

1.62   These provisions are policed by the European Commission which can offer guidance on the fine line between acceptable and unacceptable practices, as it has done, inter alia, by issuing 'block exemptions' for certain types of agreement or terms in agreements.[52] By the same token, the Commission is also empowered to fine any undertaking which contravenes the terms of Articles 101 and 102.

---

[50] See, eg, Joined Cases C-414/99, C-415/99 and C-416/99 *Zino Davidoff SA v A & G Imports Ltd and Levi Strauss & Co and Others v Tesco Stores Ltd and Others*, Judgment of the Court, 20 November 2001.

[51] See *Silhouette International Schmied GmbH & Co KG v Hartlauer Handelsgellschaft mbH* [1998] ECR I-4799.

[52] Commission Regulation (EEC) 240/96 on the application of Art 85(3) to certain categories of technology transfer agreements. (Note that Art 101 TFEU was originally Art 85 EC.)

1.63   The relevance of these provisions for IP right holders is seen most acutely in the context of licensing. IP can be exploited through licences, which are simply agreements between the right holder and third parties to determine how, when, where and for how much the third party can exploit the IP of the owner. Ordinarily, these licences are subject to domestic contract law, with the proviso that they must also accord with Articles 101 and 102. Thus, the terms of these agreements are potentially liable to scrutiny by the Commission, although the granting of block exemptions has made it clearer as to which provisions may or may not be included. Moreover, it is not the case that a refusal to enter an agreement with a third party to exploit IP is automatically a contravention of the TFEU, even though this might leave the right holder with exclusive control of its IP in the market.[53] In some rare circumstances, however, it may be abuse of a dominant position to refuse to license.[54] We discuss the margins of permissible and impermissible conduct in Chapters 20 and 21.

International obligations

1.64   We can see, then, that the EU has its own particular agenda for interfering with the exercise of IPRs and guiding their future development. However, beyond this particularised regional influence, other agendas have operated for well over a century, and today a large number of internationally-imposed obligations mould the nature and content of IPRs and ultimately determine the direction of IP law.

1.65   Although it has been the tradition of IP law to protect rights first and foremost at the national level, the international possibilities for the exploitation of IP have long been appreciated. Markets do not recognise territorial boundaries, and IP producers will always gravitate towards a potential market. And, as international trade became a more realistic possibility with the advent of the industrial revolution in the 19th century, so too industrialised nations realised that disparities between markets in terms of IP protection could have an adverse impact on the rights of their IP producers and, in turn, on their own economic interests. In a spirit of economic reciprocity, then, a number of countries sought to establish multilateral treaties to minimise these adverse effects. The first instruments to emerge were the *Paris Convention for the Protection of Industrial Property* (1883), and the *Berne Convention for the Protection of Literary and Artistic Works* (1886).

Paris Convention for the Protection of Industrial Property (1883, as revised)

The protection of 'industrial property' has as its objects patents, utility models, industrial designs, trade marks, service marks, trade names, indications of source or appellations of origin and the repression of unfair competition.

Berne Convention for the Protection of Literary and Artistic Works (1886, as revised)

The expression 'literary and artistic works' shall include every production in the literary, scientific and artistic domain, whatever may be the mode or form of its expression, such as books, pamphlets and other writings; lectures, addresses, sermons and other words of the same nature; dramatic or dramatico-musical

---

[53] *AB Volvo v Erik Veng (UK) Ltd* [1988] ECR 6211.
[54] The first landmark case is *Radio Telefis Eireann v EC Commission* [1991] ECR II-485.

works; choreographic works and entertainments in dumb show; musical compositions with or without words; cinematographic works to which are assimilated works expressed by a process analogous to cinematography; works of drawing, painting, architecture, sculpture, engraving and lithography; photographic works to which are assimilated works expressed by a process analogous to photography; works of applied art; illustrations, maps, plans, sketches and three-dimensional works related to geography, topography, architecture or science.

 Question

Why two conventions and not one? What differentiates 'industrial property' under the Paris Convention from the entities protected under the Berne Convention? Does this remain a meaningful distinction in the modern age?

1.66   Signatory countries to these conventions undertook to provide two key elements of protection. The first is *national treatment* of foreigners, which, as the name suggests, means that any individual seeking protection in a signatory country beyond their own shores must be dealt with on the same terms as if they were a national of that country. Secondly, these instruments sought to establish certain baselines of protection, as the previous definitions indicate, to ensure that the same kinds of 'property' were protected in the various party states. The obligation to provide this level of protection is, however, very broadly drafted. For example, the UK does not have a specific law to guard against unfair competition, yet the argument is made that the UK nonetheless complies with its international obligations under the Paris Convention in a piecemeal fashion, inter alia, because of the existence of common law actions such as passing off and breach of confidence.

 Discussion point For answer guidance visit www.oxfordtextbooks.co.uk/orc/waelde3e/

What does protection against unfair competition mean? Do you think that the UK maintains a defensible position in this regard? Would it be preferable to institute a specific law in this area? Reconsider the question after you have read Chapter 17.

1.67   In summary, two main themes typify international agreements on IP protection: (1) access to protection and 'national treatment' for foreigners; and (2) minimum (harmonised) standards of protection to be offered by national laws.

1.68   The Paris and Berne Conventions, and indeed many other instruments, are administered by WIPO in Geneva.[55] Disputes and compliance measures may be dealt with through the International Court of Justice.

TRIPS Agreement (agreement on trade-related aspects of intellectual property rights, 1994)

1.69   The TRIPS Agreement was included in the Accord which finalised the Uruguay Round of the General Agreement on Tariffs and Trade (GATT, 1994). The Agreement touches all the major forms of IPR and is administered by the World Trade Organization (WTO), also based in Geneva. Importantly, states which

---

[55] For more information on international treaties and agreements, see the WIPO website at http://www.wipo.org.

do not comply with the provisions of TRIPS may face proceedings before the GATT dispute settlement system and this in turn may lead to the withdrawal of GATT privileges. A variable timescale for implementing TRIPS operates to ensure that developing and least developed countries have a transitional period in which to bring their laws into compliance with the Agreement.

1.70   TRIPS is similar to the Paris and Berne Conventions in that it provides for national treatment and seeks to harmonise basic IP provisions. However, in other respects it goes far beyond its 19th-century counterparts. For example, TRIPS puts more flesh on the bones of the elements of protection required of signatory countries, as we shall see in each of the chapters to come that deal with the substantive law. Moreover, TRIPS ties these countries into many of the essential terms of the Paris and Berne Conventions, even if they are not signatories to them, thereby considerably extending the reach of these instruments.[56]

1.71   The motivation for the implementation of TRIPS is almost entirely economic. It was driven by the concerns of Western industrialised countries, and most notably the United States, which could not countenance the multi-billion dollar trade in unauthorised IP that had developed over the years, despite the existence of the Paris and Berne Conventions. One of the problems was that these Conventions had not attracted universal support, and in particular many of the countries where illicit trading was taking place were not signatories to them, and so were not subject to their terms. How then to implement a regime that could bring offending states under its influence? The answer was trade. By linking TRIPS to GATT, and so thereby bringing all signatory states under the auspices of the WTO, the relevant politicians and governments in control have been able to establish a system which is almost impossible to resist. No state in the modern world can develop without international trade; and so tight is the hold on that regime through GATT, that no state can fail to sign up, and thereby become obliged to comply with TRIPS. The real stroke of economic genius has been to link non-compliance with TRIPS to the withdrawal of GATT privileges, in the event of an adverse ruling by the WTO—which could potentially cripple a state's entire economy.[57] Finally, despite the power available for IP owners as a result of TRIPS, there has also been an increase in regional or bilateral trade agreements which require that states provide other parties with higher levels of protection than is required by TRIPS. Given the national treatment requirement, this can lead to higher levels of protection in a state's IP laws as a whole.[58] This is known as the phenomenon of TRIPS-plus. Similarly, and outside the organisations discussed, several developed countries led secret negotiations of the Anti-Counterfeiting Trade Agreement (ACTA). Activist groups, with a focus on access to knowledge and innovation, led strong challenges to this, and its content became more moderate; further, at the time of writing in 2013, it is unclear whether or not sufficient states will now choose to ratify the agreement.[59]

Other international instruments

1.72   This has clearly not been an exhaustive account of the international measures which impact on IP law. It is not intended to be. Rather, this overview should give a good idea of the influences which international measures have on the discipline. Bear these in mind as you proceed through this book. For the sake of completeness, however, note too that there are many other international instruments which exist in this realm. We will consider them where this is relevant in the forthcoming chapters.

[56] TRIPS (1994), Arts 2 and 9.
[57] For further discussion, see F Ravida, 'Influence of WTO decisions on international intellectual property' (2008) 3(5) JIPLP 314–326 and D Gervais, *The TRIPs Agreement: Drafting History and Analysis* (4th edn, 2012).
[58] D Vivas Eugui and J von Braun, 'Beyond FTA negotiations: implementing the new generation of intellectual property obligations' at 113 and P Drahos, 'Doing deals with Al Capone: paying protection money for intellectual property in the global knowledge economy' at 141 in P Yu (ed), *Intellectual Property and Information Wealth: Issues and Practices in the Digital Age. Volume 4: International Intellectual Property Law and Policy* (2007).
[59] PK Yu, 'Six secret (and now open) fears of ACTA' (2011) 64 SMU Law Review 975; discussion on ACTA FFII Blog, available at http://acta.ffii.org/?p=633; see also http://www.ustr.gov/acta (including text) and http://ec.europa.eu/trade/tackling-unfair-trade/acta/.

- *Patents*

    - Patent Cooperation Treaty, Washington 1970
    - Convention on the Grant of European Patents (European Patent Convention), Munich 1973, 2000. Protocol on Interpretation of Article 69
    - Budapest Treaty on the International Recognition of the Deposit of Microorganisms for the Purposes of Patent Procedure, 1977

- *Copyright*

    - Universal Copyright Convention 1952, revised 1971
    - WIPO Copyright Treaty, 1996, and associated Agreed Statements

- *Designs*

    - Hague Agreement Concerning the International Registration of Industrial Designs, 1925, as revised

- *Trade marks*

    - Madrid Agreement Concerning the International Registration of Marks (1891, as revised, and Protocol, June 1989)
    - Trademark Law Treaty, Geneva 1994

- *Appellations of origin*

    - Lisbon Agreement for the Protection of Appellations of Origin and Their International Registration (1958, as revised)

- *Performers' rights*

    - WIPO Performances and Phonograms Treaty, 1996, and Agreed Statements
    - Rome Convention for the Protection of Performers, Producers of Phonograms and Broadcasting Organizations (1961)
    - The Beijing Treaty on Audiovisual Performances 2012 (adopted June 2012, not yet in force)
    - Geneva Convention for the Protection of Producers of Phonograms Against Unauthorized Duplication of their Phonograms, 1971

- *Plant breeders' rights*

    - International Convention for the Protection of New Varieties of Plants (UPOV Convention 1961, as revised 1991)

- *Integrated circuits*

    - Treaty on Intellectual Property in Respect of Integrated Circuits, 1989

Intellectual property and human rights

1.73   A final influence on the possible development of IP law that we must consider comes once again from the international plane, although this time the forces at work may be pulling in different directions. The European Convention for the Protection of Human Rights and Fundamental Freedoms (1950) was a post-war initiative by the Council of Europe designed to prevent a repeat of the atrocities of the era that had gone immediately before. Its general approach was to establish fundamental, and largely negative, rights for individuals against the state: rights of non-interference. Over the years a rich and complex jurisprudence has grown around the Articles of the Convention through the work of the European Court of Human Rights in Strasbourg, but for the most part its rulings have only touched the lives of UK citizens indirectly, because successive governments had refused to make the terms of the Convention part of domestic law. All of this changed, however, with the passing of the Human Rights Act 1998, which came into full force in October 2000. The last decade has accordingly seen an explosion in speculation about the possibility of human rights having an impact in every conceivable area of law, including IP law.[60] And, as the courts of the jurisdictions in the UK continue to consider to what extent human rights arguments can affect IPRs and their enforcement, it is undeniable that this represents a potentially significant sea change in the power balance between the various institutions which shape and form this discipline. The place of human rights within the discussion of IP will be strengthened further (although with uncertain impact)[61] now that the Lisbon Treaty has entered into force as discussed (para 1.53). This includes the Charter of Fundamental Rights, Article 17(2) of which provides that 'Intellectual property shall be protected'. Further, negotiations are ongoing in 2013 for the EU to become a party to the Convention,[62] and the impact of this again remains to be seen.[63]

The existence of IP, its infringement, business and societal impact (in particular in complex areas such as health, communications and the environment), the interaction between IP and other interests, and the conflicts between IP owners, access seekers and activists, will be explored in more detail in the following chapters.

Further reading

Books

L Bently and S Maniatis, *Intellectual Property and Ethics* (1998)

WR Cornish, *Intellectual Property: Omnipresent, Distracting, Irrelevant?* (2004)

W Cornish, D Llewelyn and T Aplin *Intellectual Property: Patents. Copyrights, Trademarks and Allied Rights* (7th edn, 2010)

GB Dinwoodie and RC Dreyfuss, *A Neofederalist Vision of TRIPS* (2012)

P Drahos, *A Philosophy of Intellectual Property* (1996)

P Drahos with J Braithwaite, *Information Feudalism: Who Owns the Knowledge Economy?* (2003)

P Drahos and R Mayne, *Global Intellectual Property Rights: Knowledge, Access and Development* (2002)

G Ghidini, *Intellectual Property and Competition Law: The Innovation Nexus* (2006)

---

[60] *Ashdown v Telegraph Newspapers* [2001] 4 All ER 666. See also for a theoretical exploration of human rights in the context of copyright, STM Newman, 'Human rights and copyrights: a look at practical jurisprudence with reference to authors' rights' (2009) 31(2) EIPR 88.

[61] See N MacCormick, 'Human rights and competition law: possible impact of the proposed EU Constitution' (2005) 2(4) SCRIPTed 444 (http://www.law.ed.ac.uk/ahrc/script-ed/vol2-4/maccormick.asp) and C Geiger, 'Intellectual property shall be protected!? Article 17(2) of the Charter of Fundamental Rights of the European Union: a mysterious provision with an unclear scope' (2009) 31(3) EIPR 113.

[62] Draft Agreement on the Accession of the European Union to the Convention for the Protection of Human Rights and Fundamental Freedoms CDDH-UE (2011)16fin, available at http://www.coe.int/t/dghl/standardsetting/hrpolicy/CDDH-UE/CDDH-UE_documents/CDDH-UE_2011_16_final_en.pdf.

[63] See, eg, existing presumptions of compliance, C Banner and A Thomson, 'Human rights review of state acts performed in compliance with EC law—*Bosphorus Airways v Ireland*' (2005) 6 EHRLR 649.

MR Pugatch, *The Intellectual Property Debate: Perspectives from Law, Economics and Political Economy* (2006)

B Sherman and L Bently, *The Making of Modern Intellectual Property* (3rd edn, 2008)

U Suthersanen, G Dutfield and KB Chow (eds), *Innovation Without Patents: Harnessing the Creative Spirit in a Diverse World* (2007)

Reports

Gowers Review of Intellectual Property (HM Treasury, 2006)

I Hargreaves, *Digital Opportunity: A Review of Intellectual Property and Growth* (2011)

Report of UK Commission on Intellectual Property Rights (2002) http://www.iprcommission.org/

Articles and lectures

A Brimelow, 'Does intellectual property need a new set of wheels?' (2001) 23(1) EIPR 44

E Cameron and J Berger, 'Patents and public health: principle, politics and paradox', Inaugural British Academy Law Lecture, http://www.law.ed.ac.uk/ahrc/script-ed/docs/cameron.asp

E Derclaye 'Should patent law help cool the planet? An inquiry from the point of view of environmental law', Part 1: (2009) 31(3) 168 and Part 2: (2009) 31(5) EIPR 227

W Fikentscher, 'Intellectual property and competition—human economic universals or cultural specificities?—a farewell to neoclassics?' (2007) IIC 137

C Geiger, 'Fundamental rights—a safeguard for the coherence of intellectual property law' (2004) 35 IIC 268

EC Hettinger, 'Justifying intellectual property' (1989) 19 Philosophy and Public Affairs 31

A Kur, 'A new framework for intellectual property rights—horizontal issues' (2004) 35 IIC 1

Sir H Laddie, 'National IP rights: a moribund anachronism in a federal Europe?' (2001) 23(9) EIPR 402

K Maskus and J Reichman, 'The globalisation of private knowledge goods and the privatization of global public goods' (2004) 7 JIEL 279–320

T Rychlicki, 'GPLv3: new software licence and new axiology of intellectual property law' (2008) 30(6) EIPR 232–243

PK Yu, 'Currents and crosscurrents in the international intellectual property regime' (2004) 38 Loyola of Los Angeles Law Review 323

Ongoing updates

The IPKat blog: http://ipkitten.blogspot.com/

Part II

Copyright

Introduction

This Part of the book explains and discusses the law of copyright. It has six chapters. The first considers the scope of copyright in the UK against the background of international, EU, and comparative law on the subject as well as its historical development. This also throws light on the rationales or justifications for copyright. The chapter then discusses the subject matter of copyright, that is to say, those things—or works—which come under its protection. The second chapter goes on to explain which persons can claim the benefits of copyright (including moral rights) and the length of time for which the protection endures. The next chapter explains what constitutes infringement of copyright, and is followed by a discussion of the exceptions to copyright. A crucial point is that the forms of infringement—or restricted acts—also define how copyright may be exploited to obtain financial returns for its owner. Other persons who wish to do one or more of these acts will have to obtain the copyright owner's permission—or licence—to do so and usually that permission will come at a price unless an exception applies. The fifth of the copyright chapters examines recently introduced rights very similar to, but different from, copyright—the *sui generis* database right and performers' rights. The final chapter deals with some of the most important contemporary issues affecting the development of copyright law, including the Internet, the concept of the public domain, and the impact of human rights law.

Sources of the law: key websites

- Copyright, Designs and Patents Act 1988 as amended. The UK–IPO provides a consolidated text of the copyright sections (as at 3 May 2007) at
  http://www.ipo.gov.uk/cdpact1988.pdf

- Decisions of the courts in the various jurisdictions of the UK, for which see BAILII
  http://www.bailii.org/

- EU Copyright Directives, for which see the Commission's Internal Market Directorate General's website
  http://ec.europa.eu/internal_market/copyright/index_en.htm

- Berne Convention for the Protection of Literary and Artistic Works, for which see the WIPO website
  http://www.wipo.int/treaties/en/ip/berne/trtdocs_wo001.html

- Rome Convention for the Protection of Performers, Producers of Phonograms and Broadcasting Organizations, for which see the WIPO website
  http://www.wipo.int/treaties/en/ip/rome/index.html

- The UK–IPO website has a useful section devoted to copyright
  http://www.ipo.gov.uk/copy.htm

Copyright 1: history, rationale, and subject matter

Introduction

Scope and overview of chapter

2.1 This chapter considers the scope and subject matter of modern copyright law against a background of its historical development in the UK and the international and European contexts in which that historical development has been increasingly set since the 19th century. Having thus set the scene, the chapter examines the matter in which copyright subsists. This centres on the concept of the 'protected work', and makes use of a distinction between what are sometimes known as 'author works' (literary, dramatic, musical, artistic, and film works) and 'media works' (typographical arrangements, sound recordings, broadcasts, and adaptations).

2.2 **Learning objectives**

By the end of this chapter you should be able to describe and explain:

- the development of copyright, and its rationale;
- the subject matter that copyright protects, and the different categories of work used by the law.

2.3 The chapter explores the history and rationales of copyright, before turning to consider the subject matter which the law protects. So the rest of the chapter looks like this:

- History (2.4–2.16)
- Rationale of copyright (2.17–2.21)
- Subject matter of protection (works, fixation, originality) (2.22–2.48)
- Author works (literary, dramatic, musical, artistic, film) (2.49–2.89)
- Media works (sound recordings, broadcasts, published editions) (2.90–2.96)

History

Early history

2.4   In most European countries the origins of copyright law lie in the efforts of government to regulate and control the output of printers once the technology of printing had been invented and become established in the 15th and 16th centuries. Whereas before printing a writing, once created, could only be physically multiplied by the highly laborious and error-prone process of manual copying out, printing made it possible to have as many exact copies of a work as there were persons who wanted and could afford to buy them. This meant much more rapid and widespread circulation of ideas and information. While the state and church thought this was to be encouraged in many aspects (eg dissemination of material such as Bibles and government information), it also meant that undesirable content—dissent and criticism of government and established religion, for example—could circulate too quickly for their comfort. So, all over Europe, government established controls over printing, by requiring printers to have official licences to be in business and produce books. These licences typically gave the printer the exclusive right to print particular works for a fixed period of years, enabling him to prevent others doing so during that period. Although the official licences could only grant rights to print in the territory of the state that had granted them, and therefore could not prevent printing of the same works in other territories, they did usually prohibit the import of such foreign printings into the territory where the licence had been granted. In England, the printers (then termed 'stationers') formed a collective organisation, known as the Stationers' Company, which in the 16th century was given the power to require the entry in its register of all lawfully printed books. Further, only members of the Company could enter books in the register. As a result the Company achieved a dominant position over publishing in 17th-century England. But there was no equivalent in contemporary Scotland or Ireland.[1] However, in 1694 the English Parliament deprived the Stationers' Company of its powers of control, creating uncertainty about regulation of the printing industry at a critical juncture in British history.[2]

 Question

How was the printing of books regulated in England before 1707?[3]

2.5   In 1707 the Parliaments of England and Scotland were united in a single body as the result of the Anglo-Scottish Union finally agreed that year, after much debate. The new Parliament was enjoined to respect the separate identities of the English and Scottish legal systems, but was enabled to change the laws of both countries as part of an overall project that today might be described as the creation of a single market in the UK. An important early piece of legislation to this end was the Copyright Act of 1709,[4] which created a single regime for application in both England and Scotland. The Act marks an important shift

---

[1] On the pre-history of copyright in Scotland, see AJ Mann, 'Scottish copyright before the Statute of 1710' [2000] JR 11; also the same author's *The Scottish Book Trade 1500–1720* (2000), Ch 4 and App 1; and 'Some property is theft: copyright law and illegal activity in early modern Scotland' in R Myers, M Harris and G Mandelbrote (eds), *Against the Law: Crime, Sharp Practice and the Control of Print* (2004).

[2] See in general M Rose, *Authors and Owners* (1993); J Greene, *The Trouble with Ownership: Literary Property and Authorial Liability in England, 1660–1730* (2005).

[3] See 'Primary Sources on Copyright (1450–1900)' at http://www.copyrighthistory.org/, a digital collection of primary sources from the UK and beyond and related commentary.

[4] Often known to copyright lawyers as 'the Statute or Act of Anne', after Queen Anne, who reigned 1702–1714. The Act entered into force in 1710 and is sometimes given that date rather than 1709.

of emphasis in the law, because it gave the 'sole right and liberty of printing books', not to printers, but to the authors of the books. This is the first formal legal recognition that a reason for conferring exclusive or property rights in this area was the work of its creator or originator. It may reflect the theories of contemporary philosophers such as John Locke, who held that rights of property flowed first from the labour of the person who created the thing to be owned. But the 1709 Act also enabled the author to transfer his rights to 'assigns', who would typically be the printer, without whom the author would be unable to disseminate and profit from his creation. Further, a precondition of the right was registration of the work at Stationers' Hall; something of a disadvantage for Scottish and Irish printers, since the Hall was in London. The right lasted for 14 years from first publication and if at the end of that time the author was still alive, it was renewed for another 14 years.[5]

 Question

When was the first copyright statute passed? What changes did it make to the previous regime described in para 2.4?

2.6   The next critical stage in the early history of British copyright came from the 1730s on, as the first copyrights created under the 1709 Act began to expire. Did those who had held statutory rights to prevent unauthorised copies also have an underlying right at common law which now revived to enable them to continue to control printing and publication of their work? There was intense controversy and much litigation in both England and Scotland on this question.[6] Matters were not resolved until the great cases of *Hinton v Donaldson*[7] in Scotland in 1773 and *Donaldson v Beckett*[8] in England in 1774. In these decisions, the Court of Session and the House of Lords respectively held that there was no copyright at common law in works which had been published and enjoyed copyright under the 1709 Act. While the common law of both England and Scotland went on to develop with regard to *unpublished* works (only the author or his licensee could authorise publication), the development of copyright would henceforth be principally through statute. The common law copyright in unpublished work remained significant until the beginning of the 20th century, however, because unlike the statutory copyrights, it had no specific time limit, and lasted until lawful publication (ie it could go on forever if publication never occurred).

 Question

What was the effect of the decisions in *Donaldson v Beckett* and *Hinton v Donaldson*?

  [5] See further R Deazley, *On the Origin of the Right to Copy—Charting the Movement of Copyright Law in Eighteenth Century Britain (1695–1775)* (2004); JC Ginsburg, '"Un chose publique?" The author's domain and the public domain in early British, French and US copyright law' (2006) 16 CLJ 636.

  [6] In addition to works already cited, see WR Cornish, 'The author's surrogate: the genesis of British copyright' in K O'Donovan and GR Rubin (eds), *Human Rights and Legal History: Essays in Honour of Brian Simpson* (2000); W St Clair, *The Reading Nation in the Romantic Period* (2004); W McDougall, 'Copyright litigation in the Court of Session, 1738–1749, and the rise of the Scottish book trade' (1987) 5 Edinburgh Bibliographical Society Transactions 2–31; HL MacQueen, 'Intellectual property and the common law in Scotland c1700–c1850' in L Bently, C Ng, and G D'Agostino (eds), *The Common Law of Intellectual Property: Essays in Honour of David Vaver* (2010).

  [7] 1773 Mor 8307. Full text of the judicial opinions in the case can be found in J Boswell, *The Decisions of the Court of Session upon the Question of Literary Property in the Cause of John Hinton of London, Bookseller, against Alexander Donaldson and John Wood, Booksellers in Edinburgh, and James Meurose, Bookseller in Kilmarnock* (1774). See further MacQueen, 'Intellectual property and the common law', note 6, 33–38.   [8] (1774) 2 Bro PC 129. See further R Deazley, *Rethinking Copyright: History, Theory, Language* (2006).

2.7 The primary development of copyright after *Donaldson v Beckett* was by statute. Engravings had been given copyright by statutes in 1734 and 1766, and further Acts for this subject matter were passed in 1777 and 1836;[9] sculptures joined books as copyright subject matter in 1798;[10] and paintings, drawings, and photographs (the last a form of art recently made possible by technological development) were added by the Fine Arts Copyright Act 1862. Plays were protected against unauthorised public performance as well as printing by the Dramatic Copyright Act 1833, and public lectures were given limited protection by the Lectures Copyright Act 1835. The length of the copyright term began to increase, moved by ideas that, if the basis of copyright was the recognition and encouragement of authorship, its duration should be extended for the benefit of family and descendants who might otherwise suffer for their relative's art.[11] In 1814 the term for books became the longer of 28 years or the author's lifetime, while in 1842 there was a further extension, inspired by the lawyer-playwright Thomas Talfourd, to the longer of 42 years or the author's lifetime plus seven years. These extensions of copyright did not have an easy passage through Parliament: for example, the debates on the 1842 Act include TB Macaulay's famous criticism that copyright was 'a tax on readers for the purpose of giving a bounty to authors'.[12] In general, however, it was accepted that if authorship in literature, drama, music, and art was to be rewarded, then the protection of copyright was essential.[13]

Key points on the early history

- Modern copyright begins in the 18th century, mainly for printed books
- It is decided that copyright is primarily a statutory right, which endures only for the period laid down by the statute
- Unpublished works have a common law copyright which lasts for as long as the work is unpublished
- In the 19th century, copyright is extended to works of art and drama, and the period of protection gets longer

---

International developments: Berne Convention 1886

2.8 The major problem which domestic legislation alone could not solve was unauthorised activity outside the UK. Copyright remained, like the old licensing systems from which it sprang, entirely limited to the territory in which it was granted, leaving authors and publishers unprotected beyond their home shores. As international markets for creative output began to take off in the course of the 19th century, so states began to enter into negotiations for the mutual recognition and enforcement of foreigners' copyrights. This culminated in 1886 in the multinational arrangement known as the *Berne Convention*, although the treaty also underwent important revisions at Paris in 1896, Berlin in 1908, Rome in 1928, Brussels in 1948, Stockholm in 1967 and Paris in 1971.[14] The Convention relates to literary and artistic works, amongst which are included films, and requires its member states to provide protection for every production in the literary, scientific, and artistic domain.

---

[9] Engraving Copyright Acts 1734, 1766, 1777, and 1836.

[10] Sculpture Copyright Act 1798; replaced by Sculpture Copyright Act 1814.

[11] Particularly significant writers in this regard were William Wordsworth and Sir Walter Scott.

[12] See for a very full account of the genesis of the 1842 Act, C Seville, *Literary Copyright Reform in Early Victorian England* (1999).

[13] On the 19th-century 'crystallisation' of copyright in the UK, see B Sherman and L Bently, *The Making of Modern Intellectual Property* (1999), 111–128, 137–140.

[14] See in general S Ricketson and J Ginsburg, *International Copyright and Neighbouring Rights: The Berne Convention and Beyond* (2006); C Seville, *The Internationalisation of Copyright Law: Books, Buccaneers and the Black Flag in the Nineteenth Century* (2006).

> **? Question**
>
> When did the Berne Convention come into being, and how often has it been revised? What is the policy objective of the Convention?

The other main features of the Berne Convention which have emerged from the international activity of the last 120 years are:

- The principle of *national treatment*: each member state of the Convention would give citizens of other member states the same rights of copyright that it gave to its own citizens (Arts 3–5).

- *Minimum standards for national copyright legislation*—each member state agreed to certain basic rules which their national laws must contain, although it could if it wished increase the amount of protection given to right holders. One of these minimum rules was that copyright should arise with the creation of a work and not depend upon any formality such as a system of public registration (Art 5(2)). This entailed the end of the British system of registration at Stationers' Hall when the UK finally implemented the Berne Convention in the Copyright Act 1911. Another important Berne rule, also implemented in the 1911 Act, was that the term of copyright was to be a minimum of the author's lifetime plus 50 years.

- *A focus on the author* as the key figure in copyright law: apart from the prohibition of registration requirements and the extension of the copyright term, the Berne Convention emphasised in other ways the centrality of authorship in copyright. Its purpose was 'the protection of the rights of authors in their literary and artistic works' (Art 1), not the protection of publishers and other actors in the process of disseminating works to their public. In the 1928 revision the concept of moral rights was introduced (Art 6*bis*), giving authors the right to be identified as such and to object to derogatory treatment of their works. These rights, unlike those which have become known as the economic rights to prevent reproduction, public performance and, in due course, broadcasting, could not be transferred to others.

- The possibility of exceptions to copyright, enabling the reproduction of literary and artistic works without the right holder's prior permission. The precise nature of these exceptions was for national legislation: the guiding principle stated that such exceptions were permitted 'in certain special cases, provided that such reproduction does not conflict with a normal exploitation of the work and does not unreasonably prejudice the legitimate interests of the author' (Art 9). Free use of works was expressly permitted in the cases of quotation from lawfully published works, illustration for teaching purposes, and news reporting (Art 10).

2.9   The importance of the Berne Convention cannot be overstated. It remains the basis for international copyright relations and domestic copyright law. Originally a mainly European instrument, it now extends to most of the world, including since 1989 the United States. Under the TRIPS Agreement of 1994 (see para 2.12), states wishing to participate in international trade must join and comply with the Berne Convention.

Recent history: Copyright Acts 1911–1988; European and international law

Copyright Acts 1911–1988

2.10   As already noted, the UK implemented the Berne Convention in the Copyright Act 1911, which came into force on 1 July 1912. The Act swept away all the particular copyrights which had grown up over the previous century (see para 2.7), and replaced them with a much more general approach. It also abolished the common law copyright in unpublished works, replacing that with a statutory scheme for such material. The Act also responded to technological development by conferring a copyright on a new subject matter not mentioned in Berne, namely, sound recordings. Yet more new technology underlay the 1911 Act's replacement with the Copyright Act 1956, which came into force on 1 June 1957, and extended protection to films and broadcasts, and also to the typographical arrangements of published editions of works. Between them the two statutes brought under the umbrella of copyright works which, apart from films, were seen in Continental European systems as belonging to a distinct category of their own. They were not author works, but rather technological media works by which entrepreneurs brought such works to new audiences in a different form. While they deserved copyright-like protection, the substance of the protection did not need to be as great as with author works. The Continental European systems thus developed systems for the protection of what were termed 'neighbouring rights' quite distinct from those for author works. The approach was reinforced by the creation in 1961 of a Berne-like treaty for such neighbouring rights, the Rome Convention on the Protection of Performers, Producers of Phonograms and Broadcasting Organizations. But in the UK the 1956 Act followed the distinction between author and media works only in a modified form: one part of the Act gave copyright to literary, dramatic, musical, and artistic works, while a second part gave a somewhat modified form of what was still called copyright to sound recordings, films, broadcasts, and published editions.

Question

What are the differences in subject matter of the Berne and Rome Conventions?

2.11   The Copyright, Designs and Patents Act 1988 (CDPA 1988), which came into force on 1 August 1989, was also a response to technological development. Again new ways of creating and disseminating works—for example, computer programs, or software, and cable and satellite broadcasting—were recognised. But even more important in giving rise to the replacement of the 1956 Act were expansions in the ways by which copies might be made of works, notably photocopying, re-recording sound recordings on audio cassettes, and videoing broadcasts. Advances in copying technology meant that not only could individuals make copies for their personal or business use, but so too could so-called 'pirates', that is, persons who made copies in great quantities for commercial resale at prices significantly lower than those of the copyright owner. The Act continued to apply the concept of copyright generally to both author and media works, but it also moved towards the Continental European model by recognising moral rights for authors in literary, dramatic, musical, and artistic works and films.

Question

List and date the three UK copyright statutes of the 20th century, and give the dates when each of the Acts came into force.

Further international developments

2.12   There were important developments in the international protection of copyright in the 1990s. The TRIPS Agreement 1994 contains a number of provisions on copyright, compliance with which is required of states wishing to be members of the World Trade Organization (WTO). They have to:

- sign up to the Berne Convention, apart from its provisions on moral rights (Art 9(1));

- protect computer programs and databases (Art 10);

- provide for rental rights in at least computer programs and films (Art 11);

- where the duration of copyright is calculated other than by reference to the life of a natural person, give a minimum term of 50 years calculated from, as the case may be, the date of authorised publication or of the work being made (Art 12).

Further, TRIPS makes explicit what had previously been an underlying principle of copyright law, namely, that it protects expression rather than ideas.[15] The agreement also states that member states must 'confine' limitations or exceptions to copyright to 'certain special cases which do not conflict with a normal exploitation of the work and do not unreasonably prejudice the legitimate interests of the right holder'.[16] The verb 'confine', not found in this context in the Berne Convention, is significant, hinting as it does at a hostile attitude towards copyright exceptions and limitations. Finally, there is provision for the protection of performers, producers of sound recordings, and broadcasting organisations.[17]

 Question

What does TRIPS add to the Berne and Rome Conventions?

2.13   In 1996 two further treaties supplementing the Berne Convention were agreed at the World Intellectual Property Organization (WIPO). The WIPO Copyright Treaty (WCT) followed TRIPS in:

- providing that copyright protected only the form in which a work was expressed and not its underlying ideas (Art 2);

- requiring copyright protection for computer programs and databases (Arts 4 and 5);

- recognising rental right in relation to computer programs and films, and extending it to sound recordings (Art 7);

- adopting the language of 'confining' copyright exceptions and limitations (Art 10 WCT).

2.14   But where TRIPS was driven by concerns about international trade, the WCT was primarily concerned to respond to the problems created by the rise of the Internet, and hence it added rights to deal with distribution and public communication of works and to support the use of technological measures in the protection from unauthorised use of works recorded digitally.[18] The other treaty concluded in 1996, WIPO Performances and Phonograms Treaty (WPPT), was for the further protection of performers and producers of sound recordings, significantly supplementing the provisions of the Rome Convention 1961 (see para 2.10) in this regard.

 Question

What did WCT 1996 add to previous international agreements on copyright? What was its main policy goal?

---

[15] TRIPS, Art 9(2).   [16] TRIPS, Art 13.   [17] TRIPS, Art 14.   [18] WCT, Arts 6, 8, 11, and 12.

European developments

2.15   In the 1980s the European Union (EU)[19] began to become more interested in copyright as an element in the creation of a single market. In 1991 there began a programme of Directives on copyright, designed to harmonise the national laws of the member states in certain key areas (computer programs[20] and databases[21]) and to reduce the potential for differences to cause unjustified obstacles to the free movement of goods and services (rental rights,[22] satellite broadcasting,[23] copyright duration,[24] resale rights in works of art[25]). The international activity in the 1990s had further significant effects upon harmonisation of copyright law in the EU.[26] In particular, the WCT led to the introduction in 1997 of the first draft of what eventually became, after much debate and controversy, the Information Society (InfoSoc) Directive 2001.[27] The implementation of these Directives in the UK led to significant amendment of the CDPA 1988, generally by way of amending regulations. In addition, references for preliminary rulings on the interpretation of these Directives on copyright are regularly made by member states to the Court of Justice of the European Union (CJEU). As such, CDPA 1988 and any other UK legislation on copyright must be construed in conformity with these Directives, related CJEU jurisprudence, and relevant international agreements to which the EU is a party.[28]

 Question

What topics have been dealt with in the EU's copyright Directives?

2.16   The collection of Directives so far, have focused on approximating laws in specific areas of copyright and led to piecemeal partial harmonisation of copyright in the EU. However, recent judgments of the CJEU on copyright matters have attempted to harmonise some fundamental copyright concepts, which were previously believed to be unharmonised (see paras 2.29, 2.39, and 2.40) and as such received criticism for having 'deepened the harmonisation of copyright well beyond that which had been agreed politically.'[29] The full impact of such judgments on UK copyright law remains to be seen. At the same time, the European Commission is continuing with its harmonisation programme and evaluating further initiatives (see para 7.1). This process has made it clear that the initiative for copyright reform legislation taking effect in the UK now lies mainly in Brussels rather than Westminster.[30] An appreciation of the European developments as well as the international background is therefore vital to fully understand the present law in the UK.

---

[19] At the time called European Community.

[20] Directive 91/250/EEC on the legal protection of computer programs, repealed and replaced by Directive 2009/24/EC.

[21] Directive 96/9/EC on the legal protection of databases.

[22] Directive 92/100/EEC on rental right and lending right, repealed and replaced by Directive 2006/115/EEC.

[23] Directive 93/83/EEC on satellite broadcasting and cable retransmission.

[24] Directive 93/98/EEC harmonising the term of protection, repealed and replaced by Directive 2006/116/EC, which has recently been amended by Directive 2011/77/EU.

[25] Directive 2001/84/EC on the resale right for the benefit of the author of an original work of art.

[26] WCT and WPPT were signed by the European Union in December 1996 and ratified in December 2009.

[27] Directive 2001/29/EC on the harmonisation of certain aspects of copyright and related rights in the information society.

[28] See *SAS Institute Inc v World Programming Ltd (No 2)* [2010] ECDR 15, paras 163–168.

[29] L Bently, 'The return of industrial copyright?' [2012] EIPR 654 at 671; see also S Vousden, '*Infopaq* and the Europeanisation of copyright law' [2010] WIPO J 197 and E Rosati, 'Towards an EU-wide copyright? (Judicial) pride and (legislative) prejudice' [2013] IPQ 47.

[30] See further E Derclaye (ed), *Research Handbook on the Future of EU Copyright* (2009); MV Eechoud et al, *Harmonizing European Copyright Law: The Challenges of Better Lawmaking* (2009).

> ## Key points on modern developments
>
> - Copyright extended further, to photographs, films, sound recordings, broadcasts, and computer technology (software and databases)
> - Copyright internationalised from the late 19th century on—today there is both a global and a European dimension to law-making, meaning that scope for purely national initiatives is limited
> - There is a division apparent in most legal systems between the copyright treatment of 'author works' (covered by the Berne Convention) and 'neighbouring' or 'media works' (covered by the Rome Convention)—see further para 2.47

Rationale of copyright

2.17   Copyright first developed in the early modern period as a response to the growth of the printing technology that facilitated the rapid multiplication and distribution of copies of written works. As shown by the history just described, change in the law has continued to be driven by technological advance in the means by which works can be presented to the public at large, and protection has been extended and adapted to cover photography, cinematography, sound recording, broadcasting, cable transmissions, computer programs and, most recently, the Internet. The practical benefit of developing protections within the copyright mould is the applicability of the international regime under the Berne Convention and other treaties which ensure potentially worldwide protection for right holders.

2.18   Despite the harmonising effects of the Berne Convention and other more recent international instruments, two distinct major conceptualisations of the functions of copyright can still be identified in the world's legal systems.[31] The Anglo-American or common law tradition emphasises the *economic role of copyright*. Protection of copyright subject matter against unauthorised acts of exploitation enables right holders either to go to market themselves with a product based on the material, or to grant others, by outright transfer or, more typically, by licence, the right to do so for whatever seems an appropriate price. In the absence of copyright, which would enable free-riding by would-be users, it is unlikely that producers of the material would earn any return for their work, and without that incentive production would dry up or slacken significantly. Copyright is thus essentially a response to market failure, a means by which socially beneficial activities can be made financially worthwhile for those engaging in them. It rests ultimately upon the general or public interest in having works containing ideas, information, instruction, and entertainment made available, and in rewarding those—publishers as well as the creators of the works—who perform this function in society in accordance with the public demand for their efforts.[32] In contrast, the Continental European or civil law tradition sees copyright as springing from the *personality rights of the individual creator* of the subject matter. This perception is reflected in the name 'author-law' given to the topic by the various

---

[31] For a comparative overview see G Davies, *Copyright and the Public Interest* (2nd edn, 2003), especially Chs 5–7. See also B Sherman and A Strowel (eds), *Of Authors and Origins: Essays on Copyright Law* (1994).

[32] The economics of copyright are explored in, eg, W Landes and R Posner, *The Economic Structure of Intellectual Property Law* (2003), Chs 2–6, 8–10; R Towse (ed), *Copyright and the Cultural Industries* (2002); MA Einhorn, *Media, Technology and Copyright: Integrating Law and Economics* (2004). Many classic earlier studies are reprinted in R Towse and R Holzhauer (eds), *The Economics of Intellectual Property* (2002), vol 1 (Introduction and Copyright).

Continental systems—*droit d'auteur, urheberrecht,* and so on. Protection is given out of respect for the individual's creative act of production, and extends beyond the merely economic to the so-called 'moral rights': the right to be identified as the creator of a work, the right to have the integrity of a work preserved, and others. Copyright is thus rooted in protection of the individual personality and interests of the author as expressed in his work. Companies and organisations as such cannot be creators.

2.19   The distinction between the two conceptualisations is sometimes summarised by saying that the Anglo-American tradition is centred on the entrepreneur, the Continental one on the author. It is reflected in various rules. For example:

- where the Anglo-American tradition gives copyright protection to media works such as sound recordings and broadcasts, the Continental tradition uses a separate group of 'neighbouring rights' for these non-author works;

- where the Anglo-American tradition vests first ownership of copyright in the employer of an author making a work in the course of employment, the Continental tradition gives it to the author;

- where the Anglo-American tradition operates a relatively low threshold of 'originality' for works to enjoy copyright, based mainly upon the author's effort in not copying previous work, the Continental tradition tends to require a higher level of creativity before works will be protected.

> **? Question**
>
> Explain with illustrative examples the differences between the Anglo-American and Continental European conceptions of what copyright is for.

2.20   A further significant aspect of the distinctness of the two traditions is their stances in relation to the *copyright limitations and exceptions* allowed under the Berne Convention (see para 2.8); that is, those activities in which members of the public may engage with regard to copyright works without any authorisation from the right holders concerned. The Anglo-American tradition has traditionally allowed 'fair dealing' or 'fair use' for free in areas where it is thought that the public interest in the dissemination of information and ideas outweighs the interest of the right holder in earning reward from the exploitation of the work and the public interest in encouraging the author's activities. In contrast, although the Continental traditions typically permit private copying, the author still receives remuneration by way of levies imposed upon the sale of the equipment that enables the copying to take place. There is generally a less expansive approach to exceptions and limitations based upon wider interests than those of the author and the publisher.

2.21   The significance of such distinctions should not be overemphasised. Continental copyright laws are also a basis for market operations with regard to ideas, information, and entertainment, while, as we shall see (paras 3.4–3.30), the author plays a fundamental role in Anglo-American copyright laws, where moral rights are now also developing (paras 3.31–3.46). Membership of the Berne Convention has embraced countries from both traditions for most of its history and since 1989 has included the United States. The convergence promoted by the Convention's minimum standards has been further advanced by TRIPS and the WIPO Treaties of 1996, as well as the copyright Directives of the EU. Nonetheless the deep-seated differences in basic concepts have an effect upon international discussions, the outcomes of which occasionally reflect a somewhat uneasy compromise between the competing schools of thought.

> **Key points on rationales**
>
> - Copyright has an economic function, enabling the production of information, ideas, and entertainment to be rewarding for their authors and publishers
> - Copyright also has a non-economic function, related in some legal systems to the idea of recognising creativity as an aspect of individual personality
> - Copyright rewards individuals for their contributions; but this is offset by recognition of the interests—if not the rights—of the wider public in the free dissemination of material in certain circumstances
> - Different legal systems give different emphases to these functions, making it sometimes difficult to achieve European or global harmonisation

Subject matter

2.22   Under the CDPA 1988, as now several times amended, the following subject matter is protected by copyright:[33]

- original literary, dramatic, musical, and artistic works (literary work including computer programs, databases, and compilations other than databases);
- films;
- sound recordings;
- broadcasts;
- the typographical arrangement of published editions of literary, dramatic, or musical works.

The Act is seen to meet the requirements of the Berne Convention (protection for literary and artistic works—see para 2.8), the Rome Convention as supplemented in 1996 (protection for sound recordings and broadcasts—see para 2.10), and the WCT (computer programs and databases—see para 2.13). A number of general points may be made covering all the categories listed, before turning to the detailed law of each one.

Products may have more than one copyright

2.23   A very important point is that any product in the domain of the subject matter listed in the previous paragraph (para 2.22) is quite likely to have more than one copyright in it. Thus a book will have copyright as a literary work, but there will also be a copyright in its typographical arrangement, as would also be the case with printed dramatic scripts and musical scores. A database has copyright in the selection and arrangement of its contents,[34] but this does not affect any copyright those items of content may have in their own right. A sound recording of a piece of music will involve copyrights, not only in the sound recording as such, but also, separately, one in the music. And if the work recorded is a song, there will be a further copyright in the song lyrics.[35] A broadcast of a film or sound recording will have copyright as a

---

[33] CDPA 1988, ss 1–8.   [34] 1988 Act, s 3A.
[35] Note how CDPA 1988, s 3(1) defines 'musical work' as excluding any words intended to be spoken or sung with the music.

broadcast, but this will leave unaffected the copyrights in the film or sound recording. While the sound track accompanying a film is treated as part of the film for copyright purposes, a copyright may also subsist in the sound track as a sound recording.[36] With the advent of digital technology, the multimedia product (eg a computer game, a film on a DVD, the BBC website), which consists of digitised material combining audio, video, text, and images still and moving played through a computer, and with which the user may interact, has become commonplace, raising difficult questions about the mixture of copyrights which such a product may have.[37]

 Question

Explain what it means to say that a product may have more than one copyright, and give some examples.

Need for a work

2.24   Copyright protects works. To paraphrase TRIPS and the WCT (see paras 2.12–2.14), the concern is, not with ideas as such, but with their expression.[38] There can be difficult issues, however, in knowing when an expression, in whatever medium, reaches the level of a work capable of copyright protection. In a case about the copyright in law reports, Canadian judges argued that a work is something which generally is whole, complete, or able to stand on its own, and that

> if a production is dependent upon surrounding materials such that it is rendered meaningless or its utility largely disappears when taken apart from the context in which it is disseminated, then that component will instead be merely a part of a work.[39]

With this approach, they were nonetheless able to conclude that component parts of a law report, such as its key words and headnote, were, like the full report itself, works that attracted copyright. The idea that, when an expression is 'able to stand on its own' there is a work, presumably covers the many well-known examples of incomplete productions such as Schubert's Unfinished Symphony and Samuel Taylor Coleridge's poem 'Kubla Khan', the composition of which was famously interrupted by a person on business from Porlock, with the consequence that the poet's inspiration was lost and the work never completed.

■ *Sweeney v Macmillan Publishers Ltd* [2002] RPC 35

This complex case concerned the copyright in James Joyce's novel *Ulysses*, first published in 1922, and the publication of a new edition of that work in 1997, edited by DR. The novel was written over a long period, and considerably revised and rewritten in the process. Joyce's manuscripts and other preparatory material, such as corrected and amended typescripts and proofs, continued to exist. As originally published, the book contained many typographical errors. Some of these were corrected in later editions, which, however, also introduced new ones. Facsimiles of the Joyce manuscripts

---

[36] CDPA 1988, s 5B(2), (5).

[37] See I Stamatoudi, *Copyright and Multimedia Works: A Comparative Analysis* (2002); T Aplin, *Copyright Law in the Digital Society* (2005).

[38] The classic discussion of this distinction is the US case of *Baker v Selden* 101 US 99 (1879). See also *University of London Press v University Tutorial Press* [1916] 2 Ch 601 and J Pila, 'An intentional view of the copyright work' (2008) 71 MLR 535.

[39] *CCH Canadian Ltd v Law Society of Upper Canada* [2002] 4 FC 213 (CA) at 260 per Linden JA at para 66. See also at 308 per Rothstein JA at paras 197–199. The court's conclusion was upheld by the Supreme Court of Canada, which did not find it necessary, however, to dwell on the meaning of 'work' in this context: see *Law Society of Upper Canada v CCH Canadian Ltd* [2004] 1 SCR 339.

and other materials were published from 1975 onwards. The 1997 edition was based on a collation of all this material with the published editions, and sought the publication of the text intended by Joyce. The Joyce estate, which owned the copyright in *Ulysses* and the preparatory material, claimed infringement of copyright by the new edition. It was held that copyright subsisted in each chapter and perhaps each page or even sentence of *Ulysses* as it was written; but as each passage was incorporated into the larger work, copyright should be regarded as residing in that rather than in its constituent parts.[40] Copyright thus subsisted in Joyce's fair copy manuscript. Copyright also subsisted in earlier drafts of the work and in successive typescripts and proofs. DR had copied parts of this material, and its copyright had been infringed.

2.25   Nor is there a requirement of minimum length or substance to constitute a work: for example, musical copyright was found to exist in the four notes constituting the Channel 4 television theme.[41] More recently, newspaper headlines have been found to be independent literary works.[42] On the other hand, single words, titles, the catch-phrases of a TV personality, headings on computer menus, and individual command names in a computer program[43] have been held to be too insubstantial to be literary works.

 Discussion point For answer guidance visit www.oxfordtextbooks.co.uk/orc/waelde3e/

Can '4 Minutes 33 Seconds', by the composer John Cage, be held to be a work? In this composition, an orchestra is on stage at the outset, but does not start to play any of its instruments. Instead, the members of the orchestra silently sit on the platform for a period of just over four and a half minutes. If it is a work, does the fact that its author is generally regarded as a composer of music make the work musical? Are there any other possibilities? See further Cheng Lim Saw, 'Protecting the sound of silence in 4'33': a timely revisit of basic principles in copyright law' (2005) 12 EIPR 467.

2.26   While the general principle, that copyright protects the expression of a work rather than its ideas, is central, it is also important not to be misled as to its scope. In considering the concept, bear in mind what constitutes infringement of copyright, for example (see further paras 4.10ff). Analysis of this part of the law shows it to be misleading to say that copyright protects no more than the form of expression. Otherwise it would not be possible for the author of a book to be able to control the exploitation of his work in other media such as film and broadcasting. Such adaptations will almost certainly adopt a distinct mode of expression, yet must be authorised by the author to be legitimate.[44] The author of a two-dimensional artistic work may challenge a three-dimensional reproduction, and vice versa.[45] Editors of anthologies and collections of material produced by others have a copyright, not so much in the words gathered together by them, as in the arrangement and ordering of the material.[46] Of course this is a form of expression, but it shows that we should not take 'form of expression' in any narrow sense coloured by the idea that copyright prevents only slavish imitation. Thus a particular interpretation of historical

---

[40] Contrast *Robin Ray v Classic FM plc* [1998] FSR 622, where a catalogue was subsumed into a database, but Lightman J rejected an argument that as a result the copyright of the first work was also subsumed into that of the second.

[41] *Lawton v Lord David Dundas*, The Times, 13 June 1985. Another example might be the Intel Inside theme.

[42] *Newspaper Licensing Agency Ltd v Meltwater Holding BV* [2010] EWHC 3099 (Ch); affirmed in *Newspaper Licensing Agency Ltd v Meltwater Holding BV* [2011] EWCA Civ 890 (CA). An appeal to the Supreme Court is pending.

[43] *Navitaire Inc v EasyJet Airline Co Ltd* [2006] RPC 3.   [44] CDPA 1988, ss 16(1)(e) and 21.

[45] CDPA 1988, s 17(3). See further para 4.26.

[46] *Macmillan v Suresh Chunder Deb* (1890) ILR 17 Calc 951; *Macmillan v Cooper* (1923) 93 LJPC 113. Note also Berne Convention, Art 2(5): 'Collections of literary or artistic works such as encyclopaedias and anthologies which, by reason of the selection and arrangement of their contents, constitute intellectual creations shall be protected as such, without prejudice to the copyright in each of the works forming part of such collections.'

events has been held capable of copyright protection.[47] The best view seems to be that there is no copyright in ideas while they remain just that, but that once the ideas have been expressed in some form it would be wrong to assume that a different expression of the same ideas must necessarily be a new work with its own copyright, or cannot be an infringement of the earlier work.

 Question

Give some examples to illustrate the difference between protectable expression and unprotectable ideas.

2.27   Lord Hoffmann said the following on this topic in *Designers Guild Ltd v Russell Williams (Textiles) Ltd*:[48]

> Plainly there can be no copyright in an idea which is merely in the head, which has not been expressed in copyrightable form, as a literary, dramatic, musical or artistic work, but the distinction between ideas and expression cannot mean anything so trivial as that. On the other hand, every element in the expression of an artistic work (unless it got there by accident or compulsion) is the expression of an idea on the part of the author. It represents her choice to paint stripes rather than polka dots, flowers rather than tadpoles, use one colour and brush technique rather than another, and so on. The expression of these ideas is protected, both as a cumulative whole and also to the extent to which they form a 'substantial part' of the work. [para 24]...My Lords, if one examines the cases in which the distinction between ideas and the expression of ideas has been given effect, I think it will be found that they support two quite distinct propositions. The first is that a copyright work may express certain ideas which are not protected because they have no connection with the literary, dramatic, musical or artistic nature of the work. It is on this ground that, for example, a literary work which describes a system or invention does not entitle the author to claim protection for his system or invention as such. The same is true of an inventive concept expressed in an artistic work. However striking or original it may be, others are (in the absence of patent protection) free to express it in works of their own: see *Kleeneze Ltd v DRG (UK) Ltd* [1984] FSR 399. The other proposition is that certain ideas expressed by a copyright work may not be protected because, although they are ideas of a literary, dramatic or artistic nature they are not original, or so commonplace as not to form a substantial part of the work. *Kenrick & Co v Lawrence & Co* (1890) 25 QBD 99 is a well known example. It is on this ground that the mere notion of combining stripes and flowers would not have amounted to a substantial part of the plaintiff's work. At that level of abstraction, the idea, though expressed in the design, would not have represented sufficient of the author's skill and labour as to attract copyright protection [para 25].

2.28   Lord Hoffmann here connects the translation of unprotectable idea into copyright expression with the degree of originality, skill, and labour shown by the author, and more will be said of that later (para 2.39).[49] Clearly, each case will turn on its own facts in this area, although it can perhaps be said that the higher the level of generality, or abstraction, of the idea of a work, the less likely it is to be protected as such.[50] Lord Hoffmann also connects the expression of ideas with the nature of the work. A celebrated dictum in this regard is: 'You do not infringe copyright in a recipe by making a cake.'[51] Similarly, a literary work consisting of instructions is not infringed by making a fabric according to it.[52]

■ *Interlego AG v Tyco Industries Inc* [1989] AC 217 (PC)

Artistic copyright was claimed in engineering drawings modifying an earlier design by the same author (the Lego company). The visual impression from the two sets of drawings was much the same; the

---

[47] *Harman Pictures NV v Osborne* [1967] 1 WLR 723 (Charge of the Light Brigade); see further para 4.32.
[48] [2001] FSR 11, paras 24 and 25.
[49] See further M Spence and T Endicott, 'Vagueness in the scope of copyright' (2005) 121 LQR 657.
[50] *Plix Products v Winstone* [1986] FSR 63 per Prichard J at 92–94 (aff'd [1986] FSR 608); *Nova Productions Ltd v Mazooma Games Ltd* [2007] RPC 25 (CA), paras 31–55 (Jacob LJ).
[51] *J & S Davis (Holdings) Ltd v Wright Health Group* [1988] RPC 403 per Whitford J at 414.
[52] *Abraham Moon & Sons Ltd v Thornber & Ors* [2012] EWPCC 37.

distinction lay mainly in the technical information as to dimensions and tolerances. It was held that the later drawings were not new works for the purposes of artistic copyright: the new ideas in the second drawings were not artistic, but literary. 'Nobody draws a tolerance, nor can it be reproduced three-dimensionally' (per Lord Oliver at 258). This was important because literary copyright knows no equivalent to artistic copyright's concept of three-dimensional infringement.

Work of a relevant kind

2.29   There must be a work of a relevant kind—literary, dramatic, musical, artistic, film, sound recording, broadcast, or published edition—that is, a work which does not fit into these expressed categories under the law does not receive copyright protection or causes uncertainty about the category to which it belongs.[53] In a recent reference to the Court of Justice, a question for determination was whether a graphical user interface (GUI) could be protected by copyright as a computer program.[54] The Court held that a GUI was not a computer program. However, it noted that a GUI can, as a work, be protected under the ordinary law of copyright by virtue of the Information Society (InfoSoc) Directive, if it was the author's own intellectual creation.[55] A system, like that in the UK, which provides an exhaustive list of subject matter protected by copyright may be contrary to this case which suggests that provided a work is the author's own intellectual creation, it is capable of protection. Whether this decision will force a change in the way the UK views works capable of copyright protection remains to be seen but, in the meantime, a work must fall in the relevant categories to receive protection.

> ### Key points so far on subject matter
>
> • Copyright protects expressions rather than ideas and information as such
>
> • Before copyright can arise, there must be a *work* of a relevant kind: literary, dramatic, musical, artistic, film, sound recording, broadcast, published edition

Fixation

2.30   One way of establishing whether or not there is a work is to find a recording, or fixation, of the expression which constitutes the work.

> The *Berne Convention* says that copyright subsists in literary and artistic works 'whatever may be the mode or form of its expression' (Art 2(1)), but then allows national law 'to prescribe that works in general or any specified categories of works shall not be protected unless they have been fixed in some material form' (Art 2(2)). Note that this means that member states have a choice as to whether to require fixation.
>
> In the UK, the *CDPA 1988* provides that copyright does not subsist in a literary, dramatic, or musical work unless and until it is recorded in writing or otherwise (s 3(2)). 'Writing' includes any form of notation or code, whether by hand or otherwise, and regardless of the method by which, or medium in or on which, it is recorded (s 178). No definition of otherwise!

---

[53] CDPA 1988, s 1(1), (2).
[54] Case C-393/09 *Bezpečnostní softwarová asociace v Ministerstvo kultury* [2011] ECDR 3 (ECJ).
[55] *Bezpečnostní softwarová asociace*, note 54, paras 44–47; see further. C Handig, '*Infopaq International A/S v Danske Dagblades Forening* (C-5/08): is the term "work" of the CDPA 1988 in line with the European Directives?' [2010] EIPR 53.

2.31   The UK thus opts for an explicit requirement of fixation before any literary, dramatic, or musical work may enjoy copyright protection. The main form of fixation mentioned in the 1988 Act is writing; but the definition previously quoted is very broad and obviously capable of covering, for example, the use of shorthand.[56] In any event, writing is not the only possible method of recording literary, dramatic, and musical works, nor does the 1988 Act so limit its requirement. The electronic storage of work in digital form on discs and in computer memories is well known. Literary work means work which is spoken and sung as well as written,[57] while music and drama can be created in improvised performances as well as based upon scores and scripts. So far as concerns speech, singing, and music, the tape and cassette recorder have been familiar ways of making recordings for a long time, and film, video, and digital recording, including voice recognition software, can now be added to the list of methods of fixation sufficient to confer copyright on the work recorded. A further possibility might arise through lip-reading what a speaker is saying on a film without a sound track, as for example with closed circuit TV cameras.

2.32   The requirement of fixation still means, however, that there is no copyright in the unrecorded spoken word, ad lib stage performance, or aleatory musical composition. Since the copyright does not come into existence unless and until the recording is made, copyright confers no right on a speaker to stop people making recordings of what is said. If there is any right at all to prevent recording of one's words, it must be sought in other branches of the law.[58] However, the 1988 Act expressly provides that, for the purposes of conferring copyright on a work by recording it, it is immaterial whether the work is recorded by or with the permission of the author, that is, the speaker.[59] Thus, while I may eavesdrop on and record other people's telephone conversations without infringing copyright in what they say, as soon as the recording is made, the words have copyright and the subsequent reproduction and publication of these words elsewhere may be controlled by the speaker.[60]

 Question

What will constitute fixation of a work so that it can enjoy copyright?

■ *Norowzian v Arks Ltd (No 2)* **[1999] FSR 79; aff'd [2000] FSR 363**

N produced a film called *Joy*. It showed a man dancing to music. Use of the editing technique known as 'jump cutting' made it appear that the man was making sudden changes of position not possible as successive movements in reality. An issue in the case was whether the film was a recording of a dramatic work. Rattee J held not, in the following passage later approved by the Court of Appeal:

> Joy, unlike some films, is not a recording of a dramatic work, because, as a result of the drastic editing process adopted by Mr Norowzian, it is not a recording of anything that was, or could be, performed or danced by anyone . . . It may well be, in the case of "Joy", that the original unedited film of the actor's performance, what I believe are called "the rushes", was a recording of a dramatic work, but Mr Norowzian's claim is not in respect of copyright in them or their subject-matter. His claim is in respect of the finished film. ([1999] FSR at 87–88, approved [2000] FSR at 367).[61]

---

[56] See *Pitman v Hine* (1884) 1 TLR 82.   [57] CDPA, s 3(1).
[58] Eg the Regulation of Investigatory Powers Act 2000 or breach of confidence.   [59] CDPA 1988, s 3(3).
[60] See for further discussion HL MacQueen, '"My tongue is mine ain": copyright, the spoken word and privacy' (2005) 68 MLR 349.
[61] See further on the *Norowzian* case, A Barron, 'The legal properties of film' (2004) 67 MLR 177.

Discussion point For answer guidance visit www.oxfordtextbooks.co.uk/orc/waelde3e/

How exact or good must a recording be to confer copyright on unscripted speech (eg a lecture), drama, or music? Do a student's non-verbatim lecture notes make the lecturer's extempore words protectable? Or a bootlegger's poor-quality and unauthorised recording of a live 'jamming' session by a musician?

2.33   There is no explicit requirement of fixation in the 1988 Act with regard to artistic works, but it seems clear from the definitions within the category (see further at paras 2.69–2.86) that copyright will not exist until the work is recorded in either tangible or visible form. Similarly, films and sound recordings must both be 'recordings' on some medium from which sounds or moving images, as the case may be, can be reproduced.[62] Broadcasts, however, are electronic transmissions of visual images, sounds, or other information which need only be visible and/or audible to their intended audience.

 Question 1

What is the significance of having an explicit fixation requirement for literary, dramatic, and musical works, but not for the other categories of copyright works?

Question 2

Is it possible to have copyright works which have not been 'fixed' in the sense just discussed?

Originality

2.34   Another important test of whether or not a work protected by copyright has been created is the requirement of originality. The 1988 Act says that to have copyright, literary, dramatic, musical, and artistic works must all be original.[63] There is no statutory definition of originality, except for databases which are a sub-category of literary works (see further paras 2.39–40).[64] However, the concept has been developed through UK case law which suggests that for a work to be original, it should originate from the author and must not be a copy of a preceding work. In addition, a common theme found in case law is the test of the *skill, labour and judgment* which the author has invested in the work. Where this test is satisfied, there is likely to be a copyright in the result. But the production of a copy of a work may involve considerable labour and no little skill; yet in that case there will be no originality and no copyright (see all these themes developed further at paras 2.35–2.38, 2.41–2.44). There is no express requirement of originality as such in relation to films, sound recordings, broadcasts, and typographical arrangements of published editions,[65] but copyright does not subsist in a sound recording or film or typographical arrangement of a published edition which is, or to the extent that it is, respectively, a copy taken from a previous sound recording or film, or reproduces the typographical arrangement of a previous edition.[66]

 Question

Which kinds of work must be 'original' to enjoy copyright protection?

---

[62] CDPA, ss 5A and 5B.   [63] CDPA 1988, s 1(1)(a).   [64] CDPA 1988, s 3A(2).   [65] CDPA 1988, s 1(1)(b), (c).
[66] CDPA 1988, ss 5A(2), 5B(4), and 8(2). For broadcasts, see para 2.46.

Originality in the UK: a combination of factors

2.35   In order to be original, a work must not be a copy of a preceding work and should originate from the author. The underlying idea is still best expressed in the classic words of Peterson J:

> The word "original" does not in this connection mean that the work must be the expression of original or inventive thought. Copyright Acts are not concerned with the originality of ideas, but with the expression of thought.... The originality which is required relates to the expression of the thought. But the Act does not require that the expression must be in an original or novel form, but that the work must not be copied from another work—that it should originate from the author.[67]

Originality, in other words, is not a high standard for entry into copyright protection. It imposes no requirement of aesthetic or intellectual quality: even the most mundane of works, rehearsing old ideas and information, has copyright if expressed in the author's own way. This is reinforced by other provisions of the copyright legislation: for example, that certain artistic works are protected 'irrespective of artistic quality', or that tables and compilations are to be counted as literary works.[68] Another theme found in discussions of originality is the test of the skill, labour, and judgment which the author has invested in the work. Where this test is satisfied, there is likely to be a copyright in the result. Finally, there is the point succinctly made by Peterson J himself: 'What is worth copying is worth protecting'.[69] This is not in itself a test of the originality of the work that has been copied, but if someone has copied another's work, that tends to suggest the value of the latter and its possible need for copyright protection to ensure that the return goes to its author.

All these themes require some qualification, however. While what is worth copying is worth protecting, it is not always clear that copyright is the appropriate form of protection. With regard to ideas, 'as the late Professor Joad used to observe, it all depends on what you mean by ideas'.[70] Although copyright may not specify intellectual or aesthetic qualities as essential for its protection, nonetheless courts do assess the fitness of works to the designated categories under the legislation, such as literary or dramatic, the identification of which may involve assessment of just such qualities. Similarly, the mere expenditure of skill and labour may not be sufficient to give rise to copyright if the end result is not a work of a 'literary nature' or likewise. The appropriate general conclusion seems to be that originality is not definable in terms of a single, simple test but should rather be considered as a combination of factors, the relative importance of which may vary according to the nature of the case and the type of work in question (see paras 2.49–2.89 for specific examples of different types of works).[71]

 Question

What are the main elements of originality for copyright purposes?

No requirement of quality or merit

2.36   It is easy to misunderstand the absence of any requirement that a work possess intellectual or aesthetic merit. What is clear is that, in determining whether or not a work has copyright, the court is not called

---

[67] *University of London Press v University Tutorial Press* [1916] 2 Ch 601 at 608.   [68] CDPA 1988, ss 3(1)(a) and 4(1)(a).

[69] *University of London Press*, note 67, at 610.

[70] Lord Hailsham in *LB Plastics* at 629. Professor Cyril Joad (1891–1953) was a professor of philosophy at Birkbeck College London, who became famous through appearances on a BBC show, *The Brains Trust*, and the catchphrase with which he prefaced the answer to any question, 'Well, it depends what you mean by …' This is also quite a useful phrase for a lawyer's conversational armoury.

[71] For a discussion of the standards of originality for copyright protection, and whether all protected works have elements in common or are different in nature, see A Waisman, 'Revisiting originality' [2009] EIPR 370.

upon to judge the work on standards of good or bad in its field. This would be much too subjective to be acceptable. On the other hand, the court evaluates whether a work falls into one or other of the categories found in the copyright legislation, and this is bound to involve some effort to judge what objective qualities constitute a work of this kind.

■ *George Hensher Ltd v Restawile Upholstery (Lancashire) Ltd* [1976] AC 64

An example is the difficulty in which the House of Lords found itself in this case where it had to determine whether a rough prototype for a suite of furniture was a work of artistic craftsmanship (see further at paras 2.83–2.85). This required an understanding of how such a work might be identified—how to distinguish it from a sculpture, for example—which called for some sort of aesthetic judgement. It was held that the prototype was not a work of artistic craftsmanship.

■ *Green v Broadcasting Corp of New Zealand* [1989] 2 All ER 1056 (PC)

Similarly in this case (see further para 2.66) the Privy Council had to grapple with the question of whether a few catchphrases used constantly by the host of a television talent show (*Opportunity Knocks*) constituted a dramatic work. The phrases included: 'For [*competitor's name*], opportunity knocks!'; 'This is your show, folks, and I do mean you'; and 'Make up your mind time'. The show also used a device called the 'clapometer' to measure the levels of applause attracted by each act. It was held that this did not amount to a dramatic work.

In both these cases, the works in question were excluded from copyright, not on the ground of lack of merit, but on the ground that they lacked the intellectual qualities of the categories under which copyright was claimed. Here there is some overlap with the requirement that skill, labour, and judgment should be employed by the author to gain copyright: is the work one which needed such qualities to be brought into existence?

Skill, labour, and judgment

2.37   The expenditure of independent skill, labour, and judgment by the author is often seen as the essence of originality in the field of copyright. The amount of skill, labour, and judgment required should be sufficient and more than minimal or negligible[72] but cannot be defined in 'precise terms' as it depends on the facts of the case and is a question of degree.[73] Use of the skill, labour, and judgment test can be seen in cases of copyright in a compilation, particularly where it is of information or material which was available before the publication of the work. In such cases, it is the skill and labour of the compiler in arranging the material which receives protection.[74] If this has occurred, it is unlikely that the resulting work will be merely derivative. In *Cramp v Smythson*,[75] on the other hand, it was held that tables and information printed on part of a pocket diary had no copyright because their selection and arrangement had not required the exercise of any judgment or taste by the compiler. Behind all this lies the idea that simple copying does not involve the requisite degree of activity to justify the award of copyright. This is so even though copying may require at least labour, and often skill and judgment as well, as Lord Oliver pointed out in *Interlego AG v Tyco Industries Inc*:

---

[72] *Ladbroke v William Hill* [1964] 1 WLR 273 (HL); *Express Newspapers plc v News (UK) Ltd* [1990] FSR 359.
[73] *Macmillan & Co Ltd v K & J Cooper* (1923) 93 LJPC 113.
[74] *Macmillan & Co Ltd v K & J Cooper* (1923) 93 LJPC 113.
[75] [1944] AC 329. Compare the decision of the US Supreme Court in *Feist Publications Inc v Rural Telephone Service Co Inc* 499 US 340 (1991), where it was held that there was no copyright in a telephone directory organised by alphabetical listing of surnames. But see further paras 7.25–7.30.

Originality in the context of literary copyright has been said in several well known cases to depend upon the degree of skill, labour and judgment involved in preparing a compilation...that the amount of skill, judgment or labour is likely to be decisive in the case of compilations. To apply that, however, as a universal test of originality in all copyright cases is not only unwarranted by the context in which the observations were made but palpably erroneous. Take the simplest case of artistic copyright, a painting or a photograph. It takes great skill, judgment and labour to produce a good copy by painting or to produce an enlarged photograph from a positive print, but no one would reasonably contend that the copy painting or enlargement was an "original" artistic work in which the copier is entitled to claim copyright. Skill, labour or judgment merely in the process of copying cannot confer originality...A well-executed tracing is the result of much labour and skill but remains what it is, a tracing.[76]

2.38   In the *Interlego* case the subject of the copyright claim was the design of Lego bricks which included modifications of some technical importance in relation to earlier designs but where the visual impression was much the same. Skill and labour had been expended on the technical changes but these did not change the artistic or visual character of the drawings. Accordingly, the later drawings were not original. Another case in which it was accepted that much effort, skill, labour, and investment of money had gone into the creation of the work in question, yet its author was not entitled to a copyright, is *Exxon Corporation v Exxon Insurance*.[77] The claim was to literary copyright in the single word 'Exxon'. Here the failure was to achieve a literary work,[78] rather than originality as such, but the point to be stressed in the context of the present discussion is that *effort, skill, labour, and judgment by itself is not necessarily enough for the result to have copyright*. It would seem that, while the presence of skill, labour, and judgment will often be very important, it should not be adopted as a universal test of originality, and that it is also necessary to consider exactly what type of skill, labour, and judgment has been involved in relation to the nature of the copyright claimed.[79]

Question

Why are skill, labour, and judgment not *necessarily* enough for originality?

Author's own intellectual creation

2.39   The UK has been seen to have a different tradition than the Continent with regard to originality. Speaking very generally, Continental systems require works to manifest 'intellectual creation' and the UK test of 'skill, labour, and judgment' is generally taken to be less demanding in comparison. However, it is the 'intellectual creation' standard which has so far been applied in those EU Directives referring to the matter. The Software Directive 1991 declared in Article 1(3) that 'a computer program shall be protected if it is original in the sense that it is the author's own intellectual creation'. The UK took no action to implement the formula in its resultant legislation. The Commission noted that the UK's implementation was lacking a specific clause and whether this would lead to over-extensive protection of computer programs remained to be seen.[80] However, it took no action to suggest that this failure involved non-compliance with the Directive. The Term Directive 1993 also provided in Article 6 that 'photographs which are original in the sense that they are the author's own intellectual creation shall be protected' in accordance with the term specified in the Directive but member states were also free to provide for the protection of other photographs. As such, this resulted in no changes in the CDPA 1998 with regards to originality.

---

[76] [1989] AC 217 (PC) at 262–263.   [77] [1982] Ch 119 (CA).   [78] See further paras 2.51ff.
[79] *Interlego AG v Tyco Industries Inc* [1989] AC 217 at 262.
[80] European Commission Report on the implementation and effects of Directive 91/250/EEC, COM(2000) 199 final.

A different result occurred, however, in the implementation of the Database Directive 1996, which again used the phrase *'the author's own intellectual creation'* in defining the object of protection. This time the UK took action to implement it and s 3A of the CDPA 1988 provided that a database is to be considered original 'only if, by reason of the selection or arrangement of the contents of the database the database constitutes the author's own intellectual creation.' This meant that the test of originality *for databases* in the UK was no more the same as for other literary works. As a result, many databases which would have been protected by copyright before s 3A was introduced were no longer protected. This is why the *sui generis* database right was created, establishing a special new and additional form of protection for databases even if they did not attract copyright under the more rigorous originality test (see para 6.4). The aim was clearly to provide an alternative for those who would have had copyright in places such as the UK before the Directive. Therefore, the UK test for originality remained 'skill, labour, and judgment' for all works, except for databases which required 'author's own intellectual creation'.

2.40   These developments raise concerns at least about the lack of express implementation of the higher standard of originality with regard to computer programs, and perhaps photographs, but also whether there should be an EU-wide and comprehensive test of originality for all copyright works. A Commission Consultation Paper in 2004[81] suggested that the 'intellectual creation' standard adopted in the Directives was necessary to take account of the special features or the special technical nature of software, photographs, and databases and that apart from these categories of works, member states remained free to determine the standard of originality. It also concluded that the lack of harmonisation of the concept of originality for other categories of works was not creating a problem for the functioning of the internal market and therefore there was no need for legislative action at the time.

However, in *Infopaq v Danske Dagblades Forening*,[82] a reference made to the CJEU on infringement of the reproduction right and exceptions to copyright (both of which had been harmonised under the InfoSoc Directive), the Court of Justice, in providing guidance on such matters, also clarified the meaning of originality. It held that copyright protection under the InfoSoc Directive only applies if a work is original in the sense of 'author's own intellectual creation'. Even though the Directive does not provide for originality, and as such was not seen to be harmonising the concept, the Court reasoned as follows:

> 34 It is, moreover, apparent from the general scheme of the Berne Convention, in particular arts 2(5) and (8), that the protection of certain subject-matters as artistic or literary works presupposes that they are intellectual creations.

> 35 Similarly, under arts 1(3) of Directive 91/250, 3(1) of Directive 96/9 and 6 of Directive 2006/116 , works such as computer programs, databases or photographs are protected by copyright only if they are original in the sense that they are their author's own intellectual creation.

> 36 In establishing a harmonised legal framework for copyright, Directive 2001/29 is based on the same principle, as evidenced by recitals 4, 9–11 and 20 in the preamble thereto.

> 37 In those circumstances, copyright within the meaning of art.2(a) of Directive 2001/29 is liable to apply only in relation to a subject-matter which is original in the sense that it is its author's own intellectual creation.

Subsequent rulings of the CJEU have followed *Infopaq* to suggest that the test for originality has now been de facto harmonised for all works[83] and also provided guidance on the meaning of 'author's own

[81] European Commission Staff Working Paper on the review of the EC legal framework in the field of copyright and related rights, SEC(2004) 995.   [82] Case C 5/08 *Infopaq International A/S v Danske Dagblades Forening* [2009] ECDR 16.
[83] See Case C-393/09 *Bezpečnostní Softwarová Asociace—Svaz Softwarove Ochrany v Ministerstvo Kultury* [2011] ECDR 3, para 45; Cases C-403/08 and C429/08 *Football Association Premier League Ltd v QC Leisure, Murphy v Media Protection Services Ltd* [2012] 1 CMLR 29, para 97; Case C-145/10 *Painer v Standard Verlags GmbH* [2012] ECDR 6 at para 87; see also, E Rosati, 'Originality in a work, or a work of originality: the effects of the *Infopaq* decision' [2011] EIPR 746.

intellectual creation' in relation to computer programs, photographs, and databases (see paras 2.54, 2.75 and 2.63).[84] Consequently, an important question is whether the UK test of 'skill, labour, and judgment' has been replaced by 'author's intellectual creation' for all works?[85] In the case of *Newspaper Licensing Agency Ltd v Meltwater Holding BV*, the UK courts had an opportunity to address this issue. In the High Court, Proudman J while applying *Infopaq* noted that it 'may sit awkwardly with some provisions of English law, that many questions remain unanswered by the ECJ and that the full implications of the decision have not yet been worked out'.[86] The Court of Appeal noted that the use of the term 'intellectual creation' in the *Infopaq* decision related to the question of origin of a work and not its novelty or merit, and as such, it has not qualified the long-standing test of originality, in that the work originates from the author, established by UK case law.[87] Other recent decisions have adopted the language of 'author's own intellectual creation' interchangeably with 'skill, labour, and judgment'.[88] As such, for works other than databases, the full and clear impact, if any on the UK's test of 'skill, labour, and judgment' remains to be seen.

Derivative works

2.41   The concept of originality may be further qualified by considering the many examples of works (*derivative works*) drawing on, even copying from, other works, which nonetheless can have their own copyright. The obvious examples in the material already discussed in this section are compilations and anthologies. Other straightforward instances in the literary world would be books and articles quoting or summarising source material, as for example in a legal textbook. Originality is not simply a matter of not copying, therefore. In all the examples given, it is clear that while the author is copying, he is also exercising independent skill and labour, both in the selection of sources and quotations, and in the choice of words in which to express the material, so that the work is not entirely derivative. Less straightforward may be the cases where a new edition of a text is published. If a new copyright is to be created, the alterations to the text must be extensive and substantial. If a text is printed unaltered from a previous edition and the editorial matter consists of annotations or appendices, then again, as long as these have independent value, there will be a new copyright, independent of that of the text, if any.[89]

■ *Black v Murray* (1870) 9 M 341

B had published an edition of the poetry of Sir Walter Scott which had gone out of copyright. B published a second edition of the texts together with amendments, alterations, and editorial notes. M published what purported to be a reprint of B's first edition, but which included material taken from the second edition as well. It was held that the changes made in B's second edition had their own copyright, but that M's takings were substantial, and infringed copyright, only in relation to the editorial notes.

---

[84]   Case C-393/09 *Bezpečnostní Softwarová Asociace—Svaz Softwarove Ochrany v Ministerstvo Kultury* [2011] ECDR 3; Case C-406/10 *SAS Institute Inc v World Programming Ltd* [2012] ECDR 22; Case C-145/10 *Painer v Standard Verlags GmbH* [2012] ECDR 6; Case C-604/10 *Football Dataco v Yahoo* [2012] ECDR 10.

[85]   This question is based on the assumption that the two tests are different, see E Derclaye, '*Infopaq International A/S v DanskeDagblades-Forening* (C-5/08): wonderful or worrisome? The impact of the ECJ ruling in *Infopaq* on UK copyright law' [2010] EIPR 247. Even if the tests are different, the result as to originality might be the same in most instances, see D Rose and N O'Sullivan, '*Football Dataco v Yahoo!* Implications of the ECJ judgment' [2012] JIPLP 792.

[86]   *Newspaper Licensing Agency Ltd v Meltwater Holding BV* [2010] EWHC 3099 (Ch) at para 81.

[87]   *Newspaper Licensing Agency Ltd v Meltwater Holding BV* [2011] EWCA Civ 890 (CA) at para 20; an appeal against this decision to the Supreme Court is outstanding.

[88]   Eg tables and compilations: *Forensic Telecommunications Services Ltd v Chief Constable of West Yorkshire* [2011] EWHC 2892 (Ch); photographs: *Temple Island Collections Ltd v New English Teas Ltd* [2012] FSR 9; see also A Rahmatian, '*Temple Island Collections v New English Teas*: an incorrect decision based on the right law?' [2012] EIPR 796.

[89]   *Black v Murray* (1870) 9 M 341 (editorial material in the works of Sir Walter Scott).

2.42   Translations, adaptations, and dramatisations will attract their own copyright, even though manifestly derivative, as do arrangements, orchestrations, and transcriptions of musical works.[90] In the computer world, many programs are developed from existing ones, either by the creators themselves or by competitors engaging in 'reverse engineering', but it seems to be accepted that even when the end result is very close to the original work a new copyright has come into existence.

■ *Walter v Lane* [1900] AC 539

The House of Lords allowed *The Times* newspaper copyright in its reporter's verbatim transcript of a speech by Lord Rosebery, a leading politician of the day. Clearly the reporter's work was derivative, but its creation had involved the expenditure of individual skill and effort. Since the case was decided before originality became a statutory requirement, it has been questioned whether the copyright would be accepted now, as otherwise an audio typist would acquire rights in dictated material.[91] However, the current judicial view appears to favour the reporter's copyright established in *Walter v Lane*.[92]

? Question

Is there a relevant difference between a typist taking dictation or typing from material recorded on a dictaphone, on the one hand, and a transcriber such as the journalist in *Walter v Lane*?

■ *Eisenman v Qimron* (2000) 54(3) PD 817, [2001] ECDR 6 (Supreme Court of Israel)

Q deciphered and put together a text from 67 fragments of an ancient Dead Sea scroll known as 4QMMT. Publication was planned but not yet accomplished when S published in the archaeology journal he edited a copy of the text as edited by Q. S had been critical of the long delays in publishing the Dead Sea scrolls, and this publication formed part of his campaign. Q sued for infringement of his copyright. The defendant contended that Q's editorial labours amounted to no more than an attempt to reproduce as faithfully as possible what had been originated by the scribe who wrote 4QMMT, and therefore lacked the originality required for copyright. It was held that Q's work had copyright and that S had infringed. Q's work was original in the sense that he 'used his knowledge, expertise and imagination, exercised judgement and chose between different alternatives'.[93]

■ *Sawkins v Hyperion Records Ltd* [2005] RPC 32 (CA)

S edited the work of a late 17th/early 18th-century composer, L. The editing involved the insertion of notes missing or inaccurately recorded in L's original scores, the addition or correction of flourishes and other performing indications and the supply of figuring which, in relation to the bass line of baroque works, was the foundation of the work. The expert evidence was that without this last the works could not have been performed in a modern recording session using the original sources. HR produced CDs of the music using

---

[90]   See also Berne Convention, Art 2(3): 'Translations, adaptations, arrangements of music and other alterations of a literary or artistic work shall be protected as original works without prejudice to the copyright in the original work.' And see the UNESCO Nairobi Recommendation: the Translator's Charter (1994), available at http://www.fit-ift.org.

[91]   *Roberton v Lewis* [1976] RPC 169 per Cross J at 174–175.

[92]   See *Express Newspapers plc v News (UK) Ltd* [1990] FSR 359 per Sir Nicolas Browne-Wilkinson V-C at 365–366, preferring the views expressed in *Sands McDougall Pty Ltd v Robinson* (1917) 23 CLR 49 to those of Cross J. See further MacQueen, (2005) 68 MLR 349 at 369–373.

[93]   For an English translation of the judgments in this case and discussion of its content, see TH Lim, HL MacQueen, and CM Carmichael (eds), *On Scrolls, Artefacts and Intellectual Property* (2001). The extensive discussion of this case is critically reviewed in HL MacQueen, 'The legal definition of authorship and the scrolls' in JJ Collins and TH Lim (eds), *Oxford Handbook of the Dead Sea Scrolls* (2010).

S's editions but without a licence. It was held that HR had infringed S's copyright in the work. S's work was original, involving skill and labour over a considerable period of time, going beyond mere transcription.

Discussion point   For answer guidance visit www.oxfordtextbooks.co.uk/orc/waelde3e/

Consider whether *Walter v Lane*, *Interlego v Tyco*, and *Sawkins v Hyperion Records* are correctly decided on the originality point. See further J Pila, 'An intentional view of the copyright work' (2008) 71 MLR 535 and NP Gravells, 'Authorship and originality: the persistent influence of *Walter v Lane*' [2007] IPQ 267.

2.43   In the *Interlego* case, Lord Oliver recognised that a derivative artistic work might be original where there was *'some element of material alteration or embellishment'* in it by comparison with the previous work.[94]

■ *Baumann v Fussell* [1978] RPC 485 (CA)

A photograph of two cocks fighting each other was used as the basis of a painting. The composition of the subject matter was followed closely but the painter employed different colouring to heighten the dramatic effect of the representation. It was held that there was no infringement. It seems likely, therefore, that the painting would have been held to be original and so qualified for its own copyright.

Contrast the New York case of:

■ *Bridgeman Art Library Ltd v Corel Corp* 25 F Supp 421 (1999)

Kaplan J found that he was obliged to apply UK law in a case where the question was whether photographs of public domain works of art were the subject of copyright so that their unauthorised digitisation and inclusion in the defendants' CD-ROMs was infringement. It was held that, since the photographs aspired to create as accurate as possible a copy of the subject of the photograph, their work lacked originality under UK law and could not be protected (see further para 2.75).

Discussion point   For answer guidance visit www.oxfordtextbooks.co.uk/orc/waelde3e/

Is this decision a correct application of the concept of originality? Compare with *Eisenman v Qimron*, described previously (para 2.42). See further K Garnett 'Copyright in photographs' [2000] EIPR 229; R Deazley, 'Photographing paintings in the public domain: a response to Garnett' [2001] EIPR 229; S Stokes, 'Photographing paintings in the public domain: a response to Garnett' [2001] EIPR 354; and R Arnold, 'Copyright in photographs: a case for reform' [2005] EIPR 303.

Consider further:

■ *Antiquesportfolio.com plc v Rodney Fitch & Co Ltd* [2001] FSR 345

It was held that a photograph of a single static item was an original artistic work, because it could be said that the positioning of the object, the angle at which it was taken, the lighting, and the focus were all matters of personal judgement, albeit in many cases at a very basic level.

[94] [1989] AC 217 at 263.

Discussion point   For answer guidance visit www.oxfordtextbooks.co.uk/orc/waelde3e/

Do the auto-focus, portrait, landscape, and action shot functions in a digital camera mean that there is insufficient input from the user of the camera to make his or her photographs with the camera original for copyright purposes?

Independent but similar works

2.44   As indicated by the dictum of Peterson J quoted at the outset of this section (para 2.35), 'the Act does not require that the expression must be in an original or novel form, but that the work must not be copied from another work'.[95] Thus, if two works are similar, it does not follow that one cannot be original in the sense of copyright law. Unless there is derivation of one from another, a link between them beyond the similarity, the question cannot arise. The point is perhaps most significant in the field of artistic works, particularly paintings and photographs, where certain subjects and themes (eg representations of well-known scenes, landmarks, and buildings) are or become well-worn. Probably there is often some indirect derivation—influence may be a better word—in relation to earlier works in such cases, but it may well be difficult if not impossible to establish the absolute originality of a particular view, even in the limited copyright sense of the originator as the person who first gave expression to it.

 Question

List again all the elements to be considered in dealing with issues about originality. Which do you consider the most significant?

Key points on originality

- Literary, dramatic, musical, and artistic works must be '*original*' to attract copyright
- Originality is not a high standard, or a requirement of quality/merit/creativity/novelty
- Although individual facts and circumstances are always significant, the following factors are often cumulatively of use in assessing originality: work not copied; work is a product of author's own skill, labour, and judgment
- But derivative works may nevertheless be original

Originality in sound recordings, films, and published editions

2.45   With regard to sound recordings, films, and the typographical arrangements of published editions, there is no express requirement of originality; but no copyright arises in such a work to the extent that it reproduces another work in the same category. This is regardless of whether or not the earlier work had, or is still in, copyright. Thus a photographic reprint of an out-of-copyright book does not preclude others from making another edition of the same work using the same technique, although any additional editorial matter in the first work would have its own copyright in accordance with *Black v Murray*.[96] The

[95] *University of London Press v University Tutorial Press* [1916] 2 Ch 601 at 608.   [96] (1870) 9 M 341 (discussed at para 2.41).

matter is becoming ever more important in the film and recording industries, where digital technology has made it possible to re-record old material with greatly enhanced quality of sound and visual reproduction, with the possibility of embellishments such as colourisation of black-and-white films, or the stripping out of production effects in the original which are no longer wanted.[97] Although such re-recordings are derivative works, it may well be that the further technological input will be enough to mean that the new version is not merely a copy of the old but gains a new copyright.

 Exercise

Through use of a 'sampler', a digital recorder converts small samples of sound from other records into digits and stores them in microchips. These samples are then capable of electronic manipulation—for example, by slowing down or speeding up—and the results are then mixed to produce a new record. In effect, it is equivalent to a compilation of extracts from previous records. Quite apart from the question of the extent to which such activities infringe the copyrights in the original recordings, is the collection of samples itself a subject of copyright? (See further LC Bently, 'Sampling and copyright: is the law on the right track?' [1989] JBL 113 and 405.)

Broadcasts

2.46   The position of broadcasts with regard to requirements of originality is different from that of sound recordings, films, and typographical arrangements. The 1988 Act provides that copyright does not subsist in a broadcast which infringes, or to the extent that it infringes, the copyright in another broadcast.[98] The background to this is that merely broadcasting a programme which has already been put out has the effect of creating a new copyright. This is clear from the provisions of what is now s 14(5) of the 1988 Act, which states that 'copyright in a repeat broadcast expires at the same time as the copyright in the original broadcast'. As the subsection goes on to say, however, 'accordingly no copyright arises in respect of a repeat broadcast which is broadcast after the expiry of the copyright in the original broadcast'. It is also clear from this that only unauthorised repeats infringe the original copyright and are therefore unable to claim copyright themselves. This seems obvious, but it makes an important contrast with the forms of work discussed in the previous paragraph (para 2.45), where no copy, authorised or unauthorised, can bring a new copyright into existence.

Author works and media works

2.47   For convenience, in the remainder of this chapter, literary, dramatic, musical, and artistic works and films will be collectively referred to as '*author works*', and the other categories will be grouped as '*media works*'. The distinction has already been discussed insofar as it can be derived from the international structure of copyright: the Berne Convention for literary and artistic productions, broadly conceived (see para 2.8) and the Rome Convention for sound recordings and broadcasts (see para 2.10). The distinction rests on a number of points, of which the most important conceptually is the idea that the second group relies essentially on the operation of machinery and technology where the first depends upon one or more individuals as creator. The nature of authorship, as understood in the

---

[97] See for examples the colourisation of John Huston's film, *The Maltese Falcon* and, more recently, the removal from a 2003 re-release of The Beatles' final album, *Let It Be*, of effects added in the original by the producer Phil Spector.
[98] CDPA 1988, s 6(6).

law of copyright, is dealt with in further detail later (paras 3.4–3.30). Another element may be that in author works *content* is protected, whereas with media works it is the *medium* itself, or the *signal*, that is protected rather than the material embodied within it. So a song or music have author copyright, while the sound recording and broadcast containing them are purely media ones. Note also that the distinction has some difficulties in dealing with photographs and films, although in the law and in this book both are included in the author rather than the media work category. The point here is that anyone can get a result by wielding a camera, but does that make the person an author with protection for the content of the result?[99]

2.48   The distinction between author and media works has practical consequences in differences in the rules applying to the two groups. The first owner of the copyright in an author work is generally the author,[100] whereas in the media work it is the person by whose investment (to be conceived more widely than the kind of investment that is authorship or composition) the work was produced. Only author works need be original to be protected,[101] meaning that they must be independent forms of expression achieved through their author's judgment, skill, and labour.[102] Author works alone attract moral rights.[103] Author work copyright lasts significantly longer than media work copyright: with the former, it normally lasts for the lifetime of the author plus 70 years, while for sound recordings and broadcasts it is 50 years from making, release, or transmission, as the case may be.[104]

Key points on author and media works

- The distinction between *author* and *media* work, resting in principle on the degree of individual as opposed to technological creativity involved

- The difference in rules applying to each of the groups, explained in detail later

- The borderline nature of photographs and films in this distinction

---

Author works

2.49   The following are the categories of author work:

- literary;

- dramatic;

- musical;

- artistic;

- films.

---

[99] See for interesting discussion of this point R Arnold, 'Copyright in photographs: a case for reform' [2005] EIPR 303.

[100] In the case of films in the UK, joint authorship is attributed to the principal director and the producer (CDPA 1988, s 9(2) (ab)). Note also (1) the British concept of a computer-generated work where there is no human author (CDPA 1988, ss 9(3) and 178); and (2) that copyright in a work produced in the course of employment falls to the employer unless otherwise agreed (CDPA 1988, s 11(2)). Employment should be distinguished from a commission, where the copyright would remain with the author unless otherwise agreed.

[101] But note that there is no express requirement that a film be original (see CDPA 1988, s 1(1)(b), and para 2.45).

[102] See further paras 2.34–2.43.

[103] Apart from computer programs (CDPA 1988, s 79(2)(a)); see further para 3.38.

[104] See further paras 3.49ff, for copyright terms.

The distinctions between these groups of author works are not without importance, but in a number of recent cases the English courts have held that a work may belong to more than one of the categories. So, for example, circuit diagrams have been held to be both literary and artistic works,[105] while a film has been held to be also a dramatic work.[106] As Laddie J has pointed out, this is a different point from the one made earlier in this chapter (para 2.23), that one product may embody several copyrights:

> although different copyrights can protect simultaneously a particular product and an author can produce more than one copyright work during the course of a single episode of creative effort, for example a competent musician may write the words and the music for a song at the same time, it is quite another thing to say that a single piece of work by an author gives rise to two or more copyrights in respect of the same creative effort. In some cases the borderline between one category of copyright work and another may be difficult to define, but that does not justify giving to the author protection in both categories. The categories of copyright work are, to some extent, arbitrarily defined. In the case of a borderline work, I think there are compelling arguments that the author must be confined to one or other of the possible categories. The proper category is that which most nearly suits the characteristics of the work in issue.[107]

Exercise

Explain clearly the difference between copyright in a work and the several copyrights which may coexist in a product such as a CD. Why does this distinction matter? Consider in particular the multimedia product (eg the BBC website, a computer game), which consists of digitised material combining audio, video, text, and images still and moving played through a computer, and with which the user may interact.

2.50   From a taxonomic point of view there must be much to be said for the approach of Laddie J; what, after all, is the point of having categories if they are not mutually exclusive? And if they are not mutually exclusive, or fail to capture particular types of work adequately, should the categorisation not be abandoned or re-thought? The principle of Occam's razor might usefully be applied:[108] categories are not to be multiplied unnecessarily in copyright law, and perhaps the present UK statute is guilty of that offence (see further on this theme, paras 7.19–7.23).[109]

Literary works

2.51   The 1988 Act defines 'literary work' as follows:

> any work other than a dramatic or musical work which is written, spoken or sung, and accordingly includes a table or compilation other than a database, a computer program, preparatory design material for a computer program, and a database (s 3(1)).

This statutory definition is not exhaustive and there are a number of cases in which the courts have had to give an opinion one way or the other as a matter of impression. Standard examples of literary works protected by copyright would include novels, short stories, poetry, song lyrics, non-fiction books, and

---

[105] *Anacon Corp Ltd v Environmental Research Technology Ltd* [1994] FSR 659; *Electronic Techniques (Anglia) Ltd v Critchley Components Ltd* [1997] FSR 401; *Sandman v Panasonic UK Ltd* [1998] FSR 651.

[106] *Norowzian v Arks Ltd (No 2)* [2000] FSR 363.

[107] *Electronic Techniques (Anglia) Ltd v Critchley Components Ltd* [1997] FSR 401 at 413.

[108] For Occam's razor see http://en.wikipedia.org/wiki/Occam's_Razor.

[109] See further A Christie, 'A proposal for simplifying UK copyright law' [2001] EIPR 26; I Stamatoudi, *Copyright and Multimedia Works: A Comparative Analysis* (2002); T Aplin, *Copyright Law in the Digital Society* (2005), Ch 6; B Bandey, 'Over-categorisation in copyright law: computer and internet programming perspectives' [2007] EIPR 461.

periodical articles. But, as already noted in the discussion of originality (para 2.36), the law does not require works to possess, or even to aspire to possess, aesthetic merit before they can be the subject of copyright as literary works. Trade catalogues,[110] examination papers,[111] a grid containing 25 letters and two separate rows of five letters each,[112] and the critical apparatus or annotations attached to an edition of another work[113] may all be literary works. Moreover, while the work must have some meaning,[114] it is not necessary for it to be expressed in a conventional way, so that a work written in shorthand or in code may be a literary work.[115] A knitting guide consisting of 'various words and numerals…which constitute detailed instructions intelligible to anyone who understands the production of knitwear'[116] would presumably be a literary work.

Single words and phrases

2.52   On the other hand, the courts usually had great difficulty in according copyright to single words and phrases as literary works.

■ *Exxon Corporation v Exxon Insurance Consultants* [1982] Ch 119

Copyright was claimed in the invented single word 'Exxon', which had been developed as a new company name with great expenditure of time and money by the company in question. The court held that a literary work must be 'intended to afford either information and instruction or pleasure in the form of literary enjoyment',[117] and that this could not be the case with a single word, even though research and effort had been involved in its creation.

Similarly it has been said that in general the title of a work by itself does not have copyright,[118] while advertising slogans consisting of stock phrases or a few commonplace sentences have also been denied copyright as literary works.[119] It has been held in a number of cases that there is no copyright in the names of computer program commands, since they are merely 'triggers' for a set of instructions to be given effect by the computer.[120]

2.53   But there are also recent departures from the generally negative view of short works of this kind, which demonstrate a renewed willingness on the part of the courts to recognise copyright in phrases.[121]

■ *Shetland Times v Wills* [1997] FSR 604

The *Shetland Times* home page used its newspaper headlines as links to the material deeper within the site. The headline texts were used by *The Shetland News* website to act as the deep links on to the relative *Times* stories. But, in a prima facie view granting interim interdict, Lord Hamilton held that the headline texts had copyright, so that the actions of the *News* in copying them for reproduction on its own website was infringement. In defence of Lord Hamilton's view, the creation of a headline does involve skill and labour, in that the reader's attention has to be attracted, information about the relevant item conveyed

---

[110] *Harpers v Barry Henry & Co* (1892) 20 R 133.   [111] *University of London Press v University Tutorial Press* [1916] 2 Ch 601.
[112] *Express Newspapers plc v Liverpool Daily Post & Echo plc* [1985] FSR 306.   [113] *Black v Murray* (1870) 9 M 341.
[114] *Fournet v Pearson* (1897) 14 TLR 82.   [115] *Pitman v Hine* (1884) 1 TLR 82; *Anderson & Co v Lieber Code Co* [1917] 2 KB 469.
[116] *Brigid Foley Ltd v Ellott* [1982] RPC 433 per Sir Robert Megarry V-C at 434; see also *Abraham Moon & Sons Ltd v Thornber and others* [2012] EWPCC 37.   [117] Phrasing derived from *Hollinrake v Truswell* [1894] 3 Ch 420.
[118] *Francis Day & Hunter Ltd v Twentieth Century Fox Corp Ltd* [1940] AC 112 (PC) per Lord Wright at 123; *Rose v Information Services Ltd* [1987] FSR 254; cf *Dicks v Yates* (1881) 18 Ch D 76 per Jessel MR at 89.
[119] *Kirk v J & R Fleming* [1928–35] MCC 44; *Sinanide v La Maison Kosmeo* (1928) 139 LT 365 (CA).
[120] *Powerflex Services Pty Ltd v Data Access Corporation* (1996) 137 ALR 498 (Fed Ct Aus); aff'd (1999) 202 CLR 1 (HCA); *Navitaire Inc v EasyJet Airline Co Ltd* [2006] RPC 3 (Pumfrey J).
[121] See also P Sumpter, 'Copyright in slogans: another bald spot exposed' [2009] EIPR 287.

and (at least in the case of the tabloid press, which much favours punning and jokey headlines) entertainment provided.

■ Case C-5/08 *Infopaq International A/S v Danske Dagblades Forening* [2009] ECDR 16

For the facts of this case, which related to an electronic news-cuttings service, see para 4.20. The Court of Justice stated that 'words, considered in isolation, are not as such an intellectual creation of the author who employs them' (para 45); but 'the possibility may not be ruled out that certain isolated sentences, or even certain parts of sentences... may be suitable for conveying to the reader the originality of a publication such as a newspaper article, by communicating to that reader an element which is, in itself, the expression of the intellectual creation of the author of that article' (para 47).

■ *Newspaper Licensing Agency Ltd v Meltwater Holding BV* [2010] EWHC 3099 (Ch); [2011] EWCA Civ 890 (CA)

For the facts of this case, which related to a media-monitoring service, see para 4.20. A question for determination was whether headlines in newspapers could be literary works which would attract copyright independently of the substantive article. In the High Court, Proudman J applied *Infopaq* and held that 'headlines are capable of being literary works, whether independently or as part of the articles to which they relate. Some of the headlines... with which I have been provided are certainly independent literary works within the Infopaq test' (para 71). It was also concluded that 'a mere 11 word extract may now be sufficient in quantity provided it includes an expression of the intellectual creation of the author' (para 77). Both these conclusions were affirmed by the Court of Appeal, which rejected the argument that 'a 256 character extract would be too short and factual to give a reader more than an idea of what the article is about but with no sense of the author's intellectual creation' (paras 27–28). An appeal to the Supreme Court is outstanding.

These cases reinforce that sentences in the form of headlines or extracts from newspaper articles can be independent literary works and protected if there is sufficient originality. It also means that slightly more elaborate texts, such as notes on what will be found through using a link, or material on help menus and 'frequently asked questions' facilities could also be protected. The protection of such works, if any, must be very 'thin', however, given the necessarily limited scope of the genre.[122]

? Question

What is needed for there to be a literary work?

Computer programs as literary works[123]

2.54   The 1988 Act states that a computer program and its preparatory design material are literary works.[124] The Act does not otherwise define the meaning of computer program. Jacob LJ has pointed out that the Software Directive implemented by the 1988 Act envisages one rather than two separate copyrights in the program *and* its preparatory material.[125] In general a computer program is a set of instructions to a

---

[122] Ie, not very much variation from the first work would be required to evade a charge of infringement.
[123] See generally D Bainbridge, *Legal Protection of Computer Software* (2008); S Gordon, 'The very idea! Why copyright law is an inappropriate way to protect computer programs' [1998] EIPR 10.
[124] CDPA 1988, s 3(1)(b), (c). Note also the possibility of software patents, discussed at paras 11.33ff.
[125] *Nova Productions Ltd v Mazooma Games Ltd* [2007] RPC 25 (CA), para 28.

computer to perform certain tasks. The production of a program is a complex process involving first the expression of an analysis of the functions to be performed as a set of algorithms (often most simply represented by means of a flow chart or some other logical flow diagram); secondly, its restatement (usually by a programmer, but also often by a computer) in a computer language (the source code); and, finally, the translation by a computer running under a compiler program of the source code into a machine-readable language (the object code).

■ Case C-406/10 *SAS Institute Inc v World Programming Ltd* [2012] ECDR 22 (ECJ)[126]

This reference involved questions on copyright protection available to computer programs under the Software Directive. The Court of Justice held that the object of the protection is 'the expression in any form of a computer program which permits reproduction in different computer languages' (para 35). As such, source code and object code are clearly protectable forms of expressions. Protection includes expression in the 'preparatory design material for a computer program' which must be such that a computer program can result from it at some stage (para 36).[127] Such matter as the logic, algorithms, and programming languages lying behind the source code comprise unprotectable ideas and principles.[128] The functionality of a computer program, as well as programming language and format of data files used in a computer program, do not constitute a form of expression of that program (para 39). The Court also noted that 'keywords, syntax, commands and combinations of commands, options, defaults and iterations consist of words, figures or mathematical concepts which, considered in isolation, are not, as such, an intellectual creation of the author of the computer program' and 'it is only through the choice, sequence and combination of those words, figures or mathematical concepts that the author may express his creativity in an original manner and achieve a result, namely the user manual for the computer program, which is an intellectual creation' (paras 66–67).

The lack of a definition of a computer program is to avoid failure to cover advances in the technology.[129] Some examples of computer programs that have been protected are: a 'hardware lock' enabling a computer program to run (Australia);[130] codes embedded in microchips within the computer (United States);[131] and a video game simulating a game of pool (UK).[132] It has been held that a GUI, which enables communication between the computer program and the user, is not a form of expression of a computer program because it 'does not enable the reproduction of that computer program, but merely constitutes one element of that program by means of which users make use of the features of that program.'[133]

 Question

What is the difference between source code and object code?

---

[126] See further D Gervais and E Derclaye, 'The scope of computer program protection after *SAS*: are we closer to answers?' [2012] EIPR 565.

[127] See Case C-393/09 *Bezpečnostní softwarová asociace v Ministerstvo kultury* [2011] ECDR 3 (ECJ) at paras 34–37.

[128] Software Directive 1991, recitals 7, 13, 14, and 15 (note this is now consolidated into Directive 2009/24/EC; see *Navitaire Inc v EasyJet Airline Co Ltd* [2006] RPC 3 (Pumfrey J), for an example of denial of copyright to programming languages comprised by defined user command interfaces (despite its ad hoc character) and a collection of commands; see also *SAS Institute v World Programming* [2010] ECDR 15 (Arnold J) at para 217.

[129] This argument succeeded in the Australian case of *Apple Computer Inc v Computer Edge Pty Ltd* [1986] FSR 537.

[130] *Autodesk Inc v Dyason and Kelly* [1992] RPC 575 (HCA); criticised in *Cantor Fitzgerald v Tradition UK* [2000] RPC 95.

[131] *NEC Corp v Intel Corp* 835 F 2d 1546 (1988). See also recital 7 of the Software Directive 1991.

[132] *Nova Productions Ltd v Mazooma Games Ltd* [2006] RPC 14 (Kitchin J); aff'd [2007] RPC 25 (CA).

[133] Case C-393/09 *Bezpečnostní softwarová asociace v Ministerstvo kultury* [2011] ECDR 3 (ECJ) at para 41.

Tables and compilations

2.55 Tables and compilations may be literary works. Thus import and export lists,[134] railway timetables,[135] television programme schedules,[136] and football fixture lists[137] have been held to be literary works, as have poetry anthologies[138] and football pools coupons.[139] Character-based screen displays used for online booking of tickets on a 'ticketless' airline, providing a static framework within which the dynamic data supplied by customers caused the booking software to operate, were also held to be copyright tables, but in the same case a collection of computer programs was held not to be a compilation since there was no overall design underlying the collection, simply an accretion of material over time.[140] Similarly, a list of 33 pairs of electronic addresses allowing police to recover deleted data from mobile phones was held not to be a compilation because it was not planned, lacked overall design, and was simply an accretion of data acquired by happenstance over time.[141] The component parts of a compilation may be out of copyright, but the compilation will still enjoy copyright as such.[142] But such material has always to be subjected to the test of originality before copyright can be claimed and its construction must be shown to be the product of some skill and labour by the author.[143]

 Question

What is it that copyright protects in relation to tables and compilations?

Databases[144]

2.56 Until 1 January 1998, databases were thought to be protected under UK law as 'compilations'; but from that date the position was changed as a result of the implementation of the EU's Database Directive 1996.[145] 'Compilation' now expressly does not include databases.[146] A database is defined as:

> a collection of independent works, data or other materials arranged in a systematic or methodical way and individually accessible by electronic or other means (CDPA 1988, s 3A(1)).

This definition means that, unlike traditional compilations, database protection is not confined to collections the basic form of which is written, as distinct from other forms of expression (eg graphic). Databases include:

> literary, artistic, musical or other collections of works or collections of other materials such as texts, sounds, images, numbers, facts, and data (Database Directive 1996, recital 17).

That is, they can be *multimedia works*. So the elements of a database may be works in their own right, or simply items of information in textual, visual, or audio form. Many websites are database-driven, for example, particularly where they are interactive. But databases are not merely electronic compilations or collections; they can also be created in non-electronic media. The Court of

---

[134] *Walford v Johnston* (1846) 20 D 1160; *Maclean v Moody* (1858) 20 D 1154. [135] *Leslie v Young* (1894) 21 R (HL) 57.
[136] *Independent Television Publications Ltd v Time Out Ltd* [1984] FSR 64. For the Australian approach, see [2009] EIPR N63.
[137] *Football League v Littlewoods Pools* [1959] Ch 637. [138] *Macmillan v Suresh Chunder Deb* (1890) ILR 17 Calc 951.
[139] *Ladbroke (Football) Ltd v William Hill (Football) Ltd* [1964] 1 WLR 273 (HL).
[140] *Navitaire Inc v EasyJet Airline Co Ltd* [2006] RPC 3 (Pumfrey J).
[141] *Forensic Telecommunications Services Ltd v Chief Constable of West Yorkshire Police* [2011] EWHC 2892 (Ch).
[142] *Ashmore v Douglas Home* [1987] FSR 553. [143] See also paras 2.39–2.40.
[144] See generally E Derclaye, *The Legal Protection of Databases* (2008); T Aplin, *Copyright Law in the Digital Society: The Challenges of Multimedia* (2005), 41–73.
[145] Directive 96/9/EC on the legal protection of databases, Art 3(1), implemented in the UK by the Copyright and Rights in Databases Regulations 1997 (SI 1997/3032). [146] CDPA 1988, s 3(1)(a).

Justice has indicated that the definition of the term 'database' is intended to have wide scope and is capable of including football fixture lists,[147] telephone directories,[148] trade directories,[149] and news websites.[150]

2.57   The CDPA 1988 expressly provides for the level of originality that a database must show:

> if, and only if, by reason of the *selection or arrangement of the contents* of the database the database constitutes the *author's own intellectual creation* (CDPA 1988, s 3A(2); emphasis added).

This provision, introduced as a result of the Database Directive 1996 is generally taken to require a higher level of originality than the traditional 'skill, labour, and judgment' UK originality test (see paras 2.39–2.40). One result of this provision was that many databases which would previously have been protected by copyright in the UK were no longer protected. For this reason, the Database Directive also introduced a special, or *sui generis*, database right for the protection of databases not covered by copyright. An account of this special right is given in paras 6.4–6.20. Another consequence of the special definition of originality is to make clear that database copyright covers, not the contents of the database, but their *selection or arrangement*—that is, the way in which the contents are structured.[151] It is this structure that must be the author's *own intellectual creation* (see further para 2.63).

 Question

What is protected by the copyright (if any) in a database?

Databases and computer programs

2.58   The Database Directive provides that its protection does not apply to computer programs used in the making or operation of databases accessible by electronic means,[152] raising the sometimes difficult question of when and whether an electronically operated database might or might not also be a computer program. In *Navitaire Inc v EasyJet Airline Co Ltd*[153] Pumfrey J held that schemas or material directly entered by the compiler of a database which changed its structure by adding or subtracting fields, or adding or removing datasets, were computer programs rather than databases in their own right. On the other hand, he held with some hesitation that the metadata created by this activity, defining the fields and datasets in the database, fell to be protected, since this related to the structure and arrangement of the data in the database.

 Question

What are the differences between (1) a database and a compilation; (2) a database and a computer program?

---

[147] Case C-444/02 *Fixtures Marketing Ltd v OPAP* [2005] ECDR 3 (ECJ), paras 20–24 and 33–36.
[148] Unauthorised reproduction of telephone directories on CDROM [2002] ECDR 3.
[149] *Societe Tigest SARL v Societe Reed Expositions France* [2002] ECC 29.
[150] *SA Prline v SA Communication & Sales and Sarl News Invest* [2002] ECDR 2 (Trib de Comm); *Danske Dagblades Forening v Newsbooster* [2003] ECDR 5.   [151] Case C-604/10 *Football Dataco Ltd v Yahoo! UK Ltd* [2012] ECDR 10.
[152] Database Directive, Art 1(3). Computer programs have copyright as such (see para 2.54).
[153] [2006] RPC 3 (Pumfrey J).

Defining databases: four elements

2.59   The complex definition of a database protectable by copyright requires further analysis of four specific elements:

(1) independence of the constituent elements;
(2) systematic or methodical arrangement of the elements;
(3) individual accessibility of the elements;
(4) intellectual creation in selection and arrangement of contents.

The meaning of each of these elements can be understood from the rulings of the CJEU and guidance from the Opinions of the Advocate General.

Defining databases: (1) independence of the constituent elements

2.60   The 'data or materials must not be linked or must at least be capable of being separate without losing their informative content'.[154] So films as such are not databases, because there *is* interaction between script, music, sound recordings, and the moving images.[155] But an entry in a telephone directory can be understood standing alone, and so the directory is a database. Sports fixtures, the subject of several European Court references, provide more complex examples. Is the information, 'X v Y', an item which can be understood on its own? Is it separate from the date information without which 'X v Y' is probably meaningless? Or is 'X v Y, 1 January 2010' the single item of information which can be understood on its own and which therefore renders the whole collection of such items a potentially copyright database? The ECJ has held that the materials have to be separable from one another without their informative, literary, artistic, musical, or other value being affected; data relating to sporting activity was not precluded from recognition as a database; the date and time of, and the identity of two teams playing in, both home and away matches were covered by the concept of independent materials with autonomous informative value.[156]

Defining databases: (2) systematic or methodical arrangement of the elements

2.61   The purpose of this requirement is 'to exclude random accumulations of data and ensure that only planned collections of data are covered, that is to say, data organised to specific criteria'.[157] The arrangement required here need not be a physical one,[158] but the ECJ has stated that the condition implies that the collection should be contained in a fixed base of some kind; such a base may be technical (eg electronic, electro-magnetic, or electro-optical processes), or something else (eg an index, table of contents, or a particular plan or method of classification), to allow retrieval of any independent material contained within it.[159] Thus, the arrangement involved is *conceptual*, that is to say, it is about the way in which the contents are presented to and retrievable by the user of the database. Alphabetical, chronological, or subject arrangements will be enough (although subject to the requirement of 'intellectual creation', for which see further para 2.63).

---

[154] Case C-444/02 *Fixtures Marketing Ltd v OPAP* [2004] ECR I-10549, para 39 (AG); Case C-46/02 *Fixtures Marketing Ltd v Oy Veikkaus Ab* [2004] ECR I-10365, para 36 (AG).

[155] See also Database Directive, recital 17: 'a recording or an audio visual cinematographic, literary or musical work as such does not fall within the scope of this Directive'.

[156] Case C-444/02 *Fixtures Marketing Ltd v OPAP* [2004] ECR I-10549, paras 23 and 32–35 (ECJ).

[157] Case C-444/02 *Fixtures Marketing Ltd v OPAP*, para 40 (AG); Case C-46/02 *Fixtures Marketing Ltd v Oy Veikkaus Ab*, para 37 (AG).   [158] Database Directive, recital 21.

[159] Case C-444/02 *Fixtures Marketing Ltd v OPAP* [2004] ECR I-10549, para 30 (ECJ).

Defining databases: (3) individual accessibility of the elements

2.62   This requirement has some ambiguity. Does it mean that the works or items comprising the database must be separately retrievable by the user and, if so, how must that access work? The ECJ has stated that a means of retrieving each of a database's constituent materials, technical or otherwise (as described in the previous paragraph), was what made it possible to distinguish a protected database from a mere collection.[160] Nevertheless, this and the previous requirement do not appear to be difficult to satisfy, for example a table consisting of 33 electronic addresses was held to be systematically arranged and individually accessible by virtue of its arrangement into columns and rows.[161]

Exercise

Take a printed telephone directory or sports fixture list. When you access an item of information therein (eg a person's telephone number you want to call, a match you want to attend), is it 'individually accessible by electronic or other means' simply because you can read it and ignore the rest of what is visible on the printed page? Or is it accessible only alongside the other information on the page, and therefore not individually or separately retrievable? Compare what happens if you search an electronic telephone directory for a particular person, or a fixtures database for the match on a particular date, or for the date your team plays its local 'derby' game on its home ground. Should there be a different result according to whether the information is collected in print or electronic form?

Defining databases: (4) intellectual creation of selection and arrangement

2.63   Finally, to attract copyright the database must be the author's own intellectual creation by reason of the selection or arrangement of its contents.[162] The protection is offered to the selection and arrangement of the database, rather than to its contents as such, although the latter may attract copyright—or several copyrights—in their own right. It is irrelevant whether the collection is made up of materials from a source or sources other than the person making up the collection, materials created by that person or a combination of the two.[163] The Database Directive says that, as a rule (ie normally), the compilation of several recordings of musical performances on a CD does not attract copyright protection as a database.[164]

■ Case C-604/10 *Football Dataco Ltd v Yahoo! UK Ltd* [2012] ECDR 10[165]

It was claimed that fixtures lists of English and Scottish football leagues were protected by copyright in databases and the Court of Appeal referred questions on the interpretation of the Database Directive. The Court of Justice held that national legislation is precluded from granting database copyright under conditions which are different than that of originality as laid down in the Directive. It then provided

---

[160] Case C-444/02 *Fixtures Marketing Ltd v OPAP* [2004] ECR I-10549, paras 31–32 (ECJ).

[161] *Forensic Telecommunications Services Ltd v Chief Constable of West Yorkshire Police* [2011] EWHC 2892 (Ch).

[162] CDPA 1988, s 3A. See also for use of this formulation Council Directive on the legal protection of computer programs 91/250/EEC (now consolidated in Directive 2009/24/EC), Art 1(3); but in the implementation of this Directive the UK did not see fit to use the phrase. See paras 2.39 and 2.40.

[163] Case C-444/02 *Fixtures Marketing Ltd v OPAP* [2004] ECR I-10549, para 25 (ECJ).

[164] Database Directive, recital 19.

[165] On the effects of this ruling, see D Rose and N O'Sullivan, '*Football Dataco v Yahoo!* Implications of the ECJ judgment' [2012] JIPLP 792.

guidance on the meaning of 'author's own intellectual creation'. Copyright protection of database concerns the structure of the database; it does not concern the contents of the database or the elements constituting its contents, and does not extend to the data itself. As such, intellectual effort and skill expended on creating data is not relevant for assessment of database copyright (paras 30–33). The originality requirement for databases is satisfied when 'through the selection or arrangement of the data which it contains, its author expresses his creative ability in an original manner by making free and creative choices...and thus stamps his "personal touch"' (para 38). In contrast, it is not satisfied 'when the setting up of the database is dictated by technical considerations, rules or constraints which leave no room for creative freedom' (para 39). There is no need for the author to 'add important significance' to the data through the selection or arrangement (para 41). The fact that the author had used significant labour and skill in setting up the database may be irrelevant if the labour and skill does not express originality in the selection or arrangement of the data; this is a matter for the national court to assess (para 42). Although the Court of Appeal will have to decide whether the fixtures lists are original, the Court of Justice's guidance on 'intellectual creation' seems particularly likely to *exclude* alphabetical or chronological ordering.

The lack of intellectual creation does not mean that the collection fails to be a database, however. Rather, the database does not have copyright; but it may still be protected by the *sui generis* database right, for which see further paras 6.4–6.20.

? Question

Are the following databases: (1) newspapers; (2) websites; (3) multimedia works? If so, how far is the database covered as such by copyright?

💬 Discussion point For answer guidance visit www.oxfordtextbooks.co.uk/orc/waelde3e/

Imagine a compilation which is not a database for legal purposes, that is, is not a collection of independent works or items of information, systematically arranged and individually accessible. Would the work you have thus imagined be protectable by copyright?

Crossing categories: circuit diagrams

2.64   Electronic circuit diagrams have been held to be literary works without excluding the possibility that they also incorporate artistic works.[166] Electronic circuits incorporate a number of interconnected components, such as resistors, transistors, and capacitors, and the diagrams show the way in which these components are connected as well as stating in relation to each component the rating or value that that component should have for the circuit to work. The components themselves are shown in the diagrams by way of conventional symbols. The diagrams are not visual representations of the way the circuit is linked up in reality, but are simply 'topological', 'schematic', or 'architectural' indications of the interrelationship of the components in the completed circuit. Such diagrams may also form part of the information accompanying individual components when sold, in order to indicate the kinds of circuit in which the component in question will give its best performance.[167]

---

[166] *Anacon Corp Ltd v Environmental Research Technology Ltd* [1994] FSR 659; *Electronic Techniques (Anglia) Ltd v Critchley Components Ltd* [1997] FSR 401; *Sandman v Panasonic UK Ltd* [1998] FSR 651.

[167] An illustration of an electronic circuit diagram is in *Electronic Techniques (Anglia) Ltd v Critchley Components Ltd* at 405.

2.65 The question of category is important for this reason. The typical act of alleged infringement is the production of a circuit, and generally this will not look particularly like the original diagram. Although copyright in a two-dimensional artistic work (the diagram) can be infringed by a three-dimensional reproduction (the circuit) (see para 4.26), this will only be so if the latter is visually similar to the former. This is why artistic copyright is not very useful to stop circuits being copied. But the second circuit will incorporate the information shown in the diagram, and may well be based on a 'net list' of all the components and their interconnections in the first circuit, made from that circuit and then fed into a computer to produce the second, allegedly infringing, circuit. The production of the second circuit thus potentially involves an infringing indirect copy of the literary elements of the diagram underlying the first circuit.

 Question

To which category of copyright works do electronic circuit diagrams belong?

Dramatic works

2.66 The distinction between literary, dramatic and musical works is not of much practical significance in terms of its consequences for copyright, and this may explain a lack of definition of dramatic works. The 1988 Act defines 'dramatic work' as including a work of dance or mime.[168] It has been said that a dramatic work must be such that 'for its proper representation, acting, and possibly scenery, formed a necessary ingredient'.[169] The Privy Council has stated that a dramatic work must have sufficient unity to be capable of performance, leading to a decision that the stock phrases and other aspects of the format of a television talent show did not constitute a dramatic work in themselves, being merely accessories to the show.[170] On the other hand, where the format of a television show had been worked out in sufficient detail in a written document supported by a feasibility study, the New Zealand courts were prepared to hold that this was a dramatic work.[171] In the latest case, it was said that 'a dramatic work is a work of action, with or without words or music, which is capable of being performed before an audience.'[172] Thus a scene created to be part of the cover for a forthcoming album by the pop group Oasis was held not to be a dramatic work, since it involved no action.[173] The sequence of images produced by a computer video game was also not a dramatic work, because it varied too much each time the game was played and lacked the unity for it to be a work capable of performance.[174]

 Question

How may a dramatic work be defined for copyright purposes?

2.67 The 1988 Act omits from its definition of dramatic work some words which appeared in the 1956 Act, that the phrase does not include a cinematograph film as distinct from a scenario or script for a

---

[168] CDPA 1988, s 3(1). For an example see *Norowzian v Arks Ltd (No 2)* [2000] FSR 363 (CA).
[169] *Fuller v Blackpool Winter Gardens & Pavilion Co Ltd* [1895] 2 QB 429 per AL Smith LJ at 442.
[170] *Green v Broadcasting Corp of New Zealand* [1989] 2 All ER 1056 per Lord Bridge of Harwich at 1058.
[171] *Wilson v Broadcasting Corp of New Zealand* [1990] 2 NZLR 565.
[172] *Norowzian v Arks Ltd (No 2)* [2000] FSR 363 (CA) per Nourse LJ at 367.
[173] *Creation Records Ltd v News Group Newspapers Ltd* [1997] EMLR 444.
[174] *Nova Productions Ltd v Mazooma Games Ltd* [2006] RPC 14 (Kitchin J); point not discussed in the Court of Appeal ([2007] RPC 25).

cinematograph film.[175] Did this change mean that films, which retain their own copyright under the 1988 Act,[176] can now also be protected as dramatic works? In *Norowzian v Arks Ltd (No 2)*,[177] the Court of Appeal concluded that a film which was a work of action and which could be performed before an audience could as a result also be a dramatic work. A film might be both a recording of a dramatic work and a dramatic work in itself; sometimes it might not be a recording of a dramatic work but would nonetheless itself be a dramatic work. The questions arising from overlapping categories are reduced inasmuch as films and dramatic works both attract moral rights, have more or less the same duration of copyright[178] and enjoy the same categories of restricted acts.

Discussion point 1 For answer guidance visit www.oxfordtextbooks.co.uk/orc/waelde3e/

Is a television commercial a dramatic work? See *Marblehead Trading Ltd v The Stroh Brewery Co* 1988 GWD 20-885.

Discussion point 2

How should works which contain a musical element but are intended for stage performance or to be made as a film—for example, an opera, a ballet, or the type of entertainment known as a 'musical'—be characterised for the purposes of copyright?

Musical works[179]

2.68   A musical work is a work consisting of music, exclusive of any words or action intended to be sung, spoken or performed with the music.[180] Words written to be sung to music thus do not form part of any musical work but have their own literary or dramatic copyright. Music, it might be thought, consists of sounds other than words, recorded in writing or otherwise. At the same time, the limits of the definition of music are unclear. It seems to go beyond the notes on a score to include the combination of melodies and harmonies, the figuring of the bass, ornamentation, and performance directions.[181] Music also covers the sampling and scratching of tracks by DJs of works composed by other artists which create a new work. Another problem is the example of John Cage's '4 Minutes 33 Seconds', which has already been mentioned on the question of what constitutes a work (para 2.25): is a deliberately created silence in a concert hall, lasting for a fixed period, a musical work?[182] Most other gaps in the definition can probably be filled by the categories of literary, dramatic, and artistic work, or by sound recording copyright. Cage's work might be regarded as a dramatic one, for example inasmuch as it involves a performance before an audience.

---

[175] 1956 Act, s 48(1).   [176] CDPA 1988, s 1(1)(b).

[177] [2001] FSR 363 (CA); see para 2.32. See further A Barron, 'The legal property of film' (2004) 67 MLR 177; I Stamatoudi, 'Joy for the claimant: can a film also be protected as a dramatic work?' [2000] IPQ 117; R Arnold, 'Joy: a reply' [2001] IPQ 10.

[178] Note, however, that the only relevant author for a dramatic work is the dramatist, whereas for a film it is not only the screenplay writer and dialogue author but also the principal director and the composer of any special music, and the duration of the copyright is determined by the death of the last of these to die. A film may thus enjoy copyright for longer as such than it does as a dramatic work.

[179] See generally S Frith and L Marshall, *Music and Copyright* (2nd edn, 2004); A Rahmatian, 'Music and creativity as perceived by copyright law' [2005] IPQ 267.

[180] CDPA 1988, s 3(1).   [181] See *Sawkins v Hyperion Records Ltd* [2005] RPC 32 (CA).

[182] See Cheng Lim Saw, 'Protecting the sound of silence in 4'33": a timely revisit of basic principles in copyright law' [2005] EIPR 467.

❓ Question

What is the definition of a musical work? Can you define music?

Artistic works[183]

2.69 An artistic work is defined[184] as:

- a graphic work, photograph, sculpture, or collage, irrespective of artistic quality;
- a work of architecture, being either a building or a model for a building;
- works of artistic craftsmanship.

Graphic work, photograph, sculpture, or collage

2.70 The 1988 Act defines most, but not all, of these works:[185]

- Graphic work includes any painting, drawing, diagram, map, chart, or plan, and any engraving, etching, lithograph, woodcut, print, or similar work.
- Photograph means a recording of light or other radiation on any medium on which an image is produced or from which an image may by any means be produced, and which is not part of a film.
- Sculpture includes any cast or model made for purposes of sculpture.

Graphic works

2.71 The first point to note is that the definition of graphic work is non-exclusive, so that it may catch works other than those listed. Thus, the screen layouts of websites have been held to be graphic works, even though only recorded as such in digital code. The same case found that icons used in the displays were also graphic works, but as drawings.[186] But the Court of Appeal has held that a common feature of graphic works as defined in the 1988 Act is their static and non-moving character. So video games are not graphic works, while a series of drawings is a series of graphic works, not a single one.[187]

Paintings

2.72 The word 'painting' is not defined by the Act. There has been a judicial attempt to do so:

■ *Merchandising Corporation of America v Harpbond* [1983] FSR 32

It was held that a painting required a surface before it could be a protected work. Paint without a surface is not a painting. From this premise it was concluded that a flamboyant style of facial make-up forming part of the distinctive image of Adam Ant, a well-known popular musician, could not be a painting for

---

[183] See generally P Kearns, *The Legal Concept of Art* (1998); D McClean and K Schubert (eds), *Dear Images: Art, Culture and Copyright* (2002); S Stokes, *Art and Copyright* (2012); A Barron, 'Copyright law and the claims of art' [2002] IPQ 369; D Booton, 'Framing pictures: defining art in UK copyright law' [2003] IPQ 38; W Landes and R Posner, *Economic Structure of Intellectual Property Law* (2004), Ch 9 ('The legal protection of postmodern art').

[184] CDPA 1988, s 4(1). See further T Rychlicki, 'Legal questions about illegal art' [2008] 3 JIPLP 393.

[185] CDPA 1988, s 4(2).   [186] *Navitaire Inc v EasyJet Airline Co Ltd* [2006] RPC 3 (Pumfrey J).

[187] *Nova Productions Ltd v Mazooma Games Ltd* [2007] RPC 25 (CA).

copyright purposes.[188] Works of graffiti could, under this definition, fall within the purview of artistic works for the purposes of copyright protection.[189]

 Question

Does the fact that the surface in question in the Adam Ant case was a person's face take the work out of the judge's definition of a painting?

Drawings

2.73   The most significant of the categories of artistic work in terms of reported litigation is that of drawings. Examples of works held to be drawings include architects' plans,[190] sketches of garments,[191] engineering and machine part drawings,[192] cartoon characters,[193] and trade mark and label designs.[194] The rudimentary nature of a drawing is no objection to its being copyright; thus, for example, a drawing of three concentric rings has been held to have artistic copyright.[195] Many of the cases concerning design drawings should now be read with caution, however. While such drawings retain copyright under the 1988 Act, the scope of infringement has been severely restricted in relation to them, and the principal mode of protection is likely to be under design right. (See further Part III of this book.)

Diagrams, maps, charts, and plans

2.74   The special feature of all these kinds of work is that, while they have a strong visual dimension, at the very least literary matter also found on the work (words and numbers) is necessary for its full meaning to be comprehended or utilised. Indeed, between the 1911 and the 1956 Acts they were treated as literary works, and the appearance of the phrase 'irrespective of artistic quality' in the provision about graphic works (see para 2.81) is to be explained by the inclusion of this then new subject matter in the category of artistic works.[196] One important effect of the change, in particular with regard to plans, is that as artistic works these two-dimensional works can be infringed by three-dimensional reproductions, which would not be so if they were literary works.[197] This rule then had rather disastrous knock-on effects with regard to the protection of industrial designs (see the Online Resource Centre), and the scope of copyright infringement by three-dimensional reproductions in this context is now carefully restricted (see paras 9.81–9.93). But the rule remains in full effect outside industrial design protection.

Photographs[198]

2.75   With regard to photographs, the 1988 Act's definition (see para 2.70) is clearly intended to cover continuing development in the technology of photography. The replacement of film by digital recording as

---

[188] For more about Adam Ant, see http://en.wikipedia.org/wiki/Adam_Ant.

[189] T Rychlicki, 'Legal questions about illegal art' (2008) 3 JIPLP 393 at 396.

[190] See, eg, *Robert Allan & Partners v Scottish Ideal Homes* 1972 SLT (Sh Ct) 32.

[191] See, eg, *Howard Clark v David Allan & Co Ltd* 1987 SLT 271.   [192] See, eg, *British Leyland v Armstrong Patents* [1986] AC 577.

[193] *King Features Syndicate Inc v OM Kleeman Ltd* [1941] AC 417 (Popeye the Sailorman).

[194] *KARO STEP Trade Mark* [1977] RPC 255.

[195] *Solar Thomson Engineering v Barton* [1977] RPC 537. For the drawing see p 540.

[196] For a Singaporean case concerning copyright in an online street map, see *Virtual Map (Singapore) Pte Ltd v Singapore Land Authority and Anr* [2009] SGCA 2, noted in B Ong, 'Copyright and cartography: mapping the boundaries of infringement liability' [2009] EIPR 17.

[197] See para 4.26.

[198] See generally Y Gendreau, *Copyright and Photographs: an International Survey* (1999); C Mihalos, *The Law of Photography and Digital Images* (2004); K Garnett, 'Copyright in photographs' [2000] EIPR 229; R Deazley, 'Photographing paintings in the public domain: a response to Garnett' [2001] EIPR 229; S Stokes, 'Photographing paintings in the public domain: a response to Garnett' [2001] EIPR 354; and R Arnold, 'Copyright in photographs: a case for reform' [2005] EIPR 303.

the ordinary mode of photography well demonstrates the need for definitional flexibility of this kind. Photographs of antiques have been protected where they were taken with a view to exhibiting particular qualities such as colour, features, and other details because some degree of skill is involved in the lighting, angling, and judging of positioning in these circumstances.[199]

■ Case C-145/10 *Painer v Standard Verlags GmbH* [2012] ECDR 6

The Court of Justice held that a portrait photograph could be protected by copyright if the photograph is an intellectual creation of the author in that it reflects the author's personality, that is, the author expresses his creative abilities by making free and creative choices in the production of the photograph and stamps his 'personal touch'. Such choices can be made in several ways: 'In the preparation phase, the photographer can choose the background, the subject's pose and the lighting. When taking a portrait photograph, he can choose the framing, the angle of view and the atmosphere created. Finally, when selecting the snapshot, the photographer may choose from a variety of developing techniques the one he wishes to adopt or, where appropriate, use computer software' (para 91). The protection of the photograph is not inferior to any other work protected by copyright.

■ *Temple Island Collections Ltd v New English Teas Ltd* [2012] FSR 9 (PCC)

This case concerned two similar photos, by F and H, showing a London bus in red in the foreground in front of a black-and-white image of iconic London landmarks. Both photos had been altered using a computer program. Judge Birss QC referred to the decisions in *Infopaq* and *Painer* to state that copyright may subsist in a photograph if it is the author's own intellectual creation. The judge held that 'A photograph of an object found in nature or for that matter a building, which although not natural is something found by the creator and not created by him, can have the character of an artistic work in terms of copyright law if the task of taking the photograph leaves ample room for an individual arrangement. What is decisive are the arrangements (motif, visual angle, illumination, etc.) selected by the photographer himself or herself' (para 20). The judge viewed F's image as not a mere photograph ('an image which is nothing more than the result of happening to click his camera in the right place at the right time') but as a photographic work (where the 'appearance is the product of deliberate choices and also deliberate manipulations by the author' such as choosing where to stand, when to click, as well as changes wrought after the basic image had been recorded) and noted that although 'the image may look like just another photograph in that location but its appearance derives from more than that' (para 66).

 Discussion point   For answer guidance visit www.oxfordtextbooks.co.uk/orc/waelde3e/

Does the definition of a photograph cover the case whereby the camera records the image digitally and the photographer then adjusts the result electronically, for example to insert other images, as by putting the head of the prime minister on what is otherwise an image of a footballer; or merely editing out unwanted parts of the image captured? Is there still a photograph where the image has been digitally enhanced, for example by sharpening contrasts, or heightening/lowering colours?

Sculptures

2.76   Sculptures are plainly three-dimensional works and must be distinguished from works of architecture and of artistic craftsmanship. Casts and models for the purposes of sculpture are included in the

---

[199] *Antiquesportfolio.com plc v Rodney Fitch & Co Ltd* [2001] FSR 345.

category.[200] The vagueness of the statutory definition has been used by those seeking copyright protection for industrial designs.

■ *Wham-O Manufacturing Co v Lincoln Industries Ltd* **[1985] RPC 127**[201]

It was held that wooden model prototypes for the Frisbee toy were sculptures.[202] The New Zealand court held that sculpture could no longer be confined to the process of carving and modelling representations using natural materials, but should simply be thought of as the three-dimensional expression of an idea of its creator. The model fitted this conception, but not, the court held, the Frisbee itself. A plastic injection process for mass production could not give rise to a sculpture.

2.77   Similar arguments were rejected in English cases, which have generally construed 'sculpture' narrowly, in accordance with its ordinary dictionary meaning. These authorities were reviewed in a powerful judgment by Mann J in the 'Star Wars' case, subsequently approved in the Court of Appeal and the Supreme Court:

■ *Lucasfilm Ltd v Ainsworth* **[2009] FSR 2 (Ch D); [2009] EWCA Civ 1328 (CA); [2012] 1 AC 208 (SC)**

A established a website in 2004 selling replica helmets and body armour used in the *Star Wars* films. Working from general designs prepared by L, A had previously created the moulds used to create the various pieces of armour used in the original 1977 film for the Imperial Stormtroopers and other characters. These included white helmets as well as armour referred to as the 'cheesegrater', 'jawbone', 'X-wing fighter pilot', 'rebel troop', 'Tie fighter' helmets, and a 'chest box' worn by the Tie fighter pilots. L's claim of copyright infringement against A was met with a counterclaim to enforce A's alleged copyright in the helmets and armour as sculptures. It was held that the Imperial Stormtrooper helmet was not a sculpture within the meaning of the Act. It was a mixture of costume and prop, but its primary function was utilitarian. Mann J, at the first instance, indicated that 'while it has an interest as an object, and while it was intended to express an idea, it was not conceived, or created, with the intention that it should do so other than as part of character portrayal in the film' (para 121). Furthermore, he opined that it was not that it lacked artistic merit, but that it lacked artistic purpose. The same reasoning applied to the armour. Toy models marketed by L after the film became successful were also not deemed to be sculptures for the reason that their primary purpose was for play. The *Wham-O* decision was disapproved for similar reasons: the purpose of the model for the Frisbee was not artistic. The Supreme Court held that 'it would not accord with the normal use of language to apply the term "sculpture" to a 20th century military helmet used in the making of a film, whether it was the real thing or a replica made in different material, however great its contribution to the artistic effect of the finished film ... it was the Star Wars film that was the work of art ... The helmet was utilitarian in the sense that it was an element in the process of production of the film' (para 44).

Mann J provided the following multi-factorial approach on the meaning of sculpture:

(1) Regard was to be had to the normal use of the word.

(2) Nevertheless, the concept could be applicable to things going beyond what would normally be expected to be art in the sense of the sort of things expected to be found in art galleries.

(3) It was inappropriate to stray too far from what would normally be regarded as sculpture.

(4) No judgment was to be made about artistic worth.

---

[200] CDPA 1988, s 4(2).   [201] See also *Plix Products v Winstone* [1985] 1 NZLR 376.
[202] For more on the Frisbee, see http://en.wikipedia.org/wiki/Frisbee.

(5) Not every three-dimensional representation of a concept could be regarded as a sculpture, otherwise every three-dimensional construction or fabrication would be a sculpture.

(6) It was of the essence of a sculpture that it should have, as part of its purpose, a visual appeal in the sense that it might be enjoyed for that purpose alone, whether or not it might have another purpose as well. The purpose was that of the creator and it was this underlying purpose that was important.

(7) The fact that the object had some other use did not necessarily disqualify it from being a sculpture, but it still had to have the intrinsic quality of being intended to be enjoyed as a visual thing.

(8) The process of fabrication was relevant but not decisive. There was no reason why a purely functional item, not intended to be at all decorative, should be treated as a sculpture simply because it had been (for example) carved out of wood or stone.

The Court of Appeal approved the judge's reasoning and held that he had correctly applied his 'multi-factorial approach' (para 77) finding that 'Neither the armour nor the helmet are sculpture' (para 80). With regard to the toy stormtroopers it noted: 'We are not dealing here with highly crafted models designed to appeal to the collector but which might be played with by his children. These are mass produced plastic toys. They are no more works of sculpture than the helmet and the armour which they reproduce' (para 82). The Supreme Court, while affirming the multi-factorial approach, rejected the 'elephant test' proposed by the Court of Appeal. It stated that: 'Any zoologist has no difficulty in recognising an elephant on sight, and most could no doubt also give a clear and accurate description of its essential identifying features. By contrast a judge, even one very experienced in intellectual property matters, does not have some special power of divination which leads instantly to an infallible conclusion, and no judge would claim to have such a power. The judge reads and hears the evidence (often including expert evidence), reads and listens to the advocates' submissions, and takes what the Court of Appeal rightly called a multi-factorial approach. Moreover the judge has to give reasons to explain his or her conclusions' (para 47).

In the light of this decision,[203] earlier cases denying protection to moulds for making functional cartridges[204] and prototypes of plastic dental impression trays[205] were correct, unlike the protection given to scallop-shaped ones for use in toasted sandwich-makers.[206]

Discussion point For answer guidance visit www.oxfordtextbooks.co.uk/orc/waelde3e/

Should ice sculptures be protected as sculptures? Is the snowman you make during a white Christmas so protected?

Discussion point 2

Kinetic sculptures are sculptures with moving parts, or in which motion is incorporated as part of the design, so that the form or colour of the work may change continuously or from time to time. Does mobility or motion within the sculpture take it out of the dictionary definition of 'sculpture'? See also the case of *Komesaroff v Mickle* [1988] RPC 204, discussed later (para 2.85) for a similar issue with works of artistic craftsmanship.

[203] See further S Clark, '*Lucasfilm Ltd and Others v Ainsworth and Another*: the force of copyright protection for three-dimensional designs as sculptures or works of artistic craftsmanship' [2009] EIPR 384; A Hobson, 'Imperial stormtroopers, art works, and copyright defences' (2009) 4 JIPLP 16; J Pila 'The "Star Wars" copyright claim: an ambivalent view of the Empire' (2012) 128 LQR 15.
[204] *Metix v Maughan* [1997] FSR 718.   [205] *J & S Davis (Holdings) Ltd v Wright Health Group* [1988] RPC 403.
[206] *Breville Europe v Thorn EMI* [1995] FSR 77.

Engravings

2.78   The *Wham-O* case (para 2.76)[207] is also an authority on engravings, which the New Zealand court held the markings on the surface of the Frisbee to be, along with the plastic injection mould. Engraving is first a process of cutting or incising images into material such as wood or metal, and then using the result for the purpose of producing prints of the image.[208] In the 1956 Act it was defined to include etchings, lithographs, woodcuts, and prints, but photographs were expressly excluded.[209] Using this, it was held that an engraving included both the original engraved plate and the resulting print, and further that, given the apparent need to exclude the process of producing prints known as photography, engraving was not confined to processes involving cutting into material to produce the plate.[210] This approach enabled the court in *Wham-O* to hold that the mould was a plate and the Frisbee disc a 'print' thereof.[211]

Exercise

Compare the *Wham-O* case with *George Hensher Ltd v Restawile Upholstery (Lancs) Ltd* [1976] AC 64, discussed at paras 2.83ff. What, if any, policy reasons justify the different results reached in these cases with regard to the protection of models to be used in the mass production of consumer objects?

2.79   As already noted, however, the 1988 Act differs somewhat from the 1956 Act in respect of engravings. In particular, the word 'print' no longer appears either in juxtaposition (as with etchings, lithographs, and woodcuts) or in any definition. Nor is photography mentioned.[212] It is not clear whether this excludes the reasoning of the *Wham-O* decision, given that mere changes of expression in the 1988 Act do not necessarily entail departure from the previous law.[213] But considering the Act's overall policy of excluding copyright from the field of industrial design, it is suggested that the result in *Wham-O* should now be treated with caution, although its general discussion of both engravings and sculptures remains helpful. With regard to both categories of work, the case may be an example of a court anxious to protect the skill and labour of the plaintiff from piracy and forcing the facts rather uneasily into unsuitable concepts. Design rights probably offer more satisfactory solutions to such problems now.[214] In *Greenfield Products Pty Ltd v Rover-Scott Bonnar Ltd*,[215] an argument that a mould of a lawnmower engine was an engraving was rejected. Pincus J said:

> It is not all cutting which is engraving . . . The term does not cover shaping a piece of metal or wood on a lathe, but has to do with marking, cutting or working the surface—typically the flat surface—of an object . . . [216]

Collages

2.80   The last item specifically mentioned is the collage. A collage is an artistic equivalent to the literary compilation. The creator assembles diverse fragments of material, some of which may be extracts from other copyright or formerly copyright works, artistic and others, some of which may be incapable of copyright at all (eg a piece of string), and places them either on a single surface or in some other form of juxtaposition, often with incongruous effect. Without this specific reference in the 1988 Act, there is an obvious danger that such works may fail to attract copyright on the ground of lack of originality or the inherent

---

[207] [1985] RPC 127.   [208] For an example, see *Martin v Polyplas* [1969] NZLR 1046.   [209] 1956 Act, s 48(1).
[210] *James Arnold & Co v Miafern Ltd* [1980] RPC 397 esp at 403–404: rubber stereos for printing designs on ties held to be engravings.
[211] [1985] RPC 127.   [212] CDPA 1988, s 4(2).   [213] CDPA 1988, s 172(2).
[214] For design rights, see Part III (Chapters 8 and 9).   [215] (1990) 95 ALR 275.
[216] (1990) 95 ALR 275 at 285. See also *Talk of the Town v Hagstrom* (1991) 19 IPR 649 at 655.

nature of the material used. Collage has been held not to be constituted by ephemeral collocation, whether or not with artistic intent, of random, unrelated, and unfixed elements.[217]

Artistic quality of graphic works etc

2.81   An artistic work in any of the categories just discussed need not have aesthetic appeal or be a work of fine art in the ordinary sense, for it is provided that the copyright subsists 'irrespective of its artistic quality'.[218] The phrase 'artistic work' is rather to be taken as an indication of the methods by which the work must be produced. Some recent decisions suggest that it may be necessary to show that the work is intended to be permanent, insofar as anything can be, or at least not transient in form.[219] On the other hand, with a very simple drawing, it may be difficult to show infringement of the copyright.[220] As a consequence, however, there can be difficult questions of definition where there is some overlap with other forms of work. Although it is clear that plain lettering cannot be the subject of artistic copyright,[221] fancy lettering, for example in a greeting card, a label, or a trade mark, may well be a drawing. In relation in particular to maps, charts, diagrams and plans, lettering, words, and figures may form an integral part of the representation and would fall to be protected by artistic rather than literary copyright; but where a drawing is merely an explanatory adjunct to written material, the latter has literary copyright.[222]

Works of architecture[223]

2.82   Works of architecture are either buildings or models for buildings and do not include architects' plans, which are dealt with as drawings for copyright purposes.[224] A building includes any fixed structure,[225] and it would appear from the use of the word 'any' that no consideration need be given to the question of artistic quality in determining whether or not a work of architecture has copyright, a view supported by an *obiter* dictum of Lord Reid.[226] The meaning of 'structure' has not been judicially discussed since the passage of the 1956 Act, but in an earlier case it had been held that a garden layout including stone walls, steps, and ponds had copyright as a structure;[227] department store buildings[228] and semi-detached villas[229] have also been accorded copyright. It may be suggested that a building is an artificial structure attached to land, but difficult questions of definition can be seen by examining some of the leading cases on fixtures.[230]

 Exercise

Consider, for example, the Scottish case of *Christie v Smith's Executrix* 1949 SC 572, which raised the question whether a summerhouse which rested on specially laid foundations on land by virtue of its considerable weight was sufficiently attached to the land to be a fixture (answer: yes). Was the summerhouse also a work of architecture for copyright purposes?

---

[217] *Creation Records Ltd v News Group Newspapers Ltd* [1997] EMLR 444. See further at para 2.86.
[218] CDPA 1988, s 4(1)(a).
[219] *Merchandising Corp of America v Harpbond* [1983] FSR 32; also *Komesaroff v Mickle* [1988] RPC 204. Note that there is no explicit requirement of fixation with artistic works, unlike literary, dramatic and musical works (see paras 2.30–2.33).
[220] *Kenrick v Lawrence* (1890) 25 QBD 99.   [221] *Miller & Lang Ltd v Macniven & Cameron Ltd* (1908) 16 SLT 56.
[222] *Duriron Co Inc v Hugh Jennings & Co Ltd* [1984] FSR 1; *British Leyland v Armstrong Patents* [1986] RPC 279 per Oliver LJ at 289–296; *Interlego AG v Tyco Industries Inc* [1989] AC 217 per Lord Oliver at 264–265.
[223] See further A Adrian, 'Architecture and copyright: a quick survey of the law' (2008) 3 JIPLP 524.
[224] CDPA 1988, s 4(1)(b).   [225] CDPA 1988, s 4(2).   [226] *Hensher v Restawile* [1976] AC 64 per Lord Reid at 78.
[227] *Vincent v Universal Housing Co* [1928–35] MCC 275.
[228] *Meikle v Maufe* [1941] 3 All ER 144.   [229] *Blake v Warren* [1928–35] MCC 268.
[230] For the English and Scots law of fixtures, see *Halsbury's Laws of England*, vol 27(1), paras 143–156, and *Laws of Scotland: Stair Memorial Encyclopaedia*, vol 18, paras 578–587.

Works of artistic craftsmanship

2.83   The phrase 'artistic craftsmanship' is not defined in the 1988 Act and no single clear meaning has emerged from the cases on the subject.[231] Considering the phrase in the context of the section on artistic works as a whole, it would appear to cover works in three dimensions which are not sculptures or buildings; since the decision of the House of Lords in *George Hensher Ltd v Restawile Upholstery (Lancs) Ltd*,[232] it has also been accepted that for a work to be one of artistic craftsmanship it must be of a quality making it capable of being described as artistic. The problem which is fully but inconclusively discussed in *Hensher* is how the court may test the issue of artistic quality without becoming involved in subjective discussion of the merits of a work.

■ *George Hensher Ltd v Restawile Upholstery (Lancs) Ltd* [1976] AC 64

H produced popular suites of furniture deploying a boat-shaped theme. Expert witnesses described the shape as 'flashy', 'horrible', 'middle of the road', 'mediocre', and 'slightly vulgar', although obviously quite a good commercial design, and a 'winner' in terms of its appeal to the market.[233] R, competitors of H, produced similar-looking suites, and H sued for infringement of copyright, relying not on any right in the finished articles but in the original three-dimensional prototype of the design made before the furniture went into production. Their claim was that the prototype was a work of craftsmanship, artistic quality was not necessary for protection, and therefore the adjective 'artistic' added nothing to the legal meaning of the subject matter to be protected; accordingly the prototype fell within the scope of copyright. All the judges in the House of Lords agreed with those of the Court of Appeal that the prototype was not a work of artistic craftsmanship, but there was considerable disagreement as to the reasons why this should be so.

2.84   In *Hensher* the House of Lords rejected the view expressed by the Court of Appeal in the case, that the test was whether the work would be purchased for its aesthetic appeal rather than for its utility, but their Lordships differed among themselves about what the test should be and about whether it was a test of fact depending on the evidence or a test of law for the court. One view was that the intention of the author of the work to produce a work of art was the critical factor, and this is supported in other earlier cases.[234] A second view was to ask whether a substantial part of the public would regard the work as artistic, this being distinct from the question of whether or not the primary reason for purchasing it was its aesthetic appeal. But the most cogent speech in *Hensher* is that of Lord Simon of Glaisdale, who argued that works of artistic craftsmanship first came to be copyright subjects under the Copyright Act 1911 as a consequence of the influence of the Arts and Crafts movement of the 19th century, which emphasised the necessary connection between form and function. The phrase 'artistic craftsmanship' should therefore be construed as a whole rather than by separate examination of its constituent words. So the question to be asked of a work in which copyright was claimed under this heading is: is this the work of one who was in this respect an artist-craftsman? The artistic merit of the work was thus not an issue to be considered. The question was to be answered on the evidence, and the best evidence was likely to be that of acknowledged artist-craftsmen or those concerned with training artist-craftsmen.[235]

---

[231] See also M Rushton, 'An economic approach to copyright in works of artistic craftsmanship' [2003] IPQ 255.

[232] [1976] AC 64.

[233] Three slightly fuzzy black-and-white photographs of the plaintiff's suites are available in [1975] RPC 31 at 33–34.

[234] *Burke v Spicers Dress Design* [1936] Ch 400 per Clauson J at 407–408; *Cuisenaire v Reed* [1963] VR 719 per Pape J at 730; *Cuisenaire v South West Imports* [1968] 1 Ex CR 493 per Niel J at 574.

[235] Lord Simon's approach was preferred by the Federal Court of Australia in *Coogi Australia v Hysport International* (1999) 157 ALR 247 and by the High Court of Australia in *Burge v Swarbrick* [2007] FSR 27.

2.85   The test of the creator's intention seemed to gain ground in decisions holding that a baby's raincape and a plastic dental impression tray were not works of artistic craftsmanship.[236] But it remains far from clear exactly what works will come under this head of artistic copyright. If Lord Simon's historical analysis in *Hensher* is correct, then we should begin with articles which have some function to perform, for example furniture, crockery, cutlery, and clothing, and it should not necessarily be an objection that the article is the subject of industrial production, or that its function is industrial, or indeed merely decorative.

■ *Komesaroff v Mickle* [1988] RPC 204 (Sup Ct of Victoria)

K developed and marketed a product named 'moving sand pictures', which was made by enclosing inside glass panels a mixture of liquid, coloured sands, and a layer of air bubbles. Miniature sand landscapes were brought about when the sands trickled through the bubbles under the influence of gravity. The process could be repeated by shaking the product. M copied and commenced marketing an identical product. It was held that K's product was not a work of artistic craftsmanship because her activity did not directly bring about the sand landscapes which resulted from shaking the product, and there was no craftsmanship in what she had done.

■ *Burge v Swarbrick* [2007] FSR 27 (HCA)

The question in this case was whether a model known as a 'plug' from which a mould for a yacht hull could be derived was a work of artistic craftsmanship. Following Lord Simon in *Hensher*, the court held that artistic craftsmanship is not limited to artistic handicraft and so can include machine production items and indeed prototypes such as the 'plug'. There was no antithesis between utility and beauty. A conclusion on the question of the 'plug's' character was not controlled by the creator's intentions, but was one for objective determination by the court. Matters of visual and aesthetic appeal were but one element in the design, and were subordinated to the achievement of the purely functional aspects of the design. The determination of artistic craftsmanship turns on assessing the extent to which the work's artistic expression is unconstrained by functional considerations. The more substantial the latter, the less the scope for real or substantial artistic effort. The evidence in this case was that the designer had been constrained to such an extent that his work was not that of an artist-craftsman.

2.86   A difficult question is whether there must be an individual artist-craftsman whose concept the work is; it has been suggested that where the idea and the execution are separated there can be no work of artistic craftsmanship.[237] But this may be too restrictive, as has been held in the New Zealand case of *Bonz Group v Cooke*,[238] which involved the production of hand-knitted woollen sweaters where the designer and the hand-knitters were different persons. *Bonz Group* was applied in the English case of *Vermaat and Powell v Boncrest Ltd*,[239] which was concerned with sample patchwork bedspreads and matching cushion covers made by seamstresses to a design produced by another. It was finally held, however, that while the work of the seamstresses might have involved craftsmanship, the result was not a work of artistic craftsmanship.

■ *Lucasfilm Ltd v Ainsworth* [2009] FSR 2

See also para 2.77 for the facts of this case. Mann J held that the intention of the creator was relevant in determining whether a work was one of artistic craftsmanship. *Bonz Group (Pty) Ltd v Cooke* was approved and applied, with the judge stating that the artist and the craftsman did not have to be the same person but there had to be a proper nexus between them. The producer of the helmets in this

---

[236] *Merlet v Mothercare* [1986] RPC 115; *J & S Davis (Holdings) Ltd v Wright Health Group* [1988] RPC 403.
[237] *Burke v Spicers Dress Design* [1936] Ch 400.   [238] [1994] 3 NZLR 216.   [239] [2001] FSR 5.

case was a craftsman producing high-quality products with justifiable pride in his work. However, his works could not be described as works of artistic craftsmanship. They did not have the purpose of being aesthetically appealing. Instead, they were used to provide an impression in a film. Unlike a work of artistic craftsmanship, they were not intended to sustain close scrutiny.[240]

Discussion point 1 For answer guidance visit www.oxfordtextbooks.co.uk/orc/waelde3e/

Are the designer and the hand-knitters in the *Bonz Group* case joint authors? See paras 3.7–3.14.

Discussion point 2

Could and should a recipe constitute a work of artistic craftsmanship? See TSL Cheng, 'Copyright protection of haute cuisine: recipe for disaster?' [2008] EIPR 93.

Exercise

Consider the two following cases and how, if at all, they may be reconciled (or distinguished).

■ *Shelley Films Ltd v Rex Features Ltd* [1994] EMLR 134

SF was making a film called *Mary Shelley's Frankenstein*. RF took an unauthorised photograph of a scene from the film as it was being shot. The picture was later published in *The People* newspaper. SF claimed infringement of copyright in the actors' costumes and the set as works of artistic craftsmanship, and in the latex prostheses being worn by the star of the film (Robert de Niro), as either a sculpture or a work of artistic craftsmanship. In preliminary proceedings, all the claims of copyright were held to be arguable and an injunction was granted against RF.

■ *Creation Records Ltd v News Group Newspapers Ltd* [1997] EMLR 444

CR devised a scene (a white Rolls Royce in a swimming pool with various other props, none of them made for the purpose) to be the background for a photograph of a pop group (Oasis) to appear on the cover of their forthcoming album. An unauthorised photograph of the scene was taken and published in *The Sun* newspaper, which also intended to market the picture as a poster. CR claimed copyright in the scene as a sculpture or work of artistic craftsmanship. It was held that the scene was not a sculpture, since its making involved no carving, modelling, or other techniques of sculpture. Nor was such an assemblage of *objets trouves* a work of artistic craftsmanship, since neither subject nor result involved craftsmanship.

Films[241]

2.87 A film is:

> a recording in any medium from which a moving image may by any means be reproduced (s 5B(1)).

---

[240] There was no appeal on this point: [2009] EWCA Civ 1328 (CA); and nor was it argued before the Supreme Court: [2012] 1 AC 208 (SC).
[241] See generally P Kamina, *Film Copyright in the EU* (2002); I Stamatoudi, *Copyright in Multimedia Products: A Comparative Analysis* (2002).

Again there is apparent in this broad definition the effort of the 1988 Act to retain the ability to offer copyright protection whatever technical changes may occur in the film industry. Thus the recording embodied in a video, a CD-ROM, or a DVD, or captured by a closed circuit TV camera, has copyright just as much as if it were recorded on traditional translucent film. The sound track accompanying a film is part of the work for copyright purposes, although it may also have an independent copyright as a sound recording.[242] Computer games can be protected as films,[243] but it is very doubtful whether images consisting purely of written text and/or still pictures can ever be treated as film, even if the reader is able to move the material around on her screen by use of scroll bars, cursors, and other control mechanisms.[244]

2.88   Questions of overlap with other copyright works and subject matter may sometimes arise with films. It has already been noted that a film may be a dramatic work.[245] The definition of a photograph excludes any part of a film,[246] so that there is no possibility of a film claiming copyright as a set of photographs; but modern still cameras may include motor drive units which enable photographs to be taken in very rapid sequence. If these are capable of being shown as moving images then there may be a film for copyright purposes. The converse case is the camera which is fixed on one place, for example part of the sky or the ground, and captures images at intervals; which when played in sequence at normal speed show speeded-up and striking images of cloud movement or plant growth.

2.89   For the purposes of infringement, a photograph may be a copy of a film.[247] It would seem to follow from this, and the exclusion of parts of a film from the definition of a photograph, that a publicity poster using an image from the film would not have a copyright in that image as such. The protection would be that of a film, and it would be achieved through the concept of indirect copying (see para 4.21). It has also been suggested that a completed set of drawings intended for use in a cartoon film will by itself be a film because it is capable of being shown as a moving picture.

 Question

What is a film for copyright purposes? Is there an overlap with other categories of copyright work?

Media works

Sound recordings

2.90   A sound recording is defined as:

> … either
>
> (a) a recording of sounds, from which the sounds may be reproduced, or
>
> (b) a recording of the whole or any part of a literary, dramatic or musical work, from which sounds reproducing the work or part may be reproduced (s 5A(1)).

---

[242] CDPA 1988, s 5B(2), (5).

[243] See *Sega Enterprises Ltd v Galaxy Electronics Pty Ltd* (1997) 145 ALR 21 (Fed Ct of Australia); *Golden China TV Game Centre v Nintendo Co Ltd* 1997 (1) SA 405 (A); *Nova Productions Ltd v Mazooma Games Ltd* [2007] RPC 25 (CA). The computer program incorporated in the game will also have its own copyright as a literary work.

[244] Cf *WGN Continental Broadcasting Co v United Video Inc* 693 F 2d 622 (7th Cir, 1982), where teletext accompanying a TV programme but broadcast from a different channel was held to be an audiovisual work.

[245] See *Norowzian v Arks Ltd (No 2)* [2000] FSR 363; and see para 2.67.

[246] CDPA 1988, s 4(2).   [247] CDPA 1988, s 17(4).

Sounds in category (a) might include, for example, bird-song or sound effects for use in a dramatic production, while category (b) includes readings as well as, most importantly from a commercial point of view, music. The Act seeks to retain coverage against technical development in sound recording by providing that there will be copyright regardless of the medium on which the recording is made or the method by which the sounds are reproduced or produced.[248] Copyright subsists in every sound recording that is not a copy taken from a previous sound recording.[249] Accordingly, copyright will not subsist in the records, cassettes, and CDs as such as sold to the public, since these are merely copies of the producer's master recording. But to copy from such copies will still be infringement of the master recording's copyright.[250]

 Question

Looking at the statutory definition of a sound recording given previously, what in essence is protected by the copyright in this subject matter?

Broadcasts

2.91   This embraces both television and radio. There is no significant difference in the technology involved in radio and television broadcasting, merely in the end result, television embracing visual images as well as sound. Under the law until 2003, a distinction was drawn between the wireless technology of broadcasting and the supply of programme services by cable, but this has been dropped as a result of the implementation of the InfoSoc Directive. A broadcast is now defined as:

> an electronic transmission of visual images, sounds, or other information, either
>
> (a) transmitted for simultaneous reception by members of the public and is capable of being lawfully received by them; or
>
> (b) transmitted at a time determined solely by the person making the transmission for presentation to members of the public (CDPA 1988, s 6(1)).

The purpose of distinguishing between (a) and (b) is to accommodate the phenomenon of satellite alongside more traditional terrestrial wireless and cable broadcasting. The latter are covered by (a); (b) requires some explanation of satellite technology in broadcasting.

Satellite broadcasting

2.92   There are two main forms of satellite broadcasting:

(1) point-to-point or fixed satellite broadcasts; and

(2) direct broadcasting by satellite.

The former involves the transmission of signals to a satellite by one broadcaster, which are then transmitted to another broadcaster who includes the signals in his own transmissions. Familiar examples of this include the broadcasting by the BBC and IBA of sports events taking place in other countries, where the initial signal is sent by a broadcaster in the other country. With direct broadcasting by satellite, the signal of the originating broadcaster is transmitted through the satellite direct to the receivers of the public.

---

[248] CDPA 1988, s 5A(1).   [249] CDPA 1988, s 5A(2).   [250] See further at para 4.21.

These receivers may require special equipment to receive the signal, for example satellite dishes, and to decode it for the purposes of viewing. Signals broadcast from satellites may be encrypted or scrambled in order to ensure that only those so equipped—that is, subscribers to the service—can receive the signal in intelligible form. Sky Television provides an example of this technology currently familiar in Britain.

2.93 This simplified account of broadcasting technology helps in understanding some of the problems underlying the provisions in the 1988 Act defining broadcasting. Doubts as to whether a signal directed initially only to a satellite (the 'up-leg') could be a broadcast are removed, because it is an electronic transmission of visual images and sounds made at a time determined solely by the person making the transmission for presentation to members of the public. The purpose of the transmission is such a presentation, although as such the signal is not capable of lawful reception by the public. There were similar doubts as to whether the signal from the satellite (the 'down-leg') could be a broadcast if it was encrypted. The 1988 Act provides that an encrypted transmission shall be regarded as capable of being lawfully received by members of the public (and therefore a broadcast) only if decoding equipment has been made available to the public by or with the authority of the person making the transmission or the person providing the contents of the transmission.[251]

■ *Network Ten Pty Ltd v TCN Channel Nine Pty Ltd* (2004) 205 ALR 1 (HCA)[252]

Ten broadcast a TV programme which included short excerpts from programmes previously broadcast by Nine. Nine claimed infringement of copyright in that each visual image capable of being observed as a separate image on the TV screen was a broadcast in which copyright subsisted. Ten argued that a broadcast was constituted rather by a programme than by the images making up the programme. The importance of the point in the case was whether or not Nine's actions amounted to 'substantial' copying for the purposes of infringement. It was held that a broadcast was more than the transmission of a single image for the purposes of copyright, and that Ten's activities had to be related to Nine's programmes for the purposes of infringement. A television commercial in the middle of a programme was itself a discrete TV broadcast. Kirby J dissented on the ground that the court was going beyond the language of the copyright statute (which was similar to that of the 1956 Act in the UK).

 Question

Does the amended language of the 1988 Act make clear the answer to the question raised by this Australian case?

Teletext and Internet transmissions

2.94 The definition of broadcasting makes clear that broadcasting is not restricted to the transmission of sounds and visual images, but can include other material such as teletext information services.[253] Internet transmissions are in general *not* to be treated as broadcasts,[254] since in general they are neither transmitted simultaneously to their audience nor does the transmitter decide the time of transmission (the recipient generally does that). However, an Internet transmission can fall within the definition of a broadcast if:

---

[251] CDPA 1988, s 6(2); and see ss 6(1)(b) and 6(4).
[252] The judgment is applied by the Federal Court of Australia at (2005) 216 ALR 631.   [253] CDPA 1988, s 6(1).
[254] So the decision in *Shetland Times v Wills* [1997] FSR 604 that a website was a cable programme service could not now be reached. None of the exceptions to the general rule would have applied either.

(1) the transmission takes place simultaneously on the Internet and by other means, such as conventional TV or radio ('streaming');

(2) it is a concurrent transmission of a live event; or

(3) it is a transmission of recorded moving images or sounds forming part of a programme service offered by the person responsible for making the transmission, being a service in which programmes are transmitted at scheduled times determined by that person.[255]

Discussion point 1   For answer guidance visit www.oxfordtextbooks.co.uk/orc/waelde3e/

Consider 'podcasting', a method of distributing audio or audiovisual material on the Internet, for playback on personal computers or mobile devices at a time chosen by the user. This technique is increasingly being used by broadcasting companies to allow viewers/listeners to see/hear programmes or other material at a time convenient to them.
Is a 'podcast' a broadcast for copyright purposes?

Discussion point 2

Consider also the possibility increasingly deployed in digital broadcasting, where the viewer may 'pause and record' a programme as it is transmitted, thereby allowing him to answer the doorbell or telephone without missing any part of the programme. What are the implications for the distinction between broadcasts and other forms of transmission?

Repeats

2.95   Many broadcasts on television and radio are repeated once or more. Such repeats have a copyright separate from or additional to that of the original broadcast,[256] unless it infringes the copyright in another broadcast or in a cable programme.[257]

Published editions of literary, dramatic, and musical works

2.96   Copyright subsists in the typographical arrangement of every published edition of a literary, dramatic, or musical work.[258] A new edition is not a reprint of the work reproducing the typographical arrangement of a previous edition, but some new mode of presenting the work. The concept of 'edition' used here should be distinguished from the use of the word in describing versions of, say, a textbook, where each successive edition involves a change, not only in the typographical arrangement but also in the content of the text thus presented. The same text may be published several times, but as long as each publication adopts a different typographical arrangement, there will be separate copyrights for the publishers.[259] Equally, the text itself may be out of copyright, but there will be a copyright in the typographical arrangement of any edition which is not a reproduction, in whole or in part, of a previous typographical arrangement.[260]

---

[255] CDPA 1988, s 6(1A).

[256] See CDPA 1988, s 14(2), (5) (note duration of copyright in a repeat cannot exceed that of the original transmission).

[257] CDPA 1988, s 6(6).   [258] CDPA 1988, ss 1(1)(c) and 8(1).

[259] See further discussion of this point by Lord Hoffmann in *Newspaper Licensing Agency Ltd v Marks and Spencer plc* [2003] 1 AC 551 at paras 11 and 16.   [260] CDPA 1988, s 8(2).

■ *Newspaper Licensing Agency Ltd v Marks and Spencer plc* [2003] 1 AC 551

M&S subscribed to a press-cutting service which provided a daily supply of photocopies of items of interest appearing in national and daily newspapers. The press-cutting service had a licence from the newspapers' collecting society, the NLA. M&S copied the photocopies for distribution to individuals within its organisation, but had no licence for this. The NLA sued for infringement of a copyright in the typographical arrangement of the published editions of the newspapers. The issue was whether the copyright subsisted only in the whole newspaper, or separately in each article within the newspaper. Giving the main speech, Lord Hoffmann said: 'In my opinion, the frame of reference for the term "published edition" is the language of the publishing trade. The edition is the product, generally between covers, which the publisher offers to the public' (para 14). While the articles each had literary copyright in their own right, this did not mean that each article as printed was a separate published edition, and a newspaper a collection of such editions. Lord Hoffmann added: 'In the case of a modern newspaper, I think that the skill and labour devoted to typographical arrangement is principally expressed in the overall design. It is not the choice of a particular typeface, the precise number or width of the columns, the breadth of margins and the relationship of headlines and straplines to the other text, the number of articles on a page and the distribution of photographs and advertisements but the combination of all of these into pages which give the newspaper as a whole its distinctive appearance...I find it difficult to think of the skill and labour which has gone into the typographical arrangement of a newspaper being expressed in anything less than a full page. The particular fonts, columns, margins and so forth are only, so to speak, the typographical vocabulary in which the arrangement is expressed' (para 23).

Further reading

Books

L Bently and B Sherman, *Intellectual Property Law* (3rd edn, 2009), Chs 2, 3, 4

Copinger & Skone James on Copyright (16th edn, 2010), Chs 2, 3

WR Cornish, D Llewelyn, and T Aplin, *Intellectual Property* (7th edn, 2010), Chs 10, 11, 20

Laddie, Prescott & Vitoria on the Modern Law of Copyright (4th edn, 2011), Chs 3–9, 34

History

R Deazley, *On the Origin of the Right to Copy* (2004)

C Seville, *The Internationalisation of Copyright Law: Books, Buccaneers and the Black Flag in the Nineteenth Century* (2006)

C Seville, *Literary Copyright Reform in Early Victorian England* (1999)

B Sherman and L Bently, *The Making of Modern Intellectual Property* (1999)

Economics

MA Einhorn, *Media, Technology and Copyright: Integrating Law and Economics* (2004)

W Landes and R Posner, *The Economic Structure of Intellectual Property Law* (2003), Chs 2–6, 8–10

R Towse (ed), *Copyright and the Cultural Industries* (2002)

R Towse and R Holzhauer (eds), *The Economics of Intellectual Property* (2002), vol 1 (Introduction and Copyright)

Multimedia

T Aplin, *Copyright Law in the Digital Society: The Challenges of Multimedia* (2005)

I Stamatoudi, *Copyright and Multimedia Products: A Comparative Analysis* (2002)

Musical works

S Frith and L Marshall, *Music and Copyright* (2nd edn, 2004)

Artistic works

Y Gendreau, *Copyright and Photographs: An International Survey* (1999)

C Mihalos, *The Law of Photography and Digital Images* (2004)

S Stokes, *Art and Copyright* (2012)

Articles

Works

J Pila, 'An intentional view of the copyright work' (2008) 71 MLR 535

Originality

HL MacQueen, 'The legal definition of authorship and the scrolls' in JJ Collins and TH Lim (eds), *Oxford Handbook of the Dead Sea Scrolls* (2010)

E Rosati, 'Originality in a work, or a work of originality: the effects of the *Infopaq* decision' [2011] EIPR 746

A Waisman, 'Revisiting originality' [2009] EIPR 370

Musical works

A Rahmatian, 'Music and creativity as perceived by copyright law' [2005] IPQ 267

Artistic works

J Pila 'The "Star Wars" copyright claim: an ambivalent view of the Empire' (2012) 128 LQR 15

M Rushton, 'An economic approach to copyright in works of artistic craftsmanship' [2003] IPQ 255

T Rychlick, 'Legal questions about illegal art' (2008) 3 JIPLP 393

3

Copyright 2: first ownership, moral rights, and term

Introduction

Scope and overview of chapter

3.1 This chapter initially considers the identification of the first owner of the copyright when it comes into existence. Normally this is the author of the work; but this concept is not so easily applied to media works. This difficulty involves further analysis of the difference between 'author' and 'media' copyright works, first explored in the previous chapter. The highlighting of the author's position makes this also the appropriate chapter in which to consider the author's 'moral rights': that is, the right to be identified as the author of the protected work, and to have that work's integrity respected by others. Copyright (including moral rights) is generally a right of limited duration, however, and the final section of the chapter expounds the various periods of time for which it lasts.

3.2 **Learning objectives**

By the end of this chapter you should be able to describe and explain:

- who is the first owner of copyright in a protected work (usually the author or equivalent);
- the moral rights of the author to be identified and to have the work's integrity respected;
- how long the protection of copyright lasts in relation to each of the categories of its subject matter.

3.3 Copyright is a form of property which comes into existence with the creation of its subject matter (no registration process is required, unlike patents, trade marks, or designs), so there are some important rules to identify the first owner of the right thus created. This is usually the author with author works, and an equivalent in the case of media works. The author's moral rights to be identified and to have the integrity of a work respected are treated next, along with other rights akin to moral rights, such as the artist's resale right, the right to prevent false attribution, and the special right of privacy in relation to certain commissioned photographs. These and the other rights conferred by copyright also exist for a specified period of time, varying according to the subject matter protected. In sum, the chapter explains who is the first to benefit from the protection of copyright; some of the rights which authors gain along with first ownership; and for how long the protection lasts. So the rest of the chapter looks like this:

- First ownership (3.4–3.30)
- Author's moral rights (3.31–3.48)
- Duration of copyright and moral rights (3.49–3.61)

First ownership

Introduction

3.4   It is necessary to consider ownership of copyright in two parts:

(1) the *initial ownership* of the copyright, which in general pertains to the *author or creator* of the work in question;

(2) given that copyright is an item of property, ownership of which may be transferred and which may also endure beyond the author's lifetime, the *transfer of copyright and consequent rights*.

This section considers only the first of these issues. The second issue is covered in the chapter on exploitation of intellectual property in general (Chapter 22).

3.5   The *author* of a work is usually the *first owner* of the copyright in the work (Copyright, Designs and Patents Act 1988 (CDPA 1988), s 11(1)). There is *no requirement of registration*, in contrast with most other forms of intellectual property, and *copyright will arise automatically with the creation of the work*. An *author is the person who creates the work* (s 9(1)), a concept readily applicable to most literary, dramatic, musical and artistic works. However, the 1988 Act gives explicit definitions of who is to be taken as the author of sound recordings, films, broadcasts, and computer-generated works. Further, an *employer will be the first owner of copyright in any literary, dramatic, musical, or artistic work or film authored by an employee in the course of employment unless there is an agreement to the contrary* (s 11(2)). In these provisions can be most clearly seen the UK's attribution of authorship to the entrepreneur as distinct from the creator. Finally, there are *special rules relating to Crown and parliamentary copyright*, and copyright vested in certain international organisations.

Author of literary, dramatic, musical, or artistic work

3.6   With literary, dramatic, musical, and artistic works which are not computer-generated (for which see para 3.22), the author is the person who creates the work.[1] There is a statutory presumption that, where a name purporting to be that of the author appears on copies of a literary, dramatic, musical, or artistic work when published, or when made, the person whose name so appears is the author of the work, and that the work was made in circumstances not involving that person's course of employment, Crown or parliamentary copyright, or the copyright vested in certain international organisations. Like any presumption, this may be rebutted by contrary proof.[2] In general, the author

---

[1] CDPA 1988, s 9(1).   [2] CDPA 1988, s 104(2).

is the person by whose skill and labour, or intellectual creativity, the work took on its final material form, and the broad principle that copyright subsists, not in ideas but in the way in which ideas are expressed (see paras 2.24–2.28) should also be borne in mind. Copyright law has thus not taken up the post-modern deconstructionist critique, which rejects what it calls 'the Romantic concept of the author', and argues that works are not so much the expression of an individual as of the whole society and culture in which they are made.[3] Such analysis can be taken to undermine the individual author's claim to ownership of rights in the work and to highlight instead the claims that society as a whole is entitled to make. The foundation of copyright law remains, however, its recognition of the author's contribution against anyone or anything else.

 Question

Who may be treated as the author of a literary, dramatic, musical, or artistic work?

Joint authorship

3.7   However, the law does recognise that a work may have more than one author. There may be joint authorship of a work where it is

> a work produced by the collaboration of two or more authors in which the contribution of each author is not distinct from that of the other author or authors (CDPA 1988, s 10(1)).

Works of joint authorship are usually readily identifiable as such because the names of all authors appear on the work and no effort is made to separate their contributions. The presumption of authorship in favour of those whose names appear on copies of literary, dramatic, musical or artistic works[4] applies also to works of joint authorship. Complexities may arise where there is no express attribution to joint authors.[5] However, the essence of joint authorship is *collaboration* between the authors in the *execution* of the work.

3.8   Collaboration suggests a process of cooperation between the authors in the furtherance of a common design to produce a work and even if one carries out a larger share of work than the other, each author is required to make a 'significant contribution'.[6] However, the authors' contributions should not be separate or distinct.[7] Does collaboration require a joint intention to create a joint work? In an old case the test of joint authorship was said to be whether the authors had a 'pre-concerted joint design' so that one who improved or touched up the work of another was not a joint author of the eventual production.[8] In *Beckingham v Hodgens*,[9] however, the Court of Appeal held that the existence of a common intention to produce a joint work was not a requirement for a work of joint authorship.

---

[3] The classic analyses are: M Foucault, 'Qu'est ce qu'un auteur?' (1969) 64 Bulletin de la Société française de Philosophie 73 (translated as 'What is an author?' in JV Harris (ed), *Textual Strategies: Perspectives in Post-Structuralist Criticism* (1979)); R Barthes, 'The death of the author' in Image Music Text (1977); and J Derrida, 'Limited Inc a b c' in Limited Inc (1988). The literature in English is immense: see, eg, L Zemer, *The Idea of Authorship in Copyright* (2007). See too JC Ginsburg, 'The concept of authorship in comparative copyright law' (2003) 52 De Paul LR 1063; J Pila, 'An intentional view of the copyright work' (2008) 71 MLR 535; J Phillips, 'Authorship, ownership, wikiship: copyright in the twenty-first century' (2008) 3 JIPLP 788; WR Cornish, 'Conserving culture and copyright: a partial history' (2009) 13 Edinburgh Law Review 8; HL MacQueen, 'The legal definition of authorship and the scrolls' in JJ Collins and TH Lim (eds), *Oxford Handbook of the Dead Sea Scrolls* (2010).   [4] CDPA 1988, s 104(2).
[5] See generally L Zemer, 'Contribution and collaboration in joint authorship: too many misconceptions' (2006) 1 JIPLP 283.
[6] *Levy v Rutley* (1871) LR 6 CP 523; *Cala Homes (South) v Alfred McAlpine Homes East* [1995] FSR 818 at 834–835.
[7] *Beckingham v Hodgens* [2002] EMLR 45 (Ch D).
[8] *Bagge v Miller* [1917–23] MCC 179; see also *Levy v Rutley* (1871) LR 6 CP 523.   [9] [2003] EMLR 18.

3.9   The decision as to whether or not there is joint authorship will turn on the nature of each of the contributions, linked to the fundamental concept of copyright pertaining to the form of expression rather
than to ideas and information. Did one person supply only ideas and material which were translated
into a work by the other, or did the former's contribution amount to a part in formulating the expression, that is, authorship?

■ Brown v Mcasso Music [2005] FSR 40

M had drafted lyrics for a rap song to be used in a TV commercial. B had then amended the lyrics to give
them greater authenticity as a rap song, changing idiomatically incorrect language, using appropriate
Jamaican English to match word rhythm to the music and adding extempore exclamations. It was held
that B was a joint author of the song. His contribution to the writing was an active one, involving skill
and judgment to obtain the authentic feel of rap. Although he made use of standard elements of rap
culture, his work satisfied originality in the copyright sense (paras 2.34–2.46).[10]

Question

When may a person be identified as a joint author?

In cases where clearly one person supplies ideas and information and another puts these into literary or artistic form, the latter is author and owner of the copyright. So a person who supplied the
ideas for the plot of a play,[11] a director who added ideas during the rehearsals and development
of a play's script,[12] and a person who had had the idea of using an outline drawing of a human
hand as an indicator on a ballot paper,[13] were all held not entitled to the copyright in the resultant
works, while in *Donoghue v Allied Newspapers*[14] the ghostwriter of a jockey's memoirs was held to be
the owner of the copyright therein as the person responsible for the language in which the work
was cast.

■ Robin Ray v Classic FM plc [1998] FSR 622

RR, an individual with wide knowledge of classical music, entered a consultancy arrangement with
Classic FM under which he provided a catalogue of 50,000 items to be in the radio station's music
library, categorised in a way which would enable it to be used to establish the station's playlists. A database incorporating RR's work was established by Classic FM, which then sought to license its use by overseas radio stations without RR's consent. RR claimed copyright in the catalogue and its categorisation,
and argued that Classic FM were infringing. Classic FM replied that they were joint authors. It was held
that RR was the sole author of the catalogue; Classic FM had supplied ideas, suggestions and materials
for RR's use, but he alone composed the catalogue.

Some particular examples of joint authorship issues

3.10   There have been a number of difficult cases where parties were working together in the production of
new software.

---

[10] Leave to appeal was refused by the Court of Appeal: [2006] FSR 24.
[11] *Tate v Thomas* [1921] 1 Ch 503; also *Wiseman v Weidenfeld & Nicolson* [1985] FSR 525.
[12] *Brighton v Jones* [2005] FSR 288.   [13] *Kenrick & Co v Lawrence & Co* (1890) 25 QBD 99.
[14] [1938] Ch 106; also *Evans v Hulton & Co* (1924) 131 LT 534.

■ *Fylde Microsystems Ltd v Key Radio Systems Ltd* [1998] FSR 449

The parties were cooperating (without a contract) in the development of radios. FM wrote software for installation in KRS's radios, which the latter then sold. The parties fell into dispute over ownership of the copyright in the software. KRS admitted that F was the writer but argued that it was a joint author by setting the specification for the software, reporting errors and bugs, making suggestions as to the cause of faults, and providing technical information about the hardware in which the software had to operate. It was held that although KRS's activities involved much skill and labour, it was not of the nature of authorship, and the parties were not joint authors.

■ *Cyprotex Discovery Ltd v University of Sheffield* [2004] RPC 4[15]

The university and a company (C) were engaged together under a contract in the development for practical application of software initially created by the university. The relationship broke down and an issue emerged as to whether the parties were joint authors of the software which had been developed under the contract. It was held that the university's contribution to the new software—provision of background information about the initial software, assistance in compilation of the technical specifications of what the new software should contain, and vetting the suggestions of third party sponsors of the work—was not that of an author but of a client wishing to ensure the functionality of the new software when completed. It therefore had no claim to the copyright in the new software.

Exercise

Consider the case of two sets of solicitors negotiating and drafting written contracts on behalf of their respective clients. Is the contractual document which results a work of joint authorship or not? See David Vaver, 'Copyright in legal documents' (1993) 31 Osgoode Hall LJ 661.

3.11   Another quite common situation is the development of musical work by a group working together but developing the ideas by playing them on their instruments rather than writing them down.[16] Contrast the two following cases, where there were different results on the particular facts:

■ *Stuart v Barrett* [1994] EMLR 448

The case concerned the output of a pop group called Keep it Dark. S was the drummer and, after his expulsion from the group, he claimed joint authorship in the music of the band's songs. The music resulted from 'jamming' sessions at which, after one member of the group began with an opening phrase or series of notes, the group then played together, improvising and composing by ear; no one wrote down any notes. Thomas Morison QC held that the music was the result of joint authorship, although emphasising that there was no general rule for such group compositions. With regard to S's contribution, the judge said:

---

[15] On appeal the decision was affirmed in other grounds: [2004] RPC 44 (CA).

[16] In addition to the cases cited in the following text, see *Beckingham v Hodgens* [2003] EMLR 18 (music of the Bluebells' 'Young at heart' a work of joint authorship); *Fisher v Brooker* [2007] FSR 12 (music of Procul Harum's 'A whiter shade of pale' also a work of joint authorship); aff'd on this point [2008] FSR 26 (CA). The issue of joint authorship was not discussed when the case reached the House of Lords; *Fisher v Brooker* [2009] FSR 25 (HL). See on this latter case in the Court of Appeal, N Elsborg, 'Skip the light fandango, turning cartwheels "cross the court"' (2008) 3 JIPLP 626. See generally on authorship in musical works, R Arnold, 'Reflections on "The Triumph of Music": copyrights and performers' rights in music' [2010] IPQ 153.

I also have no doubt that in principle a drummer may claim copyright in a piece of music if, as here, he had collaborated with the other members of the group to produce an original piece of music. Whilst the player of tuned percussion might be more readily recognisable as a contributor to a musical composition than a drummer, in my judgment it would be a misinterpretation of the drummer's contribution to composition in contemporary music, whether pop or otherwise, to reject his contribution in principle. I listened to some of the tapes produced in Court and I am in no doubt about the significance of the drum part to the whole of the work. The work is given shape and drive by the drummer and a good drummer, as I accept the plaintiff is, can significantly influence the whole composition (at 460).

■ *Hadley v Kemp* [1999] EMI R 589

This case originated in the break-up of the 1980s pop-rock band Spandau Ballet. The band's music was generally attributed to GK, one of its five members; three of the others claimed joint authorship on the basis that, although GK initiated the compositions, he did not write them down but presented them aurally to the other band members, from whence the material was developed by further performance. It was held on the evidence that the compositions remained those of GK and that the contribution of the other band members to the final product were matters of performance and was not in the nature of composition (authorship).

Question

What is the distinction between the previous two cases?

3.12   Even where a person is not the originator of the whole of a work, he may still be the sole author for copyright purposes: it is 'not a question which . . . can be determined by counting' the material produced by the respective parties but 'has to be regarded as a matter of substance'.[17] The person who improves or amends another's work—as, for example, the editor of a new and updated edition of a legal textbook originally composed by someone else—would most likely have a separate copyright in his contribution to the result rather than a joint one, provided there was sufficient independent skill and labour.[18]

Discussion point 1 For answer guidance visit www.oxfordtextbooks.co.uk/orc/waelde3e/

Is this book a work of joint authorship? What do you need to know to answer this question?

Discussion point 2

The novel *Swan*, published in 1994, is said on its dust jacket and title page to be by the supermodel, Naomi Campbell. However, on the catalogue page it is said to be 'Copyright© Naomi Campbell and Caroline Upcher: The Author and the Writer have asserted their moral rights.' Who would have been the first owner of the copyright in the text of *Swan*? Who has the moral right to be identified as the author of the novel? See further at para 3.13, *Najma Heptulla v Orient Longman Ltd* [1989] FSR 598.

---

[17] *Samuelson v Producers Distributing Co* (1931) 48 RPC 580 per Romer LJ at 593.
[18] See, eg, the cases on editorial work at para 2.42: *Sawkins v Hyperion Records* [2005] RPC 32 (CA).

Problems in the spiritual world

■ *Cummins v Bond* [1927] 1 Ch 167

The plaintiff produced a literary work called *The Chronicle of Cleophas*, which was written at high speed while she was participating in seances and which all parties to the litigation believed to be a communication from 'some being no longer inhabiting this world, and who has been out of it for a length of time sufficient to justify the hope that he has no reasons for wishing to return to it' (per Eve J at 172). The defendant (who was present at the seances), transcribed, punctuated, and arranged the work, and argued that he had also contributed to the work by the silent transfer of ideas to the plaintiff during the seances. It was held that copyright belonged to the plaintiff only and was not owned jointly with the defendant. The defendant also argued that the work had no copyright as neither he nor the plaintiff was its originator. Eve J said:

> The conclusion which the defendant invites me to come to in this submission involves the expression of an opinion I am not prepared to make, that the authorship and copyright rest with some one already domiciled on the other side of the inevitable river. That is a matter I must leave for solution by others more competent to decide it than I am. I can only look upon the matter as a terrestrial one, of the earth earthy, and I propose to deal with it on that footing (at 175).

■ *Leah v Two Worlds Publishing Ltd* [1951] Ch 393

An artist produced pictures of the dead by means, as he claimed, of extra-sensory perception activated by contact with living persons who wished to have the representation made. Here it was accepted that the artist was the author of the resultant work even though 'inspired by influences of which perhaps no easy explanation can be given' (per Vaisey J at 398).

3.13   There may, however, be exceptional cases where the contribution of the person supplying material to the person actually executing the work is sufficient to allow a claim of copyright as either sole or joint author: that is to say, it goes beyond giving ideas to giving directions or instructions as to the mode of expression or execution. A straightforward example would be where someone is dictating to an amanuensis, in which case he is plainly the sole author. It also appears certain that a builder cannot claim copyright in a work of architecture, where the architect is regarded as the author.[19]

■ *Najma Heptulla v Orient Longman Ltd* [1989] 1 FSR 598 (High Court of India)

MA, a leader of the Indian independence movement, dictated his memoirs to HK, with whom he also discussed the content. MA was not confident writing in English (the language of the memoirs) and this was why he worked with HK. MA read the whole manuscript, made many corrections, and ordered a deletion. It was held that HK was not the sole author of the book. In a literary work both language and subject matter are important. Joint authorship arose where there was an intellectual contribution by two or more persons in pursuit of a pre-concerted joint design.

Nature of joint ownership: common property

3.14   In cases of joint authorship, all the authors own the copyright in the work.[20] The main consequence of joint authorship for a work is that there is only one copyright in the whole work, the duration of which is tied to the death of the last-surviving author alone.[21] The copyright is usually held by the authors as common property, subject to any circumstances or agreement to the contrary, each having a title to his own share

---

[19] *Meikle v Maufe* [1941] 3 All ER 144.   [20] CDPA 1988, ss 10(3) and 11(1).   [21] CDPA 1988, s 12(8); and see para 3.54.

which he can alienate and which passes to his estate on death.[22] It would also follow that each co-owner is entitled to share in the management of the common property, meaning in this case that the consent of all must be obtained before any licence is granted.[23] In any event, it is provided that where copyright is owned jointly any requirement of the licence of the copyright owner requires the licence of all the owners.[24] It has been held, however, that a co-author may sue for infringement of copyright without the other authors.[25]

Key points on joint authorship

- Arises where more than one person *collaborates* in the *execution* of a work (ie in formulating the expression) and the contributions are indistinguishable in the final work
- Supply of ideas/information insufficient to make one a joint author
- Improvement/amendment/editing of another's work not enough to make one a joint author
- Giving another directions/instructions as to the mode of expression may lead to one becoming at least a joint author
- Dictation makes one the sole author
- Ownership is usually common, not joint: that is, there is one copyright, each party owning a share of the whole which passes to his estate on death; each may share in management, sell the share

---

Collective works

3.15   The definition of joint authorship makes it possible to distinguish what may be called 'collective works',[26] that is, works produced by collaboration where the contributions of the collaborators are separate from each other. A common example of the latter would be a song in which the words were written by one person and the music by another.[27] In a collective work each contributor has a separate copyright as the author of his part of the work, and the terms of copyright in each part will vary according to the longevity of each contributor.

 Discussion point 1   For answer guidance visit www.oxfordtextbooks.co.uk/orc/waelde3e/

Can you give any other examples of 'collective works' which are not works of joint authorship?

Discussion point 2

What is the position where a work is produced as apparently one of joint authorship within the meaning of the CDPA 1988, but the authors indicate, perhaps in a prefatory statement, that responsibility has in fact been divided along certain lines?

---

[22] See *Lauri v Renad* (1892) 3 Ch 402; *Slater v Wimmer* [2012] EWPCC 7 (PCC) at para 89. The point is not entirely free from doubt and it still might be open, at least to a Scottish court, to hold that this was a case of joint property, in which case all the rights would ultimately accresce in the estate of the last-surviving author. Possibly, however, this would be unfair. On joint and common property, see *Halsbury's Laws of England* vol 9(2), para 122; *Laws of Scotland: Stair Memorial Encyclopaedia*, vol 18, paras 22–36.

[23] *Powell v Head* (1879) 12 Ch D 686; *Mail Newspapers v Express Newspapers* [1987] FSR 90.

[24] CDPA 1988, s 173(2).   [25] *Waterlow Publishers v Rose*, The Times, 8 December 1989 (CA).

[26] Although note that CDPA 1988, s 178 unhelpfully defines 'collective work' to include works of joint authorship as well as the category of work discussed in this paragraph.

[27] See *Redwood Music Ltd v Feldman & Co Ltd* [1979] RPC 385 esp at 400–403 (a decision on the 1911 Act).

Compilations and authorship

3.16   Compilations must also be distinguished from both collective works and works of joint authorship: compilations have copyright and the compiler is an author even though there may be several different works by other authors represented in the compilation. The borderline can be unclear: thus *Who's Who*, which is compiled from returns completed by the subjects of each entry, has been held to be a compilation rather than a collection of autobiographies with the subjects each having copyright in their own contributions.[28]

Authors of films

3.17   The authors of a film are its producer and principal director,[29] and the film will be treated as a work of joint authorship unless these two are the same person.[30]

Sound recordings

3.18   The first copyright in a sound recording is owned by the producer.[31]

Broadcasts

3.19   The first copyright in every broadcast is owned by the person making the broadcast or, in the case of a broadcast which relays another broadcast by reception and immediate re-transmission, the person making that other broadcast.[32] The person making the broadcast is the person transmitting the programme, if he has any responsibility for its contents, or any person providing the programme who makes with the person transmitting it the arrangements necessary for its transmission; a programme is any item included in a broadcast.[33] An example of a situation where the transmitter has no responsibility for the contents is when he is simply transmitting a signal received from a satellite.

Published editions

3.20   The copyright in a published edition of a literary, dramatic, or musical work belongs to its publisher.[34]

Joint authorship and the media copyrights

3.21   There is no restriction of the concept of joint authorship to literary, dramatic, musical, and artistic works. As already noted, joint authorship arises with films; and there is express provision for joint authorship in broadcasts when a person provides a programme having made arrangements with the person actually transmitting it which are necessary for the programme's transmission.[35] Joint authorship might

---

[28] *A & C Black Ltd v Claude Stacey Ltd* [1929] 1 Ch 177.

[29] CDPA 1988, s 9(2)(ab). Note that this provision resulted from implementation of EU Directives and the Court of Justice, in Case C-277/10 *Martin Luksan v Petrus van der Let* (9 February 2012), has recently confirmed that under EU law, member states must allocate initial rights in films to the principal director and cannot exclusively grant them to the producer although they have the option of laying down a rebuttable presumption of transfer of rights in favour of the producer.

[30] CDPA 1988, s 10(1A). For a discussion of the terms 'producer' and 'principal director', see *Slater v Wimmer* [2012] EWPCC 7 (PCC). On joint authorship, see paras 3.7–3.14.

[31] CDPA 1988, ss 9(2)(aa) and 11(1).   [32] CDPA 1988, ss 9(2)(b) and 11(1).   [33] For all this see CDPA 1988, s 6(3).

[34] CDPA 1988, s 9(2)(d).   [35] CDPA 1988, ss 10(2) and 6(3).

also arise with sound recordings produced by joint ventures or other collaborations over arrangements needed to make the record.

Using computers: computer-generated works

3.22   Problems may arise with computers. It is obvious that a person composing a computer program is author and (subject to the rules of employment discussed at paras 3.25–3.28) first owner of the copyright in the work. When a work is produced by a computer program, the computer can be seen as a tool or as an aid, meaning that the copyright in the work belongs to the person who employed the computer as a tool to enable this function.[36] If a computer program, such as a word-processing package, is used in the production of another work, the appropriate analogy would appear to be with a person using a pen, typewriter, or paintbrush to create something, where the copyright would plainly be in the user of the tool rather than in its maker. The 1988 Act introduces a further complication into this difficult area, the *computer-generated work*. This means that the work is generated by computer in circumstances such that there is no human author of the work.[37] In such circumstances, the author is taken to be the person by whom the arrangements necessary for the creation of the work are undertaken.[38] It seems that a distinction now requires to be made between works thus *generated* and those which are computer-*aided*. A work seems likely to be treated as computer-generated when the machine is merely provided with data by its operators which it analyses and converts into output. Where the operator has some role in the formulation of the output beyond the supply of data, then the work is more likely to be computer-aided only. The sequence of images generated in playing a computer video game has been held to be a computer- rather than player-generated work; the person playing the game was merely a player, not an author.[39] There are several grey areas, as for example whether material obtained from a database[40] by means of a user's questioning (an example of this would be a search on a particular topic in a library catalogue or in Lexis[41]) is computer- or user-generated.[42] Resort to the traditional test of whose skill and labour is more significant may be necessary in such cases. The importance of the point is that the user may well be distinct from the person by whom the arrangements necessary for the creation of the work were undertaken. With computers, relevant factors may include ownership or possession of the machine, control of access, and degree of input in terms of programming and data.

 Question

What is a computer-generated work? Can you give an example?

Anonymous and pseudonymous works

3.23   A literary, dramatic, musical, or artistic work may be composed in such circumstances that it is not possible to identify any author. The work is thus *anonymous*. Alternatively, authors may choose to use names or badges of identity other than their true names in connection with their works. The works will then be *pseudonymous*. Both are what the CDPA 1988 terms 'works of unknown authorship'.[43] In both

---

[36] *Express Newspapers v Liverpool Daily Post and Echo* [1985] FSR 306.   [37] CDPA 1988, s 178.   [38] CDPA 1988, s 9(3).

[39] *Nova Productions Ltd v Mazooma Games Ltd* [2006] RPC 14 (Kitchin J).

[40] Which will have its own copyright or database right.

[41] Especially where the user can obtain a printout of the results of the search.

[42] See M Perry and T Margoni, 'From music tracks to Google maps: who owns computer-generated works?' (2010) 26 CLSR 621.

[43] CDPA 1988, s 9(4).

cases, copyright in the work remains with the author whoever that may be, because where the identity is ascertainable by reasonable inquiry,[44] the term of copyright is determined by reference to the date of that person's death.[45] But there is a statutory presumption that, where no name purporting to be that of an author appears upon a published literary, dramatic, musical, or artistic work, and a name purporting to be that of the publisher does appear on copies of the work as first published, the person whose name appeared is presumed, until the contrary is proved, to have been the owner of the copyright at the time of publication.[46] The presumption operates even in cases where the publisher is not a party.

■ *Warwick Film Productions v Eisinger* [1969] 1 Ch 508

WFP claimed that the executor of the author of an anonymous book had assigned its copyright to them. It was held that, as WFP had not rebutted the presumption that the publisher owned the copyright, their case on this point failed. Plowman J also said that it would not have helped WFP to prove who the author was; the presumption could only be rebutted by evidence that the publishers did not own the copyright. This seems to go too far: the basic position under the Copyright Acts is that the author is the first owner of copyright and, in the case of published anonymous and pseudonymous works, if his identity can be established his date of death determines the term of the copyright. Viewed in this context, the presumption that the publisher owns the copyright must be rebuttable by evidence of who the author was.

3.24   The presumption does not deal with either the unpublished work or the work where the name that appears as author is a pseudonym, and the identity of the author is not reasonably discoverable in either case. Ownership may then hang in something of a void in both cases; but the effects of this are mitigated by the provision that where it is reasonable to assume that copyright has expired or that the author died 70 years or more before the beginning of the current calendar year, then no act can constitute infringement of copyright.[47]

 Discussion point   For answer guidance visit www.oxfordtextbooks.co.uk/orc/waelde3e/

What advice would you give to someone who wished to include in an anthology of verse a poem published in a student magazine in 1900 under the name 'John Smith', but who had no idea who John Smith was?

Employment

3.25   In general, where a literary, dramatic, musical, or artistic work is made in the course of the author's employment by another person, the employer is entitled to the copyright in the work.[48] The converse is, of course, that unless any contract under which a literary, dramatic, musical, or artistic work is made is one of employment, the author will always be the first owner of the copyright.[49] This is particularly important with respect to *commissions*, one of the two points in this area where the 1988 Act departed from its predecessor's position. Under the 1956 Act, the commissioner was the first owner of copyright in respect of a limited class of artistic works; now in every case an assignation from the author will be

---

[44] CDPA 1988, s 9(5).   [45] CDPA 1988, s 12(2).
[46] CDPA 1988, s 104(4). For an example see *Waterlow Publishers v Rose*, The Times, 8 December 1989 (CA). Note here the author's moral right to be identified as such (paras 3.35–3.38), and a person's right not to have a work falsely attributed to him (para 3.47).
[47] CDPA 1988, s 57(1).   [48] CDPA 1988, s 11(2).
[49] For the meaning of employment see *Halsbury's Laws of England*, vol 16; *Laws of Scotland: Stair Memorial Encyclopaedia*, vol 9.

needed to achieve this result.[50] The other change wrought by the 1988 Act was the removal of any claim by an employee-journalist to copyright in his work.[51]

 Question

When is an employer entitled to the copyright in an employee's work?

3.26   The 1988 Act's general provisions on the effect of employment on copyright are subject to any agreement to the contrary, and it is worth noting that there are no formal requirements with respect to such agreements.[52] Agreements can be implied from actings, as for example where universities have generally not claimed copyright in their academic employees' works even though the production of such works might be said to be in the course of employment.[53]

■ *Noah v Shuba* [1991] FSR 14 (Mummery J)

N was employed as an epidemiologist at the Public Health Laboratory Scheme (PHLS). He wrote a book entitled *A Guide to Hygienic Skin Piercing*. In accordance with the usual practice of the PHLS, under which employees retained copyright in works written by them, the book showed N as the author and copyright owner. In an action for copyright infringement which N brought against third parties, Mummery J stated *obiter* that the long-standing practice of PHLS with regard to employees' copyright works meant that N's contract contained an implied term against the application of the employment rule in the 1988 Act.

There are no express provisions on commissions as such, and so general principles will apply. If the parties agree that the commissioner is to have the copyright in the commissioned work, the agreement will have to take the form of an assignation by the author, which the 1988 Act requires to be in writing.[54]

In the course of employment

3.27   Before the employer can claim any copyright in his employee's literary, dramatic, musical, or artistic work, it must be shown to have been made in the course of the author's employment.[55]

■ *Stephenson Jordan and Harrison v Macdonald and Evans* (1952) 69 RPC 10

A former employee of the plaintiffs had published a book made up of the texts of public lectures composed and delivered by him before various audiences, and also of a report prepared by him for a client of the plaintiffs. Both parts had been written during the period of his employment. It was held that copyright in the report belonged to the employers, because the author wrote it as part of what he was employed to do; but with regard to the text of the lectures, even though the employers had encouraged the author to give the lectures and had met his resultant expenses, it was held that the employers had no copyright. An analogy was drawn between the employee and a university lecturer, and it was said

---

[50] 1956 Act, s 4(3). See CDPA 1988, Sch 1, para 11 for transitional provisions. For an example of the copyright in a commissioned work vesting in the author see *Oilfield Publications Ltd v MacLachlan* 1989 GWD 26-1128.
[51] 1956 Act, s 4(2); not replaced in CDPA 1988.   [52] CDPA 1988, s 11(2).
[53] See further on universities and copyright ownership, J Pila, 'Who owns the intellectual property rights in academic work?' [2010] EIPR 609; A Monotti with S Ricketson, *Universities and Intellectual Property: Ownership and Exploitation* (2003); C McSherry, *Who Owns Academic Work? Battling for Control of Intellectual Property* (2001); and D Bok, *Universities in the Marketplace: The Commercialisation of Higher Education* (2003) Chs 4, 5, 8, 9.
[54] CDPA 1988, s 90(3).   [55] CDPA 1988, s 11(2).

to be 'both just and commonsense' (per Lord Evershed at 18) that the latter rather than his university, had copyright in his lectures. The grounds for this view do not clearly appear in the case but it has been suggested that the employee was only employed to deliver and not to write the lectures. However, this appears inconsistent with the observation of Morris LJ that it had not been shown that the employee could have been ordered either to write or to deliver the lectures (at 24).

■ *Byrne v Statist Co* [1914] 1 KB 622

A member of the editorial staff of a newspaper made a translation into English of a speech reported in a foreign language for publication in the paper. The work was commissioned and paid for by his employers, but he carried it out in his own time and independently of his normal duties. It was held that he was the owner of the copyright, not having made the translation in the course of his employment.

■ *King v The South African Weather Service* [2009] FSR 6 (Supreme Court of Appeal, Republic of South Africa)

An employee created a computer program working both from home and in the office, over which he asserted his own copyright. His employer, a weather forecasting service, argued that the program was created 'in the course of employment' and so the copyright belonged to it. This was despite the fact that the employee's duties as a meteorologist did not include computer programming. The program assisted him in his duties to collect, collate, and transmit weather data. The court held that the creation of the program, which fitted into the service's automated weather system, had been to the advantage of the employer. The employment had been the *causa causans* of the programs. A format for the program had been prescribed by the employer which also had to approve the program prior to its installation on the system. Furthermore, the appellant's job description was initially not intended to be comprehensive and was later amended to state that work outside the terms of the contract could still be created 'in the course of employment'. The scope of the employment could change either explicitly or implicitly.[56]

 Discussion point   For answer guidance visit www.oxfordtextbooks.co.uk/orc/waelde3e/

Discuss whether a schoolteacher who writes and publishes a text for use in schools would have the copyright in it. Is there any difference in the position of the university lecturer who writes a book or articles? What about the composition of a database or a computer program by the same lecturer?

Presumption against employer

3.28   Where the name of a person purporting to be that of the author appears on a published copy of a literary, dramatic, musical, or artistic work, or on a work when it is made, it is presumed that he is the author and that he did not make that work in the course of his employment. The contrary must therefore be proved.[57]

---

[56] See further L Tong, 'South African Supreme Court of Appeal interprets "course of employment" for copyright' (2009) 4 JIPLP 323.   [57] CDPA 1988, s 104(2).

Crown copyright[58]

3.29 The monarch is entitled to copyright in every work made in the copyright area by the monarch or an officer or servant of the Crown in the course of his duties.[59] It seems that, for the most part, the position of the Crown is little different from that of any other employer, apart from the much longer duration of the copyright. It may have some unusual rights in respect of the works of former intelligence officers where these breach the lifelong duty of confidentiality owed to the Crown by such persons. According to some of the judges in *Attorney-General v Guardian Newspapers Ltd* (No 2),[60] copyright in such works may vest in the Crown even though their creation occurs after the employment has ceased and cannot in any event be said to be in the course of the author's employment. The monarch is also entitled to copyright in every Act of Parliament, Act of the Scottish Parliament, Act of the Welsh and Northern Ireland Assemblies, or Measure of the General Synod of the Church of England.[61] Finally, the monarch has copyright in works made in his private capacity. This is presumably affected by the special provisions as to the term of Crown copyrights, on the basis that such works are made by the monarch in terms of the section. Members of the royal family who make copyright works have the usual rights[62] and are not affected by any aspect of Crown copyright, since their works are not made by the monarch.[63]

Parliamentary copyright[64]

3.30 The first ownership of copyright in works made by or under the direction or control of the House of Commons or the House of Lords falls to the relevant House, or, if it made by or under the direction and control of both Houses, jointly to the two Houses.[65] The CDPA 1988 also provides that the copyright of every Bill introduced into the UK Parliament is vested in one or both of the Houses.[66] Copyright in a public Bill belongs in the first instance to the House in which the Bill is introduced, and after the Bill has been carried to the second House to both Houses jointly.[67] Copyright in a private Bill belongs to both Houses jointly.[68] Copyright in a personal Bill belongs in the first instance to the House of Lords, and after the Bill has been carried to the House of Commons to both Houses jointly.[69] Copyright in a Bill ceases when it receives Royal Assent (in which case it becomes an Act and subject to Crown copyright) or on the withdrawal or rejection of the Bill.[70] There are similar provisions for the Bills of the Scottish Parliament (first copyright belongs to the Scottish Parliamentary Corporate Body) and the Welsh and Northern Ireland Assemblies (first owner the Welsh and Northern Ireland Assembly Commissions respectively).[71]

---

[58] See further the website of the Information Management section of the National Archives, which administers Crown copyright at http://www.nationalarchives.gov.uk/information-management/our-services/crown-copyright.htm.

[59] CDPA 1988, s 163(1).

[60] [1988] 3 All ER 545 per Scott J at 567, per Dillon LJ at 621 (CA) and per Lords Keith and Griffiths at 645 and 654 (HL). The argument is dependent on notions of equitable ownership which it would be impossible to apply in the Scottish context.

[61] CDPA 1988, s 164(1); Scotland Act 1998, s 92(3). For the Bill stage, see para 3.30.

[62] *Prince Albert v Strange* (1848) 2 De G & Sm 652 (64 ER 293); aff'd (1849) 1 Mac & G 25 (41 ER 1171); *HRH The Prince of Wales v Associated Newspapers Ltd (No 3)* [2006] EWHC 522 (Ch) (Blackburne J).

[63] For a valuable discussion of the development and contemporary significance of Crown copyright, see S Saxby, 'Crown copyright regulation in the UK—is the debate still alive?' (2005) 13(3) IJL & IT 299.

[64] See generally the website of the Information Management service of the National Archives at http://www.nationalarchives.gov.uk/information-management/our-services/parliamentary-copyright.htm and N Cox, 'Copyright in statutes, regulations and judicial decisions in common law jurisdictions: public ownership or commercial enterprise?' (2006) 27(3) Statute Law Review 185.

[65] CDPA 1988, s 165(1).   [66] CDPA 1988, s 166(1).   [67] CDPA 1988, s 166(2).   [68] CDPA 1988, s 166(3).

[69] CDPA 1988, s 166(4).   [70] CDPA 1988, s 166(5). For the Crown copyright in an Act, see para 3.29.

[71] CDPA 1988, ss 166A, 166B, 166C, and 166D.

Question

Why was there no provision for Welsh Assembly copyright before the coming into force of the Government of Wales Act 2006, Sch 10, para 28?

Author's moral rights

International background[72]

3.31   As noted in the historical introduction (para 2.8), the Berne Convention developed the concept of *non-transferable (inalienable) moral rights* (to claim authorship and to object to derogatory treatment of the work prejudicial to the author's honour or reputation (Art *6bis*). Moral rights thus recognise certain non-economic interests which an author (but no one else) may continue to exercise in respect of a work even though no longer owner of the copyright or of the physical form in which the work was first created and recorded, this last being particularly important in respect of artistic works. The rights are reinforced by their recognition in the 1948 Universal Declaration of Human Rights: 'everyone has the right to the protection of the moral and material interests resulting from any scientific, literary or artistic production of which he is the author' (Art 27(2)).[73] The Berne Convention also provides (Art 14*ter*) for an author's inalienable resale right (*droit de suite*) in works of art and original manuscripts, giving him a right to a share of the proceeds of any sale of the work after the first transfer by the author. This latter right is, however, optional for Berne states.

3.32   EU Directives have nothing substantive to say about moral rights.[74] In 2001, however, a Directive was enacted on the subject of artists' resale rights (*droit de suite*), to be implemented in the member states for the benefit of living artists by 2006 and for those who had died before then by 2012 at the latest.[75] It applies only to works of art and not (unlike the Berne Convention, see para 3.31) to literary or musical manuscripts, thus taking partial advantage of the option of resale rights under the Convention. The Directive gives the artist a right to a share of the proceeds of any resale of the original of his work after the sale by the artist to a first purchaser. While the Directive's objective is primarily economic, its content owes much to moral right ideas. The Directive was enacted against British opposition, but the majority of the then EU member states already had such a system in place and perceived distortion in the European art market resulting from the variability of the national laws, as well as an injustice to the artist who gained no benefit from the value others came to place on the original of his work.

The law in the UK[76]

3.33   The two principal moral rights introduced in the UK by the CDPA 1988 are:

---

[72] See in general E Adeney, *The Moral Rights of Authors and Performers: An International and Comparative Analysis* (2006) Chs 5–7.

[73] Note also the International Covenant on Economic, Social and Cultural Rights 1966, Art 15(1): 'the States Parties to the present covenant recognize the right of everyone ... to benefit from the protection of the moral and material interests resulting from any scientific, literary or artistic production of which he is the author'.

[74] See the Database Directive 1996, recital 28 ('whereas the moral rights of the natural person who created the database belong to the author and should be exercised according to the legislation of the Member States and the provisions of the Berne Convention for the Protection of Literary and Artistic Works; whereas such moral rights remain outside the scope this Directive').

[75] EC Directive 2001/84/EC on the resale right for the benefit of the author of an original work of art.

[76] See Adeney, *Moral Rights*, note 72, Chs 13, 14.

> **Paternity:** *the right to be identified as author* of a literary, dramatic, musical, or artistic work, or as director of a copyright film (CDPA 1988, s 77).
>
> **Integrity:** the *right* of such *authors and directors to prevent derogatory treatment of their work* (CDPA 1988, s 80).

Under the heading of 'moral rights', the 1988 Act also deals with *prevention of false attributions* to one of literary, dramatic, musical, or artistic works and films,[77] and a *right of privacy in certain photographs and films*.[78] It should be noted, however, that these are not usually seen as moral rights in other legal systems, or under the Berne Convention. In contrast, the Regulations implementing the *artist's resale right* in the UK do not characterise the rights as moral rights, although many of the characteristics of such rights are present, notably their inalienability from the author of the work to which they attach (see further at para 3.34). The right is not usually included amongst the moral rights in other systems, as a result of its highly economic character.

 Question

What moral rights are now recognised in the UK?

Characteristics of moral rights

3.34   As will be explained in more detail later in the chapter, moral rights last as long as the other rights conferred by copyright (see para 3.51). This contrasts with the position in some Continental European countries, where the moral rights are of indefinite duration.[79] Being conceived as highly personal to the author, moral rights are not assignable[80]—that is, transferable to third parties—but they can be waived by an instrument in writing signed by the person giving up the right.[81] It is also not an infringement of the moral rights to do anything to which the person entitled to the right has consented.[82] In these ways, UK moral rights are significantly weaker than their Continental counterparts. Infringements of the rights are treated as breaches of statutory duty, giving rise to remedies such as injunction and damages.[83] Note that moral rights do not extend to the authors of computer programs.

 Question

May the owner of moral rights choose not to enforce them?

---

[77] CDPA 1988, s 84.   [78] CDPA 1988, s 85.   [79] Eg France (Adeney, *Moral Rights*, note 72, Ch 8); cf Ch 9 (Germany). Compare Canada, the United States, and Australia, also discussed in Adeney, Chs 11, 12, 16, 18.

[80] CDPA 1988, s 94.   [81] CDPA 1988, s 87(2)–(4).   [82] CDPA 1988, s 87(1).

[83] CDPA 1988, s 103. Note that an injunction may prohibit the doing of any act infringing the right of integrity unless a disclaimer is made dissociating the author or director from the treatment of the work (s 103(2)).

> ## Key points about moral rights in general
>
> - The main moral rights are the rights of paternity and integrity
> - These moral rights last for the same length of time as the economic rights (see para 3.51)
> - The rights are inalienable, but can be waived, while the holder may consent to acts which would otherwise be infringements

Paternity right

3.35   The precise extent of the right to be identified as the author of a copyright work varies according to the nature of the work. When it is required, the identification must be clear and reasonably prominent so as to bring the identity of the author or director to the attention of the public.[84] The right applies to the whole or any substantial part of a work.[85] Identification is required in the following circumstances:

> ### Literary and dramatic works (excluding song lyrics)
> Whenever the work is published commercially, performed in public or communicated to the public, or whenever copies of a film or sound recording including the work are issued to the public, or when any of these events occur in relation to an adaptation of the work.
>
> ### Musical work and song lyrics
> Whenever there is commercial publication or copies of a sound recording are issued to the public, or where it is the soundtrack of a film available to the public, or when any of these events occur in relation to an adaptation.
>
> ### Artistic work
> Whenever there is commercial publication or public exhibition, or when a visual image is communicated to the public, or included in a film available to the public. In the case of three-dimensional artistic works, the author must be identified when copies of graphic works representing them or photographs of them are issued to the public. The author of a work of architecture in the form of a building has the right to be identified on the building as constructed, by appropriate means visible to persons entering or approaching the building.
>
> ### Film
> Whenever the film is shown in public, communicated to the public, or copies of the film are issued to the public.

> ## Question
> When must the author of a work be identified?

---

[84] CDPA 1988, s 77(2)–(7).   [85] CDPA 1988, s 89(1).

Paternity must be 'asserted'

3.36 There is no infringement of the right of paternity unless it has been previously *asserted* by the author.[86] Assertion is by *statement in writing* to that effect, either in any assignation of copyright in the work, or in any other instrument in writing signed by the author (eg in a licence or in a warning letter to an infringer, actual or potential).[87] The requirement may well offend against the Berne Convention provision that the enjoyment and exercise of rights under the Convention (which include moral rights) shall not be subject to any formality.[88] The assertion may be general or in relation to any specified act or acts. A statement that the right has been asserted will commonly be found in the prelim pages of books, usually saying something like, 'The right of XYZ to be identified as the author of this work has been asserted in accordance with the Copyright, Designs and Patents Act 1988.' The Act contains *no requirement that paternity be asserted before the publication of a work*; but any delay in asserting the right is to be taken into account by a court in deciding whether or not to grant a remedy for breach of the right.[89]

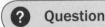 **Sawkins v Hyperion Records [2005] RPC 32 (CA)**

For the facts see para 2.42. Hyperion issued the CD of Lalande music with the statement 'With thanks to Dr Lionel Sawkins for his preparation of performance materials for this recording'. Since this did not identify Sawkins as the author of a copyright work, the attribution right was held infringed. Sawkins had previously asserted his right with a letter during pre-recording negotiations with Hyperion in which he stated that the CD sleevenotes should bear the legend '© Copyright 2002 by Lionel Sawkins'.

 Question

How and when must 'paternity' be asserted to be effective?

Exercise

Have the authors of this book asserted their rights of paternity? If not, why not?

Public exhibition of artistic works

3.37 There are some special provisions in respect of the *public exhibition of artistic works*. If the author affixes his name to the original or a copy when he parts with possession of it, he has asserted the moral right to be identified as its author against any subsequent possessors, whether or not the original identification is still present or visible on the work.[90] Further, where the author licenses the making of copies, moral rights to be identified where in pursuance of the licence there is an exhibition of a copy of the work may be asserted in the licence.[91] This affects the licensee and anyone into whose hands a copy made in pursuance of the licence comes, regardless of whether or not he has notice of the assertion.[92]

[86] CDPA 1988, s 78(1).   [87] CDPA 1988, s 78(2).   [88] Berne Convention, Art 5(2).   [89] CDPA 1988, s 78(5).
[90] CDPA 1988, s 78(3)(a) and (4)(c).   [91] CDPA 1988, s 78(3)(b).   [92] CDPA 1988, s 78(4)(d).

Exercise

A city council commissions a large bronze statue of a phoenix to stand in the city's main square, symbolising its post-industrial renaissance. The sculpture is erected and becomes a popular success. However, no information is provided at the site about the identity of the sculptor, although it is publicised in newspapers at the time of the commission and again at the unveiling ceremony. The sculptor also identifies herself as the creator on her website, and her name is mentioned in official tourist and business guides. The commissioning contract contained no provisions about identification of the sculptor at the site, but it did give the council merchandising rights such as the reproduction and sale of miniatures of the sculpture, and the marketing of T-shirts bearing its image. Now the sculptor has approached the council, requesting that she be identified at the site of the sculpture and on merchandising material. Must the council comply with this request?

Limits on the right to be identified as author or director

3.38   The right to be identified as author does not exist in respect of computer programs, the design of typefaces or computer-generated works.[93] Where copyright first vested in an employer, nothing done or authorised by him infringes the author's moral right.[94] Certain acts permitted in respect of the copyright in a work—fair dealing, for example—are not to be taken as infringements of the moral right to be identified as author.[95] The right does not apply to works in which Crown or parliamentary copyright subsists, unless the author or director has previously been identified as such on or in published copies of the work.[96] Nor does it apply to publications in newspapers, magazines, or similar periodicals, or in an encyclopaedia, dictionary, yearbook, or other collective works of reference where the work was made for the purposes of such publication.[97]

Discussion point   For answer guidance visit www.oxfordtextbooks.co.uk/orc/waelde3e/

What is the reason for these limitations on the right of paternity?

Key points about the moral right of paternity

- Paternity is the right to be identified as the author of a work
- It applies in varying ways to literary, dramatic, musical, and artistic works and films but not to computer programs
- The right must be asserted by a statement in writing
- An employer who owns the copyright in a work cannot infringe the employee-author's moral rights

Right of integrity

3.39   The author of a work or director of a film has the right to object to *derogatory treatment* of his work. This moral right does not need to be asserted in any formal way. The right applies to the treatment of the

---

[93] CDPA 1988, s 79(2).   [94] CDPA 1988, s 79(3).   [95] CDPA 1988, s 79(4), (5).   [96] CDPA 1988, s 79(7).
[97] CDPA 1988, s 79(6).

whole or any part (without a requirement that it be a substantial part) of the work.[98] Derogatory treatment will occur when there is:

> addition to, deletion from or alteration to or adaptation of a work which amounts to distortion or mutilation of the work or is otherwise prejudicial to the honour or reputation of the author or director (CDPA 1988, s 80(2)).

There must be a *treatment* of the work (in the form of addition, deletion, alteration, or adaptation) and such treatment must be *derogatory* (a distortion or mutilation that must also be prejudicial to the author's honour or reputation).[99] But a translation of a literary or dramatic work will not amount to derogatory treatment, nor will an arrangement or transcription of a musical work involving no more than a change of key or register.[100] The right affects those who:

- publish commercially, perform in public or communicate to the public, or issue to the public copies of a film or sound recording of, or including, a literary, dramatic, or musical work (CDPA 1988, s 80(3));

- publish commercially, exhibit in public, communicate to the public, show or issue to the public copies of a film including images of, an artistic work (CDPA 1988, s 80(4)(a), (b));

- issue to the public copies of a graphic work or photograph of works of architecture in the form of models, sculptures, or works of artistic craftsmanship (CDPA 1988, s 80(4)(c)). Note that the author of a building has only the right to require that his identification be removed from it in the event of derogatory treatment (s 80(5));

- show in public, communicate to the public, or issue to the public copies of, a film (CDPA 1988, s 80(6)).

If any of these activities includes a derogatory treatment of a work to which the right pertains, the right of integrity has been infringed.[101] Further, dealing in an article which infringes this right will also attract a secondary infringement liability.[102]

 Question

Identify the common features of the various situations in which the moral right of integrity may be infringed.

 Discussion point For answer guidance visit www.oxfordtextbooks.co.uk/orc/waelde3e/

How far may the right of integrity be compared to one of private censorship?

3.40   The potentially wide scope of this right can be illustrated with well-known decisions from other jurisdictions: for example, the French decision that the moral rights of the film director John Huston were infringed by the colourisation of his black-and-white film *The Asphalt Jungle*, even although the colouriser had a contractual right to do so and there was no right of integrity in Huston's home territory of the United States;[103] in a Canadian case it was held that the integrity of a sculpture in a public place was infringed by festooning it with Christmas decorations.[104]

---

[98] CDPA 1988, s 89(2).   [99] *Pasterfield v Denham* [1999] FSR 168; *Confetti Records v Warner Music UK Ltd* [2003] EMLR 35.
[100] CDPA 1988, s 80(2)(a).   [101] CDPA 1988, s 80(1).   [102] CDPA 1988, s 83.
[103] *Huston v Turner Entertainment Inc* (1992) 23 IIC 702.   [104] *Snow v Eaton Centre Ltd* (1982) 70 CPR (2d) 105 (Ont).

3.41   There have been few cases to date in the UK courts about the right of integrity, and they exhibit a cautious approach.

■ *Morrison Leahy Music Ltd v Lightbond Ltd* [1993] EMLR 144

L produced a sound recording entitled 'Bad Boys Megamix' which took bits of the music and words from five George Michael compositions (the copyright of which MLM owned) and put them together in snatches lasting from ten to 65 seconds, where the works from which they were taken lasted from three minutes, 22 seconds to six minutes, 45 seconds. It was held that it was plainly arguable that such relatively short snatches did alter the character of the original works by removing them from their original context and creating a new one.

■ *Tidy v Natural History Museum Trustees* (1995) 37 IPR 501

T, a cartoonist, produced large-scale dinosaur cartoons to hang in the museum. It was held that the right of integrity did not entitle T to prevent the republication of the cartoons on a much smaller scale in a book being published by the museum trustees.

■ *Pasterfield v Denham* [1999] FSR 168

P was commissioned by Plymouth City Council in 1988 to design promotional leaflets for the Plymouth Dome, a tourist attraction. The leaflet used devices of a satellite, a German bomber formation and a detailed cut-away drawing of the Dome's interior. In 1994, the council commissioned D to produce a new leaflet for the Dome: this included copies of the satellite and bomber formation, along with a smaller and altered version of the cut-away drawing. The alterations included the omission of features on the edge of the original drawing and a variation in colouring. It was held that these differences were so trivial that they could only be seen by close inspection, and so could not amount to derogatory treatment. Such treatment had also to be prejudicial to the author's honour or reputation as an artist; it was not enough that the artist felt aggrieved.

■ *Confetti Records v Warner Music UK Ltd* [2003] EMLR 35

The composer of a musical work called 'Burnin' sued for derogatory treatment by way of mixing it on a compilation album with rap material referring to violence and drugs. It was held that merely distorting or mutilating a work did not infringe the right of integrity; prejudice to the author's honour and reputation was also required. In giving evidence the composer made no complaint about the treatment of 'Burnin', and the court should not infer prejudice for him. The words of the rap were for practical purposes in a foreign language the content of which was not proved, and they were anyway hard to decipher. All this went against any conclusion that the treatment infringed the right of integrity.

■ *Harrison v Harrison* [2010] ECDR 12

JP had a written the first edition of a book and its second edition was edited and published by JD. JP claimed that the second edition was prejudicial to his honour or reputation. Fysh J noted that 'treatment' is a broad general concept implying a spectrum of possible acts, 'from the addition of, say, a single word to a poem to the destruction of the entire work' (para 60). The generality of the term 'treatment' is limited by the requirement of prejudice to the honour or reputation of the author to arise from such treatment. It was held that there was no infringement of the integrity right because it not enough for the author to point to a 'miscellany of arguable trivia' to substantiate a case for derogatory treatment (para 64).

■ *Delves-Broughton v House of Harlot Ltd* [2012] EWPCC 29

D took a photograph depicting a model in a forest wearing clothes supplied by H which H included in its website after cropping it, reversing the image, and removing the background. On D's claim for infringement of integrity right, it was found that considerable time and effort had been spent in the composition of the photograph for which D considered the forest to be particularly important. The judge held that the changes to the photograph amounted to distortion, that such treatment of the work was therefore derogatory and awarded £50 for it. Surprisingly, the judge noted that the changes were not prejudicial to D's honour or reputation. The approach and outcome in this case is inconsistent with earlier cases which suggest that mere distortion/mutilation is not sufficient unless such distortion/mutilation also prejudices the author's honour or reputation.

Exercise

A local authority commissions a new concert hall and paintings to be hung in its entrance hall. The paintings are unpopular and much criticised in the local media for their abstract character. Following an election leading to a change of party in control of the authority, and amidst much publicity, the council orders the removal of the paintings to storage, and their replacement with cartoons humorously depicting aspects of local life. Can either the architect of the hall or the painter object to the council's action on the basis of their rights of integrity? You may find it helpful in thinking about this problem to consider the Indian case of *Sehgal v Union of India* [2005] FSR 39.

Limits on the right of integrity

3.42   The limits on the kinds of work affected by the right of integrity are similar to those operative in the right of paternity:[105] for example, computer programs, computer-generated works,[106] publications in collective works,[107] and works where the employer, Crown, or Parliament has the first copyright.[108] There are some important further limits on the integrity right, however. It does not apply in relation to any work made for the purpose of reporting current events, since otherwise the traditional sub-editing process could be severely hampered.[109] In the case of anonymous and pseudonymous works where it is reasonable to suppose that copyright has expired,[110] no act will infringe the right of integrity if it would not infringe copyright.[111] The right is not infringed by anything done for the purpose of avoiding the commission of an offence, or complying with a duty imposed by or under an enactment.[112] Finally, anything done by the BBC for the purpose of avoiding the inclusion in a programme of anything which offends against good taste or decency or which is likely to encourage or incite crime or lead to disorder or to be offensive to public feeling will not infringe the right of integrity.[113]

---

[105] See generally CDPA 1988, ss 81 and 82, and para 3.38.
[106] CDPA 1988, s 81(2). But there is a right of integrity in a typeface.   [107] CDPA 1988, s 81(4).
[108] CDPA 1988, s 82.   [109] CDPA 1988, s 81(3).   [110] CDPA 1988, ss 57 and 66A; also see para 3.53.
[111] CDPA 1988, s 81(5).   [112] CDPA 1988, s 81(6)(a), (b).
[113] CDPA 1988, s 81(6)(c). There is no specific exemption for commercial broadcasters, which will therefore have to rely on the general exemption in respect of avoiding the commission of offences or breach of a statutory duty (see note 112).

Exercise 1

Before the 1988 Act came into force, the author of a play about the Falklands War to be broadcast on the BBC strenuously objected to the Corporation's cutting of passages that presented the Prime Minister Mrs Thatcher in an unfavourable light.[114] Would that author now be able to make a claim under the right of integrity, and would the BBC be able to plead its privileged position (described previously) in its defence?

Exercise 2

Would Elinor Glyn have been able to argue that the film satire *Pimple's Three Weeks (without the option)* infringed the moral rights in her novel *Three Weeks* (see *Glyn v Weston Feature Film Co* [1916] 1 Ch 261)?

Exercise 3

To what extent are authors able to use the right to control the way in which their works are presented to the world—for example, through distasteful association, packaging, or advertising, or through adaptations in other media which travesty their work (at least in their view)?

Exercise 4

Consider the case of *Galerie d'Art du Petit Champlain inc v Théberge* [2002] 2 SCR 336 (Supreme Court of Canada), discussed at para 4.29. Was the artist's right of integrity infringed in that case?

Exercise 5

Could an author who had become dissatisfied with the quality of his work demand its withdrawal from public circulation, on the basis that its continued availability would damage his honour and reputation?[115] Consider in this connection the old Scottish case of *Davis v Miller* (1855) 17 D 1166.

Exercise 6

Consider the case of *Hugo v SA Plon* [2007] ECDR 9 (Cour de Cassation, France) in which the moral right of Victor Hugo (1802–1885) in his famous novel *Les Misérables* (published 1862 and out of copyright) was held not infringed by the publication in 2001 of two works purporting to be sequels to the novel and using characters from it. French law requires respect for the author's name, title and work. Apart from the questions of location, term, and assertion, would it have been possible to sue on these facts for infringement of the UK moral rights of paternity or integrity?

Meaning of publishing commercially

3.43   Both the rights of paternity and integrity arise, inter alia, when a work is published commercially. Commercial publication means issuing copies of the work to the public at a time when copies made in

---

[114] Cf *Frisby v British Broadcasting Corporation* [1967] Ch 932, where a similar complaint was dealt with as a matter of interpreting the author's contract.

[115] The example is drawn from the well-known French case of *Eden v Whistler* DP 1900, I 497, where the famous artist was allowed to refuse to deliver a portrait to its commissioner, despite previously exhibiting it himself. The permission was conditional on Whistler repaying his fee and undertaking not to exhibit the painting again. On honour, see E Adeney, 'The moral right of integrity: the past and future of "honour"' [2005] IPQ 111.

advance of the receipt of orders are generally available to the public (eg through a retail outlet), or making the work available to the public by means of an electronic retrieval system.[116]

> ### Key points on the moral right of integrity
>
> - The right is to prevent derogatory treatment of copyright works when they are published or otherwise put before the public
>
> - Derogatory treatment is distortion or mutilation of a work or treatment which is otherwise prejudicial to the honour or reputation of the author
>
> - The UK courts have not given the right expansive scope in their decisions on the matter

Artists' resale rights

3.44 A further right was introduced in the UK on 14 February 2006, in implementation of the European Resale Right Directive 2001.[117] The author of a work of graphic or plastic art in which copyright subsists has a right to a royalty on any sale of a work that is a resale subsequent to the first transfer of ownership by the author.[118] The right subsists as long as the copyright subsists,[119] one effect of this being that 'only the originals of works of modern and contemporary art . . . fall within the scope of the resale right'.[120] In general, and in the fashion of a moral right, this right cannot be assigned,[121] waived,[122] or shared[123] by the author, although it can be transmitted on death, whether by will or the rules of intestate succession,[124] and the right may be transferred to a charity.[125] But the right can be exercised *only* through a collecting society.[126] The holder of the right can choose which such collecting society to mandate for this purpose,[127] but in the absence of such a transfer of management, the collecting society managing copyright on behalf of artists (eg the Design and Artists' Copyright Society (DACS))[128] is deemed mandated to manage the right[129]—that is, collect the resale royalty in return for a fixed percentage or fee of the money so ingathered.[130] The amount of the royalty is calculated in relation to the resale price,[131] the resale price being taken to be the price obtained for the sale net of any tax payable on the transaction and converted into euros at the European Central Bank reference rate prevailing at the contract date.[132] The (not especially generous) royalty rates are shown in Diagram 3.1.[133]

---

[116] CDPA 1988, s 175(2).

[117] Directive 2001/84/EC of the European Parliament and Council on the resale right for the benefit of the author of an original work of art was implemented by the Artist's Resale Right Regulations 2006 (SI 2006/346), now amended by Artist's Resale Right (Amendment) Regulations 2009 (SI 2009/2792) and 2011 (SI 2011/2873). See generally S Stokes, 'Droit de suite: an artistic stroke of genius? A critical exploration of the European Directive and its resultant effects' [2012] EIPR 305.

[118] Artist's Resale Right Regulations 2006, reg 3(1). A sale is a transfer of ownership of the work from seller to buyer under a contract in exchange for a money consideration called the price (Sale of Goods Act 1979, s 2 and reg 2 (definition of 'sale')). The author is the person who creates the work (reg 2, definition of 'author'). For a presumption that the author is the person whose name appears on the work as such, see reg 6.

[119] Reg 3(2).   [120] Resale Right Directive 2001, recital 17.   [121] Reg 7(1). Any charge on a resale right is void (reg 7(2)).

[122] Reg 8(1).

[123] Reg 8(2). Note, however, the provisions for cases of joint authorship, where resale right is owned in common unless otherwise agreed in writing (reg 5).

[124] Reg 9. The person into whose hands the right is transmitted may likewise transmit it. The Court of Justice, in Case C-518/08 *Fundación Gala-Salvador Dali v ADAGP* [2010] ECDR 13, ruled that national law provisions reserving the benefit of the right to artist's heirs at law alone, to the exclusion of testamentary legatees, is not precluded by the Directive.

[125] Reg 7(3)–(5).   [126] Reg 14(1).   [127] Reg 14(3).   [128] See the DACS website at http://www.dacs.org.uk/.

[129] Reg 14(2).   [130] Reg 14(5)(b).   [131] Reg 3(3).   [132] Reg 3(4).   [133] Schedule 1.

Diagram 3.1 Royalty rates table

Portion of the sale price	Percentage amount
From 0 to 50,000 euro	4%
From 50,000.01 to 200,000 euro	3%
From 200,000.01 to 350,000 euro	1%
From 350,000.01 to 500,000 euro	0.5%
Exceeding 500,000 euro	0.25%

A resale becomes liable to the royalty where the buyer or the seller or the agent of either is acting in the course of a business of dealing in works of art, and the sale price is not less than €1,000.[134] The persons liable to pay the royalty are the seller *and*, if acting in the course of a business of dealing in works of art, the seller's agent, the buyer's agent if there is no seller's agent, and, where there are no such agents, the buyer.[135] The liability of these parties is joint and several.[136] The liability to make the payment arises on completion of the resale.[137]

3.45 A number of other points should be made about the artist's resale right:

- The royalty is only payable on the *resale of works of art*. Works of graphic or plastic art include, for example, a picture, collage, painting, drawing, engraving, print, lithograph, sculpture, tapestry, ceramic, glassware item, or photograph.[138] The work sold must be the one which the artists created. The resale of a *copy* of a work of art is not subject to the royalty right unless it is one of a limited number made by the author or under his authority.[139]

- The royalty is only payable on a resale *after* the *first transfer of ownership of the work of art by the author*. While the author's first transfer of ownership will typically be a sale to another person, the transaction need not be for any consideration,[140] and so might be a gift. Transfer also includes transmission on death by will or by intestate succession, and disposal of the work by the author's personal representatives for estate administration purposes, as well as disposal by the administrator of the author's insolvent estate.[141]

- Where the seller previously acquired the work directly from the author less than three years before the resale *and* the sale price now does not exceed €10,000, there is no liability to a resale royalty.[142]

- There are complex *transitional* provisions. Resale royalties are not payable in respect of contracts concluded before 14 February 2006, but the right does otherwise apply to works made before that date.[143] Where the artist died before 14 February 2006, rules for determination of artist's successors are provided.[144]

- The right initially applied only to living artists. The UK took advantage of a provision in the Directive intended to enable the economic operators in those member states which did not, at the time of the adoption of the Directive, apply a resale right to adapt gradually to the right whilst maintaining their economic viability.[145] As such, resale rights transmitted on the death of the artist (as per reg 16(2) or actually transmitted on or after 14 February 2006), were not exercisable in respect of any sale where

---

[134] Reg 12(2), (3).   [135] Reg 13(1), (2).   [136] Reg 13(1).
[137] Reg 13(3). The liable person may withhold payment until evidence of entitlement to be paid the royalty is produced (reg 13(3)).
[138] Reg 4(1).   [139] Reg 4(2).   [140] Reg 12(1).   [141] Reg 3(5).   [142] Reg 12(4).   [143] Reg 16(1).
[144] Reg 16(2).   [145] Resale Right Directive, recital 17 and Art 8(2), (3).

the contract date preceded 1 January 2010.[146] The UK Government chose to extend this derogation until 1 January 2012.[147] The derogation has since expired meaning the right is now applicable to deceased artists and the Secretary of State is required to review the regulations periodically.[148]

3.46   The purpose of an artist's resale right is succinctly summarised in one of the recitals to the Resale Right Directive: 'to ensure that authors of graphic and plastic works of art share in the economic success of their original works of art…to redress the balance between the economic situation of authors of graphic and plastic works of art and that of other creators who benefit from successive exploitations of their works'.[149] Crudely, the model is one of the impecunious artist forced to sell his creations, only to see others later earning riches from dealings in those creations. As already noted, the right did not exist in the UK before 14 February 2006, but it was found in the majority of other EU member states, albeit with variable rules. The harmonisation of the Directive was thus intended to eliminate the differences found in the EU, in order to remove an obstacle to the operation of a single European market in this field. The Directive was highly contested, because the resale right is not widely found outside Europe, and there was significant concern that what is effectively a form of tax on dealings in art would drive business away from Europe to other centres such as the United States (in particular New York).[150] The UK was particularly concerned because the success of its international art market could be attributed, some thought, to the absence of any artists' resale right. More fundamentally, it can be argued against the right that those who make successful businesses through dealing in art are not necessarily merely enriching themselves on the back of the artist, but play a significant independent role in ensuring that art works generate wealth.[151]

Discussion point For answer guidance visit www.oxfordtextbooks.co.uk/orc/waelde3e/

Why should resale royalty right be limited to works of art? Why are there no equivalent right for authors of literary, dramatic, and musical works in relation to their manuscripts, as provided in the Berne Convention, Article 14*ter* (para 3.31)? (Note recital 19 of the Resale Right Directive: 'the harmonisation brought about by this Directive does not apply to original manuscripts of writers and composers').

Key points about artists' resale rights

- The aim of the right is to enable artists to take a share of the profit made by others from sales of their original art works

- The right lasts for the same period as the copyright in the work

- The right is inalienable, although it transmits on death

---

[146] See reg 17 as originally enacted in Artist's Resale Right Regulations 2006 (SI 2006/346).

[147] See reg 17 as amended by Artist's Resale Right (Amendment) Regulations 2009 (SI 2009/2792); in September 2008 the UK–IPO had published a consultation document proposing that the UK exemption be extended for a further two years and 90 per cent of respondents stated that the derogation should not be extended (http://www.ipo.gov.uk/about/press/press-release/press-release-2008/press-release-20081219.htm).

[148] Reg 17 as amended by Artist's Resale Right (Amendment) Regulations 2011 (SI 2011/2873).

[149] Resale Right Directive, recital 3.

[150] California has an artists' resale royalty right, and has lost much art business to New York. For a discussion of the impact of the resale right in the UK, see S Blakeney, 'The great debate—using artistic licence to resist the artist's resale right' [2011] Ent LR 22.

[151] J Merryman, 'The proposed generalization of the droit de suite in the European Communities' [1997] IPQ 16.

False attribution of authorship

3.47   A person has a moral right not to have a work falsely attributed to him.[152] This is the counterpart of the right to be identified as the author. There is a potential secondary liability for dealers in copies which infringe this right.[153] The right applies to the whole or any part (without any requirement of substantiality) of the work.[154]

■ Clark v Associated Newspapers Ltd [1998] 1 All ER 959[155]

The London *Evening Standard* published a series of articles entitled 'Alan Clark's Secret Election Diary' or 'Alan Clark's Secret Political Diary' set beside a photograph of Clark, a prominent Conservative politician and an author well known for the publication of his personal diaries, which were 'malicious, lecherous and self-pitying, and...enormous fun'. The *Standard* articles sought to parody or spoof the real diaries, and contained a statement that 'Peter Bradshaw...imagines what a new diary might contain'. The statement was in a font bigger than that of the main text but much smaller than the heading and title. It was held that there had been a false attribution. The statement of attribution had to have a clear single meaning, but the law did not require proof of damage, nor was there a cure for the attribution in the 'counter-messages' about Bradshaw's contribution. If 'counter-messages' are to be effective, they have to be as bold, precise and compelling as the false statement.

■ Harrison v Harrison [2010] ECDR 12

JP had a written the first edition of a book and its second edition was edited and published by JD. JP claimed that the promotion of the second edition, through testimonials on the back cover of the second edition which referred to the first edition, created the impression that both editions were, contrary to fact, written by the same author. The court held that there was false attribution of authorship because the single message to the reader from the back cover was praise for the author responsible for the creation of first edition, not the publisher who would usually produce a number of books on different subjects and, without any indication to the contrary, the reader would assume that the author of the title had not changed (para 55).

Right of privacy of certain photographs and films

3.48   A person who for private and domestic purposes commissions the taking of a photograph or the making of a film has, where copyright subsists in the resulting work, the right not to have copies of the work issued to the public, the work exhibited or shown in public or the work communicated to the public.[156] The statutory right applies in relation to the whole or any substantial part of the photograph or film.[157] Any person doing or authorising one of these acts is liable as an infringer. An example would be the display of wedding photographs in the photographer's shop window where that was not authorised contractually or otherwise.[158] The right is not infringed where the act occurs in the context of one of the permitted acts in respect of the copyright in the work.[159]

---

[152] CDPA 1988, s 84.   [153] CDPA 1988, s 84(3)–(7).   [154] CDPA 1988, s 89(2).
[155] See also on the passing off aspects of this case in Chapter 17.   [156] CDPA 1988, s 85(1).
[157] CDPA 1988, s 89(1).
[158] See also *McCosh v Crow & Co* (1903) 5 F 670 and *Pollard v Photographic Co* (1889) 40 Ch D 345.   [159] CDPA 1988, s 85(2).

Duration of copyright and moral rights

Introduction

3.49   The rights conferred by copyright generally endure for a limited period of time only. The Berne Convention provides for a *minimum* period of the author's lifetime plus 50 years for the works to which it applies (Art 7), while the Rome Convention lays down another minimum of at least 20 years for sound recordings and broadcasts (Art 14). Various formulae are used in the UK legislation, generally involving a period of either 70 or 50 years from the end of the calendar year in which a given event occurred. The present position is the result of an EU Directive first enacted in 1993 and implemented in the UK in 1995.[160] In the following paragraphs, references to the 70- or 50-year periods should be understood as references to these formulae. The use of 'the end of the calendar year' as part of the formula is to avoid disputes as to precisely when the event in question occurred. With literary, dramatic, musical, and artistic works, the copyright period is tied first to the lifetime of the author, with the 70-year period added on after his death (*post mortem auctoris*). This reflects recognition of the author's 'natural' right of property in his work, but it continues to be the period even where the copyright in the work is in other hands.[161] The extension of copyright beyond the author's lifetime was initially conceived as a form of protection for his family and descendants, but again the period applies even when the copyright has been transferred to others. With the media copyrights, there is a 50-year period, not tied to any particular lifetime, but rather to the making or publication of the work; reflecting views that works of this kind involve a lesser creative endeavour on the part of the individuals concerned; that the first owner will usually be a company, making it impossible to calculate the term by reference to a human life; and that the protection is essentially to support investment rather than creativity. The UK position parallels the rest of the EU, since the rules on copyright terms were harmonised by the 1993 Directive but, outside the Union, different copyright terms may apply in other jurisdictions. This can have the effect that a work which is in copyright in the EU may not have it in other countries, and vice versa. This can create problems for the international flow of copyright products.

Economic rights in literary, dramatic, musical, and artistic works

3.50   All literary, dramatic, musical, and artistic works, published or unpublished, enjoy the economic rights conferred by copyright—that is, the rights of reproduction, distribution, rental and lending, public performance, communication to the public, and adaptation (see further para 4.10)—until the end of the 70-year period after the author's death (see Diagram 3.2).[162]

Diagram 3.2 Author copyright table

```
                                                              70 years
   Creation ------------------------- Author's death – year end ----------- ----------- Copyright expires
```

---

[160] Directive 93/98/EEC of 29 October 1993 harmonising the term of protection for copyright and certain related rights implemented by the Duration of Copyright and Rights in Performances Regulations 1995 (SI 1995/3297). The Directive was replaced by a consolidated version, European Parliament and Council Directive 2006/116/EC which has now been amended by Directive 2011/77/EU.

[161] On economic justifications for the copyright terms see W Landes and R Posner, *Economic Structure of Intellectual Property Law* (2004), Ch 8. See also the still thought-provoking K Puri, 'The term of copyright protection: is it too long in the wake of new technologies?' [1990] EIPR 12.   [162] CDPA 1988, s 12(1).

Under the pre-1988 Act law, unpublished works could enjoy copyright for as long as they remained unpublished, which might mean in perpetuity. But under the 1988 Act there is now no possibility of a *new* perpetual copyright coming into existence. The perpetual copyrights which existed under pre-1988 legislation have had dates of expiry placed upon them (generally the end of the 50-year period from the end of the year when the 1988 Act came into force, meaning that there could be a sort of copyright bonanza on 1 January 2040).[163] There is one exception to this, found in provisions added at a very late stage of the parliamentary progress of the 1988 Act, giving the Hospital for Sick Children, Great Ormond Street, London, a right without limit of time to a royalty in respect of public performances, commercial publications, broadcasting or use in a cable programme service of JM Barrie's *Peter Pan*, notwithstanding that the copyright therein expired on 31 December 1987. Although the 1988 Act does not preserve the work's copyright in so many words, the effect is much as though it had.[164]

 Question

If the author of a book published in 2010 was born in June 1956, when will the copyright in the book expire?

Moral rights

3.51 The rights of paternity and integrity (see paras 3.35–3.43) subsist as long as copyright in the works in question, as does the artist's resale right (para 3.44). The right to prevent false attributions (see further para 3.47) subsists until 20 years after the author's or director's death.[165] This creates the curious possibility of false attribution being lawful 20 years and one day after the death of the author or the director. In these respects, UK moral rights are weaker than those of some other countries, such as France, where they are of indefinite duration.

Computer-generated works

3.52 Where a literary, dramatic, musical, or artistic work is computer-generated (see para 3.22), the copyright expires at the end of the period of 50 years from the end of the calendar year in which the work was made,[166] as there is no reason to attach the work to the lifetime of any particular person.

Anonymous and pseudonymous works

3.53 Anonymity and pseudonymity (see paras 3.23 and 3.24) affect only the period for which the copyright endures. The copyright continues until the end of the 70-year period following the end of the calendar year in which either (1) the work was made, or (2) the work was first made available to the public.[167] But if the identity of the author becomes known before the end of those periods, then the usual period of that person's lifetime plus 70 years applies.[168] Literary, dramatic, and musical works are made available to the public by performance in public or by being communicated to the public, although this definition does not exhaust the possible ways in which such works are made available to the public.[169] In the case of an artistic work, making available to the public includes exhibition in public, showing in public

---

[163] CDPA 1988, Sch 1, para 12.   [164] CDPA 1988, s 301 and Sch 6.   [165] CDPA 1988, s 86.
[166] CDPA 1988, s 12(7).   [167] CDPA 1988, s 12(3).   [168] CDPA 1988, s 12(4).   [169] CDPA 1988, s 12(5)(a).

a film including the work, and communication to the public.[170] No account is taken, however, of any unauthorised act.[171]

A person is copying and collecting with a view to publication the verses engraved on tombstones in local churchyards, most of which appear to have been erected in the 19th or early 20th centuries. The verses are otherwise unpublished and of unknown authorship. What steps should the collector take to avoid any danger of being sued for copyright infringement?

Works of joint authorship

3.54   The term of copyright for a work of joint authorship (see paras 3.7–3.14) is determined by reference, where appropriate, to the date of death of the author who died last.[172] Copyright in the jointly authored work will therefore expire 70 years from the end of the calendar year in which there occurred the death of the author who died last of the group of joint authors. Where the identity of one or more of the authors is known, and the identity of one or more is not, copyright expires 70 years from the end of the calendar year in which died the last of the authors whose identity is known.[173]

Question

When will the copyright in this book expire? How do the relevant rules affect moral rights?

Term of Crown copyright in literary, dramatic, musical, and artistic works

3.55   Where the monarch is entitled to the copyright in a literary, dramatic, musical, or artistic work, it subsists until the end of the period of 125 years from the end of the calendar year in which the work was made or, if the work is published commercially before the end of the period of 75 years from the end of the calendar year in which it was made, until the end of the period of 50 years from the end of the calendar year in which it was first so published.[174] The 125-year period is therefore a maximum which may be shortened by commercial publication during the first 75 years after the work is made. Commercial publication consists in issuing copies of the work to the public at a time when copies made in advance of the receipt of orders are generally available to the public, or when the work is made available to the public by means of an electronic retrieval system.[175] Crown copyright in sound recordings and films is of the same duration as for other owners.

Why is Crown copyright in literary, dramatic, musical, and artistic works not subject to the usual rules on duration?

---

[170] CDPA 1988, s 12(5)(b).   [171] CDPA 1988, s 12(5) proviso.   [172] CDPA 1988, s 12(8)(a)(i).
[173] CDPA 1988, s 12(8)(a)(ii).   [174] CDPA 1988, s 163(3).   [175] CDPA 1988, s 175(2).

Crown copyright in Acts and Measures

3.56   The Crown copyright in Acts of Parliament, the Scottish Parliament, and the Welsh and Northern Ireland Assemblies, and Measures of the General Synod of the Church of England subsists from Royal Assent until the end of the period of 50 years from the end of the calendar year in which Royal Assent was given.[176]

Term of parliamentary copyright

3.57   Copyright in literary, dramatic, musical, or artistic works made by or under the direction or control of the Houses of Parliament subsists until the end of the period of 50 years from the end of the calendar year in which the work was made.[177] Where copyright has subsisted in a parliamentary Bill, it ceases when the Bill receives the Royal Assent or is withdrawn or rejected or at the end of the parliamentary session.[178] There are similar provisions for Bills of the Scottish Parliament and the Northern Ireland and Welsh Assemblies.[179] If a Bill is rejected by the House of Lords but may be presented for Royal Assent by virtue of the Parliament Acts 1911 and 1949, copyright will continue to subsist in it notwithstanding the Lords' rejection.[180]

Films

3.58   Film copyright expires at the end of the period of 70 years from the end of the calendar year in which the death occurs of the last to die of (1) the principal director, (2) the screenplay author, (3) the dialogue author, or (4) the composer of music specially created for and used in the film.

If the identity of one or more of these persons is unknown, but the identity of another is not, the relevant death date is that of the last whose identity is known. If the identity of none of these persons is known, the film copyright subsists as follows:

(1)   until the end of the 70-year period from the end of the calendar year in which the work is first made; or

(2)   if, during period (1) it is made available to the public by being shown in or communicated to the public, 70 years from the end of the calendar year in which it is first so made available.[181]

In determining whether a film has been made available to the public, no account is taken of any unauthorised act.[182] Finally, if there is no principal director, screenplay or dialogue author, or composer of music specially for the film, copyright expires at the end of 50 years from the end of the calendar year in which the film was made.[183]

 Question

Remind yourself of who is to be treated as the author of a film (para 3.17). Are there any anomalies when you compare these rules with the rules about the duration of film copyright?

---

[176] CDPA 1988, s 164(2).   [177] CDPA 1988, s 165(3).   [178] CDPA 1988, s 166(5).
[179] CDPA 1988, ss 166A(2), 166B(2), 166C(2), and 166D(2).   [180] CDPA 1988, s 166(5) proviso.
[181] CDPA 1988, s 13B(2)–(4).   [182] CDPA 1988, s 13B(6) proviso.   [183] CDPA 1988, s 13B(9).

Sound recordings

3.59   The copyright in a sound recording subsists:

(1) until the end of the 50-year period from the end of the calendar year in which the work is first made; or

(2) if it is published before the end of period (1), 50 years from the end of the calendar year in which it is first published; or

(3) if, during period (1) it is not published but is made available to the public by being played in or communicated to the public, 50 years from the end of the calendar year in which it is first so made available.[184]

See Diagram 3.3.

Diagram 3.3 50 years table

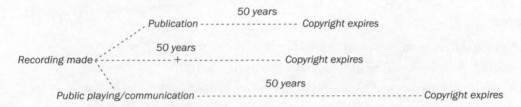

In determining whether a sound recording has been published, played in, or communicated to the public, no account is taken of any unauthorised act.[185]

In July 2008 the European Commission published a proposal for a Directive to extend the term for sound recordings from 50 to 95 years.[186] The primary incentive behind this proposal was to improve the position of performers (see paras 6.33 and 6.42), although it faced strong opposition from academics who questioned the potential for benefit to performers.[187] Although the UK was originally against any term extension,[188] it later became a strong supporter.[189] The proposal led to Directive 2011/77/EU, adopted on the 12 September 2011, which extends the term of protection for sound recordings from 50 years to 70 years and must be implemented into UK law by 1 November 2013.

Broadcasts

3.60   Copyright in a broadcast expires 50 years from the end of the year in which the broadcast is made.[190] Copyright in a repeat broadcast expires at the same time as the copyright in the original broadcast.[191]

---

[184] CDPA 1988, s 13A(2).   [185] CDPA 1988, s 13A(2) proviso.

[186] The proposal is accessible at http://eur-lex.europa.eu/LexUriServ/LexUriServ.do?uri=COM:2008:0464:FIN:EN:PDF. See further paras 7.5 and 7.43–7.47.

[187] Centre for Intellectual Property Policy & Management, Centre for Intellectual Property and Information Law, Institute for Information Law & Max Planck Institute for Intellectual Property, Competition and Tax Law, 'The Proposed Directive for a Copyright Term Extension—A Backward-Looking Package', Letter to the Commission (27 October 2008); N Helfberger et al, 'Never forever: why extending the term of protection for sound recordings is a bad idea' [2008] EIPR 174.

[188] *Gowers Review of Intellectual Property*, para 4.33 and the Government's reply to the Committee in Media Culture and Sport Report (Cmnd 718).

[189] Speech by Andy Burnham at Creator's Conference, 11 December 2008 (http://webarchive.nationalarchives.gov.uk/+/http://www.culture.gov.uk/reference_library/minister_Speeches/5685.aspx).

[190] CDPA 1988, s 14(2).   [191] CDPA 1988, s 14(5). See para 2.95 for copyright in repeats.

Published editions

3.61   The publisher's copyright in the typographical arrangement of published editions of literary, dramatic, and musical works expires 25 years from the end of the calendar year in which the edition was first published.[192]

 Discussion point   For answer guidance visit www.oxfordtextbooks.co.uk/orc/waelde3e/

Why is the publisher's copyright in its typographical arrangement so much shorter than other copyrights?

Further reading

Books

L Bently and B Sherman, *Intellectual Property Law* (3rd edn, 2009), Chs 5, 7, 10, 13.7

Copinger & Skone James on Copyright (16th edn, 2010), Chs 4, 6, 11, 20

WR Cornish, D Llewelyn, and T Aplin, *Intellectual Property* (7th edn, 2010), Chs 11.6, 12.6, 13.1

Laddie, Prescott & Vitoria on the Modern Law of Copyright (4th edn, 2011), Chs 10, 10A, 13, 21

Authorship

L Zemer, *The Idea of Authorship in Copyright* (2007)

Employment and universities

A Monotti with S Ricketson, *Universities and Intellectual Property: Ownership and Exploitation* (2003)

Moral rights

E Adeney, *The Moral Rights of Authors and Performers: An International and Comparative Analysis* (2006)

FW Grosheide, 'Moral rights' in E Derclaye (ed), *Research Handbook on the Future of EU Copyright* (2009), Ch 10

Articles

Authorship and ownership

R Arnold, 'Reflections on "The Triumph of Music": copyrights and performers' rights in music' [2010] IPQ 153

WR Cornish, 'Conserving culture and copyright: a partial history' (2009) 13 Edinburgh Law Review 8

HL MacQueen, 'The legal definition of authorship and the scrolls' in JJ Collins and TH Lim (eds), *Oxford Handbook of the Dead Sea Scrolls* (2010)

J Phillips, 'Authorship, ownership, wikiship: copyright in the twenty-first century' (2008) 3 JIPLP 788

J Pila, 'Who owns the intellectual property rights in academic work?' [2010] EIPR 609

D Vaver, 'Copyright in legal documents' (1993) 31 Osgoode Hall Law Journal 661

[192] CDPA 1988, s 15.

Crown copyright

S Saxby, 'Crown copyright regulation in the UK—is the debate still alive?' (2005) 13(3) IJL & IT 299

Parliamentary copyright

N Cox, 'Copyright in statutes, regulations and judicial decisions in common law jurisdictions: public ownership or commercial enterprise?' (2006) 27(3) Statute Law Review 185

Artists' resale rights

J Merryman, 'The proposed generalization of the droit de suite in the European Communities' [1997] IPQ 16

S Stokes, 'Droit de suite: an artistic stroke of genius? A critical exploration of the European Directive and its resultant effects' [2012] EIPR 305

Term

N Helfberger et al, 'Never forever: why extending the term of protection for sound recordings is a bad idea' [2008] EIPR 174

Copyright 3: economic rights and infringement

Introduction

Scope and overview of chapter

4.1 This chapter considers the rights which the owner of copyright enjoys while the copyright endures, apart from the moral rights discussed in the previous chapter. The rights to be considered here are usually known as '*economic rights*', because, unlike the moral rights, they may be exploited by transferring them to others or licensing others to use them for a price. The basic scheme of the Copyright, Designs and Patents Act 1988 (CDPA 1988) is to define a group of what it calls '*acts restricted by copyright*'. This concept has two functions:

- one is to define those acts by others in relation to the copyright work which the right holder can challenge and stop by *court action*;
- the other is to tell persons who wish to use works the copyright in which is owned by another whether or not that use requires the permission of the right holder. In other words, the restricted acts define the ground on which right holder and would-be user will *negotiate the terms and conditions* on which the use will be permitted.

An important point of which we need to remind ourselves constantly is that in practical terms copyright is useless to its owner unless others want to perform the various restricted acts, whereupon it becomes the basis upon which a bargain may be struck between the two sides. It may be that the owner has no wish to bargain, and expressly or impliedly gives carte blanche to users. On the other hand, the owner who does not wish to bargain may simply want to prevent anyone else from disseminating the work, in which case the would-be user's remedy, if any, lies in competition law (for which, see Chapter 21).

4.2
Learning objectives

By the end of this chapter you should be able to describe and explain:

- the general nature of the economic rights conferred by copyright upon its owners;
- the distinction between moral and economic rights;
- the specific economic rights (to make copies, issue copies to the public; rent or lend commercially to the public; perform, show or play in public; communication to the public; make adaptations).

4.3   The chapter opens with a general discussion of the rights flowing from ownership of copyright and the international framework which underpins them, noting in particular the influence upon UK law of a number of EU Directives. The chapter next elaborates upon what distinguishes economic from moral rights, before turning to the detailed rules on the former category in the CDPA 1988. So the rest of the chapter looks like this:

- International background (4.4–4.9)
- Economic rights in general (4.10–4.12)
- Economic rights and primary infringements: general principles (4.13–4 ??)
- Restricted acts and primary infringement: detail (4.23–4.67)
- Authorisation of infringement (4.68–4.75)
- Secondary infringement of copyright (4.76–4.78)

International background

Berne Convention

4.4   In addition to the non-transferable moral rights discussed in the previous chapter (paras 3.31–3.46), the Berne Convention recognises *transferable economic rights* enabling copyright owners to control the following activities in relation to their works:

- translation (Art 8);
- reproduction (Arts 9, 14);
- public performance and communication of dramatic and musical works (Arts 11, 11*ter*, 14);
- broadcasting (Art 11*bis*);
- adaptation (Art 12).

4.5   Economic rights are so known because it is essentially through these rights that copyright can become a source of income for its owner, by selling them or licensing others to perform the acts restricted by the rights. Moral rights, on the other hand, cannot be transferred to persons other than the author of the work, and are essentially linked to the author's interests in the work as an expression of an individual's personality. Resale rights admittedly occupy something of a middle ground between the economic and moral rights, in that through them the author earns an income; but this is entirely contingent on the activities of others over which the author has no control.

 Question

How may economic and moral rights be distinguished?

TRIPS and WCT

4.6   Modern international activity has, unsurprisingly, focused almost entirely on economic rights, and the TRIPS Agreement of 1994 expressly states that its members have no rights or obligations under

Article 6*bis* of Berne,[1] that is, the moral rights Article. TRIPS did require members to provide commercial rental rights in respect of 'at least' computer programs and films,[2] and this was also laid down in the WIPO Copyright Treaty of 1996 (WCT).[3] The Treaty further provided for a *distribution, or first sale, right*[4] and a *public communication right*. This was to be without prejudice to the relevant provisions of Berne.[5]

Rome Convention, TRIPS, and WPPT

4.7   Economic rights in neighbouring or media works were initially dealt with in the Rome Convention, which enables producers of phonograms (sound recordings) to authorise or prohibit direct or indirect reproduction of their products.[6] Broadcasters have likewise the right to authorise or prohibit re-broadcasting, fixation, reproduction of fixations in certain circumstances, and public communication, again in certain circumstances, of broadcasts.[7] TRIPS and the WIPO Performances and Phonograms Treaty 1996 (WPPT) restated these minimum rights for phonogram producers,[8] while the WPPT added distribution, commercial rental and 'making available to the public' rights.[9]

EU Directives

4.8   The following EU Directives contain provisions relevant to copyright ownership economic rights:

- Software Directive 2009 (Art 4);[10]
- Rental and Lending Right Directive 2006;[11]
- Satellite Broadcasting Directive 1993;
- Database Directive 1996 (Art 5);
- Information Society (InfoSoc) Directive 2001 (Arts 2–4).

Essentially these implement in Europe the policies also apparent in the development of the international instruments described in the previous two paragraphs (paras 4.6–4.7), requiring member states to have distribution, rental, and public communication rights. All made necessary significant changes to the UK CDPA 1988, as will emerge from the account of UK law later in this chapter.

4.9   A specifically European initiative is the inclusion of temporary or transient reproduction as an act restricted by copyright, which as yet has not been agreed at the global level. Attempts to include a provision of this kind in the WCT 1996 failed. First introduced in the EU in respect of software, so that copyright owners could regulate the use of programs in computers,[12] it was extended next to databases,[13] and now covers all author works, phonograms, films, and broadcasts.[14] But the UK did not have to make any change here, as the concept of infringement by transient copying had already been introduced in the 1988 Act.[15] See further at para 4.36.

---

[1] TRIPS, Art 9(2).   [2] TRIPS, Art 11.   [3] WCT, Art 7.   [4] WCT, Art 6.
[5] WCT, Art 8, referring to Berne Convention, Arts 11, 11*ter*, and 14—see para 4.4.   [6] Rome Convention, Art 10.
[7] Rome Convention, Art 13.   [8] TRIPS, Art 14(2), (3); WPPT, Art 11.   [9] WPPT, Arts 12–14.
[10] Directive 2009/24/EC amended and consolidated Directive 91/250/EEC.
[11] Directive 2006/115/EC consolidated and replaced Directive 92/100/EEC.   [12] Software Directive 2009, Art 4(1).
[13] Database Directive 1996, Art 5(a).   [14] InfoSoc Directive, Art 2.   [15] CDPA 1988, s 17(6).

Key points on international background

- The Berne Convention recognises two groups of rights:
  - the economic (basis on which copyright can be used to make money)
  - the moral (recognition of author's personality claims)
- The Berne Convention has been supplemented with respect to media works by the Rome Convention
- The economic rights have been the subject of most international activity in modern times, through TRIPS, the WCT, and the WPPT
- Much of this more recent international activity has been concerned with new technology subject matter such as computer programs and databases, and new rights such as the rental right
- Within the EU, the developing global framework has been reflected and sometimes led by initiatives embodied in Directives aimed at harmonising the laws of the member states

Economic rights in general

Primary restricted acts

4.10 There are six major exclusive economic rights arising from ownership of the copyright in any protected work. The restricted acts for which a licence must be sought if they are to be lawfully carried out by a person other than the copyright owner may be listed as follows:[16]

- copying (reproduction right);
- issuing copies of the work to the public (first sale or distribution right);
- renting or lending the work to the public (rental/lending right);
- performing, showing or playing the work in public (public performance right);
- communicating the work to the public (public communication right);
- making an adaptation of the work (adaptation right).

4.11 The restricted acts may be described as *methods of reproducing the work*. Defining their scope is important for the copyright owner in two main ways: first, in determining the areas in which generally his licence must be sought by others wishing to use the work and, secondly, in deciding when action may be taken in respect of infringement of copyright. In addition, a person who without right to do so *authorises* another to do any of the restricted acts is himself an infringer as well.[17]

 Question

List the ways in which copyright in a work may be infringed.

---

[16] CDPA 1988, s 16(1).   [17] CDPA 1988, s 16(2).

Secondary infringement

4.12   In addition, *dealing in infringing copies* of a work—for example, selling, importing or exporting copies made without the licence of the copyright owner—may also be an infringement of copyright. This type of infringement is termed *secondary infringement*, the contrast being with the *primary infringements* constituted by the six restricted acts listed previously.[18] It is unlikely that a copyright owner will grant licences to deal in infringing copies, and the nature of the infringement is distinct in various other ways, in particular in requiring that the infringer should know or have reason to believe that he was dealing in infringing copies. There is nothing comparable in respect of the primary infringements, as unauthorised performances of the restricted acts will henceforth be called. With these, liability is strict and not dependent on the knowledge or fault of the infringer.

 Question

What is the difference between primary and secondary infringement of copyright?

Economic rights and primary infringements: general principles

4.13   In this section the economic rights as defined by UK law are discussed in more detail. The principal focus is on the six restricted acts and infringing authorisation thereof, with secondary infringement given relatively brief treatment after that. The restricted acts will be considered mainly in the context of infringement of copyright (ie the primary infringements), leaving the question of exploitation by transfer and, in particular, licensing to the chapter on exploitation of intellectual property in general (Chapter 22).

4.14   The six restricted acts each attract their own law, which will be set out in detail later. But there are some concepts which are applicable to each of them, and which need to be discussed first.

General principles: (1) taking of the whole or a substantial part

Substantial part: quality of what is copied

4.15   In general and subject to some exceptions, it is not necessary that the whole of the copyright work should be taken by the infringer. Infringement may be constituted as much by the doing of an act in relation to a substantial part of a work as by the doing of such acts in relation to the whole of the work.[19] It is also specifically provided that copying in relation to a film or broadcast includes making a photograph of the whole or any substantial part of any image forming part of the work.[20] It follows that if what is done is in relation to an insubstantial part of a work there is no infringement.[21] The question of what constitutes a substantial part of a work 'depends much more on the quality than on the quantity of what he has taken';[22] hence, an extract of some 20 bars lasting about

---

[18] See CDPA 1988, ss 22–26, headed 'Secondary infringement of copyright'.   [19] CDPA 1988, s 16(3)(a).
[20] CDPA 1988, s 17(4); see *Spelling Goldberg v BPC Publishing* [1981] RPC 280 (CA).
[21] *Warwick Film Productions Ltd v Eisinger* [1969] 1 Ch 508.
[22] *Ladbroke (Football) Ltd v William Hill (Football) Ltd* [1964] 1 WLR 273 per Lord Reid at 276.

50 seconds from a musical work which took about four minutes to play was held to be a substantial part because it constituted that section which would ensure recognition of the work by the public.[23] But to be a substantial part the section taken does not have to be a copyright work in its own right: in arguments about infringement, the issue is not whether the component taken would have copyright in its own right, but rather whether that component is a substantial part of a larger, copyright, work.[24]

4.16   The emphasis on quality rather than quantity of taking does not mean that the latter has always been irrelevant, however.[25] There is some authority to the effect that separate acts of copying of what are in themselves insubstantial parts may be taken as a whole to constitute substantial taking, either as acts in relation to a serial work, such as a newspaper treated as a single copyright work, or as simply a single act spread over time.[26] Substantiality has also been tested by looking at what was the matter of consequence to users of the original work.[27]

■ Ludlow Music Inc v Robbie Williams [2001] FSR 19

In 1961 Woody Guthrie composed a song called 'New York Town', containing the line, 'Every good man gets a little hard luck sometimes'. LM owned the copyright in this work. In 1973 Loudon Wainwright III composed a parody of Guthrie's song, entitled 'I Am The Way (New York Town)', obtaining LM's permission to do so and later assigning the copyright in the parody to LM. The fourth verse of the parody consisted of the line 'Every Son of God gets a little hard luck sometime', repeated three times and followed by 'Especially when he goes around saying he's the way'. In 1998 RW composed and recorded a song entitled 'Jesus in a Camper Van', containing the lines 'I suppose the Son of God/Gets it hard sometimes/Especially when he goes round/Saying I am the way'. This was repeated, then the first two lines were repeated twice. The Wainwright parody was brought to RW's attention, but copyright negotiations between him and RW were unsuccessful.

LM sued RW for infringement. It was held that 'Jesus in a Camper Van' took its central idea, that the Son of God attracted bad luck by going around saying 'I am the way', from 'I Am The Way (New York Town)', and this was sufficiently substantial copying to be infringement.

 Discussion point   For answer guidance visit www.oxfordtextbooks.co.uk/orc/waelde3e/

Does this case go too far in its use of the concept of 'copying of a substantial part' towards protecting the idea rather than the expression of a work?

4.17   On the other hand, where the taking is only of the idea rather than the substance of the work, there is no infringement.[28] Similarly there is no protection for what is merely the style or technique with which a work is created.

---

[23] *Hawkes & Son Ltd v Paramount Film Services* [1934] Ch 593 (CA).

[24] *Ladbroke (Football) Ltd v William Hill (Football) Ltd* [1964] 1 WLR 273 per Lord Reid at 276; to like effect, Lord Hodson at 285, Lord Devlin at 290 and Lord Pearce at 293. The context is the component parts of a football pools coupon. See also *Law Society of Upper Canada v CCH Canadian Ltd* [2004] 1 SCR 339.

[25] *Sillitoe v McGraw Hill Book Co* [1983] FSR 545.

[26] *Cate v Devon and Exeter Constitutional Newspaper Co* (1889) 40 Ch D 500; *Electronic Techniques (Anglia) Ltd v Critchley Components Ltd* [1997] FSR 401. See also the provisions for such infringement of the *sui generis* database right (paras 6.15–6.16).

[27] *Express Newspapers v Liverpool Daily Post and Echo* [1985] FSR 306 per Whitford J at 311.

[28] *Williamson Music Ltd v Pearson Partnership Ltd* [1987] FSR 97.

■ *Norowzian v Arks Ltd (No 2)* [1999] FSR 79 (Rattee J) ChD; [2000] FSR 363 (CA)

A film entitled *Joy* showed a man dancing to music and produced its principal effects through the technique of 'jump cutting', 'whereby the editor excises pieces of the original film within a sequence of movements by the actor, with the result that on the edited version of the film he appears to have performed successively, without an interval, two movements that in reality could not have immediately succeeded each other . . . This gives the finished film . . . a surreal effect' (per Rattee J at 81). The allegedly infringing film was an advertisement for Guinness called *Anticipation* which used the same technique in showing a man dancing while waiting for his newly poured pint of Guinness to settle. It was held that that *Anticipation* did not infringe *Joy*. Although there was a striking similarity of style and technique, no copyright subsisted in these elements. A choreographer also gave evidence that there was no particular similarity in the dance movements of the two films.[29]

Substantial part: quality that gives the copied part its originality

4.18   Recent case law from both the UK and EU has clarified that originality of the copied part is the main test to be applied. In *Nova Productions Ltd v Mazooma Games Ltd*, Jacob LJ emphasised that a finding that there had been some copying of an earlier work was 'a starting point for a finding of infringement, not the end point'. If the copying is of 'small, unimportant details', rather than of a substantial part of the earlier work, there is no infringement.[30] The House of Lords has held that generally the role played by the component in the allegedly infringing work is irrelevant, and that substantiality is related to the qualities that give the copied work its originality, or to the skill and labour involved.

■ *Designers Guild Ltd v Russell Williams (Textiles) Ltd* [2001] FSR 11 (HL)

DGL sued RWT for infringement of the copyright in its *Ixia* fabric design by the latter's *Marguerite* design.[31] The trial judge found that *Marguerite* had been copied from *Ixia*, and that the copying had been of a substantial part. The Court of Appeal, although unable to overturn the judge's finding of fact that there had been copying, reversed his decision on the basis that there had been no copying of a substantial part: the designs were not similar enough. The House of Lords agreed that the approach of the Court of Appeal had been wrong, and that in general the question of substantiality had to be tested only in relation to the copyright work, not the allegedly infringing work. The similarity or otherwise of the two designs, while relevant to the basic question of copying, was irrelevant to substantiality. Lord Hoffmann said:

> Generally speaking, in cases of artistic copyright, the more abstract and simple the copied idea, the less likely it is to constitute a substantial part. Originality, in the sense of the contribution of the author's skill and labour, tends to lie in the detail with which the basic idea is presented. Copyright law protects foxes better than hedgehogs (para 26).[32]

Lord Scott of Foscote distinguished between cases where an identifiable part of the whole of a work, but not the whole, had been copied, and those of what he called 'altered copying', where the copying relates to the whole of a work but has not been exact but rather with modifications. He proposed that in such cases, of which the present was one, the test of substantiality should be whether the infringer had incorporated a substantial part of the independent skill and labour contributed by the original author

---

[29] See further A Barron, 'The legal properties of film' (2004) 67 MLR 177.

[30] *Nova Productions Ltd v Mazooma Games Ltd* [2007] RPC 25 (CA) at para 26.

[31] The competing designs in the case are illustrated in colour at [2000] FSR 121 at 136 and 137.

[32] 'The fox knows many things, but the hedgehog knows one big thing' (Archilocus, 7th-century BCE Greek poet). See also Isaiah Berlin, *The Hedgehog and the Fox: An Essay on Tolstoy's View of History* (1953). See further *L Woolley Jewellers Ltd v A & A Jewellery Ltd* [2003] FSR 15 per Arden LJ at 259–260.

in creating the copyright work, and that for these purposes a comparison between the two designs was legitimate, albeit that once there had been found to be copying in such cases, it was almost inevitable that it would be found to be of a substantial part as well. Lord Millett criticised Lord Scott's distinction and emphasised the irrelevance of the copied design to the issue of substantiality. Lords Bingham of Cornhill and Hope of Craighead expressed no view other than that the Court of Appeal had illegitimately taken to itself the role of the trial judge in re-deciding the issue of substantiality.[33]

Discussion point For answer guidance visit www.oxfordtextbooks.co.uk/orc/waelde3e/

What does the *Designers Guild* case tell us about the meaning of substantiality in relation to infringement? What else may be learned from the cases described in the next two paragraphs?

4.19   The House of Lords also appeared to accept the relevance of the copyright owner's skill and labour to substantiality in the later case of:

■ Newspaper Licensing Agency Ltd v Marks and Spencer plc [2003] 1 AC 551

For the facts, see para 2.96. The question was, given that the typographical arrangement copyright in a newspaper applied only to the whole newspaper, and not to individual articles within the newspaper, whether the copying of an article from the newspaper was copying of a substantial part of the newspaper's typographical arrangement. The House of Lords held that it was not. In general, the quality relevant for the purposes of substantiality was the originality of, or skill and labour in, what had been copied. In typographical arrangement copyright as applied to newspapers, what mattered was the overall appearance of the newspaper, and Lord Hoffmann, giving the only reasoned speech, found it 'difficult to think of the skill and labour which has gone into the typographical arrangement of a newspaper being expressed in anything less than a full page' (para 23).

4.20   The provision on 'substantial part' in section 16(3) of the CDPA 1988 must be construed in conformity with the Information Society (InfoSoc) Directive. The Directive in Article 2, titled 'reproduction right', does not mention 'substantial part' but prohibits reproduction 'in whole or in part' and must be interpreted in the same way throughout the EU.[34] The meaning of 'reproduction in part' has been considered by the Court of Justice of the European Union (CJEU).

■ Case C-5/08 Infopaq International A/S v Danske Dagblades Forening [2009] ECDR 16

The case concerned an electronic newspaper-cuttings firm which undertook a complex process of searching, scanning and printing for the material which it then distributed to its customers. The Court of Justice (ECJ) held that this data capture process, consisting in the particular case of storing an extract of a copyrighted work amounting to 11 words and subsequently printing it, amounted to 'reproduction in part' if the elements reproduced were an expression of the intellectual creation of their author. The Court emphasised that Article 2 had to be given a broad interpretation and stated:

> As regards the parts of a work, it should be borne in mind that there is nothing in Directive 2001/29 or any other relevant Directive indicating that those parts are to be treated any differently from the work as a whole. It follows

---

[33] For discussion of the issues raised by this case see M Spence and T Endicott, 'Vagueness in the scope of copyright' (2005) 121 LQR 657.

[34] Case C-5/08 *Infopaq International A/S v Danske Dagblades Forening* [2009] ECDR 16, paras 27–29; Cases C-403/08 and C-429/08 *Football Association Premier League Ltd v QC Leisure, Murphy v Media Protection Services Ltd* [2012] 1 CMLR 29, para 154

that they are protected by copyright since, as such, they share the originality of the whole work...the various parts of a work thus enjoy protection under Art.2(a) of Directive 2001/29 , provided that they contain elements which are the expression of the intellectual creation of the author of the work (paras 38–39).

The UK courts, in a number of cases, have considered the implications of this judgment on the assessment of 'substantial part'. In *SAS Institute Inc v World Programming Ltd*[35] Arnold J noted that the ECJ's approach in *Infopaq* is the same as that mentioned in the House of Lords decision in *Newspaper Licensing Agency Ltd v Marks and Spencer plc* and stated:

when considering whether a substantial part has been reproduced, it is necessary to focus upon what has been reproduced and to consider whether it expresses the author's own intellectual creation. To that extent, some dissection is not merely permissible, but required. On the other hand, the Court of Justice also held...that it is necessary to consider the cumulative effect of what has been reproduced (para 243).

■ *Newspaper Licensing Agency Ltd v Meltwater Holding BV* [2010] EWHC 3099 (Ch); [2011] EWCA Civ 890 (CA) Appeal to the Supreme Court outstanding

M, a commercial online media monitoring service, monitored publishers' websites using computer programs which 'scraped' content, and recorded the position of every word in every article in an index. It then provided a monitoring report, based on the customer's search terms, of content comprising article headline, opening text and an extract from the article. N, who represented a number of newspapers, claimed infringement and argued that M required an end user licence for its customers to use its services. Proudman J, with whom the Court of Appeal agreed, found that the extracts constituted a substantial part of the article and the receiving and using of monitoring reports by users was infringing. In following *Infopaq*, Proudman J stated:

It therefore seems that the ECJ is saying that no distinction is to be made between the part and the whole, provided that the part contains "elements which are the expression of the intellectual creation of the author". There is no reference to "substantial part" in art.2; the ECJ makes it clear that *originality rather than substantiality is the test to be applied to the part extracted*. As a matter of principle this is now the only real test (para 69; emphasis added).

It seems to me wrong in principle to suggest that the court must conduct some sort of assessment of whether the extract is itself novel or artistically worthwhile. That would be tantamount to determining whether the extract is itself a literary work...(para 80).

In my judgment the test of quality has been re-stated but for present purposes not significantly altered by Infopaq...The effect of the Infopaq case...is that *even a very small part* of the original may be protected by copyright if it demonstrates the stamp of individuality reflective of the creation of the author or authors of the article. Whether it does so remains a question of fact and degree in each case. It is often a matter of impression whether use has been made of those features of the article which, by reason of the skill and labour employed in its production, constitute it an original copyright work (paras 81–83; emphasis added).

It is clear that the originality of the copied part is the main test to be applied in this regard. However, *Infopaq* also requires this originality to be in the sense of 'author's intellectual creation'. Whether, and how, this affects the UK's originality test of 'skill, labour and judgment' remains to be seen (see paras 2.39–2.40).

General principles: (2) doing a restricted act directly or indirectly

4.21   The doing of a restricted act is infringement whether carried out directly or indirectly.[36] In other words, it is no answer to a claim of infringement to say that the restricted act was carried out, not in relation to the original work, but to some other work which was derived from it.

---

[35] *SAS Institute Inc v World Programming Ltd* [2010] ECDR 15   [36] CDPA 1988, s 16(3)(b).

■ *King Features Syndicate Inc v Kleeman Ltd* [1941] AC 417

Copyright in drawings of Popeye the Sailorman was held to be infringed although the defendant had copied not the drawings, but the plaintiffs' licensed dolls and brooches based on these drawings.

■ *Sony Music v Easyinternetcafé Ltd* [2003] FSR 48

Internet cafes operated by E provided a CD-burning service for customers, which could include sound recordings downloaded from the Internet by the customers. Fees were payable for this service. The owners of the copyright in sound recordings sued E for copyright infringement. It was held that E was guilty of indirect infringement by copying the copies which its customers had made. It was not an involuntary copier like an Internet service provider or the recipient of a fax. It was irrelevant that the customer might be going on to use the CD for private and domestic purposes; E was in business for commercial gain.

Reverse engineering

4.22 *'Reverse engineering'* can thus be an infringement of copyright. This involves a party working back from a finished product to the copyright work which underlies it, and then evolving a work of his own. Formerly of greatest significance in the field of industrial design (see Part III), it also raises problems for the software industry, where competitive development is commonly achieved by such endeavours in relation to the embodiment of the program in a disk.[37] Often 'reverse engineering' will be carried out through a process of *'redesign'* or *'clean-room' procedure*, where the analysis of the original product and the briefing of the designers of the new one are kept rigorously apart within the organisation carrying out the work. It has been held that a defender cannot escape liability by showing that the copy was made by a third party if the third party acted in accordance with the defender's instructions;[38] but there have been successful arguments that redesign is not copying.[39] In considering whether a restricted act has been carried out indirectly, it is immaterial whether any intervening acts themselves infringe copyright, as for example might be the case in the preparation of a redesign brief.

Question

What is the difference between direct and indirect infringement? Give an example of each form of infringement.

Key points on general principles applicable to all restricted acts

- The restrictions apply whether the act in question relates to the whole of the copyright work or only part of it

- Where the act relates to only part of the copyright work, it must be a substantial part of the work to be an infringement of the copyright

---

[37] For an example see *Autodesk Inc v Dyason and Kelly* (1990) 96 ALR 57. Note, however, that 'decompilation' of a computer program in low-level language (ie the object code) is not infringement if certain conditions are met: CDPA 1988, s 50B, implementing Software Directive 1991 now in consolidated Directive 2009/24, Art 6; discussed further at para 5.44.

[38] *Solar Thomson Engineering Co Ltd v Barton* [1977] RPC 537; *Howard Clark v David Allan & Co Ltd* 1987 SLT 271.

[39] *Merlet v Mothercare* [1986] RPC 115 (CA); *Rose Plastics GmbH v Wm Beckett & Co* [1989] FSR 113.

- Substantiality depends more on the quality than on the quantity being used; how far is the author's skill and labour appropriated? Or is the part taken the expression of the intellectual creation of the author?

- A restricted act may infringe copyright whether performed directly or indirectly, via some intermediate work

Restricted acts and primary infringement: detail

4.23   We now turn to detailed discussion of each of the restricted acts, viewed primarily through the lens of infringement actions.

(1) Copying (reproduction)

4.24   Two basics need to be established in any action for infringement based on a claim of copying:

- *similarity* of the alleged infringing work with that of the copyright owner;

- *the similarity is caused by copying* the copyright owner's work.

When are two works similar?

4.25   The starting point is the similarity of two works. In many of the most important instances of infringement, this is not a problem. The development of modern copying technology has made the production of *exact copies* in the fields of reprography, software and other digital works, and audiovisual works, increasingly easy, and this is one of the major policy issues which copyright law has to confront. From a conceptual rather than a policy point of view, however, identifying the use of such technology as potentially infringing copying is not difficult.

Works similar but not the same

4.26   Generally, problems begin to arise when *works are similar but not the same*. It is clear from the law on substantial copying (paras 4.15–4.20) that the later work need not be identical to the earlier work in order to infringe the latter's copyright, although the limits of this, given the basic principle that copyright subsists in modes of expression rather than ideas, are uncertain. The issue is perhaps most acute where it is alleged that a work has been reproduced in a different medium from the original. Copying in relation to a literary, dramatic, musical or artistic work means reproducing the work in any material form, including storing the work in any medium by electronic means.[40] This certainly includes reproduction in the form of a record or a film,[41] as well as reproduction in a broadcast or in a computer, computer disk or on the Internet. In the case of an artistic work, a version produced by representing a two-dimensional work in three dimensions is a reproduction, as is a version produced by the reverse process.[42] An example illustrating the second instance might be a photograph of a work of artistic craftsmanship.[43] Not being exhaustive, these statutory definitions are but particular instances showing the general principle that the reproduction need not be in the same form as the original to

---

[40] CDPA 1988, s 17(2).   [41] As was specifically provided in s 48 of the 1956 Act.   [42] CDPA 1988, s 17(3).
[43] If not situated in a public place—see CDPA 1988, s 62.

be an infringement. Other examples might include a painting of a photograph.[44] However, there may be a difficulty where a literary work is translated into an artistic or quasi-artistic form: for example, the conversion of statistical data into drawings and graphs. Arguably, in the absence of express provision, reproducing the literary work is confined to reproductions which have some literary form in the sense of using words.

■ *Cuisenaire v Reed* [1963] VR 719

It was held here that coloured rods used for arithmetical calculations did not reproduce a literary work describing such rods.

■ *Brigid Foley v Ellott* [1982] RPC 433

It was held here that garments did not reproduce the words and numerals constituting a knitting guide. A reproduction of a literary work must be, according to Sir Robert Megarry V-C, 'some copy of or representation of the original' (at 434).[45]

■ *Anacon Corporation Ltd v Environmental Research Technology Ltd* [1994] FSR 659

ACL were held to have both literary and artistic copyright in electronic circuit diagrams relating to an electronic dust meter. See para 2.64 for a description of electronic circuit diagrams. ERTL produced circuit boards using information derived from ACL's boards, involving the creation of a 'net list' of all the components in ACL's circuits, and the connections between them; by feeding such lists into a computer, a new circuit diagram could be produced and a scheme for producing a printed circuit board. It was held, with regard to the artistic copyright, that ACL's claim of infringement failed, because the alleged infringement did not look like the copyright work. With regard to the literary copyright, however, the claim succeeded so far as the net lists reproduced the information which was the literary work contained in the diagram. Jacob J preferred not to decide whether the ERTL circuits themselves, 'because in relation to each of the components there is also a written or coded indication of what it is' (at 663), were also infringements.

■ *Electronic Techniques (Anglia) Ltd v Critchley Components Ltd* [1997] FSR 401

Another case about infringement of copyright electronic circuit diagrams in which Laddie J too held that they were literary works but that the defendant's taking might be insufficiently substantial to be infringement.

■ *Sandman v Panasonic UK Ltd* [1998] FSR 651

A final case on whether the copyright in electronic circuit diagrams was infringed by electronic circuits. It was held that the diagrams had both artistic and literary copyright. The artistic copyright would only be infringed if the circuit reproduced from a circuit diagram was visually similar to the latter, at least when laid out on the circuit. With regard to the literary copyright, there was no equivalent to the artistic infringement of two-dimensional by three-dimensional works, but it was possible for a circuit itself to contain the content of the literary aspects of the circuit diagram.

---

[44] See *Bauman v Fussell* [1978] RPC 485.
[45] See also *Interlego AG v Tyco Industries Inc* [1989] AC 217 per Lord Oliver at 265 (PC); also *J & S Davis (Holdings) Ltd v Wright Health Group* [1988] RPC 403 per Whitford J at 414.

Discussion point For answer guidance visit www.oxfordtextbooks.co.uk/orc/waelde3e/

How may the copyright in electronic circuit diagrams be infringed?

Causal connection between two works

4.27   It is necessary to show the causal connection of copying between two works, since there may be many other explanations for a similarity between them which do not involve infringement of the right holder's copyright: for example, mere chance, a common source, the nature of the subject matter or that the claimant copied the other party's work.[46]

■ *Purefoy v Sykes Boxall* (1955) 72 RPC 89

P produced a trade catalogue containing illustrations of its products. SB's products copied P's. SB produced a catalogue of its imitative products, and P sued for infringement of the copyright in the catalogue. It was held that these facts by themselves were not enough to establish that SB's *catalogue* was a copy, direct or indirect, of P's catalogue. SB's copying of the *products* was not indirect copying of P's catalogue. (However, other evidence showed that SB had copied certain advertisements and tables in P's catalogues; there was also indirect copying, since SB had copied certain tables from sheets prepared with P's consent by its customer, H, who had supplied them to SB.)

4.28   In general, it may be said that if two works are strikingly alike, if the claimant's work predates that of the defendant, and if the latter had access to it, then the court will be ready to infer that copying took place.[47] '[I]n most copyright cases...infringement can only be established by inference because there is no evidence of anyone being present and looking over the defendants' shoulder.'[48] But before proceeding to make that inference, the court must consider when it can be displaced by other evidence.[49] However, the more strikingly similar the two works are, the more likely the proposition that there has been copying, and as such more cogent evidence is required for a rebuttal than where the similarities are less striking, this being a matter of weighing up the evidence.[50] This is not a matter of the copyright owner shifting the evidential burden to the alleged infringer but rather of making 'a prima facie case for [him] to answer'.[51]

 Question

When will a court infer that copying has taken place?

4.29   But consider the problem confronted in a Canadian case:[52]

■ *Galerie d'Art du Petit Champlain inc v Théberge* [2002] 2 SCR 336 (Supreme Court of Canada)

T, a well-known painter, assigned to a publisher the right to publish cards, posters and other stationery products for sale to art galleries. The appellant galleries had purchased copies of these licensed

---

[46]   *Corelli v Gray* (1913) 29 TLR 570 per Sargent J at 570 (Ch D).
[47]   See *Designers Guild Ltd v Russell Williams (Textiles) Ltd* [2001] FSR 11 (HL).
[48]   *Sifam Electrical Instrument Co Ltd v Sangamo Weston Ltd* [1971] 2 All ER 1074 per Graham J at 1076.
[49]   *LB (Plastics) Ltd v Swish Products Ltd* [1979] RPC 537 per Lord Wilberforce at 621.
[50]   *Mitchell v BBC* [2011] EWPCC 42, para 25.   [51]   *Francis Day & Hunter Ltd v Bron* [1963] Ch 587 per Willmer LJ at 612.
[52]   See further S Stokes, 'Copyright and the reproduction of artistic works' [2003] EIPR 486.

products and then transferred the images on them to canvas by means of a technique for lifting the ink from the card or poster and shifting it to the canvas. The end result was to leave the original card or poster blank, so that there was no increase in the overall number of reproductions. The artist sued for infringement of copyright by reproduction. By a majority of 4:3, the Supreme Court of Canada held that there was no infringement. What the galleries had done was within their rights as the owners of the physical posters and cards. Substitution of a new backing was not reproduction, which for purposes of infringement required the production of new or further copies of the original work. In this literal, physical, mechanical *transfer* no multiplication took place. The artist was asserting moral rights in the guise of economic rights.

The dissenting minority view was that copyright protected the work, and that the work in this case included its material support. Reproduction did not have to entail the multiplication of copies, since the concept included, not just reproduction of the work, but of a substantial part of the work (see paras 4.15–4.20). This made it necessary to consider reproduction qualitatively and not just quantitatively.

 Discussion point For answer guidance visit www.oxfordtextbooks.co.uk/orc/waelde3e/

Which of the competing views in the *Théberge* case do you prefer, and why? Why is the painter's moral right claim to the integrity of his work (see paras 3.39–3.43) unlikely to be successful on these facts?

Relevance of knowledge

4.30   So far as the issue of whether or not there has been infringement is concerned, it is irrelevant that the defendant did not know or was unaware of the existence of the original work (as might be the case, for example, where he was copying from a copy of it) or of the fact that the original work had copyright. All that matters is the causal chain between the original and the derivative work and that chain may have several links. Even where the defender produces a work apparently independently it has been said that he may be liable if subconscious copying can be established by the usual tests of similarity, dating and access.[53] However, the inference that subconscious copying has taken place is one to be considered on the evidence as a whole and if subconscious copying is a proper inference to be drawn in the light of all the circumstances, then it is not a presumption to be rebutted, but is a conclusion of copying.[54]

■ *Francis Day & Hunter Ltd v Bron* [1963] Ch 587 (CA)

FDH owned the copyright in a musical work 'In a Little Spanish Town' (published in 1926 and performed in a 1955 recording by Bing Crosby), and claimed that it was infringed by the conscious or unconscious taking of its first eight bars in another work, 'Why', published by B in 1959. There was considerable similarity, but the composer (Peter de Angelis) gave evidence, accepted by the judge (Wilberforce J), that he had not consciously copied or indeed heard 'In a Little Spanish Town', and that his main musical influences were Puccini, Ravel and Debussy; if he had heard 'In a Little Spanish Town', this had probably occurred when he was young. It was held that there was no infringement, although subconscious copying was a possibility which might amount to infringement. But, 'if subconscious copying is to be found, there must be proof (or at least a strong inference) of de facto familiarity with the work alleged

---

[53] *Francis Day & Hunter Ltd v Bron* [1963] Ch 587. See also *Industrial Furnaces Ltd v Reaves* [1970] RPC 605 per Graham J at 623–624.
[54] *Mitchell v BBC* [2011] EWPCC 42, para 39.

to be copied. In the present case, on the findings of Wilberforce J, this element is conspicuously lacking' (per Willmer LJ at 613).

■ *Jones v Tower Hamlets London Borough* [2001] RPC 23

J, an architect, was instructed by ADL, a property development company, to produce plans for a housing development commissioned by THLB and to be carried out by ADL. After starting work, ADL was dismissed by THLB, which continued the development but developing its own plans. J had not been paid his fees of £219,000 by ADL and remained unpaid when ADL went into liquidation. In an action against THLB, J claimed that the 'footprint' of the houses as built on the site and some interior floor plans infringed the copyright in his plans. The claim was largely rejected save in respect of a 'wrap around' bathroom partition. Although the THLB official concerned could not remember seeing J's plan for this, it was so striking that the only possible inference was that there had been copying, J's plans having possibly remained subconsciously in the official's mind.

 Question

What is the relevance of knowledge in a question about copying?

Copying and adaptation

4.31   Adaptation of a work is a form of infringement distinct from copying, applying only to literary, dramatic and musical works.[55] Adaptation is given a restricted meaning—it covers dramatisations and translations, for example—and it is specifically provided that no inference as to what does or does not amount to copying a work should be drawn from the definition of adaptation.[56] There may well be overlap, but copying is wider in scope. However, the dividing line between what amounts to a reproduction of a work and what amounts to an adaptation of a work can be unclear.[57]

■ *Hodgson v Isaac* [2010] EWPCC 37 (PCC)

H wrote an autobiography and entered into an agreement with I to make a film based on the book. Permission to use the book was later withdrawn and H claimed infringement by adaptation but the claim also referred to reproduction. I claimed that he did not need permission as the film script was not an adaptation of the book but rather based on I's own creative input. The similar elements in the two works were 'the main characters, many of the settings and contexts in which the events take place and a good number of the incidents themselves'. Birss J noted that adaptation was a more apt description of the facts here; while these elements were not quantitatively the majority of the book and there was much more in the book than the script, this was due to the different nature of the works; nature of film scripts meant they will often have fewer incidents as the scriptwriter's skill involves distilling down the essence of a story in a book to a suitable film. The judge held that the elements reproduced were not generic but a recognisable part of the story, including incidents and their interpretations, which were a key part of what made the book an original work. The fact that such elements are presented as factual rather than fictional did not make a difference and producing an autobiography is an intellectual effort of creation. Such elements together amounted to a substantial part of the book.

---

[55] See CDPA 1988, s 21 and generally paras 4.66–4.67.   [56] CDPA 1988, s 21(4).
[57] *Hodgson v Isaac* [2010] EWPCC 37, para 21.

Ideas and impressions

4.32 Even where both works are in the same medium or form of expression, it can be difficult to determine whether one reproduces another. Reproduction must be substantial rather than exact or complete,[58] and so the substance of a work must be determined in order to judge the scope of the copyright owner's rights. In some cases this has extended well beyond expression in the simple sense of words used, to touch on the ways in which information and ideas have been arranged by the author.

■ *Harman Pictures NV v Osborne* [1967] 1 WLR 723

It was held here that similarities of incidents and situations suggested that a film screenplay by John Osborne infringed the copyright in a historical book (*The Reason Why* by Mrs Cecil Woodham Smith), even though there were also many dissimilarities between the two works and both were based upon historical events (the Charge of the Light Brigade in the Crimean War).

■ *Ravenscroft v Herbert* [1980] RPC 193

R had written *The Spear of Destiny*, a non-fiction book on an ancient spear held in the Hofburg Museum, Vienna. He had researched the provenance of the spear and identified it as the one which pierced the side of Christ at the Crucifixion, and which was later used by legendary figures, and inspired Nazi Germany. The research had combined orthodox historical methods with mystical meditation. H, who had read R's book, wrote a novel called *The Spear* about what happened to the spear after the Second World War, but the prologues to each section retold the story of the Hofburg spear from the Crucifixion onwards. It was held that while a novelist might use the facts derived from a historical work, he was not entitled to adopt the language, selection and arrangement of the latter. 'In the prologues...[H] had deliberately copied the language of the plaintiff on many occasions. To a more significant extent he has adopted wholesale the identical incidents of documented and occult history which the plaintiff used in support of his theory of the ancestry and attributes of the spear, of Hitler's obsession with it and also General Patton's. He did this in order to give his novel a backbone of truth with the least possible labour to himself. In so doing he annexed for his own purposes the skill and labour of the plaintiff to an extent which is not permissible under the law of copyright' (per Brightman J at 207).

Several other cases demonstrate that where the question is whether or not one dramatic or musical or artistic work reproduces another of the same kind, account may be taken of factors other than the similarity of the respective modes of expression. With dramatic works, the essence of the copyright may be not so much in the words used as in the characterisation and sequence of incidents and events and where that is taken there is infringement of copyright.[59] With musical works, 'infringement of copyright...is not a question of note for note comparison', but falls to be determined 'by the ear as well as by the eye'.[60]

4.33 But there are limits to how far this approach can be taken, since it can make unacceptable inroads upon the basic principle that copyright does not protect ideas and information, which are available for all to use in their own work.

■ *Bauman v Fussell* [1978] RPC 485

A photograph of two cocks fighting each other was used as the basis of a painting. The composition of the subject matter was followed closely but the painter employed different colouring to heighten the

---

[58] CDPA 1988, s 16(3)(a).   [59] *Rees v Melville* [1911–16] MCC 168.
[60] *Austin v Columbia Gramophone Co Ltd* [1917–23] MCC 398 at 409 and 415, quoted with approval by Willmer LJ in *Francis Day & Hunter Ltd v Bron* [1963] Ch 587 at 608.

dramatic effect of the representation. It was held that it was appropriate to consider the different effects of each work on the viewer in assessing whether there had been an infringement of artistic copyright (answer in this case, no).

■ *Baigent v Random House Group Ltd* [2006] EMLR 16 (Peter Smith J); aff'd [2007] FSR 24 (CA)

This case was based on a claim that the best-selling novel, *The Da Vinci Code* (DVC) by Dan Brown, infringed copyright in an earlier, non-fictional work called *The Holy Blood and the Holy Grail* (HBHG), written by B and others. The claimants relied on *Ravenscroft v Herbert*, arguing that Dan Brown had used the central theme and argument of HBHG in constructing the plot of DVC, and so infringed their copyright. The evidence showed that Dan Brown had used HBHG while working on DVC, and there was some limited textual copying. It was held that DVC did not infringe any copyright in HBHG. The central theme or argument claimed for HBHG was not made out in the book itself, but was an artificial creation put together for the purposes of raising the claim. DVC did not copy any central theme of HBHG, and the textual copying was insubstantial. While the way in which facts, themes or ideas were put together could be protected by copyright, because this was the result of the skill and labour of the author, the facts, themes and ideas in themselves were open to anyone else.

■ *Allen v Bloomsbury Publishing plc* [2010] EWHC 2560 (Ch)

A, alleged that B's *Harry Potter and the Goblet of Fire* infringed an earlier work, *Willy the Wizard*, because of the similarities in plot elements in the two works: main characters are wizards and compete in a contest; they have to work out the nature of their main task; they work this out covertly in a bathroom; they complete it using information from helpers; it involves rescuing human hostages from half-human, half-animal creatures. B sought summary judgment arguing that any similarities were of a general nature and arose purely by chance. Kitchin J noted that the similarities seemed to constitute ideas which are relatively simple and abstract and was inclined to view them as ideas rather than expressions due to their high level of generality. However, the judge refused summary judgment because while A's claim had an improbable chance of success, it was not so bad as to be described as fanciful. The merits of the case were not tested further as the case was struck out after a failure to abide by an aspect of court procedure.[61]

■ *Temple Island Collections Ltd v New English Teas Ltd* [2012] FSR 9 (PCC)

This case concerned two similar photos, by F and H, showing a London Routemaster bus in red in the foreground, on a black-and-white background of Westminster Bridge and the Houses of Parliament. Both photos had been altered using a computer program.[62] The defendants had settled a previous case of infringement based on an earlier photograph. Birss J stated that photographs, as one species of artistic work, are not to be treated differently from other artistic works and, as such, infringement is not limited only to facsimile reproductions of a photograph and in an appropriate case infringement can take place by recreating a scene which was photographed (para 31). The defendant argued that the place of the picture was where many tourists stand and it was altered using a 'bog-standard bit of software'. The judge noted that:

> What falls to be considered, in order to decide if a substantial part of an artistic work has been reproduced, are elements of the work which have visual significance. What is visually significant in an artistic work is not the skill and labour (or intellectual creative effort) which led up to the work, it is the product of that activity. The fact

---

[61] *Allen v Bloomsbury Publishing plc* [2011] EWCA Civ 943.
[62] The competing images in the case are reproduced in colour at the end of the judgment.

that the artist may have used commonplace techniques to produce his work is not the issue. What is important is that he or she has used them under the guidance of their own aesthetic sense to create the visual effect in question (para 34).

The defendant also argued that their expression of the same idea was very different, in almost every respect, than the claimant's. The judge noted that:

> I have not found this to be an easy question but I have decided that the defendants' work does reproduce a substantial part of the claimant's artistic work. In the end the issue turns on a qualitative assessment of the reproduced elements. The elements which have been reproduced are a substantial part of the claimant's work because, despite the absence of some important compositional elements, they still include the key combination of what I have called the visual contrast features with the basic composition of the scene itself. It is that combination which makes...[the claimant's]...image visually interesting. It is not just another photograph of clichéd London icons (para 63).

The judge found that while images of London landmarks are free to be used, the defendant went to elaborate lengths to produce an image in which they sought lawfully to produce an image which bore some resemblance to the claimant's image but would not infringe the copyright of the claimant. The decision is seen as an unsatisfactory application of the basic principle that copyright does not protect ideas and information.[63]

 Question

How useful is the distinction between idea and expression? How does it work in relation to, say, poetry, music or art?

Computer programs and infringement

4.34   Particular problems have arisen with copyright programs. It is clearly infringement to make an exact copy of a program.[64] More complex, however, is the situation often arising as a result of 'reverse engineering',[65] where the aim of the second party is to produce a program which can perform the same functions on the same machines as the first program (ie compatibility or interoperability). This functional similarity can be achieved with quite distinct underlying codes. Thus, the reverse engineer's product may not be an exact or literal copy of the original program, and the question which arises is how far the first programmer's copyright may be pressed in challenging such non-literal copies as infringements of a substantial part of his work. In the United States, there were controversial decisions to the effect that the 'structure, sequence and organisation', and the 'look and feel' of a program might be protected by copyright, taking account of the similarity of the results (including the appearance of screen displays) produced by running the two programs in question.[66] One interlocutory decision of the English High Court hinted at a similar approach.[67] Did this carry copyright beyond the protection of expression into the protection of ideas? As already noted (paras 4.32–4.33), copyright protection is not confined to literal copying, and can extend to sequences of ideas and effects. But the Software Directive provides

---

[63] A Rahmatian, 'Temple Island Collections v New English Teas: an incorrect decision based on the right law?' [2012] EIPR 796.

[64] Note however CDPA 1988, s 50A, implementing the Software Directive 1991, now in consolidated Directive 2009/24, Art 5(2), providing that the making of a back-up copy of a computer program necessary for the purposes of lawful use is not infringement, and may not be prevented by contract (para 5.44).   [65] For this phrase, see para 4.22.

[66] Whelan Associates Inc v Jaslow Dental Laboratory Inc 797 F 2d 1222 (3rd Cir, 1986); Apple Computer Inc v Microsoft Corp 709 F Supp 925, 717 F Supp 1428 and 759 F Supp 1444 (1989, 1991); Lotus v Paperback Software 740 F Supp 37 (1990).

[67] MS Associates v Power [1988] FSR 242.

that ideas and principles which underlie any element of a computer program, including those which underlie its interfaces, are not to be protected.[68] In the United States the very broad early approach was reined back in *Computer Associates v Altai*.[69] Instead the copyright program was analysed back from its object code to its conception, to filter out those elements which had come from the public domain or which could be expressed only in one way (the merger of idea and expression). What was then left was the core of protectable expression, which could not be copied without infringing.

The scope of infringement of software copyright by copying has continued to create unresolved difficulties for the English courts, although the US 'look and feel' test has not been adopted.

■ *John Richardson Computers Ltd v Flanders* [1993] FSR 497 (Ferris J)

F worked for JRC, first as employee, then as consultant, and had contributed to the development of JRC's program for stock control in a pharmacy. F left JRC, set up on his own and produced a stock control program which JRC challenged as an infringement of the copyright in the first program. The first program had been developed for a BBC computer, the second for an IBM-compatible one. The making of the second program had not involved any use of JRC's source code, but it allegedly followed the scheme of the first, and included specific details of its particular routines. Ferris J followed *Computer Associates v Altai* in tackling the question of what would constitute infringement. As Ferris J remarked, 'this means that consideration is not restricted to the text of the code' (at 527). In the particular case, he held that F had infringed three elements of JRC's program (the line editor, the amendment routines and the dose codes).

■ *Ibcos Computers v Barclays Mercantile* [1994] FSR 297 (Jacob J)

The reliance of Ferris J on US authority was criticised by Jacob J in this case, emphasising that the wording of the US and the UK statutes was not the same. But he agreed that testing infringement was not limited to literal copying of the source code: 'That must be right: most literary copyright works involve both literal matters (the exact words of a novel or computer program) and varying levels of abstraction (plot, more or less detailed, of a novel, general structure of a computer program). I therefore think it right to have regard in this case not only to... "literal similarities" but also to... "program structure" and "design features"' (at 302). Taking this approach to a set of facts similar to the *Richardson* case, but involving accountancy packages for agricultural dealers, Jacob J held that the second program infringed the first, involving as it did both line-by-line literal copying of certain routines and substantial copying of structural elements.

■ *Cantor Fitzgerald International v Tradition UK Ltd* [2000] RPC 95 (Pumfrey J)

This case involved two inter-dealer bond brokers, C and T. A group of C ex-employees joined T, bringing with them a program which they had designed for C. This code was loaded into T's system, and was then used by the ex-employees for reference while writing and testing a system being designed for T. Copying in producing T's system was eventually admitted, but only to the extent of 2 per cent of C's system, which T submitted was insubstantial. An additional 1.3 per cent of T's code was questionable. It was held that there had been no copying of anything not admitted to be copied. Further, a computer program's only purpose was to make a machine function in a particular way. Only at a very high level of abstraction, such as its overall structure, or the allocation of functions between different programs, might the analogy with the plot of a play or novel be helpful. Copyright protected the author's skill and labour; entirely mechanical labour, involving no skill, might be saved by copying something produced only by entirely

---

[68] Art 1(2).   [69] 982 F 2d 693 (1992).

mechanical labour. Neither system in this case had anything exceptional or unusual in its overall design, and the architectural similarities were no more than might be attributable to both being written by the same programmers. The substantiality of what had been taken had to be judged in relation to the criteria for the originality of the copied work, namely the extent to which the skill and labour of the first author had been taken.

■ *Navitaire Inc v EasyJet Airline Co Inc* [2006] RPC 3 (Pumfrey J)

EJ had taken a licence from N to use their 'OpenRes' copyright software for an online 'ticketless' airline booking system and another program ('TakeFlight') for the web user interface accompanying it. EJ moved on to another web interface and B wrote for them the code for a new booking system ('eRes'). N alleged that its 'OpenRes' copyright was infringed by 'eRes'. There was no dispute that the underlying software was different, that EJ had wanted a new system substantially indistinguishable from 'OpenRes' in respect of its user interface and that 'eRes' acted upon identical or very similar inputs and produced very similar results. N argued that there was non-textual copying, akin to that involved in copying the plot of a book, or copying of the 'business logic' of the program. It was held that there was no infringement by non-textual copying. The analogy with infringement of the copyright in a plot was inapt, because a computer program did not have a theme, events or narrative flow, but was rather a series of pre-defined operations to produce a result in response to a user's requests or commands. 'Business logic' fell within the scope of unprotectable ideas and principles.

■ *SAS Institute Inc v World Programming Ltd* [2010] ECDR 15 (Arnold J); Case C-406/10 *SAS Institute Inc v World Programming Ltd* [2012] ECDR 22 (ECJ)

S developed analytical software (SAS), which consisted of an integrated set of programs and its core component (Base SAS) allowed users to write and run application programs which were written in the SAS language. W studied the SAS manuals and functioning of SAS to create competing software (WPS) which emulated much of the functionality of SAS, that is, the same inputs would generate the same outputs as SAS. There was no suggestion that W had copied the source code of SAS. S argued that the court's decision in *Navitaire*, that it is not infringement of copyright in a computer program for a competitor to engineer a program that emulates the functionality of the first, was incorrect. In addition, S claimed that W had infringed the copyright within manuals for the program, and had breached the contract of use of a learning edition. Arnold J reiterated the decision in *Navitaire* and was not persuaded that it was incorrect. The judge concluded that it W had not infringed components of SAS but the resolution of the case depended on a number of issues of interpretation of the Software Directive. As such, several questions were referred to the Court of Justice to clarify whether copyright in computer programs protected programming language, interfaces and functions.

The Court of Justice held that the source code and the object code are forms of expression which can be protected by copyright but the ideas and principles which underlie a computer program are not protected by copyright. The Court found that neither the functionality nor the programming language and the format of data files used in a computer program constitutes a form of expression of that program and are not protected under the Directive. The Court noted that: 'to accept that the functionality of a computer program can be protected by copyright would amount to making it possible to monopolise ideas, to the detriment of technological progress and industrial development' (para 40). This interpretation is generally consistent with the approach taken in UK case law.

The Court held that a lawful user of a program could, without further authorisation, observe, study or test the functionality of a program to determine underlying ideas and principles, where he is carrying out acts covered by the licence. However, the Court also held that reproduction, in a computer program or a user manual for that program, of certain elements described in the user manual for another computer program is capable of constituting an infringement if the reproduction constitutes the expression of the intellectual creation of the author of the user manual for the computer program protected by copyright (see also para 2.54). It is up to the High Court now to apply this interpretation to the facts of the case.

> **Discussion point** For answer guidance visit www.oxfordtextbooks.co.uk/orc/waelde3e/
>
> Consider the difference of view between Jacob and Pumfrey JJ as to the analogy between a computer program and the plot of a play or novel. Which view is better, and why? Is Pumfrey J's suggested approach through linking the concepts of originality and substantiality of taking a helpful one in the context of computer programs? (see also paras 4.15–4.20)

4.35   Even where the form of expression in computer language is distinct from the first version, there may still be infringement by adaptation.[70] With regard to screen displays, a problem may be the idea that a literary work (which includes a computer program) cannot be infringed by a visual representation.[71] On the other hand, the display may have an independent artistic copyright of its own, which would be infringed by substantially similar displays.

Transient copies: computer programs, databases and the Internet

4.36   Copying in relation to any description of work includes the making of copies which are transient or are incidental to some other use of the work.[72] This again has particular significance in relation to computer programs. When a program is loaded into a computer, it is generally copied from the source into the computer's random access memory and central processing unit. This may well be transient or incidental, but is nonetheless infringement unless authorised. Similarly, in accessing a database via a computer, a user may bring up momentarily on screen copies of material contained in the work. If a substantial part is taken—and again the basic test of quality rather than quantity will be important—unauthorised access to a database will infringe its copyright. This can be readily extended to a browser on the Internet who calls up a webpage on his computer screen. Theoretically it also covers the reproduction which occurs on the various computers and servers through which the various packages comprising the webpage travel as they thread their way across the networks to the user's machine. It applies to 'data scraping', the use of programs to copy data from a website or database, whether only the information available on-screen or the code which underlies it (eg an airline company having its pricing information copied and displayed by a price comparison company's website).[73] The concept of transient reproduction also embraces activities such as proxy server caching where, by deploying appropriate software technology Internet service providers, librarians, archivists and others make and store on their own servers temporary and regularly updated copies of materials contained on other servers with the purpose of making the information more readily available to their own clients by avoiding congestion at the 'live' site. Such operations may also amount to the infringing act of storage by electronic means.[74]

On creation of small transient fragments of a work, such as those in the memory of a satellite decoder or in the buffers of a streaming service, an important question for assessing reproduction is whether it is appropriate to consider the fragments on a cumulative or rolling basis. It has been held that the rolling

---

[70] See CDPA 1988, s 21(3)(a)(i) and (4), discussed later.   [71] See para 4.26.   [72] CDPA 1988, s 17(6).
[73] See F Jennings and J Yates, 'Scrapping over data: are the data scrapers' days numbered?' (2009) 4 JIPLP 120.
[74] CDPA 1988, s 17(2).

basis is not to be applied 'where the copies relied upon are successively destroyed as an inherent part of the process'; this is because what is restricted is a 'a transient copy of a substantial part of the work' and as such 'the substantial part must be embodied in the transient copy, not a series of different transient copies which are stored one after the other in the decoder box'.[75]

■ **Cases C-403/08 and C429/08 *Football Association Premier League Ltd v QC Leisure, Murphy v Media Protection Services Ltd* [2012] 1 CMLR 29 (ECJ)**

This case concerned the reception of Premier League matches, in a pub, through foreign decoders, which included the Premier League anthem, pre-recorded films showing highlights of recent matches and various graphics (for the full facts, see para 20.68). As part of the reception, transient sequential fragments of works are created within the memory of a satellite decoder and on a television screen which are immediately effaced and replaced by the next fragments. The Court of Justice was asked whether the reproduction right extends to these fragments of works (para 153).

The Court began by emphasising that the concept of 'reproduction' is to be given an autonomous and uniform interpretation throughout the EU and various parts of a work enjoy protection provided they contain elements which are the expression of the intellectual creation of the author (see discussion on *Infopaq* at para 4.20). The Court confirmed that reproduction extends to transient fragments of works within the memory of a satellite decoder and on a television screen, if those fragments contain elements which are the author's own intellectual creation. The Court also noted that:

> the unit composed of the fragments reproduced simultaneously—and therefore existing at a given moment—should be examined in order to determine whether it contains such elements. If it does, it must be classified as partial reproduction . . . it is not relevant whether a work is reproduced by means of linear fragments which may have an ephemeral existence because they are immediately effaced in the course of a technical process (para 157).

In *ITV Broadcasting Ltd v TV Catchup Ltd*[76], which concerned reproduction of films in memory buffers of a streaming service and on TV screens, Floyd J noted that the *FAPL* decision by the Court of Justice had clarified that the rolling approach is incorrect and, as such, it should not be applied to either films or broadcasts. The judge concluded that there was reproduction of substantial part of the films in the memory buffers but not on the TV screens. It is important to note here that copying of such transient fragments can be allowed as a permitted act where it is an integral and essential part of a technological process, the sole purpose of which is to enable a transmission of the work in a network between third parties by an intermediary or a lawful use of the work and the temporary copy has no independent economic significance.[77] Otherwise, the remarkable result would be that the technical basis of the operation of the Internet itself is illegal. In fact, this exception was seen as applicable in both the *FAPL* and *ITV* decisions as well as for aspects of the data capture process in an electronic-cuttings service (see further at paras 5.14–5.17).[78]

Common source material; admittedly derivative work

4.37   Difficult questions can also arise with compilations where the same generally available information or material is conveyed in a different way; but if it is shown that in fact the second work was based on the first then it will be held to infringe copyright.

---

[75] *Football Association Premier League Ltd v QC Leisure (No 2)* [2008] EWHC 1411 (Ch) at para 227.
[76] *ITV Broadcasting Ltd v TV Catchup Ltd* [2011] EWHC 2977 (Pat).
[77] CDPA 1988, s 28A, inserted after the InfoSoc Directive 2001, Art 5(1).
[78] Case C-302/10 *Infopaq International A/S v Danske Dagblades Forening* (*Infopaq II*); see also Case C-5/08 *Infopaq International A/S v Danske Dagblades Forening* [2009] ECDR 16.

■ *Alexander v Mackenzie* (1847) 9 D 748

A, a solicitor, published a work entitled *An Analysis of the Heritable Securities and Infeftment Acts with an Appendix, containing Practical Forms of the Writs and Instruments thereby introduced.* The Acts, which had been passed in 1845, were aimed at the simplification of conveyancing, and gave general directions and descriptions of the styles to be used henceforth by conveyancers. A used industry and his knowledge as a conveyancer to produce 19 new styles. A committee of the Society of Writers to the Signet (a society of solicitors in Edinburgh) prepared and circulated amongst its membership reports on the two statutes, which also had an appendix containing a number of forms. The forms were largely based on those in A's work; A, who was a member of the committee, objected to this way of proceeding. It was held that the styles, being the creation of industry and knowledge rather than a mere reproduction of what was in the statutes, were copyright subject matter; the committee's alterations in its forms were of a trivial and unimportant nature; the committee styles were presented in the same order as A's; actual copying was acknowledged; and A's copyright was infringed.

■ *Elanco Products Ltd v Mandops (Agrochemical Specialists) Ltd* [1980] RPC 213 (CA)

EP invented, patented and marketed a weedkiller. The product was accompanied by an instruction leaflet. The information contained in this leaflet was also available by way of scientific journals. When the patent expired, M brought out a competing version of the product accompanied by an instruction leaflet very similar to that of EP. When EP challenged M, the latter produced new versions of the leaflet embodying the information but which was not so similar to EP's leaflet. EP sought an interlocutory injunction and it was held that EP had an arguable case. It appeared on the evidence that M had begun by making a simple and unauthorised copy, which M had then revised. This was not sufficient to cure the copyright infringement. It would have been different if M had researched all the other available information as well as EP's leaflet before writing their leaflet; then, even if the results had been extremely similar, there would have been no infringement.

4.38   But, on the other hand, it may be admitted that the allegedly infringing work was based upon the pursuer's work, yet, because the defender put in sufficient independent skill and labour, the result was not an infringement but a new and independent work. See, for example, the case of *Bauman v Fussell* [1978] RPC 485, described at para 4.33. Again, there may be issues about whether a product emanates from the claimant's work or from a wider source upon which both products ultimately depend.

■ *JHP Ltd v BBC Worldwide Ltd* [2008] FSR 29 (Ch D)

JHP sought an injunction to prevent further publication of *The Daleks Survival Guide*, which the BBC published in 2002 as a 'secret dossier on this deadly breed of embossed exterminators'. The book was said to be in breach of the copyright in previous books, published in the 1960s, in which JHP now claimed the rights. Though the judge found that JHP did not hold the rights claimed, he went on to consider the issue of copying and substantiality had they held the rights. Any similarities between the new book and the three original ones were held to arise from the texts all referring to material in the TV series, which existed as a published artistic concept separate from the books. In any case, even if there had been copying, the quantity was insignificant.

Parodies as reproductions

4.39   A parody of another work may or may not be an infringement of its copyright as a reproduction of a substantial part thereof. Much depends upon the extent to which the parodist has put in independent skill and labour in producing the parody. 'Parody' is therefore neither necessarily an infringement of copyright, nor an independent, substantive defence to a charge of infringement.[79] The InfoSoc Directive allowed member states to provide an exception for 'use for the purpose of caricature, parody or pastiche', but unlike French law, there is still no express provision on the subject in the UK.[80]

■ *Joy Music Ltd v Sunday Pictorial Newspapers* [1960] 2 QB 60

The *Sunday Pictorial* newspaper published an adaptation of a popular rock and roll song containing the line 'Rock-a-Billy, Rock-a-Billy, Rock-a-Billy, Rock', which became in the adaptation 'Rock-a Philip, Rock-a-Philip, Rock-a-Philip, Rock'. The newspaper was satirising the social activities of HRH The Duke of Edinburgh. The owner of the copyright in 'Rock-a-Billy' sued for copyright infringement, but it was held there was sufficient input of independent new work to mean that there was no substantial copying involved.

■ *Schweppes v Wellingtons* [1984] FSR 210

W manufactured tonic bubble bath, which they marketed in a bottle with a label very similar to that on bottles of Schweppes tonic water, but under the name 'Schlurppes'. Sued for copyright infringement, W argued that their bottle was a parody. It was held that they had nonetheless copied a substantial part of the Schweppes label.

 Discussion point For answer guidance visit www.oxfordtextbooks.co.uk/orc/waelde3e/

Why did Schweppes sue in copyright rather than passing off (for which see Chapter 17)?

■ *Ludlow Music Inc v Robbie Williams* [2001] FSR 19

For the facts and decision, see para 4.16. The case further illustrates how a parody may need the licence of the owner of the copyright in the parodied work, yet also have copyright in its own right.

 Question

When will a parody infringe the copyright of the work parodied?

Abridgements as reproductions

4.40   Abridgements have received favourable treatment in England in being held not to infringe copyright, as long as the abridger does not make excessive use of the original's mode of expression.[81] It was held that an abridgement infringed copyright, however, in a Scottish case on the subject.[82] Again, therefore, it is apparent that the question of whether or not an abridgement is an infringement depends on the

---

[79] It might be defended on the basis that it was 'fair dealing…for purposes of criticism'. See CDPA 1988, s 30(1); see perhaps *Kennard v Lewis* [1983] FSR 346 (the *SDP* case). For discussions of parody see W Landes and R Posner, *Economic Structure of Intellectual Property Law* (2003), Ch 5 ('Fair use, parody, and burlesque'); C Rütz, 'Parody: a missed opportunity?' [2004] IPQ 284; M Spence, 'Intellectual property and the problem of parody' (1998) 114 LQR 594; E Gredley and S Maniatis, 'Parody: a fatal attraction?' [1997] EIPR 339.

[80] InfoSoc Directive, Art 5(3)(k); French Intellectual Property Code L.122–5(4) ('La parodie, le pastiche et la caricature, compte tenu des lois du genre'). See for further comparative material Rütz, [2004] IPQ 284, 293–307, 313–314. See also para 7.59.

[81] See *Sillitoe v McGraw Hill* [1983] FSR 545.   [82] *Murray v McFarquhar* (1785) Mor 8309.

normal principles of copyright: how much and in what way has use been made of the original work and its mode of expression?

Copying of sound recordings, films, and broadcasts

4.41   The copyright in a sound recording, film or broadcast is infringed by copying the work.[83] This can include the copying of a substantial part of the work as well as the whole,[84] and so in relation to a film or broadcast making a photograph of the whole or any substantial part of any image forming part of the work is an infringement.[85] This would cover, for example, the enlargement of one section of an image from a film or broadcast. However, film copyright may be infringed only by 'copying of the particular recording of the film'.[86] Perhaps the most important general point to note here is that 'home copying' of such works by private individuals is infringement, without any general exception being made for private use.[87] Similarly, downloading from unlicensed music or film sites on the Internet is infringement of the copyright in the sound recordings or films in question.[88] On the other hand, it is expensive as well as exceptionally difficult if not impossible to enforce this right against individual infringers, which explains the need for several other provisions.[89]

Copying in relation to the typographical arrangement of a published edition

4.42   Copying in relation to the typographical arrangement of a published edition means making a facsimile copy of the arrangement.[90] The most important example of this is photocopying or reprography, which is therefore prima facie infringement of the publisher's right, as well as that of the author of the text.[91] The scope of the publisher's protection is, however, restricted to a certain extent by provisions on the permitted acts and on licensing.[92]

> ## Key points on copying
>
> - Copying means that there must be a causal link between two works in that one is derived from the other
>
> - Copying does not have to be intentional to be infringement
>
> - The copying does not have to be exact ('literal'). It could be of the 'substance', or of the 'look and feel', or of the 'sequence of incidents', of the original work
>
> - The copy may be transient or temporary (this is especially important for computer programs, databases, and the Internet)
>
> - A work may be derivative of another work, yet not infringe, because the second work's author has used independent skill and labour to achieve the result
>
> - A parody may or may not be treated as an infringing copy—it depends on the facts of the particular case

[83] CDPA 1988, s 17(1).   [84] CDPA 1988, s 16(3)(a).   [85] CDPA 1988, s 17(4).
[86] *Norowzian v Arks Ltd (No 1)* [1998] FSR 394. See also para 63 in *Dramatico* (note 88).
[87] Note, however, the provision for 'time-shifting' in CDPA 1988, s 70, discussed at paras 5.45–5.46.
[88] *Dramatico Entertainment Ltd & others v BSkyB & others* [2012] ECDR 14 (Ch).
[89] Eg rental right (see paras 4.49–4.52); Digital Economy Act 2010 (see para 7.53).   [90] CDPA 1988, s 17(5).
[91] See for discussion of copying in relation to typographical arrangements, *Newspaper Licensing Agency Ltd v Marks & Spencer plc* [2003] 1 AC 551, discussed at para 4.19.   [92] CDPA 1988, ss 29, 36, 38–42, 130, and 136–141.

(2) Infringement by issuing to the public copies of the work

4.43   The issue to the public of the original work or of copies of the work without the authority of the copyright owner is an infringement of the copyright.[93] *Issuing to the public* means:

> putting into circulation copies not previously put into circulation in the European Economic Area by or with the consent of the copyright owner, or putting into circulation outside the EEA copies not previously put into circulation in the EEA or elsewhere.

Specifically excluded from the definition is any *subsequent* distribution, sale, hiring, or loan of such copies, or any subsequent importation of those copies into the UK or another EEA state.[94] In other words, the owner has the right to be first to produce copies of the copyright work to be available to the public, whether in the form of books, posters, records, videos, or whatever. The right is therefore sometimes described as the right of *first sale* or of *distribution*. Only the copyright owner or his licensee can put a new reproduction of the work on the market.

■ *HRH The Prince of Wales v Associated Newspapers Ltd (No 3)* [2008] Ch 57 (CA)

The Prince of Wales kept private journals of his overseas trips, and made a small number of copies for confidential circulation amongst his friends. A newspaper obtained a copy and published extracts from the journal. It was held that the previous circulation did not amount to issuing to the public, and the newspaper had infringed copyright by unauthorised issuing to the public.

4.44   The publication right exists only as far as, or is *exhausted* by, the initial sale, however. So the second-hand bookseller does not require copyright licences in order to carry on business. Generally, of course, the author will exercise the right by the grant of a licence to a commercial publisher, because it is the latter's business to put material into public circulation. Once the publisher has put copies of the work on the market, these may be dealt with freely, and no subsequent sale or other dealing with those copies can be an infringement of copyright. Those who *subsequently* issue *other* copies of the work without consent also do not infringe under this heading, because they are not trespassing on the owner's very limited right under this *first* sale provision, although they will probably infringe on other grounds, for example by copying to make the copies they propose to put into public circulation. The scope of the definition can be best exemplified from the facts of *Infabrics Ltd v Jaytex Ltd*,[95] although it was decided under the 1956 Act.

■ *Infabrics Ltd v Jaytex Ltd* [1982] AC 1

The subject matter of the copyright was an artistic work used for the decoration of fabrics. The work was applied without a licence to shirts manufactured in Hong Kong, and the defendant, unaware of the infringement, imported these into England and sold them there. His lack of knowledge made a 'secondary' infringement claim against him impossible, and the copyright owner claimed infringement by publication, arguing that this was constituted by selling the shirts and so making the work available to the public for the first time in England, regardless of whether there had been publication elsewhere. By occasionally tortured interpretation of the 1956 Act, the House of Lords was able to reject this claim that, in effect, selling goods was a form of publication. The position under the 1988 Act is now quite clear: infringement on this ground is established only when the work has

---

[93] CDPA 1988, s 18(1), (4).

[94] CDPA 1988, s 18(2). But note the provisos to the subsection, about rental and lending rights (on which see further paras 4.49–4.52), and about parallel importing in the EEA (as to which see Chapter 20).   [95] [1982] AC 1.

not been previously issued to the public anywhere in the territories to which the 1988 Act extends, and this has been proved by the claimant. Further sales or other dealings with copies subsequent to their being first put on the market with the consent of the copyright owner are generally not to be treated as infringements under this heading, because they are to be dealt with as secondary infringements only.

Issuing

4.45   The issue must take place in the copyright territory, that is, the area to which the CDPA applies. It has been held that the time and place of issue is the time and place where reproductions were put on offer to the public rather than at the point of transfer to members of the public.[96] This might be particularly significant with regard to issuing an online database to the public, or publishing on the Internet. It might be thought that the infringement occurs at the point where the database or the relevant Internet server is located. But in *Independiente Ltd v Music Trading On-line (HK) Ltd*[97] (the CD-WOW case), where a parallel importer posted infringing copies of CDs from Hong Kong to customers in the UK who made orders by way of the supplier's website, it was held that infringement by issuing to the public took place when the goods were delivered to the customer through the post. The case was strengthened by the fact that the CD-WOW website was clearly intended to attract customers in the UK. Issuing must be understood in accordance with the EU notion of 'distribution'.

■ Case C-5/11 *Criminal proceedings against Titus Alexander Jochen Donner* (21 June 2012)

The Court of Justice gave guidance on the meaning of 'distribution to the public' (under InfoSoc Directive, Art 4). Distribution is 'characterised by a series of acts going, at the very least, from the conclusion of a contract of sale to the performance thereof by delivery to a member of the public' and, in a cross-border sale, distribution may take place in a number of Member States. As such, the right may be infringed in a number of Member States (para 26). The Court noted that: 'a trader who directs his advertising at members of the public residing in a given Member State and creates or makes available to them a specific delivery system and payment method, or allows a third party to do so, thereby enabling those members of the public to receive delivery of copies of works protected by copyright in that same Member State, makes, in the Member State where the delivery takes place, a "distribution to the public"'(para 30). In these circumstances, the trader not only bears responsibility for any act carried out by him or on his behalf but acts carried out by a third parties, such as freight forwarders, may also be attributed to him, where he specifically targeted the public of the destination and was aware of the actions of the third party.

Issuing to the public and publication

4.46   Issue of copies to the public should be kept distinct from publication, which is important for other aspects of copyright such as term and qualification for protection in the UK, and receives an independent definition.[98] A key element in the constitution of publication is that it does not include publication which is merely colourable and not intended to satisfy the reasonable requirements of the public.[99] This would not apply to the right of the owner to be the first to issue copies of his work, and so private publication for limited circulation might exhaust that right, although it might not constitute publication for

---

[96] *British Northrop Ltd v Texteam Blackburn Ltd* [1974] RPC 57.   [97] [2007] FSR 21 (Ch).   [98] CDPA 1988, s 175.
[99] CDPA 1988, s 175(5).

other purposes. Nevertheless, it is probably true to say that most acts constituting publication under the 1988 Act will also constitute issuing copies to the public.

 Question

What is the difference between 'issuing to the public' and 'publication'?

The public

4.47   The question—who are the public for these purposes?—is one on which there is no direct authority, and it may be that it should be answered in the same way as it has been in the cases concerning infringement by performing the work in public.[100] However, issue to the public should be kept distinct from the other forms of infringement, in particular performance and public communication. Finally a question raised by the *Infabrics* case (para 4.44) is now answered by the 1988 Act. Issuing a substantial part of a work to the public will constitute infringement of the copyright where copies of the work have not previously been put into circulation.[101]

Issuing to the public and transient copies

4.48   The provisions on the restricted act of 'issuing to the public' make no reference to the notion of a 'transient copy'; the copies required for the purposes of the provisions may therefore be limited to those which are non-transient. This would, for example, go beyond mere 'on demand' transmission of works. If so, it would then follow that the user who accesses material and passes it on to another is not guilty of infringement under this section as long as the transmission is electronic.

Key points about issuing to the public

- The right is to be the first to sell or otherwise distribute copies of a work to the public
- A typical example is when an author licenses a publisher to publish his book
- The right does not reach second or subsequent sales: it is *exhausted* by the first transaction

(3) Rental or lending of a work to the public

4.49   The copyright owner's right to be the first to issue copies of his work to the public (paras 4.43–4.48) generally does not preclude subsequent dealing with those copies so as to make them available to the public, for example through a public library. But since the 1988 Act and its subsequent amendment as a result of the Rental Right Directive of 1992,[102] certain forms of subsequent dealing are within the scope of the restricted acts by virtue of an express provision stating that in relation to most forms of copyright work, *rental or lending of copies to the public* is an act restricted by the copyright in the work.[103] The works to which rental and lending right do *not* apply are works of architecture in the form of a building or a model for a building, works of applied art and broadcasts.[104]

---

[100] See paras 4.53–4.59.   [101] CDPA 1988, s 16(3)(a).
[102] Council Directive 92/100/EEC, now in a consolidated version, Directive 2006/115/EC.   [103] CDPA 1988, s 18A(1).
[104] CDPA 1988, s 18A(1)(b)(i), (ii). For works of applied art, see para 8.4 and Berne Convention, Arts 2(7) and 7(4).

Discussion point   For answer guidance visit www.oxfordtextbooks.co.uk/orc/waelde3e/

Why do rental and lending rights not apply to works of architecture in the form of buildings or models for buildings, works of applied art, and broadcasts?

4.50   *Rental* is:[105]

> making a copy of a work available for use, on terms that it will or may be returned, for direct or indirect economic or commercial advantage (CDPA 1988, s 18A(2)(a)).

The typical scenario where the right applies is that of a business or other organisation which has purchased authorised copies of the works in question; in order to engage in the business of rental of these copies to customers, a licence from the copyright owner is required. The primary target behind the introduction of such rights in the late 1980s was 'home copying' of records, videos, and computer programs thought to be facilitated by rental. Licences permit control of rental outlets and libraries, while royalties to the copyright owner provide some sort of compensation for the supposedly illicit copying carried out by the outlet's customers.

 Question

How does 'rental' differ from 'issuing to the public'?

4.51   *Lending* right, an innovation of the Directive, is defined similarly to rental (para 4.50), save that the restricted act is one performed *otherwise* than for direct or indirect economic or commercial advantage, *and* is carried out through an establishment which is accessible to the public.[106] Thus, a public library's lending activities now require a copyright licence, unless the book lent is within the Public Lending Right scheme set up in 1979.[107] Libraries and archives other than public libraries which are not conducted for profit and are prescribed as such by the Secretary of State, also do not infringe copyright by lending any copy of a work.[108] But if you lend a book or DVD to a friend there is no copyright infringement, since you are not an establishment accessible to the public. The power that lending right gives to copyright owners is subject to further control inasmuch as the Secretary of State may, by Order, provide that lending to the public shall be treated as licensed by the copyright owner subject only to the payment of such reasonable royalty as may be agreed or fixed by the Copyright Tribunal.[109]

 Question

How does 'lending' differ from rental?

4.52   Neither rental nor lending covers making copies available for the purpose of performance, showing, playing, or exhibiting in public (activities subject to their own regime of rights—see further at paras 4.53–4.59), or for the purpose of on-the-spot reference use, as for example in a reference library or in the reference section of a university or college library.[110]

---

[105] CDPA 1988, s 18A(2)(a).   [106] CDPA 1988, s 18A(2)(b).
[107] CDPA 1988, s 40A. Note, however, that the library of an educational establishment is generally exempted from lending right: CDPA 1988, s 36A.
[108] CDPA 1988, s 40A. The libraries in question are prescribed by regulations made by the Secretary of State (s 37(1)(a)).
[109] CDPA 1988, s 66(1). There used to be similar provisions in respect of rental.   [110] CDPA 1988, s 18A(3).

Question

How do the provisions on lending right affect your university or college library?

Key points on rental and lending

- Both are about the right to issue products to the public, on condition that the product is returned to the issuer

- Rental involves an economic return to the party issuing the product, while lending involves no economic return

- The issuer will typically be someone who has a licence to do so from the copyright owner, rather than the copyright owner itself

---

(4) Public performance, showing, and playing

4.53   Public performance of a literary, dramatic, or musical work in public infringes its copyright.[111] *Performance* includes:

> delivery, in relation to lectures, addresses, speeches and sermons; it also includes any mode of visual or acoustic presentation, including presentation by means of a sound recording, film, or broadcast of the work (CDPA 1988, s 19(2)).

Since this definition only 'includes', other things than the activities mentioned may amount to performance. It has been suggested that the meaning of performance should be confined to performing in the sense of entertaining or instructing; otherwise it might be possible to argue, for example, that the copyright in a concert programme was infringed by the performance of the items there listed.[112] The performance need only be of a substantial part of the copyright work to infringe.[113] *Playing or showing* a sound recording, film, or broadcast in public is also an infringement of copyright.[114]

Discussion point   For answer guidance visit www.oxfordtextbooks.co.uk/orc/waelde3e/

Can an artistic work be performed, played or shown in public? Why are artistic works excluded from protection under this head?

When is a performance in public?

4.54   Public performance is a 'direct representation or performance', encompassing interpretation of the works before the public that is in direct physical contact with the actor or performer of those work[115] and

---

[111] CDPA 1988, s 19(1).

[112] See *British Broadcasting Co v Wireless League Gazette Publishing Co* [1926] Ch 433 per Astbury J at 442 for the example.

[113] CDPA 1988, s 16(3)(a).   [114] CDPA 1988, s 19(3).

[115] Such as a live presentation or performance of a work, Case C-283/10 *Circ & Variete Globus Bucureşti v Uniunea Compozitorilor şi Muzicologilor din România—Asociaţia pentru Drepturi de Autor—UCMR—ADA* (24 November 2011), para 40.

is different from 'communication to the public'[116] (see para 4.63). Most of the case law on this topic has been concerned with when a performance is in public. It is clear that the performance must be addressed to an audience before any question of infringement can arise and that it is the nature of the audience which determines whether it is in public. It is not necessary that the performance be one which the public at large may attend. The test has been well put in a Scottish case:

■ *Performing Right Society v Rangers FC Supporters Club* 1974 SC 49

At one end of the spectrum there is what has been described as the domestic situation. At the other end is the situation where the promoter invites the public to attend the performance on payment of an entrance fee. In between there is a wide range of varying situations. "Domestic" has been extended to include "semi-domestic". What is the underlying reasoning behind the exclusion of domestic or quasi-domestic performances? It is to be found in the relationship between the audience and the owner of the copyright. In a situation where a person organises a private party in his own home, or in what might reasonably be deemed to be an extension of his own home, then it seems reasonable to assume that the unauthorised publication or use of the copyright work is not rebounding to the financial disadvantage of the owner of the copyright, since the selected audience is not enjoying the work under conditions in which they would normally pay for the privilege in one form or another. A performance of the work in such circumstances would ordinarily be regarded as being in private (per Lord Justice-Clerk Wheatley at 59).

 Discussion point For answer guidance visit www.oxfordtextbooks.co.uk/orc/waelde3e/
If there is no charge to attend a performance, does that make it private? See also para 4.59.

4.55   The test is the relationship between the audience and the copyright owner. The courts have held that performances in the following places were in public:

- members' clubs (*Harms (Incorporated) Ltd v Martans Club Ltd* [1926] Ch 870; *PRS v Rangers FC Supporters Club* 1974 SC 49);

- the lounge of a hotel (*PRS v Hawthorns Hotel (Bournemouth) Ltd* [1933] Ch 855);

- a factory during working hours (*Ernest Turner Electrical Instruments v PRS* [1943] Ch 167 (CA));

- a meeting of a women's rural institute (*Jennings v Stephens* [1936] Ch 469);

- performance of musical works in a record shop by playing records over a loudspeaker system (*PRS v Harlequin Record Shops* [1979] 1 WLR 851);

- a butcher's shop (*South African Music Rights Organisation Ltd v Trust Butchers (Pty) Ltd* [1978] 1 SALR 1052).

4.56   In most of these cases, attendance at the performance was restricted to certain categories of the public only. It is also apparent that it is not relevant to consider either the size of the audience or the return, if any, received by the performer. But if the audience is unrestricted and the performer is acting for profit, the performance is clearly an infringement. It has been said that 'a performance given to any audience consisting of the persons present in a shop which the public at large are permitted, and indeed encouraged, to enter without payment or invitation, with a view to increasing the shopowner's profit,

---

[116] Cases C-403/08 and C429/08 *Football Association Premier League Ltd v QC Leisure, Murphy v Media Protection Services Ltd* [2012] 1 CMLR 29, para 201. There may, however, be overlap between CDPA 1988, s 19 and s 20 in that certain activities may fall under both, *FAPL v QC Leisure* [2012] EWHC 108 (Ch) at para 63.

can only properly be described as a performance "in public".[117] The nature of the retailer's business is unimportant in deciding whether or not performances of this type are in public.[118]

■ Brown v Mcasso Music Ltd [2005] FSR 40

B and M were joint authors of a rap song which was used in a TV commercial for two months. Subsequently M made the work available on its website for nine months, in order to advertise M's services to prospective clients. After that, the work was archived on a part of the website not intended to be accessible to the public. M had only paid B for the two months' transmission in the TV commercial. It was held that the initial nine months' use of the song on the website infringed B's joint copyright, and damages of £180 were awarded. *Obiter*, however, Fysh J thought that the website archiving was not an infringing public performance.

Discussion point For answer guidance visit www.oxfordtextbooks.co.uk/orc/waelde3e/

Is website archiving of a work any other form of restricted act?

An audience of one, or of several, but at different times?

4.57 A gathering of the audience together in one place is not a necessary condition for performance in public. It has been held in Australia that playing recorded music 'on hold' to users of mobile telephones was 'in public' even though the distribution of the material was not necessarily, or even very often, simultaneous for each member of the audience.[119] The fact that the members of the audience would be quite unaware of each other, and joining and leaving the audience at various times, would not seem to be relevant. Nor would the fact that the audience might consist of only one person at any given moment. Many such cases may now be dealt with by the public communication right (paras 4.60–4.65).

Exercise

I book a venue at the Edinburgh Festival Fringe at which I advertise that I will be giving readings from my favourite 20th-century poets, most of whose work is still in copyright. But I do not seek any copyright licences. Tickets for my show cost £10 each, but none are sold and no one comes to any of my performances, which I nonetheless resolutely give in an otherwise empty room. Have I infringed the various poets' copyrights by public performance? Would it make any difference to your answer if:

(1) one night a newspaper critic came on a complimentary ticket, but did not publish any review of the show; or

(2) if the venue provided a couple of staff to man the public entrance and operate the lighting and sound systems for the show?

Performing for one's own benefit but in public places; education

4.58 It is arguable that there is no performance in public in situations where the performer is acting essentially for personal benefit or pleasure and incidentally members of the public constitute an audience which watches or listens: for example, the members' sing-song in a club[120] or labourers playing music on a radio

---

[117] *PRS v Harlequin Record Shops* [1979] 1 WLR 851 at 858.
[118] *South African Music Rights Organisation Ltd v Trust Butchers (Pty) Ltd* [1978] 1 SALR 1052.
[119] *Telstra Corporation Ltd v Australasian Performing Right Association Ltd* (1997) 191 CLR 140 (HCA).
[120] See *PRS v Rangers FC Supporters Club* per Lord Stott at 55.

at a building site.[121] The same would seem to apply to playing a sound recording on a personal stereo which can be overheard by persons close to the wearer of the equipment. Note that performance of a literary, dramatic or musical work in the course of the activities of an educational establishment (school, college, university) before an audience of teachers, pupils, and other persons directly connected with the establishment's activities[122] is not in public if the performers are teachers or pupils or if the performance is for the purpose of instruction.[123] The rule is the same for playing or showing a sound recording, film, or broadcast to such an audience in the course of instruction at an educational establishment.[124]

 Discussion point   For answer guidance visit www.oxfordtextbooks.co.uk/orc/waelde3e/

Would the old case of *Duck v Bates* (1884) 13 QBD 843, in which a performance of a dramatic work by a group of amateurs before an audience of nurses and others in Guy's Hospital, London, was held not to be in public, be followed today?

Use of apparatus for receiving visual images or sounds conveyed by electronic means

4.59   One of the most important ways of performing, playing, or showing a work may be through a television screen or radio set situated in a public place, on which a literary, dramatic, or musical work may be being performed, or a sound recording, film, or broadcast played or shown. It is provided that in such cases the person by whom the images or sounds are sent is not an infringer and, in the case of a performance, nor is any performer;[125] but there is nothing to define who is the primary infringer in such cases; or, to put it another way, who should be seeking the licence for the performance in question. The 1956 Act provided that the occupier of the premises where the apparatus was situated would be taken as giving the performance, playing, or showing if he also provided the apparatus itself.[126] This may still be the most useful guide. It should be noted, however, that an occupier of premises who merely gave permission for the apparatus to be brought on to the premises can only be liable as a secondary infringer,[127] and that where there is no charge for admission to the premises, there is no infringement of any copyright in a broadcast, or any sound recording or film included in it, by showing or playing in public a broadcast.[128] There are also special exceptions for hotels, guest houses, and similar facilities, as well as for clubs and societies where the provision of facilities for seeing or hearing broadcasts is only incidental to the organisation's main purposes.[129]

 Exercise

Does a pub or bar which has a 'big screen' on which are shown broadcasts of football matches, but which does not charge its customers for anything other than the drinks which they buy at the bar, have to have a copyright licence in respect of its displays? What is the effect of section 72(2) of the CDPA 1988 on this situation?

---

[121] See, however, *PRS v Kwik-Fit Group Ltd* [2008] ECDR 2, where it was held arguable that employees using personal radios at their place of work in such a way that members of the public and customers of the employer could hear the music being played might be guilty of infringing public performances.

[122] A parent of a pupil is not as such directly connected (CDPA 1988, s 34(3)).   [123] CDPA 1988, s 34(1).

[124] CDPA 1988, s 34(2).   [125] CDPA 1988, s 19(4).

[126] 1956 Act, s 48(6). See also *Phonographic Performance Ltd v Lion Breweries* [1980] FSR 1 (NZ).

[127] CDPA 1988, s 26(3); and see further at paras 4.76–4.77.

[128] CDPA 1988, s 72(1). See further, *FAPL v QC Leisure* [2012] EWHC 108 (Ch) where Kitchin J states that s 72(1)(c) applies not only to performance in public under CDPA 1988, s 19 but also communication to the public under s 20. See also para 4.76.

[129] CDPA 1988, ss 67 and 72(3). See also para 4.76.

Key points on public performance

Whether a performance, playing, or showing of a work is in public depends on a number of factors:

- Is the audience paying, in some form or another, to attend the performance?
- Is the person responsible for the performance engaged in a profit-making activity?
- The audience must consist of members of the public, but restrictions on who may attend do not prevent the performance being in public
- The performance need not be simultaneous for each member of the audience

(5) Public communication right

4.60　The communication to the public of the work is an act restricted by the copyright in literary, dramatic, musical, and artistic works, sound recordings, films, and broadcasts.[130] This right was introduced in implementation of the InfoSoc Directive, which in turn implemented for the EU the WCT 1996.[131]

Public communication for these purposes means *electronic transmission* (CDPA 1988, s 20(2)).

It includes:

(1) *broadcasting* the work (CDPA 1988, s 20(2)(a)).
electronic transmission of visual images, sounds, or other information,
transmitted for simultaneous reception by members of the public
capable of being lawfully received by members of the public
transmitted at a time determined solely by the person in question for presentation to members of the public (CDPA 1988, s 6(1) and see paras 2.91–2.94).

Public communication also includes:

(2) *making available* to the public of the work by electronic transmission in such a way that members of the public may access it from a place and at a time individually chosen by them (s 20(2)(b)).

 Question

What are the differences between 'broadcasting' and 'making available' in these definitions?

4.61　Although the definition of public communication uses the term 'include' to refer to the two particular cases, it is not limited to those cases alone and the term is technologically neutral.[132] *Internet transmission* is public communication under the 'making available' head, and only the copyright owner or

---

[130]　CDPA 1988, s 20(1). See further J Ginsburg, 'The (new?) right of making available to the public' in D Vaver and L Bently (eds), *Intellectual Property in the New Millennium* (2004).

[131]　See paras 4.6 and 4.8. Note also that the concept of communication to the public is not the same for related rights, eg equitable remuneration right for performers (see further at para 6.41) because it pursues somewhat different objectives. Case C-135/10 *Societa Consortile Fonografici (SCF) v Del Corso* [2012] ECDR 16, paras 73–78.

[132]　*ITV Broadcasting Ltd v TV Catchup Ltd* [2011] FSR 40, paras 45, 81.

its licensee may so transmit a work. Accordingly, those who make copyright material such as sound recordings or films available for Internet transmission without authorisation will infringe copyright under this category of restricted act. This is the chief purpose of the new right. Uploaders in peer-to-peer networks or on bulletin boards would be examples of such infringers. In the case of broadcasting, the infringer will be the person transmitting the programme, if he has responsibility to any extent for its contents, or the person providing the programme who made with the person transmitting it the arrangements necessary for its transmission.[133] An important limitation on this form of infringement applies where a wireless broadcast is included in a cable programme service by reception and immediate retransmission. Neither the copyright in the broadcast nor in any work included in the broadcast is infringed by this if the inclusion is in pursuance of certain statutory requirements under the Broadcasting Act 1990.[134]

Exercise

Consider the case of *Shetland Times v Wills* [1997] FSR 604. Would the defender's activities in this case (providing hyperlinks from his website to the pursuer's website, and bypassing the latter's home page) be an infringement of the pursuer's public communication right?

Key points on public communication right

- The right is concerned with electronic transmission of works to the public
- The right covers broadcasting and Internet transmissions of works
- The right covers both transmissions where the transmitter decides when the transmission takes place and those where the recipient decides

4.62   A number of cases have recently considered the meaning of 'communication to the public'.

■ Case C-306/05 *SGAE v Rafael Hoteles SL* [2006] ECR I-11519

S, a collecting society, claimed that provision of television sets with broadcast signals within hotel rooms owned by R required copyright licences as public communications. The ECJ stated:

> communication to the public must be interpreted broadly. Such an interpretation is moreover essential to achieve the principal objective of that Directive, which, as can be seen from its ninth and tenth recitals, is to establish a high level of protection of, inter alios, authors, allowing them to obtain an appropriate reward for the use of their works (para 36).

The ECJ held that the distribution of a signal by means of a TV to different customers in individual hotel bedrooms amounted to communication even though the mere provision of physical facilities did not. The hotel was intervening and transmitting the broadcasts to a new public consisting of a rapid turnover of guests who could decide whether to watch the TVs. In the absence of such intervention, the guests would not be able to enjoy the broadcast work although physically within that area. The Court identified hotel customers as 'a public' distinct from other 'publics', when holding that the copyright author's licence to the TV broadcasters to communicate its work to the public covered only 'direct' users of the

---

[133] CDPA 1988, s 6(3).   [134] CDPA 1988, s 73.

broadcasts, that is, 'owners of reception equipment who, either personally or within their own private or family circles, receive the programme'. This did not extend to occupants of hotel bedrooms receiving the work by way of a further transmission process inside the hotel, who were a new and different public for the work; a further licence was needed before the material could be communicated to them. A 'public' is constituted by 'a fairly large number of persons', and in determining the relevant numbers it is relevant to consider 'the fact that, usually, hotel customers quickly succeed each other' (para 38), that is, it is not a matter of 'freezing' the audience at any particular moment in time.

Moreover, whether or not customers switch on the TVs is unimportant; or, putting the point more generally, whether or not members of the public actually access the communication. The language of the Directive—'may access'—makes clear that creation of the possibility of reception of the communication is sufficient. The ECJ noted that the seemingly very wide potential liability is somewhat restricted by a statement in the InfoSoc Directive recitals: 'the mere provision of physical facilities for enabling or making a communication does not in itself amount to communication within the meaning of this Directive.'[135] Thus, according to the Court, merely installing TV sets in the bedrooms would not be enough for liability, whereas transmitting signals to be picked up by those TVs would complete the infringement. Just as it did not matter there whether or not customers switched on the TVs, whether or not they received the same communications by way of the transmission or whether they were received simultaneously or at different times, was also unimportant. But the Court noted that it is not necessary that the unlicensed communicator had to make a profit or receive some other benefit from the activity to be liable for it, but held that the hotel clearly did do so in the case before it, since it affected both the hotel's standing and the price of its rooms (para 44).[136] The view of the Commission, that profit or other benefit is not a precondition of liability, is also borne out by the absence of any reference to such a requirement in the Directive, and may also be supported, at least in the UK, by the fact that no such requirement exists in relation to public performance right either. The Court observed that the public or private nature of the place where the communication took place was immaterial. The essence of 'making available' was the recipient's ability to choose the place and time of the communication, and this would be rendered meaningless if her choice of a private place made a difference.

4.63   ■ Cases C-403/08 and C-429/08 *Football Association Premier League Ltd v QC Leisure, Murphy v Media Protection Services Ltd* [2012] 1 CMLR 29

For the facts in brief, see para 4.36. The Court of Justice held that communication to the public covers transmission of broadcasts, such as showing of football matches, on a television to customers in a pub.[137] The customers present in the pub are a new public and the publican intervenes by giving the customers access to the broadcast, without which the customers cannot enjoy them. The profit-making nature of the communication in a pub, in that it attracts an increased number of interested customers, is not irrelevant. The Court noted that communication to the public 'must be construed broadly, as referring to any transmission of the protected works, irrespective of the technical means or process used' (para 93). It requires that the work broadcast must be transmitted to a 'public not present at the place where the communication originates' per Article 23 of InfoSoc Directive (paras 200–203).[138] As such, it does not cover any activity which does not involve a 'transmission' or a 'retransmission' of a work.[139]

---

[135] InfoSoc Directive, recital 27; Case C-306/05 *SGAE v Rafael Hoteles SL* [2006] ECR I-11519, paras 45–47.

[136] AG Sharpston had felt it not necessary to decide this particular point (paras 56–57 of her Opinion).

[137] Kitchin J applied this and held that defendants had infringed the public communication right: *FAPL v QC Leisure* [2012] EWHC 108 (Ch).

[138] This differentiates it from the right of public performance (see para 4.54).

[139] Case C-283/10 *Circ & Variete Globus Bucureşti v Uniunea Compozitorilor şi Muzicologilor din România—Asociaţia pentru Drepturi de Autor—UCMR—ADA* (24 November 2011) at para 40.

■ **Case C-431/09** *Airfield NV v SABAM* **[2012] ECDR 3**

The Court of Justice considered the meaning of communication to the public but in the context of the Satellite Broadcasting Directive. It was held that a licence from the collecting society was required where a satellite broadcaster took a communication from the original broadcaster and made it available to a new public.

4.64   In the Internet context, an issue is whether an Internet service provider (ISP) can be liable as a person 'making available' infringing material even though that material is placed upon its servers by others.[140]

■ *Twentieth Century Fox v Newzbin* **[2010] ECDR 8 (Ch)**

For facts see para 4.73. The claimants contended that N made their films available to the public under section 20(2)(b) of the CDPA 1988 while N argued that its service was passive and it acted as an intermediary providing links to the sites for the films. Kitchin J held that N had intervened in a highly material way to make the films available to a new audience, being its premium subscription-paying members. Although N did not store the films, it had intervened 'by providing a sophisticated technical and editorial system which allows its premium members to download all the component messages of the film of their choice upon pressing a button, and so avoid days of (potentially futile) effort in seeking to gather those messages together for themselves' (para 125).

■ *Dramatico Entertainment Ltd & others v BSkyB & others* **[2012] ECDR 14 (Ch)**

The claimant contended that users of The Pirate Bay website communicate their copyright works to the public. Arnold J held that users of The Pirate Bay do make the works available under section 20(2)(b) of the CDPA 1988 and as such infringe claimant's copyright. They communicate them to users who have not purchased the works from an authorised source who are the new public, being 'a public which was not taken into account by the right holders when authorising the distribution of the recordings' (para 70).

4.65   Although a clearer meaning of public communication right has emerged from the case law, its application to Internet transmissions is not fully clear.[141] One issue is whether inserting hypertext links to other sites is potentially an infringement of the public communication right.[142] Hyperlinks seem to provide an intermediate case: neither a physical facility nor a transmission, but undoubtedly something which enables communication to the public. Another issue is how the right applies to Internet streaming of television broadcasts.

■ *ITV Broadcasting Ltd v TV Catchup Ltd* **[2011] EWHC 2977 (Pat)**

ITV, television broadcasters, contended that TVC's Internet-based service for live streaming of television programmes amounted to acts of communication to the public. Floyd J's provisional conclusion was that TVC had infringed the public communication right by intercepting ITV's broadcasts and underlying works and making them available via the Internet. However, the judge was not persuaded that the

---

[140] The ISP will, however, have available the defences discussed at para 4.75. For more details on ISP liability, see paras 7.51-7.53.

[141] See A Ross and C Livingstone, 'Communication to the public: Part 1' [2012] Ent LR 169 and 'Communication to the public: Part 2' [2012] Ent LR 209.

[142] A reference from Sweden on this issue to the CJEU is currently pending, Case C-466/12 *Nils Svensson v Retreiver Sverige AB*.

principle of law was clear and amongst other reasons, was concerned whether there is a 'new public' in this case:

> Whilst the decision in Airfield is consistent with the provisional view which I expressed, I am not persuaded that the principle of law engaged in the present case is rendered acte claire by Airfield. The Court's multi-factorial approach does not make it easy to distil a clear principle as to what amounts to a communication to the public in this context. The extent to which the creation of a new link from the broadcasting organisation to the subscriber is to be equated, without more, with the creation of a "new public" is not clear. It is also not clear whether the subscribers in the present case can be described as "unable to enjoy the broadcasts although physically within the catchment area", given that they are entitled to receive the original broadcast in their own homes and on their laptops without intervention from TVC. Equally it is not clear whether the audience reached by these broadcasts is an audience which is additional to the public targeted by the broadcasting organisation concerned (para 23).

The judge referred several questions to the CJEU and the case is pending at the time of writing.[143]

(6) Infringement by adaptation

4.66   Making any adaptation of a literary, dramatic or musical work infringes its copyright (see also para 4.31).[144] An adaptation is made when it is recorded in writing or otherwise.[145] Copying such an adaptation in any material form, issuing it to the public for the first time, performing it in public, broadcasting it, or further adapting it, also infringes the copyright in the original work.[146] In relation to *literary works other than computer programs or databases*, or to dramatic works, adaptation means any of the following things:

- a *translation* of the work (eg from French into English);
- in the case of a dramatic work, *conversion* into a non-dramatic work or, in the case of a non-dramatic work, a *dramatisation*;
- a *version* of the work in which the story or action is conveyed wholly or mainly by means *of pictures* in a form suitable for reproduction in a book or in a newspaper, magazine or similar periodical (CDPA 1988, s 21(3)(a)).

4.67   In relation to *computer programs and databases*, adaptation means an arrangement or altered version, or a translation.[147] Translation is given a particular meaning in relation to computer programs, where it is to include a version of the program in which it is converted into or out of a computer language or code or into a different computer language or code.[148] This is of particular importance in respect of 'reverse engineering' activities, which may well be caught by this provision if not by the prohibition on copying.[149]

 Discussion point   For answer guidance visit www.oxfordtextbooks.co.uk/orc/waelde3e/

What does 'adaptation' add to the concept of 'copying' (paras 4.24–4.42)? Is there adaptation or copying when a book is made into a film, or when a film is made into (1) a book, or (2) a play?

---

[143] Case C-607/11 *ITV Broadcasting Limited ea v TV Catch Up Ltd.*   [144] CDPA 1988, s 21(1).   [145] CDPA 1988, s 21(1).
[146] CDPA 1988, s 21(2).   [147] CDPA 1988, s 21(3)(ab), (ac).   [148] CDPA 1988, s 21(4).
[149] See para 4.22, for reverse engineering.

> **Key point on adaptation**
>
> • Adaptation deals with specific cases not clearly within the concept of 'copying'

Authorisation of infringement

4.68   The copyright in a work is infringed by:

> any person who, without the licence of the copyright owner, authorises another person to do any of the restricted acts (CDPA 1988, s 16(2)).

There cannot be infringement by authorisation unless there has been an infringement of the primary rights of the copyright owner; or to put it another way, only if authorisation comes from the copyright owner is there no primary infringement. To authorise an infringement is to 'sanction, approve, or countenance' it,[150] a formulation capable of a very wide meaning, especially when conjoined with the apparent willingness of the courts to treat indifference as capable of being authorisation.[151] However, the concept has previously been applied in a relatively restricted way, by employing a test of the degree of authority, or control, which the defender had over those who actually carried out the infringement.

■ *CBS v Ames Records and Tapes* [1982] Ch 91

The defendants owned a chain of record shops and began to operate record lending libraries in them. This facilitated infringing copying of records by borrowers from the libraries and the plaintiffs argued that this was 'countenancing' infringement in such a way as to authorise it. Whitford J refused to grant an injunction: 'an authorisation can only come from somebody having or purporting to have authority ... an act is not authorised by somebody who merely enables or possibly assists or even encourages another to do that act, but does not purport to have any authority which he can grant to justify the doing of the act' (at 105).

■ *RCA Corp v John Fairfax & Sons Ltd* [1982] RPC 91 (NSW Supreme Court)

Publishing a newspaper article or advertisement referring to the possibility of tape recording records by use of machinery does not authorise infringement because the authors cannot control what individuals do with the machinery once they have bought it.

■ *Vigneux v Canadian PRS* [1945] AC 108 (PC)

A company which rented a juke box to restaurateurs was held not to authorise infringement of the copyright in musical works by performance because it 'had no control over the use of the machine [and] ... no voice as to whether at any particular time it was to be available to the restaurant customers or not' (per Lord Russell of Killowen at 123).

---

[150] This definition of 'authorise' was first stated in *Monckton v Pathe Freres Pathephone Ltd* [1914] 1 KB 395 and *Evans v Hulton & Co Ltd* [1924] WN 130.
[151] *PRS v Ciryl Theatrical Syndicate* [1924] 1 KB 1; *Moorhouse v University of New South Wales* [1976] RPC 151 (HCA); *CBS v Ames Record & Tapes* [1982] Ch 91; *PRS v Kwik-Fit Group Ltd* [2008] ECDR 2.

■ *CBS Songs Ltd v Amstrad Consumer Electronics plc* **[1988] 1 AC 1013**

The manufacture, distribution and supply of machines capable of use by buyers for copying copyright works at high speed cannot be by themselves authorisations of infringement since, again, the manufacturer lacks control over the uses to which the machine is put, and it is also capable of legitimate use.

4.69   Compare the leading case on the US copyright law equivalent of infringement by authorisation—contributory infringement:

■ *Universal City Studios Inc v Sony Corp of America* **464 US 417 (1984) (US Supreme Court)**

It was held here that the manufacture and sale of video-tape recorders for use to copy broadcasts and films being shown on TV did not give rise to contributory infringement liability, although Sony knew that the machines were being used to commit infringements. A claim of contributory infringement would be defeated if, as in this case, the product in question was shown to be capable of substantial or commercially significant non-infringing uses. Constructive knowledge of infringing activity could not be imputed from a general awareness that the machine could be used for infringement.

 Discussion point For answer guidance visit www.oxfordtextbooks.co.uk/orc/waelde3e/

Would a UK court have reached the same decision in a case like *Sony*?

Cases finding authorisation to have taken place

4.70   The decisions just discussed may be compared with those where there has been held to be authorisation. Supply of a film of a play for exhibition at a cinema was held to authorise infringement of the copyright in the play in *Falcon v Famous Players Film Co*.[152] Ordering spare parts from a manufacturer authorised him to infringe the copyright in drawings of those spare parts.[153] The prior approval by a local authority of the list of musical works to be played on a public bandstand was held to be an authorisation of infringement.[154] In all these cases there was a direct and immediate link between the act of the defendant and the infringement which followed. They differ, too, from most of the cases cited in the previous paragraph where what was really being complained of was the fact that the defendant had created an opportunity for others to infringe which had probably, even certainly, been taken up, but specific instances of this were not brought to the court's attention.[155] However, where the complaint is about the provision to others of the opportunity to infringe and it can be coupled with the necessary degree of control over those others and specific instances of infringement, then there may be liability for authorisation.

■ *Moorhouse v University of New South Wales* **[1976] RPC 151 (HCA)**

The High Court of Australia held that a university had authorised infringement by students (and, presumably, staff) by providing photocopying facilities in the university library without adequate supervision of what was copied. A notice near the photocopiers warning against copyright infringement was insufficient to avoid liability. Specific incidents of infringing copying were established and the court stressed that authorisation might be implied from indifference to infringement where it was likely that

---

[152] [1926] 2 KB 474.   [153] *Standen Engineering v Spalding & Sons* [1984] FSR 554.
[154] *PRS v Bray UDC* [1930] AC 377 (PC).
[155] See in particular the discussion of the problem of 'home copying', which was the real issue in *CBS Songs Ltd v Amstrad Consumer Electronics plc* [1988] 1 AC 1013.

such infringement would occur. Here the university also had power to control the access of students to photocopying facilities, either by not providing them or by ensuring through supervision that no infringing copying was done and accordingly it was liable.[156]

> In a recent complaint, the Advertising Standards Authority in the UK, an independent regulator for advertising, had to unusually consider the potential for copyright infringement (ASA Adjudication on 3GA Ltd, Complaint 140713). The adjudication concerned an advert which read: 'The Brennan JB7 is a CD player with a hard disk that stores up to 5,000 CDs...It saves space and clutter and delivers near immediate access to an entire music collection...The Brennan also records from vinyl and cassette so you can enjoy your entire music collection but keep it out of the way in another room or retire it to the attic...What's the point in owning hundreds of CDs worth thousands of pounds if you never listen to them?...CDs are great but they are also inconvenient, inaccessible and a bit of a chore...Load CDs in about four minutes...One touch record from vinyl, cassette or radio.'[157] The complaint was upheld as the advertisement was misleading because it made references to the product being able to copy music and encouraged customers to do so but did not make it clear that copying was illegal without permission from the copyright owner and so it incited customers to break the law.

Notices and statements as defences against claims of authorisation

4.71   A further significant point in the *Moorhouse* case concerned the use of notices as a defence to a claim of authorisation. The university issued guides for library users which made incomplete reference to the provisions of the copyright legislation on copying and stated that a copy of the Act was available in the photocopying room. It was held that these were insufficient to rebut authorisation, but that an invitation to use copying facilities might be so restricted as to avoid liability.[158] But even the fullest possible notices will be inadequate if, despite their existence, infringing copying continues and the person able to control its occurrence remains indifferent to this.[159] The placing of copyright warning notices in the premises and on the copies of records lent was an important (but not the sole) factor in the *Ames Records & Tapes* case, where it was held that there had been no authorisation.[160] Contrast with:

■ *Law Society of Upper Canada v CCH* [2004] 1 SCR 339 (Supreme Court of Canada)

The Law Society of Upper Canada maintained its Great Library at Osgoode Hall in Toronto. The library was for reference and research and had one of the largest collections of legal material in Canada. A self-service photocopier was located in the library for the use of patrons (Law Society members, the judiciary, and other authorised researchers), alongside a notice warning that the library would not be responsible for any copies made in infringement of copyright. Law publishers challenged these practices as authorisation of infringement. It was held that the Law Society did not authorise copyright infringement. Authorisation could be inferred from indirect acts and omissions, but the authorisation of use of equipment which could be used to infringe copyright was not enough. Posting a notice warning against infringement was not an express acknowledgement that the machines would be used in an illegal manner. Authorisations should be presumed to be given to lawful acts only, this being rebuttable if a relationship or degree of control existed between the authoriser and persons who infringed copyright. This was not the case here, and there was no evidence of actual infringements. *Moorhouse* was criticised

---

[156] Compare *CBS v Ames Records & Tapes* [1982] Ch 91, where no copying machines were provided. Under the CDPA 1988, the *Moorhouse* situation would now be avoided through the limited scope of the permitted acts (see in particular CDPA 1988, ss 29 and 36–39) and reprography licensing (ss 130 and 136–141). The Copyright Licensing Agency plays a significant role here (see further at paras 22.19ff).

[157] http://asa.org.uk/Rulings/Adjudications/2011/3/3GA-Ltd/TF_ADJ_50026.aspx.

[158] *Moorhouse v University of New South Wales* [1976] RPC 151 (HCA).

[159] *Moorhouse v University of New South Wales* [1976] RPC 151 per Jacobs J at 166.

[160] *CBS v Ames Record & Tapes* [1982] Ch 91.

as shifting the balance in copyright too far in favour of the owner's rights, unnecessarily interfering with the proper use of copyrighted works for the good of society as a whole.

 Discussion point For answer guidance visit www.oxfordtextbooks.co.uk/orc/waelde3e/

Is the criticism of *Moorhouse* in this case justified? Consider the implications for Internet service provider liability, discussed in para 4.72.

Key points on authorisation

- Authorisation of infringement is sanctioning, countenancing, or approving another person's primary infringement where one has authority or control over a primary infringer

- Creating opportunities for others to infringe, for example by means of machinery, is not by itself authorisation, especially where legitimate activities are also made possible by the action

- Notices warning against infringement may be a factor in preventing authorisation, but are not usually enough by themselves

---

Authorisation and Internet file-sharing

4.72 Liability by authorisation has obvious importance for Internet service providers such as the operators of unlicensed file-sharing networks or website operators but also commercial Internet access providers, universities and other bodies which enable access to the Internet for customers, students and others by means of which infringing Internet activity can take place, whether by way of copying or the public communication right. Can such bodies be liable for authorising such infringing use? The *Amstrad* and *Ames Records & Tapes* cases held the providers of facilities not liable despite the fact that their services and products rendered infringement easy and probable;[161] the crucial factors being that lawful activity is possible with the facilities provided and that the defendants had given express warnings to customers against use for infringing copying. This may have seemed encouraging for those whose facilities enable others to make use of the Internet: the facilities are capable of many lawful as well as infringing uses, and the providers generally give warnings to users against unlawful activity with the service.

4.73 However, it is now clear that service providers and site operators on the Internet may nonetheless be liable for authorisation of infringement.

■ *Twentieth Century Fox & others v Newzbin* [2010] ECDR 8

Usenet is a worldwide Internet discussion system where users can post content such as films, which is split into lots of smaller sized components, and can retrieve such content by downloading and reassembling all of the components. N operated a website, which allowed its premium members to search and locate the content on Usenet and allowed them to download an NZB file for each content, which when run on a computer would reassemble the content from its component parts and make an infringing copy. The claimants, makers and distributors of films contended that N had authorised infringement by its members. N claimed that its website was just a search engine and content agnostic. Kitchin J first reviewed earlier case law on authorisation and noted that:

---

[161] *CBS Inc v Ames Records & Tapes Ltd* [1982] Ch 91; *CBS Songs Ltd v Amstrad Consumer Electronics plc* [1988] 1 AC 1013.

it is clear...that "authorise" means the grant or purported grant of the right to do the act complained of. It does not extend to mere enablement, assistance or even encouragement. The grant or purported grant to do the relevant act may be express or implied from all the relevant circumstances. In a case which involves an allegation of authorisation by supply, these circumstances may include the nature of the relationship between the alleged authoriser and the primary infringer, whether the equipment or other material supplied constitutes the means used to infringe, whether it is inevitable it will be used to infringe, the degree of control which the supplier retains and whether he has taken any steps to prevent infringement. These are matters to be taken into account and may or may not be determinative depending upon all the other circumstances (para 90).

The judge held that N had actively encouraged, guided and rewarded its editors to make reports on films; provided a facility which went beyond indexing and categorisation, and instead identified components of a content and saved its members the 'the very substantial task of manually locating and identifying each of them separately'; provided useful information in relation to the content; created and controlled the NZB facility which was the means of infringement; and had failed to install any filtering system.[162]

In *Dramatico Entertainment Ltd & others v BSkyB & others*,[163] Arnold J followed the four factors suggested in *Newzbin* and held that operators of the Pirate Bay website authorised its users' infringing acts of copying and communication to the public. The judge noted that the Pirate Bay provides a sophisticated and user-friendly facility and goes well beyond enabling infringement to sanctioning and approving it.

Specific situations in which operators of unlicensed file-sharing networks and site operators on the Internet may be liable for authorisation of infringement can also be understood from consideration of some of the early but important body of US case law before the Digital Millennium Copyright Act 1998 (for which see further at para 4.74). This case law focuses upon the US equivalent of authorisation, the concept of contributory infringement, and its application to cases of 'file-sharing' on peer-to-peer (P2P) networks on the Internet.[164]

■ *A&M Records v Napster* 239 F 3d 1004 (2001)

The arrival of MP3 software in the late 1990s enabled the conversion of digitally recorded (or remastered) material (in particular music) into highly compressed computer files postable on and downloadable from the Internet. Napster Inc, through its proprietary MusicShare software, allowed users to upload to the Napster servers a list of all MP3 files on the hard disk of the user's computer; search the servers, which contained master indices of the locations of music files on the hard disks of all users of the service; and download copies of the files they wanted, directly from the hard disks of other users. Napster was held to be guilty of contributory and vicarious infringement. Napster's liability was founded, not upon their own infringement of copyright, but rather upon the holding that through their provision of indices they enabled, knew of and could prevent, such infringement by others.

■ *Metro-Goldwyn-Mayer Studios Inc v Grokster Ltd* 380 F 3d 1154 (9th Cir, 2004); 545 US 913 (2005) (US Supreme Court)

The defendants distributed free software enabling users to exchange digital media via a P2P transfer network. Multiple transfers to or from other users could occur simultaneously to and from a single

---

[162] Bear in mind also that unauthorised file-sharing might also involve infringement of the public communication right by the operators (para 4.63).   [163] [2012] ECDR 14 (Ch)

[164] Under US law, contributory infringement results when someone knows of the direct infringement of another and substantially participates in that infringement, such as inducing, causing, or materially contributing to the infringing conduct. This is a common law concept in the United States, and is not found in the US Copyright Act.

user's computer. The defendants did not operate a centralised file-sharing network like that of Napster and argued that they merely provided software to users over whom they had no control. Although the lower courts held for the defendants, the Supreme Court took a different view, holding that a party who distributed a device with the object of promoting its use to infringe copyright, as shown by clear expression or other affirmative steps taken to foster infringement, is liable for the resulting acts of infringement by third parties. Documents showed that the defendants hoped to become the 'next Napster' and had sought to woo Napster customers after the closure of that service, highlighting the availability through its service of copyright material. There was no evidence that the defendants had sought to filter out copyright material from downloads or otherwise impede the sharing of such material. Contributory infringement arose through intentional inducement or encouragement of direct infringement, while vicarious infringement arose from profiting by direct infringement while declining to exercise a right to stop or limit it. Where an article was good for nothing else but infringement, its unlimited availability served no legitimate public interest. It did not follow that the possibility of non-infringing use exempted the product from liability. There was evidence of intent to induce infringement.

Note also a decision of the Federal Court of Australia on this topic, using a similar concept of authorisation as applied by courts in the UK.

■ *Universal Music Australia Pty Ltd v Sharman License Holdings Ltd* (2005) 220 ALR 1 (FCA)

This case concerned the Kazaa system of file-sharing, another service available to users free of charge. It enabled one user to share with other users any material the first user wished to share, whether or not subject to copyright, simply by placing that material in a file called 'My Shared Folder'. A user interested in obtaining a copy of a particular work, such as a musical item, could instantaneously search the 'My Shared Folder' files of other users, worldwide. If the file was located, the title would be displayed against a blue icon on the first user's computer as a 'blue file'. The work could then be downloaded onto the first user's computer. The site generated its income through advertising. It was held that the Australian operators of the Kazaa system authorised infringement of copyright by users of the service. The warnings against infringement by file-sharing placed on the Kazaa website, and an end user licence agreement under which users had to agree not to infringe copyright, were obviously ineffective to prevent, or even substantially to curtail, copyright infringements by users. The operators had long known that the system was widely used for the sharing of copyright files. Technical measures such as keyword filtering existed that would enable them to restrict, albeit not completely prevent, the sharing of copyright files. This had not been done because it would not have been in the operators' financial interest to do so. Instead, the operators included on the website exhortations to users to increase their file-sharing, including a page headed 'Join the Revolution' that criticised record companies for opposing P2P file-sharing. To the site's predominantly young audience, the effect of this would be to encourage file-sharing in defiance of the record companies, even though there was no express advocacy of the sharing of copyright files.

4.74   There have been attempts to make ISPs which provide access to the Internet liable for authorisation of infringement of its subscribers. In *Roadshow Films Pty Ltd v iiNet Ltd*,[165] the Australian Federation Against Copyright Theft (AFACT) along with a number of film and television studios were unsuccessful against the ISP iiNet which was accused of authorising copyright infringement of its subscribers who used the P2P system BitTorrent, over their Internet network. The High Court held that iiNet had no technical power to prevent its users' infringements and did not assist them in locating infringing material; it had

---

[165] [2012] HCA 16.

no control over the BitTorrent system nor hosted any infringing content; it had the contractual power to terminate the service of its users but not only would that deny them from using the Internet for non-infringing uses but they could also take their business to another ISP.

In the UK, although the ISPs which provide access to the Internet have not so far been liable for authorisation of infringement, a separate legislative measure, the Digital Economy Act 2010, was enacted to allow for imposition of obligations on Internet access providers to assist in curbing online infringement (see further paras 7.53). In addition, section 97A of the CDPA 1988[166] gives power to courts to grant an injunction against a service provider, where that service provider has actual knowledge of another person using its service to infringe copyright. Rights owners have been successful in obtaining such injunctions against internet access providers who knew that their services were used by one or more subscribers to receive infringing copies of works to block Newzbin2 and The Pirate Bay websites (para 4.73).[167]

'Safe harbours'

4.75   The Directive on electronic commerce in the EU[168] sets out an exemption from liability for intermediaries where they play a wholly passive role as mere conduits of information from third parties.[169] It also limits service providers' liability for other activities such as the storage of information provided by recipients of the service and at their request (hosting), as long as the provider does not know of the illegal activity, is unaware of facts and circumstances from which illegal activity is apparent and acts expeditiously to remove or disable access upon learning or becoming aware of the activity.[170] There is explicitly no obligation actively to screen or monitor third party content.[171] The CJEU has indicated that these provisions, when read with other relevant EU Directives, preclude an injunction against an ISP that requires it to install a system for filtering all electronic communications passing via its services or information stored on its servers by its users, which applies indiscriminately to all its users, as a preventative measure exclusively at its expense for an unlimited period.[172] In the UK, injunctions granted to Internet access providers to block the Newbin website were held not to be in contravention of the safe harbour provisions.[173]

In the United States, the Digital Millennium Copyright Act 1998 exempts the service provider from liability where it has no knowledge or information about the infringing material in its system, acts expeditiously to remove or block access to material when knowledge or information comes to hand, does not receive any financial benefit directly attributable to the infringing material and complies with certain 'notice and take-down' provisions of the Act enabling copyright owners to require the service provider to remove or block access to infringing material. For example, after *Napster I* (para 4.73), the court ordered the copyright owners to give Napster notice of specific infringing files and required Napster then to search its index continually and block all files containing the works in issue. Napster's

---

[166] Implementing Art 8(3) of the InfoSoc Directive. See also Enforcement Directive 2004/48/EC, Art 11.

[167] *Twentieth Century Fox Film Corporation & others v BT* [2011] RPC 28, [2011] EWHC 2714 (Ch); *Dramatico Entertainment Ltd & others v BSkyB & others* [2012] ECDR 14 (Ch).

[168] European Parliament and Council Directive 2000/31/EC on certain legal aspects of Information Society services, in particular electronic commerce, in the Internal Market (E-Commerce Directive), implemented in the Electronic Commerce (EC Directive) Regulations 2002 (SI 2002/2013).

[169] E-Commerce Directive, Art 12; Electronic Commerce Regulations, reg 17.

[170] See E-Commerce Directive, Art 14; Electronic Commerce Regulations, reg 19 (hosting). See also Case C-236/08 *Google France Sarl v Louis Vuitton Malletier SA* [2010] RPC 19; Case C-324/09 *L'Oreal SA v eBay International AG* [2011] RPC 27.

[171] E-Commerce Directive, Art 15.

[172] Case C-70/10 *Scarlet Extended SA v SABAM* [2012] ECDR 4 (ECJ); Case C-360/10 *SABAM v Netlog NV* [2012] 2 CMLR 18 (ECJ).

[173] *Twentieth Century Fox Film Corporation & others v BT* [2011] RPC 28, [2011] EWHC 2714 (Ch).

inability to comply with this order led to the collapse of the service in its then form (Napster has since been relaunched as a licensed subscription service).

Discussion point For answer guidance visit www.oxfordtextbooks.co.uk/orc/waelde3e/

Would the orders made against Napster in the United States have been possible under the E-Commerce Directive?

Key points on authorisation and Internet file-sharing

- The provider of a service by means of which otherwise unauthorised sharing of copyright files takes place will be liable for authorisation if it grants or purports to grant its users the right to carry out the restricted acts

- The E-Commerce Directive provides a procedure by which the provider may avoid liability by acting expeditiously to remove infringing material once aware of its existence

Secondary infringement of copyright

4.76   'Secondary' infringements[174] of copyright are distinguished from 'primary' infringements because the defender is not liable unless he knew or had reason to believe that he was handling infringing copies, or that the performances would infringe copyright.[175] The following acts in relation to infringing copies of works constitute 'secondary' infringements of copyright:

- importing otherwise than for the importer's private and domestic use;
- possessing in the course of a business;
- selling or hiring or offering or exposing for sale or hire;
- exhibiting or distributing in the course of a business;
- distribution otherwise in the course of a business to such an extent as to affect prejudicially the copyright owner.

Discussion point For answer guidance visit www.oxfordtextbooks.co.uk/orc/waelde3e/

What is the common feature of this list of secondary infringements?

4.77   Also categorised as secondary infringements are:

- providing the means for making infringing copies;
- permitting the use of premises for infringing performances;
- provision of apparatus for infringing performances.

---

[174] See the headings to the relevant sections of the CDPA 1988, ss 22–26.
[175] See ss 22, 23, 24, 25(1), and 26(2)–(4).

Where no charge is made for admission to the premises, however, there is no infringement of any copyright in a broadcast, or any sound recording or film included in it, by showing or playing in public a broadcast.[176] An audience has paid for admission to premises if (1) it has to pay for admission to *part* only of the premises; (2) it pays prices for goods or services on the premises either (a) *substantially* attributable to the facilities afforded for hearing or seeing the broadcast, or (b) exceeding those usually paid there and *partly* attributable to the facilities.[177] There are also special exceptions to copyright restrictions for hotels, guest houses, and similar facilities, as well as for clubs and societies where the provision of facilities for seeing or hearing broadcasts is only incidental to the organisation's main purposes.[178]

 Discussion point   For answer guidance visit www.oxfordtextbooks.co.uk/orc/waelde3e/

How do these rules interact with those on public performance, showing or playing as a primary infringement (paras 4.53–4.59)?

Importance of secondary infringement

4.78   Claims of secondary infringement are of great importance in preventing commercial piracy, in particular the circulation of infringing sound recordings, videos, CDs, and DVDs, where it is not possible to identify or take action against the person actually making the copies. The question of the degree and amount of knowledge required to make someone liable as a secondary infringer is one on which there is little clear authority. The 1988 Act requires that only 'reason to believe' need be shown to impose the liability.[179] The latest case law suggests that this is an objective test, requiring knowledge of facts from which a reasonable person would, after the passage of a reasonable amount of time, arrive at the relevant belief; facts giving rise only to suspicion would not be enough.[180] In practice, the safest approach where a possible infringement is discovered will be to send the defendant a warning letter as a first step; this will fix him with actual knowledge sufficient to justify action should the activities continue. The copyright owner should allow a reasonable time after receipt of the letter to enable the defender to consider his position, before further action is taken.[181]

Key points on secondary infringements

- Secondary infringements are essentially those of dealing commercially in products the making of which was a primary infringement of copyright, or which enable such products to be made

- The infringer must know or have reason to believe that infringing copies were being handled

---

[176] CDPA 1988, s 72(1). See further, *FAPL v QC Leisure* [2012] EWHC 108 (Ch) and para 4.59.

[177] CDPA 1988, s 72(2). On this test, the employer was probably not guilty of secondary infringement under this head in *PRS v Kwik-Fit Group Ltd* [2008] ECDR 2 (allowed employees to play personal radios at work so that music could be heard by customers of the employer).   [178] CDPA 1988, s 72(3).

[179] See ss 22, 23, 24, 25(1), and 26(2)–(4).

[180] *ZYX Music GmbH v King* [1997] 2 All ER 129 (CA); *Pensher Security Door Co Ltd v Sunderland City Council* [2000] RPC 249 (CA); *Vermaat and Powell v Boncrest (No 2)* [2002] FSR 21.

[181] *Van Dusen v Kritz* [1936] 2 KB 176; *Vermaat and Powell v Boncrest (No 2)* [2002] FSR 21.

Further reading

Books

General

L Bently and B Sherman, *Intellectual Property Law* (3rd edn, 2009), Chs 6, 8

Copinger & Skone James on Copyright (16th edn, 2010), Chs 7, 8

WR Cornish, D Llewelyn, and T Aplin, *Intellectual Property* (7th edn, 2010), Chs 12.1–2, 12.5

Laddie, Prescott & Vitoria on the Modern Law of Copyright (4th edn, 2011), Chs 14–19

Internet

G Westkamp, *Digital Copyright Laws in Europe: Regulating Information Access* (2011)

A Strowel (ed), *Peer-to-Peer File Sharing and Secondary Liability in Copyright Law* (2009)

Articles

Film

A Barron, 'The legal properties of film' (2004) 67 MLR 177

Art

S Stokes, 'Copyright and the reproduction of artistic works' [2003] EIPR 486

Parody

E Gredley and S Maniatis, 'Parody: a fatal attraction?' [1997] EIPR 339

F W Grosheide, 'Some observations with regard to the parody-exception in copyright law' in E Philippin et al (eds), *Mélanges en l'honneur de Francois Dessemontet* (2009), 217–232

C Rütz, 'Parody: a missed opportunity?' [2004] IPQ 284

M Spence, 'Intellectual property and the problem of parody' (1998) 114 LQR 594

Public communication right

J Ginsburg, 'The (new?) right of making available to the public' in D Vaver and L Bently (eds), *Intellectual Property in the New Millennium* (2004)

A Ross and C Livingstone, 'Communication to the public: Part 1' [2012] Ent LR 169 and 'Communication to the public: Part 2' [2012] Ent LR 209

5

Copyright 4: exceptions, technical protection measures, and contracts

Introduction

Scope and overview of chapter

5.1 This chapter first considers exceptions and limitations to the rights of the copyright owner described in the previous chapter. Copyright law establishes many such exceptions and limitations, listed in the Copyright, Designs and Patents Act 1988 (CDPA 1988) as what it calls the *'permitted acts'*. These are acts which can be carried out in relation to the copyright work *without* the owner's permission or, in some cases, which can be performed subject to terms and conditions specified by the statute rather than by the copyright owner. As a result, it is sometimes suggested that they are *user rights*. A controversial potential challenge to copyright exceptions and any concept of 'user rights' is, however, posed by the technical protection measures (TPMs) which right holders use to prevent unauthorised access to and use of copyright digital works. Arguably such TPMs are also capable of preventing use under the copyright exceptions and, indeed, when a work has fallen out of copyright altogether (eg at the expiry of its term). Yet copyright law gives protection to TPMs which makes their circumvention illegal as long as the protected work is made available by way of contractual terms. So TPMs also set up a world in which right holders and would-be users *contract* for the use of the copyright work, raising complex questions about the inter-relationship between exceptions to copyright, TPMs, and contract rights.

5.2 ### Learning objectives

By the end of this chapter you should be able to describe and explain:

- the exceptions to the rights conferred by copyright;
- the legal protection of technical protection measures placed upon digital copyright works;
- the possibilities created by technology for the creation of direct contracts between right holders and would-be users;
- the interaction between exceptions, technical protection measures, and contract law.

5.3 The chapter analyses each of the 'permitted acts', raising the question whether these exceptions can be regarded as 'user rights', and how far they may be set aside as a result of the application of the technological protection measures, or by contractual provision. So the rest of the chapter looks like this:

- The public domain and copyright exceptions in general (5.4–5.7)
- International background (5.8–5.11)
- Copyright exceptions in the UK (5.12–5.46)
- Other limitations on copyright (5.47–5.49)
- Technical protection measures and rights management information systems (5.50–5.57)
- Copyright exceptions, TPMs, RMIs, and contract (5.58–5.66)

The public domain and copyright exceptions in general

5.4 This chapter deals with what people may do with works without the authorisation or permission of the copyright owner.[1] Some material, of course, is never in copyright—for example, a single word because it is not a literary work,[2] or an unoriginal artistic work.[3] Some material which once was in copyright is no longer because the term of copyright has expired, for example sound recordings made over 50 years ago. In both cases, people are free to do all the things which in other cases copyright would restrict: that is, copy the work, issue copies to the public whether for sale, rental or commercial lending, perform the work in public, communicate it to the public, or adapt it. Some uses of copyright works do not fall within the scope of the restricted acts and may be freely carried out: for example, reselling a book of which you were the first purchaser or performing a work of music in private. This copyright-free zone is sometimes known as the *public domain*.[4] It has been argued that there is a 'virtuous circle' between copyright and the public domain, with the latter feeding the creation of new copyright works which in turn fall bit by bit into the public domain, the process becoming complete when the copyright expires.[5]

 Question

How may the 'public domain' be defined in relation to copyright?

5.5 Further, and most importantly for the purposes of this section of the chapter, people may do certain things with copyright material without the licence of the copyright owner which *would* otherwise fall within the scope of the restricted acts, for example make a copy for private study and research, perform the work in private, record a film on TV to watch it at a more convenient time,

---

[1] See in general G Davies, *Copyright and the Public Interest* (2nd edn, 2003); LMCR Guibault, *Copyright Limitations and Contracts: An Analysis of the Contractual Overridability of Limitations on Copyright* (2002); M Senftleben, *Copyright, Limitations and the Three-Step Test: An Analysis of the Three-Step Test in International and EC Copyright Law* (2004); R Burrell and A Coleman, *Copyright Exceptions: The Digital Impact* (2005).
[2] See *Exxon Corp v Exxon Insurance* [1982] Ch 119.   [3] *Interlego AG v Tyco Industries Inc* [1989] AC 217.
[4] See generally C Waelde and HL MacQueen (eds), *The Many Faces of the Public Domain* (2007), and references therein.
[5] W Davies and K Withers, *Public Innovation: Intellectual Property in a Digital Age* (Institute of Public Policy Research, 2006); see also MD de Rosnay and JC de Martin (eds), *The Digital Public Domain: Foundations for an Open Culture* (2012).

or quote a work for purposes such as criticising it or reporting the news. This is because British copyright law contains extensive and detailed provisions by which various carefully specified 'acts which would otherwise be infringements of copyright are made lawful'.[6] They are described in the CDPA 1988 under the general heading, 'Acts Permitted in Relation to Copyright Works'. Such acts do not require any licence from the copyright owner and may be freely performed by others.

5.6   The contents of the list of permitted acts reflect a legislative perception that certain interests in certain circumstances outweigh the interest in conferring and enforcing copyright. Some of the items on the list of permitted acts are grouped together as 'fair dealing', but there is no general principle that 'fair dealing' beyond the listed acts or for other than the listed purposes is allowed. (Note, however, the rather uncertain principle that copyright may be limited by what is known as the defence of 'public interest', discussed further at para 5.47.)

5.7   In this avoidance of a general principle and concentration upon a specific list of permitted acts, there is a contrast with US law, which provides a general 'fair use' defence covering purposes 'such as' criticism, comment, teaching, scholarship and research, and indicating that factors to be taken into account 'include' such matters as whether the use is of a commercial nature or for non-profit educational purposes, the amount and substantiality of the portion used in relation to the whole work, and the effect of the use upon the market or value of the copyright work.[7] The argument against such a general approach is that it creates uncertainty by contrast with the more specific approach in the UK;[8] on the other hand, the flexibility of a general approach may enable the law to deal better with changing ways of producing and exploiting copyright works. There is also a different contrast between the UK and many of the Continental laws, which tend to exclude private non-commercial copying from the scope of copyright, although a concomitant in many of these systems is levies on blank audio cassettes and reprography, the proceeds from which are routed back ultimately to copyright owners via their collecting societies.[9] Thus, the permitted use is nonetheless one for which the copyright owner ultimately receives remuneration, whether paid directly or indirectly by the user. The UK, on the other hand, has historically resisted both a general exemption for private use and the correlative deployment of levies on materials and machinery used for copying purposes.[10] The European Commission is investigating whether such levies should be introduced on a harmonised Union-wide basis.[11]

 Question

What contrasts exist between UK, US and Continental European approaches to permitted acts?

---

[6] CDPA 1988, ss 28–76.   [7] US Copyright Act 1976, s 107.

[8] For a recent discussion on whether the UK should adopt 'fair use' see I Hargreaves, *Digital Opportunity: A Review of Intellectual Property and Growth* (2011) available at http://www.ipo.gov.uk/ipreview.htm (Hargreaves Review 2011). See also para 7.57.

[9] See, eg, the French Intellectual Property Code of 1 July 1992, L122–5, L211–3, L212–10, and L311; and German Copyright Act 1965, §§ 53, 54, and 54a–h.

[10] The Hargreaves Review 2011 recommended the introduction of a private copying exemption which was followed up by a consultation and the UK Government plans to introduce a narrow private copying exception for lawfully copied content for personal use, 'Modernising Copyright: A Modern, Robust and Flexible Framework' (2012) available at http://www.ipo.gov.uk/response-2011-copyright-final.pdf. See para 7.60.

[11] See the European Commission Internal Market DG website at http://ec.europa.eu/internal_market/copyright/levy_reform/index_en.htm.

Key points on permitted acts (introduction)

- Works never in copyright, or the copyright in which has expired, are often said to be 'in the public domain'
- The permitted acts are ones which would be infringements of copyright but are made lawful by specific statutory provision
- UK law takes a specific rather than a general 'fair use' or 'private use' approach to this subject
- The UK approach is not really consistent with the idea that the permitted acts are 'user rights'

International background

Berne Convention ('three-step test'), TRIPS, and WCT

5.8   Under Article 9(2) of the Berne Convention members of the Union may:

> permit the reproduction of [literary and artistic] works in certain special cases, provided that such reproduction does not conflict with a normal exploitation of the work and does not unreasonably prejudice the legitimate interests of the author.

Article 10, under the heading 'Certain Free Uses of Works', goes on to permit quotation from work lawfully made available to the public, provided that this is 'compatible with fair practice' and is not in excess of what is 'justified by the purpose'. The Article also allows members of the Union to permit 'utilisation, to the extent justified by the purpose' of literary and artistic works by way of illustration for teaching, as long this is 'compatible with fair practice'. In both cases, the source and the name of the author must be identified. Article 10*bis* of the Convention adds 'Further Possible Free Uses of Works' for the reporting of current events. The TRIPS Agreement of 1994 notes that limitations or exceptions to copyright are to be 'confined' to 'certain special cases which do not conflict with a normal exploitation of the work and do not unreasonably prejudice the legitimate interests of the right holder'.[12] For some reason, Article 10 of the WIPO Copyright Treaty (WCT) 1996 repeats this formula no less than twice but, like TRIPS, where the Berne Convention talks of 'permitting' such acts, the WIPO Article speaks of 'confining' them. In 2000 a Dispute Panel of the World Trade Organization (WTO) issued an opinion on the scope of the three-step test, holding that section 110(5) of the US Copyright Act 1976 violated the test by allowing public performance of works received from broadcasts. All three steps had to be complied with in any copyright exception. While minor or *de minimis* departures from the test were permissible, section 110(5) did not fall into that category.[13]

 Question

The Berne Convention regulation of exceptions to copyright is sometimes known as the 'three-step test'. What are these three steps?

---

[12] TRIPS, Art 13.

[13] Report of the WTO Panel dated 15 June 2000, WT/DS160/R. See further C Geiger, J Griffiths and RM Hilty, 'Towards a balanced interpretation of the 'three-step test' in copyright law' [2008] EIPR 489.

Discussion point For answer guidance visit www.oxfordtextbooks.co.uk/orc/waelde3e/

Why do TRIPS and the WCT 1996 want to 'confine' exceptions to copyright?

European Union

5.9 The Information Society (InfoSoc) Directive 2001, the EU's implementation of the WCT 1996, made provision for what it called 'Exceptions and Limitations' to copyright. During the prolonged gestation of the Directive there was great controversy as to whether its extension of owner rights was sufficiently (or, indeed, at all) balanced by the exceptions to the restricted acts of reproduction and public communication set out in Article 5; and whether these in turn were set at naught by the rules in Article 6 supporting the use of technical measures of copyright protection in digital products, and enabling the right holder to deny access until paid by the would-be user, whether or not the proposed use fell within the scope of copyright or the exceptions. The importance of the debate was that, at least with regard to reproduction and public communication rights in the digital context, these exceptions were to replace entirely existing national rules on the subject.[14] However, all but one of the exceptions listed in Article 5 is permissive—that is, the member states may (and therefore need not) introduce them. The result is that an unharmonised scheme of exceptions and limitations continues to exist in the EU.

5.10 A generally restrictive approach to the exceptions is visible in the recitals:

> the provision of...exceptions [to copyright]...should...duly reflect the increased economic impact that such exceptions...may have in the context of the new electronic environment. Therefore the scope of certain exceptions may have to be even more limited when it comes to certain new uses of copyright works...(recital 44).

The Directive also seems to suggest that in at least some circumstances contractual provision may eliminate copyright exceptions. The fourth paragraph of Article 6(4) appears to give pre-eminence to contractual terms over the exceptions where works are made available in such a way that they may be accessed from places and at times individually chosen by users. Since this condition applies to everything found on the Internet, the provision seems to have the potential to eliminate the exceptions to copyright altogether in that context. Such apocalyptic conclusions need to be modified, however, because such elimination should only occur if a contract to that effect is *previously* in place between right holder and user. On the other hand, this reinforces the position of the right holder barring access in order to create an opportunity to establish a contractual nexus under which the user pays for his use; and it is really only against the right holder who wishes to deny access in order to be paid for the privilege that exceptions and limitations giving access regardless of the right holder's wishes are of any significance.[15]

 Exercise

Why do copyright exceptions have 'increased economic impact' in the electronic environment? Why should contract prevail over exceptions in that electronic environment?

---

[14] COM(1997) 628 final, 28 (para 2); see also recital 22 and Art 5(3)(p), the latter of which permits member states to provide for 'use in certain other cases of minor importance where exceptions already exist under national law, provided *that they only concern analogue uses* [emphasis added] and do not affect the free circulation of goods and services within the Community [now Union]'.

[15] See further C Geiger, 'From Berne to national law, via the Copyright Directive: the dangerous mutations of the three-step test' [2007] EIPR 486.

5.11   It should also be noted that the Software and Database Directives made provision for exceptions to the rights which they conferred,[16] and that these are largely unaffected by the InfoSoc Directive. The Software Directive notably lays down that most of the exceptions to copyright in computer programs—in particular, making back-up copies, decompilation and observation, studying, and testing—cannot be overcome by contractual agreement.[17] But there is nothing of this kind in the Database Directive.[18]

Copyright exceptions in the UK

5.12   The UK implemented the InfoSoc Directive provisions on copyright exceptions and limitations with effect from 31 October 2003,[19] and the following account is based upon the law as so amended (for recent proposals for changes, see paras 7.54–7.60). In negotiating and implementing the Directive, the UK Government's policy was to maintain as far as possible the previously existing regime, adjusting it as necessary. No new rights allowed under the Directive were introduced; but none of the existing rights made permissive by the Directive were eliminated, although some have been narrowed significantly in scope. The account which follows will therefore make use of authorities from the pre-Directive law as far as possible. It also deals with the implementation of the Software and Database Directives' provisions on exceptions and limitations, although only the former has truly distinct issues needing to be addressed.

(1) Making temporary copies

Introduction

5.13   As noted earlier (para 4.36), copying in relation to any description of work includes the making of copies which are transient or incidental to some other use of the work.[20] Major examples of what may therefore be infringement of copyright without the licence of the copyright owner are loading a computer program into a computer's RAM, or accessing an online database or website, where again copies are made in the RAM of the machine being used for the purpose. Indeed, the actual operation of the Internet, which involves the transmission of data in small packets from computer to computer across a network, also involves the making of temporary copies in each of the computers through which the packages are forwarded on their way. However, there are also important provisions amongst those on the permitted acts which prevent such temporary copying being infringement in certain, carefully defined, circumstances and so stop copyright becoming an impediment to perfectly reasonable, indeed often necessary, activities.

Temporary reproduction exception

5.14   The most general exception flows from the InfoSoc Directive. Copyright in author works (apart from computer programs and databases) and in typographical arrangements of a published edition, sound recordings, or films is not infringed by the making of a temporary copy which is transient or incidental, as long as:[21]

(1) the making is an *integral and essential part of a technological process,*

and

(2) the *sole purpose* is to enable *either—*

---

[16] Software Directive, Arts 5, 6; Database Directive, Arts 6, 9.
[17] Software Directive, Arts 5(2), (3), 6(1). See CDPA 1988, ss 50A, 50B(4), 50BA, and 296A, and para 5.44.
[18] However, see CDPA 1988, ss 50D(2) and 296B.   [19] Copyright and Related Rights Regulations 2003 (SI 2003/2498).
[20] CDPA 1988, s 17(6).   [21] CDPA 1988, s 28A.

(a) a *transmission of the work in a network* between third parties by an intermediary;

or

(b) a *lawful use* of the work *and*

(3) the temporary copy has no *independent economic significance*.

Diagram 5.1 Exceptions to copyright

Exceptions	Subject matter to which applicable	Relevant restricted acts
Temporary reproduction (general)	Author works apart from computer programs and databases	Temporary reproduction
Temporary reproduction (special)	Computer programs and databases	Temporary reproduction
Fair dealing (1): Non-commercial research	LDMA works	All
Fair dealing (2): Private study	LDMA works	All
Fair dealing (3): Criticism or review	LDMA works, films, sound recordings, broadcasts	All
Fair dealing (4): Reporting current events	LDMA works, films, sound recordings, broadcasts	All
Educational establishments	LDMA works	Copying; performing, playing, showing in public
Libraries and archives	LDM works	Copying; issuing to the public; lending
Disability	LDM works, broadcasts	Copying
Public administration	All; work done for public service, open to public inspection under statute, communicated to Crown in course of public business, public records	Copying; issuing to public
Incidental inclusion	All	Copying; issue to the public
Computer programs: back up; decompilation; observe, study, test; adapt for lawful use/error correction.	Computer programs	Copying; adaptation
Time-shifting	Broadcasts	Copying

Note: LDMA – literary, dramatic, musical and artistic works

This is an extremely simplified representation of the main exceptions recognised in UK copyright law, and should not be relied upon as a detailed analysis (for which the reader is referred to the text below as well as, of course, the relevant parts of CDPA 1988).

5.15 The operation of the Internet and the making of copies of packets in transmission, typically by Internet service providers, provide the clearest example of this exception in action. The technology works by the making of these copies, and its only purpose is to play a role in the transmission of the information from a website to the person accessing it. The copy has no independent economic significance, both because normally no one has any awareness of its existence and because on its own it has no utility or value to anyone; only when the packets are reunited at the accessing computer does the material become intelligible to a user.

Recital 33 of the InfoSoc Directive states that 'this exception should include acts which enable browsing as well as acts of caching to take place, including those which enable transmission systems to function effectively'. The temporary reproduction exception covers the copy made in the RAM of the recipient's computer in order for that person to see the page on the screen when that enables a 'lawful use'. Given that making a temporary copy as such is infringement of copyright, such use can only become lawful as a result of an express or implied licence from the copyright owner, or as a result of some other permitted act, such as research for non-commercial purposes, private study or certain educational uses.

5.16   It is a moot point whether the temporary reproduction exception covers what is known as 'proxy server caching', where by deploying appropriate software technology Internet service providers, universities, librarians, archivists, and others make and store on their own servers temporary and regularly updated copies of materials contained on other servers with the purpose of making the information more readily available to their local clients by avoiding congestion at the 'live' site.[22] Such copies are thus temporary, transient, and incidental, arguably form an integral and essential part of a technological process the purpose of which is to enable transmissions between other parties and lawful uses (whether licensed or permitted), while having no independent economic significance (unless perhaps users are charged for the enhanced service thus made available). The European Parliament sought to prevent the exception extending so far, but such a limitation was rejected by the Commission on the ground that if right owners' authorisation was required for cache copies, the effective operation of the Internet would be seriously hindered.[23] The InfoSoc Directive also provides that there may be exceptions for:

> use by communication or making available, for the purpose of research or private study, to individual members of the public by dedicated terminals on the premises of [publicly accessible libraries, educational establishments or museums, or by archives] of works and other subject-matter not subject to purchase or licensing terms which are contained in their collections (Art 5(3)(n)).

5.17   Two recent rulings by the Court of Justice have provided some guidance on the interpretation of the temporary reproduction exception.

■ Case C-5/08 *Infopaq International A/S v Danske Dagblades Forening* [2009] ECDR 16 (ECJ)

For the facts see para 4.20. The ECJ found that the acts of *printing* 11-word extracts from electronic news articles, carried out during the data capture process of an electronic 'cuttings' service by an agency, were not 'transient' copies. As a derogation from general principle (ie reproduction is infringement), the exception was to be interpreted restrictively and for the exception to apply, five cumulative conditions must be fulfilled (paras 54–71):

(1)   the act must be temporary;

(2)   it must be transient or incidental;

(3)   it must be an integral and essential part of the technological process;

(4)   the sole purpose of the process must be to enable a transmission network between third parties by an intermediary or the lawful use of the work or protected subject matter; and,

(5)   the act must have no independent economic significance.

---

[22]   Such operations may also amount to the infringing act of storage by electronic means.
[23]   See COM(1999) 250 final, para 4(1).

The Court also noted that a transient act of reproduction is intended to enable the completion of a tech-nological process of which it forms an integral and essential part and must not exceed what is necessary for the proper completion of that technological process. It has been held by the UK courts, following this ruling, that s 28A CDPA does not exempt users of a media-monitoring service from liability for making copies of headlines and extracts of newspaper articles while browsing the monitoring reports because the copies were not an essential or integral part of the technological process but the end which the process was designed to achieve.[24]

■ Case C-302/10 *Infopaq International A/S v Danske Dagblades Forening* (*Infopaq II*) (17 January 2012) (ECJ)

The Court of Justice found that acts of temporary reproduction carried out during the data capture proc-ess of an electronic 'cuttings' service by an agency met the requirements of the exception. The Court re-emphasised that the exemption must be interpreted strictly. There is no requirement to the effect that the acts of reproduction constituting an integral and essential part of a technological process must not initiate and terminate that process or involve human intervention (paras 29–29). The exception aims to make access to the protected works and their use possible. Acts of reproduction do not have independent economic significance if the implementation of those acts does not enable the generation of additional profit going beyond that derived from the lawful use of the work and the temporary reproduction does not modify the work in any way (paras 40–54).[25] The Court also said that if the activity meets all the criteria set down in Article 5(1) of the Infosoc Directive then it must be regarded as not conflicting with a normal exploitation of the work and must not unreasonably prejudice the legitimate interests of the rights holder (paras 55–57).

 Question

Under what conditions is temporary reproduction a permitted act rather than an infringement? Give some illustrative examples.

Temporary reproduction of databases and computer programs

5.18   The Database Directive[26] and, following it, section 50D of the 1988 Act provide in effect that tempo-rary reproduction of a database which is necessary for the purpose of access to and normal use of the contents of a database, or part thereof, by a person with a right to use the database, does not require the authorisation of the author of the database. A person will have a right to use through licence, express or implied, or by way of the generally permitted acts as far as they apply to databases. Any term or condi-tion of an agreement purporting to prohibit an act permitted under this provision of the 1988 Act is void.[27] The Software Directive[28] and, following it, section 50C of the 1988 Act also provide in effect that temporary reproduction or adaptation of a computer program necessary for a lawful user's lawful use of

---

[24] *Newspaper Licensing Agency Ltd v Meltwater Holding BV* [2010] EWHC 3099 (Ch); [2011] EWCA Civ 890 (CA); an appeal to the Supreme Court is outstanding. See para 4.20.

[25] See Case C-429/08 *Football Association Premier League Ltd v QC Leisure, Murphy v Media Protection Services Ltd* [2012] 1 CMLR 29, paras 174–178 where the reproduction taking place in the memory of a satellite decoder and its visual display were found to have no independ-ent economic significance beyond the advantage derived from mere reception of the broadcasts at issue. See also *ITV Broadcasting Ltd v TV Catchup* [2011] EWHC 2977 (Pat), paras 28–31 for reproduction taking place in the server memory of a streaming service.

[26] Database Directive, reading Art 6(1) in conjunction with Art 5(a).

[27] CDPA 1988, ss 50D(2) and 296B. For an example of a clause being held void under s 50D, see *Navitaire Inc v EasyJet Airline Co Inc* [2006] RPC 3.   [28] Software Directive, reading Art 5(1) in conjunction with Art 4(a).

the program is permitted. But, in an example of contract prevailing over exceptions (unlike the position with databases just described), a term of any contract regulating the circumstances in which the user's use is lawful, and prohibiting the copying or adaptation in question, will make those acts infringements. There are, however, a number of other acts in relation to computer programs which may be undertaken by a lawful user thereof, and which cannot be overridden by contract—making a back-up copy of the program, decompilation in terms of section 50B(2), and observing, studying, or testing the functioning of the program in accordance with section 50BA(2). And for the owner of copyright in a computer program to put it on the market without granting a licence, express or implied, to enable the purchaser to load it into a computer's RAM and run it (thereby making the purchaser a lawful user) would seem an absurd scenario.

Key points on exceptions for temporary reproduction

- The general exception, which does not apply to computer programs and databases, is for copying as an integral part of a technological process enabling either a network transmission or a lawful use of the work, and having no independent economic significance

- This is intended to allow 'browsing' on the Internet and 'caching'

- There are special exceptions for computer programs and databases, most of which cannot be contractually overridden

---

(2) Fair dealing

5.19   No fair dealing with a literary, dramatic, musical, or artistic work will constitute infringement of the copyright in the work if it is carried out for one of the permitted purposes. Fair dealing for any other purpose, or dealing which is only fair in general, is not permitted as such, and if there is not to be liability for infringement of copyright the activity will have to be shown to fall within some other category of permitted act. But dealing for one of the statutory purposes and also for some other purpose may still be fair dealing.[29] The permitted statutory purposes for all literary, dramatic, musical, and artistic works are:

- *research for a non-commercial purpose* accompanied by a sufficient acknowledgement, unless such acknowledgement is impossible for reasons of practicality or otherwise (CDPA 1988, s 29(1), as amended by 2003 Regulations);

- *private study* (CDPA 1988, s 29(1));

- *criticism or review*, whether of the work whose copyright is said to be infringed or of some other work or of a performance of a work, which is accompanied by a sufficient acknowledgement (CDPA 1988, s 30(1));

- *reporting current events* (CDPA 1988, s 30(2) and (3)).[30]

In addition, fair dealing for purposes of criticism and review and reporting current events can extend to sound recordings, films, and broadcasts. But in these cases, where current events are being reported, there is no need for a sufficient acknowledgement.[31]

---

[29] *Sillitoe v McGraw-Hill Book Co Ltd* [1983] FSR 545.
[30] Note that photographs are not included under the exception for reporting current events.
[31] See *BBC v BSB Ltd* [1992] Ch 141.

Question

Does fair dealing for purposes of non-commercial research or private study extend to films, sound recordings, and broadcasts?

Fairness and the 'three-step test'

5.20   The dealing with the copyright work must be fair; but the Act, both before and after the 2003 amendments, contains no elaboration of what is or is not fair. Contrast the list of factors to be taken into account under the fair use provisions of the US Copyright Act, which 'include' such matters as whether the use is of a commercial nature or for non-profit educational purposes, the amount and substantiality of the portion used in relation to the whole work, and the effect of the use upon the market or value of the copyright work (see para 5.7). Some of these (eg commercial use) are built into the structure of the specific exceptions in the UK, and others have emerged in the case law, as will appear from the following account. But the question of fairness is still, to at least some extent, at large. An important element now, however, is the express reference to the Berne 'three-step test' (para 5.8), not in the amended text of the 1988 Act, but in the underlying Software, Database, and InfoSoc Directives, that the exceptions and limitations are to be applied:

(1)   only in certain special cases;

(2)   not conflicting with normal exploitation; and

(3)   not unreasonably prejudicing the legitimate interests of the copyright owner.[32]

At least one implication of this must be that the impact of the activity upon the market for the right holder's work, if any, is a relevant factor in assessing the fairness of that activity and whether it should be allowed as an exception to the copyright.

Fair dealing: (a) research for non-commercial purposes[33]

Meaning of research

5.21   The meaning of the word 'research' appears never to have been judicially considered in the UK. Prior to the 2003 amendments it was linked to 'private study' but the two have now been severed, so they must each have a separate rather than a cumulative meaning. The *Oxford English Dictionary* defines research as a process of search or investigation undertaken to discover facts and reach new conclusions by the critical study of a subject or by a course of scientific inquiry; or as a systematic investigation into and study of materials, sources, and so on, to establish facts or collate information. Study, on the other hand, is more about the application of the mind to the acquisition of knowledge, or reading a book or text with close attention.[34] Research may therefore be thought of as having some end product in view, a contribution to knowledge and understanding; while study is more about acquiring knowledge and understanding that already exists. But on these definitions it must also be admitted that research is hardly conceivable without study, and that any distinction between the two is difficult

---

[32] Database Directive, Art 6(3); InfoSoc Directive, Art 5(5). The Software Directive also refers to the three-step test in permitting decompilation of computer programs (Art 6(3)): see further para 5.44.

[33] See generally Burrell and Coleman, *Copyright Exceptions*, note 1, 115–120. See also para 7.59.

[34] For these definitions see the *Oxford English Dictionary*; note also the Australian and New Zealand cases of *De Garis v Neville Jeffress Pidler* (1990) 18 IPR 292 (Fed Ct Aus); *Television New Zealand v Newsmonitor Services* [1994] 2 NZLR 91 (High Ct NZ); and *Copyright Licensing v University of Auckland* (2002) 53 IPR 618 (NZ).

to maintain. In the university context, research would be the characteristic activity of the PhD student and study that of the first-year undergraduate; but between the two levels there is a wide spectrum, indeed a progression, of activity partaking of both study and research. Thus, the undergraduate will study for exams and research for essays or dissertations, while the postgraduate will have studied for an undergraduate degree and to establish the base from which the subject of the doctoral research can be identified. The professor or lecturer, on the other hand, will research to write learned articles in scholarly journals, perhaps merely study in order to give lectures and tutorials, and be somewhere in between in writing a student textbook. It is not clear whether the professor merely keeping up to date in his field—for example, reading and making copies of new publications and filing them for possible future use—can be said to be carrying out research: on these definitions, probably not, but perhaps it amounts to private study. Whether research includes the publication of research results (ie quotation from research materials in the resulting publication) is perhaps a moot point. But it is difficult to see how one accompanies research carried out in one's own office, or in a library, archive, or gallery, with the 'sufficient acknowledgement' required by the statute. The use of that phrase with regard to the research exception (but not that for private study) at least suggests that the former *does* cover quotation from research materials (with appropriate citation) in the publication of the researcher's results.[35] The Directive talks of 'scientific research', but this does not mean that only research in what would generally be thought of as science (as opposed to arts, humanities, or social sciences) is covered; rather, it means research directed to the development of knowledge and understanding (*scientia*) in whatever discipline.

 Discussion point For answer guidance visit www.oxfordtextbooks.co.uk/orc/waelde3e/

Does the research exception extend to quotation from research materials in a subsequent publication? What is the implication of section 29(3)(b) of the CDPA 1988 in this connection?

Non-commercial purpose

5.22   The really crucial change to UK law which was made by the Directive and the 2003 Regulations was the restriction of the exception or permission for research to research carried out for a *non-commercial purpose*. Thus, for example, the copying which might have been involved in a lawyer carrying out legal research on behalf of a client now requires authorisation from—and probably the payment of a fee to—the copyright owner.[36] On the other hand, the research carried out by an undergraduate writing an essay for assessment is clearly for a non-commercial purpose, as would be that carried out by a civil servant while preparing an internal report for a government minister. Unfortunately, however, there is a large amount of ambiguity in the distinction between commercial and non-commercial research. To pursue the university context as an example: what is the position of the professor writing a learned monograph which will be published by a commercial publisher, and from which the professor will earn royalties?[37] Is it different if the product is for a professional journal or conference for which the professor will receive

---

[35] Burrell and Coleman, *Copyright Exceptions*, note 1, 117, argue the opposite view, supporting it by reference to CDPA 1988, s 29(3)(b). Guidance has been promulgated by the British Academy and the Publishers Association in April 2008, entitled 'Joint Guidelines on Copyright and Academic Research', available at http://www.publishers.org.uk/images/stories/AboutPA/Joint_Guidelines_on_Copyright_and_Academic_Research.pdf.

[36] So the comment in *Law Society of Upper Canada v CCH Canadian* [2004] 1 SCR 339, para 51 ('Lawyers carrying on the business of law for profit are conducting research') may be literally true, but that would probably not enjoy the benefit of any exception in the UK.

[37] Contrary to popular belief amongst students, academic authors do earn royalties!

a fee? Or for research which is initially published in an academic journal, for no fee, but which subsequently becomes the basis for the development of a commercial product? The language of the statute seems to suggest that the purpose of the research is to be tested at the time it is carried out, and that it is sufficient if there is 'a' non-commercial purpose, that is to say, where the researcher has multiple purposes, the presence of a non-commercial one will suffice to bring the copying involved within the scope of the exception. But the Database and InfoSoc Directives say that the 'sole purpose' must be scientific research,[38] that is, research that contributes to the development of knowledge and understanding, for it to fall within the exception.

■ *Controller HMSO and Ordnance Survey v Green Amps* **[2007] EWHC 2755 (Ch)**

In this case HMSO provided map data for a database service available to universities and the research community in the UK. Green Amps Ltd (GAL), a private company, gained unlicensed access to that service but argued that it came within the non-commercial research provision because it had used the data for a mapping tool facility in development, and their use thus had research and development status. The court held that, even if GAL's use of the mapping data had at that point only been for research, the research was for commercial purposes. Further, GAL's actions could not be described as fair dealing considering the extent and covertness of its copying.[39]

 Discussion point   For answer guidance visit www.oxfordtextbooks.co.uk/orc/waelde3e/

Does the InfoSoc Directive require the exclusion of all commercial research from the benefit of the exception for research?

 Exercise

The government commissions a private research consultancy company to investigate and report back on a social issue upon which it is proposed there should be legislation. The company will receive a substantial fee for its work. Is the company's research for government non-commercial? Would your answer be any different if the research was to be carried out by a charity active in the area where the social issue arises? Or by a law firm with expertise on it?

Research and typographical arrangements

5.23   Fair dealing with the typographical arrangement of a published edition for the purposes of research does not infringe any copyright in the arrangement.[40] The purpose of the research appears to be irrelevant in this context. The main significance of this permission would appear to be that the publisher of material which is photocopied or scanned into a computer, and who claims copyright infringement as a result, can be met with a defence of fair dealing. It is not clear, however, how much of the material can be copied on this basis; the dealing does have to be fair, and the publisher's loss of a sale, for example, might be seen as unfair in at least some contexts.

---

[38]   Database Directive, Art 6(2)(b); InfoSoc Directive, Art 5(3)(a).
[39]   See further E Derclaye, 'Of maps, Crown copyright, research and the environment' [2008] EIPR 162.
[40]   CDPA 1988, s 29(2).

Key points on the exception for non-commercial research

- UK law in this area was changed in 2003 as a result of the InfoSoc Directive

- Research, a process of search and investigation, must now be distinguished from private study

- Research for a commercial purpose is not within the exception. It is enough that there is 'a' commercial purpose; the presence of other non-commercial purposes will probably not bring the research within the exception

- The purpose is tested at the time the research is carried out

- This exception also applies to *sui generis* database right, but not to films, sound recordings, or broadcasts

Fair dealing: (b) private study

5.24   We have already defined 'study' as the application of the mind to the acquisition of knowledge (para 5.21). 'Private study' is the private study of the person dealing with the work. The fact that some third party may use the secondary work for purposes of private study does not protect the copier from a claim of infringement of copyright. Thus, the reprinting of examination papers as a collection for sale to students was not fair dealing with the examination papers,[41] nor was the publication of study aids on well-known literary works for the use of school pupils.[42] This principle is reinforced by statutory provision to the effect that copying by a person other than the student himself is not fair dealing in two cases. First is the provision of copies by librarians outside the special provisions for them found elsewhere in the 1988 Act.[43] Second is the person who makes the copy, knowing or having reason to believe that it will result in copies of substantially the same material being provided to more than one person at substantially the same time and for substantially the same purpose. This seems to ensure that the production of multiple copies cannot be justified under the heading of private study.[44] It would also seem that study carried out for another person—an employer, for example—cannot be private study. Private must mean that the study is for one's own personal purposes.

Private study and students in schools, colleges, and universities

5.25   The exception for private study is of particular importance to students undertaking education in schools, colleges, and universities.[45] There is extensive provision in the 1988 Act restricting reprography (ie photocopying, digital scanning) *by educational establishments*, which restrain what can be freely done by and on behalf of an educational establishment for the purposes of providing instruction, but *not* what can be done *by the individual receiving instruction* or, indeed, carrying out research, where the fair dealing exceptions may be relevant. An institution making and distributing photocopies or printouts to a class as a course pack can be distinguished from students copying parts of or complete works for their own study. Such copying does not fall within the scope of any of the other exceptions for educational

---

[41]   *University of London Press Ltd v University Tutorial Press Ltd* [1916] 2 Ch 601.

[42]   *Sillitoe v McGraw-Hill Book Co Ltd* [1983] FSR 545 (*The Loneliness of the Long-Distance Runner*).

[43]   CDPA 1988, s 29(3)(a); and see further para 5.39 for librarians and archivists.

[44]   CDPA 1988, s 29(3)(b). Compare s 40 (librarian exception), discussed at para 5.39.

[45]   See generally *Universities UK v Copyright Licensing Agency* [2002] RPC 36 (Copyright Tribunal), paras 31–40. For educational establishments, see CDPA 1988, s 174 and Copyright (Educational Establishments) Order 2005 (SI 2005/223).

reprography or copying by librarians, but this does not mean that the defence of fair dealing for private study is unavailable.[46]

Private study and typographical arrangements

5.26   An important provision in this context says that fair dealing with the typographical arrangement of a published edition for the purposes of private study does not infringe any copyright in the arrangement:[47] thus, photocopying can be fair dealing in relation to the publisher as well as the author of the work being copied. How much of the material can be legitimately taken for purposes of private study? In the context of photocopying, Parliament has resisted publishing lobbies seeking a quantifiable measure of how much of a work may be copied or used under this exemption, and it remains arguable that in some circumstances the whole of a work may be taken. For example, if I call up a webpage while surfing the Internet, a copy of the whole is made in the RAM of my computer, and it would be impossible to do less.

Exercise

Find out what the policies of your educational establishment are with regard to the making and distribution of copies of material for study purposes. Who, if anyone, pays for the making of these copies?

Private study and websites

5.27   Private study is probably the most obviously significant permitted act for users of websites, at any rate in the domestic context. It means that the surfer at home is making a lawful use of the work embodied in the website when a temporary copy is made in the computer's RAM by accessing the site: therefore that copy is not an infringement of copyright.[48] The private study exemption would also appear clearly applicable to the user of a website making a hard or electronic copy of the material he finds there, as long as he keeps it for private purposes; but if he prints out a copy of text or an image found on the Internet to replace a previous copy which he made but has lost or destroyed, is he within the exception? Note that the private study exception does not apply to sound recordings, films, or broadcasts, so that the unauthorised downloader can find no comfort here from claims of copyright infringement. If I want to study the music or lyrics embodied in a sound recording, I will have to do so in ways other than copying the sound recording: for example, by making copies of the musical notation or the text of the words.

Storing and making available for private study

5.28   Can the operator of a website use the private study exemption to justify putting up on his site the copyright works of others as a convenient library akin to the books on the shelves in his study? In French cases about the unauthorised inclusion of the poetry of Raymond Queneau on websites, it was held that a website unprotected by security devices and open to any visitor was in the public domain and that the copying involved in its creation could not be justified by the general exemption in French law for private reproduction.[49] UK law has no general saving for private use, and it seems likely that a British court would reach the same conclusion as the French one, albeit by the route that the private study exemption

---

[46] See CDPA 1988, s 28(4).   [47] CDPA 1988, s 29(2).   [48] CDPA 1988, s 28A, inserted by 2003 Regulations.
[49] French Intellectual Property Code of 1 July 1992, Art L122–5.

applies only to one's own study and not to making private study possible for third parties.[50] Admittedly, in the British cases the copier was supplying the copied material in the course of business, while a website producer might well not be earning any financial return from his activities; but the court would likely be concerned about the probable damage to the earnings of the copyright owner and so deem the activity unfair. The general rule that the exemption does not apply to one whose copying makes private study possible for others would seem to eliminate any possibility that this exception could be used by those who provide materials on the Internet by way of proxy server caches. British courts would also probably hold that the exception would not allow MP3.com to copy CDs into MP3 format to enable them to be accessed on the Internet for private use by customers who were already lawful users of the CDs in question,[51] or for Napster to provide lists enabling Individuals to locate and copy files of copyright music held on other people's computers.

 Exercise

Is 'bookmarking' your favourite websites, or creating hyperlinks to them from your own personal website, allowed as 'private study'?

Key points on the exception for private study

- Study, the application of the mind to the acquisition of knowledge, is distinct from research

- Private means that the study is for the student's personal purposes

- Copying or issuing material to the public for the purpose of others' private study is not within the exception

- There are a number of special exceptions for educational establishments and libraries to enable them to provide copies for others' private study

- While the exception can apply to 'web-surfers', it does not apply to sound recordings, films or broadcasts

Fair dealing: (c) criticism or review[52]

Criticism or review

5.29   Fair dealing with any kind of work, including sound recordings, films, broadcasts and cable programmes, for purposes of *criticism and review* of that, or of another, work or of a performance of a work, is also a permitted act if accompanied by a *sufficient acknowledgement*, and provided that the work has been made available to the public.[53] This gives effect to Article 5(3)(d) of the InfoSoc Directive, save that the latter refers to 'purposes *such as* criticism *or* review' (emphasis added). *Review* requires, as a minimum, some dealing with an original copyrighted work other than condensing that work into a summary. *Criticism*, on the other hand, is not solely focused on the style of a copyrighted work but can also extend to the ideas or theories that work contains.

---

[50] *University of London Press Ltd v University Tutorial Press Ltd* [1916] 2 Ch 601; *Sillitoe v McGraw-Hill Book Co (UK) Ltd* [1983] FSR 545.
[51] *UMG Recordings Inc and others v MP3.com Inc*, 2000 WL 1262568 (SD NY).
[52] See generally Burrell and Coleman, *Copyright Exceptions*, note 1, 42–62.
[53] CDPA 1988, s 30(1) as amended by 2003 Regulations.

Quantity of material quoted and reproduced

5.30   Unlike research and private study, there is nothing express to prevent the criticism/review exception extending to the making of multiple copies, but it is difficult to see how such activity could be justified under this heading. A typical example of an activity coming within the exception would be a review of a book with quotations in illustration of critical points, or a film review on a TV programme containing extracts from the film in question. Another instance would be comments upon a book in another book or article, with the use of quotations to point the criticism. The criticism need not be hostile. But how much of the original work can be used for such purposes? Lengthy extracts from the original work have been permitted where the purpose was purely to enable criticism to be made,[54] but where the purpose is not so much to provide criticism but the same information as the original work and to compete with it, the activity cannot be allowed.[55] Further, the criticism or review must be directed to the original or another work, not at the author or against the person whose activities are the subject of the original work.[56] The original or other work criticised must be a work of the kind protected by copyright, although it need not be in copyright at the time.[57]

■ *Hubbard v Vosper* [1972] 2 QB 84 (CA)

This case involved the unauthorised publication (although in a traditional rather than an electronic medium) of the works of L Ron Hubbard, founder of the Church of Scientology, together with critical commentary thereupon. The Court of Appeal found that the criticism was sufficient to make the taking of substantial extracts of the copyright material fair dealing.[58]

■ *Pro Sieben Media AG v Carlton UK Television Ltd* [1999] FSR 610 (CA)

The case concerned a German TV programme in which Mandy Allwood, then pregnant with eight foetuses as a result of fertility treatment, was interviewed with her boyfriend, both having been paid for their participation. CTV used unauthorised extracts from the German programme in another documentary attacking 'chequebook' journalism. It was held that their use was fair dealing as criticism and review rather than copying to take the right holder's market. The Court of Appeal said that the extent of use was relevant in considering fair dealing, but that relevance would depend on the circumstances of each case. Most important was the degree of competition, if any, between the two works in question. The mental element of the user was of little importance, so that a sincere belief that one was being critical in one's handling of the previous work would not be enough to make out the defence. However, the court emphasised that the phrase 'criticism or review' was of wide and indefinite scope and should be interpreted liberally.

■ *Fraser-Woodward Ltd v BBC and another* [2005] FSR 36

Photographs of a well-known footballer (David Beckham) and his family were published under licence in tabloid newspapers. The defendants used images of the newspaper pages with the photographs in a BBC TV programme, to criticise their coverage of the doings of celebrities. The copyright owner sued for

---

[54] *Hubbard v Vosper* [1972] 2 QB 84; cf *Sillitoe v McGraw-Hill Book Co Ltd* [1983] FSR 545.

[55] *Independent Television Publications Ltd v Time Out Ltd* [1984] FSR 64.

[56] *Ashdown v Telegraph Group Ltd* [2002] Ch 149 (CA).

[57] *Fraser-Woodward Ltd v BBC and another* [2005] FSR (36) 762.

[58] Cf the US case of *Religious Technology Center v Lerma*, 1996 WL 633131 (ED Va). In similar circumstances in *Religious Technology Center v Netcom On-Line Communication Service* 907 F Supp 1361 (ND Cal, 1995), however, the court held that Netcom, a service provider, might have a valid fair use defence.

infringement of the copyright in the photographs. It was held that the defendants' use was for the purposes of criticism and review of the newspapers rather than the photographs themselves. But since under section 30(1) a work could be used to criticise 'another work', the defendants' activity fell within the scope of the permitted act. The other work had to be a work itself capable of copyright protection, but it did not have to be still in copyright. The *Pro Sieben* case also showed that the ideas or philosophy underlying a certain style of journalism could be the subject of criticism within the scope of section 30(1).

■ *IPC Media Ltd v News Group Newspapers Ltd* [2005] FSR 35

The *Sun* newspaper advertised its new magazine with illustrations of the front covers of two other magazines with which it was to compete. The owners of the rival magazines sued for copyright infringement, to which the owners of the *Sun* responded with a claim of fair dealing for purposes of criticism or review. It was held that the criticism/review in this case was directed not at the claimant's *work*, but at their product. Comparative advertising was intended to advance the *Sun*'s work at the expense of the other works, and this was not fair dealing.

Discussion point 1   For answer guidance visit www.oxfordtextbooks.co.uk/orc/waelde3e/

Do you agree with the decision of the Court of Appeal in *Hubbard v Vosper*?

Discussion point 2

Why is a 'wide, liberal' approach needed for the exemption for criticism and review? How does this compare to the ECJ's idea in *Infopaq* (para 5.17) that exceptions should be approached narrowly?

Sufficient acknowledgement

5.31   A *sufficient acknowledgement* is an identification of the work in question by its title or other description and, unless the work is published anonymously or the identity of the author cannot be ascertained by reasonable inquiry, also identifying the author.[59] It is not sufficient for it to be merely possible to identify the original work and author in the activity said to be fair dealing; the acknowledgement must be such as to suggest recognition of the position or claim of the author in respect of the original work. Thus study aids on the work of well-known authors, aimed at school pupils, did not sufficiently acknowledge their position or claim even though the merest glance at the study aids revealed the works and authors in question.[60]

Public availability of work being criticised and reviewed

5.32   Under the law before 31 October 2003, it was held to be unfair to subject an unpublished work to public criticism, particularly where the author never intended to publish it.[61] Again, to use copyright documents which were confidential yet given to someone not entitled to them might be unfair even though the use is for one or more of the statutory purposes.[62] 'But after all is said and done it must be a matter of impression ... The tribunal of fact must decide.'[63] So it was not impossible for use of confidential documents to be fair dealing,[64] and public criticism of unpublished material was not automatically to be

---

[59] CDPA 1988, s 178.   [60] *Sillitoe v McGraw-Hill Book Co (UK) Ltd* [1983] FSR 545.
[61] *British Oxygen Co v Liquid Air Ltd* [1925] Ch 383; *Beloff v Pressdram* [1973] RPC 765.
[62] See *Beloff v Pressdram* [1973] RPC 765 at 787–788.   [63] *Hubbard v Vosper* [1972] 2 QB 84 per Lord Denning MR at 94.
[64] *Fraser v Evans* [1969] 1 QB 349.

regarded as unfair dealing if it had had some previous circulation.[65] The law of copyright was not to be used to restrain free speech in relation to political or religious controversy.[66] The implementation of the InfoSoc Directive has, however, led to a significant development of the law in this respect. *Only* criticism and review of a work which has been made available to the public is fair dealing. The work may have been made available by any means—by issue of copies to the public, through an electronic retrieval system, by way of public rental, lending, performance, exhibition, showing, or playing, or through public communication. However, no account is to be taken in this regard of any unauthorised act.[67] Thus, it would seem that criticism or review of unpublished material involving quotation thereof, or where the material has been obtained surreptitiously or by breach of confidence, cannot claim to be fair dealing as criticism or review.[68]

■ *Fraser v Evans* [1969] 1 QB 349

(Consider the facts of this breach of confidence case in the light of the discussion point following it.) F, a public relations consultant, submitted a report to the Greek Government under a contract expressly imposing on him alone a duty to keep his work confidential. The report came into the hands of the *Sunday Times*, apparently from Greek Government sources. *Sunday Times* journalists interviewed F and proposed to publish an article the following Sunday based on the report and the interview. F obtained an injunction *ex parte* to restrain publication as a breach of confidence. On appeal it was held that as the Greek Government owed no duty of confidence to F and did not itself seek the court's protection, F had no standing to obtain interim relief on his own behalf.

 Discussion point   For answer guidance visit www.oxfordtextbooks.co.uk/orc/waelde3e/

Supposing that both F and the Greek Government wished to prevent quotations from the report appearing in the *Sunday Times* by claiming copyright infringement, could the newspaper in defence now plead fair dealing for purposes of criticism and review?

■ *Beloff v Pressdram* [1973] RPC 765

B, a political journalist for the *Observer*, sent an internal memorandum to colleagues revealing the view of a serving Cabinet minister that another minister was the natural successor to the then Prime Minister. A copy of this memorandum was obtained surreptitiously by *Private Eye*, which published and commented on the memorandum as part of an attack on the serving Cabinet minister and on the journalist, who had previously criticised the magazine's campaign against the second minister. It was held that *Private Eye*'s actions were not fair dealing for purposes of criticism and review, although it was not the law (then) that unpublished works were outside the fair dealing defences.

 Question

How would this case be decided today? See further the following case.

---

[65] *Hubbard v Vosper* [1972] 2 QB 84.   [66] *Kennard v Lewis* [1983] FSR 346 per Warner J at 347.
[67] For all this see CDPA 1988, s 30(1A), added by 2003 Regulations.
[68] In appropriate cases, however, it might be fair dealing for the purpose of reporting current events: see further paras 5.33–5.35.

■ *HRH The Prince of Wales v Associated Newspapers Ltd (No 3)* [2008] Ch 57 (CA)

Extracts from unpublished journals of the Prince of Wales recording his impressions from his official visit to Hong Kong were published in the *Mail on Sunday* in 2005, without the Prince's consent. It was held that since the journals were unpublished, the exception for criticism and review was inapplicable. The fact that much of the *information* contained in the journals was already in the public domain made no difference.

Key points on exception for criticism and review

- This exception applies to all forms of copyright work
- The critic/reviewer must, however, provide a sufficient acknowledgement to the work in question by identifying it by its title, and also its author
- The work criticised/reviewed must be one that is publicly available
- The exception should be given a wide and liberal interpretation
- Use of a copyright work in the criticism or review of another work, even one that is not in copyright, may be justified under the exception
- But the exception does not allow one freely to criticise the author of the work as distinct from the work itself, or the person whose activities are the subject of the work's content

---

Fair dealing: (d) reporting current events[69]

5.33 Fair dealing with any work *other than a photograph* for the purpose of reporting current events does not infringe copyright, provided that it is accompanied by a sufficient acknowledgement.[70] The underlying idea here is clearly to support the circulation of news. There is no requirement like that for the criticism/review exception, that the work being reported is available to the public, although in the modern case law unauthorised takings of material subsequently quoted in news reports has been a factor in holding the publication not fair dealing.[71] Photographs are exempted altogether from the fair dealing provisions on news reporting.[72] Since news reporting is a major use of photographs in all media, the availability of a fair dealing exception in respect of these works was felt to undermine the market position of the photographer too much.

Sufficient acknowledgement

5.34 Principles similar to those discussed with regard to criticism and review (para 5.29) apply to the concept of acknowledgement in the context of reporting current events. A brief reference in a newspaper story to the fact that quoted words had been given in answer to another newspaper's questions did not constitute sufficient acknowledgement of its authorship as distinct from its copyright.[73] But no acknowledgement is required in connection with the reporting of current events by means of a sound recording,

---

[69] See generally Burrell and Coleman, *Copyright Exceptions*, note 1, 42–62.
[70] CDPA 1988, s 30(2). See also s 45(2) in relation to reporting parliamentary and judicial proceedings.
[71] See *Hyde Park Residence Ltd v Yelland* [2000] RPC 604 (CA); *Ashdown v Telegraph Group Ltd* [2002] Ch 149 (CA); and further J Griffiths, 'Copyright law after *Ashdown*: time to deal fairly with the public' [2002] IPQ 240.
[72] CDPA 1988, s 30(3).   [73] *Express Newspapers plc v News (UK) Ltd* [1990] FSR 359.

film, broadcast, or cable programme, where this would be impossible for reasons of practicality or otherwise.

Examples

5.35   A defence of reporting current events was upheld in *BBC v BSB Ltd*,[74] where extracts from BBC sports broadcasts lasting from 4 to 37 seconds and made with acknowledgement to the BBC were included without permission in BSB news programmes. The Court of Appeal in *Pro Sieben Media AG v Carlton UK Television*[75] indicated that, like 'criticism or review', reporting of current events is of wide scope and is to be interpreted liberally. In this area, the right to freedom of expression in the European Convention on Human Rights is likely to be of particular importance.[76]

■ *Newspaper Licensing Agency v Marks and Spencer plc* [2001] Ch 257 (CA)

For the facts, see para 2.96. It was held in the Court of Appeal, reversing Lightman J ([1999] RPC 536) that a company which ran a daily programme of circulating and distributing amongst its executives copies of newspaper cuttings provided by a licensed cuttings agency could maintain that this was fair dealing for the purpose of reporting current events. The Court of Appeal also held that in any event there had been no infringement by the defendants, since what was copied was not a substantial part of the original copyright work (the typographical arrangement of the *whole* newspaper, as distinct from the articles copied). On appeal the House of Lords upheld this view and therefore did not think it necessary to discuss fair dealing defences (again, see para 2.96).

■ *Hyde Park Residence Ltd v Yelland* [1999] RPC 655 (Jacob J); [2000] RPC 604 (CA)

This case was concerned with the unauthorised publication by the *Sun* in September 1998 of CCTV photographs of Princess Diana and Dodi al-Fayed, taken on the day of their deaths on 31 August 1997 at the former mansion of the Duchess of Windsor. Jacob J held that the one-year gap in time did not prevent these events continuing to be 'current', given the continuing publicity about the visit arising from statements made two days before the publication in question by Mohammed al-Fayed, tenant of the mansion and, through a security company which he controlled, owner of the copyright in the photographs. This 'liberal' approach to the definition of current events was accepted by the Court of Appeal, even although the *Sun's* actual use of the photographs was held not to be fair dealing, because the falsity of Mr al-Fayed's statements was already public knowledge, and the spread given to material itself dishonestly obtained and hitherto unpublished was excessive.

■ *Ashdown v Telegraph Group Ltd* [2002] Ch 149 (CA)

The 'liberal' approach to the currency of events was again applied by the Court of Appeal in this case. The *Sunday Telegraph* newspaper had published unlicensed extracts from the diaries of Paddy Ashdown, the former Liberal Democrat leader, shortly before they were due to be published by him as a book. The copying in question occurred in December 1999 but related to events over two years earlier. These were nonetheless arguably current events: 'In a democratic society, information about a meeting between the Prime Minister and an opposition party leader during the then current Parliament to discuss possible close co-operation between those parties is very likely to be of legitimate and continuing public interest. It might impinge upon the way in which the public would vote at the next general election' (para 64). But in the end the Telegraph Group's dealings were unfair: the publication destroyed part of the

---

[74] [1991] 3 WLR 174, 3 All ER 833.   [75] [1999] FSR 610 (CA).   [76] See further at para 5.49.

commercial value of Ashdown's diary, which he intended to publish himself;[77] much of the material covered was already in the public domain at the time of publication although the diary was previously unpublished; the material had been obtained in breach of confidence; and a substantial portion was copied, adding significant commercial value for the newspaper.

■ *HRH The Prince of Wales v Associated Newspapers Ltd* (No 3) [2008] Ch 57 (CA)

For the facts, see para 5.32. It was held that the exception for reporting current events was inapplicable. The events in question—the UK's return of Hong Kong to the People's Republic of China in 1997—were no longer current in 2005, when the extracts were published. While there was some faint light on the recent conduct of the heir to the throne and his approach to his position, the overall impression of the article was of a selection of 'choice passages' from the journal, with the revelation of the contents of the journal itself the event of interest.

■ *Media Works NZ Ltd v Sky Television Network Ltd* [2007] NZHC 924

The case concerned the broadcasting rights of the Rugby World Cup 2007, held exclusively by MWNZ. The court held that three Sky programmes entitled *The Cup* (a magazine programme), *The Crowd Goes Wild* (discussing the prospects and performance of teams and players), and *Reunion* (another magazine-style programme with rugby reviews) did not use MWNZ rugby footage for the 'purpose of reporting current events'. Furthermore, it was held that Sky's use of MWNZ footage on its programmes did not amount to fair dealing given the number of programmes and the number of times they were repeated. Sky's coverage had gone beyond public interest considerations by eroding the status of MWNZ as an exclusive broadcaster of the Rugby World Cup 2007 and negatively impacting upon MWNZ's investment in the copyright.

 Discussion point For answer guidance visit www.oxfordtextbooks.co.uk/orc/waelde3e/

Is the death of Princess Diana in August 1997 still a current event? Or the events in New York on 11 September 2001? Or the fall of the Berlin Wall in 1989?

Key points on the exception for reporting current events

- The exception applies to all copyright works except photographs
- There must be sufficient acknowledgement of the source
- The exception is to receive wide scope and a liberal interpretation
- Events may remain 'current' for some time after their occurrence, but not indefinitely

Fair dealing: fairness

5.36   Even if the dealing is shown to be for the statutory purposes, and appropriate acknowledgement has been made, the test of *fairness* remains to be satisfied. For example, to take large extracts from a work and

---

[77] And in fact did, in November 2000: *The Ashdown Diaries, vol 1: 1988–1997* (2000).

criticise only some of them may be unfair and make the dealing an infringement rather than a permitted act.[78] Insofar as it may involve criticism of someone else's work, comparative advertising is nonetheless not fair dealing because its primary purpose is to advance the critic's own work.[79] The InfoSoc Directive, in language not transposed directly into the UK legislation, says that the use should be 'in accordance with fair practice, and to the extent required by the specific purpose'.[80]

Exercise

Consider the case of a database protected by copyright (as distinct from *sui generis* database right, see paras 2.56–2.63). Do the fair dealing exceptions discussed previously apply to such databases? Has the UK properly implemented Article 6 of the Database Directive?

Educational establishments

5.37 There are a number of exceptions in favour of educational establishments (schools, further education colleges, and universities).[81] Education is clearly an area of activity for which dissemination of material amongst teachers and students is important, but the permissions and exemptions are nonetheless quite narrowly and technically drawn. So, for example, copying literary, dramatic, musical, and artistic works in the course of instruction (or its preparation) which is non-commercial is not infringement provided that the copying is:

- done by the person giving or receiving instruction;

- *not* done by a reprographic process (ie photocopying, printouts of electronically stored material, and electronic copies of such material);[82]

- accompanied by a sufficient acknowledgement unless practically or otherwise impossible.[83]

Question

What steps should be taken by a school teacher wishing to make use of the educational establishment exception to distribute copies of a copyright poem for discussion in his class?

5.38 In addition, if the work in question has been made available to the public,[84] the copying must amount to fair dealing (ie be for purposes of research, private study, criticism and review, or reporting current events). An example of a permitted use under this heading might be a teacher dictating a poem to a class; but cutting and pasting text or images from a website into a project would have to look for exemption under another head. The 1988 Act does permit reprography for non-commercial instructional purposes by educational establishments, but only subject to quite severe limitations. Reprographic copies of more than 1 per cent of any work in any quarter of a year are prohibited; and even that is not allowed if licences for such copying are available[85] and the person making the copies knew or ought

---

[78] *Hubbard v Vosper* [1972] 2 QB 84; *Sillitoe v McGraw-Hill Book Co (UK) Ltd* [1983] FSR 545.

[79] *IPC Media Ltd v News Group Newspapers Ltd* [2005] FSR (35) 752.   [80] InfoSoc Directive, Art 5(3)(d).

[81] CDPA 1988, ss 32–36A; s 174 (meaning of educational establishment); Copyright (Educational Establishments) Order 2005 (SI 2005/223). See generally Burrell and Coleman, *Copyright Exceptions*, note 1, 120–135.

[82] CDPA 1988, s 178 (definition of 'reprography').   [83] CDPA 1988, s 32(1), (2A).

[84] For the meaning of 'making available', see CDPA 1988, s 30(1A).

[85] As they commonly will be, from the Copyright Licensing Agency: see now *Universities UK v Copyright Licensing Agency* [2002] RPC 36, and see further U Suthersanen, 'Copyright and educational policies: a stakeholder analysis' (2003) 23 OJLS 585.

to have known of that fact.[86] These provisions significantly restrain what can be freely done by and on behalf of an educational establishment for the purposes of providing instruction, and are really aimed at providing a basis upon which the real needs of the educational establishment can only be met by obtaining and paying for a licence from collecting societies acting on behalf of authors and publishers. Other exemptions include:

- copying sound recordings, films, or broadcasts by making films or film sound tracks in the course of instruction in the making of films or films sound tracks;[87]

- anything done for purposes of examinations, apart from reprography of musical works for exam candidates to perform;[88]

- inclusion in educational anthologies of short extracts from published literary and dramatic works;[89]

- performing, playing, or showing works in the course of educational activities;[90]

- recording broadcasts for educational purposes.[91]

Question

Do these provisions for educational establishments go as far as Article 5(3)(a) of the InfoSoc Directive, which allows exceptions for 'use for the sole purpose of illustration for teaching... to the extent justified by the non-commercial purpose to be achieved'?

Libraries and archives[92]

5.39   A public library does not infringe lending right by lending books within the Public Lending Right scheme,[93] while prescribed libraries and archives other than public libraries, not conducted for profit and prescribed by the Secretary of State, likewise do not infringe lending right by lending any copy of a work.[94] The 1988 Act also contains extremely detailed provisions which, speaking very broadly, enable prescribed libraries and archives to supply readers with a single copy of published literary, dramatic or musical material for the purposes of private study or research, provided that the reader makes a signed declaration to that effect and pays a sum not less than the cost attributable to producing the copy.[95] This exemption is undoubtedly geared to a world of hard rather than electronic copies, and also does not seem readily applicable to making Internet material available, or storing it in advance of a specific demand, via a proxy cache on the computers or servers in the library or archive.

Discussion point For answer guidance visit www.oxfordtextbooks.co.uk/orc/waelde3e/

Why do libraries and archives receive the special provision detailed previously, but not museums and galleries?

---

[86] CDPA 1988, s 36.   [87] CDPA 1988, s 32(2).   [88] CDPA 1988, s 32(3), (4).   [89] CDPA 1988, s 33.
[90] CDPA 1988, s 34; and see paras 4.53–4.59.   [91] CDPA 1988, s 35.
[92] See generally Burrell and Coleman, *Copyright Exceptions*, note 1, 136–163.   [93] See the Public Lending Right Act 1979.
[94] CDPA 1988, s 40A. Libraries and archives are prescribed by the Secretary of State under regulations (s 37(1)(a)).
[95] CDPA 1988, ss 37–44; Copyright (Librarians and Archivists) (Copying of Copyright Material) Regulations 1989 (SI 1989/1212).

Deposit libraries

5.40   The Legal Deposit Libraries Act 2003 is the current provision under which those who publish print material in the UK can be required to deposit a copy of the publication with each of the following libraries: the British Library, the National Libraries of Scotland and Wales, the Bodleian Library, Oxford, the Cambridge University Library, and the Library of Trinity College Dublin. The deposit rights have existed since the 18th century; the purpose of the 2003 Act was to extend the deposit obligation beyond print, and in particular to works published on the Internet. In order to facilitate the capture of Internet material for the deposit libraries, the Act introduced an exception allowing them to make copies of such material for the purpose.[96]

Key points on libraries and archives

- Libraries receive some special exemptions in relation to their lending activities

- Libraries and archives are also enabled to supply readers with copies for their private study or non-commercial research, but the reader must sign a declaration and pay at least the cost of producing the copy in question

- There are six 'copyright libraries' in the British Isles, each entitled to receive a copy of every copyright work printed in the UK. This right of legal deposit is being applied to Internet material

---

Provision for disability

5.41   The InfoSoc Directive allows 'uses for the benefit of a people with a disability, which are directly related to the disability and of a non-commercial nature, to the extent required by the specific disability'.[97] As originally passed in 1988, the CDPA contained provisions enabling designated bodies to make copies of broadcasts and issue them to the public with subtitles for the deaf and hard of hearing, or otherwise modified for the special needs of those physically or mentally handicapped in other ways.[98] The 1988 Act was supplemented by the Copyright (Visually Impaired Persons) Act 2002, which allowed the making of accessible copies for the personal use of such a person, provided that he or she has lawful possession or use of a 'master copy' of the work which is inaccessible as a result of the impairment. Further, approved bodies that have lawful possession of a copy of a commercially published author work or edition may make accessible copies for the personal use of visually impaired persons.[99] Visual impairment includes not only blindness and impairment of visual function not curable to acceptable levels by the use of corrective lenses, but also physical disability preventing the person from holding or manipulating a book or from focusing or moving his eyes to the extent normally acceptable for purposes of reading.[100]

---

[96] CDPA 1988, s 44A; the 2003 Act came into force on 1 February 2004 (Legal Deposit Libraries Act 2003 (Commencement) Order 2004 (SI 2004/130)), but Regulations bringing the Internet provisions into operation were still awaited as at 30 August 2012. Details of a consultation on the Draft Legal Deposit Libraries (non-print works) Regulations 2013 can be found at http://www.culture.gov.uk/consultations/8878.aspx.

[97] Art 5(3)(b).   [98] CDPA 1988, s 74.   [99] See in general CDPA 1988, ss 31A–31F.

[100] CDPA 1988, s 31F(9). See further D Bradshaw, 'Making books and other copyright works accessible, without infringement, to the visually impaired: a review of the practical operation of the applicable, and recently-enacted, UK legislation' [2005] IPQ 335.

Public administration

5.42 Copyright is not infringed by a number of actions which are grouped under the heading of public administration.[101] Again this is permitted under the InfoSoc Directive,[102] although it talks of 'public security'[103] rather than 'public administration'. Only one example, perhaps of particular pertinence to law students and lawyers, will be given here. Anything done for the purpose of reporting parliamentary or judicial proceedings does not infringe copyright; but this does not authorise the copying of a work which is itself a published report of the proceedings (eg Hansard, a law report).[104]

Incidental inclusion

5.43 Copyright in a work is not infringed by its incidental inclusion in an artistic work, sound recording, film or broadcast:[105] for example, the inclusion in the background of an informal photographic portrait of a painting or sculpture, or its appearance in the background of a television broadcast. Alongside this rule may be mentioned another one, permitting certain acts in respect of buildings, sculptures, models for buildings, and works of artistic craftsmanship which are situated permanently in a public place or in premises open to the public: they may be made the subject of a graphic work, a photograph or film, or included in a broadcast as a visual image without their copyright being infringed thereby.[106] In neither case is the copyright infringed by the issue to the public of copies (eg videos of the broadcast), or the playing, showing, or broadcasting of such a work.[107] A musical work, words spoken or sung with music, or so much of a sound recording, broadcast or cable programme as includes a musical work or such words, is not to be regarded as incidentally included in another work if it is deliberately included[108]—for example, as part of background noise in a film or television production; thus, copyright permission will be required.

■ *FA Premier League v Panini* **[2004] FSR 1 (CA)**

P distributed an unofficial football sticker album and a sticker collection of pictures of players from Premier League clubs wearing team strips showing the Premier League logo or the logo of a Premier League club. FAPL, acting on behalf of the clubs, had granted exclusive rights to T, to use and reproduce the official team logos in stickers and albums. It was held at first instance that there was infringement. The use of the logos was not incidental, meaning casual or of secondary importance, but integral to showing the footballer in his current strip. An appeal was dismissed. 'Incidental' did not mean only unintentional or non-deliberate inclusion, and the question had to be answered by considering the circumstances in which the relevant artistic work was created. There was no necessary dichotomy between 'incidental' and 'integral'. Where a copyright artistic work appeared in a photograph because it was part of the setting in which the photographer found his subject, it could properly be said to be an integral part of that photograph. In order to test whether the use of one work in another was incidental, it was proper to ask why it had been included in the other, considering both commercial and aesthetic reasons.

---

[101] CDPA 1988, ss 45–50. See also Copyright and Rights in Databases Regulations 1997, Sch 1, for public administration exceptions to *sui generis* database right.

[102] Art 5(3)(h).

[103] On the use of public security, see Case C-145/10 *Painer v Standard Verlags GmbH* [2012] ECDR 6.

[104] CDPA 1988, s 45(2), (3). For successful uses of s 45, see *Ebden v News International Ltd* 17 May 2011 (unreported); *British Broadcasting Corporation v Hainey* [2012] SLT 476.

[105] CDPA 1988, s 31(1). See generally Burrell and Coleman, *Copyright Exceptions*, note 1, 64–66.   [106] CDPA 1988, s 62.

[107] CDPA 1988, ss 31(2) and 62(3).   [108] CDPA 1988, s 31(3).

Applying that test, it was evident that the use of the team and Premier League logos in the stickers was not incidental. Further, the defence would probably not apply to the albums since they were arguably literary works.

Question

What does 'incidental' mean in this context?

Discussion point 1 For answer guidance visit www.oxfordtextbooks.co.uk/orc/waelde3e/

Is 'incidental inclusion' really an exception to copyright? Or does it just follow from the definitions of copyright and infringement thereof?

Discussion point 2

If I take a photograph of my family against the background of a statue in a city square in order to create a striking overall image, is the sculptor's copyright infringed? Is it any different from taking a picture of a well-known actor against the background of a sculpture in his home because I think the statue symbolises something of the actor's personality?

Lawful uses of computer programs

5.44   A lawful user of a computer program (meaning someone who has a right to use it, whether under a licence or otherwise, eg under a fair dealing exception) who does the following things with the program is not infringing copyright:

- makes a *back up* copy necessary for his lawful use (CDPA 1988, s 50A);
- *decompiles* the program (ie converts it from a low-level language (object code) to a high-level one, incidentally copying it in the process), for the sole purpose of obtaining the information necessary to enable the creation of another program which will be interoperable with the original one (CDPA 1988, s 50B);
- *observes, studies, or tests* the functioning of the program to determine its underlying ideas and principles, while loading, displaying, running, transmitting, or storing the program as entitled to do (CDPA 1988, s 50BA);
- *copies or adapts as necessary for lawful use,* and so far as not contractually prohibited, in particular for the purpose of *error correction* (CDPA 1988, s 50C).

Only the last of these is subject to any overriding contractual clause; in the other three cases, such clauses are void.[109]

---

[109] CDPA 1988, s 296A.

Discussion point For answer guidance visit www.oxfordtextbooks.co.uk/orc/waelde3e/

To what extent may the exceptions for lawful use of computer programs be compared with fair dealing for purposes of private study and non-commercial research in relation to literary, dramatic, musical, and artistic works?

Time-shifting

5.45   The development of the video recorder as a consumer item has made it normal for individuals to be able to make copies of television programmes which can be viewed later at a more convenient time than that scheduled by the broadcasting authority. This is commonly known as 'time-shifting'. Such activities do not constitute infringement of copyright either in the broadcast or in any work included in it—for example, a film—as long as carried out in domestic premises for private and domestic use.[110] The provision also applies to audio taping of a radio broadcast. Similarly, the making for private and domestic use of a photograph of the whole or any part of an image forming part of a television broadcast, or a copy of such a photograph, does not infringe any copyright in the broadcast or in any film included in it.[111] Selling or otherwise dealing with a copy made under these provisions may become a secondary infringement of copyright (see paras 4.76–4.78).[112]

5.46   There would seem clearly to be no room, however, for an argument under the present legislation such as that advanced, unsuccessfully, in the *MP3.com* case in the United States:[113] that since the company's activities, in enabling CD owners to make additional copies in MP3 format, allowed users to listen to the music, not only at the time but also in the place most convenient to them ('space- or place-shifting'), a fair use defence was available. Thus, copying a computer program from one's PC to a laptop, or a CD into an MP3 player, does not fall within the scope of any current copyright exception in the UK (see further para 7.59).

 Discussion point For answer guidance visit www.oxfordtextbooks.co.uk/orc/waelde3e/

Is 'place-shifting' as legitimate as 'time-shifting'? Ought there to be such an exception to copyright?

Other limitations on copyright

Public interest and public policy

5.47   The 1988 Act saves various rights and privileges in general terms as unaffected by its provisions.[114] It is also provided that nothing in the Act affects the law on breach of trust or confidence,[115] or any rule preventing or restricting the enforcement of copyright on grounds of public interest or otherwise.[116] The *public policy* concept is that certain types of work—pornography or material published in breach

---

[110] CDPA 1988, s 70.   [111] CDPA 1988, s 71.   [112] CDPA 1988, ss 70(2), (3) and 71(2), (3).
[113] *UMG Recordings Inc and others v MP3.com Inc*, 2000 WL 1262568 (SD NY).   [114] CDPA 1988, s 171(a)–(d).
[115] CDPA 1988, s 171(e).   [116] CDPA 1988, s 171(3).

of a lifelong obligation of secrecy, for example—are undeserving of the protection of copyright.[117] A second limitation is one which allows otherwise infringing acts—or encourages dissemination—on the ground that they are in the *public interest*.[118] The scope and, indeed, existence of this defence remain uncertain,[119] although in twice affirming it in 1999 Jacob J formulated the test as being one of reasonable certainty that no right-thinking member of society would quarrel with the validity of the defence in the circumstances.[120] The public interest defence in the law of confidential information has been applied in relation to the unauthorised publication of information and material generated but kept secret by public authorities. If the authority's motivation in preventing publication is improper—for example, to conceal the failings of its officials—then an unauthorised publication, including one on the Internet, may be justified.[121]

■ *Hyde Park Residence Ltd v Yelland* [1999] RPC 655 (Jacob J); [2000] RPC 604 (CA)

Jacob J took a similar approach to copyright, holding that the public interest defence was applicable against a private individual (Mohammed al-Fayed), enabling the defendant to counter misleading public statements about how much time Princess Diana and Dodi al-Fayed had spent at the 'House of Windsor' in Paris on the day of their deaths. But this was overturned by the Court of Appeal,[122] the majority (Aldous and Stuart-Smith LJJ) holding that (1) there was no public interest defence separate from that of public policy; (2) the circumstances in which copyright would not be enforced must derive from the work itself (ie its immoral character or deleterious effects) rather than from the conduct of the owner of copyright; and (3) the considerations arising in breach of confidence cases, where the courts balanced the public interest in maintaining confidentiality against the public interest in knowledge of the truth and freedom of expression, were different from copyright ones, where property rights were involved and the legislation already provided fair dealing defences in the public interest. It should not be possible for public interest to uphold as legitimate an act that had been found, as in this case, not to be fair dealing (see para 5.35).[123] While generally agreeing with this approach, the third member of the court, Mance LJ, indicated that there might be cases where a public interest dimension did arise from the ownership of the work, although this was not such a case.[124]

■ *Ashdown v Telegraph Group Ltd* [2002] Ch 149 (CA)

The approach of Mance LJ was preferred by a subsequent Court of Appeal in this case (see para 5.35), emphasising in particular the public interest in freedom of expression under Article 10 of the European Convention on Human Rights, albeit that on the facts of the case it was held that the defence was not made out, since the newspaper had extracted from Mr Ashdown's diaries 'colourful passages...likely to add flavour to the article and thus to appeal to the readership of the newspaper...for reasons that were essentially journalistic in furtherance of the commercial interests of the Telegraph Group' (para 82) rather than in the public interest.

---

[117] See, eg, *Glyn v Weston Feature Film Co* [1916] 1 Ch 261; *Attorney-General v Guardian Newspapers Ltd (No 2)* [1990] 1 AC 109. See also A Sims, 'The denial of copyright on public policy grounds' [2008] EIPR 189.

[118] *Beloff v Pressdram* [1973] RPC 765. See generally Davies, *Copyright and the Public Interest*, note 1; Burrell and Coleman, *Copyright Exceptions*, note 1, 80–112.

[119] A Sims, 'The public interest defence in copyright law: myth or reality?' [2006] EIPR 335.

[120] *Hyde Park Residence Ltd v Yelland* [1999] RPC 655; *Mars UK Ltd v Teknowledge Ltd* [2000] FSR 138.

[121] See paras 18.56–18.59.   [122] [2000] RPC 604.   [123] See paras 55, 58, 64–67.   [124] Paras 79–83.

■ *HRH The Prince of Wales v Associated Newspapers Ltd (No 3)* **[2008] Ch 57 (CA)**

For the facts, see para 5.32. It was held that the unauthorised publication in a newspaper of extracts from the Prince's unpublished journals was not justified by any public interest defence, such as making more widely known the political views of the heir to the throne in relation to an important foreign power (the People's Republic of China). It would be rare for a case on public interest to succeed where the fair dealing defences had been found inapplicable (see also para 5.35). Public interest also rarely justified copying content rather than simply referring to the information therein.

Exercise 1

Explain the distinction between 'public policy' and 'public interest', if any. What difference does it make?

Exercise 2

Should pornography be unprotected by copyright? Does this encourage or discourage freedom of expression?

No derogation from grant

5.48   In *British Leyland v Armstrong Patents*,[125] the House of Lords declared that a copyright owner could be deprived of his rights where their exercise was in 'derogation from grant'. The context was the manufacture and supply to consumers of spare parts for cars, to which the car manufacturers took objection by means of copyright. The House found that car owners had a right to repair their vehicles, and that the car manufacturers could not exercise their copyright so as to prevent third parties enabling the owners to exercise their own separate and pre-existing rights as cheaply as possible. This was founded on the general legal principle of 'no derogation from grant', established in the context of leases, sales of goodwill and easements or servitudes. It had never been previously applied to copyright, and the reasoning of the House on the point is unsatisfactory. The Privy Council has since indicated that the principle should be interpreted very narrowly in copyright law, and that it is really based on public policy.[126] Nonetheless, it is therefore still applicable,[127] and may find some application in the context of the Internet, perhaps in relation to the questions about activities such as downloading and the construction and deployment of search engines.

Exercise

How might the 'no derogation from grant' principle apply to Internet copyrights?

---

[125] [1986] AC 577 gives the House of Lords' speeches only.

[126] *Canon Kabushiki Kaisha v Green Cartridge Co (Hong Kong) Ltd* [1997] AC 728.

[127] See in particular *Mars UK Ltd v Teknowledge Ltd* [2000] FSR 138 (Jacob J), a case about reverse engineering of computer programs and databases. The defence was rejected, however.

Human rights and exceptions to copyright[128]

5.49 In *Ashdown v Telegraph Group*,[129] the Court of Appeal held that exceptions to copyright must be read in the light of the European Convention on Human Rights. The *Sunday Telegraph* newspaper had published unlicensed extracts from the diaries of Paddy Ashdown, the former Liberal Democrat leader. The issue concerned the impact of the Article 10 right to freedom of expression upon the fair dealing defences to claims of infringement under the CDPA 1988. At first instance Sir Andrew Morritt V-C held that the fair dealing provisions of the statute in themselves satisfied the requirements of Article 10 and that there was no need to bring into play section 3 of the Human Rights Act 1998 (which requires statutes to be interpreted as far as possible in consistency with Convention rights):

> the balance between the rights of the owner of the copyright and those of the public has been struck by the legislative organ of the democratic state itself in the legislation it has enacted. There is no room for any further defences outside the code which establishes the particular species of intellectual property in question.[130]

The Court of Appeal concluded, however, that:

> rare circumstances can arise where the right of freedom of expression will come into conflict with the protection afforded by the Copyright Act, notwithstanding the express exceptions to be found in the Act. In these circumstances, we consider that the court is bound, insofar as it is able, to apply the Act in a manner that accommodates the right of freedom of expression.[131]

This view must be correct under section 3 of the Human Rights Act 1998. The court went on to observe that, at least in this case, the approach required could be fulfilled, not so much through examination of the statutory language as such, as by way of the remedies granted to enforce the legislation: in the particular case, by withholding the discretionary relief of an injunction and leaving the copyright owner to a damages claim or an account of profits.[132] Further, while the statutory defences and the judicial precedents elaborating upon their application fell to be reconsidered in the light of Article 10, this did not require the defendant to be able to profit from the use of another's copyright material without paying compensation. The political interest of the matters discussed and freedom of expression under Article 10 of the European Convention on Human Rights did not justify deliberate filleting of and selection of the most colourful passages from the Ashdown diary.

■ *British Broadcasting Corporation v Hainey* [2012] SLT 476

B sought to engage the right of freedom of expression to access photos lodged as Crown productions in H's trial for the murder of H's son. H objected on the basis of ownership of copyright in the photos. B was successful in gaining access to photos of the son only. The court suggested that the permitted act provisions in the CDPA 1988, particularly fair dealing provisions, usually provide a defence where there is a potential conflict between Article 10 rights and the rights of the copyright owner; but there are 'exceptional and rare' cases where this is not the case even if the CDPA 1988 is given a generous interpretation to accommodate the right (para 24).[133] The court also stated *obiter* that 'were it necessary to do so, the public interest in the proper and full reporting of this case is sufficient to "trump" any right of the copyright owner' (para 26).

---

[128] See generally J Griffiths and U Suthersanen (eds), *Copyright and Free Expression* (2005); P Torremans (ed), *Copyright and Human Rights: Freedom of Expression, Intellectual Property, Privacy* (2004); C Ryan, 'Human rights and intellectual property' [2001] EIPR 521; PB Hugenholtz, 'Copyright and freedom of expression in Europe' in RC Dreyfuss, DL Zimmerman, and H First (eds), *Expanding the Boundaries of Intellectual Property* (2001), 343–364.
[129] [2001] 2 WLR 967 (Morritt V-C); rev'd [2002] Ch 149 (CA).
[130] [2001] 2 WLR 967, para 20.   [131] [2002] Ch 149, para 45.   [132] [2002] Ch 149, paras 46 and 59.
[133] Citing with approval *Copinger and Skone James on Copyright* at para 3-308.

Exercise

What other ECHR rights apart from freedom of expression (Art 10) might be relevant to copyright exceptions?

Technical protection measures and rights management information systems

Introduction

Technical protection measures

5.50   In its original form, section 296 of the CDPA 1988 provided that where copies of a copyright work were issued to the public in an electronic copy-protected form—that is, could not be copied or could only be copied with poor quality reproduction—the copyright owner had a secondary infringement claim against a person dealing in any device specifically designed or adapted to circumvent the form of copy-protection employed, or publishing information intended to enable or assist persons to circumvent that form of copy-protection. The Software Directive 1991 also provided that there should be appropriate remedies in national legislation against a person putting into circulation, or possessing for commercial purposes, any means the sole intended purpose of which was to facilitate the unauthorised removal or circumvention of any technical device applied to protect a computer program.[134] The aim of this legislation was to support the pragmatic answer to the problems of protecting electronic or digital works deployed to ensure that users and consumers paid for their access and use. That answer had been provided by the technology itself: products could be locked behind technological barriers (or 'walls' or 'fences'), for example, encryption, passwords, activation codes, and so on, requiring payment and/or authorisation by electronic means before they could be opened up or set aside. Other examples operate through interaction between software and hardware: the former is encrypted and will only operate if the latter contains a device or key with which decryption is possible. Such devices protecting against unauthorised access are commonly known as *technical protection measures* (TPMs).[135]

5.51   The New York case of *Universal Studios Inc v Corley*[136] provides an explanation of one well-known such TPM, the 'content scramble system' (CSS) protecting DVDs:

> CSS is an encryption scheme that employs an algorithm configured by a set of 'keys' to encrypt a DVD's contents. The algorithm is a type of mathematical formula for transforming the contents of the movie file into gibberish; the 'keys' are in actuality strings of 0's and 1's that serve as values for the mathematical formula. Decryption in the case of CSS requires a set of 'player keys' contained in compliant DVD players, as well as an understanding of the CSS encryption algorithm. Without the player keys and the algorithm, a DVD player cannot access the contents of a DVD. With the player keys and the algorithm, a DVD player can display the movie on a television or a computer screen, but does not give a viewer the ability to use the copy function of the computer to copy the movie or to manipulate the digital content of the DVD.[137]

---

[134]   Software Directive, Art 7(1)(c).

[135]   See further G Davies, 'Technical devices as a solution to private copying' in IA Stamatoudi and PLC Torremans (eds), *Copyright in the New Digital Environment* (2000); 'Digital Rights Management', Report of an Inquiry by the All Party Internet Group (June 2006), available at http://www.apcomms.org.uk/apig/current-activities/apig-inquiry-into-digital-rights-management/DRMreport.pdf. For an international perspective, see P Akester, *A Practical Guide to Digital Copyright* (2008), Ch 6.

[136]   *Universal City Studios Inc v Corley* 273 F 3d 429 (2d Cir, 2001).

[137]   *Universal City Studios Inc v Corley* 273 F 3d 429 at 436–437 (2d Cir, 2001).

From 1989, making and supplying devices to enable such TPMs to be evaded was, as we have just seen, made equivalent to infringement of copyright itself and, in the UK, also invited criminal penalties. In the early days, the primary kind of protected work was the computer program; but databases, CDs, commercial websites on the Internet, and DVDs quickly joined the ranks of works technologically protected against unauthorised copying.

Rights management information systems

5.52   The WCT 1996 and the InfoSoc Directive 2001 contained further provisions designed to support and strengthen the rules against circumvention devices and their use, and also extended protection to 'electronic rights management information systems' (RMIs). The latter are electronic tags or fingerprints included in copies of digital products, enabling them to be traced and identified electronically wherever they may be in use, lawfully or otherwise. The systems typically identify the software, the copyright owner and the rights held by that party and the users of the work respectively. The information in the system may well often appear on the computer screen when the work is installed or run. Such systems are of particular importance in the Internet context, through which most tracing and identification activity is likely to be conducted.[138] The generic term for such systems together with TPMs is *digital rights management* (DRM). As a result of the InfoSoc Directive, UK law on the protection of DRMs has been substantially amended and added to, and it is to the present position that we now turn.

 Question

Explain the difference between technological protection measures and electronic rights management systems.

TPMs: computer programs

5.53   There are still specific provisions for computer programs since the Software Directive was not superseded on this point by the InfoSoc Directive.[139] Any device that is intended to prevent or restrict acts unauthorised by the copyright owner *and* restricted by copyright is protected. Making, dealing in or possessing for commercial purposes a circumvention device while knowing or having reason to believe that it will be used to make infringing copies makes the person in question liable as an infringer of copyright in his own right.

■ *Sony Computer Entertainment v Owen* [2002] EMLR 34 (Jacob J)

S made *PlayStation 2* computer games consoles. O imported a computer chip which bypassed the process which otherwise ensured that only authorised copies of discs could be used in the machine and which also ensured that discs purchased in one region could not be played in another. O argued that the chip could be used legitimately, for example to make back-up copies of discs, or play a disc from another licensed region. It was held, giving summary judgment for S, that (1) O's chip was a device specifically designed to circumvent the copy protection; (2) it was not a defence that the chip also enabled the machine to play software from another region; copyright was inherently territorial, and if a disc was 'for Japan only', there was no reason to suppose it was licensed for use elsewhere.

---

[138] See further P and R Akester, 'Digital rights management in the 21st century' [2006] EIPR 159; 'Digital Rights Management', Report of an Inquiry by the All Party Internet Group (June 2006), note 135.

[139] CDPA 1988, s 296 as amended by the Copyright and Related Rights Regulations 2003, reg 24.

Contrast:

■ *Kabushiki Kaisha Sony Computer Entertainment v Stevens* **(2005) 224 CLR 193 (HCA)**

This Australian case also concerned Sony's PlayStation games. Insertion of a PlayStation CD into the PlayStation console enabled the game to be played. There was an 'access code' on each CD, and a chip described as a 'Boot ROM' was located on the circuit board of the PlayStation console. In consequence of their interaction, a game could be played only with the authority of the owner or licensee of the copyright. An unauthorised copy of a Sony PlayStation CD did not replicate the access code and therefore the Boot ROM of the console denied it access. S sold 'mod chips' or 'converter chips' and installed them in PlayStation consoles. Their purpose and effect was to overcome Sony's device. It was held that Sony's device was not a 'technological protection measure' within the wording of the Australian statute. It was necessary that, in order to be a TPM within the meaning of the legislation, a device must be designed to prevent or inhibit post-access infringement of copyright. The purpose of S's chips was not to reproduce the computer games but to permit access to them. The court also decided that the temporary reproduction of the program embodying the game in the PlayStation console was not an infringement of copyright under Australian law. This probably provides an important point of distinction for a court in the UK, where unauthorised temporary reproduction *is* an infringement (see para 4.36), and it would be difficult to support a distinction between 'reproduction' and 'access'. Note, however, that the UK legislation also requires that the TPM prevent or restrict acts which are infringements of copyright, rather than access per se.[140]

In *Nintendo Co Ltd v Playables Ltd & Another*,[141] Floyd J held that both section 296 and section 296Z were infringed by the defendants who imported and sold mod chips which allowed users to play pirated games on Nintendo's consoles. Technical devices had been applied to the copyright computer programs in the games console and game cards and the sole purpose of mod chips was to circumvent them. On the question of knowledge, the court held that since it was well known that this device was used for piracy and given the minor proportion of the market represented by lawful use and the large numbers sold, the defendants did not have a realistic prospect of asserting lack of knowledge of unlawful uses.

TPMs: other copyright works

5.54   The rules are similar in respect of copyright works that are not computer programs (eg broadcasts, databases, sound recording CDs, film DVDs, websites), but wider in scope. Here there is a provision that the person who circumvents an effective technological measure, knowing or having reasonable grounds to know that he is pursuing that objective, is to be treated as a copyright infringer.[142] So now we are dealing with actual circumvention, and not just the manufacture of, dealing in or commercial possession of a circumvention device. The rules apply to protect not just technical devices, but effective technological measures applied to the work. This covers any technology, device, or component designed in the normal course of its operation to protect a copyright work, that is, to prevent or restrict acts unauthorised by the copyright owner *and* restricted by copyright.[143] These measures are 'effective' if use of the work within the scope of the acts restricted by copyright is controlled by the copyright owner through either (1) an access control or protection process such as encryption, scrambling, or other transformation of the work; *or* (2) a copy control mechanism.[144]

---

[140] For commentary on this case see T Ciro and M Fox, 'Competition v Copyright Protection in the digital age' [2006] EIPR 329.
[141] *Nintendo Co Ltd v Playables Ltd & Another* [2010] FSR 36.   [142] CDPA 1988, s 296ZA.   [143] CDPA 1988, s 296ZF(1).
[144] CDPA 1988, s 296ZF(2).

Question

What are the differences between the protection of technical protection measures for computer programs and the protection of those for other kinds of copyright work?

 Discussion point   For answer guidance visit www.oxfordtextbooks.co.uk/orc/waelde3e/

Technical protection systems being developed by the entertainment industries include ones built into the hardware used to access and copy digital works, such as DVD players and games consoles. For instance, an encryption code in the work that prohibits access is more effective if the work has to be run through a chip embedded in a computer which decrypts the work, rather than simply relying on the code itself. Are systems so constructed in the hardware subject to the protection for 'effective technological measures'? See *Sony v Ball* in the following text.

■ *Sony v Ball* [2005] FSR 9

This was another case about the territorially-based protection of Sony's *PlayStation 2*. The protection system was in two parts, one in the console and the other in the DVD carrying the game to be played. An unauthorised copy of a game would therefore not play on the console, nor would a game from a different region. B produced an electronic chip to fit the console and trick it into believing that unauthorised or foreign DVDs being played had the necessary embedded code. It was held that summary judgment could be granted to prevent sales of B's chips in the UK (but not elsewhere). It did not matter that the protection system was partly in the hardware (the console) and only partly in the software (the games DVD).[145]

There are, however, limits to the protection offered by the 'effective technological measure' provision in section 296ZF.

■ *R v Higgs (Neil Stanley)* [2008] FSR 34 (CA)

The facts were similar to those of *Sony v Ball* in the previous case. H ran a business selling 'mod chips', which circumvented the embedded codes in a games console and allowed 'pirated' games to be played. The Crown charged H under section 296ZB of the CDPA 1988. It was held that to fall within the meaning of 'effective technological measure' in section 296ZF it was not sufficient for the TPM to be merely a discouragement or general commercial hindrance to copyright infringement. Instead, the TPM either had to deny access to a copyright work or limit a person's ability to make copies of the work. A person must therefore be physically prevented from committing acts of infringement by the TPM. Based on this narrow interpretation, H's convictions were quashed.

In contrast to this, in *R v Gilham*[146] the operator of a business selling 'mod chips' that allowed counterfeit computer games to be played on consoles, failed in his appeal against conviction for copyright infringement. In this case the key question was around substantiality which the Court of Appeal understood broadly. As such, the playing of a counterfeit game was enough to constitute substantial copying of the copyright work in question.[147]

---

[145] For discussion of this and the other PlayStation cases described previously (para 5.53), see A Macculloch, 'Game over: the "region lock" in video games' [2005] EIPR 176.   [146] *R v Gilham* [2009] EWCA Crim 2293 (CA).

[147] See also *Nintendo Co Ltd & Anor v Playables Ltd & Another* [2010] FSR 36 (Ch) for an additional case where defendants providing mod chips which allowed TPMs protecting computer games to be circumvented, were also found liable for copyright infringement.

Rights management information systems

5.55 The approach to the protection of rights management systems (for the definition of which see para 5.52) is likewise to make it akin to infringement of copyright knowingly and without authority to remove or alter digital rights management information associated with a copy of a copyright work or which appears in connection with a communication of the work to the public.[148] Also caught is the person who knowingly and without authority distributes, imports for distribution or communicates to the public copies of a copyright work from which the RMI has been removed or altered. In both cases the person so acting must know, or have reason to believe, that the action induces, enables, facilitates, or conceals an infringement of copyright.[149] A crucial difference between this and the protection of TPMs is that only for the former are the circumvention wrongs tied to actual copyright infringement. Nothing similar limits the protection of TPMs; and from this it seems to follow that circumvention of such a measure not aimed at copyright infringement but at the exercise of a copyright exception, such as private study or non-commercial research, will still be caught as infringement of the TPM right. Indeed, TPMs could go even further and prevent access to a work which had either fallen out of copyright at the end of its term, or had never had copyright in the first place. None of this would apply, however, to RMI protection.

Persons enjoying the anti-circumvention rights

5.56 The people who can sue under any of the anti-circumvention rights are:

- those who have issued copies of the protected work, or communicated it, to the public;
- the copyright owner or his exclusive licensee.[150]

In addition, with regard to devices protecting computer programs, the owner/exclusive licensee of any intellectual property right in the protection device itself may take action.[151]

Dealing in apparatus for unauthorised reception of transmissions

5.57 A person who makes charges for the reception of broadcasts provided from a place in the UK, or who sends encrypted transmissions of any other description from a place in the UK, has the same rights and remedies as a copyright owner in respect of infringement against a person dealing in any apparatus or device designed or adapted to enable or assist persons to receive the programmes or other transmissions when they are not entitled to do so, or publishing information calculated so to enable or assist them.[152]

■ *BBC Enterprises Ltd v Hi-Tech Xtravision Ltd* [1990] FSR 217 (CA)

H, a manufacturer of decoders used to unscramble encrypted satellite transmissions for the purpose of television viewing, argued that this provision did not avail the BBC, operators of a satellite television service, in their efforts to stop H supplying decoders to persons who were not subscribers to the BBC service. The basis for this argument was that the provision did not in terms disentitle persons from receiving transmissions and, there being in consequence no person disentitled, H had committed no wrong in supplying decoders. Having been upheld at first instance, the argument was overturned in the

---

[148] CDPA 1988, s 296ZG(1), (3).   [149] CDPA 1988, s 296ZG(2).
[150] CDPA 1988, ss 296(2), 296ZA(3), and 296ZG(3), (4).   [151] CDPA 1988, s 296(2)(c).
[152] CDPA 1988, s 298(1), (2).

Court of Appeal, which held that the rule created a substantive right not to have transmissions received as well as the right to stop the supply of decoders.

The provisions may also be applied in relation to services provided from outside the UK.[153] There are criminal law sanctions against manufacturing, dealing in or with, or installing, maintaining, or repairing unauthorised decoders (counterfeit or stolen viewing cards, or illicit devices);[154] punishments include imprisonment and/or fines.[155]

Key points on TPM and RMI protection

- TPMs are any technological means within a copyright product designed to prevent acts restricted by copyright unless the authorisation of the copyright owner is obtained, usually by electronic means provided within the system

- RMIs are electronic systems built into digital products which record information about the identity and use of the product, thus enabling their tracing and the pursuit of unauthorised uses

- TPMs and RMIs are sometimes known generically as digital rights management (DRM) systems

- Copyright legislation prohibits circumvention of TPMs and removal or alteration of RMIs, treating these as infringements of copyright if carried out with knowledge, or reasonable grounds to know. The law is more limited with regard to computer programs

- The legislation also treats as a form of infringement manufacturing or dealing in devices designed to circumvent TPMs or in products whose RMIs have been removed or altered

---

Copyright exceptions, TPMs, RMIs, and contract

TPMs v copyright exceptions and the public domain?

5.58   The previous section (paras 5.50–5.57) has shown that producers of digital works may be able to deploy TPMs to prevent users gaining access to them. At least theoretically, this is possible even if the users in question wish to perform acts that are permitted if the works have copyright—and, indeed, even if the works never had or have passed out of copyright. Thus, technology has the potential to create protection akin to copyright for works which have never had, or have ceased to have, copyright, as well as to extend protection beyond the scope of copyright where that exists.[156] There has been little discussion in Britain to compare with a US and Canadian debate as to whether the rules on permitted acts merely

[153] CDPA 1988, s 299(1)(b). See SI 1989/2003. Note that s 299(2) was repealed by the Broadcasting Act 1990, s 179(2).
[154] On the meaning of 'unauthorised' in relation to foreign decoders, see Cases C-403/08 and C-429/08 *Football Association Premier League Ltd v QC Leisure, Murphy v Media Protection Services Ltd* [2012] 1 CMLR 29 and *Murphy v Media Protection Services Ltd* [2012] CMLR 2.   [155] CDPA 1988, s 297A.
[156] N Braun, 'The interface between the protection of technological measures and the exercise of exceptions to copyright and related rights: comparing the situation in the US and the EU' [2003] EIPR 496; W Davies and K Withers, *Public Innovation: Intellectual Property in a Digital Age* (Institute of Public Policy Research, 2006), 46–8, 84–7.

provide defences to claims of infringement or are free-standing user or public rights.[157] The difference is important because, if the permitted acts are substantive rights, then the copyright owner should not be able to prevent actions designed to exercise them. But if the permitted acts are merely defences, then they can be invoked only when the copyright owner sues for infringement. The 1988 Act does say that its provisions on permitted acts:

> relate only to the question of infringement of copyright and do not affect any other right or obligation restricting the doing of any of the specified acts (CDPA 1988, s 28(1)).

This is clearly against the notion that the permissions are to be seen as user rights.

Contracting out of the exceptions?

5.59   There has also been little British discussion of whether the fair dealing provisions prevail over contrary contractual provision, contained, for example, in a copyright licence (see paras 5.60–5.62, 7.61). To put it another way, can one contract out of fair dealing?[158] Following the case of *ProCD v Zeidenberg*[159] and the passage in 1999 of what is now the Uniform Computer Information Transactions Act, however, the matter became controversial in the United States.[160]

■ *ProCD v Zeidenberg* 86 F 3d 1447 (7th Cir, 1996)

ProCD compiled information from more than 3,000 telephone directories (which do not have copyright under US law) into a computer database. The company sold a version of the database, called SelectPhone, on CD-ROM discs in packages covered in plastic or cellophane 'shrink-wrap'. A proprietary method of compressing the data served as effective encryption too. Customers decrypted and used the data with the aid of an application program written by ProCD. This program, which had copyright, searched the database in response to users' criteria, and the resulting lists could be read and manipulated by other software, such as word-processing programs. The database cost more than $10 million to compile and was also expensive to keep current. ProCD charged consumers a much lower price for the product than commercial customers, but every box containing its consumer product declared that the software came with restrictions stated in an enclosed licence. The licence was encoded on the CD-ROM disks as well as printed in the manual; it also appeared on a user's screen every time the software ran. The licence limited use of the application program and listings to non-commercial purposes. Z bought a consumer package of the database from a retail outlet, but decided to ignore the licence. He formed a company to resell the information in the database over the Internet, at prices undercutting those of ProCD. ProCD sought an injunction against further dissemination, based on a claim of breach of the licence conditions by Z. It was held that the licence was enforceable, even although it in effect gave protection, as between ProCD and Z, to the non-copyright contents of the database. (Note that this is not a case of contract overriding copyright exceptions, but rather one of contract providing protection where there was no copyright at all.)

---

[157] The language of 'user rights' features strongly in *Law Society of Upper Canada v CCH Canadian Ltd* [2004] 1 SCR 339, following D Vaver, *Essentials of Canadian Law: Copyright Law* (2000), 171. For a different perspective see H Cohen Jehoram, 'Restrictions on copyright and their abuse' [2005] EIPR 359.

[158] See Guibault, *Copyright Limitations and Contracts*, note 1; Burrell and Coleman, *Copyright Exceptions*, note 1, 67–70, 269–270, 306–310.   [159] 86 F 3d 1447 (7th Cir, 1996).

[160] See P Samuelson and K Opsdahl, 'The tensions between intellectual property and contracts in the information age: an American perspective' in FW Grosheide and K Boele-Woelki (eds), *Molengrafica: Europees Privaatrecht 1998* (1999).

> ## Uniform Computer Information Transactions Act (UCITA)
>
> UCITA is a uniform model law for adoption in US states (so far taken up in only two states). The Act makes 'shrink-wrap' and 'click-on' licences enforceable in what it calls 'mass market transactions', that is, those involving consumers. Information transactions thus move away from the model of selling copies (the model on which copyright is based) to one of licensing information in its electronic transmission to the consumer. This may give the supplier more control of access to and use of information, whether or not the information itself and the use thereof is protected by copyright.

5.60   The un-argued assumption in the UK, however, was that fair dealing prevails over contract. But on closer examination this assumption appears ill-founded, at least as a generalisation. For example, the exception enabling educational establishments to make a limited quantity of copies of works for purposes of instruction, does not apply if a licence for such activity is available (para 5.38).[161] There is also the provision quoted previously (in para 5.58), which might be read as meaning that beyond the permitted acts may lie, unaffected, other rights or obligations restricting the doing of any of the specified acts.[162] Another example of contract prevailing over exceptions relates to the permitted act of temporary reproduction or adaptation of a computer program necessary for a lawful user's lawful use of the program: a term of any contract regulating the circumstances in which the user's use is lawful, and prohibiting the copying or adaptation in question will make those acts infringements.[163]

5.61   On the other side of the coin (ie suggesting that contract does *not* prevail over exceptions and limitations) are the following specific provisions. Any term or condition of an agreement purporting to prohibit the permitted act of temporary reproduction of a database necessary for the purpose of access to and normal use of the database contents by a person with a right to use the database is void.[164] A number of other acts in relation to computer programs which are permitted to a lawful user thereof cannot be overridden by contract: that is, making a back-up copy of the program,[165] decompilation in terms of section 50B(2) of the CDPA 1988,[166] and observing, studying, or testing the functioning of the program in accordance with section 50BA of the CDPA 1988.[167]

5.62   Overall, there seems much to support the view of Burrell and Coleman that it is:

> generally possible to contract out of the permitted acts. There is, however, a growing list of circumstances in which it is not possible to contract out of the permitted acts, Parliament and the European legislator having recognised that it ought not to be possible to exclude the exceptions in certain circumstances.[168]

They argue that such a piecemeal approach is preferable to the inflexibility which would arise from a blanket prohibition on contractual exclusion of the permitted acts.[169] It would be better, in their view, to distinguish types of fair use, those excludable by contract and those not.[170]

---

[161] CDPA 1988, s 36(3).   [162] CDPA 1988, s 28(1).
[163] CDPA 1988, s 50C, implementing Software Directive 1991 (reading Art 5(1) in conjunction with Art 4(a)).
[164] CDPA 1988, ss 50D(2) and 296B.   [165] CDPA 1988, s 50A.   [166] See further para 5.44.
[167] See further para 5.44.   [168] Burrell and Coleman, *Copyright Exceptions*, note 1, 69.
[169] Burrell and Coleman, *Copyright Exceptions*, note 1, 70.
[170] Burrell and Coleman, *Copyright Exceptions*, note 1, 269–270, 306–310.

Discussion point 1 For answer guidance visit www.oxfordtextbooks.co.uk/orc/waelde3e/

Is there a real difference between acts which are not within the scope of copyright at all, and acts which are permitted as exceptions to copyright? Is this important in the context of the idea of 'user rights'?

Discussion point 2

Can you distinguish between 'fair dealing' and 'public interest' exceptions to copyright?

Discussion point 3

How would the case of *ProCD v Zeidenberg* be decided in the UK? Are shrink-wrap and click-on licences enforceable under either English or Scots contract law?

Discussion point 4

Do you agree with the analysis of Burrell and Coleman?

Controlling TPMs and RMIs

5.63   Concerns that the legal protection of TPMs had the potential to deprive copyright exceptions of their content and value led to Article 6(4) of the InfoSoc Directive. This requires Member States to take:

> appropriate measures to ensure that right-holders make available to the beneficiary of an exception or limitation provided for in national law [in accordance with the Directive] the means of benefiting from that exception or limitation, to the extent necessary to benefit from that exception or limitation and where that beneficiary has legal access to the protected work or subject-matter concerned.

The UK has implemented Article 6(4) in the following rather complex fashion. Where the application of any effective technological measure to a copyright work other than a computer program prevents a person from carrying out a permitted act in relation to that work, then that person (or a person who is a representative of a class of persons prevented from carrying out a permitted act) may complain to the Secretary of State (ie the relevant Government minister). The Secretary of State may thereupon issue written directions to the copyright holder, with which the latter must comply. Failure to do so gives the complainant a civil right of action. The directions may be to establish whether any voluntary measure or agreement subsists with regard to the copyright work in question, *or* to ensure that the copyright owner or exclusive licensee makes available to the complainant the means of carrying out that permitted act, to the extent necessary to benefit from that permitted act. The direction can be subsequently revoked or varied. The complainant must be someone who has lawful access to the protected copyright work.[171]

5.64   The previous point only applies to certain (and not all) permitted acts.[172] This includes, for example, research and private study as well as making a copy available for a visually impaired person. It is noteworthy, however, that it does not apply to criticism, review and news reporting, despite the particular

---

[171] CDPA 1988, s 296ZE.   [172] CDPA 1988, Sch 5A, Part 1.

importance which the courts have attributed to these exceptions in the interests of freedom of speech and expression (see paras 5.30, 5.35, and 5.49).

5.65   None of this is applicable, however, where the copyright work in question has been 'made available to the public on agreed contractual terms in such a way that members of the public may access them from a place and at a time individually chosen by them'.[173] So, for example, there can be no complaint about TPMs and RMIs attached to music files downloaded from the iTunes service.[174] This would seem to suggest that the only complaint likely to be successful is one where access is completely blocked. A party making material available for a price, however exorbitant, is unlikely to be on the receiving end of government directions to change its ways. Thus it appears that in a digital network environment the exceptions and limitations to copyright may be overridden by contract, or at the least that the procedure described previously will not be available where *contract* limits the availability or use of the exceptions. The limits on this may arise from the phrase 'agreed contractual terms'. Does 'agreed' mean that the terms must in some way be negotiated ones, rather than the standard forms normally used in online transactions? If the word does not have this meaning, its use alongside 'contractual' would appear rather tautologous.

5.66   It is also worth noting that equivalent legislation in the US (Digital Millennium Copyright Act) enacts the WCT to afford TPMs legal protection. Case law suggests that even where such measures are preventing access to works for uses provided for in law by exceptions to copyright, 'fair use' is not a sufficient defence. This effectively gives TPMs legal protection even in cases where the works they are guarding are to be lawfully used, or where the works are not in fact protected by copyright.

 ### Question 1

Who may apply to the Secretary of State that the application of a TPM is preventing the exercise of an exception to copyright?

Question 2

What kinds of order may the Secretary of State make?

Question 3

What must be shown before the Secretary of State will issue an order?

---

[173] CDPA 1988, s 296ZE(10).

[174] Example suggested in W Davies and K Withers, *Public Innovation: Intellectual Property in a Digital Age* (Institute of Public Policy Research, 2006), 23.

Further reading

Books

General

L Bently and B Sherman, *Intellectual Property Law* (3rd edn, 2009), Chs 9, 11.8, 13.4–13.5

Copinger & Skone James on Copyright (16th edn, 2010), Chs 9, 15

WR Cornish, D Llewelyn, and T Aplin, *Intellectual Property* (7th edn, 2010), Chs 12 3, 12.4, 14.1, 14.2

Laddie, Prescott & Vitoria on the Modern Law of Copyright (4th edn, 2011), Ch 20

Copyright exceptions and public interest

R Burrell and A Coleman, *Copyright Exceptions: The Digital Impact* (2005)

G Davies, *Copyright and the Public Interest* (2nd edn, 2003)

LMCR Guibault, *Copyright Limitations and Contracts: An Analysis of the Contractual Overridability of Limitations on Copyright* (2002)

G Mazziotti, *EU Digital Copyright Law and the End-User* (2008)

M Senftleben, *Copyright Limitations and the Three-Step Test: An Analysis of the Three-Step Test in International and EC Copyright Law* (2004)

C Waelde and HL MacQueen (eds), *The Many Faces of the Public Domain* (2007)

Exceptions and human rights

J Griffiths and U Suthersanen (eds), *Copyright and Free Expression* (2005)

P Torremans (ed), *Copyright and Human Rights: Freedom of Expression, Intellectual Property, Privacy* (2004)

Technological protection measures and rights management information

P Akester, *A Practical Guide to Digital Copyright* (2008), Ch 6

P Akester, *Report on the Impact of Technological Accommodation of Conflicts between Freedom of Expression and DRM: The First Empirical Assessment* (2009), available at http://www.law.cam.ac.uk/faculty-resources/summary/technological-accommodation-of-conflicts-between-freedom-of-expression-and-drm-the-first-empirical-assessment/6286

Articles

Copyright exceptions and public interest

H Cohen Jehoram, 'Is there a hidden agenda behind the general non-implementation of the EU three-step test?' [2009] EIPR 408

J Espantaleon, 'Does private copying need an update in the UK?' (2008) 3 JIPLP 115

A Sims, 'Strangling their creation: the courts' treatment of fair dealing in copyright law since 1911' (2010) IPQ 192

A Sims, 'The denial of copyright on public policy grounds' [2008] EIPR 189

A Sims, 'The public interest defence in copyright law: myth or reality?' [2006] EIPR 335

Technical protection measures and rights management information systems

P Akester, 'The new challenges of striking the right balance between copyright protection and access to knowledge, information and culture' [2010] EIPR 372

P and R Akester, 'Digital rights management in the 21st century' [2006] EIPR 159

N Braun, 'The interface between the protection of technological measures and the exercise of exceptions to copyright and related rights: comparing the situation in the US and the EU' [2003] EIPR 496

G Davies, 'Technical devices as a solution to private copying' in IA Stamatoudi and PLC Torremans (eds), *Copyright in the New Digital Environment* (2000)

6

Rights akin to copyright: database right and performers' rights

Introduction

Scope and overview of chapter

6.1 This chapter considers two rights closely akin to copyright in many ways, in terms of both subject matter and the substantive contents of the rights. Both rights have also been relatively recently introduced into the armoury of intellectual property law. The rights in question are (1) the special or *sui generis* database right, which operates alongside the copyright in databases (for which see paras 2.56–2.63); and (2) performers' rights. The chapter gives an account of each of these rights, comparing them with copyright, but also underlining the differences between the regimes, and the reasons behind these differences.

6.2
> ### Learning objectives
>
> By the end of this chapter you should be able to describe and explain:
> - the special or *sui generis* database right;
> - performers' rights;
> - the ways in which each of these rights compares with copyright;
> - the reasons why these rights have been created and are distinct from copyright.

6.3 The chapter first explores the *sui generis* database right, explaining the reasons for its introduction by the Database Directive 1996 and considering in detail its exposition by the jurisprudence of the CJEU. The chapter then turns to performers' rights, again providing background to the introduction of the rights in their present form, and considering also developments now in prospect. So the rest of the chapter looks like this:

- *Sui generis* database right (6.4–6.20)
- Performers' rights (6.21–6.42)

Sui generis database right

Reasons for introduction of the *sui generis* right

6.4   The Database Directive 1996[1] not only harmonised the copyright protection of databases in the EU, but also introduced an additional, special (*sui generis*) database right to protect those commercially valuable and expensively created databases henceforth to be excluded from copyright in some member states (notably the UK) by the higher originality requirement now imposed under the Directive (see para 2.57).[2] The UK implemented the Directive in the Database Regulations 1997.[3]

Criteria for protection to arise

Database right and copyright in a database

6.5   The definition of database applying for copyright purposes (paras 2.56 and 2.60–2.62) also applies for the *sui generis* right.[4] There is no requirement of 'intellectual creation' for the database right to subsist, that is, the database contents must still be organised in a systematic or methodical way but the system or method need not be a personal intellectual creation.[5] A database enjoying copyright protection is not precluded from also enjoying database right, the relevance of this being that database right confers protection against extraction and reutilisation of the contents of the database rather than the copyright protection for the selection and arrangement of the contents (see further paras 6.12–6.16). The principal substantive ground for database right protection is the creator's substantial investment in obtaining, verifying, or presenting the contents of the database, and it is immaterial whether or not the database is also a copyright work, that is, is an intellectual creation of the compiler in its selection or arrangement[6].

?   Question

Can a copyright database also be protected by the *sui generis* right? Will a database protected by the *sui generis* right also have copyright?

Obtaining, verifying, or presenting the contents of the database

6.6   Database right arises where there has been substantial investment in 'obtaining, verifying or presenting the contents of the database'. The first question to which this has given rise is whether, if the investment is in *creating* rather than *obtaining* data, database right is excluded. In other words, must the data exist before the investment is made? The ECJ's answer to this question, in the leading cases decided in 2004, surprised many.

---

[1] Directive 96/9/EC of the European Parliament and of the Council of 11 March 1996 on the legal protection of databases.

[2] Database Directive, recitals 1–12, 38–39.

[3] Copyright and Rights in Databases Regulations 1997 (SI 1997/3032). See generally E Derclaye, *The Legal Protection of Databases: A Comparative Analysis* (2008); T Aplin, *Copyright Law in the Digital Society: The Challenges of Multimedia* (2005), 41–73.

[4] Database Regulations 1997, reg 12(1).

[5] So, eg, an arrangement of surnames in alphabetical order would attract database right provided the other criteria for protection are met.   [6] Database Regulations 1997, reg 13.

■ *British Horseracing Board v William Hill Organization Ltd* [2001] RPC 31 (Laddie J); [2002] ECDR 4 (CA); Case C-203/02, [2005] RPC 13 (ECJ); [2005] RPC 35 (CA)[7]

BHB administered British horse-racing, creating the fixture lists each year, and distributing information about races to subscribers. WHO were subscribers who used the BHB data in relation to their betting services. An issue arose between the parties about whether WHO's unauthorised use of the BHB data in its new Internet betting service infringed BHB's database right. The Court of Appeal referred the question of whether 'obtaining' covered 'creating' as well as 'compiling' to the ECJ. The Advocate General opined that 'obtaining' extended to the creation or generation of data only when 'the creation of the data took place at the same time as its processing and was inseparable from it' (para 157). The ECJ held that merely creating data did *not* amount to obtaining it, or to its verification or presentation. 'Obtaining' involved the seeking out and collecting of existing independent materials, and verification and presentation had generally to relate to such material (paras 29–34). The Court of Appeal then applied this interpretation of the law to deny the existence of database right in BHB's database, since BHB created the data rather than collecting it from existing independent sources. The decision appears to restrict considerably the scope of protection given by the *sui generis* right.[8]

 Discussion point For answer guidance visit www.oxfordtextbooks.co.uk/orc/waelde3e/

Explain why the exclusion of *creation* from *obtaining* limits the scope of *sui generis* database right.

The difficult distinction between creating data and obtaining pre-existent data can be understood through decisions regarding databases containing information about football matches in England and Scotland. The ECJ provided the same reasoning as the horse-racing case in a group of cases concerned with football fixture lists (the *Fixtures* cases)[9] meaning that organisation of football leagues by deploying sources for determining dates, times and team pairings for home and away matches involves creating data. Subsequently, fixture lists have been denied database protection in the UK.[10] However, in *Football Dataco Ltd v Sportradar*,[11] Floyd J distinguished 'fixtures data' which are created by event organisers from 'match data' such as goals which are created by the footballers and the organisers only provide the environment for them to be scored. He held that 'factual data which is collected and recorded at a live event' relating to 'events outside the control of the person doing the collection and recording is not created by that person, but is obtained by him' (para 60). Collecting and recording data fall with the ordinary meaning of 'obtaining' but 'creating' suggests creation of new information.[12] The recording of existing facts, such as the fact of a goal which is created when the ball hits the back of the net, is not the same as creating new information (para 61).

6.7   'Obtaining' data is only one of three alternative ways in which an investment may be rewarded with database right. There may still be protection by way of 'verification' and 'presentation' for the creator

---

[7] For a useful analysis of the legal outcomes of the whole litigation, see J Jenkins, 'Database rights' subsistence: under starter's orders' (2006) 1 JIPLP 467.

[8] See MJ Davison and PB Hugenholtz, 'Football fixtures, horseraces and spin-offs: the ECJ domesticates the database right' [2005] EIPR 113; T Aplin, 'The ECJ elucidates the database right' [2005] IPQ 204.

[9] Cases C-338/02 *Fixtures Marketing Ltd v Svenska Spel AB* [2005] ECDR 4 (ECJ), paras 24–31; C-444/02 *Fixtures Marketing Ltd v Organismos Prognostikon Agonon Podosfairou (OPAP)* [2005] ECDR 3 (ECJ), paras 40–47; and C-46/02 *Fixtures Marketing Ltd v Oy Veikkaus Ab* [2005] ECDR 2 (ECJ), paras 34–42 .

[10] *Football Dataco Ltd v Brittens Pools Ltd* [2010] RPC 17 (ChD), para 92; *Football Dataco Ltd v Brittens Pools Ltd* [2011] ECDR 9 (CA), paras 10–12.   [11] [2012] ECC 26 (ChD) (appeal outstanding at the time of writing).

[12] See also *British Sky Broadcasting Group plc v Digital Satellite Warranty Cover Ltd (In Liquidation)* [2012] FSR 14 (Ch D), paras 19–21.

of data *later* put into a database. So checking the accuracy, completeness and reliability of the data *once in the database* is verification, while presentation is about giving the database its function of processing information, that is, the resources used for the systematic or methodical arrangement of the data and the organisation of their individual accessibility.[13] So the concept includes materials necessary for the operation or consultation of the database by users such as thesaurus and indexation systems, as well as the structuring of the contents (the conceptual as distinct from the external format of the database). What is crucial is that, to be relevant for the establishment of *sui generis* protection, investment in verification and presentation must be subsequent to and not part of the process of creation of the data. None of this could, however, avail the creators of the data in the horse-racing and *Fixtures* cases.

 Discussion point For answer guidance visit www.oxfordtextbooks.co.uk/orc/waelde3e/

Consider the derivation of data from naturally occurring phenomena such as the weather or the genetic sequences of living creatures. Is that derivation an act of creation or obtaining for the purposes of *sui generis* database right? Read Floyd J's rationale in *Football Dataco Ltd v Sportradar* [2012] ECC 26 at 52–67 and compare the views of E Derclaye, 'Database "*sui generis*" right: should we adopt the spin-off theory?' [2004] EIPR 402, and MJ Davison and PB Hugenholtz, 'Football fixtures, horseraces and spin-offs: the ECJ domesticates the database right' [2005] EIPR 113 at 115.

Substantial investment

6.8   The investment necessary for the existence of database right need not be merely financial, but can include human, technical and professional resources as well as the expenditure of time, effort, and energy.[14] The substantiality of an investment may be measured qualitatively and/or quantitatively.[15] In her opinion in *Fixtures Marketing v Svenska*, the Advocate General said that the substantiality of an investment is to be assessed 'first in relation to costs and their redemption and secondly in relation to the scale, nature and contents of the database and the sector to which it belongs'. But she added that substantiality is not only a relative matter: 'the Directive requires an absolute lower threshold for investments worthy of protection as a sort of de minimis rule.'[16] This was justified by reference to recital 19 of the Directive, which states that, as a rule (ie usually), the compilation of several recordings of musical performances on a CD does not represent a substantial enough investment to be eligible for the *sui generis* right.[17] The difficulty is in using this rather specific example as a basis for determining what is the minimum threshold making an investment substantial, or indeed that there is such a requirement. The ECJ did not comment on this aspect of the Advocate General's Opinion.

'Spin-off' databases

6.9   Are 'spin-off' databases—databases created as a by-product or a sort of side effect of activity and investment of resources which had other aims primarily in mind—excluded from database right

[13] Cases C-338/02 *Fixtures Marketing Ltd v Svenska Spel AB* (ECJ), para 27; C-444/02 *Fixtures Marketing Ltd v OPAP*, para 43; C-46/02 *Fixtures Marketing Ltd v Oy Veikkaus Ab*, para 37; and C-203/02 *British Horseracing Board Ltd v William Hill Organization Ltd* [2005] RPC 13, paras 34–41. See also recital 20 of the Database Directive.

[14] Database Regulations 1997, reg 12(1); Cases C-338/02 *Fixtures Marketing Ltd v Svenska Spel AB*, para 28; C-444/02 *Fixtures Marketing Ltd v OPAP*, para 44; and C-46/02 *Fixtures Marketing Ltd v Oy Veikkaus Ab*, para 38.

[15] See references in note 14.

[16] C-338/02 *Fixtures Marketing Ltd v Svenska Spel AB* [2004] ECR I-10497, paras 38–39 (AG) (for both quotations).

[17] Database Directive, recital 19.

protection? For example, investing in the creation of sports fixture lists or a horse-racing calendar is not done just to build a database, but to organise and structure the season of the sport in question and provide advance information for participants, the media and potential spectators. The Advocate General took the view in the *Fixtures* cases that the Directive imposes no requirement as to the purpose for which the database is created and, in principle, spin-off databases could be protected.[18] The ECJ held that the purpose of the Directive is to promote and protect investment in data storage and processing systems and while 'spin-off' databases are not precluded from protection, investment is to be understood in relation to the creation of a database, that is, obtaining, verifying or presenting the contents of the database.[19] This is consistent with its view that creating data is not obtaining data of the kind necessary to achieve a protectable database (para 6.6). Therefore, 'spin-off' databases will not be protected by the *sui generis* right unless there is additional substantial investment directed specifically at the database, most probably in the verification or presentation of the data contained within it.

Key points on *sui generis* database right

- For databases (collections of independent data, arranged systematically, individually accessible)

- Selection and arrangement need not be intellectual creation (contrast copyright protection)

- Needs substantial investment in:
  - obtaining (*not* creating—horse-racing and football fixtures cases)
  - verifying
  - presenting

contents of database (problems of 'spin-off')

- Substantial investment financial/human/technical/professional; qualitative and/or quantitative

---

First ownership

6.10   The maker of a database is the first owner of the *sui generis* database right in it.[20] There is a presumption that a name appearing on copies of a database as its maker is the maker unless the contrary is proved.[21] The maker is the person taking the initiative in obtaining, verifying or presenting the database contents and assuming the risk of investing in those activities.[22] If, however, a database is anonymous, in the sense that it is not possible by reasonable inquiry to ascertain its maker's identity, and it is reasonable to assume that database right has expired, then extraction and re-utilisation of the database contents is not infringement.[23] There may be joint makers if two or more parties collaborate in taking the initiative and assuming the risk.[24] Where an employee makes a database in the course of employment, the employer

---

[18] C-338/02 *Fixtures Marketing Ltd v Svenska Spel AB* [2004] ECR I-10497, paras 41–45, 57 (AG).
[19] Cases C-338/02 *Fixtures Marketing Ltd v Svenska Spel AB*, paras 23–29 (ECJ); C-444/02 *Fixtures Marketing Ltd v OPAP*, paras 39–45; and C-46/02 *Fixtures Marketing Ltd v Oy Veikkaus Ab*, paras 33–39.
[20] Database Regulations 1997, reg 15.   [21] Database Regulations 1997, reg 22.
[22] Database Regulations 1997, reg 14(1).
[23] Database Regulations 1997, reg 21. On infringement of database right, see paras 6.12–6.16.
[24] Database Regulations 1997, reg 14(5).

is to be regarded as the maker in the absence of any agreement to the contrary.[25] There is also provision for Crown and parliamentary database right.[26]

Duration

6.11   The *sui generis* database right has its own special period of duration which on the face of it is much shorter than any of the main copyright terms.[27] The right lasts for 15 years from the end of the year in which the making of the database was completed, or in which it was first made available to the public if that event occurs before the end of the first period.

Diagram 6.1 Duration of database right

```
                              15 years
        Creation - - - - - - - - - - - - - - - - + - - - - - - - - - - - - - - - - - Database right expires

                                            15 years
                       Public availability - - - - - - - - - - - - - - - - Database right expires
```

However, the right can last much longer than either of these 15-year periods, because any substantial change to the contents of a database (arising, eg, from additions, deletions or alterations to its content) which would result in the database being considered a substantial new investment will qualify the database resulting from that investment for its own new 15-year period of protection. The same result might follow from a substantial investment in verification of the contents of the database.[28] A dynamic database could therefore end up with a rolling series of 15-year protections which will keep the right alive as long as the owner thinks it worthwhile to continue investment in it.[29]

Diagram 6.2 Duration of database right after substantial investment

```
                            15 years
      Creation - - - - - - - - - - - - - - - - + - - - - - - - - - - - - - - - - Database right 1 expires

                                      15 years
                   Investment 1 - - - - + - - - - Database right 2 expires

                                            15 years
                        Investment 2 - - - - - - - - - - Database right 3 expires
```

Infringement

6.12   The *sui generis* database right has its own infringement regime distinct from that of copyright. *Unauthorised extraction from or re-utilisation of all or a substantial part of the database* is prohibited.

---

[25] Database Regulations 1997, reg 14(2). In *Cureton v Mark Insulations Ltd* [2006] EWHC 2279 (QB), a case decided in the English High Court, Bean J held that a sales agent was the first owner of a customer database prepared on behalf of and paid for by its principal.
[26] Database Regulations 1997, reg 14(3)–(4A).   [27] Database Regulations 1997, reg 17 (see also reg 30).
[28] Database Directive, recital 55. On verification and substantial investment, see paras 6.7 and 6.8.
[29] See the opinion of the Advocate General in Case C-203/02 *British Horseracing Board Ltd v William Hill Organization Ltd* [2005] RPC 13, paras 143–154.

Unauthorised extraction means 'in relation to any contents of a database,... *the permanent or temporary transfer of those contents to another medium* by any means or in any form' (Database Regulations 1997, reg 12(1)).

Re-utilisation means 'in relation to any contents of a database,... *making these contents available to the public by any means*' (Database Regulations 1997, reg 12(1)).

Rental or lending of a database otherwise than for direct or indirect economic or commercial advantage through an establishment accessible to the public is not extraction or re-utilisation for these purposes;[30] but this does not apply to making available for on-the-spot reference use.[31] Payment which does no more than cover the establishment's costs gives rise to no direct or indirect economic or commercial advantage.[32] The rights are exhausted after the *first sale* of the database in the European Economic Area (EEA), as long as that sale was with the consent of the owner of the database right.[33]

Extraction and utilisation of a substantial part

6.13   The meaning of the infringement provisions of the Database Directive was considered in detail by the ECJ in *British Horseracing Board v William Hill Organization*[34] (see for facts of the case, para 6.6). The following points emerge from the Court's judgment:

- The terms extraction and re-utilisation must be interpreted in the light of the objective pursued by the *sui generis* right (para 44). The concepts of extraction and re-utilisation are intended to have a wide definition, cannot be exhaustively defined and must be 'interpreted as referring to any act of appropriating and making available to the public, without the consent of the maker of the database, the results of his investment, thus depriving him of revenue which should have enabled him to redeem the cost of the investment' (paras 51–52). The purpose of extraction and re-utilisation, whether for creating another database or a commercial or non commercial purpose, is irrelevant (paras 47–48).

- Extraction and re-utilisation can be either direct or indirect; that is, either from the database itself, or from a copy of the database (paras 52–53). The context is provided by the facts of the case, where the defendants had obtained the data, not from BHB's database, but from one of BHB's licensed distributors. Since temporary transfer of database contents is specifically included in relation to extraction, it would appear that any unauthorised access to a database would be extraction. However, the ECJ said specifically, albeit delphically, that mere consultation of a database was not an act of extraction or re-utilisation but gave no further guidance on this distinction (para 54).

- Extraction meant the transfer of contents of database to another medium and covered any unauthorised act of appropriation. It does imply removal in the sense that the contents in question must be removed from the database altogether; there is extraction even when afterwards the contents remain on the database (paras 58, 59, and 67). So, for example, a printout from a database is an extraction.[35]

- Re-utilisation is making available to the public the database contents and covers any unauthorised distribution to the public. It therefore embraces both online transmission and distribution or rental/lending of the database, and is not limited to a right to first publication of the contents (paras 58, 59, and 67). Exhaustion only arises in relation to the sale of physical copies of the database (eg on CD and DVD).[36]

- Substantiality of the part of the database extracted or re-utilised can be assessed both quantitatively and qualitatively. A quantitative measure is the volume of data extracted compared to the volume

---

[30] Database Regulations 1997, reg 12(2).   [31] Database Regulations 1997, reg 12(4).
[32] Database Regulations 1997, reg 12(3).   [33] Database Regulations 1997, reg 12(5).   [34] [2005] RPC 13.
[35] See also para 100 (AG); [2001] RPC 31, para 57.   [36] See also para 190 (AG).

of the contents of the whole database; while a qualitative measure is the scale of the investment required in relation to the material extracted or re-utilised. The intrinsic value of the data, as distinct from the cost of the investment, is not a relevant consideration for the qualitative measurement of the substantiality of a part (paras 70–72). Finally, 'it must be held,' said the Court, 'that any part which does not fulfil the definition of a substantial part, evaluated both quantitatively and qualitatively, falls within the definition of an insubstantial part of the contents of a database' (para 73).

While the ECJ only gives guidance to national courts on the interpretation of Union law, it did make the following comment on how, in the light of its opinion, summarised in the previous points, on the meaning of the infringement provisions of the Database Directive, this case should be decided. Thus, as far as concerned the quantitative measure of whether a substantial part of the database had been extracted or re-utilised:

> the materials displayed on William Hill's internet sites, which derive from the BHB database, represent only a very small proportion of that database.... It must therefore be held that those materials do not constitute a substantial part, evaluated quantitatively, of the contents of that database (para 74).

With regard to qualitative measurement:

> The intrinsic value of the data affected...does not constitute a relevant criterion for assessing whether the part in question is substantial, evaluated qualitatively. The fact that the data extracted and re-utilised by WH are vital to the organisation of the [BHB] horse races...is thus irrelevant to the assessment [of] substantial part (para 78).[37]

6.14   Several recent decisions provide guidance on the interpretation of extraction, re-utilisation and substantial part as well as proof and place of infringement.

■ Case C-304/07 *Directmedia Publishing GMBH v Albert-Ludwigs-Universitat Freiburg* [2008] ECR I-7565 (ECJ)

This case concerned alleged infringement of a university's *sui generis* database right in a list of poetry titles. D used the database as a guide to the creation of its CD-ROM entitled *1,000 poems everyone should have*, omitting certain poems, adding others and critically examining each selection made by the professor who created the original database. Despite D taking the texts of each poem from its own resources, the ECJ held that the concept of 'extraction' covered the transfer of material from a protected database to another database following an on-screen consultation of the first database and an individual assessment of the extracted contents. The Court noted that the objective of the Directive is to guarantee the maker of a database, created through substantial human, financial or technical resource investment, a return on the investment involved without unauthorised appropriation of the results at a fraction of the cost needed to design it independently. As such, extraction is to be given a wide meaning. The concept is 'not dependent on the nature and form of the mode of operation used' and covers an act of transfer of 'all or part of the contents of the database concerned to another medium, whether of the same nature as the medium of that database or of a different nature' (paras 35–36). Therefore, extraction is not limited to physical taking, and also includes taking that is preceded by the taker's critical evaluation of the material. The information 'extracted' from the database could be transferred in any way to another medium, such as manual recopying, photocopying, or downloading. It was irrelevant that the copied information was adapted into a different format. The objective pursued in the act of transfer was also immaterial.

---

[37] This and the preceding issue were not considered when the case returned to the Court of Appeal, since there it was decided that the database in question was not protected by the *sui generis* right ([2005] RPC 35).

■ **Case C-545/07 *Apis-Hristovich EOOD v Lakorda AD* [2009] 3 CMLR 3 (ECJ)**

A, which operated a legal database, claimed that L, which had been set up by two ex-employees of A, infringed its database rights by extracting without A's consent substantial parts of two modules of the database. These extracted elements, it was argued, were used by the defendants to develop a similar system. L argued that it had invested significant independent time and money in the new database. Any similarities to the two modules were argued to be due to the fact that the legal sources relied upon were publicly available. The Court held that protection could be claimed in database sub-groups provided that each sub-group qualified as a protected database. If they did, the level of extraction was compared against the amount of data in the sub-group. If they did not, the level of extraction was measured against the entire database, rather than its constituent parts. The term 'extraction' should be given a broad definition and the purpose of extraction was irrelevant, as was the unique feature of the new database. Furthermore, the Court noted that the public availability of materials did not preclude protection as long as there had been qualitative and/or quantitative substantial investment when obtaining, verifying or presenting the contents of the database. Additionally, the use of hyperlinks or other such similar features in both databases could be indicative, though not determinative, of extraction, as could such materials not available to the public.

■ **Case C-173/11 *Football Dataco v Sportradar GmbH* [2013] FSR 4 (CJ)**

F, provider of *Football live* containing data from football matches in progress in England and Scotland claimed database right infringement against S, a German company and its Swiss parent company which provided football statistics of English matches live via the Internet through its service *Sport Live Data* which held its data in a member state outside the UK and transmitted it to the public in the UK who clicked on the service. The Court of Justice noted that the database right protection, although harmonised, is provided by national law of a member state and as such acts of infringement must take place in that member state. It held that re-utilisation covers the act of sending data, previously extracted from a protected database, by means of a web server in member state A, to another person's computer in member state B, at their request, for the purpose of storage in that computer's memory and display on its screen. Such re-utilisation takes place, at least, in member state B, if there is evidence from which it may be concluded that the act discloses an intention on the part of the sender to target members of the public in member state B (para 47).

■ ***Beechwood House Publishing Ltd v Guardian Products Ltd* [2011] EWHC 22 (Patents County Court, England & Wales)**

B, a publisher of a database consisting of details of individuals associated with GP practices, put seeds—dummy or fictitious entries not belonging to real people but to addresses of its staff—in its database which led them to find out that G, a direct marketing information provider, was using information from its database for printed mail outs. Judge Birss QC held that 6,000 practice nurse records which were extracted by G for a mailing exercise, representing about 14 per cent of the database, was a quantitatively substantial part, even if it was at the lower end of what could be regarded as such. Alternatively, it was a qualitatively substantial part as the scale of human and financial investment they represented was significant.[38]

Repeated and systematic extraction/re-utilisation of insubstantial parts

6.15 Repeated and systematic extraction/re-utilisation of insubstantial parts of database contents may amount to the extraction/re-utilisation of a substantial part of those contents.[39] In the *British Horseracing*

---

[38] For another example of a successful case of database infringement, see *Forensic Telecommunications Services Ltd v Chief Constable of West Yorkshire* [2011] EWHC 2892 (Ch).

[39] Database Regulations 1997, reg 16(2), implementing Database Directive, Art 7(5). A reference to the Court of Justice on the meaning and interpretation of this provision is currently pending, C-202/12 *Innoweb BV v Wegener ICT Media BV*.

Board case,[40] Laddie J held that the defendant's daily use of the BHB database was caught by this provision, but the issue of its meaning was referred to the ECJ by the Court of Appeal. The Advocate General made clear that repetition and system are cumulative rather than alternative requirements, and imply acts at regular intervals such as weekly or monthly. The ECJ noted that the purpose of the rule was to prevent circumvention of the basic exclusive right conferred by the Directive by a series of insubstantial acts which would cumulatively cause serious prejudice to the investment of the maker of the database. It went on to hold that the prohibition affected repeated and systematic acts leading to the reconstitution of the whole database or a substantial part of it, whether or not the acts were carried out to create such a database. Third parties were also prevented from repeated and systematic making available to the public of insubstantial parts of the database.

6.16   The Directive says that the repeated and systematic acts must either (1) conflict with normal exploitation of the database, or (2) unreasonably prejudice the legitimate interests of its maker.[41] The ECJ held that this refers to serious prejudice to the database maker's investment by unauthorised acts the cumulative effect of which is (a) the reconstitution or (b) making available to the public, of the whole or a substantial part of the contents of a protected database.[42] The Court concluded that the defendant's acts in this case would not result in the reconstitution of the BHB database, or in making it available to the public, so the prohibition did not apply.

Key points on infringement of *sui generis* database right

- The right is infringed by unauthorised extraction or re-utilisation of all or a substantial part of the database

- Extraction is transfer of database contents to another medium (but removal not needed)

- Extraction and re-utilisation are to be given a wide meaning

- Re-utilisation is making database contents available to the public by any form of distribution

- Extraction/re-utilisation may be direct or indirect

- Substantiality is measured both quantitatively and qualitatively, but the intrinsic value of the data is not a factor in this assessment

- Repeated and systematic extraction/re-utilisation of insubstantial parts may cumulatively amount to extraction/re-utilisation of a substantial part

---

Exceptions

6.17   The Database Regulations 1997 provides for exceptions for non-commercial research and teaching and also a deposit library exception.[43] The provisions in the Database Directive for exceptions to the rights which it conferred[44] were left largely unaffected by the subsequent Information Society (InfoSoc) Directive. But there is nothing in the Database Directive[45] to compare with the rules in the Software Directive that contractual agreement cannot overcome exceptions to copyright in computer programs—in particular, making back-up copies, decompilation, and observation, studying, and testing.[46] So it

---

[40] [2001] RPC 31 (Laddie J); [2002] ECDR 4 (CA); Case C-203/02, [2005] RPC 13 (ECJ).
[41] Database Directive, Art 7(5); not transposed as such in the 1997 Regulations.
[42] [2005] RPC 13, para 89.   [43] Database Regulations 1997, regs 20 and 20A.   [44] Database Directive, Arts 6 and 9.
[45] However, see CDPA 1988, ss 50D(2) and 296B.
[46] Software Directive, Arts 5(2), (3), and 6(1). See CDPA 1988, ss 50A, 50B(4), 50BA, and 296A, and para 5.44.

would seem that in this area contract will prevail over exceptions. The Database Regulations do, however, make it clear that a lawful user of a database which has been made available to the public in any manner shall be entitled to extract or re-utilise an *insubstantial* part of the contents of the database for any purpose,[47] and that any term in an agreement purporting to limit this entitlement shall be void.[48] This illustrates that contract provisions may not be used to extend the scope of the *sui generis* right itself; it is infringed only by taking of a *substantial* part of the database contents (see paras 6.12 and 6.13).

Exception for non-commercial research

6.18   There is an exception permitting extraction for non-commercial research purposes from a database protected not by copyright, but by the *sui generis* database right.[49] The database must have been made available to the public, and the person making the extraction must be already a lawful user apart from the exception. The source must be acknowledged. The exception covers only extraction of a substantial part of the database, so presumably extraction of an insubstantial part, not being infringement, requires no exception. It is worth noting that the ECJ has said that mere consultation of a database is not extraction of the database.[50] No similar exception exists for the other act restricted by database right, re-utilisation.

Teaching exception

6.19   There is also an exception to allow extraction (but, again, not re-utilisation) from a database made available to the public, by one already a lawful user of the database, for the purpose of illustration for teaching and not for any commercial purpose, as long as the source is indicated.[51]

Discussion point   For answer guidance visit www.oxfordtextbooks.co.uk/orc/waelde3e/

Why do the non-commercial research and teaching exceptions apply only to extraction of content from a database and not to its re-utilisation?

Exercise

Compare the exceptions to *sui generis* database right with the exceptions to copyright in a database (see paras 5.12–5.46). Are the two systems compatible?

Key points on exceptions to *sui generis* database right

- The principal exceptions are for non-commercial research and teaching
- The exceptions are only in relation to extraction and not to re-utilisation
- It seems to be possible to exclude the exceptions by contractual agreement between the right holder and the user of the database

---

[47]   Database Regulations 1997, reg 19(1).   [48]   Database Regulations 1997, reg 19(2).
[49]   Database Regulations 1997, reg 20; implementing Database Directive 1996, Art 9. Cf the equivalent copyright exception, discussed at para 5.22.
[50]   C-203/02 *British Horseracing Board Ltd v William Hill Organization Ltd* [2005] RPC 13, para 54.
[51]   Database Regulations 1997, reg 20; implementing Database Directive 1996, Art 9.

Commission's evaluation of database right

6.20   The *sui generis* database right has met with mixed results.[52] A Commission Working Paper noted that decisions of the ECJ had substantially curtailed the right.[53] There have been problems defining key terms within the right. Furthermore, there are a number of textual ambiguities between national legislatures implementing the Directive, confusion about the parallel availability of copyright and the *sui generis* right, and consequent reluctance to use the right due to its complexity by national courts. The Commission also noted that there are difficulties understanding the legal nature of the right due to it being framed in non-legal language.

Performers' rights[54]

Historical background to performers' protection

6.21   Performers were, historically, not well protected in the UK. Only in 1925 were criminal sanctions provided by the Dramatic and Musical Performers' Protection Act 1925 against making recordings of dramatic and musical performances without consent ('bootlegging'). The law was consolidated and extended over the years, notably by encompassing performances of literary, dramatic, musical and artistic works in the Performers Protection Act 1963, and in 1972 when another Performers Protection Act extended the penalties available. The Rome Convention for the Protection of Performers, Producers of Phonograms and Broadcasting Organizations 1961 provided the international basis for such protection.

6.22   The UK Acts appeared to give rise to criminal liability, but not to any civil cause of action, for either the performer or those who held recording contracts with the performer. Despite this, in *Rickless v United Artists Corporation*[55] a civil cause of action was accorded to *performers*. In that case, United Artists made a film using out-takes from previous films in the Pink Panther series starring the late Peter Sellers. Rickless, as the owner of the rights of Peter Sellers' services as an actor, sued for infringement of section 2 of the Dramatic and Musical and Performers' Protection Act 1958 because United Artists had failed to obtain permission for its activities. The Court of Appeal upheld the lower court's ruling that the Performers Acts *did* give civil remedies to a performer whose performance had been exploited without consent, in addition to the criminal penalties under the Act. This was although earlier, in *RCA v Pollard*,[56] the Court of Appeal had found that the Acts did *not* give rise to civil remedies for *recording companies* with whom performers had exclusive recording contracts.

6.23   The Rome Convention only gives performers the possibility of 'preventing' a list of acts, rather than a right to authorise and prohibit them in advance.[57] Thus, it was argued that the approach through the criminal law could continue.[58] However, in 1977 the Whitford Committee[59] recommended that performers should be given a civil right of action for injunctions and damages, but that this should not amount to copyright. The Copyright, Designs and Patents Act 1988 (CDPA 1988) introduced two distinct rights in performances. One right was a personal, non-assignable right for performers, while

---

[52] See E Derclaye, *The Legal Protection of Databases: A Comparative Analysis* (2008).
[53] See European Commission Working Paper, First Evaluation of Directive 96/9/EC (2005). See further para 6.6.
[54] See generally R Arnold, *Performers' Rights* (4th edn, 2008).   [55] *Rickless v United Artists Corp* [1988] QB 40.
[56] [1983] Ch 135.   [57] Arts 7, 10, and 13.
[58] WR Cornish, D Llewelyn, and T Aplin, *Intellectual Property* (7th edn, 2010), para 14.30.   [59] Cmnd 6732.

the other was for those making exclusive recording contracts with performers. The latter right could be assigned.[60]

> ## Key points on historical background
>
> - Between 1925 and 1988 performers were protected against unauthorised reproduction of their performances only through the criminal law
> - A civil right of action was recognised by the courts in 1983 but the statutory change took place five years later
> - The 1988 Act creates two kinds of civil right for performers: one personal and non-assignable, the other for those making recording contracts, which is assignable

European reforms

6.24   A number of EU Directives have now further changed the position for performers. Measures affecting the position of performers are to be found in the following:

- Rental Right Directive;[61]
- Satellite and Cable Directive[62] (which applies these requirements to satellite broadcasting);
- Term Directive;[63] and
- Infosoc Directive.[64]

Each of these resulted in significant amendments to the CDPA 1988.[65]

Current law on performers' rights

6.25   A *performer* is not defined in the Act, but a *performance* means a dramatic performance (including dance or mime), a musical one, a reading or recitation of a literary work, or a performance of a variety

---

[60] Cornish, Llewelyn, and Aplin (note 58, para 14.31) argue that this in effect gave performers no entitlement to any protection of their own distinct from that of their recording company, except in relation to bootlegging.

[61] Originally Council Directive 92/100/EEC on rental right and lending right and on certain rights related to copyright in the field of intellectual property; now in a consolidated version, European Parliament and Council Directive 2006/115/EC. For a challenge to the UK implementation of the Rental Right Directive, see *Phonographic Performance Limited v Department of Trade and Industry and another* [2004] 3 CMLR 31 (ChD).

[62] Council Directive 93/83/EEC on the coordination of certain rules concerning copyright and rights related to copyright applicable to satellite broadcasting and cable retransmission.

[63] Originally Council Directive 93/98/EEC harmonizing the term of protection of copyright and certain related rights; it was replaced by a consolidated version, European Parliament and Council Directive 2006/116/EC; and has now been amended by Directive 2011/77/EU which extends the term of musical performers' rights to 70 years and provides additional rights (see para 6.33).

[64] Directive 2001/29/EC of the European Parliament and of the Council on the harmonization of certain aspects of copyright and related rights in the information society.

[65] The current law is to be found in the CDPA 1988, Part II, as amended by the Duration of Copyright and Rights in Performances Regulations 1995 (SI 1995/3297), the Copyright and Related Rights Regulations 1996 (SI 1996/2967), the Copyright and Related Rights Regulations 2003 (SI 2003/2498), and the Copyright Rights in Performances (Moral Rights, etc) Regulations 2006 (SI 2006/18). For a case about the legislation's application to pre-Act performances, see *Experience Hendrix LLC v Purple Haze Records Ltd and others* [2007] FSR 31 (CA).

act or any similar presentation.[66] There is no requirement for a performance to be in public and in any performance given by more than one person, each performer would be entitled to rights in their own part.[67]

 Question

The Edinburgh Festivals, which take place every year from July to September, see a plethora of interesting, diverse and ingenious individuals engaged in all manner of behaviour. Under the definition, would the following be performances?

- An individual dressed as a Greek Goddess standing stock still on an upturned bucket in the middle of the Royal Mile.
- A group of individuals attentively engaged in drawing collaborative pictures on the pavement.
- A group of individuals in Princes Street Gardens intently following instructions given by a keep-fit expert, the purpose of which is to teach the elderly to keep fit.
- An individual juggling with balls of fire whilst on top of a monocycle.
- A fortune teller seated in a gypsy caravan gazing into a crystal ball.
- A group of models parading around Edinburgh Castle showing off the latest collections by up-and-coming Scottish designers.
- A heated debate between Professor Alexander McCall Smith and an audience over whether the latest course of action taken by Precious Ramotswe was morally justifiable.

Categories of performers' rights

6.26   Performers' rights are divided into two main categories:

- performers' non-property rights: rights against bootlegging (recordings of live performances made without performers' consent);
- performers' property rights: rights in authorised copies of performances.

The main distinctions between the non-property and property rights are:

- non-property rights cannot be assigned, although they are transmissible on death, whereas the property rights are capable of transfer and assignation;
- infringements of non-property rights are actionable only as breach of statutory duty, whereas infringement of property rights are actionable in the same way as other property rights, including copyright.

Performers' rights in respect of live performances

Diagram 6.3 shows performers' rights in respect of live performances by reference to the CDPA 1988.

---

[66] CDPA 1988, s 180(2); on definition of a performance see D Liu, 'Performers' rights: muddled or mangled? Bungled or boggled?' [2012] EIPR 374.

[67] In *Bamgboye v Reed* [2002] EWHC 2922 (QB), it was held that a performance can be one that is made in a recording studio as there is no need for an audience.

Diagram 6.3 Performer's rights in live performances

Property rights in recordings of performances	Non-property rights against 'bootlegging'	Remuneration right	Secondary infringement rights (wrongdoer must have knowledge that recording illicit) (183–4)
reproduction (182A)	fixation and live broadcasting (182)	on any public playing or broadcasting of commercially published sound recording (182D)	showing or playing performance in public
distribution (182B)	public performance and broadcasting of recording made without consent (183)		broadcasting the performance
rental (182C)	dealings in illicit recordings (184)		importing a recording or copy for other than private or domestic use
lending (182C)			selling, hiring, distributing or otherwise dealing in copies
making available (182CA)			

The extent of performers' rights

6.27   **(1) Performers' property rights**

6.28   A performer's property rights are infringed by the following (compare with the economic rights conferred by copyright: see paras 4.23–4.67):

- **Reproduction**

By a person who, without consent, either directly or indirectly makes a copy of a recording of the whole or any substantial part of a qualifying performance.[68]

- **Distribution**

By a person who, without consent, issues to the public copies of a recording of the whole or any substantial part of a qualifying performance. The rights are exhausted once copies are placed into circulation within the EEA by or with the consent of the performer (but note consent is still required for rental or lending).[69]

- **Rental and lending**

By a person who, without consent, rents or lends to the public copies of a recording of the whole or any substantial part of a qualifying performance.[70] *Rental* means the making of a copy of a recording available for use, on terms that it will or may be returned for direct or indirect economic or commercial advantage, and *lending* means making a copy of a recording available for use on terms that it will or may be returned otherwise than for direct or indirect economic or commercial advantage through an establishment which is accessible to the public.[71]

---

[68]   CDPA 1988, s 182A.   [69]   CDPA 1988, s 182B.   [70]   CDPA 1988, s 182C.

[71]   CDPA 1988, s 182C(2)(a),(b). There are other definitions in this section. Eg, the terms 'rental' and 'lending' do not include making available for the purpose of public performance, playing or showing in public or broadcasting. In addition, the expression 'lending' does not include making available between establishments which are accessible to the public (CDPA 1988, s 182C(3), (4)).

• **Making available**

By a person who, without consent, makes available to the public a recording of the whole or any substantial part of a qualifying performance by electronic transmission in such a way that members of the public may access the recording from a place and at a time individually chosen by them.[72]

 Discussion point For answer guidance visit www.oxfordtextbooks.co.uk/orc/waelde3e/

Which of the economic rights conferred by copyright (para 4.10) is not to be found in the previous list? Why not?

(2) Performers' non-property rights

6.29   A performer's non-property rights are infringed by the following (again, compare with the economic rights conferred by copyright: see para 4.10):

• **Fixation**

By a person who, without consent:

(1) makes a recording of the whole or any substantial part of a qualifying performance directly from the live performance;

(2) broadcasts live, the whole or any part of a qualifying performance;

(3) makes a recording of the whole or any substantial part of a qualifying performance directly from a broadcast of the live performance.[73]

No damages will be awarded against a defendant who shows that at the time of the recording he believed on reasonable grounds that consent had been given.[74]

• **Distribution**

Where a recording made without consent is imported into the UK otherwise than for private or domestic use, or is exposed for sale or for hire in the course of a business.[75]

• **Public performance; communication to the public**

Where a person, without consent, shows or plays in public the whole or any substantial part of a qualifying performance, or communicates to the public the whole or any substantial part of a qualifying performance where the person knows or has reason to believe the recording was made without the performer's consent.[76]

Non-property rights and exclusive recording contracts

6.30   Where a performer enters into an exclusive recording contract with another person under which that person is entitled to the exclusion of all other persons (including the performer) to make a recording of one or more of his performances with a view to their commercial exploitation,[77] consent of *both* the person having exclusive recording rights and the performer is necessary for:

[72] CDPA 1988, s 182CA.
[73] CDPA 1988, s 182(1); prior to 2003, these rights were not infringed when the recording of a performance was made for a private and domestic use but these provisions were repealed resulting from implementation of the InfoSoc Directive (SI 2003/2498, reg 2(2), Sch 2).
[74] CDPA 1988, s 182(3).   [75] CDPA 1988, s 188(1)(a), (b).   [76] CDPA 1988, s 183(a), (b).
[77] CDPA 1988, s 185(1).

- recording of the whole or any substantial part of the performance;[78]

- showing or playing in public the whole or any substantial part of the performance;

- communicating to the public the whole or any substantial part of the performance;[79] and

- importing it into the UK otherwise than for private or domestic use, or selling or letting for hire the performance in the course of a business.[80]

Exercise

Why are performers' rights classified into property and non-property rights? Are there coherent policy objectives underlying this aspect of the law? What would you do to reform the law in this area and what would be your underlying objectives in suggesting such reform?

Restrictions on the scope of performers' property and non-property rights

6.31   The CDPA 1988 details various permitted acts in relation to performers' property and non-property rights. These may be compared with the exceptions to copyright (Chapter 5, especially at paras 5.29 and 5.37–5.38). The permitted acts relate to the question of infringement of the rights. They include such matters as things done for purposes of criticism, review, or news reporting,[81] or instruction or examination;[82] recording of broadcasts by educational establishments;[83] recording of folksongs;[84] and recording for the purpose of time-shifting.[85] The exceptions largely cover the same ground as those to be found in the 1988 Act as defences to an action of infringement of copyright.

Duration of rights

6.32   The rights conferred in relation to a performance currently expire at the end of the period of 50 years from the end of the calendar year in which the performance takes place. If a recording of a performance is released during that period, the rights expire 50 years from the end of the calendar year in which the recording is released.[86] A recording is released when it is first published, played or shown in public or communicated to the public.[87] Where a performer is not a national of an EEA state, the duration of rights is that to which the performer is entitled in the country of which he is a national provided this does not extend the period to which he would be entitled if he were an EEC national.[88] In *Sony Music Entertainment (Germany) GmbH v Falcon Neue Medien Vertrieb GmbH*,[89] the ECJ held that the term of protection of 50 years for copyright held by producers of Bob Dylan performances before 1966 captured on phonograms could apply to such work in a member state that at the time of performance gave no such protection. Such protection arose where the work was, on 1 July 1995, protected in at least one other member state and where the right holder, being a national of a non-member state, benefited at that date from the protection provided by those national provisions.

---

[78] CDPA 1988, s 186(1).   [79] CDPA 1988, s 187(1)(a), (b).   [80] CDPA 1988, s 188(1)(a), (b).
[81] CDPA 1988, Sch 2, para 2.   [82] CDPA 1988, Sch 2, para 4.   [83] CDPA 1988, Sch 2, para 6.
[84] CDPA 1988, Sch 2, para 14.   [85] CDPA 1988, Sch 2, para 17A.   [86] CDPA 1988, s 191(2).
[87] No account is to be taken of any unauthorised act (CDPA 1988, s 191(3)).   [88] CDPA 1988, s 191(4).
[89] Case C-240/07, [2009] ECDR 13. See N Owers, 'Term of protection of copyright-related rights in the EC' (2009) 4 JIPLP 321.

6.33   The duration of performers' rights was previously seen as being comparable with that for the media works in copyright (see paras 3.59–3.60) but the Term Directive 2011 is aimed at bringing performers' rights in sound recordings more in line with the protection given to authors.[90] Rights of performers, where the fixation of their performance as a sound recording is lawfully published or lawfully communicated to the public, will be extended to 70 years.[91] The rights of performers in other performances will not change.

 Discussion point For answer guidance visit www.oxfordtextbooks.co.uk/orc/waelde3e/

Why are all performers not given rights lasting for the same duration as authors of works protected by copyright? Should they be?

Moral rights

6.34   It was only with the adoption of the WIPO Performances and Phonograms Treaty 1996 (WPPT) that the question of moral rights arose for performers in the UK. Article 5 of the WPPT states:

Moral Rights of Performers

(1) Independently of a performer's economic rights, and even after the transfer of those rights, the performer shall, as regards his live aural performances or performances fixed in phonograms have the right to claim to be identified as the performer of his performances, except where omission is dictated by the manner of the use of the performance, and to object to any distortion, mutilation or other modification of his performances that would be prejudicial to his reputation.

The UK Patent Office carried out an extensive consultation exercise on the implementation of these rights,[92] asking also whether the provisions should be extended to audiovisual performers (ie those whose performances are captured in television broadcasts, films, DVDs, and the like), who are not included within the WPPT. Predictably, the responses fell into two broad camps:

• performers, authors, and film directors favoured a broad implementation of the rights and an extension to audiovisual performers;

• film and television producers, film distributors, cinema exhibitors, broadcasters, record producers, theatres, and music argued for narrow implementation restricted to the obligations under the WPPT with no extension to audiovisual performers.

The UK Regulations[93] came into force on 1 February 2006 and extend only as far as required under the WPPT, in some respects giving weaker protection to performers than might have been the case. The rights endure for the same period as the performers' economic rights.[94]

---

[90] Directive 2011/77/EU, adopted on the 12 September 2011 and to be implemented by the member states by 1 November 2013. It has not yet been implemented in the UK, but the government intends to do so soon (IPO, http://www.ipo.gov.uk/types/hargreaves.htm).

[91] Term Directive 2011, Art 1(2). While the extension will apply to performances which are still protected under the current term, it will not revive any rights which have expired.

[92] See references to the 1999 consultation at http://www.ipo.gov.uk/pro-policy/consult/consult-closed/consult-closed-2004/consult-2004-moralrights.htm.

[93] Copyright Rights in Performances (Moral Rights, etc) Regulations 2006 (SI 2006/18), amending CDPA 1988 (to which following references are made).   [94] CDPA 1988, s 205I.

Right to be identified

6.35   A performer will be given the right to be identified as performer whenever a person:

- produces or puts on a qualifying performance that is given in public;
- broadcasts live a qualifying performance;
- communicates to the public a sound recording of a qualifying performance; or
- issues to the public copies of such a recording.[95]

The right to be identified is one:

- in the case of a performance that is given in public, to be identified in any programme accompanying the performance or in some other manner likely to bring his identity to the notice of a person seeing or hearing the performance;
- in the case of a performance that is broadcast, to be identified in a manner likely to bring his identity to the notice of a person seeing or hearing the broadcast;
- in the case of a sound recording that is communicated to the public, to be identified in a manner likely to bring his identity to the notice of a person hearing the communication;
- in the case of a sound recording that is issued to the public, to be identified in or on each copy or, if that is not appropriate, in some other manner likely to bring his identity to the notice of a person acquiring a copy.[96]

However, the right to be identified will not be infringed unless it has first been asserted,[97] and is also hedged with a number of exceptions including:

- where it is not reasonably practicable to identify the performer (or, where identification of a group is permitted);
- in relation to any performance given for the purposes of reporting current events;
- in relation to any performance given for the purposes of advertising any goods or services.[98]

In addition, the right will not be infringed by an act which is covered by provisions relating to inter alia:

- news reporting;
- incidental inclusion of a performance or recording;
- things done for the purposes of examination.[99]

Right to object to derogatory treatment

A performer has a right to object where a performance:

6.36
- is broadcast live, or
- by means of a sound recording the performance is played in public or communicated to the public,

---

[95] CDPA 1988, s 205C(1).   [96] CDPA 1988, s 205C(2).   [97] CDPA 1988, s 205D(1).   [98] CDPA 1988, s 205E.
[99] CDPA 1988, s 205E(5).

with any distortion, mutilation, or other modification that is prejudicial to the reputation of the performer.[100] Again, this right is subject to a number of exceptions. Thus, it does not apply or is not infringed:

- in relation to any performance given for the purposes of reporting current events;[101]
- by modifications made to a performance which are consistent with normal editorial or production practice.[102]

A performer may also waive the rights to be identified and to object to derogatory treatment.[103]

Exercise

Compare and contrast a performer's rights of attribution and to object to derogatory treatment with those conferred on authors under sections 77–82 of the CDPA 1988 (see paras 3.31–3.43). Has the UK successfully implemented its obligations under the WPPT with respect to the moral rights of performers?

Key points on performers' moral rights

Moral rights exist for performers only in respect of their live aural performance and performances fixed in phonograms. Audiovisual performers do not have moral rights.
The moral rights conferred are:

- the right to be identified;
- the right to prevent derogatory treatment of one's performance.

Audiovisual performers

6.37   As indicated previously, the provisions in the WPPT concerning moral rights cover only performers in respect of their live aural performance and performances fixed in phonograms. This engendered a debate concerning moral rights for audiovisual performers (ie those appearing in films and TV broadcasts). WIPO convened a diplomatic conference in December 2000 to discuss the protection of audiovisual performances.[104] After nearly 12 years, in June 2012, it adopted a new international treaty, the Beijing Treaty on Audiovisual Performances[105] which will provide for moral rights of attribution and integrity to audiovisual performers. Article 5(1) of the Treaty states:

Independently of a performer's economic rights, and even after the transfer of those rights, the performer shall, as regards his live performances or performances fixed in audiovisual fixations, have the right:
(i) to claim to be identified as the performer of his performances, except where omission is dictated by the manner of the use of the performance; and
(ii) to object to any distortion, mutilation or other modification of his performances that would be prejudicial to his reputation, taking due account of the nature of audiovisual fixations.

---

[100] CDPA 1988, s 205F(1).   [101] CDPA 1988, s 205G(2).   [102] CDPA 1988, s 205G(3).   [103] CDPA 1988, s 205J.
[104] For a full discussion see S von Lewinski, 'The WIPO Diplomatic Conference on Audiovisual Performances: a first resumé' [2001] EIPR 333.
[105] It was signed on 26 June 2012 after attendance by 156 member states, six intergovernmental organisations and 45 non-governmental organisations, the highest level of participation to date at a WIPO diplomatic conference. 48 countries have signed the treaty which will enter into force once 30 eligible parties have ratified it: http://www.wipo.int/pressroom/en/articles/2012/article_0013.html.

An agreed statement in relation to Article 5 states:

> For the purposes of this Treaty and without prejudice to any other treaty, it is understood that, considering the nature of audiovisual fixations and their production and distribution, modifications of a performance that are made in the normal course of exploitation of the performance, such as editing, compression, dubbing, or formatting, in existing or new media or formats, and that are made in the course of a use authorized by the performer, would not in themselves amount to modifications within the meaning of Article 5(1)(ii). Rights under Article 5(1)(ii) are concerned only with changes that are objectively prejudicial to the performer's reputation in a substantial way. It is also understood that the mere use of new or changed technology or media, as such, does not amount to modification within the meaning of Article 5(1)(ii).

Ever since the 2000 conference, WIPO's member states, particularly the producer countries, have had concerns over the extent to which moral rights of audiovisual performers might hinder the exploitation of collective works. Hence, the agreed statement in relation to Article 5 allowing modifications consistent with the normal exploitation of a performance.

The nature of a performer's right

6.38   As will be evident from the preceding summary, the characterisation of performers' rights within the UK statutory regime now far is from clear. One writer is of the opinion that performers' rights should *not* be considered as falling under the head of copyright,[106] while admitting that, since the inclusion of performers' property rights in the legislation, those rights have now 'inched…close to copyright'.[107] Others have said that although the performers' property rights granted by the 1988 Act were not described as copyright, 'in effect a new copyright was conferred on performers'.[108]

6.39   Nor is it easy to classify performers' rights as neighbouring or media rights as traditionally understood in the UK. Although UK legislation does not formally distinguish between authorial and other works, that distinction still underlies a good part of the assumptions on which the legal framework is built. In this context, authors' rights are understood to refer to the works created by authors such as books, plays, music, and art. By contrast, neighbouring or entrepreneurial or media rights are derivative, and in general it is the investment in technical and organisational skill that is being protected, rather than the creative effort. Perhaps in response to this conundrum, performers' non-property rights which are personal and non-assignable rights have been described as 'a form of neighbouring right to copyright'.[109] The Act makes clear that the rights conferred in relation to performers are independent of any copyright in, or moral rights relating to, any work performed or any film or sound recording of, or broadcast including the performance.[110] For these reasons some have referred to performers' rights as 'related rights',[111] which is perhaps the most suitable terminology to use. Yet performers appear rather closer to authors as figures with a claim to the law's protection, and the introduction of moral rights for the former as well as the latter makes the analogy even closer.[112]

---

[106] Cornish, Llewelyn, and Aplin, note 58, para 11.02.   [107] Cornish, Llewelyn, and Aplin, note 58, para 14.36.
[108] *Copinger & Skone James on Copyright* (16th edn, 2010), para 12.04.   [109] Cornish, Llewelyn, and Aplin, note 58, para 14.32.
[110] CDPA 1988, s 180(4)(a).   [111] L Bently and B Sherman, *Intellectual Property Law* (3rd edn, 2009), Ch 13.
[112] The distinction between joint author and performer was considered in the case of *Fisher v Brooker* [2009] 1 WLR 1764 (HL); see also L McDonagh, 'Rearranging the roles of the performer and the composer in the music industry: the potential significance of *Fisher v. Brooker*' [2012] IPQ 64.

Performers' remuneration rights

6.40   An aspect of performers' rights which appears to be distinctive is the right to equitable remuneration. Two such rights are available to performers, introduced as a result of the Rental and Lending Rights Directive:

- A performer can claim equitable remuneration from the owner of the copyright in the sound recording[113] where a commercially published sound recording of a performance (but not a film) is played in public or communicated to the public otherwise than under the 'making available to the public' right.[114] The right may not be assigned except to a collecting society for the purpose of enabling it to enforce the right on the performer's behalf.[115] The amount payable is as agreed by the parties[116] or, failing agreement, application may be made to the Copyright Tribunal to determine the amount payable.[117] Any agreement purporting to exclude or restrict the right to equitable remuneration, or purporting to prevent a person questioning the amount of equitable remuneration or to restrict the powers of the Copyright Tribunal, is of no effect.[118]

- A performer retains a right to equitable remuneration where she transfers (or is presumed to transfer) her rental right in a film or sound recording to the producer.[119] Any agreement purporting to exclude or restrict the right to equitable remuneration is of no effect.[120] The right may not be assigned by the performer except to a collecting society for the purpose of enabling it to enforce the right on her behalf.[121] The Copyright Tribunal has jurisdiction to determine the amount payable failing agreement[122]

In the UK, the British Equity Collecting Society (BECS) deals with management of performers' equitable remuneration rights, including ingathering monies due from exploitation in other member states.

6.41   The meaning of communication to the public in this context has been considered by a number of recent cases. In *Phonographic Performance (Ireland) Ltd v Ireland*,[123] the Court of Justice held that a hotel was liable to pay equitable remuneration for the communication to the public of a sound recording, in addition to that paid by the broadcaster. When the hotel receives the signal and communicates that signal to guest bedrooms, it is using the sound recording 'in an autonomous way and transmitting it to a public which is distinct from and additional to the one targeted by the original act of communication', namely the hotel guests and 'derives economic benefits from that transmission which are independent of those obtained by the broadcaster or the producer of the phonograms' (para 51). In contrast, in

---

[113] CDPA 1988, s 182D.   [114] CDPA 1988, s 182CA(1).   [115] CDPA 1988, s 182D(2).

[116] CDPA 1988, s 182D(3).

[117] CDPA 1988, s 182D(5). The Tribunal may order any method of calculation and payment of equitable remuneration it may determine to be reasonable in the circumstances, taking into account the importance of the contribution of the performer to the sound recording (CDPA 1988, s 182D(6)).

[118] CDPA 1988, s 182D(7).   [119] CDPA 1988, ss 191F–191H.   [120] CDPA 1988, s 191G(5).

[121] CDPA 1988, s 191G(2), (6). The collecting society must be an organisation which has as its main object, or one of its main objects, the exercise of the right to equitable remuneration on behalf of more than one performer.

[122] Remuneration shall not be considered inequitable merely because it was paid by way of a single payment or at the time of the transfer of the rental right (CDPA 1988, s 191H(4)).

[123] Case C-162/10 *Phonographic Performance (Ireland) Ltd v Ireland* [2012] ECDR 15.

Societa Consortile Fonografici (SCF) v Del Corso,[124] the Court of Justice held that a dentist who played a radio in his surgery whilst patients were present was not liable to pay equitable remuneration. The number of persons at any time in such a surgery is very limited and while the radio may have been played for the benefit of the patients, there was no active choice on their part and it did not have an impact on the income of the dentist (paras 95–100).

Key points on equitable remuneration right

- A performer can claim equitable remuneration from the copyright owner in a commercially published sound recording of a performance (but not a film) when it is played in public or communicated to the public
- A performer retains a right to equitable remuneration where she transfers (or is presumed to transfer) her rental right in a film or sound recording to the producer
- These rights cannot be excluded by contract
- The rights are not assignable except to a collecting society

---

 ### Exercise

What other areas of copyright and related rights contain provisions for equitable remuneration? Should such schemes be extended more generally across the area of copyright and related rights? Why do we not move from the 'property' system we have at present to one which is merely a right to remuneration for exploitation?

Additional benefits for performers

6.42   The Term Directive 2011 (see para 6.33) introduces a number of additional benefits for musical performers:[125]

- A 'use it or lose it' provision: where the performer has transferred or assigned the rights in the performance to a record company, the performer will be able to request reversion of the rights, if the record company fails to commercially release the recording of the performance in sufficient quantity within the extended 20-year period of the right. Not only will this allow the performer to terminate the license agreement and license the rights to another record company, but upon such termination the copyright in the sound recording will also expire.

- A 20 per cent fund: record companies must pay 20 per cent of revenue earned during the extended 20 years of protection into a fund which will be used to pay an annual supplementary remuneration to the performers who had transferred or assigned their right to remuneration in exchange for a one-off payment. This is to ensure that such performers receive some benefit from the term extension.

---

[124] Case C-135/10 *Societa Consortile Fonografici (SCF) v Del Corso* [2012] ECDR 16.   [125] Art 1(2)(c).

Further reading

Books

General

T Aplin, *Copyright Law in the Digital Society: The Challenges of Multimedia* (2005)

R Arnold, *Performers' Rights* (4th edn, 2008)

L Bently and B Sherman, *Intellectual Property Law* (3rd edn, 2009), Ch 13

Copinger & Skone James on Copyright (16th edn, 2010), Chs 12, 18

WR Cornish, D Llewelyn, and T Aplin, *Intellectual Property* (7th edn, 2010), Chs 14.4, 20.2

E Derclaye, *The Legal Protection of Databases: A Comparative Analysis* (2008)

Laddie, Prescott & Vitoria on the Modern Law of Copyright (4th edn, 2011), Chs 12, 30

Articles

R Arnold, 'Reflections on "The Triumph of Music": copyrights and performers' rights in music' [2010] IPQ 153

D Liu 'Performers' rights: muddled or mangled? Bungled or boggled?' [2012] EIPR 374

L McDonagh, 'Rearranging the roles of the performer and the composer in the music industry: the potential significance of *Fisher v. Brooker*' [2012] IPQ 64

S von Lewinski, 'The WIPO Diplomatic Conference on Audiovisual Performances: A First Resumé' [2001] EIPR 333

Websites

The Database Right File (website maintained by the Institute for Information Law, University of Amsterdam http://www.ivir.nl/files/database/index.html)

Diplomatic Conference on the Protection of Audiovisual Performances (http://www.wipo.int/dc2012/en/)

Contemporary issues in copyright

Introduction

Scope and overview of chapter

7.1 This chapter considers a number of issues of current concern in copyright. The Director General of WIPO, Francis Gurry, noted in 2011 that copyright laws and rights holder business models should more appropriately suit the digital age:

> I am firmly of the view that a passive and reactive approach to copyright and the digital revolution entails the major risk that policy outcomes will be determined by a Darwinian process of the survival of the fittest business model. The fittest business model may turn out to be the one that achieves or respects the right social balances in cultural policy. It may also, however, turn out not to respect those balances. The balances should not, in other words, be left to the chances of technological possibility and business evolution. They should, rather, be established through a conscious policy response.[1]

The starting point for this chapter is the several recent copyright reform initiatives. Copyright featured prominently among the issues addressed by two major UK independent reviews of intellectual property in the last ten years.

The remit of the Gowers Review of intellectual property published in 2006[2] included, in particular, whether the 'infringement framework reflects the digital environment'; whether 'fair use' (sic) provisions for citizens are reasonable; and what the term of protection for sound recordings should be. This followed the Labour Party manifesto commitment with which it entered and won the 2005 general election: 'Copyright in a digital age: We will modernise copyright and other forms of protection of intellectual property rights so that they are appropriate for the digital age.'

The Hargreaves Review of intellectual property and growth was published in 2011, commissioned by the Conservative Party-led government. Prime Minister David Cameron, when launching the review, stated: 'I can announce today that we are reviewing our IP laws, to see if we can make them fit for the internet age...[the review will] focus on how the IP system can be improved to help the new business models

---

[1] See his comments at the February 2011 Blue Sky Conference in Queensland Australia at http://www.wipo.int/about-wipo/en/dgo/speeches/dg_blueskyconf_11.html. [2] *Gowers Review of Intellectual Property* (HM Treasury, 2006).

arising from the digital age.'[3] The Hargreaves Review's recommendations included the area of copyright exceptions (it rejected a US-style fair use defence but considered exemptions for format shifting, parody, non-commercial research, library archiving) and copyright licensing (it recommended establishment of a Digital Copyright Exchange and enabling licensing of orphan works).

The EU has also been at work and the Commission is continuing with its harmonisation programme. A Commission Staff Working Paper on the review of EU legislation on copyright and related rights was issued in July 2004 (henceforth 'Commission Copyright Paper 2004').[4] This assessed, in particular, whether inconsistencies between the different Directives hamper the operation of EU copyright law or damage the balance between right holders' interests, those of users and consumers and those of the European economy as a whole. The Commission Paper appeared to envisage a future 'Copyright Code' for Europe, in which the present piecemeal collection of Directives enacted at various times since 1991 would be consolidated and, presumably, the gaps between them filled. Thereafter, the EU introduced consolidated versions of the Rental Right Directive, Software Directive and Term Directive enabling easy accessibility to the law in these areas. In 2010, copyright scholars from across the EU, under the Dutch-based Wittem Group, produced a 'European Copyright Code' envisaging it to 'serve as a model or reference tool for future harmonization or unification of copyright at the European level.'[5] It is not a re-codification of the law but rather restates, with surprising brevity, the basic principles in the Berne Convention and the TRIPS Agreement with the aim of promoting transparency and consistency in European copyright law. A Communication from the Commission in 2011[6] discussed the possibility of creation of a 'European Copyright Code' which could not only comprehensively consolidate and codify the current body of EU copyright Directives but also allow examination of any need to update the exceptions and limitations.

It has been said, however, that the continuing existence of many national copyright laws within the EU makes life very complicated for would-be users of works because so many permissions have to be sought for the use. The only solution to that would be a Community Copyright Regulation replacing the existing Directives and at least partially pre-empting national systems. A reflection document on the challenges for creative content in the digital single market in the EU was issued in 2009 (henceforth 'Commission Reflection Document 2009').[7] In discussing commercial users' access to creative content online, it considered the potential benefits of a unified 'community copyright title' by means of a Regulation and suggested that its legal basis could be Article 118 TFEU as introduced by the Lisbon Treaty (see para 1.53).

The focus of the Commission on adapting copyright to the digital environment is also reflected in the *Green Paper on Copyright in the Knowledge Economy* published in 2008 (henceforth 'Green Paper 2008') which set out a number of issues connected with the role of copyright in the 'knowledge economy' on which it intended to launch consultations and focused on those exceptions to copyright most relevant for the dissemination of knowledge.[8] The Commission has also been evaluating specific initiatives and recently adopted proposals for two new Directives: on collective rights management and multi-territorial licensing of rights in musical works for online uses; and on certain permitted uses of orphan works. At the same time, recent judgments of the Court of Justice of the European Union (CJEU) on

---

[3] I Hargreaves, *Digital Opportunity: A Review of Intellectual Property and Growth* (IPO, 2011).

[4] European Commission Staff Working Paper on the review of the EC legal framework in the field of copyright and related rights, SEC(2004) 995.

[5] See the code at http://www.copyrightcode.eu/.   [6] COM(2011) 287 final.

[7] Creative Content in a European Digital Single Market: Challenges for the Future A Reflection Document of DG INFSO and DG MARKT, 22 October 2009.   [8] COM(2008) 466/3.

copyright matters have also, arguably, attempted to indirectly harmonise copyright concepts, which were previously believed to have remained unharmonised by the current piecemeal framework of copyright Directives (see para 2.16).

7.2 The present chapter surveys some of the major issues to which the initiatives just described are directed, as well as some which, perhaps significantly, are not mentioned. The importance of doing this is above all to understand why reform of copyright is such an important question at present. This also enables one to come to grips with the policy issues with which copyright law has to deal, recognising the sometimes sharply opposed views that exist on these matters. The issues chosen for discussion vary, however, in the likelihood that they will be addressed in any reform process which may flow in the coming years from the initiatives launched by the UK Government and the European Commission. At the best of times, law reform is a slow process; and the chapter shows how difficult it is in relation to copyright. The approach taken here is to consider specific issues against the general background of recent technological development (the 'digital environment'), while looking towards solutions that might be possible under a Europe-wide 'copyright code' rather than in a merely UK context. This recognises that significant reform in the future will generally stem from the EU or even more widely based international institutions.

7.3 | **Learning objectives**

By the end of this chapter you should be able to describe and explain:

- major policy issues relating to the reform of copyright law;
- the significance of the increasingly digital environment for copyright law;
- possible European solutions to some particular problems in copyright law.

7.4 The chapter begins by identifying some of the specific issues which have brought copyright reform to the forefront in recent times. What holds many of these together is the development of digital, mobile, and interactive technology as the means of delivering ideas, information, and entertainment to their users. The chapter then proceeds to look at the difficulties which this new environment presents for copyright, the rules of which were mostly created in a world where material came to users in the form of single copies or performances put on the market by intermediaries of one kind or another, such as publishers, broadcasters, and film and sound recording producers. A running theme, picking up from Chapter 5 in particular, is how far in the digital world copyright may be replaced or superseded by contract. Having thus surveyed the scene in general, the chapter turns to a number of specific topics where either the digital environment, or national differences of approach within Europe, or both, present reformers with particular challenges. Altogether, then, the rest of the chapter looks like this:

- Context (7.5–7.11)
- Purpose of copyright (7.12–7.17)
- Specific issues (7.18–7.63)

Context

7.5 Amongst the many particular developments which have brought copyright reform to the fore in the UK and Europe may be included the following:

- *File-sharing through unlicensed peer-to-peer networks*, especially with regard to sound recordings, but also in relation to computer software and games, and films as well. The music and other entertainment industries claim that this unlicensed activity is having a significant impact upon the 'legitimate' market for their products. The major developments since the phenomenon first became prominent through the Napster case in the United States in 2000–2001 (see para 4.73) are the growth of licensed downloading and streaming sites, increased numbers of actions against individual downloaders and several court decisions around the world, including the UK, against the operators and users of unlicensed file-sharing networks as infringers of copyright. The entertainment industries have also had some success in pressing for some form of liability for ISPs through whose services file-sharing takes place, partly through successful court claims, partly through negotiation with bodies representing ISPs, and partly through legislation proposed and actual. In the UK the Digital Economy Act was enacted in 2010 which provides for imposition of certain obligations on internet access providers to assist in curbing online infringement.

- *Sound recording industry pressure to replace the term for the protection of sound recordings* (currently 50 years from release) with a term the same as that in the United States (ie 95 years from the year of first publication). In July 2008 the European Commission published a proposal for a Directive to extend the term for sound recordings from 50 to 95 years. The result was a Directive in September 2011 which has increased the term of copyright in sound recordings as well as performers' rights to 70 years.

- *The Google Books Settlement*. In the United States, the Association of American Publishers and a number of authors began court action in the autumn of 2005 to stop the implementation of Google's arrangements with a number of leading academic libraries to digitise their collections of books in order to make the full texts thereof available to users of the Google service. The claim was that copyright was bound to be infringed in the execution of the scheme, even though Google and the participating libraries declared that digitisation would be confined to works either out of copyright or whose authors had not opted out of the scheme. The settlement proposed by the parties was finally rejected by the District Court for the Southern District of New York in 2011, in part due to the necessity of authors who do not want to participate having to opt out of having their books scanned, which would give Google an unfair competitive advantage. The judge recommended that the settlement be revised from opt-out to opt-in. There is yet to be an agreement on this.

- The use of *rights management information systems* (RMIs) and *technical protection measures* (TPMs) to build into products such as CDs, DVDs, databases, and websites—and also into the hardware needed to use these products—mechanisms that prevent unauthorised access and use unless and until such contractual conditions as the producer imposes (typically payment by way of credit card or fund transfer systems such as Paypal, and carefully restricted re-use of the product) are met by the would-be user. As noted previously (see paras 5.50–5.57), these mechanisms are intensely controversial.

- *The establishment of Creative Commons UK* (building on a US model), with the aim of developing forms of licence under which copyright is retained but users are given advance permission to copy and distribute the work for their own purposes, as long as due credit is given to the original work and similar conditions are imposed upon any further sub-users; this being, it is argued, the most appropriate way to support and encourage creativity and innovation in the online and digital environments. The licensor can indicate those types of use which remain restricted; but the starting point is that use is free and restrictions on use have to be stated, whereas the underpinning assumption of traditional licences is that no use is allowed unless expressly permitted. Creative Commons was inspired originally by the 'open source' movement which began in connection with computer software and was conceived in opposition to the existence of copyright in such material. The credo was that software should be made available in such a way that others might use and build upon it, especially in developing new software, as this was the best way to facilitate further such innovation. This does not necessarily mean that the software must be made available free of charge, but rather that copyright should not be used to block further development of what already exists. There is a certain irony in the fact that copyleft needs copyright in order to function. In order to grant an effective licence removing any restrictions of use, or granting wide use, copyright must subsist.[9]

- *The publication of the Adelphi Charter on creativity, innovation and intellectual property* in October 2005, calling upon governments to maintain a balance between public domain and private right, and between competition and monopoly, with regard to intellectual property rights in general; to ensure in particular that the copyright term is limited in time and does not extend beyond what is proportionate and necessary; and to facilitate a wide range of policies to stimulate access and innovation, including non-proprietary models such as open source software licensing and open access to scientific literature.

There are also widespread perceptions of copyright as complex, inaccessible, productive of difficulty and uncertainty in relation to otherwise lawful activities, and sometimes absurd. On the other hand, piracy—the unlicensed mass reproduction of copyright material such as sound recordings, films and computer games for resale at prices far undercutting those of the copyright owner—continues undoubtedly to be a serious issue for the affected industries, as it was also for most of the second half of the 20th century.

- *The Controversial Anti-Counterfeiting Trade Agreement (ACTA)*, a plurilateral agreement aimed at creating effective common enforcement standards to combat global proliferation of counterfeiting through enhanced international cooperation. The agreement was signed by a number of countries including the United States, UK, and the European Union between 2011 and 2012 and contained, amongst others, general provisions on civil and criminal enforcement especially for copyright infringement on a commercial scale and IP enforcement in the digital environment. ACTA was met with strong opposition, in particular due to mistrust developed as a result of the agreement being negotiated outside the traditional international forums on IP as well as concerns about its effect on freedom of expression and privacy. The CJEU was asked to review the compatibility of the agreement with fundamental rights. In July 2012, the European Parliament resoundingly rejected the agreement (see also 22.154).

- *European and UK initiatives aimed at adapting copyright licensing to the digital age.* In July 2012, the European Commission adopted a proposal for a Directive aimed at easing and facilitating multiterritorial and multi-repertoire musical licensing online in the EU and creating an appropriate legal framework for the collective management of rights administered by collecting societies.[10] The Commission's press release noted the need for collecting societies to adapt to requirements of management of rights in a cross-border context, in the light of the increased demand for online services providing cultural content and their borderless nature; and the need for improved governance and greater transparency in the conduct of the activities of collecting societies.[11] In the UK, the Hargreaves Review 2011 recommended the introduction of a 'Digital Copyright Exchange' which would provide a common platform for cross-sectoral licensing transactions and provide a marketplace where such licences can be bought and sold. The Government appointed Richard Hooper to

[9] See, eg, J Boyle, 'A manifesto on WIPO and the future of intellectual property' (2004) 9 Duke Law & Technology Review 1; A Guadamuz, 'Viral contracts or unenforceable documents? Contractual validity of copyleft licenses' [2004] EIPR 331.
[10] COM(2012) 372 final. [11] See http://europa.eu/rapid/press-release_IP-12-772_en.htm?locale=EN.

lead an independent review of this proposal. The second phase of this review[12] recommended the creation of a 'Copyright Hub' in the UK that is not for profit and industry-led, which will link, inter-operably, copyright-related databases and will operate on a voluntary, opt-in, and non-exclusive basis; to reduce the complexity of licensing, it will also act as an information and education source and provide a mechanism for would-be users of orphan works to demonstrate that they have done reasonable due diligence to find owners of the work.

7.6   As the examples in the previous paragraph show, a huge range of areas of activity are affected by copyright: government, entertainment, education, creativity, technology, and international development, to name but a few. These examples also show that much of the current debate has arisen in the context of the ever-expanding scope and possibilities of using digital, wireless, and mobile technologies for the creation, dissemination, and reproduction of ideas, information, and entertainment. The context for policy thinking in the areas traditionally covered by copyright has been transformed by the ability to make material available so that it is potentially always accessible to users at times and places chosen by them; especially when it has gone along with expanding possibilities of, and demand for, interactivity between suppliers and users who, starting on the basis of what already exists, may themselves become creators, developers, and suppliers of further material. It is also clear that increasing amounts of material from both the digital and pre-digital era is becoming available electronically: not only sound recordings, films, and broadcasts, but also works of art and literature of all kinds and all periods. The idea of the digital environment as a cultural jukebox, always on and available for use, shifts the traditional relationships between users and consumers, on the one hand, and creators and repositories such as libraries, archives, museums and galleries, and publishers and broadcasters, on the other. Further, because the digital environment does not know jurisdictional and national frontiers, the law's approach has to be an international one, moving beyond the traditional international approach of setting minimum standards of copyright protection (which does not entail the law and rights being the same everywhere), and according to foreigners whatever protection the national law affords its own nationals (see para 2.8).

Exercise

Can you give any other examples of copyright policy issues like those mentioned in para 7.5, arising from attempts to create, disseminate, and reproduce ideas, information, and entertainment in the digital environment?

7.7   Debate is sparked, however, by varying visions of what the Internet and, following it, the 'information superhighway' through wireless and mobile communication systems should be about. For *government and commercial interests*, it is primarily a means of economic development. Technology now provides an information, marketing, and selling device capable of reaching an ever-widening number of citizens, consumers, and buyers. All kinds of producers can in effect set up electronic shops and information resources. Some simply sell goods and services that are already available (but usually more expensively) through traditional outlets. Good examples are Amazon, the online store, offering books, CDs, and DVDs, and easyJet, offering airline services; and each contracting with customers principally by way of electronic communication across the web. eBay, the online auction site, is a slightly different example of the same thing, electronically putting sellers in contact with potential buyers of whatever they have to

---

[12] See 'Copyright works: streamlining copyright licensing for the digital age: an independent report by Richard Hooper CBE and Dr Ros Lynch' (July 2012) available at http://www.ipo.gov.uk/dce-report-phase2.pdf.

sell. In another world altogether, courts have websites where their judgments can be read and, increasingly, aspects of their process carried out.

7.8   But digital technology also creates the possibility of new types of purely electronic products and services that can be traded primarily through communication systems. Computer programs and games were the most familiar type of digital product before the Internet took off; these could now be made available on the Internet for downloading directly to computers linked to the relevant website. Familiar also by the end of the 1980s were the digital CD-ROMs which were largely replacing analogue cassettes and the still-surviving vinyl record as the primary means of disseminating recorded musical performances. The Internet opened up the possibility, soon realised by Napster and others, of the global jukebox from which music enthusiasts could at any time download to a local computer, a mobile telephone, or other device (eg an iPod) whatever took their fancy at the time. From music it was but a short step to films, aided by the arrival of broadband. Broadcasting has also moved into the digital era via 'podcasting' and 'webcasting', so that viewers and listeners can increasingly choose when to watch and hear programmes, and interrupt, pause, and replay them to suit their own rather than the broadcaster's convenience. Digitisation also enabled the rapid development of the multimedia product, combining writing, sounds, and images still and moving. Finally, the most obviously new kind of service made both necessary and possible in the digital environment was the search engine provided by such organisations as Google and Yahoo!, through which users of the Internet could find their way most speedily to the material they wanted.

7.9   The key point in all this for copyright is that, by contrast with the analogue world in which, although copying was easy, the copy was invariably less good than the original, the digital work will always copy perfectly. The downloader gets as good a version as the master copy on the original site—and gets it increasingly easily and quickly as the technology moves on. Nor does the user necessarily have to have, keep, or find space for the products involved: access by way of streaming, webcasting, and cloud-based computing may soon replace acquisition of anything other than the devices which provide the means of access. The Internet and subsequent developments in mobile communications systems thus provide a tremendous new way to reach consumers of information and entertainment products in the comfort of their own homes and social patterns. But the difficulty also facing those minded to exploit these opportunities is precisely the ease and speed of digital reproduction and transmission. How can consumers be made to pay for the material they download or receive in this way? How can pirates, those making copies and providing access for their own commercial gain without the authority of the originator, be stopped from exploiting the technology and thereby undercutting the latter's market?

7.10   A further question is raised, however, from the perspective of those who see the new technology as raising other exciting possibilities of ever greater and wider access to, and expression and circulation of, ideas and information. In this perspective, the ease and speed of digital communication and reproduction is an opportunity rather than a problem; a real step forward in allowing the realisation of both individual and societal goals. This is the perspective which lies behind the idea of 'open source', in which material is made freely available to others—'free' here meaning, as it has famously been put, 'free' as in 'free expression' rather than as in 'free beer'. By their very nature, information and ideas want to be free in the same sense as a prisoner or a caged wild animal might want. As economists point out, information and ideas are 'public goods', meaning that their availability is not diminished no matter how many people have enjoyed or employed them. Insofar as copyright is a barrier to the free flow of information and ideas, it is misused. Some go as far as to say that copyright is always such a barrier; the purpose of others, such as Creative Commons, however, is to recognise the value possessed by copyright provided that it is not used simply to obstruct otherwise beneficial further activity and creativity.

7.11   File-sharing (paras 4.72ff and 7.5) provides a good example for argument about the different perspectives. The sound recording industry sees the transfer of music recordings from user to user without charge as the main reason, apart from piracy, behind a significant decline in the sale of music CDs since 2000 (the year in which the Napster operation first took off). The industry argues that without profit its investment in new talent will necessarily decline, with the end result being less opportunity for, and so overall less, new recorded music. Those supporting a more 'open' approach argue that the sound recording industry failed to move quickly enough to meet the potential of the Internet as a means of distributing music, and that users of the unlicensed file-sharing services actually did continue to buy CDs, turning to the services only for hard-to-obtain or actually unavailable material. The sound recording industry had only itself to blame for its financial woes, having been exposed by others more innovative and better attuned to the ways in which consumers wished to acquire and use their music in the digital environment, and who made that pay in different ways (eg by selling advertising space on their services).

 Exercise

Discuss the perspectives about file-sharing in the previous paragraph with reference to the more general perspectives explained in paras 7.7–7.10. What conclusions would be drawn about the correct use of copyright here by (1) the commercial sound recording industry; and (2) advocates of an 'open' approach to the distribution and circulation of recorded music? See also W Davies and K Withers, *Public Innovation: Intellectual Property in a Digital Age* (Institute of Public Policy Research, 2006), 43–44.

Purpose of copyright

7.12   A fundamental question in thinking about these issues is the purpose, or purposes, of copyright. Only with clear ideas of what we are trying to achieve will clear, coherent and principled law emerge. We have already discussed at some length many of copyright's underlying ideas:

- The *economic role* (para 2.18)—incentivising and rewarding, in accordance with market demand, those involved in the creation and publication of certain kinds of work. Economic interests therefore include not only creators, but also entrepreneurs who convert what is created into products for the marketplace. Copyright is a response to market failure; without it, the *expression* of ideas and information, creativity and innovation would be available to all, without reward for those who invested in the creation and dissemination of the works thereby produced, either personally or financially. With copyright, the way is open for the reward of creative individuals and those who convert their creative work into products that the public will buy or otherwise spend money on.

- Protection of the *creative individual's personality rights* (para 2.18), most evident in the moral rights, and their recognition of inalienable, non-economic interests that an author (but no one else) may continue to exercise in respect of a work even though no longer owner of the copyright or of the physical form in which the work was first created and recorded. This aspect of copyright is also apparent in the copyright terms, much longer than a strict economic analysis would suggest is necessary for the fulfilment of the economic goal. There may also be a link between moral rights and the fundamental human rights that underlie many personality rights in general. Human rights to dignity and respect seem particularly apt to support the right to be identified in connection with one's work and to have that work treated appropriately by others. Copyright can also protect the individual's interest in *privacy*. There is no obligation to publish or make available one's work, and copyright serves to protect that position should that be the author's wish.

- The *rights of users, or the public domain* (paras 2.20 and 5.4). By placing various limitations upon what it protects on the producer side, copyright also protects, directly or indirectly, non-producer interests. Thus:

  - freedom of expression and information are protected by the limitation of copyright to forms of expression, as distinct from the ideas and information which are expressed;

  - copyright is not unlimited in duration, and works which fall out of copyright at the end of their term are available to all for any purpose;

  - works which fall below the threshold requirement of 'originality' do not have copyright, even if in other respects they come within one of the categories of protected work (eg being written, they are literary);

  - works which do not fit into the expressed categories of the law do not receive copyright protection;

  - copyright exceptions, whether general, for example fair dealing, or for specific types of work, for example 'time-shifting' of TV broadcasts, reflect a recognition that certain non-producer interests outweigh producer ones in at least some circumstances; or at any rate the impracticability of certain kinds of copyright enforcement; and

  - the *product* embodying the protected work can generally be dealt with freely by the first and subsequent purchasers apart from integrity/ commercial rental/lending/ public communication rights.

We might also take note of a further dimension:

- The *cultural purposes* of copyright: this dimension is apparent in the nature of what copyright protects—literary, dramatic, musical, and artistic works, films, sound recordings, and broadcasts—and also in the length of time for which it gives that protection, which, as noted later, is not necessarily (or at all) driven by economic analysis.

7.13   It is not suggested here that current UK law does anything other than reflect a mixture of these various purposes, which attempts to provide a *balance* between the different interests involved. Nor is it suggested that the present balance is satisfactory, or that it was at any time in the past. The interests inevitably come into conflict, especially those related to economic and personality interests in works, on the one hand, and those reflecting the public domain dimension, on the other. All that law-makers can do is be sensitive to all the interests involved, make choices between options from time to time and be prepared to act should it become apparent that a solution, old or new, is not working as it should, or has become inappropriate in changing circumstances.

7.14   The digital environment now raises the question whether the economic interests of the creator and entrepreneur, or of society, still actually require copyright. In the pre-digital world, an author and a person wishing to use the author's work would have very little opportunity or incentive to meet and negotiate the terms and conditions of the latter's use; hence, the need for copyright law to set down some general social bargain, as it were, and also for intermediaries such as publishers to enable works to find their markets and audiences. But in the digital environment it is potentially much easier for author and audience to find each other directly, and for them to use technology to conclude their own bespoke bargain about terms and conditions of use of the author's work. As already noted (para 5.58), TPMs and RMIs (henceforth collectively 'DRMs' (digital rights management)) can prevent access to and use of a work unless and until such contractual conditions as the producer imposes are met by the would-be user. Usually such technologies are seen by critics hostile to current legal developments in the field as the manifestation of the worst of current copyright rules, since the law protects them against circumvention by third parties even though their use can enable, not only the prevention of activities falling within the exceptions to copyright, but, indeed, the protection of works no longer or never in copyright. The position of the right owner thus appears to be considerably strengthened at the expense of the user, since money can be made even from a work without copyright, as long as it is technologically protectable. Equally, however, through contracts such as the forms provided by Creative Commons, an author can indicate in advance, as it were, those uses of the work by others which, although within the scope of copyright protection, are nonetheless permitted; further, the author can require those using this permission to apply those terms and conditions to further downstream sub-users. So in this context technology can operate in support of widespread use and later creativity with existing works. There is some evidence that in response to consumer demand right owners are beginning to explore the possibilities of DRMs enabling consumers to make use of their products other than by simply playing them (eg making additional copies to store on personal computers or playback machines). Further market pressures may lead to more such developments, particularly if different consumers might be prepared to pay variable prices for different packages of permissions made available through DRMs. Contract will therefore often be automated and 'standard form' in this context, rather than the result of individual negotiation and bargaining; especially if the Internet does develop into the global digital jukebox already referred to (para 7.6), in which the user simply has to locate the material wanted, pay, and play. But, nonetheless, given contract's enormous flexibility, can it replace copyright, and would that be a good thing?

7.15   An obvious tricky point is that it is copyright, for the most part, which, at least initially, creates the subject matter around which contracting parties can subsequently bargain. In the absence of copyright at the point of creation, there might be no room for bargaining at all. In particular, the individual author/creator without access to the means of sophisticated technological protection, dissemination and online payment methods (and such persons will continue to exist for a long time, even in the digital environment) would be at a serious disadvantage without copyright in dealing with the entrepreneur who will convert the work into a marketable product. One could, of course, try to create some sort of 'fair contract' or 'minimum terms' regime for such authors, perhaps akin to the German publishers' contract law found in that country's Copyright Act (as amended). But that instrument assumes the existence of copyright; and the 'minimum contract' that would have to be created in the absence of copyright might end up looking remarkably similar to copyright.

7.16   Further, the economic interests protected by copyright are not limited to those of the author/creator of the work and the entrepreneur who first takes it to market. Since the economic rights protected by copyright are freely transferable to third parties, the person who at any given moment owns the copyright and reaps the economic returns it gives, may well be someone who had no hand in the original production of the work or the product flowing from it. How far such investors in works may deserve the same level of protection as the originators of the work is a nice question: after all, they are risk-takers to a greater extent than those from whom they bought the rights, and they have helped to ensure that the author/creator/first producer does, indeed, earn reward from their work. Outright transfers of copyright could be banned, but licensing would still be necessary to secure the author's reward; while a licensee would certainly require some incentive in its own right to make the investment in a licence worthwhile.

7.17   Contracts, whether between the author/producer and the user of a work, or between authors and their publishers, are clearly important in the digital world. Many such contracts will be in non-negotiable standard forms provided on a 'take it or leave it basis'. In general contract law such standard contracts are well recognised as promoting economic efficiency but as also requiring policing against the potential for abuse: see, for example, the Unfair Contract Terms Act 1977 and the Unfair Terms in Consumer Contracts Regulations 1999 (implementing an EU Directive of 1994). The English and Scottish Law Commissions published a report in 2005 recommending general reforms to the law on unfair contract terms: is something more specific required for copyright contracting? There are already provisions in the copyright legislation regulating contract terms. The common law on restraint of trade and undue influence has often been deployed against publishing contracts. But copyright contracts could be more closely vetted for general unconscionability. There might be protection for copyright exceptions against contractual exclusion (see paras 5.59–5.62 and 7.61). Compulsory equitable remuneration provisions, such as already exist in relation to performers' rights (see para 6.40), could be extended to publishing contracts more generally, as in France and Germany. The jurisdiction of the Copyright Tribunal to regulate the licensing practices of collecting societies (see para 22.28) could be extended to cover the activities of all those who engage in 'mass-marketing licensing' (see para 5.59): that is, put their copyright product on the marketplace for access to anyone prepared to pay the licence fee or meet any other conditions imposed. An important question is whether contract law, consumer protection law and competition law deal adequately with copyright contracting of all kinds, a matter the detailed investigation of which lies beyond the scope of this chapter. It may be noted that, while users of copyright products can often be at least analogised with consumers, authors are often persons whose work is being consumed by their publishers; in a sense, therefore, their claim to protection from market forces is more like that of the employee in labour law than the consumer. Further, however, and like the employee who is a member of a trade union or professional association, the author has some possibility of self-protection through collective action by way of copyright management societies and pressure groups. But should copyright be displaced altogether by contract in a digital environment, specifically targeted controls over these contracts would probably become essential.

 Discussion point For answer guidance visit www.oxfordtextbooks.co.uk/orc/waelde3e/

Can contract (often automated in this context) replace copyright in the digital environment?

Specific issues

Introduction

7.18 In this section, we turn to look at some more specific issues of copyright law where reform seems necessary, likely or desirable as a result of either (1) the impetus created by the Europeanisation of the subject and international harmonisation, or (2) the impact of technological development, or, quite often, (3) both. The topics are generally treated in the order in which they were dealt with in the preceding five chapters, to facilitate the cross-reference needed in studying the section.

Categories of copyright work

7.19 The initial questions under this heading arise from the process of Europeanisation. Where Continental countries have a strong tradition of distinguishing between authors' rights and neighbouring rights in substance as well as form, and this distinction is reflected in international conventions (Berne and Rome), the UK has awarded copyright to both authors and entrepreneurial producers of works, albeit with differentiated content of rights—for example, clearly distinct copyright terms (see para 2.47). The law purports to draw its distinctions here on the basis of the nature of the work—literary, dramatic, musical, artistic, film, sound recording, broadcast, and so on—rather than by way of a distinction between works of authorship and work to do with the media in which the products of authorship are conveyed to their public (if any). In a process of European harmonisation, which of the two approaches is to be preferred? Or is there some third way? The digital environment may suggest that there should be. If increasingly all kinds of work are carried out and fixed (insofar as they are ever fixed) in digital media, is the distinction between authorship and medium increasingly obsolescent? Further, in the post-modern world of culture generally, authors and artists are rejecting past understandings of their respective disciplines and consequent self-imposed limitations, to seek more and more to cross boundaries and use the huge flexibility of digital technology to convey their message, whatever it may be, to the world?

7.20   It seems most likely, however, that for the time being the basic distinction between author and other works will continue to be drawn, if only because it also underlies some of the basic international infrastructure which will not be easily shifted. But, nonetheless, there may still be questions about the way in which UK law gives effect to the distinction. Only in the 1990s, for example, were films brought into author rather than media work protection in the UK, as a result of the Term Directive (Art 2). Also, there are major differences in substantive content between author and media works. An effect of these differences is that many *products* in the copyright domain are likely to enjoy more than one copyright—the basic media right, depending on which medium the product is using, and the right or rights which subsist in the work or works embodied in the product. Each one of these rights may then have a different owner as well as different content (see para 2.47). This variability of the copyrights which may exist in a single product can mean that while one element of the product is in the public domain, another is not. Several undesirable effects are possible: damage to the remaining copyright interest in the work in question; inhibition of perfectly lawful and appropriate free use of the product; or simply confused people. The issue is focused by the debate about the copyright term in sound recordings, the importance of which in the digital environment is already clear from the controversy about file-sharing and peer-to-peer networks (para 7.5). While the right in recordings made in, say, 1962 will expire from 1 January 2013, the rights in the recorded music and song lyrics will continue until 70 years after the deaths of the respective authors. There is thus no danger at all of a rash of unauthorised issues of copies of old recordings of Elvis Presley or Cliff Richard recordings from the 1950s and 1960s, since that would also involve copying and issuing to the public works that are still in copyright (further, copyrights that presumably would often be held by the recording companies rather than the original authors). Note, too, in the context of Europeanisation, that some EU member states treat songs as works of joint authorship between lyricist and composer, meaning that the copyright term in such material is extremely variable across the EU. The Commission Copyright Paper 2004 raises the possibility that the term for songs as a whole should always be calculated in relation to the last-surviving author.

7.21   A question of policy may therefore be whether, when a product enjoys multiple copyrights, these ought to stand and fall together, at least in relation to products of the kind in question; and this, whatever the duration of the rights may finally be.

7.22   As noted in paras 2.49 and 2.50, the categorisation of author works into literary, dramatic, musical, and artistic (not to mention the sub-categorisation within that of artistic works) is also problematic, creating the possibility of a single work of authorship being protected in more than one category, or causing uncertainty about the category to which it belongs. As noted in para 2.29, the exhaustive categories may be contrary to EU law, as the CJEU jurisprudence seems to suggest that any work is capable of protection, provided it is the author's own intellectual creation. Categorisation is also not required under the Berne

Convention: only protection of 'literary and artistic work', which includes 'every production in the literary, scientific and artistic domain, whatever may be the mode or form of its expression'. The Convention provides an illustrative list of works, while elsewhere, and only so to speak incidentally, it refers to dramatic, musical, and cinematographic works. French law speaks of 'works of the mind whatever their kind, form of expression, merit or purpose' and gives thereafter an illustrative list. This approach reduces the need to struggle with categories, albeit it may carry its own obvious uncertainties. But these uncertainties also have the attractive feature of being perhaps more flexible than narrower categories in meeting the emergence of new kinds of work. It also limits the possibility of giving the categories unnecessary or cumbersome substantive content: that is, having rules making it matter whether a work is literary or artistic, musical or dramatic.

7.23   A question of policy is therefore whether the requirement that a work falls into one of the relevant categories should continue to remain; or should there be a change in the law to make the categories illustrative only.

Fixation

7.24   As noted in paras 2.30–2.33, the Berne Convention allows national law 'to prescribe that works in general or any specified categories of works shall not be protected unless they have been fixed in some material form'. The UK in general requires fixation of a work before copyright can come into existence, leading to some peculiar, even absurd, rules, the effect of which is that while unauthorised recording of my ad lib speech or aleatory musical creation cannot be prevented by copyright, I can nonetheless control the subsequent reproduction and publication of the recording which has made those words or music the subject of copyright. Other legal systems within the Berne Union exercise their discretion to avoid the imposition of any requirement of fixation. In the UK, the requirement in relation to literary, dramatic, and musical works appears intended to serve a mainly evidential purpose, but to be cast in a right-constituting form. Consideration might therefore be given to dropping the requirement of fixation in UK law, and to leaving the question of the existence of a literary, dramatic, or musical work as a matter of evidence (in which the existence of a recorded form is always likely to be the best kind of evidence).

Originality

7.25   One of the major issues in harmonising copyright in Europe has been the different traditions of the UK ('skill, labour, and judgment' standard) and the Continent ('author's own intellectual creation' standard) with regard to originality. The question of how to choose between the two standards in developing a copyright law suitable for the digital environment seems so far to have been resolved in favour of the Continental approach, especially in the light of recent CJEU jurisprudence (see paras 2.39 and 2.40). However, what a genuinely Europe-wide and comprehensive test of originality should be remains a question suitable for investigation.

7.26   There have been relevant developments in the common law world outside England, seeming to elevate 'skill' over 'labour' in the traditional test of originality. In the United States, the standard of 'originality' was raised by the Supreme Court in 1991, in *Feist v Rural Telephone Service Company Inc*, a case concerned with whether a telephone directory enjoyed copyright. In answering the question negatively, *Feist* recast the originality requirement in US law, from a 'sweat of the brow' test to one of 'spark of creativity'. But *Feist* must be seen in the context of its own facts, namely, once again, the protection of a compilation or database. In this context, what copyright protects is, in the language of the Berne Convention, the 'selection and arrangement' of the contents of the work, and since all subscribers were included in the directory, and alphabetical listing was the only possible usable way of presenting the results, the originality of the selection and arrangement was indeed negligible.

7.27 The decision equivalent to *Feist* in Canada is *Tele-Direct (Publications) Inc v American Business Information*. The case concerned the yellow pages section of a telephone directory, and again it was held that there was insufficient originality for copyright. But a later court confined *Tele-Direct* to the compilation/database area, saying that difficulties arose there 'because such works are not likely to exhibit, on their face, indicia of the author's personal style or manner of expression'. *Tele-Direct* has also been the subject of criticism by the Federal Court of Appeal in *CCH Canadian Ltd v Law Society of Upper Canada*, a case about the copyright in law reports rather than databases. On appeal in that case, the Supreme Court took up a mid-position, emphasising that originality lay, not in either labour and 'sweat of the brow' or 'sparks of creativity', but in the author's exercise of skill and judgment.

7.28 Adoption of a higher threshold criterion of originality (or equivalent) might remove from the ambit of copyright some of the relatively trivial and ephemeral material that has been within the scope of copyright. The disadvantage would be that someone (ultimately the courts) would have to take the decision as to which side of the line any given work fell. The possibility of seeming absurdity would be replaced by perhaps dangerous uncertainty. It should be noted, moreover, that nearly all of the discussion of a higher standard in the common law world has been in the probably special context of databases where already the UK is applying the 'author's own intellectual creation' standard for copyright purposes (although not for the *sui generis* right).

7.29 An alternative approach would be to drop any threshold test whatsoever. Possibly this might sit best in a world where copyright had been displaced by contract, with the material which its producer did not want disseminated to a wider world being protected by laws of confidentiality and privacy (for which see Chapter 18). The protection afforded by contract would be relevant for any item for which a buyer was prepared to pay; that of confidentiality and privacy for material which was indeed confidential or private and which the producer was not prepared to sell or give away.

7.30 The policy issue here is the desirability of threshold tests for 'originality' such as 'skill, labour and judgment', or 'intellectual creation', in particular in the digital environment, and what the consequences would be if there was no threshold test at all.

Databases: other issues

7.31 There are still more fundamental issues about the *sui generis* right protecting databases. Since the right protects the *contents* of the database, and not just the *selection and arrangement* thereof, does it go beyond the traditional exclusion of information as such from the scope of copyright protection? Does it preclude access to that which in the past has circulated freely amongst would-be users? An example which has been much discussed is scientific information, now commonly held on databases. The Commission published a Communication on database rights in December 2005. This notes that decisions of the ECJ have limited the protection conferred by the *sui generis* right. The Commission's research suggests that the *sui generis* right has anyway failed to achieve its objective of boosting the global competitiveness of the European database industry (although the UK continues to be the leading member state in the field). Abolition of the right is accordingly one of the options under consideration by the Commission, along with amendment of the Directive to reverse the effects of the Court decisions, repeal of the whole Directive or doing nothing, simply awaiting further judicial decisions. The last always looked the likeliest outcome, and the cases that have emerged have shown a broader view being taken of the right's scope.

7.32   The policy issue that remains here, however, is fundamental: does the *sui generis* database right serve any useful purpose, and if it does, should it be amended in any way in particular?

Ownership: employment

7.33   Under UK (but not Continental) laws, where an employee creates a work in the course of employment, the employer gets first ownership of the resulting copyright. Given that the employer is an investor who is backing the production of copyright works, his gaining the copyright (at least in its economic aspects) and the return therefrom does not seem so dreadful as is sometimes suggested by those from systems more focused on copyright as reflecting more of personality rights than economic interests. The Software Directive laid down that the economic rights in a computer program should go to the employer unless otherwise provided by contract, thus pointing Europeanisation for the digital environment in a UK or Anglo-American direction; but there has been no similar provision in any subsequent Directive.

7.34   Were a European copyright law to follow the UK model and give an employer the first copyright in an employee's work, a question might arise as to how to compensate the latter for the loss of the right that would otherwise have fallen to him. Patent law provides a possible example: the employer is entitled to patent inventions by employees working in the course of their employment, but the employee has a right to participate in the economic benefit which the work brings to the employer. However, that scheme does not appear to have been regularly used and is not easy to apply. But this may also be because well-advised employers put in place suitable or satisfactory schemes of their own devising as part of the contract of employment. Another model of possible relevance is the artists' resale right, introduced into UK law on 14 February 2006 (see paras 3.44–3.46). The right guarantees the original artist a share of the returns being earned from sales of the original art work, regardless of whether the artist still owns the copyright in the work in question.

7.35   Were an employee reward scheme along this or similar lines to be introduced into copyright, the question of whether it should be a default scheme subject to contract would have to be addressed; the precedent of the Software Directive suggests that it would be such a scheme.

Ownership: orphan works

7.36   One further issue related to the ownership of copyright is of considerable practical significance. Since copyright is an unregistered right and copyright in author works extends well after the death of the author (and the date of that event may be difficult to ascertain), would-be users and re-publishers of works who wish to comply with the law frequently find it impracticable or impossible to take the necessary steps to do what they want to do lawfully, that is, find out whether a work is still in copyright and, if so, who is now the owner. At present, the law offers certain protections to such persons only where authors have made it very difficult to identify themselves, by means of anonymity or pseudonymity. These protections themselves cause certain difficulties in many cases. The British Academy identified the issue as one of significance for academic research in the humanities and social sciences, and the issue was also sharply focused in the debate about the Google Book Settlement. The US Register of Copyrights published a Report on Orphan Works on 31 January 2006, broadly recommending that 'if the user has performed a reasonably diligent search for the copyright owner but is unable to locate that owner, then that user should enjoy a benefit of limitations on the remedies that a copyright owner could obtain against him if the owner showed up at a later date and sued for infringement'; this was introduced in the Shawn Bentley Orphan Works Bill in 2008, but never passed by the House of Representatives.

The EU has taken initiatives towards finding solutions that would partially alleviate the problem of orphan works. In July 2008 the European Commission published a Green Paper entitled *Copyright in the Knowledge Economy*, which discussed orphan works within the context of the best dissemination of knowledge in the digital environment for the purposes of research, science and education, and raised the possibility of Community legislative intervention in order to ensure a harmonised cross-border approach by member states. This would build on a recommendation of the Commission, encouraging member states to create mechanisms to facilitate the use of orphan works, as well as the Final Report and Memorandum of Understanding produced by a High Level Expert Group on Digital Libraries on Digital Preservation, Orphan Works and Out-of-Print Works and signed by representatives of libraries, archives and right holders. The Memorandum contained a set of guidelines on diligent search for right holders and general principles concerning databases of orphan works and rights-clearance mechanisms, leaving detailed solutions for development at national level. In 2011, a proposal for a Directive on permitted uses of orphan works was issued which provides for common rules on the digitisation and online display of orphan works.[13] It allows certain uses to be made of orphan works by publicly accessible libraries, educational establishments, museums, archives, film heritage institutions, and public-service broadcasting organisations provided that a diligent search is carried out to identify the work as an orphan work.

7.37   In the UK, the Gowers Review 2006 supported the introduction of a copyright exception permitting the use of genuine orphan works provided the user had made a reasonable search and, where possible, given attribution. The Digital Economy Act 2010, when initially presented to Parliament in 2009, contained a provision on allowing use of orphan works but criticised by authors and photographers, among others, this clause was withdrawn before the act was passed during the 'wash-up' process ahead of the general election in April 2010. The Hargreaves Review 2011 examined the issue, further recommending that legislation should be introduced to provide for licensing of orphan works and a clearance procedure for use of individual works. The Digital Copyright Exchange, another of the Review's key proposals, is also envisaged to provide a forum which may authorise the use of such works provided that the search for the rights holder is sufficiently diligent. In July 2012, the Government stated its position in a policy statement: 'it benefits no-one to have a wealth of copyright works be entirely unusable under any circumstances because the owner of one or more rights in the work cannot be contacted. This is not simply a cultural issue; it is also a very real economic issue that potentially valuable intangible assets are not being used, and an issue of respect for copyright if they are being used unlawfully.'[14] The Government plans to bring in legislation enabling the use of orphan works after a diligent search and confirmed by an independent authorising body. It has amended the Enterprise and Regulatory Reform Bill 2012–13 to include a provision by which the Secretary of State may, by regulation, grant licences of orphan works. Whether and how the UK and EU proposals on orphan works are taken forward remains to be seen. A completely different solution to the problem of orphan works would be a copyright registration system, but that would presumably be a radical step too far, since it is inconsistent with the Berne Convention.

 Question

Ought the law to provide that where it is impossible to identify by reasonable inquiry whether a work is still in copyright or who the owner of any copyright is, the performance of the restricted acts will not be infringement of copyright provided that the original work receives due acknowledgement, attribution, and respect for its integrity in the new one?

---

[13] COM(2011) 289 final.   [14] IPO, Government Policy Statement: Consultation on Modernising Copyright, July 2012.

Moral rights

7.38 As noted in para 2.18, moral rights first developed in Continental European legal systems, and were not recognised in UK law until introduced by the Copyright, Designs and Patents Act 1988 (CDPA 1988). The Act recognised two major rights: (1) *paternity* (the right to be identified as author of a literary, dramatic, musical or artistic work, or as director of a copyright film); and (2) *integrity* (the right of such authors and directors to prevent derogatory treatment of their work). The rights belong to the author/director, and cannot be alienated, although on death they transmit as part of the decedent estate. Inalienability means that these rights cannot be the subject of commerce in themselves, but under UK law, they may be waived, albeit this requires writing. Further, the paternity right must be 'asserted' before it can apply, and it is not generally available to authors whose works are created in the course of employment. (For all this see paras 3.33–3.43.) In all these respects, the British moral rights are weaker than the systems found, for example, in some other EU member states. It is possible to imagine situations where export of a lawful product from a weak moral rights member state could be blocked in one with stronger rights. There is accordingly a clear issue of possible harmonisation. In the Continental traditions, moral rights are plainly seen as an important aspect of copyright, protecting significant interests, and these are therefore unlikely to be much watered down in a Europe-wide regulation. A significant move in a parallel area took place early in 2006, when the UK introduced artists' resale rights (*droit de suite*), following a harmonising Directive in 2001 (see paras 3.44–3.46).

7.39 However, the subject of moral rights is otherwise and in general underplayed in international negotiations, discussions, and instruments. The Commission Copyright Paper 2004, consistently with the emphasis it generally placed on the economic in European reforms, saw 'no apparent need to harmonise moral rights protection at this stage'.

7.40 That a strong moral rights regime is nonetheless in the public interest has been argued, on the following grounds:

- a trade mark-like function of assuring the public as to the origin and quality of the work;
- social reward (prestige, status, recognition) going to where it belongs;
- cultural preservation, helping to maintain the record of the country's culture;
- author empowerment in connection with the exploitation of their work.

The rights may also be considered particularly significant in an online digital world where works can be speedily and endlessly transmitted and retransmitted, readily modified and reshaped, and integrated, in whole or in part, in other works. Even if economic interests in the digital environment can be as effectively defended by way of contract as by copyright, it is much less clear that this is so with the moral rights, since it will not necessarily be the author who is making the product available to the public (contractually or otherwise). Many of the functions of moral rights identified previously could also be of great importance in a world of open access journal publishing, to ensure author recognition. After much debate, the rights are recognised in the Creative Commons licences for England and Wales, and Scotland. The right of integrity caused particular concern because it might seem to hamper the rights of users to rework existing material in their own works. The answer to this concern is that such reuse will only infringe the integrity right if it is derogatory to the earlier work, which ought not to happen very often with genuinely creative reuse.

7.41 The issue here is, then, whether in a codification or reform process moral rights should be given increased recognition as of especial significance in the digital environment. The Commission appears to think not, as its 2004 Copyright Paper says that 'no evidence exists in the digital environment either that the current state of affairs does affect the good functioning of the Internal Market'. But the good functioning of the internal market is not the only relevant consideration in the reform and restatement of copyright in Europe.

7.42   If the arguments in favour of a stronger moral rights regime in the European digital environment are accepted, then also questions may follow about the present UK position, in particular the position with regard to:

- the exclusion of employees from the paternity right in their work (para 3.38);
- the need to assert paternity right (para 3.36);
- whether waivers of moral rights should be allowed (para 3.34);
- regulation of waivers for unconscionability;
- duration (para 3.51)—it is not clear, especially in the light of some of the underlying policies referred to previously, why there should be a time limitation on any of the moral rights; on the other hand, moral rights which endure beyond an author's lifetime may be an undue limitation of the public domain, putting powers capable of amounting to censorship in the hands of people other than the person in whose interest the rights were created;
- the name of the rights, at least in the UK, where 'moral' in the context of rights tends to suggest, at least to the uninformed, 'not legal', and so to devalue their significance; 'author's personality rights', while cumbersome, might better convey what the law seeks to protect here.

Exercise

Take each of the points previously listed, and consider how if at all the present UK rules should be reformed in the light of Europeanisation of the law and the requirements of the digital environment.

Duration of rights

7.43   A number of issues relating to the term of copyright have already been identified in this chapter:

- the adoption of the Term Directive 2011 which will lead to extension of the term of protection for sound recordings and performers' rights to 70 years in the UK, which is less than the term of protection in the United States which was reflected in the original proposal by the European Commission (para 7.5);
- whether when a multiplicity of copyrights exists in one product (eg a sound recording) they should all expire together, at least as regards reproduction of similar products (paras 7.20–7.22);
- whether there should be any term at all for moral rights (para 7.43).

7.44   The initial proposal for the recent term extension in the EU appeared to be primarily motivated by the following: many of the most popular sound recordings made in the 1950s and 1960s started falling into the public domain; the belief that session musicians are outliving the current 50-year term and are left without income when their rights expire;[15] such musicians only have the protection of performers' rights

---

[15] See the opinion of the then European Commissioner, Charlie McCreevy at http://europa.eu/rapid/press-release_IP-08-240_en.htm?locale=en.

as their contribution to the musical work is insufficient to attract copyright. The preamble to the Term Directive 2011 also states that 'the socially recognised importance of the creative contribution of performers should be reflected in a level of protection that acknowledges their creative and artistic contribution.' However, the term extension proposal was widely criticised by many academics primarily on the ground that the main benefit of the extension will fall to the record labels.[16] It was also argued that given the inherent inequality of bargaining position in the relationship between the labels and the performers it is unlikely that performers will see any increase in revenue. This is something that the Commission has clearly sought to address in the additional rights created in the Directive (*see* para 6.42). Although economic analysis may not support the term extension, it is arguable that the natural rights justifications for copyright do not support a distinction between performers and authors.[17]

Question

Do you agree with the European Commissioner Michel Barnier that the recent term extension will 'make a real difference for performers?'[18]

7.45   Further, it is clear from economic studies that the precise duration of copyright is not governed by the need to incentivise production with the promise of a long-lasting reward should the product be successful. Production is generally governed by other incentives from the point of view of creative authors, and by much shorter-term calculations of likely return by copyright entrepreneurs. On the other hand, the length of copyright enables the author and the entrepreneur to take benefit from the development of new markets through changing technology (eg the emergence of the home video and DVD markets for films) and so encourages (and enables) them to take greater investment risks with new works only a very few of which will become such long-term winners. This is also true of the income generated by successful products over the lifetime of a successful product whether or not there is relevant technological change. Empirical and economic analysis of the effects of the copyright term on entrepreneurial behaviour over time could be helpful in the formation of policy in this area.

7.46   On the basis of the economic literature to date, however, it seems quite likely that such a study would show the impact of the copyright term on economic behaviour and initial decision-making about creation and publication to be negligible, whatever the length of time involved, as long as it extends beyond the period needed to ensure 'lead time' (ie the benefit of being first to market with a particular product), and consequent opportunity to earn a profit on the investment made. Much more difficult would be the question of how to measure and assess the effects of works falling out of copyright at the expiry of term. This question would be raised in particular if it was decided, for example, to create a copyright of indefinite duration to support a world in which copyright owners contracted directly and online with would-be users for access to and use of works.

7.47   What then is the value, economically, socially and intellectually, of works entering the public domain because they no longer enjoy copyright? One imagines that for the great majority of works it is nil or

---

[16] Criticism of the extension can be found in B Farrand, 'Too much is never enough? The 2011 Copyright in Sound Recordings Extension Directive' [2012] EIPR 297; *Gowers Review of Intellectual Property*, para 4.33; Centre for Intellectual Property Policy & Management, Centre for Intellectual Property and Information Law, Institute for Information Law & Max Planck Institute for Intellectual Property, Competition and Tax Law, 'The Proposed Directive for a Copyright Term Extension—A Backward-Looking Package', Letter to the Commission (27 October 2008), 8; Helfberger et al, 'Never forever: why extending the term of protection for sound recordings is a bad idea' [2008] EIPR 174.

[17] Eg see R Arnold, *Performers' Rights* (2008).

[18] M Barnier, 'Copyright: extension of the term of protection for performers' (12 September 2011) available at http://ec.europa.eu/commission_2010-2014/barnier/headlines/news/2011/09/20110912_en.htm.

negligible; is there a point of time at which the enduring value of a relatively small number of works should be taken out of the ordinary interplay of market and social conditions (by giving them a long-enduring copyright) which otherwise produces a price for them as between supplier and customer? How far can copyright be analogised with, say, the antiques, paintings, or books markets, where some (but not many) very old works can command extremely high prices despite the absence of any particular legal protection of their exclusivity? Or do old works derive their value in these markets from uniqueness or rarity, and/or associations (eg famous former owners), whereas in the digital environment it is increasingly unlikely that any manifestation of a work will have that quality of uniqueness or rarity?

Infringement: reproduction rights

7.48   Copying occurs constantly and necessarily in the digital environment: every time a program is loaded into a computer RAM, or a surfer opens up a webpage. But the provision of *copies* of works is nonetheless not what the Internet is about from the perspective of the user; rather, the key issue is that of *access* to the digital work, whether to read, view, hear, or otherwise use it. In some ways, therefore, the primary right enjoyed under copyright—the right to make (or prevent) copies of a work—is no longer as significant as it is in the non-digital, product-based world. Instead, rights like the not quite so long-established distribution, performance, and broadcasting rights appear at first sight to be of greater relevance. But the technology specificity of these rights meant that they did not quite 'fit' the online world, and accordingly we now have the public communication right, with which copyright owners have begun an assault upon those engaging in unlicensed provision of and access to material by way of their personal computers (para 4.60).

7.49   The Commission Copyright Paper 2004 raised some issues about the provisions of the various copyright Directives in relation to the reproduction right, in particular the inconsistent definition of *temporary reproduction* as between, on the one hand, the Software and Database Directives and, on the other, the Information Society (InfoSoc) Directive. It recommends that what it sees, probably correctly, as a mainly terminological difference be ironed out to ensure consistency. However, the Paper does not address the oddity that the creation of the temporary reproduction right has brought in its train the need to establish a temporary reproduction *exception*, in order to ensure that the basic mechanisms enabling the Internet to function do not constitute massive continual infringements of copyright. For this reason, this is the only copyright exception mandatory throughout the EU.

7.50   Recent CJEU jurisprudence has addressed the meaning of temporary reproduction and temporary copy exception (see paras 4.36 and 5.14–5.17). Yet, the question which might be asked is whether the temporary reproduction right is not too widely drawn for the digital environment. After all, temporary reproduction necessarily occurs whenever a digital product—be it a computer program, online database, or website—is used, and it might be thought easier to say that reproduction of this kind should not be infringement of copyright at all, save in carefully defined circumstances, that is, the reverse of the present approach.

Internet file-sharing

7.51   A number of issues relating to copyright and file-sharing have already been identified previously:

- The possibility of making individual file-sharers, both downloaders and uploaders of infringing content, liable for infringing copyright (paras 4.41 and 4.61) even though this is generally seen as an expensive option with little deterrent effect.

- The importance of liability by authorisation for making ISPs such as the operators of unlicensed file-sharing networks or website operators (paras 4.72 and 4.73).

- The attempted use of liability by authorisation to make commercial Internet access providers, which enable access to the Internet for customers, liable for infringement by its subscribers (para 4.74) and enactment of the Digital Economy Act 2010 to make internet access providers cooperate and participate in reducing unlawful file-sharing.

- Safe harbour provisions exempting or limiting liability of ISPs (para 4.75).

7.52 With regard to tackling copyright infringement online, standardisation of current and introduction of further criminal measures have been recently discussed at both EU level and beyond (paras 22.147–22.159). In the UK, criminal liability is available under section 107 of the CDPA 1988 for making or dealing with infringing articles where the person knows or has reason to believe that the article is an infringing copy (paras 22.141, 22.142, and 22.146). This includes distribution of an infringing copy, otherwise than in the course of a business to an extent as to affect prejudicially the owner of the copyright (s 107(1)(e)) which was successfully used for a recent conviction;[19] and communication of a work to the public in the course of a business, or otherwise than in the course of a business, to an extent such as to affect the right owner prejudicially (s 107(2A)) which has, so far, been unsuccessfully used.[20] Elsewhere, successful criminal cases relating to copyright infringement include the much publicised *Pirate Bay* case in Sweden, where the four individuals running the self-styled 'world's largest Bit Torrent tracker' were found guilty of contributory infringement and given substantial fines as well as prison sentences.[21] The policy issue that remains here, however, is fundamental: when can criminal measures serve a useful purpose and be justified in the digital environment, and if that is the case, how can it be ensured that they are not disproportionate and not too widely drawn?

7.53 A slightly different approach to tackling online infringement can be found in the Digital Economy Act 2010 (see para 4.74). The provisions in sections 3–18 aim to reduce illegal file-sharing through a system of cooperation between ISPs and right owners, whereby they work together to prevent and act upon copyright infringement on the ISP's network. It provides for imposition of certain obligations on ISPs requiring them to: notify subscribers of reported infringements once they receive a Copyright Infringement report from a right owner who suspects that his right has been infringed by a particular IP address, which is a subscriber of the ISP; to provide infringement lists to copyright owners on request, being a list of infringement reports made relating to a subscriber without identifying them[22] (together known as 'initial obligations'); and to take technical measures to limit Internet access of subscribers should initial obligations be ineffective and infringement continues (known as technical obligations).[23] A further provision, section 17, requiring ISPs to block websites was dropped by the government although rights owners have successfully achieved the same result through other means (see para 4.74). The Act is seen as a graduated response for reducing infringement from persistent infringers and also a mechanism to provide education and information about legitimate services for accessing copyright content online. But it has also

---

[19] Conviction by the Ayr Sheriff Court for Anne Muir, 58 years old from Scotland, who distributed music files worth £54,000, available at http://www.sln.law.ed.ac.uk/2011/05/10/first-illegal-music-file-sharing-conviction-in-scotland/.

[20] Eg *R v Rock & Overton* (2010) T20097013, Gloucester Crown Court.

[21] Note also the successful prosecution in Germany against the founder of movie-streaming website kino.to leading to a prison sentence and the pending criminal case in the United States against Kim Dotcom, the founder of a file-hosting service, Megaupload.com.

[22] To ensure compliance with the Data Protection Act 1998; right owners can apply for a court order should they want the infringer to be named.

[23] The Digital Economy Act provides for insertion of relevant provisions in the Communications Act 2003. Although the Act is in force, its provisions on copyright infringement are yet to be implemented. These obligations are to be governed and implemented by regulatory codes to be prepared by the telecoms regulator Ofcom and approved by Parliament. Ofcom published a draft 'Initial Obligations Code' in June 2012.

been controversial, partly due to strong objections to its contents by users, rights groups, and ISPs,[24] but also due to the rush to enact it in the parliamentary wash-up period. The issue here is, then, whether the graduated response mechanism is a step in the right direction to reduce unlawful file-sharing.

Copyright exceptions and defences

7.54   Both the Gowers Review 2006 and the Hargreaves Review 2011 focused considerably on copyright exceptions. Questions had certainly arisen previously about whether exceptions are actually necessary in the digital environment (with which Gowers was also specifically concerned) and can be adapted to the digital environment (with which Hargreaves was concerned). It can be argued that copyright exceptions and limitations were created because they related to areas of activity in which the creation of an efficient market in which producers and users could bargain about prices for access to and use of works seemed impossible, or at least far too costly; but if that was so, has the Internet solved the market's failure by providing an environment in which transaction costs are hugely reduced by the automation of the contracting process between supplier and consumer? And, if so, does that justify allowing contracts, supported by DRMs, to override copyright exceptions? (See further paras 7.61–7.63.)

7.55   There is also a Europeanisation question. The UK system has differed from at least some Continental ones regarding the way in which exceptions or limitations operate, with the former taking them to be rather a limit on the grant of property whilst, by contrast, the latter perceive them rather as an exception to the property right granted. Equally, there are differences in approach with the way in which they operate in domestic law, with the UK favouring relatively broadly drawn fair dealing provisions, but the Continental systems focusing rather on specific, narrow categories. How should the two approaches be reconciled? This question was still too difficult to be answered in the InfoSoc Directive of 2001, which set out a long list of possible exceptions, but gave member states the option to enact some, all or none, and thus failed to achieve any sort of harmonisation on the matter. It also made it impossible for member states to introduce new exceptions not on the Directive's list.

7.56   A starting point for policy discussion in this area may be whether we begin from an assumption of a general liberty to which copyright protection forms an exception, or a norm of copyright from which exceptions need to be carved out to protect certain other interests. The Berne Convention is itself expressed in terms of copyright protection within certain general limits (subject matter, term, restricted acts, etc), and even within these limits there are still further specific limitations (a general power to create exceptions and certain specified 'free uses', such as quotation and illustration for teaching). The recent international approach has been to restrict the scope of exceptions and limitations, in terms of what is now commonly known as the 'Berne three-step test' (it comes from Art 9(2) of the Convention). Under this test, exceptions:

- can only relate to certain special cases;
- must not conflict with a normal exploitation of the work; and
- must not unreasonably prejudice the legitimate interests of the author.

7.57   This seems at least to make a little difficult an approach like that found in the US copyright statute: a general 'fair use' defence covering purposes 'such as' criticism, comment, teaching, scholarship, and

---

[24] It also faced opposition through an attempted judicial review by UK ISPs TalkTalk and BT, on the basis that its provisions are not compatible with EU law. The Court of Appeal held that it was compatible with a number of EU Directives including the E-Commerce Directive and the Data Protection Directive. See *R (on the application of British Telecommunications Plc) v Secretary of State for Business, Innovation and Skills* [2012] 2 CMLR 23.

research, and indicating that factors to be taken into account 'include' such matters as whether the use is of a commercial nature or for non-profit educational purposes, the amount and substantiality of the portion used in relation to the whole work and the effect of the use upon the market or value of the copyright work. While it is unlikely that the US approach will ever be challenged as inconsistent with the Berne Convention, the very openness of the defence makes it vulnerable to the charge that it creates uncertainty. A proposal for such a general fair use exception to be included in the InfoSoc Directive was rejected during its negotiation. In the UK, Gowers was asked specifically to consider whether 'fair use' provisions for citizens were reasonable. Hargreaves was also asked to consider whether fair use would be beneficial in the UK, which the Hargreaves Review rejected because there are genuine legal doubts about viability of transposing fair use into the UK legal framework which is based in a European context. Instead, it recommended the use of all copyright exceptions at national level which are allowed in the EU by the InfoSoc Directive.

7.58   Another issue of uncertainty, but perhaps of growing significance, is how all this may be linked with human rights ideas about protection for, on the one hand, the moral and material interests resulting from any scientific, literary, or artistic production of which a person is author (favouring wide protection for such persons and so leaning against wide exceptions) and, on the other, freedom of expression (favouring the right of non-authors to make use of material).

7.59   There are a number of specific difficulties with the exceptions as they exist in the present law; for example:

- The greatest current controversy in the UK is the restriction of the exception for research to *research for non-commercial purposes* (see para 5.22). This sprang from the Database and InfoSoc Directives. The meaning and scope of 'non-commercial' causes much concern in university and professional research circles. In its 2003 report on Keeping Science Open, the Royal Society stated: 'We believe that the limitation of fair dealing to non-commercial purposes gives rise to uncertainty, is not useful and is complex to operate, and we recommend that it be renegotiated when the Copyright [InfoSoc] Directive is reviewed ...' The British Academy stated in its 2006 review of copyright and research in the humanities and social science: 'we believe that statutory clarification will be necessary to protect scholarship and the public interest in research.'

- Further, why are the exceptions for fair dealing for purposes of non-commercial research and private study limited to literary, dramatic, musical, or artistic works, and not extended to films, sound recordings, and broadcasts? (See paras 5.21–5.28.) The Gowers Review recommended that the exception for private copying for research should be extended to *all* content. The Hargreaves Review also suggested that current exceptions can inhibit new technology, such as text mining and gave the example of research in malaria where valuable materials cannot be mined. It recommended extension of the non-commercial research exception 'to allow use of analytics for non-commercial use' and pressing at EU level for 'an exception to support text mining and data analytics for commercial use' (section 5.26).

- The Hargreaves Review also recommended that the Government press at EU level for the introduction of 'an exception allowing uses of a work enabled by technology which do not directly trade on the underlying creative and expressive purpose of the work (this has been referred to as "non-consumptive" use)' so as to allow uses of works 'where copying is really only carried out as part of the way the technology works' (section 5.24).

- The Gowers Review also boldly recommended an exception for creative, transformative or derivative works within the Berne three-step test, to legitimise clearly the reworking of existing material for a new purpose or to give it a new meaning, and to align the law in the EU with that of the United

States. The transformative use would have to be such as not to prejudice the market or the artistic integrity of the work so used.

- Further, has the rather vague and uncertain copyright defence of 'public interest' in UK copyright law (see para 5.47) survived the InfoSoc Directive's permission for specific national exceptions in cases of minor importance concerning only analogue uses, as long as consistent with the Berne 'three-step' test—and, if so, to what extent?

- Should there be an exception in favour of 'place-shifting' for private and domestic use in relation to sound recordings akin to that already in existence for 'time-shifting' for broadcasts (ie allowing the owner of a lawful copy of a sound recording to make copies usable on other machinery, eg copy a CD held in the house to obtain a copy to keep in the car, or in a portable playing device—see paras 5.45 and 5.46). The Gowers Review recommended the non-retrospective introduction of a limited private copying exception for this purpose, confined to 'format-shifting' such as transferring a CD to an MP3 player or a video cassette to a DVD. Noting that in many other member states of the EU such exceptions were funded by levies on the sale prices of the relevant equipment, from which copyright owners were then remunerated, the Review argued that owners themselves could set sale prices at levels reflecting the additional use conferred by the new exception. The Hargreaves Review has also recommended introduction of a limited private copying exception which allows making of copies by individuals for their own and immediate family's use on different media. Not only does it correspond to what consumers are already doing but there is no strong evidence of harm done by such private copying. A private copying exception, provided that fair compensation is paid to the rights holder, is allowed within the EU framework (InfoSoc Directive, Art 5(2)(b)) although its exact nature and scope remains unclear.[25]

- Should there be an express exception for parody, at present covered only indirectly, if at all, by such exceptions as 'criticism and review' (see para 5.29)? Contrast, for example, French law; but note that in the United States 'parody' as fair use is a creation of the courts rather than something spelled out in the legislation. The InfoSoc Directive permits such an exception, and the Gowers Review recommended that it should be expressly introduced in the UK. The Hargreaves Review recommended use of parody exception allowed in the EU as it has both economic and cultural consequences in the digital environment.

- With regard to databases, the Commission Copyright Paper 2004 questioned whether differences between the exceptions to copyright and those for the *sui generis* right may mean that the former can be undermined by the rights existing under the latter. Specifically, where a copyright exception allows *use* of a database for purposes of teaching or non-commercial research, the exception for the *sui generis* right is limited to *extraction* for such purposes. This may be justified by the nature of the *sui generis* right, which extends only to extraction, and so requires an exception only in relation to that right, whereas the scope of copyright protection is wider; but at the least, there is room for confusion and uncertainty in the present law since it will not always be instantly clear to a user whether the database is protected by copyright or only by the *sui generis* right. In any event, what is the difference, if any, between 'use' and 'extraction' in this context?

---

[25] The provision has given rise to a number of CJEU decisions such as Cases C-277/10 *Martin Luksan v Petrus van der Let*; C-462/09 *Stichting de Thuiskopie v Opus Supplies Deutschland GmbH, Mijndert van der Lee and Hananja van der Lee*; C-467/08 *Padawan SL v Sociedad General de Autores y Editores de Espana (SGAE)*. Several more references remain pending. See Case C-521/11 *Amazon.com International Sales and Others*; Cases C-457/11 to C-460/11 *VG Wort and others*.

Exercise

Consider the previous list of issues in the light of the Europeanisation of the law, and also the need to create a copyright law appropriate to the digital environment. What would your solutions be, and how would you justify them?

7.60   Many of the issues about exceptions raised by the Gowers Review (but significantly, perhaps, not the matter of transformative works) were taken up in a UK IPO consultation published in January 2008. However, despite the then Government's acceptance of Gower's recommendations, it failed to adopt those exceptions. The Hargreaves Review termed this as 'a clear demonstration of the failure of the copyright framework to adapt.' The present Government, in its response to the Hargreaves Review broadly accepted the recommendations.[26] It then launched a consultation on copyright to seek views on its proposals to widen copyright exceptions, which closed in March 2012.[27] At the time of writing, the Government has proposed in the Enterprise and Regulatory Reform Bill 2012–13, a provision by which the Secretary of State would have the power to add or remove exceptions to copyright by way of regulations. The outcome of this process remains to be seen.

The European Commission, in November 2007, produced a relatively brief review of the InfoSoc Directive for the Council, the European Parliament and the Economic and Social Committee, in the course of which exceptions are discussed. The main concern of the document is to identify which of the exceptions have been taken up by the member states, how they have been implemented and how they have operated in the courts and in practice, rather than to reconsider the whole approach of the Directive. The exceptions specifically discussed, however, are those for private copying, reporting current events, quotation for criticism or review, parody, and the benefit of libraries. The Commission's Green Paper 2008 discussed copyright exceptions within the context of the best dissemination of knowledge in the online environment for the purposes of research, science, and education, emphasising in particular exceptions for libraries, archives, and teaching and research purposes.

Technical protection measures, rights management information systems, and copyright exceptions

7.61   The nature and role of TPMs and RMIs (DRMs) have been set out earlier in the chapter (see paras 7.5 and 7.12–7.14). While clearly these technical protection devices are of critical importance to the creation of markets using the new forms of distribution made possible by the Internet and digitisation, and have therefore themselves received specific legal protection alongside the reform of the law of copyright (see paras 5.53–5.57), further questions can be raised about the effect on the established copyright exceptions and limitations, especially in sectors outside the entertainment industry. For example, can the contractual conditions imposed by the right holder by means of DRMs bar access to and use of non- or otherwise out-of-copyright material, or use of the kind otherwise permissible under the exception and limitation rules? In the context of education and research (increasingly making use of digital tools and resources), should copyright owners be able to protect products with digital fences as to preclude others from exercising their fair dealing rights, or to limit or exclude those rights by

---

[26] IPO, 'The Government Response to the Hargreaves Review of Intellectual Property and Growth', August 2011.
[27] IPO, 'Consultation on Copyright', December 2011.

contract? Some provisions in the CDPA 1988 seem to exclude the possibility of contracting out of copyright exceptions, but often the law is simply silent on the matter, and it may well be that exceptions are contractually excludable unless specifically provided otherwise (see paras 5.58–5.62). That such questions are of importance is confirmed by the ambiguous provision in the InfoSoc Directive requiring member states to ensure that the exceptions for permitted acts are made available to the public where it has lawful access to the protected work. The importance of this issue is also underlined by the Hargreaves Review's recommendation for a change in the law to ensure that contracts cannot override any exceptions to copyright.

7.62   Discussion in Australia has brought out two clearly contrasting perspectives. In 2002, the Australian Copyright Law Review Committee produced a report examining the issue for Australian law, and comparing the approach taken in the EU and the United States. The Commission recommended that the Australian Copyright Act be amended to provide that an agreement excluding or modifying sections in the Act limiting copyright should be of no effect. It is noteworthy that what appears to be the first official report in this area concluded that legislative measures should be taken to preserve what the Review Committee saw as the copyright balance. Another Australian report published at much the same time argues, however, that prohibitions against contracting around the limits of copyright protection are generally undesirable. The view that such restrictions are needed overestimates the ability of the law to establish optimal rules for the protection of copyright material, at the expense of the considerable advantages to be derived from private market-based arrangements. It also over-estimates the extent to which copyright owners, operating in a competitive market, are capable of unilaterally imposing terms on end users. Insofar as private agreements may result in less than optimal outcomes, they should be dealt with under established principles of contract law, competition law, or consumer protection law. The attention of policymakers should therefore focus on examining whether existing principles of contract law, competition law, and consumer protection law are able to deal adequately with mass market agreements for the distribution of copyright material, rather than on imposing rigid prohibitions on freedom to contract. On the other hand, there may be an argument for imposing some restrictions on freedom of contract to the extent that copyright policy is directed at promoting non-economic objectives. If that is the case, it is important that the non-economic objectives be clearly specified and that any prohibitions be narrowly focused on achieving such objectives.

7.63   These issues were not directly addressed in a report on DRMs by the All Party Parliamentary Internet Group (APIG) published in June 2006. But the Committee recommended that:

- 'the Government consider granting a much wider-ranging exemption to the anti- circumvention measures in the CDPA for genuine academic research';

- 'the Office of Fair Trading (OFT) bring forward appropriate labelling regulations so that it will become crystal clear to consumers what they will and will not be able to do with digital content that the purchase' (this with regard to TPMs such as 'regional locks'—see paras 5.53 and 5.54);

- 'the Government do NOT legislate to make DRM systems mandatory'.

In the absence of evidence for use of the system of complaint to the Secretary of State that DRMs were blocking the deployment of copyright exceptions, the Committee concluded that any difficulties were being overcome by way of voluntary arrangements. The British Academy review of copyright and research in the humanities and social science, also published in the summer of 2006, concluded however that 'the effect of DRMs may be to make ineffective the existing exemptions under copyright', and recommended:

Rights holders should not generally be able to circumvent the objectives of the exemptions to the copyright act by contract or through the use of technology. The current UK law which seeks to allow access that will enable its use for research or for criticism or review through a DRM system too readily favours the upholding of the access terms prescribed by the operator of that system. The result can only be side-stepped by complaint to a Minister and consequent action to modify the system. This serious impediment to the freedom of researchers to discover material and make appropriate use of it, needs to be reviewed wherever in consequence undue constraints on scholarship and the development of new creative material arise.

A 2006 report for the Institute of Public Policy Research proposed that 'anti-circumvention provisions [should] cease to apply once copyright protection has expired.' Finally, the Gowers Review recommended that the Patent Office should take steps to make it easier for users to file complaints about DRMs by providing an accessible website for the purpose. It also recommended that the Department of Trade and Industry (now the Department for Business, Innovation and Skills) should investigate the possibility of providing consumer guidance on DRMs through a labelling convention.

 Exercise

What if any legislative action should be taken by government with regard to TPMs and RMIs? Should they be made mandatory in relation to digital works? Should it be possible for them to exclude the exercise of copyright exceptions by users of works? Should section 296ZE of the CDPA 1988 (for which see paras 5.63–5.66) be amended?

Further reading

Books

General

L Bently, *Between a Rock and a Hard Place: The Problems Facing Freelance Creators in the UK Media Market-Place* (2002)

WR Cornish, *Intellectual Property: Omnipresent, Distracting, Irrelevant?* (2004), Ch 2

WR Cornish, D Llewelyn, and T Aplin, *Intellectual Property* (7th edn, 2010), Ch 20.3

W Davies and K Withers, *Public Innovation: Intellectual Property in a Digital Age* (Institute of Public Policy Research, 2006)

C Geiger, *Criminal Enforcement of Intellectual Property: A Handbook of Contemporary Research* (2012)

PB Hugenholtz (ed), *The Future of Copyright in a Digital Environment* (1996)

Institute for Information Law, University of Amsterdam, *The Recasting of Copyright & Related Rights for the Knowledge Economy* (European Commission DG Internal Market Study, November 2006)

L Lessig, *Free Culture: How Big Media Uses Technology and the Law to Lock Down Culture and Control Creativity* (2004)

J Litman, *Digital Copyright* (2001)

G Mazziotti, *EU Digital Copyright Law and the End-User* (2008)

A Strowel, *Peer-to-Peer File Sharing and Secondary Liability in Copyright Law* (2009)

G Westkamp, *Digital Copyright Laws in Europe* (2011)

Articles

Copyright in the digital environment: current issues

C Angelopoulos, 'The myth of European term harmonisation—27 public domains for 27 Member States' [2012] IIC 567

A Barron, '"Graduated response" à l'anglaise: online copyright infringement and the Digital Economy Act (UK) 2010' [2011] 3(2) Journal of Media Law 305

A Christie, 'Reconceptualising copyright in the digital age' [1995] EIPR 522

T Cook and E Derclaye, 'An EU copyright code: what and how, if ever?' (2011) IPQ 259

T Dreier, 'Copyright in the age of digital technology' (1993) 24 IIC 481

G Grassie, 'A UK digital copyright exchange: will the pipe dream ever become a reality?' [2012] 7(1) JIPLP 23

A Rahmatian, 'The Hargreaves Review on copyright licensing and exceptions: a missed moment of opportunity' [2011] Ent LR 219

E Rosati, 'The Hargreaves report and copyright licensing: can national initiatives work per se?' [2011] EIPR 67

Part III

Design protection

Introduction

This Part follows on from the Copyright Part of the book, to consider a particular kind of work that might have been protected by copyright alone but for which there has been—sometimes instead of, sometimes as well as, copyright—a special regime or set of regimes since the 19th century. Traditionally the works in question were the designs of industrial products, meaning very broadly either the three-dimensional shape or configuration of a product, or the two-dimensional pattern, colouring or ornamentation applied to the surface of a product. The context in which this right developed was industrial and commercial; the concern was typically with the end results of mass production rather than the individual creative efforts which were seen as the essence of copyright. In any event, in the 19th century copyright had still not been generalised, and there were several different statutes each covering particular types of work—literature, sculpture, fine art, and so on. The system of design protection which was created alongside copyright survived the great generalisation of the Copyright Act 1911 because it was used and found useful in several industries. It also reflected what had become general government policy in the course of the 19th century, namely the support of good design, which was supposed to give products a competitive edge in the marketplace.

The basic form of design protection depended upon registration of the design in a public register maintained by government. In this feature design protection was like that provided by patents and trade marks, but unlike copyright from the 1911 Act on. Registration provided publicity, not only about who owned a design, but also about designs in general. Any member of the public could study design at the registry, just as inventions and trade marks could be studied. Registration continues to be a major feature of design protection down to the present day. Chapter 8 deals in detail with the present regime governing protection of designs by way of registration.

A difficulty, however, is and always has been the design that is not registered. A design may be unregistered for a variety of reasons: the designer did not know about the registration system; or chose not to register; or the design did not meet the criteria for registration laid down by the law. Many such unregistered designs might, however, attract copyright protection. This created an anomaly. Registered design protection was different from copyright protection: in particular, it was shorter in terms of time, although it gave a monopoly right rather than simple protection against copying. So the law-makers have had to make decisions about whether to allow, exclude or restrict copyright in the context of unregistered designs.

As Chapter 9 explains, views have changed from time to time on this question. By the time of the Copyright, Designs and Patents Act 1988 (CDPA 1988), the prevailing view was that, while copyright could not be excluded altogether from the field of industrial design, it should be severely restricted and the 1988 Act set out to do this, although, as we shall see later, one of the measures enacted as part of this effort (CDPA 1988, s 52) is now being repealed. The 1988 Act also introduced a new right, the UK unregistered design right, by which it was sought to give appropriately limited protection in UK law to certain unregistered designs.

A further layer of complexity came about in the 1990s when the EU set about harmonisation of national registered design laws and the creation of unitary Community registered and unregistered design protection. These steps were achieved by way of Designs Directive 98/71/EC and Community Design Regulation 6/2002/EC. However, these contained no measures to harmonise national unregistered design protection. The UK has chosen to continue with its own national unregistered design system, which is very different from the EU-wide one. Chapter 9, which considers unregistered design protection, has to deal with three different sets of rules, viz:

- copyright, insofar as it has a continuing role in this field in the UK;
- UK unregistered design right;
- Community unregistered design right.

Complexities can be caused by the multiple systems for design protection considered in Chapters 8 and 9. At the same time, with its connections to all of copyright, trade mark and patent law, there can also be difficulties in terms of positioning design law in the overall scheme of intellectual property protection. Design law has often attracted criticism for these reasons. However, with the importance of good design and of the creative economy increasingly recognised by policymakers, ongoing processes of consultation and legislative reform in the UK and with the European designs regime beginning to show its potential muscle in high-profile disputes such as the *Samsung v Apple* litigation discussed in Chapter 8, there is no doubt that design protection is undergoing something of a renaissance in terms of both legal and policy interest.

Sources of the law: key websites

- UK IPO designs pages:
  http://www.ipo.gov.uk/design.htm
- OHIM Community design pages:
  http://oami.europa.eu/ows/rw/pages/RCD/index.en.do
- European Commission designs pages:
  http://ec.europa.eu/internal_market/indprop/design/index_en.htm

Registered designs

Introduction

Scope and overview of chapter

8.1   This chapter deals with the law of registered designs, leaving the protection of unregistered designs for Chapter 9. It considers which designs may be validly registered and the nature of the rights conferred. Because of the EU legislative intervention on design laws discussed in further detail later, the rules on these matters are the same whether one is seeking registration in the UK or at EU level. We can therefore consider the substantive law pertaining to UK registered designs and Community registered designs together. The chapter does not go in detail into the practicalities and requirements of the registration process, guidance on which can be found in one of the practitioner works on the subject.

Learning objectives

8.2   By the end of this chapter you should be able to describe and explain:

- the international treaty context for contemporary design laws;
- the criteria designs must meet to be validly registered and the exclusions from protection;
- the special rules dealing with the designs of component parts of complex products and the policy issues surrounding spare parts;
- the basic elements of the registration process in the UK and for Community registered designs;
- on what grounds a design registration may be challenged as invalid;
- the rights given as a result of a valid registration, including the scope of protection against infringement and defences;
- the interaction between registered design protection and other IP rights, in particular copyright.

8.3   The chapter begins by explaining the international treaty context for design law, which is more fragmentary and less detailed than for copyright law and other IP rights. The chapter then looks at the substantive law of registered designs: what designs may be validly registered and what is excluded from protection (including the difficult problems of 'complex products' and spare parts), what is involved in the registration process, challenging the validity of a registration, the rights conferred by a valid registration and the defences available to a party sued for infringement. It will also look briefly at the interaction between registered design protection and other IP rights, in particular copyright. So the rest of the chapter looks like this:

- The international background to the current law (8.4–8.9)
- Development of UK and EU law (8.10–8.14)
- Designs that can be validly protected by registration (8.15–8.72)
- Complex products (8.73–8.78)
- Spare parts (8.79–8.89)
- Registration process (8.90–8.105)
- Declarations of invalidity (8.106–8.110)
- Rights given by registration, infringement and defences (8.111–8.121)
- Interaction with other IP rights (8.122–8.126)

The international background to the current law

8.4   Unlike for copyright, there is no international treaty stipulating detailed substantive requirements for protection of designs. Of all of the principal IP rights, designs are the least harmonised at international treaty level. The revision of the Berne Convention in 1948 opened up the possibility of copyright protection for industrial designs, including 'works of applied art' within the definition of protected 'literary and artistic works' (Art 2(1)). The expression 'works of applied art' is, however, not defined. The Berne Convention gave its members freedom to determine the extent of the application (or not) of their copyright laws to 'works of applied art' and 'industrial designs and models', the conditions under which they were to be protected (Art 2(7)) and the term of protection for 'works of applied art in so far as they are protected as artistic works', subject to a minimum of 25 years from the making of such a work (Art 7(4)). Berne adds the following, however, ensuring that a distinction is drawn between copyright on the one hand and design protection on the other, where systems for the latter exist:

> Works protected in the country of origin solely as designs and models shall be entitled in another country of the Union only to such special protection as is granted in that country to designs and models; however, if no such special protection is granted in that country, such works shall be protected as artistic works (Art 2(7)).

Thus the Berne Convention allows copyright protection for industrial designs, but tends to exclude it in favour of design laws (if available) for designs originating in countries where special non-copyright protection for designs exists.

8.5   Designs are also only briefly addressed in the Paris Convention. The Paris Convention provides that: 'Industrial designs shall be protected in all the countries of the Union' (Art 5 *quinquies*, adopted in 1958) but leaves open how that protection is to be given. Thus designs may be protected through a regis-tration system or an unregistered system or, indeed, through a combination of the two. Consistently with its general approach to industrial property protection based on registration (national treatment for non-nationals—Art 2, and see para 1.66), the Paris Convention also requires its members to allow foreigners access to national design registration systems, with an application in one Paris Convention country giving a right of priority in the others (Art 4.A(1)), meaning that the registrant can have the validity of his later filings for a particular design assessed as at the date of his first filing for that design in a Paris Convention country, provided his later filings are made within the prescribed priority period, currently set at six months for designs—Art 4.C(1).

Question

In what ways do the Berne and Paris Conventions allow designs to be protected?

8.6   The Hague Agreement Concerning the International Registration of Industrial Designs enables interna-tional design applications but, in effect, simply provides a means whereby a central deposit at the World Intellectual Property Organization (WIPO) can give rise to filings in the Agreement's member states. It contains no substantive provisions governing design protection. In 1968 the Locarno Agreement Establishing an International Classification for Industrial Designs (the *Locarno Classification*) was also concluded. The Locarno Classification (at the time of writing, in its ninth edition) consists of a series of classes and sub-classes providing indications as to the sector of goods incorporating the relevant design. Designs registries of the contracting states must include the numbers of the relevant classes and sub-classes in the official documents for the deposit or registration of designs, and, if they are officially published, in corresponding publications. However, the Locarno Agreement explicitly describes clas-sification as an administrative matter, leaving it to national laws to address the scope of protection of designs (Art 2(1)).

Question

What are the Hague and Locarno Agreements and what is their effect?

8.7   TRIPS contains two Articles on design protection (Arts 25 and 26). These deal with substantive matters of design law in some more detail than previous treaties, and may be taken to reflect an increased degree of international consensus as to the minimum content of design law. However, much is still left to the discretion of TRIPS member states. In terms of requirements for protection, the only mandatory require-ment is that members shall provide for the protection of 'independently created industrial designs that are new or original' (Art 25(1)). None of these expressions are defined. Members *may* provide that designs are not new or original 'if they do not significantly differ from known designs or combinations of known design features' (Art 25(1)). Members are also left a discretion as to whether to extend protec-tion to 'designs dictated essentially by technical or functional considerations' (Art 25(1)). In terms of the action for infringement, the only mandatory requirement is that the owner of a protected industrial design must have the right to prevent unauthorised third parties from making, selling, or importing articles bearing or embodying a design which is a copy, or substantially a copy, of the protected design, when such acts are undertaken for commercial purposes (Art 26(1)). There may be limited exceptions to design rights, as long as they do not unreasonably conflict with normal exploitation of protected industrial designs and do not unreasonably prejudice the legitimate interests of the owner, taking into account the legitimate interests of third parties (Art 26(2)). Finally, the protection must last for at least ten years (Art 26(3)).

 Question

What is the minimum content of design law under TRIPS?

> ## Key points on the international framework for design law
>
> - The international framework of design law has had, until relatively recently, very little substantive content
> - Individual states still have considerable discretion as to how to protect industrial designs
> - Protection may be by means of copyright or through a special system for the protection of designs
> - There is no need for any special system for protection of designs to be one of registration; but where a registration system exists non-nationals must be given access to it
> - TRIPS has increased the international harmonisation on the minimum content of design protection, but without limiting the options as to how it is achieved

8.8 The essence of the minimum content as found in TRIPS can be put like this:

- Protected designs are to be independently created and new or original.
- Designs dictated by technical or functional considerations do not have to be protected.
- The minimum scope of the exclusive right is to prevent third parties commercially manufacturing/selling/importing articles bearing or embodying a design which is a copy, or substantially a copy, of the protected design.
- Exceptions to design protection are allowed if they are consistent with normal exploitation and do not prejudice the owner's legitimate interests, taking into account the legitimate interests of third parties.
- Duration of protection must be at least ten years (note also previously re the Berne Convention minimum of 25 years for works of applied art insofar as protected as artistic works).

8.9 The low demands made of states by international law in the field of design protection has led to very variable national protection. However, the relatively recent achievement of the minimum standards set down in TRIPS may be the first step towards a better harmonised global picture. In the EU, as will be seen in more detail in the section immediately following, further steps were taken with the enactment of the Designs Directive in 1998 which harmonised the design registration systems of member states; enactment of the Community Design Regulation in 2002 has also created EU-wide unitary forms of protection for designs (see further paras 8.11–8.13).

Development of UK and EU law

UK law: history

8.10 Only the briefest reference to the development of registered design law in the UK is possible here; a fuller account may be found on this book's Online Resource Centre. The UK has had a registration process for the legal protection of product designs since the 18th century. The latest piece of primary legislation is the Registered Designs Act 1949 (RDA 1949) although, as we shall see, that has been extensively amended as a result of the EU harmonisation discussed in the section immediately following. For most of the 20th century before the EU intervention, UK legislation sought to exclude purely functional designs from registration. What constituted a registrable 'design' under the old RDA 1949 was very different to the present position and included a requirement of so-called 'eye appeal', now abolished. This was reflective of a preference in the UK at the time for the protection of aesthetic, rather than functional, designs. As we shall see, much has now changed as a result of the EU legislation in this field.

EU Directive and Regulation

8.11 In the late 1980s the EU began to take a serious interest in design law as part of its efforts to ensure that different national intellectual property laws did not pose unnecessary barriers to the creation of a single market in Europe. The European Court of Justice (ECJ) had held that a design registration system (in the case, the Benelux system) was 'industrial and commercial property' the rights in which might be exercised in derogation from the free movement of goods within the European Community, provided that the goods in question had not already been put on the market in the exporting member state by or with the consent of the rightholder.[1] Thus a national design right could be used to prevent the import of goods lawfully produced in one member state into another member state. However, member states' national design laws varied very considerably and a party who had rights in a design in one member state might not have had equivalent rights in another member state. There was, therefore, significant potential for divergent national designs laws to impede the free movement of goods within the single market.

> **? Question**
>
> Consider the recitals to Designs Directive 98/71/EC and Community Design Regulation 6/2002/EC. What were the main objectives of the EU legislative intervention on design protection?

8.12 Although agreement on the matter took a decade and more to achieve, the EU did finally settle on two steps with regard to the protection of industrial designs:

(1) harmonisation of the national registered design laws of member states, the harmonised regime being set out in Directive 98/71/EC on the legal protection of designs (referred to in this chapter as the 'Designs Directive' or 'DD'); and

(2) creation of two new Community design rights, both unitary rights covering the whole of the EU. This took effect by way of Regulation 6/2002/EC on Community designs (referred to here as the

---

[1] Case 144/81 *Keurkoop BV v Nancy Kean Gifts BV* [1983] FSR 381.

'Community Design Regulation' or 'CDR'). This created the Community registered design (discussed in this chapter) and the Community unregistered design (discussed in Chapter 9), both of which are together referred to as 'Community designs'.

In the UK, the effect of the Designs Directive was to require very substantial amendment of the RDA 1949, effected by way of the Registered Design Regulations 2001 (SI 2001/3949), which came into force on 9 December 2001.[2] The Community Design Regulation took direct effect in all member states without any need for transposition into national laws; applications for Community registered designs were accepted at the Office for Harmonisation in the Internal Market (OHIM) in Alicante, Spain, and at various national offices, effective from 1 April 2003.

8.13   For the purposes of the present chapter, two important points emerge about these two pieces of European legislation. First, they introduced a number of key new concepts which have required consideration and elucidation by the courts. Secondly, they created a basically unified substantive law of registered designs in the EU. The rules on the definition of protectable designs, requirements for and exclusions from protection, challenges to validity, infringement, and defences are the same for UK national design registrations and Community registered designs, meaning that they can be treated together in this chapter. Within the Community Design Regulation, subject to certain matters discussed further in Chapter 9, the substantive rules on these matters are in large part also the same between Community registered designs and Community unregistered designs, with the result that case law on national registered designs, Community registered designs and Community unregistered designs is all relevant when considering their common substantive concepts and requirements. Given this, it is necessary in the UK to follow closely not only the decisions of the UK IPO and UK courts, but also decisions emanating from OHIM, the General Court, and Court of Justice of the European Union, as well as the courts of other member states.

 Question

What was the effect upon UK law of the EU legislation on design protection?

Key points on EU developments

- The intervention of the EU in design law came about to prevent differences in national laws creating an obstacle to the single European market by preventing the free movement of goods

- There are two major European instruments:
  - Directive 98/71/EC, harmonising the national registered design laws of the EU member states
  - Regulation 6/2002/EC, creating the pan-EU unitary Community design, registered and unregistered

---

[2] A complex challenge to the constitutional validity of the 2001 Regulations was rejected by the English Court of Appeal in *Oakley Inc v Animal Ltd* [2006] RPC 9. According to the transitional provisions governing the amendment of the RDA 1949, the new law applies to all design registrations resulting from an application filed on or after 9 December 2001. Infringement of earlier-filed designs will also be governed by the new law. However, the validity of earlier-filed designs will continue to be determined on the basis of the old pre-harmonisation version of the RDA 1949.

> • The result is that there are EU-level and national systems of registered designs running in parallel which employ the same substantive legal rules on the definition of protectable designs, requirements for and exclusions from protection, challenges to validity, infringement, and defences

8.14 The discussion which follows will generally cite relevant provisions in the first instance from the RDA 1949 (as amended), supported by reference as appropriate to the Designs Directive and the Community Design Regulation.[3] In terms of case law, this chapter will focus on key developments before the General Court and the Court of Justice together with the leading UK cases. In an attempt to step away from the two dominant but markedly different approaches to design protection which had previously existed in member states' national laws (the so-called 'copyright approach' and the so-called 'patent approach'), the Designs Directive and Community Design Regulation adopted a new 'design approach'. This new 'design approach' was intended to reflect that 'the importance of design in modern societies is at least to a large extent due to the fact that it constitutes a marketing instrument' and a focus, in particular, on the 'communication relationship established between the design and the public'.[4] As we will see, this is reflected in a number of aspects of the Designs Directive and Community Design Regulation discussed in this chapter.

Designs that can be validly protected by registration

8.15 For a design to be validly registered, it must:

- fall within the definition of 'design' given by the legislation (paras 8.16–8.27);
- be 'new' and have 'individual character' (paras 8.28–8.61); and
- not fall within any of the exclusions from protection (paras 8.62–8.72).

Each of these criteria will be discussed in turn. The requirements at the first two bullet points may be described as *positive* requirements—characteristics that a design must have to be validly registered—while the exclusions are *negative* in character—either the design should be refused registration or should not have been registered or, if a registered design consists in part of such features, the right conferred by registration does not extend to those features.

Definition of 'design'

8.16 'Design' means:

the appearance of the whole or a part of a product resulting from the features of, in particular, the lines, contours, colours, shape, texture or materials of the product or its ornamentation (RDA 1949, s 1(2); DD, Art 1(a); CDR, Art 3(a)).

The essence of this definition is that a 'design' is constituted by 'the appearance of the whole or part of a *product* . . .'. However, it is the *design* in itself which is protected not its application to, or embodiment in,

---

[3] The RDA 1949 (as amended) does not always transpose the provisions of the Designs Directive into UK law *verbatim*. This chapter will generally quote the relevant provisions from the RDA 1949 and give details of the corresponding Articles from the Designs Directive and Community Design Regulation, but readers should always check the precise terms of the DD and CDR.

[4] A Kur, 'The Green Paper's "Design Approach"—what's wrong with it?' [1993] EIPR 374–378 at 376–377.

a specific product as such. As we shall see in further detail later (see para 8.116), this means that the protection conferred by the design registration encompasses use of the design for any product, whether or not the same as the product of the design right holder.

8.17   The features of appearance which may constitute a protectable design can be three-dimensional (eg contours or shape) or two-dimensional (eg colours). The lawyer is at once led to two further questions:

(1) What is a 'product'?
(2) Does 'appearance' mean that design is confined to what is visible to the human eye or may features perceived by other senses also be relevant?

'Product'

8.18   'Product' is defined as:

> any industrial or handicraft item other than a computer program; and, in particular, includes packaging, get-up, graphic symbols, typographic typefaces and parts intended to be assembled into a complex product (RDA 1949, s 1(3); DD, Art 1(b); CDR, Art 3(b)).

We will return to the issues relating to 'complex products' later (see paras 8.73–8.78).

8.19   An immediately striking feature of the definition of 'product' is its inclusion of 'handicraft items' as well as industrial items, so that the design of single or unique artisan items, including sculptures and works of artistic craftsmanship, may be protectable as well as the results of mass production processes.

8.20   The inclusion of matter such as graphic symbols within the definition of 'product' also represents a change, from a UK perspective, in the way in which this subject is approached. In the pre-Directive UK law, these might at most have been seen as designs applied to an article.[5] But now they are to be seen as products themselves. In other words, products (as well as the protectable features of their appearance) may be two-dimensional. Typefaces are also expressly included in the definition of 'product'.

> **? Question**
>
> Explain how we can tell from the legislation that two-dimensional designs are now protectable by registration.

8.21   The new law's inclusion of two-dimensional items in the definition of 'product' raises issues about overlap with other IP rights, in particular trade marks and copyright. There is, for example, no reason in principle why a logo which might primarily be thought of as a trade mark cannot also be protected as a registered design—the logo being the *design* for a two-dimensional *product* in the form of a *graphic symbol*.[6] A design could also include an artistic work painted or drawn onto a canvass or paper. The old UK law used to avoid overlaps with copyright in such circumstances by denying registration to printed

---

[5] Eg see *Apple Computer Inc v Design Registry* [2002] FSR 38 considering the registrability of computer screen icons under the old RDA 1949. Icons appearing on a computer into which they were inherently built (because they were built into the software included in the machine) were treated as designs applied to the computer, the computer being an 'article' for the purposes of the old UK RDA 1949.

[6] On the overlap with trade marks, see further A Kur, 'No logo!?' (2004) 35(2) IIC 184–186 and A Carboni, 'The overlap between registered Community designs and Community trade marks' (2006) 1(4) JIPLP 256–265.

items of a primarily literary or artistic character and in cases where the article was no more than a carrier for the design.[7] This is no longer the case in the EU designs regime, which explicitly envisages cumulation of protection with other IP rights, including trade marks and copyright, as we shall see further at paras 8.122–8.126.

 Exercise

Consider whether the following are products the appearance of which may constitute a registrable design:

- Book dust jacket
- Calendar
- Dress-making pattern
- Map
- Playing cards
- Painting
- Typographical arrangement of this book
- Computer screen icons
- A web page
- Tattoos

8.22   It also appears from the definition set out previously that products do not need to have a physically tangible form. The word 'item' which appears in the definition of 'product' is not defined but does not in itself appear to limit the concept to goods or corporeal moveables. This ties into the notion that designs for, for example, computer screen icons are registrable as designs for two-dimensional *intangible* products. Computer programs are, however, specifically excluded from the definition of 'product', although the scope of this exclusion is not wholly clear. Is it limited to the source and object codes which constitute the program itself? Or does it go further, to exclude from the designs regime the 'look and feel' of the program when in operation, such as the overall 'look and feel' of the user interface? There may also be questions about how far the word 'item' can be taken to include matter such as buildings and works of architecture. However, even the old UK law did allow registration of designs for structures such as poultry and animal sheds which were prefabricated and portable in that they were delivered to purchasers as a whole.[8]

 Discussion point 1   For answer guidance visit www.oxfordtextbooks.co.uk/orc/waelde3e/

May the design of a building be registered?

---

[7]   Registered Design Rules 1989 (SI 1989/1105), rule 26 (now repealed); *Re Littlewoods Pools Application* (1949) 66 RPC 309.
[8]   Although an air-raid shelter cast in reinforced concrete on site was denied registration under the old RDA 1949: see *Concrete Ltd's Application* (1940) 57 RPC 121.

Discussion point 2

To what extent does the definition of 'product' mean that there are overlaps between registered design and copyright subject matter?

Key points on the meaning of 'product'

- 'Product' encompasses two- as well as three-dimensional items and even intangible items such as computer screen icons
- 'Product' also includes handicraft items as well as industrial items
- The definition of 'product' increases the potential overlap between registered design protection and matter which may be the subject of copyright or trade mark protection

Appearance

8.23   *Appearance* is the second essential element in the definition of design. 'Appearance' is not defined but is said to 'result from':

> the features of, in particular, the lines, contours, colours, shape, texture or materials of the product or its ornamentation (RDA 1949, s 1(2); DD, Art 1(a); CDR, Art 3(a)).

It is important to note that the expression 'appearance', and thus the definition of 'design', contains no requirement of 'eye appeal' or aesthetic quality. Instead, the expressions 'appearance' and 'design' are neutral in terms of protecting both aesthetic and functional design features. Although difficulties may arise for some functional designs in terms of the exclusions from protection (see paras 8.62–8.71), in itself the definition of 'design' is capable of encompassing purely aesthetic and purely functional designs, as well as designs which are a mixture of both. This was a major feature of the 'design approach' adopted in the new EU design regime.[9]

8.24   An interesting question is what, if anything, is intended by the reference to 'texture and materials' in the definition of 'design'. Does this mean that how a product 'feels' as well as how it 'looks' is protectable? Or does the concept of 'appearance' imply that protection is only for design features that can be perceived visually?

8.25   Although there was some suggestion in the Commission's 1991 Green Paper on designs that the concept of design should include aspects of design perceived by the various human senses such as touch as well as sight,[10] the argument that the concept of 'appearance' in the legislation as finally enacted concentrates only on what can be seen is supported by various aspects of the Designs Directive and Community Design Regulation, including:

- the ordinary meaning of the word 'appearance', not only in English but also in the versions found in the other language versions of the Designs Directive and Community Design Regulation;

---

[9] See further A Kur, 'The Green Paper's "Design Approach"—what's wrong with it?' [1993] EIPR 374–378 and G Dinwoodie, 'Federalized Functionalism: The Future of Design Protection in the European Union' (1996) 24 AIPLA QJ 611.

[10] Green Paper on the legal protection of industrial design, European Commission, June 1991, III/F/5131/91-EN, paras 5.4.7.1 and 5.4.7.2.

- the reference in recital 11 of the Designs Directive to registration conferring protection upon design features shown *visibly* in an application; and

- the reference in recital 13 of the Designs Directive and recital 14 of the Community Design Regulation, on the assessment of a design's individual character, to 'the overall impression produced on an informed user *viewing* the design'.

As a practical matter, texture and material are also at least to some extent discernible to the eye. In any event, it has now been emphasised by the General Court and the Advocate General that registered design protection under the Designs Directive and Community Design Regulation is concerned with *visual appearance* only. In his Opinion in *PepsiCo, Inc v Grupo Promer Mon Graphic SA*, the Advocate General stated that:

> the protection of designs under the Regulation takes into account only the *visual* impression which the designs produce on the informed user.[11]

In his view, this reading of the Regulation had been 'convincingly demonstrated' by the General Court in its decision in the *Grupo Promer* case.[12] The UK courts have taken the same view. In *Gimex International Groupe Import Export v Chill Bag Co Ltd and Others* (Patents County Court, England & Wales), Judge Birss QC considered the reference to 'materials' in the definition of 'design' at Article 3(a) of the Community Design Regulation. He noted:

> it bears emphasising that Community design law is concerned with the *visual* appearance of products. The materials can only be relevant insofar as they influence the appearance of a product (emphasis added).[13]

 Exercise

Are there any arguments which you can think of to counter the view that, as a matter of principle, design laws should be solely concerned with what can be seen? Can you think of any examples where 'feel' is an important element in product design? In your view, should that element be protectable and, if so, how would you have formulated the definition of what is capable protection as a 'design'?

8.26 In general, the interpretation of 'appearance' as being about what can be seen does not mean that the features in question must at all times be visible to the customer or user. Thus, to take some examples from the old UK law, the designs of the interior of chocolate eggs,[14] or for liquid crystal displays only made visible by pressing a button on the machine containing them,[15] or of computer screen icons only visible when the related software is running on the computer,[16] should continue to be capable of being registered as they were under the old UK law. What will be important is that the designs have an 'appearance' in that they are capable of being seen.[17]

---

[11] Case C-281/10 P *PepsiCo, Inc v Grupo Promer Mon Graphic SA*, Opinion of Advocate General Mengozzi, [2012] FSR 5, para AG73 (emphasis in original).

[12] *Grupo Promer* (note 11), Opinion of Advocate General Mengozzi, para AG73. See further General Court, Case T-9/07 *Grupo Promer Mon Graphic SA v Office for Harmonisation in the Internal Market (Trade Marks and Designs) (OHIM) with PepsiCo Inc (Intervener)* [2010] ECDR 7, para 50. This aspect of the General Court's decision was not appealed to the Court of Justice in the *Grupo Promer* case: see further para 8.36.   [13] [2012] ECDR 25, para 25; see also para 58.

[14] *P Ferrero and Co SpA's Application* [1978] RPC 473.   [15] *KK Suwa Seikosha's Design Application* [1982] RPC 166.

[16] *Apple Computer Inc v Design Registry* [2002] FSR 38.

[17] Note, however, the special rules on visibility in normal use, novelty and individual character for component parts of complex products in RDA 1949, ss 1B(8)–(9), DD, Arts 3(3)–(4) and CDR, Arts 4(2)–(3) (see paras 8.73–8.78).

8.27   There is also no need for the design to be of a single fixed or rigid shape for the product; an important point, for example, for clothing, in particular dresses and skirts. The possibility of a design having multiple possible forms of 'appearance' might be important if, for example, a product looks different in use compared to when it is not in use.[18]

 Question

What features of a design are relevant to consideration of its appearance?

Key points about appearance

- Appearance is concerned with what can be *seen* in a product and not, despite the legislation's reference to 'texture or materials', with what can be perceived by other human senses

- This does not mean that the design feature in question has to be visible all the time, but that it has an 'appearance' which is capable of being perceived visually

- There are no requirements that the appearance must be aesthetic or have 'eye-appeal' and the definition of 'design' does not in itself distinguish between functional or aesthetic design features

---

The requirements of novelty and individual character

8.28   In order to be validly registered, a design must be 'new' and have 'individual character'.[19] These are separate and cumulative requirements. The determination of whether a design is new (sometimes also referred to as 'novel') and has individual character is made by way of a comparison with other designs that have been made available to the public before the 'relevant date'. This body of existing designs is sometimes referred to as the 'existing design corpus' or the 'prior art'. For registered designs, the relevant date is the date on which the application for the registration of the design was made or the priority date of that application, where priority is claimed (see para 8.5). As will be seen, the requirements of novelty and individual character impose a higher threshold for designs to meet in order to be protected than the requirement of originality in copyright law. However, the nature of the protection conferred by a registered design is also stronger than the rights conferred by copyright, justifying a more demanding regime.

Novelty

8.29   A design is 'new':

> if no identical design or no design whose features differ only in immaterial details has been made available to the public before the relevant date (RDA 1949, s 1B(2); DD, Art 4; CDR, Art 5).

8.30   To be 'new', therefore, a design must differ from previous designs at least in material details. However, what constitutes a 'material' or an 'immaterial' detail is not defined. Unlike the concept of 'individual

---

[18]   By way of illustration, for an OHIM invalidity decision on bottle carriers, the shape of which varied according to whether or not they were filled with bottles, see *Built NY Inc v I-Feng Kao*, 8 May 2006 (ICD 0000002053) (discussed in more detail at para 8.30).

[19]   RDA 1949, s 1B(1); DD, Art 3(2); CDR, Art 4(1).

character' (see paras 8.32–8.49), the definition of 'novelty' has not yet come before the General Court or Court of Justice for interpretation. The requirement of novelty has also not yet been considered in detail by the UK courts.[20] In the meantime, some guidance on the concept of novelty, and the characterisation of design details as material or immaterial, can be gleaned from examples of case law from the OHIM Invalidity Division and the OHIM Boards of Appeal:

■ **Built NY Inc v I-Feng Kao**, **OHIM Invalidity Division, 8 May 2006 (ICD 0000002053)**[21]

The design of a bottle carrier was registered as Community design no 00387584–0003 (see Figure 8.1). It was argued that this design was not novel in the light of a prior registered Community design no 000359922–0001 (see Figure 8.2). It was held that, while the two designs had many features in common, they also differed in a number of features. For example: the ratio between width and height was about 1:1.3 in the challenged design but around 1:1 in the prior design; the body part in the challenged design encompassed its bottom half and in the prior design its bottom two-thirds; the handle part in the challenged design encompassed its top half and had a trapeze shape whereas in the prior design it encompassed its top third and had a circular shape; and the hole in the handle part had a circular shape in the challenged design and an oval one in the prior design. These were not immaterial differences, so the challenge on novelty failed.

■ **Unistraw Asset Holding Pty Ltd v Felföldi Edesseggyarto Kft (OHIM Third Board of Appeal, Case R 417/2009-3) [2010] ECDR 10**

This dispute concerned an application for invalidation of a registered Community design for 'drinking straws'. The design was for a drinking straw containing a large number of small granules or pellets intended to produce a flavoured drink. It was argued that the registered Community design lacked novelty and individual character in the light of prior designs disclosed in two earlier published international patent applications. On the issue of novelty, the OHIM Third Board of Appeal found that the differences between the features of the contested registered Community design and the earlier designs shown in the patent application drawings did not go beyond immaterial details. Both showed products consisting of

Figure 8.1 Images from Community registered design no 00387584–0003

Source: Page 2, http://oami.europa.eu/pdf/design/invaldec/ICD-000002053-decision-%28EN%29.pdf

 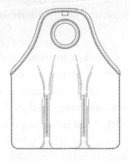 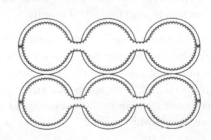

---

[20] In *Gimex* (Patents County Court, England & Wales), note 13, a novelty challenge against the registered Community design in suit failed: paras 101–104. In large part, although pleaded, the challenge was not insisted upon at trial and Judge Birss QC did not therefore have to address novelty in detail. However, he did comment in passing that he considered the design in suit to be novel over certain prior designs not reproduced in the judgment but described at para 106.

[21] A copy of the decision is available at: http://oami.europa.eu/pdf/design/invaldec/ICD-000002053-decision-%28EN%29.pdf.

Figure 8.2 Images from Community registered design no 000359922–0001

Source: Pages 3–4, http://oami.europa.eu/pdf/design/invaldec/ICD-000002053-decision-%28EN%29.pdf

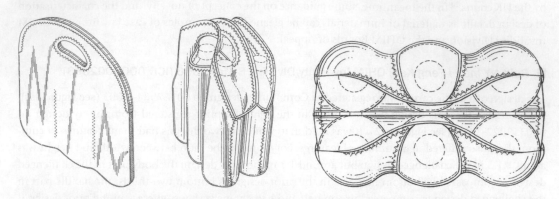

a transparent elongated hollow cylinder with conical filters at either end. The filters had a number of apertures and formed end caps at either end of the cylinder, with roughly spherical granules or pellets being readily discernible within the body of the cylinder itself. The differences between the contested registered Community design and the earlier designs were limited to minor details of the structure and appearance of the end caps and were held to be of no material relevance to the appearance of the products. The registered Community design was held invalid for lack of novelty.

■ *JA Diffusion SARL v Shanghai Creamode Distribution Co, Ltd* (OHIM Third Board of Appeal, Case R 1823/2010-3), 7 November 2011[22]

This dispute concerned a registered Community design for 'sales and display equipment'. The display unit depicted in the design registration had a cylindrical base sitting on five castors. A central column rose out of the base topped by another, slightly tapering, cylindrical unit. Arranged evenly around the central column were rings of hooks, in the form of adjustable and moveable turnstiles, from which items could be hung for display purposes. The novelty of the registered design was challenged on the basis of the alleged import and distribution within Europe of the display units. The evidence showed that, in the units imported and distributed, there were more hooks in each turnstile and that the hooks were more rounded than those shown in the contested registered Community design. However, the OHIM Board of Appeal held that these differences were immaterial and the registered Community design was invalid for lack of novelty.

8.31   As well as the question of what constitutes a material or immaterial design detail, there are also as yet unresolved issues over how to assess novelty—for example, should this be done through the eyes of the 'informed user' as in the assessment of 'individual character' (see paras 8.37–8.40) or on some other basis and, if so, what? The English courts have suggested that the perspective of the 'informed user' is not relevant to the assessment of novelty,[23] but this does not appear to be the view presently taken by OHIM.[24]

---

[22] A copy of the decision including images of the contested and prior designs is available at: http://oami.europa.eu/LegalDocs/BoA/2010/en/R1823_2010-3.pdf.

[23] *Green Lane Products Ltd v PMS International Group Ltd* [2008] FSR 28 (CA), in which Jacob LJ observed that the informed user 'plays no part' in the assessment of novelty: para 41.

[24] See OHIM's Manual on 'Examination of Design Invalidity Applications' (available at: http://oami.europa.eu/ows/rw/resource/documents/RCD/guidelines/manual/design_invalidity_manual.pdf), section C.5.2.2 (p 35).

Discussion point   For answer guidance visit www.oxfordtextbooks.co.uk/orc/waelde3e/

In the old UK design law case of *Vlisco BV's Application* [1980] RPC 509, concerning a design applied to textile goods, it was held that a simple reduction in size compared to previous designs was an immaterial difference. Do you think this approach would be applicable under the Designs Directive/Community Design Regulation? Is the increasingly small size of, for example, mobile phones, palmtop computers, and headsets for personal music players an immaterial difference in their design or not?

Key points on novelty

- To be validly registered, a design must be 'new'
- A design is 'new' if it is not identical to any previous design and differs from such designs in more than immaterial details

Individual character

8.32   A design will have 'individual character' if:

> the overall impression it produces on the informed user differs from the overall impression produced on such a user by any design which has been made available to the public before the relevant date (RDA 1949, s 1B(3); DD, Art 5(1); CDR, Art 6(1)).

In assessing the extent to which a design has individual character:

> the degree of freedom of the author in creating the design shall be taken into consideration (RDA 1949, s 1B(4); DD, Art 5(2); CDR, Art 6(2)).[25]

The recitals to the Designs Directive and Community Design Regulation add:

> The assessment as to whether a design has individual character should be based on whether the overall impression produced on an informed user viewing the design clearly differs from that produced on him by the existing design corpus, taking into consideration the nature of the product to which the design is applied or in which it is incorporated, and in particular the industrial sector to which it belongs and the degree of freedom of the designer in developing the design (DD, recital 13; CDR, recital 14).

Question

What factors must be considered according to the legislation in assessing the 'individual character' of a design?

8.33   Assessment of individual character is a more complex exercise than assessment of novelty. The concepts of 'individual character', 'overall impression', the 'informed user' and 'design freedom' were all new to the Designs Directive and Community Design Regulation and are a key part of the new 'design approach' underlying these legislative instruments. These expressions are, however, not defined. Unsurprisingly

---

[25] RDA 1949, s 1B(4) uses the expression 'author' as this is the term used in the RDA 1949 in relation to first ownership (see RDA 1949, s 2; see also para 8.92). However, the DD and CDR both refer to the 'degree of freedom of the *designer*' (DD, Art 5(2); CDR, Art 6(2)). This terminology, referring to the 'degree of freedom of the designer', is more widely used, including in UK case law, and will be used in this chapter.

given the importance of the requirement of individual character in the overall process of determining validity, the interpretation and application of these concepts have received much more by way of recent judicial attention from the General Court, Court of Justice, and higher courts in the UK.

8.34   It should be noted that the scope of protection against infringement conferred upon a design by the European regime is also dependent on the concept of 'overall impression': a protected design will be infringed by any design which does not produce on the informed user a different overall impression (see para 8.111).[26] The degree of freedom of the designer in developing the design is also to be taken into consideration in assessing the scope of protection against infringement.[27] The assessment of whether a design produces the same or a different 'overall impression' on the 'informed user' should be the same in the context of both validity and infringement. It is therefore possible to draw from validity case law in infringement cases and vice versa when dealing with 'overall impression' and related concepts, and we shall do so in this section of the chapter.

8.35   The interpretation and application of the concepts of 'individual character', 'overall impression', the 'informed user', and 'design freedom' have now been addressed in, among other cases, a series of decisions of the General Court and, in one case, an appeal from the General Court to the Court of Justice. These concepts have also been addressed in three major UK infringement cases which have reached the English Court of Appeal. This section will look first at the key cases before the General Court and Court of Justice, before turning to the leading UK case law.

General Court and Court of Justice case law

8.36   The main developments can be found in the judgments from two key appeals from OHIM to the General Court and in one of these, the *Grupo Promer* case, from the General Court to the Court of Justice:[28]

■ *PepsiCo, Inc v Grupo Promer Mon Graphic SA*, General Court, Case T-9/07 [2010] ECDR 7; Court of Justice, Case C-281/10 P [2012] FSR 5

This case concerned an invalidity challenge to a registered Community design for products described by the registrant as 'promotional items for games'. These were small round discs, more commonly known as 'pogs', 'rappers' or 'tazos'. These are often distributed as free gifts for children inside the packaging of other products. The OHIM Third Board of Appeal had dismissed the challenge to validity based on conflict with an earlier design belonging to the challenger, Grupo Promer (see Figures 8.3 and 8.4). The General Court found that the registered Community design was invalid for lack of individual character. The case was appealed to the Court of Justice which upheld the General Court's ruling.

---

[26] RDA 1949, s 7(1); DD, Art 9(1); CDR, Art 10(1).

[27] RDA 1949, s 7(3); DD, Art 9(2); CDR, Art 10(2). The English courts have also looked to DD, recital 13 and CDR, recital 14 for guidance in the context of infringement case law. Eg: *Procter & Gamble Co v Reckitt Benckiser (UK) Ltd* (CA) [2008] FSR 8, paras 15–19; *Dyson Ltd v Vax Ltd* (HC) [2010] ECDR 18, paras 39 and 44–45 and (CA) [2012] FSR 4, para 34; *Samsung Electronics (UK) Ltd v Apple, Inc* (HC) [2013] ECDR 1, para 48.

[28] The General Court has also considered individual character/overall impression in a number of further appeals from the OHIM Boards of Appeal. In terms of interpretation of the key legal concepts on individual character/overall impression, these cases essentially repeat the key aspects of the rulings in the two cases, *Grupo Promer* and *Shenzhen*, discussed in this chapter. For a regularly updated list of General Court decisions maintained by OHIM, see: http://oami.europa.eu/ows/rw/pages/RCD/caseLaw/appealsOffice.en.do.

Figure 8.3 PepsiCo Community registered design no 74463-0001

Source: Para 10, http://oami.europa.eu/ows/rw/resource/documents/RCD/case-law/jj100281_2_en.pdf

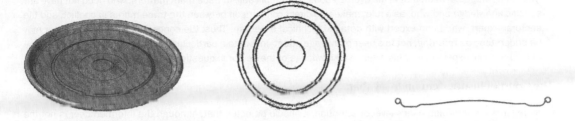

Figure 8.4 Grupo Promer Community registered design no 53186-0001

Source: Para 12, http://oami.europa.eu/ows/rw/resource/documents/RCD/case-law/jj100281_2_en.pdf

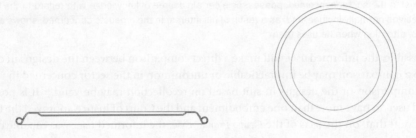

■ *Shenzhen Taiden Industrial Co Ltd v Office for Harmonisation in the Internal Market (Trade Marks and Designs) (OHIM), Bosch Security Systems BV*, General Court, Case T-153/08, 22 June 2010 (currently unreported)[29]

This dispute concerned a registered Community design for units to be used by speakers at conferences. The design was challenged for lack of individual character in the light of an earlier registered design and documentary evidence of the advertisement for sale of units made to that design. The designs in question had a similar overall shape and number of similar features including speakers, a microphone on a stem, control buttons and screen. This judgment of the General Court post-dates its own earlier decision in *Grupo Promer* but predates the decision of the Court of Justice in the *Grupo Promer* case. In *Shenzhen*, the registered Community design was found by the General Court to be invalid for lack of individual character.

In the *Grupo Promer* and *Shenzhen* cases, the General Court and Court of Justice have elaborated on a number of important concepts:

The 'informed user'

8.37   As noted previously, whether a design has individual character depends on whether it produces a different overall impression upon the 'informed user' compared to earlier designs. The 'informed user' is the first of a number of notional legal persons which we will encounter during the course of this book, others being the 'average consumer' of registered trade mark law (see para 15.58) and the 'skilled man' of patent law (see paras 11.117–11.119). The UK IPO, OHIM and the courts have to adopt the perspective of the 'informed user' when assessing the overall impression produced by a design. However, the concept of the 'informed user' is not defined in the Designs Directive or Community Design Regulation.

---

[29] A copy of the decision of the General Court, including images of the contested registered Community design and evidence of prior designs relied upon is available at: http://oami.europa.eu/ows/rw/resource/documents/CTM/case-law/jj080153_en.pdf.

8.38 The 'informed user' was the main focus of the judgment of the Court of Justice in the *Grupo Promer* case. The Court of Justice held that the 'informed user' was a concept which must be understood as:

> lying somewhere between that of the average consumer, applicable in trade mark matters, who need not have any specific knowledge and who, as a rule, makes no direct comparison between the trade marks in conflict, and the sectoral expert, who is an expert with detailed technical expertise. Thus, the concept of the informed user may be understood as referring, not to a user of average attention, but to a particularly observant one, either because of his personal experience or his extensive knowledge of the sector in question.[30]

The Court of Justice went on to say that:

> as regards the informed user's level of attention, it should be noted that, although the informed user is not the well-informed and reasonably observant and circumspect average consumer who normally perceives a design as a whole and does not proceed to analyse its various details..., he is also not an expert or specialist capable of observing in detail the minimal differences that may exist between the designs in conflict. Thus, the qualifier 'informed' suggests that, without being a designer or a technical expert, the user knows the various designs which exist in the sector concerned, possesses a certain degree of knowledge with regard to the features which those designs normally include, and, as a result of his interest in the products concerned, shows a relatively high degree of attention when he uses them.[31]

8.39 Where possible, the informed user will make a direct comparison between the designs in dispute; however, such a comparison may be impracticable or uncommon in the sector concerned in which case an indirect comparison of the designs in suit based on recollection may be valid.[32] It is possible for the 'informed user' to have more than one embodiment and the Court of Justice approved the finding of the General Court that, on the facts of the *Grupo Promer* case, the informed user was capable of being both a child in the approximate age range of 5 to 10 or a marketing manager in a company that made goods promoted by giving away 'pogs', 'rappers', or 'tazos'.[33]

8.40 In *Shenzhen*, the General Court also elaborated upon the level of technical expertise of the informed user. The General Court emphasised that 'the status of "user" implies that the person concerned uses the product in which the design is incorporated, in accordance with the purpose for which that product is intended'.[34] The General Court added that although the qualifier 'informed' suggests that the user knows the various designs which exist in the sector concerned, possesses a certain degree of knowledge with regard to their normal features and shows a relatively high degree of attention when using them:

> that factor does not imply that the informed user is able to distinguish, beyond the experience gained by using the product concerned, the aspects of the appearance of the product which are dictated by the product's technical function from those which are arbitrary.[35]

On the facts of *Shenzhen*, the General Court agreed with the OHIM Board of Appeal's characterisation of the informed user as 'anyone who regularly attends conferences or formal meetings at which the various participants have a conference unit with a microphone on the table in front of them'.[36]

---

[30] Case C-281/10 P *PepsiCo, Inc v Grupo Promer Mon Graphic SA*, Court of Justice, [2012] FSR 5, para 53.

[31] *Grupo Promer*, note 30, para 59.   [32] *Grupo Promer*, note 30, paras 55–57.

[33] *Grupo Promer*, note 30, para 54. In *Sphere Time v OHIM and Punch SAS* (Case T-68/10, 14 June 2011, currently unreported), the General Court held that, in cases in which there may be multiple embodiments of the informed user, it is sufficient for a finding of lack of individual character that only one of the relevant categories of informed user perceives the designs in suit as producing the same overall impression: para 56.

[34] *Shenzhen Taiden Industrial Co Ltd v Office for Harmonisation in the Internal Market (Trade Marks and Designs) (OHIM), Bosch Security Systems BV* (Case T-153/08, 22 June 2010, currently unreported), para 46.

[35] *Shenzhen*, note 34, paras 48–49.

[36] *Shenzhen*, note 34, paras 49–50. For some illustrative further examples of the 'informed user', see also the UK cases discussed at paras 8.47–8.48.

The degree of freedom of the designer

8.41 This was discussed at some length by the General Court in the *Grupo Promer* case.[37] The General Court explained that:

> the designer's degree of freedom in developing his design is established, *inter alia*, by the constraints of the features imposed by the technical function of the product or an element thereof, or by statutory requirements applicable to the product. Those constraints result in a standardisation of certain features, which will thus be common to the designs applied to the product concerned.[38]

On the facts of the case, the designer's design freedom was 'severely constrained' by the need for the product to fit the paradigm of a small, flat or nearly flat disc made of plastic or metal often slightly curved towards the centre so that it made a noise if the centre of the disc was pressed by a child, a design not possessing these characteristics being unlikely to be accepted by the marketplace; design freedom was also constrained by the need for the product to be inexpensive, safe for children and fit to be added to the products which it promoted.[39] Although not explicitly commented upon, these factual findings on design freedom seem to widen the scope of relevant constraints further from just the technical and statutory matters explicitly identified as relevant by the Court in the passage quoted immediately above. This was not addressed by the Court of Justice in the *Grupo Promer* appeal, but has been the subject of some discussion in the English courts (see para 8.48).[40]

8.42 In *Grupo Promer*, the General Court also explained how to take design freedom into account as part of the assessment of overall impression. It held that:

> in so far as similarities between the designs at issue relate to common features such as those described... above, those similarities will have only minor importance in the overall impression produced by those designs on the informed user. In addition, the more the designer's freedom in developing the design is restricted, the more likely minor differences between the designs at issue will be sufficient to produce a different overall impression on the informed user.[41]

In other words, similarities between designs which relate to common features dictated by design constraints will have only minor importance in the overall impression produced by the designs on the informed user, the informed user being more affected by those aspects of the designs which are not subject to design constraints. As the Advocate General explained in the in *Grupo Promer* appeal to the Court of Justice:

> The need to take account of the designer's creative freedom arises because some features of the product to which the design relates are, so to speak, 'compulsory': as a result, the designer is not free to change them and the fact that they bear similarities to the features of another design cannot be regarded as significant.[42]

However, the greater the restrictions on the designer's freedom in developing the contested design, the more it is likely that minor differences in the unconstrained aspects of the design will be enough to produce a different overall impression on the informed user.

8.43 Design freedom was also considered by the General Court in *Shenzhen*. In that case, the General Court accepted that design freedom was restricted insofar as certain features, such as a speaker and microphone,

---

[37] This aspect of the General Court's decision was unaffected by the appeal to the Court of Justice. See *Grupo Promer*, note 30, paras 39–46.

[38] *Grupo Promer Mon Graphic SA v Office for Harmonisation in the Internal Market (Trade Marks and Designs) (OHIM) with PepsiCo Inc (Intervener)*, General Court (Case T-9/07) [2010] ECDR 7, para 67.

[39] *Grupo Promer*, note 38, paras 68–70.

[40] The Advocate General in *Grupo Promer* expressed the view that design freedom should only be impacted by constraints of a strictly functional nature: *Grupo Promer*, note 30, para AG31.

[41] *Grupo Promer*, note 38, para 72.   [42] *Grupo Promer*, note 30, para AG29. See further paras AG28–32.

control buttons, and screen, were necessary in a conference unit, but held that that only concerned the presence of such features in the unit and did not have a significant impact on how those features were actually configured or on the specific form or appearance of the unit itself.[43] Evidence of design freedom could be found in the evidence of varying designs in the existing design corpus.[44] On the facts, the Court found that the degree of design freedom for conference units was relatively wide.[45] General trends in design were not relevant.[46]

Overall impression produced on the informed user

8.44   As emphasised by the General Court in *Shenzhen*, the individual character of a design is not assessed by looking at an amalgam of selected features of a number of different earlier designs. Instead, the comparison must be conducted on a design-by-design basis, comparing the overall impression produced by the registered design against the overall impression produced, in turn, by each individual earlier design relied on in support of the allegation of invalidity.[47]

8.45   The General Court's assessment of overall impression in the *Grupo Promer* case illustrates how this exercise involves a process of evaluating the visual significance to be attached to the different features of the designs in suit and assessing the relative significance of those features to form a view of the overall impression produced on the informed user. In *Grupo Promer*, the General Court examined the similarities and differences between the designs in suit. The General Court held that the fact that both designs were for small, almost flat, discs and had a rounded edge would not attract the informed user's attention because of design constraints; however, the inner concentric circle present in both designs, the raising of the rounded edges of both discs in relation to the intermediate area of the disc between the edge and the raised central area and the common respective dimensions of the central and intermediate parts of both discs were not dictated by design constraints and would attract the attention of the informed user.[48] The General Court concluded that any differences in the two designs were insufficient for the registered Community design to produce a different overall impression and that the registered Community design in dispute was invalid for lack of individual character.[49] A similar approach to analysing overall impression was taken in *Shenzhen*.[50]

UK case law

8.46   The most important UK case law on 'overall impression' is to be found in three infringement cases which have reached the English Court of Appeal. As noted previously (see para 8.34), the principles developed in relation to the assessment of overall impression should be equally applicable to infringement and validity cases; so, although these were infringement disputes, these cases are of considerable importance to this discussion of individual character and will be discussed here.

8.47   The first decision of the English Court of Appeal under the new European regime, *Procter & Gamble Co v Reckitt Benckiser (UK) Ltd*, was decided before the judgments of the General Court and Court of Justice discussed

---

43   *Shenzhen*, note 34, paras 53–54.   44   *Shenzhen*, note 34, para 55.
45   *Shenzhen*, note 34, para 62.   46   *Shenzhen*, note 34, para 58.
47   *Shenzhen*, note 34, paras 23–24.   48   *Grupo Promer*, note 38, paras 76–82.
49   *Grupo Promer*, note 38, paras 83–85. The General Court's findings on this issue were unaffected by the appeal to the Court of Justice: *Grupo Promer*, note 30, paras 76–82.
50   In *Shenzhen*, the Court held that the overall impression produced by the disputed registered Community design and the earlier designs relied upon was determined, among other features, by the shape of the bodies of the units and their hinged rectangular speakers, the panel bearing buttons and screens covered by the hinged speakers when folded down and the hinged stem microphone located on the left-hand side of the units. Other features played a less important or no role at all in assessment of the overall impression produced by the designs. The Court concluded that the disputed and earlier designs produced the same overall impression on the informed user: note 34, paras 63–75.

previously. Although helpful in its development of the law on 'overall impression' in a number of respects (but not on all matters—see the discussion immediately following and, further, on an issue pertaining specifically to infringement, para 8.111), it was also criticised for its approach to some of the key issues in suit:

■ *Procter & Gamble Co v Reckitt Benckiser (UK) Ltd* [2008] FSR 8 (CA)

The competing designs were for air freshener spray canisters. Images of the registered Community design and the alleged infringement, said by the claimant to produce the same overall impression, are shown at Figures 8.5 and 8.6.

At first instance, Lewison J had found that the designs did produce the same overall impression on the informed user. However, on appeal the Court of Appeal disagreed. The Court of Appeal's comments on the informed user (paras 15–32) and overall impression test (paras 33–35) did not have the benefit of the guidance from the General Court and Court of Justice discussed previously and should, therefore, be read subject to these more recent developments and the more recent UK case law discussed immediately following. The manner in which the Court of Appeal approached the actual comparison of the overall impressions produced by the two designs on the facts was also criticised in a number of respects, not least for its apparent reliance on matters such as how the two devices would feel when being held by the informed user.[51] However, the Court of Appeal nonetheless identified a number of helpful points of principle on design freedom and on the relationship between the scope of protection (and, thus, what constitutes the design's overall impression) and the prior design corpus which, it is suggested, remain correct and relevant. Jacob LJ observed, in particular, that:

- the 'degree of freedom of the designer' to be taken into account in assessing overall impression is an objective concept, not defined by the actual constraints specifically acting upon any particular party (para 31);
- a registered design which marks a large departure from the existing design corpus is indicative of a wide degree of design freedom (para 57); and
- protection for a strikingly novel product will be greater than for a product which is only incrementally different from the prior art; its overall impression will be 'more significant' leading to a greater potential for differences in other designs still to result in the same overall impression (para 35(iii)).

Figure 8.5 Images from Procter & Gamble Community registered design no 000097969-0001

Source: Para 4, http://www.bailii.org/ew/cases/EWCA/Civ/2007/936.html

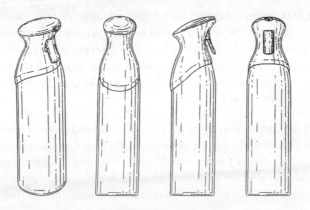

[51] See A Carboni, 'Design validity and infringement: feel the difference' [2008] EIPR 111–117 and D Stone, 'Some clarity, some confusion: 12 *P&G v Reckitt Benckiser* decisions help explain Community designs' (2008) 3(6) JIPLP 376–385.

Figure 8.6 Images of the alleged infringement in *Procter & Gamble Co v Reckitt Benckiser (UK) Ltd* [2008] FSR 8

Source: Para 19, http://www.bailii.org/ew/cases/EWCA/Civ/2007/936.html

These particular points of principle have continued to be applied in the more recent UK case law to which we now turn.

8.48   The guidance given by the General Court and Court of Justice in *Grupo Promer* and *Shenzhen* has been instrumental in the two more recent leading UK cases, *Dyson Ltd v Vax Ltd and Samsung Electronics (UK) Ltd v Apple Inc*. The two cases show an ongoing evolution in term of the sophistication and complexity of analysis of overall impression engaged in by the UK courts, as well as highlighting a number of legal questions which are unresolved at the time of writing:

■ **Dyson Ltd v Vax Ltd [2010] ECDR 18 (HC); [2012] FSR 4 (CA)**

Dyson was proprietor of a UK registered design for a bagless cyclonic vacuum cleaner. Vax was alleged to have infringed Dyson's registration by selling its own bagless cyclonic vacuum called the 'Mach Zen'. Although Dyson's registration predated the Designs Directive, the claim fell to be decided under the new regime and the key question was, therefore, whether the 'Mach Zen' produced the same overall impression on the informed user. Images from Dyson's UK design registration and corresponding views of the 'Mach Zen' are shown at Figures 8.7 and 8.8.

By the time of the first instance decision in *Dyson* the General Court had given judgment in *Grupo Promer* and *Shenzhen* and Arnold J adopted the key aspects of these decisions in dealing with the *Dyson* case.[52] Arnold J held that evidence of design freedom could come not only from the earlier design corpus, but also from designs produced after the registered design if, for example, they showed a wide variety of different designs.[53] However, in this case there were various constraints on design freedom which

---

[52] The Court of Justice had not given its judgment in *Grupo Promer* at the time.
[53] *Dyson* (HC) [2010] ECDR 18, para 37.

Figure 8.7 Images from Dyson's UK design registration no 2,043,779

Source: Annex 1, http://www.bailii.org/ew/cases/EWCA/Civ/2011/1206.html

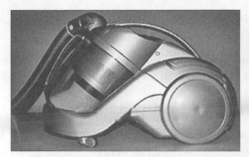 

Figure 8.8 Images of the alleged infringement in *Dyson Ltd v Vax Ltd* [2012] FSR 4

Source: Annex 2, http://www.bailii.org/ew/cases/EWCA/Civ/2011/1206.html

he accepted could be relevant to the assessment of overall impression including matters of technical functionality, the need to incorporate features common to the relevant products, economic considerations (eg price) and technical specification (eg whether the designs were for higher or lower performance products).[54] Moreover, whereas a design which was markedly different from what had gone before should normally have a wider scope of protection (as held in *Procter & Gamble*, see para 8.47), that would not be the case where the striking elements of the design were, in fact, ones where there was little design freedom because of technical constraints—this might be the case, for example, where a new design reflected new technology which also carried with it new technical requirements which had not been relevant to earlier designs.[55]

On the facts, Arnold J held that the 'informed user' was a 'knowledgeable user of domestic vacuum cleaners'.[56] In comparing the registered design and the alleged infringement, the judge considered a number of different design features including: their transparent bins; the angle at which the bins were inclined; the oversized design of the rear wheels and their spacing; and the wheel arches, operational buttons, and pedals. Although there were similarities between the designs, the judge concluded that many of these features were subject to design constraints and that the informed user would not therefore consider the similarities to be particularly significant. There were also a number of visual

[54] *Dyson* (HC), note 53, paras 33–34 and 61–62.   [55] *Dyson* (HC), note 53, paras 40–41.   [56] *Dyson* (HC), note 53, para 50.

differences between Dyson's design and the Mach Zen. The judge held that, 'standing back from the details' (para 92), Dyson's registered design and the Mach Zen produced different overall impressions. He noted also that:

> The overall impression produced by the Registered Design is smooth, curving and elegant. The overall impression produced by the Mach Zen is rugged, angular and industrial, even somewhat brutal (para 93).

Other than in relation to one point on design freedom,[57] the Court of Appeal agreed with this assessment and upheld the finding that the two designs produced different overall impressions.[58]

■ *Samsung Electronics (UK) Ltd v Apple, Inc* [2013] ECDR 1 (HC); [2013] ECDR 2 (CA)

This was the first full trial decision arising from a number of infringement claims brought by Apple in jurisdictions across Europe relation to the design of various Samsung tablet devices. Apple argued that these devices produced the same overall impression as one of its registered Community designs. Images from Apple's registered Community design and of the contested Samsung devices are available online by following the links below.

By the time of the first instance judgment, as well as the General Court decisions in *Grupo Promer* and *Shenzhen*, the Court of Justice had also given its ruling in *Grupo Promer* (see paras 8.38–8.39) on the characteristics of the informed user. Judge Birss QC applied the guidance from this body of decisions to the facts of the case.[59] He held that the informed user was a 'user of handheld (tablet) computers'.[60] He also endorsed the ruling of Arnold J in *Dyson v Vax* on the potential limiting effect of design constraints on the overall impression produced by otherwise strikingly new designs, although in *Samsung* there was some disagreement (not resolved) between the parties as to whether relevant constraints on design freedom should encompass factors other than technical ones as had been held in *Dyson*.[61]

Scan this QR code to access Apple's community design registration as well as images of the disputed Samsung devices.

Annexes A and B at
http://www.bailii.org/ew/cases/EWHC/Patents/2012/1882%28image21%29.pdf

The judge explained that, once the informed user and existing design corpus had been identified, although the case turned on 'overall impression', as a practical matter the design should be broken down into features. Each feature needed to be considered in order to give it appropriate significance or weight. Features dictated solely by technical function (see paras 8.62–8.68) should be disregarded. The remaining features should then be considered against the design corpus and from the point of view of design

---

[57] *Dyson* (CA) [2012] FSR 4. The Court of Appeal held that the assessment of design freedom should have related only to features of the registered design, not features of the 'Mach Zen' as had been the approach of the judge at first instance. However, as Arnold J's approach had had no bearing on the actual outcome of the case, this point did not affect his overall judgment: CA, paras 18–20. It remains to be seen how the UK courts would approach this issue in cases where the alleged infringement took the form of a completely different product which was subject to entirely different constraints.

[58] *Dyson* (CA), note 57, paras 21–33.   [59] *Samsung* (HC) [2013] ECDR 1, paras 33–35.   [60] *Samsung* (HC), note 59, para 66.

[61] On the facts in *Samsung*, Judge Birss QC held that it was not necessary to decide this issue: *Samsung* (HC), note 59, paras 40–41. On scope of protection and design freedom, see also paras 48–49.

 Scan this QR code to access to the judgment in *Samsung Electronics (UK) Ltd v Apple, Inc* [2013].

http://www.bailii.org/cgi-bin/markup.cgi?doc=/ew/cases/EWHC/
Patents/2012/1882.html&query=apple+and+samsung&method=boolean

freedom. Differences between the design and the alleged infringement also needed to be addressed and weighted. The aim of this exercise is to assess the significance of these matters to the informed user, so as to allow the court to decide whether the registered design and alleged infringement produce the same overall impression.[62] Judge Birss QC also commented as follows:

> How similar does the alleged infringement have to be to infringe? Community design rights are not simply concerned with anti-counterfeiting. One could imagine a design registration system which was intended only to allow for protection against counterfeits. In that system only identical or nearly identical products would infringe. The test of 'different overall impression' is clearly wider than that. The scope of protection of a Community registered design clearly can include products which can be distinguished to some degree from the registration. On the other hand the fact that the informed user is particularly observant and the fact that designs will often be considered side by side are both clearly intended to narrow the scope of design protection. Although no doubt minute scrutiny by the informed user is not the right approach, attention to detail matters.[63]

Specific features of Apple's registered Community design and the alleged infringements which were compared included: their overall form as rectangular biaxially symmetrical slabs, with four evenly and slightly rounded corners; flat unornamented transparent front surfaces; very thin rim; rectangular display screens; rear surfaces; thin profiles; and overall 'extreme simplicity' of design without features which specified orientation (paras 92–175). Ultimately, although the view of the front of Samsung's devices was 'very, very similar' to the Apple design (para 184), the judge held that the significance of that similarity was reduced in the eyes of the informed user because of a body of prior designs which appeared to form a 'family' of which both the Apple design and Samsung devices were part (para 189). As a result, the overall significance of that similarity was 'much reduced' and the informed user's attention to differences at the back and sides of the designs 'enhanced considerably' (para 189). The different degrees of thinness of the devices and the differences in detailing present on the back of the designs were 'major differences' (paras 185 and 190). It was held that there was no infringement, the judge concluding that Samsung's products:

> do not have the same understated and extreme simplicity which is possessed by the Apple design. They are not as cool. The overall impression produced is different (para 190).

This conclusion was upheld on appeal.[64]

8.49   The *Samsung* case highlights the importance of conducting the comparison of overall impression in context in the light of the full existing design corpus. On the facts of the case, the relevant design corpus included a range of different designs, including designs for products which were not computers

---

[62] *Samsung* (HC), note 59, paras 53–56.   [63] *Samsung* (HC), note 59, para 58.
[64] *Samsung* (CA) [2013] ECDR 2, paras 7–54.

(such as a child's 'Etch-A-Sketch' toy) and which had never been marketed as such (such as a display device from the film *2001: A Space Odyssey*). The judge at first instance emphasised that, while having initially been struck by how similar the Apple and Samsung designs were, those similarities did not stand out 'to anything like the same extent' after having examined the prior art and placed himself in the shoes of the informed user.[65] As part of this exercise, the judge had heard detailed evidence from experts on both sides. The English courts have tended to stress that, in designs cases, 'what really matters is what the court can see with its own eyes'.[66] In *Procter & Gamble Co v Reckitt Benckiser (UK) Ltd* Jacob LJ had said of designs cases that the 'place for evidence is very limited indeed. By and large it should be possible to decide a registered design case in a few hours... The evidence of experts, particularly about consumer products, is unlikely to be of much assistance: anyone can point out similarities and differences, though an educated eye can sometimes help a bit. Sometimes there may be a piece of technical evidence which is relevant—e.g. that design freedom is limited by certain constraints. But even so, that is usually more or less self-evident and certainly unlikely to be controversial to the point of a need for cross-examination, still less substantial cross-examination.'[67] While this may remain the case for disputes involving simple designs for basic consumer goods, whether post-*Samsung* this can still be said to be the way in which all designs cases will be resolved remains to be seen.[68]

Key points about 'individual character'

- Individual character is assessed by establishing the overall impression produced by the design compared to that produced by any design made available to the public before the relevant date

- The comparison must be against a specific earlier design, not an amalgam of different design features taken from multiple different designs

- The relevant overall impression in question is that produced on the informed user

- The informed user is more sophisticated than the 'average consumer' of trade mark law, but is not a designer, technical expert or specialist

- Assessment of the overall impression produced by a design on the informed user must take into consideration the nature of the product to which the design is applied or in which it is incorporated, the industrial sector to which it belongs and the degree of freedom of the designer in developing the design

- In assessing design freedom, relevant constraints may include the technical function of the product, statutory requirements and other objectively applicable factors

- In assessing overall impression, design features which are subject to design constraints will have less significance in the eyes of the informed user; the more design freedom is

---

[65] *Samsung* (HC), note 59, para 189.
[66] *Samsung* (HC), note 59, para 31, referring to the observations of Sir Robin Jacob in *Dyson* (CA), note 57, paras 8–9 and in *Procter & Gamble* (CA), paras 3–4 (see para 8.47).
[67] *Procter & Gamble* (CA), para 4 (see para 8.47).
[68] See further D Smyth, '*Samsung v Apple*: how does the judge become an "informed user"?' (2012) 7(11) JIPLP 776–778.

constrained, the more readily small differences between designs will produce a different over-all impression

- The assessment of the significance to the informed user of similarities in overall impression between two designs will also involve comparison of those similarities against the existing design corpus

Discussion point For answer guidance visit www.oxfordtextbooks.co.uk/orc/waelde3e/

Now that you have considered the leading case law as well as the legislative wording, what factors do you think are to be taken into account in assessing a design's 'individual character'?

What designs are 'available to the public'?

8.50 Assessing novelty and individual character is about comparing the design with designs already available to the public before the relevant date (ie the application date or priority date, as appropriate—see para 8.28). Designs have been made available to the public before the relevant date if they have been previously:

- published (following registration or otherwise);
- exhibited;
- used in trade (eg the design has already been applied to a product which is available in the marketplace);
- otherwise disclosed before the relevant date (see for all this RDA 1949, s 1B(5); DD, Art 6(1); CDR, Art 7(1)).

This is very broad and will essentially capture any placing of the earlier design into the public domain. The evidence which may be considered on this matter can be widely varied: the OHIM Invalidity Division has accepted material found as a result of a Google search, for example.[69] But it is important that the evidence be dateable: in some cases material discovered on the Internet the posting of which could not be dated has been dismissed as irrelevant.[70]

Question

Why is the dating of designs important in considering 'availability to the public'?

---

[69] Eg *Leng d'Or SA v Crown Confectionery Co Ltd*, OHIM Invalidity Division (ICD 000000388), 20 September 2005.

[70] Eg *Dryson AB v Birger Olsson*, OHIM Invalidity Division (ICD 0000000982), 17 March 2006 and *Holding C Vlemmix BV v E van Hellenberg Hubar*, OHIM Invalidity Division (ICD 000001303), 23 March 2006. For more on OHIM's practice on material sourced from the Internet, see OHIM's Manual on the 'Examination of Design Invalidity Applications' (available at: http://oami.europa.eu/ows/rw/resource/documents/RCD/guidelines/manual/design_invalidity_manual.pdf), section C.5.1.4 (pp 29–30).

8.51 In *Gimex International Groupe Import Export v Chill Bag Co Ltd and Others* (Patents County Court, England & Wales),[71] the court considered the question of whether the prior art designs against which novelty and individual character are to be assessed can include designs for products used for different purposes to the registered design. This is one of the many complexities arising from the fact that the Designs Directive and Community Design Regulation protect the design as such, without tying or limiting the protected right to any specific product; as a result, just as the scope of protection conferred by registration encompasses the use of the design on any product (see para 8.116), so too the relevant prior art can also include designs for any kind of product from any sector.

8.52 Building on the English Court of Appeal's analysis of Article 7 of the Community Design Regulation in *Green Lane v PMS* (see para 8.56), in *Gimex* Judge Birss QC confirmed that designs for products used for different purposes to the registered design are relevant prior art which must be taken into account. He held that:

> All prior designs for anything are capable of being relevant.[72]

The judge emphasised that, for a design to be valid, it must be new and have individual character over the whole of the prior art.[73] It makes no difference whether the earlier design against which it is being compared would or would not have been known to the informed user. The informed user is the user of the registered design. If the earlier design was used for a different product/purpose than the registered design, the earlier design may not form part of the informed user's general 'design awareness', but all earlier designs must nonetheless be taken into account as prior designs and assessed by the informed user for the purposes of determining novelty and individual character.[74]

8.53 An earlier disclosure will not count as part of the prior art, meaning that the design for which registration is sought could still be novel or have individual character even if conflicting with the earlier design, if the earlier disclosure:[75]

(1) Could not reasonably have become known in the normal course of business to the circles specialising in the sector concerned operating within the Community.

8.54 This 'safeguard clause' means that novelty and individual character are assessed by comparison with designs which were or could reasonably have become known in the normal course of business to circles specialised in the sector concerned within the Community; thus, for example, a disclosure in another part of the world might not affect novelty or individual character in the European context. This carve-out from the scope of the relevant prior art was introduced into the Designs Directive and Community Design Regulation as a result of lobbying by the textile industry.[76] It marks a significant difference to how the 'prior art' is defined in patent law, where there is no such carve-out and even obscure overseas disclosures are relevant (see paras 11.81–11.82).

 Discussion point For answer guidance visit www.oxfordtextbooks.co.uk/orc/waelde3e/

Who is being 'safeguarded' by this rule?

---

[71] [2012] ECDR 25.   [72] *Gimex*, note 71, para 42; see also para 72.   [73] *Gimex*, note 71, para 45.
[74] *Gimex*, note 71, para 45.   [75] For what follows see RDA 1949, s 1B(6); DD, Art 6; CDR, Art 7.
[76] *Green Lane Products Ltd v PMS International Group Ltd* [2008] FSR 28, paras 64–74.

8.55   There have been some instructive failed attempts to rely on this 'safeguard clause', both in relation to activities conducted in other parts of the world and in relation to the range and nature of industry information within the Community which those specialising in the circles concerned may be expected to know about:

■ *Crocs Inc v Holey Soles Holdings Ltd with Partenaire Hospitalier International* (OHIM Third Board of Appeal, Case R 9/2008-3) [2010] ECDR 11

In this case, the OHIM Third Board of Appeal ruled that a Community registered design for the 'Crocs' shoe lacked novelty in the light of prior sales by Crocs of 10,000 shoes in the United States, display of the 'Crocs' shoe at the Fort Lauderdale International Boat Show and disclosure of the design on the www.crocs.com website. The Board of Appeal held that the argument that these activities could not reasonably have become known in the normal course of business to the circles specialising in the sector concerned operating within the Community was 'not persuasive', commenting that:

> Exhibiting a new product at a fair, uploading it on the Internet and selling it on the marketplace—these activities having been furthermore carried out over a period of several months—are precisely the sort of activities that may become known 'in the course of business' to anybody active in the same field.[77]

■ *Unistraw Asset Holding Pty Ltd v Felföldi Edesseggyarto Kft* (OHIM Third Board of Appeal, Case R 417/2009-3) [2010] ECDR 10

In this case (see para 8.30), the OHIM Third Board of Appeal held that the publication of illustrations of prior designs in two international patent applications could reasonably be expected to have become known in the normal course of business to the circles specialising in the sector concerned within the Community even though the registrant argued that in the relevant industry sector, confectionery, it was unusual for products to be the subject of patent protection. The Board rejected this argument, noting that the two patent applications had been filed by confectionery businesses, and held that it belonged to the normal course of business of a confectionery company in the Community to monitor for such publications as they are relevant to business activities in the Community.[78]

8.56   One of the most difficult questions in interpreting and applying this 'safeguard clause' relates to the scenario in which the relevant prior art comes from within the Community (that is to say, is not 'obscure' on geographic grounds) but stems from an industry sector unrelated to that of the registered design. This scenario has been addressed by the English Court of Appeal in *Green Lane Products Ltd v PMS International Group Ltd*:

■ *Green Lane Products Ltd v PMS International Group Ltd* [2008] FSR 28 (CA)

The products in issue in this case were spiky plastic balls. PMS had imported such balls from China and sold them extensively as massage balls in the EU from 2002. Green Lane sold such balls for use in tumble driers. In August 2004, Green Lane had registered four Community designs for such balls, describing the class of products to which the designs were to be applied as 'flatirons and washing, cleaning and drying equipment'. In 2006, PMS proposed to market their products for other uses as well as massage balls, including as laundry dryer balls. Green Lane argued that PMS would infringe its Community registered designs by use of their balls for anything other than massage balls. PMS contended that Green Lane's registrations were invalid for lack of novelty in the light of PMS's earlier sales of the balls as massage

---

[77] [2010] ECDR 11, para 60.   [78] [2010] ECDR 10, paras 21–24.

balls. Green Lane responded by arguing that the prior uses by PMS 'could not reasonably have become known in the normal course of business to the circles specialised in the sector concerned' and that the 'sector concerned' means the sector for which the design was registered (ie those specialising in tumble drier balls). At first instance, Green Lane's arguments were rejected and it was held that the relevant 'sector concerned' was that consisting of or including the sector of the alleged prior art. This was upheld by the Court of Appeal. Jacob LJ said: 'the right gives a monopoly over any kind of goods according to the design. It makes complete sense that the prior art available for attacking novelty should also extend to all kinds of goods, subject only to the limited exception of prior art obscure even in the sector from which it comes' (para 79). This interpretation reduces the potential application of the 'safeguard clause' carve-out from the prior art very considerably.

> **? Question**
>
> How does the 'safeguard provision' in the Designs Directive and the Community Design Regulation compare to how we define the relevant prior art in patent law? Consider the points made by Jacob LJ about the differences between design and patent laws on this issue in *Green Lane* [2008] FSR 28. What are the pros and cons of the two different approaches?

(2) Was made to a person other than the designer, or any successor in title of his, under explicit or implicit conditions of confidentiality.

8.57   For example, a designer may create a design for a product and show it under conditions of confidentiality to potential manufacturers, potential commercial partners, or for the purposes of research and development; this will not affect the possibility of later registration of the design by the designer.

(3) Was made by the designer, any successor in title of his, or a third person as a result of information provided or action taken by the designer or any successor in title of his during the period of 12 months immediately preceding the relevant date.

8.58   The purpose of this 'grace period' is to enable exhibition or market-testing, on an open and non-confidential basis, of a design before undertaking the costs and process of registration. It will also include accidental public disclosures, where made by the designer or his successor in title in the 12-month period.

8.59   This also gives the proprietor of the design a 12-month window to register his design in cases such as where the designer authorises another party to manufacture a product according to the design and that third party places the design in the public domain in some way.

(4) Was made during the period of 12 months immediately preceding the relevant date as a consequence of an abuse in relation to the designer or any successor in title.

8.60   This might apply, for example, if a third party obtains the design by way of industrial espionage or someone to whom the design has been disclosed in confidence breaks that confidence and publishes the design.

8.61   The 12-month *grace periods* are extremely important. They cover the designer's own non-confidential disclosure by way of publication, exhibition, trade use or other disclosure. But also covered is third party disclosure, whether or not that results from the designer's own activity. However, even if the disclosure is an abuse of the designer's interests by the third party, the designer still has only a grace period of 12 months within which to file his application for registration. It is also important to remember that these grace periods only save the proprietor's design from being invalidated on the basis of the particular act of disclosure referred to in each subsection. The grace period does *not* give a general protection against other relevant disclosures in the 12-month period. So, if a competing design is placed in the public domain in that 12-month period in circumstances not covered by the provisions set out previously, that will be problematic in terms of novelty or individual character.

Key points on designs 'available to the public'

- Relevant earlier designs will be those made available to the public in any way prior to the relevant date (the filing or priority date of the registered design in question)

- This will exclude disclosures which could not reasonably have become known in the normal course of business to circles specialised in the sector concerned operating within the Community

- It will also exclude confidential disclosures and certain public disclosures in the 12-month period before the relevant date, for example if made by the designer or his successor in title or in breach of an obligation of confidentiality

---

 Discussion point   For answer guidance visit www.oxfordtextbooks.co.uk/orc/waelde3e/

Once a design has been disclosed, whether with or without the consent of the designer, what advice would you give the designer with regard to the registration of that design?

Exclusions: functionality

8.62   Rights in registered designs do *not* subsist in:

> features of appearance of a product which are solely dictated by the product's technical function (RDA 1949, s 1C(1); DD, Art 7(1); CDR, Art 8(1)).

Recital 14 of the Designs Directive and recital 10 of the Community Design Regulation explain:

> Technological innovation should not be hampered by granting design protection to features dictated solely by a technical function.

The recitals also make clear, however, that this does not entail that a design must have an aesthetic quality. An underlying policy objective here is that purely technological or technical innovation should be protected by patents, with the innovation required to meet the relatively high standards of patent-law novelty and inventiveness in order to qualify for protection rather than the lower standards of novelty and individual character required of a design. The extent to which this exclusion removes all entitlement to protection for a particular design will depend on whether, once the features dictated by technical function are discounted, the remainder of the design is still entitled to protection because that remainder meets the requirements of novelty, individual character, and so on. So, it may or may not act as a total bar to protection: whether this is the case will depend on the design in question.

 Question

Why are functional designs excluded from protection by registration?

8.63 The functionality exclusion continues what had been a well-established characteristic of previous registered design law in the UK. The old UK law had led, however, to some complex litigation around the meaning of the phrase 'solely dictated'. Two ways of construing this phrase had been considered in pre-harmonisation UK case law. The first way of construing this expression, sometimes called the 'multiplicity-of-forms' approach, provided that even purely functional designs were not excluded from protection as long as that particular design was not the *only* way of achieving the relevant function. The second way of construing this phrase, often called the '*Amp* approach' after the House of Lords decision discussed immediately below, looked not at the question of whether alternative designs could achieve the same function but instead turned on whether the design features in question were there for the purpose of function alone. This was the key pre-harmonisation decision in the UK:

■ *Amp Incorporated v Utilux Proprietary Ltd* [1972] RPC 103 (HL)

The issue in this case, heard under the old version of the RDA 1949, was the registrability of a design for electrical terminals used in washing machines. The terminals were shaped to enable them to make electrical connections. It was held that the design was dictated solely by function, even though it was possible to design the terminal in other ways in which it would still carry out its technical function. 'Dictated solely by function' did not mean that a design was unregistrable only if it was the only one possible design available to achieve the functionality in question, which had been the previous understanding of the old UK law; it meant simply that the features of the design had been adopted only for functional reasons. The features of the terminal were dictated solely by function in this sense.

8.64 The Designs Directive and Community Design Regulation do not indicate what interpretation of the words 'solely dictated by... technical function' is to be preferred. It was initially generally thought that the pre-*Amp* understanding of the law had been restored: that is, a design would be solely dictated by function when it was the *only* possible design by which the product would be able to perform its technical function. The basis of this understanding was the Green Paper of 1991 in which the Commission first proposed to legislate in the field of design protection. The Commission there indicated that because this was the approach of the majority of member states at the time it should be continued in any Europe-wide law on the matter.[79]

 Question

Can you explain the difference between the two possible meanings of 'solely dictated by... technical function'?

8.65 There had also been some contribution to the understanding of the designs law in the Opinion of the Advocate General in a trade marks case before the ECJ, *Philips Electronics NV v Remington Consumer Products Ltd* (see para 14.84).[80] That case concerned the exclusion from trade mark registration of a sign consisting exclusively of 'the shape of goods... necessary to obtain a technical result'.[81] In his Opinion, the Advocate General contrasted the wording of the trade mark exclusion with the exclusion in designs law: 'necessary' in trade mark law, he said, involved a lesser inevitability of relation between shape and function than design law's 'solely dictated'. Accordingly, in his view 'a functional design may... be

---

[79] Green Paper on the legal protection of industrial design, European Commission, June 1991, III/F/5131/91-EN, paras 5.4.6.1–5.4.6.2.
[80] Case C-299/99, [2003] RPC 2. The Advocate General's Opinion is reported at [2001] RPC 38.
[81] Trade Marks Act 1994, s 3(2)(b).

eligible for protection if it can be shown that the same technical function could be achieved by another different form'.[82] However, the ECJ made no comment on the Designs Directive in that case. This 'multiplicity-of-forms' approach to interpretation of the 'functionality' exclusion was also adopted by the English Court of Appeal in the unregistered Community design case of *Landor & Hawa International Ltd v Azure Designs Ltd*.[83]

8.66 However, a difficulty with this interpretation is that, under it, the functionality exclusion may become virtually toothless. There are very few products whose technical function is such that there is only one design which can work. One has only to visit different houses or restaurants and compare the simple everyday objects found there, such as knives, forks, spoons, glasses, and plates, to confirm that commonplace functions can be achieved in a wide variety of different ways. Cornish and Llewelyn also raise a further problem with the 'multiplicity-of-forms' approach: where a technical function can only be achieved by a limited number of designs, if the 'multiplicity-of-forms' approach is adopted all such designs could be subjected to registration (each being valid because of the alternative designs available) possibly by the same owner, thus stopping competitors making products which have the same technical function and thereby undermining the whole purpose of the legislative exclusion.[84]

8.67 Influenced by these concerns, in more recent case law of the OHIM Boards of Appeal and the UK courts, the *Amp* approach (see para 8.63) has now emerged as the preferred interpretation of the Article 7(1)/ Article 8(1) exclusion, in preference to the 'multiplicity-of-forms' approach. In *Lindner Recyclingtech GmbH v Franssons Verkstäder AB* (OHIM Third Board of Appeal, Case R 690/2007-3), after outlining the different approaches and noting the difficulties raised in Cornish and Llewelyn (see para 8.66) the OHIM Third Board of Appeal observed that:

> The approach taken in *Amp Inc v Utilux Pty Ltd* would... have the advantage of allowing the purpose of Art.8(1) CDR to be achieved. No-one would be able to shut out competitors by registering as Community designs the handful of possible configurations that would allow the technical function to be realised.[85]

In the Board's view, adoption of the *Amp* approach is supported both by a teleological (ie purposive) interpretation and by the wording of the exclusion. The Board held that the words used in Article 8(1) of the Regulation:

> do not, on their natural meaning, imply that the feature in question must be the only means by which the product's technical function can be achieved. On the contrary, they imply that the need to achieve the product's technical function was the only relevant factor when the feature in question was selected.[86]

The Board concluded:

> As long as functionality is not the only relevant factor, the design is in principle eligible for protection. It is only when aesthetic considerations are completely irrelevant that the features of the design are solely dictated by the need to achieve a technical solution. This is not, it must be stressed, tantamount to introducing a requirement of aesthetic merit into the legislation. It is simply recognition of the obvious fact that when aesthetics are totally irrelevant, in the sense that no one cares whether the product looks good, bad, ugly or pretty, and all that matters is that the product functions well, there is nothing to protect under the law of designs.
>
> It follows from the above that Art 8(1) CDR denies protection to those features of a product's appearance that were chosen exclusively for the purpose of designing a product that performs its function, as opposed to features that were chosen, at least to some degree, for the purpose of enhancing the product's visual appearance. It goes without saying that these matters must be assessed objectively: it is not necessary to determine what actually

---

[82] [2001] RPC 38, para 34.   [83] [2007] FSR 9 (CA), paras 30–43.
[84] Cornish and Llewelyn, *Intellectual Property: Patents, Copyright, Trade Marks and Allied Rights* (5th edn, 2003), p 549 as cited in *Lindner Recyclingtech GmbH v Franssons Verkstäder AB* (OHIM Third Board of Appeal, Case R 690/2007–3) [2010] ECDR 1, para 30.
[85] [2010] ECDR 1, para 31.   [86] *Lindner*, note 85, para 32.

went on in the designer's mind when the design was being developed. The matter must be assessed from the standpoint of a reasonable observer who looks at the design and asks himself whether anything other than purely functional considerations could have been relevant when a specific feature was chosen.[87]

8.68 Despite the Board of Appeal's protestations to the contrary, the *Lindner* test has been criticised for appearing to reintroduce a requirement of aesthetic character into entitlement to protection under the Designs Directive and Community Design Regulation.[88] After *Lindner*, interpretation of this exclusion from protection came before the UK courts in the English High Court decision of *Dyson Ltd v Vax Ltd*.[89] Although the approach of the Third Board of Appeal in *Lindner* was different to that of the English Court of Appeal in *Landor* (see para 8.65), in *Dyson v Vax* Arnold J held that this aspect of the ruling in *Landor* was *obiter* and, instead, adopted the interpretation of Article 7(1)/Article 8(1) set out in *Lindner*, that is, the *Amp* approach.[90] On the facts of *Dyson v Vax*, it was held that the design feature which had been challenged as excluded from protection—the transparent bin—had been chosen for a mixture of technical and aesthetic reasons and was not dictated solely by technical function. The design of the bin was therefore not excluded from protection.[91] The preference for the *Amp* approach has now also been endorsed by the OHIM Invalidity Division in *ACV Manufacturing NV v AIC SA*,[92] and *obiter* by the English High Court and Court of Appeal in *Samsung Electronics (UK) Ltd v Apple, Inc*.[93] It is, however, not clear that this will necessarily be how the case law may develop in other member states or at an EU level were a case on this exclusion to reach the General Court or Court of Justice.

 Discussion point   For answer guidance visit www.oxfordtextbooks.co.uk/orc/waelde3e/

Would the policy of protecting design primarily through the registration system be better supported by dropping the functionality exclusion altogether?

Exclusions: 'must fit' elements

8.69 The exclusion for design features 'solely dictated by... technical function' is supplemented by a 'must fit'-style exclusion, which is expressed in the following terms:

> A right in a registered design shall not subsist in features of appearance of a product which must necessarily be reproduced in their exact form and dimensions so as to permit the product in which the design is incorporated or to which it is applied to be mechanically connected to, or placed in, around or against, another product so that either product may perform its function (RDA 1949, s 1C(2); DD, Art 7(2); CDR, Art 8(2)).

 Question

What are the key elements in this exclusion? How similar is it to the 'must fit' exclusion in UK unregistered design right discussed in Chapter 9?

8.70 Recital 14 of the Designs Directive and recital 10 of the Community Design Regulation explain that 'the interoperability of products of different makes should not be hindered by extending protection to the

---

[87] *Lindner*, note 85, paras 35–36.
[88] U Suthersanen, *Design Law: European Union and United States of America* (2nd edn, 2010), para 6–015.
[89] *Dyson* (HC), note 53.   [90] *Dyson* (HC), note 53, paras 23–31.
[91] *Dyson* (HC), note 53, para 59. This aspect of Arnold J's decision was not appealed to the Court of Appeal in *Dyson*.
[92] [2012] ECDR 13, para 15.   [93] *Samsung* (HC), note 59, paras 36–38 and (CA), note 64, para 31.

design of mechanical fittings'. A simple example of when this exclusion might operate is the exhaust pipe of a car. An exhaust pipe for a given model of car is a product which must, in large part, be of certain exact dimensions and form to take its place in that model of car—that is, to be mechanically connected to, placed in, around, or against the car. This is needed for either to perform its function: the car cannot run without the exhaust pipe, and the exhaust pipe cannot discharge fumes unless connected to the car. This exclusion would operate to deny protection to those features of the design of the exhaust which necessarily had to take the exact form and dimensions required in order for the exhaust pipe to be mechanically connected to, placed in, around or against the car.

8.71   However, this 'must fit' exclusion from protection does not prevent a right in a registered design subsisting in a design serving the purpose of allowing multiple assembly or connection of mutually interchangeable products within a modular system.[94] Recital 15 of the Designs Directive and recital 11 of the Community Design Regulation offer the explanation that 'the mechanical fittings of modular products may nevertheless constitute an important element of the innovative characteristics of modular products and present a major marketing asset, and therefore should be eligible for protection'. The legislative background clarifies the provision somewhat. During the negotiations and lobbying leading up to the enactment of the Designs Directive, Denmark was anxious to protect the position of the Lego company with regard to its toy bricks, a key feature of which is the interconnecting elements. Other toy manufacturers were supportive, and the provision entered European designs law. Its scope remains unclear.

Key points on the 'must fit' exclusion

- Design protection will not subsist in features of the appearance of a product which must necessarily be reproduced in their exact form and dimensions so as to permit the product in which the design is incorporated or to which it is applied to be mechanically connected to, or placed in, around, or against, another product so that either product may perform its function

- Only those design features which are there for this purpose are excluded under this rule— other parts of the design may be validly registrable if they otherwise meet the criteria of registrability

- This exclusion is subject to an 'exclusion-from-the-exclusion' for designs serving the purpose of allowing multiple assembly or connection of mutually interchangeable products within a modular system, which are capable of registration although the scope of this provision remains unclear

---

Exclusions: public policy and morality

8.72   Rights in a registered design also do not subsist in a:

> design which is contrary to public policy or to accepted principles of morality (RDA 1949, s 1D; DD, Art 8; CDR, Art 9).

What may be contrary to public policy or accepted principles of morality is not spelled out in the legislation, and recital 16 of the Designs Directive is careful to say that 'this Directive does not

---

[94] RDA 1949, s 1C(3); DD, Art 7(3); CDR, Art 8(3).

constitute a harmonisation of national concepts of public policy or accepted principles of morality'. Thus each member state is free to bring to bear its own approach to this exclusion. The pre-Directive law of the UK also contained an exclusion of designs which, in the opinion of the Registrar, would be contrary to law or morality.[95] The limited case law on this provision probably continues to be relevant under the new rule. On the whole, the UK courts take a restrictive approach to the exclusion. For example:

■ *Masterman's Design* [1991] RPC 89 (HC)

This case concerned an application to register the design of a furry doll representing a Highlander-like figure wearing a sporran, the lifting of which revealed his genitalia. An objection on the grounds of immorality was refused, and registration allowed. The test was not whether some section of the public would be offended, but whether the design was of such a nature that its use would offend moral principles of right-thinking members of the public such that it would be wrong for the law to protect it.

 Discussion point   For answer guidance visit www.oxfordtextbooks.co.uk/orc/waelde3e/

Can you think of any immoral designs, or designs contrary to public policy?

Complex products

8.73   As a result of the European legislation, the RDA 1949 (as amended) now contains a rather complicated series of provisions dealing with what are called 'complex products'. A *complex product* is a *product* (see paras 8.18–8.22) which is:

> composed of at least two replaceable component parts permitting disassembly and reassembly of the product (RDA 1949, s 1(3); DD, Art 1(c); CDR, Art 3(c)).

There are special rules for such complex products with regard to novelty, individual character, and visibility in normal use.

 Question

What are the key elements of the definition of a 'complex product'?

8.74   It may be helpful to understanding what follows to have in mind an example of a complex product. A good one is a car. The vehicle's body will be made up of a number of parts—the basic shell, the wings, the doors, the lids of the bonnet and boot, perhaps a spoiler or fins. There will also be the engine, probably a complex product in its own right, as well as necessary attachments such as the fuel and exhaust pipes. There will be fittings—external ones, such as wheels, lights, bumpers and wing mirrors, and internal ones, such as the steering wheel, seats, dashboard and other features. The process of building a car is a process of assembling all the parts, and most if not all of these are replaceable; indeed, whole industries thrive on the business of manufacturing and supplying replacement parts for cars. At the same time, *component parts* can be distinguished from *accessories*. For example, a car

---

[95] Old version of the RDA 1949, s 43(1).

roof box or roof rack is an accessory rather than a component part. So, to draw a contrast, while the component parts of the car would be subject to the special rules described here, a roof box or roof rack would not.

 Discussion point For answer guidance visit www.oxfordtextbooks.co.uk/orc/waelde3e/

Can you give any other examples of complex products?

8.75 A design applied to or incorporated in a product which constitutes a component part of a complex product can only be validly registered if two conditions *over and above* those already stated generally (see para 8.15) are both met:[96]

- Once incorporated in the complex product, the *component part must remain visible* while the complex product is *in normal use*.

- These *visible parts* of the component part *must in themselves be new and have individual character*.

'Normal use' means use by the end user; but this does not include any maintenance, servicing, or repair work.[97]

Key points on the special requirements for component parts of complex products

- Only features of the component part that are visible during normal use of the complex product can be protected through registration, and then only if these visible features have novelty and individual character

- This rule applies *only* to designs for component parts of complex products; the requirement of visibility in normal use does *not* apply to designs generally

8.76 If we take our example of a car, let us consider the position with regard to an exhaust pipe again. We have discussed previously how the 'must fit' exclusion might affect the ability to protect an exhaust pipe through design registration (see para 8.70). The special requirements for component parts of complex products will further impact upon the registrability of an exhaust pipe design. The exhaust pipe is clearly a component part of a complex product. When the complex product—the car—is in normal use (ie being driven along, idling in traffic queues, parked or being unloaded), only a very small part of the exhaust pipe as a component part is visible. The fact that much of the pipe could be seen if its owner or a mechanic went underneath the car to inspect it (whether by lying down on the ground beneath the car, raising it on a lift, or parking it over a service pit) would be irrelevant, because that kind of maintenance or servicing activity is excluded from normal use. Likewise if the exhaust pipe had to be replaced: repair is not normal use either, and the fact that a pipe could be seen in full once removed or that the replacement was also wholly visible during the process would be irrelevant. Only the normally visible parts of the exhaust pipe are capable of entitlement to protection by registered design rights, and it is to these visible parts of the exhaust pipe that the tests of novelty and individual character have to be applied.

---

[96] RDA 1949, s 1B(8); DD, Art 3(3); CDR, Art 4(2).   [97] RDA 1949, s 1B(9); DD, Art 3(4); CDR, Art 4(3).

Probably the average visible part of an exhaust pipe does not qualify as novel or having individual character, but there are some more extravagant examples on the road—the exhaust pipes of some long-distance trucks, for instance—which might come within the scope of protection.

8.77   A good example of this sort of analysis in action can be found in a recent case before the General Court considering the design of internal combustion engines for lawnmowers. In *Kwang Yang Motor Co, Ltd v OHIM and Honda Giken Kogyo Kabushiki Kaisha* (Case T-10/08), the General Court held that the engine was a component part of the lawnmower as the overall 'complex product' into which the engine was incorporated. It was the design of the upper side of the engine only which was visible in normal use and thus only that upper side which was capable of protection, if the requirements of novelty and individual character were met:

> During the normal use of a lawnmower, it is placed on the ground and the user stands behind the lawnmower. Thus, the user, standing behind the lawnmower sees the engine from the top and therefore sees principally the upper side of the engine. It follows that the upper side of the engine determines the overall impression produced by the engine.[98]

8.78   Complications may arise where the design is for a component part which can be used in multiple different products and may be visible in some, but not all, of those different products.[99] Issues may also arise in relation to component parts which are visible some, but not all, of the time in normal use of the complex product. This was considered by the OHIM Third Board of Appeal in *Lindner Recyclingtech GmbH v Franssons Verkstäder AB* (Case R 690/2007-3). The Third Board of Appeal held that Article 4(2)(a) of the Community Design Regulation:

> does not require a component part to be clearly visible in its entirety at every moment of use. It is sufficient if the whole of the component can be seen some of the time in such a way that all of its essential features can be apprehended.[100]

In that case, the rotor element of a shredding machine was considered to remain sufficiently visible in normal use even though the rotor was spinning and largely covered by the material to be shredded: the registrant adduced sufficient evidence that the rotor would, at least to a limited degree, be visible in normal use as it was necessary for it to remain capable of observation during the shredding process.[101]

 Exercise

Discuss how far the following items may be protected as simple products in their own right, or whether they are to be seen as component parts of complex products:

- Roof rack bars
- Bicycle carriers, whether fitted to the roof or rear of a car
- Roof boxes
- Head rests
- Mud flaps
- Spoilers fitted to the car by an owner rather than as part of the original manufacturing and assembly process

---

[98] [2012] ECDR 2, para 22.
[99] See further D Musker, 'Hidden meaning? UK perspectives on invisible in use designs' [2003] EIPR 450–456.
[100] [2010] ECDR 1, para 21.   [101] *Lindner*, note 100, para 19.

Spare parts

Policy question 1: a free market in spare parts

8.79 Taking them together and looking at the issues under debate at the time of the introduction of the Designs Directive and Community Design Regulation, what are the 'complex product' and 'must fit' rules trying to achieve? The essential issue was about replacement or spare parts—components in complex products which could be replaced, either because they were exhausted (eg a spent bulb in a headlight), needed repair (eg an exhaust pipe with a hole in it), or the owner of the product wished to do so (eg replacing a conventional steering wheel with a racing one). There was clearly a significant secondary market in such components, whether because of necessary replacement and repair or otherwise. Should that secondary market be subject to the control of the manufacturers of the complex products, who could then tie in customers if the customer wanted to source a replacement or spare part? Or should designs protection not be available for such replacements and spares, potentially allowing third party providers to provide the same products at a lower price to the consumer?

8.80 The response to these issues produced in the European designs legislation is not a simple one. Complex products have produced complex law.

> **Key points on how the rules on component parts and the 'must fit' exception apply to spare and replacement parts**
>
> - In essence, the law denies protection to:
>   - those features of component parts of complex products that are not visible in normal use, and
>   - the 'must fit' elements of products that must necessarily be reproduced in their exact form and dimensions so as to permit the product in which the design is incorporated or to which it is applied to be mechanically connected to, or placed in, around or against, another product so that either product may perform its function
> - But this does not mean that spare or replacement parts are beyond protection through the registration process
> - Design features which are visible in normal use and which are not subject to the 'must fit' exclusion can enjoy the rights subsisting in a registered design if they meet the requirements of novelty and individual character

Policy question 2: repair or 'must match' parts—the 'freeze/standstill plus'

8.81 A further element in the debate about spare parts leading up to the Designs Directive and Community Design Regulation was a proposed exclusion from protection for what were, at least in the UK, called '*must match*' designs. The name came from the UK legislation on UK unregistered design right, to be discussed in detail in the next chapter. For present purposes, it suffices to note that UK unregistered design right does not subsist in:

> features of shape or configuration of an article which . . . are dependent upon the appearance of another article of which the article is intended by the designer to form an integral part (CDPA 1988, s 213(3)(b)(ii)).

This exception focuses on aesthetic aspects of design. It was designed to ensure that car body parts would not enjoy UK unregistered design rights, and followed competition investigations in the 1980s by both the UK and the European Community, the subject of which was the Ford motor company's refusal to grant licences to third parties to enable them to compete in the market for replacement body parts. A replacement car wing or door must match the remainder of the car in aesthetic terms and a refusal by a car manufacturer to license potential competitors would leave them free to control the market and set prices for such replacement parts. The denial of UK unregistered design rights for such parts in the UK was therefore part of an attempt to open up this market to competition for the benefit of consumers. The CDPA 1988 also extended this 'must match' exception into the then (but now repealed) UK registered designs law.

8.82   Although the same concerns were raised during the drafting of the European design legislation, the issues have not yet been fully resolved. The legislative history on this issue has been usefully summarised by Arnold J in *Bayerische Motoren Werke Aktiengesellschaft v Round & Metal Ltd*.[102] The original idea in the Commission's proposals for the Designs Directive and Community Design Regulation was that, three years after the first putting on the market of a product incorporating a protected design or to which such a design had been applied, the rights conferred by a registered Community design or national registered design could not be exercised to stop use of the design by third parties where the product incorporating the design or to which it was applied was part of a complex product upon whose appearance the protected design was dependent and the purpose of the third party's use was to permit the repair of the complex product so as to restore its original appearance.[103] During the debate on these proposals, the European Parliament proposed that the rightholder should receive remuneration for any repair use. However, there was no agreement from the European Council.

8.83   Ultimately, following a conciliation procedure, the so-called 'freeze plus' compromise was adopted. The recitals to the Designs Directive state that, although 'the rapid adoption of this Directive has become a matter of urgency' for a number of industrial sectors:

> full-scale approximation of the laws of the Member States on the use of protected designs for the purpose of permitting the repair of a complex product so as to restore its original appearance...cannot be introduced at the present stage.

The Designs Directive also contains Articles providing for future action which have become known as the *'freeze or standstill plus'* solution to the problem of 'must match' designs. Article 14, which is the 'freeze' or 'standstill' element, states:

> Until such time as amendments to this Directive are adopted on a proposal from the Commission in accordance with the provisions of Article 18, Member States shall maintain in force their existing legal provisions relating to the use of the design of a component part used for the purpose of the repair of a complex product so as to restore its original appearance and shall introduce changes to those provisions only if the purpose is to liberalise the market for such parts.

8.84   In the UK this was taken to require the repeal of the former 'must match' exception introduced into registered designs law by the 1988 Act. However, a new defence to claims of infringement of a UK registered design was introduced, providing that the right in a UK registered design of a component part is not

[102] [2012] ECC 28 (English HC), paras 18–46.
[103] Proposal for a European Parliament and Council Directive on the legal protection of designs, COM(93) 344 final-COD 464, 3 December 1993, Art 14 of the proposed Directive; and Proposal for a European Parliament and Council Regulation on the Community Design, COM(93) 342 final-COD 463, 3 December 1993, Art 23 of the draft Regulation. Both also proposed a requirement that the public should not be misled as to the origin of the product used for the repair.

infringed by any use of the design for the purpose of the repair of the complex product so as to restore its original appearance.[104]

8.85 Article 18 of the Directive provided the 'plus' element of the compromise. It required the Commission to submit, by three years after the deadline for member states to implement the reforms brought about by the Directive, 'an analysis of the consequences of the provisions of this Directive for Community industry, in particular the industrial sectors which are most affected, particularly manufacturers of complex products and component parts, for consumers, for competition and for the functioning of the internal market'. Within one further year any necessary changes to the Directive to complete the internal market in relation to component parts were to be proposed. Recital 19 mentioned possibilities such as a remuneration system and a limited term of exclusivity.

8.86 In 2004, the Commission issued a proposal for an amendment to the Designs Directive.[105] The Commission proposed that the market should be liberalised by removing designs protection in the 'aftermarket' for spare parts. The present 'freeze or standstill' Article 14 of the Directive was to be replaced with a provision reading as follows:[106]

(1) Protection as a design shall not exist for a design which constitutes a component part of a complex product used within the meaning of Article 12(1) of this Directive, for the purpose of the repair of that complex product so as to restore its original appearance.

(2) Member states shall ensure that consumers are duly informed about the origin of spare parts so that they can make an informed choice between competing spare parts.

8.87 This proposal has been inching its way through the formal legislative procedure of the EU, and has also been the subject of a Patent Office consultation in the UK. It remains unclear, however, where it will lead. The Commission's proposal has not been adopted and no legislation has been forthcoming, with the Designs Directive remaining as enacted.

8.88 In the meantime, the position is different in relation to the Community Design Regulation. The Community Design Regulation also takes up the 'freeze plus' position, recital 13 stating that it would not be appropriate to confer protection as a Community design on a design for a component part of a complex product upon whose appearance the design is dependent and which is used for the purpose of repairing the complex product so as to restore its original appearance, until the Council has decided on its policy in the light of the Commission's proposals. Article 110(1) of the Regulation therefore provides that, until such time as the Community Design Regulation is amended, protection as a Community design will not exist for a design constituting a component part of a complex product used for the purpose of the repair of that complex product so as to restore its original appearance—effectively the same solution as that adopted in UK registered designs law (see para 8.84).

8.89 The interpretation of Article 110(1) of the Community Design Regulation has been considered by the English High Court in *Bayerische Motoren Werke Aktiengesellschaft v Round & Metal Ltd*.[107] Arnold J confirmed that it operates as a defence to an infringement claim (rather than an exclusion from protection for designs for component parts of complex products) and applies only where the component part is used for the purpose of repair of the complex product (rather than, say, sale of the component part as part of the

---

[104] RDA 1949, s 7A(5).

[105] COM(2004) 582 final, available at: http://eur-lex.europa.eu/LexUriServ/LexUriServ.do?uri=COM:2004:0582:FIN:EN:PDF.

[106] For discussion and criticism of the Commission proposal, see J Drexl, RM Hilty and A Kur, 'Design protection for spare parts and the Commission's proposal for a repairs clause' (2005) 36(4) IIC 448–457 and J Straus, 'Design protection for spare parts gone in Europe? Proposed changes to the EC Directive: the Commission's mandate and its doubtful execution' [2005] EIPR 391–404.

[107] [2012] ECC 28.

complex product).[108] Reading Article 110(1) in line with recital 13 to the Community Design Regulation, Arnold J held that Article 110(1) is restricted to component parts which are dependent on the appearance of the complex product.[109] Although the language of Article 110(1) focuses on the actions of the repairer, it protects the supplier of the relevant parts, the repairer and the owner of the repaired product.[110] It applies to parts which are normally used for repair rather than parts normally used for upgrading the complex product.[111] Arnold J declined to refer these matters to the Court of Justice for clarification.[112]

> ## Key points on 'must match'/repair exceptions to registered designs
>
> - There is currently no exclusion in registered design law like the 'must match' exception found in UK unregistered design law (see Chapter 9)
>
> - There is also no harmonised position in the Designs Directive on the use of designs for component parts for repair of complex products so as to restore their original appearance
>
> - However, the UK RDA 1949 (as amended) and Community Design Regulation do permit use of design for a component part of a complex product for the purpose of the repair of that complex product so as to restore its original appearance

Registration process

8.90   Unlike copyright and the unregistered forms of design protection discussed in Chapter 9, protection as a registered design does not arise automatically. An application must be filed and accepted by the relevant registry. However, as we shall see, for design registrations this is much more of a formality than for other registered IP rights such as trade marks and patents.

Registration in the UK[113]

Where?

8.91   Registration is carried out by the UK Intellectual Property Office (UK IPO).

Who may apply?

8.92   The applicant must be the person claiming to be the proprietor of the design.[114] For UK registered designs, the original proprietor of a design is its 'author', defined as the person who created the design,[115] unless the design was created:

(1)   in pursuance of a commission for money or money's worth, in which case the commissioner is the original proprietor;[116] or

---

[108] *Bayerische Motoren Werke*, note 107, para 51.   [109] *Bayerische Motoren Werke*, note 107, para 57.

[110] *Bayerische Motoren Werke*, note 107, para 71.   [111] *Bayerische Motoren Werke*, note 107, paras 72–73.

[112] *Bayerische Motoren Werke*, note 107, para 76.

[113] For the detailed procedural rules, see the Registered Designs Rules 2006 (SI 2006/1975) which took effect from 1 October 2006. Useful guidance can be found on the UK IPO website at: http://www.ipo.gov.uk/types/design/d-applying.htm.

[114] RDA 1949, s 3(2).

[115] RDA 1949, ss 2(1), (3). Note also RDA 1949, s 2(4): the author of a computer-generated design is person who makes arrangements necessary for the creation of the design.

[116] RDA 1949, s 2(1A).

(2) by an employee in the course of his employment, in which case the employer is the original proprietor.[117]

If national unregistered design rights subsist in the design (see further Chapter 9), the application must be made by the owner of that unregistered design right.[118] As discussed in further detail later, it is a ground for invalidation of a UK registered design that the registered proprietor is not the actual proprietor of the design (see para 8.107). There is also provision in the RDA 1949 for the true proprietor to apply for the register to be rectified so that he becomes the registered proprietor of the design.[119]

8.93 It is important to note that ownership is one of the few substantive aspects of national registered design protection which was not harmonised by the Designs Directive. As a result, member states were free to keep their own rules on ownership. The UK rules on ownership of UK national registered designs outlined here differ from those relating to Community designs in relation to commissioned designs (see para 8.100). This can be an important issue to be aware of in practice, with the risk that UK and Community protection in a commissioned design could vest in different people unless addressed by contractual arrangement between the designer and the commissioning party. At the time of writing, the UK IPO was consulting on whether to amend the RDA 1949 so as to bring it in line with the rules on ownership in the Community Design Regulation.[120]

How?

8.94 Applications are made on a form which is accessible on the UK IPO website. There is at present no online application system. The Registered Designs Rules 2006 simplified the application procedure in several respects, including allowing multiple designs to be filed in one application and removing the requirement for two sets of representations of each design.[121] Among other requirements, the application form requires details of the owner of the design(s) being applied for, a statement of the product(s) which the design(s) are for and illustrations of the design. The illustrations need to provide an accurate and complete representation of the design for which protection is claimed and, where the design is three-dimensional, may include different views of the design from different perspectives. If there are no objections to the application, the UK IPO states that it should be registered within two months.[122] Working by extension of the case law relating to Community designs, it is clear that the statement of the product(s) which the design(s) are for does not affect the scope of protection of the design (see also para 8.116).

How much?

8.95 At the time of writing, the filing fee payable to the UK IPO is £60 for a single design or the first design in a multiple application. For every additional design included in an application which covers multiple designs, the filing fee is £40 per design. The fees are slightly different if the applicant wishes to defer publication of the design. Costs will increase if one uses a patent or a trade mark agent (since they charge their own fees for handling the application), or if the application runs into difficulties requiring professional advice.

---

[117] RDA 1949, s 2(1B).   [118] RDA 1949, s 3(3).   [119] RDA 1949, s 20, in particular s 20(1)(c).

[120] 'Consultation on the Reform of the UK Designs Legal Framework' (launched 24 July 2012), p 17 (available at: http://www.ipo.gov.uk/consult-2012-designs.pdf).

[121] See the UK IPO's Designs Practice Notice (DPN) 5/06 for further details.

[122] For timescales, guidance on how to represent a design and on other aspects of the application process, see the useful leaflet published by the UK IPO entitled 'How to Apply to Register a Design' (revised March 2010) at: http://www.ipo.gov.uk/d-howtoapply.pdf.

What happens next?

8.96   The registration procedure is much more of a formality than it once was as the UK IPO has now changed its practice to exclude any examination of and therefore any potential refusal during the examination process for lack of novelty or individual character. Essentially, an application will only be refused if it appears that the application does not comply with the relevant rules, it appears to the examiner that the applicant is not a person entitled to apply for the design or it appears to the examiner that the matter applied for does not fall within the definition of 'design', is dictated by technical function or contrary to public policy or morality.[123] There is no third party opposition procedure. When registered, the basic position is that a design is treated as registered from the date upon which the application for registration was filed.[124]

Dealing in UK registered designs and registration of transactions

8.97   A UK registered design or an application for a UK registered design is personal property (or, in Scotland, incorporeal moveable property).[125] A UK registered design or an application for a UK registered design can be assigned or transferred by testamentary disposition or operation of law, licensed or made the subject of legal security, all subject to certain formalities set out in the RDA 1949.[126] When a registered design is assigned, or otherwise transferred or licensed, the person taking an interest in the design should apply for the registration of his interest on the UK register of designs. The principal benefit of this is that third parties are deemed to have notice of these interests via the register of designs: any transmission of a UK registered design or an application is subject to any rights vested in another person of which notice has been entered on the register.[127]

Registration of Community designs

8.98   Community designs, registered and unregistered, are unitary rights, meaning that they consist of one single right which has equal effect throughout all EU member states and can only be registered, transferred, surrendered, or found invalid in respect of the whole of the EU (CDR, Art 1(3)). Applying for a Community registered design carries considerable benefits in terms of cost and ease of administration compared to applying for national design registrations in all EU member states. Another very important advantage of Community design protection is the ability of the rightholder, in certain circumstances, to apply to one court in one jurisdiction to obtain an injunction stopping infringement and granting other relief effective across the whole of the EU.[128] This brings considerable cost savings at the enforcement stage as well.

Where?

8.99   Registration is carried out at the Office for Harmonisation in the Internal Market (OHIM) at Alicante.

Who may apply?

8.100 The right to a Community design vests in the designer or his successor in title, unless a design is developed by an employee in the execution of his duties or following the instructions given by his employer in which case the right to the Community design vests in the employer unless otherwise agreed or specified in national law.[129] Unlike for UK registered designs (see para 8.92), there is no

---

[123] See RDA 1949, s 3A and UK IPO Designs Practice Notice (DPN) 1/06.   [124] RDA 1949, s 3C(1).
[125] RDA 1949, s 15A.   [126] RDA 1949, s 15B.   [127] RDA 1949, ss 15B(2) and 19.
[128] See CDR, Arts 80–83 for more details.   [129] CDR, Art 14.

provision in the Community Design Regulation vesting ownership of a commissioned design in the commissioning party. In *Fundación Española para la Innovación de la Artesanía (FEIA) v Cul de Sac Espacio Creativo SL*, the Court of Justice has confirmed that Article 14(3) of the Community Design Regulation (employee-generated designs vesting in the employer) does not apply to Community designs produced as a result of a contract for commission.[130] So, unlike UK registered designs, the right to a Community design in a design produced on commission vests in the designer. As noted previously, pending any reform of UK law, it is important to be live to this divergence in practice and to reduce the risk that ownership of UK and Community rights in a commissioned design could vest in different people by making appropriate contractual arrangements regularising ownership between the designer and the commissioning party. As for UK registered designs, it is a ground for invalidity of a Community design that the rightholder is not entitled to the Community design (see para 8.107). The Community Design Regulation also includes provision for the true proprietor to apply to be recognised as the legitimate holder of the Community design.[131] The designer, whether or not the applicant for or the holder of the Community design, has a right to be cited as such before the Office and in the register.[132]

How?

8.101   An application may be made by post, by fax, or online. An application form should be completed and must be accompanied by representations of the design claimed. The applicant can file as many designs as he wishes in one multiple application, the only condition being that the products to which the design is applied belong to the same Locarno class. This condition does not apply when an application concerns ornamentation.[133] As in the UK, the application must also contain an indication of the products intended to be incorporated or to which it is intended to be applied.[134] However, this statement does not affect the scope of protection of the design (see also, para 8.116).[135]

How much?

8.102   As at the time of writing, the basic charge for an application for a single design is a filing fee of €230 and a publication fee of €120. Thereafter, there is a reduced fee per design for the second to tenth additional designs included in a multiple filing and a further reduction per design for the eleventh design onwards included in a multiple filing. As in the UK, the fees are slightly different if the applicant requests deferment of publication.

What happens next?

8.103   The examination process before OHIM is even more of a formality than before the UK IPO. At OHIM, the examiner will check only the formalities of the application, that what is applied for falls within the definition of 'design' and that the design is not contrary to public policy or morality.[136] There is no third

---

[130] Case C-32/08, Court of Justice, [2010] RPC 13.   [131] CDR, Art 15.   [132] CDR, Art 18.

[133] CDR, Arts 36 and 37. For more detail on these points and other useful information on the application process before OHIM, see the Information and interactive flowchart published on OHIM's website at: http://oami.europa.eu/ows/rw/pages/RCD/regProcess/regProcess.en.do.

[134] CDR, Art 36(2).

[135] CDR, Art 36(6). This has been confirmed by the General Court in *Grupo Promer*, note 38, para 55 and by the English Court of Appeal in *Green Lane Products Ltd v PMS International Group Ltd* [2008] FSR 28, paras 47 and 50 (see further paras 46–63).

[136] CDR, Arts 45 and 47. See also OHIM's guidance on examination at: http://oami.europa.eu/ows/rw/pages/RCD/regProcess/examination.en.do.

party opposition procedure. When registered, the design is treated as having been registered as from the date of filing of the application.[137]

Dealing in Community registered designs and registration of transactions

8.104   The provisions relating to dealing in Community designs face potential complexities arising out of the fact that Community designs cover, and are effective in, all EU member states, all of which have their own systems of property law. Addressing this issue, Article 27 of the Community Design Regulation states that, unless otherwise provided in the Regulation, a Community design as an object of property:

> shall be dealt with in its entirety, and for the whole area of the Community

as a national design right of the member state in which, on the relevant date, the holder has his seat or domicile or, if this is not applicable, an establishment.[138] However, a Community design may be licensed for whole or part of the Community.[139]

8.105   Transfers of a Community registered design must, at the request of one of the parties (ie either side of the transaction), be entered in the register and published, before which time the new owner may not invoke the rights under the Community registered design.[140] A registered Community design may also be granted in security and all Community designs may be licensed and those transactions must likewise be registered where they relate to registered Community designs.[141] The effects of such transactions as regards third parties are governed by the law of the member state determined according to Article 27. However, transfers, grants in security and licences can only have effect in relation to third parties in all member states after their entry in the register,[142] although a transaction can have effect before registration in relation to a third party who acquires rights after its date (ie in a further, later transaction) but who at the time of acquiring the rights knows of the earlier transaction.[143]

Declarations of invalidity

8.106   As the foregoing brief account of the registration processes of OHIM and the UK IPO shows, the offices do not engage in detailed examination of applications to test their compliance with the full requirements of registrability discussed in this chapter. Nor is there any provision for third party opposition. Save in exceptional cases, the application is likely to go through to registration. However, registered designs may still be subject to challenge on the basis that, although accepted for registration, they do not meet the requirements for registrability laid down by the law. The challenge may come from a defendant when the rightholder is seeking to enforce the design in court, but it is also possible for challenges to be raised directly by application to OHIM or the UK IPO as appropriate.[144]

---

[137] CDR, Art 12.

[138] CDR, Art 27(1). Articles 27(3) and (4) go on to address the position in relation to jointly owned designs or where none of these provisions apply.

[139] CDR, Art 32(1).   [140] CDR, Art 28.   [141] CDR, Arts 29 and 32(5).   [142] CDR, Art 33(2).

[143] CDR, Art 33(2). This rule does not apply where a Community registered design or right concerning the Community registered design is acquired by way of the transfer of the whole of a company's undertaking (eg in a takeover) or by any other universal succession (eg transmission of a whole estate on death) (Art 33(3)).

[144] For invalidity applications to the UK IPO in relation to UK registered designs, see RDA 1949, s 11ZB; for invalidity applications to OHIM in relation to Community registered designs, see CDR, Arts 24 and 52.

8.107 The grounds for invalidation of a registered design are essentially the same for UK registered designs and Community designs.[145] UK registered designs and Community designs may be declared invalid on the grounds that:[146]

- the matter registered does not fall within the definition of 'design';[147]
- the design does not otherwise meet the requirements of registrability (ie that it lacks novelty or individual character or is subject to one of the exclusions from protection such as being dictated by technical function or being contrary to public policy or morality);[148]
- the design is not new or possessed of an individual character in comparison with a design made available to the public on or after the contested application for registration *but* which has priority over the contested design by virtue of earlier registration or application for registration under the RDA 1949, Community Design Registration or in an international registration designating the Community;[149]
- the registered proprietor is not the proprietor of the design;[150]
- the design involves the use of an earlier distinctive sign which provides the right to prohibit the use of that sign;[151] and
- the design constitutes an unauthorised use of a work protected by copyright.[152]

8.108 An invalidation challenge based on the grounds outlined at the first two bullet points set out in para 8.107 may be brought by any interested person.[153] Otherwise, the challenge must be brought by the owner of the earlier right relied upon or, if it is claimed that the registered proprietor is not the proprietor of the design, by the person claiming to be the true proprietor of the design.[154] If a ground of invalidity is made out, there will be a declaration of invalidity, which can be whole or partial, with an option for the proprietor to modify and maintain his design registration in amended form in certain circumstances.[155]

 Question

Who may bring an invalidity challenge and on what grounds may a design registration be declared invalid?

8.109 The General Court in *Grupo Promer Mon Graphic SA v OHIM and PepsiCo Inc* (Case T-9/07) has confirmed that the grounds of invalidity set out in Article 25 of the Community Design Regulation are exhaustive: it

---

[145] Although they are worded slightly differently.

[146] There are also additional grounds for invalidation in the UK relating essentially to the protection of Royal emblems, Olympic symbols and certain other insignia protected by the Paris Convention: RDA 1949, s 11ZA(1)(c). For similar provisions relating to Community designs, see CDR, Art 25(1)(g). See also DD, Art 11(2)(c).

[147] RDA 1949, s 11ZA(1)(a); DD, Art 11(1)(a); CDR, Art 25(1)(a).

[148] RDA 1949, s 11ZA(1)(b); DD, Art 11(1)(b); CDR, Art 25(1)(b).

[149] RDA 1949, s 11ZA(1A); DD, Art 11(1)(d); CDR, Art 25(1)(d). This provision, in essence, addresses the problem of competing designs protected under the RDA 1949 or CDR where the earlier design has not been published before the relevant date (and so cannot be relied upon as the basis for a standard challenge for lack of novelty or individual character), but nonetheless does have an earlier priority date.

[150] RDA 1949, s 11ZA(2); DD, Art 11(1)(c); CDR, Art 25(1)(c). Article 25(1)(c) of the Community Design Regulation is worded slightly differently to the broadly equivalent provision in the RDA 1949 and introduces a requirement of a court decision on ownership ('if, by virtue of a court decision, the rightholder is not entitled to the Community design under Article 14').

[151] RDA 1949, s 11ZA(3); DD, Art 11(2)(a); CDR, Art 25(1)(e).

[152] RDA 1949, s 11ZA(4); DD, Art 11(2)(b); CDR, Art 25(1)(f).   [153] RDA 1949, s 11ZB(1).

[154] RDA 1949, ss 11ZA(2), (3) and (4) and s 11ZB(5); DD, Arts 11(3) and (4); CDR, Arts 25(2) and (3).

[155] RDA 1949, ss 11ZC and 11ZD; DD, Art 11(7); CDR, Art 25(6).

is therefore not possible to apply for invalidation of a registered design on grounds not mentioned in the Directive or Regulation, such as bad faith.[156] It follows that the grounds of invalidity set out in the Designs Directive, and transposed into national law, are also exhaustive.

8.110   The General Court has, in two cases, also clarified two further specific issues arising from the language of Article 11 of the Designs Directive and Article 25 of the Community Design Regulation:

- DD, Art 11(1)(d)/CDR, Art 25(1)(d): the expression 'in conflict with' is not defined in either of these provisions. In *Grupo Promer Mon Graphic SA v OHIM and PepsiCo Inc* (Case T-9/07), the General Court confirmed that a design is 'in conflict with' a prior design within the meaning of this provision when, taking into consideration the freedom of the designer in developing the design, that design does not produce on the informed user a different overall impression from that produced by the prior design relied upon.[157]

- DD, Art 11(2)(a)/CDR, Art 25(1)(e): in *Beifa Group Co Ltd v OHIM and Schwan-Stabilo Schwanhaüßer GmbH & Co KG* (Case T-148/08), a case involving a challenge to a Community registered design on the basis of an earlier trade mark registration, the General Court confirmed that there may be grounds for invalidation where the registered design is not only the same as, but also similar to, the earlier distinctive sign. The issue is whether the owner of the earlier distinctive sign has the right to prohibit the use of its sign in the later design pursuant to the relevant law governing protection of that distinctive sign.[158]

Key points on invalidity

A registration may be challenged on the grounds that:

- The design does not meet the requirements for registration

- The design is in conflict with an earlier design protected under the RDA 1949, Community Design Regulation, or by an international registration designating the Community which had not been published as at the relevant date but which does have an earlier priority date

- The registered proprietor is not the proprietor of the design

- The use of the design could be prevented by earlier rights in copyright or trade marks

- A challenge based on the ground that the design does not meet the requirements for registration can be brought by any interested person; otherwise, challenges are limited to the true owner of the design or the owner of any earlier right relied upon

---

Rights given by registration, infringement, and defences

Exclusive right to use the design

8.111   The right conferred by registration is the 'exclusive right' to 'use' the design and:

> any design which does not produce on the informed user a different overall impression (RDA, s 7(1); DD, Arts 9(1) and 12(1); CDR, Arts 10(1) and 19(1)).

---

[156] *Grupo Promer*, note 38, para 30 (not appealed to the Court of Justice on this point).
[157] *Grupo Promer*, note 38, para 52 (not appealed to the Court of Justice on this point). Note that the transposing provision in the RDA 1949 (set out at para 8.107) does not use the wording 'in conflict with', but is intended to cover the same situation.
[158] [2010] ETMR 42, paras 50–59 and 63.

It is thus a right, not only to the registered design itself, but to any other design which produces the same overall impression on the informed user. The crucial point for present purposes—considering the scope of the rights conferred—is that *protection extends beyond the exact design registered.* 'Overall impression' and the 'informed user' are concepts we have already encountered when discussing the requirement of individual character (see paras 8.32ff). In assessing the scope of protection, as for assessment of individual character, the degree of freedom of the designer in developing his design is also to be taken into account.[159] It is now clear that the assessment of 'overall impression' is the same for validity and infringement purposes, the suggestion that this might be otherwise by the English Court of Appeal in *Procter & Gamble Co v Reckitt Benckiser (UK) Ltd* (see para 8.47) having been explicitly reversed by the English Court of Appeal in its more recent decision in *Dyson Ltd v Vax Ltd* (see para 8.48).[160] As the assessment of 'overall impression' is the same for validity and infringement, the reader is referred to the discussion of individual character/'overall impression' at paras 8.32ff for the key case law and principles.

Question

What exclusive right is conferred upon the owner of a registered design?

8.112 As the Designs Directive and the Community Design Regulation put it, the exclusive right conferred by registration confers on the proprietor:

> the exclusive right to use [the design] and to prevent any third party not having his consent from using it (DD, Art 12(1); CDR, Art 19(1)).

So the exclusive right is a basis for challenging—in court if necessary—unauthorised use of the design by others.[161] The converse of that, of course, is that the rightholder can authorise others to use the design by way of licences. But the rightholder can decide not to do so, and to exploit the exclusive right himself.

8.113 A further, fundamentally important, point is that the right to prevent third party 'use' is a very different concept from the right to prevent 'copying', which is characteristic of the scope of protection conferred by copyright. 'Copying' involves reproduction of an earlier work and a causal connection between the earlier and later works (see para 4.27). The right to prevent other parties from 'using' a design is not limited in this way and will entitle the holder of a UK registered design and Community registered design to stop 'use' of an infringing design even where that design has been developed wholly independently by the infringer, without any knowledge of the UK registered design or Community registered design relied upon. Because of this, the very strong protection conferred by a UK registered design and Community registered design— sometimes called a 'full monopoly right'—can be equated more closely to the rights conferred by a patent than those arising in copyright.

---

[159] RDA, s 7(3); DD, Art 9(2); CDR, Art 10(2).

[160] In *Procter & Gamble* (see para 8.47), Jacob LJ held that, for validity purposes, a design needed to produce a 'clearly different' overall impression compared to earlier designs to have individual character but that, for infringement purposes, a design needed only to produce a 'different' overall impression to fall outside the scope of the design relied upon; paras 10–19. The English Court of Appeal in *Dyson* has, however, now explicitly stated that its ruling in *Procter & Gamble* to the effect that these tests were different was incorrect: note 57, para 34.

[161] The references in the DD and CDR to 'the exclusive right to use [the design]' should not be understood as conferring an absolute positive right on the proprietor to use his design. In *Celaya Emparanza y Galdos Internacional SA v Proyectos Integrales de Balizamientos SL* (Case C-488/10) [2012] ECDR 17, the Court of Justice confirmed that, in a dispute relating to infringement of a registered Community design, the right to prevent use by third parties of a design which does not produce a different overall impression extends to all third parties, including the holder of a later registered Community design. The holder of a later registered Community design which produces the same overall impression as an earlier registered Community design can be sued for infringement without a need to invalidate the later registration, and will have to defend his position by proving that the earlier design does not meet the conditions for registration by seeking declaration of invalidity (paras 32–52).

8.114   The broad nature of this exclusive right is linked, in part, to the operation of the design registration system. In principle, a person who proposes to use a design can check the register to see if the same or a similar design has been registered; if it has, the person is then in a position to know that the proposed use is illegitimate. It is accordingly fair to grant a 'full monopoly' right to registered designs to prevent any use of an infringing design, whether copied or not. If, however, a design is unregistered, the only way a person can know whether someone else has already produced the same or a similar design is by finding it already in use in the market place; so, as we will see in the next chapter on unregistered design rights, it is only fair that such a person can only be liable to the existing user if he has copied the latter's design.

8.115   The concept of 'use' includes in particular but is not limited to:

> the making, offering, putting on the market, importing, exporting or using of a product in which the design is incorporated or to which it is applied, or stocking such a product for those purposes (RDA, s 7(2); DD, Art 12(1); CDR, Art 19(1)).

Much of this will typically be *commercial or trading activity*—manufacture, sale, import, export, stocking—but infringement is not limited to the commercial context. However, when we turn to the defences (see paras 8.117–8.119), we find that the right in a registered design is not infringed by an act which is done privately and for purposes which are not commercial.[162]

8.116   Finally, it is critically important to note that there is no need for an infringer's product(s) to be the same as the product(s) marketed by the rightholder or mentioned in the product statements included in the UK or Community design application forms. This was confirmed by the English Court of Appeal in *Green Lane Products Ltd v PMS International Group Ltd*, in which Jacob LJ emphasised:

> It is particularly important to realise that the scope of protection covers any use of the design for article, whatever its intended purpose. The scope provision... does not limit infringement to 'articles for which the design is registered' or anything like that. So if you register a design for a car you can stop use of the design for a brooch or a cake or a toy, or if you register a textile design you can stop its use on wallpaper, a shirt or a plate.[163]

Any use of the design, or one producing the same overall impression on the informed user, will constitute infringement whatever the product to which it is applied or in which it is incorporated. However, it remains to be fully explored in case law how far, in cases where the alleged infringement is a different product, that difference in product may impact upon the overall impressions produced by the alleged infringement and thus the question of whether the infringement produces the same overall impression as the registered design.

Key points on the exclusive right conferred by a registered design

- The scope of protection conferred by a registered design includes the registered design and any design which does not produce a different overall impression on the informed user
- The assessment of overall impression for infringement purposes is the same as for validity purposes and, as a result, the key cases and principles relating to 'overall impression' are common across infringement and validity
- The holder of a registered design can stop anyone else using the design for a product, regardless of whether or not that use is the result of copying and regardless of whether that use relates to the same product(s) as those of the holder of the registered design

---

[162] RDA 1949, s 7A(2)(a); DD, Art 13(1)(a); CDR, Art 20(1)(a).   [163] [2008] FSR 28, para 27.

Defences

8.117   The principal defences to infringement of a UK registered design and Community design cover:

- acts done privately and for non-commercial purposes;

- acts done for experimental purposes;

- acts of reproduction for the purposes of making citations or of teaching, provided that such acts 'are compatible with fair trade practice' and 'do not unduly prejudice the normal exploitation of the design', and that mention is made of the source;

- equipment on ships and aircraft which are registered in another country when these temporarily enter the relevant territory, the importation into the relevant territory of spare parts and accessories for the purpose of repairing such craft and the execution of repairs on such craft.[164]

For Community designs, Article 22 of the Community Design Regulation also preserves limited rights of prior use for third parties who had, before the relevant date, in good faith commenced use of a design included within the scope of a registered Community design or made serious and effective preparations to that end. At the time of writing, the UK IPO was consulting on whether to amend the RDA 1949 so as to include an equivalent defence to infringement of a UK registered design.[165]

8.118   Looking in more detail at the principal defences:

- **Acts done privately and for non-commercial purposes**

There is a similarly worded exception in patent law, which has caused difficulties of interpretation.[166] The acts must be both private *and* non-commercial; so a private act which was commercial would be infringement, as would a non-commercial act which was public. The difficulties in defining private and non-commercial are not inconsiderable.

- **Acts done for experimental purposes**

There is again a similarly worded exception in patent law; and once more its interpretation is open to debate.[167] In the context of designs law, experiments may occur with a view to determining the best design by which particular functions of a product may be achieved, but one can also imagine experiments being conducted to find designs which were most attractive to consumers. What sort of 'experimental purposes' are covered by the defence as compared to those, say, to test market acceptability is yet to be clarified.

- **Acts of reproduction for the purposes of making citations or of teaching**

This defence seems closer to some of those familiar from copyright law. The teaching defence certainly facilitates activities in relation to design instruction in schools, art and design colleges, and universities; however, it is not confined to activities of educational institutions and so might potentially be capable of application in an industrial or commercial context as well. The citation defence appears to cover the use of designs in publications such as books of instruction for designers and, it is suggested, textbooks for intellectual property lawyers and students. This would seem perfectly compatible with fair trade practice and not unduly to prejudice the normal exploitation of the design—indeed, not to do so at all.

---

[164]   RDA 1949, ss 7A(1)–(3); DD, Art 13; CDR, Art 20.
[165]   'Consultation on the Reform of the UK Designs Legal Framework' (launched 24 July 2012), pp 13–14 (accessible at: http://www.ipo.gov.uk/consult-2012-designs.pdf).
[166]   Patents Act 1977, s 60(5)(a); see para 11.221.   [167]   Patents Act 1977, s 60(5)(b); see para 11.222.

The source of the design has to be given in both teaching and citation activities if they are to enjoy the benefit of the defence.

8.119   Rights in registered designs are also not infringed by an act relating to a product in which a registered design is incorporated or to which it has been applied if the product has been put on the market in the European Economic Area (EEA) by the registered proprietor or with his consent (see further the discussion of exhaustion of rights at Chapter 20).[168] In addition, although not part of the harmonised regime enacted by the Designs Directive, for both UK registered designs and Community designs it is also not an infringement to use the registered design for a component part for the purpose of repair of a complex product so as to restore its original appearance (the 'must match' defence) (see paras 8.84 and 8.88).[169]

Key points on defences

UK registered designs and Community designs are not infringed by:

- acts done privately and for non-commercial purposes

- acts done for experimental purposes

- acts of reproduction for the purposes of making citations or of teaching, provided that such acts 'are compatible with fair trade practice' and 'do not unduly prejudice the normal exploitation of the design', and that mention is made of the source

- Although not part of the harmonised regime enacted by the Designs Directive, it is also not an infringement of UK registered designs and Community designs to use the registered design for a component part for the purpose of repair of a complex product so as to restore its original appearance

---

Duration of rights

8.120   The rights in a registered design last initially for five years from the date of registration (which is the date of application, see previously).[170] The right can be renewed for up to four more periods of five years, up to a maximum of 25 years in total.[171] Failure to renew leads to the right ceasing to have effect,[172] but a renewal can be made within six months of a renewal deadline subject to certain consequences.[173] It may also be possible thereafter to restore a lapsed right in a registered design in certain circumstances.[174] The renewal fees which are payable at the five-year renewal deadlines grow more expensive at each stage.

8.121   The registered proprietor of a UK registered design and a Community design can effectively abandon his registration at any time by notifying the relevant registry.[175]

Interaction with other IP rights

8.122   As discussed previously (see para 8.21), there is clear potential for overlap between entitlement to protection under the European designs regime and under other IP rights. The harmonisation effected by

---

168   RDA 1949, s 7A(4); DD, Art 15; CDR, Art 21.   169   RDA 1949, s 7A(5); CDR, Art 110(1).
170   RDA 1949, s 8(1); DD, Art 10; CDR, Art 12.   171   RDA 1949, s 8(2); DD, Art 10; CDR, Art 12.
172   RDA 1949, s 8(3).   173   RDA 1949, s 8(4); CDR, Art 13(3).   174   RDA 1949, s 8A; CDR, Art 67.
175   RDA 1949, s 11; CDR, Art 51.

the Designs Directive is limited only to national registered design protection. Article 16 of the Designs Directive states:

> The provisions of this Directive shall be without prejudice to any provisions of Community law or the law of the member state concerned relating to unregistered design rights, trade marks or other distinctive signs, patents and utility models, typefaces, civil liability or unfair competition (see also DD, recital 7).

There is equivalent provision in the Community Design Regulation (Art 96(1) and recital 31). These provisions leave open the potential for cumulation of protection for a particular design as a registered design and under such other rights, if such other protection is available.

8.123   The Designs Directive and Community Design Regulation also envisage cumulation of protection with copyright. Article 17 of the Designs Directive states:

> A design protected by a design right registered in or in respect of a Member State in accordance with this Directive shall also be eligible for protection under the law of copyright of that State as from the date on which the design was created or fixed in any form. The extent to which, and the conditions under which, such protection is conferred, including the level of originality required, shall be determined by each Member State (see also DD, recital 8).

Again, there is equivalent provision in the Community Design Regulation (CDR, Art 96(2) and recital 32).

8.124   Article 17 of the Designs Directive has been considered by the Court of Justice in *Flos SpA v Semeraro Casa e Famiglia SpA*.[176] In this preliminary reference from the Italian courts, the Court of Justice considered a number of complex issues arising from the Italian legislation transposing the Designs Directive into Italian law. Much of the detail is particular to the Italian legislation, but some points of more general significance were made in the Court of Justice's decision. The Court stressed the importance of the principle of cumulation with copyright highlighted at recital 8 of the Directive. Article 17 of the Directive relates only to designs registered in accordance with the Directive. Although the first sentence of Article 17 provides that such designs are eligible for copyright protection, the second sentence of Article 17 allows member states to determine the extent to which, and conditions under which, such copyright protection is conferred, including the level of originality required. However, the second sentence of Article 17 does not give member states a choice as to whether or not to confer copyright protection for a registered design if the design meets the conditions in that member state under which copyright protection is conferred. Controversially, the Court went on to say that it is clear from Article 17 of the Designs Directive that copyright protection *must* be conferred on all designs protected by a design right registered in or in respect of the member state concerned. It also held that the entitlement to determine the extent of copyright protection and conditions under which it is conferred does *not* include freedom to decide term of protection, as that has been harmonised at the EU level by the Term Directive (see para 3.49).[177] The *Flos* ruling has been criticised, with concerns expressed about the potential reintroduction of 'industrial copyright' in designs (as to which see further Chapter 9) as a result of the Court's interpretation of the relevant legislation as *requiring* designs to be protected by copyright rather than, as has been argued to be the underlying legislative intention of Article 17 of the Designs Directive, simply making it impermissible to deny copyright protection to a design merely because it was registered as a design.[178] It remains to see how *Flos* will be applied in subsequent cases or whether it will be confined to its particular facts.

8.125   According to the Designs Directive and Community Design Regulation, there is therefore considerable scope for a design to be protected as a registered design and in copyright at the same time. In

---

[176] Case C-168/09, 27 January 2011, [2011] ECDR 8.   [177] *Flos*, note 176, paras 32–39 in particular.
[178] See further L Bently, 'The return of industrial copyright?' [2012] EIPR 654–672.

the UK, however, the scope for infringing the copyright subsisting in such a design is significantly restricted by the effect of section 51 of the CDPA 1988. Section 51 was introduced in UK law a number of years before the Designs Directive and Community Design Regulation were enacted and, as will be discussed in greater detail in Chapter 9 (see paras 9.83–9.90), forms a key part of the provisions in the CDPA 1988 regulating the relationship between copyright, UK unregistered design right, and the extent to which copyright claims based on design drawings can be enforced in relation to industrial designs. Because section 51 of the CDPA 1988 will apply to restrict the ability to make a copyright claim based on any design drawing which falls within its scope, as a matter of UK law the copyright in many design drawings, which would otherwise have been allowed to coexist with design protection under the Designs Directive and Community Design Regulation, will not in fact be enforceable in the UK. Other copyright claims might also be affected by section 52 of the CDPA 1988, which was enacted to cut the period of enforceability in certain copyright artistic works down to 25 years in certain circumstances—although, at the time of writing, section 52 is in the process of being repealed (see paras 9.91–9.93).[179] These are all domestic matters particular to the UK. For more detail, the reader is referred to Chapter 9.

8.126   In the meantime, where UK registered design protection and copyright coexist in a design which is also an artistic work, copyright is not infringed by anything done in pursuance of an assignment or licence of the registered design granted by the person recorded on the register as its proprietor in good faith reliance on the registration, even when the person registered as the proprietor of the design was not the proprietor for the purposes of the RDA 1949.[180]

Key points on interaction with other IP rights

- The Designs Directive and the Community Design Regulation do not affect other IP rights which may coexist in a design and leave open the potential for cumulation between such other rights and the protection available for that design under the Designs Directive and Community Design Regulation

- The Designs Directive and the Community Design Regulation also provide that a protected design is eligible for copyright protection as from the date on which the design was created or fixed in any form, although the extent to which, and the conditions under which, such protection is conferred, including the level of originality required, shall be determined by each member state

- In the UK, the potential for cumulation of design protection and protection in copyright is significantly curtailed by the CDPA 1988, discussed further in Chapter 9

---

[179] See the Enterprise and Regulatory Reform Act 2013, s 74, which received Royal Assent on 25 April 2013. The repeal of CDPA 1988, s 52 will take effect on a date to be appointed by statutory instrument (Enterprise and Regulatory Reform Act 2013, s 103(3)). At the time of writing, details of when and how this repeal will be implemented are still awaited. See further para 9.93.
[180] CDPA 1988, s 53.

Further reading

Books

L Bently and B Sherman, *Intellectual Property Law* (3rd edn, 2009), Part III, Chs 25–28

WR Cornish, D Llewelyn and T Aplin, *Intellectual Property* (7th edn, 2010), Ch 15

M Howe, *Russell-Clarke and Howe on Industrial Designs* (8th edn, 2010)

Laddie, Prescott & Vitoria on the Modern Law of Copyright and Designs (4th edn, 2011)

N Pires de Carvalho, *The TRIPS Regime of Trademarks and Designs* (2006), Part II, Section 4: Industrial Designs

U Suthersanen, *Design Law: European Union and United States of America* (2nd edn, 2010)

History

B Sherman and L Bently, *The Making of Intellectual Property Law* (1999), Chs 3, 4

Articles

L Bently, 'The return of industrial copyright?' [2012] EIPR 654–672

AG de Borja, 'Exceptions to design rights: the potential impact of Article 26(2) TRIPS' [2008] EIPR 500–508

A Carboni, 'Design validity and infringement: feel the difference' [2008] EIPR 111–117

A Carboni, 'The overlap between registered Community designs and Community trade marks' (2006) 1(4) JIPLP 256–265

N Cordell and T Austen, 'European General Court highlights conflict between trade marks and designs' (2010) 5(9) JIPLP 622–624

G Dinwoodie, 'Federalized Functionalism: The Future of Design Protection in the European Union' (1996) 24 AIPLA QJ 611

J Drexl, RM Hilty and A Kur, 'Design protection for spare parts and the Commission's proposal for a repairs clause' (2005) 36(4) IIC 448–457

H Hartwig, 'European design law: reciprocity revisited' (2012) 7(11) JIPLP 827–831

H Hartwig, '*Grupo Promer v OHIM and PepsiCo* (T-9/07): the General Court's first decision on a Community design's validity—all's well that ends well?' [2010] EIPR 479–482

H Hartwig, 'The concept of reciprocity in European design law' (2010) 5(3) JIPLP 186–191

C Howell, 'Trade marks, registered designs and the monopolisation of functional shapes: a consideration of Lego and Dyson (Case Comment)' [2011] EIPR 60–62

A Kingsbury, 'International harmonisation of designs law: the case for diversity' [2010] EIPR 382–395

A Kur, 'No logo!' (2004) 35(2) IIC 184–186

A Kur, 'The Green Paper's "Design Approach"—what's wrong with it?' [1993] EIPR 374–378

M Marell, 'CJEU defines "informed user" concept in Pepsi registered Community design dispute' (2011) 25(11) WIPR 40–41

D Musker, 'Hidden meaning? UK perspectives on invisible in use designs' [2003] EIPR 450–456

D Smyth, '*Samsung v Apple*: how does the judge become an "informed user"?' (2012) 7(11) JIPLP 776–778

D Stone, 'Some clarity, some confusion: 12 *P&G v Reckitt Benckiser* decisions help explain Community designs' (2008) 3(6) JIPLP 376–385

J Straus, 'Design protection for spare parts gone in Europe? Proposed changes to the EC Directive: the Commission's mandate and its doubtful execution' [2005] EIPR 391–404

Unregistered designs

Introduction

Scope and overview of chapter

9.1 This chapter deals with the design protection available for designs that have not been registered. There are two main forms of protection: the unregistered design right established for the UK by Part III of the Copyright, Designs and Patents Act 1988 (hereafter referred to as 'UK UDR'), and the Community unregistered design right created by the Community Designs Regulation 6/2002/EC (hereafter referred to as 'Community UDR'). In contrast to the forms of registered design protection considered in Chapter 8, both of these forms of protection arise automatically if the relevant requirements are met. The chapter looks at each of these rights in turn and, building on the brief discussion at the end of Chapter 8, also considers in more detail the role still enjoyed by copyright in relation to the protection of designs in the UK and the reform ongoing at the time of writing in this area.

9.2 | **Learning objectives**

By the end of this chapter you should be able to describe and explain:

- the legal protection conferred upon unregistered designs in UK law and as Community unregistered designs, and the differences between these two systems;
- the key differences between unregistered design rights and registered design rights;
- the interaction between unregistered design rights, registered designs, and copyright.

9.3 The chapter begins by setting unregistered design protection in the international context described in more detail in the previous chapter. There then follows a detailed account and analysis of UK UDR. Thereafter, there is an assessment of the interaction with copyright in the UK. The chapter then examines Community UDR, which is different in a number of important respects from UK UDR. So the rest of the chapter looks like this:

- International context (9.4–9.8)
- Historical background to UK UDR (9.9–9.13)

- UK UDR: what is a 'design'? (9.14–9.33)
- Exclusions from protection in UK UDR (9.34–9.52)
- Original and not 'commonplace' (9.53–9.58)
- Duration (9.59–9.67)
- Rights in UK UDR (9.68–9.79)
- Assessing UK UDR (9.80)
- Interaction with copyright (9.81–9.93)
- Community UDR (9.94–9.102)

International context

9.4 In the previous chapter (see paras 8.4–8.9) we saw how the international treaty framework for the protection of designs did not require protection to be given through a registration system, and even allowed states to choose to protect designs through copyright law. Indeed, the general permissiveness of the international framework extends to enabling states to use more than one form of protection for designs. The creation of unregistered forms of design protection alongside registered designs and copyright systems by, first, the UK, and then by the EU is therefore perfectly consistent with international requirements.

9.5 We also saw in the previous chapter that if there was a registration system the Paris Convention obliged its member states to give foreigners access to that system; and, of course, the Berne Convention requires member states to provide protection under their national law for persons and works from other Berne countries (see para 2.8). However, there is no equivalent international requirement for any system of unregistered design right protection separate from copyright.

9.6 This gap was used by the UK when it created UK UDR in the late 1980s. UK UDR uses a system of *reciprocity*. Foreign nationals will only enjoy UK UDR under the rules governing 'qualification' for UK UDR protection (Copyright, Designs and Patents Act 1988 (CDPA 1988), ss 213(5) and 217–221) where their own legal system provides equivalent protection for UK nationals. The effect of this is that UK companies are able to copy foreign products entering the UK without fear of litigation on the basis of UK UDR ensuing, unless they come from countries with equivalents to UK UDR. The EU countries have been recognised as granting an equivalent protection to the designs of UK nationals, but not the United States and Japan.[1]

 Question

How does 'reciprocity' differ from the usual international principle of 'national treatment'?

9.7 The US Semiconductor Chip Protection Act 1984 was the first piece of legislation to use this technique of 'reciprocity' to gain international compliance with a system of IP rights created to protect national rights.

---

[1] CDPA 1988, s 217(3); the Design Right (Reciprocal Protection) (No 2) Order (SI 1989/1294). It has been noted that CDPA 1988, s 221 (power to make further orders as to qualification) suggests some uncertainty on the part of the UK legislature as to whether equal treatment for Paris Convention nationals is in fact needed, s 221 effectively creating scope to provide for this were it to become necessary: WR Cornish, D Llewelyn, and T Aplin, *Intellectual Property* (7th edn, 2010), para 15-45.

In this it was very successful. When the UK introduced UK UDR in 1988, it followed the US model. The qualification requirements are complex and depend, variously, upon the identity of the designer, the identity of the commissioner or designer's employer if relevant, or upon the first marketing of articles made to the design.[2]

9.8 There is no requirement of 'reciprocity' or equivalent limitation of access to Community UDR. At the time of writing, the UK IPO was consulting on whether to amend the qualification regime for UK UDR.[3]

Key points on international context

- Unregistered design rights are allowed under the international IP treaties
- There may also be more than one form of protection at a time for designs
- Under the Paris Convention, there is no requirement of national treatment outside any design registration system. Because of the UK rules on 'reciprocity' foreigners may only access UK UDR if their national laws give equivalent protection in their countries to UK nationals. There are no such restrictions on access to Community UDR

Historical background to UK UDR

9.9 The introduction of UK UDR and, at the same time, the enactment in the CDPA 1988 of provisions restricting the availability of copyright as a form of protection for designs in the UK (see paras 9.81–9.93) together represented a compromise between allowing copyright protection for designs alongside registered designs, as happened in the UK between 1968 and 1988, and only allowing registered design protection.[4] To understand UK UDR, it is necessary to find out why in the past some businesses thought copyright protection was more useful than registration of designs and why policymakers thought that this use of copyright protection was not desirable.

9.10 Once again, only the briefest reference to the development of unregistered design law in the UK is possible here; a fuller account may be found on this book's Online Resource Centre. Since the 19th century, legislation in the UK continually tried to prevent copyright protection for designs operating alongside the registration system. However, the form of the UK copyright legislation between 1956 and 1988 unintentionally allowed the courts to conclude that unregistered and unregistrable designs could be protected by copyright. This had particular importance in the car replacement part industry.

9.11 Copyright subsists in original artistic works. Artistic works include graphic works, irrespective of artistic quality, and a graphic work includes any drawing, diagram, map, chart, or plan (see paras 2.69–2.81). In relation to an artistic work, the restricted acts of copying include reproduction in any material form and the making of a copy in three dimensions of a two-dimensional work (see para 4.26). It was therefore possible to claim copyright infringement in relation to three-dimensional articles which represented

---

[2] See CDPA 1988, ss 217–221 and 255–256.

[3] 'Consultation on the Reform of the UK Designs Legal Framework' (launched 24 July 2012), p 16 (http://www.ipo.gov.uk/consult-2012-designs.pdf).

[4] Note that, at the time of writing, one of the provisions enacted to restrict the availability of copyright as a form of protection for designs in the UK, CDPA 1988, s 52, is in the process of being repealed, as discussed further at para 9.93.

indirect copies of their underlying design drawings, however simple those drawings had been. Laddie J explained the problem thus:

> In the twenty years prior to the passing of the 1988 Act, copyright lawyers found a new area in which to enforce copyright. The copyright in production drawings was argued to be infringed by the manufacture of three dimensional articles copied, directly or indirectly, from them. The era of industrial copyright had arrived. Litigation proliferated as manufacturers of mundane industrial articles and parts used the copyright in their production drawings to prevent competitors from copying their finished products derived from those drawings. Even if the copyright work consisted of no more than a drawing of two concentric circles on a piece of paper and the alleged infringement consisted of a washer made indirectly from it, copyright could be invoked to take the competing product off the market. It is hardly surprising that not everyone was persuaded that this was the proper place for copyright or that it was of benefit to industry.[5]

Ultimately, to stop this practice the House of Lords held in *British Leyland Motor Corporation Ltd v Armstrong Patents Co Ltd*[6] in 1986 that the copyright in the design drawing for a replacement part (in the case, a car exhaust pipe) could not be exercised 'in derogation from grant' to prevent repair using parts sourced from elsewhere, thereby accepting the existence of the copyright and the infringement claim based on indirect copying, but denying it any practical effect.

9.12   The problem of car spare parts as manifested by, for example, the *British Leyland* case had made apparent the need to remove impediments to a competitive market. The new law in the CDPA 1988, in effect, severely limited protection in UK law for spare parts for cars. But this has not been achieved by legislating specifically for car spare parts but instead by the use of general provisions capable of covering many other situations.

 Question

What was the underlying policy of the 1988 Act with regard to unregistered design protection?

9.13   For present purposes, the 1988 Act dealt with the problem in two key ways:

- first, by severely limiting when the copyright subsisting in certain designs and design drawings may be enforced; and

- secondly, by creating a new unregistered design right, UK UDR, of more limited effect and duration than either copyright or registered design protection.

The intention was that, as a result of the new provisions in the 1988 Act, copyright would cease to be of major significance for industrial designs, although it has not been removed altogether. The spare parts defence propounded by the House of Lords in *British Leyland* (ie no derogation from grant) was not removed in so many words and indeed section 171(3) of the CDPA 1988 provides that nothing in the Act affects any rule of law preventing or restricting the enforcement of copyright on grounds of public interest or otherwise. Given the legal doctrine of precedent, it is therefore technically still possible to plead no derogation from grant against copyright enforcement. However, the hope was that, at any rate with regard to the problem of spare parts, it would not be necessary to do so, because other provisions of the Act took care of the matter. In fact, the defence was used after the entry into force of the 1988 Act, but its death sentence was pronounced in an appeal to the Privy Council in 1997.[7]

---

[5] *Ocular Sciences Ltd v Aspect Vision Care Ltd* [1997] RPC 289 at 421.   [6] [1986] AC 577. See para 5.48.
[7] *Canon Kabushiki Kaisha v Green Cartridge Co (Hong Kong) Ltd* [1997] AC 728 (PC, appeal from Hong Kong). See para 5.48.

UK UDR: what is a 'design'?

9.14 UK UDR is dealt with in Part III of the CDPA 1988. We begin our analysis by considering the designs which may be protected by UK UDR, and noting how this differs from the definition of design already encountered in our earlier discussion of registered designs. As noted previously (see paras 9.6 and 9.7), a design also must meet the rules on qualification for UK UDR protection.

9.15 As we will see in more detail, UK UDR concentrates on the shape and configuration of the whole or part of an article. Surface decoration is not protected. There is, however, no requirement that the design should appeal to the eye, either of the customer or of anyone else.[8] Indeed, it is clear that wholly functional designs are not excluded from UK UDR.[9] So there are a number of contrasts with registered design law.

9.16 The definition of what constitutes a protectable 'design' for UK UDR purposes is set out in section 213 of the CDPA 1988, of which Jacob LJ has memorably observed:

> It has the merit of being short. It has no other ... It is not just a question of drafting (though words and phrases such as 'commonplace', 'dependent', 'aspect of shape or configuration of part of an article' and 'design field in question' are full of uncertainty in themselves and pose near impossible factual questions). The problem is deeper: neither the language used nor the context of the legislation give any clear idea of what was intended. Time and time again one struggles but fails to ascertain a precise meaning, a meaning which men of business can reasonably use to guide their conduct.[10]

Thus forewarned, let us see what we can do to render the section's meaning more comprehensible.

Definition of 'design'

9.17 For the purposes of UK UDR, 'design' means:

> the design of any aspect of the shape or configuration (whether internal or external) of the whole or part of an article (CDPA 1988, s 213(2)).

9.18 Before turning to explain the different elements in this definition, we should also take note of section 213(6) which states that:

> Design right does not subsist unless and until the design has been recorded in a design document or an article has been made to the design.

So, like copyright, the mere idea of a design is not protected; it must be expressed in some tangible form.[11]

9.19 *Design document* is defined as:

> any record of a design, whether in the form of a drawing, a written description, a photograph, data stored in a computer or otherwise (CDPA 1988, s 263(1)).

---

[8] Contrast the former requirement of 'eye-appeal' in the RDA 1949, discussed in the historical outline of the subject accessible in the 'Bonus material' on this book's Online Resource Centre.

[9] *Landor & Hawa International Ltd v Azure Designs Ltd* [2007] FSR 9, paras 10 and 16. See also D Wilkinson, 'Case closed: functional designs protected by design right' [2007] EIPR 118–122.

[10] *Dyson Ltd v Qualtex (UK) Ltd* [2006] RPC 31, para 14.

[11] *Rolawn Ltd v Turfmech Machinery Ltd* [2008] ECDR 13 per Mann J at paras 79–83. See also *Virgin Atlantic Airways Ltd v Premium Aircraft Interiors Group Ltd* [2009] ECDR 11, paras 24–25.

The scope of this definition is wide and, importantly, is not limited to 'documents' as such. The design document does not need to be a sophisticated record of the design:

■ *Lambretta Clothing Co Ltd v Teddy Smith (UK) Ltd* **[2005] RPC 6 (CA)**

It was held that a simple drawing of a track top showing its colours was a design document even although the colours were excluded from UK UDR protection as surface decoration.[12]

9.20   The role of computer technology in design work is recognised in the definition of design document. Data stored in a computer is capable of constituting a design document. Section 214(2) of the CDPA 1988 also refers to computer-generated designs.

> ## Key points on design document
>
> • There must be a design document before UK UDR can subsist
> • A design document is any record of the design and can include the article itself as well as drawings, written descriptions, or data stored in a computer

9.21   We now take each part of the definition of 'design' (see para 9.17) in turn, although not in the order in which they appear in the statutory wording.

Design of the whole or part of an 'article'

9.22   Despite the importance of component or spare parts in the history lying behind UK UDR, UK UDR is not limited to that kind of product. UK UDR applies to 'articles' of all kinds. UK UDR therefore helps the manufacturers of many different kinds of products. Products held to be protected by UK UDR have included pig fenders, slurry separators, lawnmowers, and clothing, so the reach of the right is varied and extensive.

9.23   There is no statutory definition of the meaning of the word 'article' for the purposes of UK UDR. However, there was case law on the meaning of the word 'article' for the purposes of UK registered design law under the old Registered Designs Act 1949 (RDA 1949) as it stood before its amendment to implement the harmonised European registered design regime discussed in Chapter 8:

■ *R v Registered Designs Appeal Tribunal, ex p Ford Motor Co* **[1995] 1 WLR 18 (HL)**

This case was decided under the RDA 1949 as it stood between 1989 and 2001. The issue was whether the designs of spare parts for cars had been 'applied to articles' as required by that version of the 1949 Act. As it stood at that time, the RDA 1949 defined 'article' for the purposes of registered design protection as 'any article of manufacture [including] any part of an article if that part is made and sold separately'. The House of Lords held that there was an essential difference between an item designed for incorporation in a larger article, whether as an original component or a spare part, which would not fall within this definition and which would be unregistrable, and an item designed for general use, albeit aimed principally at use with the manufacturer's own artefacts, which would fall within this definition and be registrable. In order to constitute an 'article' under the then RDA 1949, an item had to have 'an

---

[12] The significance of this was to limit how the copyright in the document might be infringed under CDPA 1988, s 51: see further paras 9.83ff.

independent life as an article of commerce' and could not be 'merely an adjunct of some larger article of which it forms part' (*per* Lord Mustill at 26).

9.24   Adopting a similar approach, there might be an argument that the expression 'article' in section 213(2) of the CDPA 1988 means that UK UDR is intended to arise for the overall design of products complete in themselves or for those parts of such a design which are not excluded by other aspects of the legislation, such as the 'must fit' and 'must match' exceptions (see further paras 9.38ff). However, it is clear from the 'must fit' and 'must match' exceptions that an 'article' which is entitled to protection in its own right in UK UDR can also be part of a larger 'article'; it has also been noted in commentary that there is no reason to import considerations from the old RDA 1949 case law into the definition of 'article' for UK UDR purposes.[13] In *Dyson Ltd v Qualtex (UK) Ltd*,[14] Mann J and the Court of Appeal had no difficulty in holding that parts for vacuum cleaners attracted UK UDR in their own right and not simply as part of the overall design of the cleaners as a whole. Similarly, in *Farmers Build Ltd v Carier Bulk Materials Handling Ltd*, it was held:

> the individual parts, combinations of parts and the parts made up into a whole machine are all 'articles' with a shape and a configuration.[15]

So in principle component parts, including spare parts, can attract UK UDR; however, this is subject to the 'must fit' and 'must match' exceptions, which are intended to exclude such articles from protection to at least some extent (see further paras 9.38ff).

'Any aspect of' shape or configuration

9.25   It is important to bear in mind that the CDPA 1988 permits UK UDR protection for 'any aspect' of the shape or configuration of an article.[16] This includes aspects of detail.[17] It has been held that this means any 'discernible' or 'recognisable' element of the shape or configuration;[18] however, the design feature need not be visually significant.[19] For example:

■ *Ocular Sciences Ltd v Aspect Vision Care Ltd* [1997] RPC 289 (Laddie J)

The products in this case were contact lenses. The designs in which UK UDR was claimed related to the front surface dimensions of the lens, the rear surface dimensions, and the edge characteristics. The lenses differed from each other only in fine dimensional details, but the plaintiffs argued that these dimensions defined the shape or configuration of the lenses. It was held that, although these differences of dimension were indistinguishable by the human eye, that did not mean that they were excluded from protection on the grounds that they were not designs.

9.26   The result of the definition at section 213(2) of the CDPA 1988 is that UK UDR may subsist in many different 'aspects' of the shape or configuration of an article, with many different 'designs', separate or

---

[13] M Howe, *Russell-Clarke and Howe on Industrial Designs* (8th edn, 2010), paras 4-007 and 4-008.

[14] [2005] RPC 19 (Mann J); aff'd [2006] RPC 31 (CA). For commentary on the significance of this case, see A Michaels, 'The end of the road for "pattern spare" parts? *Dyson Ltd v Qualtex (UK) Ltd*' [2006] EIPR 396–398 and J Sykes, 'Designs: the unregistered design right: interpretation and practical application of the must match exemption' (2006) 1(7) JIPLP 442–446.

[15] *Farmers Build Ltd v Carier Bulk Materials Handling Ltd* [1999] RPC 461 at 475. Note that it is not correct to say, as Mummery LJ did in *Farmers Build*, that 'the purpose of introducing the design right was … in the case of spare parts, to remove protection from copying completely' (at 480).   [16] CDPA 1988, s 213(2).

[17] *Dyson Ltd v Qualtex (UK) Ltd* [2006] RPC 31 (CA), para 26.

[18] *A Fulton v Totes Isotoner (UK) Ltd* [2004] RPC 16, para 31; *Dyson Ltd v Qualtex (UK) Ltd* (CA) [2006] RPC 31, paras 22–23.

[19] *Virgin Atlantic Airways Ltd v Premium Aircraft Interiors Group Ltd* [2009] ECDR 11, para 26.

overlapping in different permutations, existing in relation to the same article. As observed by Jacob LJ in *Dyson Ltd v Qualtex (UK) Ltd*:

> This is extremely wide—it means that a particular article may and generally will embody a multitude of 'designs'—as many 'aspects' of the whole or part of the article as can be.[20]

9.27   This has important tactical implications for how UK UDR cases are pleaded. As noted by the UK courts, the rightholder may tailor his definition of what he says constitutes his 'design' by reference to the particular aspects of shape or configuration of his article which he says have been copied:

> The proprietor can choose to assert design right in the whole or *any* part of his product. If the right is said to reside in the design of a teapot, this can mean that it resides in design of the whole pot, or in a part such as the spout, the handle or the lid, or, indeed, in a part of the lid. This means that the proprietor can trim his design right claim to most closely match what he believes the defendant to have taken. The defendant will not know in what the alleged monopoly resides until the letter before action or, more usually, the service of the statement of claim.[21]

It has been observed that there is a danger that the ability of the claimant to focus on parts of his design which are small in comparison to the overall article could give rise to 'a distorted impression of what the defendant has done which comes close to reversing the burden of proof.'[22] At the time of writing, the UK IPO was consulting on whether to amend the definition of 'design' for UK UDR purposes to reduce the scope for 'trimming' a claim.[23] In the meantime, the flexibility in UK UDR contrasts with the nature of protection conferred by design registration where the registered design is defined in each case by what is shown in representations filed, with no option to omit or focus down on only some of the features shown in those representations.

'Whether internal or external': visibility

9.28   UK UDR is expressly not limited to what is visible when the article in question is in use (contrast registered design protection for component parts of complex products: see paras 8.73–8.78). The design could be one which spends its entire operative life concealed within or beneath another article, as with a terminal in a washing machine, or an exhaust pipe in a car; or it could be the internal parts of a product which also has external parts, such as the shape and configuration of the inside of a car roof box. For example, in *Farmers Build Ltd v Carier Bulk Materials Handling Ltd*,[24] the designs in question included internal component parts of the disputed slurry separators.

'Shape or configuration'

9.29   At the time of the enactment of the CDPA 1988, 'shape' and 'configuration' were concepts already familiar from UK registered design law where, until the reforms to UK registered design law triggered by the Designs Directive, they were usually taken as referring to the three-dimensional aspects of a product, as distinct from two-dimensional pattern or ornamentation applied to the surface of the article. Thus, a feature of UK UDR which appeared distinctive in 1988 was that it did *not* apply to two-dimensional

[20] *Dyson Ltd v Qualtex (UK) Ltd* [2006] RPC 31 (CA), para 22.
[21] *Ocular Sciences Ltd v Aspect Vision Care Ltd* [1997] RPC 289 at 422. Note that the acceptability of this approach has been upheld by the Court of Appeal in *A Fulton v Totes Isotoner (UK) Ltd* [2004] RPC 16, where Jacob LJ comments:

> I do not fully go along with Laddie J's suggestion that what the proprietor can do is to 'trim his design right claim'. It is not really a question of 'trimming'—it is just identifying the part of his overall design which he claims has been taken exactly or substantially. And although Laddie J. was right in saying that the defendant will not know in what the *alleged* (my emphasis) monopoly resides until the letter before action or the claim form, that does not mean the defendant does not know where he stands before then. The man who copies a part of an article, exactly or substantially, will know what he has taken (para 34).

[22] *Virgin Atlantic Airways Ltd v Premium Aircraft Interiors Group Ltd* [2009] ECDR 11, para 29.
[23] 'Consultation on the Reform of the UK Designs Legal Framework' (launched 24 July 2012), pp 9–10 (http://www.ipo.gov.uk/consult-2012-designs.pdf).   [24] [1999] RPC 461.

'pattern and ornamentation'. This seemed also to be underlined by the exclusion of 'surface decoration' of an article from the scope of UK UDR. However, the UK UDR case law has blurred the distinction between the three- and the two-dimensional.

9.30   The basis for this has been the legislation's apparent distinction between 'shape' *or* 'configuration'. While shape certainly refers to three-dimensional features, it has been suggested that configuration may cover at least some two- as well as three-dimensional designs. So electronic circuit diagrams[25] have been held covered by UK UDR as 'configurations'.

■ *Mackie Designs Inc v Behringer Specialised Studio Equipment (UK) Ltd* [1999] RPC 717 (Pumfrey J)

It was held that electronic circuit diagrams were covered by UK UDR, as 'configuration' rather than shape; 'configuration' should be broadly construed to cover 'the relative arrangement of parts or elements'.

9.31   The limits of this broad approach to 'configuration' are not clear, although the case has potential analogies with mechanical engineering designs, such as pneumatic and hydraulic circuits, and chemical or process flow diagrams. Design right applies to semiconductor topographies, although these are essentially patterns fixed or etched upon semiconductor material, rather than shapes or configurations. The availability of the protection is, however, the result of express legislation, the Design Right (Semiconductor Topographies) Regulations 1989,[26] which apply the design right provisions of the 1988 Act to this subject matter.

9.32   The broad approach suggested in *Mackie* has been criticised: a merely schematic diagram[27] of something, which does not convey the physical actuality of that which is represented, cannot be the design of an article, since it could be represented by any one of several different articles. Contrast this earlier case (not discussed in *Mackie Designs*):

■ *Baby Dan AS v Brevi Srl and Another* [1999] FSR 377 (HC)

BD manufactured and sold child safety barriers in the UK, and BS distributed them in Italy. The barrier consisted of various component parts. When the distributorship ceased, BS started to manufacture child safety barriers in Italy, and the second defendant imported and sold these barriers in the UK. BD claimed that there was copying by BS and infringement by both defendants. It was held that the *relative locations* of interrelated functional parts of BD's safety barrier were not aspects of its configuration.

Discussion point For answer guidance visit www.oxfordtextbooks.co.uk/orc/waelde3e/

Refer to the discussion in paras 2.64 and 2.65 about electronic circuit diagrams and copyright, then consider how such diagrams differ from the designs of child safety barriers as revealed in the *Baby Dan* case. Why are the relative locations of the component parts of the latter not 'configuration' when electronic circuit diagrams apparently are? Can this outcome be justified?

---

[25] On the nature of electronic circuit diagrams, and the definitional problems they pose for copyright law, see paras 2.64–2.65. See also, for analysis before the cases began to come before the courts, J Reynolds and P Brownlow, 'Increased legal protection for schematic designs in the United Kingdom' [1994] EIPR 398–400.   [26] SI 1989/1100 (as amended).

[27] A well-known example of a schematic diagram, discussed in *Lambretta Clothing Co Ltd v Teddy Smith (UK) Ltd* [2005] RPC 6 (CA) at para 27, is the map of the London Underground, from which it is not possible to determine the actual geographical position of the stations or of the exact routes followed by the tunnels although one can tell what the relative positions are and the connections between them. Jacob LJ in *Lambretta* noted that 'there may well be force' in the criticism of *Mackie*: para 27.

9.33   The courts have rejected arguments that seek to reduce the definition of what constitutes 'configuration' down simply to a question of whether the design is two- or three-dimensional:

■ *Lambretta Clothing Co Ltd v Teddy Smith (UK) Ltd* [2005] RPC 6 (CA)

The article in question was L's track top, the shape of which was old (or 'retro'). The new feature was the choice of colours ('colourways')—blue for the body, red for the arms, white for the zip. L claimed T was copying and selling these tops. L claimed that the colourways were protected as configuration of the garment. It was held that UK UDR did not subsist in L's top. Giving the main judgment, Jacob LJ pointed out that the equivalent wording in the then UK registered designs law had never been interpreted such as to include colouration as 'configuration' and ruled that, even with a wide interpretation of the word 'configuration', UK UDR does not subsist in the arrangement of colours or in patterns, such as that of a patchwork quilt. Suggesting that it was 'a peripheral dead-end' to seek to analyse the issue by reference to whether the design was two- or three-dimensional (para 23), Jacob LJ remarked:

> I do not think that a debate about dimensions assists. All articles (even thin flat ones) are 3 dimensional (using the practical Euclidean view of the world—not that of modern physics). There is no reason why a 'design' should not subsist in what people would ordinarily call a 'flat' or '2-dimensional' thing—for instance a new design of doily would have a new 'shape' and could in principle have UK UDR in it.[28]

■ *A Fulton Co Ltd v Grant Barnett & Co Ltd* [2001] RPC 16 (Park J)

Outward-facing stitched seams on the edges of a rectangular box-shaped case for a compact umbrella accentuated the rectangular (rather than the more usual cylindrical) character of the product. It was held that the seams were protected as significant aspects of the shape or configuration of the case (and not excluded as surface decoration), even though only marginally three-dimensional. This was described as a 'value judgment for the court to make'.[29]

Key points on the definition of 'design'

- UK UDR can apply to 'articles' of all kinds, including component and spare parts
- UK UDR will subsist in 'any aspect', internal or external, of the shape or configuration of the whole or part of such an article; the relevant feature need not be visually significant nor is there any requirement that it be visible in ordinary use
- The words 'shape or configuration' suggest that UK UDR protects the design of three- rather than two-dimensional design features, but the concept of 'configuration' has proved controversial and difficult to define with courts reluctant to simplify the issue to a three- vs two-dimensional analysis
- Purely functional designs are not excluded from UK UDR (but note must fit/must match exclusions discussed later)

---

[28] [2005] RPC 6, para 24.   [29] [2001] RPC 257, para 79.

Exclusions from protection in UK UDR

Surface decoration

9.34 Section 213(3)(c) of the CDPA 1988 excludes 'surface decoration' from the scope of UK UDR. This exclusion is justified on the basis that generally such surface decoration will be the subject of copyright and so does not need the additional protection of UK UDR.[30] At first sight, the exclusion seems simply to reaffirm the primary concern of UK UDR with the three-dimensional rather than the two-dimensional. However, the case law shows that the position is somewhat more complex, since the exclusion has been held to affect three-dimensional features of a design in some instances:

■ *Mark Wilkinson Furniture Ltd v Woodcraft Designs (Radcliffe) Ltd* [1998] FSR 63 (HC)

This case concerned fitted kitchens. The plaintiff's kitchen units had a number of features including a painted surface, curved quadrant corners between the front and side panels, cornicing, shallow v-grooves, cockbeading, and recessed panels. It was held that surface decoration included both decoration lying on the surface of the article (such as a painted finish) and decorative features of the surface itself (such as beading or engraving), and was not restricted to features that were essentially two-dimensional. Applying this test, the painted finish, v-grooves, and cockbeading were excluded from protection as surface decoration. But the cornice, quadrant corners, and recessed panels were not excluded from UK UDR.

■ *A Fulton Co Ltd v Grant Barnett & Co Ltd* [2001] RPC 16 (HC)

It was argued that the stitched seams of the umbrella case were excluded as surface decoration. This argument was rejected. The judge emphasised that it did not follow that, because the seams existed only very slightly in three dimensions, they must be surface decoration. In the court's view (as noted previously, para 9.33), the seams were 'significant aspects' of shape or configuration and not excluded as surface decoration (para 78).

■ *Lambretta Clothing Co Ltd v Teddy Smith (UK) Ltd* [2005] RPC 6 (CA)

See previously para 9.33. T claimed that the colourways of the retro track tops were surface decoration; L responded that the colours ran right through the garment, not just its surface. This argument was rejected and it was held that UK UDR did not subsist in L's top, Jacob LJ commenting:

It is true that the parts of the garment are dyed right through, but any realistic and practical construction of the words 'surface decoration' must cover both the case where a surface is covered with a thin layer and where the decoration, like that in Brighton rock, runs throughout the article. To hold otherwise would mean that whether or not UDR could subsist in two different articles, having exactly the same outward appearance, depended on how deep the colours went. Parliament cannot have intended anything so capricious (para 30).

The court affirmed the approach of the judge in *Mark Wilkinson* (above) that surface decoration could be more than essentially flat, and could be three-dimensional.

■ *Dyson Ltd v Qualtex (UK) Ltd* [2006] RPC 31 (CA)

It was argued that ribbing on the handle and tool adaptor of the Dyson vacuum cleaner was excluded from protection in UK UDR because it was surface decoration. Jacob LJ held that the exclusion should

[30] *Dyson Ltd v Qualtex (UK) Ltd* [2006] RPC 31 per Jacob LJ at para 76.

be limited 'to that which can fairly be described as a decorated surface' (para 81). Surface features which had 'significant function' were not surface decoration (para 83). In this case, the ribbing had a functional purpose of providing a grip and was not excluded. This was, furthermore, consistent with the perception of the reasonable consumer or designer who would not have regarded the ribbing as merely a decorated surface.[31]

9.35   In *Dyson Ltd v Qualtex (UK) Ltd*,[32] Jacob LJ held that whether matter on a surface constituted surface decoration was 'a question of degree'. The judge at first instance in this case had described this as potentially a 'matter of fact and impression, or a value judgment'.[33] The judge in *Fulton v Grant Barnett* (see para 9.33) also described this as a 'value judgment'.[34] It is clear from these cases that determining whether a particular design feature is 'surface decoration' cannot be resolved simply asking whether the feature is two- or three-dimensional; instead, this will be a qualitative and fact-dependent exercise to be assessed in the individual context of each case.

 Discussion point For answer guidance visit www.oxfordtextbooks.co.uk/orc/waelde3e/

What is the difference between 'shape or configuration' and 'surface decoration'?

Key points on surface decoration exclusion

- Surface decoration is not limited to two-dimensional ornamentation of the article but can extend to three-dimensional features

- It can include features which run right through an article from its surface (eg colourways on a garment)

- If the feature has a significant functional purpose, it is unlikely to be excluded from UK UDR protection as mere surface decoration

---

Methods or principles of construction

9.36   Methods and principles of construction are excluded from UK UDR by section 213(3)(a) of the CDPA 1988. This excludes from protection the process or operation by which a shape is produced, rather than the resulting shape itself:

■ *A Fulton Co Ltd v Grant Barnett & Co Ltd* [2001] RPC 16 (HC)

In this case, the outward-facing stitched seams and box-shape of the compact umbrella case were challenged as constituting 'methods or principles of construction'. This challenge was rejected. It was held:

> It is certainly true that there are methods of construction involved in the creation of the Miniflat case … However, the design of the case is the shape or configuration produced by those methods of construction, not the methods by which that shape or configuration is produced. The fact that a special method or principle of construction may have to be used in order to create an article with a particular shape or configuration does not mean that there is no design right in the shape or configuration. The law of design right will not prevent competitors using that

---

[31] [2006] RPC 31 (CA), paras 73–84.   [32] [2006] RPC 31 (CA), para 81.
[33] *Dyson Ltd v Qualtex (UK) Ltd* [2005] RPC 19 (Mann J), para 38.   [34] [2001] RPC 257, para 79.

method or principle of construction to create competing designs ... as long as the competing designs do not have the same shape or configuration as the design right owner's design has.[35]

9.37   This exclusion does not exclude a design from protection because it has a functional purpose:

■ *Landor & Hawa International Ltd v Azure Designs Ltd* **[2007] FSR 9 (CA)**

The arrangement of zippers and piping for the expander section of a suitcase design was held *not* to be a principle or method of construction. Upholding the judge at first instance, Neuberger LJ emphasised that section 213(3)(a) does not exclude a design merely because it has a functional purpose or because every element of the design was intended to perform a functional purpose. While section 213(3)(a) might apply if the design in suit was the only way of achieving the functional purpose of the design, such that the UK UDR protection for the shape of the design in effect also granted protection for the method of its construction and would thereby stop others from using that method, that was not the case on the facts.[36]

'Must fit, must match'

9.38   The so-called *'must fit'* and *'must match'* exclusions reflect some of the problem areas relating to spare parts which developed as a result of the availability of copyright protection before the CDPA 1988. These exclusions are, however, not limited to spare parts but will apply to any design falling within their terms. Although commonly referred to as the 'must fit' and 'must match' exclusions, when interpreting and applying these provisions the Court of Appeal has cautioned that 'one must go by the actual language and not by the epithet or even the notion behind the epithet'.[37]

9.39   The 'must fit' exclusion removes from protection in UK UDR features of shape or configuration of an article which:

enable the article to be connected to or placed in, around or against another article so that either article may perform its function (CDPA 1988, s 213(3)(b)(i)).

9.40   The 'must match' exclusion removes from UK UDR features of shape or configuration of an article which:

are dependent upon the appearance of another article of which the article is intended by the designer to form an integral part (CDPA 1988, s 213(3)(b)(ii)).

 Question

What are the key elements in these definitions of 'must fit' and 'must match' designs?

9.41   Despite the legislative background, the Court of Appeal has held that it is not possible to discern any clear purposive intent in terms of whether these provisions are pro- or anti-spare parts:

I do not think it is possible to approach the provisions with any clear purposive intent in mind. Given the White Paper and the extremely complex economic arguments involved it is not possible to give a purposive construction—you need a reasonably clear idea of purpose before you can do that.... Here on the one hand

---

[35] [2001] RPC 16, para 70.   [36] [2007] FSR 9 (CA), paras 8–29.
[37] *Dyson Ltd v Qualtex (UK) Ltd* [2006] RPC 31 (CA), para 27.

Parliament refused to create a general spare parts exception, and on the other hand clearly did not intend that OEMs [original equipment manufacturers] should have absolute control over the manufacture of spares. A compromise (some might say fudge) in the form of the language actually chosen in the Act was what was done. We must construe it as it would be read by a reasonable reader. Here that means taking the language as it stands.[38]

Question

What was the main objective of the 'must fit' and 'must match' exceptions to UK UDR?

9.42   What, then, is the scope of the exceptions apart from those cases to which they were a direct response, and more generally outside the motor industry? The case law now allows us to say quite a bit more about both exceptions.

'Must fit'

9.43   A large number of the cases about 'must fit' have not involved cars or other motor vehicles. For example:

■ *Ocular Sciences Ltd v Aspect Vision Care Ltd* **[1997] RPC 289 (Laddie J)**

The defendants argued that a number of the features of the lenses in which UK UDR was claimed were present to enable the lens to fit another article—the wearer's eyeball—and to correct the wearer's vision, that is, perform its function. The plaintiffs responded that the eyeball, as a part of the human body, was not an 'article' to which the lens was to be fitted. It was held (*obiter*)[39] that any design feature falling within the criteria at section 213(3)(b)(i) was excluded from protection by the 'must fit' exception, even if it performed another function (eg if it was attractive). There was no requirement that the design feature be the only way of achieving the desired interface. There is also no requirement that the designer's intention be for the articles to fit: it is sufficient if they in fact do. In addition, the word 'article' did not have a restricted meaning, and could apply to living and formerly living things as well as inanimate objects. The back radius, diameter, 'CN bevel', and parallel peripheral carrier of the contact lenses in suit enabled them to fit against the eyeball and to perform their function of correcting vision while remaining stable in the eye. These features were excluded from UK UDR under the 'must fit' exception.

9.44   The scope of this characterisation of the human body—and, indeed, animate things in general—as articles to which other articles may be fitted raises several interesting questions. What about clothes, for example? If clothes can come within the exception, is there a relevant difference between individually tailored and off-the-peg garments? Some of the possible issues arose in the slightly different context provided by the following case.

■ *Amoena v Trulife* **(unreported, 25 May 1995) (Chancery Division, Deputy Judge Jonathan Sumption QC)**

This case concerned claims of UK UDR in breast prostheses for mastectomy patients. The aim of a prosthesis designer is to emulate the appearance of a woman's breast, not in its natural state but in a bra. The

---

[38] *Dyson Ltd v Qualtex (UK) Ltd* [2006] RPC 31 (CA), para 11.

[39] Because it was held that in any event there was no copying and thus no infringement.

shapes of bras, governed in part by fashion, are much less variable than those of breasts. It was argued that the shape of the front of the prosthesis was determined by the need to enable it to be placed in and against the bra so that both objects performed their functions. It was held, rejecting the argument, that 'must fit' was concerned with a much more precise correspondence between two articles, such as a rigid plug and socket.

9.45   Deputy Judge Sumption's approach is open to question, however, on the basis that nothing in the statutory language requires a feature to be the only way to achieve an interface between two products for it to fall within the exclusion. If a number of 'fits' are possible, in other words, the feature is still 'must fit': see *Ocular Sciences* discussed previously.[40]

Question

To what extent do articles meant to be worn with or attached to the human body fall within the 'must fit' exception?

9.46   The potential reach of this approach can be illustrated by other UK UDR disputes. In *Dyson Ltd v Qualtex (UK) Ltd*,[41] there was dispute over the handle of a Dyson vacuum cleaner. Despite the *Ocular Sciences* precedent, it was *not* argued that some parts of the handle, such as certain triggers and a catch, being designed to interface with the human finger or thumb, were excluded from UK UDR as 'must fit' features. But could they have been?

Discussion point   For answer guidance visit www.oxfordtextbooks.co.uk/orc/waelde3e/

What if any parts of an artificial human limb or joint (eg artificial knee), or of a heart pacemaker might be considered as protectable by UK UDR? Are there any other examples of such products?

9.47   It is not enough for the purposes of this exclusion that the article in suit is simply intended to be placed in, around, or against another article. The excluded design features must be such as to 'enable' the article to be so placed:

■ *A Fulton Co Ltd v Grant Barnett & Co Ltd* [2001] RPC 16 (HC)

The rectangular umbrella decision (see previously para 9.33). The judge stressed that section 231(3)(b)(i) only provides that UK UDR cannot subsist in features of shape or configuration which *enable* the article to be so placed so that either article can perform their function. In that case, the particular features which gave the umbrella case its shape (the rectangular box-shape and the outward-facing seams) were not designed to enable it to perform the function of containing the umbrella: they were so designed to 'perform the function of looking attractive and promoting sales of the product, not to perform the function of enabling the case to be placed around the umbrella' (para 75).

---

[40] [1997] RPC 289 per Laddie J at 424.   [41] [2006] RPC 31 (CA).

Exercise

Consider the application of the 'must fit' exception to the Lego brick. Bear in mind that *Interlego AG v Tyco Industries Inc* [1989] AC 217 held that the design of the original Lego brick was registrable under UK registered designs law as it then stood. Is it possible now for a design to be registrable and yet unable to attract UK UDR?

9.48   By itself, the 'must fit' exclusion does not deprive designs of UK UDR protection altogether: only the design features which enable the article to be fitted to another article in order for either article to perform their function are unprotected as a result. For example:

■ *Baby Dan AS v Brevi Srl and Another* [1999] FSR 377 (HC)

The child safety barriers case (see previously para 9.32). The barriers were made up of component parts. It was argued that this meant that there was no UK UDR protection as all such parts had to fit together to create the barrier as whole. This argument was rejected. It was held that the 'must fit' exception did not exclude the various parts of the barrier relied upon, in its embodiment not as a number of parts but as one single larger article, that is, as a barrier itself. Hence, the design of parts of the barrier, such as the cam housing and the spindle retainer, were protected.

9.49   The most significant more recent case on this exclusion is *Dyson v Qualtex* concerning spare or pattern parts for Dyson vacuum cleaners.

■ *Dyson Ltd v Qualtex (UK) Ltd* [2005] RPC 19 (Mann J); aff'd [2006] RPC 31 (CA)

While the parties agreed that large numbers of the disputed parts were affected by the 'must fit' exception—such as the stop on the main wand handle of the cleaner which interacted with the stop on the release catch and aspects of the cable winder and tools[42]—at first instance the judge ruled that many others were not: for example, airholes in the top of the head of the device's stair tool. On appeal, various points of principle emerged. First, a clearance (ie empty space) which arises as a result of the design of the two articles is capable, in principle, of forming excluded subject matter: the two articles in question do not have to touch in order for there to be a relevant interface. However, this clearance must be intended to *enable* one or other of the articles to work, not just to avoid *interfering* with the functioning of that article.[43] The exclusion will apply to features which make an article function more effectively or safely.[44] It also does not matter in what order the articles concerned are designed.[45]

 Exercise

Consider in the light of the foregoing (1) the view of Robert Englehart QC in *Parker v Tidball* [1997] FSR 680 that a leather carrying case for a mobile phone is caught by the 'must fit' exception; and (2) the contrasting view of Park J in *A Fulton Co Ltd v Grant Barnett & Co Ltd* [2001] RPC 16 that an umbrella case, designed to fit around an umbrella, is not. Which view is, in your opinion, correct as a matter of the interpretation of section 213(3)(b)(i) of the CDPA 1988? Can you reconcile these cases?

---

[42]   The full and lengthy list can be found in a schedule to Mann J's judgment.
[43]   *Dyson Ltd v Qualtex (UK) Ltd* [2006] RPC 31 (CA), paras 36 and 38.
[44]   *Dyson Ltd v Qualtex (UK) Ltd* [2006] RPC 31 (CA), paras 40–44.
[45]   *Dyson Ltd v Qualtex (UK) Ltd* [2006] RPC 31 (CA), para 46.

Key points on the 'must fit' exception

- The 'must fit' exception applies only to the interconnecting parts of the relevant article
- The relevant design features must be intended to enable the relevant article to be connected to or placed in, around, or against another article so that either article can perform its function
- The fact that the connection or placement may be effected in different ways does not prevent the relevant features of any one particular design which achieves this connection or placement being subject to the 'must fit' exception

'Must match'

9.50   This exclusion has been described as the 'aesthetic counterpart' to the 'must fit' exclusion.[46] When the CDPA 1988 was passing through Parliament in the House of Lords, it was commented:

> The must match exception is intended to prevent monopolies arising in the first place, and to preserve the benefits of competition. Although design right is only a right to prevent copying, it is quite clear that in circumstances where a competitor has no choice but to copy if he is to produce a part which will match, then if there were no must match exception he would be completely shut out of the market. This is not a question of abuse but of basic policy. And I have to say that this Government does not wish to create monopolies in this way in any sector of industry ... And we should be quite clear about this: the absence of a must match exception would enable competition in certain kinds of product to be totally frozen out. In our view that is not the way that the markets should operate.[47]

 Question

Is there an equivalent of the UK UDR 'must match' exception in the law of registered designs (see Chapter 8)?

9.51   The 'must match' exclusion is not a blanket exclusion of all accessory or spare parts. To be excluded, the relevant design features of the article in suit must be 'dependent' on the appearance of the larger article of which the article in dispute is intended to form part. However, there is no definition of what 'dependent' means or what degree of dependency is required for the exclusion to bite. As Mann J pointed out in *Dyson Ltd v Qualtex (UK) Ltd*:[48]

> most consumer goods are likely to have been produced from a designer's pen (or CAD package). If made up of more than one part (which, again, most will have been) then each of those parts is likely to have been designed with the others in mind, and to fit in.

It was argued that 'the design of each will be dependent on the appearance of the whole because that is how the designer will have intended it' (para 60). This analysis would, however, have the effect of exempting most external aspects of a product's design from UK UDR, a conclusion Mann J found unacceptably wide. Instead he took from the earlier case law, dealing with the equivalent provision in the then UK registered design law, a test of design dependency which made the 'must match' exception bite

[46] M Howe, *Russell-Clarke and Howe on Industrial Designs* (8th edn, 2010), para 4-026.
[47] Parliamentary Debates, 29 March 1988, HL, col 699.   [48] [2005] RPC 19, para 60.

only where changing the appearance of the article for which UK UDR was claimed would make the appearance of the overall article 'radically different'.[49] In assessing this, the saleability of the replacement article would be useful evidence or a cross-check, since consumers would probably not buy something which radically changed the appearance of the overall product. Applying this test, Mann J held that the design features of the Dyson vacuum cleaner handle were not caught by the 'must match' exclusion, because they could be changed without radically affecting the appearance of the vacuum cleaner, and there was no evidence to show that consumers required this utilitarian household product to retain its overall appearance.[50] The test and its application to the facts were essentially approved in the Court of Appeal. Describing the notion of 'dependency' as an 'elusive concept', Jacob LJ said:

> 'Dependency' must be viewed practically. In some cases the answer is obvious—the paradigm example being body parts of cars. In others it may be necessary to examine the position more carefully. But unless the spare parts dealer can show that as a practical matter there is a real need to copy a feature of shape or configuration because of some design consideration of the whole article, he is not within the exclusion. It is not enough to assert that the public 'prefers' an exact copy ... The more there is design freedom the less is there room for the exclusion. In the end it is a question of degree—the sort of thing where a judge is called upon to make a value judgment.[51]

Jacob LJ held that, if as a practical matter there was design freedom, then there was no dependency (para 63).

 Question

What is meant by the 'dependency' test for a 'must match' design?

9.52   The exception does not apply to 'families' of items such as dinner services and crockery sets. The requirement that, for this exclusion to apply, the replacement article should be an 'integral part' of the other article whose appearance it is to match prevents this result. Take the example of a cup and saucer in a tea set: while the two items are undoubtedly meant to 'match', neither forms an 'integral part' of the other. See also:

■ *Mark Wilkinson Furniture Ltd v Woodcraft Designs (Radcliffe) Ltd* **[1998] FSR 63 (HC)**

The kitchen furniture case (see para 9.34). It was held that the 'must match' exclusion did not apply to the plaintiff's kitchen units because the complete fitted kitchen was a series of matching articles, none of which formed 'an integral part of' the others.

 Discussion point For answer guidance visit www.oxfordtextbooks.co.uk/orc/waelde3e/

How do the UK UDR 'must fit/must match' exceptions differ from those applying to registered designs (see Chapter 8)?

---

[49] *Dyson Ltd v Qualtex (UK) Ltd* [2005] RPC 19, paras 63–64.
[50] *Dyson Ltd v Qualtex (UK) Ltd* [2005] RPC 19, para 80. However, Mann J had accepted the status of Dyson machines as 'design icons' (para 71). This may implicitly justify the view that the designers had earned the reward of UK UDR, of which they should not be deprived by giving the exceptions too wide scope.   [51] *Dyson Ltd v Qualtex (UK) Ltd* [2006] RPC 31, para 64.

> ## Key points on the 'must match' exception
>
> - The 'must match' exception catches designs of articles which are subordinate in aesthetic terms to the overall design of another article
> - However, the requirement of dependency upon the appearance of another article of which the article in question is to be an integral part restricts the scope of the exception; whether there is such a 'dependency' will be a value judgment turning on the extent to which there is design freedom or a different design would radically alter the appearance of the overall article

Original and not commonplace

9.53 Designs must be 'original' to attract UK UDR: CDPA 1988, s 213(1). A later subsection provides that:

> A design is not 'original' for the purposes of this Part if it is commonplace in the design field in question at the time of its creation (CDPA 1988, s 213(4)).

It might have been thought that this meant the test of originality in unregistered design right is *not* the same as in copyright. However, the case law shows that a two-step approach should be taken to this question, asking:

(1) *whether the design is original in the copyright sense* of being independently produced as a result of the designer's own skill and labour, and not copied from the work of another;[52] and

(2) *whether or not the design is commonplace in the design field in question*, usually resulting in a subsidiary, but necessary, further analysis of what constitutes that design field.

Most of the decisions have been concerned with step (2), that is, how to test 'commonplace-ness':

■ *C & H Engineering Ltd v F Klucznik & Sons Ltd* [1992] FSR 421 (Aldous J)

This case concerned pig fenders, devices to stop piglets leaving the sty while enabling the sow to step over into the field outside the sty. It was important that the fender be shaped so that the sow's teats were not scratched as she stepped over it. The fender in the case solved this problem by having a two-inch rounded metal tube placed around its top edge. Aldous J held first that the word 'original' in section 213(1) of the CDPA 1988 should mean the same as in copyright, namely that the design is not copied but is the independent work of the designer. The judge went on to address the section 213(4) CDPA 1988 requirement that the design not be 'commonplace'. Aldous J concluded that: 'For the design to be original it must be the work of the creator and that work must result in a design which is not commonplace in the relevant field' (at 428).

■ *Ocular Sciences Ltd v Aspect Vision Care Ltd* [1997] RPC 289 (Laddie J)

The contact lenses case (see para 9.25). The defendants argued that the lens designs were commonplace; the plaintiffs' response was that the combinations of dimensions for which UK UDR was claimed had not been used before and were not commonplace. Laddie J held that:

---

[52] On the copyright concept of originality, see paras 2.34–2.44. Although, as discussed in paras 2.39–2.40, there have been questions as to the impact (if any) on UK law of recent Court of Justice case law on the concept of 'originality' in copyright, this issue has not yet been addressed in UK UDR case law.

Any design which is trite, trivial, common-or-garden, hackneyed or of the type which would excite no particular attention in those in the relevant art is likely to be commonplace. This does not mean that a design made up of features which, individually, are commonplace is necessarily itself commonplace. A new and exciting design can be produced from the most trite of ingredients. But to secure protection, the combination itself must not be commonplace (at 429–430).

On the facts, Laddie J accepted expert evidence that there were no features to distinguish the plaintiff's designs from other lens designs available on the market. The plaintiff's designs were commonplace.

■ *Farmers Build Ltd v Carier Bulk Materials Handling Ltd* [1999] RPC 461 (CA)

The case concerned competing slurry separators. The plaintiffs' slurry separator was in part based on the designs of two earlier separators, and internally the machinery was based around 'hoppers' which the respondents argued had long been in use for agricultural machinery. It was held that the design was original in the sense of it being the independent work of the designer and not having been simply copied from the earlier machines. Counsel for the defendant submitted that all of the parts relied upon in the action and their combination as a whole were commonplace. However, it was held by the Court of Appeal that neither the parts nor the whole could be described as commonplace, even though they might involve basic articles and simple engineering principles. The requirement that a design not be commonplace was not equivalent to a requirement of 'novelty'. Having reviewed the authorities and legislative background and considered UK UDR in the round, Mummery LJ explained that the assessment of 'commonplace-ness' should be as follows (at 482–483). First, the court should compare the design of the article in which design right is claimed with the design of other articles in the same field, including the alleged infringing article, as at the time of the creation of the design in suit. Secondly, it should assess originality bearing in mind that, taking into account the functional aspect of design compared to pure works of art, one design may be very similar to, or even identical with, another design but not have been copied. To assess whether the design is commonplace, the court needs to ascertain how similar that design is to the design of similar articles in the same field of design. This is a comparative exercise which must be conducted objectively and in the light of the evidence, including evidence from experts in the relevant field on the similarities and differences, and their significance. The closer the similarity of the designs to each other, the more likely it is that the designs are commonplace, especially if there is no causal link (such as copying) which would account for the similarity. If a number of designers working independently of one another in the same field produce very similar designs, this may indicate that there is only one way of designing that article. On the other hand, if there are aspects of the design which are not to be found in any other design in the field, the court would be entitled to conclude that the design in question was not commonplace. A commonplace *article* can have an un-commonplace shape or configuration.[53]

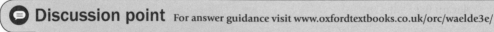

● **Discussion point**   For answer guidance visit www.oxfordtextbooks.co.uk/orc/waelde3e/

What is the difference between 'original' and 'not commonplace'?

9.54   The UK UDR requirement that a design be original and not commonplace in its design field looks like a halfway house between the copyright requirement of originality and the registered design standards of

---

[53] For a later illustration of this, see *A Fulton Co Ltd v Grant Barnett & Co Ltd* [2001] RPC 16, para 54 (umbrella cases are commonplace articles, but the rectangular shapes in suit were not a commonplace design for such articles).

'novelty' and 'individual character'. The differences with the registered design standards was stressed in *A Fulton Co Ltd v Grant Barnett & Co Ltd*,[54] where the court observed:

> A design should not be denied design right protection merely because the defendant, in researching what is often referred to as the 'prior art', discovers an obscure article which is fairly similar to the design in which design right is claimed. That would not be enough to make the claimant's design commonplace (para 52).

9.55 The assessment of whether a design is original in the UK UDR sense will relate to those aspects of the design which are left once the application of any relevant exclusions from protection has been determined. There are some further sub-questions which arise in relation to the 'commonplace' test at section 213(4) of the CDPA 1988:

The design field question: what is the 'design field' against which the design claiming UK UDR should be assessed?

9.56 In *Scholes Windows Ltd v Magnet Ltd*,[55] a case concerning historically-influenced window frame designs made in unplasticated PVC, it was held at first instance that the design field was window frames generally, including timber sash frames as well as uPVC frames. This was upheld by the Court of Appeal. Design was defined in relation to shape and configuration, not in relation to materials or the nature/purpose of the article in question, and the design field should therefore be also defined in relation to shape or configuration. In considering the design field, the court had to take account of what designs were in the field at the time of the creation of the design in question, including old designs such as Victorian window frames which were still in use and could be seen by designers and interested parties in many houses. There was no reason not to include old designs if they could fairly and reasonably still be regarded as in the design field at the relevant time. In *Lambretta Clothing Co Ltd v Teddy Smith (UK) Ltd*,[56] it was held that 'a reasonably broad approach' to the design field was called for (para 45). What mattered was the sort of designs with which 'a notional designer of the article concerned would be familiar' (para 45). In this case, the design of well-known actual sportswear (whether strictly so-called or not) would be part of the background in the mind of a designer wishing to give a garment a sporty image.

The territorial question: is the design field with which comparison is to be made limited to the UK (or possibly to England and Wales, or Scotland, or Northern Ireland, depending on which jurisdiction the parties are in), or should it extend more generally to those designs of which the designer was or could reasonably have been aware, or should designs from across the world be taken into account?

9.57 In *A Fulton Co Ltd v Totes Isotoner (UK) Ltd*[57] it was held that the design field was limited to the UK ('What relevance to the UK market has a design which is commonplace in Vanuatu?').[58] In *Dyson Ltd v Qualtex (UK) Ltd*,[59] Mann J took a broader approach in which the design field was not limited to designs marketed in the UK: 'What was, and is, important is what is apparent to those operating in the design field in question. It may be that it is hard to envisage how a design can acquire sufficient status in the field without its appearing in a marketed product, but that is matter of practicality not theory. Accordingly Mr Arnold is right to say that commonplace does not depend on marketing. It follows that he is also right to say that it does not depend on marketing *in the UK*. He accepted, however, that the design must be commonplace in the UK in the sense that UK designers in the field would have to be aware of the design to an extent sufficient to make it commonplace' (para 45). In other cases, global design fields have been used, or comparisons made with designs from other countries.[60]

---

[54] [2001] RPC 16.   [55] [2002] FSR 10 (CA).   [56] [2005] RPC 6 (CA).

[57] [2003] RPC 27 (Fysh QC); aff'd without comment on this issue [2004] RPC 16 (CA).   [58] [2003] RPC 27, para 73.

[59] [2005] RPC 19, para 45, not addressed on appeal.

[60] *Guild v Eskandar Ltd* [2001] FSR 38 (Rimer J, setting a global test in a case concerning ladies' luxury fashion, not addressed on subsequent appeal); *Spraymiser Ltd & Snell v Wrightway Marketing Ltd* [2000] ECDR 349 (in which the court made its comparison with a US design).

The whose eye question: in assessing the similarity of the design in question to other designs in the field, through whose eye is the court looking—the designer's or the customer's?

9.58   In *Farmers Build Ltd v Carier Bulk Materials Handling Ltd*,[61] Mummery LJ said that the comparative exercise must be conducted objectively, with the benefit of expert evidence in the field but, in the end, the assessment was one of fact and degree for the court. In *Lambretta Clothing Co Ltd v Teddy Smith (UK) Ltd*,[62] as noted previously the Court of Appeal said that what mattered was the sort of designs with which *a notional designer* of the article concerned would be familiar. However, the Court of Appeal took a slightly different approach in *Scholes Windows Ltd v Magnet Ltd*, approving the approach of the first instance judge in which he had made his comparison by considering the similarities and differences in the designs from the point of view of a person to whom it was ultimately intended that the design should appeal, rather than from the point of view of an expert in window design of window horns. Mummery LJ commented:

> I would reject the submission made on behalf of Scholes that the comparisons should be made from the point of view of the designer who is expert in the design field in question. Expert evidence is admissible to assist the court in the perception and appreciation of the differences and similarities in the designs compared. But it is not necessary to be an expert in the design field in question either to appreciate the similarities and differences between the designs compared or to form an opinion whether the design in which design right is claimed is 'commonplace'. At the end of the day it is for the court and not for the experts, whether they be parties or witnesses called by the parties, to determine objectively on all the evidence whether the design is commonplace.[63]

Key points on what constitutes an 'original' design for UK UDR purposes

- To be 'original', a design must possess originality in the copyright sense
- In addition, the design must also be 'not commonplace' in the 'design field in question'
- It is the 'commonplace-ness' of the design, not the article, which is to be tested

Duration

Length of protection

9.59   According to section 216(1)(a) of the CDPA 1988, UK UDR lasts for 15 years from the end of the calendar year in which the design was first recorded in a design document, or in which an article was made to the design, whichever of these is earlier in time. According to sections 216(1)(b) and (2) of the CDPA 1988, however, the duration of UK UDR is restricted if, within five years of the end of that calendar year, articles made to the design are made available for sale or hire anywhere in the world by or with the licence of the design right owner. The right will then expire ten years from the end of the calendar year in which that event occurred. Accordingly, the 15-year period is a maximum which will be reduced by commercial exploitation of the design during the first five years of its existence.

9.60   UK UDR is significantly shorter than both registered design right's maximum period (25 years) and copyright (lifetime of the author plus 70 years). This reflects a key policy decision, that UK UDR should be a lesser right in general than others available in this field. Further, the term for which there is an *exclusive*

[61] [1999] RPC 461 (CA).   [62] [2005] RPC 6, para 45.
[63] *Scholes Windows Ltd v Magnet Ltd* [2002] FSR 10 (CA), paras 48–49.

Diagram 9.1 Duration of UK UDR

```
                                    15 years
Design document/article - - - - - - - - - - - - - - - - - - - - - - - - - - - - - - - - - - - - - - - - - -EXPIRY
     made to design

        OR - - - - - - - <5yrs - - - - - - - Article lawfully - - - - - - - +10yrs - - - - - - - - - - - EXPIRY
                                             made available
                                             for sale or hire
```

right may be shortened by licences of right available during the last five years of the UK UDR term (see para 9.62). The clear policy is to encourage design registration where that is possible.

 Question

What is the maximum period of UK UDR protection?

Commencement

9.61   Three events are of importance with regard to starting time periods running:

(1) recording the design in a design document;
(2) making an article to the design;
(3) lawfully making an article made to the design available for sale or hire.

(1) or (2), whichever is the earlier, starts the 15-year period, while (3), if within five years of the earlier of (1) or (2), starts the ten-year period.

■ *Dyson Ltd v Qualtex (UK) Ltd* **[2005] RPC 19 (Mann J); [2006] RPC 31 (CA)**

The question arose as to whether taking orders for machines which had not yet been made constituted 'making available for sale'. Mann J noted that: 'One could make a logical case for saying that in the context of the Act commercial exploitation starts when articles are offered for sale, whether manufactured or not; and one could make a case for saying that it starts when articles are offered having been made, or when they are first made after an offer' (para 307). He held, however, that the natural meaning of the statutory words 'made available for sale' connoted something that was actually in existence, and that merely taking orders was not 'making available'. Prototypes or samples were not available for sale. On appeal, this approach was approved by Jacob LJ (paras 115–119).

■ *Ifejika v Ifejika* **[2012] FSR 6 (Patents County Court)**

The court rejected an argument that sales had to be on a sufficient scale to satisfy the reasonable demands of the public for the purposes of section 216(1)(b) of the CDPA 1988. It was held that there was no basis for implying into section 216(1)(b) any requirement that sales had to be on a certain scale. Any making available for sale, on any scale, is relevant for section 216(1)(b) to apply.[64]

[64] [2012] FSR 6, para 129.

Licences of right during last five years

9.62   A further limit on the duration of design right is to be found in section 237 of the CDPA 1988, which provides for licences of right to be obtainable during the last five years of the UK UDR term. In effect, this means that the design right owner can have an exclusive claim to the design for as little as only for five years after his initial exploitation of it. Diagram 9.1 illustrating duration needs to be adjusted as shown in Diagram 9.2 to take account of this.

Diagram 9.2 Duration of UK UDR with licences of right during last five years

The short term is clearly designed to foster the competitive environment. It contrasts sharply with the potential length of the protection arising through design registration and therefore encourages the use of that system.

 Question

How do licences of right promote competition?

9.63   A licence of right is one which the licensee is entitled as of right to have from the owner of the UK UDR in question, but for which negotiation about terms and conditions (including royalties) is permissible. If, however, the parties cannot agree, according to section 237(2) of the CPDA 1988 the terms will be settled by the Comptroller of Patents, Designs and Trade Marks.

9.64   An example of proceedings before the Comptroller in a licence of right case is as follows:

■ *NIC Instruments Ltd's Licence of Right (Design Right) Application* [2005] RPC 1 (Patent Office)

N had been infringing A's UK UDRs in bomb-disposal kits and, having ceased to do so, sought a licence of right (in order to limit the damages it would have to pay in respect of the infringements—see para 9.65). The parties having failed to agree terms, the matter was referred to the Comptroller. It was agreed that the Comptroller should approach the matter on the basis of what willing parties would have agreed. This was not the same as an assessment of damages that would be payable for infringement. It was held that willing parties do not negotiate by way of demands but by taking account not only of their own but also of the other side's interests, so that the agreement gives fair benefits on each side, achieving a halfway house or compromise. In the absence of comparable licences, the approach would be through splitting of the profits available to the licensee. A 50:50 split would not be appropriate outside the pharmaceuticals field (in which research and development costs greatly exceeded manufacturing ones); in the field of bomb-disposal kits, where R&D costs were unlikely to be high, the parties would have chosen a 25:75 split, with 75 per cent going to the licensee. The Comptroller also held that he would not include terms (1) prohibiting sub-licensing (no jurisdiction to do so); (2) requiring N to mark the goods as those of A (evidence that disadvantageous in the market); (3) providing a warranty that the UK UDR existed, was owned by A, and would expire on 31 December 2005 (inappropriate when licence being determined by Comptroller rather than parties); or (4) providing for termination on breach (because licensee could immediately demand a new licence). The full text of the licence imposed appears at the end of the report of the case.[65]

9.65 The availability of licences of right has one other important aspect under section 239 of the CDPA 1988. When a right owner raises proceedings for infringement of a design in respect of which a licence of right is available under the statute, the defendant may undertake to take a licence of right at any time before a final order is made in the proceedings. This may be done without any admission of liability, and has three important effects in relation to the remedies which the court may grant:

- no injunction or interdict may be granted against the defendant (in other words, he may carry on with his hitherto infringing activities);

- no order for delivery up of infringing articles or of the means of making infringing articles may be made against the defendant; and

- the amount recoverable against the defendant by way of damages or on an account of profits shall not exceed double the amount payable by him as licensee if such a licence (ie a licence of right) on those terms had been granted before the earliest infringement.

9.66 This provision does not apply to infringements committed before licences of right were available; so the situation may arise where a defendant was infringing UK UDR before and after the date on which licences of right became potentially available (ie five years before the right would have anyway expired). All relevant remedies would apply to the pre-licence availability infringements; but they would be severely restricted for the post-licence availability ones.

9.67 The potential significance of this capacity to cut down the remedies available to the right owner is well shown by the following case.

■ *Ultraframe (UK) Ltd v Eurocell Building Plastics Ltd* [2005] RPC 36 (CA)

The case concerned findings of infringement of UK UDR in kits of parts for conservatories, after which judgment the defendant offered to take a licence of right, thereby limiting the damages payable in accordance with section 239 of the CDPA 1988. The UK UDR had expired as the proceedings continued, and the claimant argued that a licence of right was no longer available. It was held that a licence of right could be obtained to restrict damages liability for infringement even after the UK UDR had expired. The licence under section 239 was a licence not of the UK UDR as such, but for the infringements that had been committed, and there was nothing in the section meaning that the undertaking had to be given within any particular period as long as there were proceedings for infringement.

---

[65] For commentary see J Reed, 'Royalties for design right "licences of right"' [2005] EIPR 298–301.

Discussion point For answer guidance visit www.oxfordtextbooks.co.uk/orc/waelde3e/

In the light of the two decisions just described, what would your advice be to a party sued for infringement of a UK UDR who wished to dispute the existence of the right, its scope in relation to his or her product, and that there had been infringement; and therefore to fight the action in all respects and continue his or her trading activities?

Rights in UK UDR

Ownership

9.68 According to section 214(1) of the CDPA 1988, the 'designer' of a design is the person who creates the design. By section 215(1), the designer is the first owner of the UK UDR in a design. There are, however, three principal circumstances in which the designer is not the owner:

(1) where a design is created in pursuance of a *commission*;
(2) where a design is created by an *employee in the course of his employment*;
(3) where a design is *computer-generated*.

9.69 In the first two cases, UK UDR belongs to the commissioner and the employer respectively.[66] 'Commission' and 'employee' are defined at section 263 of the CDPA 1988. In the case of a computer-generated design, the design right belongs to the person 'by whom the arrangements necessary for the creation of the design are undertaken'.[67] The situation should be distinguished from that where a human designer uses the computer as a tool towards the creation of the design, when it will not be computer-generated within the meaning of the Act and the other rules as to ownership, employment, and commissions will apply.

■ *Intercase Ltd v Time Computers Ltd* [2004] ECDR 8 (Patten J)

B was director, controlling shareholder, and employee of MW Ltd, a furniture manufacturing company. The company supplied worktops to a college. B designed a product called the I-Desk to deal with problems encountered with other desk styles. An issue in the case was whether B had carried out his design work in the course of his employment with MW Ltd. It was held that the test to be applied was whether the work done fell within the employee's duties, not simply whether it was done during normal office hours or with the benefit of materials provided at the employer's expense although these matters could be evidence of the work having been done in the course of employment.

■ *Bruhn Newtech Ltd v Datanetex Ltd and Another* [2012] EWPCC 17 (Patents County Court, currently unreported)

This dispute concerned rights in a product designed and made for the claimant by the defendant. The claimant argued that it owned any UK UDR in the design because the design had been commissioned from the defendant. However, a distinction was drawn between a contract commissioning a design and a contract for the supply of goods. The fact that some of the goods to be supplied had to be designed by the supplier did not make the contract a commission for the purposes of section 215(2) of the CDPA

---

[66] CDPA 1988, ss 215(2), (3).   [67] CDPA 1988, s 214(2).

1988. For there to be a commission within the meaning of that section, there had to be some fact or matter from which to infer that designs, not just goods, were being ordered and that the supplier was not to retain the freedom to reuse the design devised by him.

9.70   There are also certain more complex provisions on ownership (CDPA 1988, s 215(4)) linked to the requirement of 'qualification' for UK UDR protection (see paras 9.6 and 9.7).

 Question

Who is the first owner of UK UDR?

Infringement

9.71   The exclusive right in UK UDR is to *reproduce the design for commercial purposes*:

(1) by making articles to the design;

(2) by making a design document recording the design for the purpose of enabling such articles to be made (CDPA 1988, s 226(1)).

UK UDR is infringed by doing either (1) or (2) or by authorising another to do so without the licence of the rightholder.[68] It thus draws on two copyright concepts: reproduction (see paras 4.24ff) and authorisation (see paras 4.68ff). The requirement of a causal link of copying means that UK UDR, unlike the rights conferred by a patent or a registered design, is *not a full monopoly right in the design* in question. This is a limitation of UK UDR by comparison with the protection conferred by design registration. Again, therefore, the policy of encouraging registration of designs is apparent.

 Question

What is the difference between the nature of the exclusive right under a registered design and under UK UDR?

9.72   It is important to note that UK UDR is *a commercial right*, protecting only against copying for commercial purposes. The expression 'commercial purposes' is defined at section 263(3) of the CDPA 1988.

Key points about infringement of UK UDR

- Infringement is *reproduction* by making an article to the design, or by making design documents for the purpose of enabling such articles to be made
- The right is therefore *not a full monopoly right*, unlike registered design right
- The infringing act must be *for commercial purposes*

9.73   The exclusive rights just described are said to give rise to 'primary' infringement of UK UDR. There are also 'secondary' infringements, like those in copyright (paras 4.76ff), committed by importing

---

[68] CDPA 1988, s 226(3).

or possessing for commercial purposes or dealing in the course of a business in an article which is, and which the defendant knows or has reason to believe is, an infringing article.[69] An infringing article is one the making of which infringed UK UDR or, in the case of an imported article, would have infringed UK UDR had it been made in the UK.[70] The key distinction between primary and secondary infringements, as in copyright, is that the latter depends on knowledge where the former depends on copying, regardless of whether or not the copyist knew or had reason to know that this was infringement.

Reproduction by making articles to the design

9.74   Reproduction means copying the design, directly or indirectly, so as to produce articles 'exactly or substantially to that design'.[71] The infringing articles do not need to be the same type of articles as those of the UK UDR claimant.[72] An aspect of the copyright approach to 'reproduction' which has been used in UK UDR cases is the inference of copying based on sufficient similarity between the claimant's design and the allegedly infringing article and opportunity for the alleged copier to have access to the design. This should, however, be treated with care, as the following case illustrates:

■ *Virgin Atlantic Airways Ltd v Premium Aircraft Interiors Group Ltd* [2009] ECDR 11 (Lewison J)[73]

V alleged that UK UDR in various aspects of the design of a business-class aircraft seat had been copied. Lewison J found 'helpful' the approach of Lord Millett in the copyright case, *Designers Guild Ltd v Russell Williams* (see para 4.18) to the drawing of inferences in relation to copying: similarities had to be sufficiently close, numerous, or extensive as to be more likely the result of copying than coincidence. However, it was also necessary to bear in mind the 'warnings' of Mummery LJ in the *Farmers Build* case where he had cautioned:

> Substantial similarity of design might well give rise to a suspicion and an allegation of copying in cases where substantial similarity was often not the result of copying but an inevitable consequence of the functional nature of the design ... Copying may be inferred from proof of access to the protected work, coupled with substantial similarity. This may lead to unfounded infringement claims in the case of functional works, which are usually bound to be substantially similar to one another ... [The court] must not forget that, in the field of designs of functional articles, one design may be very similar to, or even identical with, another design and yet not be a copy: it may be an original and independent shape and configuration coincidentally the same or similar.[74]

On the facts, in *Virgin Atlantic* the UK UDR claims were rejected, the claimant failing to show copying of its designs.

9.75   Infringement of UK UDR is significantly different from infringement of copyright in another respect as well: whereas copyright is infringed by reproduction of any substantial part of a work in any material form,[75] UK UDR is infringed by making articles 'exactly or substantially to the design':

■ *L Woolley Jewellers Ltd v A & A Jewellery Ltd* [2003] FSR 15 (CA)

The product in question here was a pendant on a chain worn around the neck, with obsolete and imitation coins inserted in the pendant and held in place by 'lugs'; these could also be formed within a bezel

---

[69] CDPA 1988, s 227.   [70] CDPA 1988, s 228.   [71] CDPA 1988, ss 226(2), (4).
[72] *Electronic Techniques (Anglia) Ltd v Critchley Components Ltd* [1997] FSR 401 at 418.
[73] UK UDR was not considered when this case later reached the Court of Appeal on patent questions: see [2010] RPC 8.
[74] *Farmers Build Ltd v Carier Bulk Materials Handling Ltd* [1999] RPC 461 at 481–482.
[75] CDPA 1988, ss 16(3)(a) and 17(2); see paras 4.15ff.

(a captive ring with lugs placed over the circumference of the insert). The area around the insert contained an outline of three hearts into which the bail (through which a chain could be attached) had been inserted, while the central portion of the bail itself had been cut out in a heart shape. The first instance judge had expressed the view that the 'substantial part' test in copyright was relevant to infringement of the UK UDR in the design. It was held that this was the wrong approach. There was a difference between an inquiry whether the item copied formed a substantial part of a copyright work and an inquiry (the correct approach for UK UDR) whether the *whole* design containing the copied element is substantially the same design as the design enjoying UK UDR protection.

Question

Explain the difference between reproduction of any substantial part of a work in any material form (copyright), and making articles exactly or substantially to a design (UK UDR).

9.76   Questions arise about how to approach determining when an article has been made 'exactly or substantially' to a design. Where the design in which UK UDR is claimed is only an 'aspect' or 'part' of an article, the comparison must be with the corresponding 'aspect' or 'part' of the alleged infringement, not of the two articles as a whole.[76] In the language made familiar by registered designs law, through whose 'eye' do we judge this? The *Klucznik* case on pig fenders was the first to discuss how to approach these matters; it continues to be referred to in later cases such as *Virgin Atlantic* (see para 9.74).[77]

■ *C & H Engineering Ltd v F Klucznik & Sons Ltd* [1992] FSR 421 (Aldous J)

The allegedly infringing pig fender had a rounded tube or roll bar on top but it differed from the first fender in having flaring sides which enabled it to be stacked with other fenders. The claim of infringement failed. Although there was substantial similarity in respect of the roll bars, the overall designs of the fenders were different. Aldous J said (at 428):

> Whether or not the alleged infringing article is made substantially to the plaintiff's design must be an objective test to be decided through the eyes of the person to whom the design is directed. Pig fenders are purchased by pig farmers and I have no doubt that they purchase them taking into account price and design. In the present case, the plaintiff's alleged infringing pig fenders do not have exactly the same design as shown in the defendant's design document. Thus it is necessary to compare the plaintiff's pig fenders with the defendant's design drawing and, looking at the differences and similarities through the eyes of a person such as a pig farmer, decide whether the design of the plaintiff's pig fender is substantially the same as the design shown in the drawing.

Question

How may it be determined that an allegedly infringing article has been made to a design?

9.77   Subsequent cases have also assessed the question of whether the alleged infringement is substantially to the design through the eyes of customers, as the persons the persons 'to whom the design is directed'.[78]

---

[76] *Dyson Ltd v Qualtex (UK) Ltd* [2006] RPC 31 (CA), para 113.   [77] [2009] ECDR 11, para 32.

[78] See, eg, *Mark Wilkinson Furniture Ltd v Woodcraft Designs (Radcliffe) Ltd* [1998] FSR 63 at 74–75 (a person interested in purchasing a fitted kitchen); *A Fulton Co Ltd v Grant Barnett & Co Ltd* [2001] RPC 16 at para 89 (members of the buying public).

Problems inherent in such an anthropomorphic test may begin to emerge, however, in those cases where the key features of the design and the offending article are too fine to be picked up by anyone's unaided eye, as for example with contact lenses.[79]

> ## Key points on reproduction by making articles to the design
>
> - Infringing reproduction may be direct or indirect and relate to articles made exactly or substantially to the design
>
> - The correct approach to the question of whether an article has been reproduced 'substantially' to the design in which UK UDR is claimed is to ask whether the design containing the copied element is substantially the same as the design enjoying UK UDR (remembering that UK UDR may subsist in parts of articles only), not the copyright test of whether the element copied formed a substantial part of the original work
>
> - Similarity is tested through the eyes of the person to whom the design is directed

Reproduction of the design by making a design document for the purpose of enabling articles to be made to the design

9.78   Section 226(1)(b) of the CDPA 1988 makes it an infringement of UK UDR to reproduce the design for commercial purposes by making a design document for the purpose of enabling articles to be made to the design. There are some important differences compared to section 226(1)(a) discussed previously:

■ *Societá Esplosivi Industriali SpA v Ordnance Technologies (UK) Ltd* [2008] RPC 12 (Lindsay J)

This case arose from what was at first a joint venture between the parties to design multiple warhead systems. After the joint venture broke down, the claimant sued for infringement of UK UDR in certain warhead designs under section 226(1)(b). The judge held that, whereas infringement under section 226(1)(a) of the CDPA 1988 was enlarged by section 226(2) to cover both articles made exactly and substantially to the design in suit, section 226(2) did not apply to infringement under section 226(1)(b).[80] Section 226(1)(b) also raised questions of intention in relation to the words 'for the purpose of' making articles to the design. The judge held that this required proof that, at the material time, the infringer made the infringing record of the design with the purpose that articles should thereby be made. There was no infringement where the record of the design created by the defender had not gone beyond design study and evaluation, to manufacture or an intention to manufacture working from that record. The use of a protected document as a starting point for the making of further design documents which

---

[79] *Ocular Sciences Ltd v Aspect Vision Care Ltd* [1997] RPC 289 (Laddie J), at 424:

> The fact that the defendants' lenses also cannot be distinguished from the plaintiffs' on mere visual inspection does not prove that they are sufficiently close for the purposes of infringement. When a plaintiff relies on the most detailed and specific dimensions to support his claim to the existence of design right, he can only succeed on infringement if the defendants' designs are extremely close in design.

[80] It has been suggested that this interpretation is not supported by a closer reading of the wording of s 226 when properly analysed and that, as a matter of policy, it is 'verging on the irrational': M Howe, *Russell-Clarke and Howe on Industrial Designs* (8th edn, 2010) para 4-096.

were variations upon the protected original, even where that making had been in the course of a commercial purpose, did not in itself constitute an infringement.[81]

Exceptions to exclusive rights

9.79   There are no exceptions to UK UDR like those for registered designs (private and non-commercial use, experimental purposes, citation, and teaching—see previously para 8.118). This is because what constitutes infringement of UK UDR is much less extensive. If, for example, I wanted to use an unregistered design for the purposes of teaching design or the law on the subject, there would be no question of my infringing UK UDR since I am not making or intending to make articles to the design or making a record of the design for the purpose of enabling such articles to be made. UK UDR is also expressly limited to acts for commercial purposes, so there is no need for a private and non-commercial exception. UK UDR's exclusivity is also quite significantly limited by the availability of licences of right five years after the first marketing of the article to which the design was applied (see paras 9.62–9.67).

 Question

Why are there no exceptions to UK UDR for private and non-commercial use, experimental purposes or citation and teaching?

Assessing UK UDR

9.80   It is apparent that UK UDR is hedged around with considerable limitations and is often of uncertain scope, in respect of its subsistence, duration, and scope of protection against infringement. These uncertainties impact both on potential claimants and defendants. When the right was first introduced, it was open to question how far, if at all, commercial enterprises would seek to make use of it, since it might be seen as at best a fair-weather friend. It has also been questioned as to whether there remains a role for UK UDR now that the new Community UDR (see paras 9.94ff) has come into force.[82] Nevertheless, as shown by the now extensive case law relying on UK UDR which continues to grow, UK UDR has been and continues to be deployed, with varying degrees of success, across a wide range of industries. At the time of writing, the UK IPO was consulting on whether to abolish UK UDR. Although noting the difficulties with UK UDR and potential for the creation of uncertainties in the marketplace as third parties attempt to evaluate whether rights subsist and, if so, what may or may not constitute an infringement, the UK IPO's recommendation was to retain the right, the UK IPO noting in particular that:

> there is strong evidence to suggest that companies use UK unregistered design right as a 'default option' or 'safety net': relying on it to deal with infringement because they have not previously considered how best to protect their designs ... [L]ike it or not, many UK designers currently rely upon it for protection of their designs. To remove it now would leave them, at least to some extent, bereft of IP protection.[83]

---

[81] See further the note on this case by S Vousden, '*Societa Esplosivi Industriali SpA*: on confidences, copying designs, and company directors' [2008] EIPR 332–336. See also S Yavorsky, 'Negotiating an IP minefield: infringing design documents' (2008) 3(6) JIPLP 361–363.

[82] See, eg, E Derclaye, 'The British Unregistered Design Right: Will It Survive Its New Community Counterpart To Influence Future European Case Law?' (2003–04) 10 Columbia Journal of European Law 265.

[83] UK IPO, 'Consultation on the Reform of the UK Designs Legal Framework' (launched 24 July 2012), p 8 (http://www.ipo.gov.uk/consult-2012-designs.pdf).

Exercise

Is UK UDR useful? And how does it compare to Community UDR (paras 9.94ff)? In your view, is there a continued role for UK UDR in the overall scheme of design protection in the UK?

Interaction with copyright

9.81   We looked in Chapter 8 at the interaction between registered designs and other IP rights, including copyright. As was noted there and in the introductory sections of this chapter (see paras 9.9–9.13), there are important provisions in the CDPA 1988 which were enacted to curtail the availability of copyright claims in the UK in relation to certain designs. Alongside the creation of UK UDR, these provisions were the second key part of the move in the CDPA 1988 to remove, or at least substantially cut down, the role of copyright in relation to industrial designs. However, as we shall see, reform is presently underway in this area. In this section, we will look at these provisions of the CDPA 1988 and their present status in more detail.

9.82   To find the existence of copyright in a design requires no extraordinary application of the principles of copyright. An article may itself qualify for copyright protection if, for example, it constitutes a sculpture or a work of artistic craftsmanship. A design may also begin life as a sketch, a drawing, or a more worked-up design blueprint. All such materials may fall within the scope of copyright subject matter, typically as an artistic work. Artistic copyright can subsist in such materials, no matter how functional or simple the content recorded there, as long as there is sufficient originality. Copyright can be infringed by the making of products to the design, because the copyright in a two-dimensional artistic work could be infringed by a three-dimensional reproduction. Because copyright prevents indirect as well as direct copying, there can be infringement of the artistic work even where that is not seen and the copyist simply copies an article made to the design recorded in the artistic work. The problems caused by this were discussed previously (see paras 9.9–9.13) However, although this is the basic position, by sections 51 and 52 of the CDPA 1988, the intention was that the scope for enforcement of the copyright in certain designs should be severely cut back, with the aim of ensuring that, for the most part, copyright was to become a marginal form of protection in the industrial design field. Section 51 of the CDPA 1988 (see paras 9.83–9.90) remains in force; however, at the time of writing section 52 (see paras 9.91–9.93) is in the process of being repealed. We shall look at this further later in the chapter.

 Question

When will a product design have copyright?

Restricting copyright

Section 51 of the CDPA 1988

9.83   Section 51(1) of the CDPA 1988 provides that it is *not* infringement of any copyright in a design document or model recording or embodying a design for anything other than an artistic work or a typeface to make an article to the design or to copy an article made to the design. A design document for these purposes is defined as:

> any record of a design, whether in the form of a drawing, a written description, a photograph, data stored in a computer or otherwise (CDPA 1988, s 51(3)).

The *ejusdem generis* principle of statutory interpretation suggests that the 'otherwise' covers only two-dimensional design records like the others actually mentioned in the definition. Three-dimensional prototypes of the kind discussed by the House of Lords in *George Hensher Ltd v Restawile Upholstery (Lancs) Ltd*[84] (see para 2.83), insofar as they have copyright at all, are covered by the earlier words in the section referring to 'models' embodying a design. For the purposes of section 51, 'design' is defined as:

> the design of any aspect of the shape or configuration (whether internal or external) of the whole or part of an article, other than surface decoration (CDPA 1988, s 51(3)).

—that is, albeit slightly differently worded to incorporate in section 51(3) the exclusion of surface decoration, the kind of design that is protected by UK UDR (see paras 9.17ff).

9.84   It is important to grasp that section 51 recognises copyright in design documents (where it exists). But the usefulness of this copyright is carefully restricted because of the section 51 defence to a copyright infringement claim based on the design document. If the design is for anything other than an artistic work or typeface, it is not infringement of copyright to make an article to the design or to copy an article made to the design.

9.85   As should be apparent from this, in terms of whether the section 51 defence is available the key question is what, as a matter of copyright law, the design in question is *for*. If the design is for anything *other than* an artistic work or typeface, the effect of section 51 is that the unauthorised making of three-dimensional articles by copying either directly or indirectly from a design document cannot constitute copyright infringement. If, however, there is a design document *for an artistic work*—for example, a sketch recording the design for a sculpture or for a work of artistic craftsmanship—or for a typeface, then under section 51 there is no defence and it is possible to enforce the copyright in the design document.

9.86   It will therefore be vital to distinguish when a drawing or model is the design of an artistic work and when it is not. Only in the latter case will protection in copyright be unavailable. The most crucial things to keep in mind in approaching the question are:

- which three-dimensional works attract copyright (eg works of artistic craftsmanship and sculptures); and

- the distinction between shape and configuration on the one hand (which falls within the definition of 'design' for the purposes of s 51) and surface decoration on the other (which does not).

9.87   The operation of section 51 is well-illustrated by the *Lucasfilm* case:

■ *Lucasfilm Ltd v Ainsworth* [2009] FSR 2 (Mann J); [2010] FSR 10 (CA); [2011] 3 WLR 487 (SC)

This case was concerned with the designs for Imperial Stormtrooper helmets and armour featured in the film *Star Wars*. A had made the helmets and armour used during filming, from initial storyboard sketches and a clay model prepared for L. These were design documents and a model recording a design. The key question was therefore whether, as design documents, they were *for* items (the helmets and armour) which were, or were not, in themselves copyright artistic works. Mann J summarised his conclusions as follows:

> [Section 51] is therefore capable of barring a copyright claim in relation to the design document if it is for 'anything other than an artistic work'. If the items were not artistic works, the section works in Mr Ainsworth's favour

---

[84] [1976] AC 64.

and prevents his acts being infringements. The designs could only be for artistic works in this case if they were for a sculpture or a work of artistic craftsmanship. I have held that they were not artistic works in either of the two candidate senses. Therefore the designs were for something other than an artistic work and s.51 operates in Mr Ainsworth's favour to prevent his copying of the work being an infringement of copyright.[85]

The first instance decision was upheld on appeal to the Court of Appeal and Supreme Court, both higher courts upholding the first instance judge's characterisation of the helmets and armour as not constituting copyright artistic works of sculpture and, as a consequence, applying section 51 of the CDPA 1988 to exclude a copyright claim (see also para 2.77).

 Discussion point For answer guidance visit www.oxfordtextbooks.co.uk/orc/waelde3e/

Why do designs for artistic works retain full copyright?

9.88   Section 51 is not without its difficulties, however:

■ *Lambretta Clothing Co Ltd v Teddy Smith (UK) Ltd* [2005] RPC 6 (CA)

This is the track top case (for the facts see para 9.33). The shape of the top was not protected in UK UDR because it was not original. The key issue for section 51 purposes related to the colourways of the top. Although there was no claim in UK UDR because the colourways were excluded from UK UDR protection, there was a design document drawn by a director of the plaintiffs. So the defendants' top might have been treated as copied (indirectly) from this design document and therefore as an indirect infringement of copyright in the design document. It was held, however, that section 51 barred any claim to artistic copyright infringement. For the majority, it was not possible to divorce the colourways from the shape of the top—as noted by Jacob LJ: 'Neither physically nor conceptually can they exist apart from the shapes of the parts of the article…. If artistic copyright were to be enforced here, it would be enforced in respect of [the] whole design drawing. But that is not allowed by s51' (para 39). It is notable, however, that Mance LJ dissented, commenting as follows:

> in order 'to make an article to the design' or 'to copy an article made to the design' embodied in a drawing, it is, because of the definition in s 51(3), still necessary to conclude that the article was made, or was a copy of an article made, to the design, meaning 'the design [as embodied in the drawing] of any aspect of the shape or configuration … of the whole or part of an article, *other than surface decoration*'. Only if it was, does s 51 prevent there being any copyright infringement (para 80; emphasis added).

Therefore, Mance LJ argued, since the surface decoration was not part of the 'design' as defined by the CDPA 1988, the limitation of copyright under section 51 did not apply.

■ *Flashing Badge Co Ltd v Groves* [2007] FSR 36 (HC)

This case was about design drawings for flashing novelty badges with messages such as '40 Today', 'Let's Party', and 'Happy Birthday' presented on them in a stylised way along with images such as balloons and cakes with candles. The outline shape of each of the badges followed the outline of the relevant artistic designs. The question was whether section 51 of the CDPA 1988 applied to prevent the claimant's action for copyright infringement against an importer of virtually identical badges from China. Granting summary judgment for copyright infringement, Rimer J held that each drawing was a design document incorporating (1) a design for

---

[85] [2009] FSR 2, para 141.

an artistic work and (2) a design for something other than an artistic work, in this case an article in the nature of a badge in the same outline shape as the artistic work. Section 51 had no relevance to (1) because they were designs for artistic works. Section 51 applied only to (2), which was not an artistic work. It followed that section 51 applied, if at all, only to a copyright claim in the shape or configuration of the badge minus the surface decoration. Section 51 provided no defence in respect of an infringement of copyright in the graphic design which provided the surface decoration of the badges. Distinguishing *Lambretta*, Rimer J described *Lambretta* as a case which 'appears to have turned on its special facts'. He concluded:

> It is true that the design of the shape of the badge follows the outline of the design for the artistic work on the face of each badge. But the latter design is in the nature of a graphic design which is in no sense something which (unlike the *Lambretta* colourways) can only exist as part of the shape of the badge. It is a design which can be applied to any other substrate and which, if so applied, would enjoy copyright protection for the infringement of which s 51 would afford no defence (para 22).[86]

9.89 Overall, if section 51 operates to exclude a claim in copyright, the only claim available in terms of the scheme of the CDPA 1988 is under UK UDR if at all. However, it may well be that there is no valid or subsisting UK UDR claim (as was, eg, the case in *Lucasfilm*). The claimant may also not actually plead a UK UDR case. This does not matter—there is no requirement that UK UDR be available as an alternative to copyright. If there is no UK UDR claim and section 51 operates to exclude a copyright claim, there will be no infringement of rights at all under the CDPA 1988, whether in copyright or in UK UDR.

9.90 If section 51 operates so as to retain a claim in copyright, it is possible that there may be parallel claims in copyright and UK UDR. For example, there may be a design document for an item which is a work of artistic craftsmanship for copyright purposes and which also has an 'original' shape and configuration such as to entitle it to protection in UK UDR. In these circumstances, the scheme of the CDPA 1988 is to force the claimant to rely on his copyright claim only. Section 236 of the CDPA 1988 provides that:

> Where copyright subsists in a work which consists of or includes a design in which design right subsists, it is not an infringement of design right in the design to do anything which is an infringement of copyright in that work.

This concludes the move, in the CDPA 1988, to separate the artistic from the industrial in terms of design and copyright laws.

Key points on section 51 of the CDPA 1988

- The section restricts when copyright in a design document or model can be enforced
- The key issue is whether the design is for an item which qualifies for protection as a copyright artistic work (eg as a work of artistic craftsmanship or sculpture) or is for a typeface
- If the design document is for an artistic work or a typeface, the copyright claim will survive. If not, making an article to the design recorded in the design document does not infringe copyright

Section 52 of the CDPA 1988

9.91 Separately from section 51 of the CDPA 1988, the Act also introduced a further provision, to be found at section 52, limiting the extent to which copyright could play a role in relation to commercially exploited

---

[86] See further the note on this case by E Derclaye, *'Flashing Badge Co Ltd v Groves*: a step forward in the clarification of the copyright/design interface' [2008] EIPR 251–254.

designs. As explained in more detail in para 9.93, section 52 is in the process of bring repealed although, at the time of writing, that repeal has not yet taken effect. Section 52 of the CDPA 1988 deals with artistic works which, although not excluded from enforceability under section 51, are subsequently exploited by being made into articles by an industrial process and marketed (exposed for sale or hire) in the UK or elsewhere.[87] Section 52 provides that, at the end of the period of 25 years (a term derived from the Berne Convention provisions on works of applied art—see para 8.4) from the end of the calendar year in which such articles are first marketed, the work may be copied by making articles of any description, or doing anything for the purpose of making articles of any description, without infringing copyright in the work.

■ *Lucasfilm Ltd v Ainsworth* [2009] FSR 2 (Mann J); [2010] FSR 10 (CA); [2011] 3 WLR 487 (SC)

The defence at section 52 of the CDPA 1988 was pleaded in addition, and as an alternative to, the section 51 defence described previously. The artistic works covered by section 52 in this case were L's preliminary drawings. Mann J stated that the purpose of section 52 was to 'shorten the copyright period applicable to some copyright items which are reproduced industrially and then sold, to a period of 25 years from the date when they were first marketed' (para 144). It was held that that the designs of the Stormtrooper helmet and armour had been reproduced industrially for more than 25 years, for example as toy models of Stormtroopers. The section 52 defence therefore succeeded, in addition and as an alternative to the defence under section 51. It was held that it did not matter whether the relevant articles were made in the UK or elsewhere. The decision was affirmed by the Court of Appeal. Section 52 was not substantively addressed by the Supreme Court which disposed of the appeal on other grounds.

9.92   Section 52(4) of the CDPA 1988 empowered the Secretary of State to make orders excluding from the operation of section 52 articles of a primarily literary or artistic character. Examples are the production of books and the exploitation of a painting or a photograph by the manufacture of posters, books and posters both being commercial products which retain primarily literary or artistic character. In these cases full artistic copyright is retained.[88]

9.93   While not affecting the subsistence of copyright in an affected work, the objective of section 52 was to restrict the duration of protection for that work to a period paralleling the maximum period for a registered design (see para 8.120). As noted previously, however, section 52 is now in the process of being repealed: see section 74 of the Enterprise and Regulatory Reform Act 2013, which received Royal Assent on 25 April 2013. The repeal of section 52 of the CDPA 1988 will take effect on a date to be appointed by statutory instrument.[89] This repeal was initiated by the UK IPO in response to the ruling of the Court of Justice in *Flos SpA v Semeraro Casa e Famiglia SpA* (see previously para 8.124),[90] in particular the finding by the Court of Justice that Article 17 of the Designs Directive does not leave member states free to determine the term of protection in copyright for designs. The concern was that section 52 constitutes an impermissible restriction on copyright term in this context. However, the move to repeal section 52 has been criticised and it has been argued that repeal is not necessary, with concerns having been expressed about the correctness of *Flos* and, more widely, about the implications of *Flos* in terms of a potential return to 'industrial copyright' in designs (the difficulties engendered by 'industrial copyright' were discussed from a UK historical perspective at paras 9.9–9.13).[91] At the time of writing, details of when and

---

[87] References in s 52 to 'articles' do not include films and references to the marketing of an article are to its being sold or let for hire or offered or exposed for sale or hire: CDPA 1988, s 52(6). 'Making by an industrial process' is defined by the Copyright (Industrial Process and Excluded Articles) (No 2) Order 1989 (SI 1989/1070) as, in broad terms, the making of 50 or more articles.

[88] See the Copyright (Industrial Process and Excluded Articles) (No 2) Order 1989 (SI 1989/1070) for the full list.

[89] Enterprise and Regulatory Reform Act 2013, s 103(3).   [90] Case C-168/09, 27 January 2011 [2011] ECDR 8.

[91] See L Bently, 'The return of industrial copyright?' [2012] EIPR 654–672.

how the repeal of section 52 of the CDPA 1988 will be implemented are still awaited. However, this repeal has the potential to affect a wide range of market sectors, from character merchandising to furniture and fashion design, re-opening the potential for relevant works to be protected against copying for the much longer copyright term of life of the author plus 70 years. How repeal of section 52 will affect competition in the affected sectors remains to be seen.

Key points on section 52 of the CDPA 1988

- Section 52, as it stands in force, provides that, if an artistic work is exploited commercially within the meaning of section 52, the right to rely on copyright to prevent copying by making articles of any description is lost 25 years after first marketing of articles based on the work

- However, section 52 is in the process of being repealed; details of when and how this repeal will be implemented are, at the time of writing, still awaited

---

 ### Exercise

Modern methods of character merchandising, particularly for 'action heroes' or similar characters, often involve the presentation of a character across a variety of media— a comic or magazine centring on the character or characters, a TV series or film, models of the character, and/or other merchandise using representations of the character. Discuss (1) whether initial drawings of the characters are design documents or, instead, designs for artistic works; (2) whether protection may arise through UK UDR, copyright, or both; and (3) what the term of protection is for any rights which you think subsist. Think about the position both with section 52 of the CDPA 1988 in force and on the basis that section 52 has been repealed—how does this affect your analysis? What do you think the implications of repealing section 52 will be? You may find it interesting to reflect on the pre-CDPA 1988 'Popeye' case, *King Features Syndicate, Inc v O and M Kleeman Ltd*.[92]

Community UDR

About this topic

9.94   Now we turn to the second major form of unregistered design protection, Community UDR.[93] As explained in the introduction to Part III of this book, this form of intellectual property was introduced nearly 15 years after the UK UDR, and coexists with it, the two rights being very different from each other in a number of respects, with Community UDR being aligned much more closely with Community registered protection. Community UDR is really primarily an adjunct of the Community registered design right—recital 16 to the Community Design Regulation emphasises the utility of Community UDR to sectors where designs have a short market-life where there is no need for the longer duration of registered protection and the burdens of the filing system are a disadvantage, and Community UDR also has an important role to play where a putative registrant is relying on the grace periods discussed previously (paras 8.58–8.61) while he decides whether or not to file. In contrast, UK UDR is a fully fledged independent right. The existence of the Community UDR is expressly without prejudice to national laws relating to unregistered designs (such as UK UDR) or, indeed, to trade marks or other distinctive signs,

---

[92] [1941] AC 417 (HL).   [93] See generally VM Saez, 'The unregistered Community design' [2002] EIPR 588–590.

patents and utility models, typefaces, civil liability (ie tort or delict), and unfair competition (passing off in the UK).[94] A design protected by Community UDR may also be protected by copyright under the national laws of the member states.[95] As with registered designs, the provisions of the CDPA 1988 could apply in the UK to restrict the ways in which any coexisting copyright in the design could be infringed (see further, para 8.125).

> ### Key point on Community UDR
>
> • Community UDR is essentially a supplement to Community registered design rights, and is very different from UK UDR, being aligned much more closely with Community registered protection

> **Question**
>
> What are the major distinctions between UK UDR and Community UDR?

Designs to which Community UDR applies

9.95   The designs to which Community UDR applies and the core concepts in terms of validity and infringement are defined in the same way as for Community registered designs. Thus, the discussions of the following key points in connection with Community registered designs apply as much to Community unregistered designs as to Community registered designs:

• *Design* as the *appearance* of the whole of part of a *product* (see paras 8.16–8.27).

• Possession of *novelty* and *individual character* (see paras 8.28–8.61), the date at which this is assessed for Community UDR being the date upon which the design was first made available to the public (CDR, Arts 5(1)(a) and 6(1)(a)).

• Exclusion of *designs solely dictated by the technical function* of the product and on other grounds (see paras 8.62–8.72).

• *Complex products* (see paras 8.73–8.78).

• *Must match* or *repair* defence (see para 8.88).

• Invalidity, scope of protection, and defences (see paras 8.106–8.119).

9.96   Notice that all this necessarily implies that *Community UDR cannot apply to any design which is incapable of registration under the Community registered design system*. This is an important contrast with UK UDR which may protect designs not capable of registration. Thus, there may be unregistered designs which enjoy UK UDR in the UK but which will not have Community UDR. The best example would be a product whose design was dictated solely by function such as to be excluded from protection under the Community Design Regulation. Insofar as it was not caught by the UK UDR 'must fit' or any of the other exceptions to UK UDR protection, then that design would be protected in the UK by UK UDR, but not under the Community UDR.

---

[94] CDR, Art 96(1); see para 8.122.   [95] CDR, Art 96(2); see para 8.123.

Question

Explain why Community UDR cannot apply to a design incapable of registration as a Community registered design.

Commencement and duration of Community UDR

9.97 Unlike for Community registered designs, there is no need for the design to be registered for Community UDR to arise. Instead, according to Article 11(1) of the Community Design Regulation, Community UDR arises when the design is first made available to the public within the Community. This can be by way of publication, exhibition, use in trade, or otherwise (CDR, Art 11(2)). Article 11(2) of the Community Design Regulation also provides that a design is deemed to be been disclosed if there has been publication, exhibition, use in trade, or otherwise in such a way that, in the normal course of business, these events could reasonably have become known to the circles specialised in the sector concerned, operating within the Community. However, this does not arise if the making available occurred under explicit or implicit conditions of confidentiality (CDR, Art 11(2)).

9.98 There has been some doubt over whether, when read to together, the net effect of Articles 11(1) and 11(2) of the Regulation requires the first 'making available to the public' of the design for which Community unregistered design right is claimed to take place geographically within the territory of the Community. For example, could making a design available to the public overseas trigger the subsistence of Community unregistered design right if that event could reasonably have become known to the circles specialised in the sector concerned operating within the Community? A further provision, Article 110a(5), has been inserted into the Regulation to address this, stating that a design which has not been made public within the territory of the Community shall not enjoy protection as an unregistered Community design. Although the issue has not come before the General Court or the Court of Justice, the German Supreme Court in *Gebäckpresse*[96] has confirmed that, for Community unregistered design right to arise, first disclosure of the design must take place within the territory of the Community. A first disclosure outside the Community not only does not give rise to Community unregistered design right, but may also be novelty-destroying with regard to any subsequent attempt to claim design protection.[97]

9.99 Disclosure having occurred, the Community UDR then lasts for *three years* from the date on which the design was first made available to the public. This period is significantly shorter than both the UK UDR, even at its shortest, and Community registered design protection, which lasts for an initial period of five years and is renewable for four more such periods, so permitting a maximum period of protection of 25 years. The main purpose of this short form of protection apart from the protection of the design on its way to registration can be gleaned from recital 16 to the Community Design Regulation (see para 9.94). The best example of an industrial sector with short market-life products is the clothing fashion industry, where designs are turned over on a seasonal basis, for which registration would probably not have much point.

Rights conferred

Ownership

9.100 So far as appropriate, the same rules about ownership apply as in the Community registered design (see previously para 8.100). If an unregistered Community design is disclosed or claimed by a person not entitled

---

[96] I ZR 126/06, [2009] GRUR 79.
[97] See further A Gartner, 'Bundesgerichtshof (Pastry Press) (I ZR 126/06): the disclosure of designs outside the European Community—the Federal Supreme Court's "*Gebackpresse*" decision and its implications' [2010] EIPR 181–183.

to it, the entitled person may claim to be recognised as the legitimate holder of the design. Such a claim will become barred three years after the disclosure, unless the party making the disclosure was in bad faith.[98]

Exclusive right

9.101   Like a Community registered design, Community UDR confers on its holder the *exclusive right to use the design and to prevent any third party not having his consent from using it*, the scope of protection conferred including any design which does not produce a different overall impression on the informed user (see previously para 8.111).

9.102   However, unlike the Community registered design, which confers a full monopoly right so that the right is available even against a party who is unaware of the existence of the prior design, Community UDR only confers the right to prevent use of the design if the contested use results from *copying* the protected design (CDR, Art 19(2)). The contested use will not be deemed to result from copying if it results from an independent work of creation by a designer who may be reasonably thought not to be familiar with the design made available to the public by the Community UDR rightholder (CDR, Art 19(2)). The justification for this difference in treatment between Community registered designs and Community UDR is that a party proposing to put a design into the marketplace can check the register for any similar prior registered designs, but cannot do so for unregistered ones. Fairness requires that such a person be liable only if that person knows, or ought reasonably to know, of that prior unregistered design and right. The policy is summarised thus in recital 21 to the Community Design Regulation:

> The exclusive nature of the right conferred by the Community registered design is consistent with its greater legal certainty. It is appropriate that the unregistered Community design should, however, constitute a right only to prevent copying. Protection could not therefore extend to design products which are the result of a design arrived at independently by a second designer.

Key points about Community UDR

- Most of the core concepts and substantive legal provisions are the same as for the Community registered design

- The term of Community UDR is only three years. It is aimed at the protection of designs on their way to being registered, or with a short market-life

- The right protects only against contested uses which result from copying of the design in which Community UDR is claimed

---

 Discussion point   For answer guidance visit www.oxfordtextbooks.co.uk/orc/waelde3e/

- What is the purpose of Community UDR?

- To what products will the Community UDR typically apply?

- How do the main features of Community UDR (designs to which applicable, duration, rights, defences) compare, contrast, and interact with registered design protection?

- Likewise, how does Community UDR contrast with the UK UDR?

- Why does UK UDR continue to exist despite the introduction of Community UDR?

---

[98] CDR, Arts 15(1), (3).

Further reading

Books

General

L Bently and B Sherman, *Intellectual Property Law* (3rd edn, 2009), Chs 29, 30

WR Cornish, D Llewelyn, and T Aplin, *Intellectual Property* (7th edn, 2010), Ch 15

M Howe, *Russell-Clarke and Howe on Industrial Designs* (8th edn, 2010)

History and policy

HL MacQueen, *Copyright, Competition and Industrial Design* (2nd edn, 1995)

Articles

UK UDR

A Coulthard and L Bently, 'From the commonplace to the interface: five cases on unregistered design right' [1997] EIPR 401–411

E Derclaye, '*Flashing Badge Co Ltd v Groves*; a step forward in the clarification of the copyright/design interface' [2008] EIPR 251–254

E Derclaye, 'The British Unregistered Design Right: Will It Survive Its New Community Counterpart To Influence Future European Case Law?' (2003–04) 10 Columbia Journal of European Law 265

S Hird and M Peeters, 'UK protection for recombinant DNA—exploring the options' [1991] EIPR 334–339

A Michaels, 'The end of the road for "pattern spare" parts? *Dyson Ltd v Qualtex (UK) Ltd*' [2006] EIPR 396–398

W Pang and R Burstall, 'Sculpting an effective design protection system' (2012) 7(6) JIPLP 430–436

J Reed, 'Royalties for design right "licences of right"' [2005] EIPR 298–301

J Reynolds and P Brownlow, 'Increased legal protection for schematic designs in the United Kingdom' [1994] EIPR 398–400

J Sykes, 'Designs: the unregistered design right: interpretation and practical application of the must match exemption' (2006) 1(7) JIPLP 442–446

S Vousden, '*Societa Esplosivi Industriali SpA*: on confidences, copying designs and company directors' [2008] EIPR 332–336

D Wilkinson 'Case closed: functional designs protected by design right' [2007] EIPR 118–122

S Yavorsky, 'Negotiating an IP minefield: infringing design documents' (2008) 3(6) JIPLP 361–363

Interaction with copyright

L Bently, 'The return of industrial copyright?' [2012] EIPR 654–672

Community UDR

A Gartner, 'Bundesgerichtshof (Pastry Press) (I ZR 126/06): the disclosure of designs outside the European Community—the Federal Supreme Court's "*Gebackpresse*" decision and its implications' [2010] EIPR 181–183

C-H Massa and A Strowel, 'Community design: Cinderella revamped' [2003] EIPR 68–78

VM Saez, 'The unregistered Community design' [2002] EIPR 588–590

Part IV

Patents

Introduction

This Part of the book explores the law of patents over three chapters. Chapter 10 considers the nature of patents and patentability in the context of the various patent regimes that operate at the national, European, and international levels. We will examine current developments within these regimes against the background of the justifications that are commonly advanced for patent protection. We also consider the nature of the patent application process. Chapter 11 then explains what is required in order to obtain a patent, what it means to have a patent, and what constitutes patent infringement. Crucial to this exercise is a discussion of exceptions to patentability. An important issue in this respect is patent revocation, that is, the claim that a patent is somehow invalid and should be struck down. This is a common response to actions for infringement and we will examine how it operates together with defences for alleged infringers. Finally, Chapter 12 deals with two of the most pressing contemporary challenges to patent law, being biotechnological inventions and software patents. We will use these examples to explore how well patent law adapts to new technological advances and challenges and we will consider whether reforms to patent regimes are required.

Sources of the law: key websites

- Patents Act 1977, as amended to 1 October 2011, available at
  http://www.ipo.gov.uk/patentsact1977.pdf

- The patents related sections of the Copyright, Designs and Patents Act 1988, as amended to 1 January 2010, available at
  http://www.ipo.gov.uk/pdact1988.pdf

- European Patent Convention 2000, available at
  http://www.epo.org/law-practice/legal-texts/html/epc/2010/e/index.html

- TRIPS Agreement 1994, as amended, available at
  http://www.wto.org/english/tratop_e/trips_e/t_agm0_e.htm

- Paris Convention for the Protection of Industrial Property 1883, as amended
  http://www.wipo.int/treaties/en/ip/paris/trtdocs_wo020.html

- Patent Cooperation Treaty 1970, as amended
  http://www.wipo.int/pct/en/texts/articles/atoc.htm
- Patent Law Treaty (2000), available at
  http://www.wipo.int/treaties/en/ip/plt/trtdocs_wo038.html
- Decisions of the courts in the various jurisdictions of the UK, for which see BAILII
  http://www.bailii.org/
- WIPO Standing Committee on the Law of Patents, available at
  http://www.wipo.int/scp/en/

10

Patent regimes and the application process

Introduction

Scope and overview of chapter

10.1   This chapter examines the architecture and procedures of contemporary patent systems as they currently operate in the UK, within the European patent system, and through international agreements, instruments and procedures. The first section will lay out the framework of these patent regimes, explaining their origins and current remits. All patent regimes operate through a registration process, meaning that patent protection is only granted after rigorous consideration of the criteria for patentability as applied to each putative invention. For present purposes, a valid patent normally lasts for 20 years and provides the patent holder (the patentee) with an 'absolute' monopoly over his invention. This is the strongest of all monopolies available in intellectual property law, and it makes patent protection one of the most sought after of intellectual property rights (IPRs).

10.2
> ### Learning objectives
>
> By the end of this chapter you should be able to describe and explain:
>
> - the subject matter of patent protection and the various justifications offered for the existence of patent regimes;
> - the nature of the various patent regimes as well as their similarities and differences;
> - the current challenges for patent law and options for reform;
> - the processes and procedures for obtaining patent protection.

10.3   The chapter explains the different kinds of patent regime that exist at national, regional and international levels and helps the reader to understand those systems by setting the discussion against a background of the various arguments advanced to support patent protection.

Thereafter, we consider the registration system used in the UK to obtain a patent. Unlike copyright, patent protection does not come into existence with the creation of the relevant subject matter, but rather must be granted by an intellectual property office after an application and examination process. These processes will be described, including the issue of who is entitled to apply for, and receive, a patent. So the chapter looks like this:

- Patent regimes: past and present (10.4–10.13)
- Rationales of patent protection (10.14–10.21)
- The European dimension (10.22–10.34)
- The international dimension (10.35–10.67)
- Further reform: patent regimes in the future (10.68–10.88)
- Patent procedures (10.89–10.122)

Patent regimes: past and present

Early history

10.4   The essential features of the modern patent system can be seen in the earliest origins of that system which began, in Europe at least, as a form of state or monarch grace and favour. Monopolies over trade practices or production were initially used as a reward for loyalty or as a form of privilege, done through the grant of *letters patent* (an 'open letter') as proof that the privilege—the monopoly—had been bestowed. The first recorded patent in England was for a method of making stained glass given to John of Utynam by King Henry VI in 1449.[1] From the very beginning, however, there has been an expectation of reciprocity as between the granter of the monopoly—be it monarch or state—and the grantee. Thus the monopoly holder would be expected to undertake certain obligations to his monarch, or, as typified by the Venetian Republic, the grantee would undertake to disclose the elements of his new 'craft' in return for the privilege of a market monopoly of ten years. Venice was the first state to establish a patent system, done by decree in 1474, in an attempt to attract tradesmen to introduce products and processes not known in Venice at that time. This encouraged innovation in the Republic while avoiding conflict with the powerful guilds that held considerable sway over the markets.[2] Other states followed suit, each using the device of monopoly as the incentive to inventors to enter the social contract with the state. But the terms of this contract have been in dispute since the earliest of times, and the courts have always been willing to strike a monopoly down if the balance of interests has not been appropriately struck. Thus, in *Darcy v Allin*[3] a monopoly from Queen Elizabeth I over trade in playing cards was overturned, partly on the basis that there was no discernible advantage to the public of allowing such a state of affairs to continue. Parliament, too, has shown antipathy towards monopolies since early times, especially those which were, in effect, at the unfettered discretion of the Crown. This culminated in the 1624 Statute of Monopolies which had the general aim of preventing Crown monopolies. Section 6, however, stated:

> Provided also (and be it declared and enacted) that any declaration before mentioned shall not extend to any letters patent and grants of privilege for the term of fourteen years or under, hereafter to be made, of the sole working or making of any manner of new manufacture within this realm, to the true and first inventor and inventors of such manufactures which others at the time of making such letters patent and grants shall not use, so as also

[1] *Gowers Review of Intellectual Property* (HM Treasury, 2006), para 1.13.
[2] See CM Belfanti, 'Guilds, patents and the circulation of technical knowledge: northern Italy during the early modern age' (2004) 45 Technology and Culture 569.   [3] (1602) 77 ER 1131.

they be not contrary to the law or mischievous to the state, by raising prices of commodities at home, or hurt of trade, or generally inconvenient.

10.5   This provides an exception to the rule, and then stipulates an exception to the exception. The exception to the rule that Crown monopolies should not be granted is the proviso that the 'true and first inventor' of 'any manner of new manufacture' could receive a 14-year-long privilege over his invention, but the exception to this is that this monopoly should not be abusive or abused in ways contrary to law, state interests, trade and economic interests, or indeed, if it were 'generally inconvenient'.

 Discussion point For answer guidance visit www.oxfordtextbooks.co.uk/orc/waelde3e/

Why do you think that a period of 14 years was chosen, as opposed to 13 or 15 or some other figure?

10.6   We see, then, elements in the early history of patents which we can still recognise in our modern system. These are:

- the patent system as a mechanism to encourage innovation;
- the notion of social contract between state and patentee, with corresponding obligations on both sides;
- the centrality of monopoly to the regulation of that contract;
- the desire for a balance of interests as between society and the patentee;
- the idea that the monopoly should rightly go to the inventor of the new creation.

10.7   Other matters have changed. The law in the UK no longer talks of 'manner of new manufacture'.[4] We thus have to look elsewhere for some guidance on what constitutes an invention.[5] Patents are now granted for a maximum of 20 years, although 'in the UK typically fewer than 50 per cent of patents are renewed beyond the tenth year.'[6] The search for a just balance is, however, a constant.

10.8   It is important to note that the grant of patents remained discretionary under the Statute of Monopolies of 1624. It was not until the 19th century that procedural form and a degree of certainty of process was introduced to the British patent system. The Patent Office was not established until 1852,[7] and it did not begin thorough examination of patent applications, in the sense of a proper scrutiny of the existing art, until 1905.[8] Prior to this it was sufficient merely to lodge a specification—a description of the invention—with the Patent Office to obtain protection.[9] Reforms brought about by the Patents, Designs and Trade Marks Act 1883 introduced a more robust procedure for examining applications, but even then it was largely a matter of checking for deficiencies in the formalities of an application and for insufficiency in the description of the invention itself.[10]

---

[4] The laws in the United States, Canada, Australia, and New Zealand still refer to this concept in some form or another, betraying their colonial roots.

[5] The UK law changed with the passing of the Patents Act 1977 which brought the UK into line with the European Patent Convention 1973.

[6] See I Hargreaves, *Digital Opportunity: A Review of Intellectual Property and Growth* (2011), para 6.9, p 53. For a worldwide perspective, see World Intellectual Property Organization (WIPO), *World Intellectual Property Indicators* (2012).

[7] Patent Law Amendment Act 1852. Initially there existed Commissioners who were replaced by the Office itself in 1883. The Office is currently located in Newport, Gwent but its original home was in Southampton Buildings, London where it shared space with the Secretaries of Bankrupts and Lunatics!   [8] As a result of the Patents Act 1902.

[9] This system was introduced by the Patent Law Amendment Act 1852.

[10] Interestingly, this reflects many utility models systems which exist elsewhere in Europe, see paras 10.72ff.

10.9   There were certain adverse social consequences of such lax procedures. It meant, for example, that patents of dubious or no worth could be obtained relatively easily and then waved over competitors as a threat; it also generated considerable uncertainty as to where the boundaries of legitimate trading lay. Movements in various European countries took up against the patent system around this time,[11] and the Dutch actually abolished their system in the period 1869 to 1912. In the UK, many trade organisations railed against patents in the 18th and 19th centuries, and bodies such as the Royal Society of Arts lobbied governments against the worst excesses of patent monopolies.[12] Indeed, the Society created an alternative scheme to the patent system in an attempt to achieve the same social ends but without the restrictions that monopolies can bring. The Society offered cash *premiums* for innovations in certain areas, and published *Lists* advertising these widely. The Lists set questions or problems requiring resolution, thereby providing a partly directed policy of innovation for British society. Importantly, from 1765, no person was to be considered as a candidate for a premium if they had previously obtained a patent for the invention for which the premium was offered. The premium acted as an incentive to innovators to disclose their inventions early and to allow others to build on their expertise. No monopoly over the invention was given.

 Discussion point   For answer guidance visit www.oxfordtextbooks.co.uk/orc/waelde3e/

What are the advantages of the premium system compared to the patent system? Equally, can you think of any disadvantages?

10.10   The premium system did not survive, but the Royal Society continues its struggle against inappropriate monopolies. A contemporary example of this is the Adelphi Charter.[13] This instrument was drawn up by a distinguished group of interested individuals and parties concerned about the ever-expanding nature of intellectual property rights and the possible consequences for the public domain of their aggressive enforcement. The Charter calls on governments and other bodies to adopt new strategies for thinking about, and protecting, intellectual property and the public interest. It consists of nine statements of principle which could be taken to guide intellectual property policy in the future in ways that might result in the striking of a different balance of interests to that which exists today. Three of the principles give a flavour of the tone of the document:

(1) Laws regulating intellectual property must serve as means of achieving creative, social and economic ends and not as ends in themselves …

… (3) The public interest requires a balance between the public domain and private rights. It also requires a balance between the free competition that is essential for economic vitality and the monopoly rights granted by intellectual property laws …, and

… (9) There must be an automatic presumption against creating new areas of intellectual property protection, extending existing privileges or extending the duration of rights.

---

[11] Various countries have gone without patent systems at one time or another, see HC Wegner, *Patent Harmonisation* (1993) at 17, and E Schiff, *Industrialization without National Patents: The Netherlands, 1869–1912, Switzerland, 1850–1907* (1971).

[12] Royal Society for the Encouragement of Arts, Manufactures and Commerce: http://www.thersa.org/. The Society itself points out that in many ways the broad aim of the Society is not entirely dissimilar to that of the patent system.

[13] Royal Society of Arts Adelphi Charter: http://www.adelphicharter.org/.

Exercise

Visit the Adelphi Charter site at http://www.thersa.org/projects/past-projects/adelphi-charter to find out more. Critically assess the terms of the Charter. It is nice rhetoric, but is there much chance of it becoming reality?

10.11   The establishment of a patent registration system was a move to create a gate-keeping device. Such a system provides a relatively clear indication of thresholds that have to be met in order for patent protection to be granted, that is, that the invention must be new, involve inventive step, and be capable of industrial application. It also serves to ensure that the obligation of the applicant to disclose his invention in a way that furthers the public interest is fully discharged.[14] Moreover, and just as importantly, it is a mechanism for weeding out innovations that have been deemed not to be inventions, such as discoveries, or which are to be excluded on a number of policy grounds, for example that they offend against common decency or morality. We should be very clear, therefore, that the process of examining a patent application is not some technical box-ticking exercise. Indeed, the examination of a patent application involves the assessment of a plethora of policy considerations which are designed to reflect the policy objectives of the patent system itself. How well this is achieved is another question.

Internationalisation of patent protection

10.12   We have already seen in the context of copyright and designs that intellectual property rights started their life as creatures of national territorial effect only, meaning that protection was only afforded to innovators in their own country. The same was true, and remains true, of patents. But patents have always had an international dimension. From earliest times, part of the reason for granting a monopoly to a national was for fear that foreigners might otherwise dominate a domestic market. By the same token, as we have seen, the Venetian Republic used its own system of encouraging innovation to attract those from outside the Republic to bring new crafts and methods of manufacture to the city. Indeed, the prospect of international trade has been inherently bound up with the development of patent protection over the years. This was particularly acute in the 19th century with the advent of the Industrial Revolution and at a time when various European patent systems were developing along similar lines and cross-jurisdictional influence was common. The vagaries of international trade meant that there was a growing urgency to ensure that intellectual property was recognised and mutually protected across national boundaries for the benefit of all. Thus, just as we had the emergence of the Berne Convention in respect of copyright in 1886 (see Chapter 2), so too the international community (or much of it) foresaw an unmet need for an instrument to protect other forms of intellectual property, specifically patents, but far more broadly and crudely, *industrial property*.[15] In this way the Paris Convention of 1883 was born,[16] obliging signatory states to provide appropriate protection for the range of interests subsumed under the rubric of 'Industrial Property', being 'patents, utility models, industrial designs, trademarks, service marks, trade names, indications of source or appellations of origin, and the repression of unfair competition'.[17] This Convention says nothing specific about the substantive elements of patent law for its signatory countries—beyond the obligation to provide protection—but it did bring about various important reforms.

[14] This was one of the major criticisms of the system during the pre-registration period, see generally on this period B Sherman and L Bently, *The Making of Modern Intellectual Property Law* (1999), 101–110.

[15] Paris Convention for the Protection of Industrial Property (1883), revised at Brussels on 14 December 1900, at Washington on 2 June 1911, at The Hague on 6 November 1925, at London on 2 June 1934, at Lisbon on 31 October 1958, and at Stockholm on 14 July 1967, and as amended on 28 September 1979.

[16] There are currently 174 contracting parties to the Convention (April 2013).   [17] Paris Convention, Art 1(2).

The *main features of the Paris Convention* perform, in numerous ways, similar functions as the Berne Convention does for copyright. In other ways, it distinguishes industrial property as a class apart from copyright and its related rights. Thus:

- The principle of *national treatment* was established in the Paris Convention, ensuring that each signatory state will afford the same rights to foreigners of other signatory states as to its own nationals (Art 2). Nationals of non-contracting states are also entitled to national treatment under the Convention if they are domiciled in a contracting state or if they have a 'real and effective industrial or commercial establishment' in a contracting state (Art 3).

- An applicant enjoys a *12-month right of priority from the date of first filing of a patent in a signatory country* (Art 4). This means that no subsequent filing of related applications in other countries within this period will be invalidated by the earlier filing, nor will any publication or use of the invention affect patentability. It also means that the novelty of all such applications will be tested by reference to the period before the first filing. We discuss the significance of this later (paras 11.82ff).

- *National patents remain independent of each other*, therefore the granting of a patent in one contracting state does not oblige the other contracting states to grant a patent; a patent cannot be refused, annulled, or terminated in any contracting state on the ground that it has been refused or annulled or has terminated in any other contracting state (Art 4*bis*).

- The *focus is on the inventor* who has the right to be named as such in the patent (Art 4*ter*). The primary right holder, in the first instance, is the inventor. While this may be varied by contract or by the existence of an employer/employee relationship, such modifications to the general rule are left to domestic laws.

10.13   The Paris Convention remains of central significance in the protection of patents, and it is allied to the more recent TRIPS Agreement 1994, see paras 10.42–10.45, in that a signatory state to the latter instrument must also comply with the core provisions of the Paris Convention, notably Articles 1–12 and 19.[18]

Key points on the early history

- Contemporary patent law began as a system of grace and favour, but a central feature from early on has been the idea of the patent as a form of 'social contract' with obligations on both sides

- In return for patent protection, then, a patentee must make his invention public

- The monopolistic effects of patents have always been viewed with suspicion, and attempts to minimise these include limiting the duration of a patent (currently to 20 years in most cases)

- In the 19th century, and throughout the 20th century, the process of internationalisation of patent law gathers pace, making it today one of the most harmonised areas of law at least in terms of substantive law.

Rationales of patent protection

10.14   There is no single rationale for the patent system—indeed, some claim that it makes little sense at all. But its 400-year-long history speaks to the fact that it must be achieving some useful purpose(s), and a recent WIPO report on patenting activity worldwide reveals that 2011 was the first year in which patent filings exceeded an annual rate of 2 million and in the same year China overtook the United States

---

[18] Agreement on Trade-Related Aspects of Intellectual Property Rights (1994), Art 2.

as the largest patent office in the world.[19] Internationalisation of patent filing has grown and around 7.88 million patents were in force in 2011 and between 2009 and 2011, patent filings worldwide grew by 293,900. This, in turn, is linked to a marked rise in the use of the international application mechanism as a conduit to foreign markets.[20] Patents are, it would seem, a big success worldwide.[21]

10.15   There has, however, always been a need to justify the patent system. Its existence is not self-evidently in the public good and its approach of offering a market monopoly is not manifestly the best means to strike a balance of potentially competing interests. The interests at stake include those of inventors, their competitors, consumers, researchers, and the state itself. As we have seen, a patent is often described as a form of social contract between the patentee and the state, whereby the award of a patent monopoly is given in return for public disclosure of the invention. This reveals an irony in the way that the patent system operates: an exclusionary private property right is given in return for public dissemination of the details of the invention. Why so?

10.16   Various rationales for patents have been advanced over the years, and it is probably the case that each has held sway at one time or another in the development of patent law policy. The idea of the patent as a *reward* for inventive activity is difficult to sustain, however, because the need for a reward does not require that a monopoly be given. Rewards can take many forms such as prizes or one-off payments without any risk of adverse effects on the market.[22] Rather, the most commonly advanced rationale for the social contract approach is the *incentive* function that it is thought to represent. This is the view that the prospect of a monopoly is so attractive that it will encourage innovation and that it represents the best means to secure adequate returns for intellectual endeavour; moreover, the public disclosure requirement acts as a further spur to others to invent around a particular invention and to receive their own protection. This rationale rests on certain assumptions, however. For example, it assumes that the value of innovative activity outweighs increased costs to consumers, and that any monopolies granted will not be used to block, rather than encourage, development in a particular field.[23] It also presupposes that citizens will be in a position to pay higher costs and that the necessary infrastructures are in place to support further innovation. Neither of these last two assumptions stands for many developing countries, calling into question the rationale and value of the patent system to those countries. A World Bank publication has indicated that patent rights over high-technology products are of most value in large, middle-income, developing countries where imitation of an invention is most likely, while export decisions to poorer countries often do not depend on the existence of IPRs in those countries since the threat of imitation is lower because of lack of infrastructure.[24]

10.17   The *public disclosure* requirement in patent law should not be underestimated. It is an essential feature of the arrangement between the patentee and the state, and a patent can be struck down on grounds of *insufficiency* if adequate disclosure is not made in a patent application.[25] Adequate disclosure requires

[19] WIPO, *World Intellectual Property Indicators* (2012), p 6, available at http://www.wipo.int/export/sites/www/freepublications/en/intproperty/941/wipo_pub_941_2012.pdf.

[20] This was established by the Patent Cooperation Treaty 1970 (see paras 10.37–10.38). International applications through the PCT saw an 11 per cent growth in 2011 and the fastest since 2005, see *World Intellectual Property Indicators* (2012), note 19.

[21] See also G Scellato et al, 'Study on the Quality of the Patent System in Europe' (2011) available at http://ec.europa.eu/internal_market/indprop/docs/patent/patqual02032011_en.pdf.

[22] EC Hettinger, 'Justifying Intellectual Property' (1989) 18 Philosophy and Public Affairs 31–52.

[23] A survey funded by the European Commission found that about one-third of European patents are not used for any commercial or industrial purposes, and that one half of these are used as 'blocking' patents, ie to prevent competitors from using the protected technology, see 'Study on Evaluating the Knowledge Economy: What are Patents Actually Worth? The Value of Patents for Today's Economy and Society', Final Report, 23 July 2006, p 10. See also I Troy and R Werle, *Uncertainty and the Market for Patents* (2008).

[24] C Fink and KE Maskus (eds), *Intellectual Property and Development: Lessons from Recent Economic Research* (2005), Ch 2 by C Fink and CA Primo Braga, 'How stronger protection of intellectual property rights affects international trade flows'. See also World Bank, *Global Economic Prospects 2008: Technology Diffusion in the Developing World* (2008).

[25] Patents Act 1977, ss 14(3) and 72(1)—see further paras 11.206–11.218.

that the essential features of the invention are made public and that the means to make or reproduce the invention are revealed in a way that would enable a person skilled in the particular field ('the art') to do so.[26] The European Patent Office claims that its searchable patent databases now provide the most efficient, detailed, and up-to-date source of information in over 50 technical fields. The stringent disclosure requirements mean that 70 per cent of information contained in patents is not available anywhere else.[27]

10.18   It has also been argued that patents perform a *signalling* function, that is, indicating the innovative and productive capacity of the patent holder and signalling that he may be a sound investment for the future.[28] Patent portfolios are certainly a key consideration for venture capitalists.

10.19   *Human rights discourse* has become more prevalent in recent years both in support of, and against, the existence and exercise of IPRs. On the one hand, it is important to note that the 1948 Universal Declaration of Human Rights provides that 'Everyone has the right to the protection of the moral and material interests resulting from any scientific, literary or artistic production of which he is the author',[29] suggesting that individual creators have a human rights claim to IP. On the other hand, the UN Sub-Commission on Human Rights has pointed to the potential inherent conflict which IPRs can generate *face-à-face* other economic, social, or cultural rights and issued a Resolution to the effect that these latter rights should trump in any case of conflict.[30] But not everyone sees these two regimes as in inherent conflict.[31] Few rights, even human rights, are absolute. Limitations can be placed on the exercise of rights in an attempt either to protect the rights and freedoms of others, or to achieve an overall equitable balance of interests. In contemporary policy terms, it is clear that *balance* is the watchword of the day. The language of human rights might help us to frame the discussion, but it is unlikely to provide any universal solution.[32]

10.20   Human rights perspectives have not only had the effect of opening up dialogue about the nature of IPRs, but they have also led to a greater appreciation of relationships between the intellectual property world and other social realms. An example of this is the potential *regulation* function of the patent system. Just as the grant of a patent might encourage innovation, so it might follow that the denial of a patent might dissuade certain forms of innovation. In this sense, the patent system could be seen as a means to regulate or control undesirable inventions. Alternatively, undesirable uses of the monopoly which a patent provides might also be regulated through the patent system, for example through greater use of compulsory licences or more generous interpretations of patent defences. Little work has been done to date on the interface between patent and regulation regimes,[33] but a few cautious comments can be offered here. First, the denial of a patent in no way prohibits innovation, it merely removes an incentive. Plenty of innovative behaviour carries on without the potential of a patent, and there is no guarantee that the denial of protection will have the desired dissuasive effect. The *efficiency* of this alleged regulatory

---

[26] See generally *Kirin-Amgen v Hoechst Marion Roussel No 2* [2005] RPC 9.

[27] See the Espacenet database at http://worldwide.espacenet.com/ and EPO, *Global Patent Data Coverage* (2011).

[28] Commission on Intellectual Property Rights, Innovation and Public Health, *Public Health, Innovation and Intellectual Property Rights* (2006), 21 available at http://www.who.int/intellectualproperty/documents/thereport/ENPublicHealthReport.pdf.

[29] UN General Assembly Resolution 217A(III), UN Doc A/810, at 71, Art 27(2).

[30] UN High Commissioner for Human Rights, Sub-Commission on Human Rights, Intellectual Property Rights and Human Rights, Resolution 2000/7, 17 August 2000, available at http://www.un.org/en/rights/.

[31] See HL MacQueen, 'Towards utopia or irreconcilable tensions? Thoughts on intellectual property, human rights and competition law' (2005) 2(4) SCRIPTed 452–466 and L Helfer, 'Human rights and intellectual property: conflict or co-existence?' (2003) 5 Minnesota Intellectual Property Review 47.

[32] PK Yu, 'Reconceptualizing intellectual property interests in a human rights framework' (2007) University of California Davis Law Review 1039–1149.

[33] See GT Laurie, 'Patents, patients and consent: exploring the interface between regulation and innovation regimes' in H Somsen (ed), *The Regulatory Challenge of Biotechnology* (2007).

function is therefore open to question. Secondly, the assessment of which inventions are undesirable is a complex matter, involving ethical and moral considerations which may be beyond the competence of a patent office examiner. Moreover, given the nature of the patent system in requiring secrecy about an invention prior to applying for a patent, there will have been little or no opportunity for broader social debate about an invention, thereby raising questions about the *legitimacy* of quasi-regulatory decisions about the value, or otherwise, of a particular invention. Notwithstanding, there has been increased reliance on the exclusions provisions in patent law in recent years, especially in the field of biotechnological inventions,[34] implying that the rationale of the patent system may, once again, be changing.[35]

10.21   It matters very much which of these rationales is promoted over any other in the development and implementation of patent policy. A public interest mandate will require evidence that the dual aims of dissemination of knowledge and increased innovation can be achieved before there is any strengthening of IP rights, or indeed, the introduction of new rights. A focus on the individual inventor's claims would, however, promote new and more robust forms of protection.

 Exercise

Consider which of these, or other, rationales are operating as you read more about the different regimes and features of patent law. Are we always striking the right balance?

The European dimension

10.22   Easily the most far-reaching reforms of the 20th century for UK patent law came in the period of 'Europeanisation', which produced the European Patent Convention (EPC, 1973, as amended) after long negotiations throughout the 1960s. The Patents Act 1977 incorporated these reforms into domestic law,[36] and in doing so swept away many of the vestiges of the uniquely British regime that had gone before.[37] We have already seen, for example, that the law no longer requires proof of 'a manner of manufacture', although the reforming measures did not provide us with a replacement definition of an invention. It is now assumed that if an applicant clears the hurdles of patentability then he has produced an 'invention'.[38] The EPC harmonised the substantive law on patentability and exclusions and it now represents the position in 38 European countries.[39] Judicial attitudes in the UK towards the interpretation of patents also had to change after the 1977 Act came into force. The traditional British perspective had been towards a *literal approach* to interpreting a patentee's claims for his invention, while the European tradition (as in many other areas of law) has been to adopt a *purposive approach*, that is, to seek to interpret the law in the light of the ultimate purpose it was designed to achieve. This has been a difficult transition for the courts as we shall see in due course (paras 11.187–11.203), and there is still

---

[34] See paras 12.43ff.

[35] Cf the collective reply of German patent attorneys to the European Commission's survey on IP policy, note 23, wherein they opined (at 10) that 'there is no reason for a political debate on principles concerning patent protection in view of ethical behaviour, protection of the environment, health protection, or freedom of information'.

[36] Relevant laws in the 20th century were the Patents Acts of 1902 and 1949. European laws had, nonetheless, been approximating over the years and in many respects patent laws were very similar.

[37] Consider the early 20th-century proposals for a 'British Empire patent', see C Wadlow, 'The British Empire patent 1901–1923: the "global patent" that never was' [2006] IPQ 311.

[38] Cf the discussion on the need for an 'invention' in *Biogen v Medeva* [1997] RPC 1, especially per Lord Mustill at 31, where the door was not firmly closed on the issue but neither their Lordships nor counsel could think of a pertinent example.

[39] As of 30 April 2013.

discussion of the extent to which the UK takes its own path, despite further clarification from within the European system on how patent claims should be interpreted.[40] Most recently, the EPC has been revised and now takes the form of EPC 2000 which came into force in December 2007, and with amendments entering into force on 1 January 2011.

10.23   The EPC also established the European Patent Office (EPO), which is based in Munich, Germany, and which opened its doors on 1 June 1978 when the Convention came into force. The EPO grants 'European' patents, although this is something of a misnomer since there is no such thing (yet) as a European patent in the sense of one instrument effective throughout European territory. Rather, the EPO provides a single point of entry for the patent applicant to lodge only one application, and be subject to only one examination process, but in respect of any number of signatory countries that he might designate. If successful, the EPO grants collections of patents for the designated countries, and each patent has full effect in the country for which it was sought as if it was granted by the domestic intellectual property office.[41]

Diagram 10.1 Current internal structure of European Patent Office[42]

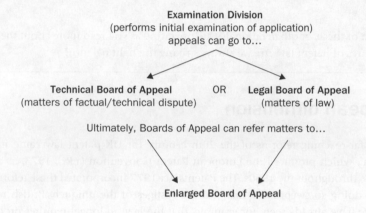

10.24   The President of the EPO can also perform a 'declaratory' function[43] and issue opinions on cases of import.[44] He or she[45] can refer questions to the Enlarged Board of Appeal to clarify matters in particular areas of law, as can Boards of Appeal.

10.25   An important feature of the European patent system is the existence of *Opposition Proceedings*.[46] These allow any party who objects to the grant of a patent—for example, on evidence that it did not, in fact, meet the criteria for patentability or because it offends *ordre public* or morality[47]—to petition the Opposition Division of the Office within nine months of publication of the grant of the patent.[48] The Division has the power to revoke the patent.[49] This mechanism has been used increasingly in recent

---

[40]   See now Art 2 to the Additional Protocol on the Interpretation of Art 69, inserted by EPC 2000.

[41]   The terminology is of European Patent (UK) or European Patent (France).

[42]   See here for up-to-date information on the Boards of Appeal: http://www.epo.org/about-us/boards-of-appeal.html.

[43]   See G3/95 *Inadmissible referral* (1996) OJEPO 169 and EPC 2000, Art 112(1)(b).

[44]   See, eg, G2/06 Comments by the President of the European Patent Office (September 2006), available at http://www.cipa.org.uk/download_files/epo_warf.pdf.

[45]   Alison Brimelow, former Director of the UK Patent Office, took over the Presidency of the EPO in July 2007 and was succeed by Benoît Battistelli from France on 1 July 2010.   [46]   EPC 2000, Part V.

[47]   EPC 2000, Art 100 outlines the grounds for opposition. These are (a) the subject matter of the European patent is not patentable within the terms of the EPC; (b) the patent does not disclose the invention in a manner sufficiently clear and complete for it to be carried out by a person skilled in the art; (c) the subject matter of the European patent extends beyond the content of the relevant application.   [48]   EPC 2000, Art 99.   [49]   EPC 2000, Art 102.

years in the context of biotechnological inventions, as we discuss in Chapter 12. It is a valuable social device which gives access to the patent system to groups who may have legitimate concerns about how well the granting authorities are striking the balance of interests at stake.[50]

10.26 Note that the EPO is a granting body only. There is no European body (as yet) on questions of infringement or enforcement. Domestic and 'European' patents are therefore enforced in individual jurisdictions. A result of this is that it can lead to the unusual scenario where a patent may be held to be valid and infringed in one country and yet invalid in another even although they relate to the very same invention.[51] This is because judicial attitudes towards interpretation of patents can vary as between jurisdictions and to that extent the harmonisation process has for a long time remained far from complete. Significant recent developments are set to change all of this.

European reforms

10.27 It is important at this juncture to clarify a point which often causes confusion. The EPC is *not* an instrument of the European Union. The European Patent Organisation is an entirely separate entity which administers the EPC through its Administrative Council. There are 38 signatory states to the EPC, including all 27 member states of the EU, as well as non-EU countries.[52] But any coordination of effort between the European Patent Organisation and the EU is on an entirely voluntary basis. It has meant, also, the reforming measures come from both camps.

10.28 Attempts to bring about closer harmonisation emanating from with the EPO included a proposal to establish a European Patent Judiciary composed of a European Patent Court and Administrative Council and with the power to settle litigation on matters of infringement over European patents.[53] Similarly, a draft Agreement to establish a European and European Union Patent Court was held to be incompatible with EU law by the Court of Justice of the European Union (CJEU) in March 2011.[54] Both, however, have effectively been overtaken by other events driven by the EU itself.

A unitary patent right for Europe?

10.29 An early initiative from the late 1950s pre-empted the negotiations towards the EPC, and this was an attempt to create a unitary patent right for the, then, European Economic Community (EEC). The rationale for such an initiative takes us back to the fundamental tensions that IPRs can create in a market: the problem for the EEC—committed as it was to a single European market—was how to prevent the exercise of national patent monopolies partitioning the market. If a single right were to subsist throughout that market then the problem of partition largely disappears. This proposal did not come to fruition, but the idea of a single European patent survived into the 1960s negotiations,[55] where two core proposals were

[50] S Harmon, 'The rules of re-engagement: the use of patent proceedings to influence the regulation of science (what the science does when the salmon comes back downstream)' (2006) 4 IPQ 378–403.

[51] *Improver Corporation v Remington Consumer Products Ltd* [1990] FSR 181.

[52] Figure accurate as at 1 April 2013.

[53] See the work of the Working Party on Litigation set up by the contracting states of the European Patent Organisation in June 1999: http://web.archive.org/web/20061018103942/http://patlaw-reform.european-patent-office.org/epla/. In particular, consider the proposals on a Draft Agreement on the establishment of a European patent litigation system (aka European Patent Litigation Agreement) (December 2005).

[54] Opinion 1/09 (Re creation of a unified patent litigation system) [2011] ECR I-1137.

[55] An early output from these negotiations was the Council of Europe Convention on the Unification of Certain Points of Substantive Law on Patents for Invention, 27 November 1963 (the Strasbourg Convention) wherein signatory states agreed the substantive criteria for invention, being novelty, inventive step, and capability of industrial application (Art 1) as well as exclusions from patentability when an invention or its publication is contrary to *ordre public* or morality (Art 2).

on the table: a European Patent Convention (to deal with harmonisation of substantive criteria and to create a centralised granting body) and a Community Patent Convention (CPC, to produce a single, truly European patent effective throughout the Community). The former, as we have seen, became a reality in 1973. A Community Patent Convention was also signed in Luxembourg in 1975,[56] but failed to receive sufficient ratifications to come into force, as did a second attempt in 1989.[57] One of the biggest problems has been that of translation. The official languages of the EPO are English, French, and German, but the EU currently has 23 official languages, and the Convention provided that a patent had to be translated into every Community language. Self-evidently, the costs of this exercise would be prohibitive, especially when one considers that it is not unusual for a patent to run to over 20 pages in length.[58]

10.30   Notwithstanding these problems, the European Commission has not been willing to give up on the idea of a unitary patent.[59] It has insisted that a single right makes economic sense, would reduce the costs of patenting, and would provide more legal certainty.[60] The EU—now a legal entity in its own right after the coming into force of the Lisbon Treaty[61]—has been emboldened as a result and stands to become a signatory to the EPC.

> ## Reminder
>
> The EU does not have authority to interfere with property rights in member states (Art 345 of the Treaty on the Functioning of the European Union (TFEU)). Any Europe-wide reforms can only *add* to national property rights, they cannot take them away.

10.31   After decades of political manoeuvring[62] and legal challenge,[63] two European Regulations were eventually adopted in December 2012 that signal the advent of unitary patent protection in the EU.[64] The 'patent package' will take forward enhanced cooperation between 25 of the 27 member states. Spain and Italy challenged the legal position[65] and Italy has indicated that it will only sign up to the Unified Patent Court Agreement (UPCA)[66] and not the two Regulations setting up the Unified Patent system. Once the Regulations have entered into force (1 January 2014 or date of entry into force of UPCA, if later), it will be possible to seek and obtain a single European patent with enforcement through the Unified Patent Court. The estimated schedule for first grants is April 2014. All would be subject to the

---

[56] Convention for the European Patent for the Common Market, 15 December 1975.

[57] Agreement relating to Community Patents, 15 December 1989.

[58] The European Commission estimated this was the average length of a patent application in its proposal for a Community patent, note 23, para 2.4.3.1.

[59] Commission's Green Paper on the Community patent and the European patent system, COM(97) 314 final, of 24 June 1997.

[60] See the EU's Industrial Property website at http://ec.europa.eu/internal_market/indprop/patent/index_en.htm.

[61] See Art 118 TFEU: 'the European Parliament and the Council, acting in accordance with the ordinary legislative procedure, shall establish measures for the creation of European intellectual property rights to provide uniform protection of intellectual property rights throughout the Union and for the setting up of centralised Union-wide authorisation, coordination and supervision arrangements.'

[62] See Council Decision of 10 March 2011 authorising enhanced cooperation in the area of the creation of unitary patent protection (2011/167/EU), available at http://eur-lex.europa.eu/LexUriServ/LexUriServ.do?uri=OJ:L:2011:076:0053:0055:EN:PDF.

[63] See Joined Cases C-274/11 and C-295/11 *Kingdom of Spain and Italian Republic v Council of the European Union*, Judgment of the Court (Grand Chamber) of 16 April 2013 dismissing all actions; not yet published. These were attempts to annul Council Decision 2011/167 of 10 March 2011 authorising enhanced cooperation in the area of the creation of unitary patent protection. It resulted in Spain and Italy not being part of the proposal for a unified patent scheme.

[64] Regulation (EU) No 1257/2012 of the European Parliament and of the Council of 17 December 2012 implementing enhanced cooperation in the area of the creation of unitary patent protection (31.12.2012 , OJ L361/1) and Council Regulation (EU) No 1260/2012 of 17 December 2012 implementing enhanced cooperation in the area of the creation of unitary patent protection with regard to the applicable translation arrangements (31.12.2012, L361/89).

[65] At the time of writing, Spain has lodged two additional complaints: Cases C-146/13 and C-147/13 *Spain v Parliament and Council*, pending.   [66] Signed by 24 member states on 19 February 2013.

supervision of the CJEU and there would be no prejudice to the jurisdiction of that court to hear referrals from domestic courts.

10.32   The passage has not been smooth and the EU is not out of the woods yet. Spain and Italy challenged the original Council cooperation approach and have also raised questions about the language provisions. Patent applications should be in one of English, French, or German. Small to medium-sized enterprises, natural persons, non-profit organisations, universities, and public research organisations having their residence or principal place of business within a member state and who must translate applications into an official language will be entitled to compensation for the costs, although the workability of this is questionable. The Max Planck Institute produced a critical report in 2012[67] suggesting, inter alia, that this will create territorial and substantive fragmentation rather that harmonisation (25 EU member states covered; two EU member states excluded; 13 non-EU EPC signatories), a risk of dysfunctional patenting practices (patentees playing the EU system off against national systems), and promotion of further uncertainty (a multi-level system across, national, European, and international levels).

 Discussion point   For answer guidance visit www.oxfordtextbooks.co.uk/orc/waelde3e/

Given the coexistence of national patents and EU patents, and roles for domestic courts as well as the divisions of the Unitary Patent Court, are we likely to see a convergence or divergence of approach to patent protection as between member states and EU bodies? In particular, would domestic courts be required to follow decisions of the Unitary Patent Court?

10.33   The issue of language remains an important and difficult issue. Within the EPC system it has been dealt with by the provisions of the *London Agreement* from 2000.[68]

This Agreement allows sigatory parties that share an official language with the EPO to waive, wholly or partially, the translation requirement under the EPC (Art 65) that a patent be filed in their national language. Countries that do not share a language with the EPO can also waive this requirement, as long as the patent has been granted in an official EPO language. The Agreement came into force in May 2008 when France ratified the Agreement. This Agreement can reduce the costs of patenting in Europe up to 45 per cent when the countries designated by the patentee have signed up to the Agreement. The approximate cost of the translation of an average length patent into one other language lies around €1,100. This results in €5,500 for five translations, which is the average number of foreign states for which protection is sought and around €30,000 for the translations which you would need to obtain patent coverage in all 38 EPC countries under the current regime.

10.34   We can sum up the European scene as follows:

European Patent Organisation

- European Patent Convention (2000)
- 38 signatory countries
- European Patent Office—grants 'European' patents for designated countries—enforced domestically
- No appeal body from signatory states
- Opposition proceedings to object to patent grant on specified grounds

European Union

- Programme of harmonising measures
- 27 members
- Unitary Patent Package pending—this will create one right enforceable throughout the Union with a single dispute settlement body—the Unitary Patents Court
- Referral possible to the Court of Justice in same way as from national courts

---

[67] Max Planck Institute for Intellectual Property and Competition Law, *The Unitary Patent Package: Twelve Reasons for Concern* (2012).
[68] European Patent Organisation, Agreement dated 17 October 2000 on the application of Art 65, EPC (London Agreement) (2001) 12 OJEPO 549. An informative guide has been produced by the EPO at http://www.epo.org/law-practice/legal-texts/london-agreement.html.

The international dimension

10.35   WIPO and the World Trade Organization (WTO) are each responsible for administering important treaties on patent protection at the international level. These perform a harmonising or approximating function for both formal and substantive aspects of patent law.

WIPO: streamlining the patent application process

10.36   Two instruments are currently administered by WIPO which considerably facilitates the process of applying for a patent.

10.37   The *Patent Cooperation Treaty* (1970, as amended) (PCT) is another product of fervent patent reform emerging from the 1960s, this time at the initiative of the United States.[69] The Treaty is designed to facilitate the process when an applicant is applying for patents simultaneously in numerous jurisdictions worldwide.[70] It is *not* a granting procedure and merely provides a conduit whereby a single application can be processed and searched by a qualified international body before being sent to national or regional intellectual property offices for full consideration. Anyone who is a national or resident of a contracting state[71] can file a single international patent application, either in his national office, or at the EPO if the state is also a signatory to the EPC, or at the International Bureau of WIPO in Geneva.[72] This single application is then subject to an 'international search' from which an international research report is prepared. This contains details of published documents that might cause problems for an invention in terms of its patentability, that is, because they may demonstrate that the invention is not 'new' (see paras 11.79ff). It is also possible for applicants to request an international preliminary examination which results in a non-binding written opinion on patentability.[73] If an applicant does not withdraw his application at this point, the report becomes a public document,[74] although the written opinion does not.

10.38   The application is then sent for consideration to national or regional offices as designated by the applicant.[75] While the results of the international search do not guarantee that an invention will be 'novel' for all purposes in the designated countries, it does provide the applicant with 'reasonable probability' of receiving patent protection, according to WIPO. Moreover, the procedure not only greatly limits costs, but it can also speed up the process for obtaining patent protection, especially in countries which do not have adequate search facilities. Applicants also have time within the PCT process—up to 18 months—to amend their application before proceeding to designated foreign offices, and, indeed, to decide whether to proceed at all, weighing up the various considerations such as appointing local patent agents, preparing translations, and paying national fees. It is also claimed that this process furthers the public interest in that the systematic publication of international reports—carried out by approved authorities[76]—means

[69]   You can read the current text of the PCT at http://www.wipo.int/pct/en/texts/articles/atoc.htm.

[70]   Full details are available at http://www.wipo.int/pct/en/.

[71]   There were 146 contracting states to the PCT as of 30 April 2013. See http://www.wipo.int/treaties/en/ShowResults.jsp?lang=en&treaty_id=6.

[72]   See further WIPO, *History of the PCT Regulations (June 19, 1970–January 1, 2009)* (2011) available at http://www.wipo.int/pct/en/texts/pdf/pct_regulations_history.pdf.   [73]   PCT, Ch II.

[74]   This is published by the International Bureau.

[75]   An application through PCT automatically constitutes an election of all contracting states in the first instance, but in reality applicants are selective about the countries they wish to target. See Rule 53.7 of the Regulations under the PCT (1 July 2011) at http://www.wipo.int/treaties/en/notifications/pct/treaty_pct_196-annex1.html#rule53.9.

[76]   International searches are carried out by approved International Searching Authorities (PCT, Art 16) and there also exist International Preliminary Examination Authorities (PCT, Art 32). Regulations under the PCT impose minimum requirements on authorities appointed by the PCT Union (Rule 36 and Rule 63). These now require that International Preliminary Examining Authorities must 'have in place a quality management system and internal review arrangements in accordance with the common rules of international preliminary examination …' and it must hold an official appointment as an International Searching Authority.

that third parties are better placed to assess the patentability of any given invention and to assess the state of the art at any given time. The importance of the quality of searches is crucial to the success and efficiency of any patent system.[77] The success of the PCT is demonstrated by the fact that it had received one million applications from around the world by the end of 2004 and exceeded two million by the end of 2011.[78]

10.39   WIPO established the *Standing Committee on the Law of Patents* in 1998 with a remit to take debate and international patent reform forward into the 21st century. The Committee's membership is broad, including all members of WIPO itself as well as non-members, and various intergovernmental and non-governmental agencies. It aims to contribute both to formal and substantive reforms of patent law, and in this regard has two core projects:

• Patent Law Treaty (2000). This treaty harmonises patent procedures and formalities for filing, obtaining, and maintaining patent protection. It entered into force on 28 April 2005 and had been ratified by 32 contracting parties as of April 2013. This includes the UK where it entered into force on 22 March 2006 and which resulted in some changes to domestic law.[79]

• Substantive Patent Law Treaty (2001–present). This draft treaty is aimed at harmonising the substantive elements of patent law, such as novelty, inventive step/non-obviousness, and industrial applicability/utility[80] with a view to streamlining of application documentation, greater legal certainty on an international level, and, as always, a reduction in costs. Negotiations are ongoing and we discuss the substance further later in the chapter (para 10.69).

10.40   The *Patent Law Treaty* (2000) mandates a maximum number of formal requirements that can be imposed on patent applications, although individual contracting parties can be more generous if they wish.[81] Important features that have been harmonised include the standardisation of requirements to obtain a filing date on the fulfilment of three criteria: (1) an indication that the elements received by the Office are intended to be an application for a patent for an invention; (2) indications that would allow the Office to identify or to contact the applicant (or both); (3) a part which appears to be a description of the invention (this part can be filed in any language or could even merely be a drawing).[82]

10.41   More than 60 countries had signed the Treaty by March 2010, indicating their intention to ratify in due course; 32 of these countries have already done so. Signatories include the United States and the European Patent Organisation on behalf of the EPO. Other countries representing the remaining members of the top five patent offices of the world[83]—China, Japan, South Korea—will doubtless follow suit. The effect of the Patent Law Treaty therefore will be near-global harmonisation of procedures for obtaining patent protection.

---

[77] This point was made very clearly by industry and patent attorneys alike in the 2006 public consultation on the future of the patent system in Europe carried out by the European Commission, see note 23.

[78] WIPO, *PCT Yearly Review: The International Patent System* (2012), 10.

[79] The UK passed the Regulatory Reform (Patents) Order 2004 to make the necessary changes to domestic law.

[80] This variation in terminology reflects current different approaches to the criteria for patentability around the globe. Thus, while European patent law talks of 'inventive step' and 'industrial applicability', US law employs the terms 'non-obviousness' and 'utility'. This is not merely a question of semantics because the terms are interpreted quite differently meaning that access to patent protection is variable (it is generally far easier in the United States). Note, that in TRIPS, Art 27(1)—which requires 'patents shall be available for any inventions, whether products or processes, in all fields of technology, provided that they are new, involve an inventive step and are capable of industrial application'—there is a caveat which provides: 'For the purposes of this Art, the terms "inventive step" and "capable of industrial application" may be deemed by a Member to be synonymous with the terms "non-obvious" and "useful" respectively.'

[81] Patent Law Treaty, Art 2. The exception to this relates to Art 5 and mandatory requirements about obtaining a filing date.

[82] Patent Law Treaty, Art 5(1), (2).

[83] These five offices account for a large majority share of all patent applications. See WIPO, *World Intellectual Property Indicators* (2012), 5 (see note 19).

WTO: the TRIPS Agreement (1994)

10.42   We have discussed the nature of the TRIPS Agreement in Chapter 1 and elsewhere in the book thus far.[84] You will recall that the Agreement on Trade-Related Aspects of Intellectual Property Rights was concluded in 1994 as part of the Uruguay Round of the General Agreement on Tariffs and Trade (GATT). It is administered by the WTO and parties to the Agreement are subject to WTO's dispute settlement system.[85] This entails the possible imposition of trade sanctions for non-compliance. The linking of obligations to protect intellectual property with the attractiveness of trade privileges available under GATT was a stroke of genius by those parties frustrated by the fact that many countries had not signed up to previous international instruments such as the Paris and Berne Conventions and were openly infringing intellectual property on an unprecedented scale. Many of these countries were, however, also developing countries desperate for increased trade to improve their economic circumstances. Few could resist the trade attractions of the Uruguay Round, and TRIPS was the bitter pill they had to swallow.

10.43   The implications for patent law from TRIPS are, first and foremost, that the agreement represents the first international measure to harmonise substantive patent provisions. Article 27(1) of TRIPS provides:

> Subject to the provisions of paragraphs 2 and 3, patents shall be available for any inventions, whether products or processes, in all fields of technology, provided that they are new, involve an inventive step and are capable of industrial application.

10.44   There are two points to note about this. First, it makes clear that there are three common criteria for patentability and, secondly, signatory states are obliged to make protection available for *any* inventions in *all* technological fields. This has required significant changes to law in numerous states which previously did not have a robust patent system or specifically excluded certain types of invention from protection, such as pharmaceuticals.[86] It has also given rise to charges against the UK or even the EU itself that continued resistance to patents in certain fields such as software can no longer be sustained and may even be illegal.

10.45   TRIPS permits, but does not require, exclusions from patentability, providing in Article 27(2) and (3) that:

> 2. Members may exclude from patentability inventions, the prevention within their territory of the commercial exploitation of which is necessary to protect *ordre public* or morality, including to protect human, animal or plant life or health or to avoid serious prejudice to the environment, provided that such exclusion is not made merely because the exploitation is prohibited by their law.
>
> 3. Members may also exclude from patentability: (a) diagnostic, therapeutic and surgical methods for the treatment of humans or animals; (b) plants and animals other than micro-organisms, and essentially biological processes for the production of plants or animals other than non-biological and micro-biological processes. However, Members shall provide for the protection of plant varieties either by patents or by an effective *sui generis* system or by any combination thereof.

Note the judicious use of the term 'may' here. These are not mandatory exclusions and were, in fact, included largely at the behest of European states and the EU which already have such provisions in their patent law (see paras 11.5-11.77). There are no such exclusions in the United States, although a surprisingly high number of countries have some form of morality exclusion in their law.

---

[84]   See generally, D Matthews, *Globalising Intellectual Property Rights: The TRIPS Agreement* (2012).

[85]   See here for an account of the Dispute Settlement System: http://www.wto.org/english/thewto_e/whatis_e/tif_e/disp1_e.htm.

[86]   China and India are obvious examples.

Patents and international development

10.46   Many discussions on reform of TRIPS have been directly bound up with the morality of the Agreement itself. The current round of negotiations are part of the *Doha Development Agenda*, and date back to the Fourth Ministerial Conference in Doha, Qatar in November 2001 with halting progress ever since. This resulted, inter alia, in the Doha Declaration which serves as the template and mandate for further negotiations in a number of subjects central to improved international trade, one of which is the protection of IPRs. The Ministerial Declaration to emerge from the Fourth Conference stressed once more the importance of balance in achieving this protection, stating in Article 17 that the implementation and interpretation give to TRIPS must be in a manner 'supportive of public health, by promoting both access to existing medicines and research and development into new medicines ...'. Further articulation of this came in a separate instrument—the Declaration on the TRIPS Agreement and Public Health[87]—which stresses the need to recognise that the WTO and TRIPS are part of the wider global, social public health crisis affecting developing and least developed countries (LDCs), most particularly in terms of securing access to affordable medicines to treat conditions such as HIV/AIDS, malaria, and tuberculosis.

10.47   All of this was prompted by an attempt by South Africa to address its own chronic public health problems through changes to patent law. The South African Medicines and Medical Devices Regulatory Authority Act 1998 allowed the Ministry of Health to 'determine that the rights with regard to any medicine under a patent granted in the Republic shall not extend to act in respect of such medicine which has been put onto the market by the owner of the medicine, or with his or her consent' (Art 15C).[88] Inter alia, this would give the South African state the power to manufacture patented pharmaceuticals under compulsory licence and/or import cheaper generic drugs from abroad. The reaction by the pharmaceutical industry and the United States was immediate, with the latter imposing economic sanctions through the removal of preferential tariff treatments (making import from the United States economically unviable). Pharma, for its part, filed a law suit against the law. The Act never saw the light of day.

10.48   The resulting international response through the WTO was the Public Health Declaration.[89] It is agreed therein that TRIPS does not and should not prevent members from taking measures to protect public health, and that WTO members have the right to use, 'to the full', the flexible provisions found in the Agreement itself to support the right to public health and promote access to medicines for all. What are these flexible provisions? These are articulated in Article 5 and include the right of each member to grant compulsory licences on the grounds that they consider appropriate, and the freedom of each member to determine its own regime of exhaustion of rights. In other words, the same mechanisms as deployed by South Africa are available under TRIPS. There are, however, certain restrictions, most notably that the compulsory licence provisions in the 1994 Agreement are solely concerned with producing drugs for a domestic market. This causes an immediate problem for countries which do not have domestic manufacturing capacity, and means, potentially, that the LDCs, which may also experience the most severe public health crises, are the ones most disadvantaged under the law. They are, indeed, doubly disadvantaged because it would also mean that another country could not rely on the provisions to come to their aid since an *export* of drugs made under compulsory licence would be a violation of TRIPS. By the same token, a solution is not immediately apparent from the perspective of developed countries which have a concern that too liberal an approach to compulsory licensing may result in their own markets being

---

[87] 14 November 2001: http://www.wto.org/english/thewto_e/minist_e/min01_e/mindecl_trips_e.htm.

[88] This is effectively a use of the 'exhaustion principle' which we discuss further in Chapter 19.

[89] Declaration on the TRIPS Agreement and Public Health, 20 November 2001, Doc No WT/MIN(01)/DEC/2.

flooded. The Declaration instructed the TRIPS Council to pursue a solution[90] which was eventually reached in August 2003.[91]

10.49   The solution is effectively a form of waiver over the obligations of members under Article 31(f) of TRIPS.[92] This provides that any compulsory licensing system should be ' authorized predominantly for the supply of the domestic market of the Member authorizing such use.' The Council Decision allows an exporting member to waive these obligations when exporting to an 'eligible importing member', being any LDC member, and any other member that has made a notification to the Council for TRIPS of its intention to use the system as an importer.[93] The waiver operates to the extent *necessary* for the purposes of production of a pharmaceutical product(s) and its export. Further conditions include notification of specific needs for drugs and the tailoring of licence terms accordingly, labelling requirements to set these products apart from others in the market, and a public disclosure requirement, via the Internet, informing of quantities and distinguishing features to be exported. The TRIPS Council plays a key role in the operation of this system: it is charged with receiving and administering all notifications and with producing an annual report on the system as a whole. This has, however, only been used once by Canada and Rwanda.[94]

10.50   A 2006 Oxfam report claimed that little had changed in the first five years after the adoption of the Doha Declaration[95] and, indeed, little has changed since. This is partly because the provisions and protections of TRIPS can be circumvented in bilateral or regional agreements between countries when there is an imbalance of bargaining power and weaker states agree to so-called TRIPS-plus obligations—tying them further into intellectual property protection—in return for economic or trade benefits. The United States relies heavily on such an approach. Oxfam called on poorer states to resist these moves and recommends that G8 countries provide the necessary technical, political, and economic support to allow poorer states to enact TRIPS safeguards.[96] It also recommended that the WTO carry out a thorough review of the impact of TRIPS on access to medicines, supported (or not) by independent studies from bodies such as the World Health Organization.

10.51   Work has nonetheless been ongoing at the WTO since the 2003 Decision. A General Council decision from 6 December 2005 will replace the 2003 decision in due course;[97] this will effectively embody the 2003 scheme permanently into the TRIPS Agreement. It is, in fact, the first official amendment of a WTO

[90] Para 6 provides: 'We recognize that WTO members with insufficient or no manufacturing capacities in the pharmaceutical sector could face difficulties in making effective use of compulsory licensing under the TRIPS Agreement. We instruct the Council for TRIPS to find an expeditious solution to this problem and to report to the General Council before the end of 2002.'

[91] General Council Decision of 30 August 2003 on the Implementation of Paragraph 6 of the Doha Declaration on the TRIPS Agreement and Public Health: WT/L/540 and Corr.1, 1 September 2003.

[92] There are, in fact, three waivers: (1) exporting countries are not bound by the provisions of Art 31(f); (2) importing countries are not bound to pay reasonable remuneration to the patent holder (this is borne by the exporter); and (3) exporting restrictions are waived for developing and least developed countries which are members of a regional trade agreement, when at least half of the members are classed as least developed countries when the export decision is made.

[93] Para 2. It is possible to notify that the system will only be used in a limited way, eg only in the case of a national emergency or other circumstances of extreme urgency or in cases of public non-commercial use. Indeed, some countries and trading blocs have notified that they will not be using the system as an importer to protect domestic markets. These include the United States, the UK, and many other European states.

[94] See WTO dedicated webpage of notifications: http://www.wto.org/english/tratop_e/trips_e/public_health_e.htm.

[95] Oxfam International, *Patents v Patients: Five Years After the Doha Declaration* (2006) available at http://policy-practice.oxfam.org.uk/publications/patents-versus-patients-five-years-after-the-doha-declaration-114562.

[96] The White Paper, *Eliminating World Poverty: Making Globalisation Work for the Poor* pointed to the need for intellectual property regimes to work better for poor people. See http://webarchive.nationalarchives.gov.uk/+/http:/www.dfid.gov.uk/Documents/publications/whitepaper2000.pdf.

[97] This will happen when two-thirds of the membership accepts the amendment. It was originally hoped that this would happen by 1 December 2007 but this deadline was not met and has been extended various times, currently until 31 December 2013—see WTO, IP/C/58, 2 November 2011. This amendment remains in limbo at the time of writing (April 2013).

Agreement.[98] The Amendment is designed to reflect the terms of the original waiver as closely as possible because there are strong political reasons not to re-open the issues. Thus, as with the 2003 waiver, any member country can manufacture and export pharmaceutical products under compulsory licence for public health reasons. Changes will be required in domestic law. The European Commission had presented a proposal for a Council Decision accepting the Amendment in April 2006 and in May 2006 the European Parliament and the Council adopted Regulation No 816/2006 on compulsory licensing of patents relating to the manufacture of pharmaceutical products for export to countries with public health problems.[99]

10.52   The Amendment[100] creates Article 31*bis* and a new annex to the TRIPS Agreement. This reiterates the core principle that it is lawful to produce pharmaceutical products under compulsory licence for export to countries lacking production capacity. It then goes on to specify further matters such as an obligation on an importing member to take 'reasonable measures' within their means to prevent re-exportation, and a duty on all members to ensure that effective legal means are in place to prevent the import of goods made under the scheme which have been unlawfully diverted to their market.[101] The annex specifies the terms for using the system and includes definitions, obligations of notification to TRIPS Council, and an ongoing duty of the Council to carry out annual reviews. Finally, an appendix to the annex lays out criteria to assess whether a country lacks manufacturing capacity such that it can rely upon the Amendment. There are 159 members of the WTO (March 2013), and fewer than a third of the member states had accepted this Amendment at the time of writing. Two-thirds of members must accept before the Amendment can replace the 2003 Decision.

10.53   It should be further noted that an additional outcome of these ongoing negotiations is that LDCs have until 2016 to provide patent protection for pharmaceuticals, and until 1 July 2013 to provide protection for other IPRs.[102]

New provision for the TRIPS Agreement, Article 31*bis*

1. The obligations of an exporting Member under Article 31(f) shall not apply with respect to the grant by it of a compulsory licence *to the extent necessary* for the purposes of production of a pharmaceutical product(s) and its export to an eligible importing Member(s) in accordance with the terms set out in paragraph 2 of the Annex to this Agreement (emphasis added).

 Discussion point   For answer guidance visit www.oxfordtextbooks.co.uk/orc/waelde3e/

How much flexibility do the words 'to the extent necessary' provide for those who would reply on this provision, or indeed, who would object to others relying on this provision?

---

[98] The Sixth Ministerial Conference which took place in Hong Kong in December 2005 reaffirmed the importance of the 2003 Council Decision and endorsed the work of the Council on an Amendment of the TRIPS Agreement, Draft Ministerial Declaration, 18 December 2005, WT/MIN(05)/W/3/Rev 2.

[99] See Proposal for a Regulation of the European Parliament and of the Council on compulsory licensing of patents relating to the manufacture of pharmaceutical products for export to countries with public health problems, COM/2004/0737 final, and ultimately, Regulation (EC) No 816/2006 of the European Parliament and of the Council of 17 May 2006 on compulsory licensing of patents relating to the manufacture of pharmaceutical products for export to countries with public health problems (2006) OJ EU, 9 June 2006, L157/1.

[100] General Council, Doc No WT/L/641, 8 December 2005, Amendment of the TRIPS Agreement, Decision of 6 December 2005.

[101] Other provisions include the prohibition on a patent holder receiving 'reasonable remuneration' from both an exporting and an importing state, the release of developing country members from Art 31(f) obligations when involved in a regional agreement with countries facing the same public health crisis, and the retention of existing TRIPS flexibilities.

[102] The 2011 Ministerial Conference in Geneva 'invited' the TRIPS Council 'to give full consideration' to a further extension of this period. A formal proposal to this effect has now been made by Haiti and Nepal on behalf of the LDCs (Doc IP/C/W/583).

10.54   Critics assessing the success of the Doha Declaration in 2006 have argued that it is largely a failure and the Doha Round should be brought to an end. It is suggested that the requirements of the system such as notification of specific type and quantity of drugs, labelling requirements, or the need to negotiate directly with the patent holder are too onerous.[103] It is essentially a protectionist system—in that it allows countries to act as exporters while blocking access to their own markets—and thereby undermines the economies of scale for developing countries with manufacturing capacity but no access to high-income markets. That said, it is acknowledged that the problem is not simply with the WTO or its Agreements. Bilateral agreements often mean that developing countries are willing to give up reliance on the TRIPS provisions for other economic advantages, such as reduced trade barriers. A 2006 World Bank report on the economics of HIV/AIDS treatment in Thailand suggested that such concessions come at significant cost.[104] It estimated that reliance on the compulsory licensing scheme could reduce the costs of second-line therapy by 90 per cent, cutting the Thai Government future budgetary obligations by US$3.2 billion to 2025 and reducing by half the costs of life-years saved under its National Access to Antiretroviral Program for People Living with HIV/AIDS. Thailand issued a compulsory licence to manufacture a generic version of the HIV/AIDS drug Efavirenz in November 2006[105] which has since been followed by several more compulsory licences for a number of different drugs.[106]

10.55   Other hurdles for developing and least-developed countries are that they are often ill-equipped to amend national laws to take full advantage of TRIPS flexibilities, and international bodies, such as UN agencies or the World Health Organization (WHO), are often under-resourced to provide the necessary technical support.

10.56   This having been said, the WHO has taken a strong interest in the issue—possibly as a direct result of the Doha Declaration—and it established a Commission on Intellectual Property Rights, Innovation and Public Health (CIPIH) in 2004.[107] Its 2006 report[108] called for a holistic approach to crises in public health: 'The market alone, and the incentives that propel it, such as patent protection, cannot by themselves address the health needs of developing countries.'[109] Furthermore, the Commission questioned whether current regimes of intellectual property protection have led to innovation or better access to medicines, particularly because market mechanisms and incentives do not lead to research and development that is directed towards the needs of developing countries. The Commission issued 60 recommendations, key among which was the call for a Global Plan to examine the challenges at each of the stages of discovery, development, and delivery of pharmaceuticals and other health products needed to secure public health. The WHO responded swiftly and the World Health Assembly adopted Resolution WHA59.24 in May 2006 calling on the Director-General to establish an Intergovernmental Working Group (IGWG) to draw up a strategy with contributions from member states and the global community.[110] A public consultation then took place by which time proposals had already started to emerge from the IGWG. The suggested elements of the strategy range across (1) prioritising and promoting R&D needs, (2) capacity building, (3) improving delivery and access, (4) securing sustainable financing, and

---

[103] Médecins Sans Frontières, Campaign for Access to Essential Medicines (1999–present) http://www.msfaccess.org/.

[104] The World Bank, *The Economics of Effective AIDS Treatment: Evaluating Policy Options for Thailand* (2006), xxxl–xl. Available at http://www.worldbank.org/.

[105] D Schuettler, 'Activists hail Thai move to make generic AIDS drug' (2006) Reuters UK, 30 November, available at http://www.reuters.com/article/healthNews/idUSBKK5661020061130.

[106] F Rozanski, *Developing Countries and Pharmaceutical Intellectual Property Rights: Myths and Reality* (2007) and CM Correa (ed), *A Guide to Pharmaceutical Patents* (2008), vols 1 and 2.

[107] WHO Resolution (WHA 56.27, 2003), see http://apps.who.int/gb/archive/pdf_files/WHA56/ea56r27.pdf.

[108] CIPIH, *Public Health, Innovation and Intellectual Property Rights* (WHO, 2006) at http://apps.who.int/iris/handle/10665/43460.

[109] CIPIH, note 108, 17.

[110] A Special Issue of the Bulletin of the World Health Organization (vol 84(5), May 2006, 337–424) is dedicated to the topic. Available at http://www.who.int/bulletin/volumes/84/5/en/index.html.

(5) instituting effective monitoring systems. A particular proposal for patents is the recommendation to promote patent pools which allow for the collective management of IPRs directed towards specific ends such as the promotion of innovation in products relating to priority diseases in developing countries. Patent pools can reduce costs and ensure uniformity of approach towards licensing, allowing countries to work together towards common goals. The IGWG presented its Global Strategy and plan of action to the World Health Assembly at its Sixty-First Meeting in 2008, which adopted the plan by resolution WHA 61.21.[111] The virtual stalemate is causing organisations such as the WHO to move towards alternative solutions. Thus in April 2012, the WHO's Consultative Expert Working Group on R&D; Financing and Coordination recommended that governments start new negotiations over a global R&D convention.[112]

Evolutionary law and policy

10.57   This ambitious WHO strategy to develop a Global Plan for addressing crises in public health demonstrates very well that although patents may be a part of the problem, they can also only be a part of the solution. Multi-level strategies will be required and part of the challenge is to understand how the operation of the world's patent systems interacts with other systems of regulation, health promotion, development, environmental protection, and even notions of justice. This approach embraces the interconnectedness of these systems and seeks solutions through those connections. Intellectual property cannot be seen as a regime in isolation. This is accepted by the WTO. The TRIPS Agreement itself required review of the provisions of Article 27(3)(b) as to the patentability of plants and animals other than micro-organisms, and essentially biological processes for the production of plants or animals other than non-biological and microbiological processes.[113] This began four years after the Agreement came into force (1999) and is ongoing.[114] The permissibility of plant and animal patents remains in dispute with lobbying on opposite sides arguing, on the one hand, that these are necessary to promote innovation and aid technology transfer and, on the other, that patenting causes problems of access, especially for farmers in gaining access to seed, excessively broad patents can lead to the misappropriation of genetic material, and that this in turn may lead to breaches under the UN Convention on Biological Diversity (CBD; see para 10.62).

Proposed solutions

10.58   These include: (1) removal of the provisions, (2) retention of the provisions with clarification as to definitions, and (3) a complete ban on plant and animal patenting. Such polar opposite views have given rise to concern that the Review remains inconclusive, and the TRIPS Council has recently moved to find common ground for agreement with a view to producing a Council Decision, but this has yielded no results so far.

---

[111] For details see WHA Resolution 61.21, available at http://apps.who.int/gb/ebwha/pdf_files/A61/A61_R21-en.pdf.

[112] WHO Consultative Expert Working Group on Research and Development (CEWG): Financing and Coordination, 'Research and development to meet health needs in developing countries: strengthening global financing and coordination' (2012) available at http://www.who.int/phi/CEWG_Report_5_April_2012.pdf.

[113] Note, however, that TRIPS, Art 27(3)(b) obliges its members to provide effective protection for plant varieties either under patent law or in some *sui generis* form (or a combination thereof). See generally, LR Helfer, *Intellectual Property Rights in Plant Varieties: International Legal Regimes and Policy Options for National Governments* (FAO, 2004), and for the European perspective, M Llewelyn and M Adcock, *European Plant Intellectual Property* (2006) and G Wurtenberger et al, *European Community Plant Variety Protection* (2006).

[114] TRIPS Council, Review of the Provisions of Art 27(3)(b), Paper IP/C/W/369/Rev 1, revised 9 March 2006, see further for a current overview of the related issues: http://www.wto.org/english/tratop_e/trips_e/art27_3b_background_e.htm.

Possible areas of consensus

10.59   These include: (1) acceptance of every member state's right to adopt appropriate regimes to protect plant varieties by an effective *sui generis* system; (2) that the TRIPS Agreement and the CBD should be implemented in a mutually supportive and consistent manner; (3) that the TRIPS Agreement, being a minimum standards agreement, does not prevent members from protecting traditional knowledge; (4) the importance of documentation of genetic resources and traditional knowledge to help better patent examination.[115]

Outstanding issues

10.60   These include: (1) the proposal to eliminate patent availability for all life forms (including micro-organisms), the need to clarify the terms in Article 27(3)(b);[116] (2) the protection of traditional knowledge;[117] and (3) consideration of ways to make the TRIPS Agreement and the CBD mutually supportive.[118] There have also been proposals to consider the ethical provisions of Article 27(2) as part of this review process given the obvious and inherent connections between the two Articles.

Beyond Doha?

10.61   The Doha Declaration further extended the remit of the TRIPS Council to consider the interconnectedness of TRIPS to other regimes.[119] Paragraph 19 requires the Council to consider the relationship between TRIPS and the CBD, as well as the challenges of protecting traditional knowledge and folklore.

10.62   World leaders agreed on a strategy for sustainable development at the World Summit in Rio de Janeiro in 1992. The CBD, signed at that time, is a central element of that strategy with three principal objectives:

(1)   the conservation of biological diversity;

(2)   the sustainable use of its components; and

(3)   the fair and equitable sharing of the benefits arising out of the utilisation of genetic resources.

10.63   There are concerns in some quarters that the provisions of the CBD and TRIPS are fundamentally incompatible. The two main arguments are, first, the TRIPS Agreement actually requires that certain genetic material—such as micro-organisms—be patentable under Article 27(3)(b), as we have seen. This therefore allows private parties to gain private property rights over material which is guaranteed by the CBD to be the exclusive sovereign domain of signatory countries.[120] Secondly, TRIPS allows patent and other IPRs over genetic material without providing that certain core provisions of the CBD—such as the need for prior informed consent and benefit sharing—are complied with.[121] While this is disputed in other quarters,[122]

[115] African Group, IP/C/W/404, p 2; Zimbabwe, IP/C/M/36/Add 1, para 201.   [116] Zimbabwe, IP/C/M/37/Add 1, para 197.
[117] African Group, IP/C/W/404, p 4.   [118] African Group, IP/C/W/404, p 5.
[119] See L Laxman and AH Ansari, 'The interface between TRIPS and CBD: efforts towards harmonisation' (2012) 11(2) Journal of International Trade Law & Policy 108-132.
[120] Eg African Group, IP/C/W/404, IP/C/W/206, IP/C/W/163, IP/C/M/40, paras 76–79; Kenya, IP/C/M/47 para 68, IP/C/M/36/Add 1, para 233, IP/C/M/28, para 144.
[121] Eg African Group, IP/C/W/404, IP/C/W/206, IP/C/W/163; Brazil, IP/C/W/228, IP/C/M/48, para 37, IP/C/M/29, paras 146 and 148; IP/C/M/28, para 135, IP/C/M/27, para 122; Brazil et al, IP/C/W/429/Rev 1, IP/C/W/356.
[122] See the summary of discussion on these issues in IP/C/W/369/Rev 1 and IP/C/W/370/Rev 1.

these issues have set the agenda for the TRIPS Council discussion in this field of reform. Opinion has largely divided along economic lines, with developing countries arguing that TRIPS should be amended to bring the two treaties into line. These arguments, in turn, split into two camps: those that argue that TRIPS should exclude genetic patents altogether (this view is mostly advanced by the African Group),[123] and those who argue that there is insufficient provision in TRIPS to achieve an appropriate balance as between the objectives of the two treaties, for example requirements of consent, disclosure of the origin of genetic material, and benefit sharing. Strong proponents of this view are Brazil and India. Options range from:

- do nothing to amend the treaties, but implement in a mutually supportive manner;

- implement in a mutually supportive manner and seek further evidence of the extent to which conflict arises in practice and might require changes to the patent system;

- accept that there is no inherent conflict but seek ways to ensure or enhance the mutual supportiveness of both Agreements (with or without amendment to TRIPS);

- accept that there is inherent conflict and amend TRIPS accordingly.

10.64 The WIPO Intergovernmental Committee on Intellectual Property and Genetic Resources, Traditional Knowledge and Folklore (IGC) reached sufficient consensus in February 2012 to produce a negotiating text for submission to the WIPO General Assembly in the same year.[124] The WIPO General Assembly then agreed 'to continue intensive negotiations and engagement in good faith, with appropriate representation, towards concluding the text(s) of an international legal instrument(s) which will ensure effective protection of genetic resources, traditional knowledge and traditional cultural expressions'. In 2013, at the time of writing, the IGC was revising its 2012 document in the light of these developments.[125]

10.65 The United States and three other nations opposed this move. The United States in particular favours national action, whereby it would be left to individual states to use national legislation and contractual arrangements to impose obligations of disclosure or benefit sharing as they see fit.[126] Disputes endure over a requirement of disclosure of genetic origin or traditional knowledge in patent applications when the invention is 'directly based' on genetic resources. Draft Article 3 of the Consolidated Document still contains possible but virtually diametrically opposed options: (1) countries shall provide in legislation a mandatory disclosure requirement, or (2) may provide in their national patent legislation a mandatory disclosure requirement, or (3) patent disclosure requirements shall not include a mandatory disclosure relating to genetic resources … unless such disclosure is material to the patentability criteria of novelty, inventive step, or enablement (see Chapter 11).[127] This must be set against a longer-standing proposal from a group of eight developing countries (including Brazil, China, and India) put forward to amend TRIPS itself with a new Article 29bis on disclosure of origin of biological resources. This proposal has been co-sponsored by several other countries since it was first drafted in May 2006.[128] The proposal states:[129]

---

[123] The Africa Group is an alliance of all African states. [124] WIPO/GRTKF/IC/19/7.

[125] See Intergovernmental Committee on Intellectual Property and Genetic Resources, Traditional Knowledge and Folklore, Consolidated Document relating to intellectual property and genetic resources, Twenty-Third Session, 4–8 February 2013, WIPO/GRTKF/IC/23/4. [126] United States, IP/C/W/257.

[127] http://www.wipo.int/edocs/mdocs/tk/en/wipo_grtkf_ic_23/wipo_grtkf_ic_23_4.pdf.

[128] Amongst others by South Africa, for a full list of countries see IP/C/W/24 add. 1–9.

[129] WT/GC/W/564, 31 May 2006 (emphasis added).

> ## Proposed Article 29*bis* TRIPS
>
> ### Disclosure of Origin of Biological Resources and/or Associated Traditional Knowledge
>
> 1. For the purposes of establishing a mutually supportive relationship between this Agreement and the Convention on Biological Diversity, in implementing their obligations, Members shall have regard to the objectives and principles of this Agreement and the objectives of the Convention on Biological Diversity.
> 2. Where the subject matter of a patent application concerns, *is derived from or developed with biological resources and/or associated traditional knowledge*, Members *shall require applicants to disclose the country providing the resources and/or associated traditional knowledge*, from whom in the providing country they were obtained, and, as known after *reasonable inquiry*, the country of origin. Members shall also require that applicants provide information including evidence of compliance with the applicable legal requirements in the providing country *for prior informed consent for access and fair and equitable benefit-sharing* arising from the commercial or other utilization of such resources and/or associated traditional knowledge …
> … 5. Members shall put in place effective enforcement procedures so as to ensure compliance with the obligations set out in paragraphs 2 and 3 of this Article. In particular, *Members shall ensure that administrative and/or judicial authorities have the authority to prevent the further processing of an application or the grant of a patent and to revoke*, subject to the provisions of Article 32 of this Agreement, *or render unenforceable a patent when the applicant has, knowingly or with reasonable grounds to know, failed to comply with the obligations in paragraphs 2 and 3 of this Article or provided false or fraudulent information.*

 Exercise

Critically assess this proposal in the light of the alternatives offered by other countries or alliances. The highlighted passages are likely to be most controversial. In particular, what do you think of the proposal to link non-disclosure to revocation or unenforceability of the patent?

10.66   The broader political question, however, is that of the legitimacy of either WTO or WIPO to initiate change in these areas. Certainly, it is only for the WTO to seek to amend TRIPS, but broader issues are at stake such as relationships with the CBD and the protection of traditional knowledge. Moreover, it was the Conference of the Parties of the CBD that invited WIPO to carry out a technical study on disclosure requirements in patent applications,[130] from which additional work has been undertaken by WIPO.[131] The IGC continues to work on its current mandate.

10.67   While WIPO probably has more technical expertise in the field, it has been argued that the WTO mandate in the Doha Declaration has a specific development remit, making it the better body to take matters forward.[132] Either way, WTO only has authority over the TRIPS Agreement, while reforms to formal aspects of patent law— such as the creation of a genetic origin disclosure requirement—will require changes to WIPO instruments such as the PCT or the Patent Law Treaty (see paras 10.39–10.41).

Further reform: patent regimes in the future

10.68   The previous descriptions of the current architecture of our patent systems did not survive the lifetime of the previous two editions of this book; nor will they survive this one. Some matters will already

---

[130] Available at http://www.wipo.int/tk/en/publications/technical_study.pdf.
[131] Full details available at http://www.wipo.int/tk/en/genetic/proposals/index.html.
[132] Eg Brazil, IP/C/M/49, para 155, IP/C/M/42, para 101, IP/C/M/36/Add 1, para 199.

have changed by the time you read this. As with all areas of intellectual property law, patent law moves fast and it is important to keep an eye on what is coming next. Here is an overview of proposed or actual reforming measures as we went to press. As previously, let us consider these at the international, European, and national (UK) levels, this time beginning where we left off in the last section with the work of WIPO.

International reforms: WIPO's ongoing programme of harmonisation

10.69   We have already seen that WIPO's Standing Committee on the Law of Patents has enjoyed success with the coming into force of the Patent Law Treaty (2000). It now hopes to bring about harmonisation in respect of a number of elements of substantive law with its draft Substantive Patent Law Treaty, discussion on which began in May 2001. The scope of the Treaty has been slowly extended over the years to cover more issues, with the result that it has been harder to reach consensus with all delegations. The first draft provisions focused on issues directly pertinent to the grant of patents, such as the definition of prior art, novelty, inventive step/non-obviousness, industrial applicability/utility, the drafting and interpretation of claims, and the requirement of sufficient disclosure of the invention. This was then expanded to a proposal that the Standing Committee on Patents consider prior art, grace period, novelty, and inventive step, and the ICG should consider sufficiency of disclosure and genetic resources.[133] Brazil, however, issued a statement[134] on behalf of the Group of Friends of Development[135] recalling that WIPO has undertaken to develop a proposal to establish a development agenda for the organisation and requesting that the continuation of the negotiations of the Treaty be on the basis of the draft treaty as a whole, including all these elements and also questions of provisions on the transfer of technology, anti-competitive practices, and the safeguarding of public interest flexibilities to ensure that appropriate balance is brought to the content of the instrument. Current work of the Standing Committee is based on a working document on issues relating to the international patent system covering the different needs and interests of all member states.[136]

European reforms: the EU and the European Patent Organisation

10.70   You will recall that the European Patent Organisation is not a body of the EU and that each institution is at liberty to pursue its own initiatives. This having been said, the 27 member states of the EU are all signatories to the EPC and it is in no one's interests for the EPO and the EU to pursue different patent agenda. In practice, the bodies work closely together to ensure complementarity. We see evidence of this in the following paragraphs.

European Union

10.71   The Green Paper on the Community patent and patent system in Europe (1997)[137] was a response to the Action Plan for the Single Market, adopted by the European Council in Amsterdam in June 1997,

---

[133] WIPO, Standing Committee on the Law of Patents, Eleventh Session, Geneva, 1 and 2 June 2005 (SCP/11/3), available at http://www.wipo.int/edocs/mdocs/scp/en/scp_11/scp_11_3.pdf.

[134] WIPO, Standing Committee on the Law of Patents, Statement Received from Brazil, Eleventh Session, Geneva, 1 and 2 June 2005 (SCP/11/4), available at http://www.wipo.int/edocs/mdocs/scp/en/scp_11/scp_11_4.pdf.

[135] The Group of Friends of Development consists of Argentina, Brazil, Bolivia, Cuba, Dominican Republic, Ecuador, Egypt, Iran, Kenya, Peru, Sierra Leone, South Africa, Tanzania, and Venezuela.   [136] http://www.wipo.int/patent-law/en/scp.htm.

[137] Green Paper of 24 June 1997 on the Community patent and the patent system in Europe, COM(97) 314 final.

and in which industrial property was highlighted as a sector where action was required to realise the full benefits of the internal market in the field of innovation. The Green Paper's aim was to initiate dialogue on the need for new initiatives in the field, and its adoption coincided with a public consultation of all interested parties. The Commission responded in turn with the publication of a Communication detailing its agenda and priorities for reform.[138]

10.72   Other initiatives, started before the Green Paper, have had variable success. A proposal to approximate laws around the Union concerning utility models was proposed after a Green Paper from 1995.[139] A utility model can be seen as a form of patent-like protection but which usually does not last as long (six to ten years) and which is subject to far less stringent criteria, especially concerning the equivalent notion of inventive step which will not require as high a level of inventiveness as we find in patent law. Utility model protection is variable around the Union, with some countries such as the UK having no such protection. The proposal[140] was not well received, and even after amendment[141] and a consultation exercise the majority of respondents (75 per cent) was against the introduction of a new scheme.[142] Arguments included a lack of clarity or agreement on the qualifying criteria, a concern that the scheme would not help small to medium-sized enterprises, as promised, but would rather open an avenue for big business to corner yet another area of the market. Moreover, it was felt that while utility model protection might be helpful for those operating in a local market it could not be justified at a Community level. Nothing has happened in this field since 2002.[143]

10.73   The Biotechnology Directive was eventually adopted in July 1998 after ten years in the European legislative process.[144] It has always been a controversial piece of law and the European Parliament in fact exercised its power of veto over a draft of the Directive in March 1995. Nonetheless, the Directive survived and has now been implemented in all member states. We discuss its implications in Chapter 12.

10.74   In 2005 the Commission issued a Communication containing a Europe-wide strategy to strengthen industrial policy.[145] IPRs are acknowledged to be of key importance in this process and it is stated that more can be done to ensure that the regulatory framework meets the needs and challenges of industries. But lessons from past failures have made the Commission cautious and it announced a dialogue on IPRs in 2006 to determine how a balance of interests can be achieved within a sound IP framework. This was followed by a Communication in 2008 in which the Commission emphasised the need to take action in the near future.[146] A public consultation on the future of patent policy that took place in 2006[147] indicated, inter alia, that the then proposal for a Community patent was unlikely to proceed in its current form and that many in industry and the patent attorney profession saw the future of successful European

---

[138] European Commission Communication, 'Promoting innovation through patents: the follow-up to the Green Paper on the Community Patent and the Patent System in Europe', 12 February 1999, available at http://ec.europa.eu/internal_market/indprop/docs/patent/docs/8682_en.pdf.

[139] Commission Green Paper of 19 July 1995 on the Protection of Utility Models in the Single Market, COM(1995) 370 final.

[140] Proposal for a European Parliament and Council Directive approximating the legal arrangements for the protection of inventions by utility model, COM(1997) 691 final, and Amended proposal, 12.07.1999, COM(1999) 309 final/2.

[141] European Commission, 'Summary report of replies to the questionnaire on the impact of the Community utility model with a view to updating the Green Paper on protection by the utility model in the internal market', SEC(2001)1307.

[142] WIPO explains utility models at http://www.wipo.int/sme/en/ip_business/utility_models/utility_models.htm.

[143] http://ec.europa.eu/internal_market/indprop/model/index_en.htm.

[144] Directive 98/44/EC of the European Parliament and of the Council of 6 July 1998 on the legal protection of biotechnological inventions, available at http://eur-lex.europa.eu/LexUriServ/LexUriServ.do?uri=CELEX:31998L0044:EN:HTML.

[145] Communication from the Commission, Implementing the Community Lisbon Programme: A policy framework to strengthen EU manufacturing—towards a more integrated approach for industrial policy, COM(2005) 474 final.

[146] Communication from the Commission: An Industrial Property Rights Strategy for Europe, COM(2008) 465/3, available at http://ec.europa.eu/internal_market/indprop/docs/rights/communication_en.pdf.

[147] 'Public Hearing on Future Patent Policy in Europe' (July 2006) available at http://ec.europa.eu/internal_market/indprop/patent/hearing_en.htm.

reform coming not from the Union, but from initiatives from the European Patent Organisation, as discussed later in para 10.75. The advent of the Unitary Patent, however, albeit unanticipated after so many years, shows that such predictions are vulnerable.

European Patent Organisation

EPC 2000

10.75 The signatory states of the European Patent Organisation met in 2000 to revisit and revise the provisions of the EPC. The aim was to modernise the Convention for the 21st century and to ensure its fitness for purpose within the European integrated economy and its compliance with international agreements, such as TRIPS. Controversial issues such as biotechnological inventions[148] and the patenting of computer programs[149] were, however, left unchanged by the 2000 Diplomatic Conference, and the view was expressed that these would require the attention of a future Conference in due course. We consider these topics separately in Chapter 12. The revised version of the Convention (EPC 2000) was adopted by the Administrative Council of the EPO on 28 June 2001 and came into force December 2007.[150] Key changes in the law were:

- **Patentability**: Article 52(1) EPC now states that 'European patents shall be granted for any inventions, in *all* fields of technology …' (emphasis added). This reflects the provisions of Article 27(1) TRIPS (see previously).

- **Exclusions**: Article 53(c) EPC now provides that methods for treatment of the human or animal body by surgery or therapy and diagnostic methods practised on the human or animal body are expressly excluded from patentability. Previously, these were considered not to demonstrate industrial applicability.[151] (See further paras 11.63ff.)

- **Novelty**: Article 54(3) EPC extends the scope of the 'state of the art' when testing the novelty of an invention. As we discuss in paras 11.79ff, an invention is only new if it was not part of the state of the art—that is, publicly available—before the patent application was filed (normally). This reform widened the scope of what constitutes the state of the art in that it now includes the content of all European patent applications filed prior to the filing date of the instant application.

- **Interpretation**: textual revisions to Article 2 of the Protocol on the Interpretation of Article 69 EPC now make it clear that the 'due account' should be taken of equivalents as part of the law in determining the extent of protection for an invention. This, however, is simply to confirm a long-standing approach and is not intended as a reform of the substantive law (see further paras 11.187ff).

- **Judicial review**: new Article 112a states that: 'Any party to appeal proceedings adversely affected by the decision of the Board of Appeal may file a petition for review by the Enlarged Board of Appeal'. This provides a limited form of judicial review in that the only grounds upon which this procedure can be used is if there was a fundamental procedural defect in Board of Appeal proceedings or if a criminal act may have had an impact on the Board's decision.

[148] This matter was not on the Conference Agenda largely because of efforts within the EU to harmonise the law on these inventions.
[149] Proposals to remove the computer program exception from the provisions of Art 52 EPC were not taken up.
[150] The Implementing Regulations of EPC 2000 are available at http://www.epo.org/patents/law/legal-texts/archive/epc2000/regulations.html.
[151] Note the text of Art 53(a) has been brought into line with TRIPS, Art 27(2) which reads: 'Members may exclude from patentability inventions, the prevention within their territory of the commercial exploitation of which is necessary to protect *ordre public* or morality'. EPC 1973 talked of '*publication* or exploitation' as being offensive to morality or *ordre public*. 'Publication' was deleted.

- **Procedure**: numerous revisions have been adopted in an attempt to streamline processes for gaining and maintaining a patent. Important changes include: (1) applicants can file in any language and do not need to submit an EPO official language translation until later in the process (Art 14(2)); (2) applicants may request 'further processing' of their application if they fail to comply with time limits (Art 121(1)); (3) the EPO will move to a system of search and examination of an application by the same examiner when previously these have been separate systems. This was designed to improve the efficiency of the Office.

- **Post-grant amendments**: EPC 1973 only allowed amendments to patent claims as part of Opposition Proceedings. Thus unilateral action could not be taken by a patentee to limit protection voluntarily and so avoid lengthy and costly litigation in cases of dispute. Article 105a EPC 2000 allows a patent proprietor to request revocation or limitation of his patent before the EPO and Article 105b(3) makes it clear that any such amendments will have effect in all countries for which the European patent was designated. This, in effect, creates a centralised amendment system. Article 138 also gives a proprietor a right to limit his claims in national proceedings questioning the validity of his patent.

10.76   The Conference also laid the groundwork for future agreements between member states on translation issues and the creation of a centralised judicial body as discussed previously. The Administrative Council is charged with the authority to revise the EPC in accordance with international treaties or EU legislation, and it has the power to conclude agreements with states, non-governmental bodies, and with documentation centres set up by virtue of agreements with such organisations.[152]

National reforms

10.77   The Patents Act 2004 embodies the most far-reaching reform to UK patent law since the passing of the Patents Act 1977, although the 1977 Act remains the primary piece of legislation in the field. The main instigation behind the 2004 Act was EPC 2000, and the reforms outlined previously came fully into force in the UK at the same time as EPC 2000 took effect (December 2007). We deal with the particular measures in domestic law in due course.

10.78   The 2004 Act also addresses certain issues about enforcement of patents and introduces a UK–IPO dispute resolution mechanism in an attempt to avoid lengthy and costly litigation. The Act makes it clear that the owner of a patent can himself apply for revocation,[153] but co-owners must act jointly if they wish to amend or revoke their patent.[154] A consultation on the 1977 Act in 2012/13 proposed changes to facilitate better working between UK–IPO and foreign offices, as well as providing easier means of providing public notice of patent rights.[155] This is all done in the spirit of improving customer service. Similarly, the Patent Opinions Service began on 1 October 2005 and offers an avenue for parties in dispute over the validity or infringement of a UK or European patent to make representations and receive a non-binding ruling from a patent examiner. It also provides an opportunity to test the strength of respective arguments before deciding whether to proceed to litigation.[156] The service costs £200 and had issued over 150 Opinions by June 2012 when a consultation on its working was launched.[157] A review

---

[152] Act Revising the Convention on the Grant of European Patents, 29 November 2000, Art 10.
[153] Patents Act 1977, s 72(4A), as amended by the Patents Act 2004, s 4.
[154] Patents Act 1977, s 36(3)(a), as amended by the Patents Act 2004, s 9.
[155] IPO, Consultation on Proposed Changes to the Patents Act 1977 (December 2012), available at http://www.ipo.gov.uk/pro-policy/consult/consult-closed/consult-closed-2012/consult-2012-patact.htm.
[156] Patents Act 1977 ss 74A–74B, as amended by the Patents Act 2004, s 13.
[157] IPO, Consultation on the Patent Opinions Service (2012) available at http://www.ipo.gov.uk/consult-2012-opinion.pdf.

carried out in 2009 suggested not only that the service filled an unmet need but that there was appetite for extending the service to other forms of intellectual property.[158]

10.79   The day-to-day business and the formal procedures of the UK–IPO are governed by the Patents Rules 2007, as amended.[159] These rules completely replaced the 1995 rules, which were in need of serious overhaul, but major reforms were held back until the publication of the *Gowers Review of Intellectual Property* in 2006 (see para 10.80). The rules had to be amended to keep pace with the UK's international obligations. More recent review was undertaken by Professor Ian Hargreaves with similar far-reaching consequences.[160]

The Gowers and Hargreaves Reviews: the future of the IP system in the UK

10.80   We have already mentioned the Gowers (2006)[161] and Hargreaves (2011)[162] reviews in previous chapters. While the remit of each was restricted to the IP system in the UK, the recommendations of both naturally included an international dimension and a view on the role of the UK Government and UK–IPO on how to achieve better IP enforcement, lower IP costs, and national and internationals system of balanced and flexible rights, while also addressing some of the vagaries of the exercise of IP rights—such as the advent of patent thickets.

International relations and associated challenges

10.81   It is recognised that while international harmonisation of patent systems has been significantly slower than in other areas of IP law, there is much that can still be achieved through closer cooperation between countries and their respective intellectual property offices. It is important to appreciate, however, that different countries may use patent laws in different ways depending on their particular needs. Gowers, for example, recommended the following:

- UK–IPO should work more closely with African patent offices to help them to take full advantage of flexibilities within the TRIPS Agreement.

- UK–IPO should encourage international reconsideration of time limits for compliance with TRIPS for least developed countries—currently 2016.

- UK Government should encourage WTO members to ratify the Amendment to Article 31*bis* on access to medicines (paras 10.51–10.53).

- UK Government and UK–IPO should pursue work-sharing agreements with other intellectual property offices, for example to avoid duplication of searches of the prior art.

Hargreaves noted and commended the lead that the UK has taken on collaborating with at least six other countries to reduce duplication of effort worldwide and attempt to speed up granting. Examples include the Patent Prosecution Highway (PPH), Vancouver Group Mutual Exploitation and Utilisation Implementation Project (UIP), and work with the US Patent and Trademark Office (USPTO) to tackle backlogs.

---

[158] IPO, Review of the Opinions Service (2010) available at http://www.ipo.gov.uk/opinion-surveyresponse.pdf.

[159] SI 2007/3291, as amended. See http://www.ipo.gov.uk/patentrules2007.pdf (consolidated 1 October 2011).

[160] I Hargreaves, *Digital Opportunity: A Review of Intellectual Property and Growth* (2011), available at: http://www.ipo.gov.uk/ipreview-finalreport.pdf. For commentary, see H Chambers, 'The Hargreaves Review: another mixed bag' (2011) 33(9) EIPR 599–603; J Smith and R Montagnon, 'The Hargreaves Review: a "digital opportunity"' (2011) 33(9) EIPR 596–599; and C Howell, 'The Hargreaves Review: digital opportunity: a review of intellectual property and growth' (2012) 1 Journal of Business Law 71–83.

[161] *Gowers Review of Intellectual Property* (HM Treasury, 2006).

[162] I Hargreaves, *Digital Opportunity: A Review of Intellectual Property and Growth* (IPO, 2011).

10.82   As we have seen previously, there has been a strong and steady growth in the number of international patent applications and this has been mirrored in the UK. However, as Hargreaves pointed out, there is an associated challenge that comes with this 'success' of the patent system. This is the problem of the so-called patent thicket: 'A current generation smartphone, for example, may well be covered by hundreds of patents owned by tens of rights holders'.[163] The problem is compounded by high numbers of patents pending and this is further exacerbated by delays in granting. For example, the EPO can now take up to ten years to grant a patent.[164] The problem is particularly acute in the computer technology sector and here there is a double disadvantage: because of the nature of the inventions and the claims to protection that are made, there is more uncertainty about validity of the patents. Furthermore, there is less evidence that patents are effective in supporting innovation in the field, and yet—despite this—there has been significant growth in patent applications since 2000 relative to other areas. For these reasons, we discuss this field of technology separately and more deeply in Chapter 12.

10.83   The uncertainty that is generated by patent thickets is driven as much by patents that have been granted as those that are pending. Moreover, the effect is disproportionately felt by smaller businesses less able to stand up to a patent action, lest it be successful. For these reasons, Hargreaves recommended: 'The Government … investigate ways of limiting adverse consequences of patent thickets, including by working with international partners to establish a patent fee structure set by reference to innovation and growth goals rather than solely by reference to patent office running costs. The structure of patent renewal fees might be adjusted to encourage patentees to assess more carefully the value of maintaining lower value patents, so reducing the density of patent thickets.[165]

10.84   In its response,[166] the Government undertook to investigate the extent of the problem and to work closely with the UK–IPO to reduce adverse effects. The UK–IPO produced a report on the topic in November 2011 showing the full complexity of the problem and how the motivations for and effects of patent practices vary significantly between sectors. Accordingly, there is no single phenomenon creating a problem for which there is one solution. Solutions will come from looking both at 'technology type' and 'stage of development'.[167] This is certainly true as a means to understand better the problem, but solutions remain elusive. The suggestion about revised fee structures only addresses the issue of the existence or possible existence of patent rights. For those who have them, can afford them' and can afford to use them as a threat, the advantages of creating thickets remain. And fee changes will do nothing to address the litigation threat-culture that largely drives the uncertainties that are at the heart of the problem.

National considerations

10.85   Various aspects of the domestic system were scrutinised by Gowers and Hargreaves, including granting procedures, training of examiners in new developments, raising awareness of firms and the public about IP and improved services for patent opinions (see previously), review of practice, fees structures, and reform of defences. In particular, Gowers encouraged the UK–IPO to play a greater and more defined role in IP policy development, for example by working more closely with industry and government departments and there has been a marked demonstration of this in the years since the report was published.

10.86   In policy terms, it was recommended by Gowers, and accepted by the Chancellor, that a Strategic Advisory Board for Intellectual Property Policy (SABIP) be established with external experts, a Secretariat, and suitable funding to advise on the future direction of IP initiatives for the UK and its wider relations. This

---

[163] Hargreaves Review, para 6.13.   [164] Hargreaves Review, para 6.9.   [165] Hargreaves Review, p 63.
[166] HM Government, Government Response to the Hargreaves Review of Intellectual Property and Growth (2011), 8.
[167] IPO, *Patent Thickets* (2011).

was established in June 2008 but was short-lived. Its work was folded into the IP Research section of the UK–IPO work package—which is committed to work with academia and industry.[168]

Implementing the Hargreaves Review

 Exercise

Follow this link to the UK–IPO website—http://www.ipo.gov.uk/types/hargreaves.htm—on how it has been following-up recommendations from the Hargreaves Review. Consider whether, and how far, the IPO can be expected to resolve many of the problems raised, given that much is about human practices around IP rights rather than with the content of the rights themselves.

Do we need new IP rights?

10.87 An interesting discussion arising in the Gowers Review is whether new rights are required to meet the needs of new and emerging technologies. The patent system has been put to the test in recent decades with the advent of biotechnologies and information technologies, including software and electronic business methods, as we see in Chapter 12. But it has also been argued that patent law sets the threshold too high for protection, necessitating a system of 'petty patents' or 'utility models' which can protect less inventive, but no less valuable, innovations.[169] Length of protection and costs are also a factor—many new technologies may have a short shelf life, thus obviating the need for protection over 20 years, while high registration, translation, and enforcement costs mean that many small to medium-sized enterprises are effectively excluded from the patent system. Hargreaves noted, for example, that fewer than 50 per cent of patents are renewed beyond their tenth year.[170] Notwithstanding, the Gowers Review rejected any special case for utility model patents, software patents, biotechnology and genetic patents, and business methods patents. In fact, it is claimed to be a strength of the system that it has not responded with the creation of new rights for new developments which would mean added complexity and increased cost.

10.88 Economics play a large part in this. Not only are there significant costs in setting up and administering new rights, but there is precious little evidence that their establishment would improve the economic situation,[171] or that they are necessary to encourage innovation.[172] Indeed, there is evidence from the United States that business method patents and gene patents can have an anti-competitive effect which de-incentivises rather than encourages innovation.[173] The UK and EPO take a harder line on these kinds of patents than the United States and the Gowers recommendation was that this should remain the position unless good economic cause can be shown to justify change. The point has been 'noted' by the UK–IPO.

 Discussion point For answer guidance visit www.oxfordtextbooks.co.uk/orc/waelde3e/

What other costs would be involved with the introduction of new IPRs? How might these new rights impact on existing rights?

---

[168] http://www.ipo.gov.uk/pro-ipresearch.htm.
[169] See paras 10.70ff for discussion of attempts in the EU to approximate laws in this area.
[170] Hargreaves Review, para 6.19.
[171] 'There seems to be no correlation between the existence of a utility model patent and innovation': Gowers Review, para 4.112.
[172] The example is given of the US software industry which 'grew exponentially without pure software patents', Gowers Review, para 4.114.   [173] Gowers Review, paras 4.118–4.121.

Exercise

Visit the UK–IPO to check which of the outstanding proposals for reform arising from these reviews have, or have not, been initiated or implemented by the time you read this chapter. For those that have not been taken up, are you convinced by the reasons given? See: http://www.ipo.gov.uk.

Patent procedures

The patenting procedure

10.89   We have already seen that there are various routes to obtaining patent registration, either via national (UK–IPO), European (EPO), or international (PCT) avenues. The net outcome is, however, always the same—patents are granted with territorial effect only in the countries for which protection was sought, and this can be a very costly process if multiple filing is contemplated.

10.90   There is therefore a great amount of strategic and economic thinking required in developing a patent strategy, including an assessment of one's actual and potential markets, a weighing-up of the costs of patenting against possible returns, a judgement on whether it is worth seeking protection in a country where imitation is unlikely, and a sense of future behaviour of competitors. Time is also against the prospective patentee. Any delay in registering an invention increases the likelihood that a rival might release their own version of the invention, thereby thwarting any chances of future protection; by the same token, seeking protection at too early a stage in the development of an invention can seriously limit the scope of monopoly obtained—the inventor is only entitled to protection for what he has actually contributed to the sum total of human knowledge (known as 'the state of the art', see further paras 11.81–11.83).

10.91   The starting point to understanding the scope and content of a patent monopoly is the patent application itself. In this section we describe the patent application process for the UK, although this largely reflects the processes of the EPO and the PCT.[174] We also consider the constituent elements of a UK patent application.

10.92   The critical event in the process of any patent application is the obtaining of its priority date. Normally, this is the date when the application is filed with the UK–IPO,[175] but crucially it can be up to 12 months earlier if a patent has been filed in another WTO country and the later application is 'supported by matter' contained in the earlier application.[176] The importance of the priority date cannot be underestimated because it is the date from which the novelty of an invention will be tested. Only if the invention was publicly available *prior* to the priority date is there a problem. It is therefore perfectly acceptable to disclose the invention after obtaining the priority date; indeed, it is common practice to begin marketing at this point or after publication of the application (see paras 10.114ff). You may have seen the term *patent pending* attached to various products. This refers to products marketed in the time period between the priority date and the grant of the patent and it puts rivals on notice of the patent application.

10.93   It is also possible to make an 'early filing' on provision of a few key pieces of information to the UK–IPO, being a written indication that a patent is sought, the identification of the person applying for the

---

[174] If the UK is designated in a European patent application the resulting patent is treated entirely as if it were a UK patent, see Patents Act, ss 77–78; Patent Rules, Part 5; EPC 2000, Art 64.

[175] Patents Act 1977, s 5(1), as amended.

[176] Patents Act 1977, s 5(2), as amended. The Comptroller also has a discretion to allow an unintentional late filing, Patents Act 1977, s 5(2A)–(2C), as amended.

patent, a description of the invention, or a reference to an earlier relevant application.[177] This mecha-nism is far short of a full application, but allows the prospective applicant up to 12 months to ponder his patent strategy and to decide if a full application is merited. It also serves to secure an early priority date for the same reasons discussed previously.

10.94   If a full application is to be made, the Patents Act 1977 lays down stringent criteria as to its form and content. Section 14(2) of the Act provides that every application must contain:

- a *request* for the grant of a patent;

- an *abstract* which gives technical information about the invention and the field to which it contrib-utes; it also serves to facilitate future searches but does not form part of the state of the art;[178]

- a *specification* which is the part of the application that contains (1) a description of the invention, (2) the claim or claims as to what has been invented and what a monopoly is sought for, (3) any draw-ings referred to in the description or claims.

10.95   The inventor must sufficiently disclose his invention in the specification to allow effective examina-tion of its suitability for a patent. The criterion is that 'the specification shall disclose the invention in a manner which is clear enough and complete enough for the invention to be performed by a person skilled in the art'.[179] If this has not happened but a patent in nonetheless granted, it can be a ground for subsequent revocation of the patent for *insufficiency*.[180] We consider this in Chapter 11 (paras 11.206–11.218).

10.96   An invention is described in words and pictures and, in the case of inventions involving living organ-isms, by a deposit of samples under the Budapest Treaty 1977.[181] Note, however, that there is no obli-gation to describe the fastest, most efficient, or most economical way to perform the invention. Such knowledge—'know how'—invariably remains out of the public domain and provides the patentee with additional commercial advantage in the exploitation of her invention.

 Exercise

The best way to make sense of these arcane terms and to understand patent applications is to read them for yourself.[182] Various patent databases exist. One of the most comprehensive is Espacenet which is maintained by the EPO: http://worldwide.espacenet.com/

10.97   Figure 10.1 shows an example of a patented invention from the United States for Animal Ear Protectors with the Patent Number US4233942.[183] Go to the Espacenet website and do a Quick Search for this patent using the Patent Number.

The first thing you will see is this picture and the *Abstract* of the patent which sums up the invention thus:

This invention provides a device for protecting the ears of animals, especially long-haired dogs, from becoming soiled by the animal's food while the animal is eating. The device provides a generally tubular shaped member for containing and protecting each ear of the animal, and a member to position the tubular member and animal ears away from the mouth and food of the animal while it is eating.

---

[177] Patents Act 1977, s 15(1).   [178] Patents Act 1977, s 14(7), as amended.
[179] Patents Act 1977, s 14(3), as amended.   [180] Patents Act 1977, s 72(1).
[181] Available at http://www.wipo.int/treaties/en/registration/budapest/.
[182] Note, procedures and processes in the EPO and through the PCT do not use the term 'specification' but, simply, 'patent application'   .[183] Also published as GB2040663(A) and FR2448289(A1).

Figure 10.1 Patent application for Animal Ear Protectors

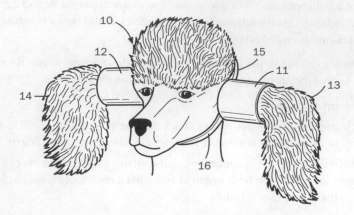

Now go to the *Description* section of the patent where we find more detail about the invention. Note, in particular, two features: (1) the applicant has described 'the prior art', that is, the existing state of knowledge before this invention, (2) the applicant describes how this invention solves a previously unsolved problem, viz, protecting the ears of long-eared animals when they eat or drink. In other words, he is explaining how this device is *new* and *inventive*. We return to the specifics of the law on these points in the next chapter. A final point to note about the description is that it must support the claims, otherwise the patent may be denied or invalidated in due course.[184]

10.98   The *Claims* are arguably the most important part of a patent. Claims serve at least two vital functions. First, they describe in technical detail the essence of the invention; secondly, they establish the limits of the monopoly that a successful applicant will eventually enjoy. You can only legitimately claim for actual technical contribution to human knowledge—to the state of the art—and any claims which exceed the boundaries of your contribution can be struck out. Overly broad claims can be a problem when a new technology emerges and patent examiners are unfamiliar with the science and so unsure about what, precisely, has been added to the state of the art.[185] Section 14(5) of the Patents Act 1977 states that:

> The claim or claims shall—(a) define the matter for which the applicant seeks protection; (b) be clear and concise; (c) be supported by the description; and (d) relate to one invention or to a group of inventions which are so linked as to form a single inventive concept.

10.99   Our invention for Animal Ear Protectors only has one claim. Here it is:

> 1. A device for protecting animal ears comprising: a pair of generally tubular protectors each of which is formed of a sheet of self-biasing material which in their free state tend to form themselves into said generally tubular protectors; each of said protectors being longitudinally openable to allow easy insertion of one of said animal ears; and positioning means for flexibly joining one end of one protector in spaced apart relationship with one end of the other protector and for securing said device to the head of said animal such that the longitudinal axis

---

[184] Patents Act 1977, s 14(5)(c).
[185] This description straddles two 'traditional' approaches to claim drafting: the 'central claiming system' whereby the objective is to define the kernel of the invention and the scope of protection flows from the precise contribution to the state of the art. This is still largely the approach in Continental Europe. It is to be contrasted with the 'peripheral claiming system' where the task is to demarcate the boundaries of the monopoly that is being claimed. This reflects more the position in the UK and the United States.

of each protector and a portion of each ear of said animal, are held generally horizontally and approximately perpendicularly to the head of said animal whereby the ends of said animal ears are separated by a distance greater than the width of the head of said animal.

10.100   There are numerous points to observe about this passage. First, consider the use of language. It may strike you as a rather convoluted way of describing two tubes placed over a dog's ears. But the purpose of claims is to describe the specific *technical* contribution that this particular invention makes to the state of the art. Indeed, it is not written with the ordinary reader in mind, but rather the audience is the person skilled in the relevant art. The drafting of patent claims is in fact a highly skilled enterprise, usually undertaken by patent agents or attorneys who specialise in particular fields of technology and who also provide advice and guidance on navigating the patent system.[186] While an applicant is not obliged to engage the services of a patent agent, the highly complex nature of the application and drafting processes indicate that it is strongly in his interests to do so.

10.101   The *precision* of the language in claims is also important because it must both distinguish the present invention from what has already been invented and describe the invention widely to secure as broad a monopoly as possible. Note the use of the term 'a pair of generally tubular protectors'—why 'generally'? Well, it may be because the applicant does not want to restrict his monopoly solely to 'tubular' protectors because then it would be easy to invent around his contribution, for example by producing square protectors. This is an issue of *interpretation* of claims and the approach of the courts to this is a matter of considerable importance, especially in infringement proceedings which we examine in the next chapter.

10.102   Most patent applications have numerous claims, and the average length of a European patent is 22 pages. The general approach is to begin with the first claim as the broadest and to claim narrower features of the invention and/or to pick out particular features of the invention in subsequent claims. In this way, if some claims are struck out, for example for being too broad, the applicant might still have a chance of receiving some, albeit narrower, protection through the remaining claims.

10.103   Let's consider another example. Do an Espacenet search for an invention relating to an insert for a cat litter box (EP1720404). Here are the first few claims:

1. An insert (1) which can be placed in a lower part (5) of a cat lavatory and is replaceable, characterised in that the blank of the insert (1) is substantially rectangular, the corners (7) of the insert (1) being sloped.

2. The insert as claimed in Claim 1, characterised in that the insert is a pouch (6).

3. The insert as claimed in either of Claims 1 or 2, characterised in that the blank of the insert (1) is substantially rectangular or square.

Question

What is *inventive* about this insert compared to all the other available cat litter accessories? How would you find out?

---

[186]   See, eg, the Chartered Institute of Patent Attorneys which was established in 1882: http://www.cipa.org.uk.

Drafting of claims

10.104   The way in which a claim is drafted is of considerable importance for the scope of protection eventually received. The previous claims in respect of the cat litter insert rely on the term 'characterised in …' to distinguish particular features of this invention from others already part of the state of the art. This is typical of the European approach. Various categories of claims exist and are used around the world. The UK has a fairly liberal approach to claim drafting and there is no prescription in law as to how claims should be drawn up.[187] In contrast, the EPO has strict guidelines about drafting[188] and does not permit all kinds of claims, as we shall see later. Moreover, the EPC Guidelines impose a fee if an application has more than 15 claims,[189] and the number of claims cannot be indefinite because 'the number of the claims shall be reasonable in consideration of the nature of the invention claimed'.[190]

10.105   It is commonly said that an invention can be a *product* or a *process*. This is reflected in the categories of claims that are most commonly used—product or process claims—and it is important to distinguish between the two because the legal effects of a patentee's monopoly can be affected by the choice of claim category.[191] A *product claim* is often characterised by a claim to a device, substance, embodiment, or compound, that is, to the physical entity making up the invention. A monopoly over the product itself is a strong one because it prevents all uses of the product by a competitor and it does not matter if the product was made by independent, non-rivalrous means. A *process claim* is as its name suggests—a claim to a means of producing something. Such claims are often characterised by language such as a method, use or system, for example a 'system for storing information'. A simple process claim is additionally useful because it extends protection to the products directly obtained by the process itself.[192]

10.106   *Product-by-process claims* are to be distinguished from the last example. These are product claims where the product is described by reference to its process of manufacture rather than by its own characteristics. For example, 'the product obtained by the process described in claim 1'. There are a couple of advantages of using such claims. One is a way of distinguishing your product from other similar products already on the market. Your monopoly will only extend to products made by your particular process, and may not therefore interfere with other products made by different means. An additional advantage of a product-by-process claim comes when it is difficult or impossible to describe your product by reference to its own characteristics, for example if you have invented a useful compound but you do not yet know its structure or composition.

10.107   Despite these benefits, product-by-process claims are frowned on by the EPO, while they have generally been acceptable in the UK. The EPO will only allow such claims when it is not possible to describe the product by any other means and when the product is patentable in its own right.[193] A product is not rendered novel merely by the fact that it is produced by means of a new process.[194] In 2005, the House of Lords ruled that 'it is important that the United Kingdom should apply the same law as the EPO' and signalled a change of practice for the UK.[195]

---

[187] *Kirin-Amgen v Transkaryotic Therapies* [2003] RPC 3 (CA) per Aldous LJ at paras 29–31.
[188] Guidelines for Examination in the European Patent Office, Part F, available at http://www.epo.org/law-practice/legal-texts/html/guidelines/e/index.htm, and Implementing Regulations to Part III of the Convention, rule 43, available at http://www.epo.org/law-practice/legal-texts/html/epc/2010/e/r43.html.
[189] Implementing Regulations, rule 45.   [190] Implementing Regulations, rule 43(5).
[191] See the comments by the EPO in T378/86 *MOOG/Change of category* [1988] OJEPO 386.   [192] EPC 2000, Art 64(2).
[193] EPO Guidelines, Part F, para 4.12, and T150/82 *IFF/Claim categories* [1984] OJEPO 309, paras 10–11.
[194] EPO Guidelines, Part F, para 4.12, and T150/82 *IFF/Claim categories* [1984] OJEPO 309, paras 10–11.
[195] *Kirin-Amgen Inc and others v Hoechst Marion Roussel Ltd and others* [2005] 1 All ER 667, [2005] RPC 9.

10.108 We may also know what a product does, that is, how its functions, without yet knowing its essential technical features, that is, how it is structured or constituted. Normally, it is the description of these technical features which is required for a successful patent application,[196] but in certain circumstances *functional claims* are acceptable 'provided that a skilled person would have no difficulty in providing some means of performing this function without exercising inventive skill',[197] and notably when the claimed features of the invention 'cannot otherwise be defined more precisely without restricting the scope of the claim'.[198]

> **Exercise**
>
> Can you think of any other advantage to drafting claims in terms of an invention's function rather than its technical features?

10.109 Article 82 of the EPC provides that a '... European patent application shall relate to one invention only or to a group of inventions so linked as to form a single general inventive concept.'[199] It is not unusual, however, and especially in the pharmaceutical and biotechnology industries, for one patent application to concern many different, yet related, embodiments of a single inventive concept. Examples include thousands of different variations on a particular chemical compound or related elements of a gene sequence. In such circumstances, patent agents will invoke *representative claims* which allow specific examples to be given of the invention's particular features which are held out to be present across the range of products claimed. It would be impractical and self-defeating for the patent system to require more specific details or separate patent applications for each and every product.

10.110 Similarly, the *Markush claim* is frequently used in the chemical industry where vast numbers of related entities can be claimed together. The distinguishing feature is that this type of claim allows 'alternatives' to be claimed as functional equivalents, that is, various permutations of different entities will produce the same inventive result and so are claimed to fall within the monopoly. This is acceptable as long as the alternatives are of a similar nature and can fairly be substituted for one another.[200] Markush claims contain symbols to refer to the sub-groups. This type of claim is named after the first inventor successfully to use it.[201]

10.111 *Swiss-type claims* were developed to get around problems of non-patentability of second or subsequent uses of existing compounds for medical treatment.[202] Consider, for example, that you find out that athlete foot cream is also good for curing acne: can you patent the product in these terms or for this second use? You cannot patent the product because it is already known and therefore not *new*. Medical use is also already known, and so what is new is the *method* of treatment, but there is a further problem because historically methods of treatment of the human or animal body have been excluded from patentability.[203] The EPO Enlarged Board of Appeal addressed this issue by following a practice first adopted by the Swiss Federal Intellectual Property Office and held that claims could be formulated in

[196] EPO Guidelines, Part F-II, para 4.5, and Implementing Regulation, rule 43(1).
[197] EPC Guidelines for Examination, Part F-IV, para 2.1.
[198] T694/92 *MYCOGEN/Modifying plant cells* [1998] EPOR 114, para 4.
[199] See also Implementing Regulations, rule 44, which requires a 'technical relationship' among all claimed inventions involving the same or corresponding special technical features.
[200] EPO Guidelines, Part F-V, para 5.   [201] Eugene Markush, US patent 1,506,316, granted on 26 August 1924.
[202] See Patents Act 1977, s 2(6) for first medical use.
[203] EPC, Art 52(4) and Patents Act 1977, s 4(2)—note, now amended as we discuss at paras 11.63ff.

a certain way to be permissible.[204] That formulation is a claim to *'use of substance X in the manufacture of a medicament for the treatment of condition Y'*. The claim, then, is to the method of manufacture not to the method of treatment. Because of the origin of the formulation, this became known as a Swiss-type claim. This legal fiction was addressed by reforms introduced by EPC 2000.[205] It is now no longer necessary to adopt Swiss-type claims because 'In the case of an invention consisting of a substance or composition for a specific use in any such method, the fact that the substance or composition forms part of the state of the art shall not prevent the invention from being taken to be new if that specific use does not form part of the state of the art.'[206] This now allows a simple claim of 'substance X for use in treatment of disease Y'.

10.112   Finally, we can consider the role of *omnibus claims*. These claims rely on references to the description of the invention in respect of their technical features and are commonly used in the UK. An example is 'A process in accordance with claim 1 substantially as described in the foregoing Example I [from the specification]'. There is, however, an express prohibition against this practice in the EPO Guidelines,[207] and therefore omnibus claims are not allowed except where 'absolutely necessary'.[208] This could be, for example, when the invention has features which can only be expressed by means of drawings or graphs defining a particular shape.

10.113   *Disclaimers* can be used to define an invention in a way that avoids problems of patentability such as non-novelty,[209] for example by expressly excluding certain features of the invention because these are already part of the state of the art.[210] But what happens if you want to disclaim features of your patent after it has been granted? This was considered by the Enlarged Board of Appeal in two cases[211] wherein it was held that post-grant disclaimers are possible in limited circumstances, namely, (1) to restore novelty by delimiting a claim against the state of the art, (2) to restore novelty by delimiting a claim against an accidental anticipation, and (3) to disclaim subject matter that is non-technical and so, non-patentable.

From preparation to application

(Note: guidance on applying for a patent is available from the UK–IPO here: http://www.patent.gov.uk/p-apply.pdf.)

10.114   Once you have completed your patent application form you can submit it to the UK–IPO for examination.

10.115   The stages in the process are:

(1) Submission of patent specification (description of invention as minimum) and application form and *request for grant of a patent* form.

(2) Receipt issued from UK–IPO with application number and confirmation of *priority date*.[212]

(3) *Request search* and file appropriate fee (£150/130 (e-Filed) for search) within 12 months. Add claims and abstract if not present.

(4) *Preliminary examination* to ensure formal requirements of the application are met and *search* of the 'prior art' to determine if invention in *new* and *inventive*. A *search report* will be prepared and sent

---

[204] G5/83 *EISAI/Second Medical Indication* [1985] OJEPO 64.   [205] Arts 53(c) and 54(4), (5) EPC 2000.
[206] Patents Act 1977, s 4A(4), as amended.   [207] Implementing Regulations, rules 43(4) and 46(6).
[208] T0150/82 *IFF/Claim categories* [1984] OJEPO 309.   [209] See EPO Guidelines, Part H-V, para 3.5.
[210] T4/80 *BAYER/Disclaimer* [1982] OJEPO 149.
[211] See G01/03 *PPG INDUSTRIES/Disclaimer* [2004] OJEPO 413 and G02/03 *GENETIC SYSTEMS CORP/Synthetic antigens* [2004] OJEPO 448.   [212] Patents Act 1977, s 15.

to the applicant highlighting any materials that may pose problems for patentability as well as other technical materials showing what has been done in the field[213] (£30/20 (e-Filed)).

(5) *Publication of the patent* happens 18 months after the priority date.[214]

(6) *Substantive examination* is a thorough consideration of the application by a skilled patent examiner to determine if it meets the requirements for patentability[215] (£100/80 (e-Filed)).

(7) *Substantive examination report* issued and period for *amendment*, if required.

(8) If all criteria are met, the patent is *granted, the application is published in its final form, and the patent certificate is sent to the patentee.*[216]

10.116 In total, it costs around £230–280 in official fees to apply for a UK patent.[217] Professional patent attorney fees will be substantially more.

Who can apply for a patent?

10.117 Anyone can apply for a patent,[218] and they do not need to be the inventor, although if this is the case they must have some entitlement in law to apply, for example through contractual arrangement, and the basis for this must be made clear at the time of application.[219] The inventor is entitled to be named both in the application and the patent.[220] It will be assumed that the applicant is entitled to apply until the contrary is proven.[221] Matters of dispute over entitlement to the patent are referred to the Comptroller in the first instance.[222]

10.118 The UK, Europe, and almost all other countries of the world apply the so-called *first-to-file* approach to patent entitlement, that is, that priority of claim depends solely on who is first to submit a complete application to the patent office. The United States, in contrast, has operated a *first-to-invent* procedure which requires a far more nuanced examination of the processes leading up to a patent application and a need to determine at what point an 'invention' occurred. This has been a two-stage process of (1) conception of the invention, and (2) reduction to practice of the invention. The best claim is that of an inventor who first conceived of the invention and then reduced it to practice and filed a patent application. Provided that he can prove this process, then he will have a stronger claim than someone who was first to file but cannot establish prior invention. But this often proved to be a difficult and costly process. After lengthy and considerable debate, the America Invents Act was passed by Congress in September 2011 and came into effect on 16 March 2013. Section 3 of the new Act now introduces a form of first-to-file into the United States, albeit that early disclosures such as presentations, demonstrations, or postings on company websites about an invention can serve a 'territory marking' function (section 102). Thus, while the US has moved substantially to the position already followed by the rest of the world, it remains to be seen whether the transition will be total or expeditious.

Discussion point For answer guidance visit www.oxfordtextbooks.co.uk/orc/waelde3e/

What are the pros and cons of first-to-invent as opposed to first-to-file?

---

[213] Patents Act 1977, ss 15A and 17.   [214] Patents Act 1977, s 16(1).   [215] Patents Act 1977, s 18.
[216] Patents Act 1977, s 18.
[217] Note: the Patents and Patents and Trade Marks (Fees) (Amendment) Rules 2010 (SI 2010/33) introduced new fees as of 6 April 2010.
[218] Patents Act 1977, s 7(1).   [219] Patents Act 1977, s 7(2).   [220] Patents Act 1977, s 13.
[221] Patents Act 1977, s 7(4).   [222] Patents Act 1977, s 8. Post-grant disputes are handled under s 37.

10.119   An application for a patent may be withdrawn at any time before the patent is granted and any withdrawal of such an application may not be revoked.[223] The publication of the patent is important for at least two reasons. First, at this time all correspondence and details of the invention are released into the public domain destroying the last vestiges of secrecy. Secondly, this is the date from which the patentee can sue for infringement.[224] If the patent is granted, the initial protection for the invention is for four years. Thereafter, the patent must be renewed annually on the payment of increasing fees up to a maximum of 20 years.[225]

10.120   A standard UK patent usually takes between two to three years to grant, but in some areas and in some other offices it is longer. For example, the EPO can take up to ten years to grant a patent. An accelerated examination and search is now available from the UK–IPO. This involves collapsing both processes and paying both fees together. This means that a patent can be granted within a few months of publication.

Post-grant amendments

10.121   Sections 27(1) and 75(1) of the Patents Act 1977, as amended, provide the Comptroller and the courts with discretion to allow the amendment of a patent once it has been granted; the former section deals with circumstances when the request is from the proprietor himself, and the latter with cases when the validity of the patent is in dispute, for example in infringement or revocation proceedings. EPC 2000 reforms found in Article 138(3) now mean that a proprietor, or consenting co-proprietors, can apply to amend or revoke a patent in *any* proceedings in which validity can be an issue, even if it is not an issue in the particular circumstances.[226] In exercising their discretion, the Comptroller and the courts must also now have regard to relevant principles in the EPC, for example Regulations made under the Convention or EPO Guidelines or rulings from the EPO Boards of Appeal or Opposition Division. This is to ensure closer approximation and consistency of approach in signatory countries.[227] The UK–IPO offers a service whereby requests for amendments are made publicly available and those who may oppose them are given notice of the application to amend.[228] You cannot apply to amend your patent in favour of more subject matter or a broader monopoly.[229] Amendments can only maintain, or more usually restrict, the scope of protection originally received.

 Discussion point   For answer guidance visit www.oxfordtextbooks.co.uk/orc/waelde3e/

What sorts of factors do you think would influence the Comptroller or court one way or another in exercising its discretion to amend a patent?

10.122   In the next chapter we consider the criteria for patentability, the exclusions, rights conferred by a patent, revocation, and defences.

---

[223] See Patents Act 1977, s 14(9).   [224] Patents Act 1977, s 69.
[225] This 20-year period is calculated from the filing date, see Patents Act 1977, s 25(1).
[226] Such circumstances are outlined in the Patents Act 1977, s 74.
[227] Patents Act 1977, s 75(5), as inserted by the Patents Act 2004, s 2(5). EPC 2000, Art 105a gives a discretion to the EPO to allow amendments to 'European' patents but not during opposition proceedings.
[228] Patent Office Amendment Service: http://www.ipo.gov.uk/p-pn-changespec.htm.
[229] Patents Act 1977, s 76(2), (3).

Further reading

Books

PW Grubb and PL Thomsen, *Patents for Chemicals, Pharmaceuticals and Biotechnology: Fundamentals of Global Law, Practice and Strategy* (5th edn, 2010)

D Matthews, *Globalising Intellectual Property Rights: The TRIPS Agreement* (2012)

MP Pugatch (ed), *The Intellectual Property Debate: Perspective from Law, Economics and Political Economy* (2006)

B Sherman and L Bently, *The Making of Modern Intellectual Property Law* (1999)

T Takenaka, *Patent Law and Theory: A Handbook of Contemporary Research* (2009)

Reports

Commission on Intellectual Property Rights, Innovation and Public Health, Public Health, Innovation and Intellectual Property Rights (2006)

European Commission, Pharmaceutical Sector Inquiry Report (2009)

Gowers Review of Intellectual Property (HM Treasury, 2006)

I Hargreaves, *Digital Opportunity: A Review of Intellectual Property and Growth* (2011)

Articles

AF Christie, 'Non-overlapping rights: a patent misconception' (2010) 32(2) EIPR 58

E Derclaye, 'Patent law's role in the protection of the environment: reassessing patent law and its justifications in the 21st century' (2009) 40(3) IIC 249

AM Imam, 'How does patent protection help developing countries?' (2006) IIC 245

R Jacob, 'Patent thickets: a paper for the European Patent Office Economic and Scientific Advisory Board meeting' (2013) 8(3) JIPLP 203–206

D Matthews, 'The Lisbon Treaty, trade agreements and the enforcement of intellectual property rights' (2010) 32(3) EIPR 104

N Moran, 'Startups, inventors cheer European Unitary Patent' (2013) 31 Nature Biotechnology 92–93

J Straus and N-S Klunker, 'Harmonisation of international patent law?' (2007) 38 IIC 907, and the reply from C Health (2008) 39 IIC 210

Patentability and infringement

Introduction

Scope and overview of chapter

11.1 This chapter is about obtaining and maintaining a patent. The first half deals with the issue of patentability and explores the criteria which are applied by an intellectual property office in examining a patent application. These are *novelty*, *inventive step*, and *industrial applicability*. Equally important, however, are the exclusions from patentability and we will begin by considering these before moving on to consider the positive criteria for patenting. The second half of the chapter concerns the rights that a patentee enjoys, the circumstances in which infringement actions might be brought, and the defences that are available to rivals.

11.2 Patent law protects inventions, but interestingly there is no legal definition of *invention*.[1] Rather, the eligibility of a new product or process for patent protection is considered in a two-step process. First, a patent examiner will consider what is *not* an invention under the law, or at least, what will not be entitled to patent protection. Well-established lists of exclusions from patentability exist in most legal systems and it is essential to understand both what is on such lists and why certain subject matter is excluded. The reasons are many and varied as we shall see. It is in these exclusions that many cultural and jurisdictional differences lie in the application of patent law. Secondly, an intellectual property office will test an invention against the positive criteria for patentability, which are *novelty* (does the invention already exist and is it in the public domain?); *inventive step* (is the invention sufficiently innovative to represent a significant move forward in the field?); and *industrial applicability* (can the invention be made or used in any kind of industry?). These criteria operate as threshold devices to determine if a particular invention makes a sufficient contribution to human knowledge and experience to merit the award of a monopoly. Article 27(1) of the TRIPS Agreement ensures that all countries are agreed that these are the relevant criteria for patentability.[2] But it is in the interpretation given to these criteria by national courts where differences emerge, and we will focus on the UK courts in this regard.

---

[1] But see the Patents Act 1977, s 125(1).

[2] TRIPS, Art 27(1): 'Subject to the provisions of paragraphs 2 and 3, patents shall be available for any inventions, whether products or processes, in all fields of technology, provided that they are new, involve an inventive step and are capable of industrial application.'

11.3

Learning objectives

By the end of this chapter you should be able to describe and explain:

- the exclusions from patentability and their underlying rationales;

- the meaning and operation of the criteria for patentability;

- the range of rights conferred on an inventor by the grant of a patent as well as the limits of those rights;

- the circumstances in which infringement proceedings can be brought and the common counterclaim of revocation;

- the available defences to an action for patent infringement.

11.4 Once granted, a patent confers on the patentee a range of rights and the monopoly is arguably the strongest within intellectual property law. But as with all intellectual property rights, limits can be placed on that monopoly such as Crown use or compulsory licences. Moreover, what can be given can also be taken away, and patents are vulnerable throughout their life to a claim for revocation, that is, that the patent should be struck from the patent register because it was erroneously granted. Infringement proceedings are often met with a counterclaim for revocation. It is therefore necessary to consider infringement and revocation together. Finally, the chapter examines the available defences to an action for patent infringement. So the rest of the chapter looks like this:

- Excluded subject matter (11.5–11.77)

- Protectable subject matter (11.78–11.140)

- Patent rights and their limits (11.141–11.170)

- Infringement proceedings (11.171–11.204)

- Revocation (11.205–11.218)

- Defences (11.219–11.232)

Excluded subject matter

11.5 The final version of the revised European Patent Convention, known as EPC 2000, was issued by the European Patent Office (EPO) in January 2007 and came into force December that year.[3] We have discussed its reforming measures in the previous chapter. Article 52(1) EPC 2000 now provides that: 'European patents shall be granted for any inventions, in all fields of technology, provided that they are new, involve an inventive step and are susceptible of industrial application.' The relevant provisions which concern non-patentable subject matter are found in Articles 52(2), (3) and 53. These provide:

Article 52(2)

The following in particular shall not be regarded as inventions within the meaning of paragraph 1:
(a) discoveries, scientific theories and mathematical methods;

---

[3] (2007) Special Edition No 1 OJEPO, available at http://archive.epo.org/epo/pubs/oj007/01_07/special_edition_1_epc_2000.pdf. See the 14th edition of the EPC here for current collection of Convention and all related instruments: http://www.epo.org/law-practice/legal-texts/epc.html.

(b)   aesthetic creations;

(c)   schemes, rules and methods for performing mental acts, playing games or doing business, and programs for computers;

(d)   presentations of information.

(3) Paragraph 2 shall exclude the patentability of the subject-matter or activities referred to therein only to the extent to which a European patent application or European patent relates to such subject matter or activities *as such* (emphasis added).

Article 53

Exceptions to patentability
European patents shall not be granted in respect of:

(a)   inventions the commercial exploitation of which would be contrary to 'ordre public' or morality; such exploitation shall not be deemed to be so contrary merely because it is prohibited by law or regulation in some or all of the Contracting States;

(b)   plant or animal varieties or essentially biological processes for the production of plants or animals; this provision shall not apply to microbiological processes or the products thereof;

(c)   methods for treatment of the human or animal body by surgery or therapy and diagnostic methods practised on the human or animal body; this provision shall not apply to products, in particular substances or compositions, for use in any of these methods.

11.6   The UK provisions equivalent to Article 52 EPC 2000 are found in section 1(2) of the Patents Act 1977,[4] while the terms of Article 53 EPC 2000 are reflected in section 1(3), (4) of, and Schedule A2 to, the 1977 Act. Schedule A2 deals with biotechnological inventions which are the subject of a European Directive[5] and which we explore in more depth in the next chapter. Finally, Article 53(c) is a new addition which is incorporated into domestic law through the Patents Act 2004 as section 4A of the Patents Act 1977.

> ❓ **Question**
>
> What is the basis for excluding the respective categories of subject matter in Article 52 as opposed to Article 53? How are they different?

11.7   As Pumfrey J stated in *Shopalotto.com's Application*:[6] '[a] moment's thought will show that it is not possible to provide an exhaustive definition of "invention". The Convention does not attempt to interpret the word but provides a list of things which are excluded, whether or not they would be regarded as inventions.'[7]

■ *Aerotel Ltd v Telco Holdings Ltd & others* [2006] EWCA Civ 1371, [2007] RPC 7

This case involved two appeals which raised issues about the interpretation of Article 52 and the approach of the British courts to considering excluded subject matter. The *Aerotel* appeal concerned a system and a method of making a telephone call from any available telephone station using a pre-paid code. An action for infringement was met with a counterclaim for revocation on the grounds that the invention was merely a method of doing business. Macrossan's invention related to an automated

---

[4] As amended by the Patents Act 2004.

[5] Directive 98/44/EC of the European Parliament and of the Council of 6 July 1998 on the legal protection of biotechnological inventions (Biotechnology Directive), available at http://ec.europa.eu/internal_market/indprop/invent/index_en.htm.

[6] [2005] EWHC 2416 (Pat), [2006] RPC 293 at para 6.

[7] There was discussion in *Biogen v Medeva* [1997] RPC 1 of the need to prove an 'invention' over and above the established criteria for patentability, while this was not entirely ruled out no example could be given of where this would be required. See further J Pila, *The Requirement for an Invention in Patent Law* (2010).

method of producing the necessary documents to incorporate a company.[8] This had been rejected by the Patent Office as unpatentable and the High Court agreed holding that it was as a method of performing a mental act by a computer.[9] The Court of Appeal similarly rejected Macrossan's appeal as a method of doing business and a claim to a computer program as such. Aerotel won, however, because the primary claim was to a new device while their second claim was to the use of the new device, and therefore not only to a method of doing business *as such*. In handing down this ruling, the Court of Appeal sought to provide a 'definitive statement' on how the UK should approach the interpretation of Article 52.

11.8   The court began by distinguishing the class of excluded matter under Article 52 from the matter mentioned in Article 53. Article 52 deals with things that are not considered to be inventions, while Article 53 is concerned with exceptions to patentability. The importance of the distinction lies in the fact that exceptions should be construed narrowly,[10] but the same does not apply to non-inventions.[11] The correct approach towards the latter is to attempt to identify the underlying policy for each exclusion and to give effect to it through interpretation, although the court could find no single principle or rationale that unifies all of the examples in Article 52. Each must be considered on its own terms.[12] Moreover, it has been confirmed to be an exercise in judgement and not something that can be reduced easily to systematic analysis.[13]

 Discussion point For answer guidance visit www.oxfordtextbooks.co.uk/orc/waelde3e/

What might be the various rationales that explain the inclusion of the specific examples in Article 52?

11.9   The approach in the UK historically has been to ask if the invention makes a 'technical contribution' to the state of the art—that is, to the sum total of human knowledge—and if so, it will be patentable as long as the contribution is not solely in the realm of excluded matter.[14] A technical contribution is one which produces a *technical effect*, and in most cases this means a real-world change in the state, operation, or function of something tangible.[15] The problem is that the term *technical contribution* suffers from an 'inherent vagueness',[16] and its utility and limits were probably best summed up by Fox LJ in *Gale's Application*:

> If you look at the case law on the subject, both here and in Munich, you will find many references to 'technical contribution', 'technical result', and so on, being touchstones by which these cases are decided. The use of the word 'technical' as a short-hand expression in order to identify patentable subject-matter is often convenient. But it should be remembered that it was not used by the framers of the Patents Act 1977 or the European Patent Convention when they wanted to tell us what is or is not an 'invention'. In any case the word 'technical' is not a solution. It is merely a restatement of the problem in different and more imprecise language. I am not claiming

---

[8] You can read Macrossan's claims at http://v3.espacenet.com/textclam?DB=EPODOC&IDX=GB2388937&F=8&QPN=GB2388937.

[9] [2006] EWHC 705 (Ch).

[10] See, eg, T19/90 *HARVARD/Oncomouse* [1990] OJEPO 376 and T356/93 *PLANT GENETIC SYSTEMS/Glutamine Synthetase Inhibitors* [1995] EPOR 357. Compare discussion at paras 12.45ff.

[11] *Aerotel v Telco Holdings Ltd and others* [2006] EWCA Civ 1371, para 12.

[12] For the impact on UK–IPO granting practice, see Practice Notice (PO: Patents Act 1977: Patentable Subject Matter) (No 1) [2007] RPC 8 and Practice Notice (PO: Patents Act 1977: Patentable Subject Matter) (No 2) [2008] RPC 15. But for comment on a different approach in the EPO, see N Gardner and P England 'European Union: patents—exclusion from patentability' (2008) 30(1) EIPR N5–6.

[13] See *Really Virtual Co Ltd v UK Intellectual Property Office* [2012] EWHC 1086 (Ch).

[14] See *Merrill Lynch's Application* [1988] RPC 1, and also *Gale's Application* [1991] RPC 305 and *Fujitsu's Application* [1996] RPC 511. But see now Practice Note (PO: Patents Act 1977: Examining for Patentability) [2006] RPC 6.

[15] In this respect the UK broadly followed the EPO, see T208/84 *VICOM/Computer-related inventions* [1987] EPOR 74, but see further paras 12.99–12.103 in Chapter 12.

[16] See *Aerotel*, note 11, para 124.

that it is wrong to decide cases with reference to the word 'technical'. It happens all the time. What I am saying is that it is not a panacea. It is a useful servant but a dangerous master.

11.10   In fact, the need to find a *technical* contribution may have been downgraded by the Court of Appeal in *Aerotel*. The court reviewed all of the existing UK and EPO rulings and opined that its ruling would be the 'definitive statement' on patentable subject matter. While confirming the authority of existing precedents,[17] the court set about 'reformulating' the test to be applied into a four-step approach. This is:

(1) properly construe the claim;

(2) identify the actual contribution;

(3) ask whether it falls solely within the excluded subject matter;

(4) check whether the actual or alleged contribution is actually technical in nature.

The fourth criterion is merely a final check which should be deployed only when the application has passed the first three criteria.[18] The presence or absence of a technical effect is therefore only a subsidiary matter which speaks to patentability rather than exclusion.[19] This approach was followed in various cases including *Astron Clinica Ltd and others v The Comptroller General of Patents*, where it was confirmed that the first three steps should answer whether the invention is excluded, with the fourth step being a final check.[20] The court reviewed the *Aerotel* test in *Symbian Ltd's Application* and came to the conclusion that the four-step test encompasses all previously employed tests and the test is intended to be equivalent to the prior case law test of 'technical contribution'.[21] It considered that it might be necessary to fuse the third and the fourth step into a single step as it is not as important *when* the technical contribution is identified, as it is to consider whether the invention makes a relevant technical contribution to the art.[22] In other words, *Symbian* confirmed that *Aerotel* is intended to be equivalent to previous rulings on the test of 'technical contribution'. Lord Walker has since noted the difference between the 'inventive concept' of a claimed invention and its 'technical contribution to the art' in *Generics (UK) Ltd & others v H Lundbeck A/S*.[23] 'Inventive concept' is concerned with the identification of the core of the invention, that idea or principle that makes the invention inventive. The 'technical contribution to the art' is concerned with the evaluation of its inventive concept—what needs to be considered is how far forward has it carried the state of the art?[24]

11.11   The UK–IPO has issued Practice Notices detailing the approach to patentable subject matter and instructing patent examiners to follow them with immediate effect.[25] The first Notice from 2006 points out that construction of the claim is necessary to establish the nature of the monopoly, and it is the actual contribution to human knowledge in terms of the substance of the invention which is important and not the form of the claim. Thus, in *Macrossan* the fact that computer hardware elements formed part of the invention did not detract from the fact that the actual contribution was merely in the realm of a computer program and a method of doing business. The third criterion is the equivalent of the term 'as such' in Article 52 EPC. It means that an application is excluded from further consideration only if the subject matter falls wholly into one or more excluded category. If, when considering the test as a whole, a patent examiner believes that it would be fruitless to conduct a search then he or she can issue a report

[17] See note 11.   [18] *Aerotel*, note 11, paras 46–47.
[19] See the ruling of the Hearing Officer in *John Lahiri Khan's Application* (BL O/356/06).
[20] *Astron Clinica Ltd and others v The Comptroller General of Patents* [2008] EWHC 85 (Pat), para 45.
[21] *Symbian Ltd's Application* [2008] EWCA Civ 1066, [2009] RPC 1
[22] *Symbian Ltd's Application* [2008] EWCA Civ 1066, [2009] RPC 1 at para 58   [23] [2009] UKHL 12.
[24] [2009] UKHL 12, para 30.
[25] Practice Notice (PO: Patents Act 1977: Patentable Subject Matter) (No 1) [2007] RPC 8 and Practice Notice (PO: Patents Act 1977: Patentable Subject Matter) (No 2) [2008] RPC 15.

to this effect.[26] This Practice Note was amended on 7 February 2008 with regards to the permissible form of a claim[27] following the *Astron Clinica Ltd and others v The Comptroller General of Patents* judgment.[28] A claim to a computer program can be allowable 'if the claim reflects the features of the invention which would ensure the patentability of the method which the program is intended to carry out when it is run.' We discuss the implications of this in Chapter 12.

11.12   In *Aerotel* the Court of Appeal acknowledged the importance of decisions from the Boards of Appeal of the EPO and that they have 'great persuasive authority' for the UK courts.[29] Notwithstanding, it did not follow the available rulings because it considered that the EPO jurisprudence is currently unstable. We explore this in the context of computer software inventions in the next chapter, but the court did suggest that its different approach would probably not make much difference in practice.[30] The court also looked beyond Europe to the United States and noted the contrasting approach to patentability where 'everything under the sun that is made by man' is patentable.[31] While this may overstate the position somewhat, it is clear that the US policy is to ensure that the categories of patentable invention are given wide scope.[32]

11.13   We have seen, however, that various examples are given in Europe of things that are not considered to be inventions and the Court of Appeal has indicated that the underlying rationales may be different depending on the example in question. Moreover, we find no real help from the *travaux préparatoires* of the EPC to assist us in understanding these exclusions.[33] We are left, then, to consider the existing case law on each example to appreciate the reasons for its exclusion from patent protection, and some additional help is provided by the EPC Guidelines for Examination.

11.14   The Guidelines provide, for example, that the list of things which are not regarded as inventions includes items which are either too abstract (eg a discovery or scientific method) and/or which are non-technical (eg aesthetic creations). An invention can be in any field of technology but it must be concrete and have technical character.[34] Let us consider each of the categories of exclusion in turn.[35]

Discoveries, scientific theories, and mathematical methods

11.15   As mentioned, this category is thought to contain items which are too abstract or indistinct to be the proper subject of patent protection. The most interesting example is, however, discoveries. Anton van Leeuwenhoek of Holland (1632–1723) is credited as being the father of microscopy. His invention of new methods to grind and polish lenses led him to be the first person to see and describe bacteria. Clearly, he did not invent those bacteria but merely discovered them using an invention. Conversely, discoveries often lead to inventions. For example, Sir Alexander Fleming (1881–1955)

[26]   Patents Act 1977, s 17(5).   [27]   Amendment available at http://www.ipo.gov.uk/p-pn.htm.

[28]   *Astron Clinica Ltd and others v The Comptroller General of Patents* [2008] EWHC 85 (Pat).

[29]   *Merrell Dow v Norton* [1996] RPC 76, per Lord Hoffmann at 82. See also *Eli Lilly & Co v Human Genome Sciences Inc* [2010] EWCA Civ 33.   [30]   But see T154/04, *DUNS LICENSING ASSOCIATES/Estimating Sales Activity*, OJ 2/2008, 46.

[31]   Famously stated by the US Supreme Court in *Diamond v Chakrabarty* 447 US 303, 100 S Ct 2204 (1980) in respect of the patentability of a man-made oil-eating bacterium.

[32]   Confirmed by the Congress Committee Reports when patents laws were being re-codified in 1952: S Rep No 1979, 82d Cong, 2d Sess, 5 (1952); HR Rep No 1923, 82d Cong, 2d Sess, 6 (1952).

[33]   J Pila, 'Art 52(2) of the Convention on the Grant of European Patents: what did the framers intend? A study of the *travaux préparatoires*' (2005) 36 IIC 755 and ED Ventose, 'In the footsteps of the framers of the European Patent Convention: examining the *travaux préparatoires*' (2009) 31(7) EIPR 353.

[34]   Guidelines for Examination in the European Patent Office, Part G-II, para 1.

[35]   It was noted in *Protecting Kids the World Over (PKTWO) Ltd, Re* [2011] EWHC 2720 (Pat); Ch D (Patents Ct) that *Aerotel* is also a helpful approach when dealing with inventions that have multiple possible exclusions, ibid para 36.

was working in 1928 on colonies of the bacterium *Staphylococcus aureus*, which can be dangerous to humans, when a batch accidentally became contaminated by a mould that killed off the bacterium. This was penicillin—the first antibiotic—and further work by Fleming and others led to production of penicillin in large, high-quality doses. A patent was eventually granted in 1948 for a method of mass production of penicillin.[36]

 Exercise

Fleming did not attempt to patent penicillin itself, but would he have been successful if he had tried? Do you think that the absence of a patent on the product contributed to the fact that it took 20 years to go from discovery to mass production?

11.16   One of the problems that has been thrown up for the biotechnology industry has been the objection that attempts to patent biotechnological products is nothing more than an attempt to patent a living thing, that is, something already pre-existing in nature and so merely a discovery. We explore the contours of these arguments in the next chapter, but the reality is that many biotechnology products are patented. Where, then, do we draw a line between a discovery and an invention? The answer is in the concept of *technical effect* which we have considered previously. If human intervention can bring about a specific technical effect or application of discovery then the embodiment of that technical effect or application can be the subject of a patent. Consider the EPO Guidelines:

> If a new property of a known material or article is found out, that is mere discovery and unpatentable because discovery as such has no technical effect and is therefore not an invention within the meaning of Article 52(1). If, however, that property is put to practical use, then this constitutes an invention which may be patentable. For example, the discovery that a particular known material is able to withstand mechanical shock would not be patentable, but a railway sleeper made from that material could well be patentable.[37]

11.17   Similarly, merely to find a naturally occurring substance is a pure discovery,[38] but if you are able to put it to some tangible use, for example as an antibiotic, then it may be patentable in respect of this particular technical effect. An invention requires some evidence of human ingenuity in realising a particular use for a discovery[39] or in making it available to the public in a form which previously it was not. An example of this last point is the case of *HOWARD FLOREY/Relaxin* before the Opposition Division of the EPO.[40] The patent in suit concerned a naturally occurring protein produced by women during childbirth to ease the passage of the child. Howard Florey had isolated and determined the chemical structure of the substance and was then able to produce it in a form which made it a marketable product, but the objection was that this remained a discovery. The Opposition Division, however, ruled otherwise holding that a newly isolated and characterised substance was not a mere discovery, but rather an industrially applicable technical solution to a pre-existing technical problem. A further relevant point in respect of a claim in the patent to the gene sequence itself was the fact that the form of the sequence claimed by the patentee was 'purer' than that found in nature and so sufficiently distinct to be patentable. These concepts are now embodied in the Biotechnology Directive which provides that 'An element isolated from the human body or otherwise produced by means of a technical process, including the sequence or

[36] W Kingston, 'Antibiotics, invention and innovation' (2000) 29(6) Research Policy 679–710.
[37] EPO Guidelines, Part G-II, para 3.1.
[38] For recent US Supreme Court confirmation, see *Mayo Collaborative Servs v Prometheus Labs, Inc* 132 S Ct 1289 (2012).
[39] The Court of Appeal in *Genentech Inc's Patent* [1989] RPC 147 confirmed that a claim to the practical application of a discovery did not relate to the discovery as such.   [40] T741/91 *HOWARD FLOREY/Relaxin* [1995] EPOR 541.

partial sequence of a gene, may constitute a patentable invention, even if the structure of that element is identical to that of a natural element.'[41] Note, in particular, that such a patent would *not* give a patentee any claim over naturally occurring elements *within* the human body.

> All of this has been confirmed by the House of Lords in *Kirin-Amgen v Hoechst Marion Roussel*[42] which summed up the current position thus:
>
> (1) to find a new substance or micro-organism in nature is a discovery and not an invention;
>
> (2) but if it is necessary to isolate and extract the substance—as will almost always be the case—then the relevant process, as well as the material obtained by this process, could both be patentable;
>
> (3) furthermore, if the material had no previously recognised existence, and can be adequately identified without reference to the process by which it is obtained, then it may be patentable per se.

11.18 We see, then, that it is possible through human endeavour to take something from an excluded category such as discovery and make it an invention and so patentable. The same is true with respect to the other two exclusions in this category when we go from the abstract to the tangible. Thus, while a scientific theory about a fifth dimension is just an example of an abstract concept and unpatentable, the application of that theory to produce a device that could dematerialise and re-materialise objects through space would be patentable, as would any related processes.[43] Similarly, a mathematical method in itself is purely intellectual and intangible, for example a shortcut method of long division, but a device which deploys this method may itself be patentable.[44] The distinction was considered by the EPO Technical Board of Appeal in *VICOM/Computer-related invention*[45] which related to an invention involving a mathematical method applied to data which resulted in an enhanced digital image on a computer. The core question was which aspects of this invention were patentable and where should the line be drawn between a mathematical method *as such* and an invention which was an application of such a method? The Board defined 'mathematical method' as something which is carried out on numbers and which produces a result in numerical form, that is, it remains in an abstract form. On this interpretation the Board rejected claims to a means of filtering data digitally on a conventional computer as they involved processes indistinguishable from a mathematical method. Conversely, the Board upheld claims to the method of using the mathematical method to process images because the output of the method was a real-world technical effect on the quality of the images. If you do no more than describe an existing property of something or even the reasons why it has that property, this will be mere discovery. Thus, in *Tate & Lyle Technology Ltd v Roquette Frères* it was not an invention to claim that maltotriitol—a known impurity in the manufacture of maltitol—can change the habit of the maltitol crystals. As the judge said: 'Roquette have explained why maltitol crystals take the habit that they do, but have not added anything else to the sum of human knowledge.'[46]

Aesthetic creations

11.19 Examples of aesthetic creations which are excluded include literary, dramatic, musical, and artistic works.[47] This should sound familiar as the realm of protection offered primarily by copyright. We have seen in the previous chapter how the international history of intellectual property protection has always drawn a division between industrial property on the one hand (Paris Convention 1883) and copyright and its related rights (Berne Convention 1886) on the other. The principal reason why aesthetic creations are

---

[41] Art 5(2) of the Biotechnology Directive, see note 5.
[42] [2005] RPC 9. The case is also known as *Kirin-Amgen Inc v Transkaryotic Therapies Inc (No 2)*.
[43] EPO Guidelines, Part G-II, para 3.2.   [44] EPO Guidelines, Part G-II, para 3.3.   [45] T208/84 [1987] OJEPO 14.
[46] [2010] FSR 1, upheld on appeal at [2010] EWCA 1049.   [47] See the Patents Act 1977, s 1(2)(b).

excluded is because they are not technical in nature and do not, normally, represent a technical contribution to our experiences. Their contribution lies elsewhere and their appreciation is usually entirely subjective. This is not to say that inventions cannot have aesthetic features, merely that those features cannot form the basis of patent protection if their sole contribution is in the realm of aesthetics. If, however, an aesthetic feature produces a de facto technical effect, then it may be patentable. The classic example that is cited in this regard is *ITS Rubber Ltd's Application*,[48] in which the main claim simply read:

> 1. A squash ball having a surface of a blue colour.

What possible difference could colour make to the functioning of a squash ball? Well, the claim was upheld on evidence that the particular colour chosen improved visibility of the ball during play. The contribution was therefore not merely aesthetic.[49] Note too that technical means which produce an aesthetic effect can be patentable even if the aesthetic effect itself cannot. For example, a machine may be set to produce a beautiful wood carving (not patentable in itself) but the new machine or the technical process used to program may be patentable. Similarly, a new printing technique to reproduce designs on fabric could be protected while the designs themselves would fall to another domain of intellectual property law. As always, the intellectual property office will be concerned not with the form of a claim but with the question of whether the essential nature of the invention is solely aesthetic or contains technical features.

 Discussion point   For answer guidance visit www.oxfordtextbooks.co.uk/orc/waelde3e/

The *ITS Rubber Ltd* case was decided under the 1949 Act. Do you think it would face any additional problems under the current legislation?

Schemes, rules, and methods for performing mental acts, playing games, or doing business, and programs for computers

11.20   Schemes, rules, and methods for performing mental acts, playing games, or doing business are similarly excluded in the first instance because of their abstract or intellectual character.[50] Much discussion in recent years has circled around the role of software and computers in this regard. Because of this and the particular vagaries of the case law, we pay particularly close attention to computer and software-implemented inventions in Chapter 12. We do no more here than lay out the general principles for exclusion.

Mental acts

11.21   Examples of methods of performing mental acts include schemes for doing arithmetic, learning to read, or speaking a new language. Similarly, a claim which merely lays out the steps for decision-making or the performance of a particular task will be rejected.

■ *Halliburton Energy Services v Smith International (North Sea) Ltd* [2006] RPC 2

This dispute before the Patent Court related to two patents concerning various features of drill bits for drilling in rock. In particular, two claims related to 'a method of designing a roller cone bit' comprising steps which involve calculating measurements and making adjustments to parameters to achieve

---

[48] [1979] RPC 318.   [49] EPO Guidelines, Part G-II, para 3.4.   [50] EPO Guidelines, Part G-II, para 3.5.

optimal effectiveness of the bit. Pumfrey J held that these claims were 'directed purely to the intellectual content of the design process and the criteria according to which decisions on the way to a design are made.' Accordingly, as framed, these were merely claims to a method for performing a mental act and would be excluded or require redrafting to take them outside the excluded category.[51]

> **? Question**
>
> Is a method of performing a mental act still excluded if it is performed by a computer rather than a human being?

■ *Fujitsu Ltd's Application* [1997] RPC 608

Applicants applied for a UK patent claiming priority from an earlier Japanese application in respect of an invention for a 'Method and Apparatus for creating synthetic crystal structure images'. The apparatus was a conventional computer programmed to allow an operator to select parameters, such as atoms or lattice vectors, to create pictorial representations of how the combined chosen structures would look. A Principal Examiner rejected the application, however, stating that it related both to a method for performing a mental act and to a program for a computer. The Court of Appeal similarly rejected the appeal stating that it is a question of fact whether a claim to an invention is to anything more than disqualified matter. It was relevant for the court that a significant amount of (human) input from an operator was required in order to carry out the task. Methods of solving a problem or providing advice remain examples of excluded methods of performing a mental act even if performed by a computer.[52]

11.22   This last point was doubted by the Court of Appeal in *Aerotel/Macrossan* but the comment was *obiter*.[53] This question was later answered in a new Practice Notice on Patentability of computer programs. The Notice followed the judgment of the Court of Appeal in *Symbian Ltd's Application*.[54] This case noted that one effect of the computer program exclusion is to prevent other excluded material becoming patentable merely by use of a computer in its implementation. The 'computerisation' of what would be a pure mental act if done without the aid of a computer would be objected to by examiners on the grounds of it being a mental act and a computer program as such.[55] Most recently, the position on the relationship between mental acts and computer programs was clarified in *Halliburton Energy Services Inc's Applications* in which it was held that the mental acts exclusion must be interpreted narrowly, that is, to involve human mental means.[56] This means that any claims to implement an invention with a computer will not fall foul of this particular exclusion, albeit that it might still be excluded as a computer program as such (see further later). A UK–IPO Practice Notice has followed suit.[57]

11.23   The EPO similarly tends to draw a distinction between mental acts which human beings can perform and automated acts which go beyond human capacity, for example in terms of the alacrity or difficulty

---

[51] Note, the objection here was to the form of the claims not to the substance of the invention which could have industrial utility, see Pumfrey J at para 218. Note also that part of this case was appealed to the Court of Appeal for lack of sufficiency and we discuss this at para 11.208.

[52] See also *Gale's Application*, para 11.33.

[53] 'we are doubtful as to whether the exclusion extends to electronic means of doing what could otherwise have been done mentally', per Jacob LJ, *Aerotel*, note 11, para 62.   [54] [2008] EWCA Civ 1066.

[55] UK–IPO, Practice Notice: Patents Act 1977: Patentability of Computer Programs (2008), [2009] Bus LR 625; also available at http://www.ipo.gov.uk/pro-types/pro-patent/p-law/p-pn/p-pn-computer.htm.

[56] [2011] EWHC 2508 (Pat), [2012] RPC 129.

[57] Practice Notice (Patents Act 1977: Patentability of mental acts), Intellectual Property Office, 17 October 2011, [2012] Bus LR 1264.

of the task.[58] Thus, method claims were allowed in *IBM/Editable document form*[59] for a method for maintaining formats of documents transferred between word processors, and in *IBM/Rotating Displayed Objects*[60] for a method ensuring high-precision rotation and manipulation of graphic images on screen. In other cases, however, text manipulation inventions have been denied protection for lack of technical contribution.[61] For example, the Technical Board of Appeal in *IBM/Document abstracting and retrieval*[62] rejected a computer system for creating and storing abstracts obtained from archives, inter alia, because the claims merely described an automated means of performing a task which could be carried out manually. It was not enough that the task was performed by technical means, that is, through a computer, the invention itself must make a technical contribution beyond that which can be done by humans.

Playing games

11.24   The rules on patentability of games were shaken up by the decision in *Shopalotto.com Ltd's Application*.[63] Strangely, the position had remained unchanged since an Official Ruling in 1926[64] despite the sweeping changes brought in by the Patents Acts of 1949 and 1977, not to mention innumerable revisions in the meantime.

■ *Shopalotto.com Ltd's Application* [2006] RPC 7

This was an appeal against a decision of the Deputy Director of the Patent Office that computer apparatus configured to provide a lottery playable via the Internet was unpatentable under section 1(2) of the Patents Act 1977. The appellant argued that he should benefit from the Official Ruling on board games handed down in 1926 and based on interpretation of the definition of an invention contained in section 93 of the Patents and Designs Acts 1907 and 1919. This was to the effect that board games are eligible for a patent if they involve apparatus for playing a game which include one or more playing pieces and a marked board together with instructions on how the game is played. The appellant argued that this should be applied by analogy to his online game. Pumfrey J made the powerful point that the 1926 Ruling cannot serve as a guide to the 1977 Act in the light of the EPC (1973). The patentability of games should be assessed in the same manner as all other potential excluded categories, and a claim which falls wholly into an established category should be excluded. Moreover, in the instant case the claimed invention was, in effect, to a general purpose computer providing a web server which makes no original contribution to the art.

11.25   The UK–IPO has since issued a Practice Notice on patentability of games.[65] This follows the judgment in *Shopalotto* and confirms that the Official Ruling from 1926 will no longer be used.[66]

Methods of doing business

11.26   Innovative ways of tackling everyday business problems are not normally patentable. These include new methods of bar-coding banking materials to improve customer services,[67] display mechanisms on buses

---

[58] See *Research in Motion UK Ltd v Inpro Licensing SARL* [2006] RPC 20 at para 186 where Pumfrey J found technical effect in 'computers running faster and transmitting information more efficiently...' On appeal: [2007] EWCA Civ 51 (although the point here made at first instance was not contested).   [59] T110/90 [1995] EPOR 185.

[60] T59/93, unreported, available on the EPO website at http://legal.european-patent-office.org/dg3/pdf/t930059eu1.pdf.

[61] T38/86 *IBM/Text clarity processing* [1990] EPOR 606.   [62] T22/85 [1990] EPOR 98.   [63] [2006] RPC 7.

[64] Official Ruling 1926(A), (1926) 43 RPC Appendix, p i.

[65] *Practice Notice 'Patents Act 1977: Patentability of games'* [2006] RPC 8, as amended in the light of the judgment in *Aerotel/Macrossan*. The current version is available at http://www.ipo.gov.uk/p-pn.htm.

[66] See too *IGT's Applications* [2007] EWHC 1341 (Ch).

[67] *Good News Pty Ltd's Application* (Patent Office Hearing Officer: BL O/124/84).

to let customers know if they are picking up or dropping off,[68] coding mechanisms to protect customers' identity,[69] a scheme to allow prisoners to trade sentence time for corporal punishment,[70] and a method to facilitate introductions between people wearing mutually recognisable artefacts, such as rings.[71] Note how under the last two examples, 'business' enjoys a wide interpretation in law and does not necessarily have to imply commercial interests.

11.27 The mantra remains the same, however: does the invention solve a technical problem rather than merely tackle a business problem?

11.28 It was previously thought that the exclusion of a method of doing business referred to the conduct of an entire business endeavour,[72] but this has been rejected by the Court of Appeal in *Aerotel/Macrossan* where it was held that there is no reason for such a narrow interpretation and that business methods should not be restricted to abstract matters or completed transactions. Double-entry bookkeeping is neither abstract nor an output of a business transaction, but it remains a method of doing business.[73] On this basis, then, the court rejected Macrossan's claim for an automatic method of providing the necessary documents to incorporate a company because this method was for the essence of the business itself, that is, to provide advice and documentation.

11.29 As we have seen elsewhere, the mere automation of a process or operation does not change its essential character. Thus in *Merrill Lynch's Application*[74] a known computer system was programmed in known computer language to provide a data-processing-based system for implementing an automated trading market for securities. The Court of Appeal held that if there was any contribution to human knowledge it was in the production of a trading system, that is, a method of doing business. Moreover, the fact that this may be an improvement on previous systems is irrelevant: 'the prohibition in section 1(2)(c) is generic; qualitative considerations do not enter into the matter.'

11.30 Methods of doing business which solve technical problems can be patentable. This was confirmed by the European Patent Office in *PENSION BENEFIT SYSTEMS/Controlling pension benefits systems*[75] which related to a computer system that performed a number of pension-related tasks, including calculations, speculation, and the control of the benefit system to ensure periodic payments to subscribers. Despite rejecting this particular appeal for want of technical character, the Technical Board of Appeal confirmed that a method claim that relates to a method of doing business can be patentable as long as it is technical, and that apparatus claims, even if they are programmed to function in a business environment, cannot be excluded because Article 52 EPC does not mention apparatus. A caveat to add to this is that it is dangerous to attempt to dress up a business method claim as an apparatus claim because the task of the patent offices and the courts is to examine the substance not for the form of the claim. Moreover, an attempt to get around a technical problem by modifying a business method—rather than by solving the problem by technical means—is insufficient to bring technical character to an invention.[76]

11.31 Many business method claims are linked to computer-implemented inventions, as the previous example demonstrates. Because of this, we continue a fuller discussion of this category of exclusion at paras 12.111ff.[77]

[68] *Crawford v Jones* [2005] EWHC 2417 (Pat).   [69] *Peter Williams' Application* (IPO Hearing Officer: BL O/038/07).
[70] *Melia's Application* (Patent Office Hearing Officer: BL O/153/92).
[71] *John Lahiri Khan's Application* (Patent Office Hearing Officer: BL O/356/06).
[72] *Macrossan's Patent Application* [2006] EWHC 705 (Ch).
[73] *Aerotel*, note 11, paras 69–70, citing the French and German texts of the EPC in support of this interpretation.
[74] [1988] RPC 1.   [75] [2002] EPOR 52.   [76] See T258/03 *HITACHI/Auction method* [2004] 12 OJEPO 575.
[77] The Court of Appeal confirmed in *Symbian Ltd's Application* [2009] RPC 1 that a business method implemented on a 'conventional computer system' would be excluded as a pure business method.

The UK–IPO Manual points out that many business arrangements implemented over the Internet have been refused protection. These include:

- a method for offering personalised financial products over the Internet;[78]
- a method of creating and distributing advertising material;[79]
- a system to allow a client to monitor progress made on a building site via the Internet;[80]
- a system for ordering food over the Internet.[81]

It seems clear that merely providing a service or assistance over the Internet will not be enough on its own to merit patent protection, but each innovation must be considered on its own merit to determine if it displays the necessary *technical effect*.

11.32   The UK–IPO has issued a Practice Notice in response to the increased number of applications relating to business method patents in recent years.[82] This provides a mechanism to invite an applicant to a hearing earlier in the application process than normal. If the application is refused it will be referred immediately to a Hearing Officer for a ruling on patentability and the applicant will be given an opportunity for an oral hearing. All other procedures are suspended at this time until the Hearing Officer gives a ruling. This need not be lengthy since the UK–IPO has articulated many times the reasons for refusal in such cases.[83] The applicant will be provided with a brief report that is intelligible and adequately explains the reasons for refusal[84] by reference to previous decisions. This procedure is designed to cut down lengthy and costly correspondence on matters which should be straightforward to settle.

Computer programs

11.33   ■ *Gale's Application* [1991] RPC 305

The applicant discovered a means of calculating a square root with the assistance of a computer and modified a silicon chip (ROM) to perform this function. He claimed the ROM chip with its particular circuitry embodying the instructions. The examiner objected that this was no more than a computer program and the case eventually made its way to the Court of Appeal. It was held that instructions to be used for the operation of a computer were not patentable. Physical alterations to the chip itself were immaterial as mere conventional means to allow the chip to perform its function—which was the ordinary running of a computer. The appeal was denied.

11.34   We have already pointed out at several junctures that patents for computer programs and computer-implemented inventions have received special attention in recent years. The current approach to their patentability is probably best summed up by Pumfrey J in *Shopalotto.com's Application*:

> The real question is whether there is a *relevant* technical effect, or, more crudely, whether there is enough technical effect: is there a technical effect over and above that to be expected from the mere loading of a program into a computer? From this sort of consideration there has developed an approach that I consider to be well established on the authorities, which is to take the claimed programmed computer, and ask what it contributes to the art over and above the fact that it covers a programmed computer. If there is a contribution outside the list of excluded

---

[78] *Accucard's Application* (BL O/145/03).   [79] *Adgistics Ltd's Application* (BLO/297/04).
[80] *Ashizawa's Application* (BL O/201/03).   [81] *Fujitsu's Application* (BL O/121/04).
[82] UK–IPO Practice Notice, 'Patent applications relating to methods of doing business', 24 November 2004, as amended, available at http://www.ipo.gov.uk/pro-types/pro-patent/p-law/p-pn.htm.
[83] See Practice Notice 'Patents Act 1977: Interpreting section 1(2)' [2002] RPC 40.
[84] See House of Lords in *South Bucks District Council and another v Porter (No 2)* [2004] UKHL 33.

matter, then the invention is patentable, but if the only contribution to the art lies in excluded subject matter, it is not patentable.[85]

11.35 This is subject to the approach now laid down by the Court of Appeal in *Aerotel/Macrossan*, although it has been emphasised that this should not make much practical difference. It is likely to mean, however, that claims to programs themselves, even if on a carrier, will fail at the third hurdle of the *Aerotel* test as specifically excluded matter. Macrossan's application failed because it was held that his contribution was the provision of a computer program which could be used to carry out his method of providing documentation. So the essence of the claim was entirely to excluded matter.[86]

11.36 A decision of the UK–IPO confirmed this and it was also one of the first decisions to apply the Court of Appeal's four-point test. In *Nintendo Co Ltd's Application*[87] the application concerned a game machine for a virtual kart race. The advance with this game lay in the fact that the computer would take over when a player crashed and run a sequence which ensured a smooth transition of the virtual vehicle back onto the track and facing in the correct direction. Existing machines did not do this. The Examiner took the view, however, that the contribution was concerned with moving the player from one game state to another and that this was executed wholly by computer program elements and therefore excluded from protection. There was accordingly no need to consider the fourth element of the test as to technical effect.[88]

11.37 In *AT & T Knowledge Ventures' Application and another*,[89] the judge offered five 'signposts' to assist in determining whether there is a technical contribution. These are (quoting the UK–IPO Patents Manual):

i) whether the claimed technical effect has a technical effect on a process which is carried on outside the computer;

ii) whether the claimed technical effect operates at the level of the architecture of the computer; that is to say whether the effect is produced irrespective of the data being processed or the applications being run;

iii) whether the claimed technical effect results in the computer being made to operate in a new way;

iv) whether there is an increase in the speed or reliability of the computer;

v) whether the perceived problem is overcome by the claimed invention as opposed to merely being circumvented.

Although these have been confirmed as non-binding,[90] their utility lies in offering practical consideration of application across the entire field.

11.38 The EPO is slightly more cavalier in these matters. It maintains[91] that while 'programs for computers' are excluded as such, if the claimed subject matter has a technical character this will be sufficient to allow patentability. And so, 'if a computer program is capable of bringing about, when running on a computer, a further technical effect going beyond these normal physical effects, it is not excluded from patentability...' This is so even if the program itself is claimed or if it is claimed in tandem with its carrier.[92] This comes very close to saying that computer programs per se are patentable. It is almost a reversal of the approach in the UK which is concerned to know if the kernel of the invention falls wholly into a category of excluded matter. The EPO made clear in *Duns Licensing*[93] that it did not approve of the approach taken in the UK. Most recently, in G03/08 A Referral by the President of the EPO to the Enlarged Board

[85] *Shopalotto*, note 6, para 9.   [86] *Aerotel*, note 11, paras 73–74.   [87] BL O/377/06.
[88] See also *Astron Clinica and others v The Comptroller General of Patents* [2008] EWHC 85 (Pat).   [89] [2009] FSR 19.
[90] See *Really Virtual Co Ltd v UK Intellectual Property Office* [2012] EWHC 1086 (Ch).
[91] EPO Guidelines, Part G-II, para 3.6.
[92] T935/97 *IBM/Computer Programs* [1999] EPOR 301 and T1173/97 *IBM/Computer Programs* [2000] EPOR 219.
[93] *DUNS LICENSING ASSOCIATES/Estimating Sales Activity* [2007] EPOR 38.

of Appeal (EBA), the EBA opined that it saw the developments in the EPO and other jurisdictions as 'a legitimate development of the law',[94] albeit that it held the referral to be inadmissible in its own terms.

 Discussion point For answer guidance visit www.oxfordtextbooks.co.uk/orc/waelde3e/

What is the underlying rationale for excluding computer programs in Europe especially when they are patentable in most other legal systems? Does the role of copyright in software protection make a difference? Can this approach be sustained?

11.39 Despite widespread patenting of inventions related to computer software throughout Europe, the *Gowers Review of Intellectual Property* (2006) recommended that the UK should maintain its policy of not extending patent rights beyond their current limits. The Review found mixed evidence of the success of 'pure' software patents, particularly from the United States where the evidence actually seems to indicate that the software industry grew exponentially in the *absence* of patent protection. Other evidence suggests that where protection is available it is used negatively to restrict competitors rather than positively to encourage further innovation.[95]

11.40 The patentability of computer programs in the UK was clarified in *Symbian Ltd's Application*, in which the Court of Appeal tried to find a way between the previous Court of Appeal authorities and the approach taken by the EPO. The main issue the court clarified was that the technical contribution of the invention to the state of the art must be considered. Whether this is done during the third or the fourth step of the test is less important. This ruling has led to a change in the UK–IPO Practice Notice for Patentable Subject Matter,[96] confirming that the four-step test will continue to be used. When dealing with computer programs, it must be considered what the program does as a matter of practical reality. Where a program results in a computer running faster or more reliably, it may be considered to provide a technical contribution even if the invention solely addresses a problem in the programming.[97] It is interesting that the UK Practice Notice confirms a point of divergence with the EPO.[98] It is not sufficient merely to include claims to computer hardware to avoid the exclusion.

Presentations of information

11.41 The concern of this exclusion is the *content* of information. No claim will be sustained if it relates solely to the expression of information or the conveyance of meaning or decisions on where and how to display information.[99] Patent law is not in the business of giving protection to pretty pictures, TV images, radio signals, books, sounds, diagrams, codes, or symbols which derive their value from the meaning they convey to human beings. Thus in *Townsend's Patent Application*[100] the problem to be solved was the thorny issue of how to ensure fair distribution of the treats found behind the doors on an advent calendar and to prevent the early-riser in the family from scoffing the lot! Mr Townsend's solution was to put markings on the doors to indicate the turn of each user to open a door. He argued that this was not

---

[94] See UK–IPO, Patents Manual, April 2013, para 1.29.7.

[95] *Gowers Review of Intellectual Property* (HM Treasury, 2006), para 4.114, available at http://webarchive.nationalarchives.gov.uk/+/http://www.hm-treasury.gov.uk/d/pbr06_gowers_report_755.pdf.

[96] Practice Notice (PO: Patents Act 1977: Patentability of computer programs) [2009] Bus LR 625.

[97] Practice Notice (PO: Patents Act 1977: Patentability of computer programs) [2009] Bus LR 625, para 5

[98] See *Dell Products LP's Application* (BL 0/321/10).

[99] *Autonomy Corp Ltd v Comptroller General of Patents, Trade Marks and Designs* [2008] EWHC 146 (Pat).

[100] [2004] EWHC 482 (Pat).

a presentation of information because the correct interpretation of the exclusion only covered *expression* of information and not *provision* of information, that is, it was restricted to *how* information is conveyed and not *what* is conveyed. It is the difference between the advent calendar being designed in the shape of a sleigh (how) and stating 'three more days to Christmas' (what). Laddie J disagreed and held that the exclusion covers both instances of presenting information on an ordinary interpretation of the provision. The calendar was refused protection.

11.42   This means that any method or means of conveying information which is characterised only by the content of the information will be excluded. It does not matter that some physical device or apparatus is used to convey the information or that such a device or apparatus can be moved around.

■ *Crawford v Jones* [2005] EWHC 2417 (Pat)

The application related to a display system for buses to indicate to passengers whether the bus was in picking-up or setting-down only mode. The claims were to Boarding and Exit Bus Indicators, being visual or audible apparatus. Notwithstanding, the application was refused, inter alia, as solely a method of presentation of information. The only advance in the art was the nature of the information displayed on the front of the bus but this was not of a technical nature.

11.43   The implication of a decision like *Crawford* is that if a presentation of information *is* of a technical nature then it might be patentable, and this is indeed true. As we now know, solving a pre-existing problem by technical means is the way to make a technical contribution. In *Cooper's Application*[101] the problem was how to fold a newspaper without hindering reading, and the successful invention was to arrange the layout of text to allow this. Similarly, in *Fishburn's Application*[102] the particular arrangement of text on a ticket meant that information was not lost when the ticket was torn and the patent was upheld. Most recently, in *Gemstar-TV Guide International v Virgin Media Ltd*[103] the dispute related to three patents relating to electronic versions of programme guides that help consumers to navigate the ever-increasing range of viewing options available. Two of the patents were revoked as involving merely presentation of information. As was said: 'The purpose of the invention is to achieve the display of information in a user-friendly way by user-friendly means' (para 45). And as Mann J confirmed: 'what achieves patentability is some real world technical achievement outside the information itself.'

11.44   These questions came into play again in *HTC Europe Co Ltd v Apple Inc*[104] involving a dispute over four patents related to mobile phone technologies. Of interest for present purposes was the feature of one of the inventions which is familiar to any user of hand-held devices: the 'sweep to unlock screen' image. It was argued that this was a mere presentation of information because it simply told the user how their gesture was progressing. This was rejected by Mr Justice Floyd who held that the particular invention did not fall foul of this particular exception: 'There is a sense in which the invention provides a technical effect outside the computer, namely an improved switch. Moreover this is a real world effect which is not limited to the presentation of information.'[105] Although this was an obvious (and therefore unpatentable) feature to produce in today's world, the invention was not caught by the particular exclusion of a simple presentation of information.

11.45   The EPO Guidelines make it clear that if the presentation of information has new technical features then there could be patentable subject matter in the information carrier, or in the process or apparatus for presenting the information, or even in the manner of presentation itself.[106] Examples include a

---

[101] 19 RPC 53.   [102] 57 RPC 245.   [103] [2009] EWHC 3068 (Ch), aff'd [2011] EWCA Civ 302.
[104] [2012] EWHC 1789 (Pat).   [105] [2012] EWHC 1789 (Pat), para 236.   [106] EPO Guidelines, Part G-II, para 3.7.

communication system using a particular code to represent characters (eg pulse code) or a gramophone record having a particular groove to allow stereo recordings. Put differently, an invention can function by presenting information and still be patentable as long as the sum and substance of that invention is not only found in the presentation of the information.

11.46   The general European approach is laid out in the decision of the Technical Board of Appeal in *KONINKLIJKE PHILIPS ELECTRONICS/Picture retrieval system*.[107] The invention related to a system of picture storage and retrieval and included a claim to a record carrier which provided recorded picture data to any part of the system and consisted of a picture access data structure which controlled the operation of the retrieval device. The data structure was the novel part of the invention but the claim to its record carrier was refused as a means of presenting information. The Technical Board of Appeal upheld the appeal against this, however, and found that the data structure provided the necessary technical nature to the invention. Moreover, it sought to draw a distinction between two types of information: cognitive data and functional data. In doing so it relied on an earlier decision of the Board in *BBC/Colour Television Signal*[108] which distinguished between the example of a TV signal solely characterised by the information per se, for example the pictures and sound, and a TV signal which is defined in terms of the TV system through which it is transmitted. Both transmit (or present) data, but the former is cognitive data which convey meaning to human beings, while the latter is functional/technical data where meaning in a human sense is irrelevant. As the Board said 'information must not be confused with meaning'. The exclusion is concerned with subject matter which merely conveys cognitive or aesthetic content directly to a human.[109] The instant invention was patentable because the record carrier was concerned with functional data and the operation of a system which produced a new technical effect. It is to be contrasted with *XEROX/Document summaries*[110] where the claimed invention related to a summary of indicators in a summary document that indicated where the section originated in the complete document. This was held to be mere presentation of information resulting from the processing of summarising and which had no connection with the technical means to produce it.

 Exercise

This decision also contains an explanation of the rationale for this particular exclusion. Look this up and then consider it against all the other possible rationales for the exclusions in Article 52 EPC.

Key points on exclusions under Article 52

- It is essential to read the provisions of the law carefully. If we look back at Article 52(2) it states: 'The following *in particular* shall not be regarded as inventions...'[111] and Article 52(3) states: 'The provisions of paragraph 2 shall exclude patentability of the subject-matter or activities referred to in that provision only to the extent to which a European patent application or European patent relates to such subject-matter or activities *as such*' (emphasis added)

- This means that the list of exclusions is *non-exhaustive*, and indeed in the UK the Secretary of State has the power to expand it (Patents Act 1977, s 1(5))

---

[107] T1194/97 [2000] OJEPO 525, [2001] EPOR 25.   [108] T163/85 [1990] OJEPO 379.
[109] See T603/89 *MARKER/Beattie* (1992) OJEPO 230 (visible marking of musical keys).   [110] T1086/07 [2012] EPOR 21.
[111] The equivalent provision in the Patents Act 1977, s 1(2), states: 'It is hereby declared that the following (*among other things*) are not inventions...'

> • The *as such* qualification is extremely important. It means that only claims which fall squarely within a category of excluded matter will be struck down. Inventions which straddle patentable and non-patentable matter can survive if the technical features meet the other criteria for patentability

11.47 There is one example of the courts excluding matter from protection for something which is not in Article 52 EPC/section 1(2) of the Patents Act 1977. In *Lux Traffic Controls Ltd v Pike Signals Ltd and Faronwise Ltd*[112] the invention related to apparatus to control traffic through a system that detected non-motion in vehicles and responded by holding the traffic lights to allow drivers more time. Although the court allowed the apparatus claims, Aldous J had this to say:

> s.1(2) of the Act comprises a non-exhaustive catalogue of matters or things which are not patentable. Although not specifically mentioned, I believe a method of controlling traffic as such is not patentable, whether or not it can be said to be a scheme for doing business. The field expressly excluded by the section concerns mere ideas not normally thought to be the proper subject for patents which are concerned with manufacturing.

11.48 This may do no more than express the common rationale underpinning many of the exclusions that abstracts, such as ideas, are not a suitable case for patenting. By the same token, it demonstrates that the categories of exclusions are not closed and policy in the future may expand the list of non-inventions. Legislative changes would, however, require to be initiated by the Secretary of State and laid before both House of Parliament for approval.

Exceptions to patentability

11.49 Let us turn now to the exceptions to patentability contained in Article 53 EPC 2000 and reproduced in section 1(3) and (4) and Schedule A2 of the Patents Act 1977.

Article 53

European patents shall not be granted in respect of:
(a) inventions the commercial exploitation of which would be contrary to 'ordre public' or morality; such exploitation shall not be deemed to be so contrary merely because it is prohibited by law or regulation in some or all of the Contracting States;
(b) plant or animal varieties or essentially biological processes for the production of plants or animals; this provision shall not apply to microbiological processes or the products thereof;
(c) methods for treatment of the human or animal body by surgery or therapy and diagnostic methods practised on the human or animal body; this provision shall not apply to products, in particular substances or compositions, for use in any of these methods.

Morality, *ordre public*, and plant and animal varieties

11.50 It has sometimes been claimed that morality has nothing to do with patent law, but this is clearly nonsense.[113] The decision whether or not to grant a patent is not some mechanistic process which merely involves a checklist of technical details. Rather, it entails many nuanced considerations and value judgements on whether the numerous criteria for patentability have been met. The entire intellectual property system is based on fundamental notions of merit and justice concerning the appropriateness or otherwise of granting protection in the form of a monopoly. This is what the morality provision in patent law is about.[114]

---

[112] [1993] RPC 107.   [113] We will not name the guilty; they know who they are.
[114] For a good analysis, see L Bently and B Sherman, 'The ethics of patenting: towards a transgenic patent system' (1995) 3 Med LR 275.

11.51   There is, however, a lot of confusion about the role and remit of the morality provision which has been fuelled in recent years by the advent of biotechnology patents.[115] Indeed, the provision had rarely been invoked before the arrival of this technology but a few decades on we have a rich literature on the topic, a series of EPO rulings and even a harmonising European Biotechnology Directive. We discuss the specifics of biotechnology in our next chapter. For now, we outline the nature of the morality provision and how it has been interpreted to date.[116]

11.52   EPC 2000 revised the text of Article 53 to bring it into line with Article 27(2) of TRIPS.[117] Previously, the provisions concerned 'inventions the publication or exploitation of which would be contrary to *ordre public* or morality'. Now the concern is with the commercial exploitation of the invention. It is arguable that much of the confusion which has surrounded the interpretation of these provisions has stemmed from a lack of clarity about the purpose of the law as well as its limits. The purpose of the law has been stated in the EPO Guidelines to be: 'to exclude from protection inventions likely to induce riot or public disorder, or to lead to criminal or other generally offensive behaviour.'[118] But the denial of a patent cannot prevent the use of an invention; it may, at best, act as a disincentive to producing it. Moreover, it is not possible to deny a patent merely because exploitation is prohibited by law.[119] Nonetheless, various groups have seized on the morality provision in an attempt to strike down patents in certain controversial areas such as animal testing or stem cell technologies or environmental impact. The strong suspicion is that the real objection is to the science not to the patent per se. If so, this use of the morality provision is largely futile.[120] The revised version of Article 53 better reflects the true limit of the patent system which is to grant a commercial monopoly. It is entirely correct, therefore, that we may have concerns about the appropriateness of *commercial* exploitation.[121] So far there have been few cases looking at the interpretation of this revised article. However, morality jurisprudence with regards to biotechnological inventions is developing rapidly.

11.53   The inherently subjective nature of morality and the increasing presumption in favour of patentability have led the patent granting institutions of Europe to interpret the morality provisions of patent law very narrowly.

■ *HARVARD/Oncomouse* [1991] EPOR 525

The EPO allowed a patent on a transgenic animal that had been bred as a research tool for cancer studies despite objections that it was immoral to patent life, especially when that life was created simply to suffer. The Examining Division held[122]—on a strictly utilitarian analysis—that the potential benefit to mankind outweighed the suffering of these animals, and as such was no bar to patent protection. Moreover, the specific wording of the claim related to 'non-human mammals' and this was deemed to be much wider than 'animal varieties' and therefore was not expressly excluded by Article 53(b). It was stated that 'An "animal variety" or "race animal" is a sub-unit of a species and therefore of even lower

[115] Y Min, 'Morality: an equivocal area in the patent system' (2012) 34(4) EIPR 261–265.
[116] See generally O Mills, *Biotechnological Inventions: Moral Restraints and Patent Law* (2005).
[117] TRIPS, Art 27: 'Members may exclude from patentability inventions, the prevention within their territory of the commercial exploitation of which is necessary to protect *ordre public* or morality, including to protect human, animal or plant life or health or to avoid serious prejudice to the environment, provided that such exclusion is not made merely because the exploitation is prohibited by their law.'
[118] EPO Guidelines, Part G-II, para 4.1   [119] See the Patents Act 1977, s 1(4) and EPC 2000, Art 53(a).
[120] This is not to deny that there may be perfectly legitimate concerns about the commercialisation of technologies.
[121] Although note the EPO Guidelines state: 'The EPO has not been vested with the task of taking into account the economic effects of the grant of patents in specific areas of technology and of restricting the field of patentable subject-matter accordingly', para 4.1.3, and see too G1/98 NOVARTIS II/*Transgenic plant* [2000] OJEPO 111, reasons 3.9.
[122] The Examining Division originally declined to consider the morality of the grant as outside its competence ([1990] EPOR 4) but was subsequently directed to do so by the Technical Board of Appeal ([1990] EPOR 501).

ranking than a species. Accordingly, the subject-matter of the claims to animals *per se* is considered not to be covered by...Article 53(b).'

11.54 Opposition proceedings were immediately instituted against the decision and these remained unresolved for a decade, during which time the patent remained in force. A resolution was eventually found in 2001 and the patent stood but its scope was restricted to 'transgenic rodents containing an additional cancer gene' rather than 'any non-human transgenic mammal';[123] it was further restricted in 2004 to cover merely 'transgenic mice'.[124] The trend towards allowing patenting was continued in *LELAND STANFORD/Modified Animal*[125] where the patent for an immuno-compromised chimera mouse was upheld and the EPO ruled that the controversial nature of the technology did not, in and of itself, act as a bar to patenting.

11.55 The provisions of Article 53 were reined in even further in *PLANT GENETIC SYSTEMS/Glutamine Synthetase Inhibitors*.[126] Here the EPO held that it was only prepared to entertain challenges on grounds of morality if actual evidence of harm to society could be demonstrated. The case concerned the patentability of crops that had been genetically modified to be resistant to herbicides, and the concern was a threat to the environment if such hybrids were released. Extending its ruling from *Oncomouse*, however, the Technical Board of Appeal sought verifiable data that the environment was at risk from the invention *before* it would apply the *Oncomouse* balancing test.[127] No evidence could be produced and the patent was granted, despite other findings that a high degree of moral opprobrium towards such inventions existed among sectors of the European population. The Board opined that survey evidence and opinion polls indicating distaste for patents over genetically modified organisms were insufficient evidence by which to judge the overall European moral tone.

11.56 It should be noted, however, that the claims in the patent to the plant itself were nevertheless revoked under Article 53(b). It was held that because the genetically altered plant could reproduce and pass on its resistance in a relatively stable manner, it qualified as a 'plant variety' and as such should be excluded from patentability. The argument that the plant was a product produced by a microbiological process was rejected because the insertion of the resistant gene was but one small part of the general process of replicating the plant.[128]

11.57 The permissibility of patenting genetically engineered plants was later considered by the EBA which held that only claims to 'plant varieties' *as such* are excluded from patent protection.[129] While this extends to genetically engineered plant varieties it does not rule out the possibility that 'plant-related products', including plants themselves, can receive patent protection. For present purposes, then, suffice it to note that the practical outcome of these plant cases is that as long as the patentee does not specifically claim a *variety* in his patent application, then a genetically engineered or otherwise 'invented' plant will not face successful challenge on the basis of Article 53.[130] As to the meaning of 'essentially biological processes'—which are excluded from patentability[131]—the EBA seemed to endorse the provisions of the Biotechnology Directive which had been adopted by the time of the decision. Article 2(2) of the

[123] By way of contrast, the Supreme Court of Canada revoked the Harvard patent over Oncomouse itself (but not the process to manufacture it) in December 2002, claiming that, 'A higher life form is not patentable because it is not a 'manufacture' or "composition of matter"': see *Harvard College v Canada (Commissioner of Patents)* [2002] SCJ No 77. This ruling cannot now be changed except by express legislation.
[124] T315/03 *HARVARD/Transgenic animal* [2005] EPOR 31.   [125] [2002] EPOR 2.
[126] *PLANT GENETIC SYSTEMS/Glutamine Synthetase Inhibitors* [1995] EPOR 357.
[127] *PLANT GENETIC SYSTEMS/Glutamine Synthetase Inhibitors* [1995] EPOR 357 at 373.
[128] The EBA refused to hold that *Oncomouse* and *PGS* were in any way inconsistent in *Inadmissible referral* [1996] EPOR 505.
[129] G1/98 *NOVARTIS II/Transgenic plant* [2000] EPOR 303.
[130] Confirmed in T775/08 *MONSANTO/Glyphosate tolerant alfalfa* [2011] EPOR 28.
[131] Note, *products*, eg plants or animals, produced by such processes are not expressly excluded, see *Oncomouse*, para 11.53.

Directive states: 'A process for the production of plants or animals is essentially biological if it consists *entirely* of natural phenomena such as crossing or selection' (emphasis added). The prospect of this being a problem for patentees in the future therefore looks slim. But, while 'microbiological processes or the products thereof' are patentable, this is not carte blanche to claim that genetically engineered processes or products always qualify, since the overarching limitation will be to assess the substance of the claims to ensure that a plant variety is not claimed. Once again, however, this is not problematic, since it directs patent attorneys to pay particular attention to the way in which claims are drafted. Whether it leads to sophistic distinctions is another matter. Two referrals to the EBA on the meaning of 'essentially biological processes' in recent years are discussed in Chapter 12.[132]

11.58   In *HOWARD FLOREY/H2 Relaxin*[133] the EPO affirmed that the morality provision should only be applied to prevent the grant of patents that would universally be regarded as outrageous. The patent in suit related to a genetically engineered human protein, H2 relaxin, which women produce during childbirth to soften the pelvis. The patent had been challenged on a number of grounds: (1) that the grant of the patent would be tantamount to slavery of women because it involved the 'dismemberment of women and the sale of their parts'; (2) that it was offensive to human dignity to use pregnant women for profit; and (3) because DNA was life itself, patenting of human DNA was intrinsically immoral.[134] The Office rejected each of these claims. DNA, it said, is not life but merely a means to carry chemical information. Moreover, the taking and modification of samples was in no way an approximation to slavery. This was particularly not so when the donors had given their free and informed consent. This, in itself, was considered enough to accord respect to human dignity. Interestingly, however, it is not clear what the women consented to, and in particular whether they were ever told of the prospect of patents being granted over material derived from them and the consequent economic potential.[135]

11.59   An example of the restrictive approach to the interpretation of the morality clause is found in *MICHIGAN STATE UNIVERSITY/Euthanasia compositions*.[136] Numerous parties objected to the patent for both product and use claims in respect of a composition for administering humane euthanasia in lower animals. Various objections were lodged, ranging from the concern that 'lower animal' could encompass 'human', that the product might be used more broadly in society, and that it was an affront to the human right to life under Article 2 of the European Convention on Human Rights. All arguments were rejected and the position confirmed that exceptions should be interpreted narrowly. In particular, objections should concern the *publication or exploitation* of the invention (interpreting EPC 1973, Art 53(a)) and therefore many arguments simply fell outside the remit of the Board, for example whether the development of the composition itself was immoral or, indeed, the act of granting it a patent is immoral. It was held that the claims were perfectly clear and unambiguous in their application to lower mammal life forms, and not humans. Moreover, the practice of humane euthanasia in animals was widely practised and accepted and so in conformity with societal notions of morality and *ordre public*.

11.60   This all culminates in the current EPO Guidelines which provide that:[137]

> A fair test to apply is to consider whether it is probable that the public in general would regard the invention as so abhorrent that the grant of patent rights would be inconceivable. If it is clear that this is the case, objection should be raised under Article 53(a); otherwise not. The mere possibility of abuse of an invention is not sufficient

[132] G2/07 and G1/08 *Essentially Biological Processes* [2011] EPOR 27. For comment prior to decision, see SJR Bostyn, 'How biological is essentially biological? The referrals to the Enlarged Board of Appeal G-2/07 and G-1/08' (2009) 31(11) EIPR 549.

[133] *HOWARD FLOREY/Relaxin* [1995] EPOR 541.   [134] *HOWARD FLOREY/Relaxin* [1995] EPOR 541.

[135] See G Laurie, 'Patents, patients and consent: exploring the interface between regulation and innovation regimes' in H Somsen (ed), *The Regulatory Challenge of Biotechnology* (2007), Ch 11.

[136] Available on the EPO website at http://legal.european-patent-office.org/dg3/pdf/t010866eu1.pdf.

[137] EPO Guidelines, Part G-II, para 4.1

to deny patent protection pursuant to Art. 53(a) EPC if the invention can also be exploited in a way which does not and would not infringe 'ordre public' and morality.

11.61 The problem of the inherent subjectivity as to what constitutes immoral conduct was tackled by the EU legislature in the Biotechnology Directive by listing four examples of inventions that should automatically be excluded. These are: (1) processes for cloning human beings; (2) processes for modifying the germ line genetic identity of human beings; (3) uses of human embryos for industrial or commercial purposes; and (4) processes for modifying the genetic identity of animals which are likely to cause them suffering without any substantial medical benefit to man or animal, and also animals resulting from such processes.[138] The Court of Justice of the European Union (CJEU) has confirmed that Article 6(2) leaves no discretion to member states with regard to the unpatentability of the processes and uses which it sets out because the very purpose of the provision is to give definition as to exclusions.[139]

11.62 These have now also been incorporated into the Implementing Regulations of the EPC as rule 23d to ensure consistency of approach as between the Union's member states and the EPO. It is very debatable whether this has resulted in any more clarity. A recent debacle concerned the patentability of human embryonic stem cell inventions which involve the destruction of human embryos for their production. This has been confirmed to be caught by the provisions of the Directive by the CJEU. We consider the decision and its implications in the next chapter (paras 12.54ff).

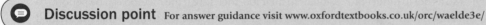

Discussion point For answer guidance visit www.oxfordtextbooks.co.uk/orc/waelde3e/

Do you consider that inventions involving the destruction of human embryos should be prohibited by the morality provisions? On what basis do you justify your response?

Exercise

Which factors do you think should be weighed in the balance in considering the morality of patents and inventions?

Methods of treatment of the human or animal body

11.63 EPC 2000 moved this provision from Article 52(4) under EPC 1973 to Article 53(c). Previously, methods of treatment were excluded from protection because they were considered not capable of industrial application,[140] and now they are specifically excluded as exceptions to patentability. This make no difference in practice but is thought to be more in keeping with the underlying reasons for such an exclusion, namely, to ensure that patents do not unduly interfere with matters of public health,[141] rather than to maintain a fiction about industrial applicability. The deep irony about this provision, however, is that it has always been accompanied by a rider that *substances* or *compositions* for use in a method of treatment or diagnosis are patentable.[142] The challenge was summed up by the Court of Appeal in *Bristol-Myers Squibb v Baker Norton Pharmaceuticals:*[143]

---

[138] Biotechnology Directive, Art 6(2). See also Sch A2 to the Patents Act 1977, as amended.
[139] C-456/03 *Commission v Italy* [2005] ECR I-5335, at points 78–79.
[140] See the Patents Act 1977, s 4(2) which was amended by the Patents Act 2004, s 1, and see now Patents Act 1977, s 4A(2).
[141] See G05/83 *EISAI/Second medical use* [1985] OJEPO 64.
[142] See now the Patents Act 1977, s 4A(2) and Art 53(c) EPC 2000.   [143] [2001] RPC 1.

[Section 4(2)—excluding methods of treatment] has the limited purpose of ensuring that the actual use, by practitioners, of methods of medical treatment when treating patients should not be the subject of restraint or restriction by patent monopolies. The difficulty is to decide whether the restraint concerns a method of treatment as opposed to that which is available for treatment.

> **Question**
>
> Why do you think that methods of treatment are unpatentable but substances or compositions are patentable? Is that not somewhat inconsistent since they are both concerned with public health?

11.64   We have to establish the parameters of this provision in order to make sense of it. Note, for example, that it does not exclude *all* methods of treating the human or animal body, only those related to 'therapy' and 'surgery'. So what do these mean? Similarly, it is only diagnostic methods which are 'practised on' the human body that are excluded. We must explore the case law to understand more.[144]

Therapy

11.65   Therapy concerns the medical treatment of disease, including cure and prevention.[145] The approach is the same whether we are considering animal or human bodies. The 'medical' or 'veterinary' nature of the treatment is an important determinant in deciding whether a claim falls foul of the provision. This is because the provision is designed so as not to hinder professionals in their job, therefore if the method can be performed by someone who does not have the specialised professional skills, it is more likely to imply that the method is patentable.[146] By the same token, if a procedure requires oversight from a professional, such as laser modification of a lenticule implanted on the cornea, then the invention will normally fall within the exclusion.[147] Irrespective of who performs it, the method must be for some therapeutic purpose, and non-therapeutic purposes are patentable. Thus, in *Schering's Application*[148] it was held that contraception is not a therapy because pregnancy is not an illness. The inclusion of some therapeutic element in a contraceptive method would, however, invoke the exclusion.[149] This has recently been confirmed by the EPO Technical Board of Appeal in *BAYER SCHERING PHARMA AG/Composition for contraception*.[150] While reiterating that contraceptive use is not therapeutic because pregnancy is not an illness, the Board stressed that the inherent features of the principal claim to reduce common side effects of contraceptive use through reduce-dose hormones *was* therapeutic. The patent failed as a result. The matter has to be decided 'exclusively on the basis of the actions carried out during such use and the effects obtained.' Disclaimers cannot avoid the reality if a therapy is encompassed by the claims. Thus the circumstances of use are also relevant. So, methods of termination of pregnancy,[151] inducing labour, and *in vitro* fertility treatment are all considered unpatentable because all must be carried out under medical supervision. Treatments to kill parasites or head lice are 'therapy'.[152]

11.66   What happens if a part of you is taken away for treatment and returned? This was considered in *Schultz's Application* before the UK Patent Office which concerned extracorporeal blood dialysis and filtration methods.[153] It was held that this method was unpatentable because there was no need for the treatment

---

[144] Because the concern of this provision is interventions designed to maintain life or improve health, it does not extend to methods that bring about death nor does it affect the patentability of methods carried out on the dead body, see T182/90 *SHELL/Blood flow* [1994] OJEPO 641.

[145] *Unilever (Davis's) Application* [1983] RPC 219.   [146] T245/87 *SIEMENS/Flow measurement* (1989) OJEPO 171.

[147] T24/91 *THOMSON/Cornea* [1995] OJEPO 512.

[148] [1971] RPC 337. The equivalent in the EPO is T74/93 *BRITISH TECHNOLOGY/Contraceptive method* [1995] OJEPO 712.

[149] T820/92 *GENERAL HOSPITAL/Contraceptive method* [1995] OJEPO 113.   [150] [2012] EPOR 23.

[151] *Upjohn (Kirkton's) Application* [1976] RPC 324.

[152] See T116/85 *WELLCOME/Pigs I* [1989] OJEPO 13. Cf *Stafford-Miller's Application* [1984] FSR 258 decided under the 1949 Act.

[153] BL O/174/84, discussed in the Examination Guidelines for Patent Applications relating to Medical Inventions in the UK Intellectual Property Office, August 2008, para 41.

to be carried out on the body itself to be excluded. That particular qualification relates only to diagnostic methods (see para 11.73). Note, however, the exclusion applies on the proviso that the human material is returned to the same human body.

11.67   *Enhancement* of the human or animal body, for example through cosmetic treatments for humans or treatment of stock animal to improve meat or milk yields, is generally not thought of as 'therapy'. Thus, hair and nail treatments are patentable,[154] as are treatments for hair loss.[155] But sometimes a method can have both cosmetic and therapeutic benefits. If the two cannot be separated out then the method is, once again, unpatentable. For example, in *L'ORÉAL/Protection against UV*[156] the method of skin protection against the effects of ageing (cosmetic) also had a physiological and beneficial effect on the skin (therapeutic) and so was held to be unpatentable.[157] In contrast, in *ROUSSEL-UCLAF/Thenoyl Peroxide*[158] it was possible to distinguish a method of cleansing the skin of comedones (blackheads) as personal hygiene (patentable) from a use of the method as a treatment for acne (unpatentable).

11.68   The EBA confirmed in G01/03 that disclaimers to exclude unpatentable methods of treatment by therapy or surgery, or methods of diagnosis practised on the human or animal body, are in principle allowable and do not constitute added matter. This is in accordance with UK Office practice. However, if claims are limited, either by disclaimer or otherwise, to patentable methods, then there must be support in the description for a non-therapeutic method, and this reflects *BAYER SCHERING PHARMA AG/Composition for contraception* discussed previously at para 11.65.

 Exercise

How would you categorise the use of skin patches to assist people in giving up smoking? Is this a therapy? Is smoking an illness? What about diet pills which can be used both by people who are morbidly obese and those who want to lose weight for aesthetic reasons?

Surgery

11.69   It must be remembered that 'surgery' in this context is a technical term of art used in patent law. It has been held to involve any non-insignificant[159] intervention on the body by operation or manipulation in an attempt to maintain the life or health of the human or animal body.[160] Unlike the previous category of therapy, the law does not draw a distinction between therapeutic and non-therapeutic interventions; it is concerned only to know if the method of intervention is surgical in nature. Thus cosmetic surgery techniques are generally excluded as well as curative surgery (but see later). Moreover, 'surgery' has enjoyed a wide definition in the sense that it has not been restricted to methods that involve a direct invasion of the body; hence the term 'manipulation' covers non-invasive techniques such as re-setting of broken bones or repositioning. Once again, however, the need for technical skill and expertise in the performance of the method is a significant factor in establishing if the exclusion applies. Thus in *Occidental Petroleum's Application*[161] it was stated that the involvement of a surgeon necessarily meant that

---

[154] See *Joos v Commissioner of Patents* [1973] RPC 79.   [155] T453/95 *Redken*, EPO, unpublished.

[156] T1077/93 *L'ORÉAL/Protection against UV* [1997] OJEPO 546.

[157] The same issue of inseparability of therapeutic and non-therapeutic applies for methods to remove plague from teeth: T290/86 *ICI/Cleaning plaque* [1992] OJEPO 414.

[158] T36/83 [1986] OJEPO 295. Similarly, see T144/85 *DU PONT/Appetite suppressant* [1986] OJEPO 30.

[159] The use of needles for the extraction of blood or administration of medicines is considered 'insignificant' for these purposes, see T182/90 [1994] OJEPO 641.

[160] T35/99 *GEORGETOWN UNIVERSITY/Pericardial access* [2000] OJEPO 447.

[161] BL O/35/84, see UK–IPO Guidelines, para 48.

the procedure was surgical in nature; by the same token, it does not follow that the absence of a surgeon means that a method is not surgical if it still requires a degree of skill in its execution, for example by a nurse.[162]

Question

Do you think that the work of tattoo or piercing artists would count as 'surgery' under the law?

11.70 The jurisprudence of the EPO has been in flux in recent years and we welcome the EBA decision from February 2010 which sought to clarify matters. Part of the problem lay is previous rulings which cast some doubt on the status of cosmetic interventions and indeed on the surgical exclusion generally. For example, in *GENERAL HOSPITAL/Hair removal method*[163] the invention concerned a method of hair removal from the skin by optical radiation and the Technical Board of Appeal felt the need to return to the *travaux préparatoires* of the EPC to determine the original purpose behind these provisions. It held that 'the intention of the legislator was that only those treatments by therapy or surgery are excluded from patentability which are suitable for or potentially suitable for maintaining or restoring the health, the physical integrity, and the physical well being of a human being or an animal and to prevent diseases.'[164] The Board opined that the therapeutic/non-therapeutic distinctions applied to 'therapy' should now also extend to 'surgery'. The appeal against exclusion was upheld on the basis that the hair removal method did not fulfil any of the purposes behind the exclusion.[165]

Discussion point For answer guidance visit www.oxfordtextbooks.co.uk/orc/waelde3e/

What would the position be in respect of breast augmentation surgery or correction of the shape of the nose? Are these always and necessarily 'cosmetic'?

11.71 The UK–IPO has stated that it will continue to follow its prior case law which draws no such distinction and is concerned only to know if the method is 'surgical'.[166] But in the particular circumstances of hair removal, this would probably not be considered as 'surgical' in the UK.[167] The EPO EBA has directly tackled this point holding that the therapeutic/non-therapeutic distinction does *not* apply in the case of 'treatment by surgery'. That is, if the claimed method is 'surgical' in nature then the exclusion will apply. The case is *MED-PHYSICS/Treatment by surgery*.[168] The main question was whether a single surgical step in an otherwise patentable method would bring the entire method under the surgical exclusion, even when the surgical step was not necessarily aimed at maintaining life and health.

---

[162] Citing *Allen's Application* (BL O/59/92) (method of inserting markers in body for NMR and CT scans).

[163] T383/03 [2005] OJEPO 159.   [164] T383/03 [2005] OJEPO 159, p 4 of judgment.

[165] See further T9/04 *KONINKLIJKE PHILIPS ELECTRONICS NV/Medical diagnostic imaging* [2007] EPOR 10, point 6 of the Reasons: where a method claim was not struck down because it was 'not a method suitable or potentially suitable for maintaining or restoring the health, the physical integrity, and the physical well-being of a human being or animal and to prevent diseases.' The claimed method allowed the use of CT scans and X-rays to gather information about positioning a catheter in patients. This simply yielded an 'intermediate result' of information to assist in treatment and did not involve treatment per se.

[166] UK–IPO Guidelines, para 47 citing *Unilever (Davis's) Application* [1983] RPC 219.

[167] See *Commonwealth Scientific & Industrial Research Organization's Application* (BL O/248/04).

[168] Case G1/07: Referral under Art 112 (1)(a) EPC by the Technical Board of Appeal T992/03 (Methods for treatment by surgery) to the Enlarged Board of Appeal; Decision of the Enlarged Board of Appeal [2010] EPOR 25.

The procedure involved a method of obtaining images of patients requiring that a contrast agent be injected into the heart. Did this invasive element prove fatal to the entire claim, even although it was in no way treatment or curative in its own right? The case throws up numerous issues, the two most important of which for present purposes are: (1) what is the purpose of the 'surgical' exclusion in patent law? and (2) what counts as 'surgical' anyway? The EBA held that the rationale for the exclusion is 'to free [medical] practitioners from being potentially hampered by patents in the application of the best possible treatment on their patients'; moreover, there is nothing in the *travaux préparatoires* or in the EPC itself to suggest that this should be limited to therapeutic or curative surgery.[169] The EBA then confirmed what it saw as the underlying principle of the law and the jurisprudence to date, viz, 'a method claim falls under the prohibition of patenting methods for treatment by therapy or surgery now under Article 53(c) EPC if it comprises or encompasses at least one feature defining a physical activity or action that constitutes a method step for treatment of a human or animal body by surgery or therapy.' It must be remembered that if a method is to be patentable it must be *neither* treatment *nor* surgical *nor* a diagnostic method (on this last point, see more later in the text). These are cumulative provisions and so even if something does not fall within the definition of 'treatment' or 'diagnostic method' it might still fall foul of the 'surgical' provision. This clearly begs the question of what is surgery? It is here that the EBA departed from existing case law in holding that the technical definition which has grown up over the years is too broad and does not appropriately reflect technical realities; these now mean that many interventions or manipulations of the human body can be carried out perfectly safely and without a (high) level of professional medical skills or risk to patients. A new concept of 'surgery' in patent law is therefore required. The EBA stopped short of providing a definition, but it did point to key elements that should be weighed in the balance at first instance. Thus the exclusion should operate to strike down claims (1) over the kinds of interventions for which the medical profession is specifically trained, (2) over physical interventions on the body which require professional medical skills, and (3) over methods which involve health risks even when carried out with requisite medical professional care and expertise. Other factors that might be of relevance include the degree of complexity involved and the degrees of intervention or risk involved but none is determinative and each case will have to be judged on its facts.

 Exercise

What are the implications of this recent ruling from the EPO? It seems both broad and narrow at the same time—broad because it upholds a wide role for the exclusion of *any* method if it involves surgery, but also narrow in that it now purports to restrict what counts as 'surgery'. Can you think of examples of interventions that might fall on either side of the line? What about the facts in the instant case? Would this count as 'surgery'?

11.72   Are there any further limitations to this exclusion? Well one further and important point dealt with by the EBA in *MED-PHYSICS/Treatment by surgery* was the role of disclaimers. The question is this: if you run the risk of falling foul of the surgery exclusion because one element of your procedure counts as 'surgery', is it possible simply to disclaim or exclude this as part of your claim for protection? The EBA confirmed that there is nothing to prevent you attempting to do so, but it will be a question of fact whether the resulting disclosure is sufficient as a matter of law. The EPC (Art 84) requires that patent claims must be clear and disclose all of the essential features of the invention needed to reproduce it.

---

[169] See BL O/058/10 in the UK–IPO in which this criterion was crucial in upholding the patentability of anti-wrinkle treatment using narrow wavelength mechanisms.

It will be a matter for first instance bodies to determine in each case whether this is so. A final point to note is that none of this affects claims to what are known as 'purely technical methods', that is, method claims about the operation of a device used in health care as opposed to claims to health-related methods which themselves involve treatment, surgery, or diagnostic methods.[170] Let us now turn to consider the last of these.

Diagnostic methods practised on the body

11.73   There has been some confusion and dispute over the years about the precise meaning of the exclusion of diagnostic methods,[171] and this has now been considered by the EBA in an attempt to bring clarity to the subject.

■ **G01/04 CYGNUS/Diagnostic methods**[172]

This case involved a referral on a point of law from the President of the EPO to the EBA. In summary, the essential question was whether 'diagnostic methods practised on the human or animal body' excluded only those claims to methods containing *all* of the procedural steps necessary to a medical diagnosis—for example, the examination phase *and* the data collection phase *and* the comparison phase *and* the discovery of deviation phase *and* the deductive clinical decision phase—or whether the exclusion applied if any *one* of these steps could be used for diagnostic purposes or related to diagnosis. It was held that:

> The method steps to be carried out prior to making a diagnosis as an intellectual exercise...are related to examination, data gathering and comparison...If only one of the preceding steps which are constitutive for making such a diagnosis is lacking, there is no diagnostic method, but at best a method of data acquisition or data processing that can be used in a diagnostic method...[173]

11.74   In other words, only claims which encompass all of the steps required to come up with a definitive diagnosis are excluded from protection. It means that methods which may represent interim steps in a differential diagnosis and which may be a value in diagnosis will be patentable in themselves as long as they do not lead directly to a diagnosis. Examples include the taking of a sample, methods of internal imaging (eg X-rays or MRI scanning), and methods for measuring temperature. This is a particularly narrow interpretation of the exclusion provisions, but one which the EBA felt able to adopt on the basis that it is a 'matter of principle' that European patents should be granted for inventions that meet the requirements of Article 52(1).

11.75   This does not mean that a claim must laboriously lay out all steps in a process; rather, it must adequately describe the invention to the extent of the monopoly claimed,[174] and if the method *in fact* allows a diagnosis to be made it will be excluded.

11.76   The exclusion is also subject to the proviso that the method is practised *on the human or animal body*. The EBA has decided that this means that the patient or animal must be present to perform the step in question. Furthermore, to be excluded *all* of the technical steps in the method must be performed on the body, but this does not include the final step of joining the dots and actually deciding on a diagnosis because this is a purely intellectual exercise and therefore not technical.[175]

---

[170] T9/04, note 165, is an example of this. If, however, there is a functional link to the effects of the device on the body this will be excluded. Once again, this will fall to be considered on the technical circumstances of each case. See further para 11.117.

[171] Compare, eg, T385/86 *BRUKER/Non-invasive measurement* [1988] EPOR 357 and T964/99 *CYGNUS/Device and method for sampling substances* [2002] OJEPO 4.

[172] [2006] EPOR 15.   [173] [2006] EPOR 15, para 6.2.2.   [174] Patents Act 1977, s 14(5)(a).

[175] See further T1197/02 *AUSTRALIAN NATIONAL UNIVERSITY/Detection of glaucoma* [2007] EPOR 9.

Exercise

Is it possible to reconcile the decisions of the Enlarged Boards of Appeal in G01/04 (diagnostic methods) and G01/07 (treatment by surgery)? Hint: read G01/07 for that EBA's own take on the issues? Do these kinds of decisions point to the need for a single body of appeal as we discuss in Chapter 10?

11.77 Finally, what about implements or other apparatus that are used for the purposes of therapy, surgery, or diagnosis—are these affected by the exclusion? Well, the exclusion relates to *method claims* and not *product claims*, and so normally medical devices should be as patentable as non-medical devices. But an invention which is characterised by its use—for example, 'in surgery'—will not be granted protection. For instance, in *TELETRONICS/Cardiac pacing*[176] the principal claim was to a method of operating a pacer in accordance with the required cardiac output while a person is exercising, and the Technical Board of Appeal held that this was, in essence, a claim involving a step that was a method of treatment. This was enough to defeat the patent and amendment at the opposition stage was not permissible. Similarly, in *EXPANDABLE GRAFTS/Surgical device*[177] it was decided that claims to products which can only be assembled inside the human or animal body by means of a surgical step are not permissible. The lesson lies in careful drafting of claims in the first place. As we discuss in para 11.72, claims to 'purely technical methods' about the operation of a device should succeed.

Protectable subject matter

11.78 Section 1(1) of the Patents Act 1977 states:

> A patent may be granted only for an invention in respect of which the following conditions are satisfied, that is to say—
>
> (a) the invention is new;
> (b) it involves an inventive step;
> (c) it is capable of industrial application;
> (d) the grant of a patent for it is not excluded by subsections (2) and (3) below...

We have already considered the extent and meaning of subsections (2) and (3). Let us now consider what we might call the 'positive criteria' for patentability. Each of these criteria sets a threshold hurdle that the prospective patentee must clear in order to secure a patent. The rationale for each criterion is different, but collectively they serve to ensure that only previously unavailable, highly innovative, and useful inventions receive patent protection.

Novelty

11.79 The policies underpinning the novelty requirement are to prevent the disutility of re-inventing of the wheel, to ensure that matter which is already in the public domain is not brought (once again) under private monopoly control, and to protect parties who have been happily using a product or process

---

[176] T82/93 [1996] OJEPO 274.   [177] T775/97 [2002] EPOR 24.

publicly from being stopped from doing so on the grant of a patent over the same or substantially the same product or process.

11.80   There are certain key questions that we must ask in order to know whether an invention will be new. These are:

(1)   What constitutes the public domain for these purposes?

(2)   How much information about an invention must have been in the public domain before this becomes a problem for patent purposes?

11.81   Novelty is covered by section 2 of the Patents Act 1977, as amended, and the equivalent provisions are found in Articles 54 and 55 EPC 2000. Section 2(1) of the 1977 Act provides that 'An invention shall be taken to be new if it does not form part of the state of the art'. The state of the art is the public domain for patent purposes. It is defined in section 2(2) as:

> The state of the art in the case of an invention shall be taken to comprise all matter (whether a product, a process, information about either, or anything else) which has at any time before the priority date of that invention been made available to the public (whether in the United Kingdom or elsewhere) by written or oral description, by use or in any other way.

11.82   This is clearly an extremely wide definition which is global in scope and which covers any manner by which information about an invention might be disclosed. Something becomes part of the state of the art on the day that it is made available to the public, and this does not even require that members of the public have actual sight of the information, merely that they can have access to the information, either freely or on payment of a fee.[178] An obscure article may, therefore, be published in a journal that no one ever reads but it would still be part of the state of the art. Moreover, this publication can be anywhere in the world and in any language. Note too, by implication, it does not matter *who* makes a public disclosure, and this includes the prospective patentee himself. This is why it is so important to keep information about an invention out of the public domain until you have secured a *priority date*. You should recall from the previous chapter that the priority date is normally the filing date of the patent application with an intellectual property office, unless an earlier filing has taken place in another office within the previous 12 months, in which case that date becomes the priority date.[179] Novelty is only tested by reference to the state of the art *prior* to the priority date.

11.83   The state of the art is forever expanding—we can only add to it; information, once added, always remains a part of it. It is dangerous to pass information to third parties without stipulating a confidentiality clause, ideally by contract; even communication to one individual can be enough to make information public.[180] Allowing the public an opportunity to examine the details of an invention in circumstances where a skilled person would become aware of the core technical features of the invention would amount to public disclosure.[181] It is even possible for something to become part of the state of the art if it is merely seen in public if a skilled person[182] on seeing it would be able to discern its core features with sufficient detail to reproduce the invention.[183] Equally, 'publicly available' is a relative term. The details of an invention must not only be physically accessible but also sufficiently intellectually intelligible

---

[178] See further the EPO Enlarged Board of Appeal in G1/92 *Availability to the Public* [1993] EPOR 241.   [179] See para 10.12.

[180] *Bristol-Myers Co's Application* [1969] RPC 146. In T482/89 *TELEMECHANIQUE/Single sale* [1992] OJEPO 646 a single sale was enough to anticipate.

[181] *Milliken Denmark AS v Walk Off Mats Ltd and another* [1996] FSR 292 (hire of mats to the public would allow an expert to discover its novel qualities and perform the invention).

[182] See *Folding Attic Stairs Ltd v Loft Stairs Co Ltd* [2009] FSR 24.

[183] See *Lux Traffic Controls Ltd v Pile Signals Ltd and Faronwise Ltd* [1993] RPC 107. Cf *Kavanagh Balloons Pty Ltd v Cameron Balloons Ltd* [2004] RPC 5.

by the skilled person using their common general knowledge. Thus Floyd J held in *H Lundbeck A/S v Norpharma SpA*[184] that 'matter may be contained in a document but so submerged in it as not to be available.' Finally, and for the purposes of testing novelty only, it is important to note that the state of the art includes the content of any patent applications designating the UK[185] published on or after the priority date of the invention in question.[186] Article 54(3) EPC 2000 makes the contents of European patent applications relevant to the state of the art.

11.84   If an invention already exists in the state of the art then we say that a subsequent patent application or invention is *anticipated*.

■ *Pall Corporation v Commercial Hydraulics (Bedford) Ltd* [1990] FSR 329

The patent in suit concerned 'hydrophilic microporous membranes' for filters. The membranes were capable of being wetted through in less than one second yet when heated to a temperature just below the softening temperature the membrane reverted to a hydrophobic material. An action of infringement was brought by the plaintiffs which was met with a counterclaim of revocation on the ground of lack of novelty. It was alleged that the plaintiff had anticipated their own invention by prior use. The plaintiff had given sight of the claimed product to a potential customer. No details of the nature or construction of the membranes were disclosed to the customer or the other suppliers represented at the test, and the nature of the membrane could not have been ascertained simply by sight of the membrane. The plaintiff also sent samples to other potential customers but these were sent under conditions of confidence and the customers knew that the membranes were experimental and secret. It was held that (1) the use of the membranes in the comparison test did not place the invention in the state of the art because the use was not a sale or supply in the course of trading nor did it make the samples available to the public; and (2) the sending of samples to potential customers in confidence did not amount to anticipation because this did not make the samples available to the public. The obligation of confidence ensured that the relevant information was kept in the private, as opposed to the public, domain.

11.85   The law of confidence can be an extremely important tool in the protection of information surrounding the development of an invention in the period prior to application and the award of a priority date. Unlike the United States which provides for 'grace periods'—the period of one year prior to filing is exempt from consideration for the purposes of testing novelty—Europe will consider everything made available to the public up to the priority date. Compare this decision with *Monsanto Co (Brignac's) Application*[187] in which a process patent was sought concerning the production of nylon having finely divided carbon black uniformly dispersed therein. Thirty or 40 copies of a *Technical Information Bulletin* containing details of pigmentation of synthetic fibres (including nylon) were given to salesmen of the company developing the process. Opposition to the grant of the patent on the ground of lack of novelty was successful because the salesmen were considered by the court to be members of the public and in the absence of a fetter on them this amounted to prior publication. No evidence was led that the brochures had in fact been distributed to customers, but this was not considered to be necessary in order for anticipation to have taken place.

---

[184] [2011] EWHC 907 (Pat).

[185] It is important to remember that this can therefore cover applications via the UK–IPO, the EPO, and/or the Patent Cooperation Treaty (PCT). In this last regard, the application must not only have been published under the PCT (Art 21) but it must also have entered the national phase for UK patents or the regional phase for European (UK) patents, ie that the necessary translation has been carried out and the appropriate fee paid: see Patents Act 1977, ss 79, 89, 89A, and 89B. The abstract of any patent application does not form part of the state of the art for these or any other purposes: Patents Act 1977, s 14(7).

[186] Patents Act 1977, s 2(3), as amended. Note, this does not apply to the test for inventive step, see Patents Act 1977, s 3, discussed at para 11.113.   [187] [1971] RPC 153.

11.86   There are strict rules about which kinds of document can anticipate an invention and in which circumstances. Many of these were established many years ago and remain relevant today.

■ *General Tire and Rubber Co v Firestone Tyre and Rubber Co* [1972] RPC 457

This was a decision by the Court of Appeal. The plaintiffs claimed infringement of their patent for oil-extended rubber by the defendants who counterclaimed for revocation of the patent, inter alia, on grounds of novelty. It was alleged that the patent had been anticipated by certain documents published prior to the priority date of 20 November 1970. The patent in suit was for a process for making a compound suitable for tyre treads by mixing synthetic rubber with oil and carbon black (a mixture referred to as 'oil-extended rubber') and for the product thus made. The earlier publications relied upon by the defendants were:

(1) a Viennese patent dated 17 May 1943 for 'Semperit (a)' (compound with carbon black for tyres);

(2) a Viennese patent dated 15 January 1945 for 'Semperit (c)' (extended synthetic rubber);

(3) an English patent dated 2 August 1944 'Wilmington' (oil and latex invention);

(4) two articles published in August 1947 and March 1950 in 'Rubber Age' (experiments using oil and carbon black to soften rubber).

It was held that:

• Alleged anticipatory matter must be interpreted at the date of its publication and without regard to subsequent events.[188]

• The alleged anticipatory material must be interpreted by a reader skilled in the relevant art at the relevant date. If the art is one having a highly developed technology, the notional skilled reader to whom the document is addressed can be a team, whose combined skills would normally be employed in that art in interpreting and carrying into effect instructions such as those contained in the document to be construed.

• Alleged anticipatory materials must be considered separately: it is not permissible to combine earlier unconnected publications to show anticipation[189] (compare with the concept of 'mosaicing' discussed later in terms of inventive step, para 11.113).

• If, in light of the previous points, the alleged anticipatory material contains a clear description of, or clear instructions to do or make something which would infringe the prospective patentee's patent if granted, the patent in suit will have been shown to lack the necessary novelty.[190]

• By corollary, if the prior publication contains a direction which is capable of being carried out in a manner which would infringe the patentee's claim, but would be at least as likely to be carried out in a way which would not do so, the patent in suit will not have been anticipated (although it might fail on grounds of obviousness, see later).

• 'A signpost, however clear, upon the road to the patentee's invention will not suffice. The prior inventor must be clearly shown to have planted his flag at the precise destination before the patentee.'[191]

---

[188] The EPO authority on this is T/396/89 *UNION CARBIDE/High tear strength polymers* [1992] EPOR 312.

[189] *British Ore Concentration Syndicate Ltd v Mineral Separation Ltd* (1909) 26 RPC 124.

[190] Endorsed by the House of Lords in *Synthon v SmithKline Beecham* [2006] RPC 10 at paras 21–25. The prior art need not disclose exactly the same invention in all its facets, see *Glaverbel SA v British Coal Corporation* [1995] RPC 255, but it must normally disclose all of the technical features of the claim which is under scrutiny.

[191] See too *Koninkijke Philips Electronics NV v Princo Digital Disc GmbH; Koninkijke Philips Electronics NV v Chin-Shou Kuo* [2003] EWHC 1598 (Ch).

- Given this, the *General Tire and Rubber* patent had not been anticipated by the prior publications. None of the publications planted a flag at the spot of GTR's invention. They were concerned essentially with different aims and different means of realising those aims.

11.87 The test to be applied is the 'notional skilled reader', and we might see this as a similar policy device to that used in tort/delict, viz, the 'reasonable man'.

11.88 The need to plant a flag in the exact spot claimed by the patent in suit means that prior publications or prior uses of matter which incidentally disclose a future invention might not anticipate the invention. In fact, the House of Lords has considered what is required for anticipation and has confirmed that this comprises two elements. (1) prior disclosure, and (2) enablement.

■ *Synthon BV v Smithkline Beecham plc* [2006] RPC 10

The dispute related to a salt of Paroxetine which is used to treat depression. Although one salt form of the compound had been marketed for some time, both parties to the dispute discovered, more or less simultaneously, another salt form which was far more suitable for pharmaceutical use (PMS). Both applied for patent protection within a few months of each other. Synthon's application referred to a group of salts of which one was PMS. Before this was published, however, Smithkline claimed priority on its own application and was successful in receiving a patent for a particular form of crystalline PMS. Synthon brought proceedings claiming that the invention had been anticipated by their own patent application on the basis of section 2(3) of the Patents Act 1977. It was held that there had been anticipation and this required the proof of two matters: first, that the Synthon application disclosed the invention which had been patented (prior disclosure) and, secondly, that an ordinary skilled man would be able to perform the disclosed invention if he attempted to do so by using the disclosed matter and common general knowledge (enablement).

11.89 This is a refinement on the approach to date.[192] The court stressed that these are two separate, albeit related, matters. As we have seen previously, a *prior disclosure* must be construed as it would have been understood by a skilled person at the date of the disclosure and not with the benefit of hindsight. Moreover, in order to anticipate, a prior disclosure must disclose subject matter such that, if performed by the skilled person, it would *necessarily* infringe the patent.[193] The prior disclosure must firmly plant the flag on the patentee's invention: 'the infringement must not merely be a possible or even likely consequence of performing the invention disclosed by the prior disclosure; it must be necessarily entailed. If there is more than one possible consequence, one cannot say that performing the disclosed invention will infringe.'[194] But note: the prior disclosure need not be expressed in the same form or by reference to the same parameters as the invention. Indeed, people do not even need to *know* what they are making[195]—the question is whether the relevant essential features of the invention are in the public domain.[196]

11.90 *Enablement* requires that the ordinary skilled person must be able to perform the invention from the information disclosed.[197] This is closely allied with the concept of sufficiency, which we discuss later in

---

[192] Followed in *Wagner International AC v Earlex Ltd* [2012] EWHC 984 (Pat); Ch D (Patents Ct); *Mölnlycke Health Care v Brightwake* [2011] EWHC 376 (Pat); Official Transcript; Ch D (Patents Ct) and *HTC Corp v Yozmot 33 Ltd* [2010] EWHC 786 (Pat); Official Transcript; Ch D (Patents Ct).

[193] See *Boegli-Gravures SA v Darsail-ASP Ltd* [2009] EWHC 2690 (Pat).

[194] *Synthon*, para 11.88, per Lord Hoffmann at para 23.

[195] T303/86 (*CPC Int*) [1989] 2 EPOR 95 (a process for the manufacture of flavour concentrates was anticipated because it could not be distinguished from known cooking and frying processes which, albeit incidentally, produced versions of the said flavour concentrates. It was irrelevant that the chefs in question had no idea that this was so).

[196] *Merrell Dow Pharmaceuticals Inc and another v HN Norton & Co Ltd and others* [1996] RPC 76.

[197] Note, Synthon made a mistake in describing PMS in its application but this was not a problem because it was held that the notional skilled person would nonetheless produce Smithkline's invention if he set out to make it using Synthon's instructions.

this chapter (paras 11.206ff). In *Synthon*, Lord Hoffmann said that he accepted that enablement meant the same thing in that case as it means for sufficiency, but he also remarked that this might not always be so because the perspective of the skilled person can change. For example, when considering sufficiency the skilled person is attempting to reproduce the invention, while in a test for novelty the prior art may have disclosed the invention but not specifically identified it—the task of the skilled person is therefore different. In similar fashion, the role of the skilled person changes depending on whether we are discussing prior disclosure or enablement. With the former, the role is to understand what is meant by the prior disclosure, while with enablement the concern is whether the skilled person can 'work' the invention. It is important, therefore, to see the two concepts as distinct.

Exercise

Can you envisage any circumstances where there would be prior disclosure but no enablement? Could the converse hold true?

11.91   The House of Lords had ruled on novelty on a number of occasions prior to this decision. Various elements of those decisions remain valid.

■ *Asahi Kasei Kogyo KK's Application* [1991] RPC 485

The patent claimed by Asahi Kasei Kogyo KK was for a human protein (Human Tissue Necrosis Factor) produced by genetic engineering and useful in the treatment of tumours. The application was rejected by the Patent Office on the grounds of lack of novelty under section 2(3) of the Patents Act 1977 because of information contained in another pending patent application filed by Dainippon. Although this second application had a filing date later than the application in suit, it claimed priority from an earlier application which disclosed and claimed the protein but did not disclose any method of preparing it. The appeal went all the way to the House of Lords.

Key dates:

- Asahi Kasei Kogyo KK filed in UK on 4 April 1985 (priority claimed United States, 6 April 1984);

- Dainippon filed European patent on 26 February 1985 (priority claimed Japan, 6 March 1984).

It was held that matter comprised in the state of the art for the purposes of sections 2(2) *and* 2(3) had to be the subject of an *enabling disclosure*, that is, there must be enough information available to allow the skilled person to reproduce the invention. This is now refined in the light of the two-part test in *Synthon*. The point remains, however, that an invention is not made available to the public merely by a published statement of its existence, unless the method of 'working' the invention is so obvious as to require no explanation. There was no anticipation because the Dainippon application did not disclose the means to make the protein.

11.92   The interpretation given to section 2(3) can lead, albeit in rare circumstances, to double patenting. Imagine the following scenario:

6 March 1984	6 April 1984	26 February 1985	4 April 1985
Japan	United States	Europe	UK
Not enabling	Priority claimed	Protein claim	Protein claim

If the UK application is not anticipated by the European application because the former can claim priority from the US application, and if the Japanese application is not an enabling disclosure, then the UK patent can be granted. However, because the European patent claims priority from the Japanese patent, the state of the art in respect of the European patent will be tested prior to 6 March 1984, and will thereby exclude the contents of the US patent application. In this way it is also possible for the European patent to be granted. The House of Lords recognised this possibility in *Asahi* but considered that it would occur only rarely.[198]

■ *Merrell Dow Pharmaceuticals Inc & another v HN Norton & Co Ltd and others* [1996] RPC 76

Merrell Dow obtained a patent in 1972 for terfenadine, an antihistamine drug. When the patent expired in 1992 other companies (including Norton) began to manufacture and sell the drug. Merrell Dow had carried out extensive research into antihistamines in the intervening period and discovered that, once ingested, terfenadine was rapidly metabolised by the human liver and a by-product was produced: an acid metabolite. It was further discovered that this acid metabolite was almost exclusively responsible for the antihistamine effects of terfenadine. Merrell Dow sought and received a patent over the acid metabolite in 1980. When after 1992 other companies began to produce terfenadine, Merrell Dow brought infringement proceedings against them in respect of the production of the acid metabolite inherent in the use of terfenadine. This was so even although the existence of the acid metabolite was not known to the companies prior to the priority date of the patent over the acid metabolite. The defendants counterclaimed that the 1980 patent had been anticipated by the use of terfenadine in clinical trials and the specification of the appellant's earlier patent which had published information on the chemical composition of terfenadine and that it should be taken for its antihistamine effect. The appeal was taken to the House of Lords.[199]

It was held that:

- The appeal was dismissed. The House emphasised the need to interpret the 1977 Act to accord with the provisions of the EPC and therefore felt able to refer to decisions of the EPO in interpreting the EPC. Although such decisions are not binding on UK courts they are highly persuasive.

- In essence, the revocation claim was based on two arguments: anticipation by use and anticipation by disclosure. Regarding the former, it was held that use only makes an invention part of the state of the art if the use itself makes information about the details of the invention available to the public. Mere use is not enough. Thus, unlike the law prior to 1977 (Patents Act 1949), secret use of a product or process prior to a patent application cannot be part of the state of the art. The ingestion of the drug by those taking part in trials did not *in se* reveal any information to the public about the existence of the acid metabolite.

- The question of anticipation by disclosure, which concerned the specification in the 1972 patent over terfenadine and its uses, revealed information which led to the production of the acid metabolite. Merrell Dow had argued that they could not anticipate that which they did not know to exist but this referred to knowledge about the chemical composition of the acid metabolite. However, one can know the same thing under many different descriptions. Section 2(2) does not confine the state of the art to the chemical composition of products. It is the invention which must be known and in this case the invention in dispute is the acid metabolite. The terfenadine patent describes a chemical

---

[198] For a discussion of the issues on double patenting, see *Synthon BV v Smithkline Beecham plc* [2003] RPC 607 and in the Court of Appeal at [2003] RPC 114. See also E Nettleton et al, 'EPO decisions: double patenting' (2009) 38(4) CIPAJ 268.

[199] Given the extensive range of patenting in the chemical field and the particularities that can arise, the UK–IPO has produced specific guidance, see IPO, Examination Guidelines for Patent Applications Relating to Chemical Inventions in the Intellectual Property Office (2012).

and its effects on the body, one such effect being the antihistamine effect (which was caused by the acid metabolite): 'an invention is part of the state of the art if the information which has been disclosed enables the public to know the product under a description sufficient to work the invention.' Lord Hoffmann concluded that: 'if the recipe which inevitably produces the substance is part of the state of the art, so is the substance as made by the recipe.' Indeed, this was supported by the EPO in T303/86 *CPC/Flavour Concentrates*[200] in which the EPO's Technical Board refused an application to patent flavour concentrates on the ground that recipes in existing cookbooks, although not containing any references to flavour concentrates, nevertheless had the effect of making them.

11.93   Although the Patents Act provides that it is an infringement of a patent relating to a product to make the product without the patentee's authority (s 60(1)(a)), the individuals who took terfenadine and therefore automatically made the acid metabolite would not be infringers by virtue of section 60(5)(a) of the 1977 Act which provides that there is no infringement in respect of acts done privately and without commercial interest.

11.94   On one view this decision is consistent with those discussed earlier, such as *General Tire and Rubber Co* which held that if alleged anticipatory material contains a clear description of, *or clear instructions to do or make*, something which would infringe the disputed patent (if valid), the disputed patent will have been shown to lack the necessary novelty.

11.95   The House of Lords' reservations on anticipation by use have since been distinguished by Pumfrey J in *Halliburton Energy Services Inc v Smith International (North Sea) Ltd*[201] in which it was stated that 'the law has always been that clear and unmistakable directions to do or make something within the claim will, if they form part of the state of the art, anticipate the claim.' The fact that *Merrell Dow* concerned a chemical produced inside the human body and so not analysable/available was thought to make a difference. In the instant case the invention was a mechanical drill bit which could serve as a 'dumb' anticipation by conveying sufficient information to enable it to be dumbly reproduced.[202] Notwithstanding, it remains the case that a prior use must give clear and precise directions to reproduce an invention before it will amount to anticipation.[203]

11.96   Disclosure in the age of the Internet has been addressed by the EPO. It has confirmed that mere sending of an email containing details of an invention is not necessarily tantamount to disclosure as such, assuming of course that this was done on a confidential basis.[204] Furthermore, the use of specific URLs to host information puts it in a rather grey area between public and private: if the URL is so straightforward to guess then this tends towards the public domain; if it is complex, then information found at its site can be as good as private data. The EPO has offered the following non-exhaustive test to consider the issues.

Where all the conditions set out in the following test are met, it can be safely concluded that a document stored on the World Wide Web was made available to the public:

(i)   If, before the filing or priority date of the patent or patent application, a document stored on the World Wide Web and accessible via a specific URL, could be found with the help of a public web search engine by using one or more keywords all related to the essence of the content of that document and

(ii)   remained accessible at that URL for a period of time long enough for a member of the public, i.e. someone under no obligation to keep the content of the document secret, to have direct and unambiguous access to the document, then the document was made available to the public in the sense of Article 54(2) EPC.

(T153/96 *PHILIPS/Public availability of documents on the World Wide Web* [2012] EPOR 40.)

---

[200] [1989] 2 EPOR 95.   [201] [2006] RPC 2; aff'd [2006] EWCA Civ 1715.
[202] See also *Evans Medical Ltd's Patent* [1998] RPC 517.   [203] *Quantel Ltd v Spaceward Microsystems Ltd* [1990] RPC 83.
[204] See T2/09 *PHILIPS/Public availability of an email transmitted via the Internet* [2012] EPOR 41.

Novelty at the margins

11.97   There are two sets of circumstances where claims to products have required a specialised approach in order to secure protection and where the perspectives of the UK and the EPO have not always been in symmetry, although the process of approximation continues unabated as we see later. These are the cases of (1) product-by-process claims and (2) selection patents.

Product-by-process claims

11.98   The UK has traditionally allowed this kind of claim whereby a product could be claimed by reference to its process of manufacture rather than by its own technical features. The claim might read, for example, 'the product obtained by the process described in claim 1'. Although this would give a more restricted monopoly through the necessary link of the product and process, it could prove useful if someone manufactured products outside the country using a patented process and then imported the products—infringement proceedings could still be brought. Moreover, such a formulation is important when it is difficult to define the product by its own characteristics, for example if you cannot discern its structure. The EPO, however, has always taken a restricted view of such claims and will only allow them when it is not possible to describe the product by any other means *and* when the product is patentable in its own right.[205] The UK has now followed suit in:

■ *Kirin-Amgen Inc and others v Hoechst Marion Roussel Ltd and others* [2005] 1 All ER 667, [2005] RPC 9

Amgen held a European patent for the production of erythropoietin (EPO) by genetic engineering (recombinant DNA technology). EPO is a protein that regulates the function of red blood cells in the body and has various therapeutic applications, including the treatment of anaemia. Hoechst developed its own method of making EPO and Amgen alleged infringement of its patent, while Hoechst argued that key parts of the patent were invalid, inter alia, for lack of novelty. In particular, claim 26 was challenged. This was to EPO as the product of the expression in a host cell of a DNA sequence according to claim 1. Claim 1 detailed a DNA sequence for use in securing the expression of EPO in a host cell, and so claim 26 was a product-by-process claim. The core novelty question was: what counts as a new product given that EPO had already been purified from urine by others? It was held that the UK has been singled out as the only signatory state to the EPC to accept product-by-process claims.[206] It is important that the UK should apply the same law as the EPO and the other member states when deciding what counts as new for the purposes of the EPC, and on the facts the product in itself was not new compared to the state of the art.

11.99   We should note, however, that the House of Lords did not consider that this change to practice for the UK would make much difference. In particular, it pointed out that a patentee can continue to rely on Article 64(2) EPC which provides that 'If the subject-matter of the European patent is a process, the protection conferred by the patent shall extend to the products directly obtained by such process.'

Selection patents

11.100   We have established that mere mention of the existence of a substance is not fatal in terms of novelty—the prior art must plant a flag at the specific spot of an invention, for example by describing not only a

---

[205] EPO Guidelines, Part F-IV, para 4.12, and T150/82 *IFF/Claim categories* [1984] OJEPO 309, paras 10–11.
[206] T150/82 *International Flavors & Fragrances Inc* [1984] OJEPO 309.

substance's existence, but perhaps also its structure, its function, its special qualities, and the means to make it.[207] This is very useful in the chemical and biotechnological industries where many thousands of substances or compounds or groups thereof may be known to exist, but where their particular properties are yet to be discovered and put to use. The refining or particularising of knowledge from the general to the specific can be achieved through *selection patents*. These concern the selection of entities from a wider known class or group and an attempt to patent them for particular qualities such as improved performance or novel use. Selection patents can be obtained provided there is no anticipation as defined earlier. For example, in *Beecham Group's (Amoxcycillin) Application*,[208] Beecham held a patent for a wide class of penicillins from which it identified nine as being particularly effective and for which a further patent was sought. The case concerned one type from the group of nine which, it had been established, was especially amenable to absorption in the blood. The question arose as to whether the mention of the penicillin in the previous patent amounted to anticipation. The Court of Appeal held that it did not because the mention in the previous patent of the penicillin did not disclose any details regarding the efficacy of the drug in humans (it concerned only mice). Similarly, in *EI Du Pont de Nemours (Witsiepe's) Application*[209] the House of Lords allowed a selection patent on a copolymer despite prior art which had suggested that copolymers of this type could be produced with a number of variants from what had already been invented in the field. Crucially, however, there was no evidence that these variants had been tried, let alone that they revealed the particular properties possessed by the invention in the instant patent. The mere raising of a possibility does not defeat novelty. The general rule which is accepted in the UK, and maybe in the EPO,[210] is that compounds are novel provided that no members of the sub-group are *specifically* described in the prior publication, even if they have been described in general terms.[211] If this has happened then even the discovery of a new property will not be enough to establish novelty. The later patent must state the precise advantage of the selected invention over the prior art, otherwise 'it is merely an arbitrary selection among things already disclosed, and will lack novelty'.[212] Moreover, the Court of Appeal has confirmed that giving clear and unmistakable directions to use the *common general knowledge* to produce a specific material is no answer to a challenge of novelty.[213]

What can be excluded from the state of the art?

11.101   The starting premise in testing novelty is that everything which is available to the public *as a matter of fact* is counted as part of the state of the art. This can be varied only in a few narrow circumstances and the onus is on the applicant to satisfy the intellectual property office or court that the exceptions should apply. These are detailed in section 2(4) of the Patents Act 1977 which provides that (a) disclosures about the invention which are made in breach of confidence[214] or unlawfully, and (b) disclosures made by the inventor at a recognised international exhibition, can be excluded from the state of the art provided that the patent is applied for within six months of the disclosure in question. The relevant date

---

[207] Arguments that an existing product or process is tantamount to an 'equivalent' are better dealt with as questions of obviousness rather than novelty since it is unlikely to be the case that all essential features have been revealed.

[208] [1980] RPC 261.   [209] [1982] FSR 303 (HL).

[210] See T658/91 *SANOFI/Enantiomer* [1996] EPOR 24 but compare with T198/84 *HOECHST/Thio-chloroformates* [1985] OJEPO 209 and T1042/92 *PFIZER/Penem* [1995] EPOR 207.

[211] See also *Dr Reddy's Laboratories (UK) Ltd v Eli Lilly and Co* [2010] RPC 9, affirming the court at first instance where the court stated that a general formula in a patent with multiple substituents chosen from lists of some length would not normally take away the novelty of a subsequent claim to an individual compound.

[212] *Ranbaxy (UK) Ltd and another v Warner-Lambert Co* [2005] EWHC 2142 (Pat) per Pumfrey J at para 64.

[213] See *Ranbaxy (UK) Ltd and another v Warner-Lambert Co* [2007] RPC 4 at para 41 quoting the court of first instance in this regard. The prior art here was an earlier co-pending application which explicitly pointed the way towards the invention under challenge and merely required the application of the common general knowledge to carry it out.

[214] See *Threeways Pressings Ltd's Application* [2012] RPC 129.

for calculation purposes is the *filing date*. The applicant must prove on the balance of probabilities that there was a breach of confidence or unlawful act leading to disclosure, or in the case of exhibition, he must provide a statement on applying for the patent that this invention has been exhibited and provide a certificate from the exhibit organisers confirming the details of this within the next four months.[215] Only exhibitions which come under the terms of the Convention on International Exhibitions (1928, as amended 1951) can count, and this is unlikely to include regular industry trade fairs. The six-month window will be helpful to an inventor who is the victim of a breach of confidence only if the invention is at a sufficient stage of development to make it worthwhile applying for a patent. At best, it may mean that a more restrictive monopoly will be granted; at worst, it might preclude patent protection altogether if the invention is only in the idea or concept phase.

 Question

What must an international exhibition do to qualify under the 1928 provisions?

Exceptions to exceptions: the case of 'medical use' patents

11.102   It has been a long-standing general principle of novelty in the UK that a known substance cannot be claimed for a new use, even if that use has never previously been described, unless the substance requires some form of transformation to make it suitable for that use. For example, a public announcement system cannot be claimed for use in attracting dogs if all that happens is that high-pitched whistle sounds are played through the system. But if the system must be technically modified to broadcast high-frequency signals inaudible to human ears then it may be patentable in respect of that use. Thus, in *IG Farbenindustrie AG's Patents* it was stated: 'no man can have a patent merely for ascertaining the properties of a known substance'.[216] The strategy in such a case is then not to attempt to claim the *product* but to claim a new *method* of using a known material.

11.103   The EPO takes a different approach. The EBA has held in two decisions[217] that a claim to a new use of a known product is possible, as long as the claim identifies the use as a technical effect and it was previously unknown to the public. The new technical effect can be the mere uncovering of a new use for the substance. For example, in G2/88 *MOBIL OIL III/Friction Reducing Additive*[218] a product originally developed as a lubricant to prevent rust was found also to have qualities to reduce friction and a patent was allowed in this respect. The advice from the UK–IPO, however, is that this approach should not be followed.[219]

11.104   But the UK recognises an exception to its general rule and this is in the realm of substances or compositions for treatment of the human or animal body.[220] We have already seen that *method* patents in this field are exceptions to patentability, but also noted that this does not apply to compounds or substances *used* in those methods. This is specifically provided for by section 4A(3) of the Patents Act 1977, which states that in relation to a method of treatment of the human or animal body by surgery or therapy, or a method of diagnosis practised on the human or animal body:

[215] See Patents Rules 2007, r 5.   [216] (1930) 47 RPC 289 at 322.
[217] G2/88 *MOBIL OIL III/Friction Reducing Additive* [1990] OJEPO 93 and G6/88 *BAYER/Plant growth regulating agent* [1990] OJEPO 114.   [218] [1990] OJEPO 93.
[219] Patents Manual (2013), para 2.14. But compare the views of L Bently and B Sherman, *Intellectual Property Law* (3rd edn, 2008) who argue that 'novelty of purpose' claims have been accepted by the UK courts, pp 469–471 quoting *obiter* comments in *Bristol*.
[220] Note this does not extend to apparatus (see para 11.77).

In the case of an invention consisting of a substance or composition for use in any such method, the fact that the substance or composition forms part of the state of the art shall not prevent the invention from being taken to be new if the use of the substance or composition in any such method does not form part of the state of the art.

11.105   We observed previously that usually the way around the 'no new use' rule is to claim a method of new use, but this could not apply in the case of methods for therapy, surgery, or diagnosis because these are already specifically excluded from protection. Section 4A(3) therefore offers a way out of the problem: it operates as an exception to an exception.

> **Discussion point** For answer guidance visit www.oxfordtextbooks.co.uk/orc/waelde3e/
>
> Look back at the definitions of the 'therapy' and 'surgery' in the previous section on method exclusions and in particular consider what we said about cosmetic methods of treatment. Are they 'therapeutic'? How does this affect the application of section 4A(3)? What about cosmetic surgery?

First medical use

11.106   A strict application of novelty from within the UK tradition should still impose limits on which medical uses can be claimed for a known substance. In particular, it would seem clear from section 4A(3) that only the first medical use can be claimed. Once a substance is deployed for a medical use this becomes part of the state of the art for any future additional medical uses and destroys novelty as a result.[221] Thus in *Bayer AG (Meyer's) Application*[222] a claim to 'Compound X for use in combating medical condition Y' was refused because compound X was already known as a therapy. But the influence from Europe is strong and the British courts are not always able to resist it.

Second medical use

11.107   Developments over the years now mean that in some circumstances a second medical use *can* be claimed. This (further) exception was invented by the EBA in G05/83 *EISAI/Second Medical Indication* in which it held that limitations to patentability should be construed narrowly—a common mantra[223]—and that legislative purpose did not overtly preclude second and subsequent uses and therefore they should be allowed. The EBA qualified this slightly, however, and required that such second or subsequent use claims should take a particular form following the practice of the Swiss Federal Intellectual Property Office. Because of this, they had been known as Swiss-type claims. The form is normally: *'use of substance X in the manufacture of a medicament for the treatment of condition Y'*, and we have seen this form of claim in the previous chapter. The focus, then, is to the method of manufacture of a new application of a known substance. This may be seen as one sophistic step too far. Nonetheless, the possibility of claiming second and subsequent medical uses has now been directly embraced by the EPO and EPC 2000 has removed the need to use Swiss-type claims.[224] Henceforth, it will be possible to claim simply 'substance X for use in treatment of disease Y'.[225]

11.108   This reform is now found in section 4A(3) and (4) of the Patents Act 1977, as amended by section 1 of the Patents Act 2004, and puts to bed any residual doubts that second medical use claims were valid in

---

[221] Note, there must be actual evidence of prior *use* of the substance to destroy novelty for later medical applications; it is not enough that a possible medical use has been discussed: see Manual, para 4A.25.

[222] [1984] RPC 11.   [223] Although see G1/07, note 167, para 3.1.   [224] This does not, however, preclude their use.

[225] See EPC 2000, Art 54(5): 'Paragraphs 2 and 3 shall also not exclude the patentability of any substance or composition referred to in paragraph 4 for any specific use in a method referred to in Article 53(c), provided that such use is not comprised in the state of the art.'

the UK.[226] In *Actavis UK Ltd v Merck*[227] the Court of Appeal held that a valid second medical use claim can be made for a new and inventive dosage regime, despite the fact that the substance in question had been used in the prior art to treat the same condition at a different dosage. In this case there was such a low expectation of a successful treatment by applying this dosage that it was a novel idea and the claim was granted.[228] Most recently, the question of whether or not second medical use claims relating to dosage regimes are patentable under the EPC 2000 has been settled by the EBA. In G02/08 *ABBOTT RESPIRATORY/Dosage regime*[229] the EBA opined that there is no reason to consider dosage regimes differently to acceptable second medical uses. More far-reachingly, however, in determining what counts as an acceptable second medical use, the EBA held that EPC 2000 (Art 54(5)) now permits the patenting of a further specific use of a known medicament *even for the same disease* as long as it is claimed in a method of therapy.[230] Swiss-type claims should no longer be used.[231]

 Exercise

Consider the implications of these decisions allowing the patenting of dosage regimes. Is there a risk that this will lead to the extension of patent protection? Consider the scenario where, through usage of a patented medicine, it becomes clear which dosage regime is most effective in the treatment of the disease and the dosage regime becomes patentable in its own right.

Inventive step

11.109   The policies underlying the inventive step requirement involve the need to show merit by reaching a sufficiently high level of inventive activity to justify the award of a strong monopoly. Also, an inventive step must demonstrate some advantage over what has gone before for the benefit of society; a departure from the prior art which has no advantages, or which represents a disadvantage, should be denied protection for lack of inventive step.[232] Finally, and as a parallel with the rationale behind novelty, the public should not be preventing from doing things which are simply obvious extensions or developments of what they were already doing.[233]

11.110   Inventive step is also referred to as non-obviousness—indeed, US law uses this term.[234] Inventive step is defined in section 3 of the Patents Act 1977, as amended, and the equivalent provisions are found in Article 56 EPC 2000. Section 3 provides:

> An invention shall be taken to involve an inventive step if it is not obvious to a person skilled in the art, having regard to any matter which forms part of the state of the art by virtue only of section 2(2) above (and disregarding section 2(3) above).

---

[226] Previously they had only been grudgingly accepted, see *Wyeth's Application* [1985] RPC 545 and *Bristol-Myers Squibb v Baker Norton Pharmaceuticals* [2001] RPC 1 in which the court refused to rule on the correctness of *Easai* but did indicate that there were 'strong reasons' to maintain the view expressed by the judges in *Wyeth* which followed *Easai* despite reservations.

[227] *Actavis UK Ltd v Merck* [2008] EWCA Civ 444.

[228] Note too in the EPO it has been stated in T1758/07 *HANKKIJA-MAATALOUS/Food additive* [2011] EPOR 2 that second and subsequent medical indications can be protected by directing claims to a process for preparing the medicament—characterised by the use of the substance or composition—rather than direct use claims.

[229] [2010] EPOR 26.

[230] See J Cockbain and Sigrid, 'Is the Enlarged Board of Appeal of the European Patent Office authorised to extend the bounds of the patentable? The G5/83 *Second Medical Indication/EISAI* and G2/08 *Dosage Regime/ABBOTT RESPIRATORY* cases' (2011) 42(3) IIC 257–271.

[231] Now followed in the UK, see IPO, Practice Notice (Patents Act 1977: Second medical use claims) [2010] Bus LR 1242.

[232] T119/82 OJEPO 5/84.   [233] *Windsurfing International Inc v Tabur Marine (GB)* [1985] RPC 59 at 77.

[234] 35 USC §103.

11.111   This raises three questions:

(1) What is the state of the art for the purposes of testing inventive step?

(2) What traits or qualities does the person skilled in the art possess?

(3) How do we know when something is 'obvious' to the person skilled in the art?

State of the art

11.112   The starting point for assessing the state of the art for inventive step purposes is the same as that we use for testing novelty, namely the definition in section 2(2) of the Patents Act 1977—so it includes virtually the sum total of human knowledge that is available to the public anywhere in the world. It does not include, however, the content of any patent applications designating the UK and filed before the priority date of the current application under scrutiny (s 2(3)).

 Question

Why are patent applications excluded from inventive step but not from novelty?

11.113   We saw that in order to defeat novelty a single piece of prior art must directly plant the flag on the applicant's invention and it is not possible to combine different pieces of prior art in order to say that something is not new.[235] This combining process is called *mosaicing* and, in contrast, it is perfectly permissible when testing inventive step as long as this is something that the person skilled in the particular art would have done. Whether this is so clearly varies from technology to technology and explains why the criterion of inventive step is something of a moveable feast—its application is very field-specific and resolution usually turns on the particular technical features of each case. The subtle relationship between inventive step and novelty was explained by Lord Hoffmann in *Synthon*: 'If performance of an invention disclosed by the prior art would not infringe the patent but the prior art would make it obvious to a skilled person how he might make adaptations which resulted in an infringing invention, then the patent may be invalid for lack of an inventive step but not for lack of novelty.'[236]

11.114   A feature of the state of the art which is not necessarily field-specific is *common knowledge*.[237] The courts will often assume that certain features, practices, or possibilities are so manifestly self-evident that they do not need to be spelled out in detail but can be assumed to be part of the skilled person's experience. This applies both to general common knowledge and to field-specific common knowledge.[238]

11.115   While it is theoretically the case that the entire sum of publicly available information is at the fingertips of the skilled person, the intellectual property office or court will ask what was the particular skilled person in the field under scrutiny likely to come across and consider together.[239] The more obscure the connections necessary across different fields, and the more documents that have to be mosaiced to come

---

[235] See too EPO Guidelines, Part G-VII, para 4: 'it is fair to construe any published document in the light of subsequent knowledge and to have regard to all the knowledge generally available to the person skilled in the art the day before the filing or priority date valid for the claimed invention.'   [236] *Synthon*, para 11.88, at para 25.

[237] For a rare instance of an appeal court overturning a trial judge's assessment of common knowledge, see *Apimed Medical Honey Ltd v Brightwake Ltd* [2012] EWCA Civ 5.

[238] On the relevance of (even highly-technical) sector standards as forming part of the common knowledge, see *Nokia v Ipcom* [2009] EWHC 3482 (Pat); confirmed on appeal [2011] EWCA Civ 6.

[239] But even publication of material a few days before the priority date can be fatal in terms of inventive step, see *Merck Sharp & Dohme Corp v Teva UK Ltd* [2011] EWCA Civ 382.

up with the invention, the more likely it is that the invention will be found to have an inventive step. Relevant factors include (1) the age of the documents, (2) the role of references in linking one document to others, (3) the proximity of fields from which the prior art comes, (4) the amount of effort or analysis required of the skilled person in identifying the relevant features in the prior art, and (5) the ubiquity of some documents in the field such that they form part of the common knowledge.[240] A good guide was offered by Lord Reid in *Technograph v Mills & Rockley*: 'In dealing with obviousness, unlike novelty, it is permissible to make a "mosaic" out of the relevant documents, but it must be a mosaic which can be put together by an unimaginative man with no inventive capacity.'[241]

11.116   The question of whether it is appropriate to look across and between technical fields is largely answered by the nature of the problem to be solved and whether the relevant skilled person would be expected to look for parallels in related fields where, perhaps, similar problems are encountered.[242] Similarly, it is also possible to consider that the skilled person might call upon the expertise of others in related fields in attempting to solve his problem. Indeed, the person skilled in the art might, in fact, be a team of different specialists and this should include those relevant to the field(s) of the invention.[243]

■ *Conor Medsystems Inc v Angiotech Pharmaceuticals Inc and another* [2008] RPC 28

This case involved a challenge on the grounds of obviousness to a patent relating to a device used in coronary surgery called a *stent*. This is implanted into diseased arteries to keep them from collapsing. The problem facing the skilled person was how to develop stents that did not cause restenosis (closure of the artery channel)—a pre-existing problem for 33–50 per cent of patients treated with existing techniques. Here it was held to be the case that the person skilled in the art and trying to solve the pre-existing problem would be a team which would include, inter alia, an interventional cardiologist and someone familiar with drugs for treating cancer. All of the experts would bring their own knowledge to the problem. In the instant case where the invention involved coating the stent with taxol (an anti-angiogenic), it was held by the Court of Appeal to be obvious that the skilled man would consider taxol to be worth testing to see what its properties were. However, the House of Lords ruled that the prior art merely mentioned taxol as one of an undifferentiated (and large) number of drugs which could be tried and this was insufficient to make it obvious that taxol would prevent restenosis. The correct question to ask was whether it was obvious to use a taxol-coated stent to prevent restenosis. The patentee had disclosed a plausible invention which, if it worked, could be patentable as long as the solution itself was not obvious. It is the technical solution which must be tested for obviousness not the question of whether it was obvious to try taxol (among many other compounds).

 Question

Could this variability in the application of the inventive step test lead to unfairness in terms of the standards to which different technologies might be held?

The qualities of the person skilled in the art

11.117   The idea of the person skilled in the art is a device used by intellectual property offices and courts to assess the merits of any given innovation. We are concerned with the notional expert and the courts will

---

[240] A good step-by-step illustration of what the skilled person might know and mosaic is found in *Ivax Pharmaceuticals UK Ltd v Akzo Nobel NV; Arrow Generics Ltd v Akzo Nobel NV* [2007] RPC 3.

[241] [1972] RPC 346 at 355.   [242] T176/84 *MOBIUS/Neighbouring field* [1986] OJEPO 50.

[243] *Schlumberger Holdings Ltd v Electromagnetic Geoservices AS* [2009] RPC 19.

hear evidence in each case on what that expert might be expected to know. He is an ordinary member of their field who is aware of everything in the state of the art[244] but, as we have seen previously, is unimaginative and with no inventive capacity (para 11.15). The range of qualities of this person was helpfully summarised for us by Jacob LJ in *Rockwater v Technip France SA and another*:[245] he is, first and foremost, a nerd (not Lord Justice Jacob)! Beyond the traits we have just discovered, he is forgetful, in that he will not join the dots between different pieces of prior art unless it is obvious to do so, and unconnected matter will drift from his memory as he moves through the literature. He can, however, have the prejudices of his field, which may be long-standing assumptions that a particular avenue of research will be fruitless. Those who prove otherwise have, therefore, a good chance of clearing the inventive step hurdle. Similarly, those who identify a problem for the first time and provide a means to overcome it should have few difficulties.[246] For example, in *Dyson Appliances Ltd v Hoover*[247] the issue of prejudice was raised and held to be relevant in determining what the skilled person would consider obvious to do. The advent of the bagless vacuum cleaner was an innovation that came from the blue—no one had even perceived a problem with conventional machines.

11.118   The skilled person is not expected to pursue avenues that he would regard as futile.[248] As the EPO Guidelines put it: 'There is an inventive step if the prior art leads the person skilled in the art away from the procedure proposed by the invention'.[249] Timing is also vitally important. We ask the skilled person to consider what was obvious at the time of the priority date and it is crucial to guard against the vagaries of ex post facto analysis—many things may appear obvious with hindsight.[250] It is not appropriate to define the class of expert so broadly that the specific knowledge and prejudices of those most closely involved in the actual field with which the patent is concerned do not form part of the prejudices and attributes of the skilled person.[251]

11.119   Evidence on what the skilled person would know or do is taken from relevant experts at first instance. Appeal courts do not have an opportunity to re-hear evidence and should not overrule a trial judge's findings of fact unless there are very good reasons to do so. The position was summed up by Lord Hoffmann in *Biogen v Medeva*:[252]

> The need for appellate caution in reversing the judge's evaluation of the facts is based upon much more solid grounds than professional courtesy. It is because specific findings of fact, even by the most meticulous judge, are inherently an incomplete statement of the impression which was made upon him by the primary evidence. His expressed findings are always surrounded by a penumbra of imprecision as to emphasis, relative weight, minor qualification and nuance (as Renan said, la vérité est dans une nuance), of which time and language do not permit exact expression, but which may play an important part in the judge's overall evaluation...Where the application of a legal standard such as negligence or obviousness involves no question of principle but is simply a matter of degree, an appellate court should be very cautious in differing from the judge's evaluation.

The test for obviousness

11.120   The criterion of 'inventive step' can be thought of as a misnomer. It is not inventive for someone to take the next logical, obvious *step* in the develop of any given field of technology, rather what is required is a *leap* forward in ways that would not be obvious to others working in the field. It is an objective test. The classic approach to this question was laid down in:

---

[244] See, eg, *WL Gore & Associates GmbH v Geox SpA* [2008] EWHC 2311 (Pat) in which the person skilled in the art was held to be a person or team with a practical interest in the functional aspects of shoe design.

[245] [2004] EWCA CIV 381, [2004] RPC 46.   [246] See, eg, *El-Tawil v Comptroller General of Patents* [2012] EWHC 185 (Ch).

[247] [2001] RPC 26.   [248] *Hallen Co v Barbantia (UK) Ltd* [1991] RPC 195.   [249] EPO Guidelines, Part G-VII, para 4.

[250] *Ferag AG v Muller Martini Ltd* [2007] EWCA Civ 15.

[251] *Mayne Pharma Ltd and another v Debiopharm SA and another* [2006] EWHC 1123 (Pat).   [252] [1997] RPC 1 at 45.

■ *Windsurfing International Inc v Tabur Marine (GB) Ltd* [1985] RPC 59 (CA)

The patent in suit claimed a wind-propelled apparatus for use on water with a sail attached to a surf-board and two arcuate booms attached to the sail—imagine an ordinary windsurf board. In an action for infringement of the patent, the defendants counterclaimed that the patent was invalid both on grounds of novelty and obviousness. The novelty issue arose from prior use of a similar device by a third party and obviousness was argued both in relation to this prior use and/or in view of a printed publication which appeared before the priority date of the patent. The publication was an article entitled, 'Sailboarding—Exciting New Water Sport' which described the basic concept as that of the patent except that the sail was square-rigged. The prior use was allegedly ten years prior to the patent application by a 12-year-old boy who had built a sailboard and used it on public waterways on summer weekends over two consecutive seasons. This sailboard differed from that claimed only in that the booms were straight and not arcuate. It was held that the patent was invalid both on grounds of novelty and obviousness. As regards novelty it did not matter that prior use was by a private individual and in a non-commercial setting. Of relevance was the extent of the public nature of the use which, in the case, was considerable even although in relative terms the public use was of short duration. Obviousness is to be tested by asking what would have been obvious to a person skilled in the particular art at the time of the priority date of the patent.

Answering the question on obviousness was held to be a four-step process:

(1) identify the 'inventive concept' embodied in the patent;

(2) impute to a normally skilled but unimaginative addressee what was common general knowledge in the art at the priority date;

(3) identify the differences, if any, between the matter cited as part of the state of the art and the alleged invention;

(4) decide whether those differences, viewed without any knowledge of the alleged invention, constitute steps which would have been obvious to the skilled man or whether they require a degree of invention.

This has been reformulated by the Court of Appeal in *Pozzoli SPA v BDMO SA*.[253] The following should be taken as an accurate reflection of the current approach and *Windsurfing* and *Pozzoli* should be read together.

The *Windsurfing/Pozzoli* approach

(1)(a) Identify the notional 'person skilled in the art'.

(1)(b) Identify the relevant common general knowledge of that person.

(2) Identify the inventive concept of the claim in question or if that cannot readily be done, construe it.

(3) Identify what, if any, differences exist between the matter cited as forming part of the 'state of the art' and the inventive concept of the claim or the claim as construed.[254]

(4) Viewed without any knowledge of the alleged invention as claimed, do those differences constitute steps which would have been obvious to the person skilled in the art or do they require any degree of invention?

---

[253] [2007] FSR 37. An explanation of this reformulation can be found at paras 15 and 16.

[254] The Patents Manual (2013) offers the following helpful instruction: 'In determining whether an invention is obvious in the light of a given document combined with common general knowledge, other documents, or instances of prior use, there are two major considerations: (i) whether the skilled person could reasonably be expected to find the document in conducting a diligent search for material relevant to the problem in hand…and (ii) whether, if he had found the document, he would have given it serious consideration' (para 3.75.1).

Question

Before reading on, ask yourself—what is the inventive concept involved with a windsurf board? Is it the sail? The boom? The board or something else?

11.121   The inventive concept in *Windsurfing* was the 'free-sail': a sail attached to an unstayed spar on one side which is connected to the board by a universal joint, that is, a joint having three axes of rotation. This allows the sail to be manipulated to power and control the board without the need for a rudder or other means. The inventive concept described in the publication was essentially that contained in the patent. The essential difference between the two was the shape of the sail: square in the publication, triangular in the patent. This, however, made no practical difference in the determination of obviousness. The prior use by the young boy was of a device essentially the same as the vehicle described in the patent in suit save that the booms were straight and not arcuate. It would have been obvious to anyone skilled in the art in 1958 on witnessing the boy's board that an improvement would be to replace the straight booms with arcuate booms. Indeed, the straight booms formed such a shape when the board was put to water.

11.122   Here is an old but valuable illustration of the importance of defining 'inventive concept'.

■ *Parks-Cramer Co v GW Thornton & Sons Ltd* **[1966] RPC 407 (CA)**

This was an appeal to the Court of Appeal concerning a patent for a device used to clean the floor around textile machines of 'fly' (or lint) by the automatic and repeated passage of an overhead vacuum cleaner having vacuum tubes extending almost to the floor. An action for infringement was brought which was met with a counterclaim alleging invalidity on grounds of obviousness. Inter alia, it was alleged that the invention was obvious because of general knowledge of the problem about the collection of fly or lint in textile factories and the existence of certain patents previously granted which were aimed at alleviating the problem. Such patents included (1) overhead devices which blew the fly onto the floor for collection and (2) suction devices aimed at the parts of the machine where most fly accumulated. None of these machines sought to deal with the problem of accumulation of fly upon the floor of the factory generally or in particular with the accumulation of fly in the aisles. Finally, (3) a number of devices were developed in an attempt to clean factory floors of fly and some were patented. They operated on the principle of directing air currents across the floor in one direction so as to blow the fly towards fixed collecting points where the fly was removed by suction into ducts or collecting chambers. None of these devices proved satisfactory in practice. On the basis of these points, it was argued by the defendants that the extension of the basic ideas disclosed by these devices and patents to using a vacuum device to clean factory floors of fly was obvious.

It was held that:

• The patent was valid. The inventive concept contained in the plaintiff's patent was this: if you pass a suction nozzle closely adjacent to the floor repeatedly at regular intervals over a fixed path along the aisles between and at the ends of rows of machines the suction will remove the fly from *the whole of the floor* and *not merely* that part of the floor which is in the relatively narrow direct track of the suction nozzle.

• It was not obvious that by passing such a machine over the floor in such a manner that the whole of the floor would be cleaned and not just a narrow tract.

- The problem which the plaintiff sought to solve had been a problem since the early 1950s. Many individuals and companies had sought to solve it but no one had been successful. It had occurred to no one that the solution lay in passing a suction tube repeatedly over a narrow track in the aisles.

- The evidence shows that the plaintiff's machine was an immediate commercial success and although this could be attributable to many other factors, this point fortified the view that it was not obvious to solve the problem in the way in which the plaintiff did.

11.123   It would appear that the inventors themselves did not even appreciate the efficacy of their invention in cleaning the whole of the floor rather than a narrow tract. Yet, not only did this not affect the validity of the patent, it aided the court in determining that the invention was not obvious: the plaintiff was very experienced in the field of cleaning devices for use in textile mills.

11.124   It has been suggested that the *Windsurfing* four-point test is merely a tool to help to decide obviousness and is not a mandatory approach,[255] but its appeal endures and it was found to have been applied by the trial judge, albeit obliquely, by the House of Lords in *Sabaf SpA v MFI Furniture Centres Ltd and others*.[256] This ruling is significant for the point that before we consider whether an invention is obvious, we must first decide what the invention is or whether it is merely a collocation, that is, the juxtaposition of devices or inventions which do not make up a unified whole. The example offered by the EPO on this point is a machine for producing sausages consisting of a known mincing machine and a known filling machine disposed side by side.[257] In *Sabaf* it was held that two features in respect of gas burners for kitchen cookers were a mere collocation, being a means to drawn air in above the burner and a way of controlling flow under the burner which did not interact with each other—there were therefore two inventions, neither of which differed significantly from the prior art in line with the *Windsurfing* structure.

The importance of the *Windsurfing/Pozzoli* structured approach[258] is to get the court in the right frame of mind to test obviousness and to avoid the trap of applying hindsight.[259]

11.125   The Court of Appeal in *Conor* best summed up the position:[260]

In the end the question is simply 'was the invention obvious?' This involves taking into account a number of factors, for instance the attributes and common general knowledge of the skilled man, the difference between what is claimed and the prior art, whether there is a motive provided or hinted by the prior art and so on. Some factors are more important than others. Sometimes commercial success can demonstrate that an idea was a good one. In others 'obvious to try' may come into the assessment. But such a formula cannot itself necessarily provide the answer. Of particular importance is of course the nature of the invention itself.

11.126   The relevance of commercial success of an invention can be a *faux ami*.[261] Numerous factors can play a role in the success of an invention in the market and many of them may have nothing to do with inventiveness. Especially when dealing with the commercial success of a product subject to anterior patent protection, one should be cautious as there is a clear reason why no one else has ever launched a similar product.[262]

[255] For an example of the court being invited to depart from *Windsurfing*, see *Cipla Ltd and others v Glaxo Group Ltd* [2004] EWHC 477 (Ch). From a comparative perspective, see *Aktiebolaget Hassle v Alphapharm* (2002) 212 CLR 411 (Australia) and *Aventis v Apotex* [2005] FC 1504 (Canada).

[256] [2004] UKHL 45, [2005] RPC 10.   [257] EPO Guidelines, Part G-VII, para 2.1.

[258] Though the modified test of *Pozzoli* is now mainly used, the *Windsurfing* approach is still valid and used occasionally, eg in *Handi-Craft Co v B Free World Ltd* [2007] EWHC 10 (Ch).

[259] *Wheatley v Drillsafe Ltd* [2001] RPC 7   [260] *Conor Medsystems Inc v Angiotech Inc and another* [2007] EWCA Civ 5, para 45.

[261] But neither is it altogether irrelevant: *Dyson Appliances Ltd v Hoover Ltd* [2002] RPC 22 'commercial realities cannot necessarily be divorced from the kinds of practical outcome which might occur to the skilled addressee as worthwhile.'

[262] *Dr Reddy's Laboratories (UK) Ltd v Eli Lilly and Co* [2008] EWHC 2345 (Pat), para 187.

Discussion point For answer guidance visit www.oxfordtextbooks.co.uk/orc/waelde3e/

How many different factors can you think of that might influence market success?

11.127 The key question in deciding if commercial success is a relevant factor in determining inventive step lies in being able to identify *why* there was commercial success and to assess whether this was because of inventiveness. In *Haberman v Jackel*[263] the invention was very simple and concerned the 'AnyWayUp Cup'—a cup especially designed to help babies to make the transition from suckling to proper feeding (UK Patent 2266045—why not try to find this on Espacenet?)

11.128 The inventiveness was said to lie in the fact that the cup sealed between sips and so avoided drips. Rival companies had similar devices which worked through various mechanisms. It was argued that Haberman had not produced anything outside the normal workshop modifications which had long been available to those in the art. It was a simple solution to a known problem using known and readily available expedients.

11.129 Laddie J laid out a list of factors that might have a bearing on a determination of obviousness:

Inventive step: some of the considerations

(1) What was the problem which the patented development addressed?

(2) How long had that problem existed?

(3) How significant was the problem seen to be?

(4) How widely known was the problem and how many were likely to be seeking a solution?

(5) What prior art would have been likely to be known to all or most of those who would have been expected to be involved in finding a solution?

(6) What other solutions were put forward in the period leading up to the publication of the patentee's development?

(7) To what extent were there factors which would have held back the exploitation of the solution even if it was technically obvious?

(8) How well has the patentee's development been received?

(9) To what extent can it be shown that the whole or much of the commercial success is due to the technical merits of the development, that is, because it solves the problem?

This is not an exhaustive list but it is a helpful guide which may point either towards or away from inventiveness.[264]

 Exercise

Consider each of these factors and the ways in which they might influence a determination of obviousness.

---

[263] [1999] FSR 683.

[264] As stated in *Generics (UK) Ltd and others v H Lundbeck A/S* [2009] UKHL 12, in the end the question of obviousness must be considered on the facts of each single case. The court must attach weight to any particular factor in taking into account all the relevant circumstances.

11.130 In the end Mrs Haberman kept her patent. She took a step forward that many others in the field could have taken during the long period during which the problem was known but did not. Nor did the simplicity of the invention defeat inventiveness; indeed, rather the opposite—if it was so straightforward then why had it not been done before? Moreover, evidence to the court suggested strongly that the tremendous commercial success of the cup was due primarily to its technical quality and contribution to the state of the art—it did not leak.

11.131 Meeting an unmet need may be evidence of inventiveness, but it is not inventive merely to take advantage of an upturn in economic circumstances which create a market not previously existing (eg by making certain materials affordable when previously they were not). Similarly, it is not because it has taken a lot of time and expense to bring a product to market that this in any sense implies inventiveness.[265]

Obvious to try

11.132 We have mentioned previously the idea of 'obvious to try' which is often offered as a gloss on the obviousness test.[266] But the Court of Appeal in *Saint-Gobain PAM SA v Fusion Provida Ltd and another*[267] opined that the obvious-to-try test really only applies in circumstances where it is more or less self-evident that what is proposed will work. In this case, however, it was not possible for the skilled person to predict success and so the invention was non-obvious. Thus, speculative inclusion of experiments in a research programme will not be defeated simply because you try—it is the obvious likelihood of success which presents a problem, not trying itself. In terms of strategy it is prudent, therefore, to lay out in the patent specification reasons why success is in doubt and far from guaranteed.[268] The House of Lords confirmed in *Conor Medsystems Inc v Angiotech Pharmaceuticals Inc*[269] that an invention can only be obvious if there is an expectation of success and noted that the expectation of success must be assessed in the light of the purpose for which the invention is intended; that is, the solution to the technical problem that it is intended to fix. Furthermore, when evaluating the reasonable expectation of success, one must consider without hindsight the attractiveness of the route at the time, taking into account all the surrounding circumstances.[270] Lord Hoffmann's views on the question of 'obvious to try without any expectation of success' are worth noting: 'This oxymoronic concept has, so far as I know, no precedent in the law of patents.'

11.133 In *Omnipharm Ltd v Merial*[271] it was clarified that: '"Obvious to try" is not an independent ground of invalidating a patent under the statute, but one of a variety of factors considered in an overall assessment of inventive step. It must be coupled with a fair expectation of success, the degree of success necessary depending on the other factors present in the individual case' (para 92). In this case, the development of 'spot-on' flea treatments for pets was not 'obvious to try' based on existing spray on treatments for the want of the element of fair expectation of success.

Reforms and the European approach

11.134 Having considered the broad approach in the UK to testing obviousness, it is important to highlight that the UK–IPO has recently conducted a consultation exercise on this criterion with a view to possible reform. The motivation for this consultation was to know if the inventive step criterion best serves

---

[265] *Teva v Gentili* [2003] EWHC 5 (Pat); [2003] EWCA Civ 1545.
[266] Its origins are found in *Johns-Manville Corporation's Patent* [1967] RPC 479.   [267] [2005] EWCA Civ 177.
[268] See *Conor Medsystems Inc v Angiotech Pharmaceuticals Inc and another* [2006] EWHC 260 (Pat).
[269] *Conor Medsystems Inc v Angiotech Pharmaceuticals Inc* [2008] RPC 28.
[270] See A Carter, '*Conor Medsystems Inc v Angiotech Pharmaceuticals Inc and others*: House of Lords judgment clarifying the assessment of "inventive step"' (2008) 30(10) EIPR 429. See also *Generics (UK) Ltd v Daiichi Pharmaceutical Co Ltd* [2009] EWCA Civ 646.
[271] [2011] EWHC 3393 (Pat); CA appeal at [2013] EWCA Civ 2.

innovation by steering a middle way through the easy and hard extremes that could otherwise be adopted. If an intellectual property office sets the inventive threshold too low this can result in trivial patents and a surfeit of protection blocking innovation, but if the hurdle is too high this may also impede innovation.[272] The consultation showed that there is no need to change the basic law on testing obviousness, as the current application of the law is broadly thought to be appropriate. It was noted, however, that it is important to make sure that practice stays in line with the high technological environments in which inventions are made and that the test is applied consistently.[273]

> ### Exercise
>
> Compare the UK approach to three alternatives considered by the UK–IPO. Should we test inventiveness by reference to:
>
> (1) The person skilled in the art, having regard to any item(s) of prior art or common general knowledge, would have arrived at the claimed invention (the European approach)?
>
> (2) Any item(s) of prior art or common general knowledge would have motivated a person skilled in the art to reach the claimed invention (the Japanese approach)?
>
> (3) Any item(s) of prior art or common general knowledge would have motivated, with a reasonable expectation of success, a person skilled in the art to reach the claimed invention (the US approach)?
>
> Which of these is a softer or harder option? What are the advantages and disadvantages of the UK maintaining its current approach?

EPO/UK differences

11.135   The EPO adopts a problem-and-solution approach. It asks what is the pre-existing technical problem and is it solved by a technical solution? The approach in the EPO and in the UK are much the same at this broad level. But the EPO has developed a three-point test which differs somewhat from the UK. Non-obviousness is determined by:

(1) determining the 'closest prior art';
(2) establishing the 'objective technical problem' to be solved; and
(3) considering whether or not the claimed invention, starting from the closest prior art and the objective technical problem, would have been obvious to the skilled person.[274]

11.136   The closest prior art often restricts the search to the same technical field as the invention and looks for the most promising point from which an obvious development towards the invention might be made. This is to be assessed on the day before the filing or priority date of the invention.[275] The objective technical problem is formulated by comparing the prior art with the distinguishing features of the invention. Occasionally, this formulation may be at odds with how the applicant has framed the problem in the patent application and this requires a reformulation of the problem in the application since the technical formulation is supposed to be the objective assessment of the problem to be solved. The technical

---

[272] See further *Gowers Review of Intellectual Property* (HM Treasury, 2006), para 5.24.
[273] The outcome of the consultation is available at http://www.ipo.gov.uk/response-inventive.pdf.
[274] EPO Guidelines, Part G-VII, para 5.   [275] EPO Guidelines, Part G-VII,, para 5.1.

problem can be interpreted broadly and may only cover an alternative means to produce the same or similar effects in the state of the art.

11.137 This test differs most significantly from the UK in its starting point of seeking (only) the closest prior art. As Pumfrey J said at first instance in *Ranbaxy*, 'its concentration on the closest prior art, which must stem from a belief that if an invention is not obvious in the light of the closest prior art it cannot be obvious in the light of anything further away. This runs the risk of offending against the principle that a skilled man must be permitted to do that which is obvious in the light of each individual item of prior art seen in the light of the common general knowledge.'[276] That said, Pumfrey J did not in the end consider that there are differences of principle at stake as between the jurisdictions.[277]

 Question

Do you agree with Pumfrey J's assessment of these approaches? Consider your answer in the light of the UK–IPO exercise discussed previously. How did the same invention fare before the EPO?

Industrial applicability

11.138 This final criterion for patentability ensures that we maintain the industrial or technical nature of inventions. The relevant section of the Patents Act 1977, as amended, is section 4(1), with the equivalent provisions being found in Article 57 EPC 2000. Section 4(1) states:

> an invention shall be taken to be capable of industrial application if it can be made or used in any kind of industry, including agriculture.

We have already covered the other provisions in sections 4 and 4A (paras 11.62ff) when we discussed methods of treatment of the human and animal body and use claims. The concept of 'industry' is construed very widely and does not necessarily involve a for-profit purpose.[278] Note that the test is whether something can be *made* or used in industry, so widening the scope further, and the requirement is only that the invention is *capable* of use in industry or agriculture; no actual evidence of effective use is required.

11.139 Something can be held to lack industrial applicability if its essential nature is aesthetic, artistic, or intellectual. There is, therefore, some overlap with the kinds of considerations we saw earlier in respect of section 1(2) of the Patents Act 1977. The two tests are, however, distinct. An example of something being denied protection was a method of initiating introductions between people in *John Lahiri Khan's Application* which was also rejected under section 1(2) as a method of doing business.[279]

11.140 Beyond this, there is little else to say about this provision. It does not cause problems in the vast majority of cases. One area which has required refinement, however, is in respect of biotechnological inventions because of the need to show the *function* of any new gene sequences or fragments unearthed during scientific research. This has been dealt with separately through the Biotechnology Directive and is the subject of recent national and European case law and we discuss all of this in detail in paras 12.47ff in the next chapter.

---

[276] [2005] EWHC 2142 (Pat), para 69.
[277] See also Jacob LJ in *Actavis UK Ltd v Novartis AG* [2010] EWCA Civ 82 and *Teva UK Ltd v AstraZeneca AB* [2012] EWHC 655 (Pat).   [278] *Chiron Corp v Murex Diagnostics Ltd and others* [1996] RPC 535 at 607.
[279] Patents Manual (2013), para 4.03 (BL O/356/06).

Patent rights and their limits

11.141   So, you have applied for your patent, your invention has not been excluded on one or more policy grounds, and you have satisfied a patent examiner that your invention is new, inventive, and of a technical nature. What now?

11.142   Your patent[280] is a right to exclude everyone from the market, even the so-called innocent infringer, for a period up to a maximum of 20 years. It is a form of *personal property* in much the same way as any other thing you own. Thus, it can be sold, assigned, licensed, mortgaged, or otherwise transferred to other parties.[281] A patent is an asset over which securities can be granted and so against which capital can be raised.

11.143   A patent will be granted initially for four years but can be extended annually for a maximum of 20 years. Supplementary Protection Certificates are available in the case of pharmaceutical inventions and agrochemicals inventions which permit an extension of the term for a further five years to compensate for the stringent regulatory approval mechanisms which these inventions are often subject to before being given access to the market.[282] The European Parliament and Council adopted a Regulation on medicines for paediatric use which includes a further six-month extension to a Supplementary Protection Certificate as an incentive to produce in the area in 2006.[283]

11.144   Like most intellectual property rights, patents are principally exploited through licences and sub-licences and, normally, these can be further assigned and mortgaged.[284] We deal with exploitation of patents in the relevant sections of Chapter 22. Patents, applications, licences, and sub-licences can vest in personal representatives on death in the same way as any other piece of personal property.[285] Some transfers of rights must be in writing and signed by or on behalf of the transferor,[286] otherwise all such transactions are void. This applies to assignments, mortgages, and transfers on death.[287] Licences do not need to be in writing and do not involve any transfer of property.[288] An assignment or an exclusive licence can give the right to bring infringement proceedings[289] or disputes over Crown use.[290] An exclusive licensee can bring independent infringement proceedings without the need to refer to the owner.[291]

---

[280]   This applies to patent applications as well.

[281]   Patents Act 1977, s 30 for England, Wales, and Northern Ireland and s 31 for Scotland where a patent is 'incorporeal moveable property'. Assignations or grants of security are subject to the provisions of the Requirements of Writing (Scotland) Act 1995.

[282]   Regulation (EEC) No 1768/92 created a Supplementary Protection Certificate for medicinal products and it entered into force on 2 January 1993. Regulation (EC) No 1610/96 of the European Parliament and of the Council, created a Supplementary Protection Certificate for plant protection products, and entered into force on 8 February 1997. The UK–IPO provides a full guide to both: UK–IPO, *Supplementary Protection Certificates for Medicinal and Plant Products: A Guide for Applicants* (2009) available at http://www. patent.gov.uk/patent/info/spctext.pdf. Disputes over SPCs arise in terms of the 'product' they are certified to cover and whether the invention and the product to be authorised are one and the same, see *Takeda Chemical Industries Ltd's SPC Applications (No 3)* [2004] RPC 3. Note, at the time of writing, the UK–IPO is considering extending its Patent Opinions Service to SPCs. For recent case law, see *Neurim Pharmaceuticals v The Comptroller-General of Patents* [2011] EWCA Civ 228 and *Actavis Group PTC EHF v Sanofi Chancery Division* [2012] EWHC 2545 (Pat).

[283]   Regulation (EC) No 1901/2006 of the European Parliament and of the Council of 12 December 2006 on medicinal products for paediatric use and amending Regulation (EEC) No 1768/92, Directive 2001/20/EC, Directive 2001/83/EC, and Regulation (EC) No 726/2004. The amendments are incorporated in Regulation (EC) No 469/2009.

[284]   Patents Act 1977, s 30(4)(a), subject to s 36(3) which deals with the need for consent of co-owners.

[285]   Patents Act 1977, s 30(3), (4)(b).

[286]   It is no longer necessary for all parties to sign as of 1 January 2005, see Regulatory Reform (Patents) Order 2004 (SI 2004/2357).

[287]   For a Scottish perspective on assignations and loss of rights to sue, see *Buchanan v Alba Diagnostics Ltd* [2004] RPC 34. For comment, see RG Anderson, '*Buchanan v Alba Diagnostics*: accretion of title and assignation of Future patents' (2005) 9(3) Edinburgh LR 457.

[288]   For discussion see *Allen & Hanburys Ltd v Generics (UK) Ltd and Gist-Brocades NV and others and the Comptroller-General of Patents* [1986] RPC 203 per Lord Diplock.

[289]   Patents Act 1977, s 30(7).   [290]   Patents Act 1977, s 58.   [291]   Patents Act 1977, s 67.

11.145   Assignations and other transfers of rights can be entered in the Register of Patents with the effect that this will give priority over someone who claims an earlier transaction if (1) the earlier transaction was not registered, and (2) the person claiming under the later transaction was unaware of the earlier transaction.[292] Moreover, assignees or exclusive licensees who register within six months of the transfer can then claim damages or an account of profits for infringements of the patent prior to the transaction.[293]

Question

What would happen if you have applied for registration but this has not taken place when someone comes forward with an earlier claim?

11.146   As well as entering specific one-to-one contracts for exploitation of a patent, a patentee has a mechanism at his disposal known as *licences as of right*.[294] We discuss these later in Chapter 22, and the principle here is largely the same: the patentee requests that an entry be made in the Register that licences are available as of right and this allows any party who wishes to take a licence on terms they are willing to accept through agreement or by intervention from the Comptroller.[295] A licensee of right can request that the patentee bring infringement proceedings to protect the invention and if nothing is done within two months can bring infringement proceedings herself.[296] A subsequent application can be made to have the patent removed from the Register in this respect, although at that stage the request can be opposed by any interested parties.[297] The UK–IPO maintains an open standards web database containing all patents issued under licence of right.[298]

Exercise

Read the relevant provisions of the law and consider the pros and cons for a patentee of relying on this scheme. Note, in particular, how signing up to the scheme affects renewal fees.

Limits on patent rights

11.147   The core unifying feature of the various limits which are imposed on the exercise of patent rights is our old friend, the public interest. At the most general level and as with other IPRs, the European principle of free movement of goods and competition law can impose limits on the way patents are exploited. We discuss these in Chapters 20 and 21 respectively.

11.148   If we accept that the whole ethos behind the patent system is to encourage inventions that become available to the public, then this end is thwarted if someone seeks and receives patent protection but then does not exploit the invention and keeps the technical details out of the public domain. For these reasons we allow *compulsory licences* under sections 48 and 53 of the Patents Act 1977. Broadly, a common criterion is that a compulsory licence cannot be sought until three years after the grant of the patent to give the patentee a fair chance to exploit the invention himself. But, if this has not happened, the law provides for two avenues to apply for a compulsory licence to the Comptroller, and the relevant avenue depends on whether the patentee is from a World Trade Organization (WTO) country or not. The criteria

---

[292] Patents Act 1977, s 33(1).   [293] Patents Act 1977, s 68.   [294] Patents Act 1977, s 46.
[295] See the Patents Manual (2007), s 46 for details on the scheme.   [296] Patents Act 1977, s 46(4).
[297] Patents Act 1977, s 47.
[298] This was following a recommendation in *Gowers Review of Intellectual Property* (HM Treasury, 2006), para 5.50.

to be met are different and we detail them in Chapter 22 in our discussion of exploitation. The important point to note for now, however, is that this scheme is rarely used and much more could be done to further the public interest in this regard. The *Gowers Review of Intellectual Property* recommended, for example, that model licence templates be established to facilitate agreements on mutually beneficial terms and obviate the need for difficult and protracted negotiation on a case-by-case basis or, indeed, the need to revert to compulsory licences at all.[299] The UK–IPO has since produced guidance *How Licensing Intellectual Property Can Help Your Business* (2008, 2011).

11.149   *Crown use* is a further limitation to a patent right.[300] This can happen when any government department or someone authorised by a government department (in writing) considers that it is in the services of the Crown to use and exploit an invention. Any act which would normally be considered an infringement is not so considered in these circumstances. 'Services of the Crown' includes supply of anything for foreign defence purposes, production or supply of specified drugs or medicines, and such purposes relating to the production or use of atomic energy or research into matter connected therewith as the Secretary of State thinks necessary or expedient.[301] Compensation is payable, however, to the patentee or exclusive licensee on the basis of the loss of profit of the contract that might have arisen for provision of the invention.[302] The Crown or its agents do not need to apply to the Comptroller to take action but any disputes will be resolved by the courts.[303]

Ownership and compensation

Ownership

11.150   We saw in Chapter 10 that anyone is at liberty to apply for a patent,[304] but who is entitled to be named as the inventor? It is important to know the answer to this because a patent is granted primarily to the inventor or joint inventors,[305] or to someone entitled to the invention by law or agreement, or ultimately a successor of either of these two categories.[306] It is the status of inventor and co-inventor that interests us here. The inventor is entitled to be named in the patent application and resulting patent even if he is not the applicant.[307] Section 7(3) of the 1977 Act states that: 'In this Act "inventor" in relation to an invention means the actual deviser of the invention and "joint inventor" shall be construed accordingly.' The test to determine inventorship is twofold: (1) what is the inventive concept? and (2) who devised that concept?[308]

11.151   You will recall from previous sections that the inventive concept is the kernel of the invention—it is the essential technical heart of the new innovation and its inventor must do more than simply proffer an initial prompt or a mere idea about where to start. That said, it is not necessary to be the one to reduce the invention to practice. If you contribute an idea that consists of the essential elements of a claim—for example, a proposal on the solution and the means to arrive at it—then this would qualify as inventorship.[309]

■ *IDA Ltd and others v University of Southampton and others* [2006] RPC 21

This was a dispute about who invented a cockroach trap. The existing art was provided by Professor Howse of Southampton University and involved a trap which worked by luring the insect into a box

---

[299] Gowers Review, paras 5.48–5.49.   [300] Patents Act 1977, ss 55–59.   [301] Patents Act 1977, s 56(2).
[302] Patents Act 1977, s 57.   [303] Patents Act 1977, s 58.   [304] Patents Act 1977, s 7(1).
[305] Patents Act 1977, s 7(2)(a).   [306] Patents Act 1977, s 7(2)(b), (c).   [307] Patents Act 1977, s 13.
[308] *Henry Brothers (Magherafelt) Ltd v The Ministry of Defence and the Northern Ireland Office* [1999] RPC 442.
[309] *Stanelco Fibre Optics Ltd's Applications* [2005] RPC 15.

with bait whereupon its feet would become contaminated with electrostatic talcum powder. This caused the insect to slip onto fly paper and die. A member of IDA, specialists in magnetic powders, read about the invention and wondered if it would work with magnetic powder—an advantage because it would not lose its 'stickiness'. He shared his idea with Mr Metcalfe in a telephone conversation and the patent in dispute was one subsequently lodged by Metcalfe in which he claimed: 'a composition comprising particles containing or consisting of at least one magnetic material.' It was held: 'This was the sole key to the information in the patent. That key was provided solely by Mr Metcalfe. Putting it another way, insofar as there is anything inventive in the patent, it was provided only by him.' It did not matter that the inventive concept was an idea because the idea provided the entire technical solution (forever-sticky magnetic powder) to the technical problem (the ongoing effectiveness of a cockroach trap).

11.152 In a dispute over entitlement to a patent, the question is simply who has an entitlement to claim to be an inventor; each claimant must establish why he has a claim to a proprietary interest in the instant patent and/or why the patentee is not entitled to it if the challenger is seeking to be named as sole inventor.[310]

Co-owners

11.153 Inventions are frequently made up by a combination of multiple features, and if different people have contributed different features towards a unitary invention then each person is considered as a co-inventor.[311]

■ *Staeng Ltd's Patent* [1996] RPC 183

The invention in question had been devised in an incremental fashion by two employees of two separate companies—one providing an initial design, the other providing an idea for improvement. It was held that this was an example of joint invention. The inventive concept lay in the use of a coiled spring to hold a cable to an adaptor—the idea of such a device came from the employee seeking to be named as sole inventor. However, the problem was solved by the other inventor, who also had expertise in the area, unlike the first employee who, it was found, would not have come up with the solution but for the role of the second employee.

11.154 Disputes such as these are resolved primarily on the basis of the evidence which the court is willing to accept. Reliable evidence of what was said, or agreed, or done, is of crucial importance. The most prudent thing to do is to begin a collaborative relationship with a written contract which addresses issues of ownership from the beginning.

11.155 The rights of co-inventors are dealt with by section 36 of the Patents Act 1977, as amended. The guiding principle is that each owner is entitled to an equal, undivided share of the property,[312] an equal share in benefits from the patent, and has an independent right to exploit the invention without the need to consult or involve co-owners.[313] This does not extend to the granting of licences, assignations, or mortgages, however, which requires the consent of all co-owners.[314] Reforms from EPC 2000 allow owners to apply to amend or revoke their own patent after grant, but in the case of co-owners this must be with the consent of all owners.[315] It is possible, however, to vary some of these rights by agreement, for example

---

[310] See *Yeda Research and Development Co Ltd v Rhone-Poulenc Rorer International Holdings Inc and others* [2008] RPC 1 on seeking to be substituted as the sole inventor.

[311] It is not enough for one party merely to follow the instructions of another, see *Stanelco Fibre Optics Ltd v Biopress Technology Ltd* [2005] RPC 319.

[312] Patents Act 1977, s 36(1).   [313] Patents Act 1977, s 36(2).

[314] Patents Act 1977, s 36(3)(b). In Scotland this also extends to the granting of a security.

[315] Patents Act 1977, s 36(3)(a), as amended by Patents Act 2004, s 9.

that one of the co-owners can grant licences unilaterally. Moreover, the Comptroller has the discretion to vary these provisions if it is thought that to do so would result in a fairer balance of interests.[316] Any disputes over who might have a valid proprietary interest in a patent are similarly determined by the Comptroller in the first instance.[317] This discretion has survived a human rights challenge when it was argued before the Court of Appeal that the discretion could not be legitimately exercised to require a co-owner to grant a licence: *Derek Hughes v Neil Paxman*.[318] The court disagreed, pointing out that it could not be the case that the legislator intended the exploitation of patents to be frustrated by deadlock situations. Moreover, there was no breach of human rights as long as the Comptroller acted rationally, fairly, and proportionately in the light of all of the circumstances. The scope of the discretionary power was not so wide as to be arbitrary.[319]

The employer/employee relationship

11.156   **Patents Act 1977, s 39**

(1)   Notwithstanding anything in any rule of law, an invention made by an employee shall, as between him and his employer, be taken to belong to his employer for the purposes of this Act and all other purposes if—

(a)   it was made in the course of the normal duties of the employee or in the course of duties falling outside his normal duties, but specifically assigned to him, and the circumstances in either case were such that an invention might reasonably be expected to result from the carrying out of his duties; or

(b)   the invention was made in the course of the duties of the employee and, at the time of making the invention, because of the nature of his duties and the particular responsibilities arising from the nature of his duties he had a special obligation to further the interests of the employer's undertaking.

(2)   Any other invention made by an employee shall, as between him and his employer, be taken for those purposes to belong to the employee.

Let's explore the elements of this provision. First, the default position is that inventions created by an employee belong to the employee and this cannot be varied by contract—such a term would be unenforceable.[320] Moreover, no one else who works with an employer, such as a consultant, need worry about their inventions (although this might give rise to problem of co-ownership, see para 11.163). It is important to know, therefore, when someone is an *employee*. This is determined on standard labour law principles[321] and the distinction is made between a contract of service (employee) and a contract of services (consultant or commissioned work).[322] Only in the specific circumstances outlined previously can an employer lay claim to an employee's invention. 'Invention' in this case does not simply mean a patentable invention, that is, one that meets the patentability criteria in this chapter, but it extends to any invention in a broad sense made by an employee and satisfying the criteria laid out earlier in section 39. So a claim may be made to an invention even if a patent will not, and could not, be sought.

---

[316] Patents Act 1977, s 37(1).

[317] Patents Act 1977, s 37(1), and Part 7 of the Patents Rules 2007 on proceedings heard before the Comptroller. Section 38 of the 1977 Act deals with the transfer of patents. Section 8 of the 1977 Act deals with the resolution of questions about entitlement to the patent which arise *before* grant.   [318] [2006] EWCA Civ 818.

[319] On the complexities of pursuing ownership in an international context and the association international private law challenges, see *Innovia Films Ltd v Frito-Lay North America, Inc* [2012] EWHC 790 (Pat).

[320] See *Electrolux v Hudson* [1977] RPC 312. See too Patents Act 1977, s 42(2) which makes unenforceable any attempt to derogate from the rights of the employee in respect of his own inventions, and Patents Manual (2007), paras 42.03–42.04.

[321] On the nature of the duty of fidelity between employee and employer, see *Helmet Integrated Systems Ltd v Tunnard and others* [2007] FSR 16.

[322] In the design case of *Ultraframe UK Ltd v Fielding* [2004] RPC 24 (see also para 9.70) it was said that a contract of service is typified by (1) circumstances where the servant has agreed that, in consideration of a wage or other remuneration, he would provide his own work and skill in the performance of some service for his master, (2) he agreed, expressly or implied, that in the performance of that service, he would be subject to the other's control in a sufficient degree to make the other master, and (3) the provisions of the contract were consistent with it being a contract of service. Control is key.

11.157   The provisions apply when an employee has invented something *either* in the course of his normal duties *or* when specific duties are assigned to him and in *both* cases the nature of those duties is such that an invention is the likely result.[323] Moreover, in other contexts when an employee has a *special obligation* to further his employer's interests then resulting inventions may also be claimed. This class of employee usually includes managers or directors with overarching responsibilities which necessarily encompass inventive activity within a business. The Court of Appeal in *Liffe Administration & Management v Pinkova*[324] ruled on the meaning of 'normal duties' under section 39(1) of the Patents Act 1977 and dismissed an employee's claim to an invention relating to an electronic trading system that he had devised while employed by Liffe. The ruling emphasised that the test under section 39(1)(a) is an objective one and that duties are not only established and set in the terms of the original contract, but may evolve over time as the job changes. It was also stated that the expectations an employer might have that an invention will result from an employee's normal duties should be directly linked to the person and the skills they possess; the reasonableness of the expectation should be judged accordingly. If a person is hired to innovate it would normally follow that the provisions of section 39(1) would be satisfied.

■ *Greater Glasgow Health Board's Application* [1996] RPC 207

A Registrar employed by the health board in the Tennent Research Institute invented an optical spacing device for use with an indirect ophthalmoscope. He conceived this idea while at home and not during his professional duties. His job description stated that his duties were clinical in nature: he had a duty to serve in the out-patient department, and this included casualty, ophthalmic, and general care of in-patients and ophthalmic surgery. His job description also included a number of other functions, which were not described as duties, and which included undergraduate and postgraduate teaching. He was also 'expected to avail himself of the facilities provided' for basic and clinical research. This having been said, his Head of Department did not consider that he was employed to carry out research. The health board argued that because of the very nature of his working environment in a research institute, he was expected to use his experiences of treating patients to produce novel forms of treatment and prevention. The patent was taken in the name of the board and the dispute arose when Dr Montgomery argued that he should be named as sole inventor. It was held that Dr Montgomery should be named as such. It was fallacious to expect that a person with clinical duties and responsibilities towards patients should necessarily be required by his contract to devise novel ways of diagnosing and treating patients. The fact that he was employed within a research institute was not, of itself, determinative of the issue. The focus must be on the terms of the employment contract as they stood, and these clearly revealed that his duties were clinical in nature and not innovative.

11.158   Another relevant factor in this case was that the creation of the invention had nothing to do with the carrying out of his duties. Dr Montgomery was a junior member of staff who spent nearly all of his time treating patients. He made the invention in his own time, he was not working to treat any particular patient or class of patients, indeed, he was concerned with the problem of eye examination generally—the invention could not be reasonably expected to result from his duties.

11.159   The importance of evidence in these cases is illustrated by *Liffe Administration and Management v Pinkava and another* which concerned inventions related to the trading of various types of financial instruments on an electronic exchange. Evidence to the court at first instance[325] showed that the inventions developed by the employee were not part of his normal duties as a product manager employed in the marketing

---

[323] An early decision is *Harris' Patent* [1985] RPC 19 which considered the pre-1977 Act position where this area was governed by the common law.

[324] [2007] RPC 30.   [325] [2006] EWHC 595 (Pat).

and product management department, but that they did arise directly from a project he was assigned to work on to develop an exchange tradable contract and this was evidenced by the nature of the initial discussions and subsequent focus of the project. The employee tried to argue that the inventions were ones unlikely to arise from the discharge of his duties, inter alia, because the employer had no history of invention. This was held not to be necessary for section 39(1) to apply, as the employer (any employer?) had a clear interest in new developments and products. It was also relevant from the evidence that the employee was known as an 'ideas man' in the firm and the expectation was that he would be creative in the discharge of his duties. This was confirmed by the Court of Appeal in dismissing the appeal.[326]

> ### Key point on employee invention
>
> • It is not sufficient merely to produce an invention which would assist an employer in tackling the problems which he faces in the course of his business or profession. This is an example of an *indirect* invention which, at best, builds on the general experience and stock of knowledge of the individual inventor, *qua* an individual and not *qua* employee. Rather, an invention which is to fall to an employer must result from the workings of an employee *qua* inventor. In other words, when his job of work *directly* requires him to invent or his duties *directly* lead him to invent; all as a *direct* consequence of doing his job of work

11.160   Consider now *Staeng Ltd's Patent* (para 11.153). The circumstances of this dispute involved, inter alia, the question of whether an employee of company H, which was soon to be taken over by company S, could be named as the sole inventor of an invention which was not part of the business of his employer. The invention in suit related to a means of securing an electrical cable sheathing to the body portion of a 'connector backshell adaptor'. Company H was not in the business of backshell adaptors, but rather was concerned with developing products for the cable industry. All technology relating to backshell adaptors had to be bought in from company S. The employee argued that it was not reasonable to imply that an individual's obligations included the making of an invention if that invention was not within the business of the employer. The employer argued that its broader business interests included backshell adaptors and, indeed, it had marketed S's adaptors as though they were its own. The employee's duties involved innovation and the seeking out of novel uses for existing products. It was held that the invention belonged to the employer. The employee had made the invention in the course of his normal duties and the circumstances were such that the invention might reasonably be expected to results from the carrying on of his duties. The intimate connection between the products produced by the employer and the invention meant that the invention was within the broad field of the employer's business. Furthermore, the position of the employee as a senior executive with knowledge and insight into the business's future interests, viz, the merger, meant he had a *special obligation* under section 39(1).

11.161   Factors which might make a difference in these cases therefore include:

• Where was the invention produced (work or home)?

• Was the invention produced during working hours?

• What is the standing of the employee within the employer's hierarchy?

• What are the specific contractual duties and which other duties can reasonably be inferred?

• What role has the employee actually assumed in the discharge of his duties?

---

[326] See also *Cinpres Gas Injection Ltd v Melea Ltd* [2008] RPC 17.

Question

Do you think it is relevant if materials from the workplace are used to create the invention?

11.162 We can easily imagine a situation where an employer might be entitled to an employee's invention, but that the employee's claim to the invention is partial because he has invented the product or process jointly with someone else who is not an employee. In such cases what should the employer do?

11.163 These questions were addressed by the Scottish Court of Session in *Goddin and Rennie's Application*.[327] In this case the patent concerned covers for circular tanks, in particular fish tanks. While the original design was conceived by G in respect of his salmon-rearing business, the design was improved by R, who was commissioned to make the net covers. Initially both contributors were named on the patent application but a dispute arose and G brought a claim that the patent application should proceed solely in the name of his company, W. The arguments were: first, R's contribution was merely ancillary to the inventive principle which had been discovered by G. Secondly, even if that were not the case, the contract of services contained an implied term that W was entitled to the exclusive benefit of what R devised in the course of his work. The court held that G was entitled to the patent in his name alone. R's contract was clearly to produce an improved design, but the contract would not make business sense unless it contained an implied term that any improved design was the property of W. This having been said, certain features of the frame for the nets had been suggested by R prior to, and separately from, the contract and as such he was entitled to the benefit of the features introduced by them. As a consequence, while G was entitled to the patent, R was entitled to an irrevocable exclusive licence, with power to sub-license in respect of the features which he had added.

11.164 This ruling in respect of the intellectual property of the commissioned person, and the authorities on which it is based,[328] reflects some of the approaches we have seen in copyright law where there has been recognition of *equitable interests* in respect of commissioned work (see paras 3.25ff). While the starting point is that a commissioned person retains the intellectual property of that which he creates, it is also true that it is illogical to enter a contract with someone to create a new entity if there is no underlying assumption that the entity will come within the control of the commissioner. It makes sound sense to read an implied clause into the contract in these circumstances. Note, however, the law does not specifically recognise equitable interests in the context. The practical answer is that the commissioned person should include an *express* term that any IPRs are to be retained if that is his intention. In practice, of course, it is unlikely that any such term will be accepted. More likely to survive is a term which specifically states that the invention is to be regarded as having been created jointly with licensing or other rights specified accordingly.

Compensation of employees for certain inventions

11.165 Sections 40 and 41 of the Patents Act 1977 provide for a compensation scheme for employees when the provisions of section 39 apply or when they have transferred their patent rights to their employer and the benefit in return is inadequate.[329] These provisions have been reformed over the years to widen the circumstances in which compensation might be paid. Thus section 40(1) now provides:

[327] [1996] RPC 141.   [328] *Bogrich & Shape Machines Ltd's Application*, 4 November 1994, unreported.
[329] S Wolk, 'Remuneration of employee inventors—is there a common European ground? A comparison of national laws on compensation of inventors in Germany, France, Spain, Sweden and the United Kingdom' (2011) 42(3) IIC 272–298.

Where it appears to the court or the comptroller on an application made by an employee within the prescribed period that—

(a) the employee has made an invention belonging to the employer for which a patent has been granted,

(b) having regard among other things to the size and nature of the employer's undertaking, the invention or the patent for it (or the combination of both) is of outstanding benefit to the employer, and

(c) by reason of those facts it is just that the employee should be awarded compensation to be paid by the employer,

the court or the comptroller may award him such compensation of an amount determined under section 41 below.

11.166   Note: compensation can be triggered when the patent *or* the invention *or* both prove to be of outstanding benefit to the employer. Previously, the scheme could only be invoked when the *patent* was of outstanding benefit. Not only was this more difficult to prove, but it necessitated that a patent was granted. As we have seen, even non-patentable inventions can be claimed by employers and even those which are patentable might sometimes be better protected by other means, for example trade secrets (see Chapter 18). This anomaly has now been rectified. Notwithstanding, a serious hurdle still faces the employee because the qualifying threshold remains the same: there must be an *outstanding benefit* to the employer. How do we know when this has happened?

■ *British Steel plc's Patent* [1992] RPC 117

In this case the employer contended that the benefit derived from the employee's invention of a new valve, for use in steel-making, should not be linked to the patented product itself but rather to the extensive development work expended on it by the employer after the application had been filed. This work had been carried out to remove what the Comptroller's hearing called 'major technical obstacles [which] stood in the way of the deployment of the rotary valve'. Thus, the employer had to incur considerable development costs before any tangible benefit accrued. This argument was, however, rejected by the hearing officer. This having been said, the employee's claim was refused because benefits had not (yet) flowed to the employer from the grant of the patent. Thus a real benefit must be shown and not merely the promise of benefit.

11.167   Is this 'just'? Were it otherwise, the paradox would arise whereby the more an employee invention departs from traditional technology the less likely it would ever be that he would receive compensation because of the necessary development costs which would be incurred by the employer.

11.168   Benefit from a patent is readily provable if the employer is in receipt of royalty payments from licensees. If, however, the employer chooses to exploit the invention himself, it becomes harder to prove.

 Discussion point   For answer guidance visit www.oxfordtextbooks.co.uk/orc/macqueen2e/

How many reasons can you think of for an increased order book?

■ *Memco-Med's Patent* [1992] RPC 403

Did the employer's sales of a patented product to a single customer amount to the creation of an outstanding benefit? In this case the lift manufacturers Otis encouraged the employer, Memco-Med, to refine an existing patent which related to door detector units and two employees undertook the task. As an incentive, Otis ordered 1,000 models of the new unit. However, the unit experienced problems and Otis changed their order to buy a new improved model. Nonetheless, in the overall period the employer earned £4 million. Unfortunately for the employees who claimed compensation, the court considered that sales were due entirely to good relations between the companies and could not be attributable to the patent, even though the new model 'stood on the shoulders' of the work done by the employees.

■ *GEC's Patent* [1992] RPC 107

The employer obtained a patent for a cockpit display unit which had been invented by their employee for use in military aircraft. The US Air Force placed substantial orders. Unfortunately, contracts could not be fulfilled because units had to be redesigned and tested. Further contracts were placed for non-patented equipment worth $75 million each. In 1986 the employer signed a main contract to supply redesigned equipment based on the patented invention. This contract was worth $72 million. The employee argued that the early sums of $75 million should be regarded as benefits deriving from the possession of a patent over the invention. It was argued that such contracts would not have been agreed but for the initial order based on the patent. It was held that the evidential burden falls on the shoulders of the employee. He was unable to discharge this given the overall size of the firm involved; in relative terms, the figures in question were not 'outstanding'.

■ *Kelly and another v GE Healthcare Ltd* [2009] RPC 12

This case is the first to award compensation to employees under section 40 of the 1977 Act. Two inventors sought a share of the profits under section 40 as compensation for the invention of a compound used in radioactive imaging which they developed while employed as research scientists. In deciding whether the patents were of 'outstanding benefit' to the company, the court took all circumstances into consideration, including the size and nature of the employer's undertaking, and came to the conclusion that the benefits of the invention went far beyond anything that could normally be expected to arise from the sort of work the employees had undertaken. The benefit was not limited to profits from sales as the resulting patents also protected the business against generic competition and were highly influential in achieving corporate deals. The patents had recently expired which allowed the court to quantify more exactly the benefit those patents had brought to the employer. Courts had shown themselves unwilling in previous cases to speculate on future benefits that patents might bring, but as that was unnecessary here, this could not bar the award of compensation.[330]

What is an 'outstanding benefit'?

(1) Benefit in question must exist at time of employee's application (future possible benefits affect quantum of compensation only).

(2) 'Outstanding' is much more than 'substantial' and 'valuable'.

(3) 'Outstanding' must be assessed in the light of all facts and circumstances. Thus, compensation is more likely from a smaller firm than a larger firm. Paradoxically, this is likely to mean that smaller firms will be liable to pay compensation which only larger firms can truly afford.

11.169 The scheme also applies when an employee retains an entitlement to his invention but has assigned it or granted an exclusive licence to his employer and when the benefit under the contract is

---

[330] See A Odell West, '*Kelly v GE Healthcare Ltd*: employee innovation in health care—deciphering ownership and the alchemy of "outstanding benefit"' (2010) 32(9) EIPR 449 and C Howell, 'Extra compensation for inventive employees: is our system equitable, unbiased and motivating?' [2011] 4 IPQ 371.

'inadequate' and it is 'just' that the employee should be awarded compensation.[331] In cases where the employer has further assigned the rights to another, the Court of Appeal has ruled that the basis of any compensation to be paid is to be calculated on the details of the actual assignee and its actual attributes, that is, there is to be no notional auction of the value of the patent because this could artificially and vastly inflate its potential worth well beyond what an assignee could ever afford.[332]

 Question

How would you assess what was 'inadequate' and 'just' in these circumstances? Could you get access to your employer's accounts to see what income had been generated?

11.170   Section 41 of the 1977 Act deals with the amount of compensation to be awarded.[333] This must obviously be decided on a case-by-case basis. The guiding parameters include the following: (1) the aim is to confer a *fair share* of the benefit of the invention and/or the patent; (2) *benefit* includes money and money's worth from exploitation of the invention and/or patent; (3) it is assessed by reference to the following, among other things; (4) nature of the employee's duties and any benefits from the invention; (5) the effort and skill he has displayed; (6) the efforts and skill of others in developing the invention; (7) the effort and skill of the employer in bringing the invention to fruition and market.

Infringement proceedings

11.171   It is all very well to have a range of sophisticated patent rights but these are worthless in the absence of a robust enforcement system. We consider broader issues of enforcement in Chapter 22; here we concentrate on enforcement of patents through infringement proceedings.

11.172   The first thing to note when you read the cases is that an action for infringement is often met with a counterclaim that the patent is invalid and should be revoked. We therefore deal with revocation in the next section. This possibility means that a patent is vulnerable throughout its life and it is a strategic question whether it is worth bringing infringement proceedings when this might result in the complete extinguishing of your property right in the long run.

11.173   If proceedings are brought, it ends up being an extremely costly business. The *Gowers Review of Intellectual Property* estimated, for example, that a firm challenging a patent can expect to pay £750,000 for a simple case, and if one loses, the costs of the other side could bring the total to over £1.5 million.[334]

11.174   This section is divided into two parts. In the first part we consider the grounds for infringement actions and the types of conduct which qualify. In the second part we consider how the courts approach the interpretation of patent claims because it is in this interpretation that we discover the fine lines between legitimate and illegitimate conduct with respect to patented inventions.

---

[331] Patents Act 1977, s 40(2).
[332] See *Shanks v Unilever plc* [2011] RPC 12. For comment, J Pila, '"Sewing the fly buttons on the statute": employee inventions and the employment context' (2012) 32(2) OJLS 265.
[333] Amended by the Patents Act 2004, s 10(3).   [334] *Gowers Review of Intellectual Property* (HM Treasury, 2006), para 3.21.

What counts as patent infringement?

11.175 Article 64(3) EPC 2000 makes it clear that infringement proceedings are to be dealt with by national law. In the UK, the principal infringing acts are laid out in sections 60(1) and 60(2) of the Patents Act 1977.

> **60(1)** Subject to the provision of this section, a person infringes a patent for an invention if, but only if, while the patent is in force, he does any of the following things in the United Kingdom in relation to the invention without the consent of the proprietor of the patent, that is to say—
>
> (a) where the invention is a product, he makes, disposes of, offers to dispose of, uses or imports the product or keeps it whether for disposal or otherwise;
>
> (b) where the invention is a process, he uses the process or he offers it for use in the United Kingdom when he knows, or it is obvious to a reasonable person in the circumstances, that its use there without the consent of the proprietor would be an infringement of the patent;
>
> (c) where the invention is a process, he disposes of, offers to dispose of, uses or imports any product obtained directly by means of that process.

11.176 So, as we can see, it is important to know what kind of invention we are dealing with because what counts as infringement depends on this and, sometimes, on the knowledge of the alleged infringer. Note, however, in the context of a product there is no knowledge requirement. This means that even the so-called innocent infringer can be liable if he carries out any of the acts detailed in section 60(1)(a) which deals with product inventions or in section 60(1)(c) which deals with process inventions which result in a product. It is irrelevant whether the infringer knew of the patent or of the lack of owner consent. This is referred to as 'absolute' liability.[335]

> **? Question**
>
> Can we justify such a draconian approach to liability?

11.177 These are all examples of *direct* infringement which involve direct dealings with the invention itself. Section 60(2) is concerned with *indirect* infringement which arises when someone facilitates a directly infringing act by supplying or offering to supply any of the means relating to an essential element of the invention, for putting the invention into effect, *and* with actual or constructive knowledge that those means are suitable for putting, and are intended to put, the invention into effect in the UK.

11.178 Note this last point. We have already established that patents are creatures of territorial effect only, and so infringement proceedings in the UK can only be brought with respect to activities within its shores. It is also trite to note that the law is only concerned with acts done during the life of the patent. Infringement proceedings can be brought for any conduct from the date the patent application is published to the end of the patent's term.[336] Those who can bring infringement proceedings include the proprietor of the patent, co-proprietors,[337] and exclusive licensees.[338]

11.179 Let us consider each of the infringing behaviours in turn.

---

[335] *Merrell Dow v Norton* [1996] RPC 76 per Lord Hoffmann at 92.

[336] Albeit that the right cannot be enforced until the patent is actually granted, see the Patents Act 1977, s 69.

[337] Each co-proprietor can do any act independently with respect to the invention which would otherwise be an infringement: Patents Act 1977, s 66, and each can bring independent infringement proceedings without the consent of the others subject to the proviso that co-owners are made parties to the proceedings, s 66(2).

[338] An exclusive licensee has the same right as the proprietor to bring infringement actions, see the Patents Act 1977, s 67(1).

Making the invention

11.180   It is clearly an infringement to make copies of someone else's existing invention, but what is the position if you buy the original item under patent and then modify it or repair it? This question was considered by the House of Lords in *United Wire Ltd v Screen Repair Services (Scotland) Ltd*[339] which involved mesh screen assemblies used in sifting and filtering machines. The defendants tried to enter the market by selling reconditioned versions of the plaintiffs' screens which had been stripped down and new mesh applied. They then tried to argue that this was mere 'repair' and not 'making' and so outside the scope of section 60(1). It was held that while 'genuine repair' is a legitimate activity, this conduct went far beyond and was equivalent to reproducing an infringing assembly. The concepts of 'repair' and 'making' are entirely distinct in patent law with the latter involving some form of manufacture. The right to repair is not an implied licence, but rather the residual right left over once the parameters of patent protection have been demarcated by the operation of section 60. In the instant case, the disassembly of the product was so extreme that it effectively ceased to exist and its reconstitution with new elements was in effect a new infringing manufacture.

11.181   The Supreme Court revisited this area in *Schutz (UK) Ltd v Werit UK Ltd*[340] and clarified the legal test as a result. The case involved a dispute over alleged infringement of a patent on large container devices for transportation of goods that included a strong frame capable of supporting rough treatment and considerable weight, into which were inserted 'bottles'—being plastic containers that were protected by the frame but which necessarily had to be changed with relative frequency because of damage or contamination. The question was whether the provision of replacement bottles by companies not holding the patent was an infringement. The judge at first instance had proposed a 'whole inventive concept' test whereby he suggested that in considering infringement under this heading the court must 'ask whether, when the part in question is removed, what is left embodies the whole of the inventive concept of the claim.' This was rejected by the Court of Appeal, but the Supreme Court upheld the finding of non-infringement. It confirmed that the meaning of 'making' necessarily is context specific and that any approach adopted by the courts involves ordinary understandable meaning and requires a careful weighing of factors. In the instant case it was relevant to ask whether the bottle was 'such a subsidiary part of the patented article that its replacement did not involve "making" a new article.' On balance, it was held that it was, being a freestanding and replaceable component that had no connection to the inventive concept as described in the patent claims. It did no substantial work to the essential features of the claimed invention.

Disposing of, offering to dispose of, or using the invention

11.182   Manifestly it is not an infringement of a patent for someone who has bought an example of an invention to sell it on as a piece of personal property—this is another example of the residual rights that the purchaser enjoys; moreover, attempts by a patent proprietor to prevent the sale and circulation of goods that he himself has placed on the market will be faced with challenges under European law because the principle of exhaustion of rights will apply as will the principle of free movement of goods (see Chapter 20). Rather, this provision concerns the commercialisation of infringing copies of an invention, and must include, at least, selling.[341]

Importing the invention

11.183   Here we are concerned with the activities of someone who imports an invention in the course of their trade, for example with a view to selling them on. A mere carrier or someone who arranges the importation on behalf of the owner of the goods is not considered to be a direct infringer because they have no

---

[339] [2001] RPC 24.   [340] [2013] UKSC 16, [2013] 2 All ER 177.
[341] *Kalman and another v PCL Packaging (UK) Ltd and another* [1982] FSR 406.

legal or beneficial interest in those goods.[342] This is true even if this person has sold the goods to the now owner outside the UK.[343] It is possible for two or more parties involved in the importation business to be jointly liable as joint tortfeasors, but this requires a common design or concerted action on all parts. The mere supplying of goods outside the jurisdiction for sale within the jurisdiction is not constitutive of joint tortfeasorship. Nor is it illegal to pass on information to domestic regulatory authorities on behalf of another party who has an intention to receive approval to sell versions of the invention on the domestic market. This does not make the third party complicit in the seller's commercial venture.[344] In keeping with the fragmented territorial nature of patent protection, the European Court of Justice has ruled that it is not possible to bring patent infringement proceedings in one state against a group of allegedly infringing parties in various different states *even if* those parties belong to the same corporate group and *even if* they have been acting in an identical or similar manner with respect to infringing activity.[345]

Keeping the invention

11.184   Once again, we are concerned here with acts done in the course of trade; acting as a mere custodian of goods does not amount to 'keeping' within the terms of the Act which has been interpreted to mean 'keeping in stock' with a view to furthering business ends. In *McDonald and another v Graham*[346] the invention in question was promotional 'Z cards' which were designed to fold out to show publicity material and to fold back down to the size of a credit card. Despite instructions to destroy any remaining copies in his possession, a business associate of the patentee was found to have a stock on his business premises. His argument that these were for private or experimental use did not hold on the evidence. Rather, he was 'keeping them in stock for the purposes of his business in order to make use of them as and when it would be beneficial to him to do so'. In contrast there was no finding of 'keeping' in *Smith, Kline and French Labs Ltd v Harbottle*[347] when a quantity of the drug Cimetidine was shipped through Heathrow on its way to Nigeria and held in British Airways' bonded warehouse under the custodianship of Harbottle. It was held that this was not an example of 'keeping' under the statutory provision. The *Oxford English Dictionary* reveals 26 nuanced meanings of this word and the correct approach for the court was to identify the mischief to be avoided and interpret the term accordingly. If the mere holding of material in a warehouse was intended to be caught by this law it would have been expressed in far stronger terms.[348]

11.185   Section 60(1)(c) confirms that a patent over a process gives monopoly control over any products derived from that process, and this can be a useful tool if, say, the process is performed outside the jurisdiction but the end products are imported into the UK—infringement proceedings could still be brought. The caveat, however, is found in the specific wording of the subsection when it talks of ' any product obtained *directly* by means of that process'.

■ *Pioneer Electronics Capital Inc v Warner Music Manufacturing Europe GmbH* [1997] RPC 757

This case involved a patented process for manufacturing CDs. The rival company's imported versions of the product certainly seemed to involve the process, but had they been 'directly' obtained? It was held that the question fell to be decided by reference to Article 64(2) EPC, the terminology of which had its origin in German law. The German authorities were consistent in their approach, taking 'directly'

---

[342] *Sabaf* in the House of Lords, note 255.

[343] Compare the trade mark case of *Waterford Wedgwood plc v David Nagli Ltd* [1998] FSR 92 in which the seller imported the goods into the UK while still retaining ownership rights. This constituted infringement.

[344] *Generics (UK) Ltd v H Lundbeck A/S* [2006] EWCA Civ 1261; aff'd [2009] UKHL 12.

[345] Case C-539/03 *Roche Nederland BV and others v Primus and another* [2006] All ER (D) 186 (Jul), OJ C 224 of 16.09.2006, p 1.

[346] [1994] RPC 407.   [347] [1980] RPC 363.

[348] This is also a more accurate reflection of the sense in which the term is employed in the Community Patent Convention, Art 29(a) and the two instruments should be read in tandem where possible.

(*unmittelbar*) to refer to the product with which the process ended. It was not correct to say that the finished disc was an identical copy of the master. The allegedly infringing devices in the instant case differed in material ways from the patented invention, notably for having gone through three further stages of production. A new and different product emerged from each stage. The Court of Appeal used the expression 'without intermediary' implying, perhaps, that the result should be immediate and precluding any possibility of further processing. But the Patent Court has more recently considered the issue and raised the possibility from German jurisprudence that it is not the number of intermediary stages which is important, but the question of whether they are material to the identity of the product—only if it emerges with the same identity as the invention will there be infringement.[349]

Indirect infringement

11.186   Section 60(2) deals with indirect or contributory infringement. It states:

> a person...also infringes a patent for an invention if, while the patent is in force and without the consent of the proprietor, he supplies or offers to supply in the United Kingdom a person...with any of the means relating to an essential element of the invention, for putting the invention into effect when he knows, or it is obvious to a reasonable person in the circumstances, that those means are suitable for putting, and are intended to put, the invention into effect in the United Kingdom.

The important issues are well illustrated in the case of *Menashe Business Mercantile Ltd and another v William Hill Organisation Ltd*[350] which also tells us something about what is meant by infringement occurring in the UK. This is because the case involved an online gaming system linked to a central computer in the Caribbean. Customers were sent software on CDs which allowed their home computers to communicate with the host computer. The patentees owned an interactive gaming system with a host computer that operated in a similar fashion to that of the defendants, but could this system be infringed when the defendants' computer was offshore? Moreover, could the supply of CDs to British customers amount to supply of the means for putting the invention into effect? It was held that the alleged infringers' host computer was 'used' in the UK by customers in a very real sense and it did not matter that it was physically located abroad. The key issue was whether persons in the UK had been supplied with the means of implementing the invention, and this was so through the supply of the CDs which allowed access to the host computer and so to the entire online gaming system. The supply of the CDs in the UK would be taken as intended to put the invention into effect and the patent was infringed.

11.187   The classic example of contributory infringement is the supply of kits for an invention which are assembled at a later date. Clearly, if you provide all of the necessary elements of an invention you are supplying the 'essential element' of the invention. By the same token, if you merely provide 'staple commercial products' which someone else takes and puts together into an infringing device or apparatus, you would not be liable for infringement, for example if you merely provide the nuts and bolts and electrical circuits. By the same token, your level of knowledge, or indeed intention to be complicit, are relevant factors in whether infringement proceedings could be brought or would succeed.[351] The relevant intention is that of the end user and not the supplier, as such.[352] Notwithstanding, a 'reasonable person' approach to what is known and likely to be understood is adopted by the courts to infer the necessary contributory infringement. Thus, in *KCI Licensing Inc and others v Smith & Nephew plc and others*[353] a supplier of a canister for use in patented wound treatment that involved 'clamp means' to prevent the escape of liquid was held to have infringed the patent even though no clamps were supplied or any suggestion made

---

[349] *Halliburton Energy Services Inc v Smith International and others* [2005] EWHC 1623 (Pat).
[350] [2003] 1 All ER 279, [2003] 1 WLR 1462.   [351] Patents Act 1977, s 60(3).   [352] *Grimme v Scott* [2010] EWCA 1110.
[353] [2010] EWCA Civ 1260.

about use of the canister by the supplier. This was so because it was obvious to a person in the hospital environment how the canister would be used and the necessary clamps were easily available.[354]

 Question

What counts as 'staple commercial products'?

Interpretation of patent claims

11.188 The question of whether there is infringement is far from straightforward when a rival has produced their own version of an invention aimed at the same technical problem and solving it in similar technical ways, perhaps with similar features. How do we know if such variants infringe an existing patent? This brings us to the complex question of *interpretation of patent claims*. We have already considered the importance of careful drafting of claims in the previous chapter, and we have made the point that it is imperative to choose the language of claims carefully because this will delineate the nature, breadth, and scope of any monopoly granted. We now turn to consider the rules that apply when these claims have to be interpreted. It is probably in the realm of interpretation that EPC 1973 brought most changes to the law in the UK. Article 69(1) EPC 1973 provided that 'The extent of the protection conferred by a European patent or a European patent application shall be determined by the terms of the claims', and the drawings and description shall also be used to interpret the claims. This remains unchanged in EPC 2000 and its UK equivalent is found in section 125 of the Patents Act 1977. Article 69 has, however, been accompanied by a Protocol on Interpretation of Article 69 because a variety of approaches were used around Europe at the time the EPC was drafted. The Protocol is designed to provide guidance to national courts on how to tackle interpretation in a uniform fashion that is in keeping with the spirit of the Convention. That spirit is grounded in the Continental legal tradition which favours a *purposive approach* to interpretation, that is, one that seeks to give effect to the underlying reasons for the particular legal provision.

11.189 This posed a challenge for the UK which had a very different tradition and was inclined to adopt a *literal approach* to claim interpretation, that is, to ask what is the literal meaning of the words used. What we have seen, then, in the last quarter century or so, is a shift of perspective among the UK judiciary in an attempt to accommodate a more purposive stance.[355] It is a matter of ongoing discussion as to how well they have fared. This process actually began before Article 69 and its Protocol came about, as we see later, but for the sake of completeness here are the principal provisions of the Protocol as embodied in EPC 2000.

Protocol on Interpretation of Article 69 EPC—Article 1

Article 69 should not be interpreted as meaning that the extent of the protection conferred by a European patent is to be understood as that defined by the strict, literal meaning of the wording used in the claims, the description and drawings being employed only for the purpose of resolving an ambiguity found in the claims.

Nor should it be taken to mean that the claims serve only as a guideline and that the actual protection conferred may extend to what, from a consideration of the description and drawings by a person skilled in the art, the patent proprietor has contemplated.

On the contrary, it is to be interpreted as defining a position between these extremes which combines a fair protection for the patent proprietor with a reasonable degree of legal certainty for third parties.

---

[354] For a discussion of the principles relevant to an assessment of damages in indirect infringements, see *Fabio Perini SpA v LPC Group plc* [2012] EWHC 911 (Ch).

[355] For a recent example of purposive interpretation in action, see *Convatec Ltd v Smith & Nephew Healthcare Ltd* [2011] EWHC 2039 (Pat), [2012] RPC 9.

11.190   This clearly eschews a literal approach (which is thought to be too narrow), but equally it does not give carte blanche to discover a patentee's true purpose or intentions (which is thought to be too broad). The expectation is that a middle course should be steered; one which seeks both certainty and fairness of outcome. It is by no means an easy task and helps to explain why patent interpretation is a complex business. It is important that we begin by laying out the parameters of Article 69 and its Protocol because, as Lord Hoffmann indicated in *Kirin-Amgen v Hoechst Marion Roussel Ltd*,[356] these embody the only compulsory question in claim interpretation, viz, 'what would the person skilled in the art have understood the patentee to have used the language of the claim to mean?' Everything else—that is, any approaches that have been developed over the years (see paras 11.194ff)—are mere guidance towards an answer to this question. But Lord Hoffmann also said that it is important to have a sense of the origins of the English (British) rules of interpretation, so let us begin with the seminal House of Lords ruling that signalled the sea-change in this field.

■ *Catnic Components Ltd v Hill and Smith Ltd* [1982] RPC 183 (HL)

Catnic were the proprietors of a patent in respect of steel lintels of considerable commercial success. The defendants decided to enter the field and to copy Catnic's lintels. Catnic served a writ on the defendants for patent infringement and as a result the latter changed the design of their lintels by slanting the rear support member at 6°–8° from the vertical, compared to that of the plaintiffs which was perpendicular to the base (see Figures 11.1 and 11.2). Claim 1 of the patent required that the rear support member 'extend vertically'. The question therefore arose as to whether the new lintels made by the defendants infringed the patent of the plaintiffs. This would not be so on a literal interpretation of the words used.

It was held that:

- The patent had been infringed. A literal interpretation of the wording of claims in a patent is not the correct approach to adopt when interpreting claims unless this is clearly the intention of the patentee. The English tradition of applying a 'pith and marrow' perspective was no longer appropriate.[357] A purposive rather than literal approach to interpretation is appropriate.

- The effect of the angulation of the rear support member was negligible as regards the load-bearing capacity of the lintel. At an angle of 6° the reduction is only 0.6 per cent. At 8° the reduction is 1.2 per cent. In other words, this had no material effect on how the lintel worked.

- The question to be asked in each case is as follows: would persons with practical knowledge and experience of the kind of work in which the invention is intended to be used, understand that strict compliance with the particular descriptive word or phrase appearing in the claim was intended by the patentee to be an essential requirement of the invention so that *any* variant would fall outside the monopoly claimed, even though it could have no material effect upon the way the invention worked?

- The question is to be answered in the negative only when it would be apparent to any reader skilled in the art that a particular descriptive word or phrase used in a claim cannot have been intended by a patentee, who was also skilled in the art, to exclude minor variations which, to the knowledge of both him and the readers to whom the patent is addressed, could have no material effect upon the way in which the invention worked.

- In this case no plausible reason was advanced why any rational patentee should want to place so narrow a limitation on his invention. To do so would render his monopoly worthless for all practical purposes.[358]

---

[356] [2005] RPC 9.

[357] The 'pith and marrow' approach was invented by Lord Cairns in *Clark v Adie* (1877) 2 App Cas 315 at 320 and involved a rather vague approach of stripping the invention down by the removal of 'immaterial' or 'non-essential' features or integers to deter what, if anything, the infringer had taken.   [358] Cf *Verathon Medical (Canada) Ltd v Aircraft Medical Ltd* [2011] CSOH 19.

Figure **11.1** Claimant's lintel

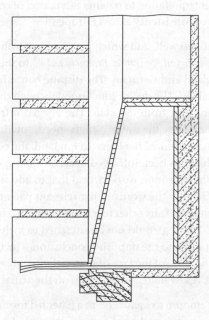

Figure **11.2** Defendant's lintel

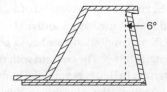

11.191   The decision has had a considerable role to play in changing the way in which patent monopolies function. It is now no longer possible (as it was pre-*Catnic*) to make minor changes in a product or process
in an attempt to evade the terms of the monopoly. This also means that improvements in efficiency or
speed of operation will not necessarily lead to a patentable invention and will infringe an existing patent
if the essential idea embodied in the patent remains unchanged. By the same token, it does not follow
that a purposive approach is necessarily more generous to the patentee. It is contingent on what the
skilled person would consider the purpose to be, and this may be fairly narrow in scope.[359]

11.192   An essential feature of this decision was the fact that the change of angulation in the rear support member made a negligible change to the load-bearing capacity of the lintel. The House of Lords was emphatic
in its assertion that the test laid down as described previously, does not apply where the variant does in
fact have a material effect upon the way in which the invention works. If this is so then the variant will
not infringe the particular claim. Furthermore, if the fact that a variant made no material difference to
the way the invention works was not obvious to a person skilled in the particular art at the date of publication of the patent, then the variant will also fall outside the claim.

---

[359] As to what and how much the skilled reader can be expected to know about the law and practice of the patent system, see *Virgin
Atlantic Airways Ltd v Premium Aircraft Interiors UK Ltd* [2009] EWCA Civ 1062.

11.193 This case began to bring the UK into line with the approaches of the EPO and other Continental patent courts which apply a purposive interpretation to patents as a matter of course.[360] This does not, however, mean that we have as yet achieved consistency across Europe.[361]

11.194 The case which illustrates this all too well, and which put the most important gloss on the *Catnic* decision, is *Improver Corporation v Remington Consumer Products Ltd*.[362] In this case litigation was conducted on the same matter in both England and Germany. The dispute concerned an electronic hair-removing device for women called the 'Epilady'. The device functioned through the use of a high-speed, rotating, arc-shaped spring which plucked hair from the skin. The alleged infringing device—the 'Smooth & Silky'—performed the same function by the use of a high-speed, rotating, arc-shaped synthetic rubber rod into which were cut slits which captured the hairs. In England, the court applied *Catnic* and came to the conclusion that the patent had not been infringed because although the variant made no material difference to the way in which the invention worked, and that to adopt the rubber rod was obvious to a person skilled in the art, the fact that the words of the relevant patent claim referred specifically to a 'helical spring' and made no mention of any other mechanism for working the invention meant that the interpretation of the term 'helical spring' could not be stretched to include a rubber rod. In the equivalent German decision, the court came to the opposite conclusion. The German court was satisfied that the patent was clearly infringed because of the lack of material difference and the obviousness of replacing the spring with a rubber rod. It saw no reason to dwell on the actual words of the patent.

11.195 This is an issue of variants which amount to *equivalents* to a patented invention. That is, although they may differ in appearance, form, or even certain technical features, there can be infringement if they amount, in essence, to the embodiment of the same inventive concept and these modifications do not bring about a material change in the way the variant works. Note, however, while it is acceptable in the UK to talk of these variants as 'equivalents' this is not to be confused with the idea of a *doctrine of equivalents* which embodies a particular test for infringement, and is often used as a shorthand to refer to the approach in the United States.[363] This does not apply in the UK, nor, indeed, do we have a general doctrine of equivalents as the House of Lords has confirmed (see para 11.98).[364] The concern with the US doctrine of equivalents is that it has been interpreted to extend protection to things beyond the boundaries of the claims which perform substantially the same function in substantially the same way to obtain the same result.[365] This is precisely what *Catnic* set out to avoid—it is the claims which delimit the scope of monopoly, nothing more, and it is bad policy to allow a monopoly beyond the scope of claims as these have been drafted. Indeed, the UK courts have been generally very wary of discussion of equivalents, but this must change because EPC 2000 added a new Article 2 to the Protocol on Interpretation of Article 69 thus:

Article 2—Equivalents

For the purpose of determining the extent of protection conferred by a European patent, due account shall be taken of any element which is equivalent to an element specified in the claims.

[360] The same purposive approach is employed in Scotland, see *Trunature Ltd v Scotnet (1974) Ltd and others* [2006] CSOH 114.
[361] The House of Lords in *Kirin-Amgen Inc v Hoechst Marion Roussel Ltd* [2005] RPC 9 took the view that the purposive approach in *Catnic* is 'precisely in accordance with the Protocol', para 48. See further P England, 'Towards a single pan-European standard—common concepts in UK and continental European patent law: Part 1: scope of patent protection and inventive concept' (2010) 32(5) EIPR 195.
[362] [1990] FSR 181.
[363] As Lord Hoffmann said in *Kirin-Amgen*, note 361, at para 37: 'it is frankly acknowledged that it allows the patentee to extend his monopoly beyond the claims.' See *Graver Tank & Manufacturing Co Inc v Linde Air Products Co* 339 US 605 at 607 (1950).
[364] Cf J Brinkhof, 'Is there a European doctrine of equivalence?' (2002) 33 IIC 911.
[365] *Festo Corp v Shoketsu Kinzoku Kogyo Kabushiki Co Ltd* 535 US 722 (2002)—US Supreme Court upholding existing approach.

11.196   The obvious question is what is meant by 'due account' and does the UK approach conform to this? Let's examine the specifics of *Improver* in more detail since they have set the tone since their inception in 1989.[366] The value of the case lies in the articulation, per Hoffmann J, of the so-called Improver Questions[367] which act as a guide to determining when a variant will infringe. These can be depicted as shown in Diagram 11.1.

Diagram 11.1 The Improver Questions

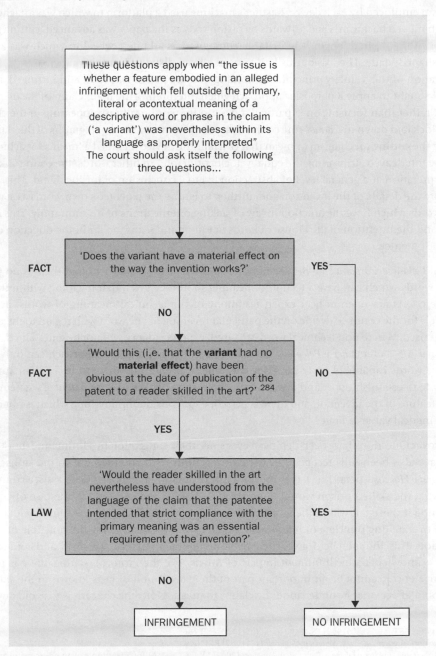

These questions apply when "the issue is whether a feature embodied in an alleged infringement which fell outside the primary, literal or acontextual meaning of a descriptive word or phrase in the claim ('a variant') was nevertheless within its language as properly interpreted" The court should ask itself the following three questions...

FACT   'Does the variant have a material effect on the way the invention works?'   YES

NO

FACT   'Would this (i.e. that the **variant** had no **material effect**) have been obvious at the date of publication of the patent to a reader skilled in the art?' [284]   NO

YES

LAW   'Would the reader skilled in the art nevertheless have understood from the language of the claim that the patentee intended that strict compliance with the primary meaning was an essential requirement of the invention?'   YES

NO

INFRINGEMENT   NO INFRINGEMENT

---

[366] Note in *PLG Research v Ardon* [1995] RPC 287 the Court of Appeal doubted if the UK approach was in conformity with interpretation of the Protocol in other European countries, especially Germany.

[367] Also known as the Protocol Questions: *Wheatley v Drillsafe Ltd* [2001] RPC 133 at 142.

11.197   The importance, then, is to consider the language of the claims as these are drafted in the specification. Contrast this with *Kastner v Rizla and another*[368] where the Court of Appeal seemed to take the purposive approach several stages further. This case involved a dispute over the patent for a device which interleaves and cuts cigarette papers for sale in small booklet form. The patent holder brought an action against market leader Rizla Ltd, for infringement of his patent and was met with a counterclaim of invalidity based, inter alia, on obviousness. The essential dispute concerned the cutting mechanism employed by each device. Kastner's machine used a platform to which was attached a knife and which moved backwards and forwards by piston rods as the paper was advanced, cutting the paper into strips of the desired length. The Rizla machine used as a knife a wheel to which was attached a crescent-shaped blade. The axis of this knife was at a fixed distance from the paper strands. It worked by application of the 'velocity principle'. In holding that the patent was valid and infringed, the Court of Appeal sought to apply a purposive approach when interpreting the main claim of Kastner's patent. However, rather than focusing on 'a particular descriptive word or phrase appearing in the claim'—as Lord Diplock laid down in *Catnic*—the court felt able to interpret several paragraphs of the claim which described the cutting mechanism to mean that *generally* the device included a 'means for achieving cutting of the interleaved strips using the equal velocity principle'. In other words, the court took the view that interpretation at a general level of abstraction led to a conclusion of infringement. This, however, is to ignore the details of the invention and, further, to ignore the patentee's own words as stated in his claim—words which have the function in law of staking out the limits of his monopoly. This approach goes beyond the intention of the House of Lords in *Catnic* and leans too far in the direction of protection of the patentee.

11.198   In *Hoechst Celanese Corporation v BP Chemicals Ltd and another*[369] it was held that there is no presumption that words which can have a technical meaning should be given that meaning within the claims. While the courts are open to hear expert testimony of the technical meaning of words, in the final analysis it is for the courts to decide on the particular meaning of any word with regard to the context in which it is used. Where non-technical words are used, expert evidence will not be entertained: *Scanvaegt International A/S and another v Pelcombe Ltd and another*.[370] The purposive approach can only apply to descriptive words capable of more than one meaning. If numerals are used in a patent application, for example to establish upper and lower limits, these must be taken as the patentee's statement of an essential feature of the invention and there is no scope for considering anything which is not caught by such a numerical value or limit.[371]

11.199   The Improver Questions have been deployed ever since their conception by Hoffmann J, but their limitations have also been fully recognised by their progenitor, as he pointed out in the House of Lords *Kirin-Amgen v Hoechst* (para 11.98): they are not a rule of law, but merely a guide to assist a court in determining what the skilled person would understand.[372] Moreover, they apply in the case of equivalents to determine if these fall within the scope of claims and they should not be confused with, or detract from, the overarching principle of interpretation laid down in *Catnic*, being the principle of purposive construction. This, the court held, gives effect to the requirements of the Protocol,[373] and Lord Hoffmann expressly acknowledged the imminent impact of Article 2 of the Protocol, stating 'there is no reason why [equivalence] cannot be an important part of the background of facts known to the skilled man which would affect what he understood the claims to mean'. Note: the concern is to avoid any concept

---

[368]   [1995] RPC 585.   [369]   [1999] FSR 319.   [370]   [1998] FSR 786.

[371]   See *Auchincloss v Agricultural & Veterinary Supplies Ltd* [1997] RPC 649.

[372]   See *Warheit and another v Olympia Tools Ltd and another* [2002] EWCA Civ 1161 for an example of an unsuccessful appeal which tried to argue that the first instance judge was wrong in law for failing to apply the Improver Questions.

[373]   *Kirin-Amgen*, note 361, para 48.

of equivalence that extends protection beyond the limits of the claims.[374] There is no objection to the idea of equivalence as such.

11.200   Lord Hoffmann accepted the limits of the Improver Questions most notably when applied to fast-moving, high-technology inventions such as genetic engineering as was the case in this appeal. The dispute concerned artificially made versions of erythropoietin (EPO)—a hormone that stimulates the production of red blood cells in the body. A crucial question in the case was what is the invention? Was it the discovery of the EPO gene sequence (a product) or the new means to make it (a process)? The trial judge held the former, but the Court of Appeal and the House of Lords opted for the latter. The problem, then, was how could Kirin-Amgen interpret their claims to a process broadly enough to cover their rival's product produced by a different and new process (gene activation) not known when Kirin-Amgen filed their patent? The Improver Questions ask a very difficult question at stage two: would it have been obvious to the person skilled in the art that the variant worked in the same way as the invention? Unless we imbue this person with considerable foresight, how can we expect them to envisage how a completely new technology would work sometime in the future? Indeed, it may not be obvious that it would work at all.[375] The Questions did not help in such cases,[376] and instead Lord Hoffmann fell back on the general principle: 'The question is always what the person skilled in the art would have understood the patentee to be using the language of the claim to mean.' On this basis, the court held that the skilled person would not have understood the claims to be sufficiently general to encompass the future technology of gene activation. Note: this is not to say that the skilled person cannot foresee future developments, it is to state that the claims must be able to encompass new developments within their original terms. Conversely, if the claims do cover the new innovation then an action for infringement will still succeed even if the new variant is inventive in its own right.

11.201   Doubts of this kind about the limits of the Questions had already been raised by the Court of Appeal[377] when a similar approach was adopted. The Questions are helpful when inventions and modifications deal with figures, measurements, and angles, as in *Catnic*, because these are measurable differences. As for other cases, the House of Lords had this to say:

> No doubt there will be patent lawyers who are dismayed at the notion that the Protocol questions do not provide an answer in every case. They may feel cast adrift on a sea of interpretative uncertainty. But that is the fate of all who have to understand what people mean by using language.[378]

The distinct impression conveyed by the House of Lords is not only that this UK approach is in keeping with Article 69 EPC and its Protocol, but that it conforms to the new Article 2 of the Protocol, namely, that 'due account' is taken of equivalents. *Plus ça change*...

  Question

Is there any need for the first two Improver Questions in the light of this ruling?

---

[374] The essence of the test is whether the skilled person can perform the invention over the entire area of claimed invention without undue burden and without the need for inventive skill, see *Novartis AG v Johnson & Johnson Medical Ltd* [2010] EWCA Civ 1039 and *Sandvik Intellectual Property AB v Kennametal UK Ltd* [2011] EWHC 3311 (Pat), [2012] RPC 23.

[375] Lord Hoffmann suggested in passing that a better way to ask the second question would be to follow the German approach and ask if the variant solves the problem underlying the invention by means which have the same technical effect, para 75. This is certainly in keeping with the underlying rational of patent protection in Europe.

[376] In fact, they lead to the unusual outcome that the answer to Q1 might be 'no' (leading to an inference of infringement) but because the technology is new and non-obvious, the answer to Q2 might also be 'no' (which implies no infringement). This was the case in *Kirin-Amgen* and also in *Union Carbide v BP Chemicals Ltd* [1999] RPC 409.

[377] In particular, see *Wheatley*, note 258, and *Pharmacia Corp v Merck and Co* [2002] RPC 775.

[378] *Kirin-Amgen*, note 361, para 71.

11.202   It has been suggested that the first two Improver Questions are merely a shortcut to answering the third question, and moreover, that an approach to asking this question which is more true to the spirit of *Catnic* is to ask 'whether it would have been apparent to the skilled addressee from the wording of the claim that a limitation to exclude the variant could *not* have been intended by the patentee.'[379]

Discussion point For answer guidance visit www.oxfordtextbooks.co.uk/orc/waelde3e/

Does it matter what way around we ask, or answer, the question?

11.203   Remember that the court must attempt to steer a middle way through claim interpretation. Here is what the House of Lords had to say on this in *Kirin-Amgen*:[380]

> the object is to combine a fair protection for the patentee with a reasonable degree of certainty for third parties. How is this to be achieved? The claims must be construed in a way which attempts, so far as is possible in an imperfect world, not to disappoint the reasonable expectations of either side. What principle of interpretation would give fair protection to the patentee? Surely, a principle which would give him the full extent of the monopoly which the person skilled in the art would think he was intending to claim. And what principle would provide a reasonable degree of protection for third parties? Surely again, a principle which would not give the patentee more than the full extent of the monopoly which the person skilled in the art would think that he was intending to claim. Indeed, any other principle would also be unfair to the patentee, because it would unreasonably expose the patent to claims of invalidity on grounds of anticipation or insufficiency.[381]

11.204   The principles of claim construction have since been summarised by Jacob LJ in *Mayne Pharma v Pharmacia Italia SpA*[382] reiterating his early account in *Technip France SA's Patent*[383] which had been approved by the House of Lords in *Kirin-Amgen*, with one exception.[384] These embody the elements discussed previously and you can read them for yourself.[385]

Exercise

Read *Mayne Pharma* for a concise summary of the UK position on claim interpretation.

Declaration or declarator of non-infringement

11.205   It is possible to apply under section 71 of the Patents Act 1977 to the Comptroller or the courts for a declaration (or declarator in Scotland) of non-infringement in respect of either past or future acts done with or to a patented invention. The procedure requires the person seeking the order first to apply to the proprietor in writing for a written acknowledgement of the declaration or declarator claimed;[386] the proprietor should also be furnished with the full particulars of the acts in question at this time.[387] Only if this acknowledgement is refused or simply not given, can the applicant then seek a formal declaration

[379] See *Telsonic AG's Patent* [2004] RPC 38 and *Merck & Co Inc v Generics (UK) Ltd* [2004] RPC 31. For commentary, see M Fisher, 'A case-study in literalism? Dissecting the English approach to patent claim construction in light of *Occlutech v AGA Medical*' [2011] 3 IPQ 283.   [380] See also *Merck & Co Inc v Generics (UK) Ltd* [2004] RPC 31.

[381] Para 47. See H Laddie, 'Kirin Amgen—the end of equivalents in England?' (2009) 40(1) IIC 3.   [382] [2005] EWCA Civ 137.

[383] [2004] RPC 46 at para 41(a)–(k).

[384] There is no presumption about the width of the claims when considering fairness to the patentee, *Kirin-Amgen*, note 361, para 33.

[385] See too, *Pozzoli SpA v BDMO SA* [2007] EWCA Civ 588, [2007] FSR 37.

[386] On the requirements, see *Mallory Metallurgical Products Ltd v Black Sivalls and Bryson Incorporated* [1977] RPC 321.

[387] An incomplete written description can be saved by accompanying drawings: *MMD Design & Consultancy Ltd's Patent* [1989] RPC 131.

or declarator from the Comptroller in the first instance. The tests for infringement in such cases are those outlined earlier. Note that while it is possible to put the validity of the patent in issue in such proceedings, a finding of invalidity does not, in itself, result in revocation of the patent. For that we have to turn to our next section which deals with this particular procedure.

Revocation

11.206   We have seen in the previous sections how an action for infringement is often met with a counterclaim for revocation. This is dealt with by section 72(1) of the Patents Act 1977, as amended, with the equivalent provisions appearing as Article 138 EPC 2000. The fact that a revocation procedure exists stands in testament to the fact that the patent granting system is not infallible. Patents may be granted when one of the exclusions or exceptions should have applied (paras 11.5–11.77), they may be granted to someone who is not entitled to the patent (para 11.150), they may be granted when the patent application does not sufficiently disclose the invention to allow it to be performed by the skilled person (and thereby discharge the public disclosure obligation), they may be granted in terms which give too broad a monopoly compared to what the invention actually contributes to the state of the art[388] (para 10.102), or they may be extended through amendment beyond the boundaries which should have been allowed (paras 10.114ff). Finally, the Patents Act 2004[389] amended the Patents Act 1977 to make it clear that it is possible to revoke a patent on the grounds that it does not comply with the provisions of new section 4A (methods of treatment and diagnosed on the human or animal body, see paras 11.63ff).

11.207   We have dealt with all of these circumstances elsewhere, and we do not need to repeat the provisions here. There is only one outstanding matter, and this is the question of *insufficiency*, that is, the challenge that the patent application does not sufficiently disclose the invention to allow it to be performed by the skilled person.[390] Article 83 EPC 2000 (and the Patents Act 1977, s 14) requires that: 'The European patent application shall disclose the invention in a manner sufficiently clear and complete for it to be carried out by a person skilled in the art.'

11.208   The rationale of this provision was explained in *Visx Inc v Nidek Co Ltd*:[391]

> The thinking behind this provision is that, as part of the quid pro quo of the monopoly granted by a patent, the patentee should give proper public disclosure of the invention: this enables the public to work the invention at the expiry of the monopoly period. The provision also exists to allow the court to revoke a patent if satisfied that the monopoly claimed by it is wider than its contribution to the art.

11.209   Questions of insufficiency have long been a part of UK patent law and the Court of Appeal has confirmed that the pre-1977 approach remains valid and equally applicable today.[392] That said, there have been few hard-and-fast rules to emerge from the courts and there has always been a desire to maintain a balance of interests between the patentee and the public and to guard against setting too high a standard for disclosure simply because the matter is inherently complex.[393]

11.210   The issue is a question of fact, dependent on the nature of the invention and the particular knowledge and skills of the notional expert.[394] These factors should be sounding bells with you—have come across

---

[388]   See in particular, *Biogen Inc v Medeva plc* [1997] RPC 1 per Lord Hoffmann at 53–54.
[389]   Para 2 of Sch 2 to the Patents Act 1977.   [390]   *Regeneron Pharmaceuticals Inc v Genentech Inc* [2012] EWHC 657 (Pat).
[391]   *Visx Inc v Nidek Co Ltd and others (No 2)* [1999] FSR 405.   [392]   *Mentor Corporation v Hollister Inc* [1993] RPC 7.
[393]   See *Halliburton Energy Services Inc v Smith International (North Sea) Ltd and others* [2005] EWHC 1623 (Pat) at paras 129–139, endorsed by the Court of Appeal at [2006] EWCA Civ 1715.
[394]   The specification must enable the invention at the date of filing, see *Biogen v Medeva* [1997] RPC 1.

them before. Can you remember in which section? Well, the House of Lords has drawn the parallel between the requirements of sufficiency and the requirements of enabling disclosure used to test novelty (para 11.88) in *Synthon BV v Smithkline Beecham*.[395] After discussing some of the historical cases,[396] Lord Hoffmann stated the following:

> In the present case the Court of Appeal was reluctant to say that the test of enablement of a prior disclosure for the purpose of anticipation was the same as the test of enablement of the patent itself for the purpose of sufficiency. But I can think of no reason why there should be any difference and the Technical Board of Appeal has more than once held that the tests are the same: see *ICI/Pyridine Herbicides* [1986] 5 EPOR 232, para 2; *COLLABORATIVE/Preprorennin* [1990] EPOR 361, para 15. In my opinion, therefore, the authorities on section 72(1)(c) are equally applicable to enablement for the purposes of sections 2(2) and (3). There may however be differences in the application of this test to the facts; for example, because in the case of sufficiency the skilled person is attempting to perform a claimed invention and has that goal in mind, whereas in the case of prior art the subject-matter may have disclosed the invention but not identified it as such. But no such question arises in this case, in which the application plainly identified crystalline PMS as an embodiment of the invention.[397]

We must, therefore, consider the authorities discussed previously as part of the novelty criterion when considering what amounts to sufficiency of disclosure.

 Exercise

Look back at the section on novelty to familiarise yourself with the relevant case law. Consider, in particular, which of the cases had an issue of insufficiency in tandem with one of novelty.

11.211   The House of Lords also laid out the beginning of the approach in *Kirin-Amgen*:[398]

> Whether the specification is sufficient or not is highly sensitive to the nature of the invention. The first step is to identify the invention and decide what it claims to enable the skilled man to do. Then one can ask whether the specification enables him to do it.

If the specification effectively claims too much for the invention, as was the case here and in *Biogen v Medeva*, then the application or patent will be invalid for insufficiency.[399] In this case the patentee was the first to isolate the genetic sequence coding for EPO but it was held that the invention was a new process for isolating EPO, not the product as such. The claims, however, sought to cover new processes *and* EPO products which could be achieved without reliance on the patented invention including those which could not have been contemplated when the patent was initially filed. Thus, the invention as disclosed did not allow the skilled person to work this range of inventions and was invalid for insufficiency.

11.212   Similarly, in *Biogen*, all that could be described (at best) was an invention for a molecule produced by crude genetic engineering techniques which exhibited antigen specificity for core and surface Hepatitis B antigens in host cells. Yet, what was claimed was an invention which covered *all* molecules displaying HBV antigen specificity produced by *any* technique using *any* host. In holding that the monopoly claimed was too broad and observing that the patent would be invalid for insufficiency, Lord Hoffmann focused on the extent to which the invention made a technical contribution to the state of the art. The technical contribution made was a way of working with HBV to produce recombinant molecules

---

[395] [2005] UKHL 59.

[396] Eg *Valensi v British Radio Corporation* [1973] RPC 337; *Mentor Corporation v Hollister Incorporated* [1993] RPC 7; and *Biogen Inc v Medeva plc* [1997] RPC 1.

[397] *Kirin-Amgen*, note 361, para 27.   [398] [2005] RPC 9.

[399] On the fuzzy edges of claims and the impact on arguments about insufficiency, see *Generics (UK) Ltd (t/a Mylan) v Yeda Research & Development Co Ltd* [2012] EWHC 1848 (Pat).

which had antigen specificity *in the absence* of knowledge about the make-up of the genetic sequence. It was confirmed that monopolies will be awarded for inventions *only* to the extent that the inventions contribute to the state of the art. In particular, if there are available ways of achieving the same result without relying on the invention (and therefore without relying on its contribution to the state of the art) then those ways fall outside the monopoly which can legitimately be claimed by the patentee of the invention in question. Here, once the sequences of the HBV genes were known, it was easily possible to produce HBV antigens without using the patentee's technique at all. In sum, what is disclosed must enable the invention to be worked *to the full extent* of the monopoly claimed. That is, if your invention embodies a principle which is capable of general application across a wide range of products, then it is permissible to claim all such products. Furthermore, Lord Hoffmann confirmed that in such cases it is not necessary for the patentee to prove that his or her principle applies in all cases—one example is sufficient to amount to an enabling disclosure. However, if the patentee claims different products or processes in the same application, each must be described by a separate enabling disclosure. Moreover, if no unifying principle links the claimed inventions together, then all that can be claimed is that which can be described.

11.213 In *Generics (UK) Limited and others v H Lundbeck A/S*[400] the validity of a patent over a novel product, the effective agent in the antidepressant drug Citalopram, was upheld and the impact of the precedent in *Biogen* was clarified.[401] The product in question was escitalopram, an enantiomer, whose separation and isolation was a non-trivial matter. The patentees claimed the product and associated processes and difficulties arose because the inventiveness of the product was claimed solely by reference to the means used to make it. As well as challenges on the grounds of novelty and inventive step, the core concern was that if this product claim stood it would provide a monopoly over the substance itself, irrespective of how it might be made, but when the patentees had only disclosed one method of production. Was this an overly broad monopoly? Had there been sufficient disclosure?

11.214 The House of Lords held unanimously that the patent was valid. At first instance the trial judge had revoked the patent, relying on *Biogen*, and on the ground that: 'The first person to find a way of achieving an obviously desirable goal is not permitted to monopolise every other way of doing so'. But the House of Lords distinguished *Biogen* not as dealing with a product claim, but rather as being concerned with an unusual product/process hybrid claim whose breadth was clearly too wide. In contrast, the court in *Generics* found the product invention to be both novel and involving inventive step because the means used to produce it was in no way obvious to a person skilled in the art. Accordingly, and as a product in itself, it was entirely in keeping with UK and EPO jurisprudence[402] that a product patent should provide a monopoly irrespective of the means to make it. Reiterating the point that a monopoly should only extend as far as the 'technical contribution' made by the teaching of the patent, the House of Lords found that the respondent's contribution was 'to make available, for the first time, a product which had previously been unavailable, namely the isolated (+)-enantiomer of citalopram. On that basis, it would appear to follow that the respondent was entitled to claim the enantiomer.'[403]

11.215 It can be seen, then, that it can matter very much how an invention is described and interpreted by the courts in giving effect to patent law. Lord Neuberger ventured the following further distinction between product claims and process (or process-type) claims:

> When considering the validity of a simple product claim...[as in *Generics*]...it may be that concentrating on the identification of the inventive step rather than the technical contribution can lead to error. 'Inventive step'

[400] [2009] UKHL 12.
[401] P Watterson, 'Appeal court reluctance: complex evidence, obviousness and related matters' (2012) 7(5) JIPLP 358.
[402] T409/91 *EXXON/Fuel Oils* [1994] OJEPO 653, para 3.3.   [403] Per Lord Neuberger at para 83.

suggests how something has been done, and, in the case of a product claim at any rate, one is primarily concerned with what has been allegedly invented, not how it has been done. On the other hand where the claim is for a process or (as in Biogen [1997] RPC 1) includes a process, the issue of how the alleged invention has been achieved seems to be more in point.[404]

The careful policing of the boundaries of the tests for patentability is now a clear policy objective advocated in many quarters.

11.216   The Court of Appeal has considered insufficiency in *Halliburton Energy Services Inc v Smith International (North Sea) Ltd and others.*[405] It confirmed that a patent for rotary cone drill bits was invalid for insufficiency because it required too much work from the skilled person to reproduce the various features of the invention. This involved claims both to the design and use of simulation systems in respect of the drill bits, and required enormously lengthy and complex calculations from the notional expert to reproduce the invention. The court held that if the patent involved an unreasonable amount of work in the light of all of the relevant circumstances, then it would be regarded as not containing an enabling disclosure.[406]

11.217   The Supreme Court has stressed once again, and most recently, that there is considerable importance in aligning UK and EPO approaches to any number of patent law questions, including sufficiency. While a national court is not bound by the decision of any EPO body, where a Board has adopted a consistent approach on any particular matter a national court would require very unusual circumstances for departing from the same position.[407]

11.218   It is possible to apply to amend claims in response to a challenge of revocation,[408] which will be considered at the discretion of the court,[409] but these amendments cannot attempt to add matter to the existing patent.[410]

11.219   A final reminder: Article 105a EPC 2000 provides that a proprietor of a patent can apply for revocation of their own instrument through a centralised procedure with effect throughout all countries for which the patent was granted. Can you find the equivalent provision in the Patents Act 1977?

Defences

11.220   Section 60(5) of the Patents Act 1977 provides a list of nine defences to an action for infringement, being acts which would be infringing but for this statutory protection. Some of these are slightly obscure and you can read them for yourself. We are going to concentrate on the four main defences:

(1) acts done privately and which are not commercial;

(2) acts done for experimental purposes;

(3) farmers' privileges;

(4) Bolar exemptions in respect of regulatory approval of generics.

---

[404] Per Lord Neuberger at para 101.   [405] [2006] EWCA Civ 1715.

[406] The EPO uses a test of 'undue effort' which is also relevant for these purposes, see T923/92 *GENENTECH/Human tPA* [1996] EPOR 275.

[407] *Eli Lilly & Co v Human Genome Sciences Inc* [2011] UKSC 51, [2012] 1 All ER 1154, [2012] RPC 6.   [408] See para 10.121.

[409] *Hsiung's Patent* [1992] RPC 497.

[410] *LG Philips Co Ltd v Tatung (UK) Ltd and others* [2006] EWCA Civ 1774. For further amendment issues see *Ratiopharm GmbH v Napp Pharmaceutical Holdings Ltd* [2009] RPC 18.

Private and non-commercial acts

11.221   This defence requires that the use of a patented invention is only for private purposes *and* non-commercial ends. 'Private' means for one's own use, and it is the opposite to 'public'; it is not a synonym for 'secret' in these circumstances.[411] The rationale is probably that such acts are of minimal or no threat to a patentee. You will recall that in *McDonald v Graham*[412] the invention concerned promotional 'Z cards', copies of which were kept by a former business partner, who then passed unlicensed copies on to a design team to consider how he might design his own version. The infringement action was in relation to 'keeping' an infringing product and this was upheld on the evidence which showed clearly that the defendant was keeping the product in stock for the purposes of his business. There was, therefore, no need for the Court of Appeal to consider the defences specifically, although it did hold that the trial judge was entitled to find on the evidence that a sufficient case was made out of use by the defendant for non-private and commercial purposes. Cases involving disputes over whether there is indeed commercial or non-commercial use would similarly turn on the evidence put to the court, and an important part of that evidence is the subjective intentions of the alleged infringer.[413]

Experimental purposes

11.222   This defence was discussed by the Court of Appeal in *Monsanto Co v Stauffer Chemical Co and another*[414] where it was decided that the word 'experiment' is an ordinary word and not a term of art of patent law, that is, it takes an ordinary meaning and not any specialised meaning for the purposes of the defence. Moreover, in contrast to section 60(5)(a), discussed previously, there is no mention of the need for experimental purposes to be non-commercial, therefore it is possible that experimental acts can be carried out which may ultimately lead to a commercial benefit. But this idea should be treated with caution, and the court drew a distinction between experiments carried out to discover a new thing, or to test a hypothesis, or even to test the parameters of an invention under new conditions, with other acts which would not fall within the defence, such as trials performed to demonstrate to a third party that a product works or work done to gather information to satisfy a third party (eg a customer or a safety regulatory body) of the workings of a product or process. Thus, in *Auchincloss v Agricultural & Veterinary Supplies Ltd*[415] it was not a defence to make and experiment with a composition designed to destroy viruses and other micro-organisms for the purposes of obtaining regulatory approval. In *Smith, Kline & French Laboratories Ltd v Evans Medical Ltd*[416] the argument was rejected that a patentee impliedly consents to experiments to test the validity of their patent; moreover, for the defence to succeed the acts in question must be done for purposes directly related to the subject matter of the patent as defined in the claims. Thus, you could not use someone's reagent invention in a trial-and-error fashion to find out if a third party's chemical invention worked efficiently. Here the direct experimentation would only be with the chemical invention.

11.223   Note, however, even if an experimental use defence applies, this would not necessarily extend to someone who supplies the means to carry out the experiment (which would otherwise be an infringing act) and they might be liable for contributory infringement.[417]

---

[411] Compare, then, the argument that 'prior use' is also an available defence, that is, that one was using the invention before it was subject to a patent. It should be self-evident to you at this stage that such a claim could only succeed if that prior use had been in secret and out of the public domain; otherwise, a patent would be invalid for lack of novelty.

[412] Para 11.183.   [413] *Smith Kline & French Labs v Evans Medical* [1989] FSR 513.   [414] [1985] RPC 515.

[415] [1997] RPC 649, and on appeal [1999] RPC 397.   [416] [1989] FSR 513.   [417] See *Monsanto* [1985] RPC 515.

11.224 There are very few examples in the case law which test the parameters of this defence, and it is an area where there is considerable diversity of approach around the world, including within Europe. Two examples illustrate the point.

11.225 The German Supreme Court has held, for example, that the equivalent provisions in German law 'in principle exempts all experimental acts as long as they serve to gain information and thus to carry out scientific research into the subject-matter of the invention' and that this even extends to research into 'possible new uses hitherto unknown',[418] and this is true *even if* there is an associated commercial purpose to the experimentation.[419] The English Patents Court has accepted this general approach but modified it slightly by suggesting that the assessment of whether 'experimental use' exists 'should involve the consideration whether the immediate purpose of the transaction in question is to generate revenue'.[420]

11.226 In stark contrast, the position in the United States was drastically clarified in *Madey v Duke University*,[421] by the US Court of Appeals for the Federal Circuit which all but reduced the effectiveness of the defence to nothing. It now only applies for 'amusement, to satisfy idle curiosity, or for strictly philosophical inquiry'; it is not available in respect of *any* activity which is 'in furtherance of the alleged infringer's legitimate business.' And in the particular circumstances of the case, this was held to extend to a university whose very 'business' is research. The presence or absence of profit motive is irrelevant and so the defence is equally unavailable to not-for-profit organisations. This is clearly a draconian measure that is open to serious question as to how it furthers the public interest. It has required, in turn, further initiatives to protect research and product development. For example, the US Supreme Court ruled in *Merck KGaA v Integra LifeSciences Ltd*[422] that there is an immunity from infringement proceedings in respect of pre-clinical research and experimentation which is 'reasonably related' to obtaining necessary information for regulatory approval before the US Food and Drug Administration. This, then, continues to exclude fundamental or other research not carried out with the intention of seeking future drug approval. It also remains unclear whether the use of research tools to develop therapeutic agents is covered.

11.227 The position in Europe remains patchy.[423] A research exemption operates across a number of European jurisdictions but in a disharmonious fashion. So what should happen in the UK? The *Gowers Review of Intellectual Property* pointed to a paper by the Department of Trade and Industry and the Intellectual Property Institute which argues that the research exemption is unclear, not widely used, and in need for reform.[424] Evidence from the United States indicates that one in six projects is stopped or never started because of intellectual property rights. In an attempt to avoid this for the UK, the recommendation is to clarify the experimental purposes defence to facilitate experimentation, innovation, and education. The proposed model is that currently operated by Switzerland which promotes the pursuit of knowledge about the object of an invention, exempts only non-commercial purposes, and specifically allows the use of the invention for teaching purposes. The UK–IPO launched a consultation in 2008 on the research exception, in which the majority of respondents indicated that clarification of the scope of the exception would be useful, especially when the judiciary would assist in providing guidance in order to give it legal weight. There was no clear evidence to suggest that the current research exception hinders

---

[418] *Klinische Versuche (Clinical Trials) I* [1997] RPC 623.   [419] *Klinische Versuche (Clinical Trials) II* [1998] RPC 423.

[420] *Corevalve Inc v Edwards Lifesciences* [2009] FSR 8, para 77.

[421] 307 F3d 1351 at 1362 (Fed Cir, 2002); petition to the Supreme Court denied 27 June 2003 (No 02-1007).

[422] 545 US 193 (2005), interpreting 35 USC §271(e)(1)—The Drug Price Competition and Patent Term Restoration Act 1984 (also known as the Hatch-Waxman Act).

[423] See generally G van Overwalle (ed), *Gene Patents and Public Health* (2007).

[424] *Gowers Review of Intellectual Property* (HM Treasury, 2006), paras 4.5–4.12. Department of Trade and Industry and the Intellectual Property Institute, *Patents for Genetic Sequences: The Competitiveness of Current UK Law and Practices* (2004).

research in the UK.[425] Most recently, a narrower consultation has sought views on exemptions in clinical and field trials for innovative drugs, and we discuss this later (paras 11.232ff).

11.228 A combination of these, and other, approaches is required to ensure a balanced and equitable way forward in the future as a host of bodies, reviews, and reports have concluded. Additional factors to be considered include the vigilance of intellectual property offices in carrying out thorough searches of the prior art, an ongoing review of the role for imaginative licensing options, and, as we have seen previously, careful application of the criteria for patentability. The Organisation for Economic Co-operation and Development (OECD) has indicated the difficulty of finding common solutions because of the complexity of the area, but it has nevertheless recommended that a multi-strategy approach should be considered at governmental level requiring, inter alia, review of the policies within the IP system itself, the manner by which patents are administered, and changing the behaviour of patentees in the way they exploit their monopolies.[426] The Organisation noted in particular that the role of compulsory licences, although not popular to date, should be revisited.[427]

Exercise

Look at the Gowers Review and the provisions of Swiss law. Critically assess this proposal to follow the Swiss model, considering the arguments that might be put from all sides on whether this is appropriate for the UK.

Farmers' privileges

11.229 New defences were introduced to the Patents Act 1977 as a result of negotiations on the Biotechnology Directive which we discuss in the next chapter. These are designed to ensure that farmers using traditional harvesting and livestock reproduction techniques are not hindered in their work by the existence and exercise of intellectual property rights relating to biological material. There are two particular defences.

11.230 Section 60(5)(g) concerns propagating material for plants, including material that may be the subject of a patent, which has been sold to a farmer by the patent owner for use in agriculture. The defence provides that the farmer may use the material for further propagation of the material on his own land without infringing any patent. This is not a catch-all provision, however; section 60(6A) of the Act provides that the defence is only available in respect of certain varieties of material, and these are detailed in paragraph 2 of Schedule A1 to the Act. Common harvest like wheat, oats, and potatoes are covered. Moreover, if use is authorised under the Act, the farmer must still pay the patent owner 'equitable remuneration' for that use, although this cannot be more than what the farmer would pay to buy more material from the owner. 'Small farmers' are exempt from this payment, being, in the case of exempted varieties, a farmer who grows plants on an area not larger than necessary to produce 92 tonnes of material.[428]

11.231 Section 60(5)(h) provides a similar scheme for farmers who breed livestock or otherwise deal in reproductive material. The law does not restrict which animal varieties can be the subject of the exemption.

---

[425] UK–IPO, 'Patent Research Exception Consultation: Summary of Responses' (2008), accessible at http://www.ipo.gov.uk/response-patresearch.pdf.

[426] OECD, *Genetic Inventions, Intellectual Property Rights and Licensing Practices: Evidence and Policies* (2002), 80.

[427] OECD, note 426, 81.

[428] Council Regulation (EC) No 2100/94 of 27 July 1994 on Community plant variety rights, Art 14(3), third indent.

The main prohibition, however, is that the farmer cannot sell on any animal or material derived from his 'use' as part of a 'commercial reproductive activity'.[429]

Bolar exemptions

11.232   Section 60(5)(i) is concerned with the conduct of clinical trials for the approval of therapeutic products based on patented inventions. It was introduced into domestic law as a result of two Directives concerning, respectively, veterinary[430] and human[431] medicinal products. These are known as 'Bolar' exemptions and they operate when generic drugs manufacturers are seeking regulatory approval for their products. They provide protection for acts done on generic medicines to demonstrate that they are bio-equivalent to a patented product; the point is, from the perspective of the generic manufacturer, it can rely on the patentee's prior regulatory approval if bio-equivalence can be shown. The problem is that while, clearly, generics can be produced once a patent expires, manufacturers do not want to have to wait until this time before carrying out trials and seeking regulatory approval. A Bolar exemption therefore works to allow this activity *before* a patent expires with a view to facilitating a wider market in generics *after* it expires. This is the European equivalent to the US Supreme Court ruling in *Merck* (para 11.226). A recent consultation by the UK–IPO acknowledges further the problems and has sought views on how the UK should proceed.[432] The consultation lays out three options:

(1)   Change UK patent law to exempt from infringement all activities required to secure regulatory approval to market innovative drugs in all countries.

(2)   Change UK patent law to exempt from infringement all activities required to secure regulatory approval to market innovative drugs in the EU and European Economic Area (EEA) only;

(3)   Change UK patent law to exempt from infringement all activities required to secure regulatory approval to market innovative drugs and also all activities necessary for health technology assessment, for example data to support assessment by the National Institute for Health and Clinical Excellence (NICE), now the National Institute for Health and Care Excellence.

11.233   The consultation had closed and a Response appeared immediately prior to completion of this edition.[433] The vast majority of responses agreed with a change in the law and the government has sanctioned this (February 2013). The UK–IPO will proceed with a Legislative Reform Order to 'exempt from infringement the activities required to secure regulatory approval to market innovative drugs, and also activities necessary for health technology assessment e.g. data to support assessment by the National Institute for Health and Clinical Excellence (NICE).' You should continue to monitor the position as part of your studies.

 Exercise

Having reached the end of this chapter, consider how many ways a person accused of patent infringement can respond—seeking a defence is only one option. What are the relative merits of any particular strategy?

---

[429]   Patents Act 1977, s 60(6B).   [430]   Art 13(6) of Directive 2001/82/EC on veterinary medicinal products.
[431]   Art 10(5) of Directive 2001/83/EC on medicinal products for human use, amended by the Directive 2004/27, Art 10(6).
[432]   UK–IPO, 'The Research and Bolar Exceptions Intellectual Property Office is an operating name of the Patent Office: A Formal Consultation on Patent Infringement in Clinical and Field Trials' (2012) available at http://www.ipo.gov.uk/pro-policy/consult/consult-closed/consult-closed-2012/consult-2012-bolar.htm.
[433]   Available at http://www.ipo.gov.uk/pro-policy/consult/consult-closed/consult-closed-2012/consult-2012-bolar.htm.

Further reading

Books

C Heath and L Petit (eds), *Patent Enforcement Worldwide* (2005)

CIPA, *Guide to the Patents Acts* (7th edn, 2011)

R Miller et al, *Terrell on the Law of Patents* (17th edn, 2011)

J Pila, *The Requirement for an Invention in Patent Law* (2010)

Reports

T Cook, *A European Perspective as to the Extent to Which Experimental Use, and Certain Other Defences to Patent Infringement, Apply to Differing Types of Research* (2006)

OECD, *Genetic Inventions, Intellectual Property Rights and Licensing Practices: Evidence and Policies* (2002)

R Sagar and A Nagarsheth, *Ownership of Employee Inventions and Remuneration: A Comparative Overview* (2006)

Articles

A Feros, 'Extending the Bolar exception to innovators?' (2013) 8(3) JIPLP 187

M Fisher, 'A case-study in literalism? Dissecting the English approach to patent claim construction in light of *Occlutech v AGA Medical*' [2011] 3 IPQ 283

G Grant and D Gibbons, 'Inventive concept—is it a good idea?' [2005] EIPR 170

EC Hettinger, 'Justifying intellectual property' (1989) 18 Philosophy and Public Affairs 31

C Howell, 'Extra compensation for inventive employees: is our system equitable, unbiased and motivating?' [2011] 4 IPQ 371

Y Min, 'Morality: an equivocal area in the patent system' (2012) 34(4) EIPR 261

A Odell West, '*Kelly v GE Healthcare Ltd*: employee innovation in health care—deciphering ownership and the alchemy of "outstanding benefit"' (2010) 32(9) EIPR 449

J Pila, 'Art 52(2) of the Convention on the Grant of European Patents: what did the framers intend? A study of the *travaux preparatoires*' (2005) 36 IIC 755

A Sims, 'The case against patenting methods of medical treatment' [2007] EIPR 43

ED Ventose, '"Farming" out an exception for animals to the method of medical treatment exclusion under the European Patent Convention' (2008) 30(12) EIPR 509

C Von Drathen, 'Patent scope in English and German law under the European Patent Convention 1973 and 2000' (2008) 39(4) IIC 384

A Von Hellfeld, 'Patent Infringement in Europe: the British and the German approaches to claim construction or purposive construction versus equivalency' (2008) 30(9) EIPR 364

P Watterson, 'Appeal court reluctance: complex evidence, obviousness and related matters' (2012) 7(5) JIPLP 358.

12

Contemporary issues in patent law

Introduction

Scope and overview of chapter

12.1 We have already identified a trend in intellectual property law and policy involving the expansion of the scope of a number of intellectual property rights and a corresponding restriction on the limitations on those rights. This trend equally typifies developments in the realm of patent law, and some contemporary examples are considered in this chapter. First, we shall examine the problem of biotechnological inventions which has proved to be a particularly controversial issue in Europe. Secondly, we shall consider the patentability of computer software and related inventions such as business method patents. The overarching aim of this chapter is to demonstrate the evolution in legal and policy thinking in these two fields as a means to assist you in making sense of developments in patent law.

12.2 **Learning objectives**

By the end of this chapter you should be able to:

- critically assess the exclusions from patentable subject matter, and in particular the meaning of the qualification *as such*;

- give an analytical account of the controversy surrounding the protection of biotechnological inventions, with particular emphasis on the role of the morality provision in European patent law;

- evaluate, by considering the strengths of opposing arguments, the acceptability of monopolies over biological material and consider strategies to temper the effects of such monopolies;

- comment in an informed manner on the application of patent law to software-related inventions, and in particular on the advisability of business method patents;

- critically compare the merits of patent and copyright protection for software products;

- assess attempts to reform patent protection for computer-implemented inventions in Europe.

Sources of law

12.3 Biotechnological inventions in most countries are not subject to special legal provisions and for the most part these have been accommodated by the standard patent law. In Europe, however, a disparity of approach existed between the member states, with some countries such as the Netherlands refusing to apply patent law to living biological material. The European Commission therefore proposed a harmonising Directive in 1988[1] as part of its wider strategy on completing the internal market.[2] The proposal proved to be one of the most controversial pieces of legislation ever to proceed through the European institutions and in 1995 it provoked the European Parliament to use its newly established power of veto for the first time over an early version of the instrument.[3] The Directive was eventually adopted in 1998[4] but, as we will see, it remains controversial and the debate on its merits is far from over.

12.4 Despite a widely held belief that patent law is a virtual irrelevancy to the protection of software in Europe, estimates indicate that tens of thousands of software-related patents have been granted over the last quarter of a century. This is notwithstanding, an express exclusion of computer programs from patent protection in the law: European Patent Convention (EPC) 2000, Article 52(2). The European Commission attempted to introduce a Directive to clarify the situation but this was defeated in the European Parliament in 2005. You can read more about it by following the link in the next box.

Web links

Directive 98/44/EC of 6 July 1998 on the legal protection of biotechnological inventions, OJ L213/13: **http://eur-lex.europa.eu/LexUriServ/LexUriServ.do?uri=OJ:L:1998:213:0013:0021:EN:PDF**

The history and defeat of the Commission Proposal on the patentability of computer-implemented inventions, COM(2002) 92 final, 20 February 2002: **http://ec.europa.eu/internal_market/indprop/comp/index_en.htm**

UK–IPO, Examination Guidelines for Patent Applications relating to Biotechnological Inventions in the Intellectual Property Office (2012): **http://www.ipo.gov.uk/biotech.pdf**

12.5 The rest of the chapter looks like this:

- Background (12.6–12.7)
- Biotechnological inventions (12.8–12.76)
- Software-related inventions (12.77–12.158)

Background

Is the scope of excluded matter narrowing?

We have already seen in Chapter 11 that certain subject matter is excluded from patent protection. This is detailed in Article 52(2) EPC 2000, with equivalent provisions in section 1(2) of the UK Patents Act 1977:

---

[1] COM(88) 496 final SYN 159, 17 October 1988; [1989] OJ C10/3.   [2] COM(85) 310 final, 14 June 1985.
[3] [1995] OJ C68, 20 March 1995.
[4] Directive 98/44/EC of the European Parliament and of the Council of 6 July 1998 on the legal protection of biotechnological inventions (Biotechnology Directive).

(2) The following in particular shall not be regarded as inventions within the meaning of paragraph 1:

    (a) discoveries, scientific theories and mathematical methods;

    (b) aesthetic creations;

    (c) schemes, rules and methods for performing mental acts, playing games or doing business, and pro-

12.6   grams for computers;

    (d) presentations of information.

(3) Paragraph 2 shall exclude the patentability of the subject-matter or activities referred to therein only to the extent to which a European patent application or European patent relates to such subject matter or activities *as such* (emphasis added).

12.7   We will concentrate on a number of these examples in this chapter, and in particular, the prohibition on patenting discoveries and the exclusion of computer programs. The most significant part of this section, however, lies in the two little words *'as such'*. The interpretation of these words by intellectual property offices and courts around Europe has had a profound impact on the scope of the exclusions from patentable inventions. The trend has been towards a narrowing interpretation of the provisions resulting in a corresponding expansion in the scope of patentable inventions in a number of controversial areas such as biotechnological inventions, computer software, and business method patents. This may be set to change, however, with new challenges brought by new technologies, such as stem cell research and also pronouncements by the European Patent Office's (EPO's) Enlarged Board of Appeal on the appropriateness of such a trend.[5] Let us consider each of these in turn.

Biotechnological inventions

12.8   The *Gowers Review of Intellectual Property* reported in 2006 that almost 20 per cent of human gene DNA sequences had been patented; 4,382 out of the 23,688 known human genes.[6] How can this be?

12.9   Several questions sit at the heart of the debate about the propriety of granting patents over genetic and biological materials. First, how can property rights be granted over genes or partial gene sequences which, after all, seem to be no more than mere discoveries? Secondly, how appropriate is it to grant a monopoly over the building blocks of life or, indeed, life itself in the form of genetically engineered organisms? Finally, if this is to happen, what is the optimal policy to ensure that research is not hindered by the grant of these patents and that individual (human and competing commercial) interests are also respected?

Biotechnology: the techniques

12.10   It is important to have a rudimentary understanding of the science that underpins biotechnology before we can embark on a study of the legal and ethical issues surrounding the patenting of biotechnological inventions.[7] You must understand some of the concepts and terminology in order to understand the legal cases.

---

    [5] G1/07 *MED-PHYSICS/Treatment by surgery* [2010] EPOR 25.

    [6] *Gowers Review of Intellectual Property* (HM Treasury, 2006), para 2.30.

    [7] See, eg, CR Harwood and A Wipat, 'Genome management and analysis: prokaryotes' in C Ratledge and B Kristiansen (eds), *Basic Biotechnology* (3rd edn, 2006), Ch 4.

12.11 Biotechnology concerns the application of scientific techniques to living organisms with a view to manipulation of these organisms. Biotechnological inventions are inventions which 'concern a product consisting of or containing biological material or a process by means of which biological material is produced, processed or used'. Biological material means 'any material containing genetic information and capable of reproducing itself or being reproduced in a biological system.'[8] Great benefits are promised in a variety of areas from this technology. For example, in the health sphere, biotechnological advances can lead to the development of new diagnostic products, medical treatments, and drugs. Genetic manipulation in farming, agriculture, and horticulture can produce more robust varieties of animals and plants that are able to resist harsh environments and provide better yield, while genetically modified foods can last longer and may even taste better and can be of considerable assistance to populations living in the developing world.

12.12 A number of techniques have been employed by the biotechnology industry. These are the most common:

- **Tissue and cell culture technology** involves the production of cell lines. These are immortal, self-replicating samples of cells grown outside the original host, which can be a bacterium, a plant, an animal, or a human being. The importance of such cell lines lies in their uniformity. Because samples in any given cell line stem from a common ancestor they have the same genetic make-up. This allows scientists to carry out highly accurate comparative tests. Cell lines are of use in the study of biological processes and play a vital role in testing the potentially harmful effects of drugs and other compounds on living matter. Stem cell lines[9] hold considerable promise in the development of therapies in their own right.

- **Hybridoma technology** is concerned with the two essential players in the human immune response: white blood cells and antibodies. The technique involves the fusion of antibody-producing white blood cells and tumour cells (myeloma). Myeloma reproduce indefinitely, and when the hybridised cell is injected into an antigen (a foreign body which provokes antibody response) an indefinite supply of antibodies is produced because of the immortal qualities inherited from the tumour cell. Hybridomas have proved to be invaluable in immune system research. The antibodies produced from this technique have also proved useful as reagents in diagnostic and other testing kits.

- **Recombinant DNA technology** is also known as genetic engineering. The processes and techniques involved in rDNA technology concern the manipulation of matter at the sub-cellular level. In this respect, genetic engineering differs from its companion technologies. DNA is the acronym for Deoxyribo Nucleic Acid. A string of DNA is contained in the nucleus of almost all living cells with the exception of very basic forms of life such as bacteria.[10] The purpose of DNA is to dictate the function of the cell in which it exists. It does this through genes. Genes are segments or *sequences* of DNA which activate the production of proteins by bringing together different combinations of amino acids in particular orders. Different genes attract different amino acids which in turn combine to produce different proteins. This is a process referred to as *coding* for a protein. Different proteins make cells function in different ways. Proteins are also known as *polypeptides*—this is a term frequently used in the case law.

---

[8] Guidelines for Examination in the European Patent Office, Part G-II, para 5.1.

[9] Stem cells have the ability to become (differentiate into) a wide variety of types of cell and as such are susceptible to manipulation towards therapeutic ends, especially in regenerative medicine. Both embryonic and adult stem cell research is undertaken, the former bringing its own ethical concerns as we shall see.

[10] Reproductive cells such as sperm and eggs each contain half the amount of genetic material necessary to make a complete organism.

- **In Silico techniques** combine genetic and bioinformatic knowledge to search and compare databases of gene sequences in an attempt to attribute function to as yet unprotected sequences based on matches with already known proteins of similar function.

12.13   The sequences of DNA known as genes are themselves composed of chemical bases. There are only four of these bases and they are known by their initial letters: A, T, C, and G.[11] Thus, a very short example of a gene sequence might look like this: AATCGAGGCTAGATC. The bases always join up across the structure of DNA in the same fashion: A with T and C with G. The entirety of genetic code necessary to create a single organism is called its genome. There are 2.9 billion base pairs in the human genome and it contains around 30,000 genes. A gene is a particular sequence of base pairs which 'codes for', that is, produces a specific protein (remember *polypeptide*). Proteins are essential to life and play a significant role in the structure and function of cells. The complete map of the human genome was finished in April 2003[12] but we still do not know what many genes do, that is, we do not know what proteins they code for and so their function remains elusive. The next great challenge for scientists is to match the genetic codes with their functional utility in order to understand better how genes work and what role they play in our bodies and the onset of disease. Remember too that gene/environment interaction considerably complicates this search to understand the determinants of disease.

12.14   Some forms of genetic disease occur when one or more bases are missing or misplaced or when genes interact with each other or the environment in adverse ways. For example, sickle cell disease is caused by one wrong letter in a sequence of bases which code for haemoglobin. Those afflicted by this disease produce red blood cells which are sickle-shaped and have a tendency to block blood vessels. This results, inter alia, in damage to surrounding tissue.

12.15   The discovery of naturally occurring enzymes in bacteria which 'cut' DNA sequences at particular locations proved to be the making of the genetic engineering industry for this allowed particular genes to be isolated from the genome of a particular specimen. Subsequent advances saw the reproduction of such samples in purer forms and greater quantities and the introduction of DNA from particular species into the genome of others. This is known as transgenics.

12.16   Recombinant DNA technology is by far the most revolutionary of the techniques employed by the biotechnology industry in recent decades. It has already produced many benefits including diagnosis testing for genetic disease, therapies, and, in rare cases, cures. Very effective research tools have also been a valuable spin-off of the Human Genome Project.

12.17   All of these developments—from the identification of full or partial gene sequences, the development of tests and vaccines based on genetic material, and the creation of genetically engineered organisms and genetic research tools—have been the subject of patent applications. A great many of these have been successful. However, the process has not been easy for the biotechnology industry, especially in Europe where a number of features of European patent law potentially place hurdles in the industry's path. In particular, a variety of objections to biotechnological patents have been raised relying on the provisions of the law and we shall consider each of these in turn.[13]

---

[11] Adenine, Thymine, Cystosine, and Guanine.

[12] You can read more about the Human Genome Project at the website of the largest contributor to the project, the Sanger Centre, at http://www.sanger.ac.uk/.

[13] See generally UK–IPO, 'Examination Guidelines for Patent Applications relating to Biotechnological Inventions in the Intellectual Property Office' (2012) available at http://www.ipo.gov.uk/biotech.pdf.

Discoveries

What is inventive about uncovering a naturally occurring gene?

12.18   One of the most frequently raised objections to biotechnological patents is the challenge that the attempt to patent a sequence of DNA, or a part thereof, is simply an attempt to patent a discovery. It is argued that it is not an invention to uncover a pre-existing and naturally occurring entity.[14] However, the terms 'discovery' and 'invention' have particular technical legal meanings in patent law which reflect fundamental policy objectives including the encouragement of innovation and the reward of endeavour. You will remember from Chapter 11 that one way to think about an invention is that it is a technical solution to a pre-existing and as yet unresolved technical problem. While discoveries and inventions both contribute new knowledge to the sum total of human understanding, an invention does so through the *application* of that knowledge, for example by making something available that was previously beyond our reach. Thus, the mere discovery of the base pair sequence of a gene cannot be the subject of a patent, but locating a previously unknown gene, determining its function, and making it accessible for further exploitation is an example of a technical solution to the pre-existing problem of the inaccessibility of the genetic product.

12.19   The US Supreme Court has recently addressed their 'product of nature' doctrine—being a version of the discovery exclusion—in two high-profile cases. In *Mayo v Prometheus*,[15] albeit not a biotech case as such, a patent on a method of drug delivery was held to be non-patentable as an example of natural law: 'the claims inform a relevant audience about certain laws of nature; any additional steps consist of well-understood, routine, conventional activity already engaged in by the scientific community; and those steps, when viewed as a whole, add nothing significant beyond the sum of their parts taken separately. For these reasons we believe that the steps are not sufficient to transform un-patentable natural correlations into patentable applications of those regularities' (judgment, at 11). A few days later, the Court sent back a challenge over gene patents held by Myriad to the district court to reconsider in the light of the *Mayo* decision. The gene patents were upheld again and the case on patentability of genes bounced back to the Supreme Court to decide the matter for once and for all. The hearing is due to begin Monday 15 April 2013 as we go to press (*Myriad v Association of Molecular Pathology*).

12.20   The position in Europe has been reached by a restrictive interpretation of the qualifier—*as such*—in the exclusions from patent law. A discovery *as such*, that is, in and of itself, cannot be patented, but the use of that discovery in bringing about a technical contribution takes it into the realm of patentable subject matter. This is illustrated most clearly in the guidelines issued by the EPO in respect of discoveries.

EPO Guidelines on discoveries

If a new property of a known material or article is found out, that is mere discovery and unpatentable because discovery as such has no technical effect and is therefore not an invention ... [i]f, however, that property is put to practical use, then this constitute an invention which may be patentable ...

To find a previously unrecognised substance occurring in nature is also mere discovery and therefore unpatentable. However, if a substance found in nature can be shown to produce a technical effect, it may be patentable. An example of such a case is that of a substance occurring in nature which is found to have an antibiotic effect. In addition, if a microorganism is discovered to exist in nature and to produce an antibiotic, the micro-organism itself may also be patentable as one aspect of the invention. Similarly, a gene which

---

[14] For arguments of this kind, see Genewatch UK at http://www.genewatch.org/.   [15] 132 S Ct 1289 (2012).

is discovered to exist in nature may be patentable if a technical effect is revealed, eg its use in making a certain polypeptide or in gene therapy.[16]

This means that an invention that happens to involve biological or genetic material can be patentable even although the material also exists in nature provided that the invention makes a technical contribution to the state of the art. This can be achieved by removing it from its natural environment and by characterising the contribution by the isolation of the substance and its new-found availability.

12.21   Patentees have also employed other techniques to ensure protection for their biotechnological inventions. These include the argument that the invention as claimed does not exist naturally in this form. For example, in the *Icos Decision*[17] the EPO held that the production of a purified and isolated nucleic acid having a sequence that does not exist in nature is not a discovery.[18]

12.22   Numerous examples of natural products have accordingly been the subject of patents. These range from sequences or partial sequences of DNA, protein molecules and recombinant DNA molecules used as research tools, to purified forms of bacteria, vitamins, and viruses. It has been argued, however, that merely to remove an entity from its natural environment and to produce it in a purer form towards an identified commercial end is insufficiently inventive and confuses the criterion of inventive step with the demonstration of function.[19] Moreover, the strength of monopoly over such an invention can be considerable. Often the breadth of a monopoly on a natural product invention can make it very difficult to invent around and this can have adverse consequences for further and future research in any number of fields requiring access to the material. This may be hindered by an unwillingness on the part of the patentee to license or by the imposition of unduly burdensome licence fees. Indeed, the threat of litigation may itself deter future research. We will return to the question of licensing in Part VIII.

12.23   For present purposes it is interesting to note that the Organisation for Economic Co-operation and Development (OECD) has produced guidelines for the licensing of genetic inventions used in health care systems.[20] These arose because of concerns about how some genetic inventions, especially those used in genetic testing, had been exploited to the detriment of patients principally because aggressive licensing practices had inhibited access to genetic tests.[21] The Recommendation lays out principles and best practices for achieving 'a balance between the delivery of new products and services, healthcare needs, and economic returns'.[22] The general spirit of the instrument is to foster openness, sharing, cooperation, and further innovation through responsible licensing practices. An OECD Recommendation

---

[16] EPO Guidelines, Part G-II, para 3.1.

[17] *Icos Decision* [2002] OJEPO 293. Available at http://archive.epo.org/epo/pubs/oj002/06_02/06_2932.pdf.

[18] It should be noted, however, that this patent failed on other grounds including lack of inventive step and lack of industrial applicability.

[19] LJ Demaine and AX Fellmeth, 'Natural substances and patentable inventions' (2003) 300 Science 1375–1376. See also MA Majumder et al, 'Ethical challenges of patenting "nature": legal and economic accounts of altered nature as property' in BA Lustig et al (eds), *Altering Nature: Concepts of 'Nature' and 'The Natural' in Biotechnology Debates* (2008), Ch 4. See also Springer Briefs in Biotech Patents, available at http://link.springer.com/bookseries/10239, notably A Huttermann, *The Limits of Patentability: Genes and Nucleic Acides* (2013), 33–44.

[20] OECD, *Recommendation on the Licensing of Genetic Inventions* (2006), Council of the OECD, 23 February 2006, (2005)149/Rev1.

[21] See B Williams-Jones, 'History of a gene patent: tracing the development and application of commercial BRCA testing' (2002) 10 Health Law Journal 123–146 and C Beauchamp, 'Patenting nature: a problem of history' (2012) Stanford Technology Law Review, available at http://ssrn.com/abstract=2152105.

[22] See further OECD, *Guidelines for the Licensing of Genetic Inventions* (2006), available at http://www.oecd.org/sti/biotechnology/licensing. See also Human Genetics Commission, 'Intellectual Property and DNA Diagnostics' (October 2010) available at http://www.hgc.gov.uk/UploadDocs/DocPub/Document/IP%20and%20DNA%20Diagnostics%202010%20final.pdf.

is by no means legally binding, but it does represent the views and political will of 34 of the most economically influential global democracies.[23]

Exercise

Critically assess the provisions of the OECD Recommendation and consider how its provisions might be implemented in practice.

Novelty

When is a naturally occurring substance new?

12.24   It might also be objected that a biotechnological invention cannot be patented because it is not new in the strict sense required by patent law because it can already be found in the natural world. You will remember, however, that novelty requires that the invention be available to the public before the priority date of the patent application. The key word here is *available*. It is not enough to anticipate an invention simply to know that a product exists in nature if it cannot also be accessed by human beings. At the very least, there must be evidence both of its availability and the means to reproduce it. Thus, in *Asahi Kasei Kogyo KK's Application*[24] the mere mention of the existence of human tissue necrosis factor in an earlier patent application in Japan was not enough to defeat the instant patent over a genetically engineered version of the protein which had been developed to assist in treating tumours. The House of Lords held that prior publication of existence does not mean that the invention is available to the public unless the method of working the invention is so obvious as to require no explanation. Mere speculation on how the invention might be useful is insufficient;[25] by the same token, the prospective patentee need not show, by experiment, that the invention actually works, merely that it is plausible that it will work.[26]

Question

Does this imply that the product must already have been produced before it will anticipate a later patent? Is it enough merely to provide instructions on how to produce it?

12.25   Remember that an invention can be either a *product* or a *process*. In the realm of biotechnological inventions, it was previously the case in the UK that the novelty of a known biological product could be derived from demonstrating the novelty of the process used to produce the product—a so-called product-by-process claim.[27] This, however, put the UK at odds with every other signatory country to the EPC, and with the jurisprudence of the EPO itself. The House of Lords has now addressed this anomaly, holding that the correct interpretation of the law is that found in Article 64(2) EPC that: 'If the subject-matter of the European patent is a process, the protection conferred by the patent shall extend to the products directly obtained by such process'[28] The only circumstances in which the EPO will consider a

---

[23] The OECD includes the United States and the UK but not China or India. Cf KS Jayaraman, 'Is India's "patent factory" squandering funds?' (2006) 442 Nature 120.   [24] *Asahi Kasei Kogyo KK's Application* [1991] RPC 485.
[25] See *Eli Lilly & Co v Human Genome Sciences Inc* [2008] EWHC 1903 (Pat).
[26] *Conor Medsystems Inc v Angiotech Pharmaceuticals Inc and another* [2008] RPC 28.
[27] See the Court of Appeal in *Kirin Amgen Inc and others v Transkaryotic Therapies Inc and others (No 2)* [2003] RPC 3.
[28] See the appeal in the House of Lords: *Kirin Amgen Inc and others v Transkaryotic Therapies Inc and others (No 2) (aka Kirin-Amgen Inc v Hoechst and others)* [2005] 1 All ER 667, [2005] RPC 9.

product-by-process claim is when the product itself is new (ie novelty is not derived from the novelty of the process), and when its novelty cannot be described in chemical or physical terms.[29] The UK–IPO has confirmed that it will now take the view that 'a claim to a product obtained or produced by a process is anticipated by any prior disclosure of that particular product per se, regardless of its method of production.'[30]

12.26   Another technique that has been used to avoid problems of novelty is to claim the artificially manufactured version of the product. Higher life forms (eukaryotics) contain segments of DNA in their genetic make-up that do not code for proteins. These segments are called *introns*. Lower life forms (prokaryotics), such as bacteria, do not contain introns.[31] Genetic engineering techniques can remove these introns leaving only the 'purified' form of the DNA, which is known as copy or complimentary DNA (cDNA). cDNA does not exist in nature and so it is argued that a claim to cDNA products is not a claim to a naturally occurring entity.[32] You should note, however, that cDNA sequences perform exactly the same function as the natural version of the same sequences.

12.27   The European Directive on the protection of biotechnological inventions confirms that patents are available for:

> An element isolated from the human body or otherwise produced by means of a technical process, including the sequence or partial sequence of a gene, even if the structure of that element is identical to that of a natural element.[33]

12.28   However, it also reiterates that patents are not available for 'the human body or its parts in their natural state or for the simple discovery of one of its elements'.[34] The equivalent provisions were incorporated into UK law by the Patents Regulations 2000.[35] The EPO Guidelines for Examination confirm that 'In principle, biotechnological inventions are patentable under the EPC',[36] while also incorporating the qualifications outlined previously.

12.29   Nonetheless, a patent based on a naturally occurring entity is always open to the claim that the entity has already been extracted from its natural environment and utilised by man. This kind of challenge has been successful in two high-profile cases: the Mexican Government and other parties secured the revocation of a patent over corn plants with improved oil composition in 2004 on the ground that the patent lacked *novelty*, that is, that maize having the characteristics described in the patent was already known and available in Mexico.[37] A similar challenge saw the defeat of the Neem Tree Oil patent in 2000 for lack of novelty based on evidence from India.[38]

Inventive step (non-obviousness)

12.30   The biggest threat to the patentability of genetic and biological material does not come from the criteria described previously but rather from the requirement that the invention demonstrate 'inventive step', that is, that it represents a non-obviousness advance in the particular field of technology compared to what was known prior to the filing of the patent. You will recall once again from Chapter 11 that this

---

[29] Remember, however, that the Patents Act 1977, s 60(1)(c) states that the protection given by a claim for a process extends to the product of that process. This provides some residual comfort to patentees. The same provision is found in Art 64(2) EPC.
[30] See Examination Guidelines for Biotech Inventions, note 13, para 14.
[31] This information is important to bear in mind when you read *Biogen v Medeva* [1997] RPC 1.
[32] *HOWARD FLOREY/Relaxin* [1995] EPOR 541.   [33] Biotechnology Directive, Art 5(2).
[34] Biotechnology Directive, Art 5(1).
[35] Patents Regulations 2000 (SI 2000/2037), incorporating Sch A2 into the Patents Act 1977.
[36] EPO Guidelines, Part G-II, para 2a.2.   [37] European Patent 0744888.   [38] European Patent 0436257.

criterion is tested by reference to the knowledge of persons skilled in the particular area.[39] In *Genentech Inc's Patent*[40] the Court of Appeal considered the validity of Genentech's patent for human tissue plasminogen activator (t-PA), a protein occurring naturally in the human body that assists in the dissolution of blood clots. Genentech was able to produce sufficient quantities of t-PA in a sufficiently pure form to market as a therapeutic agent through the application of standard recombinant DNA techniques. At least five other teams embarked on similar work at considerable expense and with a degree of uncertainty of success. Genentech was the first to succeed in establishing t-PA's genetic sequence and sought a patent for products that included t-PA produced by genetic engineering techniques and processes used in its production. Revocation of the patent was sought, inter alia, for lack of inventive step. It was held that:

- The patent was invalid for lack of inventive step. It was obvious to a person skilled in the art to set out to produce human t-PA by recombinant DNA technology. All steps taken by Genentech in establishing the composition of the relevant sequences and applying that knowledge to produce t-PA were applications of known technology towards a known end without any original step.

- The fact that at least five other teams embarked towards the same goal using the same techniques was a sign of obviousness. Being the first to succeed was not enough; but if no one else had set out to produce the invention this might be evidence that it was not obvious.

- Laborious and costly effort did not necessarily involve an inventive step even if it amounted to more than the exercise of proficiency.

12.31   In coming to this decision the Court of Appeal opined that the skilled person in such a hi-tech industry must possess a degree of ingenuity and inventiveness for otherwise they would not be part of the industry at all. Moreover, inventiveness could be assessed by reference to a research team where this is the standard working practice in a particular area.[41] It has been observed that this decision seems to set a higher standard of test of obviousness for hi-tech industries such as the biotechnology industry.[42] This could mean that problems which are encountered on the route to the end goal are more likely to be seen as everyday run-of-the-mill hiccups for the hi-tech skilled person and that their resolution is less likely to exhibit inventiveness. Invention is the norm in an industry such as biotechnology and as the law stands it is eminently sensible that the concept of the skilled person, used to test obviousness, should assume the traits of those working in the field in question. Overly zealous application of this view might, however, lead to a paradox in practice, namely, that those who make significant advances in the name of benefiting humanity and who spend considerable sums in the process, are less likely to be rewarded by the grant of a patent in recognition of their endeavour.

12.32   This, of course, depends entirely on the attitude and approach of the courts to interpreting these criteria. At the time of the *Genentech* decision there were concerns that a different standard was being laid down for the biotechnology industry and this was fuelled by the suggestion in that case that an additional requirement existed for patents involving biological material to show that there was an 'invention' over and above the basic criteria of patentability.[43] But there is no real evidence of the biotechnology industry suffering discriminatory treatment subsequent to *Genentech* and Lord Hoffmann was unconvinced by the additional criterion in delivering the House of Lords' ruling in *Biogen v Medeva*.[44] Although he did

[39] For guidance on relevant characteristics in the biotechnology field, see T455/91 *GENENTECH ET AL/Expression in yeast* [1995] OJEPO 684.   [40] [1989] RPC 147 (CA).

[41] [1989] RPC 147 (CA) at 278. Also *Schlumberger Holdings Ltd v Electromagnetic Geoservices AS* [2009] RPC 19.

[42] See too T39/93 *POLYMER POWDERS/Allied Colloids* [1997] OJEPO 134 at 149.   [43] *Genentech*, note 39, 263.

[44] *Biogen v Medeva* [1997] RPC 1.

not rule out the possibility that in the future it might be possible for a novel creation to satisfy all statutory criteria and yet not be properly describable as an 'invention', he noted that neither the draftsmen of the EPC, nor those who drew up the 1977 Act, nor indeed counsel for the defendants, could offer a single example of such a creation. For the time being, then, to satisfy the standard criteria on patentability *is* to produce an invention.

12.33   The Nuffield Council on Bioethics has called for more stringent assessments of the criteria of patentability and most notably that of inventive step.[45] The Council conjectures that many patents have been granted for so-called inventions that do not meet these rigorous requirements. Moreover, it notes that the US and European interpretations of this criterion differ slightly but to a sufficient degree to make a real difference to a prospective patentee's chances of success. Thus, while in Europe we consider the need for 'inventive step', that is, that there must be evidence of non-obvious inventiveness on the part of the inventor, the US interpretation focuses on 'non-obviousness' so that as long as the particularities of the result were not obvious to an expert then the criterion is satisfied—for example, that the precise sequence of bases that would appear in a recombinant DNA molecule would not be obvious to an expert. This latter is a lower threshold and consequently means that genetically engineered products remain, potentially at least, more easily patentable in the United States than in Europe. By the same token, it has been established in the EPO[46] and the UK–IPO[47] that it is obvious to claim a specific recombinant DNA sequence if all of the techniques necessary to produce it are known. Equally, now that many genomes have been sequenced and large-scale use of bioinformatics to find homologous sequences or polypeptides is common, the use of data mining to uncover 'new' genes or sequences will not normally be sufficient to demonstrate inventive step.[48] The corollary is that the use of non-obvious techniques, perhaps involving bioinformatics tools, can overcome this objection.

Industrial applicability (utility)

Other differences between the United States and Europe

12.34   The requirement of industrial applicability in Europe means that it must be shown that the invention can be made or used in any kind of industry, including agriculture.[49] In the United States, the equivalent criterion requires *utility*, an issue which has caused some controversy in the context of biotech patents over the years. Various attempts were made in the early 1990s to patent Expressed Sequence Tags (ESTs), being partial gene fragments with no known utility. The rationale, however, was that these might point the way to complete gene sequences and so may help to stake a claim to the full sequences once these were found. The US Patent and Trademark Office (USPTO) rejected such claims, and most notably those of the National Institutes of Health, for lack of utility: the function of the invention could not be sufficiently described. Since then, the USPTO has revised its guidelines on utility (January 2001, updated December 2008).[50] An invention now must show a 'specific and substantial and credible utility', but it should be noted that 'credible' here includes a theoretical credible use, that is, it is not necessary to show that the invention actually works in order to obtain a patent. There is therefore no specific prohibition on the patenting of ESTs, or indeed, other gene variations such as Single Nucleotide Polymorphisms (SNPs),[51] as long as the criteria for patentability are met.

[45] Nuffield Council on Bioethics, *The Ethics of Patenting DNA* (2002).
[46] T886/91 *BIOGEN INC/Hepatitis B virus* [1999] EPOR 361.   [47] *Collaborative Research's Patent* BL O/86/94.
[48] Examining Guidelines on Biotech Inventions, note 13, para 34.   [49] Patents Act 1977, s 4(1) and EPC Art 57.
[50] http://www.uspto.gov/web/offices/pac/mpep/documents/2100_2107.htm#sect2107
[51] SNPs, as their name suggests, are sequences of identical DNA that vary from the norm in only a single base pair. Despite these extremely minor differences, SNPs can be used as markers for particular genes and may play a key role in understanding the genetic basis for individual patient response to medicines.

12.35   The EC Directive on the patentability of biotechnological inventions states that full or partial gene sequences with no known function will not be patentable,[52] and this has been confirmed by the European Court of Justice (ECJ).[53] It has also been endorsed by the UK–IPO[54] and the EPO which has ruled that mere speculative function for a genetically engineered gene sequence cannot lead to the conclusion that it is capable of industrial application.[55] Indeed, the EPO indicated that uses must be 'specific, substantial and credible' to meet this criterion, thereby reflecting the wording of the US model and, potentially, approximating the legal standards on both sides of the Atlantic. Indeed, the EPO Guidelines now provide that 'the industrial application of a sequence or a partial sequence of a gene must be disclosed in the patent application. A mere nucleic acid sequence without indication of a function is not a patentable invention …'[56]

12.36   The issue of biotechnology and industrial applicability has recently been considered for the first time by the Supreme Court in the UK in *Eli Lily & Co v Human Genome Sciences.*[57] This case concerned a patent for a polynucleotide sequence which Eli Lily sought to revoke on the ground that, amongst other things, the specification failed to disclose an invention capable of industrial application. The argument was that the prediction of the uses of the sequence were purely speculative. Lower courts noted that UK jurisprudence on industrial application is limited, but that the EPO jurisprudence does provide guidance;[58] the Supreme Court confirmed that English courts ought to follow any principles of law clearly laid down by the Technical Boards of Appeal of the EPO (paras 96–102). This, however, does not preclude divergence on matters of fact based on the evidence presented to each judicial body (as happened in this case). Article 57 EPC states clearly that an invention is only patentable if it is 'susceptible of industrial application'. Any invention which does not comply should be revoked, and at national level this is according to section 72(1) of the Patents Act 1977. Central to the question of industrial application for claims to gene sequences or proteins is adequate description of their function. A patent will not be given if it is not possible to disclose how the sequence or protein can be used. Merely describing existence and structure is not enough. The Supreme Court's view in the instant case was that the law should be taken as that laid down in the jurisprudence of the Technical Board of Appeal in the EPO, albeit that this did not preclude a UK-specific different outcome (para 91). The question then for the Supreme Court was whether the first instance judge had followed the principles laid down in the EPO jurisprudence. If he had, it was not its place to displace his ruling (unless the conclusion was not one that could reasonably have been reached). In the event, the Supreme Court was not satisfied that the EPO principles had indeed been followed. It concluded that the appeal of HGS should success on the point that the claimed invention met the requirements of Article 57 EPC, viz that it displayed industrial applicability in the sense that a 'plausible' or 'reasonably credible' claimed use, or even an 'educated guess' as to function can suffice (paras 106–111).[59] This is a heavily policy-driven decision with the Supreme Court: 'Just as it would be undesirable to let someone have a monopoly over a particular biological molecule too early, because

---

[52]   Biotechnology Directive, Art 5(3) read in conjunction with recitals 23 and 24. See too Patents Act 1977, Sch A2, para 6.

[53]   Case C-377/98 *Kingdom of the Netherlands v Council of the European Union and the European Parliament* [2002] FSR 36 at para 74 of the judgment. Also see the preliminary ruling of the Court of Justice in C-428/08 *Monsanto Technology LLC v Cefetra BV* [2012] 3 CMLR 7, [2011] All ER (EC) 209, [2011] FSR 6 confirming that a DNA sequence is unpatentable in European law if it fails to perform the function described for it in the patent application, even where it had previously performed that function (or could do so again, if extracted).

[54]   Examining Guidelines on Biotech Inventions, note 13, paras 51–60 and see *Aeomica Inc* BL O/286/05 31.

[55]   *Icos Decision* [2002] OJEPO 293, http://archive.epo.org/epo/pubs/oj002/06_02/06_2932.pdf.

[56]   EPO Guidelines, Part G-II, para 5.4   [57]   [2011] UKSC 51, [2012] 1 All ER 1154, [2012] RPC 6.

[58]   For a good illustration, see T898/05 *ZYMOGENETICS/Hematopoietic cytokine receptor* [2007] EPOR 2.

[59]   For comment see T Minssen and D Nilsson, 'The industrial application requirement for biotech inventions in light of recent EPO & UK case law: a plausible approach or a mere "hunting license"?' (2012) 34(1) EIPR 689. Equally, the plausibility of a claim about the scope of a prediction in claims does not require proof that the invention works in every case, see *Regeneron Pharmaceuticals Inc v Genentech Inc Bayer Pharma AG v Genentech Inc* [2013] EWCA Civ 93.

it risks closing down competition, so it would be wrong to set the hurdle for patentability too high …'
(para 130).

12.37 These examples demonstrate how the varyingly restrictive and facilitative interpretation of the exclusions from patentability has, in turn, led to an accommodation of the particularities of biotechnological inventions in the criteria for patentability. Only the *volonté* of the intellectual property offices and the courts has brought us to this position. Yet, each is also mindful of the need to balance interests in intellectual property law, weighing up the legitimacy of the claims of the prospective patentee with the interests of competitors to invent around and compete fairly with parties enjoying a monopolistic control of sectors of the market. It is helpful in this regard to examine a few examples of how this accommodation has been reached by the British courts.

 Exercise

You might like to consider the different approaches adopted in the United States, Europe, and Japan in these comparative studies of biotechnology patent practices: **http://www.trilateral.net/projects/biotechnology.html**.

The problem of excessively broad patents

12.38 The policy concerns surrounding biotechnological inventions were first aired in the British courts in the *Genentech* case, discussed previously. Many matters were laid to rest, however, by the House of Lords in *Biogen v Medeva* which clarified the law and confirmed beyond doubt the patentability of biotechnological inventions as a matter of UK policy. The patent in *Biogen* related, inter alia, to the genetic sequence of the infective agent of the Hepatitis B virus (such an agent is referred to as displaying *antigen specificity*). Biogen was the only company to pursue this line of research and was granted a patent which was subsequently challenged. The court found that while the inventors claimed protection for *all* molecules showing Hepatitis B antigen specificity produced by *any* technique in *any* host, the actual contribution of the invention was a single means to express crude molecules displaying Hepatitis B antigen specificity in basic hosts when the relevant gene sequence was unknown. Indeed, once that sequence was uncovered—which happened very soon after the patent was first filed—there was no need to rely on the Biogen contribution, yet to uphold the patent in its original terms would have excluded much future work on the Hepatitis B virus. This is the problem of breadth of monopoly and undue scope of patent protection. It was held that the claimed monopoly was deemed to be excessively broad compared to the actual contribution that the inventors had made to the state of the art. Patent protection will only be awarded for the additional knowledge that inventors add to the sum total of human knowledge and no more.

12.39 It is a frequent problem with new and emerging technologies that early patents are granted broadly by intellectual property offices before the offices and the courts get to grips with the true nature of the technology. *Biogen* was an early attempt to keep the UK on a narrow path.

12.40 *Biogen* is also authority for the proposition that the subject matter described in the application must enable the invention to be worked *to the full extent* of the monopoly claimed. If the invention embodies a principle that is capable of general application across a wide range of products, then it is permissible to claim all such products and it is not necessary for the patentee to prove that his principle applies in all cases. However, if the patentee claims different products or processes in the same application, each must be described by a separate enabling disclosure.

Moreover, if no unifying principle links the claimed inventions together, then all that can be claimed is that which can be described.[60] It was held in *Dr Reddy's Laboratories* that where a previous patent discloses a general formula with multiple substituents chosen from lists of some length, this will not normally take away the novelty of a subsequent claim to a specific individual compound.[61]

> **Web link**
>
> You can read more about the *Biogen* case and the corresponding dispute before the EPO at the Online Resource Centre at www.oxfordtextbooks.co.uk/orc/waelde3e/

12.41   In *Kirin-Amgen v Hoechst* the House of Lords invalidated the core claims of a patent over genetically engineered Erythropoietin (EPO)—a protein found in minute levels in the body which regulates the production of red blood cells—in large part because of the unsustainability of the breadth of the claims made by the patentee.[62] The patentees claimed, in essence, *any* way of making EPO by recombinant DNA technology and the resultant forms of EPO, but their patent specification did not disclose an invention which was capable of furnishing the person skilled in the particular art with sufficient information to realise such a broad range of possibilities. Lord Hoffmann confirmed that it is possible to claim that an invention discloses 'a principle capable of general application' and accordingly to have a monopoly over the entire class of products which flow from the application of that principle, but this case was not such an example.[63] Rather, Lord Hoffmann laid down a three-point test to determine sufficiency, that is, whether the claims are sustained by the actual contribution that the invention makes to human knowledge. This is:

- What exactly is the invention?
- What does the application claim to enable the skilled man to do?
- Does the specification actually enable him to do it?

This may seem trite, but the first question is of crucial importance. The patentees sought to have the court believe that they had invented a product, a form of EPO, but their Lordships took a different view holding that they had, in fact, invented a way of making EPO, that is, a process. Moreover, the process that was revealed was not one which taught a skilled expert *any* way of making EPO by recombinant DNA technology, nor did it reveal a way of making EPO in such general terms as to cover the process used by the defendants. A further point made by the court concerns the role of the skilled expert in interpreting the language used by the applicant in drafting his claims: 'what would a person skilled in the art have understood the patentee to have used the language of the claim to mean?' In other words, the courts will use the notional expert as a device to limit ex post facto interpretations by a patentee in an attempt to broaden the scope of his monopoly. This is particularly pertinent when new technologies emerge and the patentee attempts to argue that they are also caught by his patent.[64]

---

[60]   See *Chiron Corp and others v Murex Diagnostics and others* [1996] FSR 153 in which the patent in suit claimed, inter alia, Hepatitis C virus (HCV) polypeptides, antibodies, vaccines against HCV, and methods of propagating HCV but it was shown that the principal claim as drafted 'covers an almost infinite number of polypeptides which are useless for any known purpose' (at 177).

[61]   *Dr Reddy's Laboratories (UK) Ltd v Eli Lilly and Co* [2008] EWHC 2345 (Pat), para 91, confirmed by the Court of Appeal at [2010] RPC 82.

[62]   *Kirin Amgen Inc and others Hoechst and others* [2005] 1 All ER 667, [2005] RPC 9.

[63]   For an example of this, see T 0292/85 *GENENTECH/Polypeptide expression* [1989] OJEPO 275 discussed by Lord Hoffmann at paras 112–113.

[64]   See M Fisher, 'Extracting the price of a patent: enablement and written description' [2012] 4 IPQ 262.

12.42   In another House of Lords decision their Lordships took the opportunity to clarify the law after *Biogen*. In *Generics (UK) Ltd and others v H Lundbeck A/S*[65] the House of Lords upheld the patent on a product which was for the effective agent in an antidepressant drug Citalopram (see further para 11.212). A challenge arose because the inventiveness of the product was claimed solely by reference to the means to make it. Only one such means had been disclosed but a product patent would give a monopoly that could prevent competition no matter how rival versions of the product were made. Was this an overly broad monopoly? The answer was 'no' and *Biogen* was distinguished. *Biogen* was characterised as not dealing with a product claim but rather with an unusual product/process hybrid claim whose breadth was clearly too wide. *Generics* involved a product of which the means to make it was completely non-obvious. The technical contribution was 'to make available, for the first time, a product which had previously been unavailable, namely the isolated (+)-enantiomer of Citalopram. On that basis, it would appear to follow that the respondent was entitled to claim the enantiomer.'[66] It was no offence to UK or EPO case law that the monopoly which flowed from this extended to all rival products, however made.

Key points on biotechnological inventions

Biotechnological inventions are patentable as long as you remember:

- *Discoveries*—the claim should be to the (purified) entity isolated from its natural environment and should include a description of the technical effect brought about by its application/use

- *Novelty*—prior disclosure is always a risk, but mere knowledge of the existence of a naturally occurring product is not enough. Prior availability of the claimed invention must be shown

- *Inventive step*—intellectual property offices are likely to be tougher with this criterion if policy guidance is followed; using traditional genetic engineering techniques to isolate material or bioinformatics to conduct data mining is unlikely to be inventive

- *Industrial applicability*—the function of the invention should always be disclosed but this can include a plausible promise of a function involving an educated guess

- *Broad claims*—protection will only be given for the extent of the contribution made to human knowledge and no more

---

Morality

12.43   Thus far, we have avoided mention of morality but this issue has proved to be one of the most controversial in the biotechnology patenting field. In stark contrast to the position in the United States where the Supreme Court has held that 'Congress intended statutory subject matter to include anything under the sun that is made by man',[67] Europe has long contemplated a role for moral concerns in the decision-making process about the grant of a patent.[68] Article 53 EPC 2000 provides that:

(a) inventions the commercial exploitation of which would be contrary to 'ordre public' or morality; such exploitation shall not be deemed to be so contrary merely because it is prohibited by law or regulation in some or all of the Contracting States;

(b) plant or animal varieties or essentially biological processes for the production of plants or animals; this provision shall not apply to microbiological processes or the products thereof;

---

[65] [2009] UKHL 12.   [66] Per Lord Neuberger at para 83.   [67] *Diamond v Chakrabarty* 447 US 303 at 309 (1980).
[68] Strasbourg Convention 1963. For commentary, see O Mills, *Biotechnological Inventions: Moral Restraints and Patent Law* (2005).

(Recall that this reflects Article 27 TRIPS, and has been incorporated into domestic law by amendments to the Patents Act 1977 by the Patents Act 2004.)

G2/07 and G1/08 *Essentially Biological Processes* [2011] EPOR 27

The essential question here—referred to the Enlarged Board of Appeal (EBA) for clarification[69]—is whether the selection and crossing of plants by human intervention escaped the prohibition on patentability as contained in Article 53b.

The EBA held that what had to be examined was the essence of the invention in question, taking into account the nature and overall contribution of human intervention and the extent of its impact on the results achieved. This had to be more than mere trivial interference and not be something that could occur naturally. Moreover, the significance of the intervention would be tested against traditional breeders' processes and must go beyond these. Furthermore, if the processes of manipulation introduced or significantly modified a trait in the genome of the biological subject matter that went beyond merely the result of mixing of the genes through sexual crossing, then this took the activity outside the scope of the exclusion.[70]

12.44   The morality provisions in TRIPS appear largely at the insistence of European states and as a reflection of their history, but the morality provisions in European patent law mostly lay dormant until the advent of contemporary biotechnology patenting whereupon they were aggressively invoked by parties harbouring a plethora of doubts about biotechnology, of which patenting practices are merely a small part. The debacle has largely been played out on the European stage in the Opposition Division of the EPO and more recently in the institutions of the EU.

 Exercise

Before reading any further, consider what is meant by 'inventions the commercial exploitation of which would be contrary to ... morality'. How do we know when something is immoral? Note: it is the commercial exploitation of the invention which must be immoral, not necessarily the invention itself. Why is this so? What difference does this make?

Morality case law before the EPO

12.45   We saw in the last chapter that morality provisions before the EPO have been interpreted, in the main, narrowly. This is true in respect of each category of biotechnological inventions relating to plant,[71] animal,[72] and human[73] material. The hurdle has been set very high at a level of abhorrence to the majority of the European publics, and the range of morality questions has been restricted to the term of Article 53(a)—the commercial exploitation of the invention (or previously, the publication or exploitation of the invention, EPC 1973).[74] Before we discuss more recent developments, however, we need to assess the role and impact of the Biotechnology Directive which interceded squarely in the middle of these developments.

---

[69] See also T1242/06 *STATE OF ISRAEL/Tomatoes II* [2012] EPOR 42.
[70] T775/08 *MONSANTO/Glyphosate tolerant alfalfa* [2011] EPOR 28.
[71] *PLANT GENETIC SYSTEMS/Glutamine Synthetase Inhibitors* [1995] EPOR 357.
[72] *HARVARD/Oncomouse* [1991] EPOR 525 and *HARVARD/Transgenic animal* [2005] EPOR 31.
[73] *HOWARD FLOREY/H2 Relaxin* [1995] EPOR 541.
[74] T0866/01 *Michigan State University/Euthanasia compositions*, available at http://legal.european-patent-office.org/dg3/biblio/t010866eu1.htm.

12.46   The advent of the Biotechnology Directive was one of two events in 1998 which signalled a turning point in European patent granting practice. The other was the scientific breakthrough of isolating human embryonic stem cells which hold great therapeutic promise in a number of areas including spinal cord injuries, Parkinson's disease, stroke, and transplantation therapy.[75] The Biotechnology Directive was originally proposed in 1988, but suffered a very difficult passage and was vetoed by the European Parliament in 1995. While it was eventually adopted in 1998 and contains morality provisions that broadly reflect the jurisprudence of the EPO, there was no time to incorporate any mention of human embryonic stem cell technologies. The resulting controversy has beleaguered the Directive ever since and has brought about a sea-change in attitude in the EPO. Let us begin with a consideration of the Directive itself.

The Biotechnology Directive

12.47   Objections to the European Biotechnology Directive based on moral grounds were primarily responsible for the delay in adopting the legislation; a process which, as we have noted, took ten years. Even after its eventual adoption in July 1998, the Directive was challenged before the ECJ by the Netherlands, Italy, and Norway. The Court took until October 2001 to uphold the validity of the law,[76] and eight member states were referred to the ECJ in July 2003 for failure to implement the Directive. The UK implemented the provisions of the Directive in the Patents Regulations 2000 which amended the Patents Act 1977.[77] The Commission announced in 2012 that it was establishing an expert group to prepare a report on the development and implementation of the law in this field. Watch this space.[78]

12.48   The rationale behind the Biotechnology Directive[79] was elegantly simple. Europe was lagging behind other economic areas, and in particular the United States, and unevenness of approach towards biotechnological inventions throughout the member states was at odds with the Commission's plans for completion of the internal market. The aim of the Directive is equally straightforward: to harmonise the law throughout all member states, making it clear that biotechnological inventions are patentable, subject to certain narrowly defined exceptions and limitations.[80]

12.49   Thus, for example, Article 3(1) confirms that inventions which are new, which involve an inventive step, and which are susceptible of industrial application shall be patentable 'even if they concern a product consisting of or containing biological material or a process by means of which biological material is produced, processed or used.' Moreover, Article 3(2) states that 'Biological material which is isolated from its natural environment or produced by means of a technical process may be the subject of an invention even if it previously occurred in nature'.

---

[75] JA Thomson et al, 'Embryonic stem cell lines derived from human blastocysts' (1998) 282 Science 1145.

[76] C-377/98 *Kingdom of the Netherlands v Council of the European Union and the European Parliament* [2002] FSR 36. Subsequently the EPO Technical Board of Appeal confirmed that the absence of consent to patenting from the individuals who provide human material that is used to create a patentable invention is irrelevant in European patent law, see T1213/05 *UNIVERSITY OF UTAH/Linked breast and ovarian cancer susceptibility gene*, unreported, September 2007. For comment, see A Odell-West, 'The absence of informed consent to commercial exploitation for inventions developed from human biological material: a bar to patentability?' [2009] 3 IPQ 273.

[77] Patents Regulations 2000 (SI 2000/2037).

[78] Commission Decision of 7.11.2012 on setting up a Commission expert group on development and implications of patent law in the field of biotechnology and genetic engineering, C(2012) 7686 final.

[79] A full copy of the text of the Directive is available at http://eur-lex.europa.eu/LexUriServ/LexUriServ.do?uri=OJ:L:1998:213:0013:0021:EN:PDF.

[80] See generally G Kamstra, M Döring, N Scott-Ram, A Sheard, and H Wixon, *Patents on Biotechnological Inventions: The EC Directive* (2002).

12.50   This is a direct endorsement of the policy direction that had been rigorously pursued by the EPO.[81] Indeed, the relevant provisions of the EPC were brought into line with the key Articles of the Biotechnology Directive by a Decision of the Administrative Council of the European Patent Organisation of 16 June 1999.[82] This was necessary to avoid confusion and disharmony because the Directive clearly only applies to the 27 member states of the EU, while the signatories to the EPC include these states and, currently, 11 others.[83]

12.51   Notwithstanding, the specific provisions of the Directive continue to cause controversy and their interpretation in the EPO as applied to human embryonic stem cell technologies has called into question the entire approach of European intellectual property offices towards morality clauses in patent law.

12.52   Article 6 embodies the morality provisions of the Directive. It states:

1.   Inventions shall be considered unpatentable where their commercial exploitation would be contrary to ordre public or morality; however, exploitation shall not be deemed to be so contrary merely because it is prohibited by law or regulation.
2.   On the basis of paragraph 1, the following, in particular, shall be considered unpatentable:
     (a) processes for cloning human beings;
     (b) processes for modifying the germ line genetic identity of human beings;
     (c) uses of human embryos for industrial or commercial purposes;
     (d) processes for modifying the genetic identity of animals which are likely to cause them suffering without any substantial medical benefit to man or animal, and also animals resulting from such processes.

12.53   While morality per se is left undefined, specific examples have now been included as part of a non-exhaustive list.[84] The last is a modification of the test laid down in *HARVARD/Oncomouse* albeit in a more rigorous fashion, now requiring substantial *medical* benefit to outweigh potential suffering to the animal. It remains, nonetheless, a crude felicific calculus and a questionable measure of morality from the philosophical perspective. Note too, the prohibition is now restricted to the immorality of the 'commercial exploitation' of the invention, and no longer refers to its 'publication' as was the case in Article 53 EPC 1973. This re-emphasises the fact that the moral dubiety of the patent grant should properly be focused on the way in which the monopoly is exploited.

? Question

Why were these particular examples chosen? Have any important matters been left out? Is this an appropriate measure of 'morality' for the purposes of patent law? Should the morality provision remain in European patent law?

---

[81] Eg the essence of the rulings in *Oncomouse* and *Plant Genetic Systems* is essentially reproduced in Art 4 which states:1. The following shall not be patentable: (a) plant and animal varieties; (b) essentially biological processes for the production of plants or animals. 2. Inventions which concern plants or animals shall be patentable if the technical feasibility of the invention is not confined to a particular plant or animal variety. 3. Paragraph 1(b) shall be without prejudice to the patentability of inventions which concern a microbiological or other technical process or a product obtained by means of such a process.

[82] http://archive.epo.org/epo/pubs/oj99/7_99/7_4379.pdf. Note: the Implementing Regulations are amended as of 1 April 2013, available at http://www.epo.org/law-practice/legal-texts/epc/amendments.html.

[83] There are 38 signatory states to the EPC (as at April 2013).

[84] The exclusions from patentability in the UK regulations state: 'the following are not patentable', while the Directive makes it clear that the exclusions are mere examples of exclusions. Is the UK in breach of its obligations?

Human embryonic stem cell inventions

12.54   Although Article 6 excludes uses of human embryos from patenting, it says nothing about cells or cell lines derived from embryos.[85] Nor is it clear whether the prohibition on processes for cloning human beings relates only to reproductive cloning techniques or extends to cloning to produce stem cells for therapeutic purposes.[86] Human embryo research is ethically problematic for a number of reasons, all of which centre around the moral status of this organism. The particular concern surrounding embryonic stem cell technologies is that—*at the present time*—we must both use and destroy a human embryo to produce valuable embryonic stem cell cultures. The prospect of then patenting those cultures or other products derived from embryonic stem cells is all the more problematic for many groups. Although there have been claims to have produced human embryonic stem cell lines without the destruction of embryos,[87] and while this could end the ethical debate surrounding stem cell inventions, any such method will still need further research to verify the safety and reliability of the procedure before it can be widely used; moreover, it is far from clear that such alternative methods will be scientifically equivalent to or better than embryonic stem cells. Thus the debate is far from over.

> **Exercise**
>
> The EPO has granted patents in respect of stem cell technologies which claim not to destroy embryos. Can you find these patents using the Espacenet facility?[88]

12.55   The European Group on Ethics in Science and New Technologies (EGE) reported that by 2002 over 2,000 patent applications had been lodged around the world involving both human and non-human stem cells; a quarter of which related to embryonic stem cells. Over a third of all stem cell applications had been granted, as had a quarter of those related to embryonic stem cells.[89] The EGE urged a cautious approach and recommended 'excluding the patentability of the process of creation of a human embryo by cloning for stem cells'.[90] It also stated that unmodified stem cells with no use should not be patentable, and this is in keeping with the functional approach towards biotechnological patents already outlined previously.

12.56   The EGE Opinion was, however, rejected *in toto* by the Opposition Division (OD) of the EPO when it heard the so-called 'Edinburgh Patent' case only a few months later. The patent in suit related to *animal* transgenic stem cells but numerous groups raised opposition proceedings to the grant of the patent, inter alia, on the grounds that 'animal' includes 'human' in the scientific taxonomy. In amending the

[85] Art 5(1) of the Directive provides: 'The human body, at the various stages of its formation and development, and the simple discovery of one of its elements, including the sequence or partial sequence of a gene, cannot constitute patentable inventions.'

[86] Stem cells are relatively undifferentiated cells of the same lineage (family type) that retain the ability to divide and cycle throughout postnatal life to provide cells that can become specialised and take the place of those that die or are lost.

[87] See, eg, iPS (Induced Pluripotent Stem cells) which are produced from reprogrammed adult somatic cells, argued by many to avoid the ethical dilemmas; see SA Brockman-Lee, 'Embryonic stem cells in science and medicine: an invitation for dialogue' (2007) 4 Gender Medicine 288 and LM Solomon and SA Brockman-Lee, 'Embryonic stem cells in science and medicine, part II: law, ethics, and the continuing need for dialogue' (2008) 5 Gender Medicine 3. Cf JC Watt and NR Kobayashi, 'The bioethics of human pluripotent stem cells: will induced pluripotent stem cells end the debate?' (2010) Open Stem Cell Journal 18.

[88] For some recent disputes, see T1156/09 (*Osteoblast-Neuronal cell transdifferentiation/KANEKA*) of 21.6.2012: http://www.epo.org/law-practice/case-law-appeals/recent/t091156eu1.html; T1199/08 (*Selected sperm/XY*) of 3.5.2012: http://www.epo.org/law-practice/case-law-appeals/recent/t081199eu1.html; T2464/10 (*Anticoagulant protein/IMPERIAL*) of 25.5.2012: http://www.epo.org/law-practice/case-law-appeals/recent/t102464eu1.html; T0811/11 (*Differentiated progenitor cells/ADVANCED CELL TECHNOLOGY*) of 11.7.2011: http://www.epo.org/law-practice/case-law-appeals/recent/t110811eu1.html.

[89] EGE, *Ethical Aspects of Patenting Inventions Involving Human Stem Cells*, Opinion No 16, 17 May 2002, para 1.16.

[90] EGE, note 89, para 2.5.

patent to exclude mention of human or animal embryonic stem cells, the OD interpreted the Article 53(a) EPC morality clause and the EPO equivalent guidelines to Article 6 of the Biotech Directive very broadly and in a manner which was completely at odds with the existing EPO case law. The OD noted that the provisions could be interpreted in two ways: *narrowly*, to mean that only commercial uses of human embryos *as such* are excluded from patentability, or *broadly*, to mean that human embryonic stem cells—which as we have noted can only be obtained by destroying an embryo—are also not patentable. The OD preferred the latter approach, arguing that since embryos *as such* are already protected by Rule 23(e) (equivalent of Art 5(1) of the EC Directive), a similar interpretation of Rule 23(d)(c) (equivalent of Art 6(2)(c) of the EC Directive) would be redundant and this could not have been the intention of the legislator.[91]

12.57 This approach was then followed in the Examining Division of the EPO, most notably in respect of the application of the Wisconsin Alumni Research Foundation (WARF) which was responsible for developing the first techniques to isolate human embryonic stem cells in 1998. The application was for European patents in respect of 'primate embryonic stem cells', or more particularly, embryonic stem cell cultures, that is, stem cell *products* but the application also disclosed the means to make such products, as one would expect. Thus the application disclosed a method for preparing embryonic stem cells from primate blastocysts. It was accepted, but not demonstrated in the application, that this method was also enabling of the production of human embryonic stem cells. Moreover, the sole method of production of the stem cell cultures that was described involved the use, and destruction, of embryos. The Examining Division held that all of the claims which could be extended to human embryonic stem cells were invalid on grounds of immorality. It did so on the basis of an extremely literal and broad interpretation of Rule 23(d)(c): 'European patents are not to be granted in respect of ... inventions which concern ... uses of human embryos for industrial or commercial purposes.' In sum, the Division held that: 'The use of an embryo as starting material for the generation of a product of industrial application is considered equal to industrial use of this embryo'. The rationale here is that the claimed cultures are inseparable from the means to make them. It is, therefore, in a literal sense, necessary to 'use' embryos to create the claimed invention. The message from this ruling is that the moral concern goes far beyond patenting itself and extends to general instrumentalisation. It implies that mere involvement—use—of embryos in the research and development of an invention is sufficient to bar the patentability of that invention.

12.58 The matter was referred to the EBA in November 2005 for consideration. The rulings mentioned previously represent such an extreme turnaround from previous EPO jurisprudence in this area that it leads us to wonder if the issue is not being forced from within the EPO itself to ensure that a body with standing such as the EBA brings full and final resolution to the issue. Four key questions were presented to the Board:

Embryonic Stem Cell Patents: Questions for the EPO Enlarged Board of Appeal

(1) Does Rule 23d(o) EPC apply to an application filed before the entry into force of the rule?
(2) If the answer to question 1 is yes, does Rule 23d(c) EPC forbid the patenting of claims directed to products (here: human embryonic stem cell cultures) which—as described in the application—at the filing date could be prepared exclusively by a method which necessarily involved the destruction of the human embryos from which the said products are derived, if the said method is not part of the claims?

---

[91] See G Laurie, 'Patenting stem cells of human origin' [2004] EIPR 59.

(3) If the answer to question 1 or 2 is no, does Article 53(a) EPC forbid patenting such claims?

(4) In the context of questions 2 and 3, is it of relevance that after the filing date the same products could be obtained without having to recur to a method necessarily involving the destruction of human embryos (here: eg derivation from available human embryonic cell lines)?

 Question

Before reading any further, consider how would you answer questions 2–4? By reference to what moral matters would you justify your responses?

12.59   In something of a last minute intervention, the then President of the EPO, Alain Pompidou, became involved, issuing a letter commenting on the questions put to the Board.[92] In his opinion, and contrary to practice to date,[93] Article 53 should not receive a restricted or narrow interpretation:

> A presumption in favour of a narrow interpretation of exceptions would unduly limit the significance of the moral jurisdiction under Article 53(a) and Rule23d(c) the purpose of which is the incorporation of higher ranking legal and moral principles into European patent law and would thus be in conflict with the general objective of said norms.[94]

This represents a major volte-face by the EPO.[95] There is a fear in some quarters that this direction compounds the confusions surrounding the morality provisions and result in a stifling of stem cell research around Europe. It is important to consider too the extent to which the patent system should purport to perform a regulatory function in respect of science. That is the legitimate role of state governments and it may be a role that is usurped by an unelected administrative body that is able to pass judgement on the morality of new technologies. This is particularly problematic when one considers the example of the UK, which invests millions of pounds a year in support of stem cell research. Is it acceptable that these efforts might be thwarted by the EPO?

12.60   The EBA delivered its decision in November 2008, stating that European patent law forbids the patenting of claims directed to products which, at the filing date of the application, could be prepared exclusively by a method which necessarily involved the destruction of the human embryo from which the products are derived, *even if* the method is not part of the claims.[96] Moreover, if after the filing date a method is discovered which allows the same products to be obtained without having recourse to a method which necessarily involves the destruction of human embryos, this will not 'fix' an application. There was a further issue of whether additional questions on this matter should be referred to the ECJ as it touched on the wording of the Biotechnology Directive, but it was ruled that there were no grounds for such a referral. This decision prompted the UK–IPO to reconsider its practice. It released a Practice Notice concerning Inventions involving Human Embryonic Stem Cells, which states that the Office will not grant

---

[92] G2/06 Comments by the President of the European Patent Office (September 2006) available at http://www.cipa.org.uk/download_files/epo_warf.pdf.

[93] See eg T356/93 *PLANT GENETIC SYSTEMS/Glutamine Synthetase Inhibitors* [1995] EPOR 357; T315/03 *HARVARD/Transgenic animal* [2005] EPOR 31; and G1/04 *CYGNUS/Diagnostic Methods* [2006] EPOR 15.

[94] Note 92, 37. Such a rejection of a presumption in favour of narrow interpretation of exclusions was more recently expressed by the Enlarged Board of Appeal in Case G1/07 *MED-PHYSICS/Treatment by surgery,* note 5.

[95] For British judicial angst about not giving the exclusions too wide an interpretation, see *Research in Motion UK Ltd v Inpro Licensing SARL* [2006] EWHC 70 (Pat), [2006] RPC 20, affirmed by the Court of Appeal: [2007] EWCA Civ 51.

[96] Decision G2/06 *WARF/stem cells* [2009] EPOR 15.

patents for processes of obtaining stem cells from human embryos.[97] As for the other questions referred to the EBA, since the answer to the second question was yes, the third question concerning the interpretation of Article 53 was not considered and remains open to debate. The EBA did state, however, that: 'it is important to point out that it is not the fact of the patenting itself that is considered to be against *ordre public* or morality, but it is the performing of the invention, which includes a step (the use involving its destruction of a human embryo) that has to be considered to contravene those concepts' (para 41).[98] The Practice Note was updated in 2012 to take account of the Court of Justice ruling on patentability of inventions involving embryonic material. We discuss this later at paras 12.66–12.70.

Synthetic biology

12.61   There has been growing discussion of late surrounding a new type of invention: inventions created by synthetic biology. Synthetic biology is a broad field that is hard to define, but it can roughly be seen as designing biological components, through engineering methods and principles, which have novel properties and functions that do not occur in nature.[99] A common shorthand is to talk about the creation of 'artificial life'. This type of invention has raised several concerns in the scientific and public communities.[100] From early on there have been concerns regarding biosecurity and biosafety arising from potential misuse of such technology and the risk of artificial organisms getting out of control and becoming a danger to human life. A further issue concerns the meaning and scope of 'artificial life' and the value that should be assigned to this. But these inventions also raise interesting questions where patent law is concerned, such as, do these inventions consist of patentable subject matter?; are there reasons to exclude them on reasons of *ordre public* or morality?; are they novel?; and can they satisfy the requirement of inventive step? All these issues will need further consideration and many parallels can be draw with discussions that have taken place in the context of nanotechnology and genetics.

12.62   The EU project named SYNTH-ETHICS has been addressing a variety of ethical, legal, and social aspects of synthetic biology. This might provide the basis for European policymaking in the medium to long term.[101] The first patent applications for synthetic biological inventions were filed in the United States by the Venter Institute,[102] but we will have to wait to see if these applications will go unchallenged.[103] The EGE has issued the following Recommendations:[104]

Recommendation No 16: The EGE proposes that debates on the most appropriate ways to ensure the public access to the results of synthetic biology is launched. These debates should include also what can be object of patent and what should be available through open access.

Recommendation No 17: The EU Patent Directive (98/44/EC) defines the EGE as the Body to assess ethics implications related to patents. The Group urges the European Patent Office and the National Patent Offices to

[97] UK–IPO, *Practice Notice on Inventions involving Human Embryonic Stem Cells* (17 May 2012) available at http://www.ipo.gov.uk/pro-types/pro-patent/p-law/p-pn/p-pn-stemcells-20120517.htm.

[98] For commentary, see generally A Plomer and P Torremans (eds), *Embryonic Stem Cell Patents: European Law and Ethics* (2009); P Treichel, 'G2/06 and the verdict of immorality' (2009) 40(4) IIC 450; and M Rowlandson, '*WARF/Stem cells* (G2/06): the *ordre public* and morality exception and its impact on the patentability of human embryonic stem cells' (2010) 32(2) EIPR 67.

[99] For a good definition, see M Schmidt, 'Diffusion of synthetic biology: a challenge to biosafety' (2008) 2(1–2) Systems and Synthetic Biology 1–6 at 1: 'Synthetic biologists use artificial molecules to reproduce emergent behaviour from natural biology, with the goal of creating artificial life or seek interchangeable biological parts to assemble them into devices and systems that function in a manner not found in nature.'

[100] See, eg, EGE, *Opinion 25: Ethics of Synthetic Biology* (2009).

[101] More information about this project can be found at http://synthethics.eu/index.html.

[102] For information on filings in this field see (2009) 27(12) Nature Biotech 1127.

[103] See, eg, A Rai and James Boyle, 'Synthetic biology: caught between property rights, the public domain, and the commons' (2007) 5(3) PLoS Biol PLoS Biol e58 doi:10.1371/journal.pbio.0050058 and J Calvert, 'The commodification of emergence: systems biology, synthetic biology and intellectual property' (2008) 3 Biosocieties 383.

[104] Note 100, para 4.5.

take account of Article 7 of the Patent Directive and refer contentious ethical issues of a general relevance to the EGE for consideration. This is particularly important if a class of inventions that ought not to be directly exploited commercially has to be defined.

 Exercise

Consider the possible challenges that might be created for the patent system by the advent of synthetic biology. What lessons might be learned from experiences with biotechnology patents to date?

Future action

12.63   Concern in Europe about reticence among the majority of member states to implement the Directive timeously and in full led to the establishment of a Group of Experts to monitor and advise on biotechnology and patenting in Europe, as was required by the Directive itself.[105] The remit of the Group is legal and technical aspects of biotechnological inventions. Ethical policy issues related to biotechnological patenting and social shaping are the remit of the EGE,[106] which has, inter alia, already reported on ethical aspects of patenting inventions involving human stem cells, as we have mentioned previously.[107]

12.64   The Group of Experts' programme was established in 2003 with two core issues for consideration: (1) 'the level of protection to be given to patents of sequences or partial-sequences of genes isolate from the human body'; and (2) 'the patentability of human stem cells and cell lines derived from them'. These are the two areas of most doubt and controversy to emerge from the public consultation and the Commission's negotiations with the member states.

12.65   Two reports have now been issued on the Biotech Directive and the work of the Group of Experts (2002 and 2005).[108] The first report reiterated the need to maintain competitiveness through full and proper implementation of the Directive, lest Europe lose out on the enormous potential of the biotechnology market. The report reflects the contents of a January 2002 Communication from the Commission laying out a strategy for biotechnological development and protection within the European context and its regulatory frameworks.[109] This was followed by a public consultation highlighting ongoing areas of conflict regarding the biotechnology sector, including the prospect of patenting.[110] The European Parliament has also called for greater public engagement with the issues surrounding biotechnology, including its protection by legal means.[111] The second report considered the two controversial areas of gene sequence patents and stem cell patents. It is inconclusive on both counts. The Group of Experts did not favour adopting a 'purpose-bound protection' in respect of gene patents, that is, restricting protection only to the specific use disclosed in the application, although the Commission is aware of broader ethical and economic arguments and has commissioned a survey on gene patenting practice in Europe. Another Commission survey on stem cell patents culminated in a publication which is an invaluable source of

---

[105] Art 16. See generally, http://europa.eu/legislation_summaries/internal_market/businesses/intellectual_property/l26026_en.htm.
[106] http://ec.europa.eu/european_group_ethics/index_en.htm.
[107] http://ec.europa.eu/bepa/european-group-ethics/docs/avis16en.pdf.
[108] Report from the Commission to the European Parliament and the Council, Development and Implications of Patent Law in the Field of Biotechnology and Genetic Engineering, COM(2002) 545 final, 7 October 2002, and COM(2005) 312 final, 14 July 2005, both available at http://ec.europa.eu/internal_market/indprop/invent/index_en.htm.
[109] For a summary of the strategy paper, see http://ec.europa.eu/rapid/start/cgi/guesten.ksh?p_action.getfile=gf&doc=IP/02/122|0|AGED&lg=EN&type=PDF.
[110] For the results of the public consultation, see http://www.ec.europa.eu/research/press/2006/pdf/pr1906_eb_64_3_final_report-may2006_en.pdf.
[111] http://ec.europa.eu/biotechnology/docs/com_2007_175_en.pdf.

commentary on the issues across various European perspectives,[112] and the Commission announced yet another expert group in 2012.[113] As the following development demonstrates, this is because the controversial issues are not set to go away any time soon.

12.66   *Brüstle v Greenpeace* was a dispute as to the patentability of isolated and purified neural precursor cells, processes for their production from embryonic stem cells, and their use for treatment of neural defects. Greenpeace sought revocation of a German patent for its alleged contravention of the domestic patent law embodying Article 6(1) and (2) of the Biotech Directive, which—as we have seen—states that patents may not be granted for inventions whose commercial exploitation would be contrary to *ordre public* or morality, and that, in particular, patents may not be granted for uses of human embryos for industrial or commercial purposes.

12.67   In November 2009, the Bundesgerichtshof (German Supreme Court) sent three questions to the ECJ for clarification, the first two of which are important for present purposes:

(1) What is meant by the term 'human embryos' in Article 6(2)(c)?

(2) What is meant by the expression 'uses of human embryos for industrial or commercial purposes'? Does it include any commercial exploitation within the meaning of Article 6(1), especially use for the purposes of scientific research?

12.68   Thus, the ECJ was asked to consider for the first time whether human embryonic stem cell inventions are properly described as an 'embryo' for the purposes of patent law. On this question, the ECJ fully recognised that a 'degree of sensitivity' was merited in the light of the diverse attitudes around Europe. Most surprisingly, however, it denied that it was being asked a moral question, preferring instead to characterise the issue as a matter of legal interpretation. As a term of art in EU law not referencing any domestic law, the ECJ was duty bound to provide an independent and uniform interpretation throughout Europe. It defined 'embryo' as:

(1) any human ovum after fertilisation;

(2) any non-fertilised human ovum into which the cell nucleus from a mature human cell has been transplanted; and

(3) any non-fertilised human ovum whose division and further development have been stimulated by parthenogenesis.

Although these latter entities have not been fertilised, it reasoned, they are nonetheless capable of commencing development into a human being and so must be excluded from patentability. The self-evident breadth of this conceptualisation—apparently arrived at in a morality-free zone—has been roundly criticised for its failure to take into account the underpinning value and diverse approaches to human dignity around the continent.

12.69   On the second question—whether embryos used in research represent their 'industrial and commercial uses'—the ECJ answered in the affirmative. Indeed, once again a broad exclusionary approach was adopted:

> The fact that destruction [of the human embryo] may occur at a stage long before the implementation of the invention, as in the case of the production of embryonic stem cells from a lineage of stem cells the mere production of which implied the destruction of human embryos is, in that regard, irrelevant.

[112] A Plomer and P Torremans (eds), *Embryonic Stem Cell Patents: European Law and Ethics* (2009).
[113] See http://ec.europa.eu/internal_market/indprop/invent/index_en.htm#maincontentSec.

12.70   The trend in Europe has, accordingly, been confirmed by the highest court. It might be too early to tell the likely or feared consequences, but the economic knock-on has already been signalled by the European Parliamentary Committee on Legal Affairs Draft Opinion on the Horizon 2020 Programme in which it is stated:

> The rapporteur also draws attention … to a recent judgment of the Court of Justice which states that human embryonic stem cells are not patentable. If the results of research cannot be patented, this affects the profitability of research and thus the public interest in funding it.

The rapporteur therefore proposes that research which either involves the destruction of human embryos or which uses human embryonic stem cells should be completely excluded from EU funding. It would thus be up to individual member states to decide, in line with their ethical rules, whether to fund such research from their own budgets.

 Exercise

Consider the wider implications of these decisions to exclude patent protection in respect of inventions developed using embryonic stem cells. What are the social, ethical, scientific, and economic issues at stake? In particular, where does this leave a country like the UK which actively encourages embryonic stem cell research? Do these rulings remove the incentive to research in Europe?

Monopoly concerns and licensing

12.71   It is possible to discern two main categories of objection to biotechnological inventions. There are those which find fault with the science itself and those which object to the grant of a private monopoly right over valuable resources that harbour considerable potential to further the public good. Only the latter are the proper subject of patent law. We must remind ourselves of the effect of a patent in order to appreciate the difference between the two kinds of objection. A patent merely provides a monopoly right to exclude competitors from the marketplace. It does not furnish the patentee with a right to exploit his invention—for he might be required to comply with a plethora of regulatory measures before the product or process can be introduced to the market—and it does not provide any means of curbing the way the invention might be exploited beyond limiting the impact or scope of the monopoly. We shall return to this last issue presently. For now, the point to take on board is that a patent is not a means to regulate or control developments in science, medicine, or industry. Indeed, it cannot do so. Consider the effect of a successful challenge to a patent. What are the consequences of this in terms of who can then exploit the invention? If you object to the science itself or the availability of a particular invention, will the denial of a patent further your cause? A patent is merely a right to control new information that has been contributed to the state of the art. In particular, it is only a right to prevent others from using this information in direct public competition. A biotechnology patent is not a property right over life as is so often claimed.

12.72   Sometimes, of course, free availability of the innovation is precisely what is sought and patents are seen to stand in the way of this. Consider the realm of health care where the public health benefits of freer access to medicines, therapies, diagnostic tools, or even research tools is generally considered a public good. A number of strategies have been employed to achieve this end. For example, numerous patents have been granted or are pending in intellectual property offices around the world for inventions on, or related to, the SARS virus (Severe Acute Respiratory Syndrome) and it has been reported that some applicants seek patent protection in order to provide freer access to the material, which they propose to do through the grant of non-exclusive licences at reasonable costs.[114]

Question

If the true aim is to ensure free access then why not publish results of work on the SARS virus and thereby put the knowledge in the public domain? This would effectively nix any future patents. Is there any advantage to be gained for the research community by obtaining a patent and then licensing it on liberal and generous terms, beyond, of course, a possible financial benefit for the patentee?

12.73   Other examples of more aggressive uses of monopolies and licensing provisions can easily be found. Myriad Genetics has held patents worldwide for the BRCA1 and BRCA2 breast cancer genes, and in Europe for diagnostic uses of BRCA1. The Nuffield Council on Bioethics pointed out in 2002 that because of the breadth of the patents as they were originally granted, 'there are currently no other methods of diagnosing the presence of the breast cancer susceptibility gene BRCA1 that can be used without infringing the patents'.[115] Myriad has a history of licensing its patents very restrictively and has established an exclusive market in testing in the United States. It insisted in Canada that all breast cancer screening using products derived from its patented invention be done in its own laboratories, potentially raising the costs for publicly funded bodies quite considerably. Indeed, British Columbia temporarily suspended its funding of public laboratory screening because of a fear of litigation.[116] Such measures prompted the European Parliament to issue a Resolution in October 2001 calling on the EPO to reconsider the grant of patents to Myriad Genetics over the genes,[117] and opposition proceedings instigated by the Institut Curie, the Assistance Publique-Hôpitaux de Paris, and the Institut Gustave-Roussy led to one of the patents being revoked in 2004 (EP 0699754) and the scope of the other two being severely curtailed in 2005 (EP 0705902 and EP 0705903).[118] Note, however, the reasons for these decisions were not some moral judgement on Myriad's licensing practices, but rather on technical issues of novelty and inventive step.

Discussion point   For answer guidance visit www.oxfordtextbooks.co.uk/orc/waelde3e/

As the Nuffield Council itself has asked: is it in the public interest that there is only one diagnostic test available for a particular disease? Will patents such as those that assert rights over BRCA1 inhibit further research, even in the context of other diseases? Or does the prospect of a strong reward act as a stronger incentive to innovate?

12.74   Concerns arising from this case study and others like it[119] led the Nuffield Council to recommend that intellectual property offices apply the criteria for patentability more rigorously, and indeed this may be what we have seen happen in the Opposition Division of the EPO. In particular, the Council doubted

---

[114] 'Fight over Sars Virus Genes', No 153, Patent World, June 2003, p 8.

[115] Nuffield Council on Bioethics, *The Ethics of Patenting DNA* (2002), para 5.4.

[116] L Eggerston, 'Ontario defies US firm's genetic patent, continues cancer screening' (2002) 166(4) Canadian Medical Association Journal 494.

[117] European Parliament Resolution on the Patenting of BRCA1 and BRCA2 ('breast cancer') genes (4 October 2001, B5–0633, 0641, 0651, and 0663/2001). Available at http://www.cptech.org/ip/health/biotech/eu-brca.html.

[118] On appeal the patents were upheld but in a limited form, though this narrowing of the claim will likely have no significant commercial impact, see Appeal T80/05 (November 2008).

[119] Nuffield Council, note 115, Ch 4.

that the research and development process used to isolate and purify genetic materials today is sufficiently inventive. Many of the gene cases we have considered in this chapter relate to work done many years or decades ago. Now, much of the isolation work is relatively straightforward or even routine.[120] The Nuffield Council also questioned the wisdom of granting broad patents that effectively encompass *any* use of the genetic products. It advocated the granting of use patents for diagnostic inventions whereby the monopoly only extends to the use of the invention—that is, a gene sequence—for the patentee's specific diagnostic test in relation to a single illness or condition. In this way, other uses of the same core material would not be prohibited and, it is argued, a fairer balance of interests would be reached.[121]

12.75   A two-pronged strategy is advanced here. The first ensures that the integrity of the patent system is maintained and that only truly worthy inventions receive protection, the second seeks to limit any rights that are granted and thereby delimits the scope of the corresponding monopoly. The alternative all-or-nothing approach which aims to strike patents down completely is a dangerous strategy for a number of reasons. We are constantly told that patent protection is vital to encourage research and innovation generally, especially in the medical and pharmaceutical fields where development costs can be prohibitive. If this is true, why would an organisation embark on lengthy and costly research and development if there was not some measure of reward or, indeed, an opportunity to recoup its outlays in the long run?

12.76   A more balanced approach is to consider the second arm of the Nuffield Council's recommendations, namely, to refine the scope of a patent monopoly. Other complementary strategies are also available. One such measure that is attracting growing support, although not from industry, is the prospect of an increased role for compulsory licences.[122] We consider compulsory licences in more depth in Chapter 22, but for present purposes it is sufficient to note that a compulsory licence can be sought by a third party if a patent holder refuses to grant licences for use on reasonable terms and when the patentee is not exploiting the invention himself. The first European Commission report on the Biotech Directive pointed to a possible role for compulsory licences in the biotechnological sector but envisaged no expansion in that role, for example by allowing compulsory licensing in circumstances other than three years' non-use by the patentee.[123] Other bodies have been more ambitious. The OECD has sought to move beyond anecdotal accounts about biotechnology patenting to assess the real problems and concerns on the ground.[124] It concluded that while there does not seem to be a crisis within the licensing system, a few areas do cause particular concern. These include the number and breadth of patents being granted, access to diagnostic genetic tests, and reach-through licensing whereby claims are made to future products developed using a patented invention. Reach-through clauses can cover a number of eventualities including: (1) royalties on the sales of future products; (2) options to take out exclusive or non-exclusive licences on future patents; and (3) full ownership of future inventions as a condition of the initial access.[125] The OECD recommended crucial policy guidance for a multi-strategy approach to be considered at governmental level requiring, inter alia, review of the policies within the IP system itself, the manner by which patents are administered, and changing the behaviour

---

[120] Nuffield Council, note 115, paras 3.29–3.34.

[121] Nuffield Council, note 15, para 5.24. For comment see K Liddell et al, 'Patents as incentives for translational and evaluative research: the case of genetic tests and their improved clinical performance' [2008] 3 IPQ 286.

[122] See, eg, Report from the Commission to the European Parliament and the Council, Development and Implications of Patent Law in the Field of Biotechnology and Genetic Engineering, COM(2002) 545 final, 7 October 2002, para 4.1.3; EGE, note 89, para 2.9 and the House of Commons Science and Technology Committee, *Human Genetics: The Science and the Consequences*, Third Report (6 July 1995), paras 212–14.

[123] Report from the Commission to the European Parliament and the Council, Development and Implications of Patent Law in the Field of Biotechnology and Genetic Engineering, COM(2002) 545 final, 7 October 2002, para 4.1.3.

[124] OECD, *Genetic Inventions, Intellectual Property Rights and Licensing Practices: Evidence and Policies* (2002).

[125] OECD, note 124, 92.

of patentees in the way they exploit their monopolies.[126] The OECD notes in particular that the role of compulsory licences, although not popular to date, should be revisited. It raises too the power of the threat of the compulsory licence which can, sometimes, be enough to force a patentee's hand to negotiation with potential licensees.[127] It turned this rhetoric into reality by producing an official Recommendation on Licensing Genetic Inventions.[128]

Software-related inventions

12.77   Article 52 states:

> (2) The following in particular shall not be regarded as inventions within the meaning of paragraph 1:
>   (a) discoveries, scientific theories and mathematical methods;
>   (b) aesthetic creations;
>   (c) schemes, rules and methods for performing mental acts, playing games or doing business, and programs for computers;
>   (d) presentations of information.
> (3) Paragraph 2 shall exclude the patentability of the subject-matter or activities referred to therein only to the extent to which a European patent application or European patent relates to such subject matter or activities *as such* (emphasis added)

Although the domestic and European provisions are concerned with the same end, the majority of jurisprudence in the field of patenting software-related inventions has arisen in the EPO and has thus been concerned with the interpretation of Article 52(2) EPC. For this reason, we shall use this Article as the primary reference point throughout this section.

A note on terminology

12.78   We use the term 'software-related invention' to describe inventions that employ software to perform their function and where the inventive contribution is embodied within the software itself. We avoid the term 'computer program related-inventions' to prevent confusion with the exclusion of computer programs as such, and we consider it unhelpful to employ the expression 'computer-implemented inventions', which has been deployed by the European Commission in its attempts at reform, because this does not cover all of the inventions discussed herein. The term 'software-related invention' should, therefore, be taken to encompass both (1) inventions that are described solely in terms of the software (eg the program(s) that it contains), and (2) inventions that claim products or processes whose functionality depends on software (eg computers or methods for performing certain functions or tasks).

Computer programs *as such*

12.79   Article 52(2) excludes the patenting of computer programs *as such*, and we face the problem once again of establishing what this means in practice and as a matter of law. It is instructive, however, to begin with an understanding of the logic behind this exclusion. Indeed, prospective patentees of software-related inventions have faced a double offensive from Article 52(2). First, as we have seen with biotechnological

---

[126] OECD, note 124, 80.   [127] OECD, note 124, 81.
[128] OECD, *Recommendation on the Licensing of Genetic Inventions* (2006), Council of the OECD, 23 February 2006, (2005)149/Rev1. For comparative approaches and experiences see G van Overwalle (ed), *Gene Patents and Public Health* (2007).

patents, computer programs have been objected to because they embody one or more of the pre-existing exclusions, for example it is sometimes argued that a program represents no more than an automated means to perform a mental act,[129] in the same way that it is argued that a biotechnological invention embodies little more than a discovery. However, unlike biotechnological inventions, computer programs are also the subject of a specific prohibition and can be objected to in their own right without the need to rely on other exclusions. Why is this so?

Why are computer programs excluded from patentability?

12.80   The drafting of the EPC 1973 was a long and arduous process lasting throughout the 1960s and into the early 1970s. Much of this time was taken up debating the need for, and the terms of, the exclusions from patentability. When the final version of the EPC was adopted in 1973 the specific prohibition on patenting computer programs had found its way into the instrument, but its inclusion was by no means a given.[130] Indeed, computer programs received no mention whatsoever in the outcome of the first round of negotiations. Opinion was greatly divided when the matter was eventually debated in the second round, with the UK showing most antipathy towards software-related inventions, calling them 'merely the mathematical application of a logical series of steps in a process which was no different from a mathematical method [already] excluded …'.[131] Moreover, there was concern about including a specific prohibition against computer programs lest genuinely inventive developments related to software also be excluded. Nonetheless, the provision found its way into law. The point to note, however, is the degree of ambivalence that has surrounded this particular exclusion from the start. We therefore began the modern European era of patentability with a tension over the patent protection of computer programs and a genuine desire to strike a balance between the exclusion such as it is and the imperative to protect well-deserving inventions irrespective of whether they are in some way connected to software. It is the resolution of this tension and the striking of this balance that has preoccupied the EPO ever since.

12.81   It should not be thought that because Article 52(2) EPC seems to take a double swipe at patent applications relating to software that such patents are rarely granted. Indeed, the European Commission confirmed in 2002 that over 20,000 so-called computer-implemented inventions had been granted by the EPO alone;[132] many thousands more have been awarded by national offices.[133] By corollary, commentators have indicated that only around 100 software-related inventions have experienced any problems before the EPO.[134] This gives rise to the obvious question: how is the exclusion being interpreted? In order to understand the answer to this question, it is first important to understand some essential features of computer software.

---

[129] See, eg, *Merrill Lynch's Application* [1989] RPC 561; *Gale's Application* 1991] RPC 305; *Fujitsu's Application* [1997] RPC 608; and more recently, *Aerotel Ltd v Telco Holdings Ltd* [2006] EWCA Civ 1371 and *Symbian Ltd v Comptroller General of Patents, Designs and Trademarks* [2009] RPC 1.

[130] It has even been suggested that its inclusion was a mistake, see G Kolle, 'The patentable invention in the European Patent Convention' (1974) 5 IIC 140–156.

[131] Taken from the report of discussions in October 1971. See too S Davis, 'Computer program claims: the final frontier for software inventions' [1998] 20 EIPR 429, n 11.

[132] European Commission, Proposal for a Directive of the European Parliament and of the Council on the patentability of computer-implemented inventions, COM(2002) 92 final, 20.02.2002, p 2.

[133] The overall figure from around Europe was estimated to exceed 30,000, in 2002, see 'Proposal for a Directive on the patentability of computer-implemented inventions—frequently asked questions', available at http://ec.europa.eu/internal_market/indprop/comp/index_en.htm.

[134] L Cohen, 'The patenting of software' [1999] 12 EIPR 607. For an excellent account of European software patenting law and practice, see K Beresford, *Patenting Software Under the European Patent Convention* (2nd edn, 2006).

Computer software: the functions

12.82   The World Intellectual Property Organization (WIPO) defined a computer program in 1978 as: 'a set of instructions capable, when in a machine-readable medium, of causing a machine having information-processing capabilities to indicate, perform or achieve a particular function, task or result.'[135] This definition remains broadly accurate today, in that software is essentially a means of processing information in order to control the functioning of a computer, other device, or a technical process. And, to the extent that there is a functional output from the operation of software, this technical end result may be the subject matter of a successful patent application.[136] Indeed, the Chief Executive of the UK IPO has importantly drawn attention to the fact that as many as 15 per cent of all UK patents now being granted have a software element. Although the claimed invention in such cases would not normally be the program per se, the value of the invention will nonetheless be inherently bound up with the role of the software. This highlights the central role that software plays in technological development across a wide range of fields and it should lead us to question the desirability of attempting to separate patentable and non-patentable elements of an invention. Indeed, the EPO has repeatedly stressed the need to consider inventions 'as a whole' when assessing their patentability.[137] Nonetheless, from the patentee's perspective, it is in his interests to seek protection for as many separate elements of his invention as possible, giving rise to a multiplicity of monopolies each of which can be exploited and defended against a variety of competitors. Thus, while it may be reassuring that the inclusion of a software element in an invention will not necessarily be a bar to the patentability of that invention, the prudent patentee will also seek protection for the software element itself. We present no comment at this stage on the broader acceptability of this strategy but instead offer it as one of the reasons why there has been a sustained push from the software industry to extend protection in the realm of computer programs. Indeed, the Hargreaves Review in 2011 found a significant rise in patent applications in this section in recent years, especially compared to other sectors including biotech. And yet, it was not at all clear from the evidence base that the increase also represented a corresponding rise in innovation in the area. Rather, it gave rise to a concern about patent thickets as we discussed in paras 10.82–10.84 and the recommendation from Hargreaves is that Europe should continue to resist business method patents (a significant subset of software-related patenting).[138]

12.83   A number of analogies have been used over the years to describe software, some more helpful than others. The most obvious and ubiquitous parallel that is made is between the computer code[139] and 'literary works', as these are understood in copyright law. We have already explained the rudimentary operations of computers and the software used to run them in Chapter 2 where we discuss copyright protection of

---

[135]   See WIPO Model Provisions on the Protection of Computer Software, Geneva 1978, s 1(i).

[136]   See, eg, *Raytheon Co v Comptroller General of Patents, Designs and Trade Marks* [2007] EWHC 1230 (Pat). Here the court considered that where a claimed technical contribution exists independently of whether it is implemented by a computer, in the sense that it embodies a technical process lying outside the computer, the contribution will not be a computer program as such and can therefore be the subject of a patent application. This will be so even if the only practical way of implementing the invention will be on a computer.

[137]   See, in particular, T208/84 *VICOM/Computer related invention* [1987] EPOR 74 and T26/86 *KOCH AND STERZEL/X-ray apparatus* [1988] EPOR 72.

[138]   I Hargreaves, *Digital Opportunity: A Review of Intellectual Property and Growth* (2011), available at http://www.ipo.gov.uk/ipreview-finalreport.pdf., paras 6.21–6.26.

[139]   As we explain in Chapter 2, computer code can take a variety of forms including 'source code', ie the alphanumerical code input to the computer by the programmer using an established language, and 'object code', ie the binary code read by the computer to control its functioning. Source code cannot be read by the computer and must first be converted to binary code by the computer's compiler. Both codes are potentially protectable by copyright by virtue of the inclusion of 'computer program' in the definition of 'literary work' in the Copyright, Designs and Patents Act 1988, s 3(1). While 'computer program' is not defined by the 1988 Act, TRIPS, Art 10(1) confirms that 'Computer programs, whether in source or object code, shall be protected as literary works under the Berne Convention (1971)'. Moreover, Council Directive 91/250/EEC of 14 May 1991 on the legal protection of computer programs simply states in the preamble that 'the term "computer program" shall include program in any form …'.

computer programs. But the protection that is afforded to computer code by copyright is simply in the expression of that code and does not extend to the functionality of the software, that is, to the effects that the software has when run on a computer, or to the underlying ideas and principles of the software. Yet, this is often where the true value of the software lies. It is this functionality which is the proper subject of patent protection.

 Question

What other differences can you think of between the protection afforded to software by copyright and that which might arise under patent law?

12.84   Further analogies about computer software being simply an automated means to perform mental acts vastly oversimplify the capabilities and complexities of contemporary software and probably have very little bearing on current practice, although this continues to be a problem where it has become enshrined in law. Moreover, there is no escaping the fact that the means by which software employs algorithms to perform its tasks—that is, through the application of a set of prescribed logical procedures to solve a particular problem—is in essence the deployment of mathematical formulae towards a particular end result. As we know, mathematical formulae cannot be patented but confusion has arisen because of a general failure to distinguish pure formulae, on the one hand, from the application of those formulae to produce a technical outcome, on the other. It is the same distinction that must be drawn between computer software in itself and the effects that its operation brings about.

12.85   A common concern also underpins these examples, namely, the desire to exclude mere abstracts from protection, inter alia, because these are difficult to define, impossible to police, and result in excessively broad monopolies. It has been argued that a computer program falls into this category, for where is the tangible embodiment of a computer program that consists of nothing more than a series of instructions? To the extent that these might be expressed in a written form, the program has a tangible expression which is protected by copyright. But beyond this, what *is* a computer program? This, however, simply reinforces the need to be clear about the difference between the abstract idea underlying the program and the products or processes that it influences. As Beresford has said, 'the wisest course is … to direct software claims clearly to a physical product or apparatus or a physical process'.[140]

12.86   Self-evidently, the primary effect of computer software is to make a computer work and it does this by controlling the processing of data within the computer's internal circuits. But, as the EPO Guidelines for Examination make clear, 'such normal physical effects are not in themselves sufficient to lend a computer program technical character.'[141] Rather, 'if a computer program is capable of bringing about, when running on a computer, a *further technical effect* going beyond these normal physical effects, it is not excluded from patentability' (emphasis added).[142]

12.87   The architecture of software is a central feature of its protectability. In the realm of copyright, it has been confirmed that the originality requirement can be found in the overall structure and layout of the software thereby extending the protection to non-literal aspects of the work.[143] Software architecture can

---

[140] Beresford, note 134, para 1.41.
[141] EPO Guidelines, Part G-II, para 3.6 citing T1173/97 *IBM/Computer Programs* [2000] EPOR 219. See then T22/85 *IBM/Document abstracting and retrieving* [1990] EPOR 98.   [142] EPO Guidelines, Part G-II, para 3.6.
[143] *Cantor Fitzgerald International v Tradition (UK) Ltd* [1999] Masons CLR 157; [2000] RPC 95 and *Nova Productions v Mazooma Games Ltd* [2007] RPC 25 (CA).

have a significant impact on the speed and efficiency of a program and novel architectures can result in considerable improvements in the operability of the software and the functions that it performs. To this extent, these technical features of the software may provide a means to bring about a technical effect susceptible to patent protection.

12.88   A final point to note about the central features of computer programs is that while software can only operate in the appropriate hardware, it can be stored separately in a variety of mediums such as CDs or USB sticks and it can be sent and received over the Internet or by attachment to email. In other words, software can be bought, sold, and transferred free of any hardware apparatus. This can have important implications in terms of scope of protection and infringement proceedings as we shall see later.

The development of EPO jurisprudence

12.89   We are about to embark on an account of the evolution of thinking in the EPO towards software-related inventions. To make sense of this process you need to be aware of certain key features of the EPO's approach to patentability. At the broad level, and as we discussed in Chapter 11 on patenting, a European invention must provide a technical solution to a pre-existing and technical problem. More particularly, a patentee must show that he has an invention with *technical character* in the sense that it produces a *technical effect*.

12.90   The key term here, clearly, is *technical*, and we shall explore its meaning presently.[144] But the first thing you should ask yourself is, where do these requirements come from?

Exercise

Examine Articles 52–57 EPC, the EPO Guidelines for Substantive Examination, Part G-II, and the EPC Implementing Regulations, rules 27 and 29 (all available on the EPO website).[145] Where does the need for technical character and technical effect arise in European patent law?

12.91   The need to demonstrate *technical character* and *technical effect* permeates all of the jurisprudence of the EPO. While it is not stated explicitly in the criteria for patentability in Articles 54–57 EPC, *technical effect* is used to test inventive step: has the invention made a *technical contribution* to the art? Moreover, while neither the term *technical character* nor *technical effect* appears in Article 52 EPC regarding exclusions from patentability, the need to demonstrate *technical character* has become the single most important factor is restricting the scope of these exclusions.[146] Nowhere is this more true than in the context of computer programs. Indeed, the current position can be summed up as follows:

> **SUMMARY OF EPO POSITION** As long as a software-related invention is of a technical character (in the sense of producing a technical effect) it will be eligible for patent protection. It does not matter that the essence of the invention falls into an excluded category, that is, that the technical character is found in a computer program.

---

[144] The EPO provides helpful summaries of its jurisprudence at http://documents.epo.org/projects/babylon/eponet.nsf/0/F7944E5E0AD5958DC12572BC004B2CB6/$File/clr_2006_en.pdf.

[145] Note that the Guidelines and the Implementing Regulations are updated as of 1 April 2013.

[146] Confirmed as a valid approach in T931/95 *PENSION BENEFIT SYSTEMS/Controlling pension benefits systems* [2002] EPOR 52 and see too T1227/05 *INFINEON TECHNOLOGIES/Circuit simulation I* [2010] EPOR 9.

Thus, we have the most recent version of the EPO Guidelines stating:

> The basic patentability considerations in respect of claims for computer programs are in principle the same as for other subject-matter. While 'programs for computers' are included among the items listed in Art. 52(2), if the claimed subject-matter has a technical character it is not excluded from patentability by the provisions of Art. 52(2) and (3).

What is the relationship between technical character and technical effect?

12.92   Technical character is demonstrated by bringing about a technical effect, that is, changes in the workings of apparatus, products, or processes achieved by technical means. Relevant technical effects that lend technical character to a computer program include:

(1) the control of an industrial process;

(2) the processing of data which represent physical entities; and

(3) the control of the internal functions of a computer itself or its interfaces.[147]

The EPO Guidelines further state that technical effect can be found in a computer program that:

(1) affects the efficiency or security of a process;

(2) governs the management of computer resources; or

(3) regulates the rate of data transfer in a communication link.[148]

These are mere examples and the clear message to patent attorneys who must draft claims for software-related inventions is to focus their attention on the possible technical effects which can be brought about by the computer program, for it is in these that protection will be secured.[149]

12.93   The net effect of this position is that the seemingly absolutist prohibition on the patenting of computer programs *as such* is illusory. It is no longer a matter of interpreting the provisions of Article 52 EPC (albeit narrowly), for the emphasis has shifted from considering what is *not* patentable to considering what *is* patentable, the primary requirement being that the putative invention displays technical character.[150] Of course, this does not preclude the need to show that the invention is new, involves an inventive step, and is capable of industrial application in the normal way, but it does leave us to question what, if anything, remains of the exclusion of computer programs from European patent law.

---

[147] EPO Guidelines, Part G-II, para 3.6.   [148] EPO Guidelines, Part G-II, para 3.6.

[149] Although see the comments in T1543/06 *Gameaccount* quoted in *AT&T Knowledge Ventures LP's Patent Application* [2009] FSR 19:The Board is of the firm belief, that it cannot have been the legislator's purpose and intent on the one hand to exclude from patent protection such subject matter, while on the other hand awarding protection to a technical implementation thereof, where the only identifiable contribution of the claimed technical implementation to the state of the art is the excluded subject-matter itself. It is noted that here the term 'contribution' encompasses both means (i.e. tangible features of the implementation) and effects resulting from the implementation. In that case Article 52(2) EPC would be reduced to a mere requirement as to form, easily circumvented. The Board believes it is intended as substantive in nature, whatever considerations may have been the source of this exclusion at the time of its adoption.This led the Board to conclude:It follows from the above that the mere technical implementation of excluded subject-matter *per se* cannot form the basis for inventive step. The Board concludes that inventive step can be based only on the particular manner of implementation.

[150] After T931/95 *PENSION BENEFIT SYSTEMS/Controlling pension benefits systems* [2002] EPOR 52 and T641/00 *COMVIK/Two identities* [2004] EPOR 10; followed in T588/05 *WEST DIRECT/Computer assisted telemarketing* [2010] EPOR 12.

Exercise

Before reading any further, consider whether there is any need to retain an exclusion of computer programs in Article 52 EPC. You might like to consider the discussions about possible removal of the provision at the Diplomatic Conference to revise the EPC in 2000: http://documents.epo.org/projects/babylon/eponet.nsf/0/a3d02eeebea84306c12572ae00500cdc/$file/conference_proceedings_en.pdf.

How have we arrived at this position?

12.94 We can plot the course of EPO thinking on software-related inventions in roughly three stages. First, the period from the establishment of the Office in 1978 until 1985 when the Examination Guidelines were changed in respect of computer programs. Secondly, the post-1985 period which is characterised by an increasingly liberal attitude towards these inventions when considerably fewer restraints applied, with some notable exceptions. Thirdly, the modern era, which began in 1998/99 with the two important rulings in T935/97 *IBM/Computer Programs*[151] and T1173/97 *IBM/Computer Programs*.[152] This era ushered in the effective demise of the computer program exclusion, and the final nail was put in the coffin in 2001 when the EPO revised its Guidelines to bring practice into line with the *IBM* cases. The position thereafter, as we shall see, has become unsustainable.

Stage 1: 1978–1985

12.95 We need not dwell on the national positions that prevailed prior to signing of the EPC in 1973 and the establishment of the EPO in 1978, although suffice to say that patents had been granted for software-related inventions in a variety of countries.[153] But this was set to change somewhat by virtue of the exclusion of computer programs in the EPC and the requirement of signatory states to bring their laws into line with the Convention. All eyes looked to the EPO for an indication of how patenting practice in this new era would take shape. You will recall from Chapter 10, that while national intellectual property offices and courts are not bound by the rulings of the EPO, they do consider them to be highly persuasive, and for reasons that we have already examined it is preferable to keep discrepancies to an absolute minimum. We consider the efforts of the UK in this respect later (paras 12.142–12.149).

12.96 The original version of the EPO Guidelines had this to say about computer programs:

> If the contribution to the known art resides solely in the computer program then the subject matter is not patentable in whatever manner it may be presented in the claims.[154]

Here the focus is firmly on the fact that the computer program is an example of an excluded category of invention and that if the essence of the claims in an application is to a computer program then those claims should be rejected, no matter the invention's actual technical contribution, function, or effect.

12.97 Interestingly, there is precious little evidence of an antipathetic attitude from the Examining Division of the EPO towards inventions involving computer programs during this period, and the Board of Appeal did not even hear, let alone reject, any relevant appeal during this time. Nonetheless, after consultation on the Guidelines during which time the EPO came under considerable pressure to amend the

---

[151] [1999] EPOR 301.   [152] [2000] EPOR 219.

[153] See, eg, in the UK, *Slee and Harris's Applications* [1966] RPC 194, [1966] FSR 51 ('means' for controlling a computer were held to be prima facie patentable in themselves) and *Burroughs Corporation (Perkins') Application* [1974] RPC 147, [1973] FSR 439 (computer programs having the effect of controlling computers to operate in a particular way, and which are embodied in physical form, are the proper subject matter for patent law).   [154] [1978] OJEPO 1.

provisions, the text was changed in 1985. It is possible that much of this pressure was brought to bear because of the widespread perception that the restriction on patenting was more stringent than was borne out by practice. The amended text—changed over numerous iterations—now contains the following features (April 2013):

- 'The basic patentability considerations in respect of claims for computer programs are in principle the same as for other subject-matter.'

- 'While "programs for computers" are included among the items listed in Art. 52(2), if the claimed subject-matter has a *technical character* it is not excluded from patentability by the provisions of Art. 52(2) and (3).'

- It follows also that, where the claimed subject matter is concerned only with the program-controlled internal working of a known computer, the subject matter could be patentable provided if it provides a *technical effect*.[155]

12.98   We see here a crucial shift in emphasis away from reasons to exclude protection towards reasons to extend protection to a claimed invention. The framework has thereby been established to allow the EPO more latitude in its interpretation of Article 52, a task to which it has taken with considerable gusto.

Stage 2: 1985–1998/99

12.99   The direction of EPO jurisprudence during this period was set by the first decision of the Board of Appeal to consider the exclusion of computer programs, T208/84 *VICOM/Computer related invention*.[156] This remained the most influential decision throughout this period and it continues to be a milestone of considerable significance. The case involved an appeal against the rejection by the Examining Division of claims related to (1) a method of digitally processing images with a view to enhancing their features, for example the clarity of the image, and (2) specifically designed apparatus to carry out this method. It was a particular feature of the claimed invention that all of this could be done considerably faster and more efficiently than was possible in conventional computers of the time. The inventors acknowledged, however, that the invention itself could be implemented using a suitably programmed conventional computer. The Examining Board rejected the application on the grounds that it was for a mathematical method and/or a computer program as such.

12.100   The Board of Appeal disagreed on both counts holding:

- As regards the *method* of image processing:

    (i)   Methods of processing images, including simulated images, are susceptible of industrial application under Article 57 EPC, that is, they are sufficiently technical to be the proper subject of patent law.

    (ii)   If the claim in question is directed towards a *technical process* which is carried out on a *physical entity*—here, an image (albeit one stored as an electric signal)—and that process brings about changes in that entity—here, the manipulation of the image to enhance or alter certain features—then this is a *technical effect* sufficient for the purposes of patent law.

    (iii) While it is true that such a process can be described in mathematical terms, for example the operation of a mathematical algorithm on data, the effect of this operation is not merely to produce more abstract data but rather to produce a real change in a real image and therefore there is an effect beyond the simple execution of the mathematical method.

---

[155] Note, previous editions of the Guidelines included the following statement: 'A computer program claimed by itself or as a record on a carrier, is not patentable irrespective of its content.' This has now been removed. Why?

[156] [1987] EPOR 74.

(iv) It is irrelevant that the idea underlying the invention resides in a mathematical method as long as the process that is claimed goes beyond the mere mathematical method *as such*.

(v) It is also irrelevant that the technical means used to bring about the technical effect is by way of a computer program, since the claim is to the process carried out under the control of the program and not to the program *as such*.

- As regards the *apparatus* containing the software for processing the images, it was held that:

claims which can be considered as being directed to a computer set up to operate in accordance with a specified program (whether by means of hardware or software) *for controlling or carrying out a technical process* cannot be regarded as relating to a computer program as such [157]

12.101 It is interesting and important to note that the need for specificity of claim was emphasised in *Vicom*. Thus, it was stated that:

a 'method for digitally filtering data' remains an abstract notion not distinguished from a mathematical method so long as it is not specified what physical entity is represented by the data and forms the subject of the technical process ...[158]

This was an important qualification because the original claims before the Examining Division did not specify image manipulation and spoke only of a method of 'digitally filtering ... data', which was a broad and unacceptable claim given the nature of the invention in question.

 Discussion point   For answer guidance visit www.oxfordtextbooks.co.uk/orc/waelde3e/

Does the previous comment about the exclusion of a method for digitally filtering data mean that such a claim could never succeed? Can you envisage examples where such a claim might be important to a prospective patentee? How might such a claim be successfully framed?

12.102 The net result from *Vicom* was that process *and* product claims involving both mathematical methods and computer programs became clearly patentable under the EPC. The essential lesson should be self-evident: the drafting of the claims should be to the process or product itself, emphasising the technical features used to bring about the technical effect and ensuring that any mention of a computer program (or mathematical method) is as a means to achieve the technical result not an end in itself. In particular:

- *process claims* are to a method of achieving a technical result by means of a computer program operating on appropriate hardware;

- *product claims* are to a computer, or similar device, incorporating a computer program.

Note: in both cases there is the need to link the software to hardware via the claims. This becomes important when we come to consider the third stage of EPO jurisprudence.

Successful examples that followed *Vicom* include:

(1) A method claim for processes of regulating error messages within a computer system, T115/85 *IBM/Computer related invention*.[159]

---

[157] [1987] EPOR 74 at 80 (para 15 of judgment).   [158] [1987] EPOR 74 at 90 (para 7 of judgment).
[159] [1990] EPOR 107.

(2) A method claim for maintaining formats of documents transferred between word processors, T110/90 *IBM/Editable document form*.[160]

(3) A method claim for precision rotation and manipulation of graphic images on screen, T59/93 *IBM/Rotating displayed objects*.[161]

(4) An apparatus claim for an X-ray device controlled by a computer to monitor tube voltages to ensures optimal exposure while protecting against overload, T26/86 *KOCH AND STERZEL/X-ray apparatus*.[162]

(5) An apparatus claim for a device to monitor computer components to detect the cause of, and where possible improve the speed of, the computer's reset procedure, T164/92 *BOSCH/Electronic computer components*.[163]

(6) Method and apparatus claims for a system for providing product-specific data in a service station for recognition and editing of design and function states, T1242/04 *MAN/Provision of product specific data*.[164]

 Exercise

Consider each of these judgments and identify the all-important technical effect.

12.103   It is interesting to note that in virtually all of these cases (and many more successful appeals to the Board of Appeal) the appellants amended their initial (rejected) claims after communication with the Board; indeed, this also happened in *Vicom*. Not only does this help to account for the high number of successful appeals to the Board of Appeal but it also re-emphasises the crucial point that careful drafting of claims is key.

 Discussion point   For answer guidance visit www.oxfordtextbooks.co.uk/orc/waelde3e/

Does it follow that skilful drafting can avoid Article 52 problems for any kind of method, device, or software-related invention?

12.104   In each of the previous examples the role of the computer program was as a *technical means* to realise the *technical effect* that was central to the invention. One might think as a result of these rulings that as long as a computer program is not claimed directly, sufficient protection can be gained for any software-related invention. The reality has not been quite so straightforward and a number of hurdles have remained.

12.105   You will recall that a European patent application must disclose the following:

• a *technical* problem;

• that is solved by *technical* means;

• these means make a *technical* contribution to the state of the art.

---

[160] [1995] EPOR 185.
[161] Unreported, available on the EPO website at http://legal.european-patent-office.org/dg3/pdf/t930059eu1.pdf.
[162] [1988] EPOR 72.   [163] [1995] EPOR 585.   [164] [2007] EPOR 45.

12.106   It has been confirmed many times that a computer program on appropriate hardware can provide the necessary *technical means* in this equation, as each of the previous cases demonstrates.[165] But problems remain as to what amounts to a *technical contribution* and, indeed, what is a *technical problem*? Two topics demonstrate the concerns. These are (1) software-related inventions in the field of textual processing, and (2) business method patents.

Software-related inventions and textual processing

12.107   The EPO Board of Appeal has held on a number of occasions that claims directed at processes or devices to assist the user in the processing or manipulation of text or language do not demonstrate a *technical contribution* to the art, but rather a contribution in non-technical areas such as aesthetic creations, methods of performing mental acts, or mere presentations of information. Put another way, the EPO has found that if the sole contribution is in an excluded category protection will be denied. Thus, for example, in T22/85 *IBM/Document abstracting and retrieval*[166] the Board of Appeal rejected a claim relating to a system for creating and storing abstracts from archived documents by means of a key word search because:

(1)   the claims simply outlined an excluded category, namely, schemes, rules, and methods for performing mental acts; in particular, it was considered that the claim merely described an automated means of key word search and abstract creation that could be carried out manually in essentially the same fashion;

(2)   it was insufficient merely to show that technical means, that is, a computer program running on hardware, had been used to bring about the result because the contribution itself was non-technical; and

(3)   'the true problem to be solved was that of establishing a set of rules for document abstracting and retrieval on the basis of textual properties of the documents to be handled *which problem cannot be qualified as technical*'.[167]

12.108   Similarly, in T38/86 *IBM/Text clarity processing*, the Board stated that it would 'permit patenting only in those areas in which the invention involves a contribution to the art in a field not excluded from patentability'.[168] And, although the Board recognised that the EPO will grant patents for inventions which involve both technical and non-technical features as long as a technical contribution is realised by the invention when seen as a whole, here the problem was held to be non-technical in nature—it related to the extraction of incomprehensible phrases from documents and their replacement with more comprehensible ones. This, once again, was seen as merely an automated means to execute a mental act (the act of assessing comprehensibility).

12.109   We need not see these cases, or others like them,[169] as a necessary departure from the general trend laid down in *Vicom*. Indeed, the position is well summed up in T121/85 *IBM/Spell Checker*[170] which involved

---

[165] See, in particular, *KOCH & STERZEL/X-ray apparatus*, note 137.

[166] [1990] EPOR 98.   [167] [1990] EPOR 98 at 105.   [168] [1990] EPOR 606 at 611.

[169] Other failed appeals include T52/85 *IBM/Semantically related expressions* [1989] EPOR 454 (automated editing functions to list semantically connected expressions are linguistic not technical in character), T65/86 *IBM/Text processing* [1990] EPOR 181 (automated means to correct contextual errors in a document involved no technical steps that a human being would not also perform in the same task), and T1177/97 *SYSTRAN/Translating natural languages* [2005] EPOR 13 (the use of a 'longest word-stem match' system to assist in computer translation was based on linguistic considerations and did not solve a technical problem). More recently see T528/07 *ACCENTURE/Portal system* [2010] EPOR 50 (computer system for providing a business-to-business relationship portal to facilitate the exchange of information between parties was not patentable) and T1086/07 *XEROX/Document summaries* [2012] EPOR 21 (system of indicators to solve the problem of indicating on a summary document where the summarised portions came from in the original document was merely presentation of information).   [170] Unreported.

an automatic spell checking and correction system that was denied protection by the Board of Appeal. The central passage deserves quotation in full:

> Such spelling is basically not of a technical but of a linguistic nature. A correctly spelled word represents an abstract linguistic information and a correct spelling relates therefore to the correctness of an information and not to any physical entity. A wrong spelling can be detected by performing mental acts with no technical means involved.
>
> This does not necessarily mean that a system automatically performing, instead of a human being, the same spelling checking act is excluded from patentability. Rather, this will depend on whether the manner in which it is automated, involves features which make a contribution in a field outside the range of matters excluded from patentability under Art. 52(2) in connection with Art. 52(3) EPC.

12.110 Note, once again, the stress on the need to show technicality. Has this become an overriding consideration? Consider, too, the reference to 'physical entity' which we also see appearing in *Vicom*. The indication seems to be that to bring about a change in a physical entity takes the claim more readily into the technical field, and 'physical entity' has been defined broadly to include non-tangible entities such as computer images[171] and television signals.[172]

Business method patents

12.111 Applications to patent business methods broadly come in two forms; those relating to methods of doing business involving computer software and those requiring no such input. We have already discussed the latter in Chapter 11 and therefore in this section we will focus on software-related business method patents.

12.112 Much furore has surround the prospect of business method patents of both descriptions, particularly in the context of the Internet where fears have arisen that patent thickets relating to e-commerce practices might considerably restrict the commercial viability and attractiveness of cyberspace as a place to do business. British Telecom claimed at the turn of the century that it had been granted a US patent over hyperlinking technology more than 20 years previously (US Pat No 4,873,662); it sought, and failed, to enforce rights against some US Internet Service Providers. But perhaps the most famous Internet-related business method patent involves Amazon.com, which devised a method for managing online orders and called it the 'One-Click' system (US Pat No 5,960,411). The method allows the customer to enter his personal and credit card details only once with the company and thereafter the customer can order products simply by clicking on the item on screen, whereupon Amazon can access the necessary billing information directly from the customer's account. Beyond customer convenience, the commercial advantage is that this effectively does away with the potential disincentive faced by customers who have to re-enter data for each purchase. Amazon was granted a patent on this business method in September 1999 but this was challenged by Barnes and Noble. In February 2001 the US Court of Appeals for the Federal Circuit in Washington DC lifted a preliminary injunction that had barred Barnesandnoble.com from using the one-click technology. The matter was finally settled out of court in 2002 and the patent remains in the United States. It was rejected by the EPO for lack of inventive step.

12.113 The EPO position was initially laid out in T769/92 *SOHEI/General purpose management system*[173] which concerned apparatus and method claims for a novel user interface allowing the input of management data across a broad spectrum of activities, including financial, inventory, personnel, and construction management. The advantage of the system was that it allowed the user to input all of these data via one

[171] *Vicom*, para 12.99 and T643/00 *CANON/Searching image data* [2007] EPOR 1.
[172] T163/85 *BBC/Colour Television Signal* [1990] EPOR 599.   [173] [1996] EPOR 253.

interface and for them to be processed automatically towards a variety of different ends via one medium. Previously different systems had to be learned for different spheres of management. The Examining Division rejected the application as (1) mere presentation of information, (2) a method of doing business, and (3) a computer program as such. In keeping with established case law, however, the Board of Appeal upheld the claims (albeit after amendment) on the following grounds:

- The program on the computer was merely the technical means to implement the invention and was not claimed as such; what was required was technical character and technical effect; similarly, this would not be an example of the mere presentation of information if technical character was present.

- The 'user friendly' interface allowing multiple inputs of data and the structured execution of the method for automatically processing those data on the system provided sufficient technical character.

- The subject matter was not excluded if it involved, or implied, at least one aspect or component, which was not excluded from patentability.

- No objection could be raised that the claims related only to 'doing business' because the subject matter of the claims—which could be generalised across a range of possible uses and were not necessarily restricted merely to business ends—could not be said to be merely abstract and non-technical.

12.114   Beyond reiterating the rule in *Vicom*, this decision makes it clear that it is not problematic to an application to include aspects of business management in claims, that is, non-technical features, as long as the claims cannot be taken as solely directed to those ends and, of course, further technical effect is also represented.

12.115   Similarly, in T1002/92 *PETTERSSON/Queuing System*[174] an application was allowed for a system of managing queues of people in business establishments by allocating turn-numbers and displaying free service points automatically. The objection was raised in Opposition proceedings that this was simply a method of doing business, but this was rejected by the Board of Appeal which confirmed that the central claim was to technical apparatus that solved the technical problem of efficient queue management without the need for human input and by means of the interaction of various cooperating technical components. It was stressed that just because one practical application of such a system was in the service of customers of a 'business equipment' did not mean that the claimed subject matter was a method of doing business *as such*. Moreover, while the Board accepted that one element of the claim probably was tantamount to a method of doing business—this being the means of 'deciding which particular turn-number is to be served at the particular free service point' (because it could equally be achieved by means of human intervention involving essentially the same steps)—the claim was to be viewed as a whole and a mix of technical and non-technical elements would not necessarily be excluded from patentability as long as the technical character resides in the technical elements, as was the case in the present application.

12.116   We must always bear in mind, however, that the claimed invention must be directed at a technical problem, which we have seen described in *Pettersson*, and which in *Sohei* was the problem of requiring multiple data inputs into various systems which was solved by the unique and convenient single user interface. In both cases, the fact that the invention assisted the user in the conduct of his business was incidental, and not fatal to the claim.

12.117   But, to the extent that the problem to be solved is solely a way of automating business practices, the problem to be solved here is non-technical in character and will remain unpatentable in Europe. This was held to be the case in T931/95 *PENSION BENEFIT SYSTEMS/Controlling pension benefits systems*[175] in

---

[174] [1996] EPOR 1.   [175] [2002] EPOR 52.

which the Technical Board rejected an appeal for lack of technical character. In doing so, it confirmed a number of crucial points:

- A *technical* invention does not lose its technical character simply because it is used for a non-technical purpose (eg a method of doing business).

- A method claim, as long as it is *technical*, may relate to a method of doing business and still be patentable.

- An apparatus claim, even if the apparatus is programmed for use in fields such as business or economy, cannot be an example of excluded subject matter since such products (ie apparatus) are not mentioned in Article 52(2) EPC.

12.118   Nonetheless, the appeal failed for the method claims because the claimed invention only described steps in a process for controlling a pension benefit scheme which were for administrative, actuarial, or financial purposes; typically non-technical purposes. It was not enough to point to data processing and computer means employed to execute these purposes since there was no corresponding disclosure of a technical problem requiring a solution nor of a solution that represented a technical effect. The Technical Board of Appeal later modified the earlier position in *Pension Benefit Systems* in the decision of *Hitachi* (T258/03) wherein it was held that it is not a display of technical character to circumvent a technical problem by modifying a business method as opposed to finding some truly technical means to resolve the problem.[176]

12.119   In T154/04 *DUNS LICENSING ASSOCIATES/Estimating sales activity* it was accepted that claims can contain both technical and non-technical features and this will not necessarily be fatal to the eligibility of the invention for protection. However, non-technical features will be ignored if they do not contribute to the resolution of the technical problem; indeed, there must be such a *technical* problem in the first place—this is defined as a problem which an expert in the field might be asked to solve. There was no technical problem in the instant case—it concerned merely a means to gather information about sales activities in various outlets and then to apply statistical methods to estimate future sales. This was quintessential business research and using a computer to generate the result did not make it *technical*. In similar fashion we have the Technical Board of Appeal in T388/04 *PITNEY BOWES/Undeliverable mail*[177] finding that the claims of the invention revealed 'no technical means … at all' to carry out the activities for which protection was sought (the claim was to a method of responding to a message that electronic mail was 'undelivered'). The mere possibility of using technical means to carry out the activity is not enough. Claims must specifically be directed to producing a technical effect. This has since been translated into the EPO Guidelines thus: 'A method of doing business is excluded from patentability even where it implies the possibility of making use of unspecified technical means or has practical utility.'[178]

12.120   Subsequent examples of unsuccessful business method applications include:

- Claims to a method for running 'what if' scenarios in business databases for the purposes of business planning and information modelling (lack of technical character and the reference to their use in databases was not enough), T1149/06 *IBM/Database back-solving*.[179]

- A system to estimate environmental impact had no overall technical character because the tools were typical of operational/business management, T1029/06 *TOSHIBA/Environmental impact estimation*.[180]

---

[176] The Technical Board of Appeal applied *Hitachi* in T424/03 *MICROSOFT/Data Transfer* [2006] EPOR 40 and held that 'a computer system including a memory (clipboard) is a technical means and consequently the claimed method has technical character in accordance with established case law'.

[177] [2007] OJEPO 16.   [178] Note 8, para 3.5.   [179] [2010] EPOR 3.   [180] [2010] EPOR 13.

- A system to gauge potential reduction of environmental impact of products was, in essence, a management tool to decide between investment strategies and as such lacked sufficient technical character, T1147/05 *RICOH/Environmental impact information*.[181]

We see, then, that business method patents generally receive short shrift in Europe. How does this compare with the position in the United States?

12.121   Compare and contrast the fate of Signature Financial Group Inc either side of the Atlantic when it tried to patent its data-processing system for managing financial services and portfolio returns across a variety of funds. In the EPO, the application was rejected by the Examining Division for lack of technical character. The importance of this example is the fact that it was essentially the same invention that lies at the heart of the dispute in *State Street Bank and Trust Co v Signature Financial Group*;[182] a decision that revolutionised business method patenting in the United States and set in motion a furore surrounding the practice worldwide.

12.122   In *State Street* the US Court of Appeals for the Federal Circuit upheld the claims to this data-processing system and put an end to the speculation that a business method exception applies in the United States. Indeed, it is generally acknowledged that *State Street* in tandem with *AT&T Corp v Excel Communications Inc*,[183] went further in establishing the precedent that 'pure' business methods are patentable, that is, methods not dependent on software, although neither case involved such an example. While our remit does not extend to an analysis of US law where the statutory provisions and considerations are different, the disparity of approach towards the *State Street* invention—and in particular the need in Europe to establish technical character beyond the standard criteria—indicates that prospective patentees face more hurdles in this area in Europe compared to the experience across the Atlantic.

12.123   Some comments on *State Street* are, nonetheless, of assistance in our present discussion. US law requires a 'useful, concrete and tangible result' from an invention and the means to achieve this are irrelevant.[184] Although common law exclusions have grown up over the years, for example in the realm of mathematical algorithms, formulae, or calculations,[185] there are no statutory exclusions in US law,[186] and the common law measures have been interpreted in an increasingly narrower fashion.[187] Thus, while the *State Street* invention had been rejected by the lower court because it was an 'algorithm', the Court of Appeals held that the system was a 'machine' in the proper sense of statutory subject matter, and that:

> every step-by-step process, be it electronic or chemical or mechanical, involves an algorithm in the broad sense of the term ... [and] since §101 expressly includes processes as a category of invention which may be patentable ... it follows that it is no ground for holding a claim is directed to non-statutory subject matter to say it includes or is directed to an algorithm. This is why the proscription against patenting has been limited to *mathematical* algorithms ...[188] (emphasis added).

12.124   The court went on to stress that the emphasis in patent examination should be on the essential characteristics of the subject matter and, most notably, whether it displays 'practical utility' in the sense of producing a 'useful, concrete and tangible result'. This renders an invention statutory subject matter, 'even if the useful result is expressed in numbers, such as price, profit, percentage, cost or loss.'[189] More recently, however, the approach of *State Street* was directly challenged by an en banc decision of the Court of Appeals *In re Bilski*.[190] It was suggested that the 'useful, concrete and tangible result' test should be replaced by

---

[181] [2008] EPOR 34.   [182] 149 F 3d 1368 (Fed Cir, 1998).   [183] 172 F 3d 1352 (Fed Cir, 1999).

[184] See USPTO Guidelines (2008), available at http://www.uspto.gov/web/offices/pac/mpep/mpep.htm.

[185] *Gottschalk v Benson* 409 US 63 (1972).   [186] 35 USC §101.   [187] See *In re Alappat* 33 F 3d 1526 (Fed Cir, 1994).

[188] *State Street*, note 182, at 1375.??   [189] *State Street*, note 182, at 1375.

[190] 545 F 3d 943, 88 USPQ 2d 1385 (Fed Cir, 2008).

the 'transformation-machine test': that is, it must be shown that the invention transforms the nature of an article into a different state or thing, or that it is somehow connected to apparatus or a machine. In the instant case it was not possible to satisfy such a test and this led to the denial of patent protection. The application was for a method of hedging risk in the field of commodities trading and it was argued, and accepted, that this lacked patent-eligible subject matter. It was not suggested in *Bilski* that *State Street* should be overruled but rather that the approach was incorrect. The uncertainty meant that the case was destined for Supreme Court consideration and it duly ruled in June 2010 in *Bilski v Kappos*.[191] The Court affirmed the judgment of the Court of Appeals, but revised various aspects of its decision, most particularly it clarified its own previous jurisprudence in saying: 'This Court's precedents establish that the machine-or-transformation test is a useful and important clue, an investigative tool, for determining whether some claimed inventions are processes under § 101. The machine-or-transformation test is not the *sole* test for deciding whether an invention is a patent-eligible "process"' (emphasis added). The majority held that the invention in suit was unpatentable as an 'abstract idea' in the instant case. Going forward, however, there remains dispute in the United States about what, precisely, constitutes such an abstraction—and business method patent disputes continue and patents continue to be granted.[192]

 Question

(Reminder: *Pension Benefits Systems* and *State Street* were both denied protection in Europe yet were successful in the United States.)

How approximate is the US need for 'practical utility' to the European requirement of 'technical contribution'? What impact does the continued existence of an express exclusion for methods of doing business have on European patent law and is it desirable that it should remain? How far is the US concern with an 'abstract idea' similar to the European limitation of 'as such'?

UK–IPO Guidelines

12.125   These rulings caused patent examiners in intellectual property offices around the world to sit up and take notice of the developments. Consider the current versions of the Guidelines that operate in the United States, Europe, and Japan noting that each had to be amended in the light of this case law. It is instructive to compare and contrast these provisions to gauge the different approaches.

12.126   *The US Patent and Trademark Office*

The Bilski Court underscored that the text of § 101 is expansive, specifying four independent categories of inventions eligible for protection, including processes, machines, manufactures, and compositions of matter ... ('In choosing such expansive terms ... modified by the comprehensive "any", Congress plainly contemplated that the patent laws would be given wide scope.') (quoting Diamond v. Chakrabarty, 447 U.S. 303, 308 (1980)). The Court also made clear that business methods are not 'categorically outside of § 101's scope,' stating that 'a business method is simply one kind of "method" that is, at least in some circumstances, eligible for patenting under § 101.' ... To date, no court, presented with a subject matter eligibility issue, has ever ruled that a method claim that lacked a machine or a transformation was patent-eligible. However, Bilski held open the possibility that some claims that do not meet the machine-or-transformation test might nevertheless be patent-eligible.[193]

---

[191] 130 S Ct 3218 (2010).
[192] Cf *Ultramercial v Hulu* 657 F 3d 1323 (Fed Cir, 2011) and *Dealertrack v Huber*, No 2009-1566, -1588 (Fed Cir, 20 January 2012).
[193] USPTO, Interim Guidance for Determining Subject Matter Eligibility for Process Claims in View of *Bilski v. Kappos*, available at http://www.uspto.gov/patents/law/exam/bilski_guidance_27jul2010.pdf.

Previous versions of the Guidelines instructed personnel to treat business method claims like any other process claims. In this latest version, the door is held open in the light of the *Bilski* ruling. US business method patents will be patentable as long as they meet the standard criteria for patentability and do not fall foul of the 'abstract idea' exclusion. No distinction is drawn between computer-implemented methods and so-called 'pure' business methods in themselves.

12.127 *Japanese Patent Office*

> If a matter necessary to define an invention involves any means contrary to a law of nature, the claimed invention is not considered to be a statutory invention ... If claimed inventions are any laws as such other than a law of nature (e.g. economic laws), arbitrary arrangements (e.g. a rule for playing a game as such), mathematical methods or mental activities, or utilize only these laws (e.g. methods for doing business as such), these inventions are not considered to be statutory because they do not utilize a law of nature ... On the contrary, even if a part of matters defining an invention stated in a claim does not utilize a law of nature, when it is judged that the claimed invention as a whole utilizes a law of nature, the claimed invention is deemed as utilizing a law of nature ... the characteristic of the technology is to be taken into account in judging whether a claimed invention as a whole utilizes a law of nature ... For inventions relating to a method for doing business or playing a game, since there are cases in which the claimed invention a part of which utilizes an article, apparatus, device, system, etc., is judged as not utilizing a law of nature when considered as a whole, careful examination shall be required ... There is possibility for an invention to be qualified as statutory where the invention is made not from a viewpoint of a method of doing business or playing a game but from a viewpoint of computer software-related inventions such as software used in doing business or in playing a game.[194]

The outcome in Japan is that appropriately drafted technical claims that clearly define software-related means of carrying out business practices will be considered as patentable subject matter, but that pure business methods will not be so considered.

12.128 *European Patent Office*

> Programs for computers are a form of 'computer-implemented invention', an expression intended to cover claims which involve computers, computer networks or other programmable apparatus whereby prima facie one or more of the features of the claimed invention are realised by means of a program or programs. Such claims may e.g. take the form of a method of operating said apparatus, the apparatus set up to execute the method, a readable medium carrying a program ... or ... the program itself. The examiner should disregard the claim category and concentrate on its content in order to determine whether the claimed subject-matter, considered as a whole, has a technical character. Moreover, insofar as the scheme for examination is concerned, no distinctions are made on the basis of the overall purpose of the invention, i.e. whether it is intended to fill a business niche, to provide some new entertainment, etc.[195]

The effect here then is to encourage business method-related claims to be drafted in line with software-related claims whereby they will be dealt with in the same fashion as is now represented post the *IBM* decisions (see later). 'Pure' business methods, however, should be excluded to the extent that they are merely abstract and non-technical in nature.

12.129 The approach in the UK to computer-implemented inventions, including business methods, has been revised in the light of the EPO approach and we will deal with it separately later.

Should business method patents be treated differently?

12.130 Business method patents have proved controversial for a number of reasons and in the following we recite some of the arguments that have been mounted against them.

---

[194] JPO Examination Guidelines for Patent and Utility Model in Japan (2009), Part II: Requirements for Patentability, Chapter 1: Industrially Applicable Inventions, section 1.1. See http://www.jpo.go.jp/tetuzuki_e/t_tokkyo_e/Guidelines/2_1.pdf.
[195] EPO Guidelines, Part G-II, para 3.6: http://www.epo.org/law-practice/legal-texts/html/guidelines/e/g_ii_3_6.htm

From the UK–IPO

(1) In what sense can a method of doing business be seen as an example of *industrial* property? That is, how can the protection of such a method achieve the original aims of the patent system which is to encourage *technological* innovation and development?

(2) What is a 'business method'? How can this be defined with sufficient precision to delimit clearly the scope of any patent monopoly? The problem is not just one of definition because indistinct and potentially broad claims necessarily impact on the scope of the monopoly granted. An ill-defined invention leads to an indeterminable monopoly calling its entire validity into question.

(3) A single business method could have applications across a very broad range of fields, thereby potentially leading to an excessively broad patent which might hinder rather than encourage innovation. Moreover, unlike other technical fields such as the biotechnology or pharmaceutical industries, the respective outlays in research and development costs are minimal for business methods and so the reward is disproportionate to the inventive effort. Yet the economic impact of such patents could be just as great or greater than other fields of technology.

(4) Many of the ways of doing business that form the subject of these patents have been around for a long time; a method of doing business does not become inventive simply because it is carried out on using computers or via the Internet.

(5) The prior art relating to business methods is difficult, if not impossible, to discern. This is partly because those employing effective methods kept them secret in the absence of other means of protection. It is also because of the infinite varieties of business methods that are being employed daily. If there is less evidence to reject applications this could result in an increase in patents leading to a plethora of potentially dubious monopolies. To complicate matters, patent examiners are not necessarily qualified in this field, and this too might lead to questionable and undeserving patents.

(6) To open up the categories of patentable subject matter will necessarily result in a restriction of material in the public domain.

(7) It can be very easy to infringe a business method patent leaving competitors uncertain about permissible acts and extremely vulnerable to infringement actions.

(8) Large corporations will be the ones to benefit as they are best placed to obtain and defend such patents. Small and medium-sized enterprises will lose out as a result and this will leave the relevant technical field to be ruled by technology oligarchies, none of which is in the ultimate interests of the consumer.

(9) There is simply no need for these patents because the fields where they are sought, for example the Internet, have progressed exceptionally well to date without patent protection and there is no requirement for further incentive.

(10) 'Those who favour some form of patentability for business methods have not provided the necessary evidence that it would be likely to increase innovation. Unless and until that evidence is available, ways of doing business should remain unpatentable.'

 Exercise

Evaluate these arguments along the following lines:

(1) Which are about satisfying the essential criteria of patent law?

(2) Which are practical, legal, and/or economic arguments?

(3) Which are objections that only relate to (pure) business method patents, that is, they cannot be applied to other areas such as biotechnology or software?

Stage 3: 1998/99–present

12.131   We have seen that software patenting practice in the EPO had undergone a gradual evolution towards more liberal interpretations of the EPC in the period leading up to the *IBM* decisions in 1998 and 1999, but these decisions forced further radical change by addressing two outstanding issues, namely, (1) the continuing exclusion of direct claims to the computer program, as opposed to claims to a method or apparatus run by a program, and (2) the continuing prohibition on claims to the program on a transferable medium such as a disk, as opposed to the software on some form of hardware such as a computer or similar device.

12.132   The fact that computer programs could not be claimed directly was a clear indication that the exclusion in Article 52(2) still held some sway, even if it could be drafted around in many circumstances. In *Vicom*, for instance, the Board of Appeal expressly stated that the computer program itself was not patentable.[196] The need to link any indirect software claim to hardware was embodied in the 1985 Guidelines: 'A computer program medium claimed by itself or as a record on a carrier is not patentable irrespective of its content.'[197] But this had given rise to a number of objections from the software industry. For example, it was frequently pointed out that the hardware was often an irrelevancy in the inventiveness of the claimed entity, which usually lay in the computer program itself. Moreover, these limitations had potentially serious adverse consequences for the scope of protection afforded. Effective infringement remedies could be denied to patentees with software-related patents in at least two circumstances: (1) a method claim will normally only be infringed directly by someone who runs the program, leaving a lacuna in terms of restricting suppliers of programs, (2) relatedly, if the claim is to the software in tandem with the hardware, and suppliers are to be challenged, they must supply both elements, that is, the computer with the software loaded on it. This leaves the problem of pursuing competitors who merely supply the program itself. The problem becomes all the more acute when one considers that today programs can be transferred, uploaded, and downloaded across the Internet without any need for a medium at all.[198]

The *IBM/Computer program* cases

12.133   The EPO Technical Board of Appeal set out to remedy these perceived anomalies in the *IBM/Computer program* cases. T935/97 *IBM/Computer programs*[199] and T1173/97 *IBM/Computer programs*[200] essentially embody the same ruling, delivered by the same members of an appropriately constituted Board of Appeal some seven months apart. The respective applications included (1) claims to a 'computer program product' embodying a means to alter the display of information in a text window on a computer when that window was partially obscured by a second window to ensure the information remained visible to the user (T935/97), and (2) a 'computer program product' comprising a method for resource recovery in the event of system failure (T1173/97).

12.134   *The essence of the rulings in the* IBM/Computer programs *cases*

a patent may be granted not only in the case of an invention where a piece of software manages, by means of a computer, an industrial process or the working of a piece of machinery, but in every case where a program for a

---

[196] [1987] EPOR 74 at 81 (para 18 of the judgment). Note, however, that Davis has suggested that despite this the practical effect was to allow the patenting of programs in their own right: S Davis, 'Computer program claims' [1998] EIPR 429.

[197] EPO Guidelines (1985), Part C-IV, para 2.3.

[198] But see *Menashe Business Mercantile Ltd v William Hill Organisation Ltd* [2003] 1 All ER 279 (where the supply of CDs to individuals in the UK to enable them to communicate with a host computer outside the UK and thereby to engage in an interactive casino gaming system was held to be an infringement of a patent over the said system held by the claimants. This was an example of 'supply of means relating to an essential element of the invention' under the Patents Act 1977, s 60(2) because the CD allowed UK residents to use the claimed system within the UK even though the host computer was in another country). See Chapter 11 for further comment.

[199] [1999] EPOR 301.   [200] [2000] EPOR 219.

computer is the only means, or one of the necessary means, of obtaining a technical effect ... where, for instance, a technical effect of that kind is achieved by the internal functioning of a computer itself under the influence of the said program' ... In other words, on condition that they are able to produce a technical effect ..., all computer programs must be considered as inventions within the meaning of Article 52(1) EPC, and may be the subject-matter of a patent if the other requirements provided for by the EPC are satisfied.[201]

12.135 *How did the EPO arrive at this decision and what are its consequences?*

- The Board began on safe territory, reiterating considerations that had already been laid down in previous decisions. Thus, for example, it stressed the need to view the invention as a whole, and not to attempt to draw a distinction between technical and non-technical parts of the invention or to consider elements that might fall into an excluded category. The important consideration is whether the invention so viewed displayed *technical character*. Just as importantly, however, the Board made the point that 'no importance should be attached to the specific further use of the system as a whole'. In other words, it does not matter if that system is then employed in an excluded category such as business method applications.

- The Board also re-emphasised the fact that technical character cannot be found in the normal functioning of a computer such as the generation of electrical currents by the execution of instructions given by the computer program. Rather, a *further technical effect* is required, as outlined previously.

- The full implications of the EPO's preoccupation with *technical character* are revealed in these decisions. In both rulings, the Board made the following statement:

  The exclusion from patentability of programs for computers as such ... may be construed to mean that such programs are considered to be mere abstract creations, lacking in technical character ... This means that programs for computers must be considered as patentable inventions when they have technical character.[202]

At first sight this relatively innocuous comment might seem to add nothing to the established case law. But it moves the law forward quite considerably in at least two respects. First, it speaks of 'computer programs' themselves being patentable. Secondly, given that we are dealing here with the exclusions from patentability, and considering that technical character must be shown in all cases when assessing the criteria of novelty, inventive step, and industrial applicability, where does this leave the exclusion of computer programs *as such* in European patent law? Does it not, in fact, reduce the exclusion simply to a need to satisfy the criteria for patentability and thereby collapses the distinction between excluded and patentable software-related inventions altogether? Although the Board does state that a 'computer program as such' would be one which is a non-technical program, such a program, like any non-technical invention, would fail the patentability criteria anyway.

 Question

In the light of these rulings, consider again an earlier question: is there any need for an ongoing specific exclusion of computer programs? The Board does state that the demonstration of technical character in this context can include a technical effect that is already part of the state of the art so, to this extent, technical character in this context is not synonymous with the need to show a technical contribution to the art as is required by inventive step. But what, if any, difference does this make in practice?

---

[201] T935/97, note 151, at 310.   [202] T935/97, note 151, at 309; T1173/97, note 152, at 226.

12.136   The Board also held:

- In recognition of the fact that a computer program cannot bring about a technical effect until it is run on a computer, it is sufficient to demonstrate that a computer program has the *potential* to bring about a 'further technical effect', thereby confirming the acceptance of claims to computer programs in themselves.

- The Board drew a parallel between computer hardware and a medium on which the program is stored, for example a disk, as being merely 'the material object on which the physical changes carried out by running the computer take place'.[203] Thus, not only does this remove the need to link software and hardware in claims but, arguably, it also frees computer programs claims from any tangible medium at all.[204]

- The Board sought to apply logic in defence of its rulings bringing the law to this point. It referred to the *Vicom* decision wherein it was stated that 'it would seem illogical to grant protection for a technical process controlled by a suitably programmed computer but not for the computer itself when set up to execute the control', that is, to allow the method claim but not the related apparatus claim, and by analogy the present Board found, 'it illogical to grant a patent for both a method and the apparatus adapted for carrying out the same method, but not for the computer program product, which comprises all the features enabling the implementation of the method and which, when loaded in a computer, is indeed able to carry out that method.'[205]

> **? Question**
>
> Even if this is accepted as a matter of logic, to what extent should policy be dictated by logic? What other considerations are at play here? Can 'illogical' policies ever be defended? Hint: consider the proposal from the European Commission which represented a retrenchment from this so-called 'logical' position (discussed later).

12.137   Two potential hurdles to establishing this precedent did not deter the Board of Appeal. These were the pre-existing Guidelines on Examination which, as we have seen, expressly prohibited program claims on non-hardware media, and existing case law from the EPO itself which had stressed, inter alia, that: 'exclusion under Article 52(2)(c) and (3) EPC applies to all computer programs, independently of their contents, that is independently of what the program can do or perform when loaded into an appropriate computer.' In other words, the exclusion from patentability of computer programs *as such* was a much more literal and direct interpretation of this term, and the presence or otherwise of technical character was irrelevant.[206] How, then, could the Board reconcile its policy shift with established practice? In fact, it could not do so and preferred to point out that a Board of Appeal is bound neither by the EPO Guidelines[207] nor by previous decisions of the Boards, although the present Technical Board found it easier to depart from the former rather than the latter and it expressly distinguished prior case law to the extent that it excluded all computer programs as such and irrespective of their content.[208] A possible

---

[203] See, eg, T935/97, n 151, at 312.
[204] For the possible implications of this, especially on the Internet, see R Hart, 'Computer program-related patents' [1999] CLSR 188. See also D Attridge, 'Challenging claims! Patenting computer programs in Europe and the USA' [2001] 1 IPQ 22.
[205] See T935/97, n 151, at 313.
[206] Cases include *Koch*, note 162, *IBM/Editable document*, note 160, *Bosch*, note 163, and the unreported ruling in T204/93 *ATT/System for generating software source code*.
[207] Art 23(3) EPC.
[208] T935/97, note 151, at 315. See too T1173, note 152, at 233 distinguishing the earlier case of *ATT/System for generating software source code*, note 206.

problem does, however, remain in the realm of claims relating to computer programming itself, which has been held to be akin to the performance of a mental act and so unpatentable.[209] This aspect of the prior case law was not overruled in the present cases, although there is evidence in other decisions that programming that brings about the all-important technical effect can be protected.[210] One can, however, struggle too hard to make sense of legal decisions in the mistaken belief that logic and reason are always the order of the day. The general trend is nonetheless clearly towards patentability. The EPO Guidelines were revised to conform to these rulings in 2001 and the latest version from April 2012 represents a summary of the current position, including more recent developments that occurred in the light of the ruling of the Enlarged Board of Appeal in May 2010 that arose because of the following circumstances.[211]

12.138 The *IBM* cases served as the nail in the coffin of consistency for the EPO. Boards of Appeal are not bound by each other decisions, which in itself can lead to considerable uncertainty, and this widening of approach set the scene for complete divergence in the years to come. The English Court of Appeal commented on this in *Aerotel Ltd v Telco Holdings Ltd and others*[212] and declined to attempt to follow EPO jurisprudence as it was 'mutually contradictory'.[213] In considering three post-*IBM* cases, the court concluded that there were, in fact, numerous approaches advocated by the Board of Appeal. It characterised the *IBM* approach as the 'technical effect approach' whereby the intellectual property office will ask whether the invention as defined in the claim makes a technical contribution to the known art. Since then, however, the EPO seems to have adopted a version of the 'any hardware' approach, that is, the intellectual property office asks whether the claim involves the use of, or is somehow associated with, a piece of physical hardware, however mundane (whether a computer or a pencil and paper). If this association or connection can be found then Article 52(2) will not apply. This approach was taken in three cases but each followed its own tack: *Pension Benefits*,[214] *Hitachi*,[215] and *Microsoft*.[216] The Court of Appeal characterised the approaches thus:

Three versions of the 'any hardware' approach

(1) Where a claim is to a method which consists of an excluded category, it is excluded by Article 52(2) even if hardware is used to carry out the method. But a claim to the apparatus itself, being 'concrete' is not so excluded. The apparatus claim is nonetheless bad for obviousness because the notional skilled man must be taken to know about the improved, excluded, method.

This is the *Pension Benefits* approach.

(2) A claim to hardware necessarily is not caught by Article 52(2). A claim to a method of using that hardware is likewise not excluded even if that method as such is excluded matter. Either type of claim is nonetheless bad for obviousness for the same reason as in the previous point.

This is *Hitachi*, expressly disagreeing with *Pensions Benefits* about method claims.

(3) Simply ask whether there is a claim to something 'concrete', for example an apparatus. If yes, Article 52(2) does not apply. Then examine for patentability on conventional grounds—do not treat the notional skilled man as knowing about any improved excluded method.

This is *MICROSOFT/Data Transfer*.

---

[209] *ATT/System for generating software source code*, note 206.　　[210] *Bosch*, note 163.　　[211] Note 8, paras 3.6.
[212] [2006] EWCA Civ 1371.　　[213] [2006] EWCA Civ 1371, para 25.
[214] T931/95 *PENSION BENEFITS SYSTEMS/Controlling pension benefit systems* [2001] OJEPO 441, [2002] EPOR 52.
[215] T258/03 *HITACHI/Auction method* [2004] 12 OJEPO 575, [2004] EPOR 55.
[216] T424/03 *MICROSOFT/Data transfer*, 23 February 2006, available at http://legal.european-patent-office.org/dg3/biblio/t030424eu1.htm.

12.139   The court's conclusion, beyond refusing to follow any of these (see later),[217] was to formulate questions for the Enlarged Board of Appeal to consider. A national court has no authority to refer such questions, although the President of the EPO does, and it was the sincere wish of the English Court of Appeal that the EBA consider these matters with a view to establishing, at last, some clarity and certainty for European patent law with respect to software.[218] This eventually happened in October 2008, when the President of the EPO referred the following questions to the EBA which were different from the ones posed by the Court of Appeal. The final ruling appears as G3/08 *Programs for Computers*.[219]

G03/08 *Programs for Computers* (Enlarged Board of Appeal, 2010): *Questions for the EPO Enlarged Board of Appeal*

(1) Can a computer program only be excluded as a computer program as such if it is explicitly claimed as a computer program?

(2a) Can a claim in the area of computer programs avoid exclusion under Article 52(2)(c) and (3) merely by explicitly mentioning the use of a computer or a computer-readable data storage medium?

(2b) If question 2(a) is answered in the negative, is a further technical effect necessary to avoid exclusion, said effect going beyond those effects inherent in the use of a computer or data storage medium to respectively execute or store a computer program?

(3a) Must a claimed feature cause a technical effect on a physical entity in the real world in order to contribute to the technical character of the claim?

(3b) If question 3a is answered in the positive, is it sufficient that the physical entity be an unspecified computer?

(3c) If question 3a is answered in the negative, can features contribute to the technical character of the claim if the only effects to which they contribute are independent of any particular hardware that may be used?

(4a) Does the activity of programming a computer necessarily involve technical considerations?

(4b) If question 4a is answered in the positive, do all features resulting from programming thus contribute to the technical character of a claim?

(4c) If question 4a is answered in the negative, can features resulting from programming contribute to the technical character of a claim only when they contribute to a further technical effect when the program is executed?[220]

G3/08 decision

1. In exercising his or her right of referral, a President of the EPO is entitled to make full use of the discretion granted by Article 112(1)(b) EPC, even if his or her appreciation of the need for a referral has changed after a relatively short time.

2. Different decisions by a single Technical Board of Appeal in differing compositions may be the basis of an admissible referral by the President of the EPO of a point of law to the Enlarged Board of Appeal pursuant to Article 112(1)(b) EPC.

3. As the wording of Article 112(1)(b) EPC is not clear with respect to the meaning of 'different/ abweichende/divergent' decisions, the provision has to be interpreted in the light of its object and purpose

---

[217] It further noted that the Supreme Court of Germany (Bundesgerichtshof) has also refused to follow *Hitachi*, note 215, para 29.

[218] Note, the Technical Board of Appeal in *DUNS LICENSING AUTHORITIES/estimating sales activity*, para 12.119 in the previous text, stated that the approach of the English and Welsh Court of Appeal in *Aerotel* was 'irreconcilable with the European Patent Convention', para 43.   [219] [2010] EPOR 36.

[220] For comment and criticism of the questions and, indeed, the entire approach to 'software patents' see RB Bakels, 'Software patentability: what are the right questions?' (2009) 31(10) EIPR 514.

according to Article 31 of the Vienna Convention on the Law of Treaties. The purpose of the referral right under Article 112(1)(b) EPC is to establish uniformity of law within the European patent system. Having regard to this purpose of the presidential right to refer legal questions to the Enlarged Board of Appeal the notion 'different decisions' has to be understood restrictively in the sense of 'conflicting decisions'.

4. The notion of legal development is an additional factor which must be carefully considered when interpreting the notion of 'different decision' in Article 112(1)(b) EPC. Development of the law is an essential aspect of its application, whatever method of interpretation is applied, and is therefore inherent in all judicial activity. Consequently, legal development as such cannot on its own form the basis for a referral, only because case law in new legal and/or technical fields does not always develop in linear fashion, and earlier approaches may be abandoned or modified.

5. Legal rulings are characterised not by their verdicts, but by their grounds. The Enlarged Board of Appeal may thus take *obiter* dicta into account in examining whether two decisions satisfy the requirements of Article 112(1)(b) EPC.

6. T 424/03 *Microsoft* does deviate from a view expressed in T 1173/97 *IBM*, concerning whether a claim to a program on a computer-readable medium necessarily avoids exclusion from patentability under Article 52(2) EPC. However, this is a legitimate development of the case law and there is no divergence which would make the referral of this point to the Enlarged Board of Appeal by the President admissible.

7. The Enlarged Board of Appeal cannot identify any other inconsistencies between the grounds of the decisions which the referral by the President alleges are divergent. The referral is therefore inadmissible under Article 112(1)(b) EPC.

12.140   The Enlarged Board of Appeal has, in effect, refused to recognise the problem. What is currently emerging in the EPO is a shift of focus towards novelty and inventive step, bypassing the exclusions altogether. The Office is less concerned with excluded matter as long as technical character can be found. Indeed, the advice to EPO examiners is now to move beyond a consideration of technical character and to proceed directly to consider questions of novelty and inventive step. The rationale is that in assessing inventive step the examiner must establish which technical problem has been solved by the invention. If no technical problem can be found then the implication is that no technical character is present.[221]

Key points on software-related inventions

- Software-related inventions are currently available for the following:
  - a product which carries out its function by means of a computer program
  - a method which is executed by means of a computer program
  - a computer program itself (whether or not claimed together with a product, process, or carrier medium)
- This is provided that:
  - in all cases the claimed invention demonstrates that it has technical character in the sense of being capable of producing a technical effect in the real world

---

[221] More recently, see T1244/07 *AMAZON/1-Click* [2011] EPOR 39 and T 1784/06, *COMPTEL/Classification method* [2013] EPOR 9. For commentary on decisions T1769/10 *IGT* and T1051/07 *SK Telecom* that 'appear out of step with earlier EPO case law on the patentability of computer-implemented inventions and other "mixed" inventions containing interacting technical and non-technical features', see IPKat at http://ipkitten.blogspot.co.uk/2012/06/on-threshold-of-dream-patents-and.html.

– for a computer program, it is sufficient to demonstrate that it has the potential to produce a technical effect when run on an appropriate medium or, arguably, is somehow otherwise associated with a piece of hardware, but this must be more than merely speculative

 Discussion point 1   For answer guidance visit www.oxfordtextbooks.co.uk/orc/waelde3e/

The breadth of the law now means that it is no longer necessary to claim the software and the hardware, but is it ever expedient to do so? Might there be any advantages in doing so?

Discussion point 2

In T22/85 *IBM/Document Abstracting and Retrieving* it was stated *per curiam* that: 'It cannot have been intended by the Contracting States that express exclusions from patentability could be circumvented simply by the manner in which the invention is expressed in the claim.'[222] To what extent does this remain true in the light of recent case law and the latest version of the Guidelines on Examination?

Discussion point 3

The United States does not require software-related claims to be linked to hardware, but there remains a requirement that they nonetheless be related to a carrier or some other medium (so-called Beauregard claims). It has been suggested,[223] however, that Europe has now gone beyond this in allowing direct claims to the computer program itself as long as it has at least the potential to produce a technical effect. What are the implications of this, especially for patents that might be granted in respect of the Internet?

Policy matters

12.141   A number of factors have conspired to bring Europe to this current state of affairs. These include:

- the fact that Europe has been seen to be at odds with other patent systems around the world, and most notably the United States and Japan;

- the perceived weaknesses of copyright protection for computer software which relates merely to expression, provides only thin protection compared to patents and whose duration is ridiculously long and unnecessary in a rapidly moving field like software development;

- the reality that many inventions embody computer software elements and the lack of logic perceived in protecting some elements and not others;

- the general thrust towards broadening the scope of patentable material by narrowing the interpretation of exclusions (as we have also seen with biotechnological inventions);

- a sharpening of focus on what are seen to be the crucial characteristics of patentability—for example, is there a technical effect?—accompanied by a more holistic approach to the interpretation of patent claims;

---

[222] Note 197, pp 104–105.   [223] Hart, n 204.

- the obligation under TRIPS, Article 27(1), to provide patent protection in 'all fields of technology'.[224]

Software-related inventions in the UK

12.142   The UK approach was clarified by the Court of Appeal in *Aerotel Ltd v Telco Holdings Ltd* (para 12.138). It is specifically stated by the court, however, that the approach for the future is not a departure from what has gone before, but merely a reformulation of the approach established in the trio of cases *Merrill Lynch's Application*,[225] *Gale's Application*,[226] and *Fujitsu's Application*.[227] We have covered these in Chapter 11 in our discussion of exclusions from patentability. For present purposes, suffice it to note the following features of the UK's approach prior to *Aerotel*. The ruling in *Merrill Lynch* endorsed the EPO ruling in *Vicom* to the extent that the mention of excluded matter within a claim is not fatal to its validity as long as the invention, when considered as a whole, makes a technical contribution to the art. This was not so in the instant cases, however, and the ruling is unhelpful because it does not elaborate on what is considered to be a 'technical contribution'.[228] In *Gale's Application*[229] the court rejected an attempt to link the program (for calculating a square root) to a piece of technical apparatus (a ROM chip) because the sole contribution nonetheless lay in automated instructions to perform a function that could otherwise be done by means of a mental act, that is, in an excluded category. This signalled a rider for the UK which had been outlined previously in *Merrill Lynch* and which was a departure from the position in the EPO—a contribution which falls solely within an excluded category cannot be patentable. Finally, in *Fujitsu's Application*[230] the claim was to a method and apparatus for modelling a synthetic crystal structure when designing inorganic materials for applications in chemistry and physics. The user would select key parameters and the computer would display the resulting novel structure. You will recall that *Vicom* concerned a method and apparatus claim for digitally processing and manipulating images in the design field. These inventions then appear superficially very similar. However, despite once again endorsing the EPO jurisprudence, the Court of Appeal rejected the appeal in *Fujitsu*. The distinction between the rulings is a fine but important one. The Court of Appeal read *Vicom* not to mean that claims to the digital processing of real images are always allowable, but rather that the technical contribution in that case lay in the way the enhanced image was produced. This was by means of the program technically and precisely controlling the quality of the image—a matter which was beyond human intervention. In *Fujitsu*, the user provided all necessary information to produce the final image of the combined structure. The program merely supplied a means to reproduce the image automatically and faster; a process that would in the past have been represented in substantially the same fashion by a physical model. This was insufficient to demonstrate technical contribution within the terms of UK and European patent law.

12.143   *Aerotel* purports not to disturb these rules[231] but merely to change the approach to considering exclusions.[232] That approach, now to be adopted for all such considerations, is: '(1) properly construe the claim, (2) identify the actual contribution; (3) ask whether it falls solely within the excluded subject matter; (4) check whether the actual or alleged contribution is actually technical in nature'. The House of Lords refused a request by McCrossan to appeal the case, meaning that *Aerotel* now forms the basis of

---

[224] Note, however, that while the EPO is not bound by the provisions of TRIPS, it was extremely favourably disposed to this argument in the *IBM/Computer program* rulings, notes 151 and 152.

[225] [1989] RPC 561.   [226] [1991] RPC 305.   [227] [1997] RPC 608.

[228] All was not lost, however, because they were ultimately able to amend their claims in the light of the decision and a patent was duly granted.

[229] [1991] RPC 305.   [230] [1997] RPC 608.

[231] Although the court doubted whether a method for performing a mental act executed by computer would be excluded, note 212, para 62.

[232] For shifting sands prior to *Aerotel*, see *Halliburton Energy Services Inc v Smith International (North Sea) Ltd* [2006] RPC 26 and *CFPH LLC Applications* [2006] RPC 5.

the UK approach towards patentable subject matter—although it must be read in the light of *Symbian* (para 12.146) and can be better understood in the light of newer cases.

12.144   The *Aerotel* ruling retains the rider that something which falls wholly into an excluded category is excluded *even if* it demonstrates a technical contribution. Moreover, the court said that if an application falls at the third hurdle it will not even be necessary to consider the fourth question of whether it is technical. This, then, is in stark contrast to the EPO which sets its priorities in complete contradistinction where the finding of technical contribution is a trump card. Indeed the Technical Board of Appeal has stated that *Aerotel* is 'irreconcilable with the European Patent Convention'.[233] No matter from the domestic perspective, however, because the UK–IPO issued a new Practice Notice on Patentable Subject Matter and offered examples of how the approach should be undertaken.[234] It is thought that this should rarely make a difference in practice. An early post-*Aerotel* example concerned the rejection of Sony's data structure for communicating metadata (*Sony UK Ltd* BL O/010/07). The contribution as outlined in the claims was found in the data structure whose function was to form part of the instructions in a computer network for interrogation, retrieval, and communication of metadata. As such, it was excluded as a computer program. The fourth question was not asked, begging the question why it has been retained at all.[235] Tantalisingly, however, the Hearing Office suggested that the data structure could be seen to embody a technical effect if described differently (as an apparatus) but this was not so in the claims in question. Such a remark may be worrying if it suggests that problems of exclusion can be avoided by simple alternative claim drafting.

12.145   In 2008 questions arose concerning a particular form of claim: computer program carrier claims which were not directly considered in the *Aerotel* case but thought to be excluded by its approach. These questions were answered in *Astron Clinica's Application*[236] where Kitchin J held that where claims to a method performed by running a suitably programmed computer or to a computer programmed to carry out the method were allowable, a claim to the program itself should also be allowable *provided that* the computer program implements a patentable invention. This resulted in a further Practice Notice[237] in which the UK–IPO confirmed that where a claim to a computer program is drafted to reflect the features of the invention which would ensure the patentability of the method which the program is intended to carry out when it is run, examiners would no longer object to claims to a computer program or a program on a carrier. It should be noted that the UK–IPO did not appeal this decision and instead simply pointed out that it restored the UK to its position prior to *Aerotel* with respect to claims to programs themselves.

12.146   The *Aerotel* test was reconsidered by the Court of Appeal in *Symbian Ltd.*[238] Here the court confirmed that the *Aerotel* test is intended to be, in substance, the same test that prior UK case law applied; the fundamental question to be answered remains whether there is a *technical contribution*. The patent in *Symbian* was upheld as more than a claim to a computer program 'as such' because the application disclosed a real-world effect of making a computer work better. The technical problem concerned the working of electronic libraries and how to ensure they continue to work effectively when changes are made to the library data. The invention in suit effectively provided a solution to this problem. The net result of the ruling is that a program is patentable even if it solves a problem with the running of a computer or with programming itself, including making it run faster or more reliably. It does not follow, however, that

---

[233] Note 218.

[234] *Practice Notice (Patents Act 1977: Patentable subject matter)* [2007] Bus LR 672.

[235] The fourth step has in other cases been applied regardless of a failure to meet the third step, see eg *Bloomberg LLP and Cappellini's Applications* [2007] EWHC 476 (Pat). For more information see para 11.10.

[236] *Astron Clinica Ltd and others v The Comptroller General of Patents* [2008] EWHC 85 (Pat).

[237] *Practice Notice (Patents Act 1977: Patentable subject matter) (No 2)* [2008] Bus LR 978.

[238] *Symbian Ltd v Comptroller General of Patents, Designs and Trademarks* [2008] EWCA Civ 1066.

the mere presence of computer hardware is sufficient to render a computer program patentable. On this point the UK remains divergent with the EPO. This case is helpful in providing further insight into when a 'technical contribution' is more than solely a computer program.[239] It also suggested that fusing the third and fourth step of the *Aerotel* test would help towards reconciling UK and EPO jurisprudence. The UK–IPO thereafter issued a further Practice Notice in December 2008.[240] This Notice confirms that the four-step test is the correct test for determining whether an invention falls under excluded subject matter. It further notes that when considering whether the contribution is more than solely a computer program, one must consider what the program does as a matter of practical reality. *Symbian* also confirms that other excluded material (eg business methods) cannot be rendered patentable merely by being implemented on a conventional computer system (para 27).[241]

12.147   Further guidance on how to identify technical effect in a claimed invention has been given by Lewison J in *AT&T Knowledge Ventures LP's Patent Application*.[242] Considerations are:

- whether the claimed technical effect has a technical effect on a process which is carried on outside the computer;
- whether the claimed technical effect operates at the level of the architecture of the computer; that is to say, whether the effect is produced irrespective of the data being processed or the applications being run;
- whether the claimed technical effect results in the computer being made to operate in a new way;
- whether there is an increase in the speed or reliability of the computer;
- whether the perceived problem is overcome by the claimed invention as opposed to merely being circumvented.

Note: this is all subject to the important qualification that the technical effect should not fall wholly within a category of excluded matter. This was, in fact, the problem in this case: each invention was found to be purely a method of doing business.

12.148   More recently, decisions in the UK context include:

- *Halliburton Energy Services Inc's Applications*[243] in which it was held that the mental acts exclusion in patent law must be interpreted narrowly, that is, to involve human mental activity. This means that any claims to implement an invention with a computer will not fall foul of this particular exclusion, albeit it might still be excluded as a computer program as such. A UK–IPO Practice Notice has since been issued.[244]

- *Protecting Kids the World Over (PKTWO) Ltd's Patent Application*[245] involved an electronic monitoring system to alert parents by email or text if their child has been exposed to inappropriate electronic communications. This was patentable because, following the *AT&T* signposts discussed previously, it was helpful to consider the task performed by the program and ask whether it produced a novel real-world effect. An alarm in the physical world alerting the user to activity on the computer met

---

[239] As had been noted previously by Pumfrey J in *Bloomberg LLP and Cappellini's Applications* [2007] EWHC 476 (Pat): not all 'technical effects' are relevant for the fourth step of the *Aerotel/Macrossan* test. The relevant technical effect has to be one that is more than the expected effect from the mere loading of a program on to a computer.

[240] *Practice Notice (Patents Act 1977: Patentability of computer programs)* [2009] Bus LR 625.

[241] M Kenrick, 'Software patentability—where are we, and where might we be going?' (2008) 37(7) CIPAJ 378.

[242] [2009] FSR 19, followed in *Gemstar-TV Guide International Inc v Virgin Media Ltd* [2009] EWHC 3068 (Ch).

[243] [2011] EWHC 2508 (Pat), [2012] RPC 129.

[244] Practice Notice (Patents Act 1977: Patentability of mental acts), Intellectual Property Office, 17 October 2011 [2012] Bus LR 1264.

[245] [2011] EWHC 2720 (Pat), [2012] RPC 13.

this criterion: 'The invention solved a technical problem lying outside the computer, namely how to improve on the inappropriate communication alarm generation provided by the prior art' (paras 32–35).

- *HTC Europe Co Ltd v Apple Inc, Apple Inc v HTC Corp*[246] related to various patents owned by Apple regarding their mobile touch screen devices. We have already considered aspects of this in para 11.44. Of relevance here is patent (948) that involved computer devices with inputs which were capable of responding to more than one touch at the same time. Claim 1 and 2 of the patent described a method for handling touch events on a multi-touch device. This was unpatentable as a computer program as such. In contrast, other patents relating to other features which were not excluded on this ground because they produced sufficient technical effect, viz, the slide-to-unlock feature and the zoom-image feature both solved a real-world problem with effect beyond the software itself.

- Compare, *Really Virtual Co Ltd v UK Intellectual Property Office*[247] which involved an invention relating to the manner in which a user accessed Internet services. It provided for the user to retain anonymity from the service provider while being offered services tailored to personal requirements. It was held that while the meaning of the exclusion in patent law is not readily subject to systematic analysis, the invention viewed as a whole failed to demonstrate technical contribution; moreover, this was nothing more than a method of A doing business with C using B as an intermediary to protect anonymity.

12.149   How far, then, is there a divergence between the approaches in the UK and the EPO? The European Commission cited the UK experience, and in particular *Merrill Lynch*, as a reason to harmonise the law in this area, suggesting that 'a computer program-related invention that amounts to, for example, a method of doing business … is considered unpatentable even if a technical contribution (in the terms defined in the Directive) can be found'.[248] This remains the case today. But the European Commission harmonisation measure failed, as we shall see later. Consider for yourself whether the English court decisions are moving the UK further away from, rather than towards, our Continental cousins.

European reform

12.150   The inexorable shift in patent practice over the years has led to numerous claims that the law is now unclear and uncertain. Like a red rag to a bull, this challenge has invariably attracted the attention of the European Commission, particularly when it sees any such criticism of intellectual property law to be a legitimate basis for bringing yet another area within its ever-widening harmonisation programme, as we have seen with the Biotechnology Directive. The Commission identified so-called 'computer-implemented inventions' as a priority issue following its consultation and Green Paper on the Community Patent and Patent System in Europe from 1997.[249] Responses reflecting nothing more than polarised positions prompted further consultation in 2000,[250] after which the Commission released its proposal for a Directive on the patentability of computer-implemented inventions in 2002.[251] This instrument was defeated in the European Parliament in July 2005 and it will not return. It is illuminating, however, to consider its core provisions to understand what objectors were so concerned about. It is also a very salutary lesson for intellectual property law and policymakers: while the Biotechnology Directive may

---

[246] [2012] EWHC 1789 (Pat).   [247] [2012] EWHC 1086 (Ch).

[248] Commission Proposal on the patentability of computer-implemented inventions, COM(2002) 92 final, 20 February 2002, p 10.

[249] Promoting Innovation Through Patents: Green Paper on the Community Patent and the Patent System in Europe, COM(1997) 314 final, 24 June 1997.

[250] http://ec.europa.eu/internal_market/indprop/comp/index_en.htm.   [251] COM(2002) 92 final, 20 February 2002.

have been the first example of the Parliament flexing its muscles in the legislative process, the defeat of the Computer-implemented Inventions Directive was a direct result of heavy lobbying and may indicate a real shift of power in the policy and political arena.

12.151   The usual arguments were advanced for legislative intervention at this stage: lack of legal certainty, economic instability, and the need to fulfil further potential, as well as disparities of approach among member states acting as obstacles to the operation of the internal market. The legal basis for intervention was asserted to be the same as that used for the Biotechnology Directive, namely Article 95 of the EC Treaty (now Article 114 of the Treaty on the Functioning of the European Union), which basis was robustly upheld by the ECJ in the challenge to the latter Directive.[252]

12.152   The Commission tried to hold a single line: this was an attempt to maintain the status quo while providing clarity on the legal position in Europe. There was, however, one notable exception.

12.153   The proposal began with the premise that 'computer-implemented inventions' should be treated like any other field of technology[253] and that these should be patentable as long as they demonstrate 'technical contribution', which was defined as 'a contribution to the state of the art in a technical field which is not obvious to a person skilled in the art'.[254] The focus, then, was on the criteria for patentability, and the Commission was at pains to point out that it did not seek any amendment to these criteria; the requirement of technical contribution was simply an elaboration on the criterion of inventive step. The proposal made it incumbent on patent examiners to consider the invention as a whole and to accept the presence of both technical and non-technical features in an application as long as the technical contribution was found in the technical aspects of the invention.[255] To this extent, the proposal follows the current EPO jurisprudence and also reflects the recent changes of approach in the UK (see previously).

12.154   While the focus, then, would be on member states' equivalent provisions to Article 56 EPC (criteria for patentability), there was, in fact, a general conflation between the exclusion of subject matter and these criteria throughout the instrument.[256] An important result of a shift in focus from exclusions to inventive step, however, is to remove the possibility of applications being rejected *ab initio*. Logic dictates, and practice follows suit, that an examiner will consider the exclusions before the criteria of novelty, inventive step, and industrial applicability. If it is thought that an exclusion is contained in the application it will be rejected before there is any substantive consideration, including, importantly, a search of the prior art. This could prejudice an applicant in a number of ways, as was demonstrated in the UK case of *Raytheon Co's Application*[257] where precisely this happened. This shift in emphasis would, therefore, operate in the applicants' favour. It is perhaps no coincidence that we find the UK domestic courts moving in just this direction a few weeks after the defeat of the Directive.

12.155   Notwithstanding, the proposal departed from EPO practice in one important respect in that it sought to clarify that protection should only be provided for a 'computer-implemented invention'. This was defined as:

> any invention the performance of which involves the use of a computer, computer network or other programmable apparatus and having one or more prima facie novel features which are realised wholly or partly by means of a computer program or computer programs.[258]

[252] Case C-377/98 *Kingdom of the Netherlands v Council of the European Union and the European Parliament* [2002] All ER (EC) 97.
[253] Note 251, Art 3.   [254] Note 251, Art 2(b).   [255] Note 251, Art 4(3).
[256] The same criticism could be levelled at the current version of the EPO Guidelines, note 8, and the recent changes in the UK.
[257] [1993] RPC 427.   [258] Note 251, Art 2(a).

12.156   In other words, a claim to an invention under the proposal, be it to a product (a computer or other apparatus) or a process (a method) must be linked to a computer. This would have been a return to the position under *Vicom* and a clear retrenchment from the rulings in the *IBM* decisions and subsequent case law. The concern, expressed elsewhere,[259] is that the effect of the current EPO jurisprudence might be to prevent 'reverse engineering' of elements of programs and other activities considered legitimate within the industry and important to its development.

12.157   But this seemingly cautious approach was lambasted by the European Economic and Social Committee which called upon the Commission to rethink the proposal entirely anew.[260] The Committee dismissed as 'legal casuistry' the attempt to distinguish between protection of software itself and computer-implemented inventions and warned that the proposal would nonetheless 'open the way to the future patentability of the entire software field'. The Committee went on to challenge the economic case for patents in this field and to warn of the potentially adverse impact that patenting practice might have for our knowledge-based society, and in particular the Internet and the free circulation of free/open source software. It called for a far more cautious approach still, based on more empirical evidence of the economic and employment consequences of various proposals, including leaving matters to the vagaries of the market.

12.158   This internal institutional wrangle over the proposal reflects broader, deeper divides about the issue of software patenting. These are most evident in the European Parliament where the Directive was roundly defeated by an overwhelming majority of 648:14. Open source and free software groups were particularly active in the lobbying process, arguing that the promised economic benefits were far from proven and that such a law would, rather, have a stifling and restricting effect on innovation and development. The triumph of these groups, and to an extent the triumph of the Parliament over the Commission, has led to broader questions being asked about the operation of the democratic process within the EU. Who would have thought that intellectual property could be so political?

Further reading

Books

K Beresford, *Patenting Software Under the European Patent Convention* (2000)

D Castle (ed), *The Role of Intellectual Property Rights in Biotechnology Innovation* (2009)

P England, *Intellectual Property in the Life Sciences: A Global Guide to Rights and Their Applications* (2011)

A Plomer and P Torremans (eds), *Embryonic Stem Cell Patents: European Law and Ethics* (2009)

AK Rai and ER Latty (eds), *Intellectual Property and Biotechnology* (2011)

M Rimmer, *Intellectual Property and Biotechnology: Biological Inventions* (2008)

H Somsen (ed), *The Regulatory Challenge of Biotechnology* (2007)

GA Stobbs (ed), *Software Patents Worldwide* (2009)

G van Overwalle (ed), *Gene Patents and Public Health* (2007)

[259] See, eg, Proposal for a Directive on the patentability of computer-implemented inventions—frequently asked questions at Internal Market website, at http://ec.europa.eu/internal_market/indprop/comp/index_en.htm.
[260] Opinion of the Economic and Social Committee on the 'Proposal for a Directive of the European Parliament and of the Council on the patentability of computer-implemented inventions', OJ C61/154, 14 March 2003.

Reports

Department of Trade and Industry and the Intellectual Property Institute, *Patents for Genetic Sequences: the Competitiveness of Current UK Law and Practices* (2004)

European Group on Ethics, *Ethics of Synthetic Biology* (2009)

Nuffield Council on Bioethics, *Patenting DNA* (2002)

Articles

T Aplin, 'Patenting computer programs: a glimmer of convergence?' (2008) 30(9) EIPR 379

F Bor, 'Exemptions to patent infringement—applied to biotechnology research tools' [2006] EIPR 5

S Bostyn, 'How biological is essentially biological? The referrals to the Enlarged Board of Appeal G2/07 and G1/08' (2009) 31(11) EIPR 549

S Burke, 'Justifications for patents as applied to human-animal chimeras', (2012) 34(4) EIPR 237

RS Crespi, 'The human embryo and patent law: a major challenge ahead' [2006] EIPR 569

S Gaisser et al, 'The phantom menace of gene patents' (2009) 458(7237) Nature 407

SHE Harmon, G Laurie, and A Courtney, 'Dignity, plurality and patentability: the unfinished story of *Brüstle v Greenpeace*' (2013) 38(1) EL Rev 92

CM Holman, 'Trends in human gene patent litigation' (2008) 322(5899) Science 198

A Huttermann and U Storz, 'A comparison between biotech and software related patents' (2009) 31(12) EIPR 589

G Laurie, 'Patenting stem cells of human origin' [2004] EIPR 59

K Liddell et al, 'Patents as incentives for translational and evaluative research: the case of genetic tests and their improved clinical performance' [2008] 3 IPQ 286

T Minssen and D Nilsson, 'The industrial application requirement for biotech inventions in light of recent EPO & UK case law: a plausible approach or a mere "hunting license"?' (2012) 34(10) EIPR 689

K Moon, 'The nature of computer programs: Tangible? Goods? Personal property? Intellectual property?' (2008) 31(8) EIPR 396

A Odell-West, 'The absence of informed consent to commercial exploitation for inventions developed from human biological material: a bar to patentability?' [2009] 3 IPQ 273

R Onslow, 'Software patents—a new approach' (2012) 34(1) EIPR 710

KE, Rodriguez and N Groenendjik, 'High-quality patents for emerging science and technology through external actors' (2012) 34(4) EIPR 221

M Rowlandson, '*WARF/Stem cells* (G2/06): the *ordre public* and morality exception and its impact on the patentability of human embryonic stem cells' (2010) 32(2) EIPR 67

P Treichel, 'G2/06 and the verdict of immorality' (2009) 40(4) IIC 450

G van Overwalle, 'The implementation of the Biotechnology Directive in Belgium and its after-effects. The introduction of a new research exemption and a compulsory licence for public health' (2006) IIC 889

M Varju and J Sandor, 'Patenting stem cells in Europe: the challenge of multiplicity in European Union law' (2012) 49(3) CML Rev 1007

M Yan, 'Morality—an equivocal area in the patent system' (2012) 34(4) EIPR 261

Part V

Registered trade marks

Introduction

This Part of the book explains and discusses the law of registered trade marks within their international, European, and domestic setting. Chapter 13 will explain the regulatory framework for the protection of trade marks, highlighting the international treaties and European Regulations and Directives which help to shape trade mark law within the domestic arena. It will also discuss policy trends and the jurisprudence relevant to the function of a trade mark within the consumer society. Chapter 14 will consider the definition of a trade mark and deal with the rules pertaining to registration. Chapter 15 will examine the scope of trade mark protection, infringement, and defences, bringing in current discussion on, inter alia, questions of use of a trade mark in the course of trade and comparative advertising. Chapter 16 will look at three contemporary issues in trade mark law: domain names; the use of trade marks on the Internet, in keyword advertising, and auction sites; and the related area of geographical indications.

Sources of the law: key websites

- European Union Trade Mark Directives and Community Trade Mark Regulation for which, see the Commission's Internal Market Directorate General's website
  http://ec.europa.eu/internal_market/indprop/tm/index_en.htm

- Trade Marks Act 1994 as amended (the UK–IPO Office maintains a consolidated text), see
  http://www.ipo.gov.uk/tmact94.pdf

- Decisions of the Court of Justice of the European Union/European Court of Justice (for which see the search form) at
  http://curia.europa.eu/jurisp/cgi-bin/form.pl?lang=en

- Office for the Harmonisation in the Internal Market (OHIM), for which see
  http://oami.europa.eu/

- Paris Convention for the Protection of Industrial Property, for which see the WIPO website
  http://www.wipo.int/treaties/en/ip/paris/trtdocs_wo020.html

- Madrid Agreement and Protocol, for which see the WIPO website
  http://www.wipo.int/madrid/en/legal_texts/

- The UK–IPO website has a useful section devoted to trade marks at
  http://www.ipo.gov.uk/tm.htm/

The function of a trade mark and the national, EU, and international regime

Introduction

Scope and overview of chapter

13.1 The purpose of this chapter is twofold. It is first to discuss policy tensions within trade mark law and to analyse the function of a trade mark as detailed in legislative enactments, case law, and policy papers. Through this analysis it will be explained that the function of a trade mark is far from settled. As will be seen over the ensuing chapters, the lack of harmony in relation to the function has implications for the scope of protection conferred by the law. Key aspects of the trade mark system will be introduced and comment will be made on the interaction between registered trade marks and other intellectual property rights. The second purpose is to introduce the legal regime for the protection of trade marks from an international, EU, and national perspective. Through a series of agreements, treaties, and legislation certain minimum standards for the protection of trade marks has been established as has a system by virtue of which traders can register and protect marks in many countries throughout the world.

13.2 **Learning objectives**

By the end of this chapter you should be able to describe and explain:

- the discussion surrounding the contemporary function of a trade mark;
- how registered trade marks fit in with other intellectual property rights;
- the major international, European, and national instruments concerning trade marks;
- the routes a trader might choose to register a mark.

13.3 The rest of this chapter looks like this

- Trade marks: policy issues (13.4–13.8)
- Trade marks: function (13.9–13.22)

- Trade marks and other intellectual property rights (13.23–13.28)
- The regulatory framework (13.29–13.65)

Trade marks: policy issues

13.4   Trade marks are ubiquitous. In modern society the consumer is surrounded daily by images designed to distinguish the goods and services provided by one trader from those of another. The marks are designed to indicate the origin of the goods and services. But, as will be seen in the following discussion, it is argued that a mark plays other roles, including that of a quality indicator; a means of advertising goods and services; and a vehicle for investment. These functions are increasingly reflected in provisions in trade mark law enabling the registration of a broad variety of signs, and those which seek to protect the reputation of a mark against parasitic and damaging use of the same or a similar mark by third parties.

13.5   A key theme underpinning trade mark law concerns the extent of the monopoly conferred by a registered mark. As will been seen in the next two chapters, registration of a mark does not give the trader a monopoly in either the mark, or the underlying goods and services in connection with which the mark is registered, but only a monopoly over the use of the mark in conjunction with the goods and services for which it is registered. This leads to a constant tension between traders, as proprietors of trade marks, who would like to see the scope of that monopoly construed as broadly as possible so as to reserve to themselves as much exclusivity in the market as possible, and competitors who wish to see the monopoly interpreted narrowly so as to enable them to encroach and 'free-ride' upon a successful registered trade mark. In determining where the boundaries lie, a number of interests require to be accommodated within the trade mark framework. Broadly they are of the trader, of competing traders, and of the consumer. A central question is as to how, and where, these respective interests should be taken into account and balanced. While the focus of the essential function of a trade mark remains on indicating the origin of goods and services and on consumer confusion, so the perception of the consumer is paramount. Registration and the scope of protection conferred by the mark are circumscribed by indications the consumer might find confusing, or which implicate the origin function of the mark. As the range of signs and symbols that can be registered expands, so concerns grow in some quarters as to the competitive disadvantage this may pose for other traders. The first comer may easily be able to establish a link between the more obvious mark in the mind of the consumer and the goods and services. This imposes a cost on the competing trader who will have to invest more in building a link between the less obvious mark and the consumer whilst trying to avoid allegations of consumer confusion. Once registered, and the broader functions of a mark are recognised, the interests of the consumer diminish. Consumer confusion is no longer relevant; the focus is instead on safeguarding the reputation of the mark against parasitic and detrimental uses by competing traders.

13.6   A related issue that permeates registered trade mark law is that of 'use'. A trade mark registration can be kept on the register indefinitely and so, unlike patents or copyright, a mark need not fall into the public domain after a specified time. In consequence a trade mark has to be used in order to maintain the registration. The obligation of use has been adopted in almost all jurisdictions.[1] As will be seen in the discussion in the following chapters, there are many instances in which actual and genuine 'use' of a trade mark is essential. These include the need to put a registered mark to genuine use to retain it on the trade mark register; whether a sign needs to be used 'as a trade mark' or 'in a trade mark sense' as

---

[1] See the comments by B Pretnar, 'Use and non-use in trade mark law' in J Phillips and I Simon (eds), *Trade Marks Use* (2005), 11.

opposed to descriptively; and relatedly, the extent to which the use must implicate one of the functions of a mark. These requirements seek to balance the interests of the trade mark proprietor and the competitor. Marks which are not put to genuine use will become free for competing traders as trade mark owners will not be able to stockpile marks putting competitors at a competitive disadvantage. The 'use' requirement for the purposes of infringement is vital in determining the scope of the rights granted to the trade mark holder. If any use of the same or similar mark by a competitor would infringe the registered mark whether or not that use is as a trade mark, so the rights of the owner are broader in scope than they would be if only use as a trade mark, or use which implicates one of the functions, infringed.

13.7   Case law has at times sent inconsistent signals in recognising and balancing the interests. The current provisions on registered trade marks have spawned more case law at European level than any other area of intellectual property.[2] This is not only because these central questions remain unsettled, but also because of the financial importance of trade marks to business. In 2012 Coca-Cola was valued at $77,839 million, Apple at $76,568 million, Google at $69,726 million, and Disney at $27,438 million.[3] When such sums are at issue, trade mark owners and competitors are willing to litigate in seeking to ensure that they can obtain even the smallest competitive advantage over their rivals.

13.8   While the economic aspects of trade marks and the role that they play in the consumer society have always provided key justifications for their existence,[4] an increasingly rich discussion has developed from within related areas of the law supporting trade marks and seeking to limit their power. One of these is in relation to human rights. There is an academic literature reflecting upon the role of human rights as they impact upon all aspects of trade marks—including property rights and freedom of expression.[5] Courts around the world have considered the interface between the two. In *Anheuser-Busch v Portugal*[6] the European Court of Human Rights held that trade marks and applications are possessions for the purposes of Article 1, Protocol 1 to the European Convention on Human Rights. The Advocate General made reference to balancing competing rights in *Google France v Louis Vuitton*: 'whatever the protection afforded to innovation and investment, it is never absolute. It must always be balanced against other interests, in the same way as trade mark protection itself is balanced against them. I believe that the present cases call for such a balance as regards freedom of expression and freedom of commerce.'[7] In the South African case of *Laugh It Off Promotions CC v South African Breweries International (Finance) BV*[8] freedom of expression and the censorship power which could be wielded by the owner of a trade mark came into opposition.[9] In the US case of *Mattel Inc v MCA Records Inc*, which concerned the song 'Barbie

---

[2] Jacob LJ has said in this regard that 'European trade mark law is in danger of becoming a forest of case law where everyone loses their way' (*O2 v Hutchison* [2006] EWCA Civ 1656, [2007] 2 CMLR 15 at para 35).

[3] http://www.interbrand.com/en/best-global-brands/2012/Best-Global-Brands-2012-Brand-View.aspx.

[4] A rich literature examining the economic case for trade marks and trade mark law exists. See, eg, WM Landes and RA Posner, *The Economic Structure of Intellectual Property Law* (2003); WM Landes and RA Posner, 'Trade mark law: an economic perspective' (1987) Journal of Law and Economics 268; NS Economides, 'The economics of trade marks' (1988) 78 TMR 523; RW Holzhauer, 'Jenever and jumping wild cats' in R Towse (ed), *III The Economics of Intellectual Property* (2002), 418; IPL Png and D Reitman, 'Why are some products branded and others not?' in R Towse (ed), *III The Economics of Intellectual Property* (2002), 207; SL Carter, 'The trouble with trademark' in R Towse (ed), *III The Economics of Intellectual Property* (2002), 373; S Maniatis, 'Trade mark rights—a justification based on property' [2002] 2 IPQ 123–171; H Rosler, 'The rationale for European trade mark protection' (2007) 29(3) EIPR 100–107; G Lunney, 'Trademark monopolies' (1999) 48 Emory Law Journal 367.

[5] J Davis, 'European trade mark law and the enclosure of the commons' [2002] 4 IPQ 342–367; LR Helfer, 'The new innovation frontier? Intellectual property and the European Court of Human Rights' (2008) 49 Harvard International Law Journal 1; MA Naser 'Trademarks and freedom of expression' (2009) 40 IIC 188.

[6] App No 73049/01. KD Beiter, 'The right to property and the protection of interests in intellectual property—a human rights perspective on the European Court of Human Rights' decision in *Anheuser-Busch v Portugal*' (2008) 39 IIC 714.

[7] Case 236/08 *Google France v Louis Vuitton*, AG para 102.

[8] [2005] FSR 30 (Sup Ct, SA).   [9] [2005] FSR 30 at para 15.93.

Girl' by the pop group Aqua, the court claimed that freedom of expression could be used to control the effects of trade mark protection particularly in the context of dilution where there is no requirement to show confusion.[10] In the UK in an early case considering the interface in the UK in *Miss World Ltd v Channel 4*,[11] Miss World Ltd obtained an interim injunction against C4 broadcasting a programme called Mr Miss World. During judgment the court noted that 'scope of the intervention of Article 10 in matters concerning registered trade marks is far from well worked out ... it is fair to say that it is almost completely unworked out.' Jacob LJ, in *L'Oreal v Bellure*[12] has been particularly critical of the possibility of the trade mark right to trump freedom of speech.

My own strong predilection, free from the opinion of the ECJ [European Court of Justice], would be to hold that trade mark law did not prevent traders from making honest statements about their products where those products are themselves lawful.

I have a number of reasons for that predilection. First and most generally is that I am in favour of free speech—and most particularly where someone wishes to tell the truth. There is no good reason to dilute the predilection in cases where the speaker's motive for telling the truth is his own commercial gain. Truth in the market place matters—even if it does not attract quite the strong emotions as the right of a journalist or politician to speak the truth.

Of course the right of free expression (which clearly applies in principle to expression for commercial purposes), cannot be and is not unqualified. But any suggested rule of law which stands in the way of people telling the truth, whether the context be political, commercial or otherwise, ought to be scrutinised with care and justified only on the grounds of strict necessity.

Any such scrutiny should consider not only the right of the speaker but also of his hearer. For the right of free speech extends not only to those who wish to tell the truth, but also those who would wish to hear it.[13]

Exercise

Read R Burrell and D Gangjee, 'Trade marks and freedom of expression—a call for caution' [2010] IIC 554.

Note the conclusion that the author's come to: 'Rather than looking routinely to constitutional principles to limit trade mark rights or looking to create new free speech inspired parody defences and the like, a much more productive focus, at least at this juncture, is to remain focused on the proper limits of trade mark law.'

Do you agree? Justify your response. Revisit your answer when you have completed the trade marks chapters in this book.

Question

What were the issues in the case involving the character in Figure 13.1?[14]

---

[10] 296 F 3d 894 at 905 (9th Cir, 2002).   [11] [2007] ETMR 66 (Ch).   [12] [2010] ETMR 47
[13] Paras 8–12. The relationship between trade marks and freedom of expression is discussed in R Burrell and D Gangjee, 'Trade marks and freedom of expression—a call for caution' [2010] *IIC* 554 where the authors argue not for a free speech defence to trade mark infringement but for a 'rediscovery of the fundamental principles on which trade mark protection rests' (at 557).
[14] *Ate My Heart Inc v Mind Candy Ltd* [2011] EWHC 2741 (Ch).

Figure 13.1 *Ate My Heart Inc v Mind Candy Ltd*

> **Key points on policy issues**
>
> • A key theme underpinning trade mark law is as to the extent of the monopoly conferred by the mark
>
> • The trade mark framework seeks to balance the interests of the trade mark proprietor, the competitor, and the consumer

Trade marks: function

13.9   During the 19th century, when a consumer wanted to purchase particular goods, she had to rely heavily on the expertise of the shopkeeper for advice as to the origin of the goods and their quality.[15] It was not until 1875 that a register was first introduced in the UK partly in response to the growth in international trade where an increasing variety of goods were being traded under marks normally associated with British manufacturers, such as 'Sheffield' cutlery. Now, it is said that it is the association of a trade mark with goods and services (the origin) that sells products to the consumer, rather than the expertise of the shopkeeper.

13.10   The ability to register marks brought a number of benefits to traders. Not only could marks be registered, and thus protected, prior to being used, but in addition registration reduced the burden on the trader of the need to prove goodwill and distinctiveness necessary for an action in passing off.

> **?** **Question**
>
> What do you think is, or should be, the function of a trade mark? Revisit your views once you have completed this Part and again when you have completed the chapters on trade marks.

13.11   In this symbiotic relationship between the supplier who owns the trade mark and the consumer, trade marks perform a vital function of indicating the *origin* of the goods and services being sold: in other words, the trade mark functions as a *badge of origin*. This function is at the heart of the existence of trade marks. It is noted in literature:

> The primary function of a trade mark, traditionally, has been to identify the commercial or trade origin of the goods (or services) to which it is applied.[16]

---

[15] A Vickery, 'The Woman Who Shops 'Til She Drops', BBC Radio 4, Just Looking, 3 September 2001, 09:00–09:30.
[16] S Ricketson, *The Law of Intellectual Property* (1984).

In case law:

> the essential function of the mark, which is to give the consumer or final user a guarantee of the identity of the origin of the marked product by enabling him to distinguish, without any possible confusion, that product from others of a different provenance.[17]

> Trade mark rights constitute an essential element in the system of undistorted competition which the Treaty is intended to establish and maintain. In such a system, undertakings must be able to attract and retain customers by the quality of their goods or services, which is made possible only by distinctive signs allowing them to be identified.[18] ... In that context, the essential function of a trade mark is to guarantee the identity of origin of the marked goods or services to the consumer or end user by enabling him, without any possibility of confusion, to distinguish the goods or services from others which have another origin. For the trade mark to be able to fulfil its essential role in the system of undistorted competition which the Treaty seeks to establish and maintain, it must offer a guarantee that all the goods or services bearing it have been manufactured or supplied under the control of a single undertaking which is responsible for their quality.[19]

And in formal documents:

> [A trade mark] serves to distinguish trade marked products originating from a particular firm or group of firms from the products of other firms. From this basic function of the trade mark are derived all other functions which the trade mark fulfils in economic life.[20]

Some examples of registered trade marks that fulfil this origin function include 'Tesco Everyday Value' owned by Tesco Stores Ltd,[21] and 'Rolls-Royce' owned by Rolls-Royce plc.[22] Thus when a consumer sees one of these registered marks used in conjunction with good or services, it gives an indication of the origin of those products.

13.12 However, that is not always the case. Consider the word mark 'Bambi' when it is used in conjunction with 'knitted articles of outer clothing for children', or the image shown in Figure 13.2. This was used in connection with 'articles of outer-clothing for children'.[23] Perhaps only the most astute shopper would have known that the marks were also owned by Tesco Stores Ltd. However, what is important for those who buy children's clothes is to know the *quality* of the clothes they are purchasing. And this leads to the second important function of a trade mark, a subset of the origin function, and that is that a registered trade mark indicates to the consumer the *quality* of the particular goods or services sold in connection with a particular mark.

> the relevance of the trade mark's function as a guarantee of origin lies none the less in the fact that the trade mark conveys to the consumer certain perceptions as to the quality of the marked goods. The consumer is not interested in the commercial origin of goods out of idle curiosity; his interest is based on the assumption that goods of the same origin will be of the same quality. That is how trade mark protection achieves its fundamental justification of rewarding the manufacturer who consistently produces high-quality goods.[24]

13.13 Returning to the first two examples of registered trade marks quoted previously, not only do they give an indication of the origin of goods and services, but both 'Tesco Everyday Value' and 'Rolls-Royce' conjure up images of a certain differing quality in the mind of the consumer.

> Trade marks are able to achieve that effect because they act as a guarantee, to the consumer, that all goods bearing a particular mark have been produced by, or under the control of, the same manufacturer and are therefore

---

[17] *Centrafarm v American Home Products* [1979] FSR 189.

[18] See, inter alia, Case C-10/89 *HAG GF* [1990] ECR I-3711, para 13, and Case C-517/99 *Merz & Krell* [2001] ECR I-6959, para 21.

[19] Case C-206/01 *Arsenal Football Club plc v Matthew Reed* [2003] Ch 454, [2003] 3 All ER (EC) 1, [2003] 3 WLR 450, [2003] RPC 144, paras 47–48. Also Case 102/77 *Hoffmann-La Roche* [1978] ECR 1139, para 7, and Case C-299/99 *Philips v Remington* [2002] ECR I-5475, para 30.

[20] Bulletin of the European Communities, Supplement 8/76 adopted by the Commission on 6 July 1976.

[21] CTM No 010841377.   [22] UK Trade Mark No 291969.   [23] UK Trade Mark No 1159971.

[24] Case C-10/89 *SA Cnl-Sucal NV v Hag GF AG* [1991] FSR 99 at 129–130.

Figure 13.2 Zoo

likely to be of similar quality. The guarantee of quality offered by a trade mark is not of course absolute, for the manufacturer is at liberty to vary the quality; however, he does so at his own risk and he—not his competitors— will suffer the consequences if he allows the quality to decline. Thus, although trade marks do not provide any form of legal guarantee of quality the absence of which may have misled some to underestimate their significance they do in economic terms provide such a guarantee, which is acted upon daily by consumers.[25]

This quality function has been emphasised by the House of Lords:

The quality of goods on offer is at the heart of all trading activities. As long as trading has existed, buyers have sought information and assurance about the quality of the merchandise on display. The use of trade marks is an integral part of this activity.[26]

13.14   A third function of a trade mark is that of *advertising* the goods or services sold by the trader in connection with the mark. Many traders invest not only time and effort, but also substantial sums in bringing a particular mark to the attention of the public. For many the hope will be that eventually such is the recognition of the mark on the consumer market it is then the mark that will sell the product.

[A trade mark is] a vehicle for communicating a message to the public, and itself represents financial value. This message is incorporated into the trade mark through use, especially for advertising purposes, which enables the trade mark to assume the message itself, whether informatively or symbolically. The message may refer to the product's qualities, or indeed to intangible values such as luxury, lifestyle, exclusivity, adventure, youth etc.[27]

13.15   To this end, a trade mark can also be seen as an *investment*. Much time and money is spent on building consumer awareness of a particular mark, which can itself be sold, assigned, licensed, and be the subject of a security

The fact remains that a mark also acts as a means of conveying other messages concerning, inter alia, the qualities or particular characteristics of the goods or services which it covers or the images and feelings which it conveys, such as luxury, lifestyle, exclusivity, adventure, youth. To that effect the mark has an inherent economic value which is independent of and separate from that of the goods or services for which it is registered. The messages in question which are conveyed inter alia by a mark with a reputation or which are associated with it confer on that mark a significant value which deserves protection, particularly because, in most cases, the reputation of a mark is the result of considerable effort and investment on the part of its proprietor.[28]

As with the quality function, these advertising and investment functions are considered by many as subsets of the basic function of indicating the origin of the goods and services:

It is also argued that trade marks have other functions, which might be termed 'communication', investment, or advertising functions. Those functions are said to arise from the fact that the investment in the promotion

[25] *Wagamama Ltd v City Centre Restaurants plc* [1996] ETMR 23.
[26] *Scandecor Developments AB v Scandecor Marketing AB* [2001] UKHL 21, [2001] 2 CMLR 30, [2001] ETMR 74 (Nicholls LJ).
[27] *Souza Cruz SA v Hollywood SAS*, R283/1999–3 [2002] ETMR (64) 705, para 7.
[28] *Mülhens GmbH & Co KG v OHIM* [2008] ETMR 69, para 36.

of a product is built around the mark. It is accordingly reasoned that those functions are values which deserve protection as such, even when there is no abuse arising from misrepresentations about either origin or quality. However, those functions seem to me to be merely derivatives of the origin function; there would be little purpose in advertising a mark if it were not for the function of that mark as an indicator of origin, distinguishing the trade mark owner's goods from those of his competitors.[29]

13.16   These latter functions of a trade mark (advertisement, quality, and investment) are sometimes referred to as the 'communicative functions' of a trade mark. They become particularly prominent when the scope of the protection conferred by the mark goes beyond the prevention of consumer confusion to protecting a mark with a reputation against the use of the same or similar mark in connection with the same or dissimilar goods and services. The effect on the consumer is no longer relevant. Rather, the question becomes one of whether the use by the competitor of the sign dilutes the mark in the sense of taking unfair advantage of the reputation or being detrimental to the distinctive character or reputation of the earlier mark. The focus is on the value of the mark.[30]

Current trends

13.17   In recent years there has been something of a backlash in some sectors of society against the power that it is said trade marks can have over the daily life of a consumer. This campaign has been directed primarily against brands, rather than trade marks on their own. Although there seems to be some discussion and disagreement as to the definition, the terms 'brand' and 'branding' would appear to refer to the totality of the image that is portrayed in relation to or by a product in the marketplace, and the process of getting it there. A brand has been described thus:

> The intangible sum of a product's attributes: its name, packaging, and price, its history, its reputation, and the way it's advertised.[31]

13.18   The process of branding can thus be applied to an entire corporate identity as well as to individual products and services.[32] And herein lies the nub of the controversy. In recent years companies have attempted to build whole aspirations, images, and lifestyles around a brand. Those that have achieved some success might include 'Bailey's Irish Cream', 'Pepsi Max', 'Levi' jeans, 'Absolut Vodka', and 'Lynx'. The message is that if you purchase this particular product, you too can have these experiences, this lifestyle, and this success. The effect, so it is argued, is to offer a lifestyle that is dictated by the brand-owner, but which does not necessarily reflect 'real life'. The ultimate result is that it is the companies which own these brands which determine the way we live, the choices we make, and the shape of the world in which we live.[33] This line of thinking underlies, at least in part, the activities of those involved in the anti-globalisation and anti-capitalist movement who disrupted attempts to hold meetings of G-8 leaders in, among other places, Prague, Seattle, Genoa, and Gleneagles. The law, however, does not protect brands as such, but only the constituent elements that go to making up a brand including goodwill via passing off, trade marks via trade mark law, sounds and images via copyright, and the shape of articles via design right. As

---

[29] Case C-337/95 *Parfums Christian Dior and Parfums Christina Dior BV v Evora BV* [1998] RPC 166.

[30] Case C-487/07 *L'Oréal v Bellure*. It seems that the communicative functions may extend to marks without a reputation at least in the case of comparative advertising. See para 15.129.

[31] Ogilvy at http://www.ogilvy.com/ See also *L'Oréal and others v Bellure and others* [2006] EWHC 2355 (Ch) in which a brand was described as 'a collection of intangible values as perceived by a consumer which are attributed to a name, symbol or design used to identify a product or group of products or services' (para 79).

[32] See, eg, http://www.interbrand.com.

[33] A number of books have appeared which expound this theory. These include J Bove, F Dufour, and A de Casparis, *The World is Not for Sale* (2001) and N Klein, *No Logo: Taking Aim and the Brand Bullies* (2000).

was said in *O2 v Hutchison*, 'to the extent that a brand is greater than the sum of the parts that English law will protect, it is defenceless against the chill wind of competition'.[34]

13.19 There has also been widespread criticism of the extended functions of trade marks and the complexity of the case law of the Court of Justice in this area.

■ *L'Oreal v Bellure* [2010] EWCA Civ 535

In this case, applying the ruling of the Court of Justice, Jacob LJ was particularly critical:

> We are to consider whether the functions of communication, investment or advertising are liable to be affected, even though the use 'is not capable of jeopardizing the essential function of the mark which is to indicate the origin of the goods' I am bound to say that I have real difficulty with these functions when divorced from the origin function. There is nothing in the legislation about them. Conceptually they are vague and ill-defined. Take for instance the advertising and investment functions. Trade mark owners of famous marks will have spent a lot of money creating them and need to continue to spend to maintain them. But all advertisements for rival products will impinge on the owner's efforts and affect the advertising and invest-ment function of the brand in question. No-one would say such jostling for fame and image in the market should be stopped. Similarly all comparative advertising is likely to affect the value of the trade mark owner's investment.

The Advocate General in *Interflora v Marks and Spencer*[35] made reference to criticism of the extended functions of a trade mark: 'it cannot be denied that the Court finds itself at a rather challenging situation as to the acceptability of its case law relating to Art.5 of Directive 89/104 also in view of the criticism presented by numerous academic commentators and leading national trade mark judges.' When the Court of Justice gave its judgment in the case, however, it chose to ignore the criticism and endorse its earlier case law emphasising that the extended functions were relevant to those cases which concerned infringement of identical marks as well as those where the marks were similar and those where marks had a reputation.

13.20 In a study by the Max Planck Institute for Intellectual Property and Competition Law, *Study on the Overall Functioning of the European Trade Mark System*,[36] it was pointed out that 'Although in particular *L'Oréal/ Bellure* has been welcomed by proponents of strong trade mark protection, it is undeniable that the increased focus laid on trade mark functions as an element defining the concrete ambit and scope of trade mark law has blurred the picture, notably in the double identity cases.' As such, the study recom-mends greater certainty by adding the full functions of the trade mark to the preamble and defining the ambit of trade mark law.[37]

13.21 Suffice it to say that there is no single universally accepted function of a trade mark. Although the weight of opinion tends, or at least has historically tended, towards the origin function the Court of Justice has clearly chosen to embrace the wider functions. The matter is, however, of vital importance. It not only shapes what can be registered as a trade mark, but also helps to determine the scope of protec-tion granted to the trade mark owner. It is an area of the law which is still taking shape and where the boundaries have, and will continue, to develop over time.

---

[34] [2006] ETMR 677 per Lewison J at para 7.   [35] Case C-323/09.
[36] February 2011, available at ec.europa.eu/internal_market/indprop/docs/tm/20110308_allensbach-study_en.pdf.
[37] Max Planck Institute, note 36, 103–105.

Exercise

Go into a supermarket and browse the goods on the shelves. Look at the trade marks on those products. What impressions do you get? Imagine then a supermarket full of products between which there is no differentiation. The shape of the goods and their packaging are alike. How do you make your choices?

Key points on functions of a trade mark

A trade mark is said to have the following functions:

- A badge of origin
- An indication of quality
- A means of advertising
- An investment vehicle

The latter three are sometimes referred to as the 'communicative' functions

13.22 The following chapters will examine trade marks in detail. At this juncture it is useful to note the following points:

- Registered trade marks only have a function when they are actually used in the consumer society in conjunction with particular goods or services. They do not have a life of their own. This is reflected in the fact that a registered trade mark may be expunged in whole or in part[38] from the register if it has not been used for a period of five years.[39] However, a trade mark can be assigned separately from the goodwill of the business[40] to which it refers. It is also described as personal property (in Scotland, incorporeal property).[41]

- Marks have to be registered in a particular class of the trade mark register in connection with specified goods and services for which the mark is, or will be, used. The trade mark register contains 45 classes altogether covering a diverse range of goods and services.[42] As examples, class 1 encompasses, inter alia, chemicals used in industry, science, and photography. Class 18 encompasses leather and imitations of leather, and goods made of these materials including umbrellas and parasols. Class 38 encompasses telecommunications.[43]

- The classification[44] is based on the Nice International Arrangement on the International Classification of Goods and Services,[45] an international agreement administered by World Intellectual Property

[38] TMA 1994, s 46(1), (5). See paras 14.114ff.
[39] If a registered trade mark has not been put to genuine use in the UK within five years following the date of registration, or use of the trade mark has been suspended for a continuous period of five years, registration may be revoked: TMA 1994, s 46(1)(a), (b), (c). See paras 14.114ff.   [40] TMA 1994, s 24(1).
[41] TMA 1994, s 22. The European Court of Human Rights has held that trade marks and applications are possessions for the purposes of Article 1 of Protocol 1 ECHR: *Anheuser-Busch v Portugal* (App No 73049/01). See para 13.8.
[42] The number of classes was increased from 42 to 45 on 1 January 2002: Trade Marks (Amendment) Rules 2001 (SI 2001/2832).
[43] Identification of goods and services under the Directive and the CTMR have to be clear and precise. Simply referring to a Nice classification may not be sufficient. Case C-307/10 *Chartered Institute of Patent Attorneys v Registrar of Trade Marks*. See para 14.27.
[44] TMA 1994, s 34.
[45] Full details of the classes can be found in the Trade Marks Rules 2000 as subsequently amended from time to time up to and including 2008. An unofficial consolidated version of the rules can be found on the IPO website.

Organization (WIPO). The significance of having the register divided into these classes is that an applicant will need to apply for separate registration for the mark in each category of goods or services that are relevant to the use of the mark,[46] and a separate fee is payable for each.[47]

> **Web link**
>
> You can find a copy of the Nice classification at **http://www.wipo.int/classifications/nice/en/classifications.html**.

> **Question**
>
> What Nice classes cover the following goods/services: legal advice, spades, wine, tractors, paper?

- A trader will gain protection for a trade mark in relation to the goods or services in which she deals, and for which the mark is registered. A similar mark registered in relation to a different class of goods by a different trader will not necessarily infringe the first if there is no *likelihood of confusion* between the two marks (see para 15.33 for a discussion on infringement). It follows that two or more traders can use identical marks in conjunction with similar or dissimilar goods and services, as long as the customer is not confused. For instance, the word 'Puffin' has been registered by United Biscuits (UK) Ltd, for use, among other things, in connection with coffee; tea; cocoa; sugar; rice; and tapioca all in class 30, *and* by Kalon Ltd (a company with no relationship with United Biscuits (UK) Ltd) in class 01 for adhesives, sealants, glue, bonding agents, and fillers. If, however, a consumer is likely to be confused as to the origin or the goods or services sold under a mark, then either the application for registration will be turned down, or it will be opposed by the proprietor of the first registered mark, or, if a second person uses that mark as an unregistered sign, then the proprietor of the registered mark can challenge that use.

- Extended protection is granted to marks which have a *reputation*. Infringement may occur where the use of a similar sign by a competitor, without due cause, takes unfair advantage of, or is detrimental to, the distinctive character or repute of the registered mark. This is so whether the sign is used in relation to the same or dissimilar goods or services. No consumer confusion is needed for infringement in these circumstances (for further discussion see paras 15.68ff).

Trade marks and other intellectual property rights

13.23   Trade marks find their justification in the consumer society. As discussed previously, the basic function of a trade mark is to denote the origin of particular goods or services and thus to reward the manufacturer who consistently produces goods of a particular quality using that mark. This stands in contrast with the justifications for the development of patents, copyright, and designs, each of which seeks to encourage creativity and/or innovation and to reward the creator. This in turn stimulates further creation. If a trader manages to build up a good reputation in a mark, then a reward will also come in the form of economic return as the mark may ultimately sell the products. However, it will only do so because the mark is indicating to the consumer the origin (and quality) of those goods.

---

[46] TMA 1994, s 32 deals with applications for registration. Section 34 deals with the classification of goods and marks.

[47] It is also possible to apply for registration for a series of marks: TMA 1994, s 41(1)(c). A series of trade marks is defined as 'a number of trade marks which resemble each other as to their material particulars and differ only as to matters of a non-distinctive character not substantially affecting the identity of the trade mark': s 41(2). See also Trade Marks (Fees) Rules 2008 (SI 2008/1958), r 28.

13.24 The nature of the monopoly granted by a registered trade mark also stands in contrast with the other intellectual property rights under discussion in this book. Patents give an absolute monopoly but for a limited period of time of 20 years.[48] Copyright gives a weaker monopoly, but for a longer period of up to 70 years after the death of the author.[49] Design right gives a monopoly of up to 25 years (registered designs).[50] Trade marks, by contrast, can give a monopoly for an unlimited period of time. Registration of a trade mark in the UK lasts for ten years from the date of registration.[51] Successive periods of registration thereafter for ten-year periods may be applied for with the result that, if timeously renewed, registration may be perpetual.[52] Bass plc registered the red triangle shown in Figure 13.3 on 1 January 1876.

Figure 13.3 Bass logo

It was the first mark to be registered in the UK trade mark register and is still a valid registered trade mark.

13.25 The Bass logo is registered in connection with pale ale (class 32). But the monopoly in that mark is limited in that registration does not prevent a competing trader from entering the market for beers. There are plenty of other examples of registered trade marks used in connection with beers. One example is Budweiser registered by Anheuser-Busch, Incorporated.[53] Neither does it prevent a competing trader from using a triangle in connection with other goods and services, such as that shown in Figure 13.4, which has been registered by the Society for Promoting Christian Knowledge for use in connection with, inter alia, computer programs in class 9, and printed matter in class 16.[54] Thus, a proprietor does not obtain a monopoly in the mark as such, nor in the goods and services to which it relates. The monopoly is limited to the use of the mark in connection with the same or similar goods and services for which it is registered.[55]

---

[48] For a discussion on patents, see Chapter 11. [49] For a discussion on copyright and duration of protection, see Chapter 3.
[50] For a discussion on design right, see Chapter 8. [51] TMA 1994, s 42(1).
[52] The date of registration for calculation of the period for renewal is the date of application for registration: TMA 1994, s 40(3).
[53] UK Trade Mark No 1125449. This is a rather unusual trade mark as the same word is registered by two different companies in respect of the same products—beer. This is because both companies have historically used the name, so neither has preference over the other. *Budweiser Trade Marks* [2000] RPC 906. The owners have engaged in extensive litigation as each tries to gain advantage over the other. See also UK Trade Mark No 1389680.
[54] UK Trade Mark No 2014176.
[55] This is subject to those circumstances in which the mark has a reputation. See paras 15.68ff for discussion.

Figure 13.4 Triangle

13.26   Finally, and in common with copyright, patents, and designs, the rights conferred by a mark registered in the UK register are territorial.[56] This in turn contrasts with the EU-wide rights attached to a Community mark discussed in paras 13.36–13.42.

The overlap of trade marks with other intellectual property rights

13.27   Although registered trade marks occupy a particular place within the intellectual property family, as with the other rights, there is potential for overlap between trade marks and the other areas. One such possibility is dealt with in the discussion of the Trade Marks Act 1994 (TMA 1994), section 3 in paras 14.80ff. In order to maintain the boundaries between the respective rights it is not possible to register a trade mark where the shape is necessary to give a technical result. If registration of such shapes were permitted, then trade mark law might give an extensive monopoly in an area which is regarded as the province of the law of patents. As will be understood from the discussion on this section however, the parameters are yet to be fully settled.[57] Another example is given by the Advocate General in *Dyson v Registrar of Trademarks*[58] which concerned an application to register a bagless cleaner (see para 14.9): 'in the present case, whilst Dyson may legitimately be rewarded for its research and innovation work and claim to enjoy exclusive rights to exploit its invention, I consider that such protection may be granted, in the case of a technological innovation, only through the grant of a patent and not through a trade mark.' The rationale was explained by the ECJ in *Lego Juris A/S v OHIM*[59] concerning the application to register the Lego brick as a trade mark: 'When the shape of a product merely incorporates the technical solution developed by the manufacturer of that product and patented by it, protection of that shape as a trade mark once the patent has expired would considerably and permanently reduce the opportunity for other undertakings to use that technical solution. In the system of intellectual property rights developed in the European Union, technical solutions are capable of protection only for a limited period, so that subsequently they may be freely used by all economic operators.'[60]

13.28   Registered trade marks can be used in tandem with other rights to protect different aspects of the same item. For example, the 'Work Mate' bench was protected by many patents when invented. Although patent protection has now expired, the words 'Work Mate' continue to be protected as a registered trade mark.[61] Thus, Black and Decker, the proprietors of the mark, are the only company able to market workbenches, vice benches, saw horses, and trestles, all made wholly or principally of wood, and tables, chairs, and stools, in connection with the mark 'Work Mate'.[62]

---

[56] TMA 1994, ss 9(1), 107, and 108. In *Beautimatic International Ltd v Mitchell International Pharmaceuticals Ltd* [1999] ETMR 912, [2000] FSR 267, Beautimatic International owned the registered trade mark 'Lexus'. Mitchell marketed skincare products also under the name Lexus, but which were only available outside the UK. The 1994 Act, s 10(1) was therefore not infringed as use was not 'in the UK' as required by s 9(1).

[57] For a discussion on the interaction between registered trade marks and the law of passing off, see *Inter Lotto (UK) Ltd v Camelot Group plc* [2004] RPC 9, [2003] EWCA Civ 1132.

[58] [2007] ETMR 34.   [59] Case C-48/09.   [60] Case C-48/09, para 46.   [61] UK Trade Mark No 938753.

[62] Note also the previous discussion at para 13.17 on the ways in which elements that may make up a brand can be protected—but not the brand as such.

Question

The area of registered trade marks has attracted more case law at European level than any other intellectual property right. Why do you think this is so? Note your views and return to them once you have finished this Part on registered trade marks to see if your reasoning has changed.

Key points on trade marks and other intellectual property rights

- Trade marks find their justification in the consumer society
- If renewed, a trade mark can last forever. This stands in contrast with other intellectual property rights which have limited duration

The regulatory framework

13.29   The purpose of this section is to discuss the regulatory framework in depth to provide a foundation for discussion in the ensuing chapters on substantive trade mark law. In particular, it is to enable the reader to appreciate how domestic law and procedure are shaped by both European Union and international requirements.

Institutions and measures for which they are responsible

National

UK Trade Marks Act 1994

implements Trade Mark Directive and obligations from international treaties (eg section 56 from the Paris Convention)

European

Community Trade Mark Regulation	**Trade Marks Directive**
Creation of supra national Community trade mark	Framework for protection of trade marks in member states

International

WTO	WIPO
TRIPS	**Paris Convention**
Substantive minimum standards	Substantive minimum standards
Makes reference to Paris	National treatment
National treatment	**Madrid Agreement**
Most favoured nation clause	Streamlined application process
	NB central attack

Madrid Protocol

Streamlined application process

Conversion to national applications

Trade Mark Law Treaty

Procedural rules

Singapore Treaty

Procedural rules

Nice classification

The regulatory framework: domestic and European

UK trade marks

13.30   The current legislation in the UK governing registered trade marks is contained in the TMA 1994. The TMA 1994 was introduced as a result of the EC Council Directive 89/104/EEC of 21 December 1988 to approximate the laws of the Member States relating to Trade Marks which was in turn codified as Directive 2008/95/EC of the European Parliament and of the Council of 22 October 2008 to approximate the laws of the Member States relating to trade marks.[63] The TMA 1994 repealed the earlier legislation relating to trade marks contained in the Trade Marks Act 1938[64] (the 1938 Act). The 1994 Act came into force on 31 October 1994,[65] and governs those trade marks registered in the UK Register with the UK Intellectual Property Office (IPO; or UK–IPO) in Newport, Gwent.

> **Web link**
>
> The IPO has a website at **http://www.ipo.gov.uk.**

It has a section that is devoted entirely to trade marks, giving both general information on trade marks as well as access to a database containing details of registered marks, pending applications for registration, and information on applications which have been refused.

> **Exercise**
>
> To familiarise yourself with the site and in particular the trade mark database, go to the IPO site and carry out a number of searches in the trade mark register. Can you find the Bass logo mentioned previously?
>
> You will also notice that the trade mark section of the website contains details of primary and secondary legislation affecting registered trade marks in the UK.

> **Question**
>
> What is the latest statutory instrument to have amended the TMA 1994?

---

[63] 89/104/EEC, [1989] OJ L40/1.

[64] As amended by, inter alia, the Trade Marks (Amendment) Act 1984, the Patents, Designs and Marks Act 1986, the Copyright, Designs and Patents Act 1988, and the Copyright, etc and Trade Marks (Offences and Enforcement) Act 2002.

[65] Trade Marks Act 1994 (Commencement) Order 1994 (SI 1994/2550) bringing the 1994 Act into force.

Place of application and procedure: UK

13.31 A UK trade mark has effect within the territory of the UK.[66] To apply for a UK registered trade mark, application is made to the office in Newport in Gwent (the application forms can be found on the IPO website). The application must include a request for registration, the name and address of the applicant, a statement of the goods or services in relation to which it is sought to register the mark, a representation of the trade mark,[67] and the fee, which is currently £200 for one class of goods or services and £50 for every additional class. The applicant must also include a statement that the trade mark is being used or that the applicant has a bona fide intention to use it.[68] The date of filing is the date on which all the relevant information is given to the Registrar.[69] The filling date is the one on which matters of priority under the Paris Convention may be settled[70] and those of seniority from prior use (for matters of priority and seniority see para 13.61).

13.32 When filed, the examiners at the registry examine the application on absolute grounds[71] to see if it is registerable. Absolute in this context means that the examiners examine the mark to see whether it meets the criteria for registration set out in section 3 of the TMA 1994, including whether it meets the definition of a trade mark,[72] whether it is devoid of distinctive character,[73] or has become a word commonly used in the trade.[74] Previously marks were also examined on relative grounds, which meant that the examiners looked to other marks already on the register to see if the mark should be refused registration. For instance, if there was an earlier trade mark which was identical with[75] or similar to[76] the sign, the application for registration would be refused. This was changed in 2006 after a review by the IPO in which the office noted that the Office for the Harmonisation in the Internal Market (OHIM) (the office responsible for registering Community trade marks—see paras 13.39–13.42) only undertook examinations on absolute grounds for a Community trade mark (CTM). The procedure had resulted in an anomalous situation in that it was proving easier to register a mark as a CTM than it was as a UK mark via the IPO. Because OHIM only examined on absolute grounds, it was up to the trade mark owner with an earlier right to oppose an application for registration of a confusingly similar mark. The IPO concluded that the chance of a UK applicant obtaining a national registration had decreased because of the number of earlier CTMs and that national applications were increasingly likely to fail due to the presence of earlier CTMs which had themselves not been examined on relative grounds. Hence, the change to a formal examination on absolute grounds only. However, the examiners still monitor their records on relative grounds, and then inform both the applicant and the owner of the earlier right of potential conflicts. It is now up to the owner of the conflicting right to oppose the application on relative grounds.[77] Once the application has been accepted it is published in the Trade Marks Journal.[78]

Web link

You can access the Trade Marks Journal online at the IPO website at **http://www.ipo.gov.uk/tm/t-journal/t-tmj.htm.**

[66] TMA 1994, s 108: the Act extends to England and Wales, Scotland, and Northern Ireland and to the Isle of Man.
[67] TMA 1994, s 32(2). [68] TMA 1994, s 32(3). [69] TMA 1994, s 33(1). [70] TMA 1994, s 35.
[71] This has been the practice since October 2007. See PAN 1/08 for using the Internet for searches.
[72] TMA 1994, s 3(1)(a). [73] TMA 1994, s 3(1)(b). [74] TMA 1994, s 3(1)(d). [75] TMA 1994, s 5(1).
[76] TMA 1994, s 5(2). Note that on application the grounds for a refusal under the Trade Mark Directive should not be ignored. See Joined Cases C-39/08 Bild.T-Online.de AG & Co KG v President of the German Patent-und Markenamt and C-43/08 ZVS Zeitungsvertrieb Stuttgart GmbH v President of the German Patent-und Markenamt.
[77] The legislative and administrative changes were implemented on 1 October 2007. See Practice Amendment Notice 8/07, available at http://www.ipo.gov.uk/pro-types/pro-tm/t-law/t-pan/t-pan-807.htm.
[78] TMA 1994, s 38.

Thereafter there is a three-month period during which third parties can submit observations on the application or oppose the application. If the parties do not settle any disagreement on the application there may be a hearing and determination of registerability by the Registrar.

13.33   An appeal lies from a decision of the Registrar either to an 'appointed person' or to the court.[79] If an appeal is made to an appointed person, the appointed person may refer the matter to the court if it appears that a matter of general legal importance is involved, or if the Registrar requests referral, or if such a request is made by any party to the proceedings.[80] If the appointed person hears the appeal, his decision is final.[81] If there is no effective opposition the trade mark will be registered[82] and the registration published in the Trade Marks Journal. The date of registration is the date of filing of the application[83] and is the date from which the rights of the owner are enforceable against third parties (although no enforcement action may be taken until such time as the trade mark is registered)[84] as well as the date from which the term of the trade mark is calculated.

13.34   The IPO website contains a 'Trade Marks Work Manual' giving full details of the application procedure and the forms necessary to make an application, oppose an application, appeal a decision, and other formal and administrative steps in the registration procedure. The IPO regularly issues Practice Notices which give details of changes in procedures amending existing practices as case law develops.

13.35   The website also contains statistics on trade mark applications and registrations. In 2010 26,793 applications were filed and 23,646 were registered. In 2011 this rose to 30,642 applications filed and 25,001 registered.[85]

 Question

Can you find the most recent Practice Direction? What does it concern and what prompted its promulgation?

Community Trade Marks

13.36   Not only is it possible to obtain a trade mark covering the UK, but since 1994 it has been open to traders to register a CTM, normally effective throughout the territory of member states of the EU. This was established in Council Regulation EC No 40/94 of 20 December 1993 on the Community trade mark[86] establishing the Community Trade Mark Office situated in Alicante, Spain. This came into force on 15 March 1994. The Regulation (CTMR) which governs the registration and enforcement of CTMs has been codified and can now be found as Council Regulation (EC) No 207/2009 of 26 February 2009 on the Community trade mark. The codification has entailed some changes in numbering of Articles. The codified numbering is referred to in the text and footnotes in this book but the numbering in case law is as in the original case.

Web link

The database containing applications for and information on registered Community trade marks can be found at the Alicante website at **http://oami.europa.eu/**.

---

[79] TMA 1994, s 76(2). The 'appointed person' is appointed by the Lord Chancellor after consultation with the Lord Advocate.
[80] TMA 1994, s 76(3).   [81] TMA 1994, s 76(4).   [82] TMA 1994, s 40.
[83] TMA 1994, s 40(3).   [84] TMA 1994, s 9(3).   [85] 2010/11 Annual Report.   [86] [1994] OJ L11/1.

Exercise

Familiarise yourself with the site by searching the database. Try searching for trade marks with the word 'Apple'. See what you come up with. Note that the site also contains much useful information concerning decisions made in relation to CTMs. Look under 'Case Law' and you will see that you can access decisions of the Boards of Appeal, of the General Court (formerly the Court of First Instance), and of the Court of Justice (formerly the ECJ).

Question

You were given details of the first mark to be registered in the UK trade mark register in Figure 13.3. Find the first mark that was registered as a CTM.

The main features of the Community trade mark system

13.37   By contrast with a national trade mark, a CTM is effective throughout the member states of the EU. It was the first example of a supranational EU trade mark right. Whereas prior to the introduction of the CTM, a trader who wished to have a trade mark registration in each of the member states of the EU would have had to apply to each trade mark office in each state. Now, only one application needs to be made to the office in Alicante and the one mark is effective in all member states.

13.38   It has been stated in the previous paragraph that a CTM has effect throughout all the member states within the EU.[87] However, there are circumstances in which that will not be the case, called by some the 'Emmental cheese' provisions because a hole may subsist in the unitary character of the CTM.[88] These 'holes' arise because Articles 110 and 111 of the CTMR preserve the right to invoke national or Union law to prevent the use of a later CTM in one or more member states. Annand and Norman give a number of examples of how these provisions may work in practice. Two of these are as follows:[89]

> A is the owner of a trade mark registered in France. A can oppose or apply to cancel a later conflicting CTM. Alternatively [and this is where the 'Emmental cheese' provisions arise] A can object to the use of the CTM in France by bringing an infringement action under French law before a French court.

> B is the owner of an unregistered trade mark in the United Kingdom. B can oppose or apply to cancel a later conflicting CTM. Alternatively B can bring an action in passing-off before a United Kingdom court to prevent use in the United Kingdom.

As can be seen from these examples, because the owner of the earlier right (ie the one that subsists before the application for a CTM) chooses *not* to oppose the registration of the CTM, nor to apply for its cancellation, but instead to challenge the use of the CTM within the member state in question, the CTM is valid throughout the member states *except* in the one (or ones) where the earlier right subsists. Thus, the CTM is like a piece of cheese with a hole (or holes) in it.

Place of application and procedure

13.39   This is called the Office for Harmonisation in the Internal Market (Trade Marks and Designs) or OHIM for short. This office is responsible for the registration procedures for the CTM. It maintains the public

---

[87] The unitary character of the CTM in relation to the grant of an EU-wide injunction was discussed in Case C-235/09 *Chronopost v DHL*.
[88] RE Annand and HE Norman, *Blackstone's Guide to the Community Trade Mark* (1998), 128.
[89] Annand and Norman, note 88.

registers relating to the rights and rules on applications for declaration of invalidity of the rights after registration. The CTM process is available to nationals of the EU countries, countries that are parties to the Paris Convention, and other countries granting reciprocal rights. A CTM applicant is not required to have a commercial establishment in the EU. Examiners in OHIM make decisions relating to conditions of filing of a CTM,[90] decisions on absolute grounds for refusal,[91] and refusal of a Community collective mark,[92] opposition decisions,[93] and decisions to revoke or declare invalid CTMs.[94] An appeal lies from any one of these decisions to the OHIM Boards of Appeal or in certain circumstances the Grand Board of Appeals.[95] Thereafter further appeal on specified grounds lies to the General Court.[96]

13.40   When an application has been examined, if accepted it is published in the Community Trade Marks Bulletin.[97] During a period of three months thereafter, third parties may make observations on, or oppose, the application on relative grounds. If the application is rejected it may be converted to national applications retaining the OHIM filing date[98] (but not in those member states to which the ground of refusal relates). Where there is no opposition the mark will be registered[99] using the filing date as the effective date.

13.41   The matter of enforcement of a CTM is left to national law, subject to the applicable law being that of the CTMR.[100] Each member state has designated first and second instance national courts to deal with matters of litigation concerning the enforcement of the CTM. In the UK, the High Court is the court of first instance in England, Wales, and Northern Ireland, and the Court of Session is the CTM court for Scotland.[101]

Web link

The OHIM website contains a list of cases concerning the CTM which have been heard by national courts. The first, in a British court, was delivered in 1999. To mid-2012 just under 600 cases had been disposed of in 14 different countries. For a (non-exhaustive) list have a look at **http://oami. europa.eu/ows/rw/pages/CTM/caseLaw/judgementsCTMCourtsList.en.do.**

 Question

What was the first case shown in the archive to have been heard in the English High Court? What was it about?

---

[90] CTMR, Art 36.

[91] CTMR, Art 37. Case T-317/05 *Kustom Musical Amplification, Inc v OHIM*. OHIM must inform an applicant at every stage of the process of the grounds which affect their rights and give an opportunity to present a case in reply. This obligation is not fulfilled by the mere provision of Internet links to documentation without also supplying hard copies.

[92] CTMR, Art 68.   [93] CTMR, Arts 41–43.   [94] CTMR, Arts 51–57.

[95] CTMR, Art 58. See also Council Regulation (EC) No 422/2004 of 19 February 2004 amending Regulation (EC) No 40/94 on the Community Trade Mark; Commission Regulation (EC) No 2082/2004 of 6 December 2004 amending Regulation (EC) No 216/96 laying down the rules of procedure of the Boards of Appeal of the Office for Harmonisation in the Internal Market. On the boundaries of functions between Union and domestic level, see the CFI in Case T-134/06 *Xentral LLC v OHIM* (CTMR, Art 8(1)(b); Pagesjaune. com).

[96] CTMR, Art 65.   [97] CTMR, Art 39.   [98] CTMR, Art 112.

[99] CTMR, Art 45.   [100] CTMR, Arts 14 and 101.

[101] Community Trade Mark Regulations 2006 (SI 2006/1027). Jurisdiction of these courts: CTMR, Art 96. All infringement and threatened infringement actions relating to CTMs; actions for declarations of non-infringement; claims for damages brought under CTMR, Art 9(3); counterclaims for revocation or for a declaration of invalidity of a CTM. Any other dispute relating to a CTM is heard by a national court under the terms of CTMR, Art 106.

13.42   When an application is made for a CTM, a search is carried out by the Alicante office, as with the amended practice in the UK, on absolute grounds only. The application is forwarded to national registries (including that in the UK) for searches to be carried out in those databases. If any proprietor of an existing mark wishes to oppose the registration, then it is up to them to do this, although a copy of the application is sent to those parties who may be interested.[102]

Question

Why might a trader want to have a single registration effective throughout the Community?

The advantages of the CTM over a portfolio of national marks

13.43   Procedural simplification:

- applying for a CTM greatly simplifies the procedure for trade mark owners. Only one application need be made in one language and one set of fees paid, resulting in a CTM, effective throughout the European Union;
- having a single CTM makes it much easier for trade mark owners to manage their portfolio of registered trade marks.

13.44   Single market benefits:

- Having trade marks registered in different member states by the same trader can cause problems for the internal market. Where a trade mark owner chooses different trade marks for different member states, it has the potential effect of partitioning the single market along territorial boundaries. A trade mark owner could maintain national registrations for the same mark in several member states with a view to keeping out parallel imports placed on the market by the trade mark owner or with his consent in another member state of the Union.

13.45   Over the years the problems have been dealt with in a number of ways, including the development by the Court of Justice of a distinction between the *existence* of a registered trade mark right and its *exercise*. One of the results has been that the rule has developed that once goods have been placed on the market in the EU by the trader or with the consent of the trader, the rights arising from that mark may not be used to prohibit the further movement of those goods around the Union. Another mechanism, and one of the most potent ways of overcoming the potential for fragmentation of the single European market along national territories resulting from enforcement of national trade mark rights, was to create a single registered trade mark effective throughout the Union: hence the CTM. For a discussion on the free movement of goods, see Chapter 20.

Question

Why might a trader not want a CTM but prefer instead to maintain national registrations?

---

[102] The OHIM guidelines are updated as new law and practices emerge.

13.46   The CTM is becoming increasingly important, as more and more applications for registration are made. Over 43,000 applications were filed in 1996. While there were dips in 1997, 1998, and 2008, the numbers are generally increasing. There were over 105,857 applications in 2011.[103]

The regulatory framework: international

13.47   Both WIPO and the World Trade Organization (WTO) administer international treaties pertaining to trade marks.

WIPO: Paris Convention for the Protection of Industrial Property 1883 (Paris Convention)

13.48   The Paris Convention is one of the oldest international intellectual property treaties. It deals not only with registered trade marks, but also affects, inter alia, unregistered marks, patents, and registered designs. It currently has 174 signatories.[104] The Convention is not directly effective in many countries: rather, those states which have signed the Treaty amend domestic laws to reflect the obligations imposed under the Treaty.[105] The basis of the Paris Convention is that of national treatment.[106] This means that contracting states are required to treat nationals (whether companies or individuals) of foreign contracting states as they would their own nationals. Thus, nationals of states which have signed the Convention must be able to register trade marks in the UK register and have the benefit of the law relating to those marks applied in the same way that it does to UK nationals.[107] Article 6 of the Convention provides that the conditions for filing and registration of a mark in a Convention country is to be determined according to domestic laws, but that any application in a Convention country may not be refused or registration annulled on the ground that filing, registration, or renewal of the mark has not been effective in the country of origin.

13.49   The Paris Convention provides for a system of *priority*.[108] This means that those nationals who have registered their marks in their own contracting states have a period during which they may file an application in other contracting states, and gain priority for that filing over and above other pending applications from unconnected third parties. This may be important for those entities which are attempting to protect trade marks in a number of different countries: it ensures that they may do so ahead of other pre-emptive applications. The Paris Convention *does not* provide for a central mechanism for filing trade marks. Nor does it give protection extending beyond the territory in which it is registered.

13.50   One important provision in the Paris Convention deals with unregistered marks[109] (rather than registered marks). This imposes an obligation on contracting states to protect well-known marks *even* where they have not been registered. The purpose is to protect those proprietors of well-known marks who have not commenced using their marks in a particular signatory state from activities of third parties who

---

[103] OHIM Annual report available at http://oami.europa.eu/ows/rw/pages/OHIM/OHIMPublications/annualReport.en.do. See also the statistics for national registrations in para 13.35. Case C-196/11 P *Formula One Licensing BV v OHIM*. The CTM does not replace national trade marks in member states and neither OHIM nor the General Court can rule on the registration or validity of a national mark.

[104] As of 2012.

[105] Case C-238/06 P *Develey Holding GmbH & Co Beteiligungs KG v OHIM* [2008] ETMR 20. The provisions of the Paris Convention could not be relied on directly (para 40), 'while the direct effect of the Paris Convention could flow from the cross-reference made to it by Article 2(1) of the TRIPs Agreement, such a cross-reference cannot, in the absence of the direct applicability of the TRIPs Agreement, render the Paris Convention directly applicable' (para 43).

[106] Paris Convention, Art 2.

[107] National treatment extends also to companies and individuals who are not nationals of a contracting state, but who are domiciled or have a real and effective industrial and commercial establishment in the territory of one of the countries of the Union: Art 3.

[108] Paris Convention, Art 4.   [109] Paris Convention, Art *6bis*.

might attempt a pre-emptive registration. In determining whether a mark is a well-known mark within the meaning of the Paris Convention, 'the competent authority can take into account any circumstances from which it may be inferred that the mark is well known'.[110] The Court of First Instance considered some of the requirements in *El Corte Inglés v OHIM—Abril Sánchez and Ricote Saugar (BoomerangTV)*[111] and referred to Article 2 of the Joint Recommendation concerning the provisions on the protection of well-known trade marks, adopted by the Assembly of the Paris Union and the General Assembly of WIPO at the 34th series of meetings of assemblies of the member states of the WIPO (20 to 29 September 1999).

> In determining whether a mark is a well known mark within the meaning of the Paris Convention, the competent authority can take into account any circumstances from which it may be inferred that the mark is well known, including: the degree of knowledge or recognition of the mark in the relevant sector of the public; the duration, extent and geographical area of any use of the mark; the duration, extent and geographical area of any promotion of the mark, including advertising or publicity and the presentation, at fairs or exhibitions, of the goods and/or services to which the mark applies; the duration and geographical area of any registrations, and/or any applications for registration, of the mark, to the extent to which they reflect use or recognition of the mark; the record of successful enforcement of rights in the mark, in particular, the extent to which the mark has been recognised as well known by competent authorities; the value associated with the mark.

In the instant case, limited evidence of the use of a mark (a figurative mark including the word 'boomerang') in catalogues and a photograph of balloons was insufficient to prove that the marks were well known or even recognised in Ireland, Greece, and/or the UK.

13.51   This section has been implemented in the UK in section 56(2) of the TMA 1994.[112] It was considered by Justice Arnold in the High Court in the following case.

■ *Hotel Cipriani SRL & others v Cipriani (Grosvenor Street) Ltd and others* [2008] EWHC 3032 (Ch) (affirmed on appeal)[113]

In this case Justice Arnold drew heavily on his earlier decision in *Le Man Autoparts Ltd Trade Mark Application* (0/012/05) where he sat as Appointed Person and in which extensive reference was made to *General Motors*. Reference was also made to the 1999 Joint Recommendation of WIPO. Applying these sources the judge came to the conclusion that the mark Cipriani was a well-known trade mark for hotel and restaurant services among that sector of the public.

13.52   The Paris Convention also requires Convention countries to prevent the use and registration of 'armorial bearings, flags and emblems' of the countries of the Convention,[114] to provide effective protection against unfair competition,[115] and to accept for registration any trade mark which has been duly registered in its country of origin.[116]

---

[110] *El Corte Inglés SA v OHIM* [2008] ETMR 71, para 80.

[111] Case T-420/03. The CFI was considering CTMR, Art 8(1)(a) and (b) and Art 8(5) of Regulation No 40/94.

[112] This section provides protection for proprietors of well-known trade marks which are already protected under the Paris Convention where it is proposed to use an identical or similar mark in relation to identical or similar goods where the use is likely to cause confusion. TRIPS, Art 16(2) provides that in assessing whether a mark is well known, account should be taken of the knowledge of the trade mark in the relevant sector of the public, including knowledge in the member country which had been obtained as a result of the promotion of the trade mark: TMA 1994, s 56. Section 56 provides protection to well-known unregistered marks even if there has been no trade in the UK.

[113] [2010] EWCA Civ 110, [2010] Bus LR 1465, [2010] RPC 16.

[114] Paris Convention, Art 6*ter*. This provision was recently considered in depth in Joined Cases C-202/08 P and C-208/08 P *American Clothing Associates SA v OHIM* (2009), in which the Court confirmed that there is a broad protection for state emblems. See para 14.100.

[115] Paris Convention, Art 10*bis*. It is debatable the extent to which the UK has fulfilled its obligations under this Article.

[116] Paris Convention, Art 6*quinquies*.

Exercise

Read the Paris Convention. Clarify in your own mind how the system of national treatment works.

WIPO: The Madrid Agreement and Protocol

13.53   The Madrid Agreement for the International Registration of Marks (1891) and the Madrid Protocol of 1989 are both administered by WIPO. In contrast with the Paris Convention, the Madrid Agreement and Protocol provide for a simplified mechanism for filing trade mark applications. However, and in common with the Paris Convention and by contrast with the CTM, no provision is made for a supranational right or a single application effective throughout a number of states.

- **Madrid Agreement:** the applicant must first file for or obtain a registration in the home state. Once this is done, an application may be made to WIPO for an international registration. It should, however, be noted that this is *not* an international trade mark. Rather, the application is sent to those contracting states specified in the application to WIPO. Each state specified is then responsible for individual registrations as if it had been filed directly in that country. Importantly for traders, and in common with the Paris Convention, making the home application first gives a period of *priority* as regards the applications made in the other contracting states.

- **Madrid Protocol:** the UK is a party to the Madrid Protocol 1989 (but not the Madrid Agreement). Application for registration of a mark must be made in one of the countries which have signed up to the Madrid Protocol[117] and be based on a pre-existing application or registration filed in that office. The application for international registration under the Madrid Protocol must then be made through the national office, and not directly to WIPO.[118] Once the national office has satisfied itself that the application conforms with the existing application or registration, it is forwarded to WIPO which will examine the application to confirm that it conforms to the requirements of the Protocol. When satisfied, the application is placed on the International Register of Trade Marks and details are passed to those countries named in the application. The application is then dealt with in each of the designated countries as if it had been made directly to that national office.[119] Any refusal of registration can only be based on grounds to be found in the Paris Convention.[120] If an application is made through this route and is successful, registration lasts for ten years[121] and can be renewed for further periods of ten years.[122] If a trader has registered a national trade mark, and later makes that mark the subject of an international registration under the Madrid Protocol, then the international registration replaces the national registration.[123]

- In 2004 the EC acceded to the Madrid Protocol. As a result, a CTM application or a registered CTM can be used as the basic mark for an international application and the EU can be designated in an international application via the Madrid Protocol.[124]

One of the problems with the Madrid Agreement, and why that Treaty attracted relatively few signatories, was because of the system known as '*central attack*'.[125] This means that if the home application for a trade mark is lost within five years from the date of international registration, perhaps through the national authority refusing the application, through a declaration of invalidity, or non-use for the requisite period, then all the other registrations are lost. This is not the case under the Madrid Protocol. In the

---

[117] Madrid Protocol, Art 2(1).   [118] Madrid Protocol, Art 2(2).   [119] Madrid Protocol, Art 4.
[120] Madrid Protocol, Art 5(1).   [121] Madrid Protocol, Art 6(1).   [122] Madrid Protocol, Art 7(1).
[123] Madrid Protocol, Art *4bis*.
[124] For an indication as to how the systems operate in practice, see http://oami.europa.eu/ows/rw/pages/CTM/FAQ/CTM12.en.do.
[125] Madrid Agreement, Arts 6–7(1).

event of the first registration being invalid, then the other registrations/applications may be turned into national or regional (ie CTM) applications,[126] which then stand independent of the original registration.

Exercise

Read both the Madrid Agreement and the Madrid Protocol.

Question

How many signatories are there to each? Can you find any examples of applications made under the Madrid Protocol in the UK or CTM register? How do you know which system the application has been made under?

WIPO: The Trade Mark Law Treaty

13.54   The Trade Mark Law Treaty (TLT) was signed in Geneva on 28 October 1994. The scope of this Treaty is much more limited that the other treaties discussed previously. The purpose of the TLT is to harmonise certain formalities in relation to the form and content of an application for registration and standardise the term of protection at ten-year renewable intervals. Article 1 of the TLT provides that its provisions apply to marks consisting of 'visible signs', and three-dimensional marks where contracting parties accept those for registration. The TLT does not apply to hologram marks, those 'not consisting of visible signs', for instance sound and olfactory marks, or collective, certification, and guarantee marks. The TLT goes on to make provisions for the form and content of the application (Art 3), the filing date (Art 5), and other procedural formalities such as changing a name and address (Art 10) and correcting mistakes (Art 12).

The Treaty had 53 contracting states as of November 2012.

WIPO: Singapore Treaty on the Law of Trademarks

13.55   The purpose of the Singapore Treaty on the Law of Trademarks 2006 is to update the TLT. Not long after the adoption of the TLT it became apparent that it needed to be revised largely as a result of the 'dot. com' revolution, the introduction of email, and Internet-based communications. For instance, the TLT contains provisions obliging states to accept communications in paper form. The Singapore Treaty also broadens the scope of the TLT which only covered visible marks. The Singapore Treaty encompasses any mark that a contracting party may offer. So, for example, if a contracting party protects sound marks, the provisions of the Singapore Treaty apply, but if a contracting party does not allow for sound marks, that party has no obligation to provide for them.

13.56   The Singapore Treaty is separate from the TLT. The Treaties can be joined either together or individually. Article 27 of the Singapore Treaty governs the relationship between the two and provides that, between parties that are signatories to both Treaties, the Singapore Treaty will govern. Unlike the TLT, the Singapore Treaty creates an 'Assembly of the Contracting Parties', which, among other powers, allows for modification of the treaty regulations and model forms used under the Treaty. The goal of this Assembly is to help to keep the Singapore Treaty up to date.

13.57   The Treaty was finalised in March 2006. It came into force in March 2009 and, as at November 2012, there were 29 contracting states.

---

[126] Madrid Protocol, Art *9quinquies*.

WIPO: Nice International Arrangement on the International Classification of Goods and Services

13.58   Note the comments on the Nice Agreement, a classification Treaty, in para 13.22.

WTO: Agreement on Trade-Related Aspects of Intellectual Property Rights including Trade in Counterfeited Goods (TRIPS)

13.59   The TRIPS Agreement resulted from the Uruguay Round of the General Agreement on Tariffs and Trade (GATT) discussions held under the auspices of the WTO. The Agreement, which is administered by the WTO, was passed in 1994. There are a number of points to note:[127]

- TRIPS does not provide either for its own mechanism for registration of marks, or for a mark to be registered in more than one territory (cf the CTM). TRIPS does provide for certain minimum standards in relation to trade marks (and other intellectual property rights) which must be incorporated into national laws of contracting states. For instance, contracting states must apply the Paris Convention standards relating to trade marks;[128] TRIPS also adopts a broad definition of a sign which is capable of being registered as a trade mark; requires trade mark registration to extend to marks for services;[129] and defines the rights conferred by a registered mark.[130]

- As with other international conventions, the principle of national treatment is incorporated into the TRIPS Agreement.[131]

- Unlike other international conventions and treaties, TRIPS includes a most favoured nation clause.[132] This broadly means that if any contracting state gives to any other contracting state preferential treatment, then that concession must also be given to all other contracting states.

- If a state fails to adhere to its obligations under any of the agreements administered by WIPO, then another state may bring a reference to the International Court of Justice. No such intellectual property reference has been made. By contrast, under TRIPS, failure by a state to adhere to its obligations may lead to GATT dispute settlement procedure and ultimately to sanctions withdrawing GATT privileges to that state. (For details of the enforcement procedure see paras 22.160–22.171.)

 Exercise

Read the TRIPS Agreement and, in relation to trade marks, list five key points of similarity and/or difference between the provisions found in that agreement as compared with the CTMR and the UK TMA 1994.

The interaction between the systems concerning registration

13.60   As can be seen from the previous discussion, there are a number of instruments that concern or affect the *registration* of trade marks. This has resulted in the construction of a complex framework where an application for registration of a mark in a particular trade mark register may be affected by a pending or registered mark in one of the other registers or by a claim to seniority arising from an earlier right. Full details on the registration processes and how to apply via the various routes are given in documentation available on each of the relevant websites. Each organisation maintains full and comprehensive practice

---

[127] See also the discussion in Chapter 1.   [128] TRIPS, Art 2(1).   [129] TRIPS, Art 15.
[130] TRIPS, Art 16(1).   [131] TRIPS, Art 2.   [132] TRIPS, Art 3.

manuals describing the procedures to be followed for registration. These are updated regularly to take account of the law as it develops through court decisions. It is, however, useful to be aware of the terminology that is used to manage the potentially competing claims of traders as these are often referred to in court cases.

Priority and seniority

13.61   *Priority* refers to the status a mark has on application for registration in relation to the registration systems and the Paris Convention.[133] Broadly, if a mark has already been registered or registration is applied for under one of the systems, then that mark will have priority over applications by other proprietors to register the same or similar marks in national registries or as a CTM for a period of six months from the date of the original filing of the application for registration.[134] *Seniority*, by contrast, allows a proprietor to claim the seniority of earlier national registrations in member states of the same mark when applying for a CTM.[135] The effect of a successful claim of seniority is that the trade mark proprietor can let the national registration lapse while at the same time have the same rights as if the national trade mark had continued to be registered.[136] The purpose is to permit trade mark owners to centralise ownership of trade marks in member states in a single mark (the CTM) without jeopardising rights accrued under individual trade marks.

13.62   These provisions have been incorporated into the TMA 1994 through the use of the terms 'earlier trade mark' and 'earlier right'.[137] An earlier trade mark[138] includes an existing registered trade mark (ie one that is on the UK register whether by virtue of the 1938 or 1994 Act), an international trade mark (UK) (one for which registration is applied for under the Madrid Protocol), or a CTM. All of these earlier trade marks need a date of application for registration earlier than that for the mark under consideration, taking into account any priorities[139] or the seniority of a CTM.[140] A person who is entitled to prevent the use of a trade mark is referred to in the TMA 1994 as the proprietor of an earlier right in relation to the trade mark.[141]

 Exercise

Read the Article 4 of the Paris Convention, Articles 29–35 of the CTMR, and section 6 of the Trade Marks Act 1994.

Opposition

13.63   The effect of these rules is that not only are there are a number of routes an applicant for a trade mark might choose in order to acquire registration, but also there are a series of grounds on which the registration of a mark in the UK register or CTM may be *opposed* by the proprietor of an earlier right. Opposition

---

[133] Paris Convention, Art 4.
[134] Paris Convention, Art 4C. TMA 1994, s 6(1)(c) provides for a trade mark which at the date of application for registration, in questions of the priority claimed in respect of the application, was entitled to protection under the Paris Convention as a well-known trade mark. TMA 1994, s 6(2) sets out the priority for applicants to be able to claim rights to an earlier trade mark. TMA 1994, s 35(1) provides that 'A person who has duly filed an application for protection of a trade mark in a [Paris] Convention country … has a right to priority for the purposes of registering the same trade mark under this Act for some or all of the same goods or services'.
[135] CTMR, Art 34. TMA 1994, s 6(1)(b) provides that a CTM is an earlier mark which has a valid claim to seniority due to an earlier registered trade mark or international trade mark (UK).
[136] The claim must be for the same sign, the same goods and services, and the same proprietor as the CTM: CTMR, Art 34(1).
[137] See TMA 1994, ss 5–8. This means the date and not the time of filing if two applications are made on the same day, *STAIGER Trade Mark* [2004] RPC 33, 2003 WL 23508814.   [138] See generally TMA 1994, s 6.   [139] TMA 1994, s 6(1)(a).
[140] TMA 1994, s 6(1)(b).   [141] TMA 1994, s 5(4).

refers to the right of any person to oppose the registration of a trade mark,[142] and generally occurs once the application has been accepted and published by the Registrar.[143]

13.64   Opposition grounds may include the existence of a UK, international (UK), or CTM registration; an earlier national, international, or Community pending application; a Community trade mark with a later date of application but a valid claim of prior rights from a national or international registration (stemming from Article 34 of the CTMR); the existence of a well-known mark; an existing registered mark with a reputation;[144] the use of the mark which is likely to be prohibited by any rule of law, for example passing off; the existence of an earlier copyright, design right, or registered design right;[145] or there may be a Convention priority claim[146] deriving from the Paris Convention.

 Exercise

Draw a diagram highlighting the various registration routes that can be taken by a trader who wishes to have a registered trade mark effective in the UK.

Conclusion

13.65   The international, European, and domestic framework establishes a system in which the registration of trade marks can take place within an increasingly globalised trading structure and through which existing and pending rights of traders can be managed and balanced against the demands of competitors. The system is, however, complex and the choice of route to be taken to secure registration will depend on innumerable factors including the commercial aims of the trader, the costs of obtaining registration, and the time taken for registration.

Key points on regulatory framework

- Domestic (UK) law is contained in the TMA 1994 and is shaped by European and international obligations

- The CTMR which establishes the CTM creates a supranational trade mark right normally effective throughout the territories of the member states of the EU

- WIPO administers the Madrid Agreement and Protocol, which provide for a streamlined registration process for trade marks in different countries

- The Paris Convention (WIPO) and TRIPS (WTO) both contain substantive minimum obligations regarding trade marks

- The Trade Mark Law Treaty and the Singapore Treaty contain obligations relating to procedural matters for the registration of trade marks

---

[142] TMA 1994, s 38(2). Note that the right of opposition to the registration of a CTM is limited to certain specified persons: CTMR, Art 41(1).

[143] TMA 1994, s 38(1).   [144] TMA 1994, s 5(3).   [145] TMA 1994, s 5(4)(a), (b).   [146] TMA 1994, ss 35 and 60.

Further reading

Books

R Annand and H Norman, *Blackstone's Guide to the Community Trade Mark 1998* (1998)

R Annand and H Norman, *Blackstone's Guide to the Trade Marks Act 1994* (1994)

L Bently, J Davis, and J Ginsburg, *Trade Marks and Brands: An Interdisciplinary Critique* (2011)

GB Dinwoodie and MD Janis (eds), *Trademark Law and Theory: A Handbook of Contemporary Research* (2008)

A Firth, G Lee, and P Cranford, *Trade Marks: Law and Practice* (3rd edn, 2012)

A Griffiths, *An Economic Perspective on Trade Mark Law* (2011)

Kerly's Law of Trade Marks and Trade Names (15th edn, 2009)

Max Planck Institute for Intellectual Property and Competition Law, *Study on the Overall Functioning of the European Trade Mark System* (February 2011) available at ec.europa.eu/internal_market/indprop/docs/tm/20110308_allensbach-study_en.pdf

C Morcom, A Roughton, and S Malynicz, *The Modern Law of Trade Marks* (3rd edn, 2008)

J Phillips, *Trade Mark Law: A Practical Anatomy* (2003)

N Pires de Carvalho, *The TRIPS Regime of Trademarks and Designs* (2006)

J Roberts, *International Trade Mark Classification: A Guide to the Nice Agreement* (3rd edn, 2007)

Chapters

WR Cornish, 'Intellectual property: omnipresent, distracting, irrelevant?' in *Clarendon Law Lectures* (2004), 73–110

Articles

R Ashmead, 'International classification class headings: illustrative or exemplary? The scope of European Union registrations' (2007) 2(2) JIPLP 76–88

KD Beiter, 'The right to property and the protection of interests in intellectual property—a human rights perspective on the European Court of Human Rights' decision in *Anheuser-Busch v. Portugal*' (2008) 39 IIC 714

R Burrell and D Gangjee, 'Trade marks and freedom of expression—a call for caution' [2010] IIC 554

V Di Cataldo, 'The trade mark with a reputation in EU law—some remarks on the negative condition "without due cause"' (2011) 42(7) IIC 833–845

J Davis, 'European trade mark law and the enclosure of the commons' [2002] 4 IPQ 342–367

G Dinwoodie, 'Trademarks and territory: detaching trademark law from the nation-state' (2004) 41 Houston Law Review 885

G Dinwoodie, 'Architecture of the international intellectual property system' (2002) 77 Chicago-Kent Law Review 993

A Folliard-Monguiral and D Rogers, 'Significant 2007 case law on the Community trade mark from the ECJ and the CFI' (2008) 3(5) JIPLP 291

R Ghafele, 'Trade mark owners' perspectives on the Madrid System: practical experiences and theoretical underpinnings' (2007) 2(3) JIPLP 160–169

LR Helfer, 'The new innovation frontier? Intellectual property and the European Court of Human Rights' (2008) 49 Harvard International Law Journal 1

A Horton. 'The implications of *L'Oreal v Bellure*—a retrospective and a looking forward: the essential functions of a trade mark and when is an advantage unfair?' (2011) 33(9) EIPR 550–558

N Isaacs, 'Should the United Kingdom adopt a European system for the registration of trade marks' [2006] EIPR 71–73

L Jaeschke, 'The quest for a superior registration system for registered trade marks in the UK and EU: an analysis of the current registration system in the UK, the CTM registration system and coming changes' [2008] EIPR 25

MA Leaffer, 'The new world of international trademark law' (1998) 2(1) Marquette Intellectual Property Law Review 28

L Loughlan, 'Trade marks: arguments in a continuing contest' [2005] 3 IPQ 294–308

G Lunney, 'Trademark monopolies' (1999) 48 Emory Law Journal 367

SM Maniatis, Trade mark rights—a justification based on property [2002] 2 IPQ 123–171

SM Maniatis and AK Sanders, 'A consumer trade mark protection based on origin and quality' [1993] EIPR 406–415

FW Mostert, 'When is a mark well-known?' [1997] 3 IPQ 377–383

FW Mostert, 'Is goodwill territorial or international? Protection of the reputation of a trade mark which has not been used in the local jurisdiction' (1989) 11(12) EIPR 440–448

MA Naser, 'Trademarks and freedom of expression' (2009) 40 IIC 188

H Rosler, 'The rationale for European trade mark protection' [2007] EIPR 100

F Schechter, 'The rational basis of trade mark protection' (1927) 40 Harv LR 813

S Schnell, 'The Community trade mark: unitary EU right—EU-wide injunction?' (2011) 33(4) EIPR 210–226

I Simon Fhima, 'Dilution by blurring—a conceptual roadmap' [2010] 1 IPQ 44–87

B Thompson and M Woodhouse, 'Use it or lose it!' (2006) 188 TW 22–23

A Von Muhlendahl, 'Community trade mark riddles: territoriality and unitary character' [2008] EIPR 6

J Weberndorfer, 'The integration of the Office for Harmonization in the Internal Market into the Madrid system: a first field report' [2008] EIPR 216

Definition of a trade mark and registration

Introduction

Scope and overview of chapter

14.1   Since the Trade Marks Directive and the Community Trade Mark Regulation (CTMR) were enacted, the types of signs that can be registered as trade marks have expanded. Whereas traditionally registration was limited to words, pictures, and similar signs, such is the breadth of the current legislation that all manner of two- and three-dimensional marks, sounds, gestures, and other indicia now fall under the definition of a trade mark. Many questions have been raised before the Court of Justice concerning the grounds on which registration or a trade mark should proceed or be refused by national trade mark registries and the Office for Harmonisation in the Internal Market (OHIM). As the case law develops, so it becomes possible to discern trends as to the perceived function of a trade mark; shifts in the balance among the varied interests represented within the registered trade mark framework; and fluctuations in the monopoly conferred by a mark. The purpose of this chapter is to examine the definition of a trade mark and to discuss the criteria for registration, highlighting trends in the case law which shape understanding as to the proper role of trade marks within the consumer society.

14.2   ### Learning objectives

By the end of this chapter you should be able to describe and explain:

- the definition of a trade mark and what may be registered;
- the conditions relating to graphic representation for the purposes of registration of a trade mark;
- the developing jurisprudence concerning the tests underlying the absolute grounds for refusing to register a trade mark;
- conditions under which a mark will become distinctive through use;
- details pertaining to the registration of collective and certification marks.

14.3   The rest of this chapter looks like this:

- The definition of a trade mark (14.7–14.27)

- Registration: absolute grounds for refusal (14.28–14.105)

- Collective and certification trade marks (14.106–14.108)

- Relative grounds for refusal of registration (14.109–14.112)

- Use requirements (14.113–14.126)

Preliminary matters[1]

14.4   As will be seen from a reading of the CTMR, the Trade Marks Directive, and the Trade Marks Act 1994 (TMA 1994), much of the wording dealing with the definition of a trade mark, registration, and infringement is similar if not identical. As regards the interrelationship between the CTMR and the Directive, this is because the definition and scope of what can be registered as a trade mark and the rights pertaining to a registered trade mark are intended to be the same, albeit that the geographical extent of the right differs. As was stated by the Advocate General in *SA Société LTJ Diffusion v SA Sadas*[2] concerning the parallel provisions of the Directive and the CTMR:

> [I do not] agree that a directive and a regulation which use the same criteria and the same language in parallel contexts must be interpreted differently simply because they are different in nature. On the contrary, when the Community legislature takes care to express itself in that manner—as it clearly did in the field of trade marks—the presumption is very strong indeed that the two measures are intended to be interpreted in the same way. The fact that they will be applied in different legal and factual circumstances does not detract from that presumption,'[3] and in principle, therefore, I am of the view that the relevant parallel provisions of the Directive and the Regulation fall to be interpreted in the same way.[4]

As between the Directive and the TMA 1994, this is because the purpose of the 1994 Act was, inter alia, to implement the Directive although it should be noted that the intention of the Directive is to approximate and not harmonise the laws of member states.[5] The Community trade mark regime is an autonomous system that applies independently of any national system. The legality of decisions of the Boards of Appeal must be evaluated solely on the basis of the CTMR, as it is interpreted by the EU Courts.[6] Similarly, the validity of a national trade mark cannot be called in question in proceedings for registration of a Community trade mark, only in cancellation proceedings brought in the member state concerned.[7] As the Court of Justice (formerly the European Court of Justice (ECJ)) is the final arbiter in matters of interpretation relating both to the CTMR and to the Directive, reference will be made to, and judgments drawn from, cases concerning the CTMR, the Directive, and the TMA 1994 with particular reference to the jurisprudence of the Court of Justice. Also referred to will be judgments of the General Court (formerly the Court of First Instance (CFI)) which hears appeals from the OHIM. In these circumstances the decision is highly persuasive, as is the judgment of the Court of Justice on further appeal.[8] National (UK) cases will also be incorporated into the discussion. Where a general reference is made to a court, then the new name (Court of Justice or General Court) will be used in the text. Where reference

---

[1] It was noted in paras 13.30 and 13.36 that both the Directive and the CTMR have been codified. The new provisions will be referred to in the text, but in case law the original provisions remain.

[2] Case C-291/00 [2003] ECR I-2799, [2003] ETMR 83, [2003] FSR 34.

[3] *SA Société LTJ Diffusion v SA Sadas*, para 25.   [4] *SA Société LTJ Diffusion v SA Sadas*, para 28.

[5] Trade Marks Directive, recitals.   [6] L & D SA v OHIM [2008] ETMR 62, para 58.

[7] Case T-134/06 Xentral LLC v OHIM, para 36. Case T-328/05 Apple Computer v OHIM—TKS-Teknosoft (QUARTZ). Case C-196/11 P Formula One Licensing BV v OHIM.

[8] A Firth, G Lea, and P Cornford, Trade Marks: Law and Practice (2nd edn, 2005), 3.

is made to a case or discussion of a case, the name of the court at that time (ECJ or CFI) will be used in the text.

14.5   In referring to sources of law in the text, in each heading reference will be made to the relevant section of the TMA 1994 as well as Articles of the consolidated Directive and of the CTMR where applicable. To avoid repetition, only the sections of the TMA 1994 will be referred to in the text (except where the case refers to the Directive or the CTMR). The reader is strongly urged to read the relevant provision for each section including both the codified and uncodified versions of the Directive and the CTMR as this will help considerably in understanding the discussion.

14.6   Where there are significant differences as between the application of the TMA 1994, the Directive, and the CTMR, such as the geographical extent for fulfilling the requirement of distinctiveness through use, these will be specifically drawn to the attention of the reader.

The definition of a trade mark

 Exercise

Read section 1 of the TMA 1994; Article 2 of the Directive; and Article 4 of the CTMR.

14.7   [A trade mark[9] is defined in section 1 of the TMA 1994 as:] any sign capable of being represented graphically which is capable of distinguishing goods or services of one undertaking from those of other undertakings. [The mark may] consist of words (including personal names), designs, letters, numerals or the shape of goods or their packaging.[10]

There are thus three criteria the mark must meet:

- the mark must be a sign;
- the mark must be capable of being represented graphically;
- the mark must be capable of distinguishing goods or services of one undertaking from those of another.

Sign

14.8   The requirement that the mark should be a *sign* has not proved too problematic for the purposes of registration, and many different types of signs are now accepted for registration as trade marks.

- Simple word marks that have been registered include 'Rolls-Royce' and 'Tesco'. Phrases which have been registered as trade marks include 'A Mars a day helps you work, rest and play'.[11] Many words are registered in combination with a device or a graphic such as that shown in Figure 14.1 [12]

---

[9] There is no distinction between a trade mark and a service mark under the TMA 1994.

[10] TMA 1994, s 1(1). Under the Regulation, the definition of a Community mark is much the same: 'A Community trade mark may consist of any signs capable of being represented graphically, particularly words, including personal names, designs, letters, numerals, the shape of goods or of their packaging, provided that such signs are capable of distinguishing the goods or services of one undertaking from those of other undertakings' (CTMR, Art 4).

[11] UK Trade Mark No 1438989, class 30, proprietor: Mars UK Ltd.

[12] UK Trade Mark No 2101409, classes 41 and 42, proprietor: The University Court of the University of Edinburgh.

Figure 14.1 Edinburgh Law School

EDINBURGH LAW SCHOOL

- Numbers have been registered, including the number '1010'.[13]
- Personal names (in signature form) have been registered including that of 'Marilyn Monroe'.[14]
- The shape of the packaging of goods has been registered:[15]

Figure 14.2 Coca-Cola bottle

as has the shape of goods such as the Mini shown in Figure 14.3.[16]

- Gestures: 'The Mark consists of a gesture made by a person which comprises tapping a pocket of an article of clothing worn below the waist of the person'.[17]
- Colours, such as that described in Figure 14.4.[18]
- Sounds have been registered: 'The mark consists of the sound of a dog barking'[19]; as have smells: 'The mark comprises the strong smell of bitter beer applied to flights for darts'.[20]

---

[13] UK Trade Mark No 2142860, classes 3.4.16.18 and 25, proprietor: Acheson and Acheson Limited.
[14] Trade Mark 1308828, the estate of Marilyn Monroe.
[15] UK Trade Mark No 2000546. The mark consists of a three-dimensional shape with the words 'Coca-Cola' appearing thereon, proprietor: The Coca-Cola Company. The Contour Bottle Design and Coca-Cola are registered trademarks of The Coca-Cola Company.
[16] UK Trade Mark No 2002390, classes 6, 12, 16, and 28, proprietor: Bayerische Motoren Werke Aktiengesellschaft.
[17] UK Trade Mark No 2048673, classes 29, 30, and 31, proprietor: ASDA Stores Limited.
[18] UK Trade Mark No 2009633, class 3, proprietor: Chemisphere UK Ltd.
[19] UK Trade Mark No 2007456, class 2, proprietor: Imperial Chemical Industries plc.
[20] UK Trade Mark No 2000234, class 28—flights for darts, proprietor: Unicorn Products Limited.

Figure 14.3 BMW mini

Figure 14.4 Purple colour

PURPLE as a colour applied overall to and subsisting in the goods, the colour purple being definable within chromacity coordinate parameters, according to the CIELAB system, of L between 0 and 90, A between +5 and + 100, and B between –5 and –100.

 Question

How does the registered trade mark 'The mark comprises the strong smell of bitter beer applied to flights for darts' function as a trade mark?

What other types of marks can you think of that might qualify as a trade mark under the definition given previously?

Consider the marks in the examples given. Look at the representation of the mark in the trade mark database and note the date of registration. When you have finished reading this chapter consider whether all of these would now be registrable—or whether some may now be open to challenge.

14.9   While many signs have been accepted as meeting the need to be a mark, the judgment of the ECJ in *Dyson Ltd v Registrar of Trade Marks*[21] indicates that not every sign will pass this hurdle. In this case, Dyson sought to register the shape of its vacuum cleaners in class 9 of the Nice Agreement for 'Apparatus for cleaning, polishing and shampooing floors and carpets; vacuum cleaners; carpet shampooers; floor polishers, parts and fittings for all the aforesaid goods.' A similar representation is shown in Figure 14.5.

This was accompanied by the text: 'The mark consists of a transparent bin or collection chamber forming part of the external surface of a vacuum cleaner as shown in the representation'. To see the second image, which was accompanied by the text 'The mark consists of a transparent bin or collection chamber forming part of the external surface of a vacuum cleaner as shown in the representation', have a look at the Opinion of the Advocate General which is available on the Court of Justice website at http://curia.europa.eu/.

[21] Case C-321/03 [2007] ETMR 34.

Figure 14.5 Dyson

The application was turned down by the Registry. On appeal to the High Court, that court referred a number of questions to the ECJ. Although the question referred to the Court was in relation to the conditions under which a sign can acquire a distinctive character within the meaning of Article 3(3) of the Directive where the trader had a de facto monopoly in the product bearing the sign prior to lodging an application for registration, the Court found it necessary to answer the prior question of whether the mark constituted a sign within the meaning of Article 2. The Court noted that it was common ground that the subject matter of the application was not a particular type of transparent collecting bin, but rather 'in a general and abstract manner, all the conceivable shapes of such a collecting bin.'[22] The sign was thus not specific. A consumer would not identify visually the subject matter of the application itself, but rather Dyson's graphic representations as contained in the application which, in turn, were merely examples of the application.[23] The subject matter of the application was a mere property of the product and 'does not therefore constitute a "sign" within the meaning of Article 2 of the Directive'.[24]

14.10   Thus there are certain indicia that are unregistrable because they do not constitute a sign within the meaning of the legislation.[25]

---

[22] *Dyson*, para 35.   [23] *Dyson*, para 36.   [24] *Dyson*, para 39.

[25] For further guidance on what constitutes a sign, see Practice Amendment Notice (2007) 7/07. The scrabble tile is not a sign: *JW Spear & Sons Ltd and Mattel Inc v Zynga* [2012] EWHC 3345 (Ch).

Question

Can you think of any other 'concepts' that might not meet the definition of a sign and would thus be unregistrable?[26]

Graphic representation

14.11   There have been a number of cases over recent years elaborating on the requirement for graphic representation. In the early days of the 1994 Act there was some debate as to whether sounds and smells would be registrable.[27] In a series of cases the ECJ laid down a set of criteria which the more 'unusual' types of marks, including sounds, smells, and colours must meet in order to satisfy the test of graphic representation.

Smells

14.12   The first case by the ECJ to consider an 'unusual' mark, *Sieckmann v Deutsches Patent- und Markenamt*[28] concerned a smell: a 'methyl cinnamate' scent, which the applicant had described as 'balsamically fruity with a slight hint of cinnamon' and given the formula as $C6H5–CH = CHCOOCH3$.

 Question

Do you know what 'balsamically fruity with a slight hint of cinnamon' smells like?

The question before the Court was whether Article 2 of the Directive included only signs which were capable of being represented visually, or whether it also encompassed signs that could be represented by some other means. If the latter, the question was whether the representation could include a description in words, by way of a chemical formula, or a sample. The Court held that a trade mark could consist of a sign which itself may not be capable of being perceived visually (eg a smell) provided that it could be represented graphically such as through the use of images, lines, or characters. In particular, the Court said the representation had to be:

- clear;
- precise;
- self-contained;
- easily accessible;
- intelligible;
- durable;
- objective.

These criteria have subsequently become known as the *'Sieckmann* seven'. As regards the instant application, it was not possible to register an odour by means of its chemical formula since such a formula was not representative of the odour but rather of the chemical substance itself. Neither would the

---

[26] Single colours are per se capable of being signs: *Societe des Produits Nestle SA v Cadbury UK Ltd* [2012] EWHC 2637 (Ch).
[27] H Burton, 'The UK Trade Marks Act 1994: an invitation to an olfactory occasion?' [1995] 8 EIPR 378.
[28] Case C-273/00 Sieckmann v Deutsches Patent- und Markenamt [2003] Ch 487, [2003] 3 WLR 424.

requirement for graphic representation be satisfied by a written description or by the provision of an odour sample.

14.13   Quite how these criteria will be met in the future for smells remains to be seen. A quick search on the Community trade mark (CTM) database shows that as at July 2012, no smells are currently registered. Only one smell has successfully been registered as a trade mark, which was 'The smell of fresh cut grass' in connection with tennis balls.[29] This has since expired. The application for this trade mark was filed in 1996 and was registered in 2000 (ie before the judgment in *Sieckmann*). The other six marks shown in the database at the time of writing had all been refused registration.[30] This perhaps gives an indication that it is not going to be easy to register smells as trade marks due to the difficulties of meeting the criteria set out by the ECJ.

> **Question**
>
> Do you think the mark: 'The mark comprises the strong smell of bitter beer applied to flights for darts' meets the *Sieckmann* seven criteria?

Colours

14.14   The next major case dealing with more unusual marks concerned an application to register a colour: *Libertel Groep BV v Benelux-Merkenbureau*.[31] Libertel applied to register the colour orange as a trade mark for telecommunications goods and services. The application contained an orange rectangle in the space for reproducing the trade mark, together with the word 'orange' in the space on the form for describing the trade mark. There was no reference to a colour code. When this was turned down by the office in the Netherlands, the Dutch court remitted the matter to the ECJ.

The Court held that a colour may, in respect of certain goods and services, have a distinctive character within the meaning of Article 3 of the Directive, provided that it can be represented graphically and it repeated the *Sieckmann* seven criteria: it must be clear, precise, self-contained, equally accessible, intelligible, durable, and objective. However, this could not be satisfied by reproducing on paper the colour in question as it did not satisfy the requirement for durability that was one of the requirements for graphic representation. A sample with a description or which designated the colour using an internationally recognised identification code would, however, be sufficient to constitute a graphic representation.

14.15   Further questions on the registerability of colours as trade marks were considered by the ECJ in *Heidelberger Bauchemie GmbH*.[32] These related to the registerability of two colours, blue and yellow, for a range of building products including glue, paint, and cleaning products, but where the interrelationship between the two colours was left undefined. The Court said:

> The mere juxtaposition of two or more colours, without shape or contours, or a reference to two or more colours 'in every conceivable form', as is the case with the trade mark which is the subject of the main proceedings, does not exhibit the [necessary] qualities of precision and uniformity.[33]

14.16   However, a colour combination without contours could constitute a trade mark where:

- it has been established that, in the context in which they are used, those colours or combinations of colours in fact represent a sign; and

[29]   CTM No 000428870.

[30]   Two went to appeal: El OLOR A LIMON in connection with footwear, No 001254861; the smell of ripe strawberries in connection with, inter alia, bleaching preparations, No 001122118. See also the discussion on passing off in para 17.22.

[31]   Case C-104/01 [2004] Ch 83, [2004] 2 WLR 1081.   [32]   Case C-49/02 [2004] ETMR 99.

[33]   *Heidelberger Bauchemie GmbH*, para 34.

• the application for registration includes a systematic arrangement associating the colours concerned in a predetermined and uniform way.

Thus colours may be sufficiently represented to constitute registered trade marks. Indeed, there have now been a number of colours registered as CTMs. For example, a deep cranberry colour has been registered by Deutsche Telekom for, inter alia, merchandising and finance activities[34] (the pantone number is included with the application); and purple by Cadbury Schweppes plc in connection with chocolate bars and drinks (also including the pantone number).[35]

Sounds

14.17 The ECJ has also pronounced on the registerability of sounds as trade marks. In *Shield Mark BV v Joost Kist*,[36] Shield had registered a number of marks in the Benelux registry. These included:

• a musical stave depicting the first notes of Beethoven's *Für Elise*;
• the words 'the first nine notes of Für Elise';
• the sequence of notes 'E, D#, E, D#, E, B, D, C, A';
• the word 'Kukelekuuuuu' (the Dutch word for the English 'Cock-a-doodle-do');
• the words 'a cockcrow'.

The question arose as to whether these were valid trade marks given the requirements for graphic representation.

The Court basically reaffirmed its rulings in *Libertel* and *Sieckmann* repeating the *Sieckmann* seven, and went on to say that those requirements were *not* met when the sound sign was represented by means of:

• a description such as the notes making up a musical work;
• an indication that it was the cry of an anissmal;
• a simple onomatopoeia;
• a sequence of musical notes.

However, the requirements *were* satisfied where the sign was represented by a stave divided into measures and showing, in particular, a clef, musical notes, and rests whose form indicated the relative values and, where necessary, accidentals.

14.18 This ruling contemplates that musical notes can be registered as trade marks as long as correctly represented. One example is shown in Figure 14.6.

Figure 14.6 Musical notes

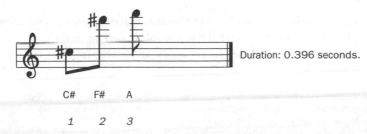

---

[34] CTM No 004636676.   [35] *Societe des Produits Nestle SA v Cadbury UK Ltd* [2012] EWHC 2637 (Ch).
[36] Case C-283/01 *Shield Mark BV v Kist (t/a Memex)* [2004] Ch 97, [2004] 2 WLR 1117, [2004] All ER (EC) 277 RPC.

The description is: 'The sound of the trade mark consists of the tones above with a deviation as noted in the chart below where each tone is defined in Hz. – n°1: 1100Hz – tone C#;n°2: 1450Hz – tone F#;n°3: 1800Hz – tone A. seconds.'[37]

14.19   More difficult will be the question of how other types of sounds, such as animal noises, might meet these criteria. 'Cock-a-doodle-doo' clearly will not do.

Question

What representations in other languages are there for the crow of a cock? Try searching on Wikipedia and you might find some of the following: Arabic, KooKooKoo-koo; Chinese, goh-geh-goh-goh; Italian, chicchirichì; Korean, k'ok'iyo; Portuguese, Cócórócócó; Swahili, KokoRikoo koo; Swedish, kuckeliku; Gujarati, kuk-de-kuk. How might you go about satisfying the criteria for graphic representation if you wanted to register an animal noise as a trade mark?

Do you think that the mark 'The mark consists of the sound of a dog barking' (para 14.8) might be open to challenge?

Taste

14.20   An application to register a taste mark was made in *Eli Lilly & Co's Community Trade Mark Application*.[38] The application, for an artificial strawberry flavour for use in pharmaceutical products, was refused by the OHIM Second Board of Appeal partly on the grounds that it did not meet the criteria for graphic representation as laid out by the ECJ. It was also thought that consumers were likely to see the taste as a means to disguise the unpleasant flavour of medicine rather than as a trade mark—in other words, there was doubt over whether it functioned as an indication of origin.[39] It is thus currently unclear as to whether tastes will be registrable as trade marks. It seems that it may be problematic to give sufficient information in an application to indicate precisely what is claimed within the parameters of the trade mark.[40]

Exercise

Go to the OHIM site and find the CTM register. Have a search around some of the more unusual marks for which registration has been applied for. What is the most unusual you can find? Has the mark been registered? How do you know? If not, do you think the mark that you have found is likely to meet the criteria for graphic representation?

The purpose of the rules

14.21   In *Heidelberger Bauchemie GmbH*,[41] the ECJ stressed that the purpose of the requirement of graphic representation is to define the mark so that it is possible to determine the precise subject of the protection so that both the authorities and the general public know what is being claimed as a mark: the authorities

---

[37] CTM No 002510345 by AB Electrolux in connection with lawnmowers and vacuum cleaners.
[38] Eli Lilly and Company's Application [2004] ETMR 4 OHIM (Second Board of Appeal).
[39] Eli Lilly and Company's Application, para 15.
[40] At the time of writing it appeared that applications had been made but turned down for a number of 'position marks' where the positioning of certain features were key (Case T-152/07 *Lange Uhren v OHIM* (figurative mark representing a watch) and Case R 846/2008-4). No further information was available at the time of writing.
[41] Case C-49/02 [2004] ETMR 99.

so that they can carry out an examination of applications and maintain a 'precise' register of trade marks; and other traders so that they know what competitors' claim and their rights.[42]

> ### Key points on graphic representation
>
> - In order to be registrable a sign should be clear; precise; self-contained; easily accessible; intelligible; durable; and objective
> - This is so the subject of protection can be determined by both the authorities charged with maintaining a register, and competitors so they know what is being claimed

14.22 An important point to note at this juncture is that although a sign may meet the tests for graphic representation, that does not of itself mean that it will be capable of being registered as a trade mark. As will be seen in the ensuing discussion, there are many other hurdles to overcome.

Service trade marks and retail trade

14.23 Service marks may be registered in connection with services. These are provided for in classes 35–45 of the Nice classification and include, inter alia, insurance and financial affairs;[43] education and the provision of training; sporting and cultural activities;[44] services for providing food and drink;[45] and medical and veterinary services.[46] Examples of service marks include 'Medacs. Giving you the option'[47] registered in classes 35 and 44 of the Nice Agreement, and the image of half a face along with the words 'Beautiful Smiles' in class 44.[48] (To see the image, go to the CTM register. The number is CTM E3275369.)

14.24 One question that has arisen is as to whether it would be possible to register a service mark for the ancillary services provided by retailers. Businesses will often provide a range of services to their customers in order to encourage the consumer to patronise their business. These may include not only the selection of the goods on offer but in addition those services that go towards consumer preferences in deciding where to shop, including the provision of such services as car parking facilities and a crèche. Arguments against permitting such registrations included the view that services were only an adjunct of the retail trade, and not the main business of the retailer. An applicant for a service mark should be in the business of providing services. In addition, there was the view that where the mark was to encompass the types of goods sold by the trader, these should be the subject of their own separate application. More recent thinking has suggested that the economic trend towards a service society necessitates a reappraisal of retail trade as a service. The purchasing decisions made by the consumer are influenced not only by the availability and price of a product, but also by other aspects such as the variety and assortment of goods, their presentation, service levels, advertising, image, and the location of the store. Services provided in connection with retail trade enable retailers to distinguish themselves from their competitors. As a result, such services ought to be eligible for protection by service marks.[49]

14.25 An application to register a service mark for retail activities was turned down under the Trade Marks Act 1938 by the Court of Appeal[50] on the ground that they were not provided for money or money's worth:

---

[42] *Heidelberger Bauchemie GmbH*, paras 28–30.   [43] Class 36.   [44] Class 41.
[45] Class 43.   [46] Class 44.   [47] UK Trade Mark No 2292972.   [48] CTM E3275369.
[49] Case C-418/02 *Praktiker Bau- und Heimwerkermarkte AG v Deutsches Patent- und Markenamt* [2006] Ch 144, [2006] 2 WLR 195, [2005] ECR I-5873, [2005] ETMR 88.
[50] In Re Dee Corporation's Application [1990] RPC 159.

the costs were only indirectly passed on to the consumer. However, the Second Board of Appeal at the OHIM allowed the registration of a figurative mark in *Giacomelli Sport SpA*[51] for the 'bringing together for the benefit of others of a variety of goods ... to enable consumers to view and buy the products' in class 35 for protective helmets and spectacles, all sporting articles, and the organisation of exhibitions in halls and showrooms for commercial or advertising purposes. The Board reasoned that the provision of a service was something over and above goods, and more in the form of labour expended to meet a particular need or want. As consumers prefer the services provided by some shops over others, so they met a certain need and were mutually beneficial to both the retailer and consumer.

14.26   This approach to permit the registration of retail service marks has been confirmed by the ECJ based on an appreciation that the provision of services by retail traders is a matter which influences consumer choice.

■ Case C-418/02 *Praktiker Bau und Heimwerkermärkte AG v Deutsches Patent und Markenamt*[52]

This case concerned a refusal by the German Patent and Trade Mark Office to register the word 'Praktiker' for the service of 'retail trade in building, home improvement, gardening and other consumer goods for the do-it-yourself sector'. The office had refused the application considering that the concept of 'retail trade' claimed did not denote independent services having autonomous economic significance but related only to the distribution of goods as such. Trade mark protection could be achieved only by applying for registration of a trade mark in respect of the goods distributed in each case. On appeal the German court referred a number of questions to the ECJ, two of which were:

* Does retail trade in goods constitute a service within the meaning of Article 2 of the Directive?
* If the answer to this question is in the affirmative:
* To what extent must the content of such services provided by a retailer be specified in order to guarantee the certainty of the subject matter of trade mark protection that is required in order to:
  (a) fulfil the function of the trade mark, as defined in Article 2 of the Directive, namely, to distinguish the goods or services of one undertaking from those of other undertakings, and
  (b) define the scope of protection of such a trade mark in the event of a conflict?

The Court saw no reason why retail services should be precluded from being covered by the concept of services under Article 2 of the Directive, pointing out that while the objective of retail trade is the sale of goods to consumers, part of that was the activity carried for the purpose of encouraging the conclusion of a transaction. This included selecting an assortment of goods offered for sale, and offering a variety of services.

Key points on retail services

* A service mark can be registered for retail services
* The specifications will need to be concise enough for third parties to be able to understand the scope of protection claimed by the mark

---

[51] [2000] ETMR 277.
[52] Case C-418/02 *Praktiker Bau- und Heimwerkermarkte AG v Deutsches Patent- und Markenamt* [2006] Ch 144, [2006] 2 WLR 195, [2005] ECR I-5873, [2005] ETMR 88.

Specification

14.27   Questions have arisen for both goods and service marks in relation to the specification in the application. This has generally been done by reference to the Nice classification. In *Praktiker Bau-* the ECJ indicated that while it was not required to specify in detail the services for which registration was sought (it would be sufficient to use general wording such as 'bringing together of a variety of goods, enabling customers to conveniently view and purchase those goods'),[53] it was necessary to specify the goods or types of goods to which those services relate.[54] The reason for this last requirement was that it would make it easier to apply the provisions in the Directive relating to conflicts with earlier trade marks and to determine the scope of the exclusive right conferred on the proprietor.[55] This requirement is likely now to be a higher one with the judgment of the ECJ in the *IP Translator* case.[56] In this, CIPA applied for registration of its services in class 41 of the Nice Agreement. This was turned down because of the breadth of the services covered in class 41 which went beyond those offered by the Institute and that the mark applied for was descriptive of the broader services. The question referred to the Court of Justice was over the degree of clarity needed in relation to an application and whether that precluded the use of class headings in the Nice Agreement. The Court stressed that the Directive required descriptions in applications to be sufficiently clear and precise to enable the competent authorities and economic operators to determine the extent of protection sought: authorities so that they could fulfill obligations in relation to examination of applications and the promulgation of the register; economic operators so that they could know the monopoly being sought by competitors.[57] The Nice classification had to be used under the Nice Agreement but not under the Directive which has its own requirements of clarity and precision. Some of the indications in the class headings of the Nice classification were too general and referred to goods and services which were too variable and thus not compatible with the function of a mark as an indication of origin. A case-by-case judgement therefore had to be made as to whether the Nice Agreement met the requirements for clarity in the Directive. An applicant had in any event to specify whether the application was to cover all of the goods and services in the class or only some, and if so, which ones.[58]

The ruling has caused quite some consternation in the IP community because of the general practice of referring to the Nice class heading in an application and expecting that the registration would cover all goods or services within the class some of which may be actually used by the trade mark owner, others of which may be purely speculative in that the trade mark owner may think of branching out into other areas in the future.

 Question

If a registered trade mark covers more goods than are dealt with by the trade mark owner in the course of trade, what is a possible outcome in terms of the validity of the mark? Revisit this question when you have finished this chapter.

---

[53] Case C-418/02, para 49.   [54] *Praktiker Bau-*, para 50.

[55] For difficulties that can arise in the intersection between the retail services and individual trade marks, see the CFI in Case T-116/06 Oakley v OHMI.

[56] Case C-307/10 *Chartered Institute of Patent Attorneys v Registrar of Trade Marks*.   [57] Paras 40–49.

[58] Paras 50–56 and 61. For comment see P Bicknell, '*Chartered Institute of Patent Attorneys v Registrar of Trade Marks*; we have not heard the last of it' (2012) 34(10) EIPR 715–719. The High Court in England has suggested that where there was a registration application for a trade mark for a shopping centre, the word 'services' should be taken to mean those that are normally provided for remuneration, as described by the EC Treaty, Art 50 (Art 57 TFEU) but it is not clear that the separate remuneration requirement could be justified in the light of the ECJ decision in *Praktiker Bau*. Land Securities plc v Registrar of Trade Marks [2008] EWHC 1744 (Pat).

Registration: absolute grounds for refusal

14.28   The grounds on which application for registration of a trade mark can be refused are set out in sections 3 and 5 of the TMA 1994. Section 3 details the *absolute* grounds for refusal of registration, whereas section 5 looks to the *relative* grounds for refusal of registration. The term 'absolute' means that a mark is incapable of being registered as a trade mark because it does not meet the definition of a trade mark,[59] is devoid of distinctive character,[60] is indicative of the characteristics of the goods or services,[61] or has become a word commonly used in the trade.[62] In other words, the grounds for refusal look to the mark itself. By contrast, the term 'relative' means that account will be taken of other marks that are already registered to see whether the sign for which registration has been applied for can be accepted. The Registrar can refuse registration on the grounds listed in section 5, if opposition on that ground is raised (successfully) by the proprietor of the earlier mark or sign.[63] Thus if there is an earlier trade mark which is identical with[64] or similar to[65] the sign, or if the registered mark has a reputation and the later registration would take unfair advantage of or be detrimental to the registered trade mark,[66] then the sign may not be registered.[67]

 Exercise

Read sections 3, 5, and 10 of the TMA 1994; Articles 3, 4, and 5 of the Directive; and Articles 7, 8, and 9 of the CTMR.

14.29   As will be seen from looking at the TMA 1994, sections 5 and 10 (Directive, Arts 4 and 5; CTMR, Arts 8 and 9) almost mirror each other in the wording. This is because if a sign may not be registered as a trade mark under section 5, then the use of that sign (albeit unregistered) in the marketplace by another trader, will inevitably infringe the registered mark. Because the sections are the same, so the same considerations apply as to whether a mark may be registered under section 5, and whether the use of the sign will infringe under section 10. Therefore these two sections will be considered together in Chapter 15.

Non-distinctive, descriptive, and customary marks

TMA 1994, section 3(1)(b), (c), (d); Directive, Article 3(1)(b), (c), (d); and CTMR, Article 7(1)(b), (c), (d)

14.30   Under these sections the following may not be registered as a trade mark:

- trade marks which are devoid of any distinctive character[68] (TMA 1994, s 3(1)(b)) (non-distinctive marks);

---

[59] TMA 1994, s 3(1)(a).   [60] TMA 1994, s 3(1)(b).   [61] TMA 1994, s 3(1)(c).
[62] TMA 1994, s 3(1)(d).   [63] See Practice Amendment Notice 8/07 on the IPO website.
[64] TMA 1994, s 10(1).   [65] TMA 1994, s 10(2).   [66] TMA 1994, s 10(3).
[67] The existence of an absolute ground must be examined on the date of filing of a (CTM) application: Case C-332/09 *Frosch Touristik GmbH v OHIM*.
[68] TMA 1994, s 3(1)(b). There are many examples under this subsection most of which do not proceed beyond the Trade Marks Registry. Eg AD 2000 Trade Mark [1997] RPC 168 (letters and numerals AD 2000); Dualit Ltd's Trade Mark Application [1999] RPC 890 (three-dimensional toaster); Jane Austen Trade Mark [2000] RPC 879 (name Jane Austen); Froot Loops Trade Mark [1998] RPC 240 (Froot Loops for breakfast cereal); Eurolamb Trade Mark [1997] RPC 279; *NMSI Trading Ltd's Trade Mark Application* (No 2449033B) [2012] RPC 7; *O2 Holdings Ltd's Trade Mark Application* (No 2481567) [2011] RPC 22. But see *32Red plc v WHG (International) Ltd* [2012] EWCA Civ 19, [2012] ETMR 14. See also the comparison with passing off in para 17.22.

- trade marks which consist exclusively of signs or indications which may serve, in trade, to designate the kind, quality, quantity, intended purpose, value, geographical origin, or the time of production of the goods or of rendering of the service, or other characteristics of the goods or service[69] (TMA 1994, s 3(1)(c)) (descriptive marks);

- trade marks which consist exclusively of signs or indications which have become customary in the current language or in the bona fide and established practices of the trade[70] (TMA 1994, s 3(1)(d)) (customary marks).[71]

Each of these sections yields to the proviso that, even though a mark may fail these tests, if it can be shown that the mark has acquired a distinctive character as a result of the *use* that has been made of it before the date of application, then the mark may be registrable.[72] So, for example, if a mark is not inherently distinctive (distinctive by nature), if it is used, and it can be shown through that use to have become distinctive (distinctive by nurture), then it will be capable of registration (see paras 14.69ff).

14.31   These subsections have spawned a good deal of case law, some conflicting. They are central to trade mark law in that, along with the provisions on graphic representation and relative grounds for refusal, application of these sections determines what can and what cannot be registered as a mark. The provisions have been described as essential to balancing the interests as between the would-be trade mark proprietor and the competing trader. The greater variety in the types of marks that can be registered, the fewer there are in the 'public domain' for competing traders to use. This is particularly so where the mark may be one that the competitor may wish, legitimately, to use in the course of her own trade, such as a descriptive term; where it is an indication of the characteristics of the goods and services on offer; or where the mark is one which is generally used to describe the characteristics of the goods.[73]

'Distinguish' and 'distinctive'

14.32   It will be noted that section 1 of the TMA 1994 1 refers to the capacity of the mark to *distinguish* goods or services of one undertaking from those of another. By contrast section 3(1)(b) talks of trade marks which are devoid of any *distinctive character*. In the early case law there was some discussion as to whether these were separate tests; in other words, whether there was a category of marks which could not distinguish between goods and services, but at the same time might have a distinctive character and vice versa. This has been judicially considered by the ECJ in *Koninklijke Philips Electronics NV v Remington Consumer Products Ltd*[74] where one of the questions put before the Court was whether there was 'a category of marks which is not excluded from registration by Art 3(1)(b), (c) and (d) and Art 3(3) of [the Directive] which is none the less excluded from registration by Art 3(1)(a) of the Directive as being incapable of distinguishing the goods of the proprietor from those [of] other undertakings'.

The Court held that was not so, saying:

there is no class of marks having a distinctive character by their nature or by the use made of them which is not capable of distinguishing goods or services within the meaning of Art.2 of the Directive

---

[69] TMA 1994, s 3(1)(c). Siemens AG's Application [1999] ETMR 146.   [70] TMA 1994, s 3(1)(d).

[71] Absolute grounds of refusal are assessed at the date of filing: Case C-332/09 *OHIM v Frosch Touristik*.

[72] When refusing registration of a mark under Art 3(1)(b) and (c) reasons must be given for each of the individual goods and services specified in the registration, see: *BVBA Management, Training en Consultancy v Benelux-Merkenbureau* [2007] ETMR 35, para 38.

[73] Case C-363/99 *Koninklijke KPN Nederland NV v Benelux-Merkenbureau*; Case C-51/10 P *Agencja Wydawnicza Technopol sp. z o.o. v OHIM*.

[74] Case C-299/99 [2003] RPC 2.

14.33   So if a mark is distinctive by nature or by nurture, it must be capable of distinguishing goods and services. This has been applied by the Court of Appeal in *West (t/a Eastenders) v Fuller Smith & Turner*[75] which concerned the registration of the trade mark 'E.S.B' for bitter beers in class 32. Referring to the judgment of the ECJ in *Koninklijke*, the Court of Appeal said that the effect of the judgment was that 'the second half of the definition of "trade mark" in section 1(1) of the Act (corresponding to Article 2 of the Directive) must be viewed as imposing no distinctiveness requirement separate from that imposed by Articles 3(1)(b), (c) and (d) and 3(3). Thus, there is no requirement that the mark be both "capable of distinguishing" and "not devoid of any distinctive character".[76]

The principles underlying the absolute grounds of refusal

14.34   There has been some discussion over recent years as to the principles underpinning the provisos in section 3 of the TMA 1994.[77] On the one hand, is the central provision of trade mark law that a trade mark must be capable, for the consumer, of distinguishing goods and services of one trader from those of another. On the other hand, is the need of competing traders to be able to use certain signs within the marketplace to compete fairly and to keep signs free from ownership to enable them to do so (the principle of availability). The debate has been as to what the underlying principles or tests are, which principle or test might be relevant to which section, and whether application of the underlying principles when applying one or other of the subsections should be independent or cumulative.

14.35   The paramount consideration when applying section 3(1)(b) is the need to ensure that a trade mark functions as an indication of origin—that a mark will be capable of distinguishing the goods and services of one trader from those of another.[78] This criterion remains important for section 3(1)(c) and (d) but both of those subsections encompass needs of competitors also—the need to keep certain marks available for competitors whether into the future (s 3(1)(c))[79] or at the point of application (s 3(1)(d)).

> Article 7(1)(c) referred to a characteristic which other traders might wish to use to designate or identify a specific feature of their goods or services so as to communicate to customers or potential customers what those goods and services were. The policy was that terms which traders might wish to use to characterise their goods and services should be freely available for use by all traders.[80]

14.36   The reason for the exclusion of customary signs from registration under section 3(1)(d) of the TMA 1994 is that while such signs may have at one time been capable of distinguishing the goods and services of one trader from those of another, they have been used in such a way, either in the normal language or in the trade, to mean those goods and services. They have thus become generic, can no longer perform a distinguishing function, and are excluded from registration.[81]

14.37   The different emphasis or weight placed on the tests will have an impact on the range of marks which are registerable. Where the emphasis is on the consumer then it is likely that a broader spectrum of marks would be registrable than if the interests of competing traders was of greater weight. A consumer

---

[75] [2003] EWCA Civ 48, [2003] FSR 44.   [76] Per Arden LJ at para 62, see also paras 34–35.

[77] Each of the grounds for refusal listed in Art 7(1) must be interpreted in the light of the general interest underlying it: Case C-51/10 P *Agencja Wydawnicza Technopol sp. z o.o. v OHIM*, para 36; Cases C-456/01 P and C-457/01 P *Henkel KGaA v OHIM*; Case C-48/09 P *Lego Juris A/S v OHIM*.

[78] Joined Cases C-53/01, C-54/01, and C-55/01 Linde AG, Winward Industries, Rado Watch Co Ltd [2003] RPC 45. Case C-90/11 *Strigl v Deutsches Patent- und Markenamt*, para 30

[79] *OHIM v Wrigley*, para 32; *Campina Melkunie*, para 38; Case C-90/11 *Strigl v Deutsches Patent- und Markenamt*, para 31; Case C-51/10 P *Agencja Wydawnicza Technopol sp. z o.o. v OHIM*.

[80] *32Red plc v WHG (International) Ltd* [2012] EWCA Civ 19, [2012] ETMR 14, [2012] RPC 19.

[81] Eg an image of a rose in connection with clothing by the Rugby Football Union: *RFU and Nike v Cotton Traders* [2002] ETMR 861.

may perceive a mark as indicating origin even though it would be in the interests of competing traders to have that mark freely available for all to use. Where the tests are cumulative, then the range of marks registerable is likely to be narrowest.

14.38   When the focus is on the distinguishing function, the ECJ has made it clear that the range of goods and services for which application has been made must be considered as must, importantly, the perception of the consumer: 'distinctive character must be assessed, first, by reference to the products or services in respect of which registration has been applied for and, second, by reference to the perception of the relevant public, which consists of average consumers of the products or services in question, who are reasonably well informed and reasonably observant and circumspect'.[82]

14.39   By contrast, when the issue is more closely allied to the interests of competing traders, so their interests come to the fore. In an early case *Windsurfing Chiemsee*,[83] concerning the name Chiemsee (the name of a lake in Bavaria), the Court stressed the need to keep certain signs free for competitors:

> Article 3(1)(c) of the Directive pursues an aim which is in the public interest, namely that descriptive signs or indications relating to the categories of goods or services in respect of which registration is applied for may be freely used by all …, Article 3(1)(c) therefore prevents such signs and indications from being reserved to one undertaking alone because they have been registered as trade marks.[84]

But the Court in the context of this case—geographical names—rejected the notion that there should be any differentiation as regards the perceived importance of keeping certain names free, thus rejecting the German doctrine of *Freihaltungsbedürfnis*.[85]

14.40   There has also been case law on whether the same test should apply to each of the subsections albeit separately considered and in terms of which the case law has developed over the years. In a case concerning the registerability of the sign 'SAT.2' for services connected with satellite broadcasting,[86] the ECJ said:

> it is important to observe that each of the grounds for refusal to register listed in Article 7(1) of the regulation is independent of the others and requires separate examination. Moreover, it is appropriate to interpret those grounds for refusal in the light of the general interest which underlies each of them. The general interest to be taken into consideration when examining each of those grounds for refusal may or even must reflect different considerations according to the ground for refusal in question.[87]

The criterion relating to marks capable of being available for competitors was relevant in the context of Article 7(1)(c) of the CTMR but not for Article 7(1)(b).[88]

---

[82] See, inter alia, Joined Cases C-53/01 *Linde AG v Deutsches Patent- und Markenamt* and C-55/01 Rado Uhren AG's Trade Mark Application; Case C-54/01 Winward Industrie Inc's Trade Mark Application [2003] ECR I-3161, [2005] 2 CMLR 44, [2003] ETMR 78, [2003] RPC 45, para 41; Case C-363/99 *Koninklijke KPN Nederland NV v Benelux-Merkenbureau* [2005] 3 WLR 649, [2005] All ER (EC) 19, para 34; Joined Cases C-473/01 P and C-474/01 P *Procter & Gamble v OHIM* [2004] ECR I-5173, para 33; Case C-25/05 P *Storck v OHIM* [2006] ECR I-5719, para 25; Case C-311/11 P *Smart Technologies ULC v OHIM*.

[83] Joined Cases C-108/97 and C-109/97 *Windsurfing Chiemsee Produktions- und Vertriebs GmbH v Boots- und Segelzubehor Walter Huber; Windsurfing Chiemsee Produktions und Vertriebs GmbH v Attenberger* [2000] Ch 523, [2000] 2 WLR 205, [1999] ECR I-2779, [1999] ETMR 585. See also Case C-53/01 Linde AG, Winward Industries and Rado Watch Co Ltd [2003] ECR I-3161, [2005] 2 CMLR 44, [2003] ETMR 78, [2003] RPC 45.

[84] *Windsurfing Chiemsee*, para 25. Case C-51/10 *Agencja Wydawnicza Technopol sp. z o.o. v OHIM*, para 37.

[85] Case C-191/01 *OHIM v Wrigley (Doublemint)* [2004] ETMR 88. On whether a sign which could be used for descriptive purposes should be excluded from registration, the Court said that was the case if 'at least one of its possible meanings designates a characteristic of the goods or services concerned' and that included whether the sign was capable of being used by other traders.

[86] Case C-329/02 *SAT.1 Satellitenfernsehen GmbH v OHIM* [2005] 1 CMLR 57, [2005] ETMR 20.

[87] SAT.1, para 25. See Case C-456/01 P *Henkel KGaA v OHIM* [2004] ECR I-5089, [2005] ETMR 44, paras 45 and 46. Joined Cases C-456/01 P and C-457/01 P *Henkel v OHIM* [2004] ECR I-5089, para 45; Case C-64/02 P *OHIM v Erpo Möbelwerk* [2004] ECR I-10031, para 39; and Case C-173/04 P *Deutsche SiSi-Werke v OHIM* [2006] ECR I-551, para 59.

[88] SAT.1, para 36. See also Case C-37/03 *BioID AG v OHIM* [2002] ECR II-5159, [2003] ETMR 60, paras 59–62.

14.41   This suggests that it is the distinguishing function that is paramount in relation to section 3(1)(b) of the TMA 1994 and the protective function that takes precedence in relation to section 3(1)(c) and (d) and that each of the tests should be considered and applied separately. But other case law suggests that the application of the tests is much more nuanced and both tests may be reflected in consideration of each subsection albeit subject to different priority and weight in application. *Windsurfing Chiemsee*, for example, noted earlier,[89] first considered the need to keep signs available for competing traders in the context of Article 7(1)(c) but then also considered that the need to show that the mark does in fact do its job as a mark remains important, the question asked being whether there was 'an association in the mind of the relevant class of persons between the geographic name and the category of goods in question'.[90] In other words, would the consumer see the mark as an indication of origin? In *Agencja Wydawnicza Technopol sp. z o.o. v OHIM* it was said that Article 7(1)(b) could be distinguished from Article 7(1)(c) 'in that it covers all the circumstances in which a sign is not capable of distinguishing the goods or services of one undertaking from those of other undertakings.'[91]

14.42   On the issue of whether the subsections should be independent or interdependent, the ECJ has, as indicated previously, stressed that each of the grounds for refusal to register listed in Article 7(1) is *independent* of the others and requires separate examination.[92] Nonetheless there is clear overlap between the scope of each of the grounds in Article 3(1)(b) and (c).[93] It has been argued that to read these subsections disjunctively may have superficial attraction in that it would appear to be logical in application. A first step would be to consider whether the sign is distinctive and functions as a badge of origin relying on the perception of the consumer. A second stage would then be to consider whether the sign should be left free for use by other traders. However, the approach has been criticised.[94] A mark which may not describe the characteristics of goods and services and thus be acceptable under (c) may *not* indicate trade origin and thus fall under (b). But if a mark falls under (c) and describes the characteristics of the goods and services, it seems hard to imagine that it might be considered by the consumer to indicate trade origin. For these reasons, it has been suggested that paragraphs (b), (c), and (d) should be considered as interdependent rather than independent and that the same tests of indicating origin and the need to leave marks free for other traders should be considered in relation to all three.[95]

Policy considerations

14.43   Much of this discussion which has arisen since the introduction of the Directive and the CTMR does so because of the wide variety of signs that may now be registered. There are only limited stocks of colours and shapes around which much of this discussion has centred. In *Libertel*,[96] discussed at para 14.14 the ECJ said of the application to register a colour:

---

[89] *Windsurfing Chiemesee.*   [90] *Windsurfing Chimesee*, para 37.   [91] Case C-51/10 P.

[92] *Eurohypo AG v OHIM* [2008] ETMR 59, para 60. In this case the Court considered a mark composed of descriptive elements 'could meet the conditions for registration where the word has become a part of everyday language and has acquired a meaning of its own. But, while that criterion is relevant in the context of Article 7(1)(c) it cannot form a basis for the interpretation of Article 7(1)(b)' (para 61).

[93] Case C-363/99 *Koninklijke KPN Nederland* [2004] ECR I-1619, para 85; Case C-90/11 *Strigl v Deutsches Patent- und Markenamt*, para 20.

[94] M Handler, 'The distinctive problem of European trade mark law' (2005) 27(9) EIPR 306–312 at 309. See also CFI, Case T-230/05 *Golf USA Inc v OHIM*, para 45.

[95] Handler, note 94. See Case T-230/05 *Golf USA Inc v OHIM*, para 45. See also Case C-90/11 *Strigl v Deutsches Patent- und Markenamt*, para 21, 'a sign which, in relation to the goods or services in respect of which its registration as a mark is applied for, has descriptive character for the purposes of Article 3(1)(c) of the directive is therefore necessarily devoid of any distinctive character as regards those goods or services, within the meaning of Article 3(1)(b) of that directive.'

[96] Case C-104/01 *Libertel Groep BV v Benelux-Merkenbureau* [2003] ETMR 63.

the fact that the number of colours actually available is limited means that a small number of trade mark registrations for certain services or goods could exhaust the entire range of colours available. Such a monopoly would be incompatible with a system of undistorted competition, in particular because it could have the effect of creating an unjustified competitive advantage for a single trader.[97]

Given the breadth of the provisions on infringement (discussed in paras 15.23–15.104) if a trader was to secure a registration for a commonly used shape or colour, so other traders might have to rely on defences to infringement if a confusingly similar colour or shape were used in trade. Questions of monopolisation apart, the discussion also reflects the continuing uncertainty as to where the respective interests of the consumer, the trade mark owner, and competitors should be taken into account in the trade mark framework.

 Exercise

Read M Handler, 'The distinctive problem of European trade mark law' (2005) 27(9) EIPR 306–312; Case C-329/02 P *SAT.1 Satellitenfernsehen GmbH v OHIM* [2005] 1 CMLR 57, [2005] ETMR 20; and Case C-109/97 *Windsurfing Chiemsee*.

What test(s) do you think should underpin the application of section 3(1)(b), (c), and (d) of the TMA 1994 and why? In assessing whether certain marks should be left free for competing traders, are public interest considerations a part of this test, or a separate test?

Key points on the test underlying the absolute grounds of refusal

- Two policy considerations underpin the absolute grounds of refusal: that of ensuring that a mark can do its job of distinguishing goods and services of one trader from those of another; and the need to keep marks free for competing traders

- Jurisprudence from the ECJ suggests that while the subsections must be read independently, they overlap and while the tests must be considered separately, both may apply to a single case

Types of marks

14.44   Subject to the previous discussion, some general comments can be made concerning the application of the absolute grounds for refusing to register a trade mark.

14.45   In determining distinctiveness under section 3(1)(b) of the TMA 1994 the overall impression given by the mark must be considered,[98] first, by reference to the goods and services and, secondly, the perception of the relevant consumers of the goods or services in question who are reasonably well informed and reasonably observant and circumspect.[99] When comparing marks, consideration must be given to notional fair use of the mark applied for.[100] In addition, the criteria are the same for all categories of

---

[97] *Libertel*, para 54. Note also Case T-97/08 *Kuka Roboter GmbH* which was an application to register orange in connection with robots. Also Cases T-282/09 and T-329/09 *Wilo Se v OHIM* (green and brown square).

[98] See in relation to a word mark, Case C-104/00 *DKV v OHIM* [2002] ECR I-7561, para 24 and, in relation to a three-dimensional mark, Joined Cases C-468/01 to C-472/01 *Procter & Gamble v OHIM* [2004] ECR I-5141; Case C-136/02 *Mag Instrument Inc v OHIM* [2004] ECR I-9165, [2005] ETMR 46.

[99] Joined Cases C-456/01 and C-457/01 *Henkel v OHIM* [2004] ECR I-5089, para 35, and Case C-173/04 *Deutsche SiSi-Werke v OHIM* [2006] ECR I-551, para 25.

[100] Compare this when considering infringement which requires consideration of the use that has actually been made of the sign in context. Case C-533/06 *O2 Holdings Ltd v Hutchison 3G UK Ltd* [2008] ECR I-4231 .

marks. Thus it is not permissible to have more stringent criteria in considering the distinctiveness of, for example, surnames (eg a search for the number of instances in which it appears in telephone books) than for any other category of mark.[101] However, and as will be seen in the following discussion, these rules have not been easy to apply at times, particularly when considering three-dimensional marks. It would appear that the perception of the ordinary consumer may differ when looking at these types of marks by comparison with words or figurative devices.

14.46   Under section 3(1)(c) of the TMA 1994 the trader needs to show that the sign is not, or may not be, used by other traders as a description of the goods or services. Such use of a sign is likely to give an unfair competitive advantage to the trader who first registered the descriptive indication as a mark. The mark need not be in current use by other traders, but it will be unregistrable if it might be so used.[102] Further, a mark should be refused registration under this head even if there are more usual ways of designating the same characteristics in the trade.[103] The kind, quality, quantity, intended purpose, value, geographical origin, or the time of production of the goods or of rendering of the service must all be regarded as characteristics of goods or services—a list which is not exhaustive. The reference to 'characteristic' means an element of the sign that is easily recognisable by the relevant class of persons as a description of one of those characteristics.[104] A sign will also be caught by this prohibition if at least one of its meanings is capable of designating a characteristic of the goods or services concerned.[105]

14.47   For the exclusion of customary signs from registration under section 3(1)(d) it is immaterial whether the sign, the subject of the application, described the properties or characteristics of the goods or services. What is important is whether the mark has become customary in the language or in the trade to designate the goods or services in respect of which registration was sought.[106]

> Article 7(1)(d) of Regulation No 40/94 must be interpreted as precluding registration of a trade mark only where the signs or indications of which the mark is exclusively composed have become customary in the current language or in the bona fide and established practices of the trade to designate the goods or services in respect of which registration of that mark is sought. Accordingly, whether a mark is customary can be assessed only, firstly, by reference to the goods or services in respect of which registration is sought, even though the provision in question does not explicitly refer to those goods or services, and, secondly, on the basis of the target public's perception of the mark.[107]

While these types of marks will be unregistrable per se, care must also be taken that a mark once registered does not become generic lest it is revoked (see para 14.123).

Three-dimensional marks

14.48   Two points may be made in relation to three-dimensional marks. The first is that such marks tend to be considered as devoid of distinctiveness, and the second, related point is the importance of the perception of the average consumer.

[101] Case C-404/02 *Nichols plc v Registrar of Trade Marks* [2005] 1 WLR 1418, [2005] All ER (EC) 1.
[102] Case C-191/01 *Windsurfing Chiemsee and Wrigley v OHIM*, para 32.
[103] Case C-363/99 *Koninklijke KPN Nederland NV v Benelux-Merkenbureau* [2005] 3 WLR 649, [2005] All ER (EC) 19.
[104] Case C-51/10 P *Agencja Wydawnicza Technopol sp. z o.o. v OHIM*, paras 49, 50.
[105] Case C-191/01 P *OHIM v Wm Wrigley Jr Co*, para 32; Case C-363/99 *Koinklijke KPN Nederland NV v Benelux-Merkenbureau*, para 97.
[106] Merz & Krell GmbH, para 41. Case T-507/08 *Psytech International Ltd v OHIM*.
[107] Case T-507/08 *Psytech International Ltd v OHIM*.

Devoid of distinctiveness

14.49 While the ECJ emphasised, in Joined Cases *Henkel KGaA v OHIM*[108] that, in principle, three-dimensional or shape marks are registrable[109] provided they are capable of being represented graphically, and of distinguishing the products or services of one undertaking from those of other undertakings,[110] a key question is as to how far the mark must be removed from the shape normally used in the trade. Often, and while registrable in principle, many three-dimensional shape signs prove to be unregistrable because, without having been used and the public having been educated that the mark is an indication of origin, they fall under the devoid of distinctiveness objection in section 3(1)(b) of the TMA 1994. In *Henkel*, the application was for the registration of the three dimensional shape of a tablet for washing machines in combination with an arrangement of colours. In these circumstances—where the shape for which registration is sought resembles the shape of the product in question—then it is likely to be considered devoid of distinctive character. 'Only a trade mark which departs significantly from the norm or customs of the sector and thereby fulfils its essential function of indicating origin, is not devoid of any distinctive character …' for the purposes of that provision.[111]

14.50 So there has to be some difference which departs significantly from the norm between the shape of the goods and the shape which is the subject of the application. Under this test, registration of the shape of a dishwasher tablet would not be permissible. However, that may not prevent the shape of a dishwasher tablet being registrable for completely different and unconnected goods and services. Nor, indeed, a shape which resembles but 'departs significantly' from the shape of a dishwasher tablet from being registrable for dishwasher tablets.

> **? Question**
>
> Why would a manufacturer of dishwasher tablets want to register the shape of a dishwasher tablets for marketing dishwasher tablets? What monopoly is the dishwasher tablet manufacturer hoping to obtain? Can you think of a shape which 'departs significantly' from the shape of a dishwasher tablet that a manufacturer of dishwasher tablets might want to register in connection with dishwasher tablets?

14.51 ■ **Case C-136/02 *Mag Instrument v OHIM* [2005] ETMR 46 (ECJ)**

This case concerned a refusal to register the shape of a torch as a trade mark. The Court emphasised that the overall impression of the mark must be considered and that the criteria for assessing distinctiveness of three-dimensional marks are no different from those applicable to other categories. However, the more closely the shape for which registration is sought resembles the shape of the product in question, the greater the likelihood of the shape being devoid of any distinctive character.[112] Only marks which depart 'significantly from the norm or customs of the sector and thereby fulfils its essential function of indicating origin, is not devoid of any distinctive character for the purposes of that provision'.[113]

14.52 A slightly different form of words was used in *August Storck KG v OHIM*[114] where the ECJ upheld the finding of the CFI that the application to register the shape of a sweet in class 30 for confectionary was unregistrable.

---

[108] Case C-456/01 *Henkel KGaA v OHIM* [2004] ECR I-5089, [2005] ETMR 44.   [109] *Henkel*, para 31.
[110] *Henkel*, para 30.   [111] *Henkel*, para 39.   [112] Mag Instrument, para 31.
[113] *Mag Instrument*, para 31. Joined Cases T-241/05, T-262/05 to T-264/05, T-346/05, T-347/05, and T-29/06 to T-31/06 *The Procter & Gamble Co v OHIM* [2007] ECR II-01549, para 44. OHIM v Erpo Möbelwerk, para 34; *Henkel*, paras 36 and 38. Case C-398/08 P *Audi AG v OHIM*; Cases C-344/10 P and C-345/10 *Freixenet SA v OHIM*.
[114] Case C-25/05.

The shape consists of a combination of presentational features which come naturally to mind and which are typical of the goods in question ... the alleged differences are not readily perceptible, it follows that the shape in question cannot be sufficiently distinguished from other shapes commonly used for sweets and that it does not enable the relevant public to distinguish immediately and with certainty the appellant's sweets from those of another commercial origin.[115]

14.53   So a second point here is that there must be differences between the way the mark would normally be used and the combination of elements which must be 'readily perceptible' from those used typically by other traders of the goods in question. This is to enable the consumer to distinguish immediately the mark from other goods in the marketplace. Many applications for three-dimensional marks have been refused because of this difficulty of showing that such marks are distinctive. Where, however, there are other distinctive features included with the shape, this may be sufficient to confer distinctive capacity on the sign.

The average consumer

14.54   As was pointed out previously (para 14.36), the ECJ has said that the criteria for distinctiveness is the same for all marks. However, and in relation to three-dimensional marks, the Court has stressed that as the average consumer is not in the habit of making assumptions about the origin of products on the basis of their shape or the shape of their packaging, in the absence of any graphic or word element it may prove difficult to establish distinctiveness.[116]

■ Case C-173/04 *Deutsche SiSi-Werke v OHIM*

In an appeal against a refusal to register three-dimensional marks for packaging for drinks, the ECJ considered that the CFI had not erred in law by holding, 'that the average consumer will see the form of drinks packaging as an indication of the product's commercial origin only if that form may be perceived immediately as such an indication'.[117] The packaging was unregistrable as a mark.[118] (If you go to the CTM register and search by proprietor (Deutsche SiSi-Werke) you will see the applications that have been refused.)

Names

14.55   Personal names are regularly used by traders in the course of trade. For example, 'Cathy Philip' for a florist; 'Sutherland's' for a hairdresser; 'Emmanuel' for a clothes designer. There is, however, a problem in showing that a name, particularly in the absence of use, is distinctive and thus registrable. In *Nichols plc v Registrar of Trade Marks*[119] concerning an appeal against a refusal to register the name Nichols for, inter alia, food and drink of the type normally sold through vending machines, the Court stressed that the distinctive character of a mark must be assessed in relation to the goods or services in respect of which registration is applied for and in relation to the perception of the relevant consumers,[120] and that no distinction is to be drawn between assessing distinctiveness of names and other categories of marks. Thus the practice of looking at telephone directories to determine how common a surname is, or of assessing how commonly surnames were used in the trade (a practice used by the UK Registry and courts) could

[115] *Storck*, para 29.
[116] *Henkel*, para 38; *Mag Instrument*, para 30; and SiSi-Werke, para 28. *Develey Holding GmbH & Co Beteiligungs KG v OHIM* [2008] ETMR 20, para 80.
[117] *SiSi-Werke*, para 30.   [118] See also Case C-98/11 P *Chocoladefabriken Lindt & Sprüngli AG v OHIM*.
[119] Case C-404/02 [2005] 1 WLR 1418, [2005] All ER (EC) 1.
[120] Citing Case C-299/99 Philips [2002] ECR I-5475, paras 59 and 63, and *Henkel*, para 50.

not be applied in assessing the distinctiveness of name marks. Neither could an application to register a name be refused because registration might give to the first comer a competitive advantage since there is no provision to that effect in the Directive.[121] However, and as with three-dimensional marks, the ECJ stressed that assessing distinctiveness for names might be more problematic than for other marks because the perception of the public differs as between categories of marks.

Combinations of words

14.56   Much case law has revolved around the question as to whether and in what circumstances combinations of words can be registered where one or both words on their own might be taken to mean the kind, quality, quantity, or intended purpose of the goods or services: in other words, a refusal would relate to section 3(1)(c) of the TMA 1994. In *Baby Dry*[122] the ECJ said that the exclusion in (c) only related to marks serving in normal usage to describe the produce or its characteristics. How different a mark must be between the application and the use of the mark in the trade has been the subject of some debate. In *Baby Dry* the Court said that 'any perceptible difference between the combination of words submitted for registration and the terms used in common parlance of the relevant class of consumers to designate the goods or services or their essential characteristic is apt to confer distinctive character on the word combination enabling it to be registered as a trade mark'.[123] The Court said that the ground for refusal must be read in the light of the defences in Article 12 and of the definition of a trade mark. In other words, another trader wanting to use the words would need to look at the defences to an action of trade mark infringement if they used the mark, in trade, to describe their own goods or services.

14.57   There was some disquiet after this decision was handed down. Not only was it thought inappropriate that other traders would need to look to defences should they wish to use these marks descriptively, notably considering the disparity that often exists as between the resources of traders in the marketplace, but in addition it was considered that the Court had failed to appreciate the strength of the monopoly the first comer would obtain over descriptive marks. Indeed, it has been stressed that to prevent trade marks from being improperly registered, the grounds for refusal of registration should be applied independently of the defences that might be available to traders accused of infringement.[124]

14.58   However, and not long after this decision, the ECJ started to place parameters around what would be acceptable in relation to descriptive marks and what would not. In *Wrigley v OHIM*[125] the ECJ said that a sign should be refused registration 'if at least one of its possible meanings designates a characteristic of the goods or services concerned.' This was so either at the time of application or if it could at some later time be so used.[126]

In attempting to draw a distinction between indications which designate a characteristic of the goods or services, and those which merely allude suggestively to those elements, Advocate General Jacobs suggested three guidelines in *Wrigley v OHIM*:[127]

- The more factual and objective the relationship between the term and the product or one of its characteristics, the more likely it is that the term may be used as a designation in trade, so that

---

[121] Case C-404/02 *Nichols plc v Registrar of Trade Marks* [2005] 1 WLR 1418, [2005] All ER (EC) 1, para 31.
[122] Case C-383/99 *Procter & Gamble Co v OHIM* [2002] Ch 82, [2002] 2 WLR 485, [2002] All ER (EC) 29, [2001] ECR I-6251 (hereafter Baby Dry).   [123] *Baby Dry*, para 40.
[124] Case C-404/02 *Nichols plc v Registrar of Trade Marks* [2005] 1 WLR 1418, [2005] All ER (EC) 1, paras 31–33.
[125] Case C-191/01 [2004] 1 WLR 1728, [2004] All ER (EC) 1040, [2003] ECR I-12447, [2005] 3 CMLR 21, [2004] ETMR 9.
[126] *Wrigley*, para 32.   [127] Case C-191/01 [2003] ECR I-12447, [2003] ETMR 88.

registration will be precluded by Article 7(1)(c); conversely, the more imaginative and subjective the relationship, the more acceptable the term will be for registration.

• The more ordinary, definite, and down-to-earth a term is, the more readily a consumer will apprehend any designation of a characteristic and the more likely the term will be not to qualify for registration as a trade mark.

• Where the characteristic designated is essential or of particular importance to the product or choice of the consumer then the case for refusing registration is compelling; where the designation is of a characteristic that is purely incidental or arbitrary, the case is considerably weaker.[128]

In applying his criteria to the word 'Doublemint' for chewing gum, the Advocate General found that the word was 'a factual, objective reference to mint flavour in some way doubled'; that it was readily perceivable as such, and that such flavour is an important feature of the product: 'the term designates a characteristic of doubled mintiness'. The Advocate General thus considered the mark to be unregistrable. While the ECJ did not make mention of the guidelines proposed by the Advocate General, as indicated previously that Court confirmed the Advocate General's view that the mark was unregistrable.

14.59   Where a neologism is created, that may not necessarily be registrable if it does not differ from the sum of its parts.

■ **Case C-265/00 *Campina Melkunie BV v Benelux-Merkenbureau* [2004] ECR I-1699, [2005] 2 CMLR 9**

This case concerned an application to register the word 'Biomild' for various foodstuffs, including milk products. The word 'Mild' means mild in the Netherlands where the applicant sought to market, inter alia, a mild-flavoured yoghurt under the mark. In giving judgment the ECJ first reiterated the general rule that 'the mere combination of elements, each of which is descriptive of characteristics of the goods or services in respect of which registration is sought, itself remains descriptive of those characteristics within the meaning of Article 3(1)(c) of the Directive even if the combination creates a neologism'.[129] However, if there was a perceptible difference between the neologism and the sum of its parts—enough to create an impression 'which is sufficiently far removed from that produced by the mere combination of meanings lent by the elements of which it is composed' then the mark may be registrable.[130] The criterion of 'sufficiently far removed' is not secondary to that of 'perceptible difference' but rather 'the existence of … a difference assumes that the combination resulting from the bringing together of the two word elements is sufficiently far removed from that produced by the simple juxtaposition of those elements'.[131]

14.60   It is possible that a mark which is descriptive of some goods or services and thus unregistrable would be registrable in connection with other goods or services because for those it would be distinctive.[132] Thus, it would not be possible to register 'giraffe' for toy giraffes, but 'Apple' for computers would be registrable.

14.61   The ECJ has also emphasised that in considering complex marks which may be made up of descriptive parts, it is essential to look at the mark as a whole and assess distinctiveness accordingly. Thus, in the

---

[128] *Wrigley*, paras 63–64.

[129] See also Case C-363/99 *Koninklijke KPN Nederland NV v Benelux-Merkenbureau* [2006] Ch 1; Case C-273/05 *OHIM v Celltech R&D Ltd*; Case C-408/08 P *Lancome Parfums et Beaute & Cie SNC v OHIN*; Case T-435/11 *Universal Display Corp v OHIM*.

[130] Case C-265/00 *Campina Melkunie BV v Benelux-Merkenbureau* [2004] ECR I-1699, [2005] 2 CMLR 9, para 43.

[131] Case T-346/07 *Duro Sweden AB v OHIM*, para 43. See also Case C-80/09 *Volker Megel v OHIM*.

[132] Case C-363/99 *Koninklijke KPN Nederland NV v Benelux-Merkenbureau* [2005] 3 WLR 649, [2005] All ER (EC) 19 EU.

appeal against the CFI's upholding of a refusal to register 'SAT.2' for satellite services on the ground that each element was descriptive (para 14.40), the Court said:

> as regards a trade mark comprising words or a word and a digit, such as that which forms the subject-matter of the dispute, the distinctiveness of each of those terms or elements, taken separately, may be assessed, in part, but must, in any event, depend on an appraisal of the whole which they comprise. Indeed, the mere fact that each of those elements, considered separately, is devoid of distinctive character does not mean that their combination cannot present a distinctive character.[133]

The Court had criticised the approach of the CFI which had been to look at each of the individual elements and when it had been determined neither were distinctive, the CFI considered the whole was not distinctive.[134] This was further considered in *OHIM v Celltech*, in which the Court confirmed that when a mark consists of a combination of elements, the mark can only be descriptive if the word combination itself is descriptive. It is not enough that each component is descriptive as where the combination creates an impression 'which is sufficiently far removed from that produced by the simple combination of those elements', such a combination may not be descriptive. It is therefore essential to look not only at the individual elements, but at the mark as a whole. The analysis of each of the elements of a mark is therefore not an essential step in this process, descriptiveness of the mark as a whole is what should be considered.[135]

 Question

Given the previous discussion, do you think the word 'BioID' would be registrable in classes 9, 38, and 42 of the Nice Agreement in connection with, inter alia, computer software including on the Internet and telecommunications? If so, why? If not, why not?[136]

Slogans

14.62 The ECJ has found slogans to be registrable. In *Audi AG v OHIM*[137] Audi sought to register the slogan 'Vorsprung durch Technik' (the German for 'Progress through technology') as a CTM in classes 9, 12, 14, 16, 18, 25, 28, 35–43, and 45. In line with earlier case law,[138] the CFI refused this as lacking in distinctive character for a large number of the classes. It was also held that the slogan was an objective message stating that technology leads to better goods. On appeal against the refusal to register the mark, the ECJ stated at that 'it is inappropriate to apply to slogans criteria which are stricter than those applicable to

---

[133] SAT.1, para 28. The Court also referred to Case C-265/00 *Campina Melkunie BV v Benelux-Merkenbureau* [2005] 2 CMLR 9, paras 40 and 41 and Case C-363/99 *Koninklijke Kpn Nederland NV v Benelux Merkenbureau* [2005] 3 WLR 649, paras 99 and 100. See also *OHIM v Celltech* [2007] ETMR 52, paras 76–80; Case C-90/11 *Strigl v Deutsches Patent- und Markenamt*.

[134] The ECJ also said in this case that 'the frequent use of trade marks consisting of a word and a number in the telecommunications sector indicates that type of combination cannot be considered to be devoid, in principle, of distinctive character' (para 44). This has been criticised. See, eg, A Folliard-Monguiral and D Rogers, 'Significant case law from 2004 on the Community trade mark from the Court of First Instance, the European Court of Justice and OHIM' [2005] EIPR 133 at 135. Those authors point to subsequent case law of the ECJ in which that Court stresses that the more closely the mark or the shape for which registration is sought resembles that most likely to be used in the trade, the greater the likelihood of the shape being devoid of distinctive character. And, 'Only a mark which departs significantly from the norm or customs of the sector and thereby fulfils its essential function of indicating origin, is not devoid of any distinctive character …' (Case C-468/01 *Procter & Gamble Co v OHIM* [2004] ECR I-5141, [2004] ETMR 88). The authors suggest that on this point, SAT.1 should perhaps be seen as a 'one-off' case.

[135] *OHIM v Celltech* [2007] ETMR 52, paras 76–80. See also, inter alia, Case C-265/00 *Campina Melkunie* [2004] ECR I1699; Case C-363/99 *Koninklijke KPN Nederland* [2004] ECR I1619; Case C-329/02 P *SAT.1 v OHIM* [2004] ECR I-8317; Case C-37/03 P *BioID AG v OHIM* [2005] ECR I7975; Case C-342/09 *Victor Guedes Industria e Comercia SA v OHIM*.

[136] Case T-91/01 *BioID AG v OHIM* [2002] ECR II-5159, [2003] ETM 60 to find the answer!   [137] [2010] ETMR 18.

[138] Case C-131/08 *Dorel Juvenile Group v OHIM* (Safety 1st); Case C-64/02 *Erpo Mobelwerk GmbH v OHIM* (Das Prinzip der Bequemlichkeit).

other types of sign',[139] however the relevant public's perception is not the same and it could be more difficult to prove distinctive character in respect of some types of marks. A requirement of imaginativeness is not appropriate.[140] The fact that a mark is laudatory does not thereby mean that it is devoid of distinctive character; neither does it mean that it cannot guarantee to consumers the origin of goods and services.[141] The fact that the mark may be primarily understood as a promotional formula is not sufficient for considering it non-distinctive. The fact that a slogan has a number of meanings, or constitutes a play on words, or is seen as imaginative or unexpected and can thus be easily remembered, are likely to mean that the mark has distinctive character. Promotional formula may not, however, be perceived as a trade mark in the absence of a striking characteristic in the structure of the sign or its overall meaning.[142]

Symbols

14.63   Applications for registration for symbols have been made, but it can be difficult to establish distinctiveness particularly for marks consisting of a single letter rather than for other word marks. What is required is an assessment as to whether the sign at issue is capable of distinguishing the different goods and services in the context of an examination, based on the facts, focusing on those goods or services.[143] In relation to an application for the symbol 'α' without any graphic modification in class 33, the ECJ noted that the test was the same as for any other mark but 'while the criteria for the assessment of distinctive character are the same for different categories of marks, it may be that, for the purposes of applying those criteria, the relevant public's perception is not necessarily the same in relation to each of those categories and it could therefore prove more difficult to establish distinctiveness in relation to marks of certain categories as compared with marks of other categories'[144] but there is no need to find a specific level of linguistic or artistic creativity or imaginativeness on the part of the proprietor of the trade mark.[145]

Numerals

14.64   Numerals too can be registered as trade marks. In *Agencja Wydawnicza Technopol sp. z o.o. v OHIM (1000)* the applicant sought to register '1000' for brochures and periodicals in class 16. This was refused under Article 7(1)(b) and (c) on the basis that the sign was descriptive as designating the extent of the contents of the publication sold in connection with the sign. The ECJ was unable to revisit this part of the General Court's findings, but did stress that the word 'characteristic' 'highlights the fact that the signs referred to in Article 7(1)(c) of Regulation No 40/94 are merely those which serve to designate a property, easily recognisable by the relevant class of persons, of the goods or the services in respect of which registration is sought.'[146] A sign can only be refused registration if it is reasonable to believe that it will actually be recognised by the relevant class of persons as a description of one of those characteristics.[147] Where the general public might believe that the sign '1000' as applied to a publication which could, for example, contain 1,000 crossword puzzles, then it was appropriate to refuse registration. The Court of Justice has thus been keen to keep the General Court's finding in *Technopol* narrowly applied by stressing that

---

[139] Para 36.   [140] Case T-138/00 *Erpo Mobelwerk GmbH v OHIM* [2001] ECR II-3739.
[141] See also Case T-175/08 *Paroc Oy AB v OHIM*, 8 February 2011 ('insulate for life'); Case T-523/09 *Smart Technologies ULC v OHIM* (Wir Machen Das Besondere); Case T-524/09 *Meredith Corp v OHIM* (Better Homes and Gardens).
[142] Case C-92/10 P *Media Saturn Holding GmbH v OHIM*, paras 51–53. See also Case T-157/08 *Paroc Oy v OHIM* ('insulate for life'); Case T-310/08 *BSH Bosch und Siemens Hausgerate GmbH v OHIM* (Executive Edition); Case T-523/09 *Smart Technologies v OHIM* (Wir Machen Das Besondere Einfach); Case T-524/09 *Meredith Corp v OHIM* (Better Homes and Gardens).
[143] Case C-265/09 P *OHIM v BORCO-Marken-Import Matthiesen*, para 38.   [144] Para 33.
[145] Case C-329/02 P *SAT.1 v OHIM* [2004], para 41.   [146] Para 50.   [147] Para 50.

where there is no possibility of a number being seen as descriptive of goods, then registration should be allowed.[148]

In applying this test the Court of Appeal in *WHG (International) Ltd, WHG Trading Ltd and William Hill plc v 32Red plc*[149] said:

> At the end of the day, the point is a very short one. In Technopol [2011] E.T.M.R. 34 , 1000 was capable of describing a feature of the goods in respect of which registration was sought, such as the number of pages or works or the number of crossword puzzles in periodicals. The bare number 32 is not descriptive of any characteristic of the services provided by the respondent. It is merely an allusion to an aspect of the game which the punter will play if he or she uses the respondent's services. The number does not in any way characterise the respondent's services in the sense of describing what will be supplied.

Geographical names

14.65   In *Windsurfing Chiemsee* (para 14.39) the ECJ made various comments in relation to the registerability of geographical indications as trade marks under Article 7(1)(c) of the CTMR. The purpose of the exclusion is that such signs should remain available not only because they may be an indication of the quality and other characteristics of the categories of goods, but in addition they may influence consumer taste because they give rise to a favourable response.[150] Registration will be refused where the name designates a specific geographical location which is already famous, or known and associated by consumers for the category of goods concerned, and where the geographical name is liable to be used by others as an indication of the geographical origin of the goods by others.[151] However, registration of a geographical name is not precluded where it is unknown to the relevant consumers as the designation of geographical origin or where, because of the place designated by the name, consumers are unlikely to believe that the category of goods concerned originates there or was conceived of there.[152] Descriptiveness of the geographical name is to be assessed by reference to the goods or services as well as by reference to the understanding which the relevant persons have of it.[153] In applying these rules the CFI found that the name 'Cloppenburg' (the name of a town in Lower Saxony in Germany) in connection with retail services falling within class 35 of the Nice Agreement to be registrable.[154]

Foreign word marks

14.66   An interesting issue arose in *Matratzen Concord AG v Hukla Germany SA*,[155] concerning the trade mark Matrazen, registered in Spain by Hukla Germany in class 20 of the Nice Agreement in respect of, inter alia, furniture such as beds, sofa-beds, camp beds, and cradles. Matratzen means mattress in German. Matratzen Concord AG, another German company, sought to have the registration revoked on the grounds that it was descriptive of the nature, quality, characteristics, or geographic origin of the products or services that it purports to distinguish. The question referred to the ECJ was whether registration of a term borrowed from the language of another member state in which it is devoid of distinctive character

---

[148] See also Joined Cases C-54/10 P and C-55/10 P *Agena Wydawnicza Technopol sp. z o.o. v OHIM* ('350', '250', '150', '222', '333', and '555'); Case T-503/09 *Cybergun v OHIM* (AK47); Case T-258/09 *i-content v OHIM* (Betwin); Case T-507/08 *Psytech International v OHIM* (16PF).

[149] [2012] EWCA Civ 19.

[150] By analogy, *Windsurfing Chiemsee*, para 26 and *Peek & Cloppenburg KG v OHIM* [2006] ETMR 33, para 33.

[151] By analogy, *Windsurfing Chiemsee*, paras 29 and 30.   [152] *Windsurfing Chiemsee*, para 33.

[153] Case T-295/01 *Nordmilch v OHIM (Oldenburger)* [2003] ECR II-4365, paras 27–34. *Peek & Cloppenburg KG v OHIM* [2006] ETMR 33, para 37.

[154] *Peek & Cloppenburg KG v OHIM* [2006] ETMR 33.   [155] Case C-421/04 [2006] ETMR 48.

or descriptive of the goods or services in respect of which registration is sought, must be refused in the member state of application. The ECJ said that this was not so and pointed out that because of linguistic, cultural, social, and economic differences between the member states, a trade mark which is devoid of distinctive character or descriptive of the goods or services concerned in one member state may not be so in another member state.

> Consequently, Article 3(1)(b) and (c) of the Directive does not preclude the registration in a Member State, as a national trade mark, of a term borrowed from the language of another Member State in which it is devoid of distinctive character or descriptive of the goods or services in respect of which registration is sought.[156]

The determining factor for registerability would be how the term would be understood by the relevant parties in the state where registration was sought. The relevant parties are the traders in, or average consumers of, the specified products.

14.67   Although it is clear that foreign word marks, generic in their own country, can be registered as trade marks in another state, this proviso that the term must be distinctive among the relevant class of traders and consumers is perhaps likely to reduce the number of such applications destined to be successful. Indeed, it has been said that the judgment 'cannot be correct' by leading commentators[157] pointing to the fact that in the UK knowledge of the main European languages is assumed. As goods move throughout the EU it is increasingly likely that traders within the relevant trade are aware of the descriptions of goods in other countries, as will the well-travelled consumer.

 Questions

Do you think that *Matratzen Concord AG v Hukla Germany SA* was correctly decided?

What do you think of the developing jurisprudence around registerability of these different signs? Do you think that the criteria are sufficiently clear to enable applicants and their advisers to determine when an application will be successful?

Key points on the types of marks that can be registered

- Non-distinctive, descriptive, and customary marks are all excluded from registration unless they have become distinctive through use

- The exclusions reflect the function of a trade mark as an indication of origin and provide a balance as between the interests of the would-be trade mark owner and competitors in the field

- The same factors are to be used in assessing the registerability of all types of marks

- For some marks a finding of distinctiveness may be difficult given that the perception of the public differs as between categories of marks

Quiz

14.68   As can be seen, the jurisprudence in relation to those aspects of registerability discussed earlier has been developing rapidly in recent years. The previous discussion has concentrated on the Court of Justice of

---

[156] *Matrazen*, para 26.   [157] WR Cornish, D Llewellyn, and T Aplin, *Intellectual Property* (7th edn, 2010), 740 fn 244.

the European Union cases. Beyond this, there are a plethora of decisions and appeals from decisions made at national and European level as to the registerability or otherwise of signs as trade marks and which base themselves on the criteria laid down by the Court.

Web links

Cases determining the registerability of marks can be researched in a number of ways. Go to the Court of Justice website at http://www.curia.europa.eu. Go to the advanced search and put trade marks in the subject matter field. This will bring up a number of hits where decisions relating to trade marks have been made at European level. Not all of the decisions concern registerability but many do and it is a useful way to find them.

You can also look at the OHIM website at http://www.oami.europa.eu. Look under case law of the Court of Justice and of the General Court.

As was mentioned previously, the OHIM website contains a database showing all the marks which have been registered. In addition, you will find on the site a database of marks which have been refused registration and the reasons for refusal (look under legal aspects on the site). If you are unsure of the contents of the particular classes of the Nice classification you can find a copy of the Treaty on the WIPO website at http://www.wipo.int/classifications/nice/en/classifications.html.

Exercise

It is now your task to investigate the decisions and cases both at EU level (OHIM and General Court) and national level (Trade Marks Registry and courts) to ascertain how this jurisprudence of the Court of Justice is applied.

Do you think the following signs would be registrable? If so why? If not, why not? Note: there are plenty of clues in the footnotes as to the correct answers—test yourself before you look at these, and don't forget to supply reasons!

- Slogan mark

    'There is a difference':
    Nice classification 23.[158]

- Word mark

    'Everything is Possible'.
    Nice classification 2, 9, 16, 35, 36, 37, 38, and 42.[159]

- Colour mark

    Where a representation of the colours and their juxtaposition is included in the application along with the description: dark brown (Pantone 411 CVC); light brown (30% Pantone 411 CVC); dark green (Pantone 611); light green (40% Pantone 611 CVC); dark blue (Pantone 291 C); light blue (45% Pantone 291 CVC).
    Nice classification 18.[160]

---

[158] App No 002694123 (n).   [159] App No 003514569 (n).   [160] CTM 003678794 (y).

- Word mark

  'DataCenterAlliance'
  Nice classification 9, 11, and 40.[161]

- Sound mark (Figure 14.7)

  Nice classification 9, 38, 41, and 42.[162]

Figure 14.7 Sound waves

- Olfactory mark

  The trade mark is a graphic representation of a particular fragrance. A lawn green note, citrus (bergamot, lemon), pink floral (orange blossom, hyacinth), musky in all shades of green and blue. Note: the graphic representation (a selection of colours) was included in the application. Nice classification 3, 5, 16, 18, and 24.[163]

- Word mark

  'Drinkfresh'
  Nice classification 29 and 30.[164]

Distinctive through use

14.69   As was indicated previously, section 3(1) of the TMA 1994 provides that each of these absolute grounds of refusal (except where a sign does not satisfy the requirement of s 1) yields to the proviso that if a sign which is unregistrable becomes distinctive through use before the application is filed,[165] then it may be registered as a mark. Evidence of the mark becoming distinctive through use after the application is irrelevant as only the period before the application is filed is taken into account.[166] It should be noted that this is not an independent right to have a trade mark registered. Rather it is an exception to the grounds for refusal listed in section 3(1)(b)–(d). The scope is therefore to be interpreted in the light of those grounds for refusal.[167]

14.70   Useful guidance on what evidence is required to show that a mark has become distinctive through use was given by the ECJ in Joined Cases *Windsurfing Chiemsee Produktions- und Vertriebs GmbH (WSC) v Boots- und Segelzubehör Walter Huber and Franz Attenberger*.[168] The Court said that the following factors could be taken into account:

[161] App No 003892262 (n).   [162] App No 000143891 (n).   [163] App No 000521914 (n).
[164] App No 003378692 (n).   [165] Case T-247/01 *eCopy Inc v OHIM* [2003] ETMR 99.
[166] *Imagination Technologies Ltd v OHIM* [2008] ETMR 10, paras 77–79; Case T-463/08 *Imagion v OHIM*.
[167] *Bovemij Verzekeringen NV v Benelux-Merkenbureau* [2007] ETMR 29, para 21.
[168] Joined Cases C-108/97 and C-109/97.

- the market share held by the mark;

- how intensive, geographically widespread, and long-standing use of the mark has been;

- the amount invested by the undertaking in promoting the mark;

- the proportion of the relevant class of persons who, because of the mark, identify goods as originating from a particular undertaking;

- statements from chambers of commerce and industry or other trade and professional associations.[169]

The important factor is whether the 'relevant class of persons, or at least a significant proportion thereof, identify goods as originating from a particular undertaking because of the trade mark'.[170] The relevant class of persons can be made up of both professionals and the general public depending on the circumstance of the case.[171] In relation to geographical marks, the ECJ has emphasised that such a mark can become distinctive through use where there has been 'long-standing and intensive use of the mark' and that the use of the mark 'is particularly well established'.[172]

Geographical extent

14.71   A question arises as to the geographical extent of the territory in which a mark may become registrable through use. For a CTM it has been said that it is necessary to show that a mark has acquired distinctiveness in all of those countries of the Union where it would be regarded as non-distinctive. Thus in *Ford Motor's Application*[173] the question arose over the registration of the word 'Options' for insurance services. It was shown that the word had acquired distinctiveness in the UK but not in France. The CFI upheld the objection to registration on the grounds that a sign must possess distinctive character throughout the Union. The CFI pointed out that the CTMR (Art 1(2)) provides that the CTM is to have 'a unitary character', which implies that 'It shall have equal effect throughout the Community'.[174] The conclusion was reinforced by Article 7(2) of the CTMR which provides that a trade mark is not to be registered 'notwithstanding that the grounds of non-registrability [laid down in Article 7(1)] obtain in only part of the Community'.[175] In *Glaverbel v OHIM*[176] concerning an application to register a piece of glass to which a design had been applied, the CFI said it was not enough that evidence was led in relation to ten of the 15 member states. It had to be shown that the mark was considered distinctive through use in each territory. Similarly, in *Diagnostiko kai Therapeftiko Kentro Athinon 'Ygeia' AE v OHIM*[177] the General Court considered the trade mark 'υγεία' (the Greek for health). The Court stated that where a mark is found not to be distinctive to customers within a linguistic area extending to multiple member states, then acquired distinctiveness must be shown in each of the territories and not just a substantial part of the linguistic area. As such, in the instant case, the applicant must show acquired distinctiveness in Greece and Cyprus.

14.72   In *Louis Vuitton Malletier v OHIM*[178] the reasoning for requiring this was explained as follows:

> The unitary character of the Community trade mark, to which the applicant refers, does not cast doubt on that finding but, on the contrary, confirms it, since it is apparent therefrom that, in order to be accepted for registration,

---

[169] *Windsurfing Chiemsee*, para 51. See also Case C-299/99 *Koninklijke Philips Electronics NV v Remington Consumer Products Ltd* [2002] ECR I-5475, [2003] Ch 159, para 60; Case C-353/03 *Société des Produits Nestlé SA v Mars UK Ltd* [2005] 3 CMLR 12, [2005] ETMR 96, [2006] FSR 2, para 31; Case C-25/05 *August Storck v OHIM*.

[170] *Windsurfing Chiemsee*, para 52.   [171] *AGC Flat Glass Europe SA formerly Glaverbel SA v OHIM* [2008] ETMR 37.

[172] *AGC Flat Glass*, para 50. See also the application in *Bovemij Verzekeringen NV v Benelux-Mekenbureau* (Benelux Trademarks Office) [2007] ETMR 29 for questions referred to the ECJ concerning geographic extent and language and para 14.74.

[173] Case T-91/99 [2000] 2 CMLR 276.   [174] *Ford*, para 23. See also Case T-318/09 *Audi AG v OHIM*.

[175] *Ford*, para 25.   [176] [2008] ETMR 37.   [177] Case T-7/10.   [178] Case T-237/10.

a sign must possess distinctive character, inherent or acquired through use, throughout the European Union ... It would be paradoxical to accept, on the one hand, pursuant to Article 3(1)(b) of Directive 2008/95/EC ..., that a Member State has to refuse to register as a national mark a sign that is devoid of any distinctive character in its territory and, on the other, that that same Member State has to respect a Community trade mark relating to that sign for the sole reason that it has acquired distinctive character in the territory of another Member State (see, by analogy, υγεία, paragraph 98 above, paragraph 53).[179]

14.73   In *Louis Vuitton Malletier* insufficient proof relating to three member states out of 15 resulted in a dismissal of the applicants claim. Information relating to market share of a sign (TDI) was found to be inconclusive of acquired distinctiveness in the absence of information concerning the economic and geographical importance of the use, its duration, and the amount of investment in promoting the sign. The fact that TDI was always used in association with another sign which had distinguishing capacity weakened the claim to the acquisition of distinctive character.[180]

The requirement is thus clearly high (and expensive) for those seeking to prove distinctiveness through use for the purposes of registration of a CTM.

14.74   The geographical extent of acquired distinctiveness differs for a national trade mark and was considered in *Bovemij Verzekeringen NV v Benelux-Merkenbureau*.[181] The question was whether the sign 'Europolis' had acquired a distinctive character in the Benelux territory. The first two questions referred to the ECJ essentially asked which territory should be taken into account in order to assess whether a sign had acquired a distinctive character through use where a member state or group of member states (such as Benelux) have common legislation on trade marks. The Court stressed that registration of a trade mark could only be allowed if it was proven that the trade mark had acquired distinctive character through use throughout the territory of the member state or, in the case of Benelux, throughout the part of the territory of Benelux in which there exists a ground for refusal.[182] The third question the Court was asked was to what extent the linguistic areas in a member state should be taken into account in assessing the acquisition of a distinctive character through use where the trade mark consisted of one or more words in the official language of a member state or of Benelux. In the instant case, the Dutch word 'polis' usually refers to an insurance contract and so the grounds for refusal existed only in that part of Benelux where Dutch is spoken. The Court ruled that it was necessary to take into account that part of Benelux where Dutch is spoken.[183]

Product marks and colours

14.75   As noted previously, although there is now the possibility of registering colours as trade marks there is a need to show acquired distinctiveness. In the case of *Cadbury Schweppes plc v Societe des Produits Nestle SA*[184] the UK Intellectual Property Office (IPO; or UK–IPO) allowed the colour purple to be registered for certain chocolate bars and chocolate drinks. It was accepted that the mark was not inherently distinctive so in order to be registered it is necessary to show acquired distinctiveness. The method of assessing acquired distinctiveness is the same as with any mark but it is noted that colours are not necessarily perceived by customers is the same way as word marks.

---

[179]   Para 100. See also Case T-318/09 *Audi AG v OHIM*; Case T-141/06 *Glaverbel v OHIM*.
[180]   Case T-318/09 *Audi and Volkswagen v OHIM*.   [181]   Case C-108/05.
[182]   *Bovemij Verzekeringen NV v Benelux-Merkenbureau*, para 23. See also Case C-25/05 P *Storck v OHIM* [2006] ECR I-5719, para 83.
[183]   *Bovemij Verzekeringen NV v Benelux-Merkenbureau*, para 26.   [184]   Unreported, 14 November 2011.

■ **Cases C-344/10 P and C-345/10 *Freixenet SA v OHIM***

This case concerned the claims by Freixenet to the colour 'golden matt' and the mark a 'white polished bottle which when filled with sparkling wine takes on a golden matt appearance similar to a frosted bottle'; and to the colour 'black matt' and the mark a 'frosted black matt bottle'.

The Court reiterated the criteria to consider for three-dimensional and 'other' marks when considering acquired distinctiveness. These included: the need for the mark to have distinctive character[185] assessed by reference to the goods and services in respect of which registration is sought and by reference to the perception of the relevant public,[186] the criteria for assessing distinctive character for three-dimensional marks are no different from those applicable to other categories of mark[187] subject to the fact that the perception of the average consumer is not necessarily the same in relation to a three-dimensional mark consisting of the shape of the product as it is in relation to a work or figurative mark so it could be challenging to establish distinctive character in relation to these marks.[188] Only a mark which departs significantly from the norm or customs of the sector fulfils the essential function of indicating origin.[189] These rules apply not only to three-dimensional marks but also to 'other' marks which are not independent of the packaging of the products it designates.[190] This means that 'marks consisting of the appearance of the packaging of the product itself that do not contain an inscription or a word element would be excluded automatically from the protection that may be conferred by the CTMR.'[191]

14.76 In the light of this consistent case law, the Max Planck Institute in its *Study on the Overall Functioning of the European Trade Mark System* recommends that the preamble of the Regulation is amended to state that shape of product marks and colours per se usually need to establish acquired distinctiveness.[192]

Distinctiveness of part of a mark

14.77 It is possible for part of a mark to become distinctive through the use of the whole of the mark. In *Société des produits Nestlé SA v Mars UK Ltd*[193] the question revolved around the slogan 'Have a break … Have a Kit Kat' and the name 'Kit Kat' which are both marks registered in the UK register in class 30 for chocolate, chocolate products, confectionery, candy, and biscuits. When Nestlé applied for registration of the words 'Have a Break' as a mark in respect of class 30 based on the acquisition of distinctive character through the use made of the whole of the mark, the Court said that the mark need not necessarily have been used independently;[194] 'of distinctive character' may be as a result both of the use as part of a registered trade mark (or of a component) and of the use of a separate mark in conjunction with a registered trade mark. In both cases it is sufficient that, in consequence of such use, the relevant class of persons actually perceive the product or service as originating from a given undertaking.[195]

[185] Joined Cases C-456/01 P and C-457/01 P *Henkel v OHIM* [2004] ECR I-5089, para 34; Case C-136/02 P *Mag Instrument v OHIM* [2004] ECR I-9165, para 29; and Case C-238/06 P *Develey v OHIM* [2007] ECR I-9375, para 79.

[186] *Henkel*, para 35; Case C-25/05 P *Storck v OHIM* [2006] ECR I-5719, para 25; and *Develey v OHIM*, para 79.

[187] *Mag Instrument*, para 30; *SiSi-Werke*, para 27; *Storck v OHIM*, para 26; and Case C-144/06 P *Henkel v OHIM* [2007] ECR I-8109, para 36.

[188] *Mag Instrument*, para 30; *SiSi-Werke*, para 28; and *Storck v OHIM*, para 27.

[189] *Mag Instrument*, para 31; *SiSi-Werke*, para 31; and *Storck v OHIM*, para 28.   [190] *Storck v OHIM*, para 29.

[191] Cases C-344/10 P and C-345/10 *Freixenet SA v OHIM*, paras 49–51.   [192] At 73.

[193] Case C-353/03 *Société des Produits Nestlé SA v Mars UK Ltd* [2005] 3 CMLR 12, [2005] ETMR 96, [2006] FSR 2.

[194] *Société des Produits Nestlé SA v Mars UK Ltd*, para 27.

[195] *Société des Produits Nestlé SA v Mars UK Ltd*, para 30.

Marks used for particular purposes

14.78   Where a sign has been used for a particular purpose prior to it being used in a trade mark manner, that use may prevent the mark from being capable of signifying trade origin if the first use still resonates in the mind of the relevant public as the sign would not be considered distinctive. So in *Score Draw Ltd v Alan Finch (CBD Trade Mark)*[196] the issue concerned a mark which had been used by the governing body for sport in Brazil, by the Brazilian football team until 1971, and had appeared on the shirts of historical football figures. In an appeal seeking to have the registration of the mark invalidated, the court said what was important was to consider whether the prior use in connection with the football teams was so ingrained in the mind of the public that it was not possible for the badge to be distinctive of origin in relation to the person putting shirts on the market carrying the sign. In the instant case, the prior use had indeed robbed the badge of its power to signify trade origin.[197]

Loss of distinctiveness

14.79   Care must be taken in establishing that a mark which has become distinctive through use has not become customary. Thus in *Alcon Inc v OHIM*[198] the question concerned the mark 'BSS' which had been used but was found to have become customary for the target public concerned and hence the use made of the mark had not been able to confer distinctive character on it.[199]

Key points on distinctiveness through use

- A mark which is not inherently distinctive may become distinctive through use before the application is filed

- This is an exception to the grounds for refusal listed in section 3(1)(b) to (d) of the TMA 1994 and not an independent right

- For a CTM it is necessary to show that a mark has acquired distinctiveness throughout the Union and is considered to be so by a significant proportion of the relevant consumers

- For a national mark it is necessary to show that it has become distinctive through use throughout the territory of the member state (or in the Benelux territory) in that part in which the objection subsists

- Part of a mark may become distinctive through the use of the whole of a mark

---

Exclusion from registration of certain shapes

TMA 1994, section 3(2); Directive, Article 3(1)(e); and CTMR, Article 7(1)(e)

14.80   Another important section dealing with absolute grounds for refusal is section 3(2) of the TMA 1994. This section provides that a sign will not be registered as a trade mark if it consists exclusively of:

---

[196]   *Score Draw Ltd v Alan Finch* (CBD Trade Mark) [2007] EWHC 462 (Ch), [2007] FSR 20.
[197]   See also Cases T-444/08 to T-448/08 *FIFA v Ferrero* concerning the words 'World Cup' which were found to be wholly descriptive and needed to be left free for competitors. Consider also the counteraction theory in the light of these cases discussed in para 15.47.
[198]   Case C-192/03 P Alcon Inc v OHIM [2004] ECR I-8993, [2005] ETMR 69. See also Case T-507/08 *Psytech International Ltd/OHIM* (16PF) (GC).   [199]   Alcon Inc v OHIM, para 31.

- the shape which results from the nature of the goods themselves;
- the shape of the goods which is necessary to attain a technical result; or
- the shape which gives substantial value to the goods.[200]

It should be noted that the ECJ has described these provisions as a 'preliminary obstacle' to registration saying: 'If any one of the criteria listed in Article 3(1)(e) is satisfied, a sign consisting exclusively of the shape of the product or of a graphic representation of that shape cannot be registered as a trade mark.'[201] In other words, if the sign falls under any one of these provisions, then it will not be registrable—and there is no need to go on to consider the other criteria as discussed previously.

14.81 The prohibitions are included because to allow registration of the shapes under contemplation would mean that a monopoly would be created in the use of the shape as a trade mark *and* in the technical or functional characteristics of the goods themselves, a monopoly that would continue for as long as registration of the mark was renewed. To allow such registrations would 'form an obstacle preventing competitors from freely offering for sale products incorporating such technical solutions or functional characteristics in competition with the proprietor of the trade mark.'[202] As it would not be in the public interest to permit registration of such shapes, it is not possible to overcome objections by showing that a shape falling under these provisions has become distinctive through use.[203]

Nature of the goods

14.82 Under section 3(2)(a) of the TMA 1994 (the shape which results from the nature of the goods themselves), it would not be possible to register the shape of a fork or a knife for cutlery as those shapes result from the nature of those implements. The first to register these shapes would have a monopoly not only over the shape as a mark, but over the shapes themselves. As was said in *Philips Electronics v Remington*:[204]

> No doubt an application to register a picture of a reel of cotton or a flag for coffee would succeed as they are not descriptive of the goods for which registration is sought; but that does not mean that a shape of an article is registrable in respect of the article shown in the application. To so hold would enable a few traders to obtain registrations of all the best designs of an article and thereby monopolise those designs. In my view a shape of an article cannot be registered in respect of the goods of that shape unless it contains some addition to the shape of the article which has trade mark significance. It is that addition which makes it capable of distinguishing the trade mark owner's goods from the same sort of goods sold by another trader.

14.83 It would appear that the exclusion is relevant to generic shapes or basic shapes. As was also said in *Phillips Electronics v Remington*: 'Subsection 2(a) has to be construed in the context of subsections (b) and (c). It is intended to exclude from registration basic shapes that should be available for use by the public at large. It is difficult to envisage such shapes, except those that are produced in nature such as bananas'. Thus, for example, the objection was not successful with regard to the shape of a three-headed rotary electric shaver which was to be registered for, inter alia, electric shavers as electric shavers do not have to be of this shape.[205]

Functional features

14.84 Similar considerations underlie section 3(2)(b), the operation of which is illustrated by the judgment of the ECJ in *Koninklijke Philips Electronics NV v Remington Consumer Products Ltd*.[206] Philips registered a trade mark consisting of a picture of a three-headed rotary electric shaver (the 208 mark). You can find

[200] Note that the Max Planck Institute study recommends abolition of this criterion (at 73).
[201] *Philips*, para 76.   [202] *Philips*, para 78.
[203] Case R 856/2004-G Lego *Juris A/S v Mega Brands Inc* (Grand Board of Appeal), 10 July 2006. Upheld by the CFI: Case T-270/06 *Lego Juris A/S v OHIM*. Case C-48/09 *Lego Juris A/S v OHIM*.
[204] [1999] RPC 809 (CA) per Aldous LJ at 818.   [205] *Philips* per Aldous LJ at 820.   [206] *Philips*.

an image of the trade mark if you look in the UK trade mark register available on the IPO website under TM (archived) No 1254208.

Web link

The web link to the mark is **http://www.ipo.gov.uk/tmcase/Results/1/UK00001254208.**

Remington marketed three-headed rotary shavers. Philips accused Remington of infringing their registered trade mark. In turn, Remington alleged that the Philips mark was invalid on a number of grounds including that it consisted exclusively of a shape which was necessary to obtain a technical result. At first instance the mark was held to be invalid and the court ordered the mark to be revoked. On appeal the Court of Appeal ordered a reference to be made to the ECJ on the ground that the case raised difficult questions of construction of the Directive.[207] In addition, similar issues had arisen in a case pending before the Swedish Court of Appeal, in which the Swedish District Court had construed the Directive differently.

In giving judgment the ECJ made a number of important points.

- To allow registration of functional characteristics of a shape 'would limit the possibility of competitors supplying a product incorporating such a function or at least limit their freedom of choice in regard to the technical solution they wish to adopt in order to incorporate such a function in their product'.[208]

- The fact that some small element of the sign does not contribute to the technical performance but may serve, either alone or in combination, an aesthetic purpose, does not save a mark from the prohibition against registration under this measure.

- There is nothing in the provision that would allow registration of the shape of goods necessary to achieve a technical result even if other shapes could achieve the same technical result: 'where the essential functional characteristics of the shape of a product are attributable solely to the technical result, Article 3(1)(e), second indent, precludes registration of a sign consisting of that shape, even if that technical result can be achieved by other shapes'.[209]

14.85 This latter point was also emphasised in *Lego Juris A/S v Mega Brands Inc*[210] (subsequently upheld by the CFI in *Lego Juris A/S v OHIM*;[211] with an appeal to the ECJ dismissed; set out later) in which the Grand Board of Appeal endorsed the finding of the Cancellation Division that if Article 7(1)(e)(ii) of the CTMR did not preclude monopolies on visual embodiments or designs of a technical solution, it would be possible to register not only the preferred embodiment of that solution (in this case of the Lego brick), but also every conceivable visual embodiment or design of that technical solution. 'This would necessarily result in a monopoly on a technical solution, so that Article 7(1)(e)(ii) CTMR would be circumvented'.[212]

14.86 While this seemed to provide a clear limitation on the registration of shape marks with technical features, the litigation concerning shavers continued[213] in *Koninklijke Philips Electronics NV v Remington Consumer*

[207] *Philips.*   [208] *Philips*, para 79.   [209] *Philips*, para 83.
[210] Case R 856/2004-G [2007] ETMR 11.   [211] Cae T-270/06 [2009] ETMR 15.
[212] Case R 856/2004-G *Lego Juris A/S v Mega Brands Inc* (Grand Board of Appeal), 10 July 2006, para 58. Case C 48/09 P *Lego Juris A/S v OHIM*, para 46.
[213] Described by Mummery LJ in the Court of Appeal in *Koninklijke Philips Electronics NV v Remington Consumer Products Ltd, Rayovac Europe Ltd* [2006] ETMR 42, [2006] EWCA Civ 16 as marathon litigation (para 1).

Products Ltd, Rayovac Europe Ltd.[214] This case concerned a different mark—the 452 mark described as the overall shape of an inverted equilateral triangle, with three heads sitting within a raised faceplate of clover leaf design superimposed on a triangle. You can find an image of this trade mark if you look in the UK trade mark register available on the IPO website under TM No 1533452[215] as well as a series of device marks (see para 14.92).

14.87 When Philips brought infringement proceedings against Remington, Remington challenged the validity of the 452 mark on the ground that it consisted exclusively of features of the shape of the goods which were necessary to obtain a technical result under section 3(2) of the TMA 1994. In giving judgment the Court of Appeal made some comments on the interpretation of the section and in particular what is meant by essential feature and exclusively.

Essential feature

14.88 A central question was whether the addition of the clover leaf feature to the invalid 208 mark made the otherwise similar 452 mark a valid trade mark: was the clover leaf design an essential feature? The High Court had found that it was not, and the mark was invalid. The Court of Appeal agreed with this saying that the important factor was the impact of the mark on the eye of the average consumer who would not dissect and examine each feature. What is key is the feature which contributes most to the overall impression. Not every feature which contributes to the overall impression is an essential feature as not all features have the same visual impact. The question of essential feature is one of fact and degree. In the instant case the High Court had been entitled to find that the clover leaf did not have such eye impact as to make it an essential feature of the mark.

14.89 The question of 'essential feature', and in particular how it should be assessed, was considered by the ECJ in *Lego Juris A/S v OHIM*.[216] The essential features are the most important elements, the identification of which must be carried out on a case-by-case basis in terms of which there is no hierarchy between the types of elements of which a sign may consist. An assessment can be carried out by a simple visual analysis or be based on a detailed examination. Once identified, it has to be considered whether they perform the technical function of the goods in question.[217]

Exclusively

14.90 In order to decide whether the shape of the goods in question is exclusively necessary to obtain a technical result, the court must consider the mark as a whole as that is how the relevant section of the public would perceive it. In *Koninklijke Philips Electronics* the trial judge, having decided that the clover leaf was not an essential feature of the mark, was entitled to conclude that the mark was in substance functional.[218] Although the point was not dealt with by the ECJ, Advocate General Leger in *Dyson Ltd v Registrar of Trade Marks*[219] (see para 14.9) took the view that the reasoning also applied to a functional feature which forms part of the appearance of a product. The functional feature in *Dyson* was the bagless vacuum cleaner. Granting a trade mark in respect of the application could extend to a multitude of shapes which that feature could take, with the result that competing undertakings could find themselves unable to determine precisely whether and how they may still use that feature.[220]

14.91 In *Lego Juris A/S v OHIM*[221] the ECJ noted that by limiting the provision to signs which consist 'exclusively' of the shape of goods which is 'necessary' to obtain a technical result,

---

[214] [2006] ETMR 42, [2006] EWCA Civ 16.   [215] Details can be found on the IPO website under TM No 1,533,452.
[216] Case C-48/09 P.   [217] *Lego Juris A/S v OHIM*, paras 65–72.
[218] *Koninklijke Philips Electronics NV v Remington Consumer Products Ltd*, Rayovac Europe Ltd [2006] ETMR 42, [2006] EWCA Civ 16), para 62.
[219] Case C-321/03.   [220] *Dyson Ltd v Registrar of Trade Marks*, para 91.   [221] Case C-48/09 P.

the legislature duly took into account that any shape of goods is, to a certain extent, functional and that it would therefore be inappropriate to refuse to register a shape of goods as a trade mark solely on the ground that it has functional characteristics. By the terms 'exclusively' and 'necessary', that provision ensures that solely shapes of goods which only incorporate a technical solution, and whose registration as a trade mark would therefore actually impede the use of that technical solution by other undertakings, are not to be registered.

Device marks

14.92   In *Koninklijke Philips Electronics NV v Remington Consumer Products Ltd, Rayovac Europe Ltd*,[222] the court also had to consider the validity of further trade marks that the claimant had registered in class 8, each of which was a two-dimensional depiction of three circles arranged within an inverted equilateral triangle.[223] You can find an image of these trade marks if you look in the UK trade mark register available on the IPO website under TM No 1203652.

Registration had been declared invalid in the High Court on the basis that the signs were functional, but even if they were not, they were not distinctive. The Court of Appeal disagreed saying the marks which had eye appeal were of an abstract, non-technical, and non-functional nature. None of them represented the shape of goods in the functional sense used in the legislation. They thus fell outwith the competition policy of the provisions and outside the scope of the functionality principle embodied in Article 3(1)(e) and section 3(2)(b) of the 1994 Act.[224] The Court of Appeal was careful to emphasise that no technical elements or details of the three-headed rotary electric shaver were depicted in the marks. Thus there was no question that the marks would give to Philips a monopoly over the technical features of three-headed razors.[225]

Substantial value

14.93   As regards the third ground, section 3(2)(c) of the TMA 1994, a shape which gives 'substantial' value to goods will not be registrable. It is suggested that the type of shape which may fall under this proviso may be the cut of a diamond[226] or the shape of a crystal decanter, each of which will add substantial value to the goods. The Court of Appeal in *Philips Electronics NV v Remington Consumer Products Ltd (No 1)*[227] said that this section:

> was aimed at preventing a trader from monopolising by way of a trade mark registration shapes which added a substantial value to the goods over other shapes, e.g. a lampshade, a telephone designed to appeal to the eye. Such designs should be protected as registered designs or the like protection, not by trade mark registration ... There may be overlap between [section 3(2)(c) and (b) of the TMA 1994] which excludes shapes necessary to obtain a technical result, but the purpose is different. The latter is intended to exclude functional shapes and the former aesthetic-type shapes. Thus the fact that the technical result of a shape is excellent and therefore the article can command a high price does not mean that it is excluded from registration by subsection (c).

14.94   In *Benetton Group SpA v G-Star International BV*[228] the ECJ emphasised that even where a mark has acquired distinctiveness through use, it may not be registered where the shape of the product adds

---

[222] [2006] ETMR 42, [2006] EWCA Civ 16.   [223] TM Nos 1 080 316; 1 087 357, 1 124 415, and 1 203 652.
[224] *Koninklijke Philips Electronics NV v Remington Consumer Products Ltd, Rayovac Europe Ltd* [2006] ETMR 42, [2006] EWCA Civ 16, para 94.
[225] *Koninklijke Philips Electronics NV v Remington Consumer Products Ltd, Rayovac Europe Ltd*, para 95.
[226] J Phillips and A Firth, *Introduction to Intellectual Property Law* (4th edn, 2001), para 21.10.
[227] [1999] ETMR 816, [1999] RPC 809.
[228] *Benetton Group SpA v G-Star International BV* [2008] ETMR 5.

substantial value to the goods, and in *Bang and Olufsen v OHIM*[229] the General Court noted that the design of speakers would be an important element in the choice made by the consumer: 'Indeed, the shape for which registration was sought reveals a very specific design and the applicant itself admits, at para.92 of the application in particular, that that design is an essential element of its branding and increases the appeal of the product at issue, that is to say, its value.'[230] Protection was thus denied. See Figure 14.8.

Figure 14.8 Bang & Olufsen loud speaker

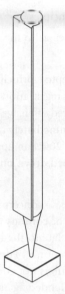

 Question 1

If in acquiring distinctiveness substantial value is added to the goods, does that mean that there is a category of signs that can never be registerable? Should the Bang and Olufsen speaker be register-able as a trade mark? If so, why? If not, why not?

Question 2

Explain in your own words why you consider it important to define the boundaries of trade mark law by excluding certain signs from being registered as trade marks based on their functional features. What marks can you think of which, if registered, would preclude other traders from entering the market in a particular sector?

Key points on the exclusion from registration of certain shapes

- If the sign falls under any one of these provisions, then it will not be registrable
- It would not be in the interests of competitors to permit registration of these shapes as it would give to the registered holder an unfair competitive advantage

---

[229] Case T-508/08 [2012] ETMR 10.   [230] Para 74.

Public policy and morality

TMA 1994, section 3(3), Directive, Article 3(1)(f), (g); and CTMR, Article 7(1)(f), (g)

14.95   Public policy and morality and public deception also have a role to play in preventing signs that might prove problematic on these grounds from being registered as trade marks.

Under section 3(3) of the TMA 1994 a mark will not be registered if it is:

- contrary to public policy or to accepted principles of morality, or
- of such a nature as to deceive the public (eg as to the nature, quality, or geographical origin of the goods or service).

What is contrary to public policy[231] or accepted principles of morality may change over time. For instance, the word 'Hallelujah'[232] was refused registration for women's clothing under the 1938 Act on the ground that is was offensive. Also considered offensive, in 1947, was the proposed use of 'Oomphies' for footwear.[233] Both would be likely to be immediately acceptable under the 1994 Act. Certain words do, however, still offend against morality. In 2001, an application to register the words 'Tiny Penis' in connection with articles of clothing was turned down on the grounds that it offended against current principles of morality.[234]

14.96   In *Basic Trademark SA's Trade Mark Application*,[235] concerning an appeal against a refusal to register the word 'JESUS' on the basis that to do so would be contrary to public policy, it was stressed that any objection on the grounds of public policy must relate to the intrinsic qualities of the mark and not to the personal qualities of the applicant for registration.[236] Further, mere offence to the public, such as that the public would consider the mark distasteful, is not enough: 'it is only in cases where it is plain that an accepted principle of morality is being offended against that registration should be denied'.[237] It is necessary to find the dividing line between distaste and outrage—where the latter is likely to undermine current religious, family, or social values amongst an identifiable section of the public.[238] Words which contain profane language will not be registrable,[239] nor will signs that glorify terrorism.[240] The standard to be applied is that of the reasonable person with normal levels of sensitivity and tolerance.[241]

■ Case R 495/2005-G *Jebaraj Kenneth trading as Screw You*

The Grand Board of Appeal had the opportunity to consider what might be contrary to public policy or to accepted principles of morality in *Jebaraj Kenneth trading as Screw You* in which an application to register the words 'Screw you' as a CTM in classes 9, 10, 25, 28, and 33 had been refused. The Grand Board started off by noting that for a CTM the grounds of non-registrability on the grounds of public

---

[231] The expression 'public policy' referred to matters of the kind covered by the French legal term 'ordre public'. *Philips Electronics NV v Remington Consumer Products Ltd* [1998] RPC 283.

[232] Hallelujah Trade Mark [1976] RPC 605.

[233] This was overturned on application to the court, and the name registered: La Marquise's Footwear Application (1947) 64 RPC 27. Apparently 'Oomphies' was derived from 'Oomph', denoting sex appeal, and had achieved significance, meaning those qualities in connection with a film actress with whom the word had originated.

[234] Ghazilian's Trade Mark Application [2002] ETMR 57.   [235] [2005] RPC 25.

[236] [2005] RPC 25; see also Case T-140/02 *Sportwetten GmbH Gera v OHIM & Intertops Sportwetten GmbH* [2006] ETMR 15, para 14.83.

[237] Ghazilian's Trade Mark Application [2002] ETMR 57, para 21.

[238] See also CDW Graphic Design Ltd's Trade Mark Application [2003] RPC 30 where the trade mark registry refused an application to register the domain name http://www.standupifyouhatemanu.com/ as a trade mark on public policy grounds. It was enough to show that the normal and fair use of such a trade mark would be likely to lead to criminal or offensive behaviour.

[239] Case R 111/2002-4 (Dick & Fanny).   [240] Case R 176/2004-2 (Bin Laden).   [241] Case R 176/2004-2.

policy and morality did not have to exist throughout the EU but that it was sufficient if they obtain in only part of the Community.[242] In the instant case, objection was taken because of the way the term was likely to be perceived in the UK and Ireland. In balancing the rights of the trader to use words and signs as trade marks, and that of the public not to be offended, and looking to the standard of a reasonable person with normal levels of sensitivity and tolerance, the Board came to the view that 'Screw You' was registrable in respect of condoms, contraceptives, sex toys (vibrators, dolls), 'artificial breasts', and 'breast pumps' of a type normally sold exclusively in sex shops.[243]

The ECJ has recognised that the concept of public policy varies from country to country and that a restrictive measure based on public policy may be based on a value not shared by all member states.[244]

 Question

Do you think that the Appointed Person allowed registration of the word 'JESUS' to proceed in Basic Trademark SA's Trade Mark Application, or do you think it was turned down?

 Exercise

Find out what marks have been refused registration as Community marks on the grounds that to do so would be contrary to public policy or to accepted principles of morality. How are the different views of morality in member states dealt with? How should they be dealt with?

Read Case T-232/10 *Couture Tech Ltd v OHIM* [2012] ETMR 5 which concerned this logo:

Figure 14.9 Case T-232/10 *Couture Tech Ltd v OHIM* [2012] ETMR 5

Why was the sign refused registration?

14.97   In *Sportwetten GmbH Gera v OHIM/Intertops Sportwetten GmbH*[245] a different question on public policy and morality arose concerning the validity of a CTM 'Intertops' registered for, inter alia, bookmaking and

---

[242] CTMR, Art 7(2). A single member state is enough. Case T-232/10 *Couture Tech Ltd v OHIM* Case [2012] ETMR 5.
[243] Note Case T-526/09 *PAKI Logistics GmbH v OHIM* in which the General Court decided, on the grounds of public policy, that the word 'Paki' should not be registered as English-speaking customers would understand it as a racially derogatory term.
[244] Case C-36/02 *Omega Spielhallen GmbH*.   [245] Case T-140/02 [2006] ETMR 15.

betting services of all kinds in class 42. The registration was challenged by Sportwetten on the basis that Intertops was not authorised to offer betting services in Germany and on that basis of non-authorisation the CTM was contrary to public policy and morality. No challenge was made alleging that either the sign or the services per se covered by the mark were contrary to public policy or accepted principles of morality. The CFI upheld the finding of the Board of Appeal in that such considerations were irrelevant when considering whether a CTM is contrary to public policy or accepted principles of morality within the meaning of Article 7(1)(f). The focus of inquiry must be on the sign in relation to the goods or services. It is also irrelevant to consider circumstances relating to the conduct of the applicant.[246]

Deceptive marks

14.98   A mark may be considered to be deceptive under section 3(3)(b) of the TMA 1994 if it suggests that the goods are made from specific materials if that is in fact not the case. An example would be the application to register the word 'Orlwoola'[247] for goods made from wool where the goods to be sold are not made solely from wool (the application was made under the 1938 Act).

14.99   In *Consorzio per la Tutela del Formaggio Gorgonzola v Käserei Champignon Hofmeister GmbH & Co KG and Eduard Bracharz GmbH*[248] the ECJ said that the prohibition presupposed the evidence of actual deceit or a sufficiently serious risk that the consumer will be deceived (ie hypothetical deceit is not enough). This was re-emphasised in *Elizabeth Florence Emanuel v Continental Shelf 128 Ltd*[249] in which the Court in dealing with the name 'Elizabeth Emanuel' in connection with a dress design business said that even if a consumer was influenced into purchasing a garment because of the name and imagining that the individual was involved in the design, the 'characteristics and the qualities of that garment remain guaranteed by the undertaking which owns the trade mark'[250] and consequently the name was not of a nature to deceive the public as to the nature, quality, or geographical origin of the product it designates. If there was an intention by the owner of the trade mark to make the consumer believe Ms Emanuel was the designer, that could be fraudulent behaviour and would be a matter for the national court but would not be deception for the purposes of Article 3.[251]

 Question

Can you think of any sign which might be refused registration on the grounds that it might be deceptive?

Marks prohibited by law and protected emblems

TMA 1994, section 3(4), (5); CTMR, Article 7(1)(h)

14.100   Further absolute grounds of refusal are to be found in section 3(4) and (5) of the TMA 1994. These relate to non-registration of marks to the extent that their use would be prohibited in the UK or by a provision of Union law and to specially protected emblems. These would include, for example, the Red Cross, the Union Jack, and any sign that would lead to indication of a connection with the Royal Family. It will be

---

[246] Case T-224/01 *Durferrit v OHIM—Kolene* [2003] ECR II-1589.   [247] (1909) 26 RPC 683 and 850.

[248] [1999] ETMR 454 (ECJ).   [249] Case C-259/04.

[250] *Elizabeth Florence Emanuel v Continental Shelf 128 Ltd*, para 48.

[251] Para 50. See also Kraft Jacobs Suchard Ltd's Application; Opposition by Nestlé UK Ltd [2001] ETMR 54 TMR; Case T-41/10 *Syndicat international des moniteurs de ski—École de ski internationale (SIMS—École de ski internationale) v OHIM*.

recalled that the Paris Convention requires Convention countries to prohibit the registration of 'armorial bearings, flags and emblems' of the countries of the Union.[252] The ECJ has confirmed that there is broad protection for state emblems.[253]

Applications made in bad faith

TMA 1994, section 3(6); Directive, Article 3(2)(d); and CTMR, Article 52

14.101   An application to register a trade mark will be refused if or to the extent that it is made in bad faith. In *Gromax Plasticulture Ltd v Don & Low Nonwovens Ltd*[254] Lindsay J said this of bad faith:

> I shall not attempt to define bad faith in this context. Plainly it includes dishonesty and, as I would hold, includes also some dealings which fall short of the standards of acceptable commercial behaviour observed by reasonable and experienced men in the particular area being examined. Parliament has wisely not attempted to explain in detail what is or is not bad faith in this context: how far a dealing must so fall-short in order to amount to bad faith is a matter best left to be adjudged not by some paraphrase by the courts (which leads to the danger of the courts then construing not the Act but the paraphrase) but by reference to the words of the Act and upon a regard to all material surrounding circumstances.[255]

14.102   Cases concerning bad faith applications have occurred where there has been an attempt to register a mark for which the applicant knows there is a competing claim,[256] where the applicant is an employee,[257] where there is an agreement to the contrary,[258] or where an application is made to register a trade mark based on an older trade mark in which there is residual goodwill.[259]

14.103   *Harrison v Teton Valley*[260] concerned the name 'China White'. The proprietors of a nightclub 'Chinawhite' had traded under the name for a number of years. As part of their business activity they discussed developing a cocktail with their bar manager—to be called China White. The bar manager informed Harrison of these developments and he proceeded to apply for registration of the name. The Court of Appeal considered that the application had been made in bad faith. The test is a combined one of dishonesty[261] and acceptable commercial behaviour observed by reasonable and experienced persons in the commercial area under consideration:[262]

> dishonesty requires knowledge by the defendant that what he was doing would be regarded as dishonest by honest people, although he should not escape a finding of dishonesty because he sets his own standards of honesty and does not regard as dishonest what he knows would offend the normally accepted standards of honest conduct.[263]

In *Harrison* the court found that on the facts of the case—that the applicant knew of the nightclub, and that a drink, China White, was sold at the club—the application was in bad faith.

---

[252] Paris Convention, Art 6ter (para 13.52). See also TMA 1994, ss 57 and 58. Case T-41/10 *Syndicat international des moniteurs de ski—École de ski internationale (SIMS—École de ski internationale) v OHIM*. The colours red, white, and blue in a circular device could not be objected to as an official emblem as there was not sufficient similarity to make a link between the mark and the French flag. Case T-397/09 *Ernst August Prinz von Hannover v OHIM* (UK emblem) the fact that the similarity between an application consisting of the coat of arms of the Hanover family can be explained by historical circumstances is irrelevant.

[253] Joined Cases C-202/08 P and C-208/08 P *American Clothing Associates SA v OHIM* (2009).

[254] [1999] RPC 367 at 379.

[255] Approved of by the Court of Appeal in *Harrison v Teton Valley Trading Co Ltd* [2004] EWCA Civ 1028, [2004] 1 WLR 2577, [2005] FSR 10.

[256] *See, eg, Harrison.*   [257] Casson's Trade Mark (1910) 27 RPC 65.

[258] Mary Wilson Enterprises Inc's Trade Mark Application [2003] EMLR 14.

[259] *Jules Rimet Cup Ltd v Football Association* [2007] EWHC 2376 (Ch).

[260] [2004] EWCA Civ 1028, [2004] 1 WLR 2577, [2005] FSR 10.   [261] *Twinsectra Ltd v Yardley* [2002] 2 AC 164.

[262] *Gromax Plasticulture Ltd v Don & Low Nonwovens Ltd* [1999] RPC 367. See also Ajit Weekly Trade Mark [2006] RPC 25.

[263] *Twinsectra Ltd v Yardley* [2002] UKHL 12, [2002] 2 AC 164, para 36.

14.104   By contrast, in *Hotel Cipriani SRL v Cipriani (Grosvenor Street) Ltd*[264] the Court of Appeal upheld the finding of the lower court that it was not bad faith on the part of one party who registered a mark when they
knew that a third party used the same mark for similar goods and services elsewhere in the Community,
a key difference being that the applicant had used that mark for many years and it was one in which they
had a reputation (Cipriani).

14.105   In *Cipriani* the Court of Appeal followed the judgment of the ECJ in *Chocoladefabriken Lindt & Sprüngli
AG v Franz Hauswirth GmbH*[265] when asked to determine a question concerning the registration as a
CTM of a chocolate bunny (Figure 14.10) and the challenge to the registration by other producers of
chocolate bunnies (Figure 14.11). In determining bad faith, the Court said that the factors to be taken
into account (which needed to be those relevant at the time of filing the application) were, in particular:

- the fact that the applicant knows or must know that a third party is using, in at least one member
state, an identical or similar sign for an identical or similar product capable of being confused with
the sign for which registration is sought;

- the applicant's intention to prevent that third party from continuing to use such a sign; and

- the degree of legal protection enjoyed by the third party's sign and by the sign for which registration
is sought.[266]

 Question

Given the ruling of the ECJ in Chocoladefabriken, do you think that Lindt's registration was allowed
to stand?

> **Key points on the exclusion of registering a trade mark based on public
> policy and morality, deceptive marks, and applications in bad faith**
>
> - Objections on the grounds of public policy must relate to the intrinsic qualities of the mark
> and not to the personal qualities of the applicant
>
> - Mere offence to the public, such as that the public would consider the mark distasteful, is not
> enough
>
> - The standard to be applied is that of the reasonable person with normal levels of sensitiv-
> ity and tolerance; for a mark to be considered deceptive there needs to be evidence of actual
> deceit or a sufficiently serious risk that the consumer will be deceived
>
> - An application made in bad faith will be refused considering both dishonesty and acceptable
> commercial behaviour observed by reasonable and experienced persons in the commercial
> area under consideration

Collective and certification trade marks

 Exercise

Read sections 49 and 50 of the TMA 1994; Article 15 of the Directive; and Article 66 of the CTMR.

---

[264] [2008] EWHC 3032 (Ch).   [265] Case C-529/07 [2009] ECR I-04893.
[266] *Chocoladefabriken Lindt & Sprüngli AG v Franz Hauswirth GmbH.* See also Case T-227/09 *Feng Shen Technology Co Ltd v OHIM.* Note
that there is no definition of bad faith in either the CTMR or Trade Marks Directive.

Figure 14.10 Lindt bunny

Figure 14.11 Franz Hauswirth bunny

14.106   The TMA 1994 provides for the registration of collective and certification marks. The Article 15 of the Directive contains permissive provisions regarding these types of marks and under the CTMR it is possible to register a Community Collective Mark, but there is no such thing as a Community Certification Mark.

> [A collective mark is defined in section 49 of the TMA 1994 as a] mark distinguishing the goods or services of members of the association which is the proprietor of the mark from those of other undertakings. [A certification mark is defined in section 50 of the TMA 1994 as] a mark indicating that the goods or services in connection with which it is used are certified by the proprietor of the mark in respect of origin, material, mode of manufacture of goods or performance of services, quality, accuracy or other characteristics.[267]

It can be seen from the definition that collective and certification marks have different objectives. *Collective* marks are designed to indicate who can use the mark, for example members of a particular association. Quality standards are not necessarily a feature of a collective mark, but may be included by way of, for example, membership rules of the particular association. By comparison, a *certification* mark is designed to indicate that the quality of the goods or services meet with certain criteria, some examples of which are set out in the definition of a certification mark.

14.107   Because the function of collective and certification marks differs from ordinary trade marks, they have special rules that govern their use. In the case of a certification mark, the applicant must not itself carry on a business involving the supply of goods or services of the kind certified,[268] and in the case of both a collective and a certification mark, the applicant must file with the Registrar regulations governing the use of the mark.[269] The regulations for collective marks must specify the persons authorised to use the mark, the conditions of membership of the association, and the conditions of use of the mark including any sanctions against misuse.[270] The regulations governing the use of a certified mark require more information including who is authorised to use the mark; the characteristics to be certified by the mark; how the certifying body is to test the characteristics and supervise the use of the mark; the fees to be paid in connection with the operation of the mark; and the procedures for resolving disputes.[271] As can be gathered from these rules, both collective and certification marks can be used by different entities: the purpose of a trader using one of these marks being either to signify membership of that group, or that certain standards are met by those who use the same mark in the marketplace.

14.108   Certification marks have been available in the UK for many years; well-known examples including the 'Woolmark' of the International Wool Secretariat.[272]

The 'Kite' mark of the British standards institute and the 'Stilton' mark.[273]

The mark shown in Figure 14.13 has been registered as a collective mark by the UK cartridge remanufacturers association.[274]

Figure 14.12 Woolmark certification mark

[267] The provisions of the 1994 Act apply to collective and certification marks, subject to Sch 1 and Sch 2 respectively.
[268] TMA 1994, Sch 2, para 4.   [269] TMA 1994, Sch 2, para 6(1) and Sch 1, para 5(1).   [270] TMA 1994, Sch 1, para 5(2).
[271] TMA 1994, Sch 2, para 6(2).   [272] UK Trade Mark No 2178977.
[273] Stilton Trade Mark [1967] RPC 173.   [274] UK Trade Mark No 2341823.

Figure 14.13 UK cartridge remanufacturers association collective mark

 Question

Can you think of any certification or collective marks you have come across?

Key points on collective and certification marks

- Collective marks are designed to indicate who can use the mark, for example members of a particular association. Quality standards are not necessarily a feature of a collective mark, but may be included by way of, for example, membership rules of the particular association

- A certification mark is designed to indicate that the quality of the goods or services meet with certain criteria, examples of which are set out in the definition of a certification mark

Relative grounds for refusal of registration

 Exercise

Read sections 5 and 10 of the TMA 1994; Articles 4 and 5 of the Directive; and Articles 8 and 9 of the CTMR.

14.109 Section 5 of the 1994 Act concerns the *relative grounds* on which an application to register a trade mark might be refused if successful opposition is raised by the proprietor of an earlier mark or sign. These grounds thus look beyond the mark itself to other marks, and other goods and services to ensure that a registration does not conflict with pre-existing rights. As mentioned previously, section 5(1)–(3) of the TMA 1994 virtually mirrors section 10(1)–(3) which relates to infringement. For registration purposes, a mark may not be registered if successful opposition is raised on the following grounds:

- it is identical to an earlier trade mark and the goods or services for which registration is sought are identical to the goods or services for which the earlier trade mark is protected;[275]

---

[275] TMA 1994, s 5(1).

- it is identical with or similar to the earlier trade mark and the application is for registration in connection with identical or similar goods and services for which the earlier trade mark is protected, and there exists a likelihood of confusion on the part of the public which includes the likelihood of association with the earlier trade mark;[276]

- it is identical with or similar to an earlier trade mark and the earlier mark has a reputation and the use of the later mark without due cause would take unfair advantage of, or be detrimental to, the distinctive character or the repute of the earlier mark.[277]

Logically, if a mark is registered, the later use of a sign in these circumstances will infringe the rights of the registered proprietor. To avoid repetition, these relative grounds for refusal will be dealt with in the next chapter when examining infringement.

14.110 The remaining parts of section 5 seek to ensure that a sign will not be registered as a trade mark looking to other factors, notably whether the registration would infringe the intellectual property rights belonging to others.[278] For instance, if the use of the mark would amount to passing off,[279] or would infringe another's copyright or design right.[280] Thus, in a case decided under the equivalent provision in the 1938 Act, *OSCAR Trade Mark*,[281] the applicant sought to register the name 'Oscar' and a picture of the Oscar statuette. The application was rejected on the grounds that the applicant did not own the copyright in the statuette and registration as a trade mark would infringe the artistic copyright.

Earlier trade mark and earlier right

14.111 It will be noted that the legislation refers to 'earlier trade mark' and 'earlier right'. As was explained in para 13.62 an earlier trade mark[282] includes an existing registered trade mark (ie one that is on the UK register whether by virtue of the 1938 or 1994 Act), an international trade mark (UK) (one for which registration is applied for under the Madrid Protocol), or a CTM. All of these earlier trade marks need a date of application for registration earlier than that for the mark under consideration, taking into account any priorities[283] or the seniority of a CTM.[284] A person who is entitled to prevent the use of a trade mark is referred to as the proprietor of an earlier right in relation to the trade mark.[285]

Consent of the earlier proprietor to registration

TMA 1994, section 5(5); Directive, Article 4(5)

14.112 All the provisions of section 5 of the 1994 Act are subject to the proviso in section 5(5) which states that where the proprietor of an earlier trade mark consents to the registration of the later mark, then registration may proceed.

Use requirements

14.113 Use provisions in the TMA 1994 arise in a number of circumstances. The Max Planck Institute in its study on the overall functioning of the European trade mark system[286] identifies eight different types of use. These are:

---

[276] TMA 1994, s 5(2).   [277] TMA 1994, s 5(3).
[278] Case C-263/09 *Edwin v Elio Fiorucci*. The holder of a name is entitled to prevent its use as a CTM where national law permits.
[279] TMA 1994, s 5(4)(a).   [280] TMA 1994, s 5(4)(b).   [281] [1979] RPC 173.
[282] See generally TMA 1994, s 6.   [283] TMA 1994, s 6(1)(a).   [284] TMA 1994, s 6(1)(b).   [285] TMA 1994, s 5(4).
[286] Available at http://ec.europa.eu/internal_market/indprop/docs/tm/20110308_allensbach-study_en.pdf

- use of the mark in the course of trade;
- use of the mark as a mark;
- use of the mark as registered or with variations not affecting its distinctive character;
- use of the mark for the goods or services for which it is registered;
- use of the mark by the proprietor or with his consent;
- use in the Community for CTMs or in the respective member state for national marks; use on exported goods is sufficient;
- use following a 'grace period' of five years from the date of registration for CTMs or from the date of the termination of the registration proceedings for national marks;
- use which is 'genuine' or justified reasons for non-use.

As has been discussed previously, a trade mark which is not inherently distinctive can become distinctive through use, and thus registrable. In addition, there are certain consequences if a registered trade mark is *not used* for a certain period of time, or if it is used in a particular manner[287] as well as questions relating to when a trade mark is *used for the purposes of infringement*. In this section the consequences of non-use will be discussed; matters relating to use for the purposes of infringement will be dealt with in the next chapter.

 Exercise

Read section 46 of the TMA 1994; Article 10 of the Directive; and Article 15 of the CTMR.

Non-use and revocation

14.114   The recitals of the Trade Marks Directive give an indication as to why a trade mark will be revoked if it is not used:

> Whereas in order to reduce the total number of trade marks registered and protected in the Community and, consequently, the number of conflicts which arise between them, it is essential to require that registered trade marks must actually be used or, if not used, be subject to revocation.

This objective reflects the basic principle that trade marks should be used, and if not used then a registration will be lost (see para 13.6).

Traders are thus precluded from stockpiling trade marks, keeping them from legitimate competitors. A concern also expressed in the recital is that the more registered trade marks on the register, the greater the potential for conflict with later applications for registration or for infringement to occur where confusingly similar signs are used by competing traders. The desire is thus to limit the potential for these conflicts.

> The purpose of revocation is to remove trade marks or parts of the specifications of trade marks where there has not been use. It is there to serve a purpose in trade; it is the Lipitor that stops the arteries of commerce being blocked with the cholesterol of unused trade marks.[288]

14.115   An applicant for a UK trade mark is required to state that they have a bona fide intention to use the mark. If the applicant does not have this intention, then the mark may be revoked on the grounds of bad faith.[289] By contrast, an applicant for a CTM does not have to state that they intend to use the mark.

---

[287] TMA 1994, s 46.   [288] Application for revocation Nirvana Trade Mark (O-030-06), para 75.
[289] TMA 1994, s 3(6).

14.116   A registered trade mark must be put to genuine use.[290] If a registered trade mark has not been put to genuine use in a form substantially similar to the registration[291] within five years following the date of registration, or use of the trade mark has been suspended for a continuous period of five years, registration may be revoked.[292] Where a proprietor of a mark has several variations, the use of a particular mark cannot be taken as use of a similar mark on account of that similarity.[293] Genuine use of a mark is to be judged against commercial criteria and must be public and outward-facing. Purely internal use does not amount to use of a mark[294] and while commercial exploitation does not need to generate a profit[295] using a mark for free 'giveaways' for the purpose of promoting other products is not genuine use.[296] Early UK cases suggested that even if there is no evidence of actual sales during the relevant five-year period, use can be shown where the mark had been employed in relation to goods offered for sale during that period,[297] and only limited use is necessary to maintain a mark on the register.[298] The ECJ has, however, indicated that token use will not be sufficient.[299] In *Ansul BV v Ajax Brandbeveiliging BV*[300] the Court said that any use must be 'consistent with the essential function of a trade mark', in this case to guarantee origin.[301] Such use must not be just internal use, but use of the mark, either by the proprietor or with consent, on the market or in relation to goods or services about to be marketed through such activities as advertising campaigns.[302] The use should be public and external.[303] Particular regard should be paid to whether the use is viewed as warranted in the economic sector concerned to maintain or create a share in the market for the goods or services. Regard must be had to the facts and circumstances relevant to establishing whether the commercial exploitation of the mark in the course of trade is real. It will not be enough to use a mark on free gifts as that does not create a commercial outlet for the goods[304] but it can be sufficient for a not-for-profit organisation to put a mark to genuine use through announcements of events, business advertising, and so on.[305]

14.117   The Court of Appeal considered the genuine use requirement in a case concerning the registered mark 'Laboratoire de la Mer'.[306] In this case the use comprised the sale of £800 worth of cosmetics containing seaweed to a firm in Banff, Scotland. There were five deliveries in 1997 where the items were packed in containers (bearing the mark) with recommended retail prices of between £5–£30. The goods were apparently to be sold by sub-agents but there was no evidence that any of the goods reached consumers. A reference was made to the ECJ asking, inter alia, for interpretation of the requirement of genuine

[290] TMA 1994, s 46(1)(a); Directive, Art 10; CTMR, Art 15. Note the questions on genuine use put to the Court of Justice in Case C-252/12 *Specsavers International Healthcase*.

[291] Case T-514/10 *Fruit of the Loom Inc v OHIM*.

[292] The period of non-use should be calculated from 'date of the completion of the registration procedure' within the meaning of Directive, Art 10(1) and must be determined in each member state in accordance with the procedural rules on registration in force in that state. See Case C-246/05 *Armin Häupl v Lidl Stiftung & Co KG* [2007] ECR I-04673.

[293] Case C-234/06 P *Il Ponte Finanziaria SpA*.

[294] *Och-Ziff Management Europe Ltd v Och Capital LLP* [2010] EWHC 2599 (Ch).

[295] Case C-442/07 *Verein Radetzky-Orden* (Radetzky).

[296] Case C-495/07 *Silberquelle* (Wellness).

[297] *Floris Trade Mark* [2001] RPC 19. But the use of a mark on goods distributed free with unrelated goods does not amount to use: Case C-495/07 *Silberquelle GmbH v Maselli-Strickmode GmbH*.

[298] *Zippo Trade Mark* [1999] RPC 173. But cf *Elle Trade Mark* [1997] FSR 529, [1997] ETMR 552.

[299] Genuine use does not include token use for the sole purpose of preserving the rights conferred by the registration: Case C-234/06 P *Il Ponte Finanziaria v OHIM* [2007] ECR I7333, para 72; Case T-191/07 *Anheuser-Busch v OHIM* [2009] ECR II-00691, para 100.

[300] Case C-40/01 [2003] ECR I-2439, [2003] RPC 40.

[301] *Ansul*, para 36.   [302] *Ansul*, para 37.

[303] Case T174/01 *Goulbourn v OHIM—Redcats (Silk Cocoon)* [2003] ECR II789, para 99; *VITAFRUIT* [2004] ECR II-2811; Case T-298/10 *Gross v OHIM*.

[304] Case C-495/07 *Silberquelle GmbH v Maselli-Strickmode GmbH* [2007] ECR I-00137.

[305] *Verein Radetzky-Orden v Bundesvereinigung Kameradschaft Feldmarschall Radetzky* [2009] ETMR 14 at 7.

[306] *Laboratoires Goëmar SA v La Mer Technology Inc* [2005] EWCA Civ 978, [2005] ETMR 114, [2006] FSR 5, 2005 WL 1801235 (CA).

use.[307] The Court noted that it had already answered the questions in *Ansul*.[308] The case was re-heard by the High Court and then appealed to the Court of Appeal.[309] That court considered that as the owner of the mark in the UK wanted to create an outlet that was sufficient to qualify as genuine use. The Court of Appeal came to the view that although internal use would not be relevant in assessing genuine use even if it was not token or sham, there was nothing in the ECJ judgment which indicated that the consumer or end user market was the only relevant market for determining whether use of a mark is genuine. In the instant case there were arm's length sales to a third party who imported the goods. The fact that the use was on the import market and was modest did not prevent that from being genuine use.

14.118   At the same time as *Laboratoire de la mer* had been progressing though the domestic courts, application was made for registration as a CTM the words 'La Mer'. Opposition was based on a likelihood of confusion with the earlier national word mark, 'Laboratoire de la mer'. The question also arose in this forum as to whether there had been genuine use of the national mark. The CFI stated that when examining whether there has been genuine use of an earlier trade mark, all relevant factors of the particular case must be considered. This assessment entails a degree of interdependence between the factors taken into account. The use of an earlier mark need not always be quantitatively significant in order to be deemed genuine and it is not possible to determine a priori and in the abstract what quantitative threshold should be chosen in order to determine whether use is genuine or not. Minimal use can be deemed genuine use, provided that this amount of use is warranted in the economic sector concerned to maintain or create a market share for the goods or services protected by the mark[310] as long as the use is 'outward-facing' and grounded in the commercial sector.

14.119   The geographical extent of genuine use was considered in *Leno Merken BV v Hagelkruis Beheer BV*.[311] The Court was asked to determine what constituted genuine use within the Community and whether use in one member state would be enough to satisfy the requirement. The applicant sought to have the earlier mark 'ONEL' revoked as it had not been used for five years. The parties agreed that ONEL had been used in the Netherlands but no proof of use was provided for any other member state. Advocate General Sharpston noted that a CTM has to be used in a manner consistent with its function otherwise protection throughout the territories of all member states would be lost. Whether a CTM has been used in one member state or several is irrelevant. 'What matters is the impact of the use in the internal market: more specifically, whether it is sufficient to maintain or create market share in that market for the goods and services covered by the mark and whether it contributes to a commercially relevant presence of the goods and services in that market. Whether that use results in actual commercial success is not relevant'.[312] Examining the genuine use requirement through this lens meant that use in one member state could be sufficient. Equally, use on a website available in all member states may not.[313]

The reason for interpreting the requirement of genuine use in the Community in this manner:

> guarantees the freedom of undertakings of all types to choose to register a mark as either a national trade mark or a Community trade mark. The Community trade mark, and its coexistence with national trade marks, were established with the objective of satisfying the needs of all market participants, and not solely those of small enterprises operating in a single Member State or small part of the internal market, or of large undertakings which are active in the whole or a large part of the internal market. Community trade mark protection must be available to all types of undertaking wishing to obtain protection of their marks throughout the territory of the 27 Member States and with the objective of using the mark in a manner that will maintain or create market share in the relevant internal market.[314]

---

[307] Case C-259/02.   [308] Case C-40/01.
[309] [2005] EWCA Civ 978, [2005] ETMR 114, [2006] FSR 5, 2005 WL 1801235 (CA).
[310] *La Mer Technology Inc v OHIM* [2008] ETMR 9, paras 57–58.   [311] Case C-149/11 (ONEL) in relation to CTMs.
[312] Para 50.   [313] Para 55.   [314] Para 58.

The Court of Justice generally agreed with the Advocate General but placed a different emphasis on the questions asked: first, saying that territorial borders should be disregarded when deciding if there had been genuine use of a trade mark in the Community and, secondly, that a 'trade mark is put to "genuine use" … when it is used in accordance with its essential function and for the purpose of maintaining or creating market share within the European Community for the goods or services covered by it.'[315]

14.120   Revocation will not occur on the grounds of non-use if there are 'proper reasons for non-use'.[316] This proviso has applied in circumstances where the registered proprietor had experienced protracted technical difficulties in setting up a satisfactory production method for a new product that has thus delayed the appearance of the product on the market for which the mark had been registered.[317] Generally, however, it would appear that lack of resources in setting up a business and using the trade mark would not amount to proper reasons for non-use as these are within the domain of the trade mark owner.[318] Other factors, outwith the trade mark proprietor's control, may constitute proper reasons.[319] A question as to whether delayed implementation of the corporate strategy being pursued by the trade mark proprietor for reasons outside the control of the proprietor might constitute proper reasons, was referred to the ECJ in *Armin Häupl v Lidl Stiftung & Co KG*[320] which also asked whether, in these circumstances, the trade mark proprietor is obliged to change his corporate strategy in order to be able to use the mark in good time. Here, the Court emphasised that in order to be taken into account any difficulties had to have a direct relationship with a trade mark making its use impossible or unreasonable. These difficulties had to be outwith the control of the proprietor of the mark. It was for the national court, when dealing with the facts of the case, to determine whether it would be unreasonable for the proprietor to change a business strategy in order to get around the difficulty.[321] It thus seems that the hurdle may be high to show non-use is reasonable.

 Exercise

Read the opinion of Advocate General Sharpston in *Leno Merken BV v Hagelkruis Beheer DV*. Do you agree with her view? What do you think of the judgment of the Court of Justice? What problems are being balanced? What challenges are thrown up and for whom?

Quality control and revocation

14.121   Revocation can also occur where the use of a mark is liable to mislead the public as to the nature, quality, or geographical origin of the goods and services for which it is registered.[322]

14.122   It will be recalled from the discussion in para 14.98 that a mark that is liable to mislead the public is precluded from registration. This section is the counterpart to the non-registerability of a mark in that if, once registered, a mark becomes likely to mislead the public then it can be revoked. The question of whether such circumstances might arise where a trade mark has been licensed to another but with no

---

[315] Case C-149/11 (ONEL). Case C-96/09 *Anheuser-Busch v Budejovický*: a geographical indication protected in a member state may prevent registration of a CTM only when it is actually used in a significant manner in the course of trade in a substantial part of that state.

[316] TMA 1994, s 46(1)(a), (b). The onus is on the registered proprietor to prove that it has made genuine use of the trade mark in suit, or that there are proper reasons for non-use. TMA 1994, s 100 and application for revocation: Nirvana Trade Mark (O-030-06).

[317] Magic Ball Trade Mark [2000] ETMR 226, [2000] RPC 439. See also the discussion at para 14.125 in relation to revocation of a trade mark and whether it must be revoked in full or part.

[318] *Ecros SA v Banco Akros SpA* Decision No 3500/2002 (9 November 2002) Opposition Division.

[319] Invermont Trade Mark [1997] RPC 125.   [320] Case C-246/05.   [321] *Armin Häupl v Lidl Stiftung & Co KG*, para 54.

[322] TMA 1994, s 46(1)(d).

provisions for quality control over the goods or services produced under the mark in the licensing agreement, was referred to the ECJ by the House of Lords in *Scandecor Developments AB v Scandecor Marketing AB*.[323] This is an interesting question which goes to the heart of the function accorded to a registered trade mark. One element of the function of a trade mark is that of quality control (paras 13.9–13.16). If a trade mark is licensed with no possibility of such control by the trade mark owner, does the trade mark still fulfil its function? If not, must the mark then be revoked? Unfortunately, the case settled before judgment was given by the ECJ and so this question remains unanswered to date.

Exercise

If the case had proceeded, how do you think the Court should have decided it? If you are in favour of licensing with no quality controls, what then do you think is the function of a trade mark?

Revocation and generic words

14.123   The proprietor of a registered trade mark should also take care that the use does not become generic. This is where the registered trade mark becomes the common name for the product or service for which it is registered. If a registered trade mark does become generic then it can be revoked.[324] Although the section refers to a mark being generic in the trade, the ECJ has said that the relevant classes of persons 'comprise principally consumers and end users. However, depending on the features of the product market concerned, the influence of intermediaries on decisions to purchase, and thus their perception of the trade mark, must also be taken into consideration'.[325] Examples of marks which have become generic in the UK include 'Thermos' for a vacuum flask and 'Escalator' for a moving staircase.[326]

14.124   The proprietor of a registered trade mark would thus be well advised to take certain self-help measures in order to ensure that his mark does not become generic. Such measure may include, for example, emphasising the mark in comparison with surrounding text; never using the mark as a noun or verb, only as a proper adjective, and using the ® symbol.[327] Proprietors of unregistered marks often add the initials TM to their marks. This may be an attempt to warn other traders that they are claiming common law rights in the sign. However, in terms of registered marks, and the TMA 1994, it has no legal significance.

Question

Can you think of any other marks that have become generic?

Exercise

Find five examples of registered trade marks, identified by the ® symbol, and five examples of unregistered signs, identified by the TM symbol. Check the trade mark register to see if the marks showing the ® are on the register.

---

[323] [2001] ETMR 74 (HL).   [324] TMA 1994, s 46(1)(c).

[325] Case C-371/02 *Björnekulla Fruktindustrier AB v Procordia Food AB* [2004] ECR I-5791, [2005] 3 CMLR 16, [2004] ETMR 69, [2004] RPC 45, para 25. The use of a mark in scientific journals is not enough to show it is generic: Case T-507/08 *Psytech International Ltd v OHIM* (16PF) (GC). 5 HTP was considered to be a common designation of a natural alternative to traditional antidepressants in respect of both health professionals and patients: Case T-190/09 *Longevity Health Products v OHIM*.

[326] 'Spork' is a generic term in the catering trade: *D Green & Co (Stoke Newington) Ltd v Regalzone Ltd* [2001] EWCA Civ 639.

[327] TMA 1994, s 95(2) provides that it is an offence to represent that a mark is registered when it is not.

The extent of revocation

14.125   If a mark is to be revoked, then the question also arises as to the extent of that revocation. Must the mark be revoked altogether, or should the mark remain and only some of the goods or services in the specification be revoked? This was considered in *Premier Brands UK Ltd v Typhoon Europe Ltd*[328] where Neuberger J said in applying this section:

> One simply looks at the list of items on the register whether or not the mark has been used in relation to or in connection with that item during the past five years. If the answer is in the affirmative then the mark can remain registered in respect of that item; if the answer is in the negative then, subject to any question of discretion the registration is revoked in respect of that item.

This test was considered too narrow in *Minerva Trade Mark*[329] where Jacob J was of the opinion that it did not deal adequately with huge classes of goods described by single phrases like 'computer software' or 'cleaning substances and preparations'. In these circumstances, the mark could be partially revoked which itself is not limited to deletion of a single specified item, but could include a category of goods within a general description.[330]

14.126   The CFI considered this in *Mundipharma AG v OHIM*[331] in which it looked at the categories and extent of use for the purposes of revocation. It said:

> it is in practice impossible for the proprietor of a trade mark to prove that the mark has been used for all conceivable variations of the goods concerned by the registration. Consequently, the concept of 'part of the goods or services' cannot be taken to mean all the commercial variations of similar goods or services but merely goods or services which are sufficiently distinct to constitute coherent categories or sub-categories.[332]

The desire is to be fair as between trade mark owner and competitor—to ensure that the proprietor is not stripped of protection with respect to all of the similar goods or services for which the trade mark has been used whilst ensuring space for the competitor in the market.[333]

 Exercise

Consider the case law on the extent of revocation in the light of the *IP Translator* case (Case C-307/10, see para 14.27). Do you think that the current jurisprudence on the principles underlying the extent of revocation will have to be rethought?

Key points on use requirements

- A registered trade mark must be put to genuine use: revocation may occur if it has not been put to genuine use within five years of registration

- Token use is not sufficient for genuine use

- Revocation will not occur if there are proper reasons for non-use

- Revocation can occur where the use of a mark is liable to mislead the public as to the nature, quality, or geographical origin of the goods and services; if the use becomes misleading and if the mark becomes generic

---

[328] [2000] FSR 767.   [329] [2000] FSR 734.

[330] See also *Mercury Communications Ltd v Mercury Interactive (UK) Ltd* [1995] FSR 850; *Decon Laboratories Ltd v Fred Baker Scientific Ltd* [2001] ETMR 46, [2001] RPC 17; *Daimler Chrysler AG v Alavi (t/a Merc)* [2001] ETMR 98, [2001] RPC 42.

[331] Case T-256/04; Case T-483/04 *Armour Pharmaceutical Co v OHIM* [2006] ECR II-4109; Case T-126/03 *Reckitt Benckiser (Espana) SL v OHIM* [2005] ECR II-2861.

[332] Case T-256/04 *Mundipharma AG v OHIM* [2007] ECR II-00449, para 24.   [333] *Mundipharma*, para 24.

Further reading

Articles

J Belson, 'Certification marks, guarantees and trust' (2004) 24(7) EIPR 340–352

J Bergquist and D Curley, 'Shape trade marks and fast-moving consumer goods' [2008] EIPR 17

O Bray, 'Vorsprung for slogans in the courts: Audi's perseverance pays off" (2010) JIPLP 5(6) 400–402

B Clark, 'The chocolate menagerie: the General Court decides on bunny, reindeer and mouse shapes' (2011) 6(6) JIPLP 361–364

T Cohen Jehoram and M Santman, 'Opel/Autec: does the ECJ realize what it has done?' (2008) 3(8) JIPLP 507

J Davis and A Durant, 'To protect or not to protect? The eligibility of commercially used short verbal texts for copyright and trade mark protection' [2011] 4 IPQ 345–370

NM Dawson, 'Bad faith in European trade mark law' [2011] 3 IPQ 229–258

A Firth, 'Shapes as trade marks: public policy, functional considerations and consumer perception' (2001) 23(2) EIPR 86–99

A Folliard-Monguiral and D Rogers, 'Community trade mark case law round-up 2006' (2007) 2(4) JIPLP 215–33

A Folliard-Monguiral and D Rogers, 'Significant 2007 case law on the Community trade mark from the ECJ and the CFI' (2008) 3(5) JIPLP 291.

A Fox 'Does the Trade Mark Harmonisation Directive Recognise a Public Interest in Keeping non-distinctive Signs Free for Use?' (2000) 22(1) EIPR 1–6

C Gielen, 'adidas v Marca II: undue limitations of trade mark owner's rights by the European Court of Justice?' [2008] EIPR 254

A Griffiths, 'Modernising trade mark law and promoting economic efficiency: an evaluation of the Baby Dry judgement and its aftermath' [2003] 1 IPQ 1–34

M Handler, 'The distinctive problem of a European trade mark' (2005) 27(9) EIPR 306–312

L Harrold, 'The genie in the bottle: brand "free riding": what's permissible and what's not?' (2008) 3(8) JIPLP 511

G Humphreys, 'Deceit and immorality in trade mark matters: does it pay to be bad?' (2007) 2(2) JIPLP 89–96

A Kamperman Sanders, 'The return to Wagamama' [1996] EIPR 521

A Kamperman Sanders, 'The Wagamama decision: back to the dark ages of trade mark law' [1996] 1 EIPR 3

DT Keeling, 'About kinetic watches, easy banking and nappies that keep a baby dry: a review of recent European case law on absolute grounds for refusal to register trade marks' [2003] 2 IPQ 131–162

P Prescott, 'Has Benelux trade mark law been written into the Directive' [1997] EIPR 99

P Prescott, 'Think before you waga finger: comment' [1996] EIPR 317

P Reeskamp, 'Is comparative advertising a trade mark issue?' [2008] EIPR 131

C Schulze, 'Registering colour trade marks in the European Union' (2003) 25(2) EIPR 55–67

I Simon, 'Trade marks in trouble' (2005) 27(2) EIPR 71–75

C Thompson and B Ladas, 'How green is my trade mark? Woolworths v BP' (2007) 29(1) EIPR 29–35

B Trimmer, 'An increasingly uneasy relationship: the English courts and the European Court of Justice in trade mark disputes' [2008] EIPR 87

P Yap, 'Honestly, neither Celine nor Gillette is defensible!' [2008] EIPR 286

15

Relative ground for refusing registration, infringement, and defences

Introduction

Scope and overview of chapter

15.1 It is essential to understand the conditions under which a registered trade mark will be infringed by virtue of unauthorised use by a third party to appreciate the scope of the rights conferred by a trade mark. If a registered trade mark is infringed easily by competing traders, so the trade mark owner will have a broad monopoly in the market. On the other hand, if a competing trader can trade using a sign that is similar to that of the registered mark and in connection with similar goods as services, so the monopoly conferred by the registered mark narrows—the greater the similarity, the narrower the monopoly. As with other areas of trade mark law there is a constant tension between the desires of the trade mark owner, those of the competing trader, and the interests of the consumer. One feature in this is the question as to whether a trade mark will be infringed only if it is used in the course of trade in a trade mark sense, or whether other unauthorised uses of a mark, such as descriptive uses, can be controlled by the trade mark owner. This in turn links to the discussion on defences to an action for trade mark infringement and the extent of permissible uses of a registered trade mark by a third party.

15.2
> ### Learning objectives
>
> By the end of this chapter you should be able to describe and explain:
>
> - the current discussions on and relevance of the debate on the use of a trade mark during trade;
> - the relative grounds for refusing to register a trade mark and those circumstances in which a trade mark will be infringed by unauthorised use by a third party;
> - the scope of defences in relation to an action for trade mark infringement.

15.3 In this chapter, having examined the concept of use in the course of trade for the purposes of infringement, discussion will move to consider the relative grounds for refusal to register a trade mark and those circumstances in which a trade mark can be infringed and consider defences to an action of infringement. (For a discussion on other trade mark uses see para 14.113ff). As was stated in the last chapter, those provisions on registration of a trade mark on relative grounds virtually mirror the provisions on infringement. The comments in relation to infringement are thus applicable to registration. The chapter will finish with an examination of the defences to an action for trade mark infringement including an analysis of comparative advertising.

So the rest of the chapter looks like this:

- Use of a trade mark for the purposes of infringement (15.4–15.22)
- Relative grounds for refusal of registration and infringement (15.23–15.104)
- Defences to an action of infringement (15.105–15.132)

Use of a trade mark for the purposes of infringement

 Exercise

Read section 9 of the Trade Marks Act 1994 (TMA 1994); Article 5(3) of the Trade Marks Directive; and Article 9(2) of the Community Trade Mark Regulation (CTMR).

15.4   Section 9 of the TMA 1994 provides that the proprietor of a registered trade mark has exclusive rights in the registered trade mark. Under the TMA 1994 these exclusive rights are infringed by the use of the trade mark in the UK without consent.[1] The acts of infringement are specified in section 10 of the TMA 1994. Infringement proceedings may be commenced on or after the date on which the mark is entered on the register.[2] This date appears on the front of the registration certificate.[3] As the rights conferred by the 1994 Act are territorial, the proprietor may only sue in respect of infringements occurring in the UK including the Isle of Man.[4] As was pointed out in para 13.34 the rights conferred by the Community trade mark (CTM) extend to all member states of the EU.

15.5   A non-exhaustive list of examples of when a sign which is identical to a registered trade mark is 'used' for the purposes of section 10 can be found in section 10(4) of the TMA 1994.

Under the 1994 Act, a sign is 'used' when a person:

- affixes it to goods or packaging;[5]
- offers to supply, stocks, or markets goods or services under the sign;[6]
- imports or exports goods under the sign;[7] or
- uses the sign on business paper or in advertising.[8]

---

[1] TMA 1994, s 9(1).   [2] TMA 1994, s 9(3)(a); CTMR, Art 9(3).

[3] Damages for infringement can be backdated and claimed from the date of the filing of the application for registration: TMA 1994, s 9(3).

[4] TMA 1994, ss 9(1), 107, and 108. An action for infringement may be brought by the proprietor of the trade mark: TMA 1994, s 14(1). An exclusive licensee may bring his own proceedings if permitted to do so by the licence: TMA 1994, s 14(1). Otherwise, a non-exclusive or sole licensee has the right to call upon the proprietor to take action, and may do so himself if the proprietor refuses or fails to do so within two months: TMA 1994, s 30(1)–(5).

[5] TMA 1994, s 10(4)(a). See Case C-119/10 *Frisdranken Industrie Winters BV v Red Bull Gmbh*, para 15.18.

[6] TMA 1994, s 10(4)(b).   [7] TMA 1994, s 10(4)(c).

[8] TMA 1994, s 10(4)(d). See also Case C-62/08 *UDV North America Inc v Brandtraders NV*.

These uses must be 'in the course of trade' which the Court of Justice has said will be found 'where it occurs in the context of commercial activity with a view to economic advantage and not as a private matter'[9] and made in the alleged infringer's own commercial communication.[10]

15.6   Section 10(5) of the TMA 1994 provides that a person who applies a registered trade mark to material which is intended to be used for labelling or packing goods, as a business paper, or for advertising goods, is to be treated as a party to any use of the material which infringes the registered trade mark. Thus, printers, advertisers, and publishers can be treated as infringers, although there is a proviso in this section that a person who so applies the mark must have known, or had reason to believe, that the application of the mark was not authorised by the licensee. In any unusual circumstances, printers, advertisers, and publishers would be well advised to obtain authorisation for the particular application from the proprietor of the registered trade mark, or warranties and indemnities from the purchaser of the services that the activities of the publishers and printers will not infringe the rights attaching to the registered trade mark.

 Question

Can you think of any other circumstances in which the use of a sign in the course of trade might infringe a registered trade mark?

Use for the purposes of infringement: case law

15.7   Under the Trade Marks Act 1938, a sign had to be used 'as a trade mark' also referred to as 'in a trade mark sense' before infringement occurred.[11] This meant that it actually had to be used as a trade mark, rather than for a descriptive purpose. Thus, for example, the travel writer who wrote an article about a fortnight's hill walking in the Lake District and gave it the title 'Wet Wet Wet' would be using that mark in a non-trade mark sense because it was actually describing the walk.[12] Whether a trade mark has to be used 'in a trade mark sense' is important as the more uses that a trade mark owner can control, the greater the scope of the monopoly that is conferred on the holder, and the correspondingly greater cost imposed both on competitors and others who may wish to use or to allude to the mark otherwise than in trade. However, it was not clear from the 1994 Act that such use was actually necessary for infringement.[13] In *British Sugar v James Robertson & Sons Ltd*[14] it was stated that use in a trade mark sense was not a necessary prerequisite to infringement. Subsequent case law from the British and European courts shows that the law is developing to tie the question of use to the function of a trade mark.

15.8   An early English case was:

■ *Trebor Bassett Ltd v Football Association Ltd* [1997] FSR 211

Trebor placed cards featuring photographs of England footballers in its packets of candy sticks. The England 'Three Lions' logo, in respect of which the Football Association owned a registered trade mark, appeared on the England football shirts worn by the players in the photographs.[15]

---

9 Case C-206/01 *Arsenal v Reed*, para 40; if, owing to their volume, their frequency, or other characteristics, the sales made on such a marketplace go beyond the realms of a private activity, the seller will be acting 'in the course of trade': Case C-324/09 *L'Oréal SA and others v eBay International AG*, para 55.

10 Joined Cases C-236/08 to C-238/08 *Google France v Louis Vuitton Malletier*, para 56.

11 *Bismag Ltd v Amblins (Chemists) Ltd* [1940] Ch 667.

12 This example is taken from the case *Bravado Merchandising Services Ltd v Mainstream Publishing (Edinburgh) Ltd* [1996] FSR 205 (OH).

13 *Wagamama Ltd v City Centre Restaurants plc* [1995] FSR 713 (Ch D).   14 [1997] ETMR 118.

15 UK Trade Mark No 1104188, class 16, proprietor: The Football Association Limited.

The Football Association alleged that Trebor had infringed its trade mark by including these cards with the pictures in which the logo was apparent. The court gave this argument fairly short shrift saying that Trebor's act of publishing and marketing these cards in conjunction with the sweets did not in any sense amount to *using the logo* in respect of the cards on which the photographs appeared. 'Trebor Basset is not even arguably using the logo … in any real sense of the word "uses" and is certainly not, in my judgment, using it as a sign in respect of its cards'.[16]

Figure 15.1 Football Association three lions logo

15.9 This case must have given some comfort to those traders where they might include a registered trade mark belonging to another as an incidental part of their own marketing strategy. An example might be a supermarket advertising its own shops, pictures of which include the interior and thus goods with registered trade marks belonging to others.

15.10 However, as indicated, the European Court of Justice (ECJ) has now had several opportunities to consider the issue. The question is not as simple as use as a trade mark or in a trade mark sense. Rather, the question is as to whether the essential function of a mark is likely to be jeopardised through the unauthorised use of the mark by the third party.

■ *Arsenal Football Club plc v Reed* [2001] 2 CMLR 23

The issue arose over the sale by Reed of souvenirs and memorabilia relating to the football club which incorporated registered trade marks 'Arsenal' and 'Gunners',[17] both marks registered by the club, and their logo, shown in Figure 15.2.

Arsenal football club argued that this use by Reed infringed their registered trade marks. The High Court, however, found that Reed's products did not state a trade origin. In other words, Reed was not using the marks *'in a trade mark sense'* but merely in association with club souvenirs—as a badge of allegiance. However, it was felt that sufficient uncertainty surrounded the issued to ask the ECJ to adjudicate on the general question as to whether a registered mark would be infringed if it was being used in such a way that did not signify trade origin.[18] The Court[19] held that it was not a defence to an action for trade mark

---

[16] *Trebor Bassett Ltd v Football Association Ltd* [1997] FSR 211 at 216. For an analysis of similar facts under the law of copyright, see *The Football Association Premier League v Panini UK Ltd* [2003] EWCA Civ 995.

[17] UK Trade Mark No 1393206, classes 6, 9, 14, 16, 18, 20, 21, 24, 26, 27, and 28, proprietor: The Arsenal Football Club Public Limited Company.

[18] The question was: 1. Where a trade mark is validly registered and (a) a third party uses in the course of trade a sign identical with that trade mark in relation to goods which are identical with those for whom the trade mark is registered; and (b) the third party has no defence to infringement by virtue of Article 6(1) of the Council Directive of December 21, 1988 to approximate the laws of the Member States relating to trade marks (89/104); does the third party have a defence to infringement on the ground that the use complained of does not indicate trade origin (i.e. a connection in the course of trade between the goods and the trade mark proprietor)? 2. If so, is the fact that the use in question would be perceived as a badge of support, loyalty or affiliation to the trade mark proprietor a sufficient connection?   [19] Case C-206/01 *Arsenal Football Club v Matthew Reed* [2002] ECR I-10273.

Figure 15.2 Arsenal Football Club logo

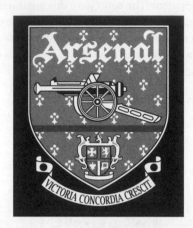

infringement to argue that a trade mark belonging to a third party was merely being used as a badge of allegiance or loyalty. That the trade mark was used in this manner did not mean that it did not affect the essential function of the mark—that of guaranteeing the identity of the origin of goods or services bearing that mark. The use of the Arsenal marks in the instant case was 'such as to create the impression that there is a material link in the course of trade' between the goods and Arsenal: 'there is a clear possibility in the present case that some consumers, in particular if they come across the goods after they have been sold by Mr Reed and taken away from the stall where the notice appears, may interpret the sign as designating Arsenal FC as the undertaking of origin of the goods'.

15.11 Ultimately, when the judgment of the ECJ was applied to the case in the Court of Appeal,[20] that court interpreted the test laid down by the ECJ as being not about trade mark use, but whether the use of the sign was likely to affect or jeopardise the guarantee of origin. In the instant case, the use of the Arsenal marks was such as to create an impression of a trade link between Arsenal and the goods: whether or not the signs were perceived as badges of affiliation was irrelevant to the function of the mark as a guarantee of origin.[21]

15.12 A somewhat different pronouncement on this question of use was made by the House of Lords in *R v Johnstone*[22] in which their Lordships came to the view that trade mark use was necessary for trade mark infringement and where the wider test of jeopardising the guarantee function was not considered. This case concerned bootleg CDs and the criminal provisions of the TMA 1994. The question was whether the fixation of the performers' names to the CDs amounted to trade mark infringement where those names were also registered trade marks. Having considered the ECJ judgment in the *Arsenal* case, the House of Lords came to the conclusion that trade mark use in the sense of the use of a mark likely to be taken as an indication of trade origin was required. Whether the use was trade mark use or not would depend on 'how the use of the sign would be perceived by the average customer of the type of goods

[20] *Arsenal Football Club plc v Reed (No 2)* [2003] EWCA Civ 696, [2003] 3 All ER 865, [2003] 2 CMLR 25, [2003] ETMR 73, [2003] RPC 39.

[21] But see the Scottish case *Dyer v Gallacher* [2006] GWD 7-136 where Gallacher was acquitted of criminally infringing the registered trade marks of Glasgow Rangers FC by selling hats and scarves bearing the word 'Rangers' or an 'RFC' monogram without any licence from the club to enable him to do so.

[22] [2003] UKHL 28, [2003] 1 WLR 1736, [2003] 3 All ER 884, [2003] 2 Cr App R 33, [2004] ETMR 2. Note *R v Boulter (Gary)* [2008] EWCA Crim 2375, [2009] ETMR 6 which involved counterfeit goods. See para 21.122.

in question'. Non-trade mark use would not amount to infringement. The majority of the House *obiter* came to the view that the use in the instant case was not trade mark use.[23]

Question

What difference does it make to the scope of the rights of the trade mark proprietor if a mark has to be used 'in a trade mark sense' before it will infringe the rights of the registered proprietor?

15.13   The matter returned to the ECJ in *Adam Opel AG v Autec AG*.[24] Opel had a registration of its trade mark not only for full-scale motor vehicles, but also for toys. The manufacturer of toy cars, Autec, affixed Opel's registered trade marks to their own toy cars. The issue was thus the use of an identical mark by Autec in connection with identical goods for which Opel had a registration. A number of questions were referred to the Court which included the following:

• Does the use of a trade mark registered also for 'toys' constitute use as a trade mark for the purposes of Article 5(1)(a) of the Trade Mark Directive if the manufacturer of a toy model car copies a real car in a reduced scale, including the trade mark as applied to the real car, and markets it?

The Court reformulated the question as whether, 'when a trade mark is registered both for motor vehicles and for toys [as it was by Opel] the affixing by a third party, without authorisation from the trade mark proprietor, of a sign identical to that trade mark on scale models of that make of car, in order to reproduce it faithfully, and the marketing of those scale models constitutes, for the purposes of Article 5(1)(a) of the directive, a use which the trade mark proprietor is entitled to prevent'.[25] As with *Arsenal v Reed*, the case concerned an identical mark used in connection with identical goods and services for which the mark was registered. The Court reiterated its judgment in *Arsenal v Reed* stating that the exclusive right under Article 5(1) of the Directive 'was conferred in order to enable the trade mark proprietor to protect his specific interests as proprietor, that is, to ensure that the trade mark can fulfil its functions and that, therefore, the exercise of that right must be reserved to cases in which a third party's use of the sign affects or is liable to affect the functions of the trade mark, in particular its essential function of guaranteeing to consumers the origin of the goods'[26] as long as the use takes place in the course of trade[27] in the context of commercial activity with a view to economic advantage and not as a private matter.[28] The affixing of an identical sign to identical goods could thus not be prohibited unless it affects, or is liable to affect, the function of the trade mark.[29] From this a key question is as to whether the function of a trade mark will be jeopardised—and that will be a matter for the national court to determine by reference to the average consumer of the type of products in question.

15.14   Another question is as to which function of a mark needs to be jeopardised. In *Adam Opel* the question was over identical marks and identical goods and services. Here it has generally been thought that the function of the mark is to guarantee origin. An issue raised by the ECJ in *Adam Opel* (although not by the parties) was what the position would be had it been claimed that the use of the Opel trade mark by Autec diluted the extended functions of a mark. Here the Court said that the affixation of a well-known mark without authorisation would be a use the proprietor could prevent if, without due cause the use

[23] See also *R v James Rupert Isaac* [2004] EWCA Crim 1082 on difficulties that can arise in showing use of a cartoon as a trade mark in an action for revocation. Also *Animated Music Ltd's Trade Mark; Application for Revocation by Dash Music Co Ltd* [2004] ETMR 79 (TMR).

[24] Case C-48/05.   [25] *Adam Opel*, para 14.   [26] *Adam Opel*, para 21.

[27] *Interflora v Marks & Spencer* [2009] EWHC 1095 (Ch).

[28] *Arsenal*, note 19, para 40. Case C-62/08 *UDV North America Inc v Brandtraders NV*, para 44.

[29] *Arsenal*, para 22.

of that sign took unfair advantage of, or was detrimental to, the distinctive character or the repute of the trade mark as a trade mark registered for motor vehicles.[30] (For discussion on the extended functions of a mark, see paras 13.12ff and 15.68ff).

15.15   The ECJ returned to this in *L'Oreal v Bellure*[31] where the issue was once again of identity of marks. In this case the Court spoke also of the functions of 'communication, investment or advertising'.[32] So it would seem that if these extended functions are implicated then there will be infringement. *L'Oreal* was in the context of comparative advertising (for a discussion see para 15.122).[33]

 Question

> Where the question of the use of a trade mark jeopardising the function of a mark arises in relation to identity of goods and services and use, should the extended functions of a mark be a relevant consideration?[34] If yes, what does this mean for the trade mark owner and the competitor?

15.16   More challengingly, the Court of Justice has been presented with a series of cases involving trade marks which have been 'sold' by Internet service providers to the highest bidder and which appear when a search request is made. The potential liability of the various parties was considered in a series of cases concerning Google.

■ Case C-236/08 *Google France Sarl v Louis Vuitton Malletier SA*

The question here was whether an entity which makes available the technical conditions necessary to use a sign and is paid to do so, uses the sign for the purposes of infringement. The Court held that the fact that the service provider allowed others to use the sign did not thereby mean that it also used the sign:

> although it is clear from those factors that the referencing service provider operates 'in the course of trade' when it permits advertisers to select, as keywords, signs identical with trade marks, stores those signs and displays its clients' ads on the basis thereof, it does not follow, however, from those factors that that service provider itself 'uses' those signs within the terms of Article 5 of Directive 89/104 and Article 9 of Regulation No 40/94. A referencing service provider allows its clients to use signs which are identical with, or similar to, trade marks, without itself using those signs.[35]

To be infringing use, it must be the alleged infringer's own commercial communication that is being challenged. So the person who would be using the mark in this scenario is the advertiser.[36] As noted previously, if the use is to be infringing use, one of the functions of a mark must also be implicated.[37]

The High Court sought to interpret the ruling of the Court of Justice in Google France in *Och-Ziff Management Europe Ltd v Och Capital LLP*.[38] The question was whether the referencing service provider used the mark, and what was meant by 'use' in this context. The High Court said:

> It seems to me that this reasoning [in Google France] may be interpreted in two ways. The first is that the referencing service provider does not use the sign 'in the course of trade' because its use is 'as a private matter' even

---

[30] Case C-48/05, para 37.   [31] Case C-487/07; [2007] EWCA Civ 936.
[32] *L'Oreal v Bellure*, para 58.   [33] See also Case C-533/06 *O2 v Hutchinson*.
[34] For a case concerning the 'use' of a mark during the course of commercial negotiations, see Case C-2/00 *Holterhoff v Freiesleben* [2002] All ER (EC) 665, [2002] ECR I-4187, [2002] ETMR 79, [2002] FSR 52. This type of nominal or referential use does not implicate the origin function of a mark.
[35] Paras 55 and 56.   [36] Para 60.
[37] Paras 77 and 78. Confirmed in Case C-91/09 *Eis.de GmbH v BBY Vertriebsgesellschaft mbH* and Case C-323/09 *Interflora Inc v Marks & Spencer plc*. This is the case even where the sign selected as a keyword does not appear in the advertisement.
[38] [2011] ETMR 1.

though it is 'in the context of commercial activity with a view to economic advantage'. In other words, 'and not as a private matter' is an additional criterion which is not satisfied in these circumstances. The second is that the referencing service provider does not 'use' the sign at all within the meaning of art.5 of the Directive and art.9 of the Regulation: it simply provides the medium for the use made by the advertiser.

The Court in the instant case preferred the second interpretation—that the sign was not used at all as a trade mark. If, however, the mark was used, then that was as a private and not infringing use.[39]

15.17   Further questions on use have been referred to the Court of Justice in *Specsavers v Asda*.[40] The case concerned an advertising campaign by Asda which made reference to Specsavers and used oval shapes similar to those registered by Specsavers.

The questions referred on use are:

a) Where a trader has separate registrations of Community trade marks for

(i) a graphic device mark;

(ii) a word mark;

and uses the two together, is such use capable of amounting to use of the graphic device mark for the purposes of art.15 of Regulation 40/94 ? If yes, how is the question of use of the graphic mark to be assessed?

b) Does it make a difference if:

(i) the word mark is superimposed over the graphic device?

(ii) the trader also has the combined mark comprising graphic device and word mark registered as a Community trade mark?

c) Does the answer to A or B depend upon whether the graphic device and the words are perceived by the average consumer as (i) being separate signs; or (ii) each having an independent distinctive role? If so, how?

The logos look like this:

Figure 15.3 CTM Nos 1321298 & 3418928

SPECSAVERS

Figure 15.4 CTM Nos 449256 & 1321348

Figure 15.5 CTM No 5608385

---

[39] Para 66.

[40] *Specsavers International Healthcare Ltd, Specsavers BV, Specsavers Optical Group Ltd and Specsavers Optical Superstores Ltd v Asda Stores Ltd* [2012] EWCA Civ 24, [2012] ETMR 17.

Question

How do you think the Court of Justice will respond? How should it respond?

15.18 There are limits on the circumstance under which a trade mark will be 'used' by a competitor. In an application for an interim injunction the High Court in *Unilever plc v Griffin*[41] held that a Marmite jar appearing in the corner of an election broadcast was political use and not use in the course of trade. The Court of Justice in *Frisdranken Industrie Winters BV v Red Bull GmbH*[42] held that where 'a service provider who, in circumstances such as those in the main action, merely fills, under an order from and on the instructions of another person, cans already bearing signs similar to trade marks and therefore merely executes a technical part of the production process of the final product without having any interest in the external presentation of those cans and in particular in the signs thereon, does not itself "use" those signs within the meaning of art.5 of Directive 89/104, but only creates *the technical conditions necessary for the other person to use them*.'[43] Here the firm sued for infringement filled cans with drink. The cans were supplied by another party and bore the name 'Bull Fighter' (among others).

 Question

Critically comment on the approach taken by the High Court in *Och-Ziff Management Europe Ltd v Och Capital LLP* in the light of the ruling of the Court of Justice in the Google cases. Do you agree with the approach taken? If yes, why do you agree? If not, why not?

Use and company names

15.19 A different question has arisen concerning the adoption of a registered word mark by an unrelated third party without authorisation as a company or business name. Would such use of the later sign amount to use as a trade mark? In *Robelco v Robeco Groep*[44] the ECJ pointed out that the harmonisation brought about by Article 5(1)–(4) of the Directive does not affect national provisions relating to the protection of a sign against use other than for the purpose of distinguishing goods or services, where the use takes unfair advantage of, or is detrimental to, the distinctive character or repute of the mark. Thus where a sign—such as a trade or company name—is used other than for distinguishing the goods or services (the origin function), it is necessary to look to the domestic law of the member states to determine the nature and extent of protection given to trade mark owners who claim to suffer damage as a result of such use.[45] This was also the conclusion of the ECJ in *Anheuser-Busch Inc v Budjeovický Budvar*[46] where the Court stressed that that the trade mark proprietor could oppose the later use of a company or business name as long as the later sign was used in the course of trade for goods. Where the mark was used otherwise than to distinguish the goods, then relief would only be available where the use of the mark took advantage of, or was detrimental to, the distinctive character or repute of the mark, and where national law provided a remedy.

[41] [2010] EWHC 899 (Ch). [42] Case C-119/10. [43] Para 30.
[44] Case C-23/01 *Robelco v Robeco Groep NV* [2002] ECR I-10913.
[45] *Robelco v Robeco Groep NV*, paras 30 and 34. Note that the Tribunal set up at the IPO to deal with the registration of opportunistic company names which might include those where trade marks belong to third parties: Companies Act 2006, s 69 and Company Names Adjudicator Rules 2008 (SI 2008/1738). For details of decisions see http://www.ipo.gov.uk/cna.htm.
[46] Case C-245/02.

15.20   Although the Court appears to have been clear in saying that where the company or trade name which is identical or similar to the trade mark is used by the third party in the course of trade to distinguish the same or similar goods and services of that third party the use could be enjoined, a question on this point was again referred to the ECJ in *SARL Céline v SA Céline*[47] by the Cour d'appel de Nancy, France.

15.21   The Court reiterated earlier case law and said that four factors had to be met:

- that use must be in the course of trade;
- it must be without the consent of the proprietor of the mark;
- it must be in relation to goods or services which are identical to those for which the mark is registered; and
- it must affect or be liable to affect the functions of the trade mark, in particular its essential function of guaranteeing to consumers the origin of the goods or services.

In the instant case the parties had agreed the names were identical. With respect to the third point, the Court considered the concept 'in relation to' as important noting that within the meaning of Article 5(1) and (2) the phrase is used for the purpose of distinguishing the goods or services in question, whereas Article 5(5) is directed at 'the use which is made of a sign for purposes other than distinguishing the goods or services …'[48] In the instant case:

> the purpose of a company, trade or shop name is not, of itself, to distinguish goods or services … The purpose of a company name is to identify a company, whereas the purpose of a trade name or a shop name is to designate a business which is being carried on. accordingly, where the use of a company name, trade name or shop name is limited to identifying a company or designating a business which is being carried on, such use cannot be considered as being 'in relation to goods or services' within the meaning of Article 5(1) of the directive.[49]

There would, however, be use in relation to goods within the meaning of Article 5(1) where a third party affixes the sign constituting his company name, trade name, or shop name to the goods which he markets[50] (see also para 15.109). Thus, use of a trade mark as a company name is not of itself infringing as it is not 'in relation to' goods and services. It is for the national court to decide in all of the circumstances whether the use should be enjoined.

Question

How do you reconcile *Robelco v Robeco Groep NV* and *Céline v SA Céline*?

Exercise

Critically consider the decisions of the company names tribunal (on the UK Intellectual Property Office (IPO; or UK–IPO) website) in the light of the judgment in *SARL Céline v SA Céline*.

15.22   As can be seen from the foregoing discussion, the place of 'use' in relation to infringement within trade mark law continues to develop.[51] While the general direction of Court of Justice jurisprudence is to tie

---

[47] Case C-17/06.   [48] *Céline*, para 20.   [49] *Céline*, para 21.   [50] *Céline*, para 22.
[51] For a detailed examination of use from a number of different perspectives, see J Phillips and I Simon (eds), *Trade Mark Use* (2005).

the question of use to the functions of a trade mark, it will take time to determine whether all functions are relevant in all cases of use and infringement and, more practically, for national courts to determine when the facts would support a finding that the functions had been jeopardised. The matter is important. The more functions that are recognised in an infringement action, and the easier it is to jeopardise a function, so the parameters of the monopoly expand. These issues are intimately linked with the balance within the registered trade mark framework as between the interests of the trader, of competitors, and of the consumer.

 Discussion point

What functions should be recognised when considering whether use by a third party is relevant to infringement? What are the parameters and what the implications and for whom?

 Question

Does permission need to be obtained from the proprietor of the trade mark to use the images of registered trade marks in this book?

Key points on use

- Court of Justice jurisprudence has developed to tie the question of use for the question of trade mark infringement to the functions of a mark
- The greater the scope for non-infringing uses by third parties, the narrower the monopoly granted by the mark and vice versa

Relative grounds for refusal of registration and infringement

 Exercise

Read sections 5 and 10 of the TMA 1994; Articles 4 and 5 of the Directive; and Articles 8 and 9 of the CTMR.

15.23   The grounds on which an action for infringement of a registered trade mark may be taken under the 1994 Act are to be found mainly in section 10 (1)–(3). As discussed previously, these provisions reflect section 5(1)–(3) of the 1994 Act which deal with the relative grounds for refusal of registration. In *LTJ Diffusion SA v Sadas Vertbaudet SA*[52] the ECJ said:

> the question submitted will be examined … solely in the light of Article 5(1)(a) of the Directive, but the interpretation adopted following that examination will also apply to Article 4(1)(a) of the Directive since that interpretation will be transposable, mutatis mutandis, to the latter provision.[53]

---

[52] Case C-291/00 [2003] ECR 1-2799.   [53] *LTJ*, para 53.

In *10 Royal Berkshire Polo Club*[54] the appointed person noted:

> Objections under section 5(2) are conceptually indistinguishable from actions under section 10(2) of the Act (Article 5(1)(b) of the Directive). They serve to ensure that trade marks whose use could successfully be challenged before the courts are not registered.[55]

These sections are therefore dealt with together in this part.[56]

Identity of goods and services and of marks

 Exercise

Read sections 5(1) and 10(1) of the TMA 1994; Articles 4(1)(a) and 5(1)(a) of the Directive; and Article 8(1)(a) and 9(1)(a) of the CTMR.

Section 5(1) of the 1994 Act provides that:

- a trade mark shall not be registered if it is identical with an earlier trade mark and the goods or services for which the trade mark is applied for are identical with the goods or services for which the earlier trade mark is protected.

Section 10(1) of the 1994 Act provides that:

- a person infringes a registered trade mark if he uses in the course of trade a sign which is identical with the trade mark in relation to goods or services which are identical with those for which it is registered.

15.24   There are some important points arising from the wording:

- There is no need to show a likelihood of confusion amongst relevant consumers for registration to be refused, or for there to be infringement of the registered mark.

- Apart from those cases dealing with use (paras 15.7–15.21), comparative advertising (paras 15.128ff), and keyword advertising (paras 16.67ff) few cases have arisen under this section as it flies against the most fundamental tenets of trade mark law: that a trade mark is an indication of origin.[57] If two or more identical marks belonging to different proprietors are registered for identical goods or services (or if the specifications for which the goods and services are registered overlap),[58] then the consumer is bound to be confused as to the origin of those goods or services. Take the example of the Bass triangle given in para 13.24. That mark has been registered by Bass plc for beer. If another company making beer were able to register an *identical* trade mark for their beer, then how could the consumer identify the origin of the particular goods in the supermarket or pub? Thus registration would not be permitted, and looking to infringement one suspects (counterfeiting aside) that if an

---

[54] *10 Royal Berkshire Polo Club Trade Mark* [2001] RPC 32.   [55] *10 Royal Berkshire Polo Club Trade Mark*, para 17.

[56] Infringement proceedings for infringement of the exclusive rights of the proprietor of a registered trade mark can only be commenced once the trade mark appears on the Register: TMA 1994, s 9(3)(a). Damages, however, can be obtained from the date of the filing of the application for registration: TMA 1994, s 9(3). An infringement of the exclusive rights attaching to a registered trade mark is actionable by the proprietor: TMA 1994, s 14(1). The exclusive rights attaching to a registered trade mark can be infringed by non-graphic use, eg orally: TMA 1994, s 103(2).

[57] One case to consider s 10(1) was *Primark Stores Ltd v Lollypop Clothing Ltd* [2001] FSR 37 (Ch D). Primark had the registered mark 'Primark' in respect of articles of clothing. Lollypop Clothing supplied a retailer with clothing apparently identical to that sold by Primark, and bearing the registered mark. Section 10(1) was thus found to be infringed.

[58] *Galileo Brand Architecture Ltd Trade Mark Application* (No 2280603) [2005] RPC 22.

identical sign is used by a third party in relation to identical goods and services, a gentle warning by the trade mark owner would be sufficient to halt the unauthorised use.[59]

 Question

The section refers to identical marks, and identical goods and services. What therefore amounts to 'identical' in this sense?

Identity of marks

15.25   The question over what amounted to identity of marks arose in *Bravado Merchandising Services v Mainstream Publishing Ltd*.[60] Bravado Merchandising Services owned the registered trade mark 'Wet Wet Wet'. It was registered for, inter alia, printed matter, books, and book covers. Mainstream Publishing produced a book about the pop group and included the name on the cover of the book albeit in a different script to the registered mark. The court held that this did not mean the marks were not identical for the purposes of this section.[61]

15.26   If absolute identity were required, then the smallest change to a mark would move the assessment of the facts from sections 5(1) and 10(1) of the TMA 1994 where *no* consumer confusion is required, and into sections 5(2) and 10(2) of that Act, where consumer confusion *is* a prerequisite of liability. Consequently, it would be more difficult and expensive for the proprietor of the registered mark to preclude registration of an 'identical' mark or to show infringement. However, subsequent cases have suggested that the test is stricter than first thought. 'Origin' has been held not to be identical to 'Origins',[62] 'Animal' not identical to 'Animale',[63] and O STORE not identical to THE O STORE.[64]

15.27   Important guidance on the identity of marks has been received from the ECJ.

■ **Case C-291/00 *LTJ Diffusion SA v Sadas Vertbaudet SA* [2003] ETMR 83, [2003] FSR 34 (ECJ)**

LTJ was in the business of design, manufacture, and marketing of clothing. They had a registered mark, 'Arthur' in France in, inter alia, class 25 for clothing.[65] Sadas, a mail order business marketing, inter alia, children's clothing, applied to register the mark 'Arthur et Felicie' in class 25. LTJ brought an action to have the Sadas mark declared invalid. The ECJ was asked how the test of identity was to be interpreted. In response the Court said that it was to be interpreted strictly. 'The very definition of identity implies that the two elements compared should be the same in all respects'.[66] That is, there would be identity between the sign and the trade mark 'where the former reproduces, without any modification or addition, all the elements constituting the latter'.[67]

15.28   So this would seem a strict test—more so than suggested in *Bravado Merchandising Services*. But the ECJ modified it somewhat when it went on to say that while the perception of identity must be assessed globally 'with respect to an average consumer who is deemed to be reasonably well informed, reasonably

[59] But the owner needs to be careful about making threats. For details, see paras 22.90ff.
[60] [1996] FSR 205 (OH).
[61] *Bravado Merchandising Services Ltd v Mainstream Publishing (Edinburgh) Ltd* [1996] FSR 205 (OH).
[62] *Origins Natural Resources v Origin Clothing* [1995] FSR 280.
[63] *H Young (Operations) Ltd v Medici Ltd* [2003] EWHC 1589 (Ch), [2004] FSR 19.   [64] Case T-116/06 *Oakley v OHIM*.
[65] TM No 17731.   [66] *LTJ*, para 50.   [67] *LTJ*, para 51.

observant and circumspect', the consumer may carry an imperfect picture with him and his attention is likely to vary as between categories of goods.[68] Insignificant changes might be missed.[69] Thus it would appear that 'identity' does not mean 'absolute' identity, but that small changes would be acceptable.

15.29   The question of identity has since been raised in the UK courts, notably in the following case.[70]

■ *Reed Executive plc and another v Reed Business Information Ltd and others*

Reed Solutions (RS) ran employment agencies and advertised job vacancies online using the domain name http://www.reed.co.uk. In 1986 RS had registered the trade mark 'Reed' for employment agency services. Reed Business Information (RBI) published magazines and journals both on and off-line some of which contained job advertisements. RBI set up the specialist job-related website, http://www.total-jobs.com. The question arose as to whether RBI's use of the word 'Reed' was an infringement of the RS registered trade mark. Referring, inter alia, to *LTJ*, the Court of Appeal held that since RBI had never used the word 'Reed' by itself but only in conjunction with other words or material, that use was not use of an 'identical mark'.

15.30   Other courts have seen fit to ignore the use of extra words if they have no trade mark significance. So in *Antoni Fields v Klaus Kobec Ltd*,[71] the addition of the word 'Limited' to the mark 'Klaus Kobec' had no trade mark significance and could be ignored.

Question

How different do you think marks could be for sections 5(1) and 10(1) of the 1994 Act to apply?

Identity of goods and services

15.31   Goods and services which are not registered in the same class of the Nice Agreement may still be considered identical for the purpose of the relative grounds for refusal of registration or for infringement. Overlapping specifications which may not co-extend will satisfy the test.[72] The inquiry is rather into what is actually being done by the trader and the applicant or alleged infringer.

■ *Avnet Inc v Isoact Ltd* [1998] FSR 16

Avnet had a registered mark 'Avnet' in class 35 for advertising and promotional services. Isoact, an Internet service provider which offered customers the opportunity to create their own webpages, used the word 'Avnet'. When Avnet argued that its trade mark was infringed under section 10(1) of the 1994 Act the court first looked to what the parties were doing—the actual 'core of what was being done'—and then examined what the defendant actually did to see if those activities fell within the requisite class. In so doing, it was found that Isoact was not providing advertising and promotional services, but simply offering the services of an Internet service provider. Therefore there was no identity between the respective services (see also the discussion in para 16.13).

---

[68] *LTJ*, para 52.   [69] *LTJ*, para 53.

[70] *Reed Executive plc and another v Reed Business Information Ltd, Reed Elsevier (UK) Ltd, Totaljobs.com Ltd* [2004] ETMR 56, [2004] EWCA Civ 159.

[71] [2006] EWHC 350 (Ch).

[72] *Galileo Brand Architecture Ltd's Trade Mark Application* (No 2280603) [2005] RPC 22. This should now be read in the light of the *IP Translator* case: Case C-307/10 *Chartered Institute of Patent Attorneys v Registrar of Trade Marks* (see para 14.27).

15.32   Other guidance has come from *British Sugar plc v James Robertson & Sons*[73] where it was argued that the word 'Treat' used by James Robertson in connection with a toffee-flavoured spread 'Robertson's Toffee Treat', infringed the trade mark 'Treat' that had been registered by British Sugar in connection with dessert sauces and syrups. The court first looked to the identity of the sign with the mark and then went on to analyse any similarity between the respective goods and services. On this point the goods were found to be *not* similar taking into account, inter alia, the uses of the products, their locations in supermarkets, and the respective food sectors into which they fell.

Key points on identity of goods, services, and marks

- Where goods/services and marks are identical it is not necessary to show consumer confusion
- When considering identity of marks the elements compared should be the same in all respects but allowance made for imperfect recollection
- When considering identity of services, the inquiry is as to what is actually done by the mark owner and applicant or alleged infringer

Similarity and confusion

 Exercise

Read sections 5(2) and 10(2) of the TMA 1994; Article 4(1)(b) of the Directive and 5(1)(b); and Articles 8(1)(b) and 9(1)(b) of the CTMR.

Section 5(2) of the 1994 Act provides that:

- a trade mark shall not be registered if because it is identical with an earlier trade mark and it is to be registered for goods or services similar to those for which the earlier trade mark is protected, or
- it is similar to an earlier trade mark and is to be registered for goods or services identical with or similar to those for which the earlier trade mark is protected,

there exists a likelihood of confusion on the part of the public, which includes the likelihood of association with the earlier trade mark.

Section 10(2) of the 1994 Act provides that:

- a person infringes a registered trade mark if he uses in the course of trade a sign where because the sign is identical with the trade mark and is used in relation to goods or services similar to those for which the trade mark is registered, or
- the sign is similar to the trade mark and is used in relation to goods or services identical with or similar to those for which the trade mark is registered,

there exists a likelihood of confusion on the part of the public, which includes the likelihood of association with the trade mark.[74]

---

[73] [1996] RPC 281.
[74] TMA 1994, s 5(2) is derived from the Directive, which is in turn based on Art 13A of the Uniform Benelux Trademarks Law of 1971.

15.33   These sections thus refer to:

Diagram 15.1 Similarity and confusion

MARK	GOODS/SERVICES	
IDENTICAL	SIMILAR	PLUS LIKELIHOOD OF CONFUSION
SIMILAR	IDENTICAL	INCLUDING ASSOCIATION = no
SIMILAR	SIMILAR	registration/infringement

15.34   The linchpin of these provisions is the notion of consumer confusion: it must be shown that a consumer would be confused if a sign is registered in connection with goods or services, where there is a similar or identical mark registered in connection with similar or identical goods or services. For cases of infringement, the rights accorded to the registered trade mark owner will be infringed if a third party uses, without authorisation, a confusingly similar sign in the marketplace in connection with identical or similar goods and services for which the earlier mark was registered.

15.35   The breadth of the monopoly conferred on the trader will depend on the notion of similarity between the marks and the goods and services. One trader might have a logo of a black cat stretching itself, and register that in connection with slippers. A competing trader might then use a picture of a black cat stretching itself in connection with gloves. Are the goods similar? They are both items of clothes but one is for use on the feet, and the other for use on the hands. If the court finds them to be similar, then the monopoly conferred by the first mark can prevent competing traders from using the same (or similar—a black cat yawing) logo in connection with a wide variety of goods and services. If on the other hand, the court finds the goods to be dissimilar, in this case slippers and gloves, so the monopoly conferred by the trade mark is defined more narrowly in relation to the goods which it covers. The same argument applies in relation to the similarity of the marks. To return to the previous example, if one trader has registered a logo of a black cat stretching in relation to slippers, would that prevent a competing trader from using a picture of a dog stretching in connection with slippers? Or a lion stretching itself in relation to slippers? If the cat, the dog, and the lion are found to be similar in trade mark terms, so the breadth of the monopoly granted to the first trader expands, in that he could prevent a variety of pictures of stretching animals being used in connection with slippers in the marketplace. The key is to decide how to determine similarity between the marks and the goods and services, and how to assess consumer confusion.

15.36   In assessing confusing similarities, the overall question to be asked is: '[are] there similarities (in terms of marks and goods and services) which would combine to create a likelihood of confusion if the earlier trade mark and the sign subsequently presented for registration were used concurrently in relation to goods or services for which they are respectively registered and proposed to be registered'?[75] The assessment must be appreciated globally[76] and depends on numerous elements.

15.37   The tests are interdependent.[77] Thus there may be a likelihood of confusion if goods or services are not so similar but there is high similarity between marks.[78] Equally, confusion may arise where a high level of similarity between goods and services offsets a lesser degree of similarity between the marks.[79] Marks

---

[75] *Naturelle Trade Mark* [1999] RPC 326 (Natrel and Naturelle). *See also Balmoral Trade Mark* [1999] RPC 297.

[76] *Sabel v Puma* [1997] ECR I-6191, para 22; Case C-425/98 *Marca Mode* [2000] ECR I-4861, para 40; *Mülhens v OHIM* [2006] ECR I-02717 (hereafter *Mülhens*), para 18.

[77] Eg *Esure Insurance v Direct Line Insurance* [2008] EWCA Civ 842, para 46.   [78] *Sabel*, para 24.   [79] *Canon*, para 19.

with a highly distinctive character, either per se or because of the recognition they possess on the market, thus enjoy broader protection than marks with a less distinctive character.[80]

Comparing the mark with the sign

15.38   There is a difference in comparing the mark with the sign in the context of an application for registration of a trade mark and that relevant to infringement.[81] As was pointed out in *O2 v Hutchison*,[82] once a mark has been registered, the proprietor may use is as she sees fit. So any application for registration of a similar sign must consider all the possible permutations in which the proprietor may legitimately use her mark. By comparison, when considering the use of a similar sign and whether that use infringes the registered mark, the analysis is limited to the circumstances characterising the use: other uses need not be considered.[83] In *Och-Ziff Management Europe Ltd v OCH Capital Ltd*[84] the High Court said that on a claim of infringement this would involve consideration of the circumstances of the use of the sign complained of, but not consideration of circumstances prior to, simultaneous with, or subsequent to the use of the sign.[85]

On the context in which use is made of the sign, the Court of Appeal in *Specsavers v Asda*,[86] another comparative advertising case, said:

> In my judgment the general position is now clear. In assessing the likelihood of confusion arising from the use of a sign the court must consider the matter from the perspective of the average consumer of the goods or services in question and must take into account all the circumstances of that use that are likely to operate in that average consumer's mind in considering the sign and the impression it is likely to make on him. The sign is not to be considered stripped of its context.[87]

15.39   In comparing similarities, the relevant comparison is between the sign and the mark ignoring extraneous material.[88]

■ *Origins Natural Resources Inc v Origin Clothing Ltd* [1995] FSR 280

The court said that section 10 of the TMA 1994 'requires the court to assume the mark of a plaintiff is used in a normal and fair manner in relation to the goods for which it is registered and then to assess the likelihood of confusion in relation to the way the defendant uses its mark, discounting external added matter or circumstances. The comparison is mark for mark …' or, 'mark for sign'.[89]

15.40   Often a third party may add extra material to a sign in an attempt to distinguish it from the registered mark. However, in a question of infringement, if it is shown that the mark and sign are confusingly similar, the defendant cannot escape liability by showing that by adding something outside the actual mark he has thus distinguished his goods from those of the proprietor.[90]

Similarities between marks

Visual, phonetic, or conceptual similarity

15.41   As regards the visual, phonetic, or conceptual similarity of the marks in question, an assessment must be based on the overall impression created by those marks and in particular their distinctive and dominant

---

[80] *Canon*, para 18; *Lloyd*, para 20; Case T-164/03 *Ampafrance v OHIM*.

[81] *Och-Ziff Management Europe Ltd v OCH Capital Ltd* [2010] EWHC 2599 (Ch), [2011] ETMR 1.

[82] Case C-533/06 *O2 Holdings Ltd v Hutchison 3G UK Ltd*.   [83] Paras 65 and 66.

[84] [2010] EWHC 2599 (Ch), [2011] ETMR 1.   [85] Para 77.

[86] *Specsavers International Healthcare Ltd, Specsavers BV, Specsavers Optical Group Ltd and Specsavers Optical Superstores Ltd v Asda Stores Ltd* [2012] EWCA Civ 24, [2012] ETMR 17.   [87] Para 87.

[88] *Rolex Internet Auction* [2005] ETMR 25.   [89] *United Biscuits (UK) Ltd v Asda Stores Ltd* [1997] RPC 513 at 535.

[90] *Julius Sämann Ltd v Tetrosyl Ltd* [2006] EWHC 529 (Ch), para 48.

components.[91] Conceptual and visual differences between two signs may counteract aural similarities between them, provided that at least one of those signs has, from the point of view of the relevant public, a clear and specific meaning, so that the public is capable of grasping it immediately[92]—known as the 'neutralisation' theory. While phonetic similarity between marks alone could create a likelihood of confusion, it is unlikely.[93]

■ **Case C-206/04 *Mülhens v OHIM***

The question was the similarity between the earlier mark:

Figure 15.6 SIR logo

and the application to register the sign 'Zirh'. The ECJ stated that the Court of First Instance (CFI) had been correct in saying that the global assessment includes the assessment of the distinctive and dominant components of the signs in question and in particular that aural similarities may be counteracted by the conceptual differences between those signs.[94]

 Question

Can you think of any other senses that might be used in assessing similarities between marks? Consider the debate as to whether taste and smell marks can be registered.

Scope of protection for weak marks or those with descriptive elements

15.42 Where a refusal to register a mark is based on an earlier mark with weak or descriptive elements, the question has arisen as to the emphasis to be placed on those elements when assessing the scope of protection.

■ **Case C-235/05 *L'Oréal SA v OHIM/Revlon*[95]**

This case before the ECJ concerned an appeal by L'Oréal against a refusal to register the mark 'Flexi Air' as a CTM in class 3 of the Nice Agreement. The application had been opposed by Revlon based on existence of the earlier word mark 'Flex' registered in France for goods covered by classes 3 and 34 of the Nice

---

[91] *Sabel*, para 23; *Lloyd*, para 25; *Mülhens*, para 19.

[92] Case C-361/04 *Ruiz-Picasso and others v OHIM* [2006] ECR I-00643, para 20; *Mülhens*, para 35.

[93] *Mülhens*, para 35; Case T-388/00 *ILS Institut für Lernsysteme GmbH v OHIM*; Case T-292/01 *Phillips-Van Heusen Corp v OHIM* (R 740/00-3). The phonetic similarity between 'Bebemil' and 'Blemil' prevailed over elements of dissimilarity. Viewed as a whole the signs were similar. Case T-221/06 *Hipp and Co v OHIM*.

[94] *Mülhens*, para 37.   [95] Case C-235/05 *L'Oréal SA v OHIM/Revlon*.

Agreement and in Sweden and the UK for goods covered by class 3. L'Oréal had argued that where the earlier mark or part of the earlier mark was non-distinctive, then it should be disregarded in assessing similarity between the marks. The Court said, however, that this was not the case. Where the earlier mark is of weak distinctive character and the products for which it is registered are identical or similar to those the subject of the application, the next step is to compare the marks to determine if they are similar. The common element between the marks should not be disregarded just because it is of weak distinctive character. There is a difference between the distinctive character of the earlier mark which determines the protection afforded to that mark, and the notion of the distinctive character which an element of a complex mark possesses. The latter is concerned with its ability to dominate the overall impression created by the mark.[96]

15.43   The Court reasoned that to accept otherwise (in other words to ignore the non-distinctive elements in assessing similarity) would be to give undue importance to the distinctive character of the earlier mark.

> The result would be that where the earlier mark is only of weak distinctive character a likelihood of confusion would exist only where there was a complete reproduction of that mark by the mark applied for, whatever the degree of similarity between the marks in question. If that were the case, it would be possible to register a complex mark, one of the elements of which was identical with or similar to those of an earlier mark with a weak distinctive character, even where the other elements of that complex mark were still less distinctive than the common element and notwithstanding a likelihood that consumers would believe that the slight difference between the signs reflected a variation in the nature of the products or stemmed from marketing considerations and not that that difference denoted goods from different traders.[97]

15.44   However it is not the case that only the distinctive element of a mark comprised of a descriptive element and a distinctive element is decisive. If a descriptive element cannot be protected as such, a specific combination of descriptive elements may be recognised as distinctive and as providing protection against a later mark having a similar construction.[98]

Scope of protection for marks with a dominant element

15.45   As will be seen from paras 15.36 and 15.41, an assessment of the similarity between the marks should be based on the overall impression created by the whole of the mark[99] and in particular their distinctive and dominant components. In relation to composite marks it is possible, in some circumstances, for the overall impression to be dominated by one or more of its component parts.[100] What, then, is the weight to be given to the dominant element when assessing the likelihood of confusion?

15.46   *Medion AG v Thomson Multimedia Sales Germany & Austria GmbH*[101] concerned the mark 'Life' registered in Germany by Medion for leisure electronic devices, and the marketing, in Germany, by Thomson of certain leisure electronic devices under the name 'Thomson Life'. The ECJ stressed that where a composite mark includes an earlier mark for identical goods, the dominance of the shared component is not the decisive test in assessing the likelihood of confusion. There may still be a likelihood of confusion where the shared element is not dominant but has an independent distinctive role in the later mark. Under those circumstances, the overall impression conveyed by the composite sign might lead the consumer to believe that the goods and services derive from economically linked undertakings. If this were the case,

---

[96] *L'Oréal*, para 43.

[97] *L'Oréal*, para 45. See also Case T-228/06 *Georgio Beverly Hills v OHIM* [2008] ECR II-00308 and Case C-353/09 P *Perfetti Van Melle SpA v OHIM* (Center Shock/Center).

[98] Case C-579/08 *Messer Group GmbH v OHIM*, paras 71–73.

[99] Case C-3/03 *Matratzen Concord v OHIM*; Case C-334/05 *OHIM v Shaker*; Case T-99/06 *Phildar v OHIM*; Case C-498/07 *Aceites del Sur-Coosur v Koipe and OHIM*, para 62.

[100] *Matratzen*, para 32.   [101] Case C-120/04.

then a likelihood of confusion would be established.[102] However, the finding that there is a likelihood of confusion should not be subject to the condition that the overall impression produced by the composite sign be dominated by the part of it represented in the earlier mark. The Court pointed out that to conclude otherwise may well deprive the owner of an earlier mark of the exclusive rights conferred by the Directive where that earlier mark was distinctive but not dominant.[103] This may be the case where the owner of a widely known mark makes a composite sign using that mark and an earlier mark which is not itself widely known.[104]

Question

Given the finding of the ECJ in *Medion*, do you think the national court should find a likelihood of confusion between 'Life' and 'Thomson Life' both used for leisure electronic devices?

Scope of protection for marks with a specific meaning

15.47   If a mark is well known in a context other than that of indicating the origin of goods and services, this can make it easier for a consumer to differentiate between the two, and thus confusion is less likely to arise. This is particularly so where the original meaning of the mark overwhelms its distinctive capacity.

■ Case C-361/04 *Ruiz-Picasso and others v OHIM*

The Picasso estate had a CTM for the word mark 'Picasso', registered in respect of, inter alia, motor cars, coaches, and vans in class 12 of the Nice Agreement. Daimler Chrysler applied for registration of a CTM for the word 'Piacro' in respect of goods and services also in class 12. Picasso opposed the application. The CFI upheld the decision of the Third Board of Appeal of the OHIM to dismiss the opposition.[105]

Picasso had relied on *Sabel*[106] and *Canon*[107] arguing that trade marks which have a highly distinctive character, either per se or because of the reputation they possess on the market, enjoy broader protection than marks with a less distinctive character. The CFI, however, said that while the word sign Picasso was well known as corresponding to the name of the famous painter Pablo Picasso, that connection was not capable of heightening the likelihood of confusion between the two marks for the goods concerned in the instant case. On appeal to the ECJ, the Picasso estate argued that the CFI had paid insufficient heed to the distinctiveness of the mark Picasso— that it had only considered the name in relation to the artist and not in connection with the goods concerned.[108] The Court, however, did not agree. The CFI had made a factual assessment and the Picasso mark was devoid of any highly distinctive mark with respect to motor vehicles.

> The reputation of the painter Pablo Picasso is such that it is not plausible to consider, in the absence of specific evidence to the contrary, that the sign PICASSO as a mark for motor vehicles may, in the perception of the average consumer, override the name of the painter so that that consumer, confronted with the sign PICASSO in the

---

[102] Case C-106/03 *Vedial v OHIM*, paras 52–54. See also Case C-512/04 *Vitakraft- Werke Wührmann & Sohn GmbH Co KG v OHIM—Krafft SA*; Case 314/05 P *Creative Technology Ltd v OHIM—José Vila Ortiz*; Case C-57/08 *Gateway Inc v OHIM*.

[103] Case C-120/04 *Medion AG v Thomson Multimedia Sales Germany & Austria GmbH* [2006] ETMR 13, para 33.

[104] See also Case T-290/07 *MIP Metro Group Intellectual Property GmbH & Co KG v OHIM*; Case C-57/08 P *Gateway Inc v OHIM*; Case T-109/07 *L'Oreal SA v OHIM*; Case C-254/09 *Calvin Klein Trademark Trust v OHIM*; Case C-51/09 *Barbara Becker v OHIM* (Barbara Becker/Becker).

[105] Case T-185/02 *Ruiz Picasso and others v OHIM—DaimlerChrysler* [2004] ECR II-01739. See also para 16.15.

[106] *Sabel v Puma* [1997] ECR I-6191.   [107] Case C-39/97 *Canon* [1999] 1 CMLR 77.

[108] Case C-361/04 *Ruiz-Picasso and others v OHIM* [2006] ECR I-00643.

context of the goods concerned, will henceforth disregard the meaning of the sign as the name of the painter and perceive it principally as a mark, among other marks, of motor vehicles.[109]

15.48   A similar issue arose in *Les Éditions Albert René v OHIM—Trucco sistemi di telecomunicazione SpA*,[110] before the CFI. Trucco applied to register the word 'Ostarix' as a CTM in connection with goods and services in classes 9 and 38 of the Nice Agreement. Les Éditions Albert René opposed the application on the basis of its earlier CTM, 'Asterix' in, inter alia, class 9 and 41. The CFI found that given that the consumer would readily associate the word 'Asterix' with the character in the cartoon series, that made it extremely unlikely that there could be any confusion in the public mind between words which were more or less similar.[111] This theory—that a clear and specific meaning of a sign may have the effect of outweighing similarities of other signs where the public is capable of grasping the meaning immediately—is known as the 'counteraction' theory.[112]

Similarities between goods and services

15.49   In assessing similarity between goods and services, that they are registered in different classes of the Nice Agreement does not thereby make them dissimilar. All relevant factors should be taken into account including the nature of the goods and services, their end users, their method of use, and whether they are in competition or complementary.[113]

15.50   In *British Sugar plc v James Robertson & Sons*[114] the judgment of the court suggested that the test to assess similarity between goods and services was distinct from the tests for assessing the similarity between the marks or the question of confusion:

- First, to consider the similarity of the sign with the mark.

- Secondly any similarity of goods and services should be assessed.

- Thirdly, the need to establish the likelihood of confusion.

15.51   Subsequent jurisprudence from the ECJ has indicated that in assessing the impact of the similarity of goods and services, the distinctiveness of the mark would be an important factor.

■ **Case C-39/97 *Canon Kabushiki Kaisha v Metro Goldwyn Mayer Inc* [1998] All ER (EC) 934, [1999] 1 CMLR 77**

MGM had applied in Germany for registration of the word 'Cannon', to be used for, inter alia, video film cassettes. This was opposed by Canon on the basis that it infringed Canon's earlier word trade mark 'Canon', registered in Germany in respect of, inter alia, picture cameras and projectors, and television filming, transmission, and reproduction devices. The German court sought a preliminary ruling from the ECJ on the following question:

- whether the distinctive character of the prior mark, 'Canon', particularly its reputation, was relevant in determining the issue of whether the similarity between the goods covered by the two marks was sufficient to give rise to a likelihood of confusion.

The Court held that in assessing the existence of a likelihood of confusion, a *lesser* degree of similarity between the products could be offset by a *greater* degree of similarity between the marks, or vice versa. The more distinctive the prior mark, either per se, or because of its market reputation, the greater the

---

[109] *Ruiz-Picasso*, para 57.   [110] Case T-311/01.   [111] *Les Éditions Albert René*, para 58.
[112] Case C-16/06 *Les Editions Albert René v OHIM*.   [113] *Canon*, para 17.   [114] [1996] RPC 281.

risk of confusion. Accordingly, the registration of a trade mark might have to be refused despite a lesser degree of similarity between the products covered where the earlier mark, particularly its reputation, was highly distinctive.

15.52   The effect of this ruling is that the more distinctive the mark and the greater its reputation, the wider the protection conferred by the trade mark over progressively more dissimilar goods. The monopoly thus granted to the trade mark owner expands (in the sense that it covers a broader range of goods and services) depending on how distinctive the trade mark is considered to be. The judgment of the Court has been criticised on the ground that no matter the distinctiveness of the mark, some point must come at which the goods and services can no longer be regarded as similar.[115]

15.53   The matter was raised again before the ECJ in *Vedial v OHIM*[116] concerning an application for registration of a composite word and figurative mark comprising the name 'Hubert' along with a picture of a chubby chef in a hat. The application was opposed by Vedial in respect of some of the products covered by the mark, namely, 'milk and milk products' in class 29 of the Nice Agreement and 'vinegar, sauces' in class 30. Their opposition was based on their earlier mark 'Saint-Hubert 41' for butters, edible fats, cheeses, and all dairy products in class 29.

15.54   The applicant had argued that the CFI had not applied the rule of interdependence between the distinctiveness of the mark and the goods and services in a clear manner. The CFI had failed to state that the alleged slight degree of similarity between the earlier mark and the mark applied for was counteracted by the high degree of similarity between the goods concerned and by the strong distinctiveness of the earlier mark.[117] The ECJ did not deal with this issue directly. It pointed out that as the CFI had made a comparison between the marks and concluded from that that there was no similarity between them, there could be no likelihood of confusion, 'whatever the reputation of the earlier mark and regardless of the degree of identity or similarity of the goods or services concerned'.[118]

15.55   Thus if there is no similarity between marks then there can be no likelihood of confusion. However, and taking into account the Court's judgment in *Canon*, a *lesser* degree of similarity between the marks can be offset by a *greater* degree of similarity between the goods, and vice versa.[119]

There remains as question as to whether there is a threshold of similarity required in relation to goods, without which, however similar the marks, there could never be confusion. The CFI has suggested that this is indeed the case in *Commercy AG v OHIM*.[120]

❓ Question 1

What do you think of the approach to link the question of similarity of goods and services with the distinctiveness of the mark? Do you think that there is a threshold of similarity required in relation to either marks or goods? Should there be?

---

[115] The test has been resisted by some: *Sihra's Trade Mark Application* [2003] RPC (44) 789 per Patten J.
[116] Case C-106/03 *Vedial SA v OHIM—France Distribution* [2005] ETMR 23.   [117] *Vedial*, para 48.
[118] *Vedial*, para 55. See also *L'Oreal SA v Bellure NV* [2006] EWHC 2355 (Ch), para 111.
[119] The case has been regularly applied. Eg Case T-112/09 *Icebreaker Ltd v OHIM*; Case T-472/08 *Companhia Muller de Bebidas v OHIM*; Case T-175/06 *Coca-Cola Co v OHIM*; Case T-363/04 *Koipe Corporacion SL v OHIM*.
[120] Case T-316/07. See also Case C-398/07 *Waterford Wedgwood v Assembled Investment Ltd*. The Court of Appeal doubted that there is a threshold of similarity required in relation to marks: *Esure v Direct Line Ltd* [2008] EWCA Civ 842.

> ## ? Question 2
>
> How do you reconcile the approach of the Court of Justice in these cases linking the question of similarity of goods and services to the distinctiveness of the mark with the case law that considers the scope of protection for weak marks or those with descriptive elements (para 15.42).

Complementarity

15.56   One of the elements to be taken into account in assessing similarity of goods is whether they are complementary.[121] Some guidance on what amounts to complementary was given in *El Corte Inglés v OHIM—Bolaños Sabri*[122] concerning an application to register the word mark 'Piranha' in stylised form as a CTM which was opposed by the owner of the Spanish 'Piranha':

> goods are complementary if there is a close connection between them, in the sense that one is indispensable or important for the use of the other in such a way that customers may think that the responsibility for the production of those goods lies with the same undertaking ...[123]

This narrow approach echoed the earlier case of *Mülhens GmbH & Co KG v OHIM*[124] concerning toiletries and where it was said that:

> this aesthetically complementary nature must involve a genuine aesthetic necessity, in that one product is indispensable or important for the use of the other and consumers consider it ordinary and natural to use these products together ...[125]

Following this reasoning, wine glasses and wine were found not to be complementary.[126]

Likelihood of confusion

Consumer perception (the relevant consumer/public)

15.57   To show there is a likelihood of confusion, there must be an association between the marks that causes the relevant consumers to believe wrongly that the goods or services come from the same or economically linked undertakings.[127] Thus there can be no objection to registration of a second trade mark under section 5(2) of the TMA 1994 or infringement under section 10(2) unless it can be shown that the public would believe goods and services come from the same producer or a linked undertaking, including licensed or joint venture arrangements,[128] or where there is a real risk that a significant number of people will believe that there is a connection between the marks.[129] Mere association, in the sense that the later mark brings the earlier mark to mind, is not sufficient (see paras 15.61–15.66).[130] The principle of availability has no relevance in determining confusion.[131]

---

[121] *Canon*, para 35.   [122] Case T-443/05.   [123] *El Corte Inglés*, para 48.
[124] Case T-150/04.   [125] Para 36.
[126] Case C-398/07 *Waterford Wedgwood v Assembled Investment Ltd*. See also Case T-487/08 *Kureha Corp v OHIM*; Case T-175/06 *Coca-Cola Co v OHIM*: to be complementary goods they would have to be closely connected in the sense that one was indispensable or important for the use of the other, applying the earlier case of Case T-169/03 *Sergio Rossi SpA v OHIM*.
[127] *Canon*, para 29. *Lloyd*, para 17; Case C-120/04 *Medion AG v Thomson Multimedia Sales Germany & Austria GmbH*, para 26; Case C-102/07 *Adidas AG v Marca Mode CV*, para 28; Case C-278/08 *Die BergSpechte Outdoor Reisen under Alpinschule Edi Koblmüller GmbH v Guni*.
[128] *Canon*, para 29; *Raleigh International Trade Mark* [2001] RPC 11; *Lloyd*, para 17; Case T-104/01 *Oberhauser v OHIM—Petit Libero (Fifties)* [2002] ECR II-4359, para 25.
[129] *Betty's Kitchen Coronation Street Trade Mark* [2000] RPC 825; *Neil King's Trade Mark Application* [2000] ETMR 22.
[130] *Sabel*, para 26.
[131] Case C-102/07 *Adidas AG and Adidas Benelux BV v Marca Mode, C&A Nederland, H&M Hennes & Mauritz Netherlands BV and Vendex KBB Nederland BV*. For a discussion on the principle of availability on registration see para 14.31.

15.58   The perception of a mark in the mind of the average consumer of the category of goods or services in question plays a decisive role in the global assessment of the likelihood of confusion.[132] The person to be considered is the ordinary consumer who may be neither too careful nor too careless; merely reasonably circumspect, well informed, and observant[133] and who normally perceives a mark as a whole and does not proceed to analyse its various details.[134] The average consumer's level of attention is likely to vary according to the category of goods or services in question[135] and is based on the perception of the group showing the lower degree of attentiveness.[136] Where the relevant public comprises groups of consumers who see the sign differently, then likelihood of confusion need only exist in respect of one group provided that it is not negligible.[137]

For instance, the consumer may give a higher level of attention when buying expensive items, such as cars, as compared with more everyday goods, such as food. That may reduce the likelihood of confusion between the marks at the moment when the consumer makes his choice.[138] There is, however, no principle that trade marks which are registered for goods of a particular value, technological advancement, or safety should enjoy greater protection. Where the value results in greater attention being paid that will reduce the likelihood of confusion between two marks, but the scope of protection of the mark is not affected.[139] The reputation of an earlier mark or its distinctive character is to be taken into consideration for the purposes of assessing likelihood of confusion and not for assessing the similarity of the signs in question which is an assessment made prior to that of likelihood of confusion.[140] Allowance must, however, be made for defective recollection and that may vary with the goods in question.[141]

Time of confusion

15.59   The relevant time at which confusion should be assessed in oppositions is when the consumer prepares to make the choice between different goods or services within the category for which the mark is registered.[142] Arguments relating to post sale confusion are relevant only when assessing infringement of trade mark rights.[143] Where a trade mark has been acquired on the basis of its distinctive character, then the relevant time to determine consumer perception is at the time when the allegedly infringing sign began to be used rather than the time the registered mark first began to be used.[144]

■ Case C-145/05 *Levi Strauss & Co v Casucci SpA*

Levi Strauss had registered its mouette (seagull) mark (similar to the one shown in Figure 15.7) in Benelux for clothes.

---

[132] *Sabel*, para 23; *Lloyd*, para 25. *Specsavers International Healthcare Ltd, Specsavers BV, Specsavers Optical Group Ltd and Specsavers Optical Superstores Ltd v Asda Stores Ltd* [2012] EWCA Civ 24, [2012] ETMR 17.

[133] *Lloyd*, para 27.   [134] *Sabel*, para 23.

[135] *Lloyd*, paras 25 and 26. Case T-400/06 *Zero Industry Srl v OHIM*, para 27.

[136] Case T-213/09 *Yorma's AG v OHIM* (Yorma's/NORMA) GC, para 25; Case T-220/09 *Ergo Versicherungsgruppe AG v OHIM* (Ergo/Urgo), para 21.

[137] Case T-22/10 *Esprit International v OHIM* (C/C), Case T-313/10 *Three-N-Products v OHIM* (Ayuuri Natural/Ayur).

[138] Case C-361/04 *Ruiz-Picasso and others v OHIM* [2006] ECR I-00643, para 40.

[139] Case T-486/07 *Ford Motor Co v OHIM* (Ca/Ka).

[140] Case C-370/10 *Ravensburger v OHIM* (Educa Memory Game/Educa); Case C-388/10 *Felix Munoz Arraisa v OHIM* (Riojavina/Rioja).

[141] *Reed Executive plc and another v Reed Business Information Ltd Reed Elsevier (UK) Ltd Totaljobs.com Ltd* [2004] ETMR 56, [2004] EWCA Civ 159.

[142] Case T-185/02 *Ruiz-Picasso and others v OHIM—DaimlerChrysler*, para 59. In Case C-412/05 *Alcon Inc v OHIM, Biofarma SA*, AG Kokott has suggested that for medicinal products available only on prescription the relevant public is health care professionals and not end consumers: para 48.

[143] *Arsenal*, para 57; Case C-361/04 *Ruiz-Picasso and others v OHIM* [2006] ECR I-00643, paras 46–48.

[144] Case C-145/05 *Levi Strauss & Co v Casucci SpA*.

Figure 15.7 Levi Strauss jeans

Casucci sold jeans on the Benelux market with a sign as shown in Figure 15.8:

Figure 15.8 Casucci jeans

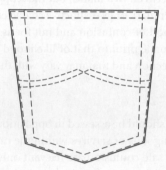

Levi Strauss sued for trade mark infringement. It lost at first instance and appealed to the Cour d'appel de Bruxelles which in turn dismissed the appeal saying that there was little difference between the two pocket designs and that Levi's sign could no longer be considered to be distinctive. The characteristics were not inherently distinctive and were now common to the products owing to their widespread use. This weakened the distinctive character of the mark. A question was referred to the ECJ asking at what point the perception of the public should be taken into account in judging the distinctiveness of a mark where that mark had been acquired on the basis of its distinctive character. The Court said that the relevant time was when the sign which infringed the trade mark began to be used. Where, at that time, the use of the sign constituted an infringement, the national court may order that the sign no longer be used. However, and where the trade mark had lost its distinctive character as a result of the failure of the proprietor to take action to stop the use of confusingly similar signs, then it would no longer be appropriate to order cessation of the use of the sign.

15.60   Initial interest confusion, a largely US doctrine which accepts that confusion can be established if a consumer is confused at the time of interest in products or services even if that confusion has gone by the time of purchase, was introduced into UK law by the High Court in *Och-Ziff Management Europe Ltd v Och Capital LLP*.[145] The case concerned financial services and the trade marks OCH-ZIFF and OCH and the use of the sign OCH Capital. The court defined initial interest confusion as 'confusion on the part of the public as to the trade origin of the goods or services in relation to which the impugned sign has been

---

[145] [2011] ETMR 1.

used arising from use of the sign prior to purchase of those goods or services, and in particular confusion arising from use of the sign in advertising or promotional materials'. In the instant case the court found that there could be an infringing use of a sign in an advertisement even if there was no sale, and the use could damage the reputation of the mark or erode its distinctiveness.[146]

Likelihood of association and confusion

15.61   It will be seen that the wording of sections 5(2) and 10(2) of the TMA 1994 refers to 'likelihood of confusion ... which includes a likelihood of association'. The question has arisen as to whether the tests suggested by the wording (confusion and association) are linked or separate. The answer matters because (as with the definition of similarity) of the effect the outcome has on the breadth of the monopoly conferred by the trade mark. If the two are linked, so the monopoly conferred by the mark is narrowed: if the two are separate, so the monopoly conferred by the mark expands. For example, you may *associate* 'Persil' and 'Ariel'. Both marks are used for soap powders in the marketplace. If association as a test was sufficient for infringement, then the later mark might not be registerable, or it might infringe the use of the former. In this way the monopoly conferred by the earlier mark would be very wide. However, you might associate 'Persil' and 'Ariel' but not *confuse* the two. If this element of confusion is a necessary part of the association test, so the mark conferred by the monopoly is kept in check.

15.62   The argument that likelihood of association is a *separate* test has its origins in Benelux trade mark law and is exemplified by such cases as *Monopoly v Anti-Monopoly*.[147] In this case, registration was refused for the mark 'Anti-Monopoly', not because the consumer would be *confused* as to the origin of the goods, but because a link would be made in the minds of the public with the trade mark 'Monopoly' due to the similarities. In other words, the consumer would *associate* the two marks.

15.63   This issue of likelihood of confusion and association has now been considered in a number of cases. In *Wagamama Ltd v City Centre Restaurants plc and others*,[148] Wagamama owned the 'Wagamama' trade mark which was registered for restaurants. City Centre Restaurants decided to open a restaurant under the name Rajamama. Wagamama sued for infringement of the trade mark and passing off. The UK court held that there had been infringement and that a case of passing off had been made out. In the judgment much discussion revolved around the phrase 'likelihood of association'. The court found that the wording of the section clearly states that there must exist a likelihood of confusion in the minds of the public, and *included in*, but not separate to, that test was a likelihood of association. Nevertheless, the court concluded that there did exist confusion in the minds of the public as to the origin of the trade mark because it was shown that the public thought that the Rajamama restaurant might be connected with 'Wagamama'.

15.64   The matter was definitively settled by the ECJ in *Sabel BV v Puma AG*.[149] The issue concerned pictures of two 'bounding felines' (large cats). One of the marks included the word 'Sabel' in addition to the picture of the running cat. The question for the ECJ amounted to whether *mere association* between two marks, through the idea of a running cat, justified refusing protection of the later mark for products similar to those covered by the earlier mark. Puma had registered their mark for, inter alia, leather goods which was the same category applied for by Sabel. The Court held that the mere association alone *was not* enough to justify a finding of a likelihood of confusion. The Court also said that the more distinctive the earlier

---

[146] *Och-Ziff*, para 101. The case has since been mentioned by the Court of Appeal in *Specsavers International Healthcare Ltd v Asda Stores Ltd* [2012] EWCA Civ 24 and *32Red plc v WHG (International) Ltd* [2012] EWCA Civ 19. See P O'Byrne and B Allgrove, 'Initial interest confusion recognized by the English courts' (2011) 6(3) *JIPLP* 147–149.

[147] *Edor Handelsonderneming BV v General Mills Fun Group*, Nederlands Jurisprudentie 1978, 83.

[148] [1995] FSR 713.   [149] Case C-251/95 [1998] 1 CMLR 445.

mark, the greater the likelihood of confusion. In the instant case, the earlier mark was not especially well known—the mere fact that the two marks were conceptually similar was not sufficient to give rise to a likelihood of confusion.[150]

15.65   This ruling was confirmed in *Marca Mode CV v Adidas AG*.[151] Adidas had a mark registered in the Benelux office consisting of three parallel stripes in connection with, inter, alia sports clothes and articles connected with sport. Marca Mode sold sports clothes in the Netherlands which bore two parallel stripes running longitudinally. When the question arose as to whether it was sufficient that consumers associated the mark, or whether there had also to be the likelihood of confusion the ECJ, referring to its judgment in *Sabel*, said that 'the concept of likelihood of association is not an alternative to that of likelihood of confusion, but serves to define its scope. The very terms of the provision exclude its application where there is no likelihood of confusion on the part of the public …'.[152] Further, the Court said that 'the reputation of a mark does not give grounds for presuming a likelihood of confusion simply because of a likelihood of association in the strict sense'.[153]

15.66   Thus it is settled that the 'likelihood of association' test is a *subset* of the 'likelihood of confusion' test. It is therefore not sufficient for a consumer to associate two marks: confusion must also be present. The monopoly in the mark is thus kept in check to this extent.

 Question

Do you think that the likelihood of association test should be a subset of the confusion test, or a separate test?

Key points on similarity and confusion

- The key tests on assessing confusion[154] have been brought together by the Trade Marks Registry and cited with approval in a number of cases including *La Chemise Lacoste SA v Baker Street Clothing Ltd*,[155] *32 RED*,[156] and *OCH–ZIFF*.[157]

  (a) the likelihood of confusion must be appreciated globally, taking account of all relevant factors;

  (b) the matter must be judged through the eyes of the average consumer of the goods or services in question, who is deemed to be reasonably well informed and reasonably circumspect and observant, but who rarely has the chance to make direct comparisons

---

[150] See also Case C-425/98 *Marca Mode CV Adidas AG and Adidas Benelux BV* [2000] All ER (EC) 694; Case T-471/09 *Dr August Oetker Nahrungsmittel v OHIM* (Buonfatti/Bonfait); *European Ltd v Economist Newspaper Ltd* [1998] FSR 283, [1998] EMLR 536, [1998] ETMR 307.   [151] [2000] ETMR 723.

[152] Case C-425/98 *Marca Mode CV Adidas AG and Adidas Benelux BV* [2000] ECR I-4861, [2000] All ER (EC) 694, para 34.

[153] *Marca Mode*, para 41.

[154] Developed from cases at the Court of Justice including: Case C-251/95 *SABEL BV v Puma AG* [1997] ECR I-6191, [1998] ETMR 1; Case C-39/97 *Canon Kabushiki Kaisha v Metro-Goldwyn-Mayer Inc* [1998] ECR I-5507, [1999] ETMR 1; Cawe C-342/97 *Lloyd Schuhfabrik Meyer & Co GmbH v Klijsen Handel BV* [1999] ECR I-3819, [1999] ETMR 690; Case C-425/98 *Marca Mode CV v Adidas AG* [2000] ECR I-4861, [2000] ETMR 561; Case C-3/03 P *Matratzen Concord GmbH v OHIM* [2004] ECR I-3657; Case C-120/04 *Medion AG v Thomson Multimedia Sales Germany & Austria GmbH* [2005] ECR I-8551, [2006] ETMR 13; and Case C-344/05 P *OHIM v Shaker de L Laudato & C SAS* [2007] ECR I-4529.

[155] (O/330/10), 9 December 2009.   [156] *32Red plc v WHG (International) Ltd* [2012] EWCA Civ 19.

[157] *Och-Ziff Management Europe Ltd v Och Capital LLP* [2010] EWHC 2599 (Ch).

between marks and must instead rely upon the imperfect picture of them he has kept in his mind, and whose attention varies according to the category of goods or services in question;

(c) the average consumer normally perceives a mark as a whole and does not proceed to analyse its various details;

(d) the visual, aural and conceptual similarities of the marks must normally be assessed by reference to the overall impressions created by the marks bearing in mind their distinctive and dominant components, but it is only when all other components of a complex mark are negligible that it is permissible to make the comparison solely on the basis of the dominant elements;

(e) nevertheless, the overall impression conveyed to the public by a composite trade mark may, in certain circumstances, be dominated by one or more of its components;

(f) and beyond the usual case, where the overall impression created by a mark depends heavily on the dominant features of the mark, it is quite possible that in a particular case an element corresponding to an earlier trade mark may retain an independent distinctive role in a composite mark, without necessarily constituting a dominant element of that mark;

(g) a lesser degree of similarity between the goods or services may be offset by a great degree of similarity between the marks, and vice versa;[158]

(h) there is a greater likelihood of confusion where the earlier mark has a highly distinctive character, either per se or because of the use that has been made of it;

(i) mere association, in the strict sense that the later mark brings the earlier mark to mind, is not sufficient;

(j) the reputation of a mark does not give grounds for presuming a likelihood of confusion simply because of a likelihood of association in the strict sense;

(k) if the association between the marks causes the public to wrongly believe that the respective goods [or services] come from the same or economically-linked undertakings, there is a likelihood of confusion.

Researching cases concerning registration and infringement on relative grounds

Web links

As with the absolute grounds for refusal to register a mark, there is a plethora of cases from the national registry, OHIM registry, OHIM Board of Appeals, and the General Court concerning in particular the relative grounds for refusing to register a mark and in addition infringement. To research these cases you can look at the databases available on the IPO website at **http://www.ipo.gov.uk**, at the OHIM website at **http://www.oami.europa.eu**, and at the Court of Justice website at **http://www.curia.europa.eu**.

[158] *32Red plc v WHG (International) Ltd* [2012] EWCA Civ 19.

Question

Do you think there are confusing similarities between the following marks? Explain your reasoning.

15.67 • EURODATA TV in, inter alia, class 35 for gathering and supply of commercial information, more especially opinion surveys and polls in the audiovisual realm, advising and assisting industrial or commercial undertakings; preparation and supply of trade statistics; marketing studies; market research and analysis; and 'M + M EUROdATA in class 35 for market research, market analysis, and trade research, services offering advice to businesses in the sphere of marketing and distribution'.[159]

Figure 15.9 HappyDog

Natürlich gesünder!

• The mark shown Figure 15.9 and HAPPIDOG both for foodstuffs for dogs in class 31.[160]

• PASH for clothing, also made of leather, belts for clothing, footwear, and headgear in class 25 and BASS for footwear and clothing[161] in class 25.

• BUD for clothing, footwear, headgear, sweatshirts, T-shirts, caps, and socks, in class 25 and BUDMEN for clothing, footwear, and headgear in class 25.[162]

Similar/dissimilar trade marks with a reputation

 Exercise

Read sections 5(3) and 10(3) of the TMA 1994; Articles 4(4)(a) and 5(2) of the Directive; and Articles 8(5) and 9(1)(c) of the CTMR.

15.68 Under section 5(3) of the 1994 Act, when originally drafted a sign would not be registered if it was identical or similar to an earlier trade mark and was to be registered in respect of goods or services which are *not* similar to those for which the earlier trade mark was registered, if the earlier trade mark had a reputation in the UK, and the use of the later mark would take unfair advantage of, or be detrimental to, the distinctive character or repute of, the earlier mark. The same provisions applied in relation to an infringement action under section 10(3) of the 1994 Act.

15.69 However, in 2003 in *Davidoff & Cie SA v Gofkid*,[163] the ECJ held that these provisions applied not only to those circumstances in which the goods were dissimilar, but also where the goods were similar or identical. In this case, Davidoff which had a registration for a stylised mark, 'Davidoff', sought to have Gofkid's mark, 'Durfee', annulled. The referring court wanted to know whether Articles 4(4)(a) and 5(2)

[159] Case T-317/01 *M+M Gesellschaft für Unternehmensberatung und Informationssysteme mbH/OHIMMediametrie SA* (R 698/2000-1).
[160] Case T-20/02 *Interquell GmbH v OHIM—Provimi Ltd & SCA Nutrition Ltd* (R 264/2000-2).
[161] Case T-292/01 *Phillips-Van Heusen Corp v OHIM* (Pash Textilvertrieb und Einzelhandel GmbH) (R 740/00-3).
[162] Case T-129/01 *Jose Alejandro SL v OHIM—Anheuser-Busch Inc* (R 230/2000-1).
[163] Case C-292/00 [2003] ECR I-389.

of the Directive were to be interpreted as entitling the member states to provide specific protection for registered trade marks with a reputation in cases where the later mark or sign, which is identical with or similar to the registered mark, is intended to be used or is used for goods or services *identical with or similar* to those covered by the registered mark. In other words, the relevant provisions of the Directive only referred to dissimilar goods and services. Were similar goods and services also covered?

The Court started off by noting that Article 5(2) of the Directive allows stronger protection to be given to marks with a reputation than that conferred under Article 5(1)[164] where the use of the sign without due cause takes unfair advantage of, or is detrimental to, the distinctive character or the repute of the mark. Where there was no likelihood of confusion, Article 5(1)(b) of the Directive could not be relied on by the proprietor of a mark with a reputation to protect himself against impairment of the distinctive character or repute of the mark.

> In those circumstances, … Articles 4(4)(a) and 5(2) of the Directive are to be interpreted as entitling the Member States to provide specific protection for registered trade marks with a reputation in cases where a later mark or sign, which is identical with or similar to the registered mark, is intended to be used or is used for goods or services identical with or similar to those covered by the registered mark.[165]

15.70   As a result of this case, the wording of the 1994 Act has been amended[166] and now reads as follows:

> A trade mark which:
>
> is identical with or similar to an earlier trade mark, shall not be registered if, or to the extent that, the earlier mark has a reputation in the United Kingdom (or, in the case of a Community trade mark, in the European Community) and the use of the later mark without due cause would take unfair advantage of, or be detrimental to, the distinctive character or the repute of the earlier trade mark.

 Question

Can you explain why you think the Court ruled that similar goods and services should be covered under this section and that protection should not just extend to those circumstances in which they were dissimilar?

15.71   Section 10(3) of the 1994 Act has been amended similarly.

15.72   As explained previously, under sections 5(2) and 10(2) of the TMA 1994 the relative grounds for refusing registration and infringement rest on the basis that there is a likelihood of consumer confusion. There is no requirement for consumer confusion in sections 5(3) and 10(3). It was the ECJ's view in *Davidoff* that the protection accorded by this provision should be stronger than that afforded where consumer confusion was a prerequisite. The concern was that if sections 5(3) and 10(3) only covered dissimilar goods and services, then the protection would in essence be weaker. Any litigant who relied on the reputation of the mark under sections 5(3) and 10(3) would only be protected if the goods were *dissimilar*. If the goods were similar, then, even though the mark might have a reputation, protection would have to be sought under sections 5(2) and 10(2).

---

[164] *Davidoff*, para 19.   [165] *Davidoff*, para 30.
[166] Trade Marks (Proof of Use, etc) Regulations 2004 (SI 2004/946). Neither the Directive nor the CTMR have been amended nor have the provisions been incorporated in the consolidated measures.

15.73   Whatever the merits or demerits of this argument, the effect was that the Court extended significantly the ambit of the measure. The judgment has been the subject of both support—J Cornwell, 'The *Davidoff v Gofkid* case' [2003] EIPR 537—and criticism—C Morcom, 'Extending protection for marks having a reputation' [2003] EIPR 279.

15.74   The *Davidoff* case has been affirmed by the ECJ in *Adidas-Salomon AG and Adidas Benelux BV v Fitnessworld*.[167]

 Exercise

Read the articles referred to in para 15.73. What do you think of the judgment of the ECJ in the *Davidoff v Gofkid* case given the clear wording of the Directive which referred to dissimilar goods and services?

15.75   Returning to the provisions of the TMA 1994, it will be seen from the wording that the requirements of sections 5(3) and 10(3) are:

- the mark must have a reputation in the UK; and
- the use of the later mark without due cause would
- take unfair advantage of; or
- be detrimental to
- the distinctive character or the repute of the earlier trade mark.

The three types of harm (also referred to as parasitism, dilution, and tarnishment) are alternative rather than cumulative conditions.[168]

Mark with a reputation

15.76   The TMA 1994 states that the mark must have a *reputation in the UK*,[169] although the sections also provide for a CTM which has a reputation in the European Union. In *General Motors Corp v Yplon SA*[170] the ECJ, in considering the extent of the reputation needed for a trade mark under the Directive held that a mark had a 'reputation' if it was *known by a significant part of the public concerned by the product or services covered by that mark*.[171] Factors to be considered would include the market share held by the trade mark, the intensity, geographical extent, and duration of its use, and the size of the investment made in promoting it. With regard to the extent of the territory in which a mark had a reputation, it need not have that reputation throughout the territory, but it is sufficient for it to be known by a significant part of the public concerned in a substantial part of that territory. In the instant case that test might consist of a part of one of the countries (Benelux) comprising that territory.[172] It is, however, not enough for a national

---

[167] Case C-408/01 [2004] ETMR 10 (ECJ).   [168] Case C-487/07 *L'Oreal v Bellure*, paras 41–42.

[169] *Wannabee Trade Mark*, 6 November, 2000 (Wannabee—insufficient reputation in the market to rely on s 5(3)).

[170] Case C-375/97 [1999] All ER (EC) 865, [1999] 3 CMLR 427.

[171] See also *Adidas-Salomon AG, Adidas Italy SpA v Gruppo Coin SpA, Oviesse* [2006] ETMR 39 Trib (Rome), para 15; Case T-8/03 *El Corte Inglés v OHIM—Pucci* [2004] ECR II-4297, para 67.

[172] The terms 'reputation', 'famous', and 'well-known' are all used in connection with trade marks, although there is little consensus on either what these terms mean, or when a mark will be considered to fall in to one or other category. Art 6*bis* of the Paris Convention gives protection to *well-known* marks used in respect of identical or similar goods (not services). The TRIPS Agreement extended the provisions of Art 6*bis* to services (Art 16(2)). Further, Art 16(3) of TRIPS extended Art 6*bis* of the Paris Convention to goods or services which are not similar to those in respect of which a trademark is registered where the use would indicate a connection between the goods and services and the owner of the registered trade mark, and provided the interests of the owner of the registered trade mark are likely to be damaged by such use.

mark if it is only known in a city and surrounding area; that is not a substantial part of the territory[173] although a substantial part could be the territory of one member state.[174]

Establishing a link

15.77   Unlike sections 5(2) and 10(2) of the TMA 1994, there is no requirement for confusion on the part of the public before registration is refused or infringement can occur.[175] A crucial point developed through case law is that the relevant section of the public establishes a *link* between the sign and the mark although the public would not necessarily be confused.[176] The absence of any similarity between the marks rules out the application of Article 8(5) of the CTMR.[177] The reputation and distinctive character of the earlier mark constitute relevant factors for the purposes of assessing whether the relevant section of the public makes a link between them.[178]

15.78   Where a mark is seen by the relevant public merely as an embellishment, that does not necessarily establish a link with the registered mark sufficient to satisfy the conditions in Article 5(2) of the Directive.[179] In *Adidas-Salomon AG & Adidas Benelux BV v Fitnessworld Trading Ltd*[180] when Adidas, the owner of the mark consisting of three vertical stripes running parallel down clothing, complained of the use by Fitnessworld of a motif consisting of two parallel stripes on clothing, it was for the national court to decide, as a finding of fact, whether the relevant public would view the sign purely as an embellishment or whether, notwithstanding that the sign was viewed as an embellishment, the relevant link was also established.[181]

15.79   In the later case of *Intel*[182] the ECJ spent some time on the notion of a link. It said that the factors to be taken into account include:

- the degree of similarity between the conflicting marks. The more similar they are the more likely it is that the later mark will bring the earlier mark with a reputation to the mind of the relevant public. But even if the marks are identical or very similar, that is not enough for a link;

- the nature of the goods or services for which the conflicting marks were registered, including the degree of closeness or dissimilarity between those goods or services, and the relevant section of the public must be taken into account when establishing a link. The marks may be registered for goods or services in respect of which the relevant publics do not overlap, in which case a link would not be established. Equally, if the goods or services are so dissimilar, the mark with a reputation may not be brought to mind;

- the strength of the earlier mark's reputation. If it is a very strong mark, the reputation may go well beyond the relevant public such that a link will be established;

---

[173] Case C-328/06 *Nieto Nuno v Fraquet*.   [174] Case C-301/07 *Pago v Tirolmilch*.

[175] Some confusion arose in an early case to consider this subsection, *Baywatch Production Co Inc v Home Video Channel* [1997] FSR 22 where it was suggested that the likelihood of confusion was an essential element for infringement of this subsection. See also *BASF v EP* [1996] ETMR 51. However, now, the ECJ in Case C-375/95 *General Motors v Yplon* [1999] 3 CMLR 427, the Trade Mark Registry in *Oasis Stores Ltd's Trade Mark Application* [1998] RPC 631, [1999] ETMR 531, the High Court in *Pfizer v Eurofood Link (UK)* [2000] ETMR 896, [2001] FSR 3, and the Court of Appeal in *BT v One in a Million* [1999] 4 All ER 476, [1999] RPC 1 have all indicated that confusion is not a necessary prerequisite.

[176] *Adidas-Salomon AG v Fitnessworld Trading Ltd* [2004] Ch 120 (ECJ), para 31. The perception of the sign must call to mind the memory of the mark: *O2 Holdings Ltd, O2 (UK) Ltd v Hutchison 3G Ltd* [2006] EWHC 534 (Ch), para 136. *Electrocoin Automatics v Coinworld* [2005] ETMR 31, [2005] FSR 7, [2004] EWHC 1498 (Ch).

[177] Case T 207/09 *Mustapha El Jirari Bouzekri v OHIM* (N Nickol/Nike).

[178] Case C-552/09 *Ferrero SpA v OHIM* (Kinderjoghurt/Kinder).   [179] *Ferrero*, para 41.

[180] Case C-408/01 [2004] Ch 120, [2004] 2 WLR 1095, [2004] ETMR 10.

[181] See also Case R 0506/2003-2 *Société des Produits Nestlé SA v Mars Inc* [2005] ETMR 37.

[182] Case C-252/07 *Intel Corporation Inc v CPM United Kingdom Ltd* [2009] ETMR 13, [2009] RPC 15.

- the degree of the earlier mark's distinctive character, whether inherent or acquired through use. The stronger a mark, the more likely it is that the relevant public will call it to mind when confronted with a later identical or similar mark. If the mark is unique, the distinctive character will be strong;

- the existence of the likelihood of confusion on the part of the public. If confusion is established, then a link is necessarily established although confusion is not required.[183]

 Exercise

Read *Adidas-Salomon AG & Adidas Benelux BV v Fitnessworld Trading Ltd* in the light of what the Court has said about a link in *Intel*. Do you think there was sufficient to establish a link in *Adidas*? Or was the use of the sign pure embellishment?

Note, however, that the existence of a link by itself is not enough. Actual and present injury, or a serious likelihood that injury will occur in the future must be proved. Hypothetical injury is not enough.[184]

Unfair advantage

15.80   Looking to recital 9 of the Directive, the purpose of these provisions is to provide 'extensive protection to those trade marks which have a reputation'. By contrast with British law, other European countries have a history of granting marks with a reputation greater protection than those without. For instance in Germany, the Federal Supreme Court,[185] said that: 'The courts have repeatedly held that it constitutes an act of unfair competition to associate the quality of one's goods or services with that of prestigious competitive products for the purpose of exploiting the good reputation of a competitor's goods or services in order to enhance one's promotional efforts'. This is sometimes more generally called 'free-riding'. What the competitor is doing here is attempting to 'take unfair advantage of' a mark with established substantial goodwill. The advantage for the third party may be a substantial saving on investment in promotion and publicity for its own mark, and it is unfair because it is done in a parasitic way.[186]

15.81   Referring to both the notion of 'advantage' and what might be unfair, the First Board of Appeal of OHIM in *Mango Sport System Srl v Diknak*[187] said this:

> As to unfair advantage, which is in issue here since that was the condition for the rejection of the mark applied for, that is taken when another undertaking exploits the distinctive character or repute of the earlier mark to the benefit of its own marketing efforts. In that situation that undertaking effectively uses the renowned mark as a vehicle for generating consumer interest in its own products. The advantage for the third party arises in the substantial saving on investment in promotion and publicity for its own goods, since it is able to 'free ride' on that already undertaken by the earlier reputed mark. It is unfair since the reward for the costs of promoting, maintaining and enhancing a particular trade mark should belong to the owner of the earlier trade mark in question.[188]

15.82   In a similar vein in *L'Oreal v Bellure*[189] the ECJ summed up the notion of unfair advantage saying:

> As regards the concept of 'taking unfair advantage of the distinctive character or the repute of the trade mark', also referred to as 'parasitism' or 'free-riding', that concept relates not to the detriment caused to the mark but

---

[183] Paras 42–58.   [184] Case T-581/08 *Perusahaan Otomobil Nasional v OHIM* (Proton Motor/Proton).

[185] *Dimple* [1985] GRUR 550.

[186] Case R 472/2001-1 (*BIBA/BIBA*) and Case R 552/2000-4 (*Cosmopolitan cosmetics/Cosmopolitan*).

[187] Case R 308/2003-1 [2005] ETMR 5.

[188] *Mango Sport*, para 19. See also Case R 1004/2000-1 *KinderCare*, para 26; *Société des Produits Nestlé SA v Mars Inc* [2005] ETMR 37 (OHIM Second Board of Appeal).

[189] Case C-487/07. See also *Specsavers International Healthcare Ltd v Asda Stores Ltd* [2012] EWCA Civ 24.

to the advantage taken by the third party as a result of the use of the identical or similar sign. It covers, in particular, cases where, by reason of a transfer of the image of the mark or of the characteristics which it projects to the goods identified by the identical or similar sign, there is clear exploitation on the coat-tails of the mark with a reputation.[190]

15.83   The concept of unfair advantage has been developing in recent years through a series of cases at the Court of Justice concerning flowers, perfumes, and Adwords. In *L'Oreal v Bellure*[191] the ECJ signalled that the concept of unfair advantage was a head of damage in its own right, not tied to the repute of the mark or detriment to the distinctive character. There is no requirement for actual economic damage or likelihood of damage to the proprietor of the mark under this head.[192] The important factor in unfair advantage is the advantage gained by the unauthorised user of the sign.

The advantage arising from the use by a third party of a sign similar to a mark with a reputation is an advantage taken unfairly by that third party of the distinctive character or the repute of the mark where that party seeks by that use to ride on the coat-tails of the mark with a reputation in order to benefit from the power of attraction, the reputation, and the prestige of that mark and to exploit, without paying any financial compensation, the marketing effort expended by the proprietor of the mark in order to create and maintain the mark's image.[193]

15.84   To determine whether the use of a sign takes unfair advantage of the distinctive character or repute of a mark, a global assessment must be undertaken which takes into account factors relevant to the circumstances of the case including the strength of the mark's reputation; the degree of distinctive character of the mark; and the similarity between the marks and the nature and degree of proximity of goods or services.[194]

 Question

Looking at the facts in *Intel*, do you think a relevant link was established in this case?

15.85   *L'Oreal*[195] concerned packaging for perfumes. One of the key questions was whether unfair advantage had been taken of the shape and packaging of perfume products. The High Court had found that certain of the packaging and bottles used for 'look-alike' perfumes infringed the registered marks as they took unfair advantage of the character or reputation of the registered marks. The court said that the extent of the similarity between certain of the packaging was deliberate. 'It "winks at" the packaging of the premium brand'.[196] The perfumes chosen as comparators were well-promoted brands which were extensively advertised. The infringing perfumes benefited from the advertising and promotion of the expensive perfumes. Thus, 'the reward for the costs of promoting, maintaining and enhancing a particular trade mark has been received by [the defendants]. That amounts to "free riding" and thus to the taking of an unfair advantage'.[197] On referring questions to the ECJ, the Court of Appeal[198] doubted the test for unfair advantage laid down in *Mango Sport v Diknak*[199] as that court had focused on advantage and not what was unfair. So the Court of Appeal formulated a question asking what amounted to unfair if advantage was taken. As indicated previously,

---

[190] Para 41.   [191] Case C-487/07.

[192] *L'Oréal*. Unlike the requirement for economic damage or likelihood of damage to the proprietor of the mark when considering detriment to distinctiveness: Case C-252/07 *Intel Corporation/CPM*.

[193] Para 50.

[194] *L'Oreal*, para 44. For early UK cases see *Oasis Stores Ltd's Trade Mark Application* [1998] RPC 631 (Ever Ready for condoms) and *Inlima SL's Application Opposition of Adidas AG* [2000] ETMR 325 (the use of the three-stripe emblem owned by Adidas and a bottle in the shape of a boot that also had three stripes).

[195] [2006] EWHC 2355 (Ch).   [196] *L'Oreal*, para 151.   [197] *L'Oreal*, para 152.

[198] [2007] EWCA Civ 968.   [199] Case R 308/2003-1 [2005] ETMR 5.

the ECJ stated that unfair advantage refers to cases where there is exploitation on the coat-tails of the mark with a reputation due to a 'transfer of the image of the mark or of the characteristics which it projects to the goods identified by the identical or similar sign …'[200] A global assessment needed to be made of all of the facts, but in the instant case where a third party might benefit from the power of attraction and prestige of a mark with a reputation without paying financial compensation and using the marketing effort expended by the proprietor of the mark with a reputation, that would amount to advantage unfairly taken of the distinctive character or repute of the mark. So the focus of the unfairness is on the benefit to the free-rider, rather than on the detriment to the trade mark owner.

15.86   In a series of cases the ECJ has refined its approach to this area of law when dealing with Adwords.

■ **Joined Cases C-236/08 to C-238/08** *Google France SARL v Louis Vuitton Malletier SA* **(*Google*); Case C-278/08** *BergSpechte Outdoor Reisen under Alpinschule Edi Kobmuller GmbH v Guni*; **Case C-558/08** *Portakabin Ltd v Primakabin BV*; **and Case C-323/09** *Interflora Inc v Marks & Spencer plc* **(*Interflora*).**

For a description of the ways in which Adwords programmes work, see para 16.47ff.

Did the practice of selling Adwords infringe trade mark law? If it did, who was liable? Were there any defences in relation to the practice? The questions were of great importance and the overwhelming majority of the revenue earned by search engines is derived from Adwords. If search engines were liable for infringing trade marks, this technology sector would have to undergo a radical change in search of a new business model.

- In the *Google* cases the ECJ found that the service provider (Google) was not using the trade mark—there could therefore be no infringement by the service provider.[201]

- Where a sign identical with a trade mark is selected as a keyword by a *competitor* of the proprietor of the mark with the aim of offering Internet users an alternative to the goods or services of that proprietor, there is a use of that sign in relation to the goods or services of that competitor.[202] So the trader who uses the Adword uses it for the purposes of trade mark law and can be liable for infringement.

- In the case of offers of imitations for sale where a third party attempts, through the use of a sign which is identical with, or similar to, a reputable mark, to ride on the coat-tails of that mark in order to benefit from its power of attraction, its reputation, and its prestige, and to exploit, without paying any financial compensation and without being required to make efforts of its own in that regard, the marketing effort expended by the proprietor of that mark in order to create and maintain the image of that mark, the advantage resulting from such use must be considered to be an advantage that has been unfairly taken of the distinctive character or the repute of that mark.[203]

- The purpose of the use of a trade mark as a keyword was to take advantage of its distinctive character and repute; the competitor derived a real advantage from the distinctive character and repute of the trade mark; and the advertiser did not, as a general rule, pay the trade mark proprietor any compensation in respect of that use. In the absence of 'due cause', such use could fall within the scope of Article 9(1)(c):

  – the use would likely be without due cause if the goods offered using the Adwords service were imitations of those sold under the trade mark. But this was not the case where the goods were simply alternatives;[204]

[200] Para 41.   [201] See para 15.16.
[202] Joined Cases C-236/08 to C-238/08 *Google France SARL v Louis Vuitton Malletier SA*, para 69.
[203] *L'Oreal*, para.49   [204] *Google France*, paras 102 and 103. *Interflora*, para 90.

> – by contrast, where the advertisement displayed on the Internet on the basis of a keyword corresponding to a trade mark with a reputation puts forward—without offering a mere imitation of the goods or services of the proprietor of that trade mark, without causing dilution or tarnishment and without, moreover, adversely affecting the functions of the trade mark concerned—an alternative to the goods or services of the proprietor of the trade mark with a reputation, such use falls, as a rule, within the ambit of fair competition in the sector for the goods or services concerned and is thus not without 'due cause' for the purposes of Article 5(2) of Directive 89/104 and Article 9(1)(c) of Regulation 40/94.[205]

15.87   A key concern was to demarcate the boundary between fair and unfair competition as described by the Court of Appeal in *Specsavers International Healthcare Ltd v Asda Stores Ltd*[206] thus:

> Specifically, the use of a trade mark as a keyword in order to advertise goods which are an alternative to but not mere imitations of the goods of the proprietor and in a way which does not cause dilution or tarnishment and which does not adversely affect the functions of the trade mark must be regarded as fair competition and cannot be prohibited.[207]

 ## Question

What do you think of the limitations concerning liability on use of a trade mark that have been developed by the ECJ in the Adwords cases? Do you think that the focus on 'due cause' is a satisfactory way of placing boundaries in this area? Are there any other areas where similar limitations might be developed in the interests of fair competition?

Detriment

15.88   The issue of the use of a sign being *detrimental* to the distinctive character or reputation of a mark has been referred to generally as 'dilution'. Dilution could be generally described as *the whittling away of the distinctive character of a trade mark* and can be used to refer to both tarnishment and blurring.[208] As with the notion of 'free-riding', and in contrast with British law, dilution has long been a part of the law of other European countries. Its purpose was considered by the German Federal Supreme Court in *Quick*.[209]

> the owner of … a distinctive mark has a legitimate interest in continuing to maintain the position of exclusivity he acquired through large expenditures of time and money and that everything which could impair the originality and distinctive character of his distinctive mark, as well as the advertising effectiveness derived from its uniqueness, is to be avoided … Its basic purpose is not to prevent any form of confusion but to protect an acquired asset against impairment.

Here the German court is referring to detriment to the distinctive character of the mark. The test looks to the impact that the use or proposed use of the second mark has on the existing mark with the reputation. Would that use be detrimental to the distinctive character or reputation of the first mark?

Detrimental to the reputation: tarnishment

15.89   The reputation of a mark can be *tarnished* where the use of the sign is detrimental to the reputation of the well-known mark. An example might be by using a phonetically similar word for household cleaner as is registered for an expensive alcoholic beverage.[210]

---

[205] *Interflora Inc*, para 91.   [206] [2012] EWCA Civ 24.   [207] Para 141.

[208] '[T]he essence [of dilution] is the blurring of distinctiveness of a mark such that it is no longer capable of arousing an immediate association with the goods or services for which it is registered and used'. *Kerly's Law of Trade Marks and Trade Names* (14th edn, 2005), para 9-118.   [209] [1959] GRUR 182.

[210] *Claeryn v Klarein* (1976) 7 IIC 420, Nederlandse Jurisprudentie 1975, 472. Also in the UK, *Inlima SL's Application for a Three Dimensional Trade Mark* [2000] ETMR 325; aff'd [2000] RPC 661.

666

15.90   As regards the detriment in *L'Oreal v Bellure*,[211] the ECJ said that this is caused where a sign is used by the third party in such a way that its power of attraction is reduced. This may be where the goods or services offered by the third party 'possess a characteristic or a quality which is liable to have a negative impact on the image of the mark'.[212]

15.91   In an earlier case, the Third Board of Appeal of OHIM had used stronger language when it said that for detriment by tarnishing it would be necessary to show that a trade mark is 'sullied or debased by its association with something unseemly'[213] and the effect should be that the power of attraction of the trade mark is affected.[214] That might happen when 'the applied for trade mark, to which the mark with reputation may be associated, is used, on the one hand, in an unpleasant, obscene or degrading context or, on the other hand, in a context which is not inherently unpleasant but which proves to be incompatible with the trade mark's image'.[215]

15.92   In *Souza Cruz SA v Hollywood SAS OHIM*[216] the Second Board of Appeal said that this might happen in three ways. Where the mark is:

(1) linked with goods of poor quality or which evoke undesirable or questionable mental associations which conflict with the associations or image generated by legitimate use of the trade mark by its proprietor;

(2) linked with goods which are incompatible with the quality and prestige associated with the trade mark, even though it is not a matter of inappropriate use of the trade mark in itself;

(3) amended or altered in a negative way.

The essence is that the mark with the reputation ceases to convey desirable messages to the public.

15.93   The UK Registry and courts considered what amounts to tarnishment in a number of cases prior to the Court's judgment in *L'Oreal v Bellure*. In *Inlima SL's Application Opposition of Adidas AG*[217] the question was over the use of the three-stripe emblem owned by Adidas and a bottle in the shape of a boot that also had three stripes which was used for alcohol. The question in relation to the refusal to register the boot concerned the extent to which detriment would be caused to the existing marks by use of the second. As the Registry pointed out: 'The applicants have alcohol included in their specification. Given the similarity of the applicants' mark to the goods of the opponents the use of the applicants mark on alcohol would, in my view, be detrimental to the opponents'.[218]

15.94   A similar line was taken in *CA Sheimer (M) Sdn Bhd's Trade Mark Application*,[219] where the question was over the proposed registration of 'Visa' for condoms, opposed by Visa International. 'I think it is a fair inference from the evidence before me that so many people are so deeply imbued with Visa International's use of the word VISA as its trade mark that Sheimer's use of the word would to a significant extent trigger recollections of Visa International and its services'.[220] But something more was needed: 'Would it also exploit the distinctive character of the earlier trade mark positively (by taking unfair advantage of it) or negatively (by subjecting it to the effects of detrimental use)'?[221] In this case it was felt that the use by Scheimer of the word 'Visa' for condoms would damage the reputation of the

---

[211] Case C-487/07.   [212] Para 40.

[213] Case R 1127/2000-3 *Elleni Holding BV v Sigla SA* [2005] ETMR 7, para 43.

[214] In *Adidas-Salomon AG v Fitnessworld Trading Ltd* [2004] Ch 120 (ECJ), AG Jacobs described it (para 38) as: 'the concept of detriment to the repute of a trade mark, often referred to as degradation or tarnishment of the mark, describes the situation where ... the goods for which the infringing sign is used appeal to the public's senses in such a way that the trade mark's power of attraction is affected'. See also *Spa Monopole v OHIM* [2005] ETMR 109 (CFI).

[215] Case R 283/1999-3, *Souza Cruz SA v Hollywood SAS* (OHIM Board of Appeal), para 85.   [216] *Souza Cruz*.

[217] [2000] ETMR 325.   [218] *Inlima SL's Application Opposition of Adidas AG* at 336.

[219] [2000] RPC 484, [2000] ETMR 1170.   [220] *Sheimer* at 502.   [221] *Sheimer* at 504–505.

Figure 15.10 Inlima's boot-shaped bottle with three stripes

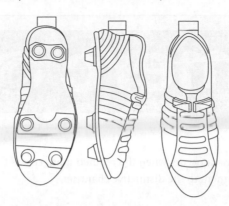

earlier trade mark because it would 'burden Visa International's use of the mark with connotations of birth control and personal hygiene … Visa International should not have to carry the burden of advertising condoms and prophylactics at the same time as it promotes its own services'.[222] Registration was thus refused.[223] Similarly, Viagrene in relation to poor quality or ineffective goods (at least where male impotence was concerned) would tarnish Viagra;[224] and the use of the 'Intel-Play' mark on inferior goods (toys) would 'almost certainly reduce the distinctive character of the Intel mark.[225]

15.95   So, in the UK, while the use (or application for registration) of a sign which is the same or similar to a mark with a reputation may be enjoined if it is used in connection with alcohol, condoms, or poor quality, ineffective, or inferior goods; the use of a sign similar to a mark with a reputation in connection with clothes aimed at mods, skinheads, and casuals would seem not to be sufficient to show detriment to the reputation of the mark.

■ *Daimler Chrysler AG v Alavi (t/a Merc)* [2001] RPC 42

Daimler brought an action under section 10(3) of the TMA 1994 against Alavi for the latter's use of the word 'Merc' for a shop selling clothes and shoes. Alavi applied for the registration of the mark in Figure 15.11 as a CTM.

This was opposed by Daimler Chrysler arguing that the use of the word 'Merc' by Alavi for the shop damaged the reputation of Daimler's marks since Alavi's business was targeted at *mods, skinheads, and casuals*, none of which groups it wished to be associated with. In other words, the claim was that the reputation of Daimler's marks would be damaged. The High Court rejected the claim saying that:

> in order to succeed … it must be shown that there is established in the mind of the relevant public a connection between the mark with which they are familiar and the disparaging use. Thus, it is not sufficient to see the work MERC, note that this is the word which one uses to refer to Mercedes cars, see the disagreeable web site and register it as disagreeable, if nothing actually rubs off on the sign MERC itself or on MERCEDES, or on Daimler Chrysler. I was not satisfied that this was the case here, and so this allegation of infringement fails.[226]

---

[222] *Sheimer* at 506.
[223] See *Mastercard International Inc v Hitachi Credit (UK) plc* [2004] EWHC 1623 (Ch), [2005] ETMR 10, [2005] RPC 21 where the question was whether the use of 'Credit Master' would be detrimental to the distinctive character or reputation of 'Mastercard'. The court found that there was insufficient similarity between the marks for the average consumer to make an association. Some proof of damage was required.
[224] *Pfizer Ltd and Pfizer Incorporated v Eurofood Link (United Kingdom) Ltd* [2000] ETMR 896, [2001] FSR 3, para 15.53.
[225] *Intel Corp Inc v Sihra* [2004] ETMR 44, [2003] EWHC 17 (Ch).   [226] [2001] RPC 42 at p 842.

Figure 15.11 Alavi's Merc mark

15.96 As is said in Kerly, tarnishment occurs when the reputed mark ceases to give desirable messages to the public and give rise to detriment to the distinctive character.[227]

Detrimental to the distinctive character: blurring

15.97 Blurring has been described as 'the gradual whittling away or dispersion of the identity and hold upon the public mind of the mark or name by its use on non-competing goods'[228] such as the use of a prestige mark in association with T-shirts and window cleaning services. In *L'Oreal* the ECJ said: 'As regards detriment to the distinctive character of the mark, also referred to as "dilution", "whittling away" or "blurring", such detriment is caused when that mark's ability to identify the goods or services for which it is registered is weakened, since use of an identical or similar sign by a third party leads to dispersion of the identity and hold upon the public mind of the earlier mark. That is particularly the case when the mark, which at one time aroused immediate association with the goods or services for which it is registered, is no longer capable of doing so …'[229] The CFI has said that there will be detriment to the distinctive character where the mark with a reputation is no longer capable of arousing immediate association with the goods for which it is registered and used.[230] The argument is thus that the original exclusive quality of the mark would be lost.[231] This will be the case where the use of the mark contributes to turning it into a generic name.[232] In *Intel* the relevant questions on this part referred to the ECJ asked whether it only applied to a unique mark; whether a first use of a mark by a third party would be sufficient; and whether the economic behaviour of the consumer had to alter to satisfy the test. The Court responded saying that a mark does not necessarily need to be unique to establish the link but the stronger the reputation of the first mark, the easier it may be to show that link; that first use of a later mark might sometimes be sufficient; and that evidence is needed of a 'change in the economic behaviour of the average consumer of the goods or services for which the earlier mark was registered consequent on the use of the later mark, or a serious likelihood that such a change will occur in the future'[233] although not relevant is whether the proprietor of the later mark gets commercial benefit from the distinctive character of the earlier mark.[234] It is for the national court to make a global assessment based on all of the factors. While these factors

---

[227] *Kerly's Law of Trade Marks and Trade Names* (15th edn, 2011), para 9-131.

[228] F Schechter, 'The rational basis of trademark protection' (1927) 40 Harv LR 813, 825. Case C-487/07 *L'Oréal v Bellure*, para 39. Case C-252/07 *Intel v CPM*, para 29.

[229] *L'Oreal*, para 39; Case C-252/07 *Intel Corp*, para 29.   [230] *Spa Monopole v OHIM* [2005] ETMR 109 (CFI).

[231] Schechter, note 228; *Parfums Givenchy SA v Designer Alternative Ltd* [1994] RPC 243 where the court considered that damage could be caused by 'erosion of distinctiveness'.

[232] *Interflora*, para 79.

[233] *Intel*, para 77. The risk of dilution is limited or non-existent where the marks are similar on account of figurative elements which have a low degree of distinctive character to the extent that they are frequently used by other operators to designate the geographic origin of goods. Case C-136/08 *Japan Tobacco Inc v OHIM* (Camelo/Camel).

[234] *Intel*, para 78.

clarify some of the criteria for this head, it will not, for instance, be easy to show that the economic behaviour of the consumer has changed due to the later use of the mark by the third party.

The concept has also been said to raise 'difficult conceptual issues'[235] and it has been suggested that where there is no tarnishment or confusion, then no real or verifiable damage would occur.[236] Bently and Sherman suggest that in order to show that the distinctive character of a mark will be blurred, it has to be shown that the earlier mark has a reputation for a limited category of goods. The result is that when the consumer thinks of the mark, they think of those goods. If a third party uses the same or similar mark for dissimilar goods or services so the 'singularity of that association' would be whittled away.[237]

15.98   A brief look at the cases in the UK that have considered this provision show some of the difficulties the courts have had in determining the parameters. In one of the first hearings on this provision in the UK Registry, *AUDI-Med Trade Mark*,[238] there was a clear concern to work out the parameters of the provision. 'Any use of the same or similar mark for dissimilar goods or services is, to some extent, liable to dilute the distinctiveness of the earlier mark. The provision is clearly not intended to have the sweeping effect of preventing the registration of any mark which is the same as, or similar to a trade mark with a reputation. It therefore appears to be a matter of degree'.[239] The Registry also indicated that it would be more difficult to show unfair advantage where the marks were descriptive ordinary words than if they were invented words. Other cases have perhaps been less clear in applying this provision. In *Premier Brands UK Ltd v Typhoon*[240] the attempted registration by Typhoon of the mark 'Typhoon' for kitchenware, was opposed by Premier Brands, which had the registration of 'TY.PHOO' for tea.[241] The court opined that: 'The use of the sign in such circumstances will lead to blurring, as it will reduce the uniqueness of the TY.PHOO mark as a brand name in the kitchen'.[242] This was, however, subject to the proviso that the association had to be such as to be 'detrimental as to the character or repute of the mark'. In this case, the existence of the association in the minds of a limited proportion of members of the public would not result in a 'lessening of the capacity of [the TY.PHOO] mark to identify and distinguish goods',[243] nor would it impinge upon 'the position of exclusivity [Premier] acquired through large expenditure of time and money', nor could it 'impair the originality and distinctive character of [the TY.PHOO] mark'.[244]

15.99   In *Julius Sämann Ltd, Julius Sämann Ltd, H Young (Operations) Ltd v Tetrosyl Ltd*[245] the High Court found a case to be made out. The question was whether the production by Tetrosyl of an air freshener in the shape of a fir tree diluted the earlier tree-shaped marks for, inter alia, air fresheners belonging to Julius Sämann Ltd. The court found that the tree marks had a substantial reputation in the UK and that there was 'a real probability that members of the public seeing the Christmas Tree product will think that it is another product in the Magic Tree range or a Christmas version of the Tree products'. On the evidence, the average consumer would make a link between the sign and the Tree marks 'and that this will inevitably damage the distinctiveness of the Tree marks. Their capacity to denote the products of the claimants exclusively will be diminished'.[246]

A question does, however, arise in relation to this case. As the sign used by Tetrosyl was both similar to Sämann's mark and used in connection with similar goods for which it was registered, it might be

---

[235] *DaimlerChrysler AG v Alavi* [2001] RPC 42, para 93.
[236] L Bently and B Sherman, *Intellectual Property Law* (3rd edn, 2009), 886.
[237] Bently and Sherman, note 236, 886. Note that there is no head of damage that would constitute 'fettering' which is said to occur when the opportunities to further exploit the commercial value of an earlier mark are limited by the registration of a later mark: see UK Trade Marks Registry *Esure/Direct Line Insurance*, 13 December 2006, para 148.
[238] [1998] RPC 863, [1999] ETMR 1010.   [239] [1998] RPC 863 at 872.
[240] [2000] ETMR 1071, [2000] FSR 767.   [241] In class 30.   [242] [2000] FSR 767 at 793.
[243] *Premier Brands* at 787.   [244] *Premier Brands* at 801.   [245] [2006] EWHC 529 (Ch).
[246] *Sämann*, para 84.

questionable whether the use by Tetrosyl of the tree mark would result in the registered mark owned by Sämann being no longer capable of arousing immediate association with the goods for which it was registered and used.[247] It may be more likely that there is confusion as to origin.

Question

Read *Julius Sämann Ltd, Julius Sämann Ltd, H Young (Operations) Ltd v Tetrosyl Ltd* [2006] EWHC 529 (Ch). Do you think that the use of the sign by Tetrosyl was:

* taking advantage,

* detrimental to the distinctive character,

* detrimental to the reputation,

of the earlier mark owned by Sämann? Justify your response.

If you want to see the registered tree mark you can find it on the trade mark database at the IPO. You could compare the case with the findings of the CFI in Case T-168/04 *L & D, SA v OHIM/Julius Sämann Ltd*, in which L&D had applied to register the same mark as a CTM. This was opposed by Julius Sämann on the basis of its earlier marks. There the CFI found that the marks and goods (apart from class 35 services) were similar, and that there was a likelihood of confusion. This was upheld by the ECJ.[248]

Without due cause

15.100   It will be noted from the legislation (and the discussion at para15.69) that the use of the sign and the taking of unfair advantage of, or being detrimental to, the earlier mark must be without *due cause*. This has been considered in the UK and, more recently, by the Court of Justice in the Adword cases. In *Premier Brands v Typhoon*[249] the court emphasised that regard should be had to the purpose of the provision which is to protect the value and goodwill of well-known trade marks from being unfairly taken advantage of or unfairly harmed. The burden of proof is on the defendant to show that the use complained of is 'with due cause' and that the taking of unfair advantage or causing of detriment are not 'without due cause'. In *Julius Sämann Ltd, Julius Sämann Ltd, H Young (Operations) Ltd v Tetrosyl Ltd*[250] the court thought that 'All of these matters point to a relatively stringent test'.[251] As noted previously, 'due cause' has been considered by the ECJ in the Adword cases (paras 15.86). Here it has been used to demarcate the boundaries between fair and unfair competition, between when a use of a trade mark will be infringing, and when it will not. The importance of the test is thus elevated to one of a 'gatekeeper' function: where a competitor uses the same or similar trade mark for goods that differ from those of the owner of the mark;

* does not dilute or tarnish the mark,

* and does not affect the functions of the mark,

the use amounts to fair competition satisfying the test of due cause. While there are clear limitations on the operation of the 'due cause' test, with the focus on fair competition, it seems that it has the potential to provide an important balance between the interests of the proprietor of the mark and those of the competitor.[252]

---

[247] See also *Och-Ziff Management Europe Ltd v Och Capital LLP* [2011] ETMR 1; *Ate My Heart Inc v Mind Candy Ltd* [2011] EWHC 2741 (Ch).

[248] Case C-488/06 P.   [249] [2000] FSR 767.   [250] [2006] EWHC 529 (Ch).   [251] *Sämann*, para 84.

[252] Note the questions on due cause referred to the Court of Justice in Case C-65/12 *Leidseplein Beheer and de Vries v Red Bull*.

Question

In what other circumstances can you envisage the test of 'due cause' being used in the interests of fair competition?

15.101   As noted previously (para 15.75), just one of these types of injury: taking unfair advantage, detrimental to the reputation, and detrimental to the distinctive character, is needed for an action.[253] When considering detriment to distinctiveness, economic damage or likelihood of damage to the proprietor of the mark needs to be shown.[254] No such requirement exists for detriment to reputation or for taking unfair advantage of distinctiveness or reputation of the mark.[255]

Question

Where are the proper boundaries between fair and unfair competition in relation to the extended functions of a mark?

The extended function

15.102   The inclusion of these provisions in domestic UK legislation marks a departure from the previous law. The provisions of the Directive are permissive: member states did not need to include them in their own laws but the UK chose to do so. As can be seen from the previous discussion, the rationales justifying protection for marks with a reputation move away from the traditional origin function, to protecting the positive reputational 'aura' associated with the mark. This echoes the extended functions of a mark examined in Chapter 13 (paras 13.12ff) As was emphasised by the Third Board of Appeal in *Elleni Holding BV*,[256] a trade mark is not only an indication of origin, but it can also serve as a communication tool. The message that the mark conveys could refer to the quality of the product 'or indeed to intangible values such as luxury, lifestyle, exclusivity, adventure, youth, etc'.[257] As these functions are recognised and protected within the scope of the mark, so the monopoly associated with the mark broadens.

15.103   No longer is it necessary that the consumer be confused under the extended functions: in other words, the mark is no longer limited to its traditional function as a badge of origin. Rather, it is the investment in the mark in its ability to communicate a message that is protected. In considering the stakeholder interests that trade mark law accommodates, by protecting marks with a reputation the focus is on the mark and the interests of the trade mark owner. As is apparent from the earlier discussion, the issue then becomes one as to the scope of that protection, and where the interests of the competing trader and of the public are to be taken into account.

15.104   As has been noted (para 15.100) Court of Appeal emphasised the need for this balance when considering the role of 'due cause'. The extension of the law in this area and the approach taken by the ECJ, coupled with the opaque boundaries and its potential effect on (unfair) competition, have been criticised by Jacob LJ, when applying the judgment of the ECJ in *L'Oreal*:[258] first, because of the impact that it may have on consumer choice and, secondly, because of the potential interference in freedom to trade:

---

[253] Case C-252/07 *Intel v CPM*, para 28.   [254] Case C-252/07 *Intel Corporation v CPM*.
[255] Case C-487/07 *L'Oréal v Bellure*.   [256] Case R 1127/2000-3 *Elleni Holding BV v Sigla SA* [2005] ETMR 7.
[257] *Elleni Holding*, para 41. See also Case R 283/1999-3 (*Hollywood/Hollywood*), paras 62–67. *Société des Produits Nestlé SA v Mars Inc* [2005] ETMR 37 (OHIM Second Board of Appeal).
[258] *L'Oréal SA v Bellure NV* [2010] EWCA Civ 535.

The ECJ's decision in this case means that poor consumers are the losers. Only the poor would dream of buying the defendants' products. The real thing is beyond their wildest dreams. Yet they are denied their right to receive information which would give them a little bit of pleasure; the ability to buy a product for a euro or so which they know smells like a famous perfume.[259]

My second reason is more specific. It is about freedom to trade—indeed, potentially in other cases, to compete honestly. (This case is *a fortiori* for the parties' respective products are not in competition with each other). If a trader cannot (when it is truly the case) say: 'my goods are the same as Brand X (a famous registered mark) but half the price', I think there is a real danger that important areas of trade will not be open to proper competition.[260]

Question

Read the ECJ judgment in Case C-487/07 *L'Oreal v Bellure* and that of the Court of Appeal in *L'Oréal SA v Bellure NV*.[261] What do you think of the arguments around consumer choice and competition made by the Court of Appeal? Where does the balance between fair and unfair competition lie? Where should it lie and how should it be dealt with in the trade mark legislation?

Exercise

For a case heard by the Supreme Court of Appeal in South Africa on matters of dilution, see *Laugh It Off Promotions CC v South African Breweries International (Finance) BV*[262] in which a parody by Laugh It Off Promotions on a T-shirt of Carling Black Label's trade mark was considered (see para 13.8). In giving judgment, the court weighed the right to freedom of speech (the parody of the trade mark) against the intellectual property rights in the mark and considered that placing the onus on the trade mark holder to adduce evidence to prove the likelihood of substantial economic harm as a result of this parody was an appropriate balance of these rights. The court found that harm to the mark had not been proven. Read and summarise the case which you will find at http://www.saflii.org/za/cases/ZACC/2005/7.html (you will find images of the T-shirt and of the beer label in the text). Give your opinion of the balance the court found between freedom of expression and trade mark rights.

Key points on similar trade marks with a reputation

- These provisions protect the extended functions of a mark
- No consumer confusion is required
- The public must establish a link between the mark with the reputation and the application or allegedly infringing sign (which must affect economic behaviour)
- The use of the later mark must be without due cause

---

[259] Para 14.   [260] Para 16.
[261] [2010] EWCA Civ 535.   [262] [2005] FSR 30 (Sup Ct, SA).

Defences to an action of infringement

Exercise

Read section 11 of the TMA 1996; Article 6 of the Directive; and Article 12 of the CTMR.

Question

When do you think a registered trade mark should be able to be lawfully used by an unconnected third party? Revisit your views once you have read this section.

15.105   Defences to an action for infringement of a trade mark are vital to balance the interests of the trade mark owner and the honest competitor. In the *Baby Dry* case[263] (discussed in para 14.56) the ECJ appeared to endorse the registration of marks that appeared to some to be no more than descriptive. In so doing, the Court linked registration to the defences for an action of infringement. What the court appeared to suggest was that although marks were not to be registered if they consisted exclusively of the characteristics of the goods or service, in the next paragraph the Court pointed out that the rights conferred by the trade mark would not permit the proprietor to prohibit a third party from using those same indications in the course of trade by reference to the defences in the Directive.[264] It appeared to commentators that, by linking the two, the Court was permitting the registration of a broader category of marks but indicating that a defence would be available for legitimate third party use. This, however, did not take account of the respective strengths of parties within the marketplace. A small trader might have had great difficulty in resisting calls by Procter & Gamble to cease using the words '*Baby Dry*' in literature describing the properties of nappies. Since then it appears that the tendency to link the two (registration and infringement) is less common. As was said in *AD2000*,[265] to protect the legitimate interests of honest traders, the first line of protection is to refuse registration of signs which are excluded under section 3 of the TMA 1994.[266] When a mark has been registered, the honest trader may then point to the defences to excuse certain legitimate uses.

The statutory provisions

15.106   Section 11 of the TMA 1994 contains provisions dealing with circumstances in which the use of a registered trade mark will not infringe the rights of the registered proprietor. The most important are in section 11(2) which contains three circumstances in which a registered trade mark will not be infringed. These are:

• the use by a person of his own name or address;

• the use of indications concerning the kind, quality, quantity, intended purpose, value, geographical origin, the time of production of goods or of rendering of services, or other characteristics of goods or services; or

• the use of the trade mark where it is necessary to indicate the intended purpose of a product or service (in particular, as accessories or spare parts).

---

[263] Case C-383/99 *Procter & Gamble Co v OHIM (Baby Dry)* [2001] ECR 1-6251, [2002] ETMR (3) (22).
[264] *Baby Dry*, paras 35 and 36.   [265] [1997] RPC 168.
[266] See also *Nichols plc's Trade Mark Application* [2003] RPC 16.

Honest practices

15.107   Use for section 11 must be 'in accordance with honest practices in industrial or commercial matters'.[267] The ECJ has said that honest practice constitutes a duty to act fairly in relation to the legitimate interests of the trade mark owner.[268] In assessing whether this condition is satisfied, account must first be taken of the extent to which the use of the third party's trade name is understood by the relevant public as indicating a link between the third party's goods and the trade mark proprietor or a person authorised to use the trade mark; and, secondly, of the extent to which the third party ought to have been aware of that. In addition, and looking at all of the relevant circumstances, it needs to be assessed whether the defendant could be regarded as unfairly competing with the proprietor of the trade mark[269] and whether the use of the sign gives rise to consumer deception or takes unfair advantage of, or is detrimental to, the distinctive character or repute of the trade mark. If it does, it is unlikely to qualify as being in accordance with honest practices.[270] Finally, a likelihood of confusion will not necessarily mean that the use is not in accordance with honest practices if there is a good reason why confusion should be tolerated.[271]

15.108   In *The Gillette Co v LA-Laboratories Ltd Oy*[272] the ECJ had the opportunity to consider what would meet the test of honest practices. Gillette had registered in Finland the trade marks 'Gillette' and 'Sensor' for, inter alia, razors and had marketed razors under this sign comprised of a handle and replaceable blades. LA-Laboratories also sold razors in Finland comprised of a handle and replaceable blades, but under the mark 'Parason Flexor'. This packaging bore a sticker stating: 'All Parason Flexor and Gillette Sensor handles are compatible with this blade'. Gillette objected to this affixing of its trade mark to the packaging. The ECJ confirmed that honest practices constitute a duty to act fairly in relation to the legitimate interests of the trade mark owner. As such, the use of a trade mark would not be in accordance with this test where:

* it is done in such a manner that it may give the impression that there is a commercial connection between the reseller and the trade mark proprietor;[273]

* where the use would affect the value of the trade mark by taking unfair advantage of its distinctive character or repute;[274]

* if the use discredits or denigrates that mark;[275]

* the third party presents its product as an imitation or replica of the product bearing the trade mark of which it is not the owner.[276]

The own name defence

15.109   With regard to section 11(2)(a) of the TMA 1994 (the 'own name defence'), it will be a matter for consideration in each case as to whether the use by a person of his own name in connection with particular

---

[267] Trade Marks Act 1994, s 11(2).

[268] Case C-100/02 *Gerolsteiner Brunnen GmbH & Co v Putsch GmbH* [2004] RPC 39; Case C-17/06 *SARL Céline v SA Céline; Bravado Merchandising Services Ltd v Mainstream Publishing (Edinburgh) Ltd* [1996] FSR 205 in which the use of the words 'Wet Wet Wet' as the title of a book was registered but third party use was in accordance with honest practices in industrial and commercial matters. *Hotel Cipriani Srl v Cipriani (Grosvenor Street) Ltd* [2010] EWCA Civ 110, para 15.111; *Och-Ziff Management Europe Ltd v Och Capital LLP* [2010] EWHC 2599 (Ch); Case C-63/97 *Bayerische Motorenwerke AG v Deenik*, para 61; Case C-100/02 *Gerolsteiner Brunnen GmbH & Co v Putsch GmbH*, para 24; Case C-245/02 *Anheuser-Busch Inc v Budejovicky Budvar np*, para 82; Case 228/03 *Gillette Co v LA-Laboratories Ltd Oy*, para 41; Case C-17/06 *Céline SARL v Céline SA*, para 33.

[269] *Gerolsteiner*, para 26; *Anheuser-Busch*, para 84; *Céline*, para 35.

[270] Case C-228/03 *The Gillette Co v LA-Laboratories Ltd Oy*, para 49; *Anheuser-Busch*, para 83; *Céline*, para 34.

[271] *Gerolsteiner*, para 25.   [272] Case C-228/03 [2005] All ER (EC) 940, [2005] 2 CMLR 62, [2005] ECR I-2337.

[273] *Gillette*, para 42.   [274] *Gillette*, para 43.   [275] *Gillette*, para 44.   [276] *Gillette*, para 45.

goods or services is in accordance with honest practices. One may question the motives of a software programmer called James Microsoft who wanted to start producing his own software and sell it under the name 'Microsoft'.[277]

15.110   In the Court of Appeal the registration by Mr Adlem of his own name for, inter alia, funeral services was considered in *IN Newman Ltd v Richard T Adlem*.[278] In the years prior to the registration Mr Adlem had carried on business as a funeral director, trading under his own name, but had sold that business along with the goodwill. Once the restrictive covenant expired he recommenced the business and registered his name Richard T Adlem. The owners of the original business objected to this registration. Mr Adlem claimed, inter alia, the own name defence.

The Court of Appeal found that the sale of the business included the goodwill and it was not open to Mr Adlem, even after the expiry of the restrictive covenant, to start a fresh business under exactly the same name. Accordingly, the trade mark registration was invalid, Mr Adlem being unable to rely on the own name defence.[279]

15.111   The own name defence applies both to individual names and to company and trade names.[280] While in principle a third party can use a trade name which is identical or similar to a trade name, the use will be subject to the condition of honest practice. As such, account should be first of the extent to which the use of the third party's trade name is understood by the relevant public as indicating a link between the third party's goods and the trade mark proprietor and, secondly, of the extent to which the third party ought to have been aware of that. Another factor to be taken into account when making the assessment is whether the trade mark concerned enjoys a certain reputation in the member state in which it is registered and its protection is sought, from which the third party might profit in selling his goods.[281] The Court of Appeal ruled in *Asprey & Garrard Ltd v WRA (Guns) Ltd (t/a William R Asprey Esquire)*,[282] that the use by William Asprey of his own name to carry out a trade the same as Asprey & Garrard did not have to be tackled because it was not William Asprey who was trading, but rather the limited company, WRA (Guns) Ltd. The court added the proviso: 'however honest his subjective intentions may be, any use of his own name which amounts to passing off cannot be in accordance with honest practice in industrial or commercial matters'. In *Hotel Cipriani v Cipriani (Grovesnor Street) Ltd*[283] the question was in whether the use of the name 'Cipriani' by Cipriani (Grovesnor Street) could be excused under the own name defence. The Court of Appeal distinguished *Asprey* arguing that the use of the trading name in that case was new. In the instant case it was open to Cipriani to use a trading name for its business that was distinct from its registered name with the limitation that this could not conflict with an existing name. The latter would not be in accordance with honest practices.

> In my judgment, the article 12(a) defence may be available in respect of a trading name, as well as the corporate name of a company, but it will depend on (a) what the trading name is that has been adopted, (b) in what circumstances it has been adopted and (c), depending on the relevant circumstances, whether the use is in accordance with honest practices.[284]

---

[277] In Case C-404/02 *Nichols plc v Registrar of Trade Marks* [2005] 1 WLR 1418 the ECJ made it clear that the fact that the effects of registration of a trade mark are limited by the own name defence has no impact the assessment of the existence or otherwise of the distinctive character of a name as a mark.

[278] *IN Newmans Ltd v Richard T Adlem* [2005] EWCA Civ 741.

[279] It is unlikely that a formal change of name (whether personal or company) to take advantage of the own name defence will be looked on favourably by the courts: *International Business Machines Corp, IBM United Kingdom Ltd v Web-Sphere Ltd, Richard de Serville, David Markson* [2004] ETMR 94, [2004] EWHC 529 (Ch).

[280] Case C-245/02 *Anheuser-Busch Inc v Budejovicky Budvar NP*, para 77; Case C-17/06 *Céline Sàrl v Céline SA*, para 31.

[281] *Céline*, para 82.

[282] [2002] FSR 31, [2001] EWCA Civ 1499. See also *Premier Luggage & Bags Ltd v Premier Co (UK) Ltd* [2002] EWCA Civ 387.

[283] [2008] EWHC 3032. See also para 14.89 and note the judgment of the Court of Appeal and ECJ.   [284] Para 72.

On the facts of the current case, the company had chosen Cipriani London as a trading name and so the use of 'Cipriani' on its own could not be justified as a trading name, even where used by employees.[285] Further, the use was not in accordance with honest practices.

For further discussion on the use of trade names see para 15.19.

The use of indications concerning, inter alia, the characteristics of products

15.112   Section 11(2)(b) of the 1994 Act is designed to allow traders to use registered trade marks where they might wish to describe some of the characteristics of their own products or services. As indicated previously, these provisions mirror the grounds for refusing registration under section 3 of the 1994 Act. An indication of the quality, etc, of goods may not be registered as a trade mark. If it is, then a third party using the mark in the course of trade in connection with its own goods or services will have a defence. For example, the maker of chairs might want to describe the fabric in which they were covered, and to do so may use a registered trade mark belonging to the maker of the fabric. As with the first subsection, however, the use must be in accordance with honest practices.

15.113   The ECJ has indicated that the use of a geographical indication may be in accordance with honest practices even where it is registered as a word mark and even if there exists a likelihood of aural confusion between the mark and the indication of geographical origin.

■ **Case C-100/02** *Gerolsteiner Brunnen GmbH & Co v Putsch GmbH* **[2004] RPC 39 (ECJ)**

This case concerned bottles of mineral water marketed in Germany under the registered trade mark 'Gerri', and bottles of Irish mineral water also marketed in Germany under the mark 'Kerry Spring' (Kerry Spring seemingly being an indication of geographical origin). The owner of the 'Gerri' mark brought trade mark infringement proceedings against the owner of the 'Kerry Spring' mark. The ECJ held that the relevant test is whether or not the use of the geographical indication is used in accordance with honest practices in industrial or commercial matters. 'The mere fact that there was a likelihood of aural confusion between a word mark registered in one Member State and a geographical indication from another Member State was insufficient to conclude that the use of the geographical indication was not in accordance with honest practices'.

15.114   This finding seemed at least in part as a result of the recognition that in a Community of then 15 states (now enlarged) there was a real possibility of phonetic similarity between a trade mark registered in one state and a geographical indication from another. Thus, the use of a geographical name as a sign can fall within this defence.

15.115   In *Adam Opel AG v Autec AG*[286] (discussed at para 15.13) questions were also referred to the ECJ concerning defences. In particular the Court was asked:

- Whether the affixation and use of a trade mark in the circumstances described is an indication of the kind or quality of the model car within the meaning of Article 6(1)(a) of the Trade Mark Directive?

- If yes: what are the decisive criteria to be applied in assessing whether the trade mark corresponds to honest practices in industrial or commercial matters?

- What is the effect of the toy manufacturer applying his own recognisable trade mark to the packaging?

---

[285] *Hotel Cipriani Srl v Cipriani (Grosvenor Street) Ltd* [2010] EWCA Civ 110.   [286] Case C-48/05.

The Court, having pointed out that the relevant provision was actually Article 6(1)(b) of the Directive, said that while it was intended to prevent the owner of a trade mark prohibiting competitors from using one or more descriptive terms forming part of the registered mark to indicate certain characteristics of their products, it was not limited to such a situation.[287] However, in the instant case, the affixation of a sign identical to a trade mark registered in respect of models of that make of vehicle in order to reproduce the vehicles was not an indication of the characteristics of the scale models but rather part of the faithful reproduction of the vehicle. In view of the answer given to this question, and the question on use, the Court found it unnecessary to reply to the other points.

15.116   Although the ECJ has suggested that the parameters of the defence in Article 6(1)(b) might be broader than suggested by the wording, the defence will not be applicable where an identical sign is used in a reproduction of an original, albeit designed for a different market, where the origin function is compromised.

> ### ❓ Question
>
> Given the ECJ's judgment in *Adam Opel AG v Autec AG* both in relation to the question of 'use' of the trade mark, and the defences, how do you think the national court should have decided the case? If the use jeopardises the essential function of the mark, and the toy manufacturer has no defence to the infringement, what does that say about the monopoly conferred by the trade mark and the function performed by the trade mark? (You might like to have a look at the opinion of the Advocate General to see what was said there.) You will remember that in *AD2000* the court said that the first line of protection for the legitimate interests of honest traders is to refuse registration of signs which are excluded under section 3 of the TMA 1994. By analogy, at what point could, or should, the legitimate interests of the honest trader be protected in this scenario?

The use of the trade mark where it is necessary to indicate the intended purpose of a product or service (in particular, as accessories or spare parts)

15.117   Section 11(2)(c) of the 1994 Act is particularly important for those who manufacture spare parts for goods, for example consumer goods, agricultural machinery, and cars. This section provides that the use of a registered trade mark will not infringe that mark where it is necessary to indicate the intended purpose of a product or service (in particular, as accessories or spare parts). It may be that a computer programmer selling computer software wants to advertise by stating 'compatible with Microsoft 95 software'. As long as the use is necessary and in accordance with honest practices such use of the registered trade mark should be permitted.

15.118   In *The Gillette Co v LA-Laboratories Ltd Oy*[288] (para 15.108) the ECJ had the opportunity to consider what was meant by 'necessary' to indicate the intended purpose of a product.[289] A use would be necessary where the trade mark was used 'to indicate the intended purpose of a product marketed by that third party where such use in practice constitutes the only means of providing the public with comprehensible and complete information on that intended purpose in order to preserve the undistorted system of competition in the market for that product'.[290]

---

[287] *Adam Opel*, para 42.   [288] [2005] 2 CMLR 62, [2005] ECR I-2337.   [289] *Gillette*, para 39.
[290] *Hasbro Inc v 123 Nahrmittel GmbH* [2011] EWHC 199 (Ch); describing a product as play-dough was not an honest use when the claimant owned the registered mark PLAY-DOH.

15.119   The Court has stressed that a trade mark can be used by a third party when advertising goods for sale. However, in relation to luxury marks the Court said in *Parfums Christian Dior SA v Evora BV*,[291] that the reseller could not act to the detriment of the trade mark owner. A balance has to be struck between the interests of resellers, on the one hand, and of the trade mark proprietors, on the other, who will always have a desire to preserve the prestige of the trade mark.

15.120   In assessing whether the defence is available, the whole circumstances of the case should be considered. If the use of the mark suggests that there is a connection between the third party and the trade mark owner, then the use is likely to be enjoined.

■ *Aktiebolaget Volvo v Heritage (Leicester) Ltd* [2000] FSR 253

Heritage had been an approved Volvo dealer, but that approval had been withdrawn. Heritage became a member of the Association of Independent Volvo Specialists, a group consisting of other motor dealers in the same situation. Heritage replaced a Volvo sign outside its premises with a new sign that read 'Independent Volvo Specialist', the word 'Volvo' being written in larger script than the other two. In addition, Heritage sent letters to customers that failed to indicate the true status of the relationship with Volvo. When challenged, Heritage argued that the use of the word 'Volvo' was necessary to describe the type of service being offered. The High Court found that while the use of the word Volvo was necessary to describe the service, such use had to be in accordance with honest commercial practices in which the *whole* circumstances of the use must be considered. Both the letters and the sign could be seen as deliberate attempts to cause confusion in the minds of its customers by indicating that a trading relationship still existed. The use was therefore *not* an honest use in the context of the motor trade.

15.121   Similarly in *Bayerische Motorenwerke AG v Deenik*,[292] the ECJ stressed that if the use of the mark makes customers believe that there is a commercial connection between that other party and the trade mark owner when in fact this does not exist, then such use would *not* be in accordance with honest commercial practices.

Question

Give three examples from your observations of the use by third parties of registered trade marks that you consider would not be deemed to be in accordance with honest commercial practices and three examples where you think it would be deemed to be in accordance with this test.

To what extent do you think that resellers and other parties should be able to use registered marks belonging to others in their businesses? Do you think that the parameters that are being hammered out represent a fair compromise between the interests of the trader and of the third party?

Key points on defences to an action of infringement

- Each of the defences (own name, use of indications concerning quality, etc, use of a mark to indicate the intended purpose) is subject to the proviso that it must be in accordance with honest practices in industrial or commercial matters

- A trader may not indicate a false commercial connection with the proprietor, take unfair advantage of the mark, or denigrate the mark

---

[291] Case C-337/95 [1998] RPC 166.   [292] Case C-63/97 [1999] All ER (EC) 235, [1999] 1 CMLR 1099.

Comparative advertising

15.122   Comparative advertising is the use of another's trade mark in advertising which compares the relative advantages and disadvantages of the products with that of the rival. In the words of the ECJ in *Pippig Augenoptik v Hartlauer*,[293] 'All comparative advertising is designed to highlight the advantages of the goods or services offered by the advertiser in comparison with those of a competitor. In order to achieve that, the message must necessarily underline the differences between the goods or services compared by describing their main characteristics. The comparison made by the advertiser will necessarily flow from such a description'.

15.123   The practice of comparative advertising has been the subject of much debate. Those who are in favour of it argue that comparative advertising is the only reasonable way in which consumers can make informed judgements about the products and services that they wish to purchase. If, in one advertisement, the relative merits and demerits of two competing products are described, the consumer has more of an opportunity to choose the best or most appropriate for themselves. Those who are against comparative advertising argue that those who engage in the practice do so for one of two reasons: either to trade off the positive reputation that is associated with the 'superior' product (eg by comparing a Skoda with a Mercedes) or to denigrate the competing product. Despite the hesitations, comparative advertising is now permitted, and the policy of the courts seems to be in favour of the practice. The boundaries of the law, however, are constantly being tested by traders.

15.124   There are two main sources for the rules on comparative advertising. One is the TMA 1994 and the other is the EC Directive on Comparative Advertising.

Trade Marks Act 1994

15.125   Under section 10(6) of the TMA 1994 a trader is given a defence for the use of a trade mark in a comparative advertising campaign. In order to take advantage of the defence the comparative advertiser must show that the trade mark is used for the purpose of identifying the goods or services of the proprietor or licensee; that the use is in accordance with honest practices in industrial or commercial matters; and that the use does not, without due cause, take unfair advantage of, and is not detrimental to, the distinctive character or repute of the trade mark.[294]

EC Directive on Misleading and Comparative Advertising

15.126   In 1997, EC Directive 97/55/EEC on Misleading and Comparative Advertising (amending an earlier Directive[295]) required member states to permit comparative advertising under the conditions in Article 3a. The provisions concerning misleading and comparative advertising were codified in Directive 2006/114/EC which came into force in December 2007.[296] The conditions for comparative advertising, which are exhaustive,[297] are set out in Article 4:

It is not misleading within the meaning of Articles 2(b), 3, and 8(1) of this Directive or Articles 6 and 7 of Directive 2005/29/EC of the European Parliament and of the Council of 11 May 2005 concerning

---

[293] Case C-44/01 [2004] All ER (EC) 1156, [2004] 1 CMLR 39, [2003] ECR I-3095, para 36. See the discussion on passing off in para 17.49.

[294] TMA 1994, s 10(6).   [295] Directive 84/450/EEC.

[296] The Directive includes provisions from the Unfair Commercial Practices Directive 2005/29/EC. Case C-44/01 *Pippig Augenoptik v Hartlauer* [2004] All ER (EC) 1156, [2004] 1 CMLR 39, [2003] ECR I-3095.

[297] Case C159/09 *Lidl SNC v Vierzon Distribution SA*, para 22.

unfair business-to-consumer commercial practices in the internal market ('Unfair Commercial Practices Directive') if:

- it compares goods or services meeting the same needs or intended for the same purpose;

- it objectively compares one or more material, relevant, verifiable, and representative features of those goods and services, which may include price;

- it does not discredit or denigrate the trade marks, trade names, other distinguishing marks, goods, services, activities, or circumstances of a competitor;

- for products with designation of origin, it relates in each case to products with the same designation;

- it does not take unfair advantage of the reputation of a trade mark, trade name, or other distinguishing marks of a competitor or of the designation of origin of competing products;[298]

- it does not present goods or services as imitations or replicas of goods or services bearing a protected trade mark or trade name;

- it does not create confusion among traders, between the advertiser and a competitor, or between the advertiser's trade marks, trade names, other distinguishing marks, goods or services and those of a competitor.

Comparative advertising is defined as 'any advertising which explicitly or by implication identifies a competitor or goods or services offered by a competitor.'

15.127   The ECJ has said that the test, as regards the comparative nature of advertising, is that it identifies, explicitly or by implication, a competitor or goods or services offered by a competitor. It is sufficient that a representation be made in any form which refers, even by implication, to a competitor or to the goods or services on offer.[299]

Web link

You can find a copy of the codifying Directive 2006/114/EC at http://www.eur-lex.europa.eu/ LexUriServ/site/en/oj/2006/l_376/l_37620061227en00210027.pdf.

The relationship between the Trade Marks Act and Comparative Advertising Directive

15.128   In *O2 Holdings Ltd, O2 (UK) Ltd v Hutchison 3G Ltd*[300] (see also the discussion in para 15.38) the question arose as to whether, to be non-infringing under the TMA 1994, a comparative advertisement must also comply with the Comparative Advertising Directive. The High Court came to the conclusion that the Directive harmonised those circumstances in which comparative advertising is permitted, 'whether comparative advertising is lawful is to be determined "solely" in accordance with the Directive.' On the relationship between section 10(6) of the TMA 1994 and the Directive, the court concluded that the 1994 Act: 'must be interpreted as permitting comparative advertising, so long as it is conducted in accordance with honest practices, as those practices have been defined for the purposes of the Comparative

---

[298] In Case C-59/05 *Siemens AG v VIPA Gesellschaft für Visualisierung und Prozeßautomatisierung GmbH*, the ECJ found, in the circumstances of the case, that the use by a competing supplier of a manufacturer's distinguishing mark known in specialist circles does not take unfair advantage of the reputation of the distinguishing mark.

[299] Case C-112/99 *Toshiba Europe v Katun Germany* [2001] ECR I-7945, paras 29–31. See also the opinion of the AG in Case C-381/05 *De Landtsheer Emmanuel SA v Comité Interprofessionnel du Vin de Champagne*, para 28. The use of a strapline 'Be a real specsaver' was not a comparative advertisement but an infringing use of a mark. *Specsavers International Healthcare Ltd v Asda Stores Ltd* [2012] EWCA Civ 24.

[300] *O2 Holdings Ltd, O2 (UK) Ltd v Hutchison 3G Ltd* [2006] ETMR 55, [2006] EWHC 534 (Ch).

Advertising Directive. Accordingly, in my judgment the defence under s.10(6) [of the TMA 1994], in the case of comparative advertising, is the same defence as the defence under the Comparative Advertising Directive itself'.[301]

When in the Court of Appeal, that court considered the defences in Article 6(1)(b) of the Directive rather than section 10(6) of the TMA 1994. While it was considered that the former dovetailed with the provisions in the Comparative Advertising Directive in that any comparison would be an indication concerning the kind, quality, quantity, etc of the goods or service, and that any advertisement that was not compliant with Article 3a of the Comparative Advertising Directive would not be in accordance with honest practices, section 10(6) was called 'a pointless provision' which 'should be repealed as an unnecessary distraction in an already complicated branch of the law'.[302]

Questions from the *O2* case were referred to the ECJ.[303] In dealing with the Directive and the Comparative Advertising Directive the Court said that in order to reconcile the protection of registered marks and the use of comparative advertising, Article 5(1) and (2) of Directive 89/104 and Article 3a(1) of Directive 84/450 mean that the proprietor of a registered mark may not prevent use by a third party of an identical or similar sign in a comparative advertisement which satisfied the conditions of Article 3a(1)[304] which is an independent ground of defence.[305] However, where there is a likelihood of confusion through the use of the sign in the comparative advertisement, then the conditions in Article 3a(1) could not be met.

Comparative advertising and the function of a mark

15.129   This jurisprudence on the interrelationship between the Comparative Advertising Directive and the Trade Marks Directive deals also with the function of the mark and whether that is jeopardised. So in *L'Oreal v Bellure*[306] the same question arose but this time in relation to identical marks rather than similar marks as in *O2*. The ECJ noted the interrelationship between the Trade Marks Directive and Comparative Advertising Directive laid out previously. It went on to state that the exclusive right under Article 5(1)(a) was conferred to ensure that the trade mark can fulfil its functions.

> These functions include not only the essential function of the trade mark, which is to guarantee to consumers the origin of the goods or services, but also its other functions, in particular that of guaranteeing the quality of the goods or services in question and those of communication, investment or advertising.[307]

So it would seem that the extended functions of a mark are relevant to determine infringement where marks and goods/services are identical—at least in comparative advertising cases. In the instant case it was for the referring court to decide whether the comparative advertising in question was such as to affect one of the extended functions.

 Exercise

Read the *O2* and *L'Oreal* cases. What do you think of the view the various courts have come to on the interrelationship between the practice of comparative advertising, the Comparative Advertising Directive, the Trade Mark Directive and section 10(6) of the TMA 1994?

---

[301] *O2 Holdings*, para 170.   [302] *O2 Holdings*, para 58.
[303] Case C-533/06 *O2 Holdings Ltd v Hutchison 3G UK Ltd* [2008] 3 CMLR 14, [2008] ETMR 55, [2008] RPC 33.
[304] *O2 Holdings* (ECJ), paras 45 and 51.   [305] *L'Oreal*, para 25.
[306] Case C-487/07.   [307] Para 58.

15.130   Once again, there had been cases which arose in front of the British courts before the *O2* and *L'Oreal* cases in which they showed themselves willing to accept the practice of comparative advertising albeit within certain parameters.[308]

■ ***Barclays Bank plc v RBS Advanta*** **[1996] RPC 307**

RBS Advanta advertised a new credit card and in the advertisement made adverse comparisons with Barclaycard and in so doing used the registered trade mark. The court refused to grant an injunction considering that the primary objective of section 10(6) of the 1994 Act was to allow comparative advertising as long as the use of the competitor's mark would be considered honest by a reasonable audience. Honesty was to be tested against what was reasonably to be expected of advertisements for that kind of goods or services by the relevant public.

■ ***Vodafone Group plc and Vodafone Ltd v Orange Personal Communications*** **[1997] FSR 34**

Orange launched an advertising campaign which proclaimed that Orange users saved £20 per month in comparison to Vodafones's equivalent tariffs. The court found that the advertisement was neither malicious nor false. It was shown that the calculation of the figures used was fair and the advertisement was not misleading. Accordingly, the claim for trade mark infringement failed.

15.131   It can be seen how important this question of fairness is in connection with comparative advertising. One case that might be considered to be on the margins is *British Airways plc v Ryanair Ltd*.[309] An advertisement by Ryanair headed 'Expensive BA _ _ _ _ DS' and 'Expensive BA' was found to constitute honest comparative advertising. In considering the actual wording of the slogan itself, the court found that this amounted to no more than vulgar abuse.

15.132   There are those traders who overstep the boundaries, and the courts have shown themselves willing to step in to moderate the practice particularly where false representations may be made in the comparison.

■ ***Emaco Ltd v Dyson Appliances Ltd*** **[1999] ETMR 903**

Both parties alleged trade mark infringement in relation to a flyer and graph in which vacuum cleaners manufactured by the other party were described unfavourably. The court found that although neither the graph nor the flyer had been published maliciously, they both contained a number of false representations and were thoroughly misleading. On an objective test this was 'otherwise than in accordance with honest practices in industrial or commercial matters'.[310]

Key points on comparative advertising

- The provisions permitting Comparative Advertising are to be found in Directive 2006/114/EC
- Courts seem generally in favour of comparative advertising where it is considered honest by a reasonable audience

---

[308] Note also from the ECJ Case C159/09 *Lidl SNC v Vierzon Distribution SA*. Price comparisons can be used for comparative advertisements.

[309] [2001] ETMR 24, [2001] FSR 32.

[310] See also *Cable & Wireless plc v British Telecommunications plc* [1998] FSR 383. On price comparisons see Case C-356/04 *Lidl Belgium GmbH & Co KG v Etablissementen Franz Colruyt NV; Kingspan Group plc and another v Rockwool Ltd [2011] EWHC 250 (Ch). Note also the reference pending to the Court of Justice in Case C-657/11 Belgian Electronic Sorting Technology.*

Further reading

Books

J Phillips (ed), *Trade Marks at the Limit* (2006)

Reports

OHIM Boards of Appeal, Case law overview of cases decided during 2007, available at http://oami.
europa.eu/en/office/aspects/pdf/BoACaseLaw2007_en.pdf

Articles

JN Adams, 'Court endorses rent seeking: *Arsenal Football Club v Reed* (*Adidas-Salomon AG v Fitness Trading Ltd* en passant)' [2004] 1 IPQ 114–120

G Anagnostaras, 'The application of the harmonised standards on comparative advertising: some recent developments' (2007) 32(2) EL Rev 246–259

Z Ballantyne, 'Legal loophole: UK companies may not be able to rely on their well-known marks under the Paris Convention' (2002) 24(8) EIPR 415–417

M Boote, 'What's in a Name?' (2006) 28(6) EIPR 349–352

A Breitschaft, '*Intel, Adidas* & Co—is the jurisprudence of the European Court of Justice on dilution law in compliance with the underlying rationales and fit for the future?' [2009] EIPR 497 1

A Carboni, 'Two stripes and you're out! Added protection for trade marks with a reputation' (2004) 26(5) EIPR 229–233

N Dawson, 'Famous and well-known trade marks usurping a corner of the giant's robe' [1998] 4 IPQ 350–382

A Folliard-Monguiral, 'Coexistence in Community trade mark disputes: conditions and implications' (2006) 1(11) JIPLP 703–713

A Folliard-Monguiral and D Rogers, 'Community trade mark round-up 2011' (2012) 7(5) JIPLP 319

A Folliard-Monguiral and D Rogers, 'Community trade mark round-up 2010' (2011) 6(5) JIPLP 302

A Folliard-Monguiral and D Rogers, 'Significant 2009 case law on the Community trade mark from the Court of Justice of the European Union and the General Court' (2010) 5(5) JIPLP 306

A Folliard-Monguiral and D Rogers, 'Significant 2007 case law on the Community trade mark from the ECJ and the CFI' (2008) 3(5) JIPLP 291

A Folliard-Monguiral and D Rogers, 'Community trade mark case law round-up 2006' (2007) 2(4) JIPLP 215–233

A Griffiths, 'The trade mark monopoly: an analysis of the core zone of absolute protection under Art.5(1) (a)' [2007] 3 IPQ 312–349

S Harper and D Curley, 'Bubble confusion—the O2 decision' (2006) 28(9) EIPR 499–504

V McEvedy, 'Keywords and resales and other fair and referential uses' [2012] 3 IPQ 149–172

FW Mostert, 'When is a mark well-known?' [1997] 3 IPQ 377–383

H Norman, 'Time to blow the whistle on trade mark use' [2004] 1 IPQ 1–34

M Rimmer, 'The black label: trade mark dilution, culture jamming and the no logo movement' (2008) 5(1) SCRIPTed 70, available at http://www.law.ed.ac.uk/ahrc/script-ed/vol5-1/rimmer.asp

C Rutz, 'After *Arsenal* and *Electrocoin*: can the opinions on trade mark use be reconciled?' (2005) 36(6) IIC 682–705

N Shemtov, 'Trade mark use in Europe: revisiting *Arsenal* in the light of *Opel* and *Picasso*' (2007) 2(8) JIPLP 557

I Simon, 'Nominative use and honest practices in industrial and commercial matters—a very European history' [2007] 2 IPQ 117–147

I Simon, 'Embellishment: trade mark use triumph or decorative disaster' (2006) 28(6) *EIPR* 321–328

I Simon, 'Trade marks in trouble' (2005) 27(2) EIPR 71–75

I Simon Fhima, 'Exploring the roots of European dilution' [2012] 1 IPQ 25–38

I Simon Fhima, 'Dilution by blurring—a conceptual roadmap' [2010] 1 IPQ 44–87

WH Tatham, 'WIPO resolution on well known marks: a small step or a giant leap' [2000] 2 IPQ 127–137

B Thompson and M Woodhouse, 'Use it or lose it!' (2006) 188 TW 22–23.

P Yap, 'Making sense of trade mark use' (2007) 29(10) EIPR 420–427

Contemporary issues in trade mark law

Introduction

Scope and overview of chapter

16.1   This chapter will give an overview of three topical areas; the first is trade marks and domain names; the second is the use of trade marks on the Internet and in connection with keyword advertising and auction sites; and the third is in the related area of geographical indications. The purpose is to highlight the contemporary tensions and trends in these areas.[1]

Trade marks and domain names

Introduction

16.2   The purpose of this part of the chapter is to discuss the interaction between trade marks and domain names. While trade marks have been around for a long time, domain names have attracted public attention only since the rise in popularity of the Internet. The legal interface between trade marks and domain names has been the subject of much analysis and resulted in one of the earliest legal 'clashes' at the interface between traditional IP and the rise of new technologies. When the potential for conflict between the two first arose, there was the possibility of a wave of cross-border litigation as trade mark owners and domain name holders battled for the control of domain names. In the event, an alternative dispute resolution mechanism was established which, in terms of dealing with a large number of domain name disputes and keeping these disputes out of the courts, has been a great success. Some cases are still litigated in UK courts, primarily by reference to the law of passing off and trade marks. The area remains one of intense practical importance given the numbers of disputes that are still heard via the dispute resolution mechanism coupled with the increase in the numbers of domain names available for registration with the introduction of significant numbers of new gTLDs (generic Top Level Domains) which are due to become live in 2013 and beyond. At international policy level, its importance is illustrated by the fact that domain names are regularly on the agenda at the World Intellectual Property Organization (WIPO).[2]

---

[1] Trade marks and personality merchandising is now dealt with in Chapter 19.

[2] Eg the General Assembly meeting agenda for October 2009. The Standing Committee on the Law of Trade Marks, Industrial Designs and Geographical Indications regularly reports on trade marks and the internet generally, and trade marks and domain names in particular. Eg the 24th Session, Geneva, 1–4 November 2010.

16.3   Having explained the basis for the disputes between trade marks and domain names and considered how the law of trade marks has been applied by domestic courts to these disputes, the alternative dispute mechanism developed to cope with disagreements over domain names and trade marks will be described followed by discussion on future developments.

The rest of this part contains the following sections:

- What is a domain name? (16.5–16.6)
- The registration of a domain name as a trade mark (16.7–16.8)
- Conflicts over domain names and trade marks (16.9–16.11)
- Resolution of disputes (16.12–16.27)

16.4

Learning objectives

By the end of this part of the chapter you should be able to describe and explain:

- the constituent parts of a domain name;
- how conflicts arise between trade marks and domain names;
- the application of trade mark law to domain name disputes in the British courts;
- the operation of the UDRP to domain name disputes.

What is a domain name?

16.5   A domain name is part of the address of the location of a site on the Internet. For instance, harrods.com is the domain name of the London department store, Harrods. The portion of the address taken by 'harrods' is sometimes the part that equates to the registered (or unregistered) trade mark of the person seeking to use the domain name: for instance, 'virgin' or 'caesars-palace'. The next part is the top level domain (TLD)—.com, .net, and .org are all gTLDs. Until 2000 these were the main generic gTLDs. Over the ensuing years new gTLDs were approved by the Internet body Internet Corporation for Assigned Names and Numbers (ICANN), for example aero, .biz, .cat, .com, .coop, .info, .jobs, .mobi, .museum, .name, .net, .org, .pro, and .travel. Agreement has been reached on the introduction of new gTLDs, including Internationalised Domain Names (IDNs) (those which use local language characters or equivalents). The process for selecting these has started although it is as yet unknown how many may result—with some estimates suggesting there could be many thousands of new gTLDs and IDNs created over the coming years.[3] There are also Country Code Top Level Domains (ccTLDs) which include .uk, .de, and .fr and more recently a .eu domain.[4] Different rules apply to registration of a domain name in the gTLDs[5] and the ccTLDs.[6]

---

[3] There were 1,930 applications for new gTLDs as of September 2012.

[4] For information see http://www.eurid.eu/en/. The reservation of the domain name 'galileo.eu' by the Commission was challenged by Galileo Lebensmittel GmbH but the application was declared inadmissible by the ECJ on the ground that the applicant was not directly and individually concerned: Case C-483/07 P *Galileo Lebensmittel GmbH & Co KG v Commission of the European Communities*. A licensee may not register an .eu doman on behalf of an organisation registered and carrying on business outwith the EU: Case C- 376/11 *Pie Optiek*.

[5] For Nominet's rules see http://www.nominet.org.uk/uk-domain-names/registering-uk-domain/choosing-domain-name/rules.

[6] For links to the eligibility criteria in each of the gTLDs, see http://www.icann.org/udrp/.

16.6   The .com, .net, and.org gTLDs are 'open' in the sense that any business or individual can make an application to register a domain name using those gTLDs. The policy is broadly to register on a first comem first served basis. It is, however, different for the newer or sponsored gTLDs, each of which has a number of rules attached to registration. For instance, the .biz gTLD must be used primarily for bona fide business or commercial purposes and not exclusively for personal use; while the .name gTLD is intended to be for individual use. Most registries operate dispute resolution policies in the event of a conflict between the holder of a trade mark and the holder of a domain name. Those who register in the gTLDs all operate the same dispute resolution policy[7] which is known as the ICANN Uniform Domain Name Dispute Resolution Policy (UDRP)[8] and has been in operation since late 1999. Nominet, the register for the .uk ccTLD, has had a dispute resolution procedure in place since December 2001, the terms of which were updated in July 2009.[9]

Web links

You will find much information about ICANN at **http://www.icann.org**.

Each domain name is maintained by a registry (eg .name is managed by www.nic.name, .uk is managed by Nominet www.nominet.org.uk). Applications for registration of a domain names are made by competing registrars. To become a registrar for the gTLDs, accreditation is required from ICANN. There are also resellers of domain names (go to Google and type in 'domain name reseller' for examples) which may also offer hosting facilities to clients. You can check to see if a domain name is registered in a number of the cc or gTLDs by going to **http://www.internic.net/whois.html** or **http://www.whois.net**.

 Exercise

Try seeing if SCRIPT is available as a domain name in any of the gTLDs.

The registration of a domain name as a trade mark

16.7   The question of whether an Internet address which includes 'www' (as opposed to a domain name) can be registered as a Community trade mark (CTM) has been considered by OHIM. In *Nationsbanc Montgomery Securities LLC's Application*[10] the application by Nationsbanc to register http://www.prime-broker.com in connection with goods and services in class 9 (computer hardware and software) and class 42 (online services) was refused on the grounds that it was devoid of distinctive character. The appeal was dismissed. It was found that the trade mark as a whole represented an email address. The element 'www' represented the 'world wide web' and '.com' a top level domain name. The whole sign was likely to be seen by the relevant public as an electronic mail address for a broker engaged in the services set out in the application and not in any way distinctive.

---

[7] http://www.icann.org.   [8] For the policy, see http://www.icann.org/udrp/.

[9] Substantive changes included clarification of the wording to make it clear that rights can exist in descriptive terms that have acquired a secondary meaning; confirmation that some activities are not in and of themselves abusive registration; the introduction of a likelihood of confusion factor and made clear that threatened use of a domain name may be evidence of an abusive registration.

[10] [2000] ETMR 245.

16.8 Despite this ruling, domain names have been registered as CTMs, albeit with added material rendering the domain name distinctive, such as http://www.bigsave.com shown in Figure 16.1.[11]

Figure 16.1 www.bigsave.com

The UK International Property Office (IPO; or UK–IPO) issued a Practice Amendment Notice[12] (a statement of the practice that will be followed at the IPO) in which they said that subject to the usual criteria of the Trade Marks Act 1994 (TMA 1994 Act), the Office will permit domain names to be registered as trade marks. The TLD part of the domain name (.com or .uk) is, however, considered to be totally non-distinctive. Therefore consideration is given to whether the remainder of the mark is descriptive or non-distinctive. If that is the case, then registration may be refused under section 3(1)(b) of the TMA 1994.

As a result of this policy, a number of domain names have been registered as illustrated in Figure 16.2. For instance:

Figure 16.2 www.bags123.com

with the text 'www.bags123.com'.[13]

> ### Key point on registering a domain name as a trade mark
>
> • A domain name can be registered as a trade mark although the gTLD or ccTLD will be considered non-distinctive

Conflicts over domain names and trade marks

16.9 Disputes over ownership of domain names have arisen for a number of reasons. A domain name has been considered as akin to a trade mark (whether registered or unregistered). Therefore those who

---

[11] CTM No 1632140, proprietor: Bigsave.com Ltd.

[12] PAN 1/08. See BL O/008/07 Application by FSTC Ltd Foundation for Science Technology and Civilisation, for the mark MuslimHeritage.com, and the decision of the Second Board of Appeal Case R 338/2006-2, DNI Holdings Ltd for the mark Sportsbetting.com.

[13] In class 35. Interestingly, the specification is 'The bringing together, for the benefit of others, of a variety of goods, enabling customers to conveniently view and purchase those goods from an Internet website specialising in the marketing of luggage, fashion handbags, and leather goods'. UK TM No 2268716, proprietor: Boros Leathergoods Ltd.

own the mark for the non-Internet business will wish to use the same name on the Internet: it is seen as a valuable addition to the branding of goods and services, or of the business as a whole. However, as discussed previously, trade mark law is territorial whereas the Internet is global. Therefore different businesses trading under the same mark in various parts of the world may have what they consider to be the same legitimate claim to a particular domain name. As no two domain names can be identical, only one business can have a particular name. 'prince.com' is a good example in that it was the subject of a dispute between Prince plc in the UK and Prince Sports Inc in the United States. Prince plc registered the domain name first and was challenged by Prince Sports Inc.[14] The name remained with Prince plc. This type of dispute might be viewed as 'domain name envy'.

16.10   Disputes have also arisen where Internet users, with a degree of entrepreneurial spirit, have registered domain names which are the same as or very similar to the trading name or registered trade mark of a company that is well known or famous, or which has a reputation. Generally the intent has been to do one of two things. One option might be to offer it to the owner of the registered trade mark or trading company in return for some payment. Alternatively, if it is a name that is similar to a well-known name, such as porschegirls.com, the intention might be to use the domain name in an effort, not necessarily to confuse, but to draw people to the site. In other words, to draw on the magnetism that attaches to the mark. The name that has been given to this type of activity is 'domain name hijacking' or more commonly *'cyber-squatting'*. Parallels can be seen with the notion of dilution discussed in Chapter 15.

16.11   And finally, there are the disputes where the owners of trade marks who have aggressively pursued policies to prevent other Internet participants from using any rendition of a name that includes or alludes to their registered trade mark, in some cases quite unjustifiably. This is sometimes termed *reverse domain name hijacking*.

 Question 1

There is a Mrs McDonald who lives in the Highlands of Scotland and operates a small bed and breakfast. McDonald is also the name of an electrical distributor in Florida, of a garden centre in France, and of a multi-national corporation which sells, among other things, beefburgers. Who should own the domain name mcdonald.com?

Question 2

What are the most common types of disputes that arise as between domain names and trade marks?

Resolution of disputes

16.12   There have been remarkably few domain name disputes that have been referred to the UK courts for resolution. This may be for a number of reasons:

- First, many domain names disputes which arise concerning the gTLDs are referred to the ICANN UDRP (discussed later). For disputes concerning the ccTLDs, many registrars operate

---

[14] *Prince plc v Prince Sports Group Inc* [1998] FSR 21.

dispute resolution policies of their own (eg Nominet in the UK). Some ccTLD registrars have adopted the UDRP on a voluntary basis.

- Secondly, one of the earliest cases, *BT v One in a Million*[15] made clear the disapproval of the court of the practice of *cyber-squatting*. This may have resulted in similar cases being settled out of court.

- Finally, it is very expensive to take a case to court. Either of the parties to a potential dispute may not have the means to fund expensive litigation. By comparison, using the ICANN UDRP or one of the cc dispute resolution procedures is relatively cheap.[16]

Resolution of disputes in British courts

Trade Marks Act 1994, section 10(1)

16.13   Of those disputes that have been heard in the UK courts, section 10(1) of the TMA 1994 was considered in *Avnet Inc v Isoact Limited (Avnet)*[17] (see also the discussion of this case in para 15.31). Avnet Inc, a US company, ran a business selling goods by catalogue and in so doing carried advertisements for different manufacturers.[18] It registered the trade mark 'Avnet' in the UK in class 35 for advertising and promotional services. Isoact Ltd, by contrast was an Internet service provider with a particular interest in aviation. It used the words 'Aviation Network' and 'Avnet' in connection with its interests. Isoact Ltd registered the domain name 'avnet.co.uk' and allowed customers to display their own advertisements on their site.

Avnet argued that Isoact infringed its registered trade mark by using the word 'avnet' in its domain name. Section 10(1) of the TMA 1994 was relied upon as the ground of infringement. So Avnet Inc argued that the sign used by Isoact was *identical* to its registered mark and used in connection with *identical* goods and services. Jacob J disagreed with Avnet. Judgment was given purely by looking to the terms of what was covered by the registration of the mark 'Avnet'. Jacob J decided that in substance Isoact were not providing advertising and promotional services within class 35 of the Trade Mark Register, but rather provided the services of an Internet service provider. These activities would (if registered) probably fall within class 42. In other words, the services provided were different. Therefore there was no infringement under section 10(1) and Isoact had a right to keep and use the domain name.

16.14   For anyone who alleges infringement of their trade mark through the use by another of a domain name, and relying on section 10(1) of the TMA 1994, the specification of the goods and services in connection with which the mark is registered is going to have to be identical with that used in connection with the domain name. If this is not the case, there will be no infringement under section 10(1).

 Question

Would the mark have to be absolutely identical with the domain name for section 10(1) of the TMA 1994 to be relevant, or might slight variations in the mark and the name be permitted? See paras 15.25ff for a discussion on what is meant by the identity of marks.

---

[15] [1999] 4 All ER 476, [1999] RPC 1.
[16] Where they do reach court now it is generally part of a wider dispute; eg *Evans and Evans v Focal Point Fires* [2009] EWCH 2784 (Ch); *Toth v Emirates & Anor* [2012] EWHC 517 (Ch).
[17] [1998] FSR 16.
[18] Jacob J doubted that this activity actually fell within class 35 of the Trade Mark Register and thought the activity was more akin to retail sales, but did not decide the point.

Trade Marks Act 1994, section 10(2)

16.15   Section 10(2) of the TMA 1994 was considered in *Phones4U Ltd v Phone4u.co.uk Ltd*[19] albeit, for the reasons explained later, it was found that there was no infringement of this section. Phones4U Ltd had been in business for a number of years. Mr Heykali, who had no connection with Phones4U Ltd, registered the domain name phone4u.co.uk. Phones4U Ltd alleged passing off and trade mark infringement. The High Court had found that passing off had not been established—a finding which was overturned in the Court of Appeal. Infringement of the registered trade mark was also considered. Phones4u Ltd had registered its trade mark in 1999[20] in the form of a logo. It included the statement that 'the mark is limited to the colours red, white and blue'. The key question was the effect of this limitation.

Section 13 of the 1994 Act describes the limitation of a mark as follows:

(1) An applicant for registration of a trade mark, or the proprietor of a registered trade mark, may—
  (a) disclaim any right to the exclusive use of any specified element of the trade mark, or
  (b) agree that the rights conferred by the registration shall be subject to a specified territorial or other limitation; and where the registration of a trade mark is subject to a disclaimer or limitation, the rights conferred by section 9 (rights conferred by registered trade mark) are restricted accordingly.
(2) Provision shall be made by rules as to the publication and entry in the register of a disclaimer or limitation.

The reason for including the limitation was that when the application was made for registration, the Registry had taken the view that the sign was not distinctive in black and white. The addition of the limitation made the non-distinctive sign distinctive for the purposes of registration. The Court of Appeal found that section 13 meant that the rights in the logo mark were limited to the colours red, white, and blue.[21] As a result, there was no infringement of section 10(2) of the TMA 1994 by the registration of the domain name Phone4u.co.uk. Had the limitation not been included, then the registered mark would have been infringed. The Court of Appeal noted that where a mark had been registered through the inclusion of a limitation to make that mark distinctive, but later and through use the mark gained a broader distinctive appeal (distinctive through use), then the mark with wider rights could be registered.[22]

16.16   This holding clearly places quite a significant restriction on marks subject to a limitation where it is alleged, as in this case, that the registration and use of a similar domain name infringes the registered mark under section 10(2) of the TMA 1994. Although the courts seem willing to find passing off to be proved in these type of domain name cases (as was the position in the instant case), trade mark owners may want the comfort of being able to rely on the law of registered trade marks. As a result, where marks have been registered with a limitation, owners would do well to consider whether the mark has sufficient acquired distinctiveness to make a further application for registration of the mark without the limitation.

16.17   Section 10(2) of the TMA 1994 was also considered in *Ellerman Investments Ltd v Elizabeth C-Vanci*[23] where, in an application for summary judgment, the court found that domain names including ritzypoker.co.uk, ritzypoker.net, ritzpoker.org, ritzpoker.info, and ritzpoker.biz to be confusingly similar to the claimant's registered trade mark 'Ritz' registered as a UK and CTM for, inter alia, gaming services.

---

[19] [2006] EWCA Civ 244, [2007] RPC 5. See the discussion on passing off and domain names at para 17.62.
[20] No 2185824 as of the date 8 January 1999.
[21] See also the discussion on limitations and disclaimers in the High Court in *L'Oréal SA and others v Bellure NV and others* [2006] EWHC 2355 (Ch), paras 84–90. *Nestlé SA's Trade Mark Application* [2005] RPC 5, [2004] EWCA Civ 1008. *Imagination Technologies Ltd v OHIM* [2008] ETMR 10, in which the CFI stated that where a mark contains an element that is not distinctive and its inclusion might give rise to doubts about the scope of protection, the OHIM may request as a condition of registration that the applicant disclaims rights to the element (para 63).
[22] Para 57.   [23] [2006] EWHC 1442 (Ch).

Trade Marks Act 1994, section 10(3)

16.18   Section 10(3) of TMA 1994 has been considered in a number of cases including *BT v One in a Million*[24] and *Global Projects Management Ltd v Citigroup Inc and others*.[25]

16.19   In *One in a Million*[26] a number of domain names including marksandspencer.com, bt.org, and britisht-elecommunication.net were registered by, among others, One in a Million. These they, inter alia, offered for sale to the claimants. The case was decided primarily by looking to the law of passing off, and by some extension of existing principles the court determined that by registering the domain names the defendants had created *instruments of fraud*.[27] Thus the domain names had to be handed back to the trade mark and brand owners. The judgment has been criticised.[28] It is said that the bounds of the tort of passing off were extended—by implication possibly too far; and that it is not at all clear that even if a case of passing off is made out, that would necessarily provide the remedy required.

In dealing with section 10(3), the court was relatively brief as to its application of the law to the facts. In the High Court it had been said that on the detriment requirement under section 10(3): 'It seems to me to be equally clear that the defendant's use of it is detrimental to the trade mark, if only by damaging the plaintiff's exclusivity'. This was confirmed in the Court of Appeal where it was said 'The domain names were registered to take advantage of the distinctive character and reputation of the marks. That is unfair and detrimental'. There was thus infringement under this section.

16.20   Although the case did not do much to aid understanding of the law of trade marks in relation to these types of disputes, consideration was given to the ruling in the following case.

■ *Global Projects Management v Citigroup* [2005] EWHC 2663 (Ch)

In this case the High Court was faced with a scenario where an individual registered citigroup.co.uk after an announcement had been made concerning the merger of two financial companies to form Citigroup Inc. The court referred extensively to *BT v One in a Million*, but went further in that it found against Global Projects Management even though no attempt had been made to sell the domain name to Citigroup or anyone else, nor was there any evidence of a track record of cyber-squatting (as there had been in *BT v One in a Million*). The court said that the mere registration and maintenance in force of a domain name which led people to believe that the holder of the domain name was linked with a person was enough to make the domain name a potential 'instrument of fraud' and amounted to passing off.[29] As with *BT v One in a Million*, the court did not consider infringement of section 10(3) in detail merely saying that: 'It is admitted that Citicorp is the holder of registered trade marks of which one is the name and mark "Citigroup", and that GPM, by virtue of obtaining and maintaining in force the citigroup.co.uk domain name, has used or may use a sign which is similar to the registered mark, and which is used in relation to services that are not similar to those for which the trademark is registered. Thus far, paras (b) and (c) of s.10(3) are satisfied'.[30] The court noted that interesting arguments had been raised to suggest that not all of the rest of the conditions in section 10(3) were satisfied, but that the arguments were contrary to

---

[24] [1999] 4 All ER 476, [1999] RPC 1.   [25] [2006] FSR 39, [2005] EWHC 2663 (Ch).

[26] [1999] 4 All ER 476, [1999] RPC 1.

[27] See also *Radio Taxicab (London) Ltd v Owner Drivers Radio Taxis Services* [2004] RPC 19 (Ch D), 12 October 2001, Chancery Division TLC 1024/00; *Phones 4U Ltd v Phone4U.co.uk Internet Ltd* [2005] EWHC 334 (Ch); *Easyjet Airline Co Ltd v Dainty (t/a EasyRealestate)* [2002] FSR 6 (Ch D).

[28] See, eg, C Thorne and S Bennett, 'Domain dames—Internet warehousing: Has protection of well-known names on the Internet gone too far?' [1998] *EIPR* 468.

[29] *Global Projects Management Ltd v Citigroup Inc* [2006] FSR 39, [2005] EWHC 2663 (Ch), para 40.

[30] *Global Projects Management*, para 58.

the holding in *One in a Million*. It therefore found that Citigroup were entitled to summary judgment on this claim.

16.21   The courts have made clear their dislike of these practices but have not really elaborated on how section 10(3) of the TMA 1994 is relevant to the facts. How, for instance, could the section be relevant when the trade mark was not actually *used* (eg offered for sale), but merely registered? To what extent does mere registration of the domain name *free-ride* upon or *dilute* an existing mark with a reputation?

16.22   What is interesting is reliance on the creation of an *instrument of fraud* as a basis of liability rather than registered trade mark law. Clearly, registered trade mark law can only be relevant where there is a registered trade mark in existence. Nevertheless, in both *One in a Million* and *Global Projects Management*, the courts found much safer ground in the related area of passing off. This does have the merit that there is less need to stretch the boundaries of trade mark law in directions to which it may be little suited. That is not, however, to say that trade mark law is not used in negotiations between parties arguing for transfer or retention of a domain name.[31]

Key points on resolution of disputes in British courts

- Section 10(1), (2), and (3) of the TMA 1994 have all been used by the courts as a basis for settling domain name disputes
- The proper boundaries for finding of infringement of section 10(3) of the TMA 1994 in domain name disputes are at present unclear

---

 Question

How do you think traditional trade mark law, and in particular s 10(3) of the TMA 1994, should apply to domain name disputes, if indeed it should?

Resolution of disputes under the ICANN UDRP

16.23   A reason why not many disputes may have been heard in the courts is because numerous cases are referred for resolution to the ICANN UDRP (or to one of the cc dispute resolution registrars). As mentioned previously, the ICANN UDRP applies to domain names registered in the gTLDs.[32] The rules governing dispute resolution were drawn up as a result of a document initially prepared by WIPO following a series of meetings with interested parties around the globe and then amended by ICANN.

The important part of the dispute policy is to be found in Article 4 (where 'you' have registered the domain name that is contested by the complainant).

---

[31]   For a case basing itself on free speech arguments, see *Patel v Allos Therapeutics Inc* 2008 WL 2442985 (Ch).

[32]   Individual countries may, however, elect to use one of the arbitration providers under the ICANN UDRP and to apply the terms of the UDRP to registrations in their ccTLDs. Eg Trinidad and Tobago .tt and Ecuador .ec (http://www.wipo.int/amc/en/domains/cctld/index.html).

4 a. Applicable Disputes. You are required to submit to a mandatory administrative proceeding in the event that a third party (a 'complainant') asserts to the applicable Provider, in compliance with the Rules of Procedure, that

(i) your domain name is identical or confusingly similar to a trademark or service mark in which the complainant has rights; and

(ii) you have no rights or legitimate interests in respect of the domain name; and

(iii) your domain name has been registered and is being used in bad faith.

In the administrative proceeding, the complainant must prove that each of these three elements are present.

b. Evidence of Registration and Use in Bad Faith. For the purposes of Paragraph 4(a)(iii), the following circumstances, in particular but without limitation, if found by the Panel to be present, shall be evidence of the registration and use of a domain name in bad faith:

(i) circumstances indicating that you have registered or you have acquired the domain name primarily for the purpose of selling, renting, or otherwise transferring the domain name registration to the complainant who is the owner of the trademark or service mark or to a competitor of that complainant, for valuable consideration in excess of your documented out-of-pocket costs directly related to the domain name; or

(ii) you have registered the domain name in order to prevent the owner of the trademark or service mark from reflecting the mark in a corresponding domain name, provided that you have engaged in a pattern of such conduct; or

(iii) you have registered the domain name primarily for the purpose of disrupting the business of a competitor; or

(iv) by using the domain name, you have intentionally attempted to attract, for commercial gain, Internet users to your web site or other on-line location, by creating a likelihood of confusion with the complainant's mark as to the source, sponsorship, affiliation, or endorsement of your web site or location or of a product or service on your web site or location.[33]

16.24   Each of the competing registrars authorised to register domain names in the gTLDs[34] must sign up to this dispute resolution process.[35] Those who register domain names then agree to be bound when registering a domain name. At the time of writing, four providers are accredited as recognised to hear disputes arising under this dispute resolution process:[36] WIPO, the National Arbitration Forum (NAF), the Asian Domain Name Dispute Resolution Centre (ADNDRC), and the Czech Arbitration Court.[37] In December 2001 eResolution withdrew from providing services under the UDRP followed by CPR (the International Institute for Conflict Prevention and Resolution) in January 2007.

 Question

Why did eRes withdraw from providing arbitration services under the ICANN UDRP?

- Have a look at:

- M Geist, 'Fair.com?: an examination of the allegations of systemic unfairness in the ICANN UDRP', **http://aix1.uottawa.ca/~geist/geistudrp.pdf** and 'Fundamentally Fair.com? An update on bias allegations and the ICANN UDRP', **http://aix1.uottawa.ca/~geist/fairupdate.pdf**.

---

[33] http://www.icann.org/udrp/udrp-policy-24oct99.htm.

[34] For details see http://www.icann.org/registrar-reports/accredited-list.html.

[35] A full list of these registries can be found at http://www.icann.org.   [36] http://www.icann.org.

[37] The ADR.eu Centre is attached to the Czech Arbitration Court. For a hearing concerning the .eu domain, see *Game Group plc v First Internet Technology Ltd* Case 04014 ADR [2007] ETMR 78.

- M Mueller, 'Rough justice: an analysis of ICANN's Uniform Dispute Resolution Policy', **http://www.acm.org/usacm/IG/roughjustice.pdf**.

- MS Donahey, 'The UDRP: fundamentally fair, but far from perfect' (2001) 6(34) Electronic Commerce & Law Reports (August 29), available at **http://www.scottdonahey.com/ Publications/UDRP_far_from_perfect.pdf**.

- See also A Kur, 'A study on the UDRP' at **http://www.zar.kit.edu/DATA/projekte/ udrp_705937a.pdf**.

16.25 While statistics giving details of the absolute numbers of proceedings are difficult to come by, WIPO holds statistics on the cases heard through their system which show increases year on year in the number of domain names in dispute to 2010 where the numbers may be levelling,[38] with 2,627 to the date of writing in 2012 (September) involving an average of 1.76 domain names per case.[39] These names included generic names such as Allocation, concierge, and cello, place names such as Barcelona and Heathrow, personal names such as BillyConnolly, Madonna, and Juliaroberts, business names such as BankofNewZealand and Easyjet, and additions such as Directlinesucks, Easymaterial, and Nokiagirls.

Web link

WIPOs Arbitration and Mediation Centre have developed a most useful search tool for domain name disputes available at **http://www.wipo.int/amc/en/domains/search/legalindex.jsp**.

In addition, WIPO has compiled an overview of WIPO Panel Views on selected UDRP questions available at **http://www.wipo.int/amc/en/domains/search/overview/**.

16.26 Looking to the cases, a number of broad factors can be suggested which tend to militate against the respondent and, if found, could mean that the domain name is transferred to the complainant— although it should be noted that there are inconsistencies in approach. Important factors (UDRP, Art 4) include whether the respondent has offered the domain name for sale: this is likely to be frowned upon, particularly if the sum is large.[40] Registering more than one domain name can be seen as an indication of the intention to profit from that name.[41] Failure to develop a website using the name can also cost the respondent the name, being seen as an indication of bad faith.[42]

16.27 While it is not the intention to discuss the cases in detail, it should be noted that the process represents an interesting exercise in Internet self-regulation—a solution to a global problem that was escalating, and which appeared to have no reasonable resolution on a national basis. Taking the disputes away from individual territories and trade mark laws has meant that a body of decisions has been developed specific to these disputes, however difficult it may be to draw consistent lessons. As noted, disputes may still be referred to national courts, and indeed a number are so referred resulting in a body of decisions which are interesting for their insights into the interaction between the UDRP process and the approach of national courts. One suspects that there would be more were the costs not prohibitive.

---

[38] But this is before the introduction of the new gTLDs. See para 16.4.
[39] See http://www.wipo.int/amc/en/domains/statistics/.
[40] billyconnolly.com; chickhere.com; hotmetal.com; topdog.com; herstyle.com; bridgetjones.com.
[41] nicholekidman.com (2) danmarino.com (50) clickhere.net (250) jimihendrix (2000).   [42] zero.com, timekeeper.com.

Exercise

Investigate at least ten different decisions made by the arbitrators in the domain name disputes in each of the following categories. Choose the cases from at least three different dispute resolution providers.

Categories:

- Generic names (eg Allocation, concierge, cello)
- Place names (eg Barcelona)
- Personal names (eg BillyConnolly, Madonna)
- Business names (eg BankofNewZealand, Easyjet)
- Additions (eg Directlinesucks, Easymaterial, Nokiagirls)

Do you consider that there is consistent application of the rules in the UDRP?

Key points on resolution of disputes under the ICANN UDRP

- The number of disputes over domain names referred to the ICANN UDRP suggests that the system has been successful in minimising the volume of disputes referred to national courts
- The dispute resolution process is intended to be limited to bad faith abusive domain name registrations

The continuing importance of domain names and the issues that arise under the dispute settlement processes can be seen when considering the prominence WIPO gave to this subject in its General Assembly in Geneva in September to October 2009 where it devoted some time to considering the current state of play[43] which preceded a conference held by WIPO, '10 Years UDRP—What's next?' The contributions to the conference suggest that participants considered that the system is working but there are several areas which could be much improved including such matters as reverse domain name hijacking; matters of identity of participants; and the ever vexed question of what will happen when new gTLDs are introduced.[44]

Exercise

Read the presentations and papers from the conference '10 Years UDRP—What's next?'[45] What do you think are the most pressing problems to be faced in the UDRP over the next decade? How would you solve them?

---

[43] WIPO paper WO/GA/38/12.

[44] For full details of the conference and copies of the presentations, see http://www.wipo.int/amc/en/events/workshops/2009/10yrs-udrp/program/index.html.

[45] Available at http://www.wipo.int/amc/en/events/workshops/2009/10yrs-udrp/index.html.

The use of trade marks on the Internet and in connection with keyword advertising and auction sites

Introduction

16.28   The use of registered trade marks on the Internet raises many different questions over the inter-action of such use with registered trade mark law. One issue concerns the coexistence of marks when the same or similar mark registered for the same or similar goods is used by traders based in different countries, but where that trade mark becomes accessible in other countries by virtue of being used on webpages. Difficulties which have arisen but are less prevalent now due to the changes in the way that searches are carried out on the Internet are where trade marks are used by an unauthorised third party in metatags or in banner advertisements. More recent challenges have concerned the use of trade marks in keyword advertising campaigns and on social media. This part will discuss some of the cases that have arisen in the British courts dealing with coexistence of trade marks on the Internet; touch on the response of the courts to the use of trade marks as meta tags and in banner advertisements; briefly comment on the keyword advertising disputes which have also been dealt with in para 15.86ff and introduce some challenges for trade marks in other social media. Chapter 22 deals with questions of jurisdiction and choice of law in cross-border IP disputes including those involving trade marks.

This part contains the following sections

- Territorial scope of protection: accessibility and disclaimers (16.30–16.41)
- Keyword advertising (16.42–16.53)
- Auction sites (16.54–16.56)

16.29

> ### Learning objectives
>
> By the end of this chapter you should be able to describe and explain:
>
> - why and in what circumstances conflicts can arise over the use of trade marks on the Internet;
> - the response of the British courts to coexistence of marks on the Internet and the suggestions made by WIPO to enable coexistence of marks on the Internet;
> - how the courts have applied trade mark law to metatags, banner advertisements, and to keyword advertising.

Territorial scope of protection: accessibility and disclaimers

16.30   The scope of protection available under a trade mark is, as with any other intellectual property rights, limited to the geographical territory where protection has been obtained. The main consequence of this principle of territoriality is that a domestic court would only be able to find an infringement in the case of a domestic right being infringed. In other words, an infringing act may occur on the Internet, yet in order to be actionable, have to manifest itself as a right that subsists within the territory in respect of which action is taken. It follows from that, that there should be no automatic case of *infringement* if an identical or similar mark is used on the Internet as such. However, where different owners own identical or similar marks in different countries, and those marks are accessible in the territory where the 'competing' mark is registered, then infringement could occur. For example, if the owner of mark 'X' in country A advertises on the Internet, and mark 'X' is owned by a different person in country B for the same goods, then conflicts are likely to arise, especially if courts view mere *accessibility* of a trade mark on the Internet as infringing use.

16.31   According to EU jurisprudence, where there are the same or similar marks owned by different persons, there is no right of importation of goods bearing the mark from member state A to member state B.[46] As was pointed out by the ECJ in *IHT International Heiztechnik v Ideal Standard:*[47]

> There is no unlawful restriction on trade between member states within the meaning of Arts. 30 and 36 where a subsidiary operating in Member State A of a manufacturer established in Member State B is to be enjoined from using as a trade mark the name 'Ideal Standard' because of the risk of confusion with a device having the same origin, even if the manufacturer is lawfully using that mark in his country of origin under a trade mark protected there, he acquired that trade mark by assignment and the trade mark originally belonged to a company affiliated to the undertaking which, in Member State A, opposes the importation of goods bearing the trade mark 'Ideal Standard'.[48]

16.32   How then can valid and competing claims between unrelated traders be reconciled when those traders wish to use their registered marks on websites?

Two avenues have been suggested:

- the first deals with accessibility or use of a trade mark on the Internet, and whether mere accessibility would amount to infringement;

- the second is whether there might be room to argue for the use of disclaimers in the event that claims appear irreconcilable.

Accessibility and use of a trade mark on the Internet: British case law

16.33   In relation to the first avenue it has been suggested that the mere use of a trade mark on a website should not be sufficient to qualify as 'use' under domestic trade mark law, and thus the trade mark in the country of importation (or accessibility) would not be infringed. The relevant infringement provisions in the TMA 1994 state: 'A person infringes a registered trade mark if he *uses* in the course of trade ...' (emphasis added).[49] Thus, where 'Fairy' was a registered trade mark for washing-up liquid in the UK register and was also registered by an independent trader in the United States, also for washing-up liquid, and both advertised their products over the web, the mere accessibility of the same word in connection with the same products on websites available in the UK (in the case of the US trader) and in the United States (in the case of the British trader) would not, of itself, constitute infringement of the trade mark.

---

[46] Neither is there a right to import goods from outwith the territory of the EU and re-sell over the Internet even where the trade mark may not be seen until after the sale (1) *Kabushiki Kaisha Sony Computer Entertainment (Also T/A Sony Computer Entertainment Inc;* (2) *Sony Computer Entertainment Europe Ltd (collectively 'Sony') v Nuplayer Ltd* [2006] FSR 9, [2005] EWHC 1522 (Ch).

[47] Case C-9/93 *IHT International Heiztechnik v Ideal Standard* [1994] 3 CMLR 857, [1994] ECR I-2789, [1995] FSR 59.

[48] Case C-9/93 *IHT International Heiztechnik v Ideal Standard* [1994] 3 CMLR 857, [1994] ECR I-2789, [1995] FSR 59.

[49] Trade Marks Act 1994, s 10(1), (2), (3).

16.34   A number of UK cases have concerned this question of *use* (see also the discussion of these cases in para 23.32, note 61).

■ *1.800 Flowers Inc v Phonenames Ltd* [2000] ETMR 369, [2000] FSR 697[50]

This case concerned an appeal against a decision to register the trade mark '800 FLOWERS' in class 35 for flowers and floral products. The applicant (a US corporation) had argued that the trade mark had been used in the UK by its use on a website. The court considered that merely because an Internet website could be accessed from anywhere in the world, did not of itself mean that it should be regarded as having been *used* everywhere in the world. *Use*, for trade mark purposes, depended on all the circumstances of a particular case, particularly the intention of the owner of the website and the understanding that a person using the Internet would gain from reading the website. On the facts of this case, the applicant's use of the mark on its website did not sufficiently constitute evidence of the requisite intention to use the mark in the UK:

> So I think that the mere fact that websites can be accessed anywhere in the world does not mean, for trade mark purposes, that the law should regard them as being used everywhere in the world. It all depends upon the circumstances, particularly the intention of the website owner and what the reader will understand if he accesses the site. In other fields of law publication on a website may well amount to a universal publication, but I am not concerned with that.[51]

■ *Euromarket Designs Inc v Peters* [2001] FSR 20 (Ch D)

This case concerned an alleged act of infringement of a registered trade mark in the UK by the use of a sign by the defendant on a website emanating from Ireland. A US company had a UK and CTM for 'Crate & Barrel' in class 21.[52] The defendant, Peters, ran a store in Dublin called 'Crate & Barrel'. The defendants advertised their shop in Dublin on a website. It was alleged that two kinds of goods sold in the Irish store, a hurricane lamp and a beaded coaster, fell within the specification of the pursuer's trade mark.

The question turned on whether the sign 'Crate & Barrel' on the defendant's website had been *used* in the UK. The court considered that an apt analogy was to consider peering down a telescope towards Dublin, and being invited to visit the shop in Dublin. This would not amount to *use* in the UK. This was different to other Internet selling activities, such as those carried out by Amazon.com, which had gone out actively seeking worldwide custom. In those circumstances, a sign would be 'used' on a website.

16.35   The merit of taking the approach that the courts have in these cases is that it allows trade mark owners to use the Internet as a method of dissemination of information on products without immediately running the risk of infringing trade mark rights in other territories where the same or similar trade mark exists, and which is owned by an independent entity.[53]

16.36   A different approach was taken by the Outer House of the Court of Session in *Bonnier Media v Smith and Kestrel*[54] in which the court seized jurisdiction over a company and individual based in Mauritius who

---

[50] Upheld on appeal—*1-800-Flowers Trade Mark* [2002] FSR 12 (CA). See also *CB Richard Ellis Inc v Groupement Carte Bleue* [2002] RPC 31; *Starbucks (HK) Ltd v British Sky Broadcasting Group plc* [2012] EWHC 3074 (Ch); *L'Oréal SA v eBay International AG* [2009] EWHC 1094 (Ch), paras 402–412.

[51] The point on use was upheld on appeal [2002] FSR 12 (CA).   [52] UK Trade Mark No 1331917.

[53] See also *KK Sony Computer Entertainment and another v Pacific Game Technology (Holding) Ltd* [2006] EWHC 2509 (Pat).

[54] [2002] ETMR 1050. See also *Mackie T/A 197 Aerial Photography v Askew* 2009 SLT (Sh Ct) 146.

carried on business in, inter alia, Greece. Smith and Kestrel had registered a number of domain names which included the word 'business a.m.', a word which formed part of Bonnier Media's registered trade mark in the UK. They then offered to sell these domain names to Bonnier Media. In asserting jurisdiction the court said:

> the person who sets up the website can be regarded as potentially committing a delict in any country where the website can be seen, in other words in any country in the world. It does not follow that he actually commits a delict in every country in the world, however … a website should not be regarded as having delictual consequences in any country where it is unlikely to be of significant interest.[55]

16.37   Going beyond questions of use, the difficulties that could arise in balancing competing interests were touched upon in *Speechworks Ltd v Speechworks International Incorporated*[56] also heard in the Outer House of the Court of Session. The application by Speechworks Ltd was for an interim interdict in respect of trade mark infringement. Speechworks Ltd, a Scottish company, held a registered trade mark for the mark 'Speechworks' in class 9 covering computer programs and apparatus. It came to their notice that Speechworks International Incorporated, a multinational company based in the United States, was also using the word Speechworks in respect of computer programs both in the UK and on its website. It transpired that the US company had been using the Speechworks sign for a number of years prior to its being registered by the Scottish company and that its use of the word had been known in the UK prior to its registration. In the event, interim interdict was denied as the court considered that the case should be heard at full trial prior to the grant of any relief. However, the court did consider the territorial reach of any relief order that might be granted saying 'I would add that if I had been minded to pronounce an interim interdict extending only to Scotland, I would have asked for further submissions on the manner in which the defenders' use of the name "SpeechWorks" in their website could be accommodated'. The court thus had in mind the need for some arrangement whereby dual use of the identical trade mark might coexist. In the event, it would appear that the case has not been litigated further—perhaps because the Scottish company did not have the resources to pursue its claim.

The use of disclaimers to facilitate competing uses by equally entitled proprietors

16.38   A second means of reconciling competing rights might be to allow for a disclaimer to be used in cases where business is done. If there are two competing identical trade marks, such as 'Ritz' for a hotel business in Paris and 'Ritz' for a hotel business in Barcelona, and those trade marks are owned by different entities, can the one be prevented from soliciting business in the other country? Under present trade mark law, the trade marks are identical, and therefore there would be infringement where one was soliciting business in the territory of the other. To solve this conundrum it may be appropriate to introduce the use of disclaimers. If 'Ritz' Barcelona' and 'Ritz' Paris made it clear that they were not associated with each other through the use of a disclaimer then there would be no infringement.

16.39   It is acknowledged that such a rule would be inconsistent with established trade mark principles in many jurisdictions.[57] There may also be questions as to the extent to which the use of such disclaimers might be considered anti-competitive and/or disguised restrictions on trade. Nonetheless, if trade marks are to coexist on the Internet, and trade is to be facilitated rather than hampered, then these avenues might help to alleviate the difficulties faced by traders.

---

[55] *Bonnier Media*, para 19.   [56] [2000] ETMR 982 (OH).
[57] Note the general discussion on 'use of a trade mark' in Chapter 15.

> **Key points on territorial scope of protection: accessibility and disclaimers**
>
> - The accessibility of trade marks on websites requires legitimate interests of owners to be balanced
> - The accessibility of a trade mark on a website may not necessarily amount to use in another territory
> - Suggestions have been made that disclaimers might be utilised to resolve conflicts

International strategies

16.40   In 1988 WIPO published a study concerning the use of trade marks on the Internet. This study was wide ranging in its terms, and covered not only registered trade marks, but also unregistered rights. The report summarised a number of possible principles for discussion, notably concerning use of trade marks on the Internet.[58]

On the question of *use*, WIPO suggested:

> There seems to be a general understanding that the mere appearance of a sign or a mark on the Internet is not sufficient to establish a connection between that sign or mark and a given territory. Many comments suggest that a relationship between a sign used on the Internet and a given territory is only established through commercial use of that sign in respect of that territory or, as it was expressed in one comment, whether the sign used on the Internet has 'commercial effect' in a territory.

The report went on to outline a number of factors which could contribute to a finding of use. These included servicing of customers in the particular territory or country; entering into other commercially motivated relationships with persons in the particular territory or country; and actual visits to the website for which or on which the sign is used from persons in the particular territory or country.[59]

16.41   The report resulted in a joint recommendation being issued by WIPO concerning provisions on the protection of marks and other industrial property rights in signs on the Internet.[60] As the document states, the purpose of the recommendation is to provide a clear legal framework for those trade mark owners who wish to use their trade marks on the Internet. Use is one of the key factors. A sign will be treated as being used in a member state only if it has commercial effect within that state. The recommendation proposes some tests that would point to this result. These include the level and character of commercial activity of the user in relation to the member state including whether the user is servicing customers in the member state; whether the user has stated that he does not intend to deliver to the member state; and whether post sale activities are directed at the member state.[61] The recommendation also suggests the adoption of a conflict avoidance procedure whereby the legitimate owner or licensee of a conflicting sign in another member state would not be liable until such time notification of infringement was given. Once served, suitable action to ensure there was no conflicting use should be taken to avoid further conflict. Finally, the recommendation suggests that remedies should be proportionate to the commercial effect of the use of the mark in that state and should not be so wide as to have the effect of prohibiting

---

[58] WIPO Standing Committee on the Law of Trade Marks Industrial Designs and Geographical Indications, Study concerning the use of trade marks on the Internet, Second session, SCT/2/9. Available on the WIPO website.

[59] WIPO, note 58, Summary, p 14.

[60] This was adopted by the General Assembly at the meetings 24 September to 3 October 2001.

[61] For a full list see the Joint Recommendation, Art 3.

future use of the sign on the Internet. While the recommendation has not been formally adopted or implemented into domestic laws, it has been referred to in national case law.[62]

 Question

Read the case law referred to earlier and the Joint Recommendation. What rules do you think should govern the coexistence of legitimate trade marks on the Internet?

Keyword advertising

16.42   As noted previously, the law in relation to banners and metatags and the implications for trade marks is largely of historical significance due to the changes in the way that search engines now operate on the Internet. It is, however, instructive to consider the law in this area to see how judicial thinking has developed over the years in relation to the challenges at the interface between trade marks and digital use and exploitation. In the case of *Reed Executive plc v Reed Business Information Ltd*[63] the Court of Appeal made some observations on the interaction between trade mark infringement, banners, and metatags. Reed Executive (RE) had registered the word 'Reed' for employment agency services in class 35. They also operated a website at reed.co.uk. An unconnected business, Reed Business Information (RBI), ran a recruitment website called totaljobs.com.

RBI used the word 'Reed' as follows:

- on their website they used the words 'Reed Business Information' with their logo and the statement 'Contact Reed Business Information if you would like to advertise your company's job vacancies';
- as metatags leading to the totaljobs.com site;
- in banner advertising on search engine home pages linking to the totaljobs.com site.

RE sued for trade mark infringement and passing off, arguing that RBI's activities amounted to a use of a sign identical or similar to their mark which was likely to lead to public confusion.

The banner argument

16.43   At first instance the court had found that when the banner was triggered by the word 'Reed', RE's trade mark was infringed. The Court of Appeal disagreed saying that the banner itself referred only to total-jobs, there being no visible appearance of the word 'Reed'. The appearance of the banner when a search for Reed or Reed jobs was undertaken could not amount to infringement of the registered trade mark as there was no consumer confusion.

> The idea that a search under the name Reed would make anyone think there was a trade connection between a totaljobs banner making no reference to the word 'Reed' and Reed Employment is fanciful. No likelihood of confusion was established.[64]

The court also raised the question (but did not answer it) as to whether the use of the word Reed by the search engine at the instance of RBI would amount to use 'in the course of trade'; a matter which would have been considered had the basis for trade mark infringement been on identity of marks rather than

---

[62] Case C-324/09 *L'Oreal SA v eBay International AG*, para 129; *Hotel Cipriani Srl v Cipriani (Grosvenor Street) Ltd* [2009] EWHC 3032 (Ch).

[63] [2004] ETMR 56.   [64] *Reed*, para 140.

similarity. The court simply noted that: 'It may be that an invisible use of this sort is not use at all for the purposes of this trade mark legislation—the computers who "read" sets of letters merely "look for" patterns of 0s and 1s—there is no meaning being conveyed to anyone—no "sign"'.[65]

The metatag argument

16.44 Metatags which are used by search engines to index Internet content may never be visible to the eye. RBI had used the words 'Reed Business Information' in their metatags and RE alleged that this amounted to trade mark infringement in that there would be consumer confusion. The Court of Appeal disagreed indicating that even if the use of a mark as a metatag amounted to trade mark use, there was no consumer confusion: causing a site to appear in a search result does not suggest any connection with anyone else.

16.45 As on the matter of banner use, interesting questions were raised but not answered by the court:

- Does metatag use count as use of a trade mark?
- If it does, is there infringement if the marks and goods or services are identical?
- If metatag use does amount to infringement, do any of the defences such as the own name defence apply?

On matters of use, and given the Court of Justice's jurisprudence in this area, the question arising now would be likely to be framed to ask whether the use implicated one of the functions of a mark (paras 15.4ff).

 Question

How would you have answered these points? Give reasons for your views. Consider the case law on Adwords—discussed later. How well did the metatag and banner cases anticipate the issues that arise with Adwords and the way that the Court of Justice has dealt with them?

16.46 As the technology as moved on, so have the business models deployed by stakeholders which in turn have resulted in new and different forms of disputes over the use made of trade marks by third parties. On the one hand is the desire of the trade mark owner to keep control of all uses of their trade mark in relation to internet usage. On the other, is the business model on which search engines and other intermediaries depend—that of the income generated through keyword advertising. As an example, in 2011 96 per cent of Google's revenue came from its advertising programmes (US$37.9 billion).[66]

The mechanics of keyword advertising

16.47 Every time a search engine is used to find something on the Internet, it not only returns results pertinent to the search terms entered by the user, but it also displays small advertisements, also called sponsored links, most commonly above or beside the actual search results. The display of these advertisements is by no means random. Rather, each advertisement is associated with certain keywords and is triggered every time the search term(s) match one of the keywords. It is the advertisers who specify the keywords. The advertiser can also indicate where those advertisements should be placed on the search page, whether at

---

[65] *Reed*, para 143.   [66] 31 December 2011, Google Annual Report.

the top or along the right-hand side. Revenue comes from the advertisers who pay to the search engine a specified amount each time an Internet user clicks on a sponsored advertisement (click through). The ranking of the advertisements on the page depends on a combination of factors. For Google, it includes other advertisers' bids; the quality score of advertisements in any particular search calculated by the click through rate; the relevance of the advertisers' text and keywords; and account history. The minimum bid for a keyword takes into account the quality of the landing page (where the user gets to when she clicks on the advertisement) including the relevancy and originality of the content.[67]

16.48   Key to the legal disputes is that search engines permit advertisers to 'buy' keywords that are the same as or similar to trade marks registered by third parties. So when a user searches for 'coca cola', advertisements for 'Pepsi-Cola' might appear if Pepsi-Cola has bid on the 'coca cola' trade mark. This, it is argued by the trade mark owners, causes consumer confusion, dilution of the trade mark, unfair competition (passing off), and leads to misleading advertising. Search engines, on the other hand, argue that their business model does not make use of the trade mark, and even if it did, it does not lead to consumer confusion or to the dilution of well-known trade marks. Further, if there is a problem for trade mark law it is the advertisers who are responsible as it is they who choose the keyword, not the search engine.

16.49   In the UK, an early case looking at these arguments was *Wilson v Yahoo!*,[68] which concerned the CTM 'Mr Spicy' which Mr Wilson had registered in classes 29, 30, and 42 of the CTM register. Mr Wilson brought an action against Yahoo! arguing that when 'Mr Spicy' was typed into Yahoo!'s search bar the first return to come up was for Sainsbury's and 'Delicious meal ideas for all occasions www.sainsbury's.co.uk, food news, inspiration and recipes from Sainsbury's on-line', and the second for Pricegrabber where the entry began with the word 'spicy' followed by 'www.pricegrabber.co.uk, compare prices on a variety of products at Pricegrabber' (as at 14 December 2006). The High Court was asked about, and dealt with, the question of use as a trade mark. According to the court:

> The trade mark in this case is not used by anyone other than the browser [Internet user] who enters the phrase 'Mr. Spicy' as a search query in the defendants' search engine. In particular, the trade mark is not used by [Yahoo!]. The response of the defendants to the use of the trade mark by the browser is not use of the trade mark by the defendants. That is enough to decide the case in the defendants' favour.[69]

The High Court went on to apply the ECJ's ruling in *Arsenal* saying:

> In my judgment, this case, very comfortably and clearly, comes within paragraph 54 of the decision in that case; that is, Mr. Wilson is not able to prohibit the use of the words 'Mr. Spicy' even when they are being applied to goods identical to those for which the mark is registered if that use cannot affect his own interest as proprietor of the mark having regard to its functions. That is satisfied here.[70]

Thus there was no infringement. It is notable in the instant case that the advertisers had only paid for 'spicy' as a descriptive term.[71] Yahoo!'s service, however, functioned so as to display the advertisement every time an Internet user searched for the term 'spicy' or any other phrase containing it. This is why Morgan J came to the conclusion that only the Internet user searching for 'Mr. Spicy' used this term and therefore Mr Wilson's trade mark, but not the advertiser or the search engine provider. *Wilson v Yahoo!* is therefore not a typical case of keyword advertising and it cannot be assumed that UK courts would thereby reject the notion of use as a trade mark if the search engine had sold a distinctive third party trade mark as a keyword.

---

[67] See the instructions at http://www.google.co.uk/intl/en/ads/. See also the description by J Grimmelmann, 'Rescuecom Oral Argument Report' (laboratorium.net, 4 April 2008) available at http://laboratorium.net/archive/2008/04/04/rescuecom_oral_argument_report.
[68] *Wilson v Yahoo! UK Ltd* [2008] EWHC 361 (Ch), [2008] ETMR 33.
[69] *Wilson*, para 64.   [70] *Wilson*, para 65.   [71] *Wilson*, paras 31 and 68.

16.50   More important have been the series of cases referred for a preliminary ruling to the Court of Justice from courts in a number of different member states. These are:

- From France, *Google v Viaticum*, *Google v CNRRH*, and *Google v Louis Vuitton Malletier*[72] each involving the search engine Google (rather than individual advertisers);

- From Austria, *BergSpechte v trekking.at*, a case in which the trade mark owner sued an advertiser who offered competing services;[73]

- From the *Hoge Raad der Nederlanden* questions in *Portakabin v Primakabin*, a dispute between a trade mark owner and an advertiser;[74]

- From the German *Bundesgerichtshof* in the *bananabay* case, a conflict between trade mark owner and advertiser;[75]

- From the UK *Interflora Inc v Marks & Spencer plc*[76] also a conflict between a trade mark owner and advertiser.

16.51   On trade mark matters most ask whether the use of a third party trade mark by the search engine is an infringing use for the purposes of Article 5(1)(a) and (b) of the Trade Mark Directive and Article 9(1)(a) and (b) of the Community Trade Mark Regulation. In addition, questions include whether the trade mark owner's exclusive right is infringed 'regardless of whether the accessed advertisement appears in the list of hits or in a separate advertising block and whether it is marked as a "sponsored link"';[77] where an identical sign is used for similar goods and services or a sign similar to the trade mark is used for identical or similar goods and services (ie those envisaged in Art 5(1)(b) of the Directive) 'is the fact that the advertisement is marked as a 'sponsored link' and/or appears not in the list of hits but in a separate advertising block sufficient to exclude any likelihood of confusion?'[78] whether it made a difference in this regard if the advertiser offered similar or identical goods or services (1) in the advertisement itself and (2) on the site to which Internet users are directed when clicking on the sponsored link.

16.52   The cases have been analysed in para 15.86ff. The key findings of the Court of Justice are:

- In the *Google* cases the ECJ found that the service provider (Google) was not using the trade mark—there could therefore be no infringement by the service provider.

- Where a sign identical with a trade mark is selected as a keyword by a *competitor* of the proprietor of the mark with the aim of offering Internet users an alternative to the goods or services of that proprietor, there is a use of that sign in relation to the goods or services of that competitor.[79] So the trader who uses the Adword uses it for the purposes of trade mark law and can be liable for infringement.

- In the case of offers of imitations for sale where a third party attempts, through the use of a sign which is identical with, or similar to, a reputable mark, to ride on the coat-tails of that mark in order to benefit from its power of attraction, its reputation, and its prestige, and to exploit, without paying any financial compensation and without being required to make efforts of its own in that regard, the

---

[72] Cass comm, 20 mai 2008, *Sté Google France c Sté Viaticum et Sté Luteciel*; Cass Comm, 20 mai 2008, *Sté Google c Sté CNRRH et autres*; Cass comm, 20 mai 2008, *Sté Google France et Sté Google Inc. c Sté Louis Vuitton Malletier*. These cases were joined for hearing in the Court of Justice (Cases 236/08 to 238/08).

[73] OGH (20.05.2008 – 17 Ob 3/08b); the decision can be found at http://www.ris.bka.gv.at/Jus/.

[74] Hoge Raad der Nederlanden (12.12.2008 – C 07/056 HR); available at http://zoeken.rechtspraak.nl/.

[75] BGH *bananabay* (22.01.2009 – I ZR 125/07); available at http://www.bundesgerichtshof.de/index.

[76] Case C-323/09.

[77] Case C-278/08 *Die BergSpechte Outdoor Reisen und Alpinschule Edi Koblmüller GmbH v Günter Guni and trekking.at Reisen GmbH*, reference for a preliminary ruling [2008] OJ C223/30.

[78] *BergSpechte Outdoor Reisen und Alpinschule*.

[79] Joined Cases C-236/08 to C-238/08 *Google France SARL v Louis Vuitton Malletier SA*.

marketing effort expended by the proprietor of that mark in order to create and maintain the image of that mark, the advantage resulting from such use must be considered to be an advantage that has been unfairly taken of the distinctive character or the repute of that mark.[80]

- The purpose of the use of a trade mark as a keyword was to take advantage of its distinctive character and repute; the competitor derived a real advantage from the distinctive character and repute of the trade mark; and the advertiser did not, as a general rule, pay the trade mark proprietor any compensation in respect of that use. In the absence of 'due cause', such use could fall within the scope of Article 9(1)(c):
  - the use would likely be without due cause if the goods offered using the Adwords service were imitations of those sold under the trade mark. But this was not the case where the goods were simply alternatives;[81]

  - by contrast, where the advertisement displayed on the Internet on the basis of a keyword corresponding to a trade mark with a reputation puts forward—without offering a mere imitation of the goods or services of the proprietor of that trade mark, without causing dilution or tarnishment and without, moreover, adversely affecting the functions of the trade mark concerned—an alternative to the goods or services of the proprietor of the trade mark with a reputation, such use falls, as a rule, within the ambit of fair competition in the sector for the goods or services concerned and is thus not without 'due cause' for the purposes of Article 5(2) of Directive 89/104 and Article 9(1)(c) of Regulation 40/94.[82]

16.53   When this clutch of cases was referred to the Court of Justice, it was argued by some to threaten the viability of the search engine as a business model: if a search engine cannot raise revenue via keyword advertising, the search engine will cease to exist. As can be seen from the judgments, that was an overly simplistic approach to the complexities involved in keyword advertising, and the very different and multi-varied questions that can and do arise with regard to the place of and potential liability in relation to unauthorised use of trade marks in relation to that activity. The Court of Justice has sought to demarcate infringing from non-infringing uses of trade marks through nuanced references to use and references to 'without due cause' and in so doing to enable practices and business models to survive and develop in ways that would never have been envisaged by the original drafters of the legislation Whether this will lead to the certainty that some participants seek is a moot point.[83] In any event, as technological advances continue, so will the legal challenges.

> ### 📖 Exercise
>
> Read the Adword cases by the Court of Justice. What is your opinion of the judgments? Do you think that a good balance has been attained between the rights of the trade mark holder and the interests of the competitor in what is a new and different type of competitive relationship between the stakeholders? What of the interests of the consumer?

Auction sites

16.54   Questions have arisen in recent years as to the liability of auction sites for trade mark infringements committed by their users. As the number of auction sites has grown, so has the potential for disputes. The

---

[80] *L'Oreal*, para 49.   [81] *Google France*, paras 102 and 103. *Interflora*, para 90.   [82] *Interflora*, para 91.

[83] See S Ott and M Schubert, 'It's the Ad text, stupid: cryptic answers won't establish legal certainty for online advertisers' (2011) 6(1) JIPLP 25–33.

key question is who should be liable for monitoring infringements of trade marks. On the one hand, it is argued that the trade mark owner is best placed to do so as they have knowledge of their goods. On the other hand, it is argued that the auction site is best placed to deal with infringements because they can filter advertisements and stop infringements. It is also argued that auction sites, like ISPs, are entities that should generally not be liable for unlawful activity conducted online as they are a mere conduit for the activities of others. Trade mark owners dispute this passivity pointing to services offered by the sites such as advertising and endorsement.

16.55   The question has been litigated in courts around the world.[84] The Court of Justice had the opportunity to consider the question when the UK referred the case of *L'Oreal v eBay International AG*.[85]

■ Case C-324/09 *L'Oreal v eBay*

L'Oreal sought a ruling that:

- eBay and its users infringed L'Oreal's trade marks when if offered for sale products bearing the mark including counterfeit goods, non-EEA **(European Economic Area)** products; testers and unboxed products;

- eBay was liable for trade mark infringement when it bought keywords corresponding to its trade marks from Internet referencing services;

- even if eBay was not liable for infringing its rights, an injunction should be granted under Article 11 of the Enforcement Directive.

The Court ruled as follows:

The sale of goods online must take place in the context of a commercial activity for the individual to be liable. Where offers for sale of goods not put on the market in the EEA are targeted at consumers within a territory of the EEA then EU trade mark rules apply. Testers marked 'not for sale' are not put on the market. Where packaging has been removed the trade mark owner may oppose the resale where information, including the identity of the manufacturer, is missing or where the image of the product and related the reputation of the mark is damaged.

Where eBay used keywords corresponding to L'Oreal's trade marks to promote its own service, that is not use in relation to identical goods and services. Where, however, eBay uses keywords to promote its users' postings, that is in relation to identical goods or services.

Where an auction site just enables its customers to display signs corresponding to trade marks on its website it does not use the signs. The use is by the customers. Under Article 14(1) of the E-Commerce Directive, the liability of service providers in relation to hosting third party information is restricted. However, where the operator plays an active role which gives it knowledge or control over the data relating to offers for sale and optimises the presentation of offers for sale, it can no longer rely on that exemption. Neither can it rely on the exception where it was aware of facts or circumstance in which a diligent operator should realise that online offers for sale were unlawful and has failed to act promptly to remove the information.

On Article 11 of the Enforcement Directive and the request for an injunction where rights have been infringed and to prevent future infringements, national courts must be able to order a website operator to take measures which bring to an end and which prevent future infringements.

---

[84] US *Tiffany v eBay* 600 F 3d 93 at 103 (2010); *L'Oreal v eBay International AG* [2009] ETMR 53; France: *LVM v eBay*, Commercial Court of Paris RG no 2006077799; *Belgium: Lancome Parfums v eBay*, Case A/07/06032.
[85] [2009] ETMR 53.

16.56 There was a great deal of anxious blogging following this judgment. There was consensus that it was strongly favourable to trade mark owners, requiring auction sites and other online marketplace operators to monitor users' postings. In confirming that the provider is not shielded from liability by Article 14 where they have played an active role in the promotion of their users' goods and/or have, or should have, knowledge about infringing activities, the question will now be as to the breadth of the injunction that the national courts will be willing to grant.[86] The Court of Justice stressed that the injunction must be effective, proportionate, and dissuasive and must not create barriers to legitimate trade. There will need to be a fine balance in the grant of the injunction if online marketplaces are to continue to ply their trade while at the same time the ruling in relation to enforcement of the trade marks is implemented.

 Exercise

At the time of writing the case had not been re-heard by the UK court. How do you think that court will deal with the grant of the injunction? How will eBay (and other online operators) need to change their behaviour to accommodate the order? Where do you think that the balance between the business models of online marketplace sites and the rights and interests of trade mark owners should lie? What of consumer interest?

 Question

Consider other social media such as Twitter and Facebook. How are trade marks used in relation to these media? How might trade marks be infringed and by whom? What other types of Internet-related activities might raise trade mark concerns? What of virtual worlds such as Second Life? In all of these consider the balance that needs to be struck between the interests of the trade mark owner, the competitor, and the consumer. Do you think that the legal framework regulating trade marks is appropriate for the digital age?

Geographical indications

Introduction

16.57 Geographical indications (GIs) are a form of intellectual property[87] rooted in agricultural policy and designed to highlight a link between the natural geographical advantages or the reputation associated with a place and the foodstuffs produced in that place. There are treaties at international level dealing with GIs although the most developed regime is at EU level. This was enhanced as part of the reform of the Common agricultural Policy designed to mark a move from mass produced to quality food products. A series of bilateral treaties has extended the protection between various countries.

16.58 On the one hand, a GI serves to give the consumer information as to the quality of the produce marketed under the GI. But critics see a danger in that if protection is overbroad and tied to reputation,

---

[86] For two other cases where injunctions against service providers have been considered, see under the E-Commerce Directive 2000/31 Case C-70/10 *Scarlet Extended SA v Societe Belge des Auteurs, Compositeurs et Editeurs SCRL (SABAM); Twentieth Century Fox Film Corp v British Telecommunications plc* [2011] EWHC 1981 (Ch).

[87] *Consorzio del Prosciutto di Parma v Asda Stores Ltd* [2002] FSR 3, para 6.

innovation may be hampered. The GI may become a means to shield against competition from new entrants to the market[88] rather than a genuine means for indicating the quality and provenance of a product.

Scope of this part

16.59   In this part, having considered some of the terminology used when referring to GIs, the scheme of protection at international level will be briefly described followed by an examination of the EU Regulation on the protection of geographical indications and designations of origin for agricultural products and foodstuffs. In its original form this Regulation came into force in 1993.[89]

The rest of this part looks like this:

- Terminology (16.61–16.62)
- International protection (16.63–16.67)
- The EU regime (16.68–16.94)

16.60   **Learning objectives**

By the end of this chapter you should be able to describe and explain:

- the terminology and definitions used in connection with GIs;
- the framework of international and regional protection;
- the EU regime from the protection of geographical indications and designations of origin.

Terminology

16.61   A number of different expressions are used to define GIs, each of which has different characteristics. The common factor is that all are designed to give protection to indications which have some link with a location. While there is no definition of a GI in the Paris Convention for the Protection of Industrial Property (the Paris Convention), that instrument refers to indications of the source of the goods, and to locality, region, and country.[90] Similarly, the Madrid Agreement for the Repression of False or Misleading Indications of Source on Goods 1891 (the Madrid Agreement) refers to indications of the country or place of origin.[91] Extrapolating from these provisions it has been said that 'an indication of source can be defined as an indication referring to a country, or to a place in that country, as being the country or place of origin of a product'.[92]

---

[88] T Josling, 'The war on terror: geographical indications as a transatlantic trade conflict' (2006) 57 Journal of Agricultural Economics 537.
[89] Originally Regulation No 2081/92 of 14 July 1992 as amended several times and most recently replaced by Council Regulation (EC) No 510/2006 of 20 March 2006 on the protection of geographical indications and designations of origin for agricultural products and foodstuffs. This followed a WTO Panel decision on the compatibility of Regulation 2081/92 with the national treatment clause in TRIPS.
[90] Paris Convention, Art 10(1), (2).   [91] Madrid Agreement, Art 1.
[92] WIPO Standing Committee on the Law of Trademarks, Industrial Designs and Geographical Indications, Sixth session, Geneva, 12–16 March, 2001, *Geographical Indications: Historical Background, Nature of Rights, Existing Systems for Protection and Obtaining Effective Protection in Other Countries* available at http://www.wipo.int/edocs/mdocs/sct/en/sct_6/sct_6_3.pdf.

16.62   For the purposes of the TRIPS Agreement, GIs are defined as 'indications which identify a good as originating in the territory of a Member, or a region or locality in that territory, where a given quality, reputation or other characteristic of the good is essentially attributable to its geographical origin'.[93] The Lisbon Agreement for the protection of appellations of origin and their international registration (the Lisbon Agreement) talks of appellations of origin. These are 'the geographical name of a country, region, or locality, which serves to designate a product originating therein, the quality and characteristics of which are due exclusively or essentially to the geographical environment, including natural and human factors'. Regulation 510/2006 refers to designations of origin as being the name of a region, place, or country used to describe an agricultural product or foodstuff originating in that place and which exhibits characteristics due to the environment, and to geographical indications as the name of a region where there is a particular quality attributable to the origin and the production, processing, or preparation taking place in that area.

> ### Key point on terminology
>
> - The extent of protection for a GI will depend on the scope of protection under each of these instruments and is linked to the definition to be found in the instrument

International protection

16.63   There is patchwork protection for GIs at international level. The Paris Convention and the Madrid Agreement both provide for the seizure of goods on importation where there is a false indication as to the source of the goods, irrespective of the intent of the user.

> ### Web links
>
> The Madrid Agreement is administered by WIPO and can be found at **http://www.wipo.int/treaties/en/ip/madrid/**.
>
> The Paris Convention, also administered by WIPO, can be found at **http://www.wipo.int/treaties/en/ip/paris/**.

16.64   The Lisbon Agreement, by contrast, established a registration system for appellations of origin. Where an appellation of origin is protected in a signatory state to the Treaty, this can be used to apply for international registration via WIPO.[94] This means that the Lisbon system of registration is only applicable to appellations of origin where they are already protected on the national level in the country of origin. Application must be made by an administrative body on behalf of the group entitled to use the appellation. When an application for registration is made, other member states which are a party to the agreement have 12 months to indicate whether they are able to protect the appellation in their home country. If no objection is lodged, the appellation must be protected for as long as it

---

[93] TRIPS, Art 22(1).

[94] WIPO held a conference in 2009 on the subject of GIs during which there was detailed examination of the Lisbon Agreement. See WIPO Symposium, Bulgaria, June 2009, 'Perspectives for Geographical Indications', WIPO/GEO/SOF/09/1.

is protected in the country of origin. Once registered, the Lisbon Agreement requires an appellation to be protected against misleading use even if a consumer may not be confused or deceived by such use. The agreement also requires member states to protect against imitation of the appellation of origin even where the origin of the product is indicated or where it is accompanied by terms such as 'kind', 'type', 'make', or 'imitation'. Examples of appellations of origin registered under the Lisbon Agreement include 'Bordeaux' for wine, 'Noix de Grenoble' for nuts, 'Tequila' for spirit drinks, and 'Jaffa' for oranges.

Web links

You will find the Lisbon Agreement at **http://www.wipo.int/lisbon/en/legal_texts/lisbon_agreement.html.**

You can also search the Lisbon Register on the WIPO website at **http://www.wipo.int/ipdl/en/search/lisbon/search-struct.jsp.**

16.65   The TRIPS Agreement contains measures relating to geographical indications which apply to all products (not just agricultural products and foodstuffs). The Agreement requires member states to prevent the use of any means that indicates or suggests that a good originates in a geographic area other than the true place of origin such that it misleads the public as to the geographical origin.[95] It also requires member states to protect against a use that constitutes an act of unfair competition within the meaning of Article 10*bis* of the Paris Convention.[96] For wines and spirits, and as with the Lisbon Agreement, member states must also protect against the use of a GI where products do not originate in that location even where the true origin of the goods is indicated (ie they are literally true) although they falsely represent to the public that the goods on which they are used come from a different territory,[97] or where the GI is used in translation or accompanied by expression such as 'kind', 'type', 'style', 'imitation', or the like.[98]

16.66   As can be seen, these instruments exhibit differences in approach to the protection of GIs. From the prohibition of the use of false and deceptive indications of source (Paris Convention and Madrid Agreement) to a more general prohibition of the use of GI which constitutes an act of unfair competition within the meaning of Article 10*bis* of the Paris Convention (TRIPS Agreement). The discussion in the following section will examine the EU approach.

16.67   There are also a number of bilateral agreements in the field of GIs most notably dealing with wines. For example, bilateral agreements between the EU and other countries include the Australia EU Agreement (Concerning the Conclusion of an Agreement between the European Community and Australia on Trade in Wine)[99] and and an Agreement between the European Community and the United States of America on Trade in Wine.[100] Such agreements may provide for a prohibition on the use of a GI not having that origin, or provide for changes to the local laws to protect GIs within the territory.[101]

---

[95] TRIPS, Art 22(2)(a).   [96] TRIPS, Art 22(2)(b).   [97] TRIPS, Art 22(4).   [98] TRIPS, Art 23(1).
[99] 94/184/EC [1994] OJ L86/1.   [100] [2006] OJ L87/2.
[101] For an ECJ case on the compatibility of a bilateral agreement between two individual countries with Regulation 2081/92, see Case C-216/01 *Budejovicky Budvar Narodni Podnik v Rudolf Ammersin GmbH* [2005] 1 CMLR 56, [2003] ECR I-13617, [2004] ETMR 21 There was a second attempt at clarifying the questions asked of the ECJ at Case C-478/07 *Budejovický Budvar, národní podnik v Rudolf Ammersin GmbH.*

> ## Key points on international regime
>
> - Patchwork protection exists for GIs at international level
> - The instruments take varying approaches to definitions of protected subject matter and scope of protection

The EU regime

16.68   The EU operates four systems for the protection of geographical indications: for wines;[102] spirit drinks;[103] agricultural products and foodstuffs (which will be examined later);[104] and for agricultural products and foodstuffs for Traditional Specialties Guaranteed (TSGs).[105] National laws of member states apply to all non-agricultural geographical indications. In its *Communication on agricultural product quality policy* adopted on 28 May 2009, the Commission announced its intention to bring together the different systems into a single register. A draft Regulation was promulgated in 2010.[106]

> ### Web link
>
> Regulation 510/2006 can be found at **http://eur-lex.europa.eu/LexUriServ/site/en/oj/2006/ l_093/l_09320060331en00120025.pdf.**

16.69   Regulation 510/2006 protects designations of origin and GIs of foodstuffs and agricultural products as stipulated in the Annex:

- foodstuffs:
  - beers
  - beverages made from plant extracts
  - bread, pastry, cakes, confectionery, and other baker's wares
  - natural gums and resins
  - mustard paste
  - pasta

- agricultural products:
  - hay
  - essential oils
  - cork
  - cochineal (raw product of animal origin)
  - flowers and ornamental plants
  - wool

---

[102] Regulation (EC) No 479/2008 on the common organisation of the market in wine.
[103] Regulation (EC) No 110/2008 on the definition, description, presentation, labelling and protection of geographical indications of spirit drinks. See Joined Cases C?4/10 and C?27/10 *Bureau national interprofessionnel du Cognac v Gust Ranin Oy* discussing 'Cognac'.
[104] Regulation (EC) No 510/2006 on the protection of geographical indications and designations of origin for agricultural products and foodstuffs.
[105] Regulation 509/2006.   [106] Regulation on agricultural product quality schemes, COM(2010) 733 final.

- wicker
- scutched flax.

The Regulation does not apply to wine-sector products (except wine vinegars) or to spirits.[107]

Protected designations of origin and protected geographical indications

16.70 Regulation 510/2006 provides for the protection of Designations of Origin (DO) and GIs. Once these are registered they are called Protected Designations of Origin (PDO) and Protected Geographical Indications (PGI) respectively.

A designation of origin is defined in Article 2:

(a) the name of a region, a specific place or, in exceptional cases, a country, used to describe an agricultural product or a foodstuff:

- originating in that region, specific place or country,
- the quality or characteristics of which are essentially or exclusively due to a particular geographical environment with its inherent natural and human factors, and
- the production, processing and preparation of which take place in the defined geographical area;

A geographical indication is also defined in Article 2 as:

(b) the name of a region, a specific place or, in exceptional cases, a country, used to describe an agricultural product or a foodstuff:

- originating in that region, specific place or country, and
- which possesses a specific quality, reputation or other characteristics attributable to that geographical origin, and
- the production and/or processing and/or preparation of which take place in the defined geographical area.

The purpose of giving protection to PDOs and PGIs is said to be twofold. It is intended both to protect producers of the products from unfair competition and to protect consumers from being misled by the application to products of false or misleading descriptions.[108]

16.71 There are both similarities and distinctions between the definitions.

- PDO: the characteristics must be essentially or exclusively due to the geographical environment.

- PGI: the quality, reputation, or other characteristics must be attributable to the geographical origin—that is, a reputation based link.

- PDO: the production, processing, and preparation must take place in the defined geographical area.

- PGI: the production or processing or preparation must take place in the defined geographic area.

In *Consorzio del Prosciutto di Parma v Asda Stores Ltd*[109] it was said that 'A PDO is similar to a PGI except that the causal link between the place of origin and the quality of the product may be a matter of reputation rather than verifiable fact'.

---

[107] Regulation 510/2006, Art 1.

[108] *Consorzio del Prosciutto di Parma v Asda Stores Ltd* [2002] FSR 3, para 58.

[109] *Consorzio del Prosciutto di Parma v Asda Stores Ltd* [2002] FSR 3, para 8. See also Case C-343/07 *Bavaria NV, Bavaria Italia Srl v Bayerischer Brauerbund eV*, for mention of the link between 'on the one hand, the geographical origin of the product and, on the other hand, a specific quality of that product, its reputation or another characteristic of the product, attributable to that origin ...' (para 107).

Traditional geographical or non-geographical names

16.72   Article 2(3) of Regulation 510/2006 also protects certain traditional geographical or non-geographical names which designate an agricultural product or a foodstuff and which originates in a region or a specific place, and fulfils the conditions in the definition of a designation of origin.

16.73   Protection of a non-geographic name was considered in *Germany v Commission of the European Communities*[110] where the question was over the protection of the word 'feta'. The ECJ accepted that the word feta was derived from the Italian word 'fetta', meaning 'slice', which had entered the Greek language in the 17th century and that 'feta' is not the name of a region, place, or country. However, where the produce came from a 'geographical environment with specific natural and human factors and which is capable of giving an agricultural product or foodstuff its specific characteristics' and where homogenous natural factors distinguished it from the areas adjoining it, that would be sufficient to fall under the criterion in Article 2(3).[111]

> ### Key point on non-geographical names
>
> • A non-geographic name can be protected as a PDO if it originates in a geographical environment which gives it specific characteristics

Generic names

16.74   Regulation 510/2006 prohibits the registration of generic names. A name that has become generic means:

> the name of an agricultural product or a foodstuff which, although it relates to the place or the region where this product or foodstuff was originally produced or marketed, has become the common name of an agricultural product or a foodstuff in the Community.[112]

The Regulation sets out a series of non-exhaustive factors to be taken into account in determining whether a name has become generic. These include factors concerning the existing situation in the member states and in areas of consumption; and the relevant national or Union laws.

16.75   The generic character of a name was considered by the ECJ in *Germany v Commission of the European Communities*[113] where the Court noted that the fact that a product has been lawfully marketed under a name in some member states may constitute a factor which must be taken into account in the assessment of whether that name has become generic.[114] Other factors to be considered were listed by the Court when considering the PDO 'Parmigiano Reggiano' and the user of the name 'Parmesan'. These included the places of production of the product both inside and outside the member state where the name was registered; the consumption of the product and how it is perceived by consumers both in and beyond the member state; and any national legislation relating to the product.[115] In *Bavaria NV, Bavaria Italia Srl v Bayerischer Brauerbund eV*,[116] the Court said that 'as regards a PGI, a name becomes generic only if the direct link between, on the one hand, the geographical origin of the product and, on the other hand, a specific quality of that product, its reputation or another characteristic of the product,

---

[110] Case C-465/02 *Germany v Commission of the European Communities* [2005] ECR I-9115, [2006] ETMR 16.
[111] *Germany v Commission*, para 50.   [112] Regulation 510/2006, Art 3(1).
[113] Case C-465/02 [2005] ECR I-9115, [2006] ETMR 16.   [114] *Germany v Commission*, para 79.
[115] Case C-132/05 *Commission of the European Communities v Germany*.   [116] Case C-343/07, para 107.

attributable to that origin, has disappeared, and that the name does no more than describe a style or type of product'.[117]

16.76   Regulation 510/2006 provides that a protected name may not become generic.[118]

Plant varieties, animal breeds, homonymous names

16.77   Regulation 510/2006 provides that a name may not be registered as a DO or a GI where it conflicts with the name of a plant variety or an animal breed and as a result is likely to mislead the consumer as to the true origin of the product.[119] As regards homonymous names (words having the same name or designation), the Regulation provides that a name which is wholly or partially homonymous with that of a name already registered can be registered after having due regard to local and traditional usage and the actual risk of confusion. Where a consumer will be misled into believing that products come from another territory then the name may not be registered even if the name is accurate as far as the actual territory of origin is concerned. In addition, there must be sufficient distinction between the homonym and the name already on the register having regard to the need to treat producers equitably and not mislead consumers.[120]

The specifications

16.78   Article 4 of Regulation 510/2006 contains the specifications with which a PDO or PGI must comply. These specifications set out the information used to determine whether a name should be registered; once registered, it sets out the standard with which users must comply if they wish to use the PDO or PGI; it also determines the scope of protection accorded by the PDO or PGI.[121]

The list of what must be contained in the specifications, which is not exhaustive, includes the following:

(1) the name of the agricultural product or foodstuff comprising the designation of origin or the geographical indication;

(2) a description of the agricultural product or foodstuff, including the raw materials, if appropriate, and principal physical, chemical, microbiological, or organoleptic characteristics of the product or the foodstuff;

(3) the definition of the geographical area;

(4) evidence that the agricultural product or the foodstuff originates in the defined geographical area;

(5) a description of the method of obtaining the agricultural product or foodstuff and, if appropriate, the authentic and unvarying local methods as well as information concerning packaging, if the applicant group within the meaning of Article 5(1) so determines and gives reasons why the packaging must take place in the defined geographical area to safeguard quality or ensure the origin or ensure control;

(6) details bearing out the following:

(i) the link between the quality or characteristics of the agricultural product or foodstuff and the geographical environment or, as the case may be,

---

[117] *Bavaria*, para 107. See also Case C-446/07 *Alberto Severi v Regione Emilia Romagna*.   [118] Art 13(2).
[119] Art 3(2).   [120] Art 3(3)(a), (b).
[121] L Bently and B Sherman, *Intellectual Property Law* (3rd edn, 2009), 985.

(ii) the link between a specific quality, the reputation, or other characteristic of the agricultural product or foodstuff and the geographical origin;

(7) the name and address of the authorities or bodies verifying compliance with the provisions of the specification and their specific tasks;

(8) any specific labelling rule for the agricultural product or foodstuff in question.

The specification has been described as a 'discursive document'.[122] Not everything that is contained in the specification is protected. Only those matters that impact upon the quality of the product[123] are relevant to the scope of protection.

Key points on specifications

The specifications are central to the protection of GIs.

- They set out the information used to determine whether a name should be registered

- Once registered the specifications set out the standard with which users must comply if they wish to use the PDO or PGI

- The specifications determine the scope of protection accorded by the PDO or PGI

16.79   One of the key questions that arises is as to the definition of the geographical area (Art 4(2)(c)), in particular where it is the reputation of the product that is to be protected (PGI) rather than a product tied to the particular characteristics of the local environment (PDO). This question arose in the *Melton Mowbray pork pie* case in which a number of questions were referred to the ECJ relating to the geographical scope.[124]

When Melton Mowbray pork pie was registered as a PGI, Northern Foods objected as it was a producer of the pies but was based outwith the geographical area in the specifications. It argued that there had never been a consistent recipe for pork pies; that the pork pies had, since at least the mid-1800s, been made outside the area detailed in the specifications; and, in any event, Melton Mowbray was considered as a generic name for a quality pork pie. When the objections were turned down, Northern Foods sought judicial review. The High Court[125] found that Melton Mowbray pork pie satisfied the definition of a PGI on account of it being a convenient shorthand term for a geographical area shown through historical analysis to be the place most likely to have been where the pies were produced in the 1900s. The High Court found that the defined geographical area for the purposes of Articles 2(2)(b) and 4(2) of the Regulation may be different from a named specific place or region where the foodstuff originated. Permission to appeal was granted as was a stay of the proceedings for a referral to the ECJ.

The following questions were referred to the Court:

Where the specification in an application for a protected geographical indication (PGI) in respect of 'Melton Mowbray Pork Pies' made pursuant to Council Regulation 2081/92/EEC on the protection of geographical indications and designations of origin for agricultural products and foodstuffs ('the Regulation') defines the relevant geographical area pursuant to Article 4(2)(c) of the Regulation as 'the town of Melton Mowbray and its surrounding region bounded as follows:'

---

[122] *Consorzio del Prosciutto di Parma v Asda Stores Ltd* [2002] FSR 3, para 29.

[123] Bently and Sherman, note 121, 994.

[124] *R (On the application of Northern Foods plc) v Department for Environment, Food and Rural Affairs and the MMPPA Minute of Order* (14 March 2006).

[125] *R (On the application of Northern Foods plc) v Department for Environment, Food and Rural Affairs* [2005] EWHC 2971.

- to the North by the A52 from the M1 and the A1 and including the city of Nottingham;
- to the East by the A1 from the A52 to the A45 and including the towns of Grantham and Stamford;
- to the West by the M1 from the A52 and the A45; and
- to the South by the A45 from the M1 and the A1 and including the town of Northampton.

1. are the requirements of Article 2(2)(b) of the Regulation capable of being satisfied insofar as the proposed PGI would apply to products produced and/or processed and/or prepared in places other than that whose name appears in the PGI;
2. if so, what criteria must be applied in delimiting the defined geographical area referred to in Articles 2(2)(b) and 4(2)(c) of the Regulation?[126]

Where protection is based on specific geographical characteristics, such as the type of soil or the quality of water, geographical origin may be demarcated by those particular qualities. However, and where protection is based on reputation 'constructed around cultural, historical or socioeconomic moorings rather than scientifically verifiable natural features',[127] the danger is that the monopoly conferred by the PGI has arbitrary boundaries. The justifications for the monopoly (consumer information and quality associated with provenance) become hard to sustain and a GI may be seen as no more than a commercially and politically expedient monopoly.

Unfortunately, the reference was withdrawn.[128] On the EU granting PGI status for Melton Mowbray pork pies, Northern Foods had been given a period of five years to transfer production thus prompting Northern Foods to drop its action and withdraw the reference. PGI protection for Melton Mowbray has now been granted.[129]

Exercise

Read Dev S Gangjee, 'Melton Mowbray and the GI pie in the sky: exploring the cartographies of protection' [2006] 3 IPQ 291–309, and the questions that were referred to the Court of Justice. If the application had proceeded, how do you think the Court should have answered these questions? From your analysis, what do you consider to be the justifications for protection of a GI under the European regime? What should the justifications for protection be?

Preparation of foodstuffs

16.80   Of historic interest is the question that arose in relation to the way in which the foodstuff is prepared and whether the preparation, such as the grating of cheese or the slicing of ham, could be limited to the region. These issues came before the Court of Justice in *Consorzio del Prosciutto di Parma, Salumificio S Rita SpA v Asda Stores Ltd*[130] concerning the slicing of Parma ham, and in *Ravil SARL v Bellon import SARL, Biraghi SpA*[131] concerning the grating of Grana Padano cheese.

In *Consorzio*, Asda sold Parma ham bought from Hygrade which in turn sourced the ham boned but not sliced from an Italian producer, a member of the Consorzio. Hygrade sliced and packed the ham. The

---

[126] Case C-169/06.
[127] Dev S Gangjee, 'Melton Mowbray and the GI pie in the sky: exploring the cartographies of protection' [2006] 3 IPQ 291–309 at 300.
[128] 'Transitional relief granted to Northern Foods in Melton Mowbray Pork Pie battle' (3 November 2006).
[129] Commission Regulation (EC) No 566/2009 of 29 June 2009 entering a name in the register of protected designations of origin and protected geographical indications (Melton Mowbray Pork Pie (PGI)).
[130] Case C-108/01 *Consorzio del Prosciutto di Parma, Salumificio S Rita SpA v Asda Stores Ltd* [2003] 2 CMLR 21, [2003] ECR I-5121, [2004] ETMR 23.
[131] Case C-469/00 *Ravil SARL v Bellon import SARL, Biraghi SpA* [2003] ECR I-5053, [2004] ETMR 22.

packaging bore the words 'ASDA A taste of Italy PARMA HAM Genuine Italian Parma Ham'. Consorzio argued that the slicing and packaging was contrary to the rules and the specifications applicable to Parma ham. The following question was referred to the ECJ:

> does Council Regulation (EEC) No 2081/92 read with Commission Regulation (EC) No 1107/96 and the specification for the PDO 'Prosciutto di Parma' create a valid Community right, directly enforceable in the court of a Member State, to restrain the retail sale as 'Parma ham' of sliced and packaged ham derived from hams duly exported from Parma in compliance with the conditions of the PDO but which have not been thereafter sliced, packaged and labelled in accordance with the specification?

The Court started off by pointing out that by requiring the slicing and packaging to be carried out in the region of production, the intention is to allow the persons entitled to use the PDO to keep under their control one of the ways in which the product appears on the market. In particular, it aimed at safeguarding the quality and authenticity of the product, and consequently the reputation of the PDO.[132] Where it has been sliced and packaged outside the region, there was a greater risk to the quality and authenticity of the product than there would be had this been done within the region.[133] Therefore the Regulation (No 2081/92) did not preclude the use of a PDO from being subject to the condition that operations such as the slicing and packaging of the product take place in the region of production, where the condition enters the specification.[134]

16.81   The Regulation was subsequently amended[135] to include Article 4(2)(e):

> (e) a description of the method of obtaining the agricultural product or foodstuff and, if appropriate, the authentic and unvarying local methods as well as information concerning packaging, if the applicant group within the meaning of Article 5(1) so determines and gives reasons why the packaging must take place in the defined geographical area to safeguard quality or ensure the origin or ensure control.

As can be seen in para 16.78, this is also included in Regulation 510/2006.

 Question

If adequate notice is given to economic operators, do you think that the specifications could extend to the slicing of ham in restaurants and delicatessens? Have a look at *Consorzio Del Prosciutto di Parma v Asda Stores Ltd* [2002] FSR 3, Lord Scott of Foscote at 62.

Procedure for registration

16.82   Articles 5 to 7 of Regulation 510/2006 detail the procedure for registration. The application may be made by a group of producers and/or processors or, subject to certain conditions, a natural or legal person. The application must include the specification and be addressed to the member state in which the geographical area concerned is located. When the member state is satisfied that the requirements have been fulfilled, the application is forwarded to the Commission. Within six months the Commission will

---

[132] Case C-108/01 *Consorzio del Prosciutto di Parma, Salumificio S Rita SpA v Asda Stores Ltd* [2003] 2 CMLR 21, [2003] ECR I-5121, [2004] ETMR 23, para 65.

[133] *Consorzio del Prosciutto di Parma*, para 76.

[134] *Consorzio del Prosciutto di Parma*, para 50. In the event, Consorzio could not stop Asda using the name for Parma ham sliced outside the region because the PDO had been registered under the fast-track procedure in Regulation 2081/92 which only required the publication of limited information about the conditions pertaining to the PDO. As the information in relation to slicing and packaging had not been published, 'this could not be relied on as against economic operators, as it was not brought to their attention by adequate publicity in Community legislation' (para 99).

[135] Added by Regulation 692/2003, Art 1(1) (8 April 2003) OJ L 99/1.

check whether the application includes all the particulars required. If the Commission concludes that the name qualifies for protection, a notice will be published in the Official Journal. Member states have six months to lodge objections. If none are forthcoming, the name is entered on the Register of protected designations of origin and protected geographical indications and published in the Official Journal.

> **Web link**
>
> To consult the Register of PDOs and PGIs (and traditional speciality guaranteed). See the Register at **http://ec.europa.eu/agriculture/quality/schemes/index_en.htm.**

16.83   Any operator marketing agricultural product or foodstuffs conforming to the corresponding specification[136] may use the registered name and the logo associated with the PDO[137] or PGI illustrated in Figures 16.3 and 16.4.

Figure 16.3 Protected designation of origin logo

Figure 16.4 Protected geographical indication logo

Scope of protection

16.84   Article 13 details the scope of protection of a PDO or PGI as follows:

1. Registered names shall be protected against:

(a) any direct or indirect commercial use of a registered name in respect of products not covered by the registration in so far as those products are comparable to the products registered under that name or in so far as using the name exploits the reputation of the protected name;

---

[136] Regulation 510/2006, Art 8(1).
[137] New logo as from 1 May 2009 (subject to transnational provisions until 1 May 2010). Commission Regulation (EC) 628/2008.

(b) any misuse, imitation or evocation, even if the true origin of the product is indicated or if the protected name is translated or accompanied by an expression such as 'style', 'type','method', 'as produced in', 'imitation' or similar;

(c) any other false or misleading indication as to the provenance, origin, nature or essential qualities of the product, on the inner or outer packaging, advertising material or documents relating to the product concerned, and the packing of the product in a container liable to convey a false impression as to its origin;

(d) any other practice liable to mislead the consumer as to the true origin of the product.

16.85   As can be seen, the scope of protection is broad. A registered name is protected against both direct and indirect commercial use where the products are comparable to the products registered under the name. In assessing the scope, much will depend on the interpretation of a 'comparable product'. The more dissimilar the product, the greater the scope of protection conferred by the registration. In addition, a registered name is to be protected where the use would exploit the reputation of the protected name. Here the scope of protection will depend on what amounts to exploiting the reputation—matters that resonate with the issues that arise in the protection of well-known marks with a reputation and the use of a sign where that takes advantage of the reputation (see the discussion in para 15.76). Protection against misuse, imitation, or invocation even if the true origin of the product is stated, would cover uses such as 'Beacon Fell traditional Lancashire cheese made in Somerset', or 'tastes like white Stilton Cheese', or perhaps 'raised using the same methods as Scotch beef'.

16.86   In relation to what constitutes evocation, the ECJ said that this 'covers a situation where the term used to designate a product incorporates part of a protected designation, so that when the consumer is confronted with the name of the product, the image triggered in his mind is that of the product whose designation is protected'.[138] Further, for evocation there is no need to show a likelihood of confusion as between the products. In addition, evocation may take place even where no Union protection extends to the parts of that designation which are echoed in the term or terms at issue.[139] The case in hand concerned the name Cambozola used for 'soft blue cheese' and whether it infringed the PDO 'Gorgonzola'. The Court concluded that:

> Since the product at issue is a soft blue cheese which is not dissimilar in appearance to Gorgonzola, it would seem reasonable to conclude that a protected name is indeed evoked where the term used to designate that product ends in the same two syllables and contains the same number of syllables, with the result that the phonetic and visual similarity between the two terms is obvious.[140]

Key points on scope of protection

- Protection extends to both direct and indirect commercial use where the products are comparable to the products registered under the name

- Evocation occurs where the consumer, when faced with a product, thinks of the product whose designation is protected

---

Cancellation

16.87   Under Article 12 of Regulation 510/2006 where the Commission takes the view that compliance with the conditions of the specification for an agricultural product or foodstuff covered by a protected name

---

[138] Case C-87/97 *Consorzio per la Tutela del Formaggio Gorgonzola v Käserei Champignon Hofmeister GmbH & Co KG, Eduard Bracharz GmbH* [1999] 1 CMLR 1203 (ECJ), para 25. See also Case C-132/05 *Commission v Germany*, para 44.

[139] *Consorzio per la Tutela del Formaggio Gorgonzola*, para 26.

[140] *Consorzio per la Tutela del Formaggio Gorgonzola*, para 27.

is no longer ensured, it can initiate a cancellation procedure published in the Official Journal. Detailed rules are laid out in the Regulation as to the procedure to be followed. Any natural or legal person having a legitimate interest may also request cancellation of the registration, giving reasons for the request.

16.88   A request for cancellation of a PGI, 'Newcastle Brown Ale', was made by Scottish and Newcastle plc.[141] The reasons for the cancellation request were twofold. The first was that production at the site in Newcastle-upon-Tyne named in the PGI specification was no longer commercially viable. The second was that the PGI, which was requested by a single producer, was granted on condition that the producer may not prevent others within the area from producing the products in accordance with the specification. The specification, however, included ingredients (the strain of yeast, the blend of water and salt) which were secret to Scottish and Newcastle plc. No other producer was thus entitled to use the name without the consent of Scottish and Newcastle, which made it clear that they would not make public details of the ingredients, nor given consent to any other producer to use them.[142]

 Exercise

Given the requirements of the specifications discussed previously, why do you think Newcastle Brown Ale was accorded PGI status without disclosing the raw materials that determined the nature of the beer?

Conflicts between PDOs, PGIs, and trade marks

16.89   Regulation 510/2006 provides for the possible (and inevitable) conflicts that could arise as between PDOs, PGIs, and registered trade marks. Article 3(4) of the Regulation states that a DO or GI is not to be registered if there exists a trade mark, and in the light of the reputation, renown, and length of time for which the trade mark has been used, registration of the DO or GI is likely to mislead consumers as to the identity of the product.

16.90   Article 14(1) of the Regulation deals with competition between applications for registration and stipulates that a trade mark application which, if registered and used within the same class of product would infringe the PDO or PDI, will not be registered where the application for registration is submitted after the date of submission of the application of the registration of the PDO or PGI.[143]

16.91   Article 14(2) provides that where a PDO or PGI is registered and there exists a trade mark which has been applied for, registered, or established by use before the date of protection of the PDO or PGI, or 1 January 1996, then the trade mark may continue to be used notwithstanding the registration of the PDO or PGI.[144]

Regulation 2081/92 and TRIPS

16.92   In 1999 the United States (joined by Australia) contended that Regulation 2081/92, as amended was not in conformity with the EC's obligations under the TRIPs Agreement. Specifically, the allegation was

---

[141] OJ 18.11.2006, C280/13.

[142] The cancellation came into effect in August 2007. Commission Regulation 952/2007.

[143] Relatedly, CTMR, Art 7(1)(j) provides that trade marks for wines or spirits which contain or consist of a geographical indication shall not be registered. See Case T 237/08 *Abadía Retuerta, SA v OHIM* where the General Court refused to register the mark 'CUVEE PALOMAR'. Palomar is a region in Spain.

[144] For a discussion on PDOs, PDIs, and trade marks under Regulation No 2081/92, see Case C-343/07 *Bavaria NV v Bayerischer Brauerbund eV*.

that the Regulation did not provide national treatment with respect to GIs and did not provide sufficient protection to pre-existing trade marks that are similar or identical to a GI. The Word Trade Organization (WTO) Panel[145]agreed with the United States and Australia on the matter of national treatment for the following reasons:

- registration of a GI from a country outside the EU was contingent upon the government of that country adopting a system of GI protection equivalent to the EC's system and offering reciprocal protection to EC GIs; and

- the Regulation's procedures required applications and objections from other WTO members to be examined and transmitted by the governments of those members, and require those governments to operate systems of product inspection like EC member states. Therefore, foreign nationals do not have guaranteed access to the EC's system for their GIs, unlike EC nationals.

The Panel did, however, find that a system of GI protection that requires product inspection is not inconsistent with WTO obligations; and that although the Regulation permits the registration of GIs where they conflict with a prior trade mark, the Regulation qualifies as a 'limited exception' to trade mark rights.

16.93   As a result, the EC implemented Regulation 510/2006. However, this would not have appeared to have satisfied the concerns of either Australia or the United States. Specifically, the anxiety would appear to relate to the interaction between trade marks and GIs. Regulation 2081/92 provided for the continued use of trade marks that acquire rights before the submission to the EC of a registration application for a conflicting GI.[146] In Regulation 510/2006 the wording has been changed from 'or the date of submission to the Commission of the application for registration of the designation of origin or geographical indication' to 'or before 1 January 1996'. The argument is that this leaves any additional trade marks acquiring rights after 1 January 1996 potentially vulnerable. The matter appears to be still under discussion between the respective authorities.

Development and reform of the system

16.94   Geographical indications remain on the policy agenda at international (WTO[147] and WIPO[148]), regional (EU),[149] and national levels. Arguments continue between proponents and opponents as to the benefits or otherwise of geographical indications, a divide which tends geographically to be East/West rather than the more usual North/South. The arguments—legal, economic, social, and political—echo those which reverberate around the broader IP framework.

---

[145] WT/DS290/R.   [146] Regulation 2081/92, Art 14(2).

[147] Although progress at the time of writing seemed stalled. A Jessen, 'Geographical indications negotiations in the WTO—the unfulfilled mandate' (2012) 26(9) World Intellectual Property Report 35–37.

[148] For an indication of the current discussions, see the papers made available in connection with Worldwide Symposium on Geographical Indications, Lima, 22–24 June 2011, available at http://www.wipo.int/export/sites/www/freepublications/en/geographical/798/wipo_pub_798.pdf.

[149] Proposal for a Regulation on agricultural product quality schemes, COM(2010) 733 final.

Further reading

Domain names

M Boote, 'What's in a name?' (2006) 28(6) EIPR 349–352

S Chapman and J Holmen, 'New gTLDs—protection or threat for IP owners?' (2006) 28(6) EIPR 315–320

W Chik, 'Lord of your domain, but master of none: the need to harmonize and recalibrate the domain name regime of ownership and control' (2008) 16(1) IJL & IT 8–72

HA Deveci, 'Domain names: has trade mark law strayed from its path?' (2003) 11(3) IJL & IT 203–225

F Gurry, 'Internet domain name disputes' (2006) 17(2) EBL Rev 413–416

G Jacobs, 'Internet specific collisions of trade marks in the domain name system—an economic analysis based on US law' (2006) 37(2) IIC 156–179

C McLeod, 'WIPO: trade and service marks—rights in domain name' [2006] 17(6) Ent LR N56–57

D Mac Sithigh, 'More than words: the introduction of internationalised domain names and the reform of generic top-level domains at ICANN' (2010) 18(3) IJL & IT 274–300

SM Maniatis, 'Trade mark law and domain names: back to basics' (2002) 24(8) EIPR 397–408

A Marinkovic, 'Domain names: towards a new form of IP right' [2011] JIPLP 632

T Varas, 'Sealing the cracks: a proposal to update the anti-cybersquatting regime to combat advertising-based cybersquatting' (2008) 3(4) JIPLP 246

C Wilson 'Internationalised domain names: problems and opportunities' (2004) 10(7) CTLR 174–181

Trade mark use on the Internet, keyword advertising, and auction sites

A Bain, 'Is it an infringement of trade mark law for the operator of an online marketplace (such as eBay) to allow counterfeit goods to be sold? As a matter of policy, should it be?' (2011) 33(3) EIPR 162–168

D Bainbridge, 'Infringement of trademarks on web pages' (2003) 19(2) CLSR 124–130

D Bainbridge, 'Trademark infringement, the Internet and jurisdiction' (2003) 1 JILT at http://www2.warwick.ac.uk/fac/soc/law/elj/jilt/2003_1/bainbridge/

T Bednarz, 'Keyword advertising before the French Supreme Court and beyond—calm at last after turbulent times for Google and its advertising clients?' (2011) 42(6) IIC 641–672

L Curtis, 'Shades—of grey trade mark law and the world wide web' (2004) 6(5) ECL&P 5–7

R Garnett, 'Cross-border internet trade mark litigation: towards a model of co-existence and parallel use' (2006) 28(4) EIPR 213–219

T Headdon, 'Beyond liability: on the availability and scope of injunctions against online intermediaries after L'Oreal v Ebay' (2012) 34(3) EIPR 137–144

A Kur, 'Use of trade marks on the internet—the WIPO recommendations' (2002) 33(1) IIC 41–47

Geographical indications

Book

D Ganjee, *Relocating the Law of Geographical Indications* (2012)

Articles

D Ampollini, 'Cheese for thought for the European Court of First Instance' (2008) 3(1) JIPLP 16

M Bicskei, K Bizer, K Sidali, and A Spiller, 'Reform proposals on the geographical indications of the European Union for the protection of traditional knowledge' (2012) 3(2) WIPO J 222–236

M Blakeney, 'Geographical indications and trade' (2000) 6(2) Int TLR 48–55

R Chesmond, 'Protection or privatisation of culture? The cultural dimension of the international intellectual property debate on geographical indications of origin' [2007] EIPR 379

GE Evans, 'The simplification of European legislation for the protection of geographical indications: the proposed Regulation on Agricultural Product Quality Schemes' (2012) 34(11) EIPR 770–786

GE Evans, 'The comparative advantages of geographical indications and Community trade marks for the marketing of agricultural products in the European Union' (2010) 41(6) IIC 645–674

GE Evans and M Blakeney, 'The protection of geographical indications after Doha: quo vadis?' (2006) 9(3) JIEL 575–614

D Gangjee, 'Say cheese! A sharper image of generic use through the lens of feta' [2007] *EIPR* 172

D Gangjee, 'Melton Mowbray and the GI pie in the sky: exploring cartographies of protection' [2006] 3 IPQ 291–309

M Handler, 'The WTO geographical indications dispute' (2006) 69(1) MLR 70–80

C Heath, 'Parmiggiano Reggiano by another name—on the ECJ's Parmesan decision' (2008) 39 IIC 951

T Kongolo, 'Any new developments with regard to GIs issues debated under WTO?' (2011) 33(2) EIPR 83–90

V Mantrov, 'Protection norms of indications of geographical origin in the applicable EU regulations—recent changes and the need for further unification' (2012) 43(2) IIC 174–202

B O'Connor, 'The EC need not be isolated on GIs', Opinion: [2007] EIPR 303

B O'Connor, 'The legal protection of geographical indications' [2004] 1 IPQ 35–57

D Rangnekar, 'Geographical indications: a review of proposals at the TRIPS Council: extending Article 23 to products other than wines and spirits', UNCTAD–ICTSD 'Project on Intellectual Property Rights and Sustainable Development'

J Reed, 'Feta: a cheese or a fudge? *Federal Republic of Germany v Commission*' (2006) 28(10) EIPR 535–538

N Resinek, 'Geographical indications and trade marks: coexistence or 'first in time, first in right' principle?' [2007] EIPR 447

AF Ribeiro de Almeida, 'The TRIPS Agreement, the bilateral agreements concerning geographical indications and the philosophy of the *WTO*' (2005) 27(4) EIPR 150–153

M Ricolfi, 'Is the European IGs policy in need of rethinking?' (2009) 40 IIC 123

S Stern, 'Are GIs IP?' (2007) 29(2) EIPR 39–42

W Van Caenegem, 'Registered GIs: intellectual property, agricultural policy and international trade' (2004) 26(4) EIPR 170–181

Part VI
Common law protection of intellectual property

Introduction

The various forms of intellectual property discussed in the previous chapters have all had their roots in statute. This Part of the book turns to consider the protection afforded to certain forms of intellectual property which have their base in common law: that is, the law developed in the decisions of the English and Scottish courts over the centuries with the assistance of jurists analysing those judgments in textbooks and treatises. There are two main forms of common law protection: *passing off*, which can be most readily equated with registered trade marks, and *breach of confidence*, which has close links to both copyright and patents. It is important to emphasise that despite these relationships with statutory intellectual property, the common law protections each have their own independent character and scope. A further point is that English and Scots law in the two fields, while very similar, are not necessarily identical and may still develop in slightly different ways. Yet it must also be borne in mind that the rights also have close relationships with other pieces of legislation, particularly regarding information and human rights, as will be explored in this Part.

The chapter on *passing off* explores the three elements which have classically been taken to amount to the legal wrong in question (tort or delict)—goodwill, misrepresentation, and damage—as well as the defences which may be available to the person defending an action based upon such a claim. The chapter then moves to consider contemporary issues that have arisen in the modern law of passing off.

The chapter on *breach of confidence* examines the history and basic principles of the law of confidence in the two main jurisdictions in the UK, with reference to personal information, national security, and employment and post-employment scenarios, the relationship between trade secrets and innovation, a balance between the public interests in preserving confidence and in disclosure, and the impact of the Human Rights Act 1998.

These are followed by a chapter exploring information control and intellectual property. This discusses developments within the passing off and breach of confidence frameworks, in particular combined with human rights, the consequences for the protection of personal privacy, and the more commercial implications for the protection and exploitation of publicity and personality. This last section also looks to trade marks.

Sources of the law: key websites

- Because common law rights arise without registration, and are based upon court decisions, it is necessary to refer to the court websites for freely accessible source material on the Internet. These are most conveniently gathered together on the British and Irish Legal Information website:
  http://www.bailii.org/

- Also important in respect of breach of confidence are decisions of the European Court of Human Rights, for which see the court website
  http://www.echr.coe.int/echr/homepage_EN/

Reference will also be made to the following legislation and instruments:

- Human Rights Act 1998
  http://www.legislation.gov.uk/ukpga/1998/42/contents

- Data Protection Act 1998
  http://www.legislation.gov.uk/ukpga/1998/29/contents

- The European Convention on Human Rights 1950
  http://www.hri.org/docs/ECHR50.html

- TRIPS
  http://www.wto.org/english/tratop_e/trips_e/t_agm0_e.htm

17

Passing off

Introduction

Scope and overview of chapter

17.1 This chapter considers the action of passing off, the means by which one trader may prevent another from misleading customers by representing (or 'passing off') goods or services as emanating from the former party. Although conceptually this part of the law is closely linked to statutory trade mark law, and offers protection to unregistered trade marks which are nonetheless badges of identity in the marketplace, in some ways passing off goes further than trade mark law, and extends to other acts of what could be termed unfair competition.

17.2 **Learning objectives**

By the end of this chapter you should be able to:

- define and explain the scope of the action of passing off;
- define and explain each of the principal elements of passing off, namely, goodwill, misrepresentation, and damage;
- differentiate passing off from other, closely related aspects of intellectual property protection, such as registered trade marks;
- understand and explain the use of passing off to control and protect in evolving areas;
- discuss the relationship between passing off and concepts of unfair competition.

17.3 After an introductory discussion, the chapter analyses the leading judicial definitions of passing off, from which emerge the key elements of goodwill, misrepresentation, and damage. These elements are then taken in turn for more detailed discussion, and some specific issues are considered. The chapter concludes with discussion of key issues regarding the future of passing off, in particular in relation to the Internet and its possible development as a law against unfair competition. So the chapter looks like this:

- Overview of passing off (17.4–17.8)

- Definitions (17.9–17.12)

- Goodwill (17.13–17.34)

- Misrepresentation (17.35–17.56)

- Damage (17.57–17.60)

- Defences (17.61)

- The Internet, passing off, and instruments of fraud (17.62–17.68)

- Unfair competition and passing off (17.69–17.72)

Overview of passing off

17.4   The action of 'passing off' is well established in the various jurisdictions of the UK, having first developed in English common law and then been received in the early 19th century in the Scottish courts.[1] Today there is little if any difference in the two laws on the subject. The usual question in passing off actions is whether in marketing goods or services one party has employed an identifying device or badge associated in the market with another party or parties. In its most typical form the action concerns the use of words or names as trade marks.

> The remedy which the law gives to a person who has used a particular name in trade is that he is entitled to prevent others from using the same name in such a way as is likely to mislead the public into thinking that the business or the goods so described is or are the business or goods of the claimant.[2]

However, as long ago as 1842 Lord Langdale MR suggested that the action was of broader scope than merely the misleading use of names:

> A man is not to sell his own goods under the pretence that they are the goods of another man; he cannot be permitted to practise such a deception, nor to use the means which contribute to that end. He cannot therefore be allowed to use names, marks, letters or other indicia, by which he may induce purchasers to believe, that the goods he is selling are the manufacture of another person.[3]

In modern times, and especially in England, the action has been applied to stop a variety of forms of passing off, using not only names, but also a wide variety of other ways in which traders enable customers to identify their products and distinguish them from those of competitors. One way of thinking about passing off is as a form of protection for unregistered trade marks;[4] but the scope of protection offered by the common law extends beyond trade marks as such. This will be seen throughout this

---

[1]   See on English law, C Wadlow, *The Law of Passing Off: Unfair Competition by Misrepresentation* (4th edn, 2011); H Carty, *An Analysis of the Economic Torts* (2010), Ch 8; M Spence, 'Passing off and the misappropriation of valuable intangibles' (1996) 112 *LQR* 472. On the development of English law, see H Carty, 'The development of passing off in the twentieth century' and C Morcom, 'Leading cases in passing off' both in N Dawson and A Firth (eds), *Trade Marks Retrospective* (2000). For Scots law, see EM Clive, 'The action of passing off: its scope and basis' 1963 JR 117.

[2]   *Kinnell v Ballantyne* 1910 SC 246 per Lord President Dunedin at 251.

[3]   *Perry v Truefitt* (1842) 6 Beav 66 at 73 (49 ER 749 at 752). Note that although Lord Langdale refers only to selling goods, it is clear that passing off also applies to the supply of services. There seems no reason why it should not also apply to the supply of incorporeals and of land and buildings.

[4]   Trade Marks Act 1994, s 2(2): 'No proceedings lie to prevent or recover damages for the infringement of an unregistered trade mark as such; but nothing in this Act affects the law relating to passing off.'

chapter, although it should also be borne in mind that passing off and trade marks are often part of the same action, and courts and parties in some cases have acknowledged that on the facts, success in a trade mark action would mean that there will also be passing off.[5]

Basis of action: misrepresentation and goodwill

17.5 At one time Scots and English lawyers flirted with the idea that the right to prevent passing off arose because the claimant or petitioner had by exclusive appropriation acquired a right of property in his marketing device. This theory became discredited because it was unacceptable to suppose that there could be rights of property in names or words, or that use alone could create such property rights. In England, the action came to be seen as based rather on two elements:

- the existence of trading *goodwill* or reputation, the desire of customers to buy from one trader rather than another, which was conceived of as a right of property of the first trader, especially as it had market value in the buying and selling of the business itself;

- the invasion of that right of property by means of a *misrepresentation*.

Marketing devices are an important element in goodwill because their use enables customers to identify the products of particular traders and to distinguish them from those of competitors. The association between device and trader means that use of the device by another may mislead the customer, who believes he is obtaining the goods and services of one trader while in fact receiving those of another. The typical injury for which the action of passing off provides a remedy is therefore loss of custom to a competitor, while the wrong which leads to the injury is the false statement by the competitor. In Scotland, 'the action for passing off is based on the general right which everyone possesses not to have published about him or his goods, statements which are both untrue and prejudicial to his pecuniary interests.'[6]

> **? Question**
>
> What are the key concepts in passing off? Consider also the evolving debates on their underlying foundation, see H Carty, 'Passing off: frameworks of liability debated' [2012] IPQ 106. Revisit this issue once again at the end of your study of this chapter.

17.6 As a result of its being rooted in the protection of goodwill, passing off is no longer confined to the case of one trader representing his goods as those of another. Wherever there is a misrepresentation damaging goodwill—for example, creating injurious associations in the public mind—there may be a claim for passing off. This is not to say that passing off has become a general law of unfair competition such as is found in various European jurisdictions. Like other items of property, the value of goodwill may fluctuate or even be destroyed as a result of the operations of the market, without giving its owner any legal remedies; the element of misrepresentation is the key which unlocks the door.

[5] See *Yell Ltd v Giboin, Zagg Ltd* [2011] EWPCC 009, *Schutz (UK) Ltd v Delta Containers Ltd* [2011] EWHC 1712 (Ch). Cf *Westwood v Knight* [2011] EWPCC 008, paras 53–56 and 156; *Specsavers International Healthcare Ltd v Asda Stores Ltd* [2012] ETMR 17, para 9.
[6] Clive, note 1, at 134.

> **Key points on general development of passing off**
>
> - Passing off starts with the idea that one person may not represent his goods or services as those of another and so gain business which should have gone to that other
>
> - In modern law, passing off is seen as protecting trading goodwill against misrepresentations in general, and this has been a basis for extending the scope of the action considerably
>
> - A question therefore arises about the extent to which passing off is becoming a law against unfair competition generally, similar to actions of this kind found in other European countries

International background

17.7   Since passing off is a long-established common law matter, it has been less affected than other areas of intellectual property by international conventions. But it has been taken to satisfy the Paris Convention requirement for protection against unfair competition.

Paris Convention Article 10*bis*

(1)   The countries of the Union are bound to assure nationals of such countries effective protection against unfair competition.

(2)   Any act of competition contrary to honest practices in industrial or commercial matters constitutes an act of unfair competition.

(3)   The following in particular shall be prohibited:
1.   all acts of such nature as to create confusion by any means whatever with the establishment, the goods, or the industrial or commercial activities, of a competitor;
2.   false allegations in the course of trade of such a nature as to discredit the establishment, the goods, or the industrial or commercial activities, of a competitor;
3.   indications or allegations the use of which in the course of trade is liable to mislead the public as to the nature, the manufacturing process, the characteristics, the suitability for their purpose, or the quantity, of the goods.

In other countries, particularly in Europe, unfair competition is a civil wrong actionable at the hand of competitors, and is certainly wider in scope than passing off. But as passing off has developed and extended its scope, so questions have been raised as to whether it is moving in the direction of an unfair competition action or, indeed, as to whether an unfair competition action should be introduced by statute, to bring the UK closer to its European neighbours. This issue is discussed later in this chapter (paras 17.69ff).

17.8   The Paris Convention also requires the countries of the Union to protect 'well-known' marks from other member countries by refusing or cancelling registrations or, more importantly for passing off, prohibiting their use by way of reproduction, imitation, or translation, when liable to cause confusion.[7] This was implemented in the UK by section 56 of the Trade Marks Act 1994, and has had an important effect on the law of passing off, to be discussed further below (para 17.16).

---

[7] Paris Convention, Art 6*bis*.

Definitions

17.9 A classical definition of passing off was given in the House of Lords by Lord Oliver in the 'Jif Lemon' case, *Reckitt & Coleman Products v Borden Inc*,[8] when he outlined what had to be shown for a party to succeed in a passing off action as follows:

> *First*, he must establish a *goodwill or reputation* attached to the goods or services which he supplies in the mind of the purchasing public by association with the identifying 'get-up' (whether it consists simply of a brand name or a trade description, or the individual features of labelling or packaging under which his particular goods are offered to the public, such that the get-up is recognised by the public as distinctive specifically of the plaintiff's goods or services. *Second*, he must demonstrate a *misrepresentation* (whether or not intentional) leading or likely to lead the public to believe that goods or services offered by him are the goods or services of the plaintiff. Whether the public is aware of the plaintiff's identity as the manufacturer or supplier of the goods and services is immaterial, as long as they are identified with a particular source which is in fact the plaintiff. For example, if the public is accustomed to rely upon a particular brand name in purchasing goods of a particular description, it matters not at all that there is little or no public awareness of the identity of the proprietor of the brand name. *Third*, he must demonstrate that he suffers or, in a quia timet action, that he is likely to suffer *damage* by reason of the erroneous belief engendered by the defendant's misrepresentation that the source of the defendant's goods or services is the same as the source of those offered by the plaintiff (emphasis added).

This definition, with its trilogy of *goodwill, misrepresentation,* and *damage,* provides an excellent basic structure for an account of the typical case of passing off, where one trader simply sells goods or services in the guise of another trader's goods or services. Hence, it will be used to provide the principal headings in this chapter.

 Question

What does Lord Oliver add to our list of key passing off concepts (cf para 17.5)?

17.10 But as already mentioned, passing off has extended well beyond the typical case with which it began. While Lord Oliver's three elements remain at the heart of this extension, they require some further elaboration. That can be found in an earlier leading House of Lords case, *Erven Warnink v Townend*,[9] the 'Advocaat' case, still probably the most important decision on the extended version of passing off. Lords Diplock and Fraser gave the following definitions in their speeches:

Lord Diplock said (at 742):

> [It is] possible to identify five characteristics which must be present in order to create a valid cause of action for passing off:
>
> (1) a misrepresentation
> (2) made by a trader in the course of trade,
> (3) to prospective customers of his or ultimate consumers of goods or services supplied by him,
> (4) which is calculated to injure the business or goodwill of another trader (in the sense that this is a reasonably foreseeable consequence), and
> (5) which causes actual damage to a business or goodwill of the trader by whom the action is brought or (in a quia timet action) will probably do so.

---

[8] [1990] RPC 341, [1990] 1 WLR 491, 1 All ER 873.   [9] [1979] AC 731, [1979] 3 WLR 68.

Lord Fraser said (at 755–756):

It is essential for the plaintiff in a passing off action to show at least the following facts:

(1) That his business consists of, or includes, selling in England a class of goods to which the particular trade name applies;

(2) That the class of goods is clearly defined, and that in the minds of the public, or a section of the public, in England, the trade name distinguishes that class from other similar goods;

(3) That because of the reputation of the goods, there is goodwill attached to the name;

(4) That he, the plaintiff, as a member of the class of those who sell the goods, is the owner of goodwill in England which is of substantial value;

(5) That he has suffered, or is really likely to suffer, substantial damage to his property in the goodwill by reason of the defendant's selling goods which are falsely described by the trade name to which the goodwill is attached.

17.11   These two statements are not easily reconciled in all respects. Lord Fraser appears to confine passing off to the misuse of trade names in relation to goods, while Lord Diplock speaks simply of misrepresentations in the course of trade, without limiting the ways in which such misrepresentations may be made. It has long been clear, however, that services may be passed off as well as goods (see para 17.4) and that the form which the misrepresentation may take includes statements other than trade names. Lord Fraser's stress on activity and goodwill in England is also important but it is not thought that by this he meant to indicate that the law would be different in Scotland. In general it appears best to treat his remarks as directed entirely at the very special kind of case which he was then deciding, namely, one involving misuse of a trade name in which many traders, some from outside the UK, shared goodwill, and not as intended to restrict the scope of the action in other cases, or in Scotland. Lord Diplock's definition, on the other hand, comprehends not only such trade name cases but also all the other situations in which passing off has been held to have taken place.

 Exercise

What are the differences between (1) Lord Oliver's definition of passing off and (2) those of Lords Diplock and Fraser; or between the definitions of Lords Diplock and Fraser? Does it matter and, if so, why? What do the definitions have in common? Consider this exercise now, and again when you have completed your study of this chapter.

Business context

17.12   The three definitions by Lords Oliver, Diplock, and Fraser have in common that passing off must take place in a business context. Although 'business context' has been widely interpreted in the courts to include, for example, charities,[10] in some cases an action has failed because the context has not been one of commercial activity. In *Kean v McGivan*[11] an action on behalf of a political party regarding the use of the initials 'SDP' failed because the plaintiff was not carrying on a business. Similarly, it may not be possible to prevent another person using the name of one's house.[12] Trade associations such as the Scotch Whisky Association can only sue in respect of their own trading activities as distinct from those of their members, although the members may sue together as individual organisations.[13]

---

[10] See, eg, *British Diabetic Association v Diabetic Society Ltd* [1995] 4 All ER 812.   [11] [1982] FSR 119.

[12] *Day v Brownrigg* (1878) 10 Ch D 294.

[13] See *Consorzio Prosciutto di Parma v Marks & Spencer* [1991] RPC 351; *Chocosuisse Union des Fabricants Suisses de Chocolat v Cadbury* [1999] RPC 826. It is assumed that similar rules would apply in Scotland.

Discussion point   For answer guidance visit www.oxfordtextbooks.co.uk/orc/waelde3e/

Can you conceive of circumstances in which use of the name of another person's house might be passing off? Is a political party any less in business than a charity? What about a school? Or a university?

Key points about the definition of passing off

There are three major elements to be established in a passing off action:

(1) goodwill

(2) misrepresentation

(3) damage

This must all occur in a business context

Goodwill

Definition of goodwill[14]

17.13   It is essential that the party claiming passing off should enjoy goodwill before any action can succeed.

Goodwill is 'the attractive force which brings in custom', or, 'whatever adds value to abusiness by reason of situation, name and reputation' (*IRC v Muller & Co's Margarine Ltd* [1901] AC 217 per Lord Macnaghten at 223 and per Lord Lindley at 235).

These definitions focus attention first on the existence of *customers* as the starting point for understanding the concept, and explain goodwill as that composite of *elements which leads to customers choosing to give their business to a particular trader, or to acquire that trader's product*. Reputation as such is not enough; customers must be attracted to the business as a result of particular element(s) of a trader's activities. Court actions may involve several different sets of goodwill.[15] For there to be protectable goodwill in a device, it must be established that in the relevant market there is an association between it and a particular trader or class of traders. This association requires to be established by evidence. The trader's actual identity need not be known to the public, as long as the device is known to distinguish his product or services in the market.[16] The test for the existence of goodwill is less demanding than that of distinctiveness in relation to registered trade marks.[17] A modest amount of goodwill can suffice.[18]

---

[14] See further H Carty, 'Passing off and the concept of goodwill' [1995] JBL 139.

[15] See also discussion in the fashion context in *Westwood v Knight*, note 5, paras 152, 163, 176–177, 184–186, 202, and 205–207.

[16] *Birmingham Vinegar Brewery Co v Powell* [1897] AC 710; *Hoffmann-La Roche v DDSA* [1969] FSR 410.

[17] *Phones 4U Ltd v Phone4U.co.uk Internet Ltd* [2006] EWCA Civ 244, [2007] RPC 5. For the registered trade mark test of distinctiveness, see paras 14.28ff.

[18] *Lumos Skincare Ltd v Sweet Squared Ltd* [2012] EWPCC 22, paras 38–39.

Question

How may goodwill be defined?

17.14   In general the public's *association* of device with trader should *arise from use* of the device. The period of use need not have been long—three weeks was sufficient to justify the granting of an interlocutory injunction in one English case,[19] a few hours in an Australian one.[20] Publicity prior to the launch of a business may in exceptional circumstances create sufficient goodwill to permit the raising of an action of passing off.[21] Goodwill may survive the cessation of use if there is an intention appropriately manifested to return to business,[22] but if the goodwill is disposed of when the business is abandoned, then there can be no claim of subsequent passing off.[23] The purchaser of goodwill is entitled to protect it by actions of passing off, even against the former owner.[24] Goodwill may be lost over time where there is a cessation or significant reduction in activity and reputation.[25]

■ *Knight v Beyond Properties Pty Ltd* [2007] FSR 34 (Ch)

'Mythbusters' was the title of a series of primary school-age children's books published in the first half of the 1990s. From late 2003, 'Mythbusters' was used by others as the title for a 'dads and lads' TV series. The author of the book series sued the TV producers for passing off. The claim was dismissed. Although the title 'Mythbusters' was capable of generating exclusive goodwill, and the claimant had established a reputation in the UK sufficient to attract passing off protection between 1993 and 1996, it thereafter diminished so that it was no longer significant by 2003.

■ *Wise Property Care Ltd v White Thomson Preservation Ltd* [2008] CSIH 44

In 1976 W and T set up a company called WTP Ltd, carrying out business in property preservation services. In 1983 W and T went their separate ways, trading respectively as WTP (Northern) Ltd (WTPNL) and WTP (Southern) Ltd in different regions of Scotland. W was joined in WTPNL by his three sons, E, G1, and G2. In 2002 the sons left and set up a new company called White Preservation Ltd (WPL); E left this in 2004. In 2005 W retired and WTPNL was dissolved. In 2006 G1 and G2 sold the business and assets of WPL to Wise Property Care Ltd; Wise successfully ran the business until late 2007 as 'White Preservation, a division of Wise Property Care Ltd'. WPL's name was first changed to 'Gragav Ltd', then the company was dissolved. Wise separately set up a company called WPL but it never traded. In 2007 E set up a new company called WTP Ltd, adopting the business get-up of his father's former company and undertaking to honour its guarantees. The court accepted that in effect E was reviving a dormant business. Wise sued E's company for passing off. Interim interdict was granted on the balance of convenience. Wise had built up goodwill in the 'White Preservation' name; the companies were trading in the same business and region; consumers were confused, although local property professionals such as solicitors were not; and WTP Ltd was effectively a newcomer or interloper, the interests of which should be given less weight than those of the established business. Note that although the defender was a 'newcomer', it was in fact the only one of the two companies

---

[19] *Stannard v Reay* [1967] RPC 589.   [20] *Fletcher Challenge v Fletcher Challenge Pty* [1982] FSR 1.

[21] *BBC v Talbot* [1981] FSR 228; *My Kinda Bones v Dr Peppers Stove Co* [1984] FSR 289.

[22] *Norman Kark Publications Ltd v Odhams Press Ltd* [1962] 1 WLR 380; *Ad-Lib Club Ltd v Granville* [1972] RPC 673.

[23] *Star Industrial v Yap Kwee Kor* [1976] FSR 256 (PC).

[24] *Melrose Drover Ltd v Heddle* (1902) 4F 1120; see also *Cowan v Millar* (1895) 22R 833.

[25] *Alexander Fergusson & Co Ltd v Matthews McClay & Manson Ltd* 1989 SLT 795, but residual goodwill can remain, see *Westwood v Knight*, note 5, para 216.

involved which had within its operation a member of the W family which had given its name to the business acquired by the pursuers.[26]

Goodwill and reputation: the problem of foreign goodwill

17.15 There are two problems:

(1) the goodwill which a trader here may enjoy abroad, and

(2) that which a foreigner may have in this country.

It is clear with regard to (1) that a home trader may protect foreign goodwill by means of the action of passing off.[27] However, as far as concerns (2), a complex series of English cases arising before the Trade Marks Act 1994 established that where there was *reputation but no trading activity in England* no action lay.[28] The usual situation was that of a well-known foreign trader whose distinctive indicia had been adopted by another party in England. The foreign plaintiff's passing off action would succeed only if he could show business activity generating goodwill in England; merely being known there will not suffice. Business activity did not necessarily mean having a place of business in England, but might arise through export or other activities, or through the fact that English customers went to the claimant in the latter's country.[29]

■ *Hotel Cipriani SRL v Cipriani (Grosvenor Street) Ltd* [2009] RPC 9, [2010] RPC 16

The Community trade mark 'Cipriani' was used for hotels in Venice, Lisbon, and Madeira by HC, members of the Orient Express Hotels Group. CGSL used the name on a sign for their restaurant in London. It was held that the claimant had to own goodwill in the UK, rather than a mere reputation in the UK. In demonstrating this, it was immaterial whether or not HC had a branch in the UK or traded through intermediaries (provided the importers or distributors did not own the goodwill). In the case of a claimant providing services abroad, as here, it was sufficient to establish UK goodwill that the services were booked by customers in the UK.

17.16 It is submitted that with the development, not only of European and international markets in many fields of business in general, but also of cross-border e-commerce by way of the Internet, it would be unfortunate if the law did not recognise that goodwill may cross national frontiers, and fail in consequence to grant appropriate protection.[30] The consequences of this have been managed, however, by the enactment in section 56 of the Trade Marks Act 1994 of the 'well-known mark' protection under the Paris Convention; under this, mere reputation is enough for the foreign trader to be able to protect its badge of identity in this country.[31]

[26] For comment on this case, see CW Ng, 'A common law of passing-off? English and Scottish perspectives' (2009) 13 Edin LR 134.

[27] See further, para 17.47.

[28] *Anheuser-Busch Inc v Budejovicky Budvar* [1984] FSR 413; note Lord Fraser's speech in *Advocaat*, with its reference to trade in England.

[29] See also *Peter Waterman v CBS* [1993] EMLR 27 and *Jian Tools v Roderick Manhattan Group Ltd* [1995] FSR 924.

[30] See also *Plentyoffish Media Inc v Plenty More Lip* [2012] RPC 5 and the recognition of international goodwill in the Australian case of *ConAgra v McCain Foods (Australia)* (1992) 23 IPR 193 (Fed Ct Aus). Cf *Yell Ltd v Giboin, Zagg Ltd*, note 5, paras 162–170 regarding the extent to which a website is directed at the UK. See D Rose, 'Season of goodwill: passing off and overseas traders' [1995] EIPR 356.

[31] Note, however, *Microsoft Corporation's Applications* [1997–8] Information Technology Law Reports 361, in which 'Windows' was held not to be a well-known mark, at least in May 1991.

England and Scotland

17.17   Since England and Scotland are independent legal systems, each is a foreign country in the other's legal system, and the problem of foreign goodwill thus takes on a particular character in this context. In *Flaxcell v Freedman*[32] a London trader using the name 'Dirty Dick's' was held entitled to interdict a Glasgow trader from trading as 'Dicky Dirts', but there was mail order business in Scotland for the London company. In *Pegasus Security Ltd v Gilbert*[33] an English company commencing business in Scotland obtained interim interdict against an existing Scottish business which had been using a similar name. In both cases it was established that the English trader had goodwill in Scotland despite not having an actual place of business there.

Regional or local goodwill

17.18   Just as goodwill may cross national boundaries, so it may not extend over the whole country but instead be confined to a particular locality. It is not clear whether protection in such cases is also confined to the locality in question, so that another trader may set up in another area using the same badges of identity as the first. In the leading English decision, the plaintiffs' operations were local in character but they were nonetheless granted an injunction covering the whole country.[34] There are other cases, however, where only restricted injunctions were obtained.[35] There seems to be no Scottish discussion in point, but the grant of a limited interdict in an appropriate case would seem consistent with the general principles of passing off.

The question of what constitutes an appropriate case is difficult, however. A business which can only offer services at a fixed location, such as a hotel, club, or restaurant, can nonetheless develop widespread goodwill as the result of passing custom, although its existence may be difficult to prove or disprove.

Key points on goodwill

- Goodwill is about bringing in customers, and in the law of passing off is to be distinguished from mere reputation

- Goodwill is increasingly recognised as an international phenomenon, so that foreign traders may be able to raise actions of passing off in England and Wales or Scotland. The 'well-known mark' provision of the Paris Convention, enacted in this country by section 56 of the Trade Marks Act 1994 has been important in this development

- Traders in this country may also be able to raise actions in this country in respect of passing off abroad

- Goodwill may also be regional or local in character

Product goodwill: 'extended passing off'

17.19   The classical definitions of goodwill as the attractive force which brings in custom do not refer directly to what has been termed *'product goodwill'*, that is, *the reputation which a product has, as distinct from its*

---

[32] 1981 SLT (Notes) 131.   [33] 1989 GWD 26–1186.   [34] *Chelsea Man Menswear Ltd v Chelsea Girl Ltd* [1987] RPC 189.
[35] *Brestian v Try* [1958] RPC 161 (CA).

manufacturer or seller. Passing off nevertheless now protects goodwill of this kind, by finding that certain named products—typically, but not exclusively, alcoholic drinks—are associated with particular characteristics in the marketplace and form a reason why they are bought. This goodwill will be damaged if products without these characteristics can be marketed under the name of the genuine article.[36] But the goodwill in such cases, unlike that protected by classical passing off, is not limited to one trader; instead it is shared by all who produce goods having the characteristics in question, and all have the right to claim passing off protection. Because the protection reaches further in this way, this is often known as *'extended passing off '*. It is to this form of passing off that the definitions of Lords Diplock and Fraser in the *Advocaat* case, quoted at para 17.10, are now typically applied.

Question

How does our previous definition of goodwill (para 17.13) now need to be revised?

Examples of product goodwill recognised by the courts in extended passing off actions include the following.

(1) Champagne

'The region in which the Champagne vineyards are found is about 100 miles east of Paris around Rheims and Epernay, where there is a chalky, flinty soil and the climate is subject to extreme variations of heat and cold.

It appears that these factors give to the wine its particular qualities.... [S]ince 1927 the Champagne Viticole district has been strictly limited by [French] law, and only certain vineyards are allowed in France to use the name 'champagne'.... The wine is naturally sparkling wine made from grapes produced in the Champagne district by a process of double fermentation which requires a considerable amount of care.... [I]n the UK ... champagne is a wine specially associated with occasions of celebration so that (in addition to sales to persons who regularly buy wine), it is purchased on such occasions from time to time by many persons who are not in the habit of buying wine for consumption and are not educated in the nature or qualities of different kinds of wine.'

(*Bollinger v Costa Brava Wine Co Ltd* [1961] 1 WLR 277 per Danckwerts J at 281–282)

(2) Scotch whisky

'"Scotch whisky" as a description has obtained a particular standing.... It may only be applied to a spirit distilled in Scotland from a mash of cereal grain saccharified by the diastase of malt. To such a spirit many individual brand names are applied but, irrespective of that, all producers satisfying the conditions applicable are entitled to describe their product as "Scotch whisky" and to take action to protect the advantages conferred by such a right from improper use of that trade description.'

(*John Walker & Sons v Douglas McGibbon* 1972 SLT 128 per Lord Avonside at 128)[37]

(3) Harris Tweed

'Harris Tweed means a Tweed made from pure virgin wool produced in Scotland, spun, dyed and finished in the Outer Hebrides and handwoven by the Islanders at their own homes in the Islands of Lewis, Harris, Uist, Barra, and their several purtenances and all known as the Outer Hebrides.'

---

[36]   See further S Naresh, 'Passing off, goodwill and false advertising: new wine in old bottles' (1986) 45 CJ 97.
[37]   Regarding 'pure malt', see Burness, 'Scottish Law December/January' IHL 2004, 116 (Dec/Jan), 87–88.

(Harris Tweed Association 1934 definition of Harris Tweed, approved in *Argyllshire Weavers Ltd v A Macaulay Tweeds Ltd* 1965 SLT 21 per Lord Hunter at 33)

(4) Advocaat

'The composition of Dutch advocaat (and therefore, in effect, of all the advocaat sold in England) is regulated by Dutch law and consists of hens' eggs, sugar flavouring and spirit. The spirit used is called in Dutch "brandewijn". Brandewijn is ethyl alcohol derived from grain or molasses. It is not the same as brandy which, at least in modern English usage, means a spirit derived from grapes.'

(*Erven Warnink BV v J Townend & Sons (Hull) Ltd* [1979] AC 731 per Lord Fraser at 749)

(5) Swiss chocolate

'The term "Swiss chocolate" is the designation which has been used, save for very minor exceptions, only on chocolate made in Switzerland in accordance with Swiss food regulations. Subject to the restrictions imposed by these regulations, those chocolates have been made to very different recipes. They taste different from each other and are no doubt of different qualities inter se. Notwithstanding these differences, together they have acquired a reputation for quality.'

(*Chocosuisse Union des Fabricants Suisses de Chocolat v Cadbury Ltd* [1998] RPC 117 per Laddie J at 135; aff'd [1999] RPC 826)

(6) Vodka

'Vodka has, on the judge's findings in this case, become known and recognised for its distinctive qualities as a particular kind of alcoholic drink. Why then, one asks, should it not be entitled to the same protection as champagne given that it satisfies the criteria which the House of Lords has laid down in ADVOCAAT?'

(*Diageo North America Inc v Intercontinental Brands (UCB) Ltd* [2011] RPC 2 per Patten LJ at para 52, aff'g *Diageo Noth America Inc v Intercontinental Brands (UCB) Ltd* [2010] RPC 12)

In the *Chocosuisse* case, Laddie J pointed out that the protection of product goodwill was not available only to 'superior' products.[38] What mattered was the public's *perception* of a distinctive quality about the product, and this was regardless of whether there was any difference in quality and ingredients between goods sold under the name and competing goods. This was upheld by the Court of Appeal in the *Diageo Vodka* case. The key issue in *Diageo* is distinctiveness.

 Discussion point   For answer guidance visit www.oxfordtextbooks.co.uk/orc/waelde3e/

Can you think of any other products on the market in which the goodwill attaches to the product, whoever and no matter how many, manufacture it? From a commercial point of view, what features might the products mentioned be thought to have in common, and how important are they for the protection given?

---

[38] [1998] RPC 117 at 128–129.

Exercise

Consider the Parma Ham case (*Consorzio del Prosciutto di Parma v Marks & Spencer plc* [1991] RPC 351), in which a claim of passing off was rejected, and discuss whether in the light of the European Court of Justice (ECJ) decision, Case C-108/01 *Consorzio del Prosciutto di Parma v Asda Stores Ltd* [2003] ECR I-5121, Parma ham should now be held to enjoy product goodwill for the purposes of protection by actions of passing off in the UK. And what about Feta cheese? (See Case C-465/02 *Germany v Commission of the European Communities* [2006] ETMR 16 (ECJ).)

Key points on product goodwill

- Some products may enjoy goodwill in their own right, as possessing certain characteristics no matter which trader produces and sells them
- Examples include champagne, Scotch whisky, Swiss chocolate, and vodka
- Such goodwill in a product's descriptive name can be protected by actions of passing off, even though it does not belong to any one trader and is instead shared by many

Other types of shared goodwill: (1) groups of companies

17.20   Issues about the possibility of shared goodwill may arise in contexts other than those of product goodwill. In *Habib Bank Ltd v Habib Bank AG Zurich*,[39] it was held that the English subsidiary of a multinational group of companies had the exclusive rights in England to the goodwill in the group's 'Habib' name, so that when it became independent it was able to sue its former holding company for passing off when the latter used the 'Habib' name in England. Similarly, in *Scandecor Development v Scandecor Marketing*,[40] the UK subsidiary of an international business originating from Sweden was held to own exclusive goodwill in England in the name 'Scandecor', so that it was able to resist successfully an attempt to stop it doing so by the company which had taken over the holding company in Sweden. But in *Revlon Inc v Cripps & Lee*,[41] the English subsidiary of a multinational group (Revlon) was unable to prevent the defendant's importation of products manufactured by the US parent company in the group and marked with the Revlon name. It was held that the public, being unaware of the Revlon group's internal structure, did not distinguish amongst the various companies, and that the sale of the imported products was not passing off by the defendants. It is not clear, however, whether this means that the goodwill in the group name is shared amongst the members of the group and, if so, what the nature of each company's property right is. The changing approach to foreign goodwill described previously may also have implications in this context, especially given

[39] [1981] 1 WLR 1265 (CA).   [40] [1999] FSR 27.   [41] [1980] FSR 85 (CA).

that there is no need for public awareness of the precise identity of the person using the badge of identity in issue.

 Question

How may a group of companies share goodwill?

Other types of shared goodwill: (2) franchises

17.21   Franchising operations, under which a franchisor licenses other traders (franchisees) to make use of particular formats under which to do business—for example, in restaurants and dry-cleaning—present similar problems. Clearly the initial goodwill is that of the franchisor, but a successful franchisee (which will be a legally independent undertaking) may be able to generate further goodwill at his particular outlet. Does that goodwill belong to the franchisor, the franchisee, or to both of them, and can it be protected by an action for passing off? The problem is even more acute where the franchisor has no goodwill in England or Scotland when he first licenses his franchisees there. Clearly the activity of the franchisees is what generates the protectable goodwill in this country. It is suggested, nonetheless, that in general the franchisor is the owner of the goodwill. Finally, such case law as there is on conflicts between franchisor and franchisee has held for the former's right to sue the latter for passing off when the licensee attempts to break away and trade independently under the same indicia.[42] Again, a particular problem is where a foreign franchisor seeks to grant franchises within a particular jurisdiction, but finds that the name or other indicia which constitute the franchise have already been appropriated by someone in that market. A number of cases where the franchisor's action has failed illustrate the point that goodwill, not just mere reputation, is required to found an action of passing off.[43]

 Question

How do franchisor and franchisee share goodwill?

Key points on shared goodwill

- In certain circumstances the action of passing off can be used to protect goodwill which is shared by a number of different persons (eg groups of companies and the group name)

- This aspect of the law is often linked to problems of foreign goodwill and reputation in this country

---

[42] *JH Coles Pty Ltd v Need* [1934] AC 82; *British Legion v British Legion Club (Street) Ltd* (1931) 48 RPC 555.
[43] *Athletes Foot Marketing Associates Inc v Cobra Sports Ltd* [1980] RPC 343; *Wienerwald Holding AG v Kwan Wong Tan and Fong* [1979] FSR 381 (Hong Kong). For a Scottish example of a foreign franchisor encountering difficulty of this kind, see *Salon Services (Hairdressing Supplies) Ltd v Direct Salon Services Ltd* 1988 SLT 417.

Focusing the goodwill: protectable devices

17.22   Traders turn customer satisfaction with their goods and services into repeat business—and so good-will—by enabling the customer to recognise the product again, and to distinguish it from competing products by the use of some device in association with the product. The range of devices which the law has been prepared to recognise as constituting badges of identity in the marketplace now stretches very widely, and carries passing off well beyond the scope of traditional trade mark law.[44] In this section of the chapter, we will consider the range of devices which the law has recognised as badges of identity for the purposes of passing off actions, and some of the rules which limit the scope of the protection offered. In particular, we will consider:

- words (including personal, geographical and business names, titles, and invented words);
- get-up (the packaging or dress in which goods are presented to the public);
- use of personalities and characters; and
- advertising techniques and themes.

Protectable devices: words

17.23   The cases show a series of distinctions which the courts have evolved to enable them to test whether a word may be protected by passing off action. The central issue is the trader's freedom to use the language, in particular to provide the customer with a description of the goods or services being offered. No one should be able to claim an exclusive right to use words in use in ordinary English language, unless there is very good reason (ie deception or confusion of customers) to allow them to do so.[45] The courts have thus come up with some distinctions to help to determine when there is such an exclusive right.

'Invented' or 'fancy' words

17.24   Invented or fancy words are much easier to protect by means of the action of passing off because it is more likely that such words will be distinctive of the party making the claim—can be contrasted with *words already established in the English language.*

Examples of invented words:

(1)   Kodak

(2)   FiloFax

(3)   Linoleum

(4)   Adidas

Descriptive or self-laudatory words with secondary meaning through use

17.25   This covers *merely descriptive or self-laudatory words*, giving rise to no rights of exclusive use, and those which, *although descriptive, have acquired a secondary meaning through use*, whereby they serve to distinguish the goods or services of a particular trader in the market and whose use by others may as a result constitute passing off.

---

[44] In *L'Oreal SA v Bellure NV* [2007] RPC 14 at para 164, however, Lewison J states that the smell of a perfume does not form part of its goodwill protectable by the action of passing off, though the Court of Appeal took a different approach: *L'Oreal SA v Bellure NV* [2008] RPC 9 at para 127; contrast registered trade marks: para 14.12.

[45] See, eg, *Reddaway v Banham* [1896] AC 199; in Scotland *Cellular Clothing Co v Maxton & Murray* (1899) 1 F (HL) 29; *Bile Bean Manufacturing Co v Davidson* (1906) 8F 1181; *Kinnell v Ballantine* 1910 SC 246; *Salon Services (Hairdressing Supplies) Ltd v Direct Salon Services Ltd* 1988 SLT 417; *Fine & Country Ltd v Okotoks Ltd* [2012] EWHC 2230 (Ch).

Examples of descriptive words acquiring secondary meanings:

(1) Camel hair (for belts) in *Reddaway v Banham* [1896] AC 199

(2) Special Brew (for beer) in *Carlsberg v Tennant Caledonian Breweries Ltd* [1972] RPC 847

(3) Oven chips (to be oven-cooked rather than fried) in *McCain International v County Fair Foods* [1981] RPC 69

(4) Mothercare (shop and clothing for expectant mothers and young children) in *Mothercare v Penguin Books* [1988] RPC 113

Example of descriptive words without secondary meaning:

(1) Office Cleaning Services as the name of a company providing office cleaning services (*Office Cleaning Services Ltd v Westminster Window and General Cleaning Cleaners Ltd* (1946) 63 RPC 39)

Where words are merely laudatory, however, it may be extremely difficult to show that any secondary meaning has arisen.

Personal and geographical names

17.26   In general, no one can claim an exclusive right in personal and geographical names but, again, a particular name (including a surname, nickname, or an assumed name) or a geographical location or descriptor may, like ordinarily descriptive words, acquire a *secondary meaning through use* in a particular trading context. The name adopted does not have to be the name of a person concerned with the business in order to gain protection, and its scope may extend to the names of fictional characters, although the scope of this protection is unclear.

Examples of personal and geographical names acquiring secondary meaning:

(1) 'Scotch' in the context of whisky (note also its use in the context of adhesive tape, however)

(2) 'Grant' in *William Grant & Sons Ltd v Glen Catrine Bonded Warehouse Ltd* 2001 SC 901 (whisky, vodka, gin)

(3) any number of distillery locations, all in the context of whisky (see, eg, *Highland Distilleries Co plc v Speymalt Whisky Distributors Ltd* 1985 SC 1 (Bunnahabhain, Islay); *William Grant & Sons Ltd v William Cadenhead Ltd* 1985 SC 121 (Glenfiddich))

(4) 'Swiss' in the context of chocolate in *Chocosuisse Union des Fabricants Suisses de Chocolat v Cadbury Ltd* [1998] RPC 117

Titles

17.27   Titles, whether of books, TV and radio programmes, newspapers, magazines, or websites, may again often consist of words and names in use in ordinary language all the time. But if it can be shown that distinctiveness has been acquired in the marketplace, then exclusive rights may be asserted by way of passing off.

Examples of protected titles:

(1) *The Times* newspaper in *Walter v Ashton* [1902] 2 Ch 282 (the newspaper could stop sales of Times bicycles)

(2) *EastEnders* TV programme (*BBC v Celebrity Centre* (1988) 15 IPR 333—an injunction granted to stop book entitled *A to Z of East Enders*)

Contrast:

(1) *GTG Sports Publications Ltd v Fitness Shop (Publications) Ltd* 1983 SC 115 (magazines on Scottish rugby: the title *Scottish Rugby* held not distinctive, being merely descriptive of the magazine contents, and so *Rugby Scotland* could not be stopped)

Note also cases about English newspapers adopting the titles of Scottish ones. In the two leading cases the English courts refused to grant injunctions to the Scottish plaintiffs on the grounds of lack of confusion between the newspapers concerned (*George Outram v London Evening Newspapers* (1911) 28 RPC 308—*Evening Times* in Glasgow and London; *D & C Thompson v Kent Messenger* [1975] RPC 191—*Sunday Post* in Scotland and south-east England). Would this happen now with the Internet?

Business names

17.28 Business names may often consist of personal names, descriptive words, or invented words, or some combination of these. Again, if distinctiveness in the marketplace is achieved, then the name may be protected by way of passing off. The cases illustrate this with regard to clubs, hotels, restaurants, professional associations, and musical bands, as well as those of partnerships and companies.

Examples of distinctive business names:

(1) Annabel's in *Annabels v Shock* [1972] RPC 838 (club)

(2) The Drifters in *Treadwell's Drifters Inc v RCL Ltd* 1996 SLT 1048 (musical group)

(3) Radio Rentals in *Radio Rentals Ltd v Rentals Ltd* (1934) 51 RPC 407 (shop/supplier)

But it may be very difficult to show distinctiveness in certain words in certain contexts: for example, 'International' in the case of hotels (*Park Court Hotel Ltd v Trans-World Hotels Ltd* [1970] FSR 89) or 'Salon Service' for hairdressing supplies (*Salon Services (Hairdressing Supplies) Ltd v Direct Salon Services Ltd* 1988 SLT 414).

Abbreviations and combinations of letters and numbers

17.29 If ordinary words might be thought normally open for use by all, this is even more so for the individual letters which go to make them up; and also numerals. But in a world where acronyms and short, eye-catching abbreviations or combinations of letters and numbers are ever more important badges of identity, passing off can be used to protect such identifiers if they have become distinctive.

Examples of distinctive abbreviations, initials, and numerals:

(1) CA in *Society of Accountants in Edinburgh v Corporation of Accountants* (1893) 20R 750

(2) BMA in *British Medical Association v Marsh* (1931) 48 RPC 565

But not:

(1) FCUK in *French Connection v Sutton* [2000] ETMR 341

17.30 What appears to be most important overall, therefore, is the creation or acquisition of distinctiveness in the marketplace of a word or combination of words (or letters and numerals). But the distinctiveness thus created or acquired can also be lost.[46] So a trader who invents a word for a product will have to be vigilant to prevent its use by other traders for similar products, since if this is not stopped the word

---

[46] *Burberry v Cording* (1909) 26 RPC 693.

will cease to be distinctive of the original product and become a *generic* term for all products of that particular kind. A well-known example is the word 'Linoleum' for a certain type of floor-covering, originally manufactured under a patent and using the name Linoleum by the patent holder alone. But once the patent had expired, other manufacturers moved into the market, also using the name Linoleum. The former patent holder's attempt to stop this was unsuccessful, on the grounds that the word had become a generic term for floor-covering of this type, and had ceased to be distinctive of the original manufacturer.[47]

 Question

Explain how an initially distinctive product name may become 'generic'. How can passing off actions help to prevent this?

17.31   On the other hand, in many extended passing off cases, initially descriptive words came once again also to indicate goods of a particular quality or set of characteristics in that context, so many traders making goods of that quality or with those characteristics could use the name without its necessarily losing its secondary and distinctive meaning.[48]

Key points about descriptive words and secondary meanings

- The use of ordinary words in the English language as part of a business identity can become associated with a particular trader in the marketplace, so that exclusive use can be claimed by way of the action for passing off. The words are then said to have acquired a 'secondary meaning'

- Just as words can acquire a secondary meaning, so they can lose it if the trader fails to defend its exclusivity in the marketplace

- Even invented words can become generic, that is, descriptive of all goods or services of a particular kind, if their exclusivity is not defended quickly enough

 Discussion point   For answer guidance visit www.oxfordtextbooks.co.uk/orc/waelde3e/

Why do extended passing off cases (the ones about product goodwill—para 17.19) allow for the protection of a generic name for a product? What is the difference from cases where words are held to be merely descriptive or to lack a secondary meaning associating it with a particular trader?

Protectable devices: get-up

17.32   Get-up is *'the dress in which the goods are offered to the public'*.[49] If distinctive of the goods, a feature by which customers distinguish the product from those of competitors, it may be protected by an action of

---

[47] *Linoleum Manufacturing Co v Nairn* (1878) 7 Ch D 834.
[48] *Erven Warnink v Townend* [1979] AC 731. Compare para 14.107.
[49] *John Haig & Co v Forth Blending Co* 1954 SC 35 per Lord Hill Watson at 38.

passing off. Get-up will usually be the packaging of the goods, either in whole or in part. Some examples are as follows. ·

(1) The *whole packaging* such as:

- the Coca-Cola or the Haig 'Dimple' bottles in *Coca Cola v Barr* [1961] RPC 387; *John Haig & Co v Forth Blending Co* 1954 SC 35;

- the lemon-shaped container of lemon juice in *Reckitt & Colman Products v Borden Inc* [1990] 1 All ER 873.

(2) Some feature of the packaging:

- colouring in *Hoffmann-La Roche v DDSA* [1969] FSR 410 (black and green colours of Librium capsules);

- stylised typeface of writing appearing on the goods in *Carrick Jewellery Ltd v Ortak* 1989 GWD 35–1624;

- the combination of some features of a vacuum cleaner, the name 'Henry', black bowler hat top, smiley face, and nose of hole for hose in *Numatic International Ltd v Qualtex UK Ltd* [2010] RPC 25.

However, the *shape of the product itself* generally *cannot* be a badge of identity and goodwill, although some part thereof may be. An example of a product shape denied protection was Cadbury's chocolate flake in *Cadbury Ltd v Ulmer GmbH* [1988] FSR 385.

 Exercise

Consider the distinction between 'get-up' and the shape of the product in the light of the cases where a container gives shape to an otherwise formless product, as in the drinks and lemon juice decisions. See the comments of Lord Oliver in *Reckitt & Colman Products v Borden Inc* [1990] RPC 341 at 410, [1990] 1 WLR 491 at 503, [1990] 1 All ER 873 at 884. Consider also that three-dimensional items, like the Coca-Cola bottle, could not be protected under the UK Trade Marks Act 1938, although they can be protected under the UK Trade Marks Act 1994 (see para 14.8). How does this influence your view of the cases?

Key points about get-up

- Passing off will protect distinctive packaging, or distinctive aspects of the packaging, of goods

- But the shape of the *product itself* cannot generally be a basis for a claim, although some distinctive part of the product may be

---

17.33   Features of the way in which goods or services are offered to the public, other than packaging or shape, could be protected by the action of passing off: for example, the ambience or decor of a restaurant,[50] or the nature of 'back-up' services offered by authorised dealers in the goods of particular manufacturers,[51] or the conduct of business over the Internet in a particular format and style.[52] The smell of a fine fragrance has been held not to form part of its goodwill protectable by passing off. In the Court of Appeal

---

[50] See *My Kinda Town v Soll* [1983] RPC 407.   [51] *Sony v Saray* [1983] FSR 302.   [52] *easyJet v Dainty* [2002] FSR 111.

in that case, Jacob LJ said that a fragrance might be a source of goodwill, 'but that does not mean that anyone who seeks to emulate the fragrance is guilty of any wrong.'[53]

■ *easyJet v Dainty* [2002] FSR 6

In this case, the judge (at p 114) described the way in which easyJet and the other 'easy-' businesses carried in their image:

> the following distinctive combination of features. First of all, the name 'easy' together with another word which alludes to the service in question being offered, so as to form one new word, such as the word 'easyJet' in the case of the airline, or 'easyRentacar' in the case of the third claimant. Secondly, the word 'easy' in this formulation is in lower case in the case of every one of the uses of the combination. Thirdly, in every combination the first letter of the second word is displayed as a capital letter so that easyJet has a capital J, easyEverything a capital E and easyRentacar a capital R. Fourthly, in every case the get-up is against a bright orange background with plain white lettering except on occasions where the colouring is reversed so that the background is white and the lettering is in the same distinctive orange colour, as has usually been associated with the product in question.... [O]ne of the distinctive features is that business is either with, to do with, or conducted over the Internet so that the evidence suggests something of the order of 75, sometimes 81% of bookings on an individual day might be done and conducted over the Internet, ... But it is a highly Internet organised business and this is a matter which also needs to be taken into account.

Key point on business image

- Passing off can protect the equivalent of 'get-up' for services, the image of a business

---

Advertising themes and techniques

17.34   In *Cadbury Schweppes Pty Ltd v Pub Squash Co Pty Ltd*[54] Cadbury marketed their non-alcoholic soft drink 'Solo' in Australia with a theme of rugged masculine endeavour, showing dynamic young men quenching the thirst arising from their activities by drinking 'Solo'. Pub Squash began to market their rival soft drink product with a similar campaign. Cadbury's claim that this was passing off was rejected by the Privy Council because the original advertising campaign had not achieved exclusive goodwill for them. But Lord Scarman stated one effect of the *Advocaat* case as follows:[55]

> the tort is no longer anchored, as in its early nineteenth century formulation, to the name or trade mark of a product or business. It is wide enough to encompass other descriptive material, such as slogans or visual images, which radio, television or newspaper advertising campaigns can lead the market to associate with a plaintiff's product, provided always that such descriptive material has become part of the goodwill of the product. And the test is whether the product has derived from the advertising a distinctive character which the market recognises.

---

[53] *L'Oreal SA v Bellure NV* [2007] RPC 14 (Lewison J) [2008] RPC 9 (CA), para 127.   [54] [1981] 1 WLR 193 (PC).
[55] *Cadbury Schweppes* at 200.

> **Key point on advertising themes**
>
> • The *Pub Squash* case recognises the possibility of an advertising theme or slogan being part of the image of a business protectable by way of passing off

Misrepresentation

17.35   Passing off provides a remedy for *misrepresentation*, appropriating, or otherwise diminishing the goodwill of another trader. A misrepresentation is a false statement of fact. In passing off, the false representation is that the goods or services in which the defendant trades are those of the claimant, or in some way have a business connection with the claimant, or have the particular qualities of the claimant's goods or services. It is comparatively easy to determine that this is what the defendant has done when he uses exactly the same device as the claimant in connection with an identical or similar product,[56] or even a similar name[57] but even there it must be clear that the claimant's goodwill will be damaged.

■ ***Mothercare UK Ltd v Penguin Books Ltd* [1988] RPC 113 (CA)**

The claimant, a well-known retailer of goods for mothers, babies, and small children, failed to establish that the use of the phrase 'Mother Care' in the title of a controversial book would lead the public to take the book as a publication of the retailer.

Yet even when the defendant has *copied* the claimant's badge of identity, passing off will not provide a remedy unless the latter's goodwill has been damaged.[58]

 Question

What is the typical misrepresentation in a passing off case?

17.36   Generally, the representation is of a more subtle kind than exact reproduction of a badge of identity, with either the nature of the defendant's statement, or the nature of the goods or services provided by him, or the way in which the defendant conducts himself in relation to the goods and services, or some combination of these things,[59] being different in some way from that of the claimant. The key factor is *the way in which the market reacts to the defendant's activities*. It must be shown that there has been, or that there is likely to be, *confusion about the existence of a trading link between the defendant's product and the claimant* as a result of what the defendant has done. In approaching this question it is important to remember that the confused public need not be aware of the claimant's actual identity (see para 17.13).

---

[56] See, eg, *Kinnell v Ballantine* 1910 SC 246 ('Horseshoe' for boilers); *Carlsberg v Tennant Caledonian Breweries Ltd* [1972] RPC 847 ('Special Brew' for lager); *Thistle v Thistle Telecom Ltd* 2000 SLT 262 ('Thistle' in relation to telecoms hardware and services); *Future Publishing Ltd v Edge Interactive Media Inc* [2011] ETMR 50 ('Edge' in relation to computer games).

[57] See *Woolley v Ultimate Products Ltd* [2012] EWHC 339 (Ch) regarding 'Henley' and 'Henleys', paras 37–41 and 42 regarding damage, aff'd on appeal *Woolley v Ultimate Products Ltd* [2012] EWCA Civ 1038.

[58] See, eg, *County Sound plc v Ocean Sound plc* [1991] FSR 367; *Arsenal Football Club plc v Reed* [2001] RPC 922.

[59] See, eg, *Specsavers International Healthcare Ltd v Asda Stores Ltd* [2011] FSR 1, paras 190–192.

■ *United Biscuits (UK) Ltd v Asda Stores Ltd* [1997] RPC 513

Asda began to market 'Puffin' biscuits to compete with UB's 'Penguin' biscuits. Asda were careful to design their packaging to avoid deception of customers, but at the same time sought to match, or challenge, or parody, the 'Penguin' style, using the image of the relevant bird and the name in black lettering alongside on the packaging, as well as similar colours and wrapping materials. See the report at p 516 for colour images of the competing wrappers. It was held that there was passing off, in that customers might be led by the similarities of get-up to suppose that the two biscuits came from the same manufacturing source.

17.37 The courts have adopted an increasingly broad approach to what kinds of misrepresentation constitute passing off, although a narrower approach in a situation akin to 'Puffin/Penguin' was taken in *Mars UK Ltd v Burgess Group plc*. This involved advertisements for cat food, and greater regard was had to differences in colour and packaging.[60]

■ *Lang Brothers v Goldwell* 1980 SC 237

This case held that it was misrepresentation to attach indicia of Scottishness (appearance on the bottle label of the name 'Wee McGlen', a tartan background, and a thistle device, and the deployment in newspaper advertisements of a caricature of a be-tartaned Scotsman) to a whisky-based product not wholly produced in Scotland.

■ *Associated Newspapers plc v Insert Media Ltd* [1991] FSR 380

A business which inserted advertising material between the pages of national newspapers without the authority of the newspaper publishers was held to misrepresent that such authority had been obtained.

■ *British Sky Broadcasting Group plc v Sky Home Services Ltd* [2007] FSR 14 (Briggs J)

The claimant BSB provided extended warranty services under the name 'Sky Repair Protection Plan' in respect of satellite broadcast reception equipment on which its Sky satellite broadcasts were viewed. The defendant SHS also marketed and supplied extended warranty contracts using corporate names including the word 'Sky' or confusingly similar words. Held that there was passing off by way of implied misrepresentations, including failure of the SHS salesforce to correct the misapprehensions held by customers as to their links with BSB. BSB had held a de facto monopoly in their services and, in entering such a market, SHS had a duty to take care that their marketing methods did not convey the implicit message of a connection with the existing monopolist.

17.38 It is no longer the law that the misrepresentation should have been fraudulent. In England, once passing off was explained as a protection of property in goodwill, the importance of fraud waned as an element in the action, although it is still occasionally mentioned. Fraud was never important in Scotland. Intention to deceive may make proof of confusion and damage to goodwill easier, but intention not to deceive, as in the *Puffin/Penguin* case (para 17.36), will not prevent a successful action of passing off if, nevertheless, customers are confused.

17.39 This will of course very much depend on the facts of the case; the intention of the trader, even a decision to 'live dangerously' will not necessarily lead to a finding of passing off. Issues can arise in particular

---

[60] [2004] EWHC 1912 (Ch), in particular para 33.

from two different perspectives; first, a decision by a marketing department to try to work alongside, while still within the law, the product, service, or advertising campaign, say, of another.[61] The second issue is the use of descriptive words or geographical and personal names. With regard to the use of one's own name in relation to one's business, it is no longer (if it ever was) the law that there is a right to use one's own name which can be used to fend off a claim of passing off: 'a man is entitled to carry on his business in his own name so long as he does not do anything more than that to cause confusion with the business of another, and so long as he does it honestly.'[62]

Again, the claimant will have a remedy if the defendant's statement falsely suggests a trading connection between them, even if in other respects the defendant's statement is a true description of his goods or services.

Consider the following cases.

■ *Dunlop Pneumatic Tyre Co v Dunlop Motor Co* 1907 SC (HL) 15

The Court of Session and the House of Lords agreed that car dealers were entitled to use their surnames as a business name, even though it was already the company name of the tyre manufacturer claimants.

■ *Parker-Knoll Ltd v Knoll International Ltd* [1962] RPC 265 (HL)

Parker-Knoll, manufacturers of furniture, became so named after the English company Parker & Sons purchased a springing system for chairs invented by Wilhelm Knoll. Wilhelm's nephew, Hans Knoll, developed Knoll International as an international furniture business from the United States, and sought to enter the UK market. It was held that Knoll International could not enter the UK furniture market using the word 'Knoll', even though it was the personal name of their founder. A name may be used as a mark under which a person's goods are sold so that the name comes to mean goods sold by that person and not those of anyone else, even when that other has the same name.

■ *BIBA Group v Biba Boutique* [1980] RPC 143

An individual may not be free to use her nickname if that name is already associated in the public mind with an existing trader.

■ *John Haig & Co Ltd v John D D Haig Ltd* 1957 SLT (Notes) 36

A man may be unable to give his name to his company if that name is already associated in the public mind with an existing trader in a relevant market. Here the new trader manufactured whisky liqueur chocolates, which was too close to the existing trader's whisky business.

---

[61] 'Living dangerously' can be particularly relevant here, see *Specsavers International Healthcare Ltd v Asda Stores Ltd*, note 59, para 193, and note 5, paras 71 and 115–116 (although the appeal before it did not involve passing off), discussed in respect of passing off in *Fine & Country Ltd*, note 45, paras 177(9), (10) and 179.

[62] *Joseph Rodgers & Sons Ltd v WN Rodgers & Co* (1924) 41 RPC 277 per Romer J; approved in *Parker-Knoll Ltd v Knoll International Ltd* [1962] RPC 265 (HL), discussed in *Asprey & Garrard Ltd v Wra (Guns) Ltd and Asprey* [2002] ETMR 47, paras 41–45 and quoted in *Reed Executive plc v Reed Business Information Ltd* [2004] RPC 40 (CA) per Jacob LJ at para 109, see also *IN Newman Ltd v Richard T Adlem* [2006] FSR 16, paras 46–47.

■ *Office Cleaning Services Ltd v Westminster Window & General Cleaners Ltd* (1946) 63 RPC 39 (HL)

The plaintiffs, who traded as 'Office Cleaning Services', were held unable to prevent the defendants carrying on business as 'Office Cleaning Association'. The term 'office cleaning' described the nature of the activity carried on and only a small differentiation between the two names was therefore required to avoid passing off.

Question

To what extent may a trader use his own name in business?
Is fraud or intent to deceive a necessary element of the misrepresentation required for passing off?

Key points on misrepresentation

- The misrepresentation is a statement that the goods or services in which the defendant trades are those of, or have a business connection with, the claimant, or have the particular qualities of the claimant's goods or services

- The misrepresentation must have damaged the claimant's goodwill by causing confusion in the marketplace for the goods or services

- The misrepresentation need not have been fraudulent

- Traders are not entitled to use descriptive terms or their personal names as those of their businesses if that would cause confusion with another's business

Discussion point

Review the range of findings of misrepresentation in *Westwood v Knight* [2011] EWPCC 008, paras 157–158, 168, 190–191, 200, 202, 204, 212, and 220–221.
Is this what you would have expected given the cases discussed previously?
Do you agree with the findings regarding Knight's conduct as a whole, paras 222–226?
Compare *Specsavers International Healthcare Ltd v Asda Stores Ltd* [2011] FSR 1, paras 190–192.

Confusion and misrepresentation

17.40   Confusion amongst the public as to the source of the goods or services, or as to their qualities in appropriate cases, is at the heart of passing off. The key factor is *the way in which the market reacts to the defendant's activities*. It must be shown that there has been, or that there is likely to be, *confusion about the existence of a trading link between the defendant's product and the claimant* as a result of what the defendant has done. It is not necessary that the whole of the public is confused, while it is not fatal to a claim that many members—even the majority[63]—of the public are not confused by the defendant's conduct. What matters is that there is, or there is likely to be, confusion amongst significant numbers of the public in

---

[63] See, eg, *Chocosuisse Union des Fabricants Suisses de Chocolat v Cadbury* [1998] RPC 117, [1999] RPC 826.

the market where the parties operate.[64] Intention is again not required, but if there is a decision to 'live dangerously' this can form part of the analysis of the likely response of consumers.[65]

■ *Clark v Associated Newspapers* [1998] 1 All ER 959

The London *Evening Standard* carried a weekly parody of the famous diaries of Alan Clark, a well-known Conservative MP. The articles were entitled 'Alan Clark's Secret Political Diaries'.
Each article had a photograph of Clark and a byline indicating that it was in fact written by a journalist imagining how Clark would be recording events. It was held that this was passing off even though many readers would not be misled; but as an evening paper read by commuters on their homeward journeys, a substantial number would be confused, and that was enough. See also para 3.47 on moral rights and para 19.43 regarding personality aspects of this case.

■ *Topps Company Inc v Tom Hannah Agencies Ltd* 1999 GWD 40–1957

This was a case about children's confectionery. Lord Nimmo Smith said: 'I have to consider what impression might be made on a child who goes into a typical corner shop clutching a 50p coin and gazes up at the whole range of confectionery on display, all competing by various forms of get-up and other attraction for the child's attention and purchasing power.'

It is permissible to lead evidence that members of the public have been confused. So, for example, in *Great North of Scotland Railway Co v Mann*,[66] which concerned the names of hotels, there was evidence that customers seeking one hotel had been taken to the other. In *Chill Foods (Scotland) Ltd v Cool Foods Ltd*,[67] a letter from a supplier was used as evidence that there was confusion between the parties as a result of their similar trading names. In *Phones 4U Ltd v Phone4U.co.uk Internet Ltd*,[68] emails from customers to the defendant's website showed that these people thought they were communicating with the claimant's business, even after visiting the website.

■ *D Jacobson & Sons Ltd v Globe GB Ltd and another* [2008] EWHC 88 (Ch)

G marketed footwear by the name of 'Globe Finale', 'Globe Wedge', and 'Globe Motto'. DJ, who owned the IP rights in Gola footwear, alleged, inter alia, that G was passing off the Gola footwear brand. The Globe shoes featured a stripe design on the sides similar to that featured on the Gola footwear. Held that there was passing off. Copious evidence in the form of, inter alia, consumer surveys, advertisements, and the product's long history was relied upon to reach the conclusion that DJ's shoes enjoyed significant goodwill and a strong reputation. The side design on G's shoes was held to misrepresent to the public that they were DJ's shoes. While there was no evidence of actual loss or damage resulting from confusion generated by the Globe footwear, the confusion that resulted between the two brands put DJ's goodwill at risk as it could not control G's use of the designs.

■ *Diageo North America Inc v Intercontinental Brands (UCB) Ltd* [2011] RPC 2; aff'g *Diageo North America Inc v Intercontinental Brands (UCB) Ltd* [2010] RPC 12

In this case discussed at para 17.19, the court held, affirmed on appeal, that the use of 'vodkat' on a drink which was not vodka would confuse customers. The court at first instance gave examples of how this could possibly be avoided: (1) if the product is prominently described on the front label as 'a mixure

[64] For an argument about the point of time at which confusion must take place in order to be legally actionable, see P O'Byrne and B Allgrove, 'Post-sale confusion' [2007] 2 JIPLP 315.
[65] *Fine & Country Ltd*, note 45, para 180.   [66] (1892) 19R 1035.   [67] 1977 SLT 38.   [68] [2007] RPC 5 (CA).

of fermented alcohol and vodka'; (2) it was in a get-up not reminiscent of vodka; (3) shops had been instructed to display the product well away from vodka; and (4) the product has been advertised and promoted in a way which educated the public as to the nature of the product (first instance, para 167; this issue was not under appeal).

17.41 Where it is averred that the passing off consists of supplying one type of goods when another type has been asked for, the evidence gleaned from placing 'trap orders' may also be accepted by the courts. A systematic survey of the public may be used as evidence of the confusion caused by the defendant's activities,[69] but will often be subject to methodological challenge, since it is usually produced at the behest of one or other or the contending parties. Expert evidence may also be led to help the court to understand such matters as the nature of the marketplace and the attention which the typical customer gives to aspects of the appearance of a product in that marketplace.[70] Further, in *Arsenal Football Club plc v Reed*,[71] which concerned the sale of unlicensed merchandise bearing Arsenal insignia outside the club's ground, Laddie J suggested that the club could have set up a mock stall with the type of products sold only by the defendant and then interviewed customers to find out their motives and beliefs when purchasing Arsenal memorabilia. But the decision on whether or not there is confusion is ultimately for the judge.[72] In the *Arsenal* case, Laddie J was unwilling to infer confusion in the absence of evidence that it existed, because the defendant had been trading in the way complained of for 30 years, quite openly and extensively.[73]

 Question

What level of public confusion must be shown for misrepresentation and a claim of passing off to be made out?

17.42 In many cases, the claimant will be seeking to prevent the defendant's activities, not on the basis that the public is already confused, but rather because of concern that the public is *likely* to be confused if the defendant's activities are allowed to continue unchecked. In testing the likelihood of confusion, two points must be borne in mind. One is the conditions in the market where the parties operate. 'Thirsty folk want beer, not explanations.'[74] Accordingly the differences between the devices of claimant and defendant, or any disclaimers which may be attached to the defendant's product, should only be given the degree of attention which the typical customer would use. Conversely, it can suffice for there to be initial instance confusion, even if the confusion has passed by the time of sale, although this will depend very much on the facts.[75]

---

[69] See, eg, *Coca-Cola v Struthers* 1968 SLT 353; *Neutrogena Corporation v Golden Ltd* [1996] RPC 473; *Chocosuisse*, note 13; *Numatic*, see para 17.31; *Lumos Skincare Ltd v Sweet Squared Ltd*, note 13, para 87(5), (6).

[70] See, eg, *Reckitt & Colman*, see para 17.19; *Chocosuisse*, note 13.

[71] [2001] RPC 922.   [72] See, eg, *Woolley v Ultimate Products Ltd* (CA), note 57, paras 43 and 47.

[73] Arsenal did not appeal against Laddie J's judgment on passing off. The case proceeded to other courts on issues about registered trade marks infringement: see further [2003] RPC 9 (ECJ); [2002] EWHC 2695 (Ch, Laddie J); [2003] RPC 39 (CA); and paras 15.10ff. But note the *obiter* comment of Aldous LJ in the Court of Appeal that he was unconvinced by Laddie J's rejection of the passing off claim ([2003] RPC 39, para 70).

[74] *Montgomery v Thompson* [1891] AC 217 per Lord Macnaghten at 225.

[75] *Och-Ziff Management Europe Ltd v Och Capital LLP* [2011] FSR 11, paras 155–157.

■ *Haig & Co v Forth Blending Co* 1954 SC 35

This case concerned the use of 'dimple'-shaped bottles for whisky. The defender's labelling was different from the pursuer's and the bottles were closed with corks rather than patent stoppers. There was little likelihood of confusion while the bottles remained unopened. But the whisky was sold in pubs, with the bottles open and a pourer attached to the top. With evidence that even barmen might confuse the rival products in the atmosphere of a pub, it was held that the defender's bottle was likely to cause confusion sufficient to amount to passing off.

■ *Reckitt & Coleman Products v Borden Inc* [1990] RPC 341, [1990] 1 WLR 491, [1990] 1 All ER 873

This case concerned the lemon-shaped containers of lemon juice sold typically in supermarkets. The shape, size, and colour of the containers were the same, but the neck-labels on the two products were different, and the word 'Jif' was embossed on the side of the plaintiffs' container. For colour photos of the competing 'lemons', see [1990] RPC at 343. There was evidence that members of the public picking up the defendants' lemon juice from open shelves in supermarkets would think that they were getting Jif lemon juice. The trial judge, Walton J, had said: 'One is typically dealing with a shopper in a supermarket, in something of a hurry, accustomed to selecting between various brands when there is such a choice, but increasingly having to choose in relation to a wide range of items between the supermarket's "own brand" and one other brand, and no more' ([1987] FSR 505 at 512). Lord Oliver said: 'The crucial point of reference for the shopper requiring Jif juice is the natural lemon-shape and size which had for many years, with only immaterial exceptions, been utilised solely by the respondents in the context of this particular trade' ([1990] 1 WLR 491 at 503).

17.43 The second point is, however, the consideration that if the defendant's activities would confuse or deceive only 'a moron in a hurry',[76] or 'a very small, unobservant section of society',[77] then there is no passing off. The court must adopt the stance of the reasonable person in all the circumstances (personified in one Scottish case as 'the average citizen of Kilmarnock'[78]) and consider the likelihood of his being confused. But it is important also to remember the diversity of customers in the marketplace, and that reasonableness is not some absolute objective standard in this context.[79]

■ *Taittinger SA v Allbev Ltd* [1993] FSR 641

This was a decision about passing off a carbonated, non-alcoholic soft drink as champagne by naming it 'Elderflower Champagne', selling it in outlets which also sold champagne, in bottles of the same shape, size, and colour as champagne, with labels and wired corks like those used for champagne. 'Elderflower Champagne' sold for £2.45 per bottle, while champagne was normally three or four times that amount at the time. It was held that there was passing off. The average person would not be deceived. 'But there is another section of the public. There is the simple unworldly man who has in mind a family celebration and knows that champagne is drunk for celebrations. He may know nothing of elderflower champagne as an old cottage drink. Seeing "Elderflower" on a label with below the word "Champagne" he may well suppose that he is seeing champagne. Since the simple man I have in mind will know little of champagne prices, he is likely to suppose that he has found champagne at a price of £2.45. I do not mean that I now refer to any majority part of the public or even to any very substantial section of the public, but to my mind there must be many members of the public who would suppose that the defendants'

---

[76] *Morning Star Co-operative Society v Express Newspapers* [1979] FSR 113 per Foster J at 117.
[77] *Newsweek Inc v BBC* [1979] RPC 441 per Lord Denning MR at 447.
[78] *Dunlop Pneumatic Tyre Co v Dunlop Motor Co* 1907 SC (HL) 15 per Lord James of Hereford at 17.
[79] See also discussion in *Fine & Country Ltd*, note 45, paras 75–82.

"Elderflower" is champagne' (per Sir Mervyn Davies at 654). In the Court of Appeal, Peter Gibson LJ quoted this passage and added (at 667): 'It seems to me at least as likely that a not insignificant number of members of the public would think it had some association with champagne, if it was not actually champagne … It is right not to base any test on whether a moron in a hurry would be confused, but it is proper to take into account the ignorant and unwary.'

See also:

■ *Chocosuisse Union des Fabricants Suisses de Chocolat v Cadbury Ltd* [1998] RPC 117

This was a passing off action by manufacturers of Swiss chocolate against the UK company Cadbury, which was marketing a new chocolate product called 'Swiss Chalet'. The report has five pages of slightly fuzzy black-and-white photos of the chocolate wrappers at issue in this case. It was held that there was sufficient confusion for passing off. 'I think it is clear that for many people, including some of those for whom the words Swiss chocolate mean a product of quality from Switzerland, the prominent use of the famous Cadbury name and get up will be enough to prevent them thinking that Swiss Chalet is a Swiss chocolate. Furthermore there are very many for whom the origin or connections of Swiss Chalet will be irrelevant.… Many people, and particularly those who are more observant, would not be confused. For them the words "Swiss Chalet" will signify nothing but a pretty sounding name for a bar of chocolate … However, I have come to the conclusion that there are some who will be struck by the largest and most prominent word on the defendant's packaging, namely "Swiss", and think it is a reference to an attribute of the product itself. I think it is likely that some will think that it is an indication that the product is Swiss chocolate … It is likely that the number who think that will be smaller than the number for whom there will be no confusion but, in my view, it is still likely to be a substantial number' (per Laddie J at 143).

In the Court of Appeal, Chadwick LJ said that the conclusion, in the previous paragraph, of Laddie J on the evidence before him 'cannot be regarded as perverse' ([1999] RPC at 838) (see also para 17.19).

Key points on confusion

- The confusion required must involve significant numbers of the public in the market where the parties operate

- Confusion may be shown by a variety of forms of evidence (eg surveys, trap orders)

- Likelihood of confusion is also a basis for preventive action

- The court must take account of conditions in the world where the goods or services are bought and sold—pubs, supermarkets, etc

- The approach should not be from the perspective of either the sophisticated or the stupid person; but the ignorant and unwary can be taken into account

---

'Common field of activity'

17.44   It has sometimes been said that there can be no relevant confusion between the parties unless both are trading in a 'common field of activity'. The phrase was first used by Wynn Parry J in *McCulloch v May*,[80]

---

[80] [1947] 2 All ER 845. This case is considered regarding personality at para 19.45.

to define what he thought was an essential element for a successful passing off action. He went on to hold that, because there was no common field of activity between the radio broadcaster plaintiff (known as Uncle Mac) and the cereal manufacturer defendant, it was not passing off for the latter to use the name of the former's radio character (Uncle Mac) in connection with his product Puffed Wheat. The concept has been applied in a number of subsequent English cases, notably those relating to character and personality merchandising, which is considered in more detail in Chapter 19.[81] But it has also been criticised.[82] Probably it is best explained in the words of Oliver J in *Lyngstad v Anabas*: 'not a term of art … a convenient shorthand term for indicating … the need for a real possibility of confusion'.[83] This seems to be the present approach of the English courts, and although passing off actions may fail on the factual basis that there has been no confusion between two different types of business, it is clear that a common field of activity between the parties is not an essential element in law.[84] It is not referred to as such in the classic definitions of passing off (see paras 17.9–17.12), and indeed appears to have been rejected by Lord Diplock in *Advocaat*.[85]

17.45 The cases which recognise the variety of types of damage which can be done to goodwill apart from deprivation of customers—for instance, association with activities tending to lower a trader's reputation—provide good examples of situations where there has been no common field of activity.[86]

■ *Lego System A/S v Lego M Lemelstrich Ltd* [1983] FSR 155

A passing off action was successfully brought by a toy manufacturer against the manufacturer of irrigation equipment, concerning the use of the name 'Lego'. Falconer J held that the Lego name was so well known that even on irrigation equipment it was bound to be associated with the plaintiffs, whose goodwill might be damaged in respect of any move that they might make into the defendants' line of business. A distinction was drawn between the use of household names and other less well-known names and it was said that with regard to the former the absence of a common field of activity would probably be irrelevant.

17.46 The Scottish courts have not evolved any 'common field of activity' test. There have been cases where the fact that the parties were engaging in different types of business has led the court to hold no passing off.[87] But this has clearly been on the basis that no confusion had been shown, rather than on the assumption that there was a substantive rule precluding the possibility of passing off.

> ### Key point on 'common field of activity'
>
> • It is not necessary that the parties to a passing off action be in the same field of business

---

[81] See *Wombles Ltd v Wombles Skips* [1975] FSR 488.
[82] See J Phillips and A Coleman, 'Passing off and the common field of activity' (1985) 101 LQR 242.
[83] [1977] FSR 62 at 67.
[84] See *Stringfellow v McCain Foods* [1984] FSR 413; *Miss World v James Street* [1981] FSR 309; *Mirage Studios v Counter-Feat Clothing* [1991] FSR 145.
[85] [1979] AC at 741–742.
[86] See *Dr Barnardo's Homes v Barnardo Amalgamated Industries* (1949) 66 RPC 103; *Annabels v Schock* [1972] RPC 838.
[87] *Dunlop Pneumatic Tyre Co v Dunlop Motor Co* 1907 SC (HL) 15 (tyre manufacturer and motor dealer); *Scottish Union & National Insurance* 1909 SC 318 (marine insurance and fire and life insurance); *Scottish Milk Marketing Board v Drybroughs* 1985 SLT 253 (milk products and beer); *Pebble Beach Co v Lombard Brands Ltd* 2002 SLT 1312 (golf course and whisky marketing).

Deception in foreign markets

17.47   It is possible to sue any party in the UK (whether England or Scotland) who is involved as an exporter of the means of practising the deception in the foreign country, such as raw materials, distinctive shapes of bottles, and labels. This follows from *Johnston & Co v Orr-Ewing & Co*,[88] in which the House of Lords held that an exporting business might restrain another from passing off its goods as the plaintiff's in a foreign market. The wrong lay, not in the actual misrepresentation in the foreign market, but in export of the goods from England, enabling the misrepresentation and deception in the foreign market. This has since been applied in several Scottish and English cases concerning the use of the trade name 'Scotch Whisky' in overseas markets, in which it was held that producers of Scotch whisky were entitled to prevent the export of whisky to be used abroad in the production and sale of blended drinks under the name 'Scotch Whisky'.[89]

Can A supply goods which enable B to pass other goods off as C's?

17.48   Despite the case law noted previously on deception on foreign markets, it seems in general not to be passing off for a trader to supply another trader with the means enabling the latter to pass off other goods as those of a third trader. Examples of the situation might include the supply of labels, containers, or raw materials which the second trader requires to pass off his goods. Such supply may be a civil wrong in extreme circumstances, such as where the supplier knew of his customer's intentions or has actively participated in the customer's deceptive marketing; but there is no obligation to ensure that supplies are not used deceptively.[90]

Substitution selling as passing off

17.49   The simple case of passing off involves the defendant passing off his own goods and services as those of the claimant. This includes responding to a customer's order for particular goods of another trader by sending one's own, unless the customer is aware of what is done.[91] However, the law also provides a remedy where an intermediary between manufacturer or producer and the ultimate consumer, such as a retailer or publican, is responsible for presenting the goods or services as those of the claimant. It is passing off, for example, to sell beer as Bass when it is not.[92] The problem which a claimant may have to overcome here is the passage of his product name into the language as a generic term for that particular type of goods.[93]

> ### Key point on substitution selling
>
> • Supplying your own goods in response to an order of another's may be passing off

[88] (1882) 7 App Cas 219.

[89] *John Walker v Ost* [1970] RPC 489; *John Walker v Douglas McGibbon* 1972 SLT 128; *John Walker & Sons Ltd v Douglas Laing & Co Ltd* 1993 SLT 156 (decided 19 October 1976); *White Horse Distillers Ltd v Gregson Associates Ltd* [1984] RPC 61; *William Grant & Sons Ltd v Glen Catrine Bonded Warehouse Ltd* 1995 SLT 936; aff'd 2001 SC 901, 2001 SLT 1419. Choice of law is considered in more detail in Chapter 23.

[90] *Paterson Zochonis Ltd v Merfarken Packaging Ltd* [1983] FSR 273.

[91] *Purefoy Engineering Co Ltd v Sykes Boxall & Co Ltd* (1955) 72 RPC 89. Sending a catalogue or statement about the substitution with the goods comes too late; the customer should be told in advance.

[92] *Bass v Laidlaw* (1886) 13R 898; *Thomson v Robertson* (1888) 15R 880; *Thomson v Dailly* (1897) 24R 1173; *Bayer v Baird* (1898) 25R 1142; (1898) 6 SLT 98; *Bass v Laidlaw* (1908) 16 SLT 660.

[93] See, eg, *Havana Cigar & Tobacco Factories Ltd v Oddenino* [1924] 1 Ch 179 ('Corona' describes shape and size of cigars generally).

Inverse passing off: A passes off B's goods as his own

17.50 English law has had some difficulty with the situation where the defendant, instead of representing his goods or services to be those of another, claims that goods and services in fact produced by another come from him.

■ *Lucasfilm Ltd v Ainsworth* [2009] FSR 2

For the facts of this case (the 'Star Wars' case), see also paras 2.77 and 2.86. It illustrates well the distinction between classic and inverse passing off. L relied on the goodwill and reputation generated by the film, asserting that this extended to the business of licensing toys, models, and other goods reproducing facets of the film, including the fictional characters in the film and their costumes. L's claim in passing off stemmed primarily from publicity on A's website which stressed the authenticity of his products (see para 172):

> Andrew Ainsworth and Shepperton Design Studios created the original helmets and armour for the greatest sci-fi fantasy film of all time. Now, almost 30 years on and for the FIRST time ever, YOU can own an exclusive 1:1 collectible replica of the original movie helmets. **Made by the original prop-maker from the original moulds** (*emboldening in original*). Produced and endorsed by Andrew Ainsworth at Shepperton Design Studios, these unique props offer collectors a rare opportunity of owning some of the most iconic designs of modern cinema. These unique collectibles are the ONLY helmets ever produced from the original moulds used to create the screen-used helmets ... (para 172).

L argued that this would mislead members of the public into thinking that it had licensed or somehow approved the manufacture and sale of the helmets and armour. Furthermore, it was claimed that members of the public would be misled into thinking that A was the creator or designer of the helmets and body armour. Finally, L alleged that A's claims amounted to inverse passing off because he was passing off L's work as his own. It was held that A's website did not either expressly or impliedly suggest that A had the consent of L. References to authenticity were to the products' fidelity to the original designs. Despite A claiming incorrectly that he had been the original creator of the designs, this did not amount to misrepresentation about licensing. As there was no relevant misrepresentation, the claim in passing off failed. The inverse passing off claim also failed. A had not pretended that L's goods actually belonged to him, or that the goods he was selling were L's. His statement as to the origin of the goods was true. Though it was false to state that the creation of the original design was A's, this did not amount to a misappropriation of L's goodwill sufficient to satisfy the requirements of a claim of passing off as any misstatement made related only to A himself and not the goods he was selling. Note that this part of the case was not the subject of the appeals which are discussed at paras 9.87, 9.91, 23.18.

■ *Bristol Conservatories v Conservatories Custom Built* [1989] RPC 455

The parties each supplied conservatories. CCB's salesmen showed photographs of BC's conservatories to potential customers, inducing them to think that they were CCB products. It was held at first instance that representing another's goods as your own was not passing off; but the decision was reversed in the Court of Appeal: there was passing off, but because CCB were representing that their own products were of the same quality as BC's (see para 17.51), rather than because the photographs showed CCB products.

There is Scottish authority that this kind of inverse passing off is actionable as such.[94]

---

[94] *Henderson v Munro* (1905) 7F 636.

Question

What is the difference between substitution selling (para 17.49) and 'inverse passing off'?
Is representing another's goods or services as yours passing off? See further on this H Carty, 'Inverse passing off: a suitable addition to passing off?' [1993] EIPR 370.

Passing off one quality of goods or services for another

17.51   The discussion thus far has been concerned with cases where there were misrepresentations as to the trading source of goods or services. Misrepresentations as to the quality of goods or services may also constitute passing off, even when the trading source is accurately represented.

■ *Spalding v Gamage* (1915) 32 RPC 273 (HL)

The plaintiffs manufactured and sold the 'Improved Sewn Orb' football. The defendants obtained a supply of the plaintiffs' rejected moulded balls, and sold them as 'Improved Sewn Orbs'. The House of Lords held that this was passing off.

■ *Lang Brothers v Goldwell* 1980 SC 237

It was held that misleading indicia of a Scottish origin—the appearance on the bottle label of the name 'Wee McGlen', a tartan background, and a thistle device, and the deployment in newspaper advertisements of a caricature of a be-tartaned Scotsman—used in the marketing of a whisky-based drink in fact manufactured in England, was passing off. This case goes further than many, however, as it is not clear that the quality in question was necessarily an exclusive part of the petitioners' goodwill. (Cf *Wee McGlen Trade Mark* [1980] RPC 115.)

 Discussion point   For answer guidance visit www.oxfordtextbooks.co.uk/orc/waelde3e/

How may this form of passing off be linked to the 'extended' form of the action (para 17.19; see also para 17.56)?

17.52   A recurrent problem in this area of passing off concerns *parallel importing*, where goods are sold by the manufacturer under the same trade mark in several countries around the world, and then some sold in one country are imported to another for re-sale there, usually at a price lower than that at which they are sold ordinarily in the importing country. Where there is a difference in quality between the imported and the 'home' goods, the English courts have held that putting the imports on the market may be passing off.[95] But where the goods are of the same quality, then it is irrelevant that the imported goods were made by another company in the same group as the company raising the action in this country; no deception as to source or quality can be said to have occurred.[96] Claims for passing off have also been rejected when products which have been re-boxed to comply with regulations for sale in another country, and sold only under a generic name; this was found to be an accurate name and there was no misrepresentation and also no evidence of confusion.[97]

[95] *Wilkinson Sword v Cripps & Lee* [1982] FSR 16; *Colgate-Palmolive v Markwell Finance* [1989] RPC 497.
[96] *Revlon Inc v Cripps & Lee* [1980] FSR 85.
[97] *Boehringer Ingelheim KG v Swingward Ltd* [2004] 3 CMLR 3, paras 55–59 and see paras 20.5ff.

17.53   It is also possible to pass off services as having qualities which they do not possess. Thus, it is passing off for a retailer to state that he is an authorised dealer in a particular product when he is not and is unable to offer the services which such a dealer should do.[98] The quality in question might be that of being connected to or under the control of the claimant, where that party enjoys a good reputation of some kind. Thus the British Legion, a charitable organisation for the benefit of First World War veterans, could prevent a local social club calling itself 'British Legion Club (Street)' when it had no connection with the Legion.[99] But the representation must be such as to suggest a connection in which the claimant has responsibility for or control over the quality of what the defendant offers. This can also apply to goods, as the following, more recent cases show.

■ *Harrods v Harrodian School* [1996] RPC 697

Harrods, the well-known London department store, sued a school which was operating from a site known as 'The Harrodian Club' (because the store had once run a social club there for its employees under that name). The aim of the action was to stop the school calling itself 'The Harrodian School'. It was held that there was no passing off. Millett LJ said (at 713): 'It is not in my opinion sufficient to demonstrate that there must be a connection between the defendant and the plaintiff, if it is not a connection which would lead the public to suppose that the plaintiff has made himself responsible for the quality of the defendant's goods or services. A belief that the plaintiff has sponsored or given financial support to the defendant will not ordinarily give the public that impression.'

■ *Arsenal Football Club plc v Reed* [2001] RPC 922

R had sold merchandise outside the Arsenal football club ground for about 30 years. The merchandise bore insignia associating it with the club, such as its name, nickname ('the Gunners'), its crest, and a logo of a cannon. From about 1987 the club began to license traders (but not R) to use these insignia on merchandise, which was then marketed as 'official' club merchandise. The club sued R in passing off to prevent his continued unlicensed operations. It was held that there was no passing off. Use of the Arsenal insignia did not carry any message of trade origin. Some fans wanted to purchase only 'official' merchandise, but it did not follow that all Arsenal memorabilia would be taken by fans to have come from or be licensed by the club. There would have to be something more than the mere use of the insignia to make that statement, and here R actually made clear that his activities were unofficial.[100]

 Discussion point   For answer guidance visit www.oxfordtextbooks.co.uk/orc/waelde3e/

Consider the previous cases in the light of *Irvine v Talksport* [2002] 2 All ER 414 after you have explored paras 19.18ff). Are they mutually consistent?

---

[98] *Sony v Saray* [1983] FSR 302.   [99] *British Legion v British Legion Club (Street)* (1931) 63 RPC 555.

[100] Note, however, the *obiter* comment of Aldous LJ in the Court of Appeal that he was unconvinced by Laddie J's rejection of the passing off claim ([2003] RPC 39 at para 70), commented upon by S Middlemiss and S Warner, 'Is there still a hole in this bucket? Confusion and misrepresentation in passing off' (2006) 1 JIPLP 131 and C Wadlow, 'One more outing for *Arsenal*: a case of dilution or one for restitution?' (2006) 1 JIPLP 143. See further note 73.

> **Key points on misrepresentations about the quality of one's goods or services**
>
> - Falsely representing one's goods or services as possessed of qualities associated in the market with another trader may amount to passing off
> - This can include cases where the representation (express or implied) is that the claimant exercises some form of quality control over the defendant's goods or services

Comparative advertising

17.54   It is generally legitimate for a manufacturer or retailer marketing goods or services to make comparisons of his product with others, or to draw attention to the compatibility of his product with that of another trader, for example as a replacement or an additional part. In no sense is the advertiser stating that his goods come from another trading source. Indeed, the whole purpose of comparative advertising in particular is to differentiate competing products in the public mind.

But if the comparison involves making specific and false claims of equivalent or greater quality for the advertised product, or false denigration of the quality of its rival, then the damage to the competitor's goodwill arising from the misrepresentation may be remedied through passing off.

■ *McDonald's Hamburgers Ltd v Burger King UK Ltd* [1986] FSR 45; aff'd on other points [1987] FSR 112

McDonald's sold hamburgers called 'Big Macs'. Burger King advertised their competing product (the 'Whopper'), using the slogan 'It's Not Just Big Mac'. Evidence showed that the public thought this meant that Big Macs were available at Burger King and that they could go to Burger King stores for them. It was held that, as the defendant's advertisement referring to the plaintiff's hamburgers had failed adequately to distinguish the two products from each other, there was passing off. The decision is not so much about false comparisons, however, as about the borderline between comparing products and representing that they come from the same trade source.

■ *Kimberly Clark v Fort Sterling* [1997] FSR 877

FS promoted their 'Nouvelle' toilet roll with the phrase, 'Softness guaranteed (or we'll exchange it for Andrex)'. It was held that this was passing off; there was a misrepresentation in that the statement would induce customers to think, wrongly, that Nouvelle was an Andrex brand.

Comparative advertising can also involve trade mark law, see paras 15.122ff.

Professional associations

17.55   Somewhat akin to the cases on misleading representations as to quality of goods and services are the decisions holding that misleading use of initials and letters which indicate membership of professional associations is passing off, for example BMA for the British Medical Association.[101] Thus, in Scotland members

---

[101] *British Medical Association v Marsh* (1931) 48 RPC 565.

of the Corporation of Accountants Ltd and the Corporation itself were held not entitled to use the letters 'CA' and 'MCA' as an abbreviation of the qualification to be obtained from the Corporation, since the public associated them with the qualification of the members of the Society of Accountants in Edinburgh.[102]

Exercise

Consider whether pre-sale misrepresentations can be remedied in passing off. See B Allgrove and P O'Byrne, 'Pre-sale misrepresentations in passing off: an idea whose time has come or unfair competition by the back door?' (2006) 1 JIPLP 413.

Key points on misrepresentations as to quality

- While comparative advertising is generally legitimate, specific and false claims of equivalent or greater quality for one's own goods or services, or false denigration of a competitor's, can be passing off
- False use in business of initials and letters indicating a status or membership of a professional association is passing off

Improper use of descriptive class designation: extended passing off

17.56   A very particular type of misrepresentation is found in the 'product goodwill' or 'extended passing off' cases, where what is protected is the goodwill attached to products of a particular kind rather than to a specific trader (see para 17.19). In such cases, the representation is that the product in question belongs to a particular class of goods, and arises through the use of a name for that class which is recognised by the public as identifying goods of that class and no others. The development of the law began in *Bollinger v Costa Brava Wine Co*.[103]

■ *Bollinger v Costa Brava Wine Co* [1961] 1 Ch 262

The producers of champagne sought and obtained an injunction to prevent the defendants from marketing a sparkling wine as 'Spanish Champagne'. The judge held that the word 'Champagne' could be used accurately only of sparkling wines produced in the Champagne district of France and that this was how it had come to be understood in the market. The inaccurate application of the name to a drink which lacked the necessary characteristics was therefore a misrepresentation which injured the goodwill of the genuine trader, and so constituted passing off.

Bollinger was approved and applied in a number of subsequent cases: for example, regarding the use of 'Sherry',[104] and 'Scotch whisky',[105] as well as further cases on 'Champagne'.[106] In *Argyllshire Weavers v*

---

[102] *Society of Accountants in Edinburgh v Corporation of Accountants* (1893) 20R 750; *Corporation of Accountants v Society of Accountants in Edinburgh* (1903) 11 SLT 424.
[103] [1961] 1 Ch 262.   [104] *Vine Products v Mackenzie* [1969] RPC 1.
[105] *John Walker & Sons v Henry Ost* [1970] 1 WLR 917; *John Walker v Douglas McGibbon* 1972 SLT 128; *Lang Brothers v Goldwell* 1980 SC 237.
[106] *Bulmer (HP) Ltd v Bollinger (J) SA* [1978] RPC 79; *Taittinger SA v Allbev Ltd* [1993] FSR 641.

Macaulay Tweeds,[107] it was held that mill-spun tweed could not be marketed as Harris tweed. Full confirmation of *Bollinger*'s place in the law was finally given by the House of Lords in *Erven Warnink v Townend* (the *Advocaat* case):[108]

■ *Erven Warnink v Townend* [1979] AC 731

This case concerned the use of 'Advocaat' as a name for an alcoholic drink. An English firm was enjoined from marketing its product as 'Keeling's Old English Advocaat', since the drink was made up, not of brandewijn, egg yolks, and sugar, but rather of dried egg powder mixed with Cyprus sherry. It was also ruled that a name's lack of geographical connotations was immaterial to this form of misrepresentation; the action lay because the defendant's product was not made up of the correct ingredients, not because the correct ingredients came from a particular locality.

Since the *Advocaat* case, the most important decisions are *Taittinger SA v Allbev Ltd*[109] (the *Elderflower Champagne* case), *Chocosuise Union des Fabricants Suisses de Chocolat v Cadbury*[110] (regarding Swiss chocolate), and *Diageo North America Inc v Intercontinental Brands (UCB) Ltd*[111] (regarding vodka). In the *Elderflower Champagne* case, where the eponymous product was sold at a very low price but in a get-up akin to that of real champagne, it was held that the misrepresentation was either that the drink was champagne or that it was in some way associated with the French champagne houses. In *Chocosuisse* it was held that 'Swiss chocolate' was a designation of a particular class of chocolate which could only be used by manufacturers of chocolate made in Switzerland in accordance with certain standards laid down by regulation in that country, meaning that its use on a non-conforming product was a misrepresentation. In the *Diageo* case, the court found that applying 'Vodkat' 'plainly suggests that the product either is vodka or a version of vodka or contains or is made from vodka'.[112]

> ### Key point on misrepresentation in extended passing off cases
>
> • In such cases the representation is that the product in question belongs to a particular class of goods, and arises through the use of a name for that class which is recognised by the public as identifying goods of that class and no others

Damage

Damage to goodwill

17.57   The courts have recognised a variety of ways in which the goodwill of a trader may be damaged by the representations of another trader in connection with his goods and services. The most obvious form of damage is loss of custom, actual or potential, arising from confusion. Closely related to this is the attraction of custom by the defendant using the goodwill associated with the claimant. It may not be possible to show that the customer bought goods from the defendant which he would otherwise have bought from the claimant—for example, because the parties do not trade in the same field—but, nonetheless, an action of passing off will lie if the customer will associate the goods with the claimant to his potential

107 1965 SLT 21.   108 [1979] AC 731.   109 [1993] FSR 641.   110 [1998] RPC 117; aff'd [1999] RPC 826.
111 [2010] RPC 12, see para 17.40.   112 *Diageo*, note 111, para 167.

detriment.[113] In *Knight v Beyond Properties Pty Ltd*,[114] the 'Mythbusters' case (for the facts see para 17.14), it was recognised that the claimant might have been able to claim for loss of opportunity to convert his books into a TV series had the evidence supported that as a real possibility (which it did not).

■ *Annabel's (Berkeley Square) Ltd v Shock* **[1972] RPC 838**

Annabel's was a well-known nightclub. S started an unconnected escort agency under the same name. It was held that there was passing off. Escort agencies did not have a good public image and, while S's agency was above reproach, it was inevitable that the two businesses would be associated in the public mind and that the nightclub's good reputation would be damaged, attracting to it the wrong kind of goodwill.

17.58 Damage to trading relationships with business customers, suppliers, distributors, and retailers, which have been recognised as part of goodwill, can also result from passing off activities, and so be a basis for action.[115] For an action to succeed, however, only one of the categories of damage which has been discussed must be established.[116]

Key points on main forms of damage relevant to passing off

The main traditional forms of damage relevant to passing off are:

- Loss of custom, actual and potential
- Attraction of custom by defendant using claimant's goodwill
- Damage to claimant's reputation, and thence goodwill, through false associations
- Damage to claimant's trading relations

Dilution of a name

17.59 The defendant's activities may have the effect of diminishing goodwill by lessening the distinctive associations and reputation of the claimant's device ('dilution').[117] This has been especially important in the product goodwill cases (paras 17.19 and 17.56), where the action of passing off has been used to ensure that a name retains a particular meaning in the market and cannot be attached to any other product.[118] Here, again, it may well not be possible to show that the claimant has been deprived of custom, but the reputation of his product is endangered by the defendant's activities and so there can be a remedy. This kind of damage is often referred to as 'dilution'. The scope of dilution as a kind of damage has been the subject of controversy in the courts.[119]

---

[113] See, eg, *Eastman Photographic Materials Ltd v Griffiths Cycle Corp* (1898) 15 RPC 105; *Walter v Ashton* [1902] 2 Ch 282; *Harrods Ltd v R Harrod Ltd* (1924) 41 RPC 74; *Dr Barnardos Homes v Barnardo Amalgamated Industries* (1949) 66 RPC 103; *Annabels (Berkeley Square) Ltd v Schock* [1972] RPC 838; *Dash Ltd v Philip King Tailoring Ltd* 1988 GWD 7–304 (rev'd on other points 1989 SLT 39); *Phones4u Ltd v Phone4u.co.uk Internet Ltd* [2007] RPC 5.

[114] [2007] FSR 34 (Ch).

[115] See, eg, *Chelsea Man Menswear Ltd v Chelsea Girl Ltd* [1987] RPC 189; *Highland Distilleries Co plc v Speymalt Whisky Distributors Ltd* 1985 SC 1; *Associated Newspapers plc v Insert Media Ltd* [1991] FSR 380.

[116] *Woolley v Ultimate Products Ltd* (CA), note 57, para 48.

[117] See, eg, *Rolls Royce v Dodd* [1981] FSR 517.

[118] See above all *Erven Warnink v Townend* [1979] AC 731; also *Macallan-Glenlivet plc v Speymalt Whisky Distributors Ltd* 1983 SLT 348; and *Highland Distilleries Co plc v Speymalt Whisky Distributors Ltd* 1985 SC 1.

[119] See further H Carty, 'Heads of damage in passing off' [1996] EIPR 487; A Murray, 'A distinct lack of goodwill' [1997] EIPR 345.

■ *Taittinger SA v Allbev Ltd* [1993] FSR 641

This was the so-called *Elderflower Champagne* case (see paras 17.43 and 17.56). In this case, only some of the public would be deceived by the defendant's use of the name 'Elderflower Champagne' that his product was champagne. But the judges of the Court of Appeal all thought that the damage extended beyond loss of custom to the blurring or erosion of the uniqueness attendant upon the word 'champagne'; to a gradual debasement or dilution not demonstrable in figures of lost sales, but diminishing the goodwill. The clearest statement was by Sir Thomas Bingham MR (at 678): 'Any product which is not Champagne but is allowed to describe itself as such must inevitably, in my view, erode the singularity and exclusiveness of the description Champagne and so cause the first plaintiffs damage of an insidious but serious kind…. [A] reference to champagne imports nuances of quality and celebration, a sense of something privileged and special. But this is the reputation which the Champagne houses have built up over the years, and in which they have a property right. It is not in my view unfair to deny the defendants the opportunity to exploit, share or (in the vernacular) cash in on that reputation, which they have done nothing to establish. It would be very unfair to allow them to do so if the consequence was, as I am satisfied it would be, to debase and cheapen that very reputation.'

But contrast Millett LJ in:

■ *Harrods Ltd v Harrodian School Ltd* [1996] RPC 697

An action by the well-known London department store, Harrods, to prevent a school from trading as the 'Harrodian School' was unsuccessful (see para 17.53). On damage and the possibility of dilution of the Harrods name, Millett LJ said (at 716): 'To date the law has not sought to protect the value of the brand name as such, but the value of the goodwill which it generates; and it insists on proof of confusion to justify its intervention. But the erosion of the distinctiveness of a brand name which occurs by reason of its degeneration into common use as a generic term is not necessarily dependent on confusion at all…. I have an intellectual difficulty in accepting the concept that the law insists upon the presence of both confusion and damage and yet recognises as sufficient a head of damage which does not depend upon confusion.

 Question

How far, if at all, does 'dilution' differ from the more traditional forms of damage recognised in passing off actions?
Does the concept of dilution blur the distinction between 'goodwill' and 'reputation' (para 17.13)?

Key points on dilution as a form of damage

- Dilution is a form of damage in which the defendant's activities in some way weaken or diminish the distinctive associations and reputation of the claimant's marketing device (typically a name), without necessarily depriving the claimant of customers

- Dilution appears to be important in 'product goodwill' or 'extended passing off' cases, but has also been deployed in the false endorsement case to protect the personal reputation of a public figure

- Dilution is a controversial form of damage, since it seems to weaken the requirement of goodwill and lead passing off into the protection of reputation

Damage need only be prospective

17.60 It is clear law that in general damage (of whatever kind) need not have been actually suffered before the action is brought. An injunction or an interdict can certainly be obtained because the likelihood of damage is reasonably anticipated. It has been said that there is a presumption of damage in cases where the defendant has sold goods as those of the claimant.[120] In cases of fraud, the burden of proving damage will be light.[121]

Defences

17.61 All the requirements of passing off as discussed so far in this chapter may be present, yet the party sued may have a defence. Some defences are of course implicit in the requirements of passing off which have been discussed, for example lack of goodwill, absence of confusion, that one is making honest use of one's own name. But there are some defences in passing off which arise even if all the other requirements of the claim are met. The scope of some of these is rather uncertain: for example, parody, as when it was held that there was no passing off by title in a film called 'Alternative Miss World' satirising the well-known beauty competition.[122] But a defence of parody was of no avail in *Clark v Associated Newspapers Ltd*,[123] where the parodist had not done enough to prevent confusion as to the authorship of the work amongst readers; while in *Irvine v Talksport Ltd*[124] the suggestion that the manipulated picture of Irvine listening intently to a radio marked with Talksport insignia would be seen as a joke by its intended audience was rejected by the court. One of the most important defences in practice is *delay*—technically known as acquiescence, or taciturnity and *mora*—on the part of the person raising the action of passing off: that is to say, despite knowing of the other party's activities, taking no steps to prevent them for a significant period of time. Thus, for example, in *Bulmer v Bollinger*[125] champagne houses were unable, after 18 years of use, to prevent cider being marketed as 'champagne perry'. In *Arsenal Football Club plc v Reed*,[126] the defendant traded openly outside the Arsenal ground for 30 years, and in such circumstances, especially when there was no evidence of actual confusion in the marketplace for the goods in question, the failure of the club's passing off action was unsurprising. An important discussion of the defence is in the following Scottish case, where it was rejected.

■ *William Grant & Sons Ltd v Glen Catrine Bonded Warehouse Ltd* 2001 SC 901

WG sought to prevent GC from using the name 'Grant's' in connection with the sale of gin, vodka, and other alcoholic drinks. WG had been selling whisky products under the name 'Grant's' since the 1920s, and gin and vodka since 1963. GC began using the name on gin in 1972 and on vodka in 1974. From 1986 GC's sales began to increase dramatically. GC believed they could use the name 'Grant's' as it had been the name of a company they acquired in 1972. GC defended WG's claim of passing off on the basis of acquiescence. The action was raised in 1992, although there had been communication between the parties since WG became aware of GC's activities in 1986. It was held that WG were not barred by acquiescence from a remedy for passing off. GC had exploited the name 'Grant's', not because they believed WG had consented, but because they believed they had a historical right to use the name. Further, acquiescence was being invoked to bar action in respect of future wrongs (ie continued passing off), but the evidence did not justify an inference that WG had consented irrevocably to GC passing their products off

---

[120] See *Draper v Trist* (1939) 56 RPC 429.   [121] *Bulmer v Bollinger* [1978] RPC 79.
[122] *Miss World v James Street* [1981] FSR 309.   [123] [1998] RPC 261.   [124] [2003] EWCA Civ 423.
[125] [1971] FSR 405.   [126] [2001] RPC 922.

as WG's in the future. Knowledge was not the same as acquiescence. The court, although relying principally on Scottish authorities on personal bar (anglicé estoppel),[127] found support for its approach in the English case of *Farmers Build Ltd v Carier Bulk Materials Handling Ltd* [1999] RPC 461 (see para 9.24).

 Question

What constitutes acquiescence or delay sufficient to prevent a party succeeding in a passing off action?

Key points on defences

- A defendant who can show that his activity went on for many years unchecked before the raising of the action has a good defence against an action of passing off
- The technical names for this defence are *acquiescence, taciturnity, mora*, and *delay*
- It follows that claimants should take prompt action when they learn of possible passing off

The Internet, passing off, and instruments of fraud

17.62   An important development in the use of passing off came in its use to control the phenomenon known as 'cyber-squatting'. This is an example of a commercial practice made possible by the Internet, and is also revealing about the sluggish response of major British companies to the trading potential of the Internet. Domain names identifying and locating organisations on the Internet are a crucial part of what is needed to do business there. There is a non-official, self-regulatory system for allocating domain names, which operates on a first-come, first-served basis (see paras 16.2ff). In the 1990s, businesses were established which registered domain names comprising well-known trade marks and corporate and other names without the consent of the person owning the trade mark or goodwill in the name in question. These businesses then offered the domain names to the owners of the trade marks or goodwill, usually for very substantial sums, but typically did not themselves make much, if any, commercial use of the domain name on the Internet. It was far from clear that this activity constituted infringement of any trade mark rights there might be in the name, although the phrase 'cyber-squatting' conveyed a sense that the businesses concerned had occupied the name without permission, and only because the real owners had left this particular part of their property vacant. So the owners turned to the law of passing off as a way of evicting the squatters. They gained their way in *British Telecommunications plc v One in a Million Ltd*.[128]

■ *British Telecommunications plc v One in a Million Ltd* [1999] 1 WLR 903 (CA)

One in a Million were dealers in domain names who had registered the following names; ladbrokes.com; sainsbury.com; sainsburys.com; j-sainsbury.com; marksandspencer.com; cellnet.net; bt.org; virgin.org. Other dealers who were co-defendants in the case had registered marksandspencer.co.uk;

---

[127] On this aspect of the case, see E Reid, 'Acquiescence in the air' 2002 JR 191.   [128] [1999] 1 WLR 903 (CA).

britishtelecom.co.uk; britishtelecom.net, and britishtelecom.com. They were sued for passing off by Marks & Spencer plc, J Sainsbury plc, Virgin Enterprises Ltd, British Telecommunications plc, Telecom Cellular Radio Ltd, and Ladbrokes plc. The Court of Appeal held that there was passing off and that the plaintiffs were entitled to *quia timet* injunctions. Analysis of previous case law showed that an injunction could be granted against a defendant equipped with or intending to equip another with an instrument of fraud. A name which would, by reason of its similarity to the name of another, inherently lead to passing off, is such an instrument. The court could infer an intention to appropriate goodwill or enable others to do so, even if there was a possibility that such appropriation would not take place (the importance of this point being that there was little evidence that the 'cyber-squatters' intended actually to trade under the domain names or to sell the names to anyone other than the plaintiffs, although there were threats, express or implied, to do so contained in the communications between them and the owners).

17.63 The decision builds on earlier cases, mostly concerned with exporting material which would be used in the destination country to pass off goods as coming from a particular source in this country (para 17.47). In general, supply of the means by which another trader might pass off goods or services—for example, providing materials for bottling or labelling—is not passing off unless there is fraud or at any rate intention and knowledge on the part of the supplier (see para 17.48). The difficulty in the *One in a Million* case is that the domain names held by the cyber-squatters were of very little value in the hands of anyone other than the cyber-squatters and the companies whose names had been used. Had the cyber-squatters attempted themselves to trade under the domain names, or sold them to third parties so to trade, then there would have been passing off in the ordinary sense. So it is difficult to see how the cyber-squat is really analogous to the earlier 'instruments of fraud' cases. The decision is also difficult to reconcile with the classic definitions of passing off by Lords Diplock, Fraser, and Oliver quoted at the outset of this chapter (see paras 17.9 and 17.10). The court clearly did not like the behaviour of the cyber-squatters, in particular the threatening way in which they advanced their offers to sell the domain names to the well-known companies; but in order to remedy that wrong, the law of passing off was probably extended further than ever before.

 Question

What is cyber-squatting? Does this activity constitute passing off as usually understood?

17.64 The courts of both England and Scotland have, however, followed the *One in a Million* decision without much quibble.[129] Scottish cases, all unreported, have dealt with cyber-squatting in relation to the domain names for Scottish Widows, the leading insurance company, and Haggis Backpackers, an Edinburgh touring hostel. In *easyJet v Dainty*,[130] the defendant registered the domain name 'easyRealestate.co.uk' and set up a website offering estate agency services; but he did no significant business through the site. He attempted to interest easyJet in his proposition, made use of 'easy ' style livery on the website, and ultimately attempted to sell his domain name to easyJet while threatening to sell to third parties. He was held liable for passing off, which was constituted in both its traditional form and in its 'instruments of deception' form. The judge ordered that the defendant's domain name be transferred to easyJet.[131]

---

[129] For critical commentary, see C Thorne and S Bennett, 'Domain names—Internet warehousing: has protection of well known names on the Internet gone too far?' [1998] EIPR 468; C Colston, 'Passing off: the right solution to domain names?' [2000] LMCLQ 523; H Carty, 'Passing off and instruments of deception: the need for clarity' [2003] EIPR 188.

[130] [2002] FSR 6. See also *Easygroup IP Licensing Ltd v Sermbezis* [2003] All ER (D) 25 (car rental websites).

[131] See also *Yell Ltd v Giboin, Zagg Ltd*, note 5, paras 185–189.

In *Phones 4U Ltd v Phone4U.co.uk Internet Ltd*,[132] the defendant commenced Internet trading under the domain name as well as offering it for sale after learning of the claimant's existence and use of the trade name; the Court of Appeal thought this not materially different from the *One in a Million* case.[133]

17.65   *One in a Million* was distinguished, however, in *French Connection v Sutton*.[134] French Connection, a chain of fashion stores, began in 1997 to use the word FCUK in a widespread advertising campaign as well as registering it as a trade mark. Sutton, an Internet consultant, registered 'FCUK.com' as a domain name, and set up a website at which he would advertise his consultancy. This was challenged by French Connection on the basis of the *One in a Million* case, and the evidence showed that Sutton had subsequently tried to sell his domain name to the company. However, Rattee J refused summary judgment, on the basis that FCUK was not a household name—or, indeed, the name of anything—in any way like the names involved in the *One in a Million* case; Sutton's website had offered services quite different from those of French Connection; and the registration of FCUK as a domain name had not been merely for the purpose of extracting money from French Connection but had rather been to draw the attention of Internet users to Sutton's site:

> According to the defendant's evidence, the letters FCUK together in that order was a well-known alternative used by people on the Internet as a means of circumventing various filters which were imposed by certain Internet Service Providers to prevent the use of the expletive FUCK in the material placed on the Internet. It is also the defendant's evidence that at the time he registered his domain name and, I think, still, FCUK is also known to a certain class of Internet users as indicating pornographic subject matter … [H]e thought that it might improve the level of custom for [his] business if he attracted to it unsuspecting persons interested in accessing a pornographic site.[135]

17.66   In *Lifestyle Management Ltd v Frater*,[136] however, Frater used doman names which were very similar to those of the claimant. The court found, applying *One in a Million*, that this was 'deceptive use' of the name with 'acquired goodwill' to 'damage the owner of the name'.

17.67   Other use has been made of the instrument of fraud to address new forms of conduct. In *L'Oreal SA v Bellure NV*,[137] the claimants complained of the defendants' importation, distribution, and sale of what were alleged to be copies—'smell-alikes'—of the former's perfumes, and argued that the defendants' products were instruments of fraud and deception, making their activities passing off. The argument was supported by the way in which the products were advertised on the Internet, albeit by third parties as well as by their names and packaging. The claim was rejected by Lewison J: to be an instrument of deception the product had to be so inherently defective that its mere existence made it passing off waiting to happen. The names and packaging of the defendants' products did not fall into that category, while third party advertising could not be laid at the defendants' door.

17.68   A further issue about passing off on the Internet was raised in *Reed Executive plc v Reed Business Information Ltd* involving metatags.[138] RE, an employment agency which had been in business using the name 'Reed' since 1960, operated a website—reed.co.uk. RBI were publishers who had used the Reed name since 1983 and who in 1999 began to run a recruitment website called 'totaljobs.com'. There was visible use of the word 'Reed' on the site, and also invisible use, as the word 'Reed' had been used as a metatag in the creation of the site. Metatags are elements of the HTML language used to provide structured metadata about a webpage, that is, data about the material contained in the webpage. Metatags permit discovery

---

[132] [2007] RPC 5 (CA). See also *Tesco Stores Ltd v Elogicom Ltd* [2007] FSR 4 (Ch).
[133] See also *Westwood v Knight*, note 5, paras 232–235.   [134] [2000] ETMR 341.   [135] *French Connection*, note 134, at 345.
[136] [2010] EWHC 3258 (TCC), para 11.
[137] [2007] RPC 14; aff'd on instruments of deception and the activities of third parties [2008] RPC 9 (CA), paras 128–132.
[138] [2003] RPC 12 (Pumfrey J); aff'd [2004] RPC 40 (CA).

of the website by search engines such as Google and Yahoo!, and also the generation of various forms of web advertising.[139] There was some evidence of confusion between the two websites in the *Reed* case, and RBI had made efforts by the date of trial to remove both visible and invisible uses of the word 'Reed'. Pumfrey J held that, while the visible uses of 'Reed' could constitute passing off, this was not so for the invisible metatags. The Court of Appeal held that there was no passing off at all, pointing to evidence that had been led about the results of searches under the phrase 'Reed jobs'. Jacob LJ said of this evidence:

> In all cases where totaljobs was listed, it came below the Reed employment site in the search results (which, as is usual, included many other results, irrelevant to both sides). Obviously anyone looking for Reed Employment would find them rather than totaljobs. I am unable to see how there could be passing off. No one is likely to be misled—there is no misrepresentation. This is equally so whether the search engine itself rendered visible the metatag or not.[140]

 ## Question

What are metatags? Why do they create problems relevant to the law of passing off? What is the law on these problems as a result of the cases discussed previously?

 ## Discussion point

What do you think will be the next Internet issue in which passing off is used—for example, Twitter tags? Do you see this as a natural progression, or an unwarranted expansion of the doctrine?

Unfair competition and passing off

17.69 As pointed out at the beginning of this chapter (para 17.7), passing off is as near as the laws of England and Scotland come to having a law of unfair competition such as is commonly found in the laws of other member states of the EU, and it is usually taken to satisfy the requirements of the Paris Convention in this regard. It has sometimes been suggested that the expansion of passing off from the simple case of representing one's goods as those of another and thereby damaging that other's goodwill, means that it would be better to speak now of unfair competition rather than passing off. A particularly strong instance of this development has been the growth of protection of product goodwill, with its ability to prevent dilution of a valuable reputation in trade. But other developments, such as the broadening concept of misrepresentation, the decreasing emphasis on confusion, and the recognition of 'dilution', are taking the law increasingly towards a basis in *misappropriation* of another's *reputation* (as distinct from goodwill), to enable one to reap profit and enrichment where another has sown the seed.[141] Laddie J has gone as far as to say that the 'underlying principle' of passing off is 'the maintenance of what is currently

---

[139] See further A Murray, 'The use of trade marks as meta tags: defining the boundaries' (2000) 8 IJLIT 263.

[140] [2004] RPC 40 (CA), para 147. For further comment see R Sumroy and C Badger, 'Infringing "use in the course of trade": trade mark use and the essential function of a trade mark' and S Maniatis, 'Trade mark use on the Internet' both in J Phillips and I Simon (eds), *Trade Mark Use* (2005), paras 10.29–30, 15.18–21.

[141] A Kamperman Sanders, *Unjust Enrichment: The New Paradigm for Unfair Competition Law?* (1996).

regarded as fair trading',[142] while Aldous LJ, unconvinced by Laddie J's rejection of the claim of passing off in the *Arsenal* case, suggested at the same time that the modern extensions of passing off meant that it was 'perhaps best referred to as unfair competition'.[143] If we consider the prohibitions listed in Article 10*bis*(3) of the Paris Convention:

1. all acts of such nature as to create confusion by any means whatever with the establishment, the goods, or the industrial or commercial activities, of a competitor;
2. false allegations in the course of trade of such a nature as to discredit the establishment, the goods, or the industrial or commercial activities, of a competitor;
3. indications or allegations the use of which in the course of trade is liable to mislead the public as to the nature, the manufacturing process, the characteristics, the suitability for their purpose, or the quantity, of the goods

—then we can see that passing off is capable of dealing with all three. Indeed, passing off goes further in several respects. It would not be straightforward to say, for example, that the use of passing off to prevent false endorsement or cyber-squatting comes squarely within these prohibitions. In *L'Oreal SA v Bellure NV*[144] the Court of Appeal was invited to develop a tort of unfair competition, either because the present law was in derogation from the Paris Convention or as an evolution of the common law. The court held (correctly, it is submitted) that there was no derogation from the Convention and vigorously rejected the argument that it could develop passing off to become a tort of unfair competition. Given that competition was not only lawful but also the mainspring of the economy, it was for Parliament rather than the judges to legislate for restraints upon competition. Jacob LJ was highly critical of the concept of misappropriation as the means of further developing the law; he thought it 'very unhelpful ... at best muddling and at worst tendentious'.[145]

 Exercise

Consider how each of the three prohibitions in the Paris Convention article on unfair competition is dealt with by the law of passing off.

17.70   There are those, however, who argue that passing off still does not go far enough to deal with all forms of unfair competition in the marketplace. During the parliamentary passage of what is now the Trade Marks Act 1994, the following additional section was proposed, although ultimately the amendment was withdrawn:

> After Clause 56, insert the following clause:
>
> **Unfair Competition**
>
> (1) Where any goods of the proprietor of a trade mark bearing the trade mark are associated in the course of trade with any label, packaging or container having an overall appearance of a distinctive character, it shall be an act of unfair competition, actionable as such, for any person in the course of trade to supply or offer to supply any such goods with or in any label, packaging or container which is similar in overall appearance,

---

[142] *Irvine v Talksport Ltd* [2002] 2 All ER 414, para 17.

[143] *Arsenal Football Club plc v Matthew Reed* [2003] RPC 39, para 70; commented upon by S Middlemiss and S Warner, 'Is there still a hole in this bucket? Confusion and misrepresentation in passing off' (2006) 1 JIPLP 131, and C Wadlow, 'One more outing for *Arsenal*: a case of dilution or one for restitution?' (2006) 1 JIPLP 143.

[144] [2008] RPC 9 (CA).

[145] *L'Oreal*, note 144, para 160. See further L Harrold, 'The genie in the bottle: brand "free riding": what's permissible and what's not?' (2008) 3 *JIPLP* 511 and T Alkin, 'Should there be a tort of "unfair competition" in English law?' (2008) 3 JIPLP 48.

whether by reason of name, shape, colour, design or any combination thereof or otherwise, to the overall appearance of that of the proprietor's goods if the use of the label, packaging or container either—

(a) is likely to cause confusion, which includes a likelihood of association with the proprietor or the proprietor's goods; or

(b) without due cause takes unfair advantage of, or is detrimental to, the distinctive character or repute of the appearance of the proprietor's goods or trade mark.

17.71   In March 2000 Lord McNally laid a Copyright and Trade Marks Bill before the House of Lords, which was again withdrawn, but which contained a clause described as follows by the noble Lord:[146]

> Clause 3 seeks to tighten up the currently weak laws on competitive imitation. It is intended to prevent business from dressing up products so as to resemble competing goods, thereby taking unfair advantage of the original's reputation for quality and safety and investment in innovation and marketing. Such legislation is necessary because the imitation is designed deliberately to mislead consumers by stealing the identity and reputation of the rival product. When I was at the Retail Consortium I noted that it was not only the back-street trader who indulged in such copycat retailing. I believe that to steal a brand image is unfair to the initiator who over decades may have made an investment to win customer confidence in a particular product. At the moment, imitation is governed by passing-off law that dates from the 18th and 19th centuries. It is very vague and has proved ineffective in providing protection to rights owners. The required standard of proof under passing-off law is extreme and gives copycats immense freedom to copy designs in a way that misleads consumers. It is unrealistic to ask industry to fight legal actions and to lose just to prove a point. The lack of legal cases demonstrates the difficulty in bringing actions. I am proposing that courts are in the best position to decide what constitutes imitation. The Bill also gives the wronged party a chance to seek damages in cases where imitation is proven. The present laws, like so many others in this area, present a barrier to innovation by industry and consumers continue to be deceived.

 Exercise

What difference, if any, would the amendment to the Trade Marks Bill have made to the law of passing off? Comment on Lord McNally's criticism of the law of passing off. Should there be a law of unfair competition to prevent imitative trading even if customers are not confused between the competing products?

17.72   While the idea of replacing passing off with a more general law against unfair competition is attractive in some ways—in bringing the law in the UK into line with that of our fellow member states of the EU, in stopping the need to strain the basic concepts of passing off to meet new forms of unfair trading, and in enabling those who invest time, creativity, and labour in generating products and services attracting goodwill to gain appropriate rewards without quite so much risk of free-riding by less innovative or would-be competitors—there are countervailing arguments.[147] Perhaps the most potent is that, while a law of unfair competition would be justified ultimately as a protection of consumers, it would be administered through the courts and by way of litigation involving, not the consumer directly, but rather the suppliers competing for the consumer's custom. It is not immediately clear that this would be the most efficient or effective way of protecting the consumer from unfair trading practices. Again, a law of unfair competition might be overly inhibiting upon the free play of market forces and competition generally, and the most effective form of consumer protection is arguably a competitive marketplace.

---

[146] *Parliamentary Debates*, House of Lords, vol 610, 17 March 2000, cols 1888–1889. The whole debate on the Bill can be found at cols 1885–1906.

[147] See especially H Carty, *An Analysis of the Economic Torts* (2010), Chs 8, 11.

Further reading

Books

General

L Bently and B Sherman, *Intellectual Property Law* (3rd edn, 2009), Chs 31–34

H Carty, *An Analysis of the Economic Torts* (2nd edn, 2010), Ch 11

WR Cornish, D Llewelyn, and T Aplin, *Intellectual Property* (7th edn, 2010), Ch 17.1

C Ng, L Bently, and G D'Agostino, *The Common Law of Intellectual Property* (2010)

C Wadlow, *The Law of Passing Off: Unfair Competition by Misrepresentation* (4th edn, 2011)

Articles

General

H Carty, 'The common law and the quest for the IP effect' [2007] IPQ 237

M Spence, 'Passing off and the misappropriation of valuable intangibles' (1996) 112 LQR 472

Development of the law

EM Clive, 'The action of passing off: its scope and basis' 1963 JR 117 (Scots law)

Goodwill

S Naresh, 'Passing off, goodwill and false advertising: new wine in old bottles' (1986) 45 CLJ 97

D Rose, 'Season of goodwill: passing off and overseas traders' [1995] EIPR 356

C Wadlow, '*Hotel Cipriani v Cipriani (Grosvenor Street) Ltd* [2010 EWCA 110; [2010] R.P.C. 16: the Court of Appeal draws the line on whether a foreign business has an English goodwill or not' [2011] EIPR 54

PJ Yap, 'Foreign traders and goodwill hunting: passed over or passing off?' [2009] EIPR 448

Misrepresentation

J Griffiths, 'Misattribution and misrepresentation: the claim for reverse passing off as "paternity" right' [2006] IPQ 34

J Phillips and A Coleman, 'Passing off and the common field of activity' (1985) 101 LQR 242

Passsing off and new challenges

J Davis, 'Passing off and joint liability: the rise and fall of "instruments of deception"' [2011] EIPR 204

Unfair competition

A Breitschaft, 'The future of the passing-off action in the law against unfair competition—an evaluation from a German perspective' [2010] EIPR 427

J Davis, 'Why the United Kingdom should have a law against misappropriation' (2010) 69(3) CLJ 561

C Wadlow, 'Passing off at the crossroads again: a review article for Hazel Carty, An Analysis of the Economic Torts' [2011] EIPR 447

Breach of confidence

Introduction

Scope and overview of chapter

18.1   This chapter considers contemporary law and policy relating to the protection of confidential information. This has its own important place within the legal and innovation landscape, and is also intertwined with IP.[1] The chapter begins with an overview of confidential information, including its legal basis and international relevance. The chapter summarises some key cases to give examples of the issues which arise, and the approaches which are adopted by the court. The chapter then reviews the action for breach of confidence. This has a long history, which is traced through scenarios involving personal secrets, national security, employment, post-employment, and regulation. The controversial impact of the action on the public domain and the public interest defence, are also considered.

18.2   After discussing the parties who may in fact be involved in the action, the chapter then discusses the evolving relationship between secrecy and innovation, and the impact of other forms of information control, including the Human Rights Act 1998 (HRA 1998), which is considered from the personal information perspective in Chapter 19. Finally, the international perspective is explored. Note that this chapter will not consider questions of remedy save in respect of Springboard orders, nor will it discuss the grant of injunctions in the light of section 12 of the HRA 1998. These are considered in Chapter 22.[2]

18.3
> ### Learning objectives
>
> By the end of this chapter you should be able to describe and explain:
>
> - when information can be confidential, such as to be the subject of the action;
> - when the courts will find that there is an obligation not to disclose information, or other basis for information not to be disclosed;

---

[1] Consider *Vestergaard Frandsen A/S v BestNet Europe Ltd* [2011] EWCA Civ 424, para 56 when the Court of Appeal considers, in the context of remedy, that a claim for misuse of technical trade secrets is a claim to enforce an IP right.
[2] See in particular paras 22.87, 22.88, 22.101ff, and 22.105.

- who can complain about use of confidential information, and against whom;

- industries and situations where breach of confidence questions arise frequently;

- the place of confidence and secrecy in innovation;

- the relationship between breach of confidence and IP in the commercial and adversarial contexts;

- have an understanding of other information-related legislation which can be relevant to confidential information and IP;

- the impact on the HRA 1998 on breach of confidence (quite apart from its role in relation to personal information); and

- the international perspective.

18.4   So the rest of the chapter looks like this:

- Overview (18.5–18.14)

- Elements of action (18.15–18.54)

- Defences (18.55–18.63)

- Parties to action (18.64–18.66)

- Confidence and IP (18.68–18.71)

- Secrecy and innovation (18.72–18.76)

- IP and other information regulation (18.77–18.80)

- The impact of the HRA on breach of confidence (18.81–18.84)

- International perspectives and approaches (18.85–18.86)

- Conclusions and the future (18.87)

Overview

Basics

18.5   Breach of confidence prevents use and disclosure of confidential information, if there is an obligation of confidence. The obligation might arise under a contract, say of employment, or may be implied. The obligation could be implied from the circumstances of receipt of information (eg through eavesdropping, or finding documents marked 'confidential' in a dustbin), or from the relationship between the parties involved in disclosure of information (solicitor/client or wife/husband). However, not all confidential information will be protected in all circumstances; and not all information which people might wish to keep secret (say, a celebrity bad hair day captured in the street and then posted on a social networking site) will be considered to be confidential.

18.6   The HRA 1998 created a new role for breach of confidence, with courts moulding a cause of action which the House of Lords in 2004 termed 'misuse of private information'. This provided new protection in the privacy field, although the House of Lords stressed that there was still no overarching action for breach of privacy.[3] This action is not explored here, and is considered in Chapter 19.

---

[3] *Campbell v MGN Ltd* [2004] 2 AC 457, [2004] UKHL 22, paras 11 and 14.

When will a claim succeed?

18.7   It is not always enough for a person complaining to establish these initial requirements. Other factors often need to be taken into account. For example, in employment cases there is a careful balance between protecting trade secrets of the employer (eg proposals for developing new products, marketing plans, customer lists, and source codes) after the employee has left, and the ability of the employee to move on and utilise their acquired skill and knowledge. Freedom of expression is also relevant, as part of the long-established public interest defence, which has been considered particularly important in national security cases. This defence required a balancing of the countervailing public interests in, first, the continuing confidentiality of material and, secondly, the disclosure proposed.

18.8   The HRA 1998 provided a different basis for freedom of expression to be considered. By relying on the protection set out in Article 10 of the European Convention on Human Rights (ECHR) for freedom of expression, courts have developed a more methodical approach. The question is: would the restriction on freedom of expression involved, by preventing publication of the information, be proportionate? This test is now used in respect of all aspects of breach of confidence. It will be interesting to observe how this use of human rights together with breach of confidence develops. Could human rights (eg to life and expression under the ECHR) be relied upon by a company wishing access to details of a new secret (and unpatented) cancer drug or climate change technology?[4] Could the innovator rely on their own rights to privacy?[5]

Confidence and IP

18.9   Protection of information by breach of confidence differs importantly from protection conferred by IP rights. IP protects the expression of an idea, an invention as claimed, or a design. In contrast, breach of confidence protects the basic underlying information. Thus, use of information in creating a valuable new product might be in breach of confidence, even if there is no IP infringement, because of differences between 'old' and 'new' products. Likewise, removing customer lists and business plans (rather than copying them) might avoid copyright infringement—but their use in a new venture could be in breach of confidence.

18.10   Further, by relying on trade secrets, rather than seeking patent protection, it would be possible for an inventor to have permanent control[6] over the use of the technology. This would not prevent third party reverse engineering attempts[7] or independent development. However, the almost mythical status according to the Coca-Cola formula suggests that it is not always possible to discover that which others wish to keep secret.

The international angle

18.11   Confidential information is covered by two international agreements:

   • TRIPS, Article 39(1) and (2) which provide that undisclosed information shall be protected in particular situations (similar to those explored here); and Article 39(3) which provides that undisclosed data submitted for regulatory clearance shall be protected against unfair commercial use.

---

[4] See discussions about the activities of Myriad in the United States in relation to cancer work, souces at http://www.bionews.org.uk/page.asp?obj_id=204459.

[5] See T Aplin, L Bently, P Johnson, and S Malynicz, *Gurry on Breach of Confidence. The Protection of Confidential Information* (2nd edn, 2012) ('Gurry'), 184–186.   [6] See para 18.31.

[7] See para 4.22 regarding reverse engineering and copyright.

- Paris Convention, Article 10*bis*—which provides that there shall be protection from unfair competition, including by acts contrary to honest practices in industrial and commercial matters.

What is breach of confidence (legally)?

18.12   The legal nature of breach of confidence in the UK jurisdictions is unclear.[8] Some argue that as information can be property (or intellectual property),[9] the action is one of property.[10] Others argue the action to be based on contract, the English concept of equity[11] (which does not exist in Scotland), or something else again.[12] This debate is likely to continue.

18.13   Notwithstanding this uncertainty, and its reflection in court decisions,[13] the set of principles considered in this chapter has emerged. Most of these come from decisions of the English courts. However, there is also strong authority for the existence of a general obligation of confidence in Scots law, which is at least similar to that in England.[14] Further, the UK-wide impact of the HRA 1998 suggests that, at least at the outset of an action, the same principles should be considered in each jurisdiction. It also suggests that there may be some convergence between decisions.

How does it work in practice? Some important examples

18.14   ■ *Coco v AN Clark Engineers Ltd* [1968] FSR 415, [1969] RPC 41 (Ch D)

Coco designed a moped engine and then negotiated with Clark about its manufacture. These discussions broke down and Clark designed an engine very similar to Coco's. In proceedings for breach of confidence (copyright was not alleged), it was held that for an action in breach of confidence to succeed, there must be (1) a contract imposing an obligation of confidence or information received in circumstances where the reasonable person would think they were under an obligation of confidence, and (2)

---

[8] See general consideration of the Scots position in *Laws of Scotland: Stair Memorial Encyclopaedia*, vol 18, Part II, paras 1451 et seq ('Stair') and also Gurry, note 5, Ch 4; and WR Cornish, D Llewelyn, and T Aplin, *Intellectual Property: Patents, Copyright, Trade Marks and Allied Rights* (7th edn, 2010), Part 3.

[9] See Senior Courts Act 1981, s 72 and Law Reform (Miscellaneous Provisions) (Scotland) Act 1985, s 15 and consideration in the Report of the UK Commission on Intellectual Property Rights, 'Integrating Intellectual Property Rights and Development Policy' (http://www.iprcommission.org/), *R v Licensing Authority, ex p Smith Kline & French Laboratories Ltd (No 1)* [1990] 1 AC 64 at 79–80, 88 ('SKF'). For an analysis of property in respect of virtual worlds which have information and intellectual property as their base, see FG Lastowka and D Hunter, 'The Laws of the Virtual Worlds' (2004) 92 Calif L Rev 1 (January).

[10] Although see the finding that it is not a general cause of action in relation to information: eg *White v Withers LLP* [2008] EWHC 2821 (QB).

[11] See consideration by the Court of Appeal in *Napier v Pressdram Ltd* [2009] EWCA Civ 443, paras 16–19 and *Commissioner of Police of the Metropolis v Times Newspaper* [2011] EWHC 2705 (QB), para 106.

[12] See consideration in N Witzleb, 'Justifying gain-based remedies for invasions of privacy' (2009) 29(2) OJLS 325–363. A different Scots' cause of action, the *actio in iniuriam* has also been considered in respect of non-information privacy. See HL MacQueen, 'Searching for privacy in a mixed jurisdiction' (2006) 21 Tulane European & Civil Law Forum 73.

[13] There are frequent references in cases to protection of property in information, this seems almost a form of shorthand, eg *Roger Bullivant Ltd v Ellis* [1987] FSR 172, headnote para 2, *SBJ Stephenson v Mandy* [2000] FSR 286, headnote 2, 298, referring to *Printers & Finishers Ltd v Holloway* [1965] 1 WLR 1 at 5. See overview in *Force India Formula One Team Ltd v 1 Malaysia Racing Team* [2012] EWHC 616 (Ch), including from the perspective of the appropriate approaches to remedies paras 215–224, 377–394, and 424. For a wider analysis of differing rationales, see Gurry, note 5, Ch 3.

[14] *Lord Advocate v Scotsman Publications Ltd* 1989 SLT 705 at 708 and 1988 SLT 490 ('Scotsman Second Division') at 503. See also Stair, note 8. Scottish courts have been reluctant, however, to accept that the position would necessarily always be so, given the evolving nature of the field: *Quilty v Windsor* 1999 SLT 346 at 347 and 355. See also para 20.92, note 91 regarding the independent approach of the Scottish courts.

use of the information. The court was willing to find an obligation of confidence, but was not satisfied that there was use of confidential information. Undertakings regarding future use were provided.

■ *Roger Bullivant Ltd v Ellis* [1987] FSR 172 (CA)

An employee moved to a rival and took with him a copy set of index cards with customer details from his former employer. Some of the information in the cards was publicly available, and the employee would have remembered some of it anyway. However, as the cards had been taken, an injunction was granted preventing use of the information for a reasonable period.

■ *London Regional Transport v Mayor of London* [2001] EWCA Civ 1491, 2001 WL 825728, [2003] EMLR 4 (CA)

This concerned proposed disclosure of a report critical of Private Public Partnerships in respect of the London Underground. The Court of Appeal balanced the interests of non-disclosure of confidential and commercially sensitive information, and the interests of the public in being informed as to serious problems with this method of funding. It carried out a careful balance, considering the pressing and recognised social need for restriction of any right; whether the proposed restriction was greater than necessary; and whether there were logical reasons for it. Ultimately, a proposed compromise with some information blanked out was found to be acceptable.

■ *Forensic Telecommunications Services Ltd v The Chief Constable of West Yorkshire Police and Stephen Hirst* [2011] EWHC 2892 (Ch)

This case involves claims for misuse of confidential information in respect of lists of information relating to mobile phone models to enable information to be obtained from the memories of mobile phones. The Security Service (and not the police) had a licence to use the list. The list was obtained by Hirst from Forensic, for a limited purpose, and then he posted it on a police website. Arnold J found there to be a misuse of confidential information. The list had the necessary quality of confidence, having been collated through the exercise of skill, judgement, and labour outside the public domain; in the circumstances, a reasonable person would have appreciated that the information was confidential.

 Exercise

Devise a scenario which you think might involve breach of confidence in the context of an innovation business. You might get some ideas from other exercises in this chapter.

The next section reviews in more detail the traditional action for breach of confidence.

Elements of action

18.15   The starting point is the three-step test set out in *Coco v Clark* considered previously:[15]

- information to be of a confidential nature;

---

[15] The decision, treated as a landmark, built on existing authorities, particularly *Saltman Engineering Co Ltd v Campbell Engineering Co Ltd* (1948) 65 RPC 203—see *Coco v Clark* [1968] FSR 415 at 419.

- information to be communicated in circumstances of confidence such that the reasonable man in the position of the recipient would realise that the information was given to him in confidence;

- unauthorised use of the information—(possibly) to the detriment of the confider.

What type of information is protected?

18.16   Over the years, cases have dealt with all manner of information: from the highly personal about individuals, through sports, trade, business, and technical information, ideas for television shows, and political and historical information about government, and indeed DNA.[16] The essential question is whether the information is confidential. Whether this is so is, perhaps surprisingly, not always clear and cases can involve detailed analysis of the facts, which might seem to suggest little of interest in other cases.[17]

 Discussion point   For answer guidance visit www.oxfordtextbooks.co.uk/orc/waelde3e/

Write down three types of information you think of as confidential. Review your answer after reading the next sections.

Nature of information

18.17   Not all information can be confidential. From decided cases, it can be discerned that to qualify information need not be complex[18] or of commercial value,[19] although some form of creativity[20] would likely be required. Courts have been reluctant to protect mere 'tittle tattle';[21] but some personal information, such as private diaries and details of sexual activities, has been found confidential.[22] Although, as noted, claims are frequent in the employment context, not all details of workplace activities will be confidential.[23]

Already in the public domain?

18.18   The content of information (isolated or in combination)[24] or its value[25] likely must not be public knowledge. Yet, unlike with patents, absolute novelty is not required—the key is the level of accessibility of the information. Note that in *Imerman v Tchenguiz and others*,[26] Imerman stored confidential information

---

[16] Regarding the lack of confidentiality of a community resource, see discussion in 'India: International Covenant on Economic, Social and Cultural Rights (1966) art. 11—*Emergent Genetics v Shailendra Shivan*' [2012] IIC 355—finding, with regard to the Indian Constitution, that there should not be any common ownership or control of what should be the common resource of the community (hybrid seeds); and so they could not be confidential.

[17] See, eg, *Force India*, note 13, paras 36–200 and *Jones v IOS (UK) Ltd In Liquidation)* [2012] EWHC 348 (Ch).

[18] *Cranleigh Precision Engineering Ltd v Bryant* [1965] 1 WLR 1293 at 1310; *Coco v Clark*, note 15, 420.

[19] *Nichrotherm Electrical Co Ltd v Percy* [1956] RPC 272; aff'd [1957] RPC 207. See Gurry, note 5, 162–163.

[20] *Coco v Clark*, note 15, 419–20.

[21] *Coco v Clark*, note 15, 421. It has been argued, however, that this point was made to avoid awarding relief, rather than to avoid confidential status—*Stephens v Avery* [1988] 2 WLR 1280, [1988] 2 All ER 477, [1988] FSR 510, [1988] Ch 449 at 454 finding wholesale revelation of sexual activity not to be tittle-tattle.

[22] See *Cadell Davies v Stewart* (1804) Mor App Literary Property No 4 June 1, 1804 FC; *Argyll v Argyll* [1967] Ch 302; *Stephens v Avery*, note 21; *X (HA) v Y* [1988] 2 All ER 648, [1988] RPC 379; *Barrymore v News Group Newspapers Ltd* [1997] FSR 600; *Mosley v News Group Newspapers Ltd* [2008] EWHC 1777 (QB), [2008] EMLR 20, paras 5, 6, and 105–108.

[23] *Tillery Valley Foods v Channel Four Television Corporation* 2004 WL 1074218 (films of frozen meals for hospitals made by someone working undercover as employee), para 11.

[24] *Coco v Clark*, note 15, 420. *Saltman*, note 15, 215.

[25] See on this issue generally, Gurry, note 5, 148–151.   [26] [2010] EWCA Civ 908.

on a server that was accessible to Tchenguiz as the controller of the server. The Court of Appeal held that 'confidentiality is not dependent upon locks and keys or their electronic equivalents.'[27] A claim in confidence has in the past survived publication of the information overseas.[28] However, this approach would likely not be taken now, given increased global communication technologies.

18.19   Information might still be confidential even if it is published to a finite group, say passengers on an aeroplane, or a small number of readers.[29] In *BBC v HarperCollins Publishers Ltd*[30] regarding the identity of 'The Stig' in a well-known television programme, the court held that even where an 'information has been published, the nature of the publication or the places where the publication is available or the period for which the published information was available might lead a court to conclude that the information was not "so generally accessible" to have lost its confidential character.' There, however, the information had become generally accessible (through 13 different publications), so it could no longer be considered as confidential.[31] When more than one person is involved in the subject matter of information (say, a sexual relationship) and only one wants to disclose it, the other might still claim the information to be confidential. Both attitudes will be relevant to the court.[32] Information shared with a friend in confidence will be confidential to that friend.[33]

18.20   If information has been disclosed for limited, specified purposes, it will remain confidential in respect of other purposes. The Prince of Wales providing confidential access to his diaries to his authorised biographer did not mean that they were no longer confidential.[34] If information is disclosed as part of a project, then when the project is completed the information must be treated as confidential.[35]

18.21   *Speed Seal Products v Paddington ('Speed Seal')*[36] suggested that confidentiality was lost only if information was published with the consent of the person to whom an obligation of confidence was owed. This case drew heavily, however, from a decision which although it involved published information, was more likely based on breach of fiduciary duty.[37] The House of Lords considered the issue in *Attorney General v Guardian Newspapers Ltd (No 2) ('Spycatcher')*.[38] The case concerned the diaries of a former member of the security services, Peter Wright, which had already been published abroad. The House of Lords indicated that it might have been prepared to grant an injunction against Wright (who was not a party). However, some Law Lords suggested that this would not have been based on breach of a continuing obligation of confidence.[39]

---

[27] *Imerman*, note 26, para 79. See also *Force India*, note 13, regarding relative confidentiality, paras 217–222, 259–264.

[28] *Franchi v Franchi* [1967] RPC 149 regarding publication in foreign patent.

[29] Gurry, note 5, 151–155. See also *Woodward v Hutchins* [1977] 1 WLR 760, [1977] 2 All ER 751, 764 (disgraceful conduct of pop-stars on aeroplane might have been confidential, if there had been slightly different facts), and *McKennitt v Ash* [2006] EWCA Civ 1714, regarding memoirs of a friend of a Canadian folk singer; singer had herself previously published some of the information privately, paras 79–80. Compare *Scotsman*, note 14, which left open whether small number of copies distributed privately meant the work was not confidential.

[30] [2010] EWHC 2424 (Ch), [2011] EMLR 6   [31] *BBC v HarperCollins*, note 30, paras 51ff.

[32] *A v B plc* [2002] EWCA 337, 2003 QB 195 (CA), paras 43(iii), 79–80.   [33] *Ash* (CA), note 29, paras 29–32.

[34] *HRH Prince of Wales v Associated Newspapers Ltd (No 3)* [2006] EWCA Civ 1776, [2008] Ch 57, [2007] 3 WLR 222, paras 21, 43.

[35] See *Torrington Manufacturing Co v Smith & Sons (England) Ltd* [1966] RPC 285; *Regina Glass Fibre Ltd v Werner Schuller* [1972] FSR 141, [1972] RPC 229.

[36] *Speed Seal Products Ltd v Paddington* [1986] 1 All ER 91, [1985] 1 WLR 1327 at 1332–1333.

[37] *Cranleigh*, note 18, 93. *Speed Seal* was agreed with by *Scotsman Second Division*, note 14, at 491–4.

[38] [1988] 3 WLR 776 at 785–786, 789, 791, 795–796, 809, 817.

[39] Other possibilities considered were Crown copyright, profiting from own wrong and Springboard. See *Spycatcher*, note 38, 786, 796, compare 791, 809–812, 818. Injunction was granted only against Peter Wright and connected parties. Regarding Crown copyright, see also para 3.29.

18.22   In 2009, in a long-running dispute involving a mosquito net, Arnold J considered that there was no general principle that injunctions could be granted in relation to breach of confidence once information was in the public domain.[40]

18.23   The confidentiality of photographs has given rise to a lot of discussion. A photograph may be confidential even if it has been published, has the same subject as a photograph proposed to be published, or was taken in public. The fact that one can take a photograph in public does not mean one can publish it, if the subject matter is clearly controlled. For example, photographs of the set for the album cover of the band Oasis were confidential, as there was a clear indication that photography was not permitted.[41]

18.24   In *Douglas v Hello!*[42] regarding photographs of the wedding of Michael Douglas and Catherine Zeta-Jones, a freelance photographer managed to attend the wedding and take photographs to sell to *Hello!* magazine. The wedding party permitted no unofficial photography, and had an exclusive deal with *OK!* magazine. There, special treatment was considered by the Court of Appeal to be appropriate for photographs (as opposed to other information potentially in the public domain) because of the invasive nature of photographs, and impact of their re-publication.[43] The photographs were found to disclose private information, and the fact that there was a contract for publication of other photographs of the wedding did not change this.[44] Further, the publisher which had entered into a contract to publish the photographs was considered by the House of Lords to have the right to control the information in the photographs.[45]

18.25   Information disclosed in open court or read by the judge is not confidential.[46] However, confidentiality is not lost if hearings do not take place in open court, or are behind a locked door, with restricted access to information ('confidentiality clubs'), and excerpted judgments.[47] This can lead to practical problems; how can a case proceed properly without proper consideration of the information, regard to transparency, and also the need to respect information which remains confidential, as is frequently seen in technology cases?[48] It should also be borne in mind that much more fundamental conflicts can arise from the disclosure of confidential information, say, in asylum and public law cases.[49]

---

[40] *Vestergaard Frandsen A/S v BestNet Europe Ltd* [2009] EWHC 1456 (Ch), [2010] FSR 2 at first instance notably paras 22, 68–76 (note that the appeal did not consider this point). Compare para 18.62 and *Northern Rock plc v The Financial Times Ltd* [2007] EWHC 2677 (QB), in particular paras 15, 19–20, 25; *Attorney-General v Blake* [2001] 1 AC 268 (HL), [2000] 3 WLR 625; *Schering Chemicals Ltd v Falkman Ltd* [1982] QB 1 including an overview of earlier cases, see pp 36, 37, 39, 40 and per Lord Denning at pp 15–17, 21–22.

[41] In *Creation Records Ltd v News Group Newspapers Ltd* [1997] EMLR 444, paras 461–464 and *Shelley Films Ltd v Rex Features Ltd* [1994] EMLR 134 at 148–149 it is unclear whether the basis for order preventing further publication was confidentiality or to prevent a springboard benefit—see paras 18.62ff.

[42] *Douglas and others v Hello! Ltd (No 3)* [2005] EWCA Civ 595, [2005] 3 WLR 881.

[43] *Campbell*, note 3, paras 31, 73–75, *Douglas v Hello!*, note 42, headnote 1, and paras 85–88, 105–108 (referring paras 40–41, 77–80 to *Theakston v MGN Ltd* [2002] EWHC 137, [2002] EMLR 22 when injunction had been granted regarding photos but not words, and also referring to *Von Hannover v Germany* (App No 59320100) [2004] EMLR 21, (2005) 40 EHRR 1, para 59). See further *Mosley*, note 22, paras 16–23. Note also special rules in respect of photographs regarding moral rights, see para 3.48 and discussions regarding photos and personality at para 19.17.

[44] *Douglas v Hello!*, note 42, para 95. See paras 16.19ff regarding circumstances in which image can be protected.

[45] And as such, to treat them as any other trade secret. The decision of the House of Lords is reported at *OBG Ltd v Allan* [2007] UKHL 21, [2002] 1 AC 1, [2007] 2 WLR 920, see paras 117–122, 278, 307, 310, 325–329, cf 255–259, 298–300. For detailed consideration of different approaches taken by the House of Lords, see G Black, '*Douglas v Hello!*—An OK! result' (2007) 4(2) SCRIPTed 161 @ http://www.law.ed.ac.uk/ahrc/scripted/vol4-2/editorial.asp and more detailed discussion in Chapter 19 where.

[46] Including where only read by the judge in advance, and not referred to in court; *Smithkline Beecham Biologicals SA v Connaught Laboratories Inc (Disclosure of Documents)* [2000] FSR 1. See also *Crossley v Newsquest (Midlands South) Ltd* [2008] EWHC 3054 (QB).

[47] See *EPI Environmental Technologies Inc v Symphony Plastic Technologies plc* [2006] EWCA Civ 3, 2006 WL 421838, [2006] 1 WLR 495 for an example of a redacted judgment.

[48] See *Samsung Electronics Co Ltd v Apple Retail UK Ltd* [2012] EWHC 2277 (Pat), 2012 WL 3062452 and brief decision in *Omnipharm Ltd v Merial* [2011] EWHC 3064 (Pat). See also Gurry, note 5, 415–424.

[49] *R v Secretary of State for Home Department, ex p S* [2012] EWHC 955 (Admin).

Government information

18.26   For government information to be confidential, the government must satisfy the court that the public interest in confidentiality exceeds the public interest in the information being available.[50] This is a special hurdle, given the importance of government information being available.

> ## Key points on when information is confidential
>
> - Not all information can be confidential
> - It is possible for information to be confidential if there has been limited sharing or some disclosure
> - There is a special public interest test in respect of government information

What *is* the information?

18.27   An important legal and practical question is whether, and how well, the information can be identified.[51] If it cannot be clearly identified and distinguished from other information, the court will be unable to determine if it is in fact confidential; also, any court order could not be set out with sufficient clarity.[52] This raises two different problems for the party complaining: the necessary detail might not be available (eg if information was communicated orally or developed in someone's head); and overspecification might reveal more than had previously been known by the other side.[53]

> ## Key point on identifying the information
>
> - It is important to specify information, to enable liability to be determined and remedy to be properly framed

Exercise

The following is a list of scenarios. Split them into three groups: is this information confidential: YES, NO, MAYBE? Is further information required?

- The formula for a new product which had been kept locked in a safe.
- The formula for an industry-staple product,which was launched years ago, is easy to reverse engineer—but is locked in a safe.
- Next year's exam papers.
- Details of the proposed use of illegal immigrants as guinea pigs for unlicensed drug tests.

---

[50] *Spycatcher*, note 38, 783, 785, 796, 807 and in *Australia Cth v Jonathan Fairfax & Sons Ltd* (180) 147 CLR 39 and *Smith Kline & French Laboratories (Australia) v Secretary to the Department of Community Services and Health* [1990] FSR 617, paras 21–22, 29. See also Gurry, note 5, 189–193.

[51] *Inline Logistics v UCI Logistics* [2002] RPC 32. For an example of a case where information was not identified with the necessary precision, see *FSS Travel & Leisure Systems v Johnson* [1999] FSR 505 (CA) at 513.

[52] Compare, however, the broad approach to framing of order preventing future disclosure in *Levin v Farmers Supply Association of Scotland* 1973 SLT (Notes) 43 at 44. Detail considered important, however, in *Ocular Sciences Ltd v Aspect Vision Care (No 2)* [1997] RPC 289 at 359. This case is considered in respect of unregistered design rights at paras 9.43 and 9.45.

[53] The importance of detail in identifying the claim and evidence can be seen, eg, in *Force India*, note 13, paras 267ff where lack of detail had some negative consequences.

Discussion point For answer guidance visit www.oxfordtextbooks.co.uk/orc/waelde3e/

Is posting on an Internet chat site the equivalent of speaking to a friend on the phone? How appropriate are established principles given new technology?

An obligation: circumstances of confidence

When will the obligation exist?

18.28   An obligation of confidence is required for breach of confidence.[54] The obligation can be based on contract, but it need not be. *Coco v Clark* set out an objective test to be applied when there is no contract; would the reasonable man realise that the information was given in confidence: how would the circumstances of receipt of information impact upon the conscience of the reasonable person?[55] There have been cases questioning whether a subjective test might also be appropriate given the reference to 'conscience'. However, so far this has not proved significant in identifying obligations.[56]

18.29   Accordingly, there might be an obligation when a confidentiality agreement is signed as part of a research and development project. Issues can arise even if there is a contract, for example in *Vestegaard Frandsen and others v Bestnet Europe and others*[57] the Court of Appeal found that strict liability could not be considered as an implied term of a contract of employment, particularly regarding information which an individual had never had. Examples of obligations in less formal situations are information obtained after hacking into a password-protected website,[58] during a heart-felt confession from a friend,[59] or by using illegal means to listen to phone calls.[60]

Scope

18.30   Even if there is an obligation, its scope must be established in each case. For example, it might be acceptable to use, but not disclose, information.[61] In 2001 in relation to disclosure of anonymised medical data by pharmacists to marketing companies, the Court of Appeal said the key question as to scope was the conscience of the reasonable pharmacist.[62]

---

[54] See also Gurry, note 5, Ch 7.

[55] *Coco v Clark*, note 15, 419–425, see also *Spycatcher*, note 38, 805; *Kavanagh Balloons Pty Ltd v Cameron Balloons Ltd* [2004] RPC 5, para 46 and *Napier*, note 11, para 42.

[56] This was considered in *Carflow Products (UK) Ltd v Linwood Securities (Birmingham) Ltd* [1996] FSR 424 at 424, 429. Cf Arnold J at first instance, *Vestegaard Frandsen A/S v BestNet Europe Ltd* [2009] EWHC 1456 (Ch), [2010] FSR 2 discussed at note 1, para 24, and the different approach taken by the Court of Appeal in *Vestergaard*, para 48 . See also *Commissioner of Police of the Metropolis v Times Newspaper* [2011] EWHC 2705 (QB), paras 107–121 and para 18.46.

[57] *Vestergaard*, note 56, paras 47–50.

[58] Although merely encrypting information, without more, has been held not to create an obligation of confidence: *Mars UK Ltd v Teknowledge Ltd (No 1)* The Times, 23 June 1999 (Ch D). See J Watts, 'Copyright: reverse engineering and encryption' (1999) 21(9) EIPR N158.

[59] Eg *Stephens*, note 21, 451, 453, 456.

[60] In *Francome v Mirror Group* [1984] 2 All ER 408, [1984] 1 WLR 892. Compare *Malone v Commissioner of Police of the Metropolis (No 2)* [1979] 2 All ER 620, [1979] 2 WLR 700 (information obtained from official wire tap was not a breach of confidence). See also paras 18.53 and 18.54. Compare the finding that the making of a complaint to the Law Society, and its investigation, did not give rise to an obligation of confidence: *Napier*, note 11, paras 48–49, 52–57.

[61] *Coco v Clark*, note 15, 419 and 421. See Gurry, note 5, 664–673.

[62] *R v Department of Health, ex p Source Infomatics (No 1)* [2001] QB 424, [2000] 2 WLR 940 (CA), para 31.

Discussion point   For answer guidance visit www.oxfordtextbooks.co.uk/orc/waelde3e/

Plans for the University of Edingow to take over the University of Glasburgh (which are being met with riots in the streets) are posted on a blog clearly described as 'Private to Members of the University of Edingow', but require no password. Ross, a student at Sydbourne, finds the information and sends it to Hamish at a newspaper. Was Ross under an obligation of confidence? If so, how wide was this obligation?

Key points on bases of obligation of confidence

- Obligation can arise under contract
- Obligation can arise from circumstances of receipt, assessed (likely) using an objective test
- Scope of an obligation is to be assessed in each case, using an objective test

Duration

18.31   Provided the information in question remains confidential, the obligation is infinite. Contractually imposed obligations (if they are not otherwise objectionable) can continue after the contract term[63]— provided the information does remain confidential. This is one appeal for business of relying on confidential information, rather than, say, patents[64] in respect of vaccines or copyright[65] in respect of customer lists.

18.32   With government information, the obligation depends upon the public interest balance, and so the obligation may cease if this balance changes.[66] Different balances have been reached in respect of members of the security services[67] and government ministers.[68]

Question

Would you prefer patents or confidential information for your business?

Key point on duration

- There is no time limit, provided the information remains confidential

---

[63] *Lady Archer v Williams* [2003] EWHC 1670, [2003] EMLR 38, para 47. Regarding the likely limited impact of a breach of the contract, see *Rock Refrigeration Ltd v Jones* [1997] 1 All ER 1 (CA) and *Campbell v Frisbee* [2002] EWHC 328 (Ch), EWCA (Civ) 1375, [2002] EMLR 31.

[64] See paras 11.79, 11.137ff and S Nisar, 'Pre-filing disclosure of an invention is found to be in breach of an equitable obligation of confidence' (2012) 7(7) JIPLP 485–486.

[65] See paras 3.49ff.   [66] See para 18.26, *Douglas v Hello!*, note 42, para 104.

[67] *Spycatcher*, note 38, 782, 790–791, 794, 808; *Scotsman*, note 14, 709 (lifelong obligation of confidence).

[68] *Attorney General v Jonathan Cape Ltd* [1976] QB 752, [1975] 3 WLR 606 (diaries of Cabinet discussions can be published after a decent interval).

18.33   Two categories merit further consideration: particular types of obligation (including, importantly, employment) and indirect recipients of information.

Special relationships

Employment

18.34   There is an obligation of confidence during a period of employment. If the contract is silent the court will imply an obligation, on the basis of good faith and fidelity. The nature of the obligation will vary;[69] however, courts have implied terms preventing injury to employers' interests.[70] Courts have found that this would cover disclosure of secret information to competitors[71] or to a trade union.[72]

18.35   Regarding preparations for the period after employment, courts have implied terms preventing making or memorising lists of customers[73] (although there are difficulties of proof if the information was publicly available)[74] or soliciting customers to join a new venture.[75] Not all preliminary activity will necessarily be prohibited: it is a question of fact and degree.[76] Courts have also extended the same approach to uses of new technologies, for example regarding use of the names from a LinkedIn account.[77] A statement that 'I did it at home, I know these people anyway and they think of me, not my (former) employer' is unlikely to work.

18.36   After the employment term has ended, courts will imply a further, more limited, obligation. According to the leading case. *Faccenda Chicken Ltd v Fowler*,[78] former employers must not use or disclose information which is a trade secret or which in all the circumstances is so confidential that it requires the same level of protection.

18.37   *Faccenda* suggests that a trade secret must not be the skill, know-how, and general knowledge of the employee.[79] Decided cases suggest that it will also depend upon:

- the nature of the employment (if an employee frequently works with confidential information, eg in a locked lab);[80]

---

[69] *Faccenda Chicken Ltd v Fowler* [1987] Ch 117, [1986] 3 WLR 288, [1986] FSR 291 at 302.

[70] Including work done outside office hours—see *Hivac Ltd v Royal Park Scientific Instruments Ltd* [1946] 1 Ch 169. Note also the Public Interest Disclosure Act 1989 and Gurry, note 5, Ch 11.

[71] *Printers & Finishers*, note 13, and *Bullivant*, note 13.   [72] *Bents Brewery v Hogan* [1945] 2 All ER 570.

[73] *Robb v Green* [1895] 2 QB 315; *Faccenda*, note 69, 302; *Bullivant*, note 13, 175–181; *JN Dairies Ltd v Johal Dairies Ltd* [2009] EWHC 1331 (Ch).

[74] See also *Bullivant*, note 13, 183. Followed in *Bradford & Bingley plc v Holden* [2002] EWHC 2445, [2002] WL 31962007 but compare *Universal Thermosensors v Hibben* [1992] 1 WLR 840 and *Stephenson*, note 13, 298. See also *Sectrack NV v Satamatics* [2007] EWHC 3003 (Comm).

[75] *Faccenda*, note 69, 302, *Bullivant*, note 13.

[76] See also *ABK v Foxwell* [2002] EWHC 9, 2002 WL 499040; *Churchill Retired Living Ltd v Luard* [2012] EWHC 1479 (Ch), and the Law of Society of Scotland's Guidelines, 'Social Media—Advice and nformation for the Legal Profession', at http://www.lawscot.org.uk/rules-and-guidance/section-e/division-b-the-management-of-files,-papers-and-information/advice-and-information/social-media-%E2%80%93-advice-and-information-for-the-legal-profession.

[77] *Hays Specialist Recruitment (Holdings) Ltd et al v Ions et al* [2008] EWHC 745 (Ch), regarding the positon in the United States, see T Snow (28 January 2012) Social Media, Esq, 'Who Owns Your LinkedIn Account? Before Phonedog, there was *Eagle v Edcomm*', at http://www.socialmediaesq.com/2012/01/28/who-owns-your-linkedin-account-before-phonedog-there-was-eagle-v-edcomm/ and T Snow (8 January 2012) Social Media, Esq, 'Who Owns Your Twitter Account: The Phone Dog case', at http://www.socialmediaesq.com/2012/01/08/phonedog-who-owns-your-twitter-account/, for links and discussion

[78] Followed in Scotland in *Harben Pumps (Scotland) Ltd v Lafferty* 1989 SLT 752.

[79] *Faccenda*, note 69, 303, *FSS Travel*, note 51, 516 and see *Lansing Linde v Kerr* [1991] 1 All ER 418, [1991] 1 WLR 251 (CA). *Faccenda*, 306 left open the question of whether it would be breach of confidence if the employee simply passed on or sold information, rather than used it themselves. See also *Crowson Fabrics Ltd v Rider* [2007] EWHC 2942 (Ch), [2008] FSR 17.

[80] *Faccenda*, note 69, 304.

- the nature of the information (possibilities include secret processes or designs,[81] and customer lists);[82]

- whether the employer impressed the confidentiality of the information on the employee (eg locked doors, training sessions, or is information openly available and discussed);[83]

- whether the information could be readily isolated from other information;[84]

- whether there would be real or significant harm if the information were disclosed.[85]

18.38   Given some uncertainties in applying these principles in practice, an employer could choose to be proac-tive and clarify information status in the contract; it might also include a clause preventing the employee working in the same field, possibly in the same geographic area, for a period. These clauses, known as restrictive covenants, will not be implied into contracts. They are also scrutinised carefully by courts.[86]

18.39   *Faccenda* provides that a restrictive covenant will not be enforced unless the protection sought was rea-sonable and necessary to protect trade secrets or prevent abuse of personal influence over customers.[87] It is a difficult balance. Is an employer protecting legitimate business information which cannot be erased from memory, and might require a special protection for a time? Or is the employer placing an unreasonable restriction on the employee's ability to work elsewhere, exploiting their skill and know-how?[88] Laddie J was more succinct in *Polymasc Pharmaceuticals v Charles*:[89] is the clause 'too greedy'?[90]

18.40   It should also be borne in mind that in a case involving Formula 1 motor-racing technology, Arnold J was of the view that the same approach should be taken both to independent contractors and to employees.[91] Further, competition law concerns, considered in more detail in Chapter 21, can also be relevant here. In *Jones v Ricoh UK Ltd*[92] it was held that a very extensively drafted confidentiality agree-ment was in breach of of Article 101 of the Treaty on the Functioning of the European Union (TFEU) and was void.[93]

Key points on employment relationship and beyond

- There is an obligation of confidence in the course of employment

- After employment, there is an obligation not to disclose trade secrets or equivalent

- Restrictive covenants are only enforced to the extent reasonable and necessary, balancing the interests of employer and employee

- Problem areas are new product ideas, business plans, know-how sets and customer lists, social media connections, and accounts

---

[81] *Faccenda*, note 69, 303–304, *Littlewoods Organisation Ltd v Harris* [1978] 1 All ER 1026, [1977] 1 WLR 1472.

[82] See also *AT Poeton (Gloucester Plating) Ltd v Horton* [2001] FSR 14.   [83] *Faccenda*, note 69, 305.

[84] *Faccenda*, note 69, 305. See also *FSS Travel*, note 51, 316.   [85] *Lansing*, note 79, 270.

[86] This was stressed by the Court of Appeal in *Faccenda*, note 69, 304–305. Regarding garden leave as well as or instead of a restric-tive covenant, see *GFI Group Inc v Eaglestone* [1994] FSR 535 (but compare *Provident Finance Group v Hayward* [1989] 3 All ER 298). In relation to England and Wales, the Fraud Act 2006, s 4, may also have some impact: see consideration in B Allgrove and S Sellers, 'The Fraud Act 2006: is breach of confidence now a crime?' (2009) 4(4) JIPLP 278–282.   [87] *Faccenda*, note 69, 303–304.

[88] *Lock International plc v Besurick* [1989] 1 WLR 1260, [1989] 3 All ER 373; *Balston v Headline Filters Ltd (No 2)* [1990] FSR 385 (CA). See also *Hinton & Higgs (UK) Ltd v Murphy* 1989 SLT 450, *Bullivant*, note 13, *Basic Solutions Ltd v Sands* [2008] EWHC 1388 (QB); *Wrn Ltd v Ayris* [2008] EWHC 1080 (QB), [2008] IRLR 889; *Mantis Surgical Ltd v Tregenza* [2007] EWHC 1545 (QB); and *Thomas v Farr plc and Hanover Park Commercial Ltd* [2007] EWCA Civ 118, [2007] ICR 932, [2007] IRLR 419.

[89] [1999] FSR 711 at 719.   [90] See also Gurry, note 5, Ch 12.   [91] *Force India*, note 13, paras 234, 235.

[92] [2010] EWHC 1743 (Ch).   [93] *Jones v Ricoh*, note 92, paras 39–49.

Exercise

Katie is headhunted to join Eversogood Ltd. Katie has been in charge of developing a new chocolate bar for FunFunFun Ltd. FunFunFun gave her no support, she worked on her own, and wrote nothing down. On joining Eversogood, Liz, her line manager, offered a team of researchers to develop a new chocolate bar. Being conscientious, Katie shared some ideas with her new team and, as some of them are overseas, they have started sharing ideas about this on Twitter, as it is so much quicker than the slow (but secure) corporate intranet. They developed a much improved third generation product. Discuss.

Other special situations

18.41   Obligations of confidence exist where there is a particular relationship, as, for example, between professional adviser and client or doctor and patient.[94] Difficulties can arise when professionals move or firms merge—although the obligations do continue.[95]

18.42   There are often specific restrictions on when information obtained on a particular statutory or regulatory basis, can be used or passed to others. This could involve information obtained pursuant to, for example, the Police and Criminal Evidence Act 1984 or the Banking Act 1987, or for regulatory product clearance.[96] The outcome in each case will depend on the proposed conduct, the wording of the legislation, and the function of the regulator.

18.43   There is an obligation of confidence in marriage and in stable relationships. The scope and, indeed, existence of this declines with the level of involvement,[97] and even if there is an obligation within a marriage, one partner can still enjoy rights of privacy as against the other.[98]

Key points on special situations

- Obligation within marriage or equivalent
- Obligation between professional adviser and client

Question

Does your best friend owe you an obligation of confidence? Consider in the light of *McKennitt v Ash* [2008] QB 73, [2007] 3 WLR 194.

---

[94] See Gurry, note 5, Ch 9 regarding particular relationships and responsibilities: consultants and contractors, licensing, bankers, ministers of religion, doctors and other health professionals, lawyers and other professionals, personal intimate relationships, and fidicuaries.   [95] See *Surface Technology v Young* [2002] FSR 25.

[96] Compare *SKF*, note 9, 70–78, 81–82, 84–85, 86–87, 89–90 and on the same facts *SKF Australia*, note 50. Regarding international perspectives more generally, see paras 18.85.

[97] *Argyll*, note 22, 322, 329–330. Post-HRA 1998 authorities are also relevant here: *A v B plc*, note 32, paras 11(xi), 29, 43, 47; *Ash* (CA), note 29, paras 29–30, *Theakston*, note 43, paras 57–61, 74, 76; and *Mosley*, note 22, paras 105–109. These are considered in more details in paras 19.9ff.   [98] *Imerman*, note 26, paras 54–71, 80–89.

Indirect recipient

18.44   An employee might take information with them to a new employer, but may be unable to use the information without the colleagues and resources available with that new employer. Or a memory stick left in a laptop found on a bus might mean nothing to the 'finder', who then passes it to a friend in the IT industry. What is the position of these new recipients? This distinction can be important in practice—as the real concern of the original holder of the information might be what another business might do with it.

18.45   The principles in *Coco v Clark* apply here: would a reasonable person believe that the information was received subject to an obligation.[99] Third parties were considered in *Spycatcher*,[100] suggesting an obligation of confidence not only in:

> those cases where a third party receives information from a person who is under a duty of confidence in respect of it, knowing that it has been disclosed by that person to him in breach of his duty of confidence, but also to include certain situations, beloved of law teachers—where an obviously confidential document is wafted by an electric fan out of a window into a crowded street, or where an obviously confidential document, such as a private diary, is dropped in a public place, and is then picked up by a passer-by.

18.46   The more intervening recipients there have been in respect of the information, the less likely it is that there will be an obligation:[101] say, a former employee tells a new colleague who later takes information to a third employer, or the finder on the bus passes it to a colleague with a plausible explanation. The key test for such recipients has been held to be dishonest conduct. Carelessness, stupidity, or naivety (eg believing the explanation without question) would not suffice.[102]

18.47   If there is no obligation, there can be no liability. However, if someone is subsequently told that information is confidential, there will be an obligation from that time.[103]

Key point on indirect recipients of confidential information

- Indirect recipients may be subject to obligations of confidence

---

 Exercise

Go back to Hamish, Ross, and Edingow (in the Discussion point following para 18.30). Is Hamish under an obligation of confidence? What about Hamish's editor? Draw a diagram setting out when there will be obligations of confidence, noting relevant factors.

---

[99] In *Shelley*, note 41, the photographic agency was found to have knowledge of restrictions so was under an obligation not to publish, 149–151.

[100] *Spycatcher*, note 38, 806.

[101] See Gurry, note 5, 263–65.

[102] *Thomas v Pearce* [2000] FSR 718 (CA) at 719, 721 which includes careful analysis of objective and subjective tests. See also *Carflow*, note 56.

[103] See, eg, *Surface Technology*, note 95. It is likely, given the equitable nature of the obligation, that even if someone pays for information, there will still be an obligation if there is the necessary knowledge: *Stephenson Jordan & Harrison Ltd v Macdonald & Evans* (1952) 69 RPC 10 at 16. See also *Burrows v Smith* [2010] EWHC 22 (Ch).

Relevant conduct

What is required?

18.48   There must be some conduct for there to be a breach of confidence. The conduct can be of the old fashioned kind, for example giving a file to a competitor or a journal (or, indeed, leaving it on the bus) or more contemporary, for example Lewis Hamilton's 2012 use of Twitter in making available what has been said to include confidential Formula 1 team information.[104]

18.49   However, the nature of the breach is closely tied to the scope of the obligation; not all activities in relation to relevant information will constitute a breach. Thus, it can be breach of confidence to use or disclose information, including doing more with information than that to which the subject consented.[105] The disclosure of anonymised medical information by pharmacists to marketing companies was not a breach of their obligation of confidence. The interest of the subject was held to be in not being identified, rather than in the confidentiality of the underlying information.[106]

Detriment

18.50   It is unclear whether, for there to be breach of confidence, there must be detriment which is suffered as a result of the disclosure. The requirement is suggested in *Coco v Clark*.[107] However, that case involved commercial secrets, where it is more likely that detriment would follow, so its consideration would seem uncontroversial. In other situations, say, disclosure to a new colleague who does not act on the information, there may be no detriment; and if the essence of the action is the obligation not to use, it would seem that 'loss' should not be required when there is use.[108] Discussions, in particular in *Spycatcher* (where it was noted that the necessary detriment could be a wider loss of morale of the security services), suggest that a broad approach may be taken by the courts.[109]

Intention

18.51   There is no requirement of intention. Thus acts in good faith, unconscious use, and drawing on information obtained in long-forgotten circumstances, can still be in breach of confidence.[110]

Risk of use and disclosure

18.52   Breach of confidence is, as noted, a particular concern for solicitors[111] and accountants. Clients are often concerned if their former adviser moves firms. There have been a number of cases on Chinese walls and confidentiality proposals, seeking orders that, for example, a partner does not go into the office for the duration of a particular matter, to remove the risk of use or disclosure of confidential information. If proposals for avoiding use or disclosure of such information are clear, robust, and avoid the possibility of interaction, the court will be likely to refuse orders.[112] The more ad hoc the arrangements, the more the

---

[104] A Benson, 'Lewis Hamilton's tweet has not caused us much harm—McLaren', BBC Sport, 3 September 2012, at http://www.bbc.co.uk/sport/0/formula1/19464220.

[105] *Cornelius v De Taranto* (2001) 68 BMLR 62 involved overly wide disclosure of medical information in the circumstances.

[106] *Source*, note 62, paras 34–35.   [107] *Coco v Clark*, note 15, 425.   [108] See consideration in Stair, note 8, para 1477.

[109] *Spycatcher*, note 38, 782, 785, 786, 800, 802, 806—the basis for the decision is unclear. The book had already been published. In *Scotsman Second Division*, note 14, 497, 500–501, 504–505 similar arguments of 'non-contents detriment' failed to prevent an injunction.

[110] *Seager v Copydex Ltd (No 1)* [1967] FSR 211 at 212, 221, 224; *Terrapin Ltd v Builders Supply Co (Hayes) Ltd* [1967] RPC 375 at 390. Gurry, note 5, 673–676.

[111] Including in respect of those who are not their clients. For consideration of this in relation to ACS:Law and its actions against alleged infringers of IP through downloading, see S Webb, 'The strictest confidence' (2011) 21(Jan) Sol 10–11.

[112] *Koch Shipping v Richards Butler* [2002] EWCA Civ 1280, 2002 WL 1446111 (CA).

potential for interaction,[113] the closer the nature of transaction is to what had been done in the past and if there is information which might be relevant when acting for a new client,[114] then the burden will shift. The second firm must establish there is no risk that there will be use; it is then more likely that the court would make an order. Courts have considered these principles in cases involving in-house professional advisers but have concluded that the more general employment position, regarding movement of workers set out in *Faccenda* and the restrictive covenant cases, continues to apply.[115]

Regulatory powers

18.53   As noted, the scope of regulatory and statutory obligations in respect of information varies, as does what will constitute breach. Information obtained by the police under the Police and Criminal Evidence Act 1984 cannot be handed over to others without a subpoena.[116] Rather, it should be held for the purposes for which it is seized: investigation of crime.[117] Information can in some cases be passed to other bodies for public purposes, however this should be done with care to avoid 'The dossier of private information … the badge of the totalitarian state'.[118] Information held under the Banking Act 1987 cannot be passed on to any person—including as part of discovery and disclosure in civil litigation. The same information could be passed on, however, if it were also or later obtained through other means.[119]

18.54   Pharmaceutical companies (usually, but not necessarily, patent owners), supply confidential test data to medicines regulators to obtain regulatory clearance. It has been held that the regulator may use this data to assess whether clearance should also be granted to another company in respect of a generic product (usually for launch after the patent term). Courts considered that this use of information was consistent with the regulator's function in respect of public safety, and that requests for the data to be held as confidential could not be taken as preventing such use.[120] However, the court stressed that the regulator may not disclose the data to anyone else.

Key points on conduct

- What will constitute a breach is closely linked with the scope of the obligation
- The requirement of detriment is unlikely to be a stumbling block
- There is no element of intention
- Problems arise frequently for professional advisers and regulators

---

[113] *Young v Robson Rhodes* [1999] All ER 524.

[114] *Prince Jefri Bolkiah v KPMG* [1999] 2 WLR 215, [1999] 2 AC 222 (HL) (Chinese walls criticised as ad hoc); and the court considered that a 'wait and see' approach or undertaking cannot suffice). See also *Marks & Spencer v Freshfields Bruckhaus Deringer* [2004] EWCA Civ 741, 2004 WL 1174253 (CA), [2005] PNLR 4, aff'g [2004] 1 WLR 2331 and *Winters v Mishcon de Reya* [2008] EWHC 2419 (Ch). As suggested in this case, regard should be paid in this context to other regulatory rules, eg of the Financial Services Authority; see also A Henderson, 'Confident about confidentiality? Civil claims for the misuse of price sensitive information' (2003) 24(4) Comp Law 116–118.

[115] See decision of the Court of Appeal in *Caterpillar Logistics Services v Huesca de Crean* [2012] EWCA Civ 156, compare *Generics (UK) v Yeda Research and Development Co Ltd* [2012] EWCA 726, paras 28–40 and compare confidential Appendices para 42–89 and 97–107.

[116] *Marcel v Commissioner of Police of the Metropolis* [1992] Ch 225, [1992] 2 WLR 50 (CA). The court considered that the original document owners should be told of the subpoena. In *Re Barlow Clowes Gilt Managers* [1992] Ch 208, [1992] 2 WLR 36, this was considered regarding information disclosed to liquidators and the scope for disclosure to directors of a company.

[117] *Marcel*, note 116, 233–5. See also *Bunn v BBC* [1998] 3 All ER 552, [1999] FSR 70 finding that a statement made to the police attracted confidentiality, as there was a strong public interest in encouraging full disclosure to the police.

[118] *Marcel*, note 116, 235 et seq.

[119] *Price Waterhouse v BCCI (In Liquidation) (No 3)* [1997] 3 WLR 849, [1998] Ch 84 at 93–94, 97–99, 102–105, re the Banking Act 1987, s 82(1).

[120] *SKF*, note 9, 64–65, 68, 78–82, 84–85, 88–90. See also on the same facts *SKF Australia*, note 50.

Defences

18.55 Even the combination of confidential information, obligation, and use does not mean that an action will succeed. There are several defences, the most significant being that disclosure is in the public interest.[121]

Public interest defence

18.56 The roots of the public interest 'defence' lie in the concept of 'no confidence in iniquity'[122]—such information could not be confidential, so no other questions arose. In the 1970s and 1980s, however, starting with *Fraser v Evans*,[123] this concept developed into broader defence of 'just cause for breaking confidence'. The House of Lords in *Spycatcher*[124] said:

> although the basis of the law's protection of confidence is that there is a public interest that confidences should be preserved and protected by the law, nevertheless that public interest may be outweighed by some countervailing public interest which favours disclosure ... It is this limiting principle which may require a court to carry out a balancing operation, weighing against the public interest in maintaining the confidence against a countervailing public interest favouring disclosure.

18.57 The application of the public interest defence and balancing act has been criticised as open to 'idiosyncracy'.[125] The public interest defence was an important weapon for the free press, but its application was invariably controversial.[126] Further, disclosure in the public interest did not necessarily mean disclosure to the press. The police or a regulator would likely be deemed more appropriate by courts;[127] however, this would depend on the nature of the information and those involved.[128] This issue played an important part in legal consideration of disclosures by Wikileaks in 2010, although that involved the disclosure of all material online without an (apparent) consideration of public interest.[129]

18.58 There are interesting examples of how a careful balance of interests was carried out in the medical field. In 1988 identification of doctors being treated for AIDS was found not to be in the public interest, given the countervailing interest in encouraging seeking of treatment and in the confidentiality of medical records.[130] However, in 1989, the doctor–patient relationship was overridden by the public interest in public safety. A report on mental health regarding a person suffering from schizophrenia was sent ultimately to the Home Secretary and this was held not to be breach of confidence.[131]

18.59 Finally, the public interest defence might be available if public bodies are discharging their public function—for example, phone tapping by the police.[132]

---

[121] See consideration of the public interest in respect of copyright infringement at para 5.47.

[122] *Gartside v Outram* (1856) 26 LJ Ch 113 at 114, *Beloff v Pressdram* [1973] 1 All ER 241, [1973] FSR 33 (this case is considered in respect of copyright at para 5.32).

[123] [1968] 3 WLR 1172, [1969] 1 QB 349 at 362 (this case is considered in respect of copyright at para 5.32). Followed in *Hubbard v Vosper* [1972] 2 WLR 389, [1972] 2 QB 84 (CA) (regarding publication of the confidential works of the Church of Scientology).

[124] *Spycatcher*, note 38, 807. See also 785, 794–795, 798, 800–801, 812. See also *Scotsman*, note 14, 709, 710, 712–713.

[125] *SKF Australia*, note 50, 663.   [126] See Gurry, note 5, 683ff.

[127] *Initial Services Ltd v Putterill* [1967] 3 WLR 1032, [1968] 1 QB 396, 405; *Malone*, note 60, 376–378; *Francome*, note 60, 898. See also *Butler v Board of Trade* [1970] 3 WLR 822, [1971] Ch 680 at 690 regarding the public interest in availability of information to authorities for use in criminal proceedings.

[128] *Lion Laboratories v Evans* 1985] QB 526, [1984] 3 WLR 539.

[129] See Legal Eagle, 'Wikileaks and the brave new world of freedom of information' (1 December 2010), at http://skepticlawyer.com.au/2010/12/01/wikileaks-and-the-brave-new-world-of-freedom-of-information/.

[130] *X v Y*, note 22, 395–396. See also the decision of the ECtHR in *I v Finland* (2009) 48 EHRR 31.

[131] *W v Egdell* [1989] 2 WLR 689, [1989] 1 All ER 1089.   [132] *Malone*, note 60, 362, 367.

> **Key points on public interest defence**
>
> - This has developed from 'no confidence in iniquity' to a careful balance of important public interests in both confidence and disclosure
> - The identity and function of both parties may be important

Unclean hands

18.60   If breach of confidence is based in equity, the complainant must, in accordance with standard principles, come with 'clean hands', having behaved properly themselves in respect of the relevant information. If not, the court may in its discretion refuse relief—even if the public interest did not favour disclosure.[133]

Prior knowledge

18.61   A more apparently mundane defence is that the information received in confidence was already known.[134] It is difficult to distinguish between two sets of information and similar problems to those considered previously in the employment context might arise here.[135]

Springboard

18.62   If someone subject to an obligation discloses or uses information in breach of this, and the information is then in the public domain,[136] are they free to use it? Special rules can apply, although they have not gone unchallenged.[137] This is called the springboard doctrine: preventing (at least for a short period) persons who have breached confidence from getting a headstart on others, and by avoiding doing preparatory work. This doctrine could apply to new theories and product designs, and also to lists of customer details. An early and still helpful summary of the doctrine is:[138]

> a person who has obtained information in confidence is not allowed to use it as a springboard for activities detrimental to the person who made the confidential communication, and springboard it remains even when all the features have been published or can be ascertained by actual inspection by any member of the public.[139]

18.63   The controversial question is how long one must be subject to restraint when others can use the information freely. The aim is not to punish but to protect and to prevent unfair advantage;[140] and situations will vary, with courts reluctant to impose permanent restrictions.[141] A key question is how easily the information could have been obtained?[142] Much will depend, however, on the view of the court—sinister behaviour is never viewed kindly:[143] 'having made deliberate and unlawful use of the plaintiff's

---

[133] See *Stephenson Jordan*, note 103, 196 and *Church of Scientology v Kaufman* [1973] RPC 627, [1972] FSR 591. Note that there is no doctrine of equity in Scotland, see para 18.12.

[134] See, eg, *Johnson v Heat and Air Systems Ltd* (1941) 58 RPC 229.   [135] See also Stair, note 8, para 1486.

[136] Note debate considered in paras 18.19–18.21 as to whether the information does enter the public domain.

[137] See *OSI*, note 52, 401 and *Vestergaard*, note 1/note 40, notably paras 67–93.

[138] See also Scottish case, *Levin*, note 52, and Gurry, note 5, 643–653.

[139] *Terrapin Ltd v Builders Supply Co (Hayes) Ltd* [1960] RPC 128 at 130.

[140] *Bullivant*, note 13, headnote paras 3, 183ff; *Sun Valley Foods Ltd v Vincent* [2000] FSR 825; and *UBS Wealth Management (UK) Ltd v Vestra Wealth LLP* [2008] EWHC 1974 (QB), [2008] IRLR 965.   [141] *Bullivant*, note 13, 183–184, 186–187.

[142] See, eg, *Hibben* which concerned a small market, and information could have been obtained from trade journals.

[143] Eg *Bullivant*, note 13, 181; *Holden*, note 74.

property, he cannot complain if he finds that the eye of the law is unable to distinguish between those he could, if he chose, have contacted lawfully and those he could not.'

 Exercise

Back at Eversogood they are doing well in the market, building on Katie's good relationships with the supermarkets' area sales managers. They all went to university together and keep in touch through industry training courses. Just yesterday, however, Katie realised that she had left her FunFunFun contacts book in the bottom of her handbag. Eversogood's in-house legal counsel Graeme is concerned. Discuss.

Parties to action

Who can raise an action?

18.64   As the essence of the action is an equitable obligation, only the person to whom that obligation is owed can raise the action. If work generating information is carried out pursuant to a commission, the commissioner is owed the obligation.[144]

18.65   If protection of information, or information, is perceived as a property right as considered at the outset,[145] there might be scope for a wider basis of complaint.[146] As discussed earlier in this chapter, this issue remains unclear. It is also discussed further in relation to *Douglas v Hello!* in Chapter 19.

Against whom

18.66   Consistent with the analysis so far, the action can be raised against the person in breach of an obligation of confidence (even if they were not aware of the obligation). Persons inducing such conduct will also be liable as will those engaging in it through a common design. As cases move further down the line, care must be taken to focus on what has actually been done—arguments that 'they must have known' are unlikely to succeed.[147] If there is conduct in the course of employment, the employer could be vicariously liable.

18.67   The greater threat may come from a subsequent employer who uses, or it is feared may use, the information. But unless they are under an obligation applying the tests set out there, they cannot be sued.

Key points on parties to action

- The person to whom obligation is owed can sue
- The person in breach of obligation and/or employer or person inducing conduct can be sued

---

[144] *Fraser v Evans*, note 123, *Apps v Weldite Products Ltd* [2001] FSR 39, para 102.   [145] See para 18.12.
[146] See also Gurry, note 5, 316–317.   [147] *Force India*, note 13, paras 345–367.

Question

Once confidential information is disclosed, can a complaint be brought by anyone against anyone, anywhere, anytime? Would the answer be different if there was a patent?

Confidence and IP

Policy

18.68 The policy relationship between trade secrets, IP, and innovation is controversial. The UK Intellectual Property Office (UK–IPO) refers to use of trade secrets to protect innovation.[148] There is also an argument that if too many restrictions are placed on patents (eg compulsory licences,[149] exceptions,[150] intervention by competition law),[151] innovators wishing to control their work will choose not to patent,[152] and will instead rely on trade secrets. This means that details of valuable innovation could be permanently outside the public domain.[153] However, this is also the very challenge made in respect of IP, for example in the Report of the Royal Society of 2003, 'Keeping Science Open', and the 2009 Manchester Manifesto.[154] There are increasing claims that companies will look to control information rather than seek IP with its limits[155]—it will be interesting to note how this develops (you will have the chance to make this decision yourself later).

> **Key point on policy**
>
> • Trade secrets and their treatment are an important part of the innovation debate

Relative scope of protection

18.69 A change of jobs, or an inquiry[156] or demonstration[157] which come to nothing (and, of course, breakdowns in collaborations)[158] frequently lead to the development of a second set of products which are similar to existing ones. There may not be IP infringement, but there might still be breach of confidence—or vice versa—as different tests and principles are applied. But if both causes of action are available, it is quite legitimate for them to be pursued together.[159]

---

[148] See http://www.ipo.gov.uk/p-need-secret.htm.   [149] See para 12.76.   [150] See paras 11.219ff.

[151] Considered in Chapter 21.

[152] See analogous developments discussed in relation to copyright, and a movement to more openness on the part of some, at para 7.5. See also B Perens, 'Innovation goes public' (2008) 14(2) CTLR 36–40.   [153] See also Gurry, note 5, 77–88.

[154] http://royalsociety.org/policy/publications/2003/keeping-science-open/   and   http://www.isei.manchester.ac.uk/TheManchesterManifesto.pdf.

[155] See, eg, for introduction AmeriKat post on IPkat (9 January 2012), 'Letter from AmeriKat I Google and the "broken" patent system, *Oracle v Google, Pystar v Apple* and more'. at http://ipkitten.blogspot.co.uk/2012/01/letter-from-amerikat-l-google-and.html.

[156] *Harrison v Project & Design Co (Red Car) (No 1) Ltd* [1978] FSR 81. An individual developed a chair lift and disclosed it to a company which visited. The company then did further work and patented its own product.

[157] In *Carflow*, note 56, 429 no obligation was identified on the facts, and the court found one would be unusual in that industry.

[158] *Collag Corp v Merck* [2003] FSR 16; *Inline Logstics*, note 51. Note if one collaborator leaves the others, that one person will have no right to control how remaining collaborators deal with the information, if the information was part of the relationship: *Murray v Yorkshire Fund Managers* [1998] 2 All ER 1015, [1998] 1 WLR 951 at 956, 957, 959–961.

[159] *HRH Prince of Wales v Associated Newspapers Ltd* [2006] EWHC 522 (Ch), [2006] ECDR 20, [2008] EMLR 3, para 183 (not considered in *HRH Prince of Wales* (CA), note 34, see para 83, given the rest of the decision); see also *British Sky Broadcasting Group plc v Digital Satellite Warranty Cover Ltd (In Liquidation)* [2012] FSR 14—breach of confidence was conceded, but the action proceeded in respect of database rights, trade marks and passing off, see para 6.6. Compare the fate of an action for breach of confidence after a patent entitlement dispute was struck out: *Markem Corp v Zipher Ltd* [2005] EWCA Civ 267, [2005] RPC 31, paras 111, 124, 126, 132.

18.70 Examples of this are in *Creation* (regarding photo shoots for an album cover for the band Oasis) and *Shelley* (regarding a set for the film *Frankenstein*). In both cases it was clear that the event was private, and that there was to be no photography, even though it was possible to observe. Regarding *Frankenstein*, the court in *Shelley* considered it to be arguable that there was copyright in costumes, prostheses for an actor, and the set, and that there was a serious question in respect of breach of confidence.[160] In *Creation*, although there was no copyright in the assembled scene to be photographed,[161] the court held it to be an occasion of confidence.[162] Further, in a case involving wheelchair lifts,[163] there was a breach of confidence in respect of the initial idea, but no IP infringement because of the redesign which had taken place.

18.71 Breach of confidence can be helpful in respect of embryonic ideas—from books to products to research projects—to enable them to develop fully, such that copyright might become relevant.[164] There have been other cases involving television shows[165] and nightclubs. However, these 'ideas' can only be the subject of the action if the original information as communicated was developed, precise, original, and identifiable.[166] Secondly, the necessary obligation of confidence may be unlikely if there are discussions over dinner, in an industry where it is standard practice to share ideas openly without restriction,[167] or indeed where IP protection, rather than confidence, might be more reasonably expected.[168] As this covers a broad spectrum, the second element of breach of confidence might be problematic.

Key points on relative scope of protection

• There can be no IP infringement, but yet breach of confidence, in respect of the same facts

• Breach of confidence can protect ideas and early stage innovation before it will be protected by IP

Exercise

Read *Cantor Fitzgerald International v Tradition UK Ltd* [2000] RPC 95.[169] What do you think of the reasoning and approach to different bases of claim. Compare it with *Coco v Clark*. Has anything changed with technology?

Secrecy and innovation

Existing practice

18.72 The classic examples of the Coca-Cola formula and, in Scotland, the Irn Bru recipe, are often used as examples of how businesses can survive based on secrecy. As has been seen throughout this chapter, it

---

[160] *Shelley*, note 41, 142–148.   [161] *Creation*, note 41, 448.   [162] *Creation*, note 41, 452–454.

[163] *Harrison*, note 156. See also *Seager*, note 110, 225.

[164] See Gurry, note 5, 172; also *Prince Albert v Strange* (1849) H & T 1 protecting misuse of ideas in etchings.

[165] Consistent with early decisions protecting plots of plays—*Gilbert v Star Newspaper Company Ltd* (1894) 11 TLR 4.

[166] *De Maudsley v Palumbo* [1996] FSR 447, [1996] EMLR 460 at 467–470 (nightclub); *CMI Centers for Medical Innovation v Phytopharm plc* 1998 WL 1076631, [1999] FSR 235 (vaccine); *Collag*, note 158 (pesticides); *Bailey v Graham* [2011] EWHC 2098 (Ch) (jerk sauce).

[167] *Palumbo*, note 166, 464, 471; *Bailey*, note 166; and *Carflow*, note 56. Compare *IBCOS Computer Ltd v Barclays Mercantile Highland Finance Ltd* [1994] FSR 275 at 286 when an obligation of confidentiality was imposed in respect of source code, as this was usually regarded as confidential in the industry.

[168] *Carflow*, note 56, 430.   [169] Considered in respect of copyright at para 4.34.

is a real challenge for businesses actually to keep information secret. Court orders can be combined, payments made, but from a practical perspective, the damage is done. It is this which means that few businesses follow the Barr's and Coca-Cola Company's route.

 Exercise

If you started a new businesses, would you rely on trade secrets rather than IP? Do you think you would have given the same answer ten years ago? What do you think your funders might say?

18.73   The position is, of course, rarely as clear-cut as this. As has been seen previously,[170] there are many situations in which breach of confidence can form part of a dispute alongside different IP rights. Innovators and their advisers may also choose to take a combined approach to IP and confidence. They may protect some by patents, some by database, some by copyright, and choose to keep secret the commercially valuable bits which make the whole thing work. The place of secrecy in innovation is well recognised from the policy perspective.[171] The European Commission committed to launching a survey in October 2012 exploring the misappropriation of trade secrets and it will be interesting to note how this develops.

Know-how and confidentiality agreements

18.74   Part of the responses to the October 2012 survey will doubtless involve confidential information, in its guise as 'know-how'. It is know-how which enables those pursuing a non-IP route to share and exploit their developments: subject, of course, to the essential problem noted previously that once information is disclosed, it is, generally, uncontrollable.[172] This is important because, just as is discussed in Chapter 23 in respect of IP, frequently innovators choose to share their technology and expertise to make money, or must obtain or be permitted to use the IP of others so that they can make products with their own information.

18.75   Non-disclosure agreements are advisable,[173] although there is of course the question of how to identify the know-how which is the subject of the agreements. This might lead to confidential attachments to agreements, named individuals who are to have access to particular information, and regimes for recording, storing, and destroying information.[174]

18.76   Competition issues might also arise in respect of know-how and collaboration agreements,[175] or reliance on trade secrets in the case of dominance.[176] These are considered in Chapter 21, in conjunction with competition implications for IP. As will be seen there, however, the European Commission in its investigation of Microsoft paid little regard to the fact that information sought to be disclosed was secret. This is consistent with its broad approach to the case: the information should be disclosed, because of

---

[170] See paras 18.69ff.

[171] Eg the European Commission held a conference on 29 June 2012, 'Trade Secrets: Supporting Innovation, Protecting Know How', available at http://ec.europa.eu/internal_market/iprenforcement/conferences/index_en.htm#maincontentSec.

[172] See paras 18.19–18.21, 18.61–18.63.

[173] See draft agreement from April 2007, available at http://www.ipo.gov.uk/cda.pdf.

[174] Similar indeed to the arrangements in court actions: see para 18.25.

[175] See paras 20.34–20.35ff regarding potentially relevant Block Exemptions.

[176] *EC Commission v Microsoft* at p 55 n 249 via http://ec.europa.eu/competition/sectors/ICT/microsoft/index.html discussed at paras 21.57ff and consideration by the Court of First Instance: *Microsoft Corp v Commission of the European Communities* [2007] ECR II-3601, paras 273, 280, 285, 289, 667, 681, 689, 692–693 regarding the extent to which trade secrets should be treated in the same way as IP rights, and the consequences of this regarding possible intervention by competition. See I Eagles and L Longdin, 'Microsoft's refusal to disclose software interoperability information and the Court of First Instance' (2008) 30(5) EIPR 205–208.

competition issues and the fact that it was the subject of IP or was secret did not matter. It will be interesting to note if this approach persists about the trade secrets inquiry introduced earlier.

> ## Key points on commercial impact
>
> • Confidential information can be the subject of research and development agreements
> • It is rare for businesses to rely wholly on confidentiality to protect their innovation—but they can

IP and other information regulation

18.77   Control and use of information lies at the heart of breach of confidence. These questions are also addressed, from different perspectives, in the Data Protection Act 1998, the Regulation of Investigatory Powers Act 1998, the Freedom of Information Act 2000, and the Freedom of Information (Scotland) Act 2002, environmental information regulations and legislation, and developments relating to e-commerce and new technologies.[177] These matters cannot be considered in-depth here, and details of further reading are included at the end of this chapter, but it is important to bear them in mind. It is also important to consider that this framework of legislation underpins the growth of ubiquitous privacy policies (which remain mainly unread on most websites).[178]

18.78   Here, it is helpful to note that data protection and breach of confidence, both of which relate to the protection and control of information, can be complementary, as can be seen from their consideration in many cases.[179] Other pieces of legislation can also be relevant to confidentiality, for example the Audit Commission Act 1988. The Court of Appeal considered this in *R (Veolia EA Nottinghamshire Ltd) v Nottinghamshire County Council*, in a case which has some similarities to *London Regional Transport* (para 18.14).[180] *Veolia* involved an application by a member of the local electorate to the council to copy documents relating to the provision of waste management services to the council. Veolia objected on the basis that they contained pricing information protected by a confidentiality clause in the contract. In an application for judicial review, the Court of Appeal found that obligations to disclose under the legislation had to be read down to exclude confidential information, because of rights to a private life and protection of property, within the ECHR.

18.79   A different approach was taken by the Court of Justice when considering obligations imposed by a Regulation on the shipment of waste[181] (the crucial point there was the extent of the obligations of an intermediary). The Court of Justice considered that disclosure obligations must be met even if this

---

[177] See also Gurry, note 5, 579–589 and 605–624.

[178] See, eg, Google Privacy Policy last modified 27 July 2012, at http://www.google.co.uk/intl/en/policies/privacy/ and, at a more global level, the Recommendations of the OECD Council concerning Guidelines Governing the Protection of Privacy and Transborder Flows of Personal Data (C(80)/58/FINAL) at http://www.oecd.org/internet/interneteconomy/oecdguidelinesontheprotectionofprivacyandtransborderflowsofpersonaldata.htm.

[179] See, eg, *Campbell, Re C's Application for Judicial Review* [2009] UKHL 15, [2009] 1 AC 908, and *Bluck v Information Commissioner* EA/2006/0090 (2007) 98 BMLR 1, [2008] WTLR 1; Information Commissioner's guidance on data protection at http://www.ico.gov.uk/for_organisations/data_protection/the_guide.aspx. Discussion about the relationship between IP and data protection can be found in the Article 29 Working Paper Group Report 105 (2005) Data Protection and Intellectual Property.

[180] [2010] EWCA Civ 1214.

[181] Regulation 1013/2006 of 14 June 2006 on shipments of waste, OJ 2006 L97, Art 18 of which did refer to business secrets, was found not to apply in this context.

would involve the disclosure of trade secrets.[182] Yet, when considering the Directive on public access to environmental information, in the context of trade secrets, innovation, and requests for information in respect of environment and pesticides, the Court of Justice considered that there must be a balance between the public interest in disclosure, and the private interest in non-disclosure must be carried out in each case.[183] There is also a complex relationship between freedom of information, confidentiality, and IP;[184] the first aims to require the disclosure of information, the others to control it in different ways. Legislation has sought to balance these,[185] but there is inevitable uncertainty which has once again led to litigation.[186] As this increases, it is likely that this will become an increasingly important source in the study of breach of confidence.

18.80 For example, the obligation to disclose environmental information under the Environmental Information Regulations 2004 has an exception which refers to IP. The meaning of this was raised in a case involving disclosure of information relating to the location of mobile phone masts. A reference was made in 2010 to the Court of Justice by the Supreme Court and a decision is awaited.[187] Regarding freedom of information more broadly, in July 2012 the Information Commission issued guidance stating that IP could not restrict disclosure under the Freedom of Information Act.[188] This restricted approach to the impact of IP as a means of preventing disclosure of information is consistent with the Open Government Licence for public sector information.[189]

Key points on IP and other information regulation

- When working with or studying information, one cannot look merely to one doctrine
- One cannot assume that two regimes will operate in the same manner and without conflict

---

Exercise

Think back to the scenario you devised on in the previous Exercise box regarding breach of confidence in an innovation business. What other forms of regulation might be relevant? How could you find this out (and remember competition).

---

[182] Case C-1/11 *Interseroh Scrp and Metals Trading GmbH v Sonderabfall-Management-Gesellscahe Rheinland-Pfalz mbH*—preliminary reference from German court.

[183] Case C-266/09 *Stichting Natuur v College voor toelating van gewasbeschermingsmiddelen en biociden* regarding Council Directive 2003/4/EC.

[184] There is also a complex relationship between freedom of information and data protection legislation, considered by the House of Lords in a case arising from a decision of the Scottish Information Commissioner—*Common Services Agency v Scottish Information Commissioner* [2008] UKHL 47.

[185] See Freedom of Information Act 2000, ss 40 (personal information), 41 (confidential information), and 43 (commercial interests); and Freedom of Information (Scotland) Act 2002, ss 33 (commercial interests), 36 (confidentiality), and 38 (personal information).

[186] Regarding 'commercial interests', see *Cabinet Office v Information Commissioner* (EA/2010/0031), September 2010 and *Visser v Information Commissioner* (EA2011/0188), 1 March 2012; regarding 'confidentiality', see *Moss v Information Commissioner* (EA/2011/0081), 28 February 2012.

[187] *Office of Communications v Information Commissioner* [2010] UKSC 2 regarding the Environmental Information Regulations 2004, reg 12(5)(c). These implement Directive 2003/4/EC on public access to environmental information and there are also the Environmental Information (Scotland) Regulations 2004. For more general guidance, see http://www.ico.gov.uk/for_organisations/environmental_information.aspx.

[188] See guidance at http://www.ico.gov.uk/news/e-newsletter/previous/201207.aspx. See also the Freedom of Information Act 2000, s 43, regarding commercial interests, and the Freedom of Information (Scotland) Act 2002, s 33. Regarding environmental information, see also http://www.ico.gov.uk/news/e-newsletter/previous/201207.aspx.

[189] See http://www.nationalarchives.gov.uk/doc/open-government-licence/ and see Chapter 22.

The impact of the HRA on breach of confidence

18.81   What is the possible impact of the HRA 1998 on breach of confidence other than in respect of private information, which is discussed in depth in Chapter 19? As is explored there, the HRA 1998 provides a new role in UK court actions for the right in Article 8 ECHR to a private life and the right in Article 10 to freedom of expression. This can be seen from the approach of the Court of Appeal in 2006 when considering the publication of diaries of the Prince of Wales which commented on the handover of Hong Kong in *HRH Prince of Wales v Associated Newspapers Ltd (No 3)*.[190] The Court of Appeal stressed that the HRA 1998 and breach of confidence are strongly intertwined, and summarised the framework of the action as follows:

> (a) there must be (i) confidential information and a relationship of confidence, (ii) private information in respect of which there was reasonable expectation of privacy in the light of article 8[191] or (iii) both; and
>
> (b) each of these must then be balanced against article 10.[192]

> **Article 10 ECHR**
>
> (1) Everyone has the right to freedom of expression. This right shall include freedom ... to receive and impart information and ideas without interference by public authority and regardless of frontiers ...
>
> (2) The exercise of these freedoms, since it carries with it duties and responsibilities, may be subject to such formalities, conditions, restrictions or penalties as are prescribed by law and are necessary in a democratic society ... for the protection of the reputation or rights of others, for preventing the disclosure of information received in confidence ...

18.82   The issue of most interest for this chapter, is the impact of Article 10 on the defences which were discussed previously (paras 18.55–18.61). The Court of Appeal in *HRH Prince of Wales v Associated Newspapers Ltd (No 3)* had reviewed the public interest defence which had been developed in the UK before the HRA 1998. The Court of Appeal considered this defence to be more limited than that required by Article 10, and that there must rather be a balance on a proportionate basis.[193]

18.83   This impact of the HRA on breach of confidence is supported by the earlier decision of the Court of Appeal in *London Regional Transport*[194] in 2001, which was summarised in para 18.14.[195] In *LRT*, the Court of Appeal considered[196] that Article 10 was central to breach of confidence. Article 10 provided a methodical approach based on proportionality,[197] and that this approach was more familiar to lawyers than the open flexibility of the pre-HRA public interest defence.[198] The key questions were: was there a

---

[190]   *HRH Prince of Wales* (CA), note 34, paras 64–65. Note consideration of this case in respect of copyright at paras 4.43, 5.32, and 5.35. See also *HRH Prince of Wales v Associated Newspapers Ltd* [2007] EWHC 1685 (Ch) which brought that matter finally to an end.

[191]   Which is discussed in Chapter 19.

[192]   *HRH Prince of Wales* (CA), note 34, para 65. Regarding contract and equitable obligations, see also *Societa Esplosivi Industriali SpA v Ordnance Technologies (UK) Ltd (formerly SEI (UK) Ltd)* [2007] EWHC 2875 (Ch), [2008] 2 All ER 622, [2008] RPC 12, para 42.

[193]   *HRH Prince of Wales* (CA), note 34, paras 32, 54–55.   [194]   [2001] EWCA Civ 1491 ('*LRT*').

[195]   The Court of Appeal in *HRH Prince of Wales* (CA), note 34, did so when considering the weight to be accorded to contract (see paras 56–60).   [196]   *LRT*, note 194, para 55.

[197]   *LRT*, note 194, para 57.

[198]   *LRT*, note 194, para 57. This defence had been analysed previously in *LRT* by Robert Walker LJ (see paras 29, 34–40), when there had been reference to ad hoc decisions and the risk of 'idiosyncracy' identified in *SKF Australia*, note 50, 663.

pressing and recognised social need for the restriction on any right; was the proposed restriction greater than necessary; and were there logical reasons for it.[199]

18.84   Yet, despite the key role of Article 10, the terminology of the 'public interest' persists in post-HRA case law.[200] It remains to be seen how this field develops.

> ### Key points on the impact of the HRA on breach of confidence
>
> - Article 10 ECHR is an important part of an action for breach of confidence, irrespective of the starting point and type of information
> - Article 10 is a wider counter to confidence than the pre-HRA public interest defence
> - Article 10 will be assessed in a more methodical manner than the pre-HRA public interest defence
> - But references to 'the public interest' continue to appear

Exercise 1

Big Bad Oil Co funds research by Car Co to prove that green fuel could never work. Car Co finds that it would. An environmental charity uses surveillance devices to record discussions between Big Bad Oil Co and Car Co about this; the charity then gives the information to the UK Government. The information cannot now be verified as records have been destroyed in a fire. Big Bad Oil want to sue the charity. Discuss.

Exercise 2

Article 10 ECHR has prevailed over confidentiality obligations in some cases. Could an argument based on the ECHR right to life and/or Article 10, as suggested previously, indeed lead to pharmaceutical companies being obliged to disclose new work, even if they choose not to patent it?

International perspectives and approaches

18.85   Courts in the UK have not considered TRIPS and the Paris Convention in any depth.[201] This is perhaps not surprising, given the strong (even if unclear) base of the breach of confidence action quite apart from

---

[199] LRT, note 194, paras 57–58. See examples in *Ashworth Hospital Authority v MGN Ltd* [2002] UKHL 29 [2002] 1 WLR 2033 (HL), paras 61–72; *Mersey Care NHS Trust v Ackroyd (No 2)* [2006] EWHC 107, [2006] EMLR 12, paras 105–107, 120–127 and the decision of the Court of Appeal [2007] EWCA Civ 101, [2008] EMLR 1, [2007] HRLR 19, paras 9–39, 62–72, 76–82, 90 (regarding disclosure of identity of a source under the Contempt of Court Act 1981 regarding the medical records of Moors murderer Ian Brady); *Commissioner of Police of the Metropolis v Times Newspaper* [2011] EWHC 2705 (QB), paras 94–105; see also *Veolia*, note 180 when regard is had to human rights in the context of decisions under the Audit Commission Act 1998.

[200] *Harrods Ltd v Times Newspaper Ltd* [2006] EWCA Civ 294, para 27; *Deloitte & Touche LLP v Dickson* [2005] EWHC 721 (Ch), paras 63–76; and *Tillery*, note 23, paras 8, 15–16, 18.

[201] For a scholarly analysis, see NP de Carvalho, *The TRIPS Regime of Antitrust and Undisclosed Information* (2008), Section 7; J De Werra, 'What legal framework for promoting the cross-border flow of intellectual assets (trade secrets and music)? A view from Europe towards Asia (China and Japan)' [2009] 1 IPQ 27–76.

these principles. Countries have taken a range of approaches to meeting the obligations set out in TRIPS and the Paris Convention.[202] The notes to TRIPS do make it clear that it considers the Paris Convention provisions to encompass breach of confidence. It will be interesting to note how this develops if more businesses did choose to keep information secret, rather than embrace IP and its accompanying international regime.

18.86   Issues have arisen in respect of Article 39(3) of TRIPS and its requirement that undisclosed data submitted for regulatory clearance shall be protected against unfair commercial use. Attempts by Canada to reduce levels of exclusivity in respect of this data were found to be inconsistent with TRIPS,[203] and free trade agreements frequently require greater protection to be extended to regulatory data.[204]

 Discussion point   For answer guidance visit www.oxfordtextbooks.co.uk/orc/waelde3e/

Do you think that the breach of confidence (with its human rights modifications) and the accompanying information legislation, result in the UK meeting its obligations under TRIPS and the Paris Convention? Devise a scenario when the UK could be challenged at the World Trade Organization (WTO) Dispute Settlement Body (see note 203) in respect of Article 39

Key points on international perspectives

- Paris and TRIPS provide a relevant backdrop to breach of confidence
- The UK (probably) complies with them
- This area might become important in the future, particularly regarding regulatory data

Conclusions and the future

18.87   Previous proposals for codification of the law of confidence[205] were not followed up. If codification should again be considered, the proposals would at least be significantly reviewed given the HRA 1998. The HRA 1998 has had a major impact on breach of confidence. The established cases and dilemmas remain, such as ex-employees' skill and know-how, customer lists, and the relationship with copyright. Cases such as *LRT* and *HRH Prince of Wales* confirm a greater willingness on the part of courts to look to Article 10 ECHR when considering if there is a breach of confidence. This suggests that there will be an ongoing role for human rights and breach of confidence in considering control of information; and this will sit aside the other forms of information regulation which have been introduced. And as discussions continue regarding the shape of breach of confidence, it still has an important role as part of the innovation landscape.

---

[202] See report by Hogan Lovells, 'Report on Trade Secrets for the European Commission' (2012), at http://ec.europa.eu/internal_market/iprenforcement/documents/index_en.htm.

[203] WTO DS 114, http://www.wto.org/english/tratop_e/dispu_e/cases_e/ds114_e.htm.

[204] For an overview, see L Brazell, 'The protection of pharmaceutical products and regulatory data. EU enlargement update' (2002) 24(3) *EIPR* 155–1161. See also note 16.

[205] The Law Commission of Scotland, 'Report on Breach of Confidence' (Report 90, 1984); and, in England, the Law Commission (Report 110, 1981) (which also proposed an offence of misuse of trade secrets in 1997) http://www.lawcom.gov.uk/misuse_trade.htm). See also 'Calcutt Report on Privacy and Related Matters' (Cmnd 1102, 1990).

Further reading

Books

T Aplin, L Bently, P Johnson, and S Malynicz, *Gurry on Breach of Confidence: The Protection of Confidential Information* (2nd edn, 2012)

RC Dreyfuss and K Standburg, *The Law and Theory of Trade Secrecy: A Handbook of Contemporary Research* (2011) (a US perspective)

C Phipps and R Toulson, *Confidentiality* (2nd edn, 2006)

DW Quinto and SH Singer, *Trade Secrets Law and Practice* (2nd edn, 2012) (a US perspective)

DW Snyder and DS Almeling, *Keeping Secrets: A Practical Introduction to Trade Secret Law and Strategy* (2012)

P Stanley, *The Law of Confidentiality. A Restatement* (2008)

Overviews of breach of confidence

L Bently and B Sherman, *Intellectual Property* (3rd edn, 2009), Chs 44, 45, 46

WR Cornish, D Llewelyn, and T Aplin, *Intellectual Property: Patents, Copyright, Trade Marks and Allied Rights* (7th edn, 2010), Part 3

Articles and chapters

Privacy and human rights

T Aplin, 'The development of the action for breach of confidence in a post-HRA era' [2007] 1 IPQ 19–59

Legal status

M Conaglen, 'Thinking about proprietary remedies for breach of confidence' [2008] 1 IPQ 82–109

J Glover, 'Is breach of confidence a fiduciary wrong? Preserving the reach of judge-made law' (2001) 21(4) Legal Studies 594–617

Commercial secrets

T Aplin, 'A right of privacy for corporations?' in P Torremans, *Intellectual Property and Human Rights. An Enhanced Edition of Copyright and Human Rights* (2008)

T Aplin, 'Commercial confidences after the Human Rights Act' (2007) 29(10) EIPR 411–419

S Becthold and F Hoffler, 'An economic analysis of trade-secret protection in buyer-seller relationships' (2011) 27(1) JLE&O 137–158

H Carty, 'An analysis of the modern action for breach of commercial confidence: when is protection merited?' [2008] 4 IPQ 416–455

CDL Hunt, 'Rethinking surreptious takings in the law of confidence' [2011] IPQ 66–85

J Lang, 'The protection of commercial trade secrets' (2003) 25(10) EIPR 462–471

N Searle, 'The criminalization of the theft of trade secrets: An analysis of the Economic Espionage Act,' (2012) 2(2) *IP Theory* (article 2), available at http://www.repository.law.indiana.edu/ipt/vol2/iss2/2

Regulatory data and article 39 TRIPS

P Ganguli, 'Complying with article 39 of TRIPS ... a myth or evolving reality?' (2003) 25(4) World Patent Information 329–333

S Gilotta, 'Disclosure in securities markets and the firm's need for confidentiality: theoretical framework and regulatory analysis' (2012) EBOR 46

A Taubman, 'Unfair competition and the financing of public-knowledge goods: the problem of test data protection' (2008) 3(9) JIPLP 591–606

J de Werra, 'How to protect trade secrets in high tech sports? An intellectual property analysis based on experiences at the America's Cup and in the Formula One Championship' [2010] EIPR 155

Scotland

Laws of Scotland: Stair Memorial Encyclopaedia (1993), vol 18, Part II, paras 1451 *et seq*

R Goldberg, 'Breach of confidence' in *Delict* (Scottish Universities Law Institute, 2008)

Other information regimes

D Altaras, 'The Environmental Information Regulations 2004—an update' [2010] JPL 310

VO Benjamin, 'Interception of internet communications and the right to privacy: an evaluation of some provisions of the Regulation of Investigatory Powers Act against the jurisprudence of the European Court of Human Rights' (2007) 6 EHRLR 637–648

G Black, 'Data protection' in *Stair Memorial Encyclopaedia* (2010)

P Carey, *Data Protection. A Practical Guide to UK and EU Law* (3rd edn, 2009)

L Edwards and C Waelde, *Law and the Internet* (3rd edn, 2009), Part IV 'Privacy, Data Protection and Cybercrime'

H Fenwick, *Civil Liberties and Human Rights* (4th edn, 2007), Chs 4, 5, 6, 7, 8, 9, 10

R Jay and A Hamilton, *Data Protection Law and Practice* (3rd edn, 2007)

I Lloyd, *Information Technology Law* (2011), Chs 1–7, 22–23

J Macdonald QC, R Crail, and C Jones, *The Law of Freedom of Information* (2nd edn, 2009)

D Mac Sithigh '"I'd tell you everything if you'd pick up that telephone": political expression and data protection' [2011] EHRLR 166

KM Rogers, *The Internet and the Law* (2011), Chs 7, 8

S Sakrouge, K Minett, D Preiskel, and J Saras, 'Monitoring employee communications: data protection and privacy issues' [2011] CTLR 213

J Wadham, K Harris, and G Peretz, *Blackstone's Guide to the Freedom of Information Act* (2011)

Useful websites

Pangloss blog http://blogscript.blogspot.com/

Light Blue Touchpaper blog http://www.lightbluetouchpaper.org/

UK Information Commissioner's Office http://www.ico.gov.uk/

Control of information, reputation, and intellectual property

Scope and overview of chapter

19.1   This chapter considers the extent to which individuals should be able to prevent others referring to them and their activities and, conversely, to what extent should individuals and companies be able to commercialise and control a reputation which they have built. These topics are both legally important and of contemporary societal interest. They build upon the discussion of trade marks in Chapter 16, of passing off in Chapter 17, and of commercial information, human rights, and statutory forms of information control in Chapter 18.

19.2   These issues have been explored using practical labels such as privacy, merchandising, and endorsement, and more legal terms such as personality and publicity; yet the meaning of and distinction between these can be unclear.[1] Accordingly, this chapter focuses on the two essential elements of information and reputation. It will explore the different means by which the law enables businesses and individuals to commercialise and protect their reputation, and details of their personal activities. It will also explore justifications for this from the intellectual property perspective.

19.3   In summary, in the UK there is an action for misuse of private information, which arose from a combination of breach of confidence and the Human Rights Act 1998 (HRA 1998). Trade marks can be obtained for a name, a signature, or the image (as in picture) of a person, if this has a distinctive character; but not if they are merely descriptive and 'image carriers'. Trade mark registrations can then be used to control merchandising. Passing off can prevent misrepresentation through merchandising practices, if the personality (be it real or fictional) has established goodwill; reputation is not enough. An important element in acceptance of this by courts has been the awareness of the public that official merchandising does occur. Passing off can also address false endorsement. If there is an agreement which relates

---

[1] There is an extensive literature focusing on the protection of personality: H Carty, 'Passing off and the concept of goodwill' (1995) *JBL* 139–154; D Howarth, 'Privacy, confidentiality and the cult of celebrity' [2002] *CLJ* 264; H Carty, 'Advertising, publicity rights and English law' [2004] *IPQ* 209; T Frazer, 'Appropriation of personality—a new tort?' (1993) 99 *LQR* 281; P Jaffey, 'Merchandising and the law of trade marks' [1998] *IPQ* 240; G Scanlan, 'Personality, endorsement and everything' [2003] *EIPR* 563; G Davies, 'The cult of celebrity and trade mark: the next installment' (2004) *1*(2) *SCRIPTed* 230; NR Whitty and R Zimmermann (eds), *Rights of Personality in Scots Law: A Comparative Perspective* (2009).

to confidential information (as was the case with the wedding photographs of Michael Douglas and Catherine Zeta-Jones), then the parties to that agreement can sue others if there is a breach of confidence—thus, *OK!* magazine could sue *Hello!* magazine. Otherwise, however, there is no right in respect of image (in the sense of reputation, rather than photograph), notwithstanding the plethora of image rights agreements involving, say, sporting celebrities. Gaps exist, therefore, in the protection conferred in respect of information and reputation. As discussed in Chapter 18 in relation to information regulation, Chapter 3 in respect of moral rights, and Chapter 15 in respect of trade marks with a reputation and dilution, some other avenues exist under the intellectual property umbrella, and some other opportunities are referred to within this chapter. The result in the UK is, however, an incomplete patchwork. This is not so elsewhere, notably in Guernsey which introduced new legislation in 2012.

19.4

Learning objectives

By the end of this chapter you should be able to describe and explain:

- the evolving right to personal privacy and its base in human rights, particularly in respect of photographs;
- the obtaining and dealing with trade marks in respect of well-known personalities;
- the relationship between passing off and merchandising;
- the extent to which individuals and businesses can and do control the use of their image through endorsement and sponsorship;
- how rights to control image and information can be transferred.

 Exercise

Develop a situation which could involve at least two of privacy, character merchandising, unauthorised endorsement, and use of image. Form your views on how the law should apply to it. Review it after you have completed your work on this chapter.

19.5   So the chapter looks like this:

- How does it work in practice—some important examples (19.6)
- Personal privacy (19.7–19.25)
- Merchandising (19.26–19.47)
- Endorsement and sponsorship (19.48–19.54)
- Control of (public) image (19.55–19.57)
- Conclusions (19.58)

How does it work in practice—some important examples

19.6   As will be seen from the summaries of the following important cases, the points explored in this chapter are not new.

■ *Campbell v MGN Ltd* [2004] 2 AC 457[2] (HL)

This involved the newspaper publication of a photograph of supermodel Naomi Campbell in a public place, leaving a confidential Narcotics Anonymous meeting. The House of Lords considered breach of confidence in conjunction with the obligations imposed on the court by the HRA 1998, and found that this was in this context better named 'misuse of private information'. The House of Lords held that the photographs were private information. The right for this to be respected was then balanced against rights to freedom of expression, considering the nature of expression involved and of the information, and the extent to which Campbell was a public figure. The House of Lords split 3:2[3] in favour of Campbell. Significant weight was attached to her seeking medical treatment, and it was considered that restriction on freedom of expression in such circumstances was necessary and proportionate.

■ *In the matter of Application No 2323092B to register a trade mark in Class 16 by Sir Alexander Chapman Ferguson*, Trade Mark Decision O/26605

The application by Alex Ferguson, the then manager of Manchester United football club, to register his name in, inter alia, class 16 (printed matter; posters; photographs; transfers; stickers; decalcomanias; stickers relating to football) was turned down. The registration of a famous name could take place where the consumer would believe that the goods bearing the name are under the control of one undertaking. However, the use of a name or image of a famous person on posters, photos, stickers, and figurines would merely be seen as descriptive of the subject matter of those goods; these items are merely 'image carriers'[4] and as such cannot be registered.

■ *Mirage Studios v Counter-Feat Clothing Co Ltd* [1991] FSR 145

The defendants applied the images of the Teenage Mutant Ninja Turtles, cartoon characters that are humanoid creatures with some of the features of turtles (notably half-shells), to their clothing products—without having a licence to do so from the creators of the characters. Browne-Wilkinson V-C held that this was passing off. A substantial section of the public knew that the reproduction of well-known characters on goods was generally licensed by the originators of the characters; the public would therefore assume that the goods so marketed had the approval of the originators for quality, and that the images used came from the originators rather than being copies. The public would therefore be misled by such unlicensed reproductions.

■ *Irvine v Talksport Ltd* [2002] 2 All ER 414 (Laddie J), [2003] EWCA Civ 423

A promotional brochure for Talksport contained a manipulated image of the racing driver Eddie Irvine apparently listening to the radio station. Irvine had no connection with the radio station. It was held that this was a representation of an endorsement of the radio station by Irvine, and constituted passing off.

■ *OBG Ltd v Allan, Douglas v Hello! and others* [2007] UKHL 21

Michael Douglas and Catherine Zeta-Jones were married in New York and entered into an exclusive agreement with *OK!* magazine to publish the photographs of their wedding. *OK!* paid Douglas and

---

[2] For other references of case reports see para 18.5, n 3.

[3] The House of Lords claimed to be united, however, on the questions of principle they considered. See *Campbell v MGN Ltd* [2004] 2 AC 457, para 36, per Lord Hoffmann.

[4] *In the matter of Application No 2323092B to register a trade mark in Class 16 by Sir Alexander Chapman Ferguson*, Trade Mark Decision o/26605, para 19

Zeta-Jones £1 million, and in return it was made clear to the many guests that cameras were not to be brought to the wedding; an obligation of confidence was imposed in respect of all photos of the wedding. However, *Hello!* magazine obtained photographs of the wedding from a freelance photographer who infiltrated the wedding. The House of Lords found that *OK!* (quite apart from Douglas and Zeta-Jones) had an action against *Hello!* for breach of confidence.

 Exercise

Can you identify common themes from these cases?

Personal privacy

Before the HRA 1998[5]

19.7   It is not a 21st-century phenomenon for individuals to wish to control references to their private life and activities. Using the established doctrine of breach of confidence discussed in Chapter 18, on several occasions courts in England have found details of extramarital affairs, private artwork, sexual activities, or photographs to be confidential, and for there to be obligations of confidence.[6] In a 1903 Scottish case, *M'Cosh v Crow*,[7] the court found that a photographer was not entitled to display in his window photographs of children which had been taken with their consent. One of the judges, referring to English cases, argued that the relationship between the photographer and the customers was a confidential one. How widely can this extend? There is a continuum between private diaries kept under lock and key, details of sexually transmitted disease, an illegitimate child of a campaigner for family values, a trip to the shop in old clothes by a minor celebrity, or a visit to the park of a stereotypical family of four.

19.8   In 1988 in *Spycatcher*,[8] discussed in Chapter 18, the House of Lords stated that 'the right to personal privacy is clearly one which the law should in this field seek to protect'.[9] This did not mean, however, that it did so protect. A 1990 report[10] recommended against the introduction of a statutory tort of infringement of privacy. But when a photographer gained unauthorised access to a hospital in the early 1990s and photographed a celebrity patient,[11] the law was found to have no means of response,[12] and there was no action for breach of privacy.[13]

---

[5] T Aplin, L Bently, P Johnson, and S Malynicz, *Gurry on Breach of Confidence: The Protection of Confidential Information* (2nd edn, 2012) ('Gurry'), 194–200.

[6] *Prince Albert v Strange* (1849) 1 H & T 1; *Argyll v Argyll* [1967] Ch 302; *Stephens v Avery* [1988] 2 WLR 1280, [1988] 2 All ER 477, [1988] FSR 510, [1988] Ch 449; *X (HA) v Y* [1988] 2 All ER 648, [1988] RPC 379 (see also paras 18.17 and 18.29).

[7] (1903) 5 F 670.   [8] *Attorney General v Guardian Newspapers Ltd (No 2)* [1988] 3 WLR 776 ('*Spycatcher*').

[9] *Spycatcher*, note 8, 782.   [10] Calcutt Report on Privacy and Related Matters (Cmnd 1102, 1990).

[11] *Kaye v Robertson* [1991] FSR 62.

[12] There was voluntary regulation of print media by the Press Complaints Commission which continues (http://www.pcc.org.uk/) (also discussions are ongoing on this respect as this book goes to press (see para 19.13). Courts are unwilling to intervene in its operation and to grant judicial review: see, eg, *R (On the application of Ford) v Press Complaints Commission* [2001] EWHC Admin 683, 2002 EMLR 5.

[13] The limits of the action in respect of non-information matters are evident in the House of Lords decision, *Wainwright v Home Office* [2003] UKHL 53, [2004] 2 AC 406 regarding strip searching of prison visitors. The UK was subsequently found to have been in breach of its ECHR obligation by the ECtHR, *Wainwright v United Kingdom* (App No 12350/04) (2007) 44 EHRR 40. See also *Peck v United Kingdom* (App No 44647/98) [2003] EMLR 15, (2003) 36 EHRR 41 and consideration in M Bhogal, 'United Kingdom privacy update 2003' (2004) 1(1) *SCRIPTed* 205, at http://www.law.ed.ac.uk/ahrc/script-ed/docs/privacy_comment.asp. The UK was again found to have failed to comply with its obligations under Art 8 ECHR in *Copland v United Kingdom* (App No 62617/00) (2007) 45 EHRR 37, regarding the monitoring by a public body of an employee's phone calls and Internet usage.

Key points on the pre-Human Rights Act 1998 position

- Some private information was considered confidential for the purposes of breach of confidence
- Obligations of confidence have been identified when there is no pre-existing relationship
- But there was still a gap and no legislation was proposed

The HRA 1998, actions between persons, and opportunities for privacy

19.9   This section will trace the significant impact of the HRA 1998 on breach of confidence, and the impact of the combination on the protection of personal privacy.[14] The HRA 1998 did not actually incorporate the European Convention on Human Rights (ECHR) into the laws of the UK. However, it created possibilities for the use of human rights in combination with existing causes of action. Section 6 of the HRA 1998 prohibits a public authority (stated to include a court) from acting in a manner incompatible with Convention rights when, essentially, an alternative approach is available.[15] Convention rights are defined to include Article 8 ECHR, the right to respect for private life, and its exceptions. This would seem to cover situations such as publication of photographs of private events. However, another Convention right is Article 10 ECHR, which was discussed in Chapter 18. This protects freedom of expression, with its own exceptions. The combination of Articles 8 and 10 (which include breach of confidence)[16] with the existing action for breach of confidence is a constant theme in the ongoing development of claims relating to information privacy.

Web links

Here is the link to the text of the ECHR in its entirety: **http://conventions.coe.int/Treaty/en/Treaties/Html/005.htm** and to the HRA 1998: **http://www.opsi.gov.uk/acts/acts1998/19980042.htm**

Article 8 ECHR

(1) Everyone has the right to respect for his private and family life, his home and his correspondence.

(2) There shall be no interference by a public authority with the exercise of this right except such as is in accordance with the law and is necessary in a democratic society in the interests of national security, public safety or the economic well-being of the country, for the prevention of disorder or crime, for the protection of health or morals, or for the protection of the rights and freedoms of others.

---

[14] Gurry, note 5, 200–222.   [15] See also para 5.49 regarding interpretation of legislation.

[16] In *Douglas and others v Hello! Ltd (No 3)* [2005] EWCA Civ 595, [2005] 3 WLR 881 the Court of Appeal confirmed that the action for breach of confidence, although still evolving with the human rights perspective, was also sufficiently precise to come within the prescribed by law restriction on free expression in Art 10, see paras 141–151.

> **Article 10 ECHR**
>
> (1) Everyone has the right to freedom of expression. This right shall include freedom ... to receive and impart information and ideas without interference by public authority and regardless of frontiers ...
>
> (2) The exercise of these freedoms, since it carries with it duties and responsibilities, may be subject to such formalities, conditions, restrictions or penalties as are prescribed by law and are necessary in a democratic society ... for the protection of the reputation or rights of others, for preventing the disclosure of information received in confidence ...

19.10   The ECHR is addressed to states, not individuals and companies.[17] Early concerns that this would therefore be of limited impact between private entities, were not realised. Articles 8 and 10 ECHR have had a central role in the privacy-related decisions between private entities; and as new social media make it easier for anyone to publish information about another, the opportunities this can provide will continue to be important.[18] Important cases establishing the place of Articles 8 and 10 ECHR when courts consider breach of confidence are the decision of the Court of Appeal in *A v B plc* in 2002 (regarding publication of the extramarital activities of a footballer),[19] the House of Lords in *Campbell* in 2004,[20] and the Court of Appeal in *Douglas v Hello!* in 2005 regarding the claims of Douglas and Zeta-Jones as individuals.[21] Further, in 2004 the European Court of Human Rights (ECtHR) in *Hannover* (regarding photographs taken of Princess Caroline of Hannover, mainly in public places) found that states might have positive obligations to introduce measures for exploration by individuals amongst themselves.[22]

> **Key point on HRA and individual actions**
>
> • National courts can use Articles 8 and 10 ECHR when considering actions for breach of confidence

 Question

What are the limits on the Article 10 right to freedom of expression which might encourage privacy seekers?

---

[17] See, eg, G Phillipson, 'Transforming breach of confidence? Towards a common law right of privacy under the Human Rights Act' (2003) 66 *MLR* 726.   [18] *Applause Store Productions Ltd v Raphael* [2008] EWHC 1781 (QB).

[19] *A v B plc* [2002] EWCA 337, [2003] QB 195.   [20] *Campbell*, note 3, paras 17–18, 49, 50.

[21] *Douglas v Hello!*, note 16, paras 47–49. Article 8 ECHR was also considered by the Scottish Court of Session in *Martin v McGuiness* 2003 SLT 1424, when a declaration was sought that the conduct of a private investigator was unlawful. The action, which sought, inter alia, to use the Scots claim of *actio iniuriarum* and Art 8 ECHR failed; there were *obiter* statements that maybe there should now be an action for privacy, but that this was not a live issue in the case.

[22] *Hannover v Germany* (App No 53920/00) (2005) 40 EHRR 1, paras 57 and 72. Considered also in 2006 in *McKennitt v Ash* [2006] EWCA Civ 1714, paras 9–11 and *Reklos v Greece* [2009] EMLR 16, para 35.

Misuse of private information

19.11   So how did Articles 8 and 10 combine with breach of confidence and to what end? The key development came in 2004 when the House of Lords considered the question in *Campbell*.[23] Although different approaches are adopted by Law Lords, key principles can be extracted for present purposes. There was still no overarching claim for invasion of privacy,[24] but breach of confidence could and did deal with personal information.[25] Pursuant to existing case law, the necessary relationship of confidence, at the core of the action as discussed in Chapter 18, might be identified in personal information cases, but it was 'awkward' to have to distinguish information from relationship.[26] Accordingly, in *Campbell* the House of Lords considered that breach of confidence in this field would be better referred to as misuse of private information.[27] The correct first question to be posed was whether the information was private. Information would be private if there was a reasonable expectation of privacy.[28] If there is a reasonable expectation of privacy, then Article 8 is engaged.

 Discussion point   For answer guidance visit www.oxfordtextbooks.co.uk/orc/waelde3e/

> Lord Hoffmann in *Campbell* considered there to have been a 'shift in the centre of gravity' of breach of confidence regarding personal information, based not on extended duties of confidence and good faith but on autonomy and dignity.[29] Do you agree? Review your answer after you have considered subsequent cases, which are discussed in the following section.

The reasonable expectation of privacy

19.12   The House of Lords in *Campbell* considered that it would usually be obvious when there was a reasonable expectation of privacy.[30] Yet case law suggests that the 'reasonable expectation of privacy' will frequently give rise to uncertainty. The ECtHR in *Hannover* in 2004 considered that private life within Article 8 covered physical and psychological integrity; and that, even in public, public figures might engage in private acts in respect of particular zones of life.[31] The Court of Appeal in *Douglas v Hello!* in 2005 considered that the test must cover information personal to the person possessing it, which they do not intend to be shared with the general public; and that this might be clear from the nature or form of the information.[32]

19.13   This suggests clearly that the expectation can exist not only in respect of public figures engaging in private acts, but also the more average person in the street. It might seem less likely that the media would be interested in such persons—but the growth of social networking, mentioned previously, means that boundaries between the private and the public become blurred (eg blogging has been found to be a public activity, and that the identity of bloggers was not information in respect of which there is a reasonable expectation of privacy).[33] There is also the potential for all lives to come into the media spotlight without having sought it, as was the experience, say, of the parents of murdered schoolgirl Milly Dowler.

---

[23] See also *A v B plc*, note 19, paras 4, 6, 9, 11(vi), (vi), (xii), and (xiii). The Court of Appeal did not, however, address ECHR authorities. The Court of Appeal in 2006 held *A v B plc* not to be binding on it in respect of how to conduct the balance in a case on similar facts: *Ash* (CA), note 22, paras 60–63.   [24] Unlike the position in the United States: see *Campbell*, note 3, para 11.
[25] *Campbell*, note 3, paras 43–45, 47, 51, referring to *Albert*, note 6, and *Spycatcher*, note 8.   [26] *Campbell*, note 3, paras 14, 49.
[27] *Campbell*, note 3, para 14.   [28] *Campbell*, note 3, paras 20–21.   [29] *Campbell*, note 3, para 51.
[30] *Campbell*, note 3, paras 21, 22, 92–94, 135 (and referring to *Australian Broadcasting Corporation v Lenah* (2001) 208 CLR 199, para 42, which has been considered at first instance, see paras 22, 93, 135, 166).
[31] *Hannover*, note 22, para 50. In England, see also *X v Persons Unknown* [2006] EWHC 2783 (QB), [2007] EMLR 10, [2007] HRLR 4.
[32] *Douglas v Hello!*, note 16, para 83. The Court of Appeal had reviewed authorities which had developed the concept of protection of some information on the basis on its nature (see paras 63–69, referring to *Spycatcher*, note 8, and *Venables v News Group Newspapers Ltd* [2001] Fam 430). The Court of Appeal went on to apply this approach in *Ash* (CA), note 22, paras 12–14.
[33] *The Author of a Blog v Times Newspapers Ltd* [2009] EWHC 1358 (QB), [2009] EMLR 22, paras 2–11, 33.

The extent to which the existing court process can protect their privacy effectively is one of the issues considered by the Leveson Inquiry,[34] which reported in 2012.[35] Key issues arise in particular in respect of children and relationships.

19.14   An important decision regarding when there might be an expectation of privacy is that of the Court of Appeal in 2008 in *Murray*,[36] regarding the publication of a photograph of the son of JK Rowling, the author of the Harry Potter books. The photograph was taken, without consent, with a long-range lens when the child was being pushed along an Edinburgh street in his buggy. This is a photograph, of an individual, who is not a celebrity. The court at first instance[37] considered this to be an attempt by JK Rowling to exercise her own rights, and held that she could not have rights in respect of walking down the street. Yet the Court of Appeal considered that her son David had his own rights, that he had a reasonable expectation of privacy,[38] and that these may, in some circumstances, be greater than those of his well-known mother. The Court of Appeal stressed that the reasonable expectation of privacy must always be assessed on the basis of the facts of each case and there could be no guarantees of privacy,[39] but that the following questions could be taken into account:

the attributes of the claimant, the nature of the activity in which the claimant was engaged, the place at which it was happening, the nature and purpose of the intrusion, the absence of consent and whether it was known or could be inferred, the effect on the claimant and the circumstances in which and the purposes for which the information came into the hands of the publisher.[40]

19.15   In addition to information relating to children, another area which has received much attention is personal and sexual relationships. Cases suggest that the details of the existence of intimate relationships (as well as information obtained in the course of them) may be private, but this varies with the degree of stability;[41] sexuality, in circumstances where there was evidence that others knew of the position, was not found to be information in respect of which there was a reasonable expectation of privacy.[42] This area is likely to continue to be a fruitful source of case law over the years.

19.16   Some other guidance can be extracted from English decisions (there are as yet no Scottish ones on point). Information will not be private if it is generally accessible (to be more flexibly applied than in respect of commercial information);[43] or if it relates to a criminal act (there is uncertainty here—drug taking might be private, but domestic violence or tax evasion would not be),[44] although Article 8 was engaged by the

[34]   http://www.levesoninquiry.org.uk/. For other discussion of the public interest and journalism, see *Mosley v News Group Newspapers Ltd* [2008] EWHC 1777 (QB), [2008] EMLR 20, paras 135–169; *Flood v Times Newspapers Ltd* [2009] EWHC 2375 (QB), [2010] EMLR 8; the ECtHR in *Financial Times Ltd v United Kingdom* (App No 821/03) [2010] EMLR 21, (2010) 50 EHRR 46; *LNS v Persons Unknown* [2010] EMLR 16, paras 72–73; and *Commissioner of Police of the Metropolis v Times Newspaper* [2011] EWHC 2705 (QB), paras 115 et seq, regarding the Data Protection Act 1998, s 32.

[35]   Note also previous UK consultations regarding the media and privacy; the UK Government gave a negative response (Cm 5985, 2003) to the Fifth Report of the House of Commons Culture, Media and Sport Select Committee on Privacy and Media Intrusion (HC 458-1, 2003) and its recommendation of the introduction of a new privacy law against media intrusion. See, eg, Uncorrected Evidence 275, http://www.publications.parliament.uk/pa/cm200809/cmselect/cmcumeds/uc275-xv/uc27502.htm.

[36]   *Murray v Express Newspapers plc* [2008] EWCA Civ 446, (2009) Ch 481.

[37]   *Murray v Express Newspapers plc* [2007] EWHC 1908 (Ch), [2007] ECDR 20, [2007] EMLR 22 reviewed in paras 13 and 44 of *Murray*, note 36.   [38]   *Murray*, note 36, para 12.

[39]   *Murray*, note 36, paras 14–20, 27 37, 45, 55–58.

[40]   *Murray*, note 36, para 36. Note the approach taken to an older child in *Spelman v Express Newspapers* [2012] EWHC 355 (QB), paras 35, 46, 53–56 although this decision focuses mainly on whether it is appropriate to grant an injunction.

[41]   See, eg, *A v B plc*, note 19, paras 11(xi), 29, 43, 47; *Theakston v MGN Ltd* [2002] EWHC 137 (QB), [2002] EMLR 22, paras 59–65, *Ash* (CA), note 22, paras 29–30 and see para 18.46; *Mosley*, note 34, paras 24, 98–104; *Ferdinand v MGN Ltd* [2011] EWHC 2454 (QB), para 53, 54, 58; *CC v AB* [2006] EWHC 3083 (QB), 2006 WL 3485386, [2007] EMLR 11 suggests that interests of spouses and children also to be taken into account.

[42]   *Trimingham v Associated Newspapers Ltd* [2012] EWHC 1296 (QB), paras 292–294, 305, 309–310, also 311–319 regarding photographs.

[43]   *McKennitt v Ash* (1st instance) [2005] EWHC 3003, [2005] EMLR 10, [2005] WL 3804441, para 81. See also application of test in *Ash* (CA), note 22, paras 21–23.

[44]   *A v B* [2005] EWHC 1651, [2005] EMLR 36, para 32.

police taking photographs, and keeping them, of a person's participation at a demonstration.[45] Sensitive personal data under the Data Protection Act 1998,[46] such as data relating to race, health, sexual orientation, and political and religious beliefs, has also been viewed as private for these purposes.[47]

Key points on reasonable expectation of privacy

- Depends on the facts (but see *Murray*)
- Even public figures can have an expectation
- Less likely to apply to publicly available information
- More likely to apply to details of sexual relationship/long-standing ones
- Beware of social networking

Pictures and images

19.17   *Campbell, Murray,* and *Hannover* all involve photographs. The impact of a photograph as a form of communicating information, rather than just using words, was discussed in Chapter 18 regarding the extent to which published photographs could still be confidential. The importance of photographs was also considered by the ECtHR in 2009 in *Reklos v Greece.*[48] A photograph was taken of the face of a newborn baby in a supposedly secure unit.[49] The ECtHR considered that the right to private life was, again, not 'susceptible to exhaustive definition',[50] but the ECtHR stressed that it did cover rights to identity, personal development, and personality; and image was considered to be one of the key parts of personality.[51] This was confirmed in a further case before the ECtHR in 2012 involving Princess Caroline of Hannover:[52] the image is 'one of the chief attributes of ... personality, as it reveals the person's unique characteristics and distinguishes the person from his or her peers. The right to the protection of one's image is thus one of the essential components of personal development. It mainly presupposes the individual's right to control the use of that image, including the right to refuse publication thereof.'[53]

Key point on image

- Publishing a photograph of someone raises special issues for privacy

---

 Exercise

Review the scenario you developed in the Exercise following para 19.4. Would there be a reasonable expectation of privacy?

---

[45] Decision of the Court of Appeal, *Wood v Commissioner of Police of the Metropolis* [2009] EWCA Civ 414, [2010] EMLR 1, paras 16–46, notably paras 45–46 (and regarding the breadth of what could be private and the importance of personal autonomy, see paras 19, 21); cf *Wood v Commissioner of Police of the Metropolis* [2008] EWHC 1105 (Admin), [2008] HRLR 34, [2009] CrimLR 376.

[46] Section 2.

[47] *Green Corns Ltd v Claverly Group Ltd* [2005] EWHC 958 (QB), [2005] EMLR 31, esp paras 62–64.   [48] See note 22.

[49] *Reklos*, note 22, para 37.   [50] *Reklos*, note 22, para 39.

[51] *Reklos*, note 22, paras 40–43. For consideration of the parent/child relationship and its impact, see A Carter-Silk and C Cartwright-Hignett, 'A child's right to privacy: "out of a parent's hands"' (2009) 20(6) *EntLR* 212–217.

[52] *Von Hannover v Germany* (App Nos 40660/08 and 60641/08) [2012] EMLR 16 (ECtHR, Grand Chamber).

[53] *Von Hannover*, note 52, para 96. See further discussion on this issue more generally in Gurry, note 5, 301–309.

19.18   It should be borne in mind that action for misuse of private information has not replaced breach of confidence. This was stated clearly by the Court of Appeal in *HRH Prince of Wales v Associated Newspapers Ltd (No 3)* in 2006, discussed in Chapter 18. The Court of Appeal dismissed arguments that there were now two actions for breach of confidence;[54] rather, information would be either private, engaging Article 8, or confidential and subject to an obligation of confidence, or both, as relevant factors to assessing each overlapped,[55] as in *Campbell*[56] and as in *HRH Prince of Wales v Associated Newspapers Ltd (No 3)*).[57] These bases for non-disclosure of information were then to be balanced with Article 10 and its limits.

Impact of Article 10

19.19   The previous discussion could lead to an identification of information in respect of which there is a reasonable expectation of privacy, and so Article 8 is engaged and relevant. But this is, of course, not the end of the story. Article 8 must then be balanced with Article 10,[58] to establish whether the disclosure and publication is in fact misuse of private information. *Campbell* provides that the balance is to be rational, fair, and not arbitrary.[59] Each right is to be afforded equal weight at the outset,[60] and to be encroached upon no more than is necessary and proportionate.[61] The weight accorded to freedom of expression will vary with the facts, with some forms of expression deserving greater weight—political and educational speech receiving more than celebrity gossip.[62]

19.20   Carrying out this balance can be difficult, as can be seen from decisions at the ECtHR involving Princess Caroline of Hannover. The ECtHR in *Hannover* in 2004 indicated that the interests of the free press would prevail over Article 8 rights if publication contributed to debate in the general interest. The ECtHR was quite prescriptive as to when this would be so: it considered that there was a fundamental distinction between details of public figures in respect of their official functions, and details of their private lives; only in respect of the official functions should the press be a watchdog in the general interest.[63] A second set of cases was then raised by Princess Caroline of Hannover, and these reached the ECtHR again.[64] They involved a photograph of Princess Caroline and her husband walking down the street in St Moritz and photographs with her father Prince Rainier of Monaco, in the context of a discussion of his health. The German court had balanced Article 8 and Article 10 (a change in its practice from the early decisions), and considered that there was a distinction between information about which people might be merely curious and information contributing to debate. In 2012, the ECtHR found that Germany's approach was not unreasonable, that there is a margin of appreciation for states to take their own approaches to balancing Articles 8 and 10, and that 'there was a zone of interaction'[65] which, even if in public, might

---

[54] [2006] EWCA Civ 1776, [2008] Ch 57, [2007] 3 WLR 222, *HRH CA*, paras 64–5, referring to New Zealand case *Hosking v Runting* [2004] NZCA 34.

[55] *HRH CA*, note 54, para 28.   [56] *Campbell*, note 3, para 53.

[57] [2006] EWCA Civ 1776, [2008] Ch 57, [2007] 3 WLR 222, paras 13, 14, 26, 28, 41, and 42. See also *Ash*, note 22, paras 15–18.

[58] *Campbell*, note 3, paras 29, 85–86, 105, 167; *Ash*, note 22, paras 11, 46–47; and *Douglas v Hello!*, note 16, para 53.

[59] *Campbell*, note 3, paras 115, 167. Regarding balancing in more extreme factual circumstances, see also *X (formerly known as Mary Bell v SO)* [2003] EWHC 1101 (QB), [2003] EMLR 37; *S (A Child) (Identification: Restrictions on Publication)* [2004] UKHL 47, [2005] 1 AC 593, [2004] 3 WLR 1129; *Re Attorney General's Reference (No 3 of 1999)* [2009] UKHL 34 [2009] 3 WLR 142, [2009] EMLR 23, [2009] HRLR 28; and *Flood*, note 34.

[60] *Campbell*, note 3, para 55, *Hannover*, note 22, paras H9, H24, 11, 13, 18, 58–64, 69, 76–79.

[61] *Campbell*, note 3, paras 139–141, *Ash*, note 22, para 46. In MGN Ltd v United Kingdom (App No 39401/04) (2011) 29 BHRC 686 (ECtHR) the ECtHR found that there had been no breach of Art 10 by the finding of the House of Lords in *Campbell*, but found that Art 10 ECHR could be violated, if disproportionate success fees are imposed on the defendant, as this could put pressure on defendant not to defend their case in court.

[62] *Campbell*, note 3, paras 148–149. See also *LNS*, note 34, paras 68–69.

[63] *Hannover*, note 22, para H20, 63–65. Reference was made to Resolution 1165 (2005) 40 EHRR 1, at *Hannover*, para 67. The resolution is considered in respect of the English courts at para 18.84.

[64] *Hannover v Germany* (App nos 40660/08 and 60641/08) (2012) 55 EHRR 15.   [65] *Hannover* (2012) note 64, para 95.

involve private life; that freedom of expression extended to ideas that offend or shock; that the press has an essential role in a democratic society; and that regard should be had to the nature of the report, the prior conduct of the person involved, the nature of publication, and circumstances of the photos.[66]

19.21   The *Hannover* decisions are important, as under the HRA, courts are required to have regard to ECtHR decisions. English courts have also looked to Resolution 1165 of the Council of Europe (passed in the aftermath of the death of the Princess of Wales, regarding the relationship between Article 8 and Article 10 ECHR).[67] However, courts in the UK are not obliged to follow the ECtHR decisions,[68] and where there is a conflict between decisions of the House of Lords and the ECtHR, the House of Lords (and now the Supreme Court) must be followed.[69] The extent of enthusiasm of English courts referring to ECtHR decisions in their judgments suggests scope for further synergy in development in this area at national level and at the ECtHR.

19.22   Even with ECtHR guidance, the carrying out of this balance is difficult and hard to predict. The Court of Appeal has rejected an argument[70] that once a person reveals information about one zone in their life, they have a lower expectation of privacy in that zone,[71] and also that particular weight should be had to the Article 8 rights of children when balancing those rights.[72] Courts have considered it relevant if information is being disclosed to correct a 'false image' (used in this case in respect of a reputation, rather than a photograph) which has been created in respect of a person—say, regarding Naomi Campbell's distaste for drugs,[73] or in respect of arguments that a footballer had now embraced family values.[74] This can lead a court down unexpected paths—the court was relieved not to need to decide whether or not the captain of the English men's football team needed to a role model.[75] The court in *LNS v Persons Unknown*,[76] another case involving footballers and sexual indiscretions, rejected the argument that conduct of one person in private must be unlawful, before another person should be permitted to criticise it in public on the basis of freedom of expression, since 'not all conduct that is socially harmful is unlawful'.[77]

19.23   The Court of Appeal in *HRH Prince of Wales v Associated Newspapers Ltd (No 3)* provided helpful guidance for the balancing act including, as considered in Chapter 18, the ongoing impact of an obligation of confidence. The court should take into account whether in all the circumstances it was in the public interest that the obligation of confidence should be breached. Was a fetter on free expression necessary in a democratic society, was disclosure justifiable and proportionate in the light of obligations of confidence? Regard should be had to the nature of the information; the nature of the relationship (including whether there was a contract); and whether in all the circumstances it was legitimate for the information to be kept confidential or whether it was in the public interest for it to be made public.[78] If there was no contract, the question under Article 10 remained on whether a fetter on free expression was necessary in a democratic society; and whether disclosure was proportionate.[79] In both situations, the Court of Appeal once again obtained important guidance from ECtHR decisions, in particular *Fressoz v France*[80] and the 2006 decision in *Editions Plon v France*.[81]

---

[66] *Hannover* (2012), paras 102–113.
[67] See *Campbell*, note 3, paras 53, 107–110, 113–122, 140; *Ash*, note 22, pays particular regard to these decisions and the need to respect them, paras 37–42, 58–66; and *Mosley*, note 34, paras 18, 21, 99–109.
[68] HRA 1998, s 2.   [69] *Murray*, note 36, para 20   [70] Based on *A v B plc*, note 19.   [71] *Ash*, note 22, 53–55.
[72] *ETK v News Group Newspapers Ltd* [2011] EWCA Civ 439, paras 14ff, in particular 19.
[73] *Campbell*, note 3, see eg para 24.   [74] *Ferdinand*, note 41, paras 64, 65, 66, 69,   [75] *Ferdinand*, note 41 paras 87, 89–91.
[76] *LNS*, note 34.   [77] *LNS*, note 34, paras 99–104; see also *Ferdinand*, note 41, paras 63, 64.
[78] *HRH* CA, note 54, paras 67–69 and see paras 30–31, 61–63 and 66–68 regarding CA, note 54.
[79] *HRH* CA, note 54, para 67.
[80] (2001) 31 EHRR 2, (1999) 5 BHRC 654.   [81] *Editions Plon* (2006) 42 EHRR 36, paras 49–53.

19.24   Like *London Regional Transport v Mayor of London* discussed in Chapter 18, this is another example of the ongoing importance of the term 'the public interest' in litigation in the HRA era.[82] As noted by the Court of Appeal in *McKennitt v Ash*, is it 'perhaps inevitable'[83] that these references to the public interest will continue, both in language and breadth of analysis. Yet the substance of the cases considered suggests that even if references to 'public interest' continue (and this is particularly likely in the context of remedies, as considered in Chapter 22, given references to it in section 12 of the HRA), final outcomes will be reached on an ECtHR and Article 10-based approach[84]—irrespective of the basis of claim or type of information.[85]

 Discussion point   For answer guidance visit www.oxfordtextbooks.co.uk/orc/waelde3e/

A style magazine publishes pictures of a supermodel leaving what is tipped to be the new fashionable beauty salon. She is not happy as she has just signed a contract with a competitor. Discuss.

Key points on the impact of Article 10

- Article 8 and Article 10 start with equal weighting
- Depends on facts and proportionality, but could look to:
  - nature of report
  - prior conduct of person involved
  - nature of publication
  - circumstances of the photos
  - genuine debate or curiosity
  - correction of false image
  - obligation of confidence
  - public interest

19.25   **Case study**

Mosley involved the publication of details of the participation of Max Mosley, the President of the FIA, the world motorsports body, in group consensual sexual activity. This was said to have a Nazi theme, which was of particular interest as Mr Mosley's father had been the leader of the British fascist party. The English court considered that there was a reasonable expectation of privacy in respect of participation in consensual sexual acts on private property.[86] When considering the Article 10 ECHR arguments, the court focused on the public interest in publication on these facts,[87] and concluded that however distasteful some might

---

[82] See also *LNS*, note 34, 62–63, 70 et seq and *Ferdinand*, note 41, para 68.

[83] *Ash* (CA), note 22, para 53.

[84] See also references in *Campbell*, note 3, 56, 63, 85 (referring to *Spycatcher* then noting in para 86 change since HRA, and also paras 106–110, 116 referring to ECtHR authorities and 142–143).

[85] *Douglas v Hello!*, note 16, paras 113–119. See also Gurry, note 5, 699–716 regarding defences.

[86] Despite the subject matter, the court did not consider this to be a 'landmark' case: see *Mosley*, note 34, para 234. But note K Hughes, 'Case comment. Horizontal privacy' (2009) 125 *LQR* 244–247.

[87] *Mosley*, note 34, paras 10–15.

consider Mr Mosley's activities to be, and despite arguments of criminal and depraved conduct, there was no public interest in publication.[88]

Mosley then raised an action at the ECtHR claiming that UK law was in breach of Article 8 ECHR since it does not provide for a legal duty for newspapers to contact a person before publishing private information related to that person. The ECtHR considered the chilling effect that could arise from this, doubts as to its effectiveness, and the wide margin of appreciation, and considered that Article 8 did not require a legally binding pre-notification requirement.[89]

Key points on personal privacy

- There is no overarching claim of invasion of privacy
- Breach of confidence covers personal information, although it is better termed misuse of private information
- Central question (1): is there information in respect of which there is a reasonable expectation of privacy—if so, Article 8 is relevant
- Central question (2): is it proportionate for disclosure of information to be prevented given Article 10 rights
- A careful balance of Articles 8 and 10 is required—weight of Article 10 will vary with the type of expression, and the weight of Article 8 will vary with the context—public figures still have private lives
- Decisions of the ECtHR and the Council of Europe Resolution are highly influential

Merchandising

Introduction

19.26 This section moves from individuals wishing to keep information secret, to situations when companies or individuals wish to control the use which they and others can make of their commercial reputation and, colloquially, their brand. Merchandising can apply to real-world personalities—a well-known sportsman such as the footballer David Beckham or a popular singer such as Elvis Presley—or entirely fictitious, for example cartoon or puppet characters in a television series such as *The Simpsons* or *In the Night Garden*.

19.27 Merchandising might involve putting on the market a variety of products bearing the name or image of the person or character, or reproducing the image in either two-or three-dimensional form. This form of marketing is known as *spin off* or *character merchandising* when applied to fictional characters or entities, *personality merchandising* when the character is a real person. The boundary between character and personality merchandising may become blurred when, for example, the personality of an actor well known in a particular role is exploited in this sort of way.

---

[88] *Mosley*, note 34, paras 24–25, 110–134, 170–171, 233. Regarding controversy after this decision, see Memorandum submitted by the Master of the Rolls to the Department of Culture, Media and Sport Select Committee (the Committee) in its investigation into Press Standards, Privacy and Libel Uncorrected Evidence 67, May 2008, paras 12–39, http://www.publications.parliament.uk/pa/cm200910/cmselect/cmcumeds/memo/press/contents.htm.

[89] *Mosley v United Kingdom* (App No 48009/08) (2011) (53) EHRR 30, in particular para 132.

Question

What is merchandising? You may find the following helpful: HE Ruijsenaars, 'Legal aspects of merchandising: the AIPPI Resolution' [1996] 6 EIPR 330.

Trade marks

19.28   What if a fan of David Beckham took a photograph of his idol as the fan was walking down the street, and applied that picture to the front of a T-shirt to be sold on market stalls. If a photograph of David Beckham had been registered as a trade mark in connection with articles of clothing, that fact might prevent any picture of him being applied to a T-shirt by another: one picture of David Beckham is likely to be similar to another.

Question

Read this last example again. What defence from registered trade mark law might the T-shirt vendor have in the given circumstances? You could have a look at paras 15.105ff.

Exercise

Choose the name of a well-known celebrity. Search both the UK register and the Community trade mark (CTM) register to see if you can find any registered trade marks consisting of or including that name.

19.29   Signatures of celebrities, both alive and dead, have been registered as trade marks in the UK. Thus, the example is given in Figure 14.1 of Marilyn Monroe's signature, registered in class 3 in connection with cosmetics; soaps; shampoos; and foamable preparations for the bath.[90]

Question

When you see the signature of Marilyn Monroe what do you think of?

19.30   So a signature might be distinctive for the purposes of trade mark law[91] because of the script used and thus registerable. However, the registration of celebrity names as such has proved more problematic and has been called into question since the appeal in *Elvis Presley Enterprises Inc v Sid Shaw Elvisly Yours*.[92] This is an excellent example of the legal arguments and policy dilemmas which arise in this field.

19.31   The Court of Appeal upheld the decision to overturn registrations of a variety of styles of the name 'Elvis Presley'. The court decided that a celebrity name was not registerable as a trade mark as it was not

---

[90] UK Trade Mark No 1308828, the estate of Marilyn Monroe.

[91] In *Elvis Presley Enterprises Inc v Sid Shaw Elvisly Yours* [1999] RPC 567 the Court of Appeal found Elvis Presley's signature to be distinctive but was not registered because opposition based on a confusing similarity to an earlier mark used by a third party merchandiser succeeded.

[92] *Elvis*, note 91, see also *Corsair Toiletries's Application* [1999] ETMR 1038 ('Jane Austen' for toiletries refused because it lacked distinctiveness).

distinctive. The court appeared aware of the broad monopoly power that could be conferred on traders if celebrity names could be registered as trade marks. In the words of Simon Brown LJ:

> there should be no *a priori* assumption that only a celebrity or his successors may ever market (or licence the marketing of) his own character. Monopolies should not be so readily created.

19.32   The *Elvis Presley* case dealt with the law as it stood under the Trade Marks Act 1938, discussed in Chapter 13. Would the same result be achieved had the 1994 Act been in operation? Some writers argue not. Nonetheless, it has been followed in the decision by the trade mark registry to turn down the application to register the name 'Diana, Princess of Wales' as a trade mark.[93] In refusing the application, the registry emphasised that a name unique to a particular person did not of itself have distinctive character as a trade mark. The essential function of a trade mark was to guarantee that the items bearing it had originated under the control of a single undertaking responsible for their quality. Unless, therefore, such control could be shown, the use of a famous name to endorse a product was not a trade mark use. It would thus seem that the better known the personality, the less likely it is that a name will be registered as a trade mark because the name is not considered distinctive in the trade mark sense, as was seen in the 'Alex Ferguson' case considered previously.[94] But note the CTM registration for 'Usain Bolt' (E9787581)—does it depend on the nature of the underlying person and the means by which they have become known?

19.33   There are many examples, however, of the names of living and dead well-known personalities becoming distinctive and being registered as trade marks: Gucci, Dior, Versace, and Naomi Campbell[95] are all examples.

 ### Exercise 1

Note the story in *The Guardian*, 14 October 2006, in which it was reported that the former Beatle, Paul McCartney applied to register the name 'McCartney' for a wide range of products including vegetarian foods and meat products. Apparently the application in respect of the meat products was defensive to give McCartney protection against the name being used in connection with products of which he does not approve. Was the application successful? Might a registration be subject to challenge at a later date? If so, on what grounds?

Exercise 2

Have a look at the Trade Marks Registry Works Manual, Chapter 3. What does it say about the registration of: famous names, badges of allegiance, names of deceased individuals or defunct groups, pictures of famous persons?

Web link

Don't forget that you can find the Trade Marks Registry Works Manual on the UK Intellectual Property Office (UK–IPO) website at **http://www.ipo.gov.uk**.

---

[93] *Diana, Princess of Wales Trade Mark* [2001] ETMR 25. See also C Waelde, 'Commercialising the personality of the late Diana, Princess of Wales: censorship by the back door?' in N Dawson and A Firth (eds), *Perspectives on Intellectual Property: Trade Marks Retrospective* vol 7 (2000).

[94] See also from Germany a decision in relation to a picture of Marlene Dietrich, discussed in F Traub, 'German courts reject trade mark application for portrait of Marlene Dietrich' [2009] *EntLR* 111.   [95] International Madrid (UK) Case M706887.

> ### Key points on signature and name of celebrities and trade marks
>
> * The signature of a celebrity may be considered as sufficiently distinctive for registration as a trade mark
> * Where the name of a celebrity is seen as purely descriptive of the subject matter of goods it will be unregisterable as a trade mark

19.34 Even if registration can be obtained, case law suggests that the names of celebrities and other well-known people will have a more limited scope of protection than other trade marks (see also para 15.42). Consider the following.

■ Case C-361/04 *Ruiz-Picasso v OHIM* [2006] ECR I-643

An application was made by DaimlerChrysler to register 'Picaro' for vehicles.[96] This was objected to by the estate of Picasso, owners of the Picasso CTM registered for vehicles shown in Figure 19.1.

The European Court of Justice rejected the appeal and found that where the meaning of at least one of the two signs at issue is clear and specific so that it can be grasped immediately by the relevant public, the conceptual differences observed between those signs may counteract any visual and phonetic similarities between them.[97] When confronted with the word sign 'Picasso', the relevant public inevitably sees in it a reference to the painter and that, 'given the painter's renown with that public, that particularly rich conceptual reference is such as greatly to reduce the resonance with which, in this case, the sign is endowed as a mark, among others, of motor vehicles'.[98]

Figure 19.1 Picasso mark

19.35 Thus it would appear that when the names of well-known people have been registered as trade marks, the better known the name the narrower the scope of protection will be granted as against similar marks, and the lower the distinguishing capacity of the mark in relation to the goods for which it is registered.[99]

❓ Question

To what extent do you think the well-known status of a name will be able to displace any likelihood of confusion between the name and the use of the name as a mark?

---

[96] CTM App No 000927764.   [97] [2006] ECR I-643, para 20.   [98] *Picasso*, note 97, para 27.
[99] See also Case C-16/06 P *Les Editions Albert Rene Sarl v OHIM* [2009] ETMR 21 and Case C-51/09 P *Barbara Becker v Harman International Industries* [2010] ETMR 53, regarding compound name and well-known surname.

19.36   What of the future dealings with trade marks? *Elizabeth Florence Emanuel v Continental Shelf*[100] concerned the assignation, by Elizabeth Emanuel a well-known fashion designer, of the trade mark bearing her name along with a crest made up of two 'E's back to back. After ownership of the trade mark had then changed hands several times, Ms Emanuel opposed a proposed amendment to the registered trade mark and applied for revocation of it on the ground that to let the mark stay on the register would be to deceive the public within the meaning of Article 3(1)(g) of the Directive (see paras 14.95ff).

19.37   It was argued that a significant proportion of the relevant public would believe that use of the trade mark indicated that the individual remained involved with the design or creation of the goods in relation to which the mark was used, and so using the name mark in a business in which the individual was not concerned would be deceptive. The Court did not accept this argument. The Court ruled that a trade mark which corresponds to the name of the designer and first manufacturer of the goods is not, for that reason, liable to revocation on the ground that that mark would mislead the public. This was particularly so where the goodwill associated with that mark has been assigned together with the business making the goods to which the mark relates.[101]

19.38   Although this might seem an odd result if the view is taken that a consumer might be confused that the named individual designer had not actually had a hand in designing the goods, it undoubtedly reflects what happens in commercial life, and which will be discussed in more detail later regarding passing off. To what extent, for example, does Naomi Campbell have a hand in developing perfumes sold under her name? As the Advocate General had argued: 'a user is aware of the possibility of divergences between personal names used as trade marks and the participation of those persons in the production of the goods or the provision of the services which they cover: All consumers know that a fashion designer is entitled to transfer his or her business at any time'.[102]

19.39   Consider, however, that in 2012 the Court of Justice considered a new CTM application for 'Elio Fiorucci'. The individual Elio Fiorucci, who had owned Fiorucca SpA and has been very well known as a designer in the 1970s, objected, including with reference to protection of well-known names by Italian law. The Court of Justice found that the right to a name of the individual Elio Fiorucci applied not only to use in a commercial context, but also to personality.[103]

Key point on well-known name trade marks

- The better known a name, the more likely it is that any confusion due to visual, aural, or conceptual similarities as between similar names may be displaced

- An assignation of a trade mark consisting of the name of a well-known celebrity is not liable to be revoked purely on the ground that the celebrity no longer remains involved with the business carried on under the mark. But the celebrity might be able to have an impact on future applications

---

[100] Case C-259/04 [2006] ECR I-3089, [2006] ETMR 56.

[101] Note that according to the UK tax authorities, an unregistered trade mark does not exist as a separate asset and is not capable of assignment separate from the goodwill of the business in which it is used (see HMRC CG68210 and TCGA92/S21 (1)).

[102] *Emanuel*, note 100, AG Opinion, para 63.

[103] *Edwin Co Ltd v Office for Harmonisation in the Internal Market (Trade Marks and Designs) (OHIM), Elio Fiorucci* [2011] ETMR 45, see paras 19, 20, 39, 65, 67.

19.40   As well as the name of a well-known personality, one might (whether the celebrity himself or a third party) want to protect the celebrity image—in the sense of a picture, what the celebrity looks like. Early cases suggested that registration would be permissible on the ground that an image is distinctive. As was said in 1897:

> it is difficult to suppose anything could be more distinctive than the portraiture of the man who was professing to be the manufacturer of that particular article.[104]

Pictures of celebrities have been registered as trade marks, such as that of Eric Cantona[105] and Damon Hill.[106] To see the picture of Eric Cantona look at the UK trade mark register under Trade Mark No 2120277 and for Damon Hill the number is 2036489.

19.41   However, the UK–IPO refused to register images of the late Diana Princess of Wales as trade marks.[107] Applications were made to register 52 different images for a wide variety of goods and services. Unfortunately, the reasoning behind the refusal has not been made public, so one can only speculate as to what it might have been. In trade mark terms, the registry may have decided that the images were not distinctive. Diana was, after all, one of the most photographed people in the world for a number of years. Another ground for refusal might have been that there was no trade connection between the images and the goods and services they were to be registered in connection with: the intention might merely have been to indicate sponsorship, such as the use of her name on tubs of margarine, rather than trade origin. Equally, there may have been a lack of any form of quality control over those products and services: an argument similar to that used to turn down the application to register her name as a trade mark.

 Question

Why do you think that the application to register the image of the late Diana Princess of Wales as a trade mark was turned down by the Trade Mark Registry?

 Exercise

Have a look at the Trade Marks Registry Works Manual, Chapter 3 at http://www.ipo.gov.uk/ tmmanual-chap3-add-archive.pdf. What does it say about the registration of pictures of famous persons?

19.42   It thus appears that neither the name (as opposed to the signature) nor the image of a well-known celebrity will be accepted in the UK for registration as a trade mark for certain goods unless the mark has acquired distinctiveness through use. For some goods the signs will be unregisterable. For those names and images that are already registered it may be that in any dispute with a third party the scope of protection will be narrow or the registration vulnerable to being declared invalid as being merely

---

[104] *Rowland v Mitchell* (1897) 14 RPC 37.
[105] UK Trade Mark No 2120277, classes 16 and 25, proprietor: Eric Cantona c/o Manchester United plc.
[106] UK Trade Mark No 2036489, classes 6, 9, 16, 25, and 28, proprietor: Damon Hill Grand Prix Limited.
[107] http://news.bbc.co.uk/1/hi/uk/272380.stm. The application was to register 52 images of Diana and was turned down by the Patent Office in February 1999. The reasons for declining the application have not been made public (except for journalistic reporting). It is understood that had the Fund decided to appeal the decision, then the reason for the initial refusal would have been publicly available. See also A Story, 'Owning Diana: from People's Princess to private property', http://webjcli.ncl.ac.uk/1998/issue5/story5. html.

descriptive of the goods for which it is registered. The more famous you are, the harder it might be to obtain a trade mark.

> ### Key points on trade marks and the image of a celebrity
>
> - The name and image of a celebrity can be registered as trade marks in certain circumstances
> - For some goods, the signs will be unregisterable as they will not be considered as indicating origin

> ### Exercise
>
> Should a well-known personality be able to protect elements of her personality as a registered trade mark? What justifications would you give? And what elements of her personality? If it were possible, what effect might this have on the availability of consumer goods in the marketplace?

Passing off

19.43   Passing off has been used when misrepresentations have been made in respect of authors, artists, or their work. It has been passing off for the author of any creative work to attach to it the name of another author, perhaps especially if that name is a *nom de plume*;[108] the author of a highly successful dramatic sketch was able to prevent a film being publicised as a version of his sketch;[109] and there may be passing off if the fanciful name of a musical band is used by another band.[110] When the London *Evening Standard* published a satire of the diaries of Alan Clark, a well-known and controversial political figure, this was found to be passing off; not enough had been done by the newspaper to remove the possibility of confusion in the mind of the typical reader.[111]

19.44   A greater variety of approaches has been taken in respect of merchandising. A court in Hong Kong held that an author may claim goodwill in a fictional character, and that a film producer who has a licence to use the story creating the character can also build up goodwill in it, which may be protected by a passing off action.[112] The 'Crocodile Dundee' cases in Australia[113] illustrate how the image of an actor and his character may coalesce. Paul Hogan played the character Crocodile Dundee in a series of films which he also wrote. These cases involved the defendants' sale of goods making use of the 'Crocodile Dundee' name and image, and the Australian courts held that Hogan himself could bring an action for passing off.

19.45   Yet, save in the *Ninja Turtles* case (1991) discussed previously, the English courts have been reluctant to recognise that the use of characters or personalities can be stopped by their originator, especially if they have not yet commenced trading operations using them. The argument is that goodwill, as distinct

---

[108] *Marengo v Daily Sketch* (1948) 65 RPC 242 (HL). Note also the right to prevent false attribution in the Copyright, Designs Patents Act 1988, s 85 (see para 3.47) and the right in Art 15(1)(c) of the International Covenant on Economic, Social and C Rights of everyone to benefit from protection of moral and material interests from any literary or artistic production of are the author.   *(The*

[109] *Samuelson v Producers Distributing Co* [1932] 1 Ch 201.

[110] *Hines v Winnick* [1947] 1 Ch 708 (Doctor Crock and his Crackpots); *Treadwell's Drifters Inc v RCL Ltd* Drifters).

[111] *Clark v Associated Newspapers Ltd* [1998] 1 All ER 959. See also para 3.47 on the moral right aspects

[112] *Shaw Bros v Golden Harvest* [1972] RPC 559.

[113] *Hogan v Koala Dundee* (1988) 12 IPR 508; *Hogan v Pacific Dunlop* (1989) 12 IPR 225.

from reputation, is necessary before there can be a claim of passing off. Examples of unsuccessful claims include the following:

- Uncle Mac, children's radio character in *McCulloch v May* (1948) 65 RPC 58;
- Sherlock Holmes in *Conan Doyle v London Mystery Magazine Ltd* (1949) 66 RPC 312;
- Wombles of Wimbledon in *Wombles v Womble Skip* [1977] RPC 99;
- ABBA pop group in *Lyngstad v Anabas* [1977] FSR 62;
- Teletubbies in *BBC Worldwide v Pally Screen Printing* [1998] FSR 665.

19.46   Even where the character or personality is already being used under licence to market goods, English judges have found that the use of the image is not seen by the public as a representation of a connection with, or authorisation by, the originator of the character or individual in question. If there is a false claim of authorisation—for example, a claim that the merchandise is 'official'—then, but only then, may there be a misrepresentation.[114] This use of such wording can lead to some complex arguments and, indeed, can be a double-edged sword.[115] In 1997, the pop band 'The Spice Girls'[116] sought an application for an injunction to prevent an unauthorised trader selling 'Spice Girls' sticker collections. The court rejected arguments that the absence of the word 'unofficial' was sufficient to influence the public's perception of the origin of the goods.

> ## Key point on character and personality merchandising—passing off
>
> - Although passing off is now recognised as reaching the unauthorised use of fictional characters and real persons in the marketing of products, the English courts have been reluctant to allow the action unless the claimant is actually trading using the character/personality in question, or where there is a false claim by the defendants that their use is authorised or 'official'

> ## Exercise
>
> Consider the case of *Taverner Rutledge v Trexapalm* [1977] RPC 275. Is it anomalous that in this case the UK licensees of the originators of 'Kojak' lollipops found themselves unsuccessfully defending a passing off action brought by an unlicensed trader who had reached the English market first with his own 'Kojakpops'? 'Do you think this could happen now in our Internet world?

19.47   In policy terms, the approach so far of the English courts in the law of passing off fails to recognise the extent to which 'character' and 'personality' merchandising has become an established form of trading supported by complex licensing arrangements, all of which will be baseless unless the law is prepared to ~ecognise the goodwill which does attach to characters even before they have been employed in a mer- ⌐ising context.[117] This raises a question which was seen in the early discussion of privacy discussed

114   Elvi~
2 S 413.
115   See also ~
official Arsenal m~ks [1997] RPC 543 per Laddie J at 558. This would also cover the Scottish case of *Wilkie v McCulloch* (1823)
116   *Halliwell v Pann*
117   See further H Car~ ~lc v Reed* [2001] RPC 922 (Laddie J), where the defendant who made clear that his goods were *not*
~ not to have engaged in passing off.
~997 (Ch D).
~sing and the limits of passing off' (1993) 13 *Legal Studies* 289.

previously and will be seen throughout the rest of this chapter; gaps between commercial reality and individual wishes and the existing legal protection. Is this a concern?

Summary of key points on merchandising

- Passing off can prevent some forms of merchandising
- Trade marks can provide the right to control the use of name, signature, and image (picture) in some cases
- The protection which exists stems from established principles—there is no dedicated comprehensive protection which applies to merchandising in its many forms

---

Endorsement and sponsorship

Passing off and false endorsement

19.48   There is an important distinction between character and personality merchandising and endorsement, as Laddie J explained in the English decision *Irvine*, which was summarised previously:[118]

> When someone endorses a product or service he tells the relevant public that he approves of the product or service or is happy to be associated with it. In effect he adds his name as an encouragement to members of the relevant public to buy or use the service or product. Merchandising is rather different. It involves exploiting images, themes or articles which have become famous.... It is not a necessary feature of merchandising that members of the public will think the products are in any sense endorsed [by the personalities or characters concerned].

19.49   The early view of the English courts was that, even if there was appropriation of goodwill by the false endorsement, the business being made by the defendant from its activities was not custom that would otherwise have gone to the person represented as making the endorsement.[119] English courts have looked in the past to defamation to address this type of scenario, for example when a champion amateur golfer was portrayed with a Fry's chocolate bar in an advertisement for that product, implying that he had been paid for an endorsement of the product, which was inconsistent with this amateur status.[120] By contrast, in the early Scottish decision of *Wilkie v McCulloch*,[121] a firm was stopped from representing that its ploughs were made under the inspection and authority of an individual who had developed a new kind of plough. In more recent times, the Australian courts also took a rather different approach in *Henderson v Radio Corporation Pty Ltd*.[122] The unauthorised appearance of a photograph of two well-known professional ballroom dancers on the sleeve of a dance music record was held to constitute passing off as a misrepresentation of the dancers' endorsement of the record.[123] And in the United States, the singer and comedian Bette Midler was held able to prevent unauthorised imitation and use of her v   e in television commercials.[124]

---

[118] [2002] 2 All ER 414, [2002] FSR 60, para 9.   Brown LJ.
[119] *McCulloch v May* (1948) 65 RPC 58; *Elvis Presley Trade Marks* [1999] RPC 567 at 597 pe   f New South Wales).
[120] *Tolley v Fry* [1931] AC 333.   [121] (1823) 2S 413.   [122] [1969] RPC 218 (Hi
[123] See also *Campomar Sociedad Limitada v Nike International Ltd* (2000) 46 IPR 48
[124] *Midler v Ford Motor Co Inc* 849 F 2d 460 (1988).

Exercise

How far does and should the law of passing off go in offering protection to aspects of individual personality against use by others constituting misrepresentation? What aspects of personality in addition to name, designation, and voice used in one's trade or profession might be covered? Is this the same as your approach in respect of trade marks?

19.50   A significant change in approach was taken in England by Laddie J in *Irvine*, which was approved by the Court of Appeal.[125] Eddie Irvine, the leading Formula 1 racing driver, was shown in a promotional brochure for Talksport Radio wearing his Ferrari racing gear and apparently listening intently to a radio marked with the Talksport insignia. This was, however, the result of manipulation of a photograph (lawfully acquired for reproduction by Talksport) which actually showed Irvine using a mobile telephone. It was held that this was passing off. Laddie J said (at para 39):

> it is common for famous people to exploit their names and images by way of endorsement. They do it not only in their own field of expertise but, depending on the extent of their fame or notoriety, wider afield also. It is common knowledge that for many sportsmen, for example, income received from endorsing a variety of products and services represent a very substantial part of their total income. The reason large sums are paid for endorsement is because, no matter how irrational it may seem to a lawyer, those in business have reason to believe that the lustre of a famous personality, if attached to their goods and services, will enhance the attractiveness of those goods or services to their target market. In this respect, the endorsee is taking the benefit of the attractive force which is the reputation or goodwill of the famous person.

19.51   The link between false endorsement and passing off was confirmed in a case involving the use of a picture of a jar of Marmite, a British product which one is often said to love or hate, in relation to advertisements by the British National Party. They stated 'Love Britain Vote BNP'. The court accepted that Unilever would probably succeed at trial in an action for passing off because of the false endorsement.[126]

Key point on endorsement

- *Irvine* is authority that false endorsement is passing off because endorsement is established as a lucrative way in which personalities may exploit their fame

Discussion point   For answer guidance visit www.oxfordtextbooks.co.uk/orc/waelde3e/

Do you agree that the endorsement of a well-known personality can be a source of goodwill? Does Article 8 ECHR (privacy) require the protection of such goodwill? Whose goodwill—the trader ~ose products are endorsed or the personality doing the endorsing? And consider how your co~ ~ions here relate to your views formed earlier regarding privacy in the light of Article 8 ECHR a~ ~he HRA.

---

[125] See further M Learmouth, 'Ed~
[126] *Unilever plc v Griffin* [2010] EWH~ ~OK? Product endorsement and passing off' [2002] *IPQ* 306.
from an interim hearing.   ~aras 20–22; note that there is no reference to *Irvine* although it is a short judgment

Intellectual property and sponsorship agreements

19.52 As considered by Laddie J in *Irvine*, well-known personalities, characters, and businesses will frequently enter into agreements regarding the use of their name and image. Examples might be the sponsorship agreement entered into by Samsung in respect of the London 2012 Olympic Games, which led to wide fears about the fate of one's 'iPad' if one were to be spotted using it; and agreements between David Beckham and Armani in relation to underwear between 2007 and 2012 worth £20 million,[127] between the Murray family (Andy, Jamie, and Judy) and Highland Spring from 2006 to 2011 worth £1 million,[128] and the agreement between Andy Murray and Rado regarding a watch, which led to visible concern when he could not find the watch after winning the US Open in 2012.[129]

19.53 Yet, as seen previously in the discussion of passing off, endorsement, and trade marks, the legal basis for this may be slim. As also noted in respect of passing off, the courts remain rather sceptical of the place of commercial reality and benefiting from one's profile. An important example comes from the decision in *LNS*,[130] which involves the publication in a newspaper of the fact of a sexual relationship involving the then English men's football captain, John Terry, with the partner of another member of the team. For present purposes, the court had concerns about the material put before it, and considered that the main priority of Terry's business advisers was not privacy but the damage to commercialisation and sponsorship opportunities which could result.[131] This was perhaps understandable, given arguments that the sexual indiscretions of Tiger Woods led to him, and his sponsors, losing a significant amount of money.[132]

19.54 Whatever the attitude of the law, contracts involving image continue to exist, and give rise to their own disputes, such as *Proactive Sports Management v Rooney and others*.[133] The agreement, which was entered into when Wayne Rooney was very young, was ultimately found to be unenforceable as being in restraint of trade (see para 22.15); but no issues arose as to whether or not there was such a thing as image rights.[134]

Exercise

Look up *Proactive Sports Management v Rooney* [2010] EWHC 1807 (QB) (It is very long ...) Review the list of image rights extracted from the agreement, in paras 53 and 187 of the judgment, and details of brand development activities in paras 198 and 221–223. Reflect on this in the light of your work in this chapter so far.

Key point on sponsorship

• Image rights lie at the heart of commercially valuable contracts

[127] Olympics, Paralympics and London Olympics Association Rights (Infringement Proceedings) Regulations 2010 (SI 2010/2477); London Olympic Games and Paralympic Games Act 2006; D Cran and S Griffiths, 'Ambush marketing: sporting behaviour or fair play' (2003) *EntLR* 293, P Johnson, *Ambush Marketing and Brand Protection* (2011).

[128] http://www.heraldscotland.com/business/company-news/highland-spring-rises-to-top-of-uk-market.17355793.

[129] http://www.forbes.com/sites/paigereddinger/2012/09/11/tennis-champ-andy-murray-loses-watch-in-moment-of-victory/.

[130] See note 34.   [131] *LNS*, note 34, paras 39, 49–52, 97 et seq, 127, 131.

[132] See CR Knittel and V Stango, 'Celebrity endorsements, firm value and reputation risk: evidence from the Tiger Woods scandal' (9 February 2012), http://web.mit.edu/knittel/www/papers/tiger_latest.pdf; and G Golden, 'How much has Tiger Woods lost in endorsements' (11 August 2011), http://www.celebritynetworth.com/articles/entertainment-articles/how-much-has-tiger-woods-lost-in-endorsements/. For suggestions regarding future agreements, see S Boyd, 'Image rights contracts: morality clauses' (2011) *EntLR* 133.

[133] [2010] EWHC 1807 (QB).

[134] For an example of other disputes which can arise in relation to a sponsorship agreement, including the removal of a sponsor's name as part of a rebranding process and the extent to which this was a repudiatory breach, see *Force India Formula One Team Ltd v Etihad Airways PJSC* [2010] EWCA 1051, [2011] ETMR 10.

Control of (public) image

19.55   The English courts took a different approach to the impact of agreements regarding confidentiality and the photographs. As discussed in Chapter 18 and previously, despite the size of it, the Court of Appeal found that the wedding of Michael Douglas and Catherine Zeta-Jones. was a private wedding, and that photographs of it were confidential. Douglas and Zeta-Jones succeeded in an action for both breach of confidence and misuse of private information when *Hello!* magazine published unauthorised photographs. The issue of present interest, also touched on in Chapter 18 (see para 18.24), is whether or not *OK!* could sue *Hello!*

19.56   The Court of Appeal has found that it could not. The House of Lords[135] found, however, that Douglas, Zeta-Jones, and *OK!* had entered into agreement that each picture taken of the wedding would be a separate piece of information which *OK!* would have the exclusive right to publish—quite apart from the other pictures which had been published by *OK!*[136] So, *OK!* could sue *Hello!* Yet although this case confirms that celebrities can trade in their reputation or image, the focus must be on the trading, the contract,[137] and confidential information, rather than reputation, image,[138] and the market value of the information.[139]

Lord Hoffmann stated that:

> There is in my opinion no question of creating an 'image right' or any other unorthodox form of intellectual property. The information in this case was capable of being protected, not because it concerned the Douglases' image any more than because it concerned their private life, but simply because it was information of commercial value over which the Douglases' had sufficient control to enable them to impose an obligation of confidence.[140]

There have still been arguments that this risks turning information into a property right.[141] Conversely, there are both economic and dignitary-based justifications for celebrities to be able to control their reputation and public image.[142]

> ### Key point on agreements and control of information
>
> - There can be agreements that information is confidential. The parties to this can sue others if they publish it. This is not an image right

19.57   Other countries have different approaches to control of public image and personality. In New York, legislation provides that one should not use the name, portrait, or picture of a living person without consent.[143] In California, one should not use the name, voice, signature, or photograph without prior consent.[144] Germany has a law on 'personality rights',[145] though freedom of expression can prevail over

---

[135] *OBG Ltd v Allan* [2007] UKHL 21, [2002] 1 AC 1, [2007] 2 WLR 920 ('*Hello!* (HL)').

[136] *Hello!* (HL), note 135, per Lord Hoffmann at paras 122, 123 although compare Lord Nicholls at paras 257–259.

[137] *Hello!* (HL), note 135, per Lord Hoffmann at para 117.

[138] Although Lord Nicholls notes that the claim of Douglas and Zeta-Jones is based on image, *Hello!* (HL), note 135, paras 252–253.

[139] *Hello!* (HL), note 135, per Lord Walker at para 299.   [140] *Hello!* (HL), note 135, para 124; see also paras 118, 120.

[141] *Hello!* (HL) note 135, per Lord Walker at para 300.

[142] See Gurry, note 5, 348–356 and G Black, *Publicity Rights and Image: Exploitation and Legal Control* (2011).

[143] New York Civil Rights Law, art 5.   [144] California Civil Code, section 3344.

[145] Arts 1(1), 2(1), and 5(1), (2) Grundgesetz, and s 823(1) German Basic Law; see development prior to the 2012 *Hannover* decision, discussed at *Von Hannover* (2012), note 64, paras 41–45, 115–17, 123.

these (with more regard had to the personality rights of those under 18).[146] German copyright law requires that there must be consent to the publication of an image, but not if the publication involves an issue important to contemporary society.[147] Closer to home, Guernsey (which is not part of the UK) passed image rights legislation in 2012.

> ## Web links
>
> For a comparative project examining elements of personality protection carried out by SCRIPT, the AHRC Research Centre for Studies in Intellectual Property and Technology Law comprising responses to personality case studies from a number of different jurisdictions and a wiki containing a variety of information on the protection of personality, see **http://www.law.ed.ac.uk/ahrc/ files/92_pppcasestudiesfinaljan07.pdf**. Although this is no longer a live project, there is a still a lot of useful material to guide you in future work.

>
> ## Discussion point
>
> Should there be an image right in the UK? If so, what would it look like? You might find the Guernsey legislation, an interesting mix of copyright and trade mark law, a useful starting point. Guernsey Image Rights (Bailiwick of Guernsey) Ordinance, 2012.

Conclusions

19.58 The protection conferred in the UK in respect of control of information and reputation is very piecemeal. There is a right of privacy in respect of private information, and the decisions of ECtHR will have a key role in developing this—save where a contrary approach has been taken since the HRA 1998 by the House of Lords, now the Supreme Court. The position is more controversial and less clear in respect of what can broadly be termed a personality right. Personality merchandising is a common feature of daily commercial life, and much money is made by individuals and organisations through these activities; but it does not thereby follow that the individual has an enforceable right in respect of their personality, at least from the perspective of the arguments in favour of intellectual property, which were discussed in Chapter 1. It cannot, for example, be argued that a property right is necessary to encourage creativity because an ability to exploit personality tends to be a by-product of another facet of the personality— such as being a film star or famous athlete. Granting a 'personality' or 'image' right would add nothing more to the innovation/incentive/reward cycle. It also begs the question as to who precisely has created the 'celebrity'. Is it the individual or the inevitable media attention that attaches itself to certain 'personalities'? For now, the starting point for study and work in relation to reputation and information should not be what seems right, or commercial reality, but established principles of IP and rationales for them.

---

[146] See decision of the Federal Constitutional Court BVerG, 1 BvR 2499/09, 1 BvR 2503/09 (Jan 2012).
[147] Law in Copyright in Arts, ss 22 and 23.

Further reading

Books

John Adams, Julian Hickey, and Guy Tritton, *Merchandising Intellectual Property* (3rd edn, 2007)

H Beverley-Smith, *The Commercial Appropriation of Personality* (2002)

H Beverley-Smith, A Ohly, and A Lucas-Schloetter, *Privacy, Property and Personality: Civil Law Perspectives on Commercial Appropriation* (2005)

G Black, *Publicity Rights and Image: Exploitation and Legal Control* (2011)

E Christie Reid, *Personality, Confidentiality and Privacy in Scots Law* (2010)

S Smith, *Image, Persona and the Law* (2008)

M Warby, N Moreham, and I Christie (eds), *Tugendhat and Christie: The Law of Privacy and The Media* (2nd edn, 2011)

Articles

K Assaf Zakharov, 'The scope of protection of trade mark image—including comments on a recent decision of the Israeli Supreme Court' (2005) 36(7) IIC 787–808

E Barendt, 'Balancing freedom of expression and privacy: the jurisprudence of the Strasbourg Court' [2009] 1 JML 49–72

G Black, 'Privacy considered and jurisprudence consolidated: *Ferdinand v MGN Ltd*' [2012] EIPR 64

G Black, 'Publicity and image rights in Scots law' (2010) 14(4) Edin LR 364–384

H Carty, 'The common law and the quest for the IP effect' [2007] IPQ 237

J Coad, '*Reynolds, Flood* and the King's new clothes' (2011) 22(1) EntLR 1–10

F Hofmann, 'The right to publicity in German and English law' [2010] IPQ 325

J Klink, '50 years of publicity rights in the United States and the never ending hassle with intellectual property and personality rights in Europe' [2003] 4 IPQ 363–387

J Mitchiner, 'Intellectual property in image—a mere inconvenience' [2003] 2 IPQ 168–203

R Moosavian, 'Charting the journey from confidence to the new methodology' [2012] EIPR 324

N Moreham, 'The right to respect for private life in the European Convention on Human Rights: a re-examination' (2008) 1 EHRR 44–79

R Mulheron, 'A potential framework for privacy? A reply to *Hello!*' (2006) 69(5) MLR 679–713

L O'Leary, '"If it moves out there, we sell it": Super League and the intellectual property of rugby league players' (2011) 32(4) ECLR 178–185

B Pillans, 'Private lives in St Moritz: *Von Hannover v Germany* (no 2)' (2012) Comms L 63

T Pinto, 'A private and confidential update—not for publication' (2007) 18(5) EntLR 170–177

E Reid, 'Case comment. No sex please, we're European: *Mosley v News Group Newspapers Ltd*' [2009] Edin LR 116

A Schreiber, 'Confidence crisis, privacy phobia: why invasion of privacy should be independently recognised by English law' [2006] 2 IPQ 160–192

A Taubman, 'Is there a right of collective personality?' (2006) 28(9) EIPR 485–492

Websites

Bloomberg BNA Intellectual Property Blog Personality rights, publicity privacy http://www.bna.com/blogs_subtopic.aspx?category=Personality%20rights%2C%20publicity%20rights%2C%20privacy&blogid=12884902340

Hacked Off http://hackinginquiry.org/about-2/

Leveson Inquiry http://www.levesoninquiry.org.uk/

Part VII

Intellectual property, free movement of goods, and competition law in Europe

Introduction

This Part of the book has two chapters. The first chapter explains and discusses the interaction between free movement of goods and intellectual property rights and the second the interaction between intellectual property rights and EU competition law.

There are four fundamental freedoms prescribed in the Treaty of Rome: freedom of movement of goods, persons, services, and capital. The goal is to establish the common market of the Union: there should not be any trade barriers or obstacles as between the member states. However, in the domain of IP, the exercise of the rights can, and do, pose problems for the free movement of goods and thus the creation of the common market. A key theme in Chapter 20 is as to how the tensions between the exercise of intellectual property by right holders and the achievement of a common market have been reconciled. Intellectual property rights also confer a right to control on the holder, albeit one carefully crafted to provide a balance between innovation and other public interest goals. But sometimes the exercise of IP rights can produce unexpected outcomes, conferring on the holder an over-strong monopoly through which the right holder may occupy a position of strength which may in turn hamper competition in the marketplace; or owners of intellectual property rights may enter into agreements which may not, ultimately, be to the benefit of consumers. Chapter 21 contains a discussion on when EU competition law may be used to curb the anti-competitive effects of the exercise of intellectual property rights within the marketplace.

Sources of the law: key websites

- Consolidated versions of the founding treaties of the European Community (now Union)
  http://eur-lex.europa.eu/en/treaties/index.htm

- For the case law of the Court of Justice of the European Union/ECJ and General Court/CFI see
  http://www.curia.europa.eu/
- For decisions of the courts in the various jurisdictions of the UK, see BAILII
  http://www.bailii.org/
- For a full list of the various notices issued by the Commission relating to competition rules, see
  http://ec.europa.eu/competition/antitrust/legislation/entente3_en.html
- For details of the notices and communications issued by the Commission in relation to the modernisation of EU competition rules and procedures, see
  http://ec.europa.eu/competition/antitrust/overview_en.html
- The Technology Transfer Block Exemption Regulation ((EC) No 772/2004 of 27 April 2004)
  http://eur-lex.europa.eu/LexUriServ/LexUriServ.do?uri=CELEX:32004R0772:EN:NOT

Free movement of goods and intellectual property rights

Introduction

20.1 The purpose of this chapter is to discuss the European rules on the free movement of goods as they impact on intellectual property rights.

There are four fundamental freedoms in European Union trade law: the freedom of movement of goods, persons, services and capital. The achievement of these freedoms is prescribed in the Treaty of Rome as a means to establish the common market of the Community (and now the Union): there should not be any trade barriers or obstacles as between the member states.

However, in the domain of intellectual property, the existence and exercise of the rights can, and do, pose problems for the free movement of goods and thus the creation of the common market. How then should the aim of establishing and maintaining a common market be reconciled with the existence and exercise of intellectual property rights?

20.2 ### Learning objectives

By the end of this chapter you should be able to describe and explain:

- the competing interests and pressures that underlie this area of the law;
- what is meant by 'consent' as it relates to free movement of goods and how it operates in particular cases;
- when a trade mark proprietor might have a legitimate interest to oppose the free circulation of goods;
- the rules on international exhaustion;
- the differences between free movement of goods and services.

Scope and overview of chapter

20.3   The first part of this chapter explains the tensions that arise between the aims of creating a common market and intellectual property with particular reference to the Treaty provisions relevant to this area, and then moves to examine the competing interests that underlie this area. The next part will focus on case law development, and in particular how the European Court of Justice (ECJ) has sought to reconcile the tensions between the owner of the intellectual property right (IPR) and the parallel importer. A particularly important facet in this is the notion of consent by the intellectual property owner to the placing of the protected goods on the market. While the IP owner will often not be able to oppose the movement of protected goods once they have been placed on the market, there are circumstances in which the IP owner will have legitimate reasons to prevent further dealings. These will be examined in the next part of the chapter. Discussion will then move to the concept of international exhaustion and examine whether exhaustion applies only within the EU, or whether it extends beyond the borders of the territory. Finally, the chapter will consider the free movement of services with a particular focus on how those rules differ from the free movement of goods. As will be seen, the majority of the cases have arisen in relation to registered trade marks. Note that there have been changes to the names of and Article numbers within key European treaties and institutions. When these are discussed, as indicated in the Preface, the present names (eg Article 34 TFEU) will be used) will be used, unless it is clearer to use the term in place at the time, when discussing arguments made in a case.

So the rest of the chapter looks like this:

- Tensions between the aims of the common market and those of intellectual property (20.4–20.10)
- Free movement of goods: case law development (20.11–20.32)
- Legitimate reasons for using a trade mark to prevent further dealing (20.33–20.47)
- International exhaustion (20.48–20.65)
- Free movement of services (20.66–20.72)

Tensions between the aims of the common market and those of intellectual property

20.4   The purpose of Article 34 of the Treaty on the Functioning of the European Union (TFEU) (ex Art 28 of the EC Treaty (EC)) is to ensure that restrictions to be found within member states that would inhibit the free movement of goods throughout the Community, and thus the creation of a common market, are prohibited.

> Quantitative restrictions on imports and all measures having equivalent effect shall be prohibited between Member States.

This is subject to certain provisos to be found in Article 36 TFEU (ex Art 30 EC). These include measures that would restrict the free movement of goods justified on the grounds of the protection of industrial and commercial property.

> The provisions of Articles 34 and 35 shall not preclude prohibitions or restrictions on imports, exports or goods in transit justified on grounds of public morality, public policy or public security; the protection of health and life of humans, animals or plants; the protection of national treasures possessing artistic, historic or archaeological value; or the protection of industrial and commercial property. Such prohibitions or restrictions shall not, however, constitute a means of arbitrary discrimination or a disguised restriction on trade between Member States.

Early case law concerning Article 34 TFEU (ex Art 28 EC) showed a determination by the ECJ to prioritise the goal of the creation of a single market. In 1979 in *Cassis de Dijon*[1] the ECJ laid down the general rule:

> In the absence of common rules, obstacles to movement within the Community resulting from disparities between the national laws relating to the marketing of a product must be accepted in so far as those provisions may be recognized as being necessary in order to satisfy mandatory requirements relating in particular to the effectiveness of fiscal supervision, the protection of public health, the fairness of commercial transactions and the defence of the consumer.[2]

One of the difficulties the Court has faced in application of Article 28 (ex Art 28 EC) to the intellectual property sphere is Article 345 TFEU (ex Art 295 EC).

> This Treaty shall in no way prejudice the rules in Member States governing the system of property ownership ...

The rules granting IPRs to those entitled is a system of property ownership. The task for the Court was thus to reconcile these tensions.

Overview of the competing interests

20.5   The essence of an IP right is that it gives to the owner a monopoly in the subject matter of the right for a defined period of time. In addition, and as has been explained in preceding chapters, the rights are mostly limited to a single territory. Thus, the owner of a particular IP right in one territory (eg a trade mark, patent or copyright) could use that right to prevent goods bearing the same or a similar mark, an invention which would infringe the patent, or a work protected by copyright, from entering another territory in which the right subsists. That is so even if the IP right is owned by the same person in the two different territories.

For example, if Company X has a registered trade mark in country A, and the same registered trade mark for the same goods in country B, the nature of the right conferred by the trade mark could enable Company X to prevent goods sold in country B from being imported into country A and sold there. Thus the owner of the IP right could partition the market by virtue of the ownership of the right in the various different territories.

This partitioning of the market could lead to price differentials as between the territories. In country A, Company X could sell the product for £10, but in country B for £5. An entrepreneur (parallel importer) might look at these price differentials and decide that if the goods were bought in country B and imported into country A, the goods could be sold below the price normally charged in country A whilst still giving the parallel importer a profit. If Company X, as the right holder, were able to prevent the importation of the goods into country A, so the common market would be partitioned. This could lead to consumers paying different prices for the same goods depending on where they were purchased.[3]

20.6   The rules on free movement of goods, as they have been developed at European level, are designed to avoid this outcome whilst taking into account Article 345 TFEU (ex Art 295 EC). This has been achieved primarily by the ECJ (now Court of Justice) looking behind the monopolistic nature of IPRs to the

---

[1] Case 120/78 *Rewe-Zentral AG v Bundesmonopolverwaltung fur Branntwein* [1979] ECR 649.
[2] *Rewe-Zentral*, para 8.
[3] There are, of course, many reasons, from the perspective of the IP owner, why the goods may be put onto the territories at different prices. Each national market has its own characteristics: the tax system; regulatory requirements (in particular in the pharmaceutical industry); costs of manufacture; exchange rate fluctuations; etc. WR Cornish, D Llewelyn and T Aplin, *Intellectual Property: Patents, Copyright, Trade Marks and Allied Rights* (7th edn, 2010), paras 1–48, 19–02.

reason for their existence and the specific subject matter. It was argued that the reason for the existence of IPRs is to obtain an economic return. Therefore, right holders are given the exclusive right to place the goods which are the subject of the IPR on the market within the Community for the first time; thereafter the right holder is unable to prevent further circulation of those goods throughout the Community. The right holder is then said to have *exhausted* the rights associated with the IP right. However, it is important to note that the rights are only exhausted in relation to further movement of those goods throughout the market, and not in respect of other rights associated with the IP.

Policy arguments

20.7   Application of the rules on free movement of goods and their interface with IP takes place against a background containing diverse views—political, social, and economic—as well as differing national regulatory regimes designed to achieve domestic goals but which can conflict with European strategies. At its most basic the exhaustion rule states that where goods which are the subject of the IPR are put on the market within the European Economic Area (EEA) by the right holder or with his consent, then the right holder may not object to movement of the physical object around the territory of the EEA. Right holders can however stop the import of goods into the EEA where those goods have been placed on the market outwith the Community.

The market

20.8   An IP owner will often argue that maintaining price differences as between territories is an essential part of any business strategy. In some circumstances, there may be no choice, for instance in the case of pharmaceuticals the price may be set by the national regulatory authority. In other cases, consumers in one jurisdiction may be more willing to pay more for goods than in others: some freedom for the IP owner to cross-subsidise costs as between jurisdictions may be seen as fundamental to economic survival. Other factors, such as labour and material costs, also have a bearing on the eventual price to be charged to the consumer. In addition, IP owners (in particular, trade mark proprietors) like to control the way in which their goods are presented and sold to the consumer. If this control is absent, so the brand image may be undermined as where luxury items are sold in what are perceived to be shoddy surroundings. If that happens, then the IP owner may be discouraged from developing new products. This in turn will reduce consumer choice.

Parallel traders on the other hand team up with the consumer to argue that the exhaustion rule actually benefits consumers. In a market with no barriers, prices will fall and so consumers pay less for the goods.

As between the IP owner and the parallel trader, the conflicts arise because of the profits that can be made from moving goods from one market (the cheaper market) to another (the more expensive market). Who should profit from the differential in prices? Should the IP owner be able to maintain the price differences? Or should the parallel trader be able to take advantage of them to their financial benefit?

The governments

20.9   But just as there are disagreements between those who operate within the markets, so there are disagreements at a political level. One conflict looks to the domestic interests of the member states. To what extent should governments be able to rely on national interests in any one sector (such as health care) to undermine the fundamental goal of the creation of a single market? Another discussion looks to the Community as a whole. Should the exhaustion rule only apply within the Community, or should a broad, international rule of exhaustion be favoured? If consumer interests are at the forefront of thinking, then that might (but not necessarily) call for a rule of international exhaustion if the effect would be a reduction in prices. If, on the other hand, it is the interests of economic entities within the Community together with promoting investment within its boundaries that is of prime concern, then is it not preferable to maintain barriers at the boundaries of the territory?

The theorists

20.10   And then there are the theoretical and philosophical underpinnings of the various IPRs. The exhaustion rule applies to all IPRs, although, and as will be discussed later, it is in the realm of patents, and in particular trade marks, that most problems arise. The application of an exhaustion rule to the exercise of IPRs raises the question as to how the existence of the right is justified, and whether a tension arises as between the justification of the right and the rules on free movement of goods. For those IPRs which rest on the incentive/innovation/reward theories, should the owner not be the one to have control over movement of protected goods so that the reward can be gained in the manner in which the IP owner anticipated? But what of those IPRs, notably trade marks, where the existence of the right is as a guarantee of origin to the consumer? What justification could there be for the right holder to control movement of goods to which the mark has been affixed once they have been placed on the market anywhere in the world with the consent of the right holder? And why should the exhaustion rule operate in the context of tangible articles embodying the IP, but not in relation to transient rights such as the performance right in copyright?

 Question 1

As will be noted in the following discussion, many of the cases which have shaped this area of the law have concerned trade marks, with patents coming in second place. Fewer cases have been brought in the domain of copyright. Why might this be the case? Revisit your answer when you have finished this chapter.

Question 2

Which countries are members of the EEA and not the EU?

Key points on the goals of free movement of goods

- The rules on free movement of goods seek to reconcile the tensions between Articles 34, 36, and 345 TFEU (ex Arts 28, 36, and 295 EC).

Free movement of goods: case law development

20.11   Through a series of cases starting in 1971, the ECJ and national courts sought to develop rules which balance the interests of the IP holder with those of the parallel trader and the creation of a common market.

Some of the terms that are used in case law in this area include:

- Existence
- Exercise
- Specific subject matter
- Exhaustion
- Free movement of goods

 Exercise

Explain what you think might be meant by these terms. Revisit your definitions when you have completed this chapter.

Note that the numbering of the relevant Articles has changed twice: Article 34 TFEU (ex Art 28, ex Art 30); Article 36 TFEU (ex Art 30, ex Art 36); and Article 345 TFEU (ex Art 295, ex Art 222). Again, the Article numbering which applies following the changes made by the Treaty of Lisbon will be used in this chapter except where the discussion relates to historical events and/or where quotations from cases are used in the text.

20.12   The first case to consider the interaction between IPRs and the free movement of goods was *Deutsche Grammophon GmbH v Metro SB Grossmarkte GmbH & Co*.[4] Deutsche Grammophon (DG) produced records. In Germany it supplied them under the 'Polydor' mark to retailers. In the agreement with the retailers DG not only controlled retail prices but also required an undertaking from the retailers that they would only import goods from elsewhere with the agreement of DG which would only be given if the retailers agreed to sell the goods at the maintained price. DG exported records to a subsidiary in Paris. These goods were re-exported and imported into Germany where Metro, not part of DG and not part of the distribution chain, sold them below the price fixed in Germany.

Diagram 20.1 *Deutsche Grammophon GmbH v Metro SB Grossmarkte GmbH & Co*

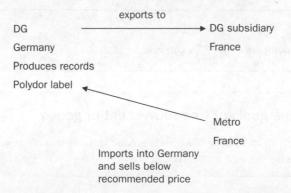

The effect of this was to undermine the system that DG had put into place to maintain retail prices in Germany. The case was ultimately referred to the ECJ. In passing judgment the Court said:

> the Treaty does not affect the existence of the industrial property rights conferred by the national legislation of a member-State, the exercise of these rights may come within the prohibitions of the Treaty. Although Article 36

---

[4] [1971] CMLR 631.

permits prohibitions or restrictions on the free movement of goods that are justified for the protection of industrial and commercial property, it only allows such restrictions on the freedom of trade to the extent that they are justified for the protection of the rights that form the specific object of this property.[5]

20.13 So here we see the ECJ making a distinction between the existence of an IP right, the exercise of that right, and the specific object or subject matter of the right. These have been further developed in subsequent case law.

Existence, exercise, and specific subject matter

20.14 In *Centrafarm v Sterling & Winthrop*[6] the ECJ was faced with questions concerning the movement of patented drugs between the Netherlands and the UK. Sterling held parallel patents for a drug in the Netherlands and the UK and had placed drugs protected by the patent on both markets. Centrafarm, without the permission of Sterling, purchased the patented drugs in the UK and imported them into the Netherlands where prices were higher. This was challenged by Sterling.

Diagram 20.2 *Centrafarm v Sterling & Winthrop*

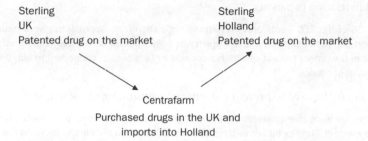

The ECJ said that the use of an exclusive right granted by a patent to prevent imports was an exercise of rights which was incompatible with the provisions of the Treaty on free movement of goods.

The specific subject matter of industrial property is to reward the creative effort of the inventor. The inventor thus has the exclusive right to use an invention with a view to manufacturing industrial products and to put them into circulation for the first time either directly or by way of a grant of a licence to a third party. In addition the inventor has the right to oppose infringements.[7] Any derogation from the principle of free movement of goods is not justified where the product, protected by the right, has been put onto the market by the patentee himself or with his consent.[8]

So in this case the ECJ alluded to the specific subject matter of industrial property as being the economic reward that can be obtained from exploitation. However, once that has been obtained—through putting the goods on the market for the first time—the right to prevent further circulation is exhausted. In addition, the ECJ mentioned consent. This is central to the concept of free movement of goods: the goods must have been placed on the market by the right holder or with his consent. Subsequent case law has helped to refine what is meant by consent.

20.15 It should be noted that the existence/exercise dichotomy has been criticised by commentators who have pointed out that it is not the exercise of rights that inhibits the free movement of goods, but measures to be found in national legislations. Further, the existence of an IPR could be considered worthless unless

[5] *Deutsche Grammophon*, para 11. [6] [1974] ECR 1147. [7] *Centrafarm* note 6, para 9. [8] *Centrafarm* note 6, para 11.

the owner is able to exercise it. It is a concept that has been less mentioned in the more recent case law, where focus is on the specific object or the specific subject matter of the right.[9]

> **Question**
>
> What have courts said to be the specific subject matter of different IP rights? Do you agree? How does this relate to the pharmaceutical cases you will consider later, and also the underlying justifications for IP discussed in Chapter 1?

Consent

20.16   A central feature in this area relates to the notion of consent. The ECJ has repeatedly said that where protected goods have been placed on the market by the right holder or with the consent of the right holder, then no objection may be made to further movement of the goods throughout the territory of the common market.

For example and in relation to patents:

> Articles 30 and 36 of the EEC Treaty prevent national legislation from applying to give a patentee the right to prohibit the import and marketing of a product which was legally placed on the market of another member-State by the proprietor of the patent himself or with his consent or by a person connected to him by a relationship of legal or economic dependence.[10]

The justification lies in the need to prevent the artificial partitioning of the market:

> In fact, if the patentee were able to prohibit the import of products covered by the patent which had been marketed in another member-State by him or with his consent he would be enabled to partition the national markets and thus to put into effect a restriction on trade between member-States without such restriction being necessary to ensure that he obtains the substance of the exclusive rights arising under parallel patents.[11]

20.17   Consent by the proprietor of a trade mark to marketing goods in the EEA by a third party who has no economic link may be implied where it can be inferred from facts and circumstances prior to, simultaneous with, or subsequent to the marketing where it can be unequivocally demonstrated that the proprietor has renounced his exclusive rights.[12]

Common origin and consent

20.18   An early case which concerned coffee and the Hag trade mark, originally held by one proprietor but later by different proprietors for different territories, is *Van Zuylen Freres v Hag AC*.[13] The Hag mark was owned both in Germany and in Belgium by the same company. During the war, the Belgian mark was

---

[9] Cornish, Llewelyn and Aplin, note 3, para 19-05. Note also that for these issues to arise at all there must be what appears to be an infringing act (eg selling, making). In the copyright case, Case C-456/06 *Peek & Cloppenburg KG v Cassina SpA* [2008] ECR I-2731 the ECJ found that the display and use of items in a shop did not infringed an IP owner's distribution right (Art 4(1) of the InfoSoc Directive 2001/29), as the relevant provision required transfer of ownership which did not occur here (see para 36).

[10] Case C-19/84 *Pharmon v Hoescht BV* [1985] ECR 2281 ECJ, para 22.   [11] *Pharmon* note 10, para 23.

[12] Case C-324/08 *Makro Zelfbedieningsgroothandel e.a. v Diesel Spa* [2009] ECR I-10019. See also para 20.54.

[13] [1974] ECR 731.

Diagram 20.3 *Van Zuylen Freres v Hag Ac*

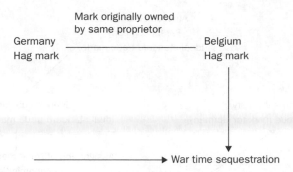

sequestrated and ownership passed to a third party. The owner of the Hag mark in Germany wanted to import coffee bearing the mark into Belgium.

The ECJ found that by virtue of the fact that the mark was originally held by one proprietor (a common origin), entitled the German owner, Van Zuylen, to market the goods in the Benelux countries.

There was much disquiet amongst commentators as a result of this case.[14] If the facts—where the trade mark had been passed to a third party and there remained no control with the original owner—entitled the owner to market goods bearing the mark in the country, why not then permit any unconnected third party to market goods in a country where the same (or similar) IPR might belong to a totally independent unconnected third party?

20.19   The ECJ had a chance to revisit its judgment in 1990 in *SA CNL-Sucal NV v Hag GV*.[15] By this time CNL owned the Hag mark for its business in Belgium. CNL sought to import its products bearing the Hag mark into Germany. The ECJ, reversing its earlier judgment, said that CNL had no right to go into the German market. No consent had been given by the German proprietor of the trade mark.

20.20   This more sophisticated appreciation of the function of a trade mark was further refined in *IHT Internationale Heiztechnik GmbH v Ideal Standard GmbH*[16] (Ideal Standard) where a question arose over the import of bathroom accessories from France into Germany. The Ideal Standard trade mark was owned by a US firm. This firm had subsidiaries in both Germany and France which held the trade marks for those territories. The Ideal Standard trade mark in France was assigned to a third party which had no legal or economic ties with either the US firm or with the German subsidiary of the US firm. IHT then sought to import goods bearing the mark from France into Germany. The German subsidiary objected and brought proceedings for infringement.

The ECJ said that the German subsidiary could indeed keep the goods bearing the trade mark from being imported into Germany. A trade mark is a guarantee of quality. There was no control by the German subsidiary or the US parent company over the goods manufactured by the French assignee under the Ideal Standard trade mark. The division of the mark through the assignment had the effect of depriving the original proprietor (the US firm) of any form of quality control over the goods manufactured under the mark.

> This principle known as exhaustion of rights applies where the owner of the trade mark in the importing State and the owner of the trade mark in the exporting State are the same or where even if they are separate persons they

---

[14] Cornish, Llewelyn and Aplin, note 3, para 19-06.   [15] [1990] ECR I-3711.   [16] [1994] ECR I-2789

Diagram 20.4 *IHT Internationale Heiztechnik GmbH v Ideal Standard GmbH*

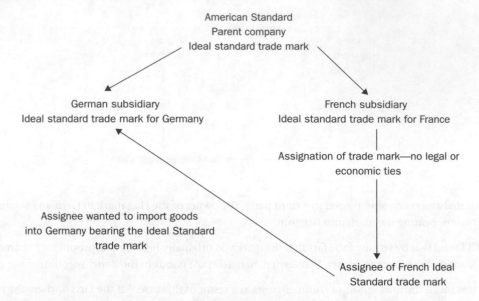

are economically linked. A number of situations are covered: products put into circulation by the same undertaking, but a licensee, a parent company, a subsidiary of the same group or by an exclusive distributor.[17]

Specifically relating to trade marks, the ECJ said in *Ideal Standard* that the decisive factor is whether the trade mark owner has the possibility of control over goods to which the mark is affixed to the country of exportation and the quality of goods that were placed on the market. If it did have such control, then it would be seen as having consented to the marketing.

 Exercise

What would have been the position if the agreement between the French subsidiary and the French assignee was not at arm's length thus enabling both the German subsidiary and the French assignee to keep goods belonging to the other out of their respective territories? Consider *Consten and Grundig v Commission* (1966) ECR 299 in para 21.23 and *Doncaster Pharmaceuticals Group Ltd v The Bolton Pharmaceutical Company Ltd* [2006] EWCA Civ 661 in para 21.74.

20.21 Consent thus refers to the consent by the right holder to the placing of the protected goods onto the common market for the first time. However, and as can be seen from *Ideal Standard*, consent is not limited to that given by the right holder as such, but extends also to circumstances where a right holder and the person placing the goods on the market, are economically linked.

---

[17] *Ideal Standard*, para 34.

Differing levels of protection in member states and no consent

20.22   Circumstances arise in which there may be differing levels of protection for IPRs in member states, or protection may exist in one country but not in another. If the owner of the IP right has not consented to the marketing, then he may invoke his right to prevent importation into the country where the right exists.

20.23   In *EMI Electrola GmbH v Patricia Im-und Export*[18] the sound recording right in Cliff Richard's songs was extant under German law but had expired in Denmark. Patricia attempted to import the sound recordings from Denmark into Germany.

Diagram 20.5 *EMI Electrola GmbH v Patricia Im-und Export*

Cliff Richard songs

Germany	Denmark
Sound recording right extant	Sound recordings right expired
Owned by EMI	Patricia sought to import into Germany

The Court held that as the copyright owner, the manufacturer, and importer were unconnected parties, no consent had been given to the marketing of the recordings in Germany. EMI could invoke its copyright in the sound recording in Germany to prevent the importation as its rights had not been exhausted.

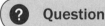

? Question

This case led to the enactment of an EU Directive. Which one?[19]

20.24   A not dissimilar set of circumstances arose in *Sony Music Entertainment (Germany) GmbH v Falcon Neue Medien Vertrieb GmbH*[20] but with the twist that copyright was argued to subsist with respect to US recordings made before 1 January 1966 by Bob Dylan. Sony sought to enjoin Falcon from copying and distributing two Bob Dylan songs in Germany. Falcon argued that those songs were never subject to copyright protection in Germany. The ECJ ruled that 'the term of protection laid down in Directive 2006/116 [the Directive on the term of protection of copyright and related rights] is also applicable ... where the subject matter at issue has at no time been protected in the Member State in which the protection is sought'. This is so because the Bob Dylan recordings were subject to copyright protection in the UK, which affords protection to US recordings made before 1 January 1966. According to the court, since the US recordings of Bob Dylan's songs were protected in at least one member state (the UK), Sony, as the current rights holder, could sue for copyright infringement in any member state (eg Germany) even though the recordings were never protected under the national copyright laws of Germany.[21]

---

[18] [1989] ECR 79.

[19] See also *Warner Bros v Christiansen* [1988] ECR 2605 dealing with the rental of videos in Denmark which had been manufactured in the UK where no rental right subsisted.

[20] Case C-240/07 [2009] ECR I-263.

[21] Regarding criminal prosecutions in one member state relating to goods which are not the subject of copyright in another member state, see the decision of Court of Justice in Case C 5/11 *Titus Alexander Jochen Donner* [2012] ECDR 18.

Different levels of protection in member states and consent

20.25 The ECJ has also considered circumstances in which no protection exists in one country but the owner has consented to the marketing of products protected by IP.

20.26 In *Merck & Co Inc v Stephar BV*,[22] Merck put drugs on the market in Italy, a country in which no patent protection for the drugs could be obtained at the relevant time. Merck did have a patent for the drugs in the Netherlands. Stephar purchased the drugs in Italy and sought to import them into the Netherlands. Merck invoked its patent rights in the Netherlands to prevent the importation. Merck acknowledged that it had consented to the marketing of the drugs in Italy, but argued that since no patent protection could be obtained there, it should not be seen as having exhausted its rights.

Stephar purchased in Italy and sought to import into Netherlands. The ECJ said that since consent had been given to the marketing of the drugs in Italy, Merck could not invoke its patent to prevent their importation into the Netherlands.

Diagram 20.6 *Merck & Co Inc v Stephar BV*

Merck	Merck
Italy—no protection possible	Netherlands—patent protection
Drugs on the market with consent	

⟶

20.27 This view was subsequently reaffirmed in *Merck & Co v Primecrown Ltd*.[23] Merck held patents in the UK for drugs which they also marketed in Spain and Portugal where protection was not obtainable. The price of the drugs was fixed by the respective governments. Merck argued that they had ethical obligations to place the drugs on the market in these countries to meet the requirements of the population. However, the ECJ did not find this argument sufficient to change the rule in *Merck v Stephar*. The Court pointed out that any anomalies that existed as between member states arising from differences in protection in the territories were disappearing with the harmonisation programme. The Court did note that if legal compulsion exists which requires marketing in a particular country, then the patent owner would not be deemed to have consented to the marketing.[24] However, ethical considerations did not provide sufficient certainty to determine when an IP owner is deprived of the power to determine how to market a product. Against this backdrop it is interesting to note the new approaches taken to this question in the accession agreements for new member states, for example that of Poland.[25]

 Question

What do you think of the argument deployed by Merck that it had ethical obligations to place the drugs on the territories in which no protection existed? Could ethical obligations ever give sufficient basis to enable an IP owner to argue successfully that there was no consent in relation to the marketing of a product?

---

[22] [1981] ECR 2063.   [23] [1996] ECR I-6285.

[24] See also *Pharmon* note 10 where drugs produced under a compulsory licence were not subject to exhaustion; also Case C-24/67 *Parke Davis & Co v Probel & Centrafarm* [1968] ECR 55 where goods were placed on a market without the consent of the trade mark owner where no protection existed.

[25] This was considered in *Merck Canada Inc v Sigma Pharmaceuticals plc* [2012] EWPCC 18.

Consent and the pharmaceutical industry

20.28 Both of the *Merck* cases involved the pharmaceutical industry. Health care is a domain in which much governmental regulation exists in member states in relation to prices, packaging, and availability of drugs and many other aspects of the industry. The ECJ has long held that price differences as between member states resulting from governmental measures make no difference to the rules on exhaustion and the goal of attaining a common market.[26] But questions continue to be raised and referred to the ECJ in this area. One concerning the interaction between competition law and free movement of goods first arose in *Syfait v GSK*.[27] The Greek Government requires that medicines sold in Greece are so sold at the lowest price prevailing on the European market. GSK supplied wholesalers with drugs but found that many batches were being onward sold by parallel traders in other territories where the price was higher. GSK decided to limit the supply of these products to the Greek wholesalers to the quantities needed to fulfil local need. The question arose as to whether it was an abuse of a dominant position (Art 82 EC [ex 86], post Lisbon Art 102 TFEU) for GSK to refuse to fill the wholesalers' orders where the intention was to limit parallel trade.[28]

In the event, the ECJ declined jurisdiction, as the questions had not been referred by a competent tribunal within the meaning of Article 234 of the EC Treaty (post Lisbon Art 267 TFEU). The Advocate General Francis Jacob's Opinion is, however, of interest.

The Advocate General noted that an intention to restrain parallel trade would probably be a reason to condemn a refusal to supply, but that in certain circumstances it might be permitted. There were instances where parallel trade might result in inadequate supplies being available. Because parallel importers sourced products from the cheapest country, pharmaceutical companies might delay or stop the supply of drugs in countries where the price was lowest. The benefits of parallel trade would go to the wholesalers in the countries were prices were limited at the lowest level and not to the patients or to those paying for their treatment. It was thus the effect of the national law in fixing the price that would be paid for the drugs that segregated the market and not, in the instant case, the behaviour of GSK.

20.29 The same questions were referred to the Court by the Efetio Athinon in Joined Cases *Sot. Lelos Kai Sia EE and others v Glaxosmith-Kline Aeve Farmadeftikon Proionton (formerly Glaxowellcome Aeve)*[29] (see also para 21.55) The ECJ ruled that a dominant undertaking that refuses to meet ordinary orders from wholesalers in order to put a stop to parallel exports carried out by those wholesalers from one member state to another abuses its dominant position; it is for the national court to decide whether the orders are ordinary. A company could however counter, in a reasonable and proportionate manner, orders where the supplies were destined for the parallel market. So it is clear from this ruling that a company may act to limit orders where parallel markets are being supplied, the key difficulty being to determine what might be ordinary, and in the event that it is thought that an order does not fall within this category, the need to respond in a reasonable and proportionate manner. As with repackaging cases, there is much grey area between what is permissible from the perspective of the company and what it not. It is likely that there will be further case law to clarify the boundaries.[30]

[26] Case C-15/74 *Centrafarm v Sterling* (1974) ECR 1147.
[27] *Synetairismos Farmakopoion Aitolias & Akarnanias (Syfait) and others v GlaxoSmithKline plc* [2005] ECR I-4609.
[28] For discussion on EU competition law under Art 101 TFEU (ex Art 81 EC), see Chapter 21.
[29] Joined Cases C-468/06 to C-478/06 [2008] ECR I-7139.
[30] For a case concerning competition, copyright, and conditional access services, see para 20.68.

> **❓ Question**
>
> Read the Opinion of the Advocate General in *Syfait v GSK* [2005] ECR I-7139 (also [2005] 5 CMLR
> 1) and of the ECJ in the *Sot. Lelos Kai* case. Read also Chapter 21 on competition law. Do you think
> it should be permissible for an entity in a dominant position to limit supply in order to prevent
> parallel trade? What weight should be placed on the right of a company to take reasonable and pro-
> portional steps to protect its own commercial interests? Who benefits from this, and who might be
> prejudiced? Should the rule be limited to the pharmaceutical industry or be more widely applicable?

Licence terms and consent

20.30   A question arises as to the interaction between licence terms and consent. Specifically whether exhaustion applies where a licensee of a trade mark places goods on the market in contravention of the
licence terms.

■ Case C-59/08 *Copad SA v Christian Dior Couture SA* [2009] ECR I-34210

Christian Dior (Dior) entered into a trade mark licence agreement with Societe industrielle lingerie
(SIL) to manufacture and distribute luxury corsetry goods bearing the Christian Dior trade mark. In
contravention of an express provision in the licence agreement, SIL sold goods bearing the Christina
Dior trade mark to Copad, which operated discount stores and was outside Dior's selective distribution network. Dior sued SIL and Copad for trade mark infringement. The ECJ ruled that a 'licensee who
puts goods bearing a trade mark on the market in disregard of a provision in a licence agreement does
so without the consent of the proprietor of the trade mark where it is established that the provision in
question is included in those listed in art.8(2) of ... [the Trade Marks] Directive'.[31]

The list in Article 8(2), which the Court said was exhaustive, provides:

> The proprietor of a trade mark may invoke the rights conferred by that trade mark against a licensee who contra-
> venes any provision in his licensing contract with regard to its duration, the form covered by the registration in
> which the trade mark may be used, the scope of the goods or services for which the licence is granted, the terri-
> tory in which the trade mark may be affixed, or the quality of the goods manufactured or of the services provided
> by the licensee.

Thus, if a breach of contract falls within Article 8(2), consent will be considered to have been withdrawn
and the licensee will infringe the trade mark.

Absence of consent

20.31   There have been examples of cases where no consent by or on behalf of the IP owner has been given and
hence the IP owner can prohibit the movement of the goods. One example is given previously (para
20.23) in *EMI Electrola v Patricia*.[32] Another example was in *Terrapin (Overseas) Ltd v Terranova Industrie
CA Kapferer & Co.*[33] The question there was whether the German firm, Terranova Industrie, could prevent the importation into Germany from Britain of prefabricated houses bearing the mark 'Terrapin'.

---

[31] Case C-59/08 *Copad SA v Christian Dior Couture SA* [2009] ECR I-3421, para 51.   [32] [1989] ECR 79.
[33] Case C-119/75 [1976] ECR 1039 (ECJ). See also Case T-168/01 *GlaxoSmithKline Services Unlimited v Commission of the European
Communities* [2006] 5 CMLR 29 for a differential pricing system for drugs in Spain and questions of competition law.

The German firm had registration of the mark 'Terranova' in Germany for construction materials. Thus, both the marks and the goods were similar. As there had never been a connection between the firms (unlike in the *Hag* situation), the ECJ ruled that the German firm could indeed keep the products bearing the Terrapin mark out of Germany. This is consistent with the basic principles of trade mark law. Indeed, the ECJ pointed out that 'If in such a case the principle of the free movement of goods were to prevail over the protection given by the respective national laws, the specific objective of industrial and commercial property rights would be undermined'. Protection thus had to be ensured for the 'legitimate use' of the rights conferred by national laws.[34]

20.32   Where the right owner has been required to place goods on the market as under a compulsory licence, in contrast with the ethical points discussed previously, the goods will not be seen as having been placed on the market by or with the consent of the IP owner who will be able to prevent further movement of the goods.

■ **Case C-19/84 *Pharmon v Hoescht* [1985] ECR 2281**

Hoescht held a drug patent in the UK and the Netherlands. A compulsory licence was obtained in the UK by DDSA Pharmaceuticals Ltd to manufacture the drug in the UK, but subject to a prohibition on export. DDSA ignored the prohibition and sold the drug to Pharmon which intended to market it in the Netherlands. Hoescht challenged this on the basis of its patent in the Netherlands. As Hoescht had not consented to the manufacture and marketing in the UK, there was no consent, and thus the sale of the drugs in the Netherlands could be prevented.

> It should be emphasised in this respect that when the competent authorities in a member-State, ... grant a compulsory licence to a third party which allows him to carry out manufacturing and marketing operations which the patentee would normally have the power to prohibit, the patentee cannot be regarded as having consented to the actions of the third party. In fact, the holder of the patent is deprived by such an official act of his right to decide freely on the conditions under which he will place his product on the market.[35]

> **Key points on consent**
> - Consent by the right holder is fundamental to free movement of goods
> - Consent means consent to placing goods on the common market for the first time, thereafter the right holder may not object to further distribution of those goods

Legitimate reasons for using a trade mark to prevent further dealing

20.33   A key question is as to when a trade mark proprietor may legitimately oppose the further dealing with goods placed on the market with their consent.

[34] *Terrapin*, note 33, para 7.   [35] *Terrapin*, note 33, para 26.

The wording of Article 7.2 of Directive 2008/95/CE to approximate the laws of the member states relating to trade marks[36] is:

> Paragraph 1 shall not apply where there exist legitimate reasons for the proprietor to oppose further commercialisation of the goods, especially where the condition of the goods is changed or impaired after they have been put on the market.[37]

The issue of legitimate reasons has arisen in two broad areas. The first concerns repackaging, most notably in the pharmaceutical industry, and the second concerns advertising where the IP is used by a third party in a promotional campaign.

The pharmaceutical industry, trade marks, and repackaging by parallel importers

20.34   The pharmaceutical industry is one of the main industries at the centre of cases on repackaging and parallel imports. When drugs are imported from one member state into another, the parallel importers often repackage, re-box, or over-sticker the drug containers. The majority of the following cases deal with the pharmaceutical industry—although it should be noted that the rulings are not limited to that industry and would appear to apply whenever the facts are relevant within other industry sectors.[38]

Some terminology:

- *Repackaging*: a parallel importer acquires a product placed on the market, replaces the container in which the products were sold, and reaffixes the trade mark before marketing.

- *Re-labelling*: a parallel importer replaces the outer packaging and reaffixes another trade mark, under which the very product is sold in the member state where it is going to be marketed.

- *Re-boxing*: a parallel importer retains the original internal packaging but adds a new exterior carton printed in the language of the member state of importation.

- *Over-stickering*: a parallel importer retains the original internal and external packaging but adds an additional external label printed in the language of the member state of importation.

- *De-branding*: a parallel importer sells the goods after their original trade marks have been removed and not replaced.

 Exercise

Have a look at the article by N Gross and L Harrold, 'Fighting for pharmaceutical profits: the decision of the ECJ in *Boehringer Ingelheim v Swingward*' [2002] EIPR 497 to get an idea of what the packages look like once some of these activities have occurred.

20.35   Parallel importers argue that such actions are necessary for the drugs to be accepted in the member state of importation. National rules and consumer expectation may require drugs to be purchased and presented in a particular way and in specified quantities. However, repackaging and re-labelling invariably

---

[36] Version 2008/95/EC consolidated version previously First Council Directive 89/104/EEC of 21 December 1988 to approximate the laws of the member states relating to trade marks (Trade Marks Directive).

[37] This was implemented in the UK as the Trade Marks Act 1994, s 12(2). Corresponding provisions exist in the Council Regulation (EC) No 207/2009 of 26 February 2009 on the Community trade mark (Codified version), Art 13.

[38] *Loendersloot (F) Internationale Expeditie v George Ballantine & Son Ltd* [1997] ECR I-6227.

involve the affixing of the drug company's trade mark back onto the repackaged product or the removal altogether of that trade mark. In addition, the trade mark of the parallel importer may be affixed to the packaging.

20.36   It will be recalled that the Trade Mark Directive provides that a trade mark owner can prevent a third party from using, in the course of trade, a sign which is identical or similar to the registered mark.[39] Use includes fixing the sign to the goods or other packaging, importing the goods, and offering the goods for sale or putting them on the market.[40] Thus, the drug companies argue that the activities of the parallel importers constitute an infringement of their trade marks and that they may legitimately oppose such activities. As regards re boxing and over stickering, the trade mark proprietors argue that the parallel importers are not only free-riding on the goodwill they have built up but, in addition, and when the parallel importers use their own generic name for a drug on the packaging, this gives them an advantage when the patent expires in that the generic name can easily be substituted as the name of the drug.

20.37   There have been many cases brought before the ECJ dealing with repackaging.[41] Four of the key ones are *Hoffmann-La Roche v Centrafarm*;[42] *Bristol-Myers Squibb v Paranova*;[43] *Loendersloot v Ballantine*;[44] and *Upjohn v Paranova*.[45]

From these cases it is apparent that a trade mark owner may legitimately oppose the further marketing of a pharmaceutical product where the importer has repackaged the product and reaffixed the trade mark unless:

- the reliance by the trade mark owner on the IP right to oppose the marketing of the repackaged goods contributes to the artificial partitioning of the markets between member states (ie the repackaging must be necessary for market access). This may be the case where the trade mark owner places identical drugs on the market in different member states but in different packaging;

- it is shown that the repackaging has not affected the original condition of the goods. Such might be the case where new instructions in the language of importation are added to the goods;

- the new packaging includes information on who repackaged the product and the name of the manufacturer in legible print;

- the presentation of the repackaged product is not such as to be liable to damage the reputation of the trade mark and of its owner; and

- the parallel importer gives notice to the trade mark owner before the repackaged product is put on sale and, on demand, supplies him with a specimen of the repackaged product.

Thus, the parallel importer who repackages the goods and re-applies the mark will need to satisfy these conditions if there is to be no infringement.

Artificial partitioning of the market

20.38   One of the key questions concerns when the reliance on the IP right by the owner might contribute to the artificial partitioning of the market between member states. There have been a number of cases elaborating on those circumstances where the result may be such artificial partitioning and in particular where repackaging might be necessary for market access.

---

[39] Trade Mark Directive, Art 5.   [40] Trade Mark Directive, Art 5(3).
[41] See Jacob LJ in *Boehringer Ingelheim v Swingward Ltd* [2004] ETMR 65, [2004] EWCA Civ 129.
[42] Case C-102/77 [1978] ECR 1139.   [43] Joined Cases C-427/93, C-429/93 and C-436/93, [1996] ECR I-3457.
[44] Case C-349/95 [1997] ECR I-6227.   [45] Case C-379/97 [1999] ECR I-6927.

Test of necessity

20.39   In *Bristol-Myers Squibb v Paranova*[46] the ECJ stressed that the power of the trade mark owner to oppose the marketing of repacked products should be limited only insofar as the repackaging is necessary to market the product in the member state of importation.[47] The justification is the risk inherent in the change that is brought about by the repackaging during which there could be interference with the original product. Thus the repackaging must be necessary to enable the marketing of the product, but is limited to what is necessary in order to ensure that the legitimate interests of the right owner are safeguarded.

20.40   The meaning was explored in *Upjohn v Paranova*.[48] Paranova marketed an antibiotic under the name 'Dalacin C' in all member states except Denmark, Germany, and Spain. In these countries it used the name 'Dalacin', and in France it used 'Dalacine'. Paranova justified the differences by reference to the rules pertaining to registration of trade marks in the various countries. Upjohn bought goods in both Greece and France, repackaged them under the name Dalacin, and marketed them in Denmark. A reference was made to the ECJ asking when it was necessary to repackage the drugs.

The ECJ said that the test of necessity would be satisfied where:

> the rules or practices in the importing Member States prevent the product in question from being marketed in that State under its trade mark in the exporting Member State. This is so where a rule for the protection of consumers prohibits the use, in the importing Member State, of that trade mark used in the exporting Member State on the ground that it is liable to mislead consumers. In contrast, the condition of necessity will not be satisfied if replacement of the trade mark is explicable solely by the parallel importer's attempt to secure a commercial advantage.[49]

20.41   Thus where products purchased by the parallel importer cannot be placed on the market in the member state of importation in their original packaging by reason of national rules or practices relating to packaging, or where sickness insurance rules make reimbursement of medical expenses depend on a certain packaging or where well-established medical prescription practices are based, inter alia, on standard sizes recommended by professional groups and sickness insurance institutions, repackaging would be necessary.[50] It would not, however, be necessary where the parallel importer can reuse the original packaging for the purpose of marketing in the member state of importation by affixing labels to that packaging.[51]

Necessity, consumer preferences, poor quality packaging, and minimum intervention

20.42   Consumer preference on a particular market might result in repackaging being necessary. *Boehringer Ingelheim v Swingward Ltd*[52] concerned a variety of different methods of repackaging: the inclusion of English language information sheets; replacing of the trade mark onto the boxes and leaflets; the inclusion, with the trade mark, of packaging which was distinctive of the parallel importer; and the use of the generic name of the drug but not the trade mark. The ECJ held that replacement packaging of drugs is objectively necessary if, without such repackaging, effective access to the market or to a substantial part of the market would be hindered as the result of strong resistance from a significant proportion of consumers to re-labelled drugs.[53]

---

[46] Joined Cases C-427/93, C-429/93 and C-436/93 [1996] ECR I-3457.
[47] *Bristol-Myers Squibb*, note 46, para 56.   [48] Case C-379/97 [1999] ECR I-6927.   [49] *Upjohn*, note 48, para 43.
[50] Note 48, paras 53 and 54.   [51] *Bristol-Myers Squibb*, note 46, para 55.
[52] Case C-143/00 [2002] ECR I-3757.   [53] *Boehringer Ingelheim*, note 46, para 54.

When this ruling was applied by the High Court it was found that the respective trade marks had been infringed.[54] This resulted in a further appeal and cross-appeal being taken to the Court of Appeal.[55] That court found that the High Court had been wrong to suggest that the ECJ had created an irrebutable presumption that repackaging was prejudicial to the specific subject matter of the trade mark right. The Court of Appeal found that there was a strong resistance to the purchase of over-stickered drugs as it had a less neat and professional look than repackaging. Re-boxing was therefore necessary.

20.43 On the extent of repackaging and whether the necessity test applies only to the act of repackaging or whether it also extends to the presentation of the repackaged product in particular where the reputation of the mark might be damaged, some conflicting views arise. In *Bristol-Myers Squibb v Paranova*[56] the ECJ recognised that where repackaging was poor and untidy, the reputation of the mark might suffer. Poor presentation could thus be a legitimate reason to oppose the further circulation of goods. In *Glaxo Group v Dowelhurst*[57] Laddie J suggested that repackaging was only to be tolerated to the extent that it could be shown to inflict the minimum possible damage on the mark. By contrast, in *Paranova AS v Merck*[58] the EFTA Court said that once it was shown that repackaging was necessary the importer has the right to repackage. Thereafter the focus should be on whether the mark's ability to guarantee origin or its reputation was compromised.

20.44 As a result a second reference was made to the ECJ in *Boehringer Ingelheim KG v Swingward Ltd.*[59] The ECJ's judgment appeared to make parallel importing more onerous for parallel importers than had been thought might be the case in the aftermath of the Advocate General's Opinion in this case.[60] While the ruling has clarified some matters, for instance that the conditions in *Bristol-Myers Squibb* apply to re-labelling, re-boxing, and over-stickering—other elements of the judgment will no doubt provoke further debate—for instance as to what is meant by an 'inappropriately repackaged product' which could damage the reputation of a trade mark.

- The Court started by noting that the specific subject matter of a mark is to guarantee the origin of the product bearing the mark and that repackaging by a third party without authorisation is likely to create real risks for that guarantee of origin.[61] Case law has indicated that it is the repackaging which is in itself prejudicial to the specific subject matter of the mark and it is not necessary in that context to assess the actual effects of the repackaging by the parallel importer.[62] However, opposition to repackaging contributes to artificial partitioning of the market where it is necessary to enable the product to be marketed in the importing state.[63] A change brought about by repackaging may be prohibited unless it is necessary to enablethe marketing of the products and the legitimate interests of the proprietor are safeguarded.[64] Notice must be given that a repackaged product is being put on sale.[65]

- The ECJ noted that in the instant case the packaging of the pharmaceutical products and instruction leaflets had been altered for importation into the UK. In some cases, labels identifying the parallel importer had been added but the trade mark and languages other than English were visible. Other products had been re-boxed and the trade mark reproduced and in yet others, which were re-boxed, the trade mark was not visible but the generic name was and in others the trade mark inside the box

---

[54] [2003] EWHC 2109 (Ch).   [55] [2004] ETMR 65, [2004] EWCA Civ 129.   [56] Note 46.
[57] [2000] FSR 529.   [58] Case E-3/02.
[59] Case C-348/04. Reference for a preliminary ruling by the Court of Appeal (England & Wales) (Civil Division), 17 June 2004, in the case of *Boehringer Ingelheim KG v Swingward Ltd* [2004] 3 CMLR 4.
[60] Case C-348/04 *Boehringer Ingelheim KG v Swingward Ltd* [2007] ECR I-3391, Opinion of AG Sharpston.
[61] *Boehringer Ingelheim*, note 59, para 14.   [62] *Boehringer Ingelheim*, note 59, para 15.
[63] *Boehringer Ingelheim*, note 59, para 18.   [64] *Boehringer Ingelheim*, note 59, para 19.
[65] *Boehringer Ingelheim*, note 59, para 20.

was over-stickered with information on the parallel importer and the generic name. The information leaflet, written in English, contained the trade mark.

- *The concept of repackaging*: the ECJ considered that both re-labelling and re-boxing are prejudicial to the specific subject matter of the mark and create a risk to the guarantee of origin.[66] A change may thus be prohibited unless it is necessary for marketing and the legitimate interests of the trade mark owner are safeguarded.[67] Thus, if the requirements set out in *Bristol Myers Squibb* are met, the proprietor may not oppose further commercialisation whether through repackaging or over-stickering.

- *The manner and style of repackaging*: the key question was whether the requirement that repackaging was necessary was directed at the fact of repackaging rather than the manner and style of that repackaging. Here the ECJ considered that the necessity test is directed only at the fact of repackaging and the choice of style of repackaging and not to the manner or style in which it is repackaged.[68]

- *The presentation of the repackaged product and the reputation of the mark*: here the ECJ noted that the five conditions to be fulfilled include the condition that the presentation of the repackaged product must not be such as to be liable to damage the reputation of the trade mark and of the proprietor: it must not be defective, of poor quality, or untidy.[69] In addition, an inappropriately repackaged product could damage the reputation of the mark where it detracted from the image of reliability and quality attaching to the product and the confidence it could inspire in the public.[70]

- *The circumstances in which the reputation of the trade mark may be damaged*: de-branding, co-branding, over-stickering such as to obscure the trade mark, a failure to state that the trade mark belongs to the proprietor or where the name of the parallel importer is printed in capital letters, are in principle liable to damage the reputation of the trade mark. These are questions of fact for the national court.[71]

- *Burden of proof*: it is for the parallel importer to prove the existence of the conditions under which parallel importation is permitted and which, if fulfilled, would prevent the proprietor from opposing further commercialisation of the products. Where it must be shown that the repackaging does not affect the original condition of the product in the packaging, the parallel importer must furnish evidence which leads to a reasonable presumption that is the case. That applies also to the presentation of the repackaged product in that it must not be such as to damage the reputation of the trade mark. The parallel importer must furnish initial evidence. It is then for the trade mark owner to prove that the reputation of the owner and that of the trade mark have been damaged.

In applying the judgment of the ECJ, Jacob LJ found that 'the defendants have complied with BMS condition 4 and in particular that their activities by way of re-boxing and re-labelling have not caused and will not cause damage to the reputation of the claimants' trade marks.'[72]

---

[66] *Boehringer Ingelheim*, note 59, para 29.   [67] *Boehringer Ingelheim*, note 59, para 30.

[68] See also Case C-276/05 *Wellcome Foundation v Paranova* [2008] ECR I-10479 in which the ECJ ruled that 'the condition of necessity is directed only at the fact of re-packaging the product inter alia by re-boxing it, and not the presentation of that new packaging'.

[69] *Boehringer Ingelheim*, note 59, para 40.

[70] *Boehringer Ingelheim*, note 59, para 44. In Case C-276/05 *Wellcome Foundation v Paranova* [2008] ECR I-10479, the ECJ held that in cases where the 'repackaging of the pharmaceutical product is necessary for its further marketing in a Member State of importation, the presentation of the packaging should be assessed only against the condition that it should not be as to be liable to damage the reputation of the trade mark or that of its proprietor' (para 30).

[71] See note 70.   [72] [2008] EWCA Civ 83, para 67.

Discussion point   For answer guidance visit www.oxfordtextbooks.co.uk/orc/waelde3e/

In *Boehringer Ingelheim* Jacob LJ gave his view of the current state of trade mark law:
Notwithstanding the two references to the ECJ and its answers, each 'side' (there are several claimant drug companies as claimants and two parallel importers as defendants) claims to have won.
That is a sorry state of affairs. European trade mark law seems to have arrived at such a state of
uncertainty that no one really knows what the rules are, outside the obviously core case of straightforward infringement (the use of a mark as a trade mark for the defendant's goods which is the
same as or confusingly similar to a plaintiff's registered mark registered for the same or similar
goods). Big brand owners want bigger rights; smaller players, no change or less. The compromises
which have emerged have very fuzzy lines. So it is that in this case, notwithstanding two references
(and a host of cases about relabelling parallel imports going back at least 30 years, see *Hoffmann-La
Roche v Centrafarm*, Case 102/77 [1978] ECR 1139), there is still room for argument.[73]
Do you agree with Jacob LJ? How would you suggest the law be clarified in this area?

 Question

What will be necessary? Consider *Boehringer Ingelheim Pharma GmbH & Co KG v Munro Wholesale
Medical Supplies Ltd* 2004 SC 468, [2004] ETMR 66.

Notice

20.45   As can be seen earlier (para 20.37), to comply with the conditions the parallel importer must give notice
to the trade mark owner and supply samples of the packaging. The ECJ has said that it is for the parallel importer to give notice.[74] In *Boehringer v Swingward*[75] the ECJ said that on the evidence before it a
period of 15 days would seem reasonable where the parallel importer chose to give notice by supplying
a sample of the repackaged product. The Court did, however, say that the period was purely indicative
and it was open to the parallel importer to allow a shorter time, and to the proprietor to ask for a longer
time to react than that proffered by the parallel importer.[76] Where a parallel importer has not given prior
notice, every importation of the product is in infringement until notice is given. The sanction should be
proportionate and effective and may be treated in the same manner for those circumstances in which
the goods were spurious.[77] It is for the national court to assess in the light of the circumstances whether
the proprietor has had a reasonable time to react to the intended packaging.

Comment on repackaging cases

20.46   The number of cases to come before the courts dealing with trade mark infringement, parallel imports,
and repackaging appears to have prompted a growing sense of frustration amongst the judiciary. In the
Court of Appeal in *Boehringer Ingelheim v Swingward Ltd*,[78] Jacob LJ highlighted the assumption made

[73] *Boehringer Ingelheim* (CA), note 72, para 2.   [74] Case C-102/77 *Hoffmann-La Roche v Centrafarm* [1979] ECR 1139, para 12.
[75] Case C-143/00 [2002] ECR I-3759.
[76] Case C-143/00 *Boehringer Ingelheim*, para 57. In Case C-400/09 *Orifarm and others v Merck & Co Inc* [2012] 1 CMLR 10 the Court
of Justice found that it sufficed for new packaging to indicate the undertaking which had instructed it and assumed responsibility for
it, rather than the actual repackager.
[77] Case C-348/04 *Boehringer Ingelheim KG v Swingward Ltd* [2007] ECR I-3391, para 64.
[78] [2004] ETMR 65, [2004] EWCA Civ 129.

in the cases that the reaffixing of the trade mark to the goods, unless permitted by free circulation rules, infringes the registered trade mark. He pointed out that most people would not assume that a mark would be infringed simply by reaffixing the original trade mark to the goods or using a mark when marketing the goods. Such practices are a daily occurrence in commerce where shopkeepers use signs to advertise goods which bear the trade mark of another and second-hand goods are sold by reference to the trade mark.

> Sometimes I think the law may be losing a sense of reality in this area—we are, after all, only considering the use of the owner's trade mark for his goods in perfect condition. The pickle the law has got into would, I think, astonish the average consumer.[79]

Jacob LJ suggested that the law of registered trade marks was being stretched to deal with conduct that would more happily sit under general unfair competition rules: 'There is more than one way to skin a cat'.[80] In her Opinion, Advocate General Sharpston indicated that after 30 years of case law on repackaging of pharmaceutical products, 'it should be possible to distil sufficient principles to enable national courts to apply the law to the constantly replayed litigation between manufacturers and parallel importers'.[81] Whether these comments will have any impact on the number of cases brought before the courts remains to be seen. That there are so many cases to come before the courts is perhaps an indication of the commercial importance of these fine distinctions that are being litigated between the parties.

 Question

What do you think of the suggestion by Jacob LJ that trade mark law might not be relevant to the activities of parallel importers? Revisit the functions of a trade mark. Are the arguments of the trade mark proprietors justified by reference to these functions?

Use of marks in advertising

20.47   As can be seen from the previous discussion, a concern of trade mark proprietors as goods are repackaged is for safeguarding the reputation of their marks. This also arises in the context of advertising. If a parallel importer wishes to re-sell the goods, then they would want to use the mark in advertising them. Where the re-seller makes those goods available to a different market, for instance where luxury goods are re-sold in supermarkets, then the trade mark owner may wish to control the way in which they are advertised over concern for the reputation of the mark. The question then arises as to whether the trade mark owner has a legitimate reason to do so: is safeguarding the reputation of the mark a legitimate reason for opposing certain styles of advertising? Such an issue arose in *Parfums Christian Dior SA v Evora BV*.[82] Dior owned trade marks for, inter alia, perfumes sold to the luxury market. Evora owned a chain of chemist shops in which it sold Dior products which were parallel imports. Evora carried out a promotion and in the literature it showed pictures of the packaging and of the bottles. Dior argued that such literature did not present the goods in the way that they wished: it did not conform to the prestige image Dior was keen to promote so brought an action for trade mark infringement.

The ECJ considered that the damage done to the reputation of a mark might be a legitimate reason to enable the proprietor to oppose further commercialisation.[83] However, a balance had to be struck

---

[79] *Boehringer Ingelheim* (CA), note 72, para 79.   [80] *Boehringer Ingelheim* (CA), note 72, para 20.
[81] Opinion of AG Sharpston, Case C-348/04 *Boehringer Ingelheim KG v Swingward Ltd* [2007] ECR I-3391, para 3.
[82] Case C-337/95 *Parfums Christian Dior SA v Evora BV* [1997] ECR I-6013.   [83] *Parfums Christian Dior*, note 82, para 43.

between the legitimate interests of the trade mark owner from a re-seller using the mark in such a manner that might damage the mark, and the re-seller's legitimate interest in being able to re-sell the goods in question by using advertising methods which are customary in his sector of trade.[84] Where luxury goods were resold, the re-seller should try to prevent the advertising from affecting the value of the mark by detracting from the aura of luxury.[85]

The ECJ did go on to note that where the re-seller used advertising methods common in the trade, even if those were not the methods the trade mark owner would have used, that was not a legitimate reason for the trade mark owner to oppose the use of the mark by the re-seller unless it could be established that the use would seriously damage the reputation of the mark. As an example, such damage could occur where the re-seller put the mark on an advertising leaflet in a context which would detract from the aura of luxury.[86]

Key points on legitimate reasons

- A trade mark owner may legitimately oppose further marketing of a pharmaceutical product where the importer has repackaged the product and reaffixed the trade mark unless the points in para 20.37 arise

- A court will look to see if the repackaging by the parallel importer is necessary

- A trade mark owner may oppose the use of a mark by an advertiser if the reputation of the mark is likely to be damaged

International exhaustion

20.48   It will be recalled that Article 7(1) of the Trade Mark Directive provides that a 'trade mark shall not entitle the proprietor to prohibit its use in relation to goods which have been put on the market in the Community under the trade mark by the proprietor or with his consent'.

This would appear to limit the operation of the exhaustion doctrine to the Community (now Union). Is this then a minimum standard, or are member states free to apply a doctrine of international exhaustion?

TRIPS, Article 6 leaves this open to signatory states:

   nothing in this Agreement shall be used to address the issue of the exhaustion of intellectual property rights.

 Question

If one member state applied the doctrine of international exhaustion, what impact would this have on the movement of goods throughout the Union where goods are imported from outwith the EEA and placed on the market in that member state?

20.49   The ECJ had a chance to rule on the question of international exhaustion in 1988.[87]

---

[84] *Parfums Christian Dior*, note 82, para 44.
[85] See also Case C-59/08 *Copad SA v Christian Dior Couture SA* [2009] ECR I-3421, note 82, para 37, and see para 20.30.
[86] *Parfums Christian Dior*, note 82, para 46.
[87] Although note also early and clear consideration in Case C-51/75 *EMI Records Ltd v CBS United Kingdom Ltd* [1976] ECR 811.

■ **Case C-355/96** *Silhouette International Schmied GmbH & Co KG v Hartlauer Handelsgesellschaft GmbH* **[1998] ECR I-4799**

Silhouette (S) manufactured designer spectacles under its trade mark, 'Silhouette'. It sold a number of outdated designs to a Bulgarian company on the condition that they would only be sold in Bulgaria and the former Soviet Union states. Hartlauer, an Austrian retailer, obtained some of these frames and sold them in their shops. S claimed that their trade mark had been infringed.

Diagram 20.7 *Silhouette International Schmied GmbH & Co KG v Hartlauer Handelsgesellschaft*

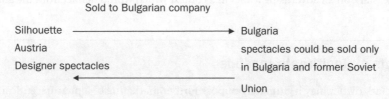

Sold to Bulgarian company

Silhouette ⟶ Bulgaria

Austria spectacles could be sold only

Designer spectacles in Bulgaria and former Soviet

⟵

Union

Hartlauer—purchased in Bulgaria and imported into Austria

The Court, proceeding on the basis that no consent had been given to the sunglasses to be sold in Austria, held that national rules which provided for exhaustion of rights in respect of goods which were put onto the market outwith the EC by the proprietor or with his consent, were contrary to Article 7(1). A member state had no discretion in this. The Court took the view that the Directive provided for full harmonisation of those rules which affect the functioning of the internal market.[88] Member states are thus not free to apply a regime of international exhaustion.[89]

20.50 Parallel importers have sought to argue around the rule on international exhaustion by stating that the mark owner had consented to the importation of goods into the Union.

Consent and batches of goods

20.51 In *Sebago Inc and Ancienne Maison Dubois v GB Unic SA*,[90] GB Unic imported shoes from El Salvador into Belgium bearing the 'Sebago' trade mark and sold them in retail outlets. GB Unic argued that whenever a trade mark owner consented to the placing of goods onto the market bearing a trade mark, then that consent extended to all goods of that type. In giving judgment, the ECJ said that consent in the sense of Article 7(1) of the Trade Marks Directive must relate to each individual item in respect of which exhaustion is pleaded. A trade mark owner does not place a whole stock of goods on the market through the act of selling one batch.

---

[88] Case C-355/96 *Silhouette International Schmied GmbH & Co KG v Hartlauer Handelsgesellschaft GmbH* [1998] ECR I-4799, para 23.

[89] In an Advisory Opinion in Case E-9/07 *L'Oréal Norge AS v Per Aarskog AS and others*, and reversing its earlier Advisory Opinion in Case E-2/97 *Mag Instrument Inc v California Trading Company Norway* [1997] EFTA Ct Rep 129, 2008 ETMR 60 the EFTA Court said that 'Article 7(1) of the Trade Mark Directive is to be interpreted to the effect that it precludes the unilateral introduction or maintenance of international exhaustion of rights conferred by a trade mark regardless of the origin of the goods in question.'

[90] Case C-173/98 [1999] ECR I-4103.

Implied consent

20.52   In a number of joined cases[91] concerning, inter alia, perfume and jeans, an argument arose over implied consent.

■ Case C-414/99 *Zino Davidoff v A&G Imports* [2002] All ER (EC) 55

Zino Davidoff (ZD) wanted to prevent the import into England of goods bearing the marks 'Cool Water' and 'Davidoff Cool Water' which had been marketed with consent in Singapore. A&G argued that by marketing the goods in Singapore, ZD had given implied consent to their free circulation. The chain of distribution included a standard agreement in terms of which distributors undertook not to sell any products outside their assigned territories. However, no such term was imposed on distributors further down the chain. In the High Court, Laddie J had held that the rule of Community exhaustion did not prevent trade mark owners from consenting to importation. Interpretation of the contract under the applicable law (in this case English law) meant that consent could be implied. There was a rebuttable presumption that, in the absence of full and explicit restrictions being imposed on purchaser at the time of purchase, the proprietor is treated as consenting to the goods being imported into and sold in the EEA.[92] When the case reached the ECJ, the Court ruled that consent could be implied:

- only where the facts and circumstances were such that the proprietor could be considered to have unequivocally demonstrated to have renounced his right to oppose the subsequent importation of those goods into the EEA.

Consent could not be implied from:

- the failure of the proprietor to communicate to subsequent purchasers of the goods that he did not consent to their subsequent importation into the EEA;
- the fact that there was nothing on the goods to suggest that they were not to be imported into the EEA;
- the fact that the proprietor had transferred ownership without imposing any restrictions.

In addition, the Court said that it was irrelevant that the importer was unaware that the proprietor objected to their importation, or that authorised retailers had not imposed on their purchasers any contractual restrictions even if those retailers were aware of the proprietor's objection.

20.53   The Court of Appeal had the opportunity to consider when implied consent might be relevant in *Mastercigars Direct Ltd v Hunters & Frankau Ltd*.[93] This appeal concerned the importation into the UK of cigars from Cuba by Mastercigars. The Cuban company, Corporacion Habanos, had an exclusive UK distributor, Hunters & Frankau. It was claimed that a consignment of cigars were counterfeit and infringed the trade mark in that no consent had been given to the placing of the goods on the market

---

[91] Joined Cases C-414/99, C-415/99 and C-416/99 *Zino Davidoff SA v A&G Imports Ltd; Levi Strauss & Co Levi Strauss (UK) Ltd v Tesco Stores Ltd, Tesco plc; Levi Strauss & Co, Levi Strauss (UK) Ltd v Costco Wholesale UK Ltd* [2002] Ch 109, [2002] 2 WLR 321, [2002] All ER (EC) 55. See also *Honda Motor Co Ltd v Neesam* [2008] EWHC 338 (Ch).

[92] See note 91, para 38.8. At the same time *JOOP! GmbH and Zino Davidoff SA v M&S Toiletries Ltd* [1999] 2 CMLR 1056 was heard in the Scottish Court of Session—an almost identical case. Lord Kingarth noted that not only would the approach taken in the High Court mean that unless the trade mark owner blocked every avenue, he could be held as having consented to importation (an almost impossible task) but, in addition, making the issue of consent dependent on the law of contract would offend against the purpose of harmonisation in the Directive and lead to uncertainty in application. It was unclear whether the reference to presumed consent would be applied in the same way in Scotland as in England.

[93] *Corporacion Habanos SA v Mastercigars Direct Ltd* [2007] EWCA Civ 176, [2007] ETMR 44.

in the EEA. As no express consent had been given to the importation of the cigars, the key question was as to whether consent could be implied. In order to show implied consent, the factors had to 'demonstrate unequivocally' that the trade mark proprietor had renounced any intention to enforce his rights. Unequivocal is not about the standard of proof; a proved act which is consistent with consent and consistent with its absence is not enough to draw the conclusion that goods had been marketed with the consent of the trade mark owner.[94]

The facts of the case—and in particular that when cigars were sold in Cuba they were sold by encouraging sales of up to $25,000, a level far too high for individual use, and that the purchaser was given appropriate customs documentation—showed that the sellers must have known that they would be used for onward resale in the end market. This was sufficient on the facts to demonstrate implied consent.

On who should give consent, the Court of Appeal said that it is insufficient for consent to be given by a licensee or connected company. What matters is the 'point of control' shown through actual knowledge and the actual practical control or right to exercise that control by the trade mark owner.[95] In this case Corporacion Habanos exercised that control through the sale of cigars in retail outlets in Cuba.

20.54   It has also been found that consent cannot be inferred from the placing on the goods of the 'CE' symbol for regulatory approval in the EU, on goods put on the market outside the EEA.[96] However, the Court of Appeal's ruling in *Mastercigars Direct* suggests that the standard is by no means insurmountable on the evidence.[97]

> **Question**
>
> *Mastercigars* gives an example of certain facts that will be taken to 'unequivocally demonstrate' that a trade mark proprietor had consented to importation of goods into the EEA. Can you think of other examples?

When are goods placed on the market?

20.55   For a trade mark owner's rights to be exhausted, goods must be put on the market within the EEA by or with the consent of the trade mark owner. What is meant by being 'put on the market' was considered by the ECJ in *Peak Holding AB v Axolin-Elinor AB*.[98] Peak Holding granted the right to use the trade mark, 'Peak Performance', to Peak Performance Production AB (PPP) in Sweden. Certain goods were offered for sale in PPP's shops within the EU but were not sold. PPP sold these to a French company. The agreement contained a clause prohibiting the French company from selling more than 5 per cent of the goods in France. Of the remainder, the only European countries that could be supplied were Russia and Slovenia. None of the goods actually left the EEA. A large number of items were subsequently offered for sale in Sweden through Factory Outlet (FO). When sued for trade mark infringement, FO argued that PPP's rights had been exhausted by the sale to the French company and that the clause which prohibited resale in the EEA was of no effect.

---

[94] *Mastercigars Direct*, note 93, para 19.   [95] Note 93, para 30.

[96] *Roche Products Ltd v Kent Pharmaceuticals Ltd* [2006] EWCA Civ 1775.

[97] For other UK cases, see *Kabushiki Kaisha Sony Computer Entertainment Europe Ltd v Nuplayer Ltd* [2005] EWHC 1522 (Ch); *Sony Computer Entertainment Ltd v Electricbirdland Ltd* [2005] EWHC 2296 (Ch); *Hewlett-Packard Development Co LP v Expansys UK Ltd* [2005] EWHC 1495 (Ch); *KK Sony Computer Entertainment and another v Pacific Game Technology (Holding) Ltd* [2006] EWHC 2509 (Pat). Note that the ECJ dealt with implied consent to marketing within the EEA in Case C-324/08 *Makro Zelfbedieningsgroothandel e.a. v Diesel Spa* (see para 20.17). For further discussion see para 20.17.

[98] Case C-16/03 [2004] ECR I-11313.

The ECJ was asked:

- Had PPP had put the goods on the market by importing them into the EU and offering them for sale in their shops?

If the answer was in the negative:

- Had the goods had been put on the market and the rights exhausted when they were sold to the French company? If this was the case, what was the impact of the restriction on resale in Europe?

The ECJ confirmed that an actual sale of goods to a third party within the EEA resulted in putting the goods on the market in the EEA. However, where the goods are imported, or offered for sale in the proprietor's shops or in those of an associated company but without actually selling any of the goods, the rights in respect of those goods are not exhausted.[99] This is because at this stage the economic value of the mark in respect of the goods has not been realised. The ECJ went on to say that any transaction which transfers the right to dispose of the goods amounts to putting the goods on the market in the EEA regardless of any agreement prohibiting resale within the EEA. This is because the sale itself is enough to realise the economic value of the mark. Any third party acquiring the goods could not be sued for infringement of the trade mark.[100] It will be for the national court to apply the ruling of the ECJ to the facts of the case.

 Question

Consider perfume testers which are made available without transfer of ownership to contractually bound intermediaries when there is marking to this effect on the tester. How should this relate to 'put on to the market' within the meaning of Article 13(1) of Regulation 207/2009 and Article 7(1) of Directive 2008/95/EC? Do you think the decisions in Case C-59/08 *Copad SA v Christian Dior Couture SA* (see para 20.30) and Case C-127/09 *Coty Prestige Lancaster Group GmbH v Simex Trading AG* [2010] ETMR 41 are correct?

20.56   There are circumstances in which public opinion might support attempts by a trade mark owner to prevent the circulation of goods within the EEA. In *Glaxo Group Ltd v Dowelhurst Ltd*[101] Glaxo had sold pharmaceuticals within the EEA at cheap rates based on the understanding that they would only be used for humanitarian purposes in Africa. The drugs were sold to a Swiss company which sold them on to a parallel importer. The drugs then found their way onto the UK market where the importer was sued for trade mark infringement. Much of the discussion in the court revolved around the question of when goods were put onto the market in the EEA (some clarity in relation to this question now exists given the ruling of the ECJ in *Peak Holding v Axolin-Elinor* (para 20.55)). Given the facts of the *Glaxo* case, it seems possible that the consignment of drugs was sold within the EEA and thus subject to the rules on exhaustion—which was the view taken by the Court of Appeal. However, it is unlikely that the arguments will be further aired in court as the case between the parties settled.[102] That does not detract from the fact that at times it may be just to enable right holders to control the movement of their products without fear of falling on the wrong side of complex and often unsettled rules in relation to free movement and

---

[99] *Peak Holding*, note 98, paras 40–44.   [100] *Peak Holding*, note 98, paras 54–56.
[101] *Glaxo Group Ltd v Dowelhurst Ltd* [2004] EWCA Civ 290, [2005] ETMR 104.
[102] http://news.bbc.co.uk/1/hi/uk/4476329.stm.

exhaustion within the EU.[103] And it is a reminder, like the *Merck* cases, paras 20.26–20.27, of the frequent distinction between law, ethics, and humanitarian questions.

Consent and goods in transit

20.57 A question as to whether a trade mark proprietor had to consent to goods being brought into the EC for transit or customs storage arose in *Class International BV v Colgate-Palmolive Co and others*.[104] The Beecham group owns the 'Aquafresh' Community trade mark for, inter alia, toothpastes. Class International, a parallel importer, brought into Rotterdam a container load of toothpaste products bearing the 'Aquafresh' trade mark, purchased from Kapex International, a South African undertaking. The Beecham group believed them to be counterfeit but a subsequent examination showed they were genuine goods. The ECJ said that the trade mark owner could not stop (ie consent was not needed) the goods being brought into the EC for the purposes of transit or customs storage. '"Importing" … requires introduction of those goods into the Community for the purposes of putting them on the market therein.'[105] Neither could the proprietor stop the goods from being offered for sale in a third county unless it was clear that they would subsequently be put on the market in the Community.[106]

20.58 A related question arose in *Montex Holdings Ltd v Diesel SpA*.[107] Here, Diesel objected to the transit through Germany of goods destined for Ireland bearing the Diesel mark. The goods had been assembled in Poland; there was no trade mark protection for the Diesel trade marks in Ireland. Referring to *Class International*, the ECJ held that a trade mark owner could only prohibit transit of goods through a member state in which the mark was protected and placed under the external transit procedure if the goods were subject to the act of a third party whilst in this procedure which would necessarily entail their being put on the market in the member state of transit.[108] A theoretical risk that the goods could fail to reach their destination and that they would be marketed fraudulently in the state where trade mark protection existed, was insufficient to reach the conclusion that the transit infringed the rights of the trade mark proprietor.[109]

20.59 A further twist arose in *Nokia Corporation v Her Majesty's Commissioners of Revenue & Customs*.[110] In this case Her Majesty's Commissioners of Revenue & Customs (HMRC) refused to continue to detain a consignment of allegedly counterfeit mobile phones and accessories bearing the Nokia trade mark that HMRC had seized at Heathrow Airport and which were in transit from Hong Kong to Colombia. In order for there to be infringement of allegedly counterfeit goods under the Counterfeit Goods Regulation, the goods must in fact infringe someone's trade mark in the territory in question.[111] The court also said that the mere risk that the goods may be diverted into the internal market is not enough to constitute infringement. In coming to this conclusion, the court exposed a gap in the law which would prevent these allegedly counterfeit goods from being seized. The Court of Justice then found that the mere presence of goods under suspensive customs procedure did not mean that they were 'counterfeit goods';

---

[103] For other initiatives impacting on this area, see C Davies, '*Glaxo v Dowelhurst—a new twist in the tale!*' [2005] EIPR 127. Consider also the possibility that a court might decline to grant an injunction (see Chapter 22) and also *Biogen Inc v Medeva plc* [1993] RPC 475 at 487.

[104] Case C-405/03 [2005] ECR I-8735.   [105] *Class International*, note 104, para 34.

[106] See also *Eli Lilly and Co and another v 8PM Chemist Ltd* [2008] EWCA Civ 24. In Case C-115/02 *Administration des Douanes, Droits Indirects v Rioglass SA* [2003] ECR I-12705, the ECJ held that where goods lawfully manufactured in one member state are in transit in the Community with the destination being a non-member country, that does not involve any marketing of the goods in question.

[107] Case C-281/05 [2006] ECR I-10881. Cf the Dutch case *Sisvel v Sosecal* (18 July 2008), see discussion on IPKat (31 July 2008) http://ipkitten.blogspot.co.uk/2008/07/mp4-players-stopped-in-their-tracks.html.

[108] Case C-281/05 *Montex Holdings Ltd v Diesel SpA* [2006] ECR I-10881, para 23.

[109] *Montex Holdings*, note 108, para 24.   [110] [2009] EWHC 1903 (Ch), [2010] FSR 5.   [111] *Nokia*, note 110, para 49.

there must be a proven intention to put them on the market in the EU. Examples of relevant factors were failure to state the destination of goods and failure to cooperate with the authorities.[112]

Parallel importing and the burden of proof

20.60   The ECJ has said that the burden of proof lies on the person alleging consent to prove it, and not for the trade mark owner to prove its absence. This left parallel importers in something of a quandary. If a parallel importer had to prove consent to marketing within the EEA, then that may involve giving information on the distribution system through which the goods had been sourced. Once the trade mark owner had details of that source, then they could act to close it—thus leaving the parallel importer without supplies. The question over who should bear the burden of proof and at what stage in the proceedings has been the subject of further consideration.

■ **Case C-244/00 *Van Doren + Q GmbH v Lifestyle + Sportswear Handelsgesellschaft GmbH* [2003] ECR I-3051, [2003] 2 CMLR 6**

Van Doren (VD) was the exclusive German distributor of goods bearing the 'Stussy' trade mark, owned by a Californian company. VD sued Lifestyle for selling goods bearing the trade mark in Germany. VD alleged that those goods were first put on the market in the United States. No consent had been given to their distribution in Germany. Lifestyle argued that the trade mark rights had been exhausted because the goods were sourced in the EEA where they had been put on the market by the trade mark owner or with his consent. As German law provides that exhaustion operates as a defence to trade mark infringement, it was for the parallel importer to prove where the goods were sourced.

The ECJ held that a rule of evidence that required a defendant relying on a plea of exhaustion to prove the conditions existed for the defence to be successful, was consistent with Community law.[113] However, that rule might have to be qualified.

- It was for the parallel importer to show that there would be a real risk of partitioning the markets if the burden of proof lay on him. This would be particularly so where the trade mark owner operated an exclusive distribution system.

If he was successful then:

- it was for the trade mark owner to establish that the products were placed on the market outside the EEA by him or with his consent.

If such evidence was forthcoming:

- the burden shifted back to the parallel importer to prove the trade mark owner's consent to subsequent marketing of the products in the EEA.[114]

20.61   Although this ruling provides some guidance, questions remain. For instance: what evidence would be required to show there is a real risk of market partitioning? Would it be enough to show that the trade mark owner operates an exclusive distribution system? Might price differences as between member states be sufficient? Suffice it to say that there will no doubt be more references to the ECJ before clarity is achieved.

20.62   A question over what a trader might have to do to show that reasonable steps had been taken to ascertain that goods had been placed on the market in the EU arose in the English High Court in *Sun Microsystems Inc v Amtec Computer Corporation Ltd*.[115] Amtec was sued by Sun for trade mark infringement in relation

---

[112] Joined Cases C-446/09 and C-495/09 *Nokia Corporation v Her Majesty's Commissioners of Revenue and Customs* [2012] ETMR 13.
[113] *Nokia* (ECJ), note 112, para 36.   [114] *Nokia* (ECJ), paras 41 and 42.   [115] [2006] EWHC 62 (Ch), [2006] FSR 35.

to servers that Amtec had purchased from a Danish intermediary. It transpired that the servers had not been put onto the market in the EEA by Sun or with Sun's consent. In seeking to discharge their burden of proof, Amtec argued that the Danish intermediary was known as a reputable European source of Sun products and that a term in the contract as between Amtec and the Danish intermediary had stipulated that the goods should be of EU origin (which they were). Amtec also believed that the goods had originally been supplied by a distributor known to be an authorised seller of Sun products—thus adding to the belief that they had originally been put on the market with the authorisation of Sun. When the servers arrived, they were in boxes marked with the words 'Origin: United Kingdom' and the servers themselves had UK serial numbers. On investigation of the facts it transpired that the servers had not actually been put on the market in the EU by Sun or with their consent (they were destined for Israel) and Amtec accepted that they had infringed Sun's trade marks but said that it had occurred innocently.

The court found that this was no defence to trade mark infringement saying:

> There is no requirement of knowledge on the part of an infringing trader that he is infringing. To put that proposition another way, lack of knowledge is not a defence to infringement proceedings;

> It is not a defence for the trader to show that he took all reasonable steps open to him to establish that goods were put on the market by, or with the consent, of the trade mark proprietor.[116]

The court did, however, limit the scope of the injunction recognising that, without Sun's assistance, Amtec could do nothing to ensure that the goods it acquired had been placed on the market in the EEA with the consent of Sun.[117]

 Question

Consider the cases and the decision of the Supreme Court in *Oracle America Inc v M-Tech Data Ltd* [2012] UKSC 27. This declined an open approach taken to consent and free movement as has been suggested by the Court of Appeal in that case, considered that the law was clear, and declined to make a reference to the Court of Justice. Would a reference be helpful? And do you agree with the robust approach to the power of the trade mark owner taken by the Supreme Court?

Should there be a system of international exhaustion?

20.63   An issue that has troubled policymakers within the EU for many years is whether a system for international exhaustion should be introduced. The debate has focused on trade marks and was galvanised after the judgment of the ECJ in *Silhouette* in 1998 (para 20.49). In order to obtain a clearer picture of the economic aspects of a possible change to the exhaustion regime, the Commission commissioned a study in 1999 from the NERA Institute in London. The conclusions of that study are as follows.

- The short-term effects on consumer pricing of a change of exhaustion regime would vary from small (less than 2 per cent price reduction) for certain products to 'negligible' (0 per cent price reduction) for other products.

- The long-term effects of a change of exhaustion are more difficult to predict. It is, however, likely that the marginal, positive effect on consumer pricing in the long run will disappear.

---

[116] *Sun Microsystems*, note 115, para 21.   [117] For discussion on the scope of the injunction, see para 22.117.

- A change in the exhaustion regime may have an impact not only on pricing but, for example, also on product quality, product availability, after-sales services, and employment in Europe.
- Trade mark policy has only a marginal effect on parallel trade: other elements like distribution arrangements, transport costs, health and safety legislation and technical standards, and labelling differences may have a greater, and more direct, impact.

20.64   In June 2000 a Communiqué was issued by the Commission indicating that, taking into account the findings in the report, there was to be no change to the rule of Community exhaustion.

Web link

You will find the Communiqué from Commissioner Bolkestein on the issue of exhaustion of trade mark rights, 7 June 2000, at **http://ec.europa.eu/internal_market/indprop/docs/tm/comexhaust_en.pdf.**

20.65   In May 2003 the issue was revisited, resulting in a Commission Working Paper, 'Possible abuses of trade mark rights within the EU in the context of Community exhaustion'.[118]

Web link

You will find this document on the Commission's Industrial Property section of the Europa website at **http://ec.europa.eu/internal_market/indprop/tm/index_en.htm.**

Set against the question as to whether the Community should move to a system of international exhaustion, the paper sought to identify whether there were any abuses of trade mark rights, to explain how they might have been addressed, and to identify deficiencies that may exist in the current legal provision.

Having examined selective distribution systems, abuse of a dominant position involving trade marks, and trade mark infringements, the conclusion of the report was that there was no evidence of deficiencies in the current legal provision relating to possible abuses of trade marks within the EU. It is still unlikely, several years on, that there will be any changes to the rules on Community-wide exhaustion in the near term. As a result, it is likely that the case law discussed previously, regarding the limits of Community-wide exhaustion, will continue to grow.

Key points on international exhaustion

- The exhaustion doctrine is limited to the Community
- Consent relates to batches of goods put onto the market and not to goods of a particular type
- The level for showing consent appears high and suggests a positive renunciation of the right to oppose importation

[118] SEC(2003) 575.

- Importing requires introduction of goods into the Community for the purposes of putting them on the market
- The burden of proving consent may shift between the parallel importer and the trade mark owner

Free movement of services

20.66   The doctrine of exhaustion, as discussed previously, applies to the right to control distribution. Within copyright it does not, however, apply to the right to rent, to perform, or to show a copy of a work in public. Here the specific subject matter of the right is to obtain a return from the exercise of the right which includes performance of a work. In *Coditel v Cine Vog (No 1)*[119] the owner of the copyright in a film, Le Boucher, granted cinema and television rights in Belgium to Cine Vog for a period of seven years. During this period a German version of the film was transmitted by cable into Belgium by Coditel. Cine Vog sued Coditel for an infringement of their exclusive rights. The ECJ held that 'the right of a copyright owner and his assigns to require fees for any showing of a film is part of the essential function of copyright in this type of literary and artistic work'[120] and accepted that the copyright owner could place geographic restrictions on the exploitation of performing rights.

20.67   Similar questions were raised in respect of the rental right[121] and the sound recording right[122] which received comparable rulings from the ECJ.

 Question

Explain why there is a distinction between the movement of goods around the Community and the movement of services. What policy goals underlie this distinction?
What Treaty provision deals with services?

20.68   As always, the law continues to evolve—most notably when challenged by new technologies. The law came under pressure with questions going to the heart of the interactions between copyright, free movement of goods and services, and competition law, which is discussed in Chaper 21,[123] in *Murphy v Media Protection Services*[124] joined with *FA Premier League v QC Leisure and others*.[125] The new technology in question was decoders and the issue was the receipt of broadcasts of football matches via a decoder supplied by a supplier to the UK, where the broadcaster had the IP right to broadcast within a defined territory which did not include the UK. Murphy purchased the decoder and used it to show the matches within licensed premises in the UK. The sale of the decoder in the third country was subject to the restriction that it could only be sold to a person who had an address in that country and was subject to an export ban as between the manufacturer and broadcaster. There was a criminal prosecution of the pub landlady

---

[119] Case C-62/79 [1980] ECR 881.   [120] *Copitel*, note 119, para 14.
[121] Case C-158/86 *Warner Bros v Christiansen* [1988] ECR 2605.   [122] Case C-402/85 *Basset v Sacem* [1987] ECR 1747.
[123] Media law is also relevant to the cases in that they involve the broadcasting of live football matches.
[124] Case C-429/08 [2008] EWHC 1666 (Admin).
[125] Case C-403/08, joined with Case 429/08 in order of the President of the Court 3 December 2008, *Football Association Premier League Ltd v QC Leisure, Murphy v Media Protection Services Ltd* [2012] 1 CMLR 29.

(*Murphy*), and a civil *FA Premier League* action against the supplier of a decoder.[126] The key issue for this chapter (see also Chapters 2, 4, 5, and 21) is the decision of the Court of Justice regarding the UK copyright legislation and the free movement provisions in the Treaty, and the meaning of illicit device, in Directive 98/84/EC (the Conditional Access Directive), which provides that member states cannot restrict the free movment of illicit devices.[127]

20.69   The Court of Justice took a narrow approach. Member states could preclude the use of decoding devices from another member state which had only been authorised for use in that other member state, those obtained using a false name, those put on the market only for private purposes, or those obtained in breach of contract.[128] Regarding the UK legislation dealing with the decoders, the Court of Justice found that the restrictions on decoding could not be justified. Legislation which conferred absolute territorial exclusivity did impose a restriction on free movement of services.[129] As a result, it can be permitted only if it is objectively justified in a proportionate manner. While the protection of IP, or indeed encouraging attendance at football matches, could meet this test, the broadcasters had already made a payment to the IP owner,[130] and encouraging attendance at games could be pursued by a contractual restriction on broadcast times by others.[131] The specific subject matter of IP was the right to exploit commercially IP, by granting licences in return for payment. This did not mean that the IP owner must get the highest possible remuneration, just what is reasonable, given the person who enjoys or wishes to enjoy the service.

 Exercise

Do you agree with the decision of the Court of Justice in *Murphy* and *Premier League*? After you have completed your work in IP as whole, draw of diagram of all the different IP issues which have arisen in this case. Do the findings fit together? Should they?

Exhaustion and the Infosoc Directive

20.70   The Directive on the harmonisation of certain aspects of copyright and related rights in the information society[132] (InfoSoc Directive) makes it clear that community exhaustion applies with respect to the movement of tangible copies of works incorporating copyright material.

Recital 28 of the Directive states:

> Copyright protection under this Directive includes the exclusive right to control distribution of the work incorporated in a tangible article. The first sale in the Community of the original of a work or copies thereof by the rightholder or with his consent exhausts the right to control resale of that object in the Community. This right should not be exhausted in respect of the original or of copies thereof sold by the rightholder or with his consent outside the Community.

---

[126] Copyright, Designs and Patents Act 1988 (as amended), ss 297 and 298.

[127] 'Illicit device' is defined in Art 2(e): 'illicit device shall mean any equipment or software designed or adapted to give access to a protected service in an intelligible form without the authorisation of the service provider.'

[128] *Football Association Premier League*, note 125, paras 62–74.

[129] Which is approached from the perspective of services, rather than goods, as goods were secondary on the facts (see para 83).

[130] *Football Association Premier League*, note 125, paras 93–95, 102–121, *Coditel* (see para 20.66) was distinguished.

[131] Paras 122–124.

[132] Directive 2001/29/EC of the European Parliament and of the Council of 22 May 2001 on the harmonisation of certain aspects of copyright and related rights in the information society.

Article 4(2) provides:

> The distribution right shall not be exhausted within the Community in respect of the original or copies of the work, except where the first sale or other transfer of ownership in the Community of that object is made by the right holder or with his consent.

However, where a work protected by copyright is delivered online, then the rights are not exhausted as expressed in recital 29:

> The question of exhaustion does not arise in the case of services and on-line services in particular. This also applies with regard to a material copy of a work or other subject-matter made by a user of such a service with the consent of the rightholder ... Unlike CD-ROM or CD-I, where the intellectual property is incorporated in a material medium, namely an item of goods, every on-line service is in fact an act which should be subject to authorisation where the copyright or related right so provides.

20.71   Thus, the act of uploading a work on to the Internet does not exhaust the right, nor does the act of downloading. Permission is thus needed to download (a reproduction), print (a reproduction), or further distribute any copies of a work obtained from the Internet. Even where a copy of a work has been printed down, exhaustion will not occur in relation to the printed copy; thus the copy could not, for example, be lent for commercial gain or resold to a third party. The matter becomes one of the terms of the contract as between the copyright owner and the downloader. (For a discussion on the interaction between copyright and contract, see Chapter 5.)

20.72   A case concerning the validity of Article 4(2) and whether it precludes member states from retaining international exhaustion in domestic legislation was referred to the ECJ by a Danish court, *Laserdisken ApS v Kulturministeriet*.[133] On the second point the ECJ held that, in conformity with recital 28, and Article 4(2) of the Directive, it is not open to member states to provide for a rule of exhaustion other than the Community-wide exhaustion rule.[134] On the first question, on the validity of the measure, the ECJ found that it was consistent with obligations to be found in the EC Treaty, and other international obligations (including the WIPO Copyright Treaty and the WIPO Performances and Phonograms Treaty, both of 1996).

Laserdisken had also argued that the maintenance of a Community-wide principle of exhaustion was anti-competitive, contrary to the principle of proportionality and breached the right to freedom of expression.[135] None of these arguments were accepted by the ECJ.

 Question

Do you think that arguments concerning cultural diversity and freedom of expression should hold sway over a rule that precludes international exhaustion?

Key point on free movement of services

- Copyright gives to the owner the right to control distribution of a work incorporated in a tangible article. First sale in the Community exhausts that right within the Community. There is no exhaustion in respect of the rights to rent, show, or perform a work in public, nor by online distribution.

---

[133] Case C-479/04 [2006] ECR I-8089.   [134] *Laserdisken*, note 133, para 24.
[135] Note that an argument against a finding of infringement based on human rights had also been advanced, unsuccessfully, by Tesco in *Levi Stores v Tesco Ltd* [2003] RPC 18.

Further reading

Book

C Stothers, *Parallel Trade in Europe: Intellectual Property, Competition and Regulatory Law* (2007)

Articles

I Avgoults, 'Parallel imports and exhaustion of trade mark rights: should steps be taken towards an international exhaustion regime?' (2012) 34(2) EIPR 108–121

AEL Brown, 'Post-harmonised Europe: united, divided or unimportant' [2001] 3 IPQ 275–286

T Cottier, 'The exhaustion of intellectual property rights—a fresh look' (2008) 39 IIC 755

D Edward, 'Trade marks, descriptions of origin and the internal market: the Stephen Stewart Memorial Lecture 2000' [2001] 2 IPQ 135–145

S Enchelmaier, 'The inexhaustible question—free movement of goods and intellectual property in the European Court of Justice's case law, 2002–2006' (2007) 38(4) IIC 453–470

A Feros, 'Free movement of pharmaceuticals within the EU—should rights be exhausted regionally' [2010] EIPR 486

N Gross and L Harrold, 'Fighting for pharmaceutical profits: the decision of the ECJ in *Boehringer Ingelheim v Swingward*' [2002] EIPR 497 and see also [2003] EIPR 582

V Korah, 'The exhaustion of patents by sale in a member state where monopoly profit could not be earned' (1997) 18(4) ECLR 265–273

HL MacQueen, 'International exhaustion of trade mark rights: a Scottish contribution to the debate' [2000] 4 IPQ 357–366

Y Marinova 'The European Court of Justice on external parallel trade: interpreting the law or constructing an implied trade mark infringement' [2009] 2 IPQ 254–280

K Maskus, 'The curious economics of parallel imports' (2010) 2(1) WIPO J 123–132

G Petursson and P Dyrberg, 'What is consent? A Note on Davidoff and Levi Strauss' (2002) 27(4) ELRev 464–471

IA Stamatoudi, 'From drugs to spirits and from boxes to publicity (decided and undecided cases in relation to trade marks and copyright exhaustion)' [1999] 1 IPQ 95–113

Intellectual property and EU competition law

Introduction

21.1   It will have been apparent from reading previous chapters that there is an unending tension between those who would argue for expansion of intellectual property rights (IPRs) on the ground that such are needed to encourage creators, and those who seek to limit, and even to roll back, the parameters of the rights on the ground that over-strong rights can harm innovation. Wherever these boundaries lie, those parts within them give to the right holder exclusive rights to deal with the subject matter in the market.

21.2   It will be recalled that one of the underlying justifications for the grant of IPRs is that innovation will be encouraged. The monopoly granted by the IPRs has been carefully crafted to ensure that, despite the extent of the right, competition will thrive in the marketplace ultimately for the benefit of consumers and users. But sometimes the exercise of IPRs can produce unexpected outcomes: perhaps an over-strong monopoly is acquired due to the popularity of a particular product protected by IPRs, the rightholder may then occupy a position of strength which may hamper competition in the marketplace; or owners of IPRs may enter into agreements which may not, ultimately, be to the benefit of consumers. Competition law, operated at national (UK) and European Union level, may then be used to regulate the behaviour of these entities in the marketplace.

Scope and overview of chapter

21.3   The purpose of this chapter, concentrating on EU competition law, is to provide an overview of some of the more common circumstances in which the Commission and the Court of Justice may intervene to regulate the exercise of IPRs by undertakings within the common market. The focus is on EU competition law as there is no international regime of competition rules. TRIPS authorises members to provide for national competition rules within certain limits,[1] but does not oblige them to do so. Accordingly competition law (called antitrust in the United States) emanates from regional and national rules which, in the UK, are now modelled on the EU provisions.

---

[1] TRIPS Agreement, Arts 8(2), 31, and 40.

21.4   **Learning objectives**

By the end of this chapter you should be able to describe and explain:

- the tension between the application of competition law and the exercise of IPRs and how that relates to the underlying justifications for the grant of IPRs;

- those circumstances in which competition law may be applied to moderate the exercise of IPRs in the relevant market;

- clauses in IP licensing agreements between undertakings that might be permissible in terms of EU competition law and those which are not;

- the conditions under which a refusal to supply products protected by an IP right might constitute an abuse of a dominant position by the right holder;

- the ongoing debate concerning the relevance of competition law to the exercise of IPRs.

21.5   The rest of the chapter looks like this:

- Theory of competition (21.6–21.10)
- Competition law and IP (21.11–21.19)
- Intellectual property and agreements between undertakings: Article 101 TFEU (21.20–21.42)
- Intellectual property and abuse of a dominant position: Article 102 TFEU (21.43–21.56)
- *Commission v Microsoft* (21.57–21.69)
- EU competition law in the UK courts: Eurodefences (21.70–21.77)

Theory of competition

21.6   Competition law seeks to regulate the behaviour of firms in the marketplace. In capitalist economies there is a belief that where there is competition between firms, this will ultimately be of benefit to consumers. This is because firms will:

- be unable to charge artificially high prices;
- continuously innovate to create new goods;
- make available those products necessary to meet consumer demand.

There is a theory that consumer welfare is maximised when there is *perfect competition*. In this model, available resources are *allocated efficiently*. This means that the consumer can buy the goods that they wish to buy, for the price they are prepared to pay, with this price not being above the marginal cost of production of the goods. Firms also work to *productive efficiency*. This means that the manufacturer makes goods for as low a cost as possible, while still making a profit. Such market conditions foster innovation or *dynamic efficiency* in which the firm is constantly striving to create new, and better, products to meet consumer demand.

21.7   At the heart of this economic analysis of competition, which as will be seen, is important to competition law, lies the concept of *market power*. If any one firm (or number of firms acting in concert) has the ability to reduce output and raise prices without concern that competitors might enter the market and fill consumer demand at lower prices, then the firm is said to be able to exercise market power. A single firm which can act substantially independently of its competitors and without regard to consumers is said to be able to exercise monopoly power and to be a *monopolist*. Two or more firms which, consciously or subconsciously, act in furtherance of a common goal in pursuit of which they deviate from competitive behaviour are termed *oligopolists*. Firms which collude to alter the competitive structure of a market to their own advantage by, for example, fixing prices or limiting production, are said to form a *cartel*.

 Question

Can you think of any flaws that might exist in this theory of perfect competition?
Can you think of any firm which you think is a monopolist through ownership and/or exercise of IPRs? Analyse your response. Why have you thought of the particular firm? What factors have you considered important in your decision? Try and think of a second example from a different industry sector. Did you approach the exercise the same way? Revisit these questions once you have finished this chapter and see if your analysis changes.

Workable competition

21.8   There are many flaws in the theory of perfect competition. Not only does it presuppose that decisions are made rationally by those decision-makers responsible for directing corporate strategy and behaviour in the marketplace, but it also assumes that consumers have perfect knowledge of market conditions and will also make rational decisions when it comes to purchases.

21.9   The deficiencies have led to the development of a theory of 'workable' or 'effective competition':[2]

> Effective competition does connote the idea … that firms should be subject to a reasonable degree of competitive constraint, from actual and potential competitors and from customers, and that the role of a competition authority is to be that such constraints are present on the market.[3]

The goal of EU and UK competition policy would appear to be predicated on this notion of effective competition[4] and is to maintain competition within the internal market.

Cartels and monopolies

21.10   In order to maintain a state of effective or workable competition, competition law is directed towards dealing with abuses that can occur to upset that state. These include:

- preventing agreements between firms that have the effect of restricting competition between them;
- checking behaviour by monopolists who might abuse their dominant position and prevent new competition emerging;
- ensuring workable competition is maintained between oligopolists;
- monitoring mergers between independent firms the effect of which may be to concentrate the market and diminish competitive pressures.[5]

---

[2] R Whish and D Bailey, *Competition Law* (7th edn, 2012), 17–18.   [3] Whish and Bailey, note 2, 18.
[4] WR Cornish, D Llewelyn, and T Aplin, *Intellectual Property: Patents, Copyright, Trade Marks and Allied Rights* (7th edn, 2010), paras 1-39–1-47.   [5] Whish and Bailey, note 2, 26.

This chapter will consider the first two of those as they relate to the exercise of IPRs and as regulated by Articles 101 and 102 TFEU (ex Arts 81 and 82 EC). Note that the Article numbering which applies following the changes made by the Treaty of Lisbon will be used in this chapter except where the discussion relates to historical events and/or where quotations from cases are used in the text.

Competition law and IP

21.11   As IP laws confer on the owner exclusive rights, so the owner can prevent competition in relation to the subject matter of the right. However, there is a constant tension between the grant of those exclusive rights and the application of competition law. The aim is to find the balance between IPRs and competitive markets. On the interaction between IP and competition law, the Commission has stated:

> The fact that intellectual property laws grant exclusive rights of exploitation does not imply that intellectual property rights are immune from competition law intervention. Articles 81 and 82 are in particular applicable to agreements whereby the holder licenses another undertaking to exploit his intellectual property rights. Nor does it imply that there is an inherent conflict between intellectual property rights and the Community competition rules. Indeed, both bodies of law share the same basic objective of promoting consumer welfare and an efficient allocation of resources. Innovation constitutes an essential and dynamic component of an open and competitive market economy. Intellectual property rights promote dynamic competition by encouraging undertakings to invest in developing new or improved products and processes. So does competition by putting pressure on undertakings to innovate. Therefore, both intellectual property rights and competition are necessary to promote innovation and ensure a competitive exploitation thereof.[6]

Exercise

Familiarise yourself with the terms of both Articles 101 and 102 TFEU. Consider the mischief they are aimed at and see if you can think of any examples where they might apply to the exercise of IPRs.

21.12   Some concepts are common in any discussion of competition law. The purpose of this next section is to introduce some of these to assist the reader in understanding this chapter.

The relevant market

21.13   The term *market* is usually understood as the place where business is done between companies. As was discussed previously, in a state of workable competition, firms will compete against each other in this market to the ultimate benefit of consumers. If a number of firms enter into an agreement which upsets competitive market conditions, or a monopolist is able to, and does, act independently of either competitors or consumers, then the market is said to be distorted.

21.14   But it is only behaviour on the *relevant market* that is taken into account when looking to the behaviour of these entities. This immediately leads to questions as to how the relevant market should be defined. The starting point is generally to look at those products which are in competition. But within these confines if a market is defined too widely, then it is unlikely that anti-competitive conduct will have an

---

[6] Commission Notice, Guidelines on the application of Article 81 of the EC Treaty to technology transfer agreements, OJ 2004/C 101/02; the Commission also issued a Report on Competition Policy 2008, COM(2009) 374.

adverse effect. For example, if there is an agreement between manufacturers to increase the retail price of wine, this would be unlikely to affect competition in the manufacture, distribution, and sale of all drinks, both alcoholic and non-alcoholic. A narrowing of this definition might look to alcoholic drinks. Narrowing it still further might concentrate on wines; or wines from a particular region. But taking a definition that is overly narrow can be equally problematic. For instance, raising the price of one brand of children's clothing might be considered an abuse of a dominant position if the market is defined as that particular brand.

■ Case C-22/78 *Hugin Kassaregister AB and Hugin Cash Registers Ltd v Commission of the European Communities* [1979] ECR 1869[7]

In this case the relevant market was defined very narrowly. Hugin made cash register machines in London and had a 13 per cent share of the cash register market; Lipton, a small firm in South East England serviced the registers. Hugin wanted to get into the servicing market and as part of that strategy it refused to supply spare parts to Liptons. In looking to the relevant market, both the Commission and the European Court of Justice (ECJ) found that it was in spare parts for the machines (although ultimately the Court found that there was no effect on interstate trade). Had the market been defined as that of the product (the cash register) *and* the spare parts, then Hugin would not have been dominant.

21.15   The Commission has published a Notice on Market Definition.[8] This sets out the factors that are taken into account in defining the relevant market. The Commission focuses on demand and supply product substitutability and potential competition. To determine the relevant market it is necessary to investigate both the relevant product market and the relevant geographical market. The relevant product market includes those products which are regarded as interchangeable or substitutable by the consumer. This may be because of the characteristics of the products, the price, and intended use. The relevant geographical market refers to the area in which the businesses are involved in the supply and demand of products or services.

> ### Web link
>
> Read the Commission's Notice on Market Definition, which can be found at
> **http://europa.eu/legislation_summaries/competition/firms/l26073_en.htm.**

Intra brand competition

21.16   Competition exists at different levels between businesses in the marketplace. A manufacturer may produce a particular product, for example soap powder. Wholesalers who purchase the soap powder from the manufacturer, and retailers who sell the soap powder to the consumer may then compete with each other in the downstream market. This is called *intra brand* competition—competition between distributors of the same brand. Here the goods are the same and therefore quality is an irrelevant factor. The price at which the product is sold, availability on the market, and the conditions under which it is sold may however be important. For example, the soap powder may be sold at a lower price in a discount supermarket as compared with a more upmarket store, but often without the amenities and services that the latter provides.

---

[7] Similar issues arose in Case T-30/89 *Hilti AG v Commission of the European Communities* [1991] ECR II-143.

[8] Commission Notice on the definition of the relevant market for the purposes of Community competition law, OJ 1997/C 372.

Inter brand competition

21.17   *Inter brand* competition is where competition exists between suppliers of competing products, for example two differently branded soap powders. Such competition is normally between different firms that have developed brands or labels for their products in order to distinguish them from other brands sold in the same market segment, although sometimes the same manufacturer may develop a number of differently branded products of the same kind. Ariel versus Persil is an example of inter brand competition. Consumers are interested in the quality and the price of the goods as well as, for many products, after-sales service.

Horizontal agreements

21.18   A horizontal agreement is one between two or more actual or potential competitors, operating at the same level of the production or distribution chain. Such an agreement may cover, for example, research and development, production, or purchasing. Horizontal agreements may restrict competition where they involve price fixing or market sharing, or where the market power resulting from the horizontal cooperation causes negative market effects with respect to prices, output, innovation, or the variety and quality of products, for example if those involved in an industry agree that one technology is to be used for a particular purpose. On the other hand, horizontal cooperation can be a means to share risk, save costs, pool know-how, minimize inefficient duplication, increase consumer choice, and launch innovation more quickly. In particular for small and medium-sized enterprises, cooperation can be an important means to adapt to the changing marketplace.[9]

Vertical agreements

21.19   A vertical agreement is one entered into between two or more undertakings each of which operates at a different level of the production or distribution chain. Vertical agreements tend to be less able to affect other parties and thus foreclose competition on the relevant market. However, where either party has a large market share in the relevant market, vertical agreements can affect third parties who supply the same or substitutable goods. An example would be an agreement between a distributor and a manufacturer which prevented other manufacturers from competing to sell goods to that distributor. The effect may be to foreclose competition in the downstream market.

Intellectual property and agreements between undertakings: Article 101 TFEU

21.20   Article 101 TFEU concerns agreements between undertaking which have the object or effect of preventing, restricting, or distorting competition within the common market, and which may affect trade

---

[9] For discussion of IP and competition issues relating to the development of technology standards, see M Lemley, 'Intellectual property rights and standard-setting organizations' (2002) 90 California Law Review 1889. Regarding IP, standards, and previous competition investigations, see the ETSI webpage on IP with policies and rules (Annex 6, revised November 2011), available at http://www.etsi.org/WebSite/AboutETSI/IPRsInETSI/IPRsinETSI.aspx, European Union Press Release, 'Antitrust: Commission accepts commitments from Rambus lowering memory chip royalty rates—Frequently Asked Questions' (9 December 2009), available at http://europa.eu/rapid/pressReleasesAction.do?reference=MEMO/09/544&format=HTML&aged=1&language=EN&guiLanguage=en, and P Treacy and S Lawrance, 'FRANDly fire: are industry standards doing more harm than good?' (2008) 3(1) JIPLP 22.

between member states. The interpretation and application of this Article is central in determining the acceptable boundaries of agreements and the clauses they contain entered into between parties which relate to the exploitation of IP, through licensing, and also horizontal and vertical agreements.

Article 101 TFEU (ex Art 81 EC)

1. The following shall be prohibited as incompatible with the common market: all agreements between undertakings, decisions by associations of undertakings and concerted practices which may affect trade between Member States and which have as their object or effect the prevention, restriction or distortion of competition within the common market, and in particular those which:
   (a) directly or indirectly fix purchase or selling prices or any other trading conditions;
   (b) limit or control production, markets, technical development, or investment;
   (c) share markets or sources of supply;
   (d) apply dissimilar conditions to equivalent transactions with other trading parties, thereby placing them at a competitive disadvantage;
   (e) make the conclusion of contracts subject to acceptance by the other parties of supplementary obligations which, by their nature or according to commercial usage, have no connection with the subject of such contracts.

2. Any agreements or decisions prohibited pursuant to this Article shall be automatically void.

3. The provisions of paragraph 1 may, however, be declared inapplicable in the case of:
   – any agreement or category of agreements between undertakings;
   – any decision or category of decisions by associations of undertakings;
   – any concerted practice or category of concerted practices,

which contributes to improving the production or distribution of goods or to promoting technical or economic progress, while allowing consumers a fair share of the resulting benefit, and which does not:
   (a) impose on the undertakings concerned restrictions which are not indispensable to the attainment of these objectives;
   (b) afford such undertakings the possibility of eliminating competition in respect of a substantial part of the products in question.

21.21   The Commission has said that, in the context of the single market programme, the objective of Article 101 TFEU (at that time Art 81 EC) is to protect competition on the market as a means of enhancing consumer welfare and of ensuring an efficient allocation of resources.[10] It will be noted from the text of the Article that agreements which are prohibited by Article 101 TFEU are void Article 101(2) TFEU. However, Article 101(3) TFEU provides that the provisions of Article 101(1) TFEU may be declared inapplicable in specified circumstances—in other words, an agreement would not be in breach of Article 101(1) TFEU. This Article will be discussed later.

Article 101 TFEU and licensing agreements

21.22   A common way of exploiting intellectual property is through a licensing agreement (paras 22.8ff). The holder of a patent might not have the financial resources to develop and exploit the patent, and so may enter into an agreement with a third party. A singer may need the help of a record company to record, market, and distribute recordings of performances, or of a collecting society to ingather sums due for the performance of that song in public. Such an agreement with one entity may well foreclose the IP owner from dealing with other parties, at least within the scope of the first arrangement, and thus be restrictive of competition as regards third parties. Equally, a licensing agreement may be pro-competitive. A licensee is permitted to do something that would otherwise be an infringement of another's rights.

---

[10] Guidelines on the application of Article 81(3) of the Treaty, 2004/C 101/08.

The owner will get a financial return while others can improve efficiency in terms of both manufacture and distribution of the products. The question then is as to when and where might the prohibitions on anti-competitive conduct found in Article 101(1) TFEU apply to licensing agreements concerning IP to render an agreement void and unenforceable?

As will be seen from the text of Article 101 TFEU, an agreement is not within its scope unless:

- it has the object or effect of preventing, distorting, or restricting competition. Where an agreement has the object of preventing competition, for example through absolute territorial exclusivity, then there will be no need to examine the economic effect of the agreement in the market. Where it is not intended to foreclose competition, then the effect of the agreement in the market will have to be analysed; this can be a difficult exercise; see, for example, *GlaxoSmithKline Services Unlimited v Commission of the European Communities* [2009] ECR I-9291;
- it may affect trade between member states. Trade must be affected to an appreciable extent. To help businesses assess whether Article 101 TFEU (ex Art 81 EC) may be applicable, the Commission has published a Notice on Agreements of Minor Importance which sets out the market share thresholds below which an agreement will be regarded as *de minimis*.[11] These are set at 10 per cent market share for agreements between competitors and to 15 per cent for agreements between non-competitors.

It should also be noted that any type of agreement between two or more entities might fall under Article 101 TFEU. An agreement does not have to be in writing and can extend to 'informal' understandings (concerted practices) between undertakings in the market, for instance an understanding not to enter the territory of another competitor.

Web link

For a series of model licensing agreements see
http://www.innovation.gov.uk/lambertagreements/index.asp?lvl1=2&lvl2=0&lvl3=0&lvl4=0.

 ## Exercise

The agreements refered to in the Web link have been prepared by the Lambert Committee which was charged with developing model agreements for use where one of the parties to the agreement is an educational institution. Read through some of the agreements to familiarise yourself with the type of provisions to be found in these documents. In what ways do you think Article 101(1) TFEU might need to be considered? Revisit your answer when you have finished this section.

ECJ case law, Article 101 TFEU, and IP agreements

21.23   In the early development of case law on the application of Article 81(1) EC to IP licences, the ECJ followed a fairly restrictive approach to what it considered may fall foul of the Treaty. This was a consequence of the pursuit of the goal of bringing about a free market between member states. This approach tended

---

[11] Commission Notice on agreements of minor importance which do not appreciably restrict competition under Article 81(1) of the Treaty establishing the European Community (de minimis), OJ 2001/ C 368/13.

to be followed irrespective of broader economic benefits that may have been brought about through an agreement. In so doing, the ECJ developed a distinction between the *existence* and *exercise* of an IPR which in turn led to a consideration of the *specific subject matter*. The existence/exercise dichotomy, which term was also discussed in paras 20.14ff, can be seen in *Consten & Grundig v EEC Commission*.

■ Case C-56/64 *Consten & Grundig v EEC Commission* [1966] ECR 299

A German manufacturer, Grundig, made electrical goods in Germany. Grundig entered into an agreement with Consten, a French distributor, whereby Consten would distribute Grundig's products in France under both Grundig and Gint trade marks. The intention was to grant Consten absolute territorial protection for the distribution of Grundig's products in France. Grundig sought to achieve this by:

• imposing certain terms on other wholesalers and distributors including re-export bans and express terms prohibiting distribution of Grundig products in France; and

• entering into a licence agreement which authorised the exclusive use by Consten of Grundig's trade mark, Gint, in France which would be assigned to Consten once the agreement came to an end.

The Commission condemned these agreements as a breach of what is now Article 101(1). Both parties sought annulment of the Commission decision.

The ECJ said:

• Article 101 (as it is now) applies to both horizontal and vertical agreements.

• An agreement between a manufacturer and distributor who are not in competition might have an adverse effect on competition between one of them and a third party. It is thus distortive of competition to make an agreement designed to insulate national markets.

Importantly for present purposes, the Court went on to say that the injunction contained in the contested decision to refrain from using rights in national trade mark law in order to set an obstacle in the way of parallel imports *does not affect the grant* of those rights, but only *limits their exercise* to the extent necessary to give effect to the prohibition under what is now Article 101.

Points to note:

• The Court considered the licensing of the trade mark a material factor in the attempt to ensure for Consten absolute territorial exclusivity. This caused the agreement to fall foul of what is now Article 101. (Note, however, that the approach to territorial exclusivity has changed over time—see, for example, the *Nungesser/Maize Seeds* case discussed later.)

• The purpose of registration of the trade mark in France was to increase the protection against parallel imports into France of Grundig products. In other words, it was to give Consten its own means of repelling the parallel imports of genuine Grundig products from other member states.

21.24   In *Windsurfing International v Commission*,[12] the Commission and the ECJ used the concept of *specific subject matter* to determine the compatibility of what is now Article 101 TFEU with a patent licensing agreement.

■ Case C-193/83 *Windsurfing International v Commission* [1986] ECR 611

Windsurfing invented a rig for a sailboard. Patents were applied for in several countries including Germany. Windsurfing entered into a number of agreements with licensees in Germany.

---

[12] Case C-193/83 [1986] ECR 611.

The provisions in the licence included:

- Clauses tying patented goods to unpatented goods. The patent itself only covered the rig. The licence tied exploitation of the rig to exploitation of the sailboard. In other words, if a licensee wanted a licence to manufacturer and sell the patented rig mechanism, they also had to manufacture and sell the sailboard.

- Royalties were to be calculated on the basis of sales of final assembled goods. This included both patented and unpatented products.

- A requirement to fix patent attribution and the logo to both patented and unpatented goods.

- A 'no-challenge' clause.

The Commission and then the ECJ found that a number of these clauses went beyond the *specific subject matter* of the patent. In other words, there was an attempt by the patentee to extend the patent monopoly.

The ECJ said:

> the clauses contained in the licensing agreements, in so far as they relate to parts of the sailboard not covered by the German patent or include the complete sailboard within their terms of reference, can therefore find no justification on grounds of the protection of an industrial property right.[13]

21.25 Little use was made of the existence/exercise and specific subject matter doctrine by either the Commission or ECJ during the 1990s. One of the leading writers in this area, Tritton, suggested that: 'It is probable it will be relied on in the future in Article 81 to the extent that [clauses in licences] which are related to the specific subject matter of an IPR will be permissible without further analysis'.[14] Such clauses may include an obligation to pay royalties and relate to quality control.

 Question

What is a 'no-challenge' clause? Why might this be relevant to the interface between IP and competition?

 Exercise 1

Compare the emergence of the existence/exercise/specific subject matter doctrines used in the application of Article 101 TFEU to IP agreements with those developed in relation to the free movement of goods (see Chapter 20, in particular para 20.14).

Exercise 2

Consider ways in which you think agreements between undertakings dealing with IP might fall under the prohibitions in Article 101 TFEU. Might or should this extend to evolving forms of sharing, such as Creative Commons licences discussed at para 7.5. Revisit this question at the end of your work in this chapter.

---

[13] *Windsurfing*, point 36.   [14] G Tritton, *Intellectual Property in Europe* (2nd edn, 2002), para 8-062.

21.26   The Court of Justice and the ECJ have also used an economic-based approach (often termed a *'rule of reason'*, particularly in the United States) in its application of Article 101 TFEU and its predecessors to IP agreements. Broadly this consists of an economic analysis of an agreement on the relevant market. If the agreement has pro-competitive effects which outweigh the anti-competitive effects, then it should not be prohibited by competition laws.[15]

This approach can be seen in *Nungesser v Commission*[16] otherwise known as the *Maize Seed* case in which the central question was whether an exclusive licence of plant breeders' rights infringed what is now Article 101(1).

■ Case C-258/78 *Nungesser v Commission* [1981] ECR 45

A French Institute developed varieties of maize seeds for which it held plant breeders' rights in French and German law. By a series of agreements the German rights were partly licensed and partly assigned to a German undertaking. The French Institute agreed to ensure absolute territorial exclusivity for the production and sale of the seeds in Germany. It did so by pursuing the following strategy:

The French Institute agreed:

- not to license another undertaking in Germany to produce or sell the seeds;
- not itself to produce the seeds in Germany; and
- not itself to export seeds to Germany, and to obtain agreement from other licensees in other territories that they would not export seeds to Germany.

The Commission took a rigid view of what is now Article 101(1) and held that the grant of exclusive rights contravened its provisions. When the case was heard by the ECJ, the Court took a different approach. The ECJ sought to reconcile the objectives of free competition between member states and the wider competitive benefits of exclusive licences of IP rights. It did so by drawing a distinction between:

- *'open exclusive licences'* where exclusive rights are granted for one territory; and
- *'closed licences'* in terms of which steps are taken to ensure there is no competition from entities in other territories.

The ECJ said that open licences were acceptable. Some exclusivity may be essential to encourage a potential licensee to invest in a new product. Therefore the agreement not to license another German undertaking and not to produce the seeds in Germany itself were acceptable. However, that part of the agreement by virtue of which the French Institute was to seek agreement from other licensees not to import into Germany was void as it affected the position of third parties such as parallel importers.

21.27   Often, however, cases do not include detailed economic reasoning. Joined Cases *Murphy v Media Protection Services*[17] and *FA Premier League v QC Leisure and others*[18] were criminal and civil actions respectively concerning the supply of decoders and receipt of broadcasts of football matches (see also para 20.68 and discussion in chapters 2, 3, and 5). One part of the cases involves agreements between the manufacturer and broadcaster to place an export ban on the decoders to be in contravention of the competition rules on market sharing in Article 101. The court making the reference to the ECJ considered

---

[15] For an in-depth discussion on the problems caused by segmentation of the internal market, see the European Commission's 'Online Commerce Roundtable Report on Opportunities and barriers to online retailing' at http://ec.europa.eu/competition/consultations/2009_online_commerce/roundtable_report_en.pdf.

[16] Case C-258/78 [1981] ECR 45.   [17] Case C-429/08 [2008] EWHC 1666 (Admin).

[18] Case C-403/08. Joined with Case 429/08 in order of the President of the Court, 3 December 2008.

in detail the *Nungesser* arguments, economics, and issues arising from open and closed licensing.[19] The Court of Justice engaged in more limited discussion of economics and case law. It found that such an exclusive licence between an IP owner and a broadcaster regarding decoding devices was a restriction prohibited by Article 101.[20]

21.28   Yet, the economic balancing approach which has been seen throughout these cases, now after some hesitation seems to be pursued by the Commission:

> The aim of the Community competition rules is to protect competition on the market as a means of enhancing consumer welfare and of ensuring an efficient allocation of resources. Agreements that restrict competition may at the same time have pro-competitive effects by way of efficiency gains. Efficiencies may create additional value by lowering the cost of producing an output, improving the quality of the product or creating a new product. When the pro-competitive effects of an agreement outweigh its anti-competitive effects the agreement is on balance pro-competitive and compatible with the objectives of the Community competition rules. The net effect of such agreements is to promote the very essence of the competitive process, namely to win customers by offering better products or better prices than those offered by rivals.[21]

 Exercise

Can you see any drawbacks in the adoption of an economic rule of reason approach? How easy or difficult do you think it is for companies operating in the marketplace to carry out a detailed economic analysis of the effect of an agreement in the relevant market? Might this depend on the industry sector?

Article 101(2) TFEU

21.29   If an agreement falls within Article 101(1) TFEU then it is void. A national court may determine if a particular clause is severable and those parts of the agreement not caught may continue.

Article 101(3) TFEU

21.30   Even if an agreement does fall under Article 101(1) TFEU, it may be exempted under Article 101(3). This Article exempts agreements which improve production or distribution of products, or which contribute to technical or economic progress. This is subject to the proviso that consumers must gain a share of the benefit. However, any restrictions should only be such as are indispensable and not eliminate competition in respect of a substantial part of the products in question.

21.31   A new procedural regime came into force on 1 May 2004 for the application of Article 81(3) EC (now Art 101(3) TFEU). Under the old regime,[22] application could be made to the Commission for exemption under this Article unless the agreement fell within one of the block exemption Regulations (discussed

---

[19] *Football Association Premier League Ltd v QC Leisure* [2008] EWHC 1411 (Ch), [2008] 3 CMLR 12, paras 336–368.

[20] Cases C-403/08 and C429/08 *Murphy v Media Protection Services Ltd, Football Association Premier League Ltd v QC Leisure* [2012] 1 CMLR 29, paras 134–146 and AG paras 243–251. See discussion in J Anderson, 'The curious case of the Portsmouth publican: challenging the territorial exclusivity of TV rights in European professional sport (Case Comment)' (2011) 11(3) International Sports Law Review 53–60, in particular from 55.

[21] Commission Notice, Guidelines on the application of Article 81 of the EC Treaty to technology transfer agreements, OJ 2004/C 101/02, para 33; see also the discussion in Chapter 22 on collective licensing and Article 101 regarding *Re CISAC Agreement Case* (COMP/C2/38.698) [2009] 4 CMLR 12, which has been appealed to the General Court, Case T-442/08 *CISAC v Commission*. For an informal report on the hearing, see http://chillingcompetition.com/2011/10/20/hearing-in-cisac-v-commission-and-more/.

[22] Council Regulation No 17/62 of 6 February 1962.

later). In 2004 a Regulation came into force under which Article 81(3) became directly applicable.[23] Under this, it is for businesses to self-assess whether an agreement falls under Article 101(1) TFEU. A ruling on the legality of an agreement will only be required if a dispute or complaint arises. At that point, national competition authorities and national courts will have concurrent jurisdiction with the Commission including the right to rule on the legality of an agreement under Article 101(3) TFEU.

 Question

What does direct applicability mean?

21.32 Alongside this new procedure the Commission issued a set of guidelines which set out the Commission's interpretation of the conditions for application of the exception contained in Article 101(3) TFEU, and to provide guidance on how the Commission will apply Article 101 TFEU in individual cases. In so doing the Commission has indicated that it will weigh the pro- and anti-competitive effects of agreements between undertakings.

> The assessment under Article 81 ... consists of two parts. The first step is to assess whether an agreement between undertakings, which is capable of affecting trade between Member States, has an anti-competitive object or actual or potential anti competitive effects. The second step, which only becomes relevant when an agreement is found to be restrictive of competition, is to determine the pro-competitive benefits produced by that agreement and to assess whether these pro-competitive effects outweigh the anti-competitive effects.[24]

Web link

The Commission has issued a raft of Notices and Communications resulting from their programme designed to update and modernise EU competition (antitrust) rules and procedures. These can be found at **http://ec.europa.eu/competition/antitrust/legislation/legislation.html**.

Note in particular the Guidelines on the application of Article 81(3) of the Treaty (2004/ C 101/08). The Commission has also issued a number of Notices on vertical and horizontal agreements which set out the principles that will be used in assessing the impact of these agreements on the relevant market and thus whether the agreement would be within Article 101(3). Details of the 2011 EU Guidelines in respect of horizontal agreements follow.[25]

Web link

For the Guidelines on the applicability of Article 101 of the Treaty on the Functioning of the European Union to horizontal co-operation agreements, OJ C 11, 14 January 2011, see **http://eur-lex.europa.eu/LexUriServ/LexUriServ.do?uri=CELEX:52011XC0114(04):EN:NOT**. For a full list of the various Notices issued by the Commission relating to competition rules, see **http://ec.europa.eu/competition/antitrust/legislation/entente3_en.html**.

---

[23] Council Regulation (EC) No 1/2003 of 16 December 2002 on the implementation of the rules on competition laid down in Articles 81 and 82 of the Treaty; for a 2009 report on Regulation 1/2003 and enforcement, see COM(2009) 206.

[24] Commission Notice, Guidelines on the application of Article 81(3) of the Treaty, OJ 2004/C 101/08, para 11.

[25] Regarding their approach to standards, see S Sattler, 'Standardisation under EU competition rules—the Commission's new horizontal guidelines' (2011) 32(7) ECLR 343–349.

Block exemption Regulations

21.33   The Guidelines may not always be the most important instruments to consider in relation to agreements. The Commission (acting on delegated authority from the EU Council of Ministers) may, pursuant to Article 101(3) TFEU, issue block exemptions relating to the licensing and sharing of IP. A block exemption specifies those conditions under which certain types of agreements are exempted from the prohibition laid down in Article 101(1) TFEU. When an agreement fulfils the conditions set out in a block exemption regulation, the agreement is automatically valid and enforceable. Block exemption regulations exist in a number of sectors including for vertical agreements,[26] vertical restraints,[27] research and development (R&D) agreements,[28] technology transfer agreements,[29] and car distribution agreements[30] and have become a valuable tool for businesses.

The most important for current purposes is the Technology Transfer Block Exemption Regulation.

Technology Transfer Block Exemption Regulation

21.34   The initial IP block exemptions promulgated by the Commission dealt separately with the licensing of patents[31] and know-how.[32] These block exemptions were replaced in 1996 by one instrument, the Technology Transfer Block Exemption (TTBE),[33] covering technology transfer agreements generally. Following extensive consultation the TTBE was replaced by a revised Technology Transfer Block Exemption Regulation, the TTBER, which came into force in 2004[34] and which is accompanied by its own very important set of guidelines[35] on the application of Article 101 TFEU to technology transfer agreements.

21.35   The TTBER is relevant to undertakings which enter into technology transfer (licensing) agreements where those agreements deal with patents, know-how, software copyright, or a mixture of these IPRs. The TTBER also covers those agreements which include other IPRs, as long as those are not the primary object of the agreement.[36]

21.36   The TTBER distinguishes between licensing arrangements between competitors and non-competitors: the question is whether the agreement restricts actual or potential competition that would have existed without the agreement.[37] Competing undertakings (horizontal agreements) may benefit from the exemptions only where the combined market share[38] of the parties does not exceed 20 per cent of

[26] Commission Regulation (EU) No 330/2010 on the application of Article 101(3) of the Treaty on the Functioning of the European Union to categories of vertical agreements and concerted practices, OJ L102, 23.4. 2010.

[27] Commission Notice, Guidelines on Vertical Restraints, OJ 2010/C 130/01.

[28] Commission Regulation (EU) No 1217/2010 on the application of Article 101(3) of the Treaty on the Functioning of the European Union to certain categories of research and development agreements, OJ L 335, 18.12.2010.

[29] Commission Regulation (EC) No 772/2004 of 27 April 2004 on the application of Article 81(3) of the Treaty to categories of technology transfer agreements.

[30] Commission Regulation 461/2010 on the application of Article 101(3) of the Treaty on the Functioning of the European Union to categories of vertical agreements and concerted practices in the motor vehicle sector, OJ L129, 28.5.2010.

[31] Regulation 2349/84, OJ 1984 L219, amended by Regulation 151/93, OJ 1993 L21/8 and Regulation 2131/95, OJ 1995 L214/6.

[32] Regulation 556/89, OJ 1989 L61, amended by Regulation 151/93, OJ 1993 L21/8.

[33] Regulation 240/96, OJ 1996 L31/2.

[34] TTBER, note 29. At time of going to press, this is under review.

[35] Guidelines on the application of Article 81 of the EC Treaty to technology transfer agreements, 2004/C 101/02 (TTBER Guidelines).

[36] TTBER, note 29, Art 1(b).   [37] TTBER Guidelines, note 35, para 12.

[38] Market share is defined in terms of presence of the licensed technology on the relevant technology market and includes the licensor's and all its current licensees' share of the market. TTBER, Art 1(j).

either a relevant technology market or a relevant product market;[39] non-competing undertakings (vertical agreements) may benefit from the exemptions only where the market share of each party does not exceed 30 per cent on the relevant technology and product markets.[40] If parties have a market share in excess of that specified, then any contractual restrictions will be subject to analysis.

The Regulation works on the premise that any clauses which are not forbidden are exempt. Two classes of restrictions are set out and detail those clauses that would, or might (unless severable), cause the agreement to be non-exempt.

Hardcore restrictions[41]

21.37   Hardcore restrictions will, if included, mean that the agreement falls outwith the TTBER.[42] These are based on the nature of the restriction and have, through experience, been found to be anti-competitive.[43] They vary depending on whether the agreement is one between competitors or non-competitors.

- Where the parties are competitors, then prohibited clauses include:
    (a) the restriction of a party's ability to determine its prices when selling products to third parties—for instance, by setting the exact price at which the products can be sold, or the range of prices with maximum rebates;
    (b) the limitation of output, except limitations on the output of contract products imposed on the licensee in a non-reciprocal agreement or imposed on only one of the licensees in a reciprocal agreement;
    (c) the allocation of markets or customers except:
        (i) the obligation on the licensee(s) to produce with the licensed technology only within one or more technical fields of use or one or more product markets,
        (ii) the obligation on the licensor and/or the licensee, in a non-reciprocal agreement, not to produce with the licensed technology within one or more technical fields of use or one or more product markets or one or more exclusive territories reserved for the other party,
        (iii) the obligation on the licensor not to license the technology to another licensee in a particular territory,
        (iv) the restriction, in a non-reciprocal agreement, of active and/or passive sales by the licensee and/or the licensor into the exclusive territory or to the exclusive customer group reserved for the other party,
        (v) the restriction, in a non-reciprocal agreement, of active sales by the licensee into the exclusive territory or to the exclusive customer group allocated by the licensor to another licensee provided the latter was not a competing undertaking of the licensor at the time of the conclusion of its own licence,
        (vi) the obligation on the licensee to produce the contract products only for its own use provided that the licensee is not restricted in selling the contract products actively and passively as spare parts for its own products,
        (vii) the obligation on the licensee, in a non-reciprocal agreement, to produce the contract products only for a particular customer, where the licence was granted in order to create an alternative source of supply for that customer;
    (d) the restriction of the licensee's ability to exploit its own technology or the restriction of the ability of any of the parties to the agreement to carry out research and development, unless such latter restriction is indispensable to prevent the disclosure of the licensed know-how to third parties.
- Where the parties are not in competition then prohibited clauses include:
    (a) the restriction of a party's ability to determine its prices when selling products to third parties, without prejudice to the possibility of imposing a maximum sale price or recommending a sale price, provided that it does not amount to a fixed or minimum sale price as a result of pressure from, or incentives offered by, any of the parties;

---

[39] TTBER, note 29, Art 3(1).   [40] TTBER, note 29, Art 3(2).   [41] TTBER, note 29, Art 4.
[42] TTBER, note 29, Art 4(1), (2).   [43] TTBER Guidelines, note 35, para 74.

(b) the restriction of the territory into which, or of the customers to whom, the licensee may passively sell the contract products, except:

(i) the restriction of passive sales into an exclusive territory or to an exclusive customer group reserved for the licensor,

(ii) the restriction of passive sales into an exclusive territory or to an exclusive customer group allocated by the licensor to another licensee during the first two years that this other licensee is selling the contract products in that territory or to that customer group,

(iii) the obligation to produce the contract products only for its own use provided that the licensee is not restricted in selling the contract products actively and passively as spare parts for its own products,

(iv) the obligation to produce the contract products only for a particular customer, where the licence was granted in order to create an alternative source of supply for that customer,

(v) the restriction of sales to end users by a licensee operating at the wholesale level of trade,

(vi) the restriction of sales to unauthorised distributors by the members of a selective distribution system;

(c) the restriction of active or passive sales to end users by a licensee which is a member of a selective distribution system and which operates at the retail level, without prejudice to the possibility of prohibiting a member of the system from operating out of an unauthorised place of establishment.

 Exercise

Read the TTBER and the Guidelines. Explain why these particular clauses are considered to be restrictive of competition and thus prohibited in IP agreements.

Excluded restrictions

21.38 The TTBER also contains excluded restrictions.[44] These are clauses that do not fall under the TTBER and thus require individual assessment as to their pro- or anti-competitive effect. Their inclusion in an agreement does not prevent the TTBER applying to the rest of the agreement. Excluded restrictions include:

- obligations on the licensee to grant exclusive licences-back (or assignments back) of severable improvements or new applications to the licensor or a third party. A severable improvement is one which can be exploited without infringing the licensed technology. The underlying concern is that such grant-backs will reduce the licencee's incentive to innovate as severable improvements cannot be exploited;[45]

- no-challenge clauses—although the licensor can include a provision for termination of the licence in the event that a challenge to the validity of the intellectual property right is made;

- obligations limiting the ability of the licensee to exploit its own technology;

- restrictions on either party's R&D activities.

 Question

What do you understand to be the differences between hardcore and excluded restrictions, and why does the treatment of the latter differ to the former?

---

[44] TTBER, note 29, Art 5.   [45] TTBER Guidelines, note 35, para 109.

21.39   The Guidelines state that analysis of the potential anti-competitive effect of an agreement should focus on the actual or potential competition that would have existed without the agreement. An example is given relating to inter-technology competition where two undertakings established in different member states cross-license competing technologies and undertake not to sell products in each other's home markets. Potential competition existing prior to the agreement is thus restricted. Equally, where a licensor places obligations on his licensees not to use competing technologies, the technology belonging to third parties would not be used. The result is that actual or potential competition that would have existed in the absence of the agreement is restricted.

21.40   On intra-technology competition a licensor might restrict its licensees from competing with each other. Any potential competition that could have existed between the licensees is restricted. Examples of restrictions would include vertical price fixing and territorial or customer sales restrictions between licensees.[46]

> ## Web link
>
> The TTBER Guidelines contain useful guidance on the types of agreements that would be covered by the TTBER, and also on how agreements outside the TTBER should be evaluated. This can be important to agreements involving cross-licensing between several parties owning different sets of IP which is relevant to the making and development of one product, as the TTBER applies only to agreements between two parties. The TTBER Guidelines can be found at
> **http://eur-lex.europa.eu/LexUriServ/LexUriServ.do?uri=OJ:C:2004:101:0002:0042:EN:PDF.**

Consequences of an agreement being in breach of Article 101(1) TFEU

21.41   If an agreement is in breach of Article 101(1) TFEU and does not benefit from the block exemption or come within Article 101(3) then:

- the agreement is automatically void and unenforceable;
- the Commission can impose a fine on the parties;[47]
- in the UK, directors of companies risk being disqualified under section 204 of the Enterprise Act 2002.

> **Exercise**
>
> Construct a decision tree showing the steps that need to be taken to ascertain whether clauses in an IP licensing agreement would fall within the parameters of the TTBER and explain the questions that would need to be asked at each step.

21.42   A number of concerns have been expressed over the application of the TTBER. These include the following.

---

[46] TTBER Guidelines, note 35, Part 2.
[47] See Guidelines on the method of setting fines imposed pursuant to Article 23(2)(a) of Regulation No 1/2003, 2006/ C 210/02.

- The need for parties (and their advisers) to assess their relevant market share to see if they can benefit from the block exemption.

- Agreements which are initially exempt can cease to be so if the market shares of the parties increase. This might occur if cutting edge technology is involved.

- The regime will be implemented by national courts and competition authorities. This may lead to inconsistencies in approach.

- The Commission can withdraw the benefit of the block exemption if it considers that it offends Article 101(1) TFEU. This could lead to uncertainty for the parties.

 Question

Can you think of any other difficulties that may be experienced with the application of the TTBER? What advantages do you think the TTBER provides?

Key points on intellectual property and agreements between undertakings: Article 101 TFEU

- Article 101 TFEU concerns agreements between undertakings which have the object or effect of preventing, restricting, or distorting competition within the common market, and which may affect trade between member states

- The TTBER is relevant to undertakings which enter into technology transfer (licensing) agreements where those agreements deal with patents, know-how, software copyright, or a mixture of these IPRs

- Where an agreement contains hardcore restrictions, it will fall outwith the TTBER

- The pro- and anti-competitive effect of excluded restrictions need to be assessed on a case-by-case basis

---

Intellectual property and abuse of a dominant position: Article 102 TFEU

21.43   Article 102 TFEU concerns the prevention of abuse of market power by undertakings which occupy a dominant position within the common market.

> Article 102 TFEU (ex Art 82 EC)
>
> Any abuse by one or more undertakings of a dominant position within the common market or in a substantial part of it shall be prohibited as incompatible with the common market insofar as it may affect trade between Member States.
>
> Such abuse may, in particular, consist in:
>   (a) directly or indirectly imposing unfair purchase or selling prices or other unfair trading conditions;
>   (b) limiting production, markets or technical development to the prejudice of consumers;
>   (c) applying dissimilar conditions to equivalent transactions with other trading parties, thereby placing them at a competitive disadvantage;

(d) making the conclusion of contracts subject to acceptance by the other parties of supplementary obligations which, by their nature or according to commercial usage, have no connection with the subject of such
   contracts.

21.44   All IPRs give some form of exclusive right to the owner. But it does not follow that the IP owner occu-
pies a dominant position and is able to exert market power. Market power implies that a consumer will
have no choice but to deal with the dominant entity—the monopolist: in other words, that there will
be no substitutes for the product or services on offer by the monopolist. That is often not the case for
the subject matter of IP. If the price of a painting by a favoured artist exceeds what most can afford, then
another less well-known but more affordable artist may find favour; if the price of a patented remedy for
a headache increases, then alternative therapies may have to be found; if the price of a well-advertised
branded product exceeds reasonable expectations, then the consumer may look for other varieties. The
extent to which alternatives cannot be found or will not find favour with a consumer may depend on,
for example, technical advances or fashion.[48]

21.45   However, it is with the expansion of both the scope and subject matter of IPRs to cover, for example, new
technological advances used by consumers in daily life, medicines essential to human health, and to
compilations of information that cannot be obtained elsewhere that increasing attention is now being
focused on the extent to which Article 102 TFEU may, in particular, be used to require the owner of an
IP right to license its IP to a third party.

Dominant position

21.46   Article 102 TFEU refers to undertakings which occupy a dominant position. A dominant position relates
to a position of economic strength enjoyed by an undertaking on the relevant market: the key test is
that an entity must be able to hinder the maintenance of effective competition and be able to act to
an appreciable extent independently of competitors and consumers, without loss of customers and/or
competitor activity in response.[49] A dominant position in and of itself does not cause an entity to fall
under the prohibition in Article 102 TFEU.[50] However, when that dominant position is *abused*, perhaps
by foreclosing effective competition on the relevant market brought about by the firm having the power
to behave to an appreciable extent independently of its competitors, customers, and ultimately of its
consumers, then Article 102 TFEU may be brought into play.

21.47   Generally, abuse has been described as conduct by a dominant firm which seriously and unjustifiably
distorts competition or causes it further to weaken.[51] This is an objective test, and may impose burdens
on dominant undertakings not faced by others.

ECJ case law

21.48   In the early cases, the ECJ made it clear that mere ownership of an IPR, and exercising it, for example to
gain higher prices, would not necessarily involve a breach of Article 82 EC (now Art 102 TFEU).[52]

---

[48] Cornish, Llewelyn, and Aplin, note 4, para 1-45.
[49] Case 27/76 *United Brands Co v Commission of the European Communities* [1978] ECR 207, para 65.
[50] Case C-78/70 *Deutsche Grammophon v Metro* [1971] ECR 487 and Case C-52/07 *Kanal 5 Ltd v Föreningen Svedska Tonsättares Internationella Musikbyrå (STIM) UPA* [2008] ECR I-9275, paras 21.25ff.
[51] See C Bellamy and G Child, *European Community Law of Competition* (5th edn, 2001), 717.
[52] Case C-24/67 *Parke, Davis v Probel* [1968] ECR 55. See also Case C-78/70 *Deutsche Grammophon*, note 50.

■ **Case C-24/67 *Parke Davis v Probel* [1968] ECR 55**

The ECJ considered whether the exercise of patent rights could be an abuse of a dominant position. Parke Davis, a US company, held a patent in the Netherlands for a certain chemical process. Probel delivered chloramphenicol to the Netherlands which had been sold freely in Italy. Parke Davis used its patent to complain.

The ECJ held:

- the existence of IPRs are not affected by Article 82;
- the exercise of rights cannot fall under Article 82 in the absence of abuse of a dominant position;
- a higher sale price does not necessarily constitute abuse.

The Court went on to say:

> For this prohibition to apply it is thus necessary that three elements shall be present together: the existence of a dominant position, the abuse of this position and the possibility that trade between Member States may be affected thereby. Although a patent confers on its holder a special protection at national level, it does not follow that the exercise of the rights thus conferred implies the presence together of all three elements in question. It could only do so if the use of the patent were to degenerate into an abuse of the abovementioned protection.[53]

Thus, the mere exercise of IPRs does not constitute an abuse. However, the exercise of IPRs when used as an instrument of abuse, and where trade between member states may be affected, may be prevented under this Article.

Article 102 TFEU and the refusal to supply

21.49   One of the most interesting areas in which the interaction between Article 102 TFEU and the exercise of IPRs has occurred in relation to the refusal to supply. When, if at all, can the owner of an IPR be required to supply a third party on the basis that a refusal to supply would amount to the abuse of a dominant position? IPRs, after all, by their nature give to the owner exclusive rights. Could, or should, the application of competition law be used to limit the exercise of the right? Or should the IP owner have the absolute right, within the parameters of the monopoly, to decide not to license that right to a third party?

■ **Case C-238/87 *Volvo v Veng* [1988] ECR 6211**

A refusal to license was considered in *Volvo v Veng*. Volvo held the design right in the UK over front wings for cars. Veng imported panels into the UK from Italy and Denmark where they had been manufactured without Volvo's consent. Volvo alleged infringement of its UK registered designs. Veng's defence was that Volvo's refusal to grant a licence was an abuse of a dominant position when Veng was willing to pay a reasonable royalty for a licence.

The question for this discussion that was put before the ECJ related to Volvo's refusal to grant a licence to others. Was this an abuse of a dominant position?

The ECJ said:

> It must also be emphasised that the right of the proprietor of a protected design to prevent third parties from manufacturing and selling or importing, without its consent, products incorporating the design constitutes the very subject-matter of his exclusive right. It follows that an obligation imposed upon the proprietor of a protected design to grant to third parties, even in return for a reasonable royalty, a licence for the supply of products

[53] *Parke, Davis*, note 52, para 4.

incorporating the design would lead to the proprietor thereof being deprived of the substance of his exclusive right, and that a refusal to grant such a licence cannot in itself constitute an abuse of a dominant position.[54]

So a refusal in and of itself would not be an abuse of a dominant position as a refusal to license others is part of the *'very subject-matter'* of an IP right. There has to be something more. The question is what more is needed? The ECJ went on to indicate those circumstances in which the exercise of an IP right may go beyond the subject matter of an IP right, and thus constitute an abuse of a dominant position:

> the exercise by the proprietor of an exclusive right in a registered design in respect of car body panels my be prohibited by Article 82 if it involves, on the part of an undertaking holding a dominant position, certain abusive conduct such as the arbitrary refusal to supply spare parts to independent repairers, the fixing of prices for spare parts at an unfair level, or a decision no longer to produce spareparts for a particular model even though many cars of that model are still in circulation, provided that such conduct is liable to affect trade between Member States.[55]

21.50   The examples given by the Court are interesting, and can be seen as related to the prohibitions laid down in Article 102 TFEU. So, for example, a decision no longer to produce spare parts for a particular model even though cars of that model were still in circulation would certainly prejudice consumers and thus fall under Article 102(b) TFEU. Nevertheless, the mere refusal to license a third party (as opposed to an arbitrary refusal to supply spare parts to independent repairers) did not, at this stage, amount to an abuse of a dominant position.

 Question

Why might a refusal to license be a contentious issue both for the IP owner and for the third party seeking the licence? In what circumstances (if any) could you imagine a refusal to license constituting an abuse of a dominant position?

21.51   Despite the position taken by the ECJ in *Volvo v Veng*, the question as to when and if a refusal to license a third party might amount to an abuse of a dominant position has come up in subsequent case law. In 1995, for the first time, the ECJ held that in *exceptional circumstances* a refusal to license might constitute an abuse of a dominant position. The case in which this arose was *RTE and ITP v Commission* (*'Magill'*).

■ Joined Cases C-241/91 P and C-242/91 P *RTE and ITP v Commission* (*Magill*) [1995] ECR I-743

Television programmes were (and are) broadcast by different companies in the UK and Ireland, and only they held the details of the programmes to be broadcast each week. They disseminated weekly listings of their own output. Given the low level of originality in each jurisdiction the listings were protected by copyright. Magill, a Dublin company, put out a publication listing channels received in most Irish households. Almost immediately it was sued for copyright infringement. Magill complained to the Commission which found the conduct of the Irish broadcasters to be an abuse of a dominant position. The Commission ordered them to supply all third parties with weekly listings in advance.

The ECJ upheld the decision of the Commission saying:

• mere ownership of an IP right cannot confer a dominant position;

---

[54] *Volvo v Veng* [1988] ECR 6211, para 8.   [55] *Volvo v Veng*, note 54, para 10. See also *CICRA v Renault* [1988] ECR 6039.

- in the absence of harmonisation the conditions for granting protection of IPRs is a matter for national rules;

- the exclusive right of reproduction is part of the author's right so that a refusal to grant a licence, even if it is the act of an undertaking holding a dominant position, cannot in itself constitute abuse of a dominant position;

- however, the exercise of an exclusive right by the proprietor may in *exceptional circumstances* involve abusive conduct.

The ECJ emphasised that the television companies were the only sources of the basic information on programme scheduling which is the indispensable raw material for compiling a weekly television guide. This meant that viewers who wished to obtain information on the available programmes had no choice but to buy the weekly guides from each TV company. The refusal of the companies to provide the basic information by relying on national copyright provisions thus prevented the appearance of a new product for which there was a consumer demand. Such a refusal constituted an abuse under Article 82 EC for which there was no justification.

The ECJ set out those *exceptional circumstances* in which a refusal to license may constitute an instrument of abuse. These are where there is:

- no actual or potential substitute for the product for which a licence is sought;

- demand for a product which is not provided by the rights owner;

- no objective justification for the refusal to license;

- interference in an adjacent/secondary market.

> **Discussion point**   For answer guidance visit www.oxfordtextboks.co.uk/orc/waelde3e/
>
> Can you think of any other examples in which these exceptional circumstances might apply to require the owner of an IP right to license that right to a third party?

21.52   *Magill* was considered by the Court of First Instance (CFI) in *Tierce Ladbroke v Commission*.[56] This involved the refusal to grant a copyright licence to enable the showing of films of horse races in betting shops. The CFI found that the refusal was acceptable as it did not concern a service which was essential for the exercise of the activity in question (betting). Neither did the refusal prevent the emergence of a new product.[57]

21.53   The matter has been considered again by the ECJ in *IMS Health v NDC Health*.

■ Case 418/01 *IMS Health v NDC Health* [2004] ECR I-5039

IMS delivered sales data and other information on pharmaceutical services to pharmacies in Germany using a 'brick like' structure. This structure divided Germany into 1860 areas, or 'bricks', corresponding to a particular geographical area. This structure, which had been developed by IMS with the assistance of its clients, was delivered free of charge to pharmacies and doctors' surgeries. It became the de facto standard for delivery of this type of pharmaceutical information. The structure was also protected

---

[56] Case T-504/93 P *Tierce Ladbroke v Commission* [1997] ECR II-923.
[57] See also Case C-7/97 *Oscar Bronner GmbH & Co KG v Mediaprint* [1998] ECR I-7791.

by copyright. NDC developed its own structure derived from that of IMS. At the request of IMS the German court prohibited NDC from using any structure derived from that belonging to IMS. However, the court also sought clarification from the ECJ as to whether a right holder's refusal to grant a licence constituted an abuse of a dominant position in circumstances where clients would reject any alternative competing pharmaceutical information unless they were delivered in the same way as the IMS product.

The ECJ, after referring to *Volvo AB v Veng*[58] and *Magill*,[59] reiterated that an exclusive right of reproduction forms part of an IP owner's rights. A refusal to grant a licence, even by a dominant undertaking, could not, of itself, constitute an abuse of Article 82 EC except in *exceptional circumstances*. The Court also repeated what it had said in earlier cases concerning the three cumulative criteria that must be met for a refusal to be regarded as abusive:

- the undertaking which requested the licence must intend to offer new products or services not offered by the owner of the copyright and for which there is a potential consumer demand; in other words, the refusal must prevent the emergence of a new product for which there is potential demand; it must not merely duplicate existing goods or services;

- the refusal cannot be objectively justified;

- the refusal must be such as to exclude competition on a *secondary market*. In this case it was for the national court to determine whether the brick structure constituted an *indispensable* factor in the downstream supply of regional pharmaceutical sales data. For the instant case the court said the test was whether the refusal reserved to IMS the market for the supply of pharmaceutical sales data in the member states by eliminating all competition in that market.

21.54   The judgment of the ECJ has led to considerable uncertainty in a number of areas. One question relates to what is meant by 'indispensable'. The ECJ said that determining whether a product was indispensable was a matter for the national court to determine, in the light of the evidence submitted to it. The national court must consider whether there are products or services which constitute alternative solutions. The ECJ gave some guidance as to the factors that may be taken into account in the instant case:

> account must be taken of the fact that a high level of participation by the pharmaceutical laboratories in the improvement of the 1860 brick structure protected by copyright, on the supposition that it is proven, has created a dependency by users in regard to that structure, particularly at a technical level. In such circumstances, it is likely that those laboratories would have to make exceptional organisational and financial efforts in order to acquire the studies on regional sales of pharmaceutical products presented on the basis of a structure other than that protected by copyright. The supplier of that alternative structure might therefore be obliged to offer terms which are such as to rule out any economic viability of business on a scale comparable to that of the undertaking which controls the protected structure.[60]

This begs the question as to whether the outcome would have been the same had the outside organisations not been involved in the creation of the brick structure but the product had still achieved significant market penetration due to the innovation of the right holder. In other words, how critical is the engagement of third parties in the process of developing a system protected by an IP right, and does engagement make it more likely that a refusal to license the system would amount to abuse? While the creation of a new system (with or without the assistance of third parties) might be expensive, how expensive might it have to be before a compulsory licence might be granted? The ECJ referred to 'any economic viability'. But what may be economically viable for some third parties may not be economically viable

---

[58] See note 54.   [59] See para 21.51.   [60] *IMS*, see para 21.53.

for others. This, in turn, raises the question as to whether the test for economic viability depends on the entity seeking the licence.

Other questions also arise over what is meant by 'new products' and which markets should be supplied. It is unclear whether it is sufficient that these products have different characteristics from those on offer or whether something more is needed. Certainly the ECJ referred to new products as those not offered by the owner and for which there was a consumer demand, but also indicated that the party seeking the licence should not intend to limit itself essentially to duplicating the goods or services already offered on the secondary market.[61]

21.55   The decision of the ECJ in *Sot. Lelos Kai*[62] challenged once again the interface between competition and IP law. The case involves the pharmaceutical market and also concerns free movement of goods (see also para 20.29).

■ **Joined Cases C-468/06 to C-478/06** *Sot. Lelos Kai Sia EE and others v Glaxosmith-Kline Aeve Farmadeftikon Proionton (formerly Glaxowellcome Aeve)* **[2008] ECR I-7139**

In this case, the ECJ was faced with the following question: 'whether there is an abuse of a dominant position contrary to Art. 82 EC if a pharmaceutical company occupying such a position on the national market for certain medicinal products refuses to meet orders sent to it by wholesalers on account of the fact that those wholesalers are involved in parallel exports of those products to other Member States'.[63] The ECJ looked into whether GSK had an objective justification for its refusal to supply medicinal products. With respect to GSK's argument that parallel trade brings minimal benefits to ultimate consumers, the ECJ ruled that 'even in Member States where the prices of medicines are subject to State regulation, parallel trade is liable to exert pressure on prices and, consequently, to create financial benefits not only for the social health insurance funds, but equally for the patients concerned, for whom the proportion of the price of medicines for which they are responsible will be lower'.[64] The ECJ, however, noted that state regulation still remains an important factor in determining whether there is an objective justification for the refusal to supply, and, despite its dominant position, a pharmaceutical company may nevertheless take reasonable and proportional steps to protect its own commercial interests. The Court said that:

> Thus, although a pharmaceuticals company in a dominant position in a Member State where prices are relatively low cannot be allowed to cease to honour the ordinary orders of an existing customer for the sole reason that that customer, in addition to supplying the market in that Member State, exports part of the quantities ordered to other Member States with higher prices, it is none the less permissible for that company to counter in a reasonable and proportionate way the threat to its own commercial interests potentially posed by the activities of an undertaking which wishes to be supplied in the first Member State with significant quantities of products that are essentially destined for parallel export.[65]

21.56   It should be borne in mind, however, that the ECJ in *IMS* stated that for there to be abuse, it was 'sufficient' for the three-step cumulative test discussed previously (see paras 21.51ff). This might not, therefore, be the only test. In the light of this, and also given its importance when considering the application of competition law in the technology sector, the litigation between the European Commission and Microsoft in *Commission v Microsoft* deserves special mention.

---

[61] For further discussion on the 'new product' requirement, see H Meinberg, 'From *Magill* to *IMS Health*: the new product requirement and the diversity of intellectual property rights' [2006] EIPR 398.
[62] Joined Cases C-468/06 to C-478/06 [2008] ECR I-7139.   [63] *Sot. Lelos Kai*, note 62, para 28.
[64] *Sot. Lelos Kai*, note 62, para 56.   [65] *Sot. Lelos Kai*, note 62, para 71.

Commission v Microsoft

The case

21.57   Microsoft has been pursued by competition authorities in both the United States and the EU over alle-gations of abuse of its dominant position. The case in the United States concerned the bundling of Microsoft's Internet Explorer browser with its Windows desktop operating system, settled in 2002.[66] In 1998 Sun Microsystems lodged a complaint with the European Commission alleging that Microsoft had abused its dominant position in the desktop operating system market. Sun Microsystems argued that Microsoft's refusal to supply interface information to allow it to create workgroup server operat-ing systems that would interoperate with Microsoft's Windows desktop and server operating systems amounted to an abuse of Microsoft's dominant position.

Competitors and interoperability

21.58   If a competitor in the market wishes to make a computer program that interoperates with an existing program, then it is essential for that competitor to obtain information with regard to the interface of the existing program. Thus, if a programmer wished to develop a spreadsheet program that would inter-operate with Microsoft Word such that information could be passed between the two programs, then the programmer would need to know details of the interface to enable him to develop an interoperable program. (See para 5.44.) Sun Microsystems wanted to develop workgroup server operating systems that would interoperate with Microsoft's PC operating system. But Microsoft refused to supply the neces-sary information. The Commission found that Microsoft had abused its market power by deliberately restricting interoperability between Windows PCs and non-Microsoft workgroup servers.

21.59   In March 2004 (just before the decision of the ECJ in *IMS* was delivered) the Commission found that Microsoft had abused its dominant position, imposed a fine of €497.2 million, and required certain undertakings from Microsoft concerning future behaviour. When considering the case, the Commission stated that all circumstances should be taken into account, and that it was not limited by the *Magill* test.[67] In addition to the fine (imposed in part for this abuse and in part for the tying discussed later), Microsoft was required to disclose complete and accurate information concerning the interface sufficient to allow those developing non-Microsoft workgroup servers to achieve full interoperability with Windows PCs and servers. This remedy was designed to allow competition to open up in the market for workgroup servers. Where the information is made available to parties in the European Economic Area (EEA), then Microsoft is entitled to reasonable remuneration. In addition, the information that is disclosed must be updated each time Microsoft places a new version of the relevant products on the market.

Bundling and customers

21.60   The investigation was expanded in 2000 to consider the effects of the bundling of Microsoft's media player with its Windows 2000 PC operating system. The Commission decision also required Microsoft to offer PC manufacturers a version of the operating system without its media player. This gives the PC manufacturer the choice of whether to install Microsoft's media player onto the desktop, or that of another manufacturer. The decision thus lies first with the PC manufacturer, but through that the cus-tomer is able to decide which products to take. The Commission said Microsoft could offer a bundled

---

[66]   *US v Microsoft Corp* 231 F Supp 2d 144 (DCC 2002).

[67]   Commission Decision relating to a proceeding under Article 82 of the EC Treaty (Case COMP/C-3/37.792 *Microsoft*) March 2004, available at http://ec.europa.eu/competition/sectors/ICT/microsoft/index.html, para 558.

version of its operating system with its media player, but was prohibited from using commercial, technological, or contractual terms (eg discounting) designed to make the unbundled version of Windows less attractive or which compromised its performance.

Review of the discussion

21.61 Microsoft sought judicial review of the decision. Interim proceedings were brought before the CFI, when it was argued that Microsoft should not need to comply with the decision before the appeal.[68] The President of the CFI held that the submissions made by Microsoft were not, on the face of it, unfounded and the prima facie case for granting the stay was satisfied. However, he went on to find that Microsoft had not proved that the stay was a matter of urgency in the sense that the company would be caused irreparable harm if refused. As these conditions for granting the stay were cumulative (the prima facie case and the urgency), Microsoft's application was dismissed.

■ **Case T-201/04 *Microsoft Corp v Commission of European Communities* [2007] ECR II-3601**

In the substantive decision on the judicial review, the CFI found that Microsoft had:

- refused to supply its competitors with 'interoperability information' or to permit them to use the information to develop products which competed with its own on the group server operating system market; and

- it had engaged in the tying of Windows Media Player with the Windows PC operating system affecting competition on the media player market.

The refusal to supply the interoperability information

21.62 The CFI noted that while undertakings are, as a rule, free to choose business partners, in some circumstances a refusal to supply by a dominant undertaking can constitute an abuse of a dominant position unless it is objectively justified. For this, the CFI considered that it should apply the *IMS* test which was by then available. The three preconditions were that:

- the refusal must relate to a product or service indispensable to the exercise of an activity on a neighbouring market;

- the refusal must be such as to exclude any effective competition on that market;

- the refusal must prevent the appearance of a new product for which there is demand.

The CFI found the Commission was correct in finding these conditions satisfied. The information protocols were indispensable for the development of a new product for which there was unmet consumer demand and without which there was a risk of elimination of viable competition. There was no objective justification for the refusal even on the basis of intellectual property. It agreed with the Commission's view that the points it had made regarding the need to balance innovation incentives was part of the objective justification. It was a not new test, as Microsoft had alleged.

21.63 In making this finding the CFI did, however, expand on the *IMS* criteria in two ways: first that it considered that a 'risk' rather than a likelihood of elimination would suffice and that competition should be 'viable'; and, secondly, that the need for a new product was not the only relevant requirement but men-

---

[68] Case T-201/04 *Microsoft Corp v Commission of the European Communities* [2007] ECR II-3601.

tioned also technical development. What precisely is meant by these is currently the subject of intense academic debate and will no doubt resurface in the courts in due course.

The tying (bundling) of Windows Media Player and Windows client PC operating system

21.64   The CFI upheld the part of the Commission decision relating to the bundling of Windows Media Player. The CFI agreed that Microsoft had a dominant position on the client PC operating systems market; that there was separate consumer demand for media players; that different companies were present in the market supplying the products; and that consumers continue to acquire competing media players separately. However, a consumer could not acquire the Windows operating system without simultaneously acquiring Windows Media Player. Through this there was a significant risk that competition would be weakened in such a way that an effective competitive structure could not be ensured in the near future. Microsoft had demonstrated no objective justification for this bundling. Consequently, the remedy imposed by the Commission was proportionate. Microsoft retained the right to continue to offer the version of Windows bundled with Windows Media Player and was required only to make it possible for consumers to obtain the operating system without that media player, a measure which does not mean any change in Microsoft's current technical practice other than the development of that version of Windows.

 Exercise

Read in full the judgment of the ECJ in *IMS* and the decision of the CFI in the *Microsoft* case. What factors strike you in the discussions concerning secondary markets?

Do you think it correct that Microsoft be compelled to grant what is in effect a compulsory licence of its IP and to what extent do you think this would be consistent with the compulsory licensing provisions in the Berne Convention and in TRIPS?

Could the points made by the Commission regarding innovation balancing be pursued or are they too uncertain? Consider S Vezzoso, 'The incentives balance test in the EU Microsoft case: a pro-innovation "economics-based" approach?' (2006) 27(7) ECLR 382–390.

Read Microsoft's arguments concerning Article 6 of the Software Directive (Directive 91/250) (as it was then) that were made before the Commission and the CFI. You will recall that the Article is designed to require owners of programs to disclose interfaces where competitors wish to develop a competing but interoperable program. What was Microsoft's interpretation of those provisions in this case? What is your view? Consider also S Weston, 'Software interfaces—stuck in the middle: the relationship between the law and software interfaces in regulating and encouraging interoperability' (2012) 43(3) IIC 427–450.

Essential facilities doctrine

21.65   Although the term 'essential facility' has not been used by the EU Courts, some have argued that the application of competition law to IP borrows heavily from the doctrine of essential facilities.[69] The concept of an essential facility developed in relation to physical infrastructure—for instance, a port or an electricity network could be regarded as an essential facility. It is 'a facility or infrastructure

---

[69] See, eg, Whish and Bailey, note 2, 697–711; for discussion from the US perspective, see H Hovenkamp, MD Janis, and MA Lemley, 'Unilateral refusals to license' (2006) 2(1) JCL&E 1.

which is necessary for reaching customers and/or enabling competitors to carry on their business'.[70] A facility is considered essential if it cannot be duplicated, or its duplication would be very difficult or expensive. If access to an essential facility is denied this may be considered as an abuse of a dominant position, especially where it inhibits competition in a downstream market. Given that the ECJ has not explicitly embraced the terminology, it is difficult to know the extent to which it could be argued as applicable to IP cases, although *Magill* and *IMS* suggest that it is, albeit called by a different name.[71]

The proper boundaries between IP rights and the application of Article 102 TFEU

21.66   Given the finding of the ECJ in *IMS*, *Sot. Lelos I*, and *Microsoft*, are an increasing number of cases likely to come before the Court of Justice (and national courts) concerning refusal to license IPRs? If this is to be the case, where do the proper boundaries lie between compulsory licensing of an IPR and the grant and exercise of that right? As was stated at the outset of this chapter, the boundaries of IP have been expanding, drawing more and more subject matter within their scope, and thus within the exclusive domain of the right holder. Exploitation of IPRs also becomes increasingly complex, with the potential for tier upon tier of rights to be bound up in the ultimate delivery of a product or service to an end user. Ultimately, and as has been suggested in *Magill* and *IMS*, those rights can prove detrimental to the emergence of competition in secondary markets.

21.67   This is all the more so where one (or more) of those IPRs emerges as an industry 'standard', enabling the right holder to prevent the emergence of any form of competition in a secondary or related market; indeed, this may also be considered an essential facility, discussed previously. Standards can arise formally through agreement, as noted in the discussion of horizontal agreements para 21.32, and through behaviour in the market, as was the case in *IMS*. IMS took the time and effort to liaise with customers to tailor a product that would meet their needs, which in turn meant that this structure became the accepted standard in the industry, thus potentially making it more likely that compulsory licensing will be ordered to allow others to compete in the secondary markets with IMS's own customers. A danger is that the overuse of competition law to require the licensing of IPRs might inhibit innovation.

21.68   At this point the tension between competition law and the exercise of IPRs becomes palpable. *Should* competition law be used in this way to define the exercise of IPRs? If a response to this question is 'no', then the further question arises as to the proper role of IP law: what is it that IP law is seeking to achieve, and does the law as it is currently constituted achieve those aims? *Sot. Lelos Kai* illustrates that there are circumstances in which a company may take reasonable and proportional steps to protect its commercial interests, even where that might be construed as being an abuse of a dominant position, as long as it takes place within recognised parameters. As relations between business in the marketplace become ever more complex, the question becomes as to how many exceptions might need to be developed to the general rule or whether the shape of the general rule, and indeed the shape of the IP right, should be rethought.

[70] See 'Glossary E' prepared by the European Commission DG Competition at http://ec.europa.eu/competition/publications/glossary_en.pdf; see the decision of the European Commission *in B & I Line plc v Sealink Harbours Ltd and Sealink Stena Ltd* [1992] 5 CMLR 255.

[71] Although note its place in *Oscar Bronner*, note 57, AG paras 35–52, and see also the discussion by the High Court in *Attheraces v British Horseracing Board* [2005] EWHC 1553 (Ch) in which pre-race data were considered an essential facility.

21.69   The European Commmission issued guidance in 2009 regarding its future enforcement priorities.[72] Echoing the discussion of the rule of reason at the start of this chapter, the guidance focuses on an economic approach, and also not only on protecting the consumer but on developing the market.[73] The guidance states that it will see refusal as a priority if the refusal relates to a product or service that is objectively necessary to be able to compete effectively on a downstream market, the refusal is likely to lead to the elimination of effective competition on the downstream market, and the refusal (in response to an actual request, although the refusal may be constructive, rather than actual) is likely to lead to consumer harm. The guidance refers to *Magill* and *IMS* and the need for a new product and technical development but does also suggest a wider willingness to intervene.[74] This would be consistent with more proactive steps which have been taken by the Commission in respect of other IP-related issues, for example the European Commission's inquiry into the pharmaceutical industry from 2008–9[75] and its investigation of AstraZeneca regarding regulatory behaviour and misleading representations, in respect of which there is an ongoing appeal in 2012.[76]

Exercise

Review the underlying justifications for IP as found in Chapter 1. What do you think the position should be as regards compulsory licensing in cases such as *Magill*, *IMS*, and *Microsoft* and ongoing regulatory action from the Commission?

What conclusions can you drawn from the future of innovation industries from the Opinion of the Advocate General Mazak (15 May 2012) in AstraZeneca, **http://eur-lex.europa.eu/LexUriServ/ LexUriServ.do?uri=CELEX:62010CC0457:EN:HTML.**

Key points on intellectual property and abuse of a dominant position: Article 102 TFEU

- Article 102 TFEU regulates the abuse of market power by undertakings which occupy a dominant position within the common market

- In IP-related cases, questions relating to abuse of a dominant position have arisen in connection with a refusal to supply (license) a product protected by an IPR

- The boundaries of those 'exceptional circumstances' in which a compulsory licence will be granted are still being tested

---

[72] 'Communication from the Commission—Guidance on the Commission's Enforcement Priorities in Applying Article 82 of the EC Treaty to Abusive Exclusionary Conduct by Dominant Undertakings' (24 February 2009), 2009 OJ C45/7.

[73] Communication from the Commission, note 72, paras 5–8, 19–22; AC Witt, 'The Commission's guidance paper on abusive exclusionary conduct—more radical than it appears?' (2010) 35(2) ELRev 214–235.

[74] Communication from the Commission, note 72, paras 75 et seq.

[75] For details of report and ongoing activity in respect of patent settlements, see http://ec.europa.eu/competition/sectors/ pharmaceuticals/inquiry/.

[76] Commission Decision of 15 June 2005 relating to a proceeding under Article 82 of the EC Treaty and Article 54 of the EEA Agreement (Case COMP/A. 37.507/F3), available at http://eur-lex.europa.eu/LexUriServ/LexUriServ.do?uri=CELEX:32006D0857:EN:NOT; Case T-321/05 *AstraZeneca AB v European Commission* [2010] ECR II-2805.

EU competition law in the UK courts: Eurodefences

21.70   The main distinction between the application of EU competition law and UK competition law is that there is no threshold requirement that trade between member states be affected for UK competition law to be relevant.[77] In the UK, the Competition Act 1998 which came into force on 1 March 2000 is closely modelled on Articles 101 and 102 TFEU. Chapter I of the Act contains a prohibition on anti-competitive agreements while Chapter II prohibits abuse of a dominant position in a market.

> ### Web link
>
> Information about the UK competition regime can be found at **http://www.oft.gov.uk/** and **http://www.oft.gov.uk//OFTwork/competition-act-and-cartels/competition-law-compliance/**.

21.71   A current trend is towards increasing use of competition law in the IP field, not only by third parties seeking access to IP belonging to another, but also by IP owners raising infringement of European competition law as a defence in an action for infringement of IP belonging to another (using competition law as a shield—sometimes referred to as a Eurodefence). These tactics are coming to the fore in a number of cases in the English courts in which IP is a factor.[78]

21.72   Some cases clearly have no prospect of success and the defences are dismissed in summary judgment. This can be because there is no link at all between the alleged anti-competitive conduct (say, high pricing of unrelated technology or products) and the alleged infringement. This was particularly so in the first cases in which arguments were advanced.[79] Courts have stressed the need for a nexus between the alleged anti-competitive agreement and the proceedings in the context of an IP infringement action where defences based on breach of Community (now Union) law were raised. The identification of a nexus remains a key challenge, for instance in *Sportswear Co v Ghattaura*[80] the court found that the necessary nexus[81] was absent.[82] Other cases have shown more openness to arguments and guidance as to what might be accepted.

21.73   One of these is *Intel Corporation v Via Technologies Inc and others*[83] in which the application of both EU and UK competition law to patent licences was considered. At the heart of the case were questions concerning Intel's Pentium chip technology and Via's efforts to license the technology for their own products. Intel began two actions alleging that Via had infringed a number of Intel's patents. In defence Via raised matters concerning Intel's behaviour and what were then Articles 81 and 82 EC (and the corresponding provisions of the Competition Act 1998). Prior to remitting the case back to the High Court for trial, the Court of Appeal made some interesting observations on what was then Article 82. It said that for Article 82 to be infringed it was not necessary for an entity occupying a dominant position to entirely exclude a new product from the market. If this was otherwise, then a licence could be granted to a third party who never took any action in terms of the licence (in other words, just sat back and did not do what was permitted under the licence). The facts in the instant case might constitute 'exceptional circumstances'

---

[77] For recent and ongoing consultations, see http://www.bis.gov.uk/Consultations/competition-regime-for-growth and http://www.bis.gov.uk/Consultations/consultation-private-actions-in-competition-law.

[78] Eg *Intel Corporation v VIA Technologies Inc and Ors* [2002] EWCA Civ 1905, [2003] FSR 33, para 20.

[79] See, eg, *Philips Electronics NV v Ingman Ltd* [1998] 2 CMLR 839, [1999] FSR 112.   [80] [2006] FSR 11.

[81] *Sportswear*, note 80, paras 14–18. The court referred to *Sandvik Aktiebolag v KR Pfiffner (UK) Ltd* [2000] FSR 17 and *Intel Corp v Via*, note 78.

[82] Another example where a Eurodefence was considered to have no prospect of success is *Microsoft Corporation v Ling and others* [2006] EWHC 1619 (Ch).   [83] [2002] EWCA Civ 1905, [2002] All ER (D) 346, [2003] FSR 33.

but would depend on the findings of fact made at the trial.[84] Further, if a term was included in a licence agreement that went beyond the terms necessary for the licensee to exploit the subject matter of the IPR, it would have to be justified on its own merits and not because of its inclusion in an IP licence.[85] Finally, Via might have a defence under Article 82 if Intel would only grant licences breaching Article 81 and that was part of abusive conduct by Intel. The Court of Appeal did not want to limit when there could be exceptional cases given the ongoing uncertainty in the area, but given the stage of the action, it declined to make a reference to the ECJ which would be helped in this respect.[86]

21.74   A second case in which a 'Eurodefence' was allowed to proceed to trial in the English courts is:

■ *Doncaster Pharmaceuticals Group Ltd v The Bolton Pharmaceutical Co Ltd* [2006] EWCA Civ 661, [2007] FSR 3

This case concerned the trade mark 'Kalten', pharmaceutical products, and the movement of these from Spain into the UK—parallel importing as discussed in Chapter 20. The mark was originally held by AZ in both territories and under which it sold pharmaceutical products. In 2001 the mark was assigned to Teofarma along with the product licence in Spain. In 2004 AZ assigned the UK mark to Bolton and entered into an agreement whereby the mark was to be used solely in connection with the marketing, promotion, sales, and distribution of the pharmaceutical product having certain contents and in accordance with the product specification. Doncaster had been engaged in buying the drugs in Spain, repackaging them under the Kalten mark, and importing them into the UK. Bolton claimed trade mark infringement as against Doncaster. In response Doncaster argued that the rights had been exhausted by the placing of the drugs on the market in Spain. Bolton argued that this was not a case in which the rights had been exhausted. On the basis of *IHT Internationale Heiztechnik GmbH v Ideal Standard GmbH*[87] (discussed in para 20.20), they argued that there was no continuing economic linkage between Bolton, Teofarma, and Astra Zenica such that AZ could exercise any form of quality control over the products. While at first instance summary judgment was granted, this was overturned by the Court of Appeal which noted that this was not a case where there was a bare assignment of the mark but rather the assignment was accompanied by the product agreement and know-how licences. This had the effect of keeping a link with AZ which could give to AZ the possibility of control. This could result in Bolton being unable to enforce the mark as against Doncaster in the UK.

21.75   In future cases the actual facts, rather than the structure of agreements, will be key; it will be for the trial court to determine if there is a market sharing agreement supporting the assignation of the trade marks which would render the assignments void under Article 101 TFEU.[88] This openness was also seen in another parallel importing case, *Sun Microsystems v M-Tech* discussed in para 20.62.[89] This involved the import to the UK from the United States of computer hardware disk drives against the backdrop of a large secondary market in the EEA. A network of agreements was argued to be in breach of Article 101. The Court of Appeal declined to limit the free movement and IP principles to those which had already been established, and found there to be an arguable connection between the competition and IP arguments. In 2012 the Supreme Court took a much narrower approach. It rejected arguments based on free

---

[84] The court referred to Cases C-241/91 P and C-242/91 P *Radio Telefis Eireann v EC Commission (Magill)* [1995] All ER (EC) 416; Case 238/87 *Volvo (AB) v Erik Veng* [1988] ECR 6211; Case T-504/93 *Tierce Ladbroke SA v European Commission* [1997] ECR II-923; Case C-7/97 *Bronner (Oscar) GmbH & Co KG v Mediaprint Zeitings- und Zeitschriftenverlag GmbH & Co KG* [1998] ECR I-7791; and Case T-184/01R *IMS Health Inc v European Commission* [2001] ECR II-2349 considered at paras 21.49–21.54.

[85] Case 193/83 *Windsurfing International Inc v European Commission* [1986] ECR 611 considered at para 21.24.

[86] *Intel v Via*, note 78, paras 48–51.   [87] Case C-9/93 [1994] ECR I-2789.   [88] *Ideal Standard*, note 87, para 59.

[89] *Sun Microsystems Inc v M-Tech Data Ltd* [2010] EWCA Civ 997, [2011] FSR 2.

movement and agreements, considered that the agreements delivered no nexus, and, as there was no arguable defence in EU law, declined to make a reference to the Court of Justice.[90]

21.76   Another significant case discussed at paras 20.68–20.69, para 21.27 and in chapters 2, 3, and 5, is *FA Premier League Ltd v QC Leisure and others*[91] which, along with *Murphy v Media Protection Services Ltd*,[92] concerns the importation and use of 'illicit' decoder cards. In *FA Premier League* the defendants raised a Eurodefence arguing that obligations imposed in the licence on foreign broadcasters to undertake to 'procure' that non-UK decoder cards were not authorised or enabled by the licensee or any sub-licensee or distributor, agent, or employee of such persons, so as to enable anyone to view the foreign broadcaster's transmission outside the latter's territory, was incompatible with what was then Article 81 EC. The court said that this point could proceed to trial.[93] In *Murphy*, the criminal action, the national court had agreed that if Ms Murphy so wished she could put forward arguments of the impact of what were then Articles 28–30 and 49 EC and Article 81 EC on the grounds that 'the Respondent's case is effectively founded on an agreement or a network of agreements imposing restrictions unlawful and void under Art.81 EC'.[94]

When the the Court of Justice considered a reference,[95] it found in the joined cases that the exclusive licence and the provisions regarding decoding devices were a restriction prohibited by what was by then Article 101 TFEU.[96] Following this, the national court in *FA Premier League* provided a declaration that the agreements were incompatible with Article 101 TFEU.[97] Murphy's conviction was quashed.[98]

21.77   While there are a rising number of cases in the English courts in which Eurodefences are raised, the success of these strategies still does remain to be seen. Perhaps with fierce enforcement powers, sophisticated investigation techniques, and growing experience in the courts in respect of Eurodefence arguments, anti-competitive behaviour (with an appropriate link to the infringing conduct) will be increasingly difficult to mask, prompting more challenges in the future. Yet the stance of the Supreme Court in *M-Tech*, and the lack of a reference to the Court of Justice, means that uncertainty will continue. It should also be borne in mind that a much narrower approach has been taken to abuse arguments in respect of the raising of an action itself, really requiring the action to be vexatious,[99] than has been seen regarding Eurodefences where the focus is on the nexus.

 Question

Should Eurodefences, and claims relating to the raising of an action, involve the same tests as those applying to the refusal to license cases?

---

[90] *Oracle America Inc (formerly Sun Microsystems Inc) v M-Tech Data Ltd* [2012] UKSC 27, [2012] 1 WLR 2026, paras 7–32 (in particular 30–32), 36.   [91] [2008] EWHC 44 (Ch).
[92] [2007] EWHC 3091 (Admin).   [93] [2008] EWHC 44 (Ch), paras 38–39, 57–59.
[94] Note 92, para 45 noting that these points had not been argued before the court. See also *Football Association Premier League Ltd and others v LCD Publishing Ltd* [2007] EWHC 3171 (Ch) in which the court allowed LCD Publishing to furnish further and better particulars of a restraint of trade and competition defence to the terms of an agreement which prohibited pictures being published in magazines which were devoted to one football player or to one club.
[95] Regarding references to ECJ, see *Football Association Premier League Ltd v QC Leisure* [2008] 3 CMLR 12, paras 365–368.
[96] Joined Cases C-403/08 and C-429/08 *Murphy v Media Protection Services Ltd* [2012] 1 CMLR 29, paras 134–146.
[97] *Football Association Premier League Ltd v QC Leisure* [2012] 2 CMLR 16. paras 97–99.
[98] *Murphy v Media Protection Services Ltd* [2012] EWHC 466 (Admin), [2012] 3 CMLR 2, paras 8–10, see also para 12.
[99] Case T-111/96 *ITT Promedia NV v Commission of the European Communities* [1998] ECR II-2937; *SanDisk Corp v Koninklijke Philips Electronics NV* [2007] EWHC 332 (Ch), [2007] FSR 22, but cf *Intel v Via*, note 78, para 26.

Further reading

Books

SD Anderman (ed), *The Interface between Intellectual Property Rights and Competition Policy* (2007)

S Anderman and H Schmidt, *EU Competition Law and Intellectual Property Rights. The Regulation of Innovation* (2011)

S Bishop and M Walker, *The Economics of EC Competition Law: Concepts, Applications and Measurement* (3rd edn, 2010)

P Roth and V Rose, *Bellamy and Child, European Community Law of Competition* (2012 Pack, 6th edn plus ongoing updates)

E Rousseva, *Rethinking Exclusionary Abuses in EU Competition Law* (2010)

R Whish and D Bailey, *Competition Law* (7th edn, 2012)

Chapters

AEL Brown, 'Intellectual property: competition and the Internet' in L Edwards and C Waelde (eds), *Law and the Internet* (3rd edn, 2009)

Reports

European Commission, Fraunhofer Fokus, and Dialogic, 'Study on the interplay between standards and intellectual property rights (IPRs)' (2011), available at http://ec.europa.eu/enterprise/policies/european-standards/files/standards_policy/ipr-workshop/ipr_study_final_report_en.pdf

Articles

A Andreangeli, 'Interoperability as an "essential facility" in the Microsoft case—encouraging competition or stifling innovation' (2009) 34(4) ELRev 584–611

D Bailey, 'Restrictions of competition by object under Article 101 TFEU' (2012) 49(2) CML Rev 559–599

B Batchelor, 'Application of the technology transfer block exemption to software licensing agreements' (2004) 10(7) CTLR 166–173

J Drexl, 'IMS Health and Trinko—antitrust placebo for consumers instead of sound economics in refusal-to-deal cases' (2004) 35(7) IIC 788

I Eagles and L Longdin, 'Microsoft's refusal to disclose software interoperability information and the Court of First Instance' (2008) 30(5) EIPR 205–208

H First, 'Microsoft's tenth anniversary' (2008) 39(4) IIC 381–383

PA Geroski, 'Intellectual property rights, competition policy and innovation: is there a problem?' (2005) 2(4) SCRIPTed 422, available at http://www.law.ed.ac.uk/ahrc/script-ed/vol2-4/geroski.asp

G Ghidini, 'Intellectual property and competition law—the innovation nexus (Conde Gallego)' (2008) 39 IIC 879

F Houwen and R Neville, 'Risky business: current challenges in the relationship between competition law and copyright' (2009) 8(1) Comp LJ 18–36

D Howarth and K McMahon, '"Windows has performed an illegal operation": the Court of First Instance's judgment in the *Microsoft v Commission*' (2008) 29(2) ECLR 117–134

D Kallay, '*Levi Strauss v Tesco*: at a difficult juncture of competition, IP and free trade policies' (2002) 23(4) ECLR 193–199

B Ong, 'Anti-competitive refusals to grant copyright licences: reflections on the IMS saga' (2004) 26(11) EIPR 505–524

C Petrucci, 'Parallel trade of pharmaceutical products: the ECJ finally speaks—comment on *GlaxoSmithKline*' (2010) ELRev 275

D Ridyard, 'Compulsory access under EC competition law—a new doctrine of convenient facilities and the case for price regulation' (2004) 25(11) ECLR 669–673

C Stothers, 'Who needs intellectual property? Competition law and restrictions on parallel trade within the European Economic Area' (2005) 27(12) EIPR 458–466

A Stratakis, 'Comparative analysis of the US and EU approach and enforcement of the essential facilities doctrine' (2006) 27(8) ECLR 434–442

J Temple Lang, 'Defining legitimate competition: companies' duties to supply competitors and access to essential facilites' (1994) 18 FILJ 439

P Treacy and T Heide, 'The new EC Technology Transfer Block Exemption' (2004) 25(9) EIPR 414–420

Part VIII
Exploitation, enforcement, remedies, and cross-border litigation

Sources of the law: key websites

- The UK–IPO website has a section devoted to enforcement, available at
  http://www.ipo.gov.uk/types/copy/c-manage/c-useenforce/c-enforce.htm

- The European Commission website has a section dealing with counterfeiting and piracy, available at
  http://ec.europa.eu/taxation_customs/customs/customs_controls/counterfeit_piracy/index_en.htm

- and one devoted to enforcement at
  http://ec.europa.eu/internal_market/iprenforcement/index_en.htm

- For the Gowers Review, see
  http://www.hm-treasury.gov.uk/media/583/91/pbr06_gowers_report_755.pdf

- For the Hargreaves Review, see
  http://www.ipo.gov.uk/ipreview.htm

- The text of the Brussels Regulation can be found at
  http://europa.eu./legislation_summaries/justice_freedom_security/judicial_cooperative_in_civil_matters/133054_en.htm

- Details about the Hague Conference on Private International Law and the text of the Convention can be found at
  http://www.hcch.net/index_en.php

Exploitation of intellectual property rights, enforcement, and remedies

Introduction

Scope and overview of chapter

22.1 Exploitation of intellectual property rights (IPRs) takes place within the context of a general framework of legislative and regulatory initiatives reflecting the policies of any particular country (eg employment and health and safety laws). Beyond that, a number of specific rules arise in the sphere of IPRs. These include rules on assignments; general contract rules determining fairness as between parties to a bargain; controls on licensing within specific pieces of IP legislation; measures on compulsory licensing and controls on collective licensing. As well as being aware of the rules within which exploitation takes place, a right holder will want a means of enforcing the right and a remedy should the right be infringed by a third party. The intellectual property system provides for a web of civil, criminal, and administrative rules and procedures which can be used in the event of an infringement.

22.2 The first half of this chapter will discuss specific examples of exploitation practices and controls on those practices primarily within the domains of copyright, patents, and trade marks, and highlight a number of topical exploitation strategies focusing on the policy and regulatory issues that arise. The second half will discuss enforcement procedures and remedies available to an intellectual property right holder in the event of an infringement of a right highlighting the tensions that arise in crafting remedies appropriate to a transgression.

For an explanation of the application of the rules on free movement of goods and of EU competition law on exploitation practices, see Chapters 20 and 21.

22.3 ### Learning objectives

By the end of this chapter you should be able to describe and explain:

- the rules on assignment for registered IPRs;

- common exploitation strategies used for copyright, patents, and trade marks;

- the regulatory controls on exploitation and their purpose;

- circumstances in which compulsory licences might be granted for the exploitation of IPRs;

- emergent exploitation strategies in the light of expansion of the scope and subject matter of IPRs;

- the matrix of civil and criminal enforcement procedures and remedies available for infringement of IPRs;

- recent developments and proposals on enforcement and remedies emanating from the EU and how these fit into, and may complement, the current framework;

- the measures to be found in TRIPS and their contribution to global intellectual property enforcement.

22.4   The rest of the chapter looks like this:

- Assignment (22.5–22.7)

- Licensing (22.8–22.66)

- Contemporary exploitation strategies (22.67–22.84)

- Enforcement and remedies (22.85–22.172)

Assignment

22.5   The owner of an IPR may choose to assign that right to a third party. An assignment (known as assignation in Scotland) is the transfer of ownership of an IPR from one party to another.[1] When an IPR is assigned, the assignee stands in the shoes of the assignor and can deal with the right as they wish.[2]

22.6   Different rules apply for assignment of an IPR, requiring care to ensure that an assignation is valid. An assignment of a Community trade mark (CTM) must be in writing and signed by or on behalf of all of the parties to the transaction.[3] An assignment of a patent must be signed by the assignor or mortgagor.[4] Where a patent or application for a patent is owned by more than one party all the co-owners must consent to the assignment.[5] Only the assignor need sign an assignment of copyright and a UK trade mark,[6] and a prospective copyright owner can assign future copyright.[7] A trade mark can be assigned without a corresponding assignment of goodwill or business,[8] but the owner of an unregistered mark can only assign that mark along with the goodwill of the business. For UK trade marks owned by more than one party, each co-owner can only assign their share, and then only if the others consent to the assignment.[9]

---

[1] In *Siemens Schweiz AG v Thorn Security Ltd* [2008] EWCA Civ 1161, [2009] Bus LR D67 the Court of Appeal, in relation to the Patents Act 1977, s 33(3) said 'The term "assignment" is inherently capable of more than one meaning. It may refer to the passing of ownership or, where parties may only transfer property by executing a particular form it can mean that instrument as executed in relation to particular property … there is no reason why the word "assignment" should not receive a wide meaning in section 33(3)' (para 88).

[2] For matters of contract interpretation see *JHP Ltd v BBC Worldwide Ltd and another* [2008] EWHC 757 (Ch).

[3] Community Trade Mark Regulation (CTMR), Art 17(3).

[4] Patents Act 1977, s 30(6) amended by SI 2004/2357, art 10.   [5] Patents Act 1977, s 36(3).

[6] Copyright, Designs and Patents Act 1998 (CDPA 1988), s 90(3), Trade Marks Act 1994 (TMA 1994), s 24(3). See also Registered Designs Act 1949, s 15B.   [7] CDPA 1988, s 91(1).   [8] TMA 1994, s 24(1); CTMR, Art 17.   [9] TMA 1994, s 23(4).

Assignment of a trade mark can be partial, that is, in respect of some of the goods covered by the trade mark registration, limited geographically, or limited in manner of use,[10] whereas a CTM must be dealt with 'in its entirety and for the whole area of the Community'.[11]

 Question

> What is the policy that underlies the rule that a CTM be dealt with 'in its entirety and for the whole area of the Community' while dealing with a national UK trade mark may be in respect of some but not all of the right?

Registration

22.7   An assignment of an unregistered right, such as copyright and unregistered design right, does not require to be registered to be effective. Indeed, there is no register on which assignment could be placed. By contrast, assignments of registered rights, such as patents and trade marks, can, but need not, be registered. However, it would appear that it is policy to encourage registration. This is apparent from the rules that lay down the consequences of non-registration.

- *Registered designs*: if no entry has been made on the design register, then any document recording an assignation may not be admitted as evidence of title unless the court otherwise directs.[12] An assignation of a registered Community design must be entered in the register to permit the successor in title to invoke the rights arising from the registration of the Community design.[13] As with CTMs, Community designs are unitary and so can only be assigned for the whole Community.

- *Trade marks*: if a transaction concerning a UK trade mark is not registered, it will be ineffective as against a person acquiring a conflicting interest in or under the mark who does not know of the transaction.[14] An assignee who does not register within six months of the transaction in respect of acts of infringement that occur prior to registration cannot recover costs in the event that the mark is infringed.[15] As regards a CTM, as long as the transfer has not been entered on the CTM register the assignee may not invoke the rights arising from registration of the CTM.[16]

- *Patents*: registration gives the registrant priority against anyone who has an earlier unregistered right as long as the registrant had no notice of the earlier right;[17] (as with trade marks) cost or expenses are withheld from assignees who do not register within six months of the transaction in respect of acts of infringement that occur prior to registration.[18]

 Question

> Why do you think there are different rules on execution of assignations and consequences of non-registration for the various registered IPRs? Do you think this area of the law should be rationalised?

---

[10] TMA 1994, s 24(2).   [11] CTMR, Art 16(1).   [12] Registered Designs Act 1949, s 19(5).
[13] Community Design Regulations, Art 28(b).   [14] TMA 1994, s 25(3).   [15] TMA 1994, s 25(4).
[16] Art 17(6). On registration of licences, see *Jean Christian Perfumes Ltd v Thakrar* [2011] EWHC 1383 (Ch). The TMA 1994 provides that: a licence under a United Kingdom registered trade mark was not effective unless it was in writing and signed by or on behalf of the grantor, so that an oral licensee of a UK trade mark lacked standing to sue for infringement, since Regulation 40/94, which was of direct effect, raised no formalities with respect to licences of Community trade marks, an oral licensee of a Community trade mark might bring proceedings for infringement if he had the consent of the proprietor.
[17] Patents Act 1977, s 33. *Schutz (UK) Ltd v Werit UK Ltd* [2011] EWCA Civ 927, [2012] FSR 2.
[18] Patents Act 1977, s 68 as amended by SI 2006/1028.

> **Key point on assignment**
>
> • Different rules exist for the assignation of the various IPRs and registration (where applicable) of those assignations. Care must be taken to ensure the correct rules are followed

Licensing

General

22.8 Licensing is a central feature of the exploitation of intellectual property. An IP owner may not have the resources or the expertise to exploit a work protected by intellectual property. For instance, the inventor of a new type of ceramic kettle may need to enter into a licensing agreement with a manufacturer to develop the product and bring it to the market. A music band may need the help of a record label to produce and market a song. Literary authors may need the assistance of a collecting society to enable them to monitor use of a work and to receive a return from exploitation. If the owner of the IPR does not assign the work, then he will need to enter into a licence to permit such exploitation and management of the right.

Licences can be exclusive, non-exclusive, or sole. An exclusive licence means that the owner licenses a third party to carry out some or all of the restricted acts to the exclusion of all others including the owner. A non-exclusive licence permits the owner to license as many other people as he wishes to carry out the same act. A sole licence permits the owner of the IPR to exploit the right as well as the person to whom he has licensed the work.[19]

> **Exercise**
>
> Imagine scenarios where these different types of licence might be used and consider why it might be appropriate to use one type of licence rather than another in any given set of circumstances. Consider the interests that require to be met when making a choice.

22.9 Licences for some IPRs, notably copyright, tend to cover some but not all of the rights pertaining to a particular work. For example, the author of a book might license the right to one publisher to publish the book in hardback, but another publisher may be granted the serial rights. One director might be given permission to turn a work into a play, another to turn the work into a film.[20] Patents tend to be exploited in a more unitary fashion, the right to exploit the bundle of rights protected by a patent being given to one or more parties.[21] Under the Trade Marks Act 1994, a trade mark licence may be limited to one or more class of goods or services and limited in respect of territory. However, there is an important caveat in that if a trade mark becomes liable to deceive through such licensing practices, it may be revoked.[22]

---

[19] For a complex case on the construction of a trade mark licence, see *Leofelis SA and Leeside srl v Lonsdale Sports Ltd, Trade Mark Licensing Co Ltd and Sports World International Ltd* [2008] EWCA Civ 640.

[20] Note that both the rules on free movement of goods and competition law will prevent the licensing of rights that have the effect of partitioning the market. For more information see Chapters 20 and 21.

[21] See later in the discussion on Genetic Inventions, Intellectual Property Rights and Licensing Practices: OECD, para 22.55.

[22] Discussed in para 14.122.

Assignment or licence?

22.10 Sometimes a question can arise as to whether a document is an assignment or a licence. In a case involving rights to the song 'A Whiter Shade of Pale', the House of Lords stated that in order for there to be an implied assignment: '(a) it would have been obvious to the [assignor] (as well as [the record company]) that his interests in the musical copyright was being, or had to be, assigned to [the record company], or, which may amount to the same thing, (b) the commercial relationship between the parties could not sensibly have functioned without such an agreement'.[23] The House of Lords ruled that there was no implied assignment and that the recording contract merely granted the record company the right to exploit the original recording.[24]

22.11 If a reverter clause is present in an agreement, a question may arise as to whether the agreement is a licence or an assignation. In *JHP Ltd v BBC Worldwide Ltd*[25] the court reviewed the authorities. In *Chaplin v Frewin*[26] an agreement in a publishers' contract whereby the publishers should, during the legal term of the copyright, have the exclusive right of producing, publishing, and selling a work in volume form in any language throughout the world was held to be an assignment of copyright. In *Messager v BBC*[27] the composers and authors of an opera granted to the proprietor of the theatre the sole and exclusive right of representing a play, in which it was provided that the copyright in the music of the play should remain the property of the composer and in certain events the right of representation should 'revert to and become again the absolute property of [the composer and the authors]'. The court in that case said that there had been use of 'inept language in which to describe the mere cessation of a licence and ... much more apt to describe the reversion to the licensors of rights which had been assigned'. The court in *JHP* came to the conclusion that 'the concept of reverter (rather than of termination or cessation) is strongly suggestive of the assignment or a transfer of a property right that does not depend for its existence on the very agreement which contains the reverter provision itself. But ... there is no general principle that a reverter clause automatically indicates an assignment'.[28]

Copyright

Copyright contract practices UK: the music company and the musician

22.12 Perhaps the most well-known examples of controls on copyright licences as between the author and exploiter arise in the entertainment field, most particularly in the music sector. Recording companies have long argued that their business model is predicated on the success of a minority of musicians. The financial return that the companies receive from this minority enables them in turn to engage other musicians. To ensure that the record company can profit from the future success of the few, it is in the interests of the record company to enter into a relationship with a musician for as long as possible. Equally, the record company will not want to be bound to the unsuccessful musician, and in particular it does not want to be under any obligation to publish and distribute music that may not have found favour in the market. This has caused some problems where record companies have signed musicians in the early stages of their career, and where the musicians have not had the benefit of independent advice in relation to the contract into which they entered. General principles of contract law have, in some circumstances, been called upon to give relief to the musician.

---

[23] *Fisher v Brooker and another* [2009] UKHL 41, [2009] 1 WLR 1764, para 50.
[24] *Fisher v Brooker*, paras 78 and 79.   [25] [2008] EWHC 757 (Ch).   [26] [1966] Ch 71.   [27] [1929] AC 151.
[28] See also *Crosstown Music Co 1 LLC v Rive Droite Music Ltd* [2010] EWCA Civ 1222. A provision in an assignment of copyright allowing automatic reverter of the rights to the assignor on a future event, namely an unremedied material breach of contract by the assignee, was a valid partial assignment within the CDPA 1988, s 90(2).

Restraint of trade

22.13   In *Schroeder Music Publishing v Macaulay*,[29] Macaulay entered into a standard form agreement with Schroeder Music Publishing in which he agreed to assign the copyright in his works to the publisher for five years and, if the royalties exceeded £5,000, for a further five-year period. However, Schroeder was not required to exploit the works. The House of Lords held that this agreement was invalid as it was in restraint of trade. Lord Reid was particularly concerned as to the one-sided nature of the contract which assigned the copyright in the work to the publisher, but which did not require the publisher to exploit that work:

> it appears to me to be an unreasonable restraint to tie the composer for this period of years so that his work will be sterilised and he can earn nothing from his abilities as a composer if the publisher chooses not to publish. If there had been … any provision entitling the composer to terminate the agreement in such an event the case might have had a very different appearance. But as the agreement stands not only is the composer tied but he cannot recover the copyright of work which the publisher refuses to publish.[30]

22.14   Although a contract dealing with image rights rather than music, this concern with the one-sided nature of a contract arose again in *Proactive Sports Management Ltd v Rooney*.[31] Here, the footballer Wayne Rooney had entered into an agreement with Proactive when he was 17 for the exclusive exploitation of his image rights. The Court of Appeal agreed with the High Court that the lack of independent legal advice for Rooney, coupled with the one-sided nature of the contract which Rooney could not terminate for eight years and the unusual nature of the agreement in the industry, meant that it was unreasonable in restraint of trade. As the agreement was unenforceable, the management company could not recover commission arising after the termination of the contract.

22.15   The doctrine is, however, not without its limits. Georgios Panayiotou (aka George Michael) challenged his contract with Sony Music Entertainment[32] from which he wanted to resile on the ground that it was in restraint of trade. The history between the parties was complex, and a number of changes to their contractual relationship had occurred during the 1980s, the last of which was in 1988. The High Court refused to set aside the agreement largely because it was considered that to do so would be contrary to public policy.

 Question

Compare and contrast the factors that amounted to restraint of trade in *Schroeder Music Publishing* and *Proactive Sports Management*. If you were a company looking to enter into a contract for the exploitation of rights belonging to an individual, how might you draft an agreement that would meet these concerns? Prepare a checklist of other steps that you would take to avoid running the risk of claims that the contract is in restraint of trade.

Undue influence

22.16   In *O'Sullivan and another v Management Agency*[33] Gilbert O'Sullivan had entered into various contracts with a management agency and publishing company without receiving any independent advice. The Court of Appeal held that the onus was on those asserting that the agreements were valid to show that

---

[29] [1974] 1 WLR 1308, [1974] 3 All ER 616. See also *Elton John v James* (1983) [1991] FSR 397.
[30] [1974] 1 WLR 1308 at 1315.   [31] [2011] EWCA Civ 1444.
[32] *Panayiotou and others v Sony Music Entertainment* [1994] EMLR 229.   [33] [1985] QB 428.

they had been entered into with full information as to the nature of the transaction—which was not so in this case.[34]

 Question

Despite these examples, there have been few other cases in which the contractual arrangement between a musician and a record company has been challenged in court. Why do you think this is the case? When considering this question you might like to browse the Musicians' Union website at http://www.musiciansunion.org.uk/. What activities does the Musicians' Union undertake on behalf of its members?

22.17 It is not only in the music industry that difficulties may be encountered due to the inequality of bargaining power as between the author and the exploiter. To assist, a number of different societies representing the interests of the author have developed style agreements that an author can use in negotiations. For instance, the Writers' Guild has negotiated a raft of agreements applicable as between their members and organisations such as the BBC, ITV, and the Producers Alliance for Cinema and Television (PACT); Equity does the same for performers with respect to the exploitation of performances in, for example, cinema and on television.

Web links

A number of the Writers' Guild agreements can be found at **http://www.writersguild.org.uk** and the Equity agreements at **http://www.equity.org.uk/**.

Copyright, performers, and equitable remuneration

22.18 In some jurisdictions measures can be found within copyright and related rights legislation which are protective of the author. For example, in Germany the Copyright Act provides that an author is entitled to reasonable remuneration for the exploitation of a work, to be judged by the standard of the prevailing levels in the industry.[35] In UK law, by contrast, there are few statutory controls on contracts negotiated between individual authors and exploiters in the field of copyright and related rights. An exception is in relation to the rental right in a film or sound recording belonging to the author or performer. When the right is voluntarily or is presumed to be transferred to a producer,[36] the author or performer has a right to equitable remuneration.[37]

This right cannot be transferred or waived although it can be assigned to a collecting society or may transfer by testamentary disposition or operation of law. The level of remuneration is to be determined by agreement or, failing agreement, by the copyright tribunal. Thus the author or performer has an unwaivable right to benefit from successful exploitation of the work, albeit in these relatively narrow areas. (See also para 6.40.)

---

[34] The doctrines of restraint of trade and undue influence may be subject to acquiescence: *Zang Tumb Tuum Records Ltd v Johnson* [1993] EMLR 61. [35] German Copyright Act, Arts 32 and 36.

[36] CDPA 1988, s 93A; CDPA 1988, s 191(G)(1).

[37] A performer also has a right to equitable remuneration where a commercially published sound recording is played in public or otherwise communicated to the public (CDPA 1988, s 182D). Note also the Beijing Treaty on Audiovisual Performances agreed July 2012 which gives states the option to provide for royalties or equitable remuneration to be paid to performers irrespective of the transfer of their rights to the producer (Art 12.3).

Exercise

Do you think that a right to equitable remuneration should be extended in the area of copyright? For instance, if a literary work becomes a best-seller, should the author, who might have assigned or licensed exclusive rights to the publisher, be entitled to benefit from the financial success of the work? Would a system such as that to be found in Germany where the copyright law provides that an author may benefit from financial success of a work be appropriate for the UK? (For information see WR Cornish, 'The author as risk-sharer' (2003) 26(1) Columbia Journal of Law and the Arts 1.) Note also the European Directive on the resale right for the benefit of the author of an original work of art.[38]

Copyright and compulsory licences

22.19   International obligations under the Berne and Rome Conventions mean that compulsory licences will be granted in respect of the exploitation of copyright in only limited circumstances under UK law. The Berne Convention allows for the grant of compulsory licences for jukeboxes, and mechanical licences for musical works, both subject to conditions. However, the UK does not take advantage of either of these relaxations.[39] Under the Rome Convention compulsory licences may only be granted as regards broadcasting or communication to the public of phonograms.[40]

22.20   A topical challenge to the narrow scope of compulsory licences in copyright law is currently being considered in the context of 'orphan works'. If an author wishes to use a substantial part of an existing protected work in a new work, then permission must be obtained from the owner of the copyright. However, tracing copyright owners can be a complex, costly, and time-consuming activity particularly where a work may be out of print, the copyright may have devolved amongst countless heirs, or the work may simply have been forgotten about. Where an owner cannot be located after reasonable inquiry, some term the work an 'orphan work'. Orphan works have been the subject of intense discussion at international, European, and national policy-making levels in recent years. One of the earliest investigations took the form of an inquiry by the US Copyright Office. During the course of this investigation much evidence was submitted on behalf of copyright owners arguing that the introduction of a scheme which would permit the use of protected works without permission, even where the author could not reasonably be traced, would amount to the imposition of a compulsory licence and thus contrary to international obligations. The Copyright Office sought to avoid this outcome by suggesting a limitation on remedies: where a work is used after a reasonable inquiry during which the owner could not be traced, damages for commercial use would be limited to reasonable compensation for the use.

Web links

Have a look at the US website discussing this issue at **http://www.copyright.gov/orphan/**. Look in particular at the comments submitted by Paul Goldstein and Jane Ginsburg at **http://www.copyright.gov/orphan/comments/OW0519-Goldstein-Ginsburg.pdf**.

What do they say about orphan works and compulsory licences?

[38] Directive 2001/84/EC of the European Parliament and of the Council of 27 September 2001 on the resale right for the benefit of the author of an original work of art.

[39] The jukebox licence: Berne Convention, Art 11*bis* (2), and the mechanical licence: Berne Convention, Art 13.

[40] Rome Convention, Art 12.

22.21   At international level, at the World Intellectual Property Organization (WIPO) orphan works have been discussed in the context of proposals for a treaty for exemptions and limitations for libraries and archives.[41] In the EU, after extensive consultation, a Directive exists which allows certain uses of orphan works;[42] in the UK, the Hargreaves Review proposed establishing licensing and clearance procedures for orphan works—a suggestion subsequently investigated further in the Hooper Report;[43] the UK Government has proposed amendments in the Enterprise and Regulatory Reform Bill that would permit commercial and non-commercial use of orphan works and create a body to license the use. At the time of writing, none of the legislative proposals have been implemented and there remain significant differences in opinion as to the shape or scope that the permissions to use orphan works should take.

 Exercise

Read the WIPO proposals, the Directive, and the UK Government and US Copyright Office proposals. List the similarities and differences in the proposals and consider the arguments put forward by interested stakeholders. What action, if any, do you consider should be taken in relation to orphan works and at what level of policy-making?

22.22   In tandem with attempts to develop legislative frameworks, there have been a number of informal initiatives to deal with orphan works. One example is the Accessible Registries of Rights Information and Orphan Works towards Europeana (ARROW) database. Funded by the European Commission, this was created as a repository of sources of information in Europe to determine whether a work is in or out of print, locate the right holders or collective management organisations to obtain permission to use the rights, or to declare the work is an orphan work. Although still in a pilot stage, the database has been attracting increasing attention as a tool that could ease significantly the challenges posed of locating right holders.[44]

Collective licensing

22.23   Exploiting works protected by copyright can cause practical problems for both the copyright owner and the prospective licensee. A copyright owner can find it difficult to keep track of third parties who wish to exploit those works in one form or another. Similarly, a licensee may wish to incorporate a large number of works protected by copyright into their repertoire, but have difficulty in tracing the copyright owners to obtain permission. For example, educational establishments and businesses often make copies of published literary works which do not fall under the fair dealing provisions in the copyright legislation[45] and broadcasters frequently use musical works which are protected by copyright. In order to facilitate the management of these rights, collecting societies were introduced.[46] Authors of works protected by copyright are able to assign or license their rights to the collecting societies (or the collecting society will

---

[41] WIPO SCCR Twenty–Third Session, Geneva, 21–25, 28 and 29 November and 2 December 2011.

[42] Brussels, 24.5.2011, COM(2011) 289 final, 2011/0136 (COD). For part of the preparatory work see i2010 EU High Level Expert Group (Copyright Subgroup), 'Final Report on Digital Preservation, Orphan Works and Out-of-Print Work', 3 June 2008.

[43] *Copyright Works: Streamlining Copyright Licensing for the Digital Age*. An independent report by Richard Hooper CBE and Dr Ros Lynch, July 2012 See also Digital Britain Final Report June 2009 (ISBN: 9780101765022). This followed on from the recommendation in the *Gowers Review of Intellectual Property* that a proposal should be put to the European Commission to introduce a provision on orphan works in the form of a Directive.

[44] http://www.arrow-net.eu.   [45] See Chapter 5.

[46] M Kretschmer, 'Access and Reward in the Information Society: Regulating the Collective Management of Copyright' (2007) http://eprints.bournemouth.ac.uk/3695/1/CollSoc07.pdf.

act as agent on their behalf) which then manage the rights on behalf of their members. Thus, the authors are saved from having to spend a lot of time on administration, and those who wish to exploit the works have one place from which they can seek permission to use them.

22.24   Examples of collecting societies currently operating in the UK include the Copyright Licensing Agency (CLA) and the PRS for Music (formerly the Performing Right Society (PRS) and the Mechanical Copyright Protection Society (MCPS)). Different societies operate in different ways. PRS for Music, which represents composers, authors, and publishers of music, has copyright assigned to it and administers licences and enforces copyright as the owner of the copyright. Royalties are distributed to the members in proportion to the use made of a particular work. In contrast, the MCPS was authorised by the composer, author, or publisher of a work to license the recording of the work on his behalf—there was no assignment of the copyright.

22.25   In 2008 a consultation was carried out on proposed changes to exemptions from public performance rights in sound recordings and performers' rights managed by the PPL (originally called Phonographic Performance Limited).[47] The consultation considered two exemptions in the CDPA 1988 which applied to rights managed by the PPL:

- where charitable bodies play CDs or other recorded music if certain conditions are met; and
- where not-for-profit bodies play radios or TVs if the broadcasts include recorded music and the audience has not been charged entry.

After consultation, the Government repealed the exemptions,[48] giving right holders exclusive rights over the public playing of sound recordings in all the circumstances which were exempt and removed the right of the Secretary of State to refer PPL licences or licensing schemes to the Copyright Tribunal. PPL granted charitable organisations a 'grace period' for complying with the new rules, stating that licences would not be required during 2011. Licences are not needed for certain occasions—including worship and weddings. If, however, recorded music is played on the premises for other events, such as coffee mornings, then a licence is needed.

Web links

Have a look at the websites of the CLA **http://www.cla.co.uk/**, PRS for Music **http://www.prsformusic.com**, and PPL **http://www.ppluk.com**. Can you envisage any regulatory problems that might arise in their management and administration? Can you find any similar organisations in other jurisdictions?

Oversight of activities of collecting societies: the UK

22.26   Because collecting societies occupy a powerful role, both in relation to the authors of the works, and in relation to users, some oversight of their activities has been found to be essential. If a collecting society manages a number of copyright works on behalf of their copyright owners, the collecting society may refuse to license the work to a particular individual or group, or it might seek to extract unreasonable royalties. These dangers were recognised after the first collecting society, the Performing Right Society

---

[47] See http://www.ppluk.com.
[48] CDPA 1988, s 128A repealed by Copyright, Designs and Patents Act 1988 (Amendment) Regulations 2010 (SI 2010/2694).

which came into being in 1914, had been in operation for a number of years. As a result, a regulatory framework for the oversight of collecting societies has been developed.

22.27 The Competition Commission has oversight of the activities of a society in relation to matters that might operate against the public interest.[49] If the Commission determines the existence of such matters, for example conditions in licences which restrict the use of a work by the licensee[50] or a refusal of the copyright owner to grant licences on reasonable terms,[51] there are powers to cancel or modify the conditions and to provide licences in respect of the copyright to be made available as of right.[52] One example of a reference to the Monopolies and Mergers Commission (MMC) (the predecessor of the Competition Commission) concerned the PRS (discussed previously).[53] The MMC found that a number of the rules which the Society had in place operated against the interests of its members. The PRS was required to alter its rules in accordance with the recommendations in the report.

22.28 The Copyright Tribunal exists to monitor the activities of collecting societies.[54] Thus, for instance, those parties who wish to take a licence from the collecting society but who feel that the terms are unfair or where the society might have refused to grant them a licence, may take a complaint and have it heard by the Tribunal.[55]

■ CT 71/00, CT 72/00, CT 73/00, CT 74/00 and CT 75/01 *Universities UK (formerly the Committee of Vice Chancellors and Principals) v The Copyright Licensing Agency (Intervenors: Design and Artists Copyright Society)* [2002] RPC 36

In this case, universities in the UK asked the Copyright Tribunal to rule on the terms of the Higher Education Copying Accord promulgated by the CLA and which allows, inter alia, students in higher education institutions to make copies, up to a certain amount, of published works during the currency of their educational courses. Negotiations had broken down on matters concerning both the scope of and the fee for the licence. The Copyright Tribunal made an order referring to both of these matters: the course pack provision (which had required separate negotiation each time a 'course pack' was provided to a class of students), so disliked in education, was to be abolished, artistic works were to be included in the licence, and the fee was to be set at £4.00 per full-time enrolled student.

 Exercise

Have a look at the final decision of the Copyright Tribunal. What do you think of the outcome of the hearing? What price do you think should be paid to authors and publishers for photocopying materials for educational purposes? What difference (if any) do you think digitisation might make to the debate?

---

[49] CDPA 1988, s 144.   [50] CDPA 1988, s 144(1)(a).   [51] CDPA 1988, s 144(1)(b).

[52] CDPA 1988, s 144 specifies what powers are available under s 41(2), 55(2), 66(6), 75(2), 83(2), 138(2) 147(2) or 160(2) of, or para 5(2) or 10(2) of, Sch 7 to the Enterprise Act 2002 in the event of an adverse finding by the Competition Commission.

[53] A report on the supply in the UK of the services of administering performing rights and film synchronisation rights (Cmnd 3147, 1995).

[54] See CDPA 1988, ss 118–122. See also the discussion in para 7.17. *In Respect of the Appeal of Phonographic Performance Ltd v The Appeal of the British Hospitality Association and Other Interested Parties* [2008] EWHC 2715 (Ch), 2008 WL 4975450. Also CT 4/05 *CSC Media Group Ltd v Video Performance Ltd* [2010] EWHC 2094 (Ch); CT 116/10 *Archive Media Publishing Ltd v MCPS*—the first decision on the small applications track in the streamlined Copyright Tribunal; *PPL v British Hospitality Association* [2010] EWHC 209 (Ch).

[55] Eg Copyright Tribunal Interim Decision CT 84-90/05 confirming that songwriters, composers, and publishers should receive 8 per cent of gross revenues from online music service providers for on-demand services including downloads and subscription streaming services, 6.5 per cent of revenues for interactive webcasting services, and 5.75 per cent for non-interactive webcasting.

Oversight of collecting societies' activities: the EU

22.29 Collecting societies are to be found in most jurisdictions and whereas, to date, they have tended to be largely concerned with activities within a particular territory,[56] they have operated between territories by means of reciprocal agreements. EU competition law has been applied to collecting societies by both the European Court of Justice (ECJ) and by the Commission. Three broad issues have been addressed: the relationship between collecting societies and users;[57] the relationship between collecting societies and their members (right holders);[58] and the reciprocal relationship between different collecting societies.[59]

22.30 On the relationship between collecting societies and users, the ECJ has ruled that as a dominant under-taking, a collecting society cannot refuse—under Article 82 of the EC Treaty (EC) (now Art 102 of the Treaty on the Functioning of the European Union (TFEU))—to license a user in its own territory without a legitimate reason (for a discussion on Art 102 TFEU and a refusal to supply, see paras 21.49ff). Neither may collecting societies engage in collective action, the effect of which is to refuse to license the use of their repertoires to users in other territories arguing that it would be impractical to set up a monitoring system in another territory.[60] The ECJ has also been vexed as to the differences in administrative costs of running a society and the level of royalties remitted to right holders as between societies located in different member states. It has been suggested that it may be the lack of competition in the market that leads to this result.[61]

22.31 On the relationship between collecting societies and right holders, both the Commission and the ECJ have had the opportunity to consider different aspects of the relationship. The Commission has said that a collecting society in a dominant position is not permitted to exclude members from other member states;[62] and that a requirement that an author assign all rights to a society, including online exploitation rights, amounts to an abuse of a dominant position in that it is the imposition of an unfair trading condition.[63] The ECJ has held[64] that mere application of a remuneration model on commercial broadcasters that is tied to the revenues of those television stations is not an abuse of a dominant position provided that the royalties are 'proportionate overall to the quality of musical works protected by copyright actually broadcast or likely to be broadcast ...'.[65] On the claim that it was an abuse of position to apply a different royalty calculation for commercial television stations and the public service broadcaster, STV, the ECJ ruled that the imposition of a different manner of computing the royalties could possibly be an abuse of a dominant position 'if it applies with respect to those companies dissimilar conditions to equivalent services and if it places them as a result at a competitive disadvantage, unless such a practice may be objectively justified'.[66]

---

[56] In Case C-425/07 P AEPI Elliniki Etaireia pros Prostasian tis Pnevmatikis Idioktisias AE v Commission of the European Communities [2009] 5 CMLR 2 the ECJ upheld a Commission Decision rejecting the complaint made by AEPI that Greece and the three main Greek collective management bodies (Erato, Apollon, and Grammo) were in breach of Arts 81 and 82 EC. In refusing the complaint, the Commission stated that:
the alleged infringement is unlikely to seriously impede the proper functioning of the common market, given that all the parties involved are established in Greece and pursue their activities in that country alone. It is not foreseeable that that situation will change, that is to say, that the three ... bodies will start to pursue their activities in other countries in the near future ... The case does not, therefore, present the level of Community interest necessary for the Commission to open an investigation (para 11).
[57] Case 395/87 Ministere Public v Tournier [1989] ECR 2521.
[58] Re GEMA No 1 [1971] CMLR D35; Case C-127/73 BRT v SABAM [1974] ECR 313.
[59] Case C-395/87 Ministère Public v Tournier [1989] ECR 2521; Cases C-110/88, 241/88 and 242/88 Lucazeau v SACEM, 13 July 1989 [1989] ECR 2811.
[60] Op cit, note 42.   [61] Op cit, note 42.
[62] GEMA I, Decision of 20.06.1971, OJ L134/15; GVL, Decision of 29.10.1981, OJ L370/49.
[63] Banghalter et Homem Christo v Sacem (Case COMP/C2/37.219), Decision of 06.08.2002.
[64] Case C-52/07 Kanal 5 Ltd v Föreningen Svenska Tonsättares Internationella Musikbyrå (STIM) UPA [2009] 5 CMLR 18.
[65] Para 41.   [66] Para 48.

22.32 On reciprocal agreements between collecting societies, in 1989 the ECJ concluded that reciprocal representation agreements as such do not fall under Article 81 EC (now Art 102 TFEU) provided they were not accompanied by concerted action or exclusivity.[67] One area in which reciprocal agreements have been discussed at length is the music industry as attempts are made to streamline the licensing processes which enable cross-border exploitation of music over many varied platforms. This is discussed at paras 22.43ff.

22.33 Regulation of collecting societies within Europe is challenging because of the different directorates involved. These are DG Market; DG Information Society and Media; DG Education and Culture; and DG Competition. The Commission has been actively considering the wider framework for the collective management of copyright and related rights over a number of years. In 2004[68] it was suggested that the regulation of collecting societies under general competition rules should be complemented by a legislative framework and that the following areas should be the target of regulation.

The establishment and status of collecting societies

22.34 Collecting societies are formed using a number of different business models including both for and not for profit and using both corporate and charitable vehicles. Given that these societies have responsibilities with regard to the economic, cultural, and social functions they fulfil, the Commission suggested there should be common rules as regards their establishment and status including in relation to the persons who may establish a society; the status of the society; the economic viability of a society; and the representation of right holders within the society.

The relation of collecting societies to users

22.35 The Commission suggested societies should be under an obligation to publish their tariffs and to grant licences on reasonable terms with redress for the user, for instance through the courts or a specially constituted tribunal being available in the event of a dispute.

The relation of collecting societies to right holders

22.36 On the relationship between collecting societies and right holders, the Commission emphasised principles of good governance, non-discrimination, transparency, and accountability which would apply to the acquisition of rights, the conditions of membership, and to representation within the society.

External control of collecting societies

22.37 Finally, and on the external control of collecting societies, practice diverges between the member states. The Commission called for harmonisation of the public control of collecting societies.

22.38 While initiatives concerning the regulation of collective licensing in general have been under consideration, the specific challenges posed by the regulation of collective licensing in the music industry have been of particular moment. Over recent years the Commission has investigated and made a number of decisions on music licensing. In 2001 the Commission investigated an agreement concerning simulcasting proposed by the International Federation of the Phonographic Industry (IFPI).[69] The IFPI brokered an agreement between a number of collecting societies from within Europe and beyond, each of which concerned the administration of the neighbouring rights of their record producer members for the purposes of broadcasting and public performance. This included the licensing of rights in sound recording

---

[67] Case C-395/87 *Ministère public v Tournier* [1989] ECR 2521; Cases C-110/88, 241/88 and 242/88 *Lucazeau v SACEM*, 13 July 1989 [1989] ECR 2811.

[68] Communication from the Commission to the Council, the European Parliament and the European Economic and Social Committee, *The Management of Copyright and Related Rights in the Internal Market*, COM/2004/0261 final.

[69] Commission Decision of 8 October 2002 relating to a proceeding under Article 81 of the EC Treaty and Article 53 of the EEA Agreement (Case COMP/C2/38.014) (IFPI simulcasting). OJ C 231/18–C 231/21 (17 August 2001).

of their members to users, determining tariffs, collecting and distributing royalties, and monitoring use.[70] As simulcasting involves the simultaneous transmission by radio and TV stations via the Internet of sound recordings[71] and this crosses boundaries, the scope and the extent of the licences had to be rethought, most notably to provide for the fact that the signals would be transmitted into several territories at the same time. A new multi-repertoire and multi-territorial licence was proposed. IFPI, on behalf of the collecting societies, sought an individual exemption under Article 81(3) EC. After some hesitation and the imposition of requirements that would ensure that competition between the collecting societies would extend to pricing,[72] and that there would be sufficient transparency in the relationship between the societies and their users by splitting the copyright and administrative fees,[73] the Commission granted an exemption under Article 81(3) EC until 31 December 2004 which has now expired.

22.39   This was followed in 2005 by consideration by the Commission of the terms of the 'Santiago Agreement' also concerning collective exploitation of music.[74] In terms of the agreement, each society could grant non-exclusive licences for the communication right from the repertoires of other societies. The society responsible for granting the licence would be the one in the country in which the content provider had its economic seat or which corresponded to the URL of the country of the website where the content provider is incorporated. The Commission believed that this arrangement would lead to an 'effective lock up of national territories'. Although just the one collecting society could grant rights for several different states (ie a one-stop shop for the user) the content provider would have no choice as to which collecting society to use: thus, there would be no competition between the collecting societies. After extensive consultations, the Commission issued a Notice[75] indicating that as the parties had agreed to undertake, amongst other things and for a period of three years, 'not to be party to any agreement on licensing of public performance rights for online use with other copyright management societies containing an economic residency clause',[76] a condition designed to meet the competition concerns.

 Exercise

Do you think the concerns of the Commission in relation to the Santiago Agreement are valid? What sort of conditions might you want to see in an agreement between collecting societies to encourage competition?

22.40   The most recent decision by the Commission concerning anti-competitive practices of music collecting societies is *Re CISAC Agreement*.[77] Broadly, the decision stipulates that the collecting societies may no longer apply a membership clause whereby authors are prevented from choosing or moving to another

---

[70] Commission Decision, note 69, para 2.   [71] Commission Decision, note 69, para 2.
[72] Commission Decision, note 69, para 120.   [73] Commission Decision, note 69, para 121.
[74] V Dehin, 'The future of legal online music services in the European Union: a review of the EU Commission's recent initiatives in cross border copyright management' (2010) 32(5) EIPR 220; I Brinker and T Holzmuller, 'Competition law and copyright—observations from the world of collecting societies' (2010) 11 EIPR 553.
[75] Notice published pursuant to Art 27(4) of Council Regulation (EC) No 1/2003 in Cases COMP/C2/39152—BUMA and COMP/C2/39151—SABAM (Santiago Agreement COMP/C2/38126) (2005/C 200/05).
[76] Commission Notice, note 75, para 9.
[77] Case COMP/C2/38.698 [2009] 4 CMLR 12. See also Case T-411/08 R *Artisjus v Commission of the European Communities* [2009] 4 CMLR 8 where interim measures were sought from the CFI by Artisjus, a Hungarian collective management association, to suspend the operation of the Commission's Decision on the CISAC Agreement case on the ground that 'the system of reciprocal representation agreements … might be destroyed completely and the present network of those agreements disappear if the model envisaged by the Commission were applied' (para 38). The application was dismissed due to lack of urgency and the appeal finally dismissed by the ECJ in Case C-32/09 *Artisjus v European Commission* [2010] 5 CMLR 20.

collecting society. Neither may the territorial restriction which prevents a collecting society from offering licences to commercial users outside their domestic territory be applied. These territorial restrictions tend to include an exclusivity clause which contains authorisation by one collecting society in favour of another to administer its repertoire on a given territory on an exclusive basis and thus results in segmentation of the market on a national basis. As such, a commercial user wishing to offer a pan-European media service could not obtain a licence which covers several member states, but has had, up to now, to negotiate with each individual national collecting society. At the time of writing the decision is under appeal.

22.41   In tandem with these decisions, in 2005 the Commission produced a Study on a Community Initiative on the Cross-Border Collective Management of Copyright and an impact assessment on Reforming Cross-Border Collective Management of Copyright and Related Rights for Legitimate Online Music Services.[78] It was suggested that there were three options: do nothing; allow wider reciprocal agreements; or allow rights holders to appoint an EU-wide collecting society. This was followed by a Recommendation the purpose of which was to facilitate cross-border music licensing.[79] As a result, major music publishers withdrew the mechanical online rights for their Anglo-American repertoire from the traditional system of collective management and offered them individually on a pan-European basis thus fundamentally changing the shape of online music licensing.[80] This was followed by Commission Communication of 3 January 2008 on Creative Content Online in the Single Market[81] in which it was sought to identify and address the most pressing challenges related to the distribution of online creative content,[82] and a Reflection Document in 2009 on Creative Content in a European Digital Single Market: Challenges for the Future. The Reflections which included comment on music, publishing, video, and audiovisual content, saw the Commission determined to pursue a strategy which takes into account both the culturally rich and diverse online content market and the need for a reasonable return for right holders. This was followed in 2010 by a Communication called 'A Digital Agenda for Europe' which proposed a framework on collective rights management; and in 2011 a Green Paper on the Online Distribution of Audiovisual Works in the European Union: Opportunities and Challenges towards a Digital Single Market. The purpose was to enhance content industries by the creation of a single digital market via online multi-territorial licensing.

22.42   For the music industry this has so far culminated in the Commission proposing a Directive on collective management and multi-territorial licensing.[83] The proposal has two key aims: first, to promote transparency and governance of collecting societies, including requirements on reporting and increased control by right holders over their activities; and, secondly, to encourage multi-territorial and multi-repertoire licensing of authors' rights in the EU. In essence, the Commission seems to be proposing a consolidation of the governance issues that have arisen in the series of court cases; and focusing on one means of cross-border licensing—what is called a European passport.

---

[78] SEC(2005) 1254.

[79] Commission Recommendation of 18 October 2005 on collective cross-border management of copyright and related rights for legitimate online music services (2005/737/EC). Subsequently the subject of significant criticism from the European Parliament. See, eg, European Parliament resolution on collective cross-border management of copyright and related rights for legitimate online music services, 15 September 2008.

[80] For details, see 'Creative Content in a European Digital Single Market: Challenges for the Future', Response from the Intellectual Property Foresight Forum to the Reflection Document of DG INGSO and DG MARKT of 22 October 2009.

[81] COM(2007) 0836.

[82] For a judgment of the ECJ concerning the enforcement of music copyright on the Internet and the disclosure of personal information about the infringers, see Case C-275/06 *Productores de Música de España v Telefónica de España SAU*.

[83] COM(2012) 372 final.

Web link

You will find an overview of the developments in online music licensing in 'Collecting societies and cultural diversity in the music sector' (study for the European Parliament, DG Internal Policies, Policy Department B, Brussels, June 2009)[84] at **http://www.europarl.europa.eu/committees/en/ studiesdownload.html?languageDocument=EN&file=28328.**

You will see that one of the conclusions is that there is no 'truly multi-territorial and multi-repertoire system in place. Repertoire fragmentation is one of the principal results of EU action in the field of music rights management.'[85]

Exercise

Consider the 2012 proposal by the Commission for a Directive in this area. What do you think of the licensing proposals? Can you devise a system which would result in a multi-territorial and multi-repertoire system of licensing of content protected by copyright while respecting traditional forms of copyright ownership and exploitation and encouraging competition? Are there differences between music and other content that might warrant different treatment?

Collective and individual licensing and digitisation

22.43 Beyond the challenges associated with the scope of online licences and the governance of collecting societies, it is interesting to speculate as to how the business models for online collective and individual licensing might develop. One of the advantages of digital rights management is that it facilitates one-to-one licensing. Hence, it makes it easier for the right holder to reach out directly to the user, and to enforce rights (and payments) against the user without necessarily needing to employ the assistance of an intermediary. The dissemination of literary works over the Internet where they are used in educational establishments is a case in point. In traditional hardcopy form a licence has been needed from the CLA to make copies for educational use—and, indeed, it still is. However, more and more publishers are making their works directly available to the user subject to payment and various terms and conditions. Along the way, those successful digital publishers (such as Sweet & Maxwell (Westlaw) and Butterworths (Lexis) in the legal domain) have acquired the rights to make available portfolios of works from other publishers. In some ways these publishers now become their own collecting societies, except that they are not subject to the controls of the Copyright Tribunal. That is not, however, to say that competition law may not be applied to their activities. On this last point, in 2001 the Secretary of State for Trade and Industry referred to the Competition Commission for investigation and report under the merger provisions of the Fair Trading Act 1973 the proposed acquisition of Harcourt General, Inc by Reed Elsevier plc.[86] Three aspects of the merger were considered as they may have caused some public interest concerns:

---

[84] IP/B/CULT/IC/2008_136.

[85] Page 10. Note also the earlier comment, 'Music copyright: study on a community initiative on the cross-border collective management of copyright' at http://ec.europa.eu/internal_market/copyright/management/management_en.htm. For a discussion on, inter alia, the difficulties encountered in cross-border exploitation of music because of the territorial nature of the rights, see 'The Recasting of Copyright & Related Rights for the Knowledge Economy' IViR (the Institute for Information Law at the University of Amsterdam), November 2006 available at http://ec.europa.eu/internal_market/copyright/docs/studies/etd2005imd195recast_report_2006.pdf.

[86] Reed Elsevier plc and Harcourt General, Inc. A report on the proposed merger presented to Parliament by the Secretary of State for Trade and Industry, July 2001.

- arrangements for providing customers with access to electronic versions of science, technology, and medical (STM) journals;

- arrangements under which other access mechanisms would be able to establish links with Reed Elsevier's and Harcourt's electronic platforms; and

- the pricing of annual subscriptions to STM journals.[87]

While two of the reporting group did find these aspects to be of some worry, they did not consider that they would operate against the public interest. By contrast, the third member of the group did consider the merger would operate against the public interest. Although the merger did proceed, interesting observations were made in the report with regard to competition in this market and which may have implications for future dealings in this area.

22.44   Another area where competitive pressure is resulting in changing business models and alleged anti-competitive practices is in the e-book market. It seems that in order to try to protect revenues, a number of publishing houses (including Hachette, HarperCollins, Macmillan, Simon & Schuster, and Penguin[88]) may together with Apple have engaged in collusive practices to maintain the price of e-books.[89] This follows a move away from the traditional model of setting prices in the publishing business, under which the publisher would sell wholesale to the seller, and the seller would then determine the price of the book to the consumer. The move has been to a model in which the seller acts as the agent of the publisher and receives a percentage of each sale. This is in large part the publishers' response to the increasing strength of Amazon in the e-book marketplace, and it is a move that may have facilitated collusive behaviour. Whether or not the charges will be pursued or those charged will all settle remains to be seen. There is no doubt, however, that the shape of the business models and modes of exploitation will continue to change over coming months and years.

 Exercise

What do you think is the future of licensing as regards the dissemination of literary works over the Internet? How do you see this segment of the market developing?

Individual online licensing schemes

22.45   The opportunities for making creative works available over the Internet, coupled with the uncertain nature of the fair dealing provisions in copyright law have led to a proliferation of licensing schemes applicable for the dissemination and re-use of creative works. These initiatives are interesting in that they operate within the existing copyright framework but are designed to meet the challenges imposed by what many perceive to be the opaque boundaries of the law on re-use of works protected by copyright.

Creative Commons

22.46   Perhaps the best known of these is Creative Commons (CC). The aim of this licensing scheme is to offer a limited range of licences containing restrictions and permissions that can be used by authors

---

[87] Report, note 86, para 1.7.

[88] Simon and Schuster, HarperCollins, and Hachette settled with the US Department of Justice in September 2012 for $69 million. See http://www.guardian.co.uk/books/2012/sep/07/ebook-price-fixing-judge-settlement.

[89] Both the US Department of Justice and the EU Commission have been investigating allegations of price fixing against Apple and a number of other publishers. See http://www.bbc.co.uk/news/business-17681137.

and artists. Started in the United States it has now become international with licences offered in over 70 jurisdictions with more in preparation, and several others in prospect. In the UK, licences are available for England and Wales and for Scotland.

Creative Commons offers several licences enabling authors (or other right holders) to select which rights they wish to reserve and which they wish to offer.[90]

> Six different licences are available:
>
> CC BY Attribution: lets others distribute remix, tweak, and build upon the work.
>
> CC BY-SA Attribution-ShareAlike: lets others remix, tweak, and build upon a work for commercial purposes as long as the author is attributed and the new creation is licensed under identical terms.
>
> CC BY-ND Attribution—NoDerivs: allows for commercial and non-commercial redistribution as long as the work is attributed and passed on unchanged.
>
> CC BY-NC Attribution–NonCommercial: lets others remix, tweak, and build on the work for non-commercial purposes.
>
> CC BY-NC-SA Attribution—NonCommercial—ShareAlike: lets others remix, tweak, and build on for non-commercial purposes as long as the original is attributed and the new work is licensed on identical terms.
>
> CC BY-NC-ND Attribution—NonCommercial-NoDerivs: allows download and sharing of the work as long as attributed.[91]

22.47   For a licensing system that is used in relation to millions of copyright protected works around the world, it is surprising that there seem to be very few court cases on any aspect of the licence. While there were doubts when the licences were first drafted as to whether courts would recognise them as valid, there seems not to have been a problem. Where there has been an infringement of a licence term, the court, no matter the jurisdiction, has found in favour of upholding the licence.[92]

Other schemes

22.48   Other licensing schemes, some of which have been trialled and some of which were established to meet similar ends, include AE ShareNet[93] run by a non-profit company in Australia to streamline the licensing of IP within the education sector; the Creative Archive[94] licence which was used by the BBC to make available programmes from its archive (the pilot ended in 2006); and BC Commons[95] (offered by the BC (British Columbia) Campus organisation in Canada) for post-secondary institutions developing online content.

Each of these was conceived of and developed in response to the complexities which arise when licensing digital content online. Each aimed to make the process of licensing works simple and efficient and, importantly, to set out clearly the parameters on re-use.

The CC licence scheme is undoubtedly the largest and the one that has outlasted the others

---

[90] For a critique of Creative Commons see N Elkin-Koren, 'What contracts cannot do: the limits of private ordering in facilitating a Creative Commons' (2006) 74 Fordham L Rev 375.

[91] For full details see http://creativecommons.org/licenses/.

[92] See, eg, *Le Tribunal de Premiere Instance de Nivelles*, Belgium 09-1684-A (Lichôdmapwa v. L'asbl Festival de Theatre de Spa), September 2010; *Curry v Audax* [2006] ECDR 22. For a list of cases see http://wiki.creativecommons.org/Case_Law.

[93] http://www.aesharenet.com.au/.   [94] http://creativearchive.bbc.co.uk/.   [95] http://solr.bccampus.ca/cms2/.

Exercise

Go to the Creative Commons webpage and have a browse around it. How may works licensed under a CC licence do you think are available today?

Key points on copyright licensing

- The doctrines of restraint of trade and undue influence can sometimes control copyright licensing practices
- Equitable remuneration is available for authors or performers who transfer the rental right in a sound recording or film
- Compulsory licences may be granted in respect of copyright in only very limited circumstances laid down in the Berne and Rome Conventions
- Collective licensing is a notable feature in copyright exploitation
- Collecting societies are subject to regulatory oversight by the Competition Commission, the Copyright Tribunal, and competition law
- The EU is currently considering the regulation of collecting societies
- Several licensing schemes have emerged in recent years to facilitate the licensing of digital works protected by copyright, the most well known of which is Creative Commons

Patents

Exploitation

22.49   In contrast with works protected by copyright, patents tend to be exploited in a unitary fashion where the licensee is given the right to exploit the bundle of rights that make up the patent. As this mode of exploitation makes the relationship between the patent owner and the licensee easier to manage, collecting societies do not exist in this area. Rather, the terms of the bargain will be the subject of negotiation between the parties. However, it has long been realised that the terms of a licence may have anti-competitive impacts, and so competition law regulates certain clauses that may be found in exploitation agreements. Chapter 21 contains a discussion of the application of the Technology Transfer Block Exemption Regulation to, inter alia, patent agreements.

Compulsory licences

22.50   In contrast with copyright, patent law does contain provisions for compulsory licences. They are included because it is considered to be in the public interest for an invention protected by a patent to be worked. A patent could be misused if it was not worked or licensed, in particular where there was a demand that was not being met. UK law was amended in 1999 to take account of the measures to be found in TRIPS[96] which contains obligations concerning compulsory licences. The UK Patents Act 1977[97] now contains two different procedures for the grant of compulsory licences. One of these is for World Trade Organization (WTO) proprietors, and the other for non-WTO proprietors. A WTO proprietor is a person

---

[96] Patents and Trade Marks (WTO) Regulations 1999 (SI 1999/1899).   [97] Patents Act 1977, s 48.

who is a national of, or domiciled in a country which is a member of the WTO, or who has a real and effective industrial or commercial establishment in a WTO country.[98] There are fewer occasions on which a compulsory licence will be granted in respect of a WTO proprietor as compared with a non-WTO proprietor.

22.51   For example, those grounds on which a compulsory licence will be granted in respect of a WTO proprietor include circumstances where:

- the demand for a patented product in the UK is not being met on reasonable terms;[99]
- the owner's failure to license a patent on reasonable terms has a blocking effect on future improvements;[100]
- the failure to license a patent on reasonable terms unfairly prejudices the establishment or development of commercial or industrial activities in the UK;[101]
- as a consequence of terms in the licence the manufacture, use, or disposal of materials in the UK not protected by the patent or the development of industrial activities in the UK is unfairly prejudiced.[102]

22.52   A compulsory licence will be granted in respect of a non-WTO proprietor in circumstances where:[103]

- the patented invention is capable of being commercially worked in the UK but is not being so worked, or not worked to the fullest extent as is reasonably practicable;[104]
- the patented invention is a product and the demand in the UK is not being met on reasonable terms, or is being met by way of importation from a country that is not a member state of the WTO.[105]

22.53   Few applications are made for compulsory licences. Most commentators do not see this as indicating that the provisions are not working. Rather, the fact that the measures are present in the law may serve as a necessary backdrop against which patent owners license third parties in circumstances where they might otherwise be tempted to refuse.[106]

 Question

Do you think that this last proposition is correct? Justify your response.

Access to medicines: compulsory licences

22.54   For a discussion on access to medicines and compulsory licences, see paras 10.48ff.

Genetic inventions, patents, and licensing practices

22.55   Remaining with public health, but moving away from compulsory licences, interesting issues have been raised over the ways in which patented genetic inventions are licensed. Concern has been expressed, in both the public and private sectors, as to the impact of granting patents over DNA sequences, and the consequent effect that might have for researchers, firms, and clinical users on legal access to genetic inventions. To explore these issues, the Organisation for Economic Co-operation and Development

---

[98] Patents Act 1977, s 48(5)(a), (b).   [99] Patents Act 1977, s 48A(1)(a).   [100] Patents Act 1977, s 48A(1)(b)(i).
[101] Patents Act 1977, s 48A(1)(b)(ii).   [102] Patents Act 1977, s 48A(1)(c).   [103] Patents Act 1977, s 48B.
[104] Patents Act 1977, s 48B(a).   [105] Patents Act 1977, s 48B(b).
[106] Note also the Patents and Plant Variety Rights (Compulsory Licensing) Regulations 2002 (SI 2002/247).

(OECD) Working Party on Biotechnology held an expert group meeting—'Genetic Inventions, IPR, and Licensing Practices'[107]—in early 2002. The aim of the group was to:

- assess the impact of patents on genetic inventions and on access to the information and technologies covered by DNA patents;
- discuss the challenges patents on genetic inventions pose for scientists, industrialists, and medical practitioners.[108]

22.56   The workshop came to a number of interesting conclusions. Not only was it found, perhaps contrary to popular perception, that the patentability of genetic inventions is not fundamentally in question among the users of the system whether from the public or private sectors or from the medical establishment, but also that the evidence available to the group did not suggest a systematic breakdown in the licensing of genetic inventions. Whereas fears were expressed as to the potential for licensing practices to over-fragment patent rights, block exploitation, and result in monopoly positions being abused, these appeared not to be borne out in practice.

Some perceived problems did, however, seem to have substance in practice. This was particularly so where the number and breadth of gene patents being issued was considered alongside the rise of patents with reach-through claims. Other areas included problems arising over access to diagnostic genetic tests, although the cause of the problems appears not to have been fully explained.

 Question

What is a reach-through claim?

22.57   The Report concluded that continued monitoring of patenting and licensing of genetic inventions is necessary, as is the collection and analysis of economic data. The purpose of such research would be to ensure that access does not become a problem in the future. However, as regards the present, it was suggested that more rigorous and data-intensive studies of licensing practices should be carried out prior to embarking on any significant reform of the present system.[109]

22.58   As a follow-up, the OECD drafted a series of 'Principles for the licensing of healthcare genetics'.[110] Noting that research thrives on collaboration and that getting the most out of the genetics revolution will rely increasingly on efficient and effective exchange between those researching and developing new innovations, the guidelines are drafted to try to facilitate licensing grounded in economic principles, to eliminate excessive transactions costs, and on a basis which ultimately will serve the interests of society, shareholders, and other stakeholders.[111]

Web link

Look at the OECD Report which can be found at **http://www.oecd.org/dataoecd/42/21/2491084.pdf**.

Do you agree with the conclusions? What measures do you think might be necessary at international, EU, or domestic level to ensure that all interests are taken into account?

---

[107] OECD, Genetic Inventions, Intellectual Property Rights and Licensing Practices: Evidence and Policies, 2002 available at http://www.oecd.org/dataoecd/42/21/2491084.pdf.

[108] OECD, note 107, 77.   [109] OECD, note 107, 77.   [110] 23 February 2006, C(2005)149/REV1.

[111] OECD, note 100, para 8.

> ## Key points on patent licensing
>
> - Compulsory licensing provisions exist for patents, the extent of which depends on whether the proprietor is a member of the WTO
>
> - Concerns over exploitation of patents in the health care domain have resulted in the promulgation of a series of Principles designed to facilitate licensing

Trade marks

Exploitation

22.59   Trade mark licensing has been said to underpin 'a multi-billion dollar activity that pervades the ways in which goods and services are distributed, marketed and sold, both domestically and internationally'.[112] The proprietor of a trade mark may itself sell goods or services under the mark. Equally, it may devise any number of different trading mechanisms that would permit subsidiaries, related companies, and third parties to manufacture, distribute, and sell goods bearing that mark. A well-known exploitation strategy is by way of franchising where an independent business is permitted to use the trade mark under strict conditions often extending to the 'look and feel' of the business: McDonald's, Dyno-Rod, and Kall Kwik are all examples of this model.[113] Another is merchandising, where third parties are licensed to make goods and services available bearing (usually) a well-known mark, such as Coca-Cola or Disney. In each of these examples a trade mark licensing agreement would need to be negotiated to permit the lawful use of the mark.

22.60   The Trade Marks Act 1994 does not contain express provisions concerning licensing of a trade mark by the right holder to a third party. In other words, the trade mark owner is, subject to competition law, free to license the mark in any way she likes. However, it is possible under the Trade Marks Act 1994 to revoke a trade mark if its use becomes generic or deceptive.[114] The power of revocation was discussed in paras 14.99ff. To avoid such an outcome, the trade mark owner may want to exert control over the use of the trade mark by a licensee. For instance, quality control mechanisms might be included in a licence agreement detailing how the mark is to appear on packaging and providing for the quality of the goods to be sold in association with the mark. If a trade mark owner chooses not to include any provisions regarding the quality of the goods sold under a licence and so has no control over the licensee in this respect (known as a bare[115] licence), the question has arisen as to whether this would be objectionable in that it may deceive potential customers. (For further discussion see para 14.122, *Scandecor Developments AB v Scandecor Marketing AB and others.*[116])

Compulsory licences

22.61   There are no compulsory licensing provisions in trade mark law.[117]

[112] N Wilkof, *Trade Mark Licensing* (1995), 1.
[113] For termination of a franchise and a non-compete clause, see *ChipsAway International Ltd v Errol Kerr* [2008] EWHC 1887 (Ch); *Pirtek (UK) Ltd v Joinplace Ltd* [2010] EWHC 1641 (Ch).   [114] TMA 1994, s 46.
[115] A bare licence is one under which the owner of the trade mark has no power to control the quality of the good sold.
[116] [2001] UKHL 21.
[117] For completeness sake it should be noted that compulsory licences are available for both registered designs; Registered Designs Act 1949, s 10; and for plant breeders' rights: Community Plant Variety Rights (CVPR) Regulation 2100/94/EC, Art 29.

Trade mark licensing and EU competition law

22.62   The Technology Transfer Block Exemption Regulation (TTBER),[118] discussed in Chapter 21 on competition law, may be relevant to licence agreements which include elements dealing with licensing of trade marks, but only where the trade mark licence is not the primary object of the agreement. Also of relevance may be the Vertical Agreements Block Exemption.

The Vertical Agreements Block Exemption[119]

22.63   The Vertical Agreements Block Exemption Regulation (VBER) exempts agreements falling within its terms from the application of Article 101(1) TFEU.

Article 2.3 provides that for an IP licensing agreement to be exempt the provisions must comply with the following conditions. They must:

- relate to use by the buyer of IPRs;
- not constitute the primary object of the agreement;
- be directly related to the use, sale, or resale of the goods or services by the buyer or its customers; and
- in relation to the contract goods or services, not contain restrictions that have the same object or effect as vertical restraints which are not exempted under the block exemption.[120]

22.64   The exemption provided for in Article 2 of the VBER will not apply where the market share of the supplier or buyer exceeds 30 per cent of the relevant market or where the agreement contains one or more of the 'hardcore restrictions' found in Article 4. These include restrictions on:

- the ability of the licensee to determine its sale price;
- the territory into which the licensee can sell or customers to whom the licensee can sell;
- active or passive sales by members of a selective distribution system operating at the retail level;
- cross-supplies between distributors operating at the same level of trade;
- the resale of components to retailers outwith the distribution chain.

22.65   A number of these are subject to provisos. So, for example, on the matter of determination of sale price, the licensor can impose a maximum sale price or recommend a sale price; and on the matter of restricting active sales, these can be limited where a second licensee has been granted exclusive territory for the same products.

22.66   The VBER also contains a number of excluded obligations in Article 5 which will not benefit from the exemption if contained in a licensing agreement. That would not, however, prevent the VBER applying

---

[118] Commission Regulation (EC) No 772/2004 of 27 April 2004 on the application of Article 81(3) of the Treaty to categories of technology transfer agreements.

[119] Commission Regulation (EU) No 330/2010 of 20 April 2010 on the application of Article 101(3) of the Treaty on the Functioning of the European Union to categories of vertical agreements and concerted practices entered into force on 1 June 2010 and replaced Commission Regulation (EC) No 2790/1999 of 22 December 1999 on the application of Article 81(3) of the Treaty to categories of vertical agreements and concerted practices.

[120] For a fuller discussion on the applicability of the VBER to intellectual property agreements, see the Guidelines on Vertical Restraints (2010/C 130/01).

to the remainder of the agreement. These excluded restrictions include any direct or indirect non-compete obligation during the currency of the agreement, the duration of which is indefinite or exceeds five years; any non-compete obligation after the expiry of the agreement; and obligations not to sell competing brands in a selective distribution system.

> ### Key points on trade mark licensing
>
> - There are no compulsory licensing provisions in trade mark law
> - Both the TTBER and the VBER may apply to licensing practices in the trade mark arena

Contemporary exploitation strategies

22.67 As will have been seen from the previous discussion, policy and regulatory responses to exploitation strategies have been developing over the years. Much of the regulatory oversight has been in response to the potential and actual anti-competitive impacts of exploitation in the marketplace and in response to the real (or perceived) ways in which exploitation could operate against the public interest. Self-regulatory initiatives are also apparent, particularly in relation to exploitation of copyright.

Over recent years there have been other notable developments in the IP sector. This section will examine the debate in relation to access to data, the database right, and competition law; and the exploitation of public sector information.[121]

Access to data, the database right, and competition law

22.68 The application of competition law to the exercise of the *sui generis* database right is an area in which a number of issues are raised. The database right has been discussed in Chapter 6. Neither the Database Directive nor UK law contain any compulsory licensing provisions as regards the database right. Compulsory licensing provisions were contained in an early draft,[122] but did not enter the final text.

22.69 While case law from the Court of Justice has suggested that the existence of the database right is more elusive than thought[123] and not as strong as was anticipated by many commentators and does not go as far as to protect information per se, nonetheless the owner of the database right is placed in a strong position vis-à-vis third parties particularly so where the owner is the sole source of the information

---

[121] Another interesting area concerns patent pools and trolls. See S Subramanian, 'Patent trolls in thickets: who is fishing under the bridge?' (2008) 30(5) EIPR 182–188.

[122] Proposal for a Council Directive on the Legal Protection of Databases, COM (92)24 final, Brussels, 13 May 1992, OJ 1992 C156/4, Art 8(1), (2). The draft text read:

(1) Notwithstanding the right provided for in Article 2(5) to prevent the unauthorized extraction and re-utilization of the contents of a database, if the works or materials contained in a database which is made publicly available cannot be independently created, collected or obtained from any other source, the right to extract and re-utilize, in whole or substantial part, works or materials from that database for commercial purposes, shall be licensed on fair and non-discriminatory terms. (2) The right to extract and re-utilize the contents of a database shall also be licensed on fair and non-discriminatory terms if the database is made publicly available by a public body which is either established to assemble or disclose information pursuant to legislation, or is under a general duty to do so.

[123] Case C-203/02 *British Horseracing Board v William Hill Organisation Limited CA* [2004] ECR I-10415; Case C-338/02 *Fixtures Marketing Ltd v Svenska Spel AB* [2004] ECR I-10497; Case C-444/02 *Fixtures Marketing Ltd v Organismoss Prognostikon Agonon Podosfairou AE* [2004] ECR I-10549; Case C-46/02 *Fixtures Marketing Ltd v Oy Veikkaus AB* [2004] ECR I-10365.

within the database or where, economically, it may not be viable for the third party to collate that information independently.[124] Merely because the contents of the database do not attract the database right it does not thereby follow that access can be gained to the contents. Tariffs, technological protection measures, and contract may all be common features surrounding access to databases.

Tariffs

22.70   That charges may be made for access to data contained within a database whether or not the database right subsists, was acknowledged by the ECJ in *British Horseracing Board v William Hill*.[125]

> The fact that a database can be consulted by third parties through someone who has authorisation for re-utilisation from the maker of the database does not … prevent the maker from recovering the costs of his investment. It is legitimate for the maker to charge a fee for the re-utilisation of the whole or a part of his database which reflects, inter alia, the prospect of subsequent consultation and thus guarantees him a sufficient return on his investment.[126]

Access may come at a high price, particularly for first comers, to reflect the lack of control thereafter. The purpose of the database right is to reward investment, so charging for access to information that has been collated and made available in a useful form would seem a sensible reward. However, it would seem that only the market will determine the price of access, which may mean that for many access may be unaffordable.

Technological protection measures

22.71   As with creative works, technological protection measures are likely to be used to guard access to the content of a database, allowing access only to those who have fulfilled relevant criteria laid down by the maker and use for only those purposes specified by the maker. See paras 5.50ff.

Contract

22.72   Contract terms could be imposed on the 'first-taker' of data from a database to prevent the data being passed on to third parties. The maker may also try to impose contractual conditions concerning use and ongoing control of the data whether by that third party or by another with whom the third party might contract: in other words, the maker may use contract to exert control over downstream innovations.

22.73   The inclusion of compulsory licensing provisions within the Database Directive and thus into the laws of member states may have alleviated a number of these concerns—although the debate over control of the re-use of data by contract would no doubt continue. The failure to include the provision now means that it will be left to competition law to regulate the behaviour of makers.

 Question

> Do you think that the absence of compulsory licensing provisions covering the *sui generis* database right will cause problems? If so, what measures would you introduce to deal with them?

22.74   There have been interesting developments in the horse-racing field in the aftermath of the decision by the ECJ in the database cases. The Court of Appeal gave its judgment in *British Horseracing Board v William Hill*[127]

---

[124] On the scope of 'extraction', see Case C-304/07 *Directmedia Publishing GmbH v Albert-Ludwigs-Universitat Freiburg*; Case C-545/07 *Apis-Hristovich EOOD v Lakorda AD*; Case C-604/10 *Football Dataco Ltd and others v Yahoo! UK Ltd and others*.

[125] [2005] EWCA Civ 863 (hereafter *BHB*).   [126] *BHB*, para 57.   [127] [2005] EWCA Civ 863.

in the light of the decision by the ECJ. The Court unanimously agreed that the *sui generis* database right did not subsist in the database compiled by the British Horseracing Board (BHB): the information contained in the database was created by BHB and did not exist as independent materials. This ruling, in conjunction with the uncertainty caused by the references to the ECJ, caused several of the organisations to which BHB supplied data to challenge the terms of their licence agreements with the result that BHB threatened to cease supplying these third parties with data. The major concern appeared to be the price charged by BHB for the use of the data. The basis of the challenges, bolstered by the absence of any form of IPR in the data, was under competition law, both UK and EU.

Victor Chandler (International) Ltd (VCI) (a bookmaker) took the view that their agreement with BHB for the supply of racing data was unenforceable given the ruling by the ECJ.[128] VCI stopped paying for data as was required under its agreement with BHB claiming the prices charged were excessive and the agreement void. BHB sought damages from VCI for breach of contract making it clear that unless the data was paid for, the agreement to supply the data (via the intermediary company, PA Ltd) would be terminated.

VCI sought an order preventing the cessation of supply of the data, claiming that BHB was abusing its dominant position under the Competition Act 1998[129] and Article 82 EC (now Art 102 TFEU). The application was dismissed by the High Court. Laddie J held that, irrespective of the decision by the ECJ, BHB was entitled to continue to charge for the service for compiling the pre-race data and making it available to VCI. In addition, for an abuse of a dominant position to subsist, it was unfair prices, and not high prices, that constituted the relevant criterion. The instant case showed no basis on which it could be claimed that the prices charged by BHB were unfair.

22.75   A similar challenge, also using competition law, was made in a second case, *Attheraces Ltd v The British Horseracing Board Ltd*.[130] Attheraces challenged the basis on which BHB charged for data; BHB in turn threatened to cease supplying Attheraces. On the contravention of competition law, Attheraces alleged that BHB's threat to cease supply was an abuse of dominance contrary to section 18 of the Competition Act 1998 and Article 82 EC (now Art 102 TFEU) and that the fees for the licence were excessive, unfair, unreasonable, and discriminatory and in themselves abuses of BHB's dominance. The High Court[131] found the BHB did indeed occupy a dominant position in the market for the supply of UK pre-race data to those in the horse-racing industry outside of the UK and Ireland, and that BHB had abused that position by charging excessive and unfair prices which bore no relation to the cost to BHB of its database plus a reasonable return. However, the Court of Appeal, while agreeing with the assessment of dominance, disagreed that BHB abused its position. On the issue of excessive pricing, the Court of Appeal found that the method of ascertaining the economic value of the data—its competitive price based on cost plus—was too narrow in that it did not take sufficient account of the value of the pre-race data to Attheraces and that it tied the costs allowable in cost plus too closely to the costs of producing the pre-race data.

22.76   As *Attheraces v BHB* did not concern excessive pricing of a work or product protected by an intellectual property right (the *sui generis* database right did not exist in the part of the BHB database under discussion), it is a matter for speculation whether the same conclusion would have been reached had the database right subsisted. It is possible that competition law will be used with increasing frequency to challenge price and other licensing terms for the supply of data most particularly where the holder of the data is in the public sector.[132]

---

[128] *BHB Enterprises plc v Victor Chandler (International) Ltd* [2005] EWHC 1074 (Ch).
[129] Competition Act 1998, s 18.   [130] [2007] EWCA Civ 38.   [131] [2005] EWHC 3015 (Ch).
[132] See, eg, OFT Report, 'The commercial use of public information (CUPI)', December 2006, OFT861; OPSI report on its investigation of a complaint, 'Intelligent Addressing and Ordnance Survey' (SO 42/8/4).

Exercise

Have a look at the database licences available at **http://www.opendatacommons.org/**. What do these licences seek to do, and do you think they meet their goals?

Exploitation of public sector information

22.77   In June 2002, the Commission presented a proposal for a Directive on the re-use and commercial exploitation of public sector documents (subsequently changed to public sector information).[133] The purpose of this proposal was to form the basis on which information created by the public sector could be used by third parties, the intention being that such re-use of information will contribute to the eEurope Action Plan in particular in the areas of eGovernment and digital content.[134] The Directive was adopted on 17 November 2003[135] and the UK implementing Regulations entered into force on 1 July 2005.

The purpose of the measure is set out in recital 8. It is to provide:

> A general framework for the conditions governing reuse of public sector documents ... in order to ensure fair, proportionate and non-discriminatory conditions for the re-use of such information.

22.78   The Directive does not affect the existence of IPRs in public sector information, or the way in which public sector bodies can themselves exercise their IPRs. It does, however, set boundaries on the exercise of those rights vis-à-vis third parties. Further, the Directive does not require public sector bodies to permit the re-use of information, but where such a body does so, it will be subject to the obligations to be found in the Directive.[136]

22.79   At first glance the measure seems to be wide in scope. 'Document' is defined in the Directive to mean 'any content whatever its medium (written on paper or stored in electronic form or as a sound, visual or audiovisual recording) and any part of such content'.[137] However, the coverage is narrowed both by reference to the type of documents to which the Directive applies, and to the body to whom it applies. Thus, it does not apply to the supply of documents generated by an activity falling outside the scope of the public task of the public sector body, to documents in which third parties hold IPRs, or to documents containing personal data unless the re-use of such data is permitted under Union or national law. Neither does it apply to documents which can be dealt with by public sector broadcasters and their subsidiaries, to those held by educational and research establishments such as universities, research facilities, archives, and libraries, nor to those held by cultural establishments such as museums, libraries, archives, orchestras, operas, ballets, and theatres.[138]

22.80   Where a public sector body does allow the re-use of documents and a request is made for re-use then it should be supplied through electronic means where possible and appropriate,[139] within 20 days where possible,[140] on non-discriminatory conditions,[141] and on a non-exclusive basis.[142] The information can be charged for, but the total income should not exceed the cost of producing, reproducing, and disseminating the information, together with a reasonable return on investment.[143]

---

[133] Proposal for a Directive of the European Parliament and of the Council on the re-use and commercial exploitation of public sector documents, COM(2002) 207 final, Brussels, 5.6.2002, 2002/0123 (COD). Subsequently changed to 'public sector information', COM(2003) 119 final, 2002/0123 (COD).
[134] eEurope 2002 Action Plan, 'An Information Society for All' (COM(2000) 330 final).
[135] Directive 2003/98/EC of the European Parliament and of the Council of 17 November 2003 on the re-use of public sector information (Re-use Directive).   [136] Re-use Directive, Art 3.
[137] Re-use Directive, Art 2(3).   [138] See generally Re-use Directive, Art 1(2).   [139] Re-use Directive, Art 4.
[140] Re-use Directive, Art 4(2).   [141] Re-use Directive, Art 10.   [142] Re-use Directive, Art 11.   [143] Re-use Directive, Art 6.

22.81   It is clear from the wording of the Directive that it does not impose compulsory licensing measures in relation to public sector information. There is no compulsion for public sector bodies to grant licences to third parties,[144] and member states are merely 'invited to stimulate public sector bodies to make the information available for re-use'.[145]

22.82   In December 2011 the Commission presented an 'Open Data Package' with three aspects: a Communication on open data;[146] a proposal for a revised Directive;[147] and a review of the Commissions approach to open data.[148] On the Directive, key changes would be to include new bodies in the scope of application of the Directive such as libraries (including university libraries), museums, and archives; to limit the fees that can be charged by the public authorities to the marginal costs as a rule; to introduce independent oversight over re-use rules in the member states; and to make machine-readable formats for information held by public authorities the norm.

22.83   In the UK, a body—the Office of Public Sector Information (OPSI)—was established, now merged with the National Archives.[149] Its remit was to uphold rights under the Re-Use Regulations.[150] An Open Government Licence and Open Parliament Licence have been developed for licensing information falling under the Re-use Regulations.[151] These are not mandatory licences but can be chosen as the licensing route by public sector bodies.

22.84   In recent years there have been some significant changes in the way the UK Government holds and manages public sector information. Driven by the belief that significant economic gains are to be had through the liberalisation of public sector information, the Government is developing a myriad of pathways for the opening up and re-use of this resource underpinned by transparent, easily understood, and non-discriminatory licensing terms. Public sector data has been of particular interest to the Government after its publication of a White Paper in 2012: 'Open Data: Unleashing the Potential'.[152]

Web link

For the report 'Open Data: Unleashing the Potential', see **http://data.gov.uk/sites/default/files/Open_data_White_Paper.pdf**.

Exercise

Could intellectual property rights be exercised by public sector bodies in a manner inconsistent with the aims of the Directive? If so how, and to what extent? Note also Case C-138/11 *Compass-Datenbank GmbH v Republik Österreich*.

---

[144] For a judgment of the Court of Justice concerning a question as to whether it was anti-competitive for the Austrian state, citing the database right to refuse access to public sector information collated under a statutory obligation to a third party wishing to make commercial re-use of that information, see Case C-138/11 *Compass-Datenbank GmbH v Republik Österreich*. The Court of Justice found that the state did not, in these circumstances act as an undertaking for the purposes of Art 102 TFEU.

[145] Proposal for a Directive of the European Parliament and of the Council on the re-use and commercial exploitation of public sector documents, COM(2002) 207 final, Brussels, 5.6.2002, 2002/0123 (COD), p 10 referring to the general principle in Art 3.

[146] Brussels, 12.12.2011, COM(2011) 882 final.   [147] Brussels, 12.12.2011, COM(2011) 877 final.

[148] Commission Decision of 12 December 2011 on the reuse of Commission documents (2011/833/EU).

[149] OPSI replaced Her Majesty's Stationery Office (HMSO).

[150] OPSI merged with the National Archives (TNA) in 2006. The Advisory Panel on Public Sector Information (APPSI) advises ministers and OPSI under the Re-Use Regulations.

[151] http://www.nationalarchives.gov.uk/information-management/our-services/click-use.htm.

[152] Cm 8353. Similar open strategies are being pursued with regard to the dissemination of publicly funded research See *Accessibility, Sustainability, Excellence: How to Expand Access to Research Publications*, Dame Janet Finch, June 2012.

Enforcement and remedies

22.85 Of importance to a right holder is a means of enforcing a right and a remedy if the right is infringed—each of which should be appropriate to a particular transgression. For instance, an owner of copyright faced with an enterprise churning out pirated copies of a music CD, is most likely to want the production of the unlawful CDs halted, the copies destroyed, and the transgressor subject to criminal penalties. The right holder might like to bring a civil action for damages or account of profits, but whether such an enterprise would be in a position to pay might be a moot point. By contrast, the owner of a patent, where the subject of the patent has been unlawfully worked by another, is likely to want to receive damages for the wrong, as well as an order prohibiting such conduct in the future. On the other side of the coin, it is equally as important that the enforcement procedure and remedy should be proportionate to the infringement. If the user of a protected work or invention unintentionally infringes the right, it would seem disproportionate if criminal sanctions were imposed where an order prohibiting the continued infringement and discretionary damages would suffice.[153]

22.86 To deal with the variety of intellectual property infringements that can occur, a raft of enforcement procedures and remedies have been developed and which can be deployed to assist the right holder in appropriate circumstances. These can be found in obligations in international agreements (TRIPS, Part III), at European level (eg in the measures for combating counterfeiting and piracy as well as the EU Enforcement Directive), and at national level in the measures both within the respective intellectual property statutes, in general rules and procedures pertaining to court actions, and at common law.

22.87 The majority of enforcement procedures are civil. IPRs are private rights; hence, it is for the owner to take action where infringement occurs. Civil cases generally need no knowledge on behalf of the infringer and require that a case be proved on the balance of probabilities. By contrast, criminal cases require knowledge on behalf of the infringer, proof beyond reasonable doubt, and may not carry the same remedies as those available in civil disputes. As civil litigation over intellectual property disputes becomes ever more complex, lengthy, and expensive, so the use of alternative dispute resolution systems is increasing in importance. Perhaps the best known is that for domain name disputes (see paras 16.23ff). Beyond that there exist a number of specialised intellectual property mediation and arbitration services which may be used in this field.

22.88 In response to the increased incidence of counterfeiting and piracy, a raft of criminal procedures have been introduced and developed over the past years. In the areas of copyright, performers' rights, and trade marks, civil actions are boosted by criminal sanctions for those cases in which infringement is carried out on a commercial scale, such as the use of trade marks on counterfeit goods, or the production of pirated copies of CDs and DVDs. Recognising that counterfeiting and piracy extend well beyond individual jurisdictions and to combat what some perceive to be organised crime, a number of measures updated over recent years now exist at European level to deal with infringers and infringing goods. These are enforced and supplemented by way of a network of administrative procedures in terms of which enforcement agencies (eg trading standards departments and customs and excise officers) are charged with apprehending intellectual property infringers.

22.89 At international level, and as between states, TRIPS contains enforcement procedures expedited by way of its Dispute Resolution System. This allows one state to take action against another if the TRIPS obligations have either not been implemented, or have been incorrectly implemented into the domestic law of contracting states.

---

[153] Although note that damages are not available for innocent infringement of a number of IPRs. See para 22.121.

Suspected infringements: unjustified threats

22.90   If an IP owner suspects that there has been an infringement of an IPR it can be easy to issue threats alleging infringement. This can be particularly damaging to a small or developing business that may not have the resources to respond or to take advice as to whether there has been an infringement. To give some protection, each industrial property right (patents,[154] trade marks,[155] registered designs,[156] and unregistered design right[157]) provides a remedy for those who receive groundless threats of infringement proceedings.

Unjustified threats and trade marks

22.91   An example from the domain of registered trade marks illustrates both the procedure and some of the pitfalls that can trap the unwary. If a claimant wants to bring an action for unjustified threats, it must be shown that an actionable threat has been made, that the claimant is aggrieved, and that the threat was groundless. The relief to which a claimant is entitled (in the absence of a successful action for infringement) includes a declaration that the threats are unjustifiable,[158] an injunction against the continuation of the threats,[159] and damages in respect of any loss sustained by the threats.[160]

22.92   Unjustified threats can be made in a number of ways. Often it is by way of letter and some thought should be given to the contents.

■ *L'Oréal (UK) Ltd and Golden Ltd v Johnson & Johnson* [2000] ETMR 691, [2000] FSR 686[161]

This case illustrates the type of content to which courts will take exception. L'Oréal launched a range of shampoos for children called 'L'Oréal Kids'. They used the words 'No Tears' on the packaging. Johnson's owned registered trade marks for 'No More Tears' for baby shampoos. Solicitors for L'Oréal wrote to Johnson & Johnson seeking confirmation that no proceedings would be raised in the UK. Johnson replied that while they had not received instructions to commence infringement proceedings, they could offer no comfort as to future litigation. The letter included the following text:

> No decision has yet been made on whether to make a claim of trade mark infringement. You should, however, be aware that, at the same time as L'Oreal is commencing use of the mark, others in the UK market who had been using the mark ... have now agreed to respect Johnson & Johnson's position and are stopping their use ... Our clients do, after all, have six years in which they could commence proceedings ... Bearing this in mind, we cannot give L'Oreal comfort at this stage and accordingly we must reserve all of Johnson & Johnson's rights.

Calling the letter a 'work of a master of Delphic utterances' the court found it to constitute a threat of legal proceedings on the basis that it would be understood as such by the ordinary recipient. According to the judge, the author of the letter was one who 'uses all his skill to say everything and nothing and to convey an enigmatic message which has the same effect on the recipient as a threat ...'[162]

---

[154] Patents Act 1977, s 70 as amended by Patents Act 2004, s 12.
[155] TMA 1994, s 21. Note also para 6 of the Community Trade Mark Regulations 2006.
[156] Registered Designs Act 1949, s 26. See also para 22.88 for Community registered and unregistered design right.
[157] CDPA 1988, s 253.   [158] TMA 1994, s 21(2)(a).   [159] TMA 1994, s 21(2)(b).   [160] TMA 1994, s 21(2)(c).
[161] Design right: *Frayling v Premier Upholstery Ltd and others* (6 November 1998, unreported). Trade marks: *Prince plc v Prince Sports Group Ltd* [1998] FSR 21.
[162] See also *Samuel Smith Old Brewery (Tadcaster) v Lee (t/a Cropton Brewery)* [2012] FSR 7; *Best Buy Co Inc v Worldwide Sales Corp Espana SL* [2011] EWCA Civ 618, [2011] Bus LR 1166, [2011] FSR 30.

Question

As an adviser to Johnson & Johnson how would you have drafted the letter to L'Oréal in order to avoid liability?

Unjustified threats and patents

22.93   In 2004 the Patents Act 2004 amended the Patents Act 1977 in a number of ways.[163] First, as the law stands now, where a patent owner who thinks he has a valid patent and on that basis approaches an alleged infringer will not be liable for unlawful threats if his patent turns out to be invalid as long as he had no reason to suspect that the patent was invalid when the approach to the alleged infringer was made. Secondly, a patent holder can discuss both primary and secondary infringing acts with an alleged infringer without necessarily leading to a claim for unjustified threats. Thirdly, if the patent owner, despite using best endeavours, cannot locate the primary infringer, he may approach the alleged secondary infringer without being found liable for making unjustified threats to the retailer.

The current law represents a subtle shift in the provisions in favour of the right holder, most notably that the patent owner may now approach an alleged secondary infringer without being liable for making unjustified threats.[164] It remains to be seen whether this will cause problems for retailers—there has been insufficient case law at present to determine the impact of the changes.[165] Much may turn on the interpretation of the phrase 'best endeavours'.

Groundless threats and design rights

22.94   Section 253 of the CDPA 1988 contains measures dealing with groundless threats for unregistered design right, and section 26 of the Registered Designs Act 1949 for registered design right. These have been extended to Community registered and unregistered design rights in the Community Design Regulations 2005[166] (the Regulations). Regulation 2 of the Regulations allows anyone aggrieved by a threat of proceedings for an infringement of a Community design to bring an action for (a) a declaration the threats are unjustifiable; (b) an injunction against the continuance of the threats; and (c) damages. There is an exception for threats relating to primary infringing (making or importing).[167]

22.95   A case on the groundless threats provisions arose in *Quads 4 Kids v Campbell*[168] illustrating the many ways in which unjustified threats may be made. eBay operates a policy whereby IP owners may notify eBay of alleged infringements of IPRs by way of filling in an online form. On receipt of a notice eBay will remove the allegedly infringing items, and then inform the seller. Campbell notified eBay in this way of the sale of quad bikes by Quads 4 Kids which Campbell alleged infringed his Community design right. An interim injunction was sought to stop Campbell interfering with Quad

---

[163] Patents Act 1977, s 70 as amended by Patents Act 2004, s 12.
[164] *Zeno Corporation (incorporated under the laws of the state of Texas, USA, & formerly known as Tyrell Inc), Adept Scientific plc v BSM-Bionic Solutions Management GmbH, Riemser Arzneimittel AG* [2009] EWHC 1829 (Pat), Patents Act 1977, s 50(5)(b): a finding of unjustified threats was upheld. *LB Europe Ltd (t/a DuPont Liquid Packaging Systems) v Smurfit Bag In A Box SA* [2008] EWHC 1231 (Ch): the appropriate level of damages if a patentee made groundless threats of patent infringement to a competitor's customer.
[165] For a case where allegations of infringement made to a retailer were upheld, see *Zeno Corp v BSM-Bionic Solutions Management GmbH* [2009] EWHC 1829 (Pat), (2009) 32(10) Intellectual Property Decisions 32070.
[166] SI 2005/2339.   [167] Community Design Regulations 2005 (SI 2005/2339), reg 2.5.
[168] [2006] EWHC 2482 (Ch).

4 Kids' business of selling quad bikes on eBay. Campbell took no further proceedings with regard to infringement action against Quad 4 Kids once the goods had been removed from eBay. The court had to decide whether the submission of the online form could be regarded as a threat to bring infringement proceedings.

The court said that the test to apply was whether a reasonable person, in the position of the person allegedly threatened, would have understood that he might have been subject to infringement proceedings at some point in the future. Filling in of eBay's form did not necessarily mean that infringement proceedings were a possibility. However, the effect in this case was to enable Campbell to stop Quads 4 Kids from selling bikes by completing the form. The proper test was thus whether eBay would have understood that it could be subject to future infringement proceedings if it had not adopted the policy of removing any allegedly infringing items. As the answer to that was affirmative, the balance of convenience meant the injunction should be granted.

Other intellectual property rights

22.96   There are no unjustified threats provisions for other IPRs such as copyright, passing off, database right, and breach of confidence. It is, however, possible to apply for a declaration that a threat of legal action of any kind is unjustified.

■ *Point Solutions Ltd v Focus Business Solutions Ltd* [2006] FSR 31

This case concerned an application by Point for a declaration that its computer software did not infringe the copyright in the source code produced by Focus. Focus had not commenced a claim for copyright infringement, but Point alleged that Focus had alleged, both expressly and by implication, that Point's software infringed Focus's copyright through correspondence between the parties, and by statements to clients of Point. The court found that while Point had established that Focus had made the assertions, there was insufficient evidence to establish that Point had developed the software independently, no evidence that there was any impact on Point's business, and a concern that a grant of declaratory relief would foreclose a future claim for Focus. The declaration was thus refused. The judgment was affirmed on appeal.[169]

 Exercise

Do you think there should be unjustified threats provisions in copyright law? If so, why? If not, why not?

22.97   The unjustified threats measures are currently under consideration by the Law Commission which will publish a consultation paper in February 2013. The purpose is to consider whether to repeal, reform, or extend the provisions taking into account the balance between the interests of the IP owner and those

---

[169] *Point Solutions Ltd v Focus Business Solutions Ltd* [2007] EWCA Civ 14. For a declaration of non-infringement in relation to the Community design, see *Samsung Electronics (UK) Ltd v Apple Inc* [2012] EWHC 889 (Ch).

who stock or purchase affected goods. Despite the wishes of some, the consultation will not consider copyright.

Key points on unjustified threats

- Unjustified threats actions are available for trade marks, patents, and registered and unregistered design right

- The test is whether a reasonable person, in the position of the person allegedly threatened, would think that he might be subject to infringement proceedings at some point in the future

---

Preparing a case: obtaining evidence—freezing (Mareva) and search (Anton Piller) orders

22.98   If an infringement of an IPR is suspected, then it will be imperative for the owner to gather evidence of that infringement. In common with other areas, in intellectual property cases it would be easy for a defendant to destroy much needed evidence, particularly if in digital form, or to move assets abroad should it be feared that action is pending. To counter this problem, the courts in England and Wales have developed two types of orders: a search order, authorising a search of the defendant's premises and to photograph, seize, or copy allegedly infringing material; and a freezing order, freezing the assets of the defendant.[170]

Although these types of orders can be of vital importance to a claimant to allow him to gain the evidence needed to prove a case, or to ensure that the illicit proceeds made from pirated copies of works are not lost prior to trial, they are potent orders, and so checks and balances exist to ensure they are granted only when appropriate and that their terms are not exceeded.

22.99   There are three essential pre-requisites for the grant of a search order:

- There must be a strong prima facie case.

- The damage, potential or actual, must be serious for the applicant.

- There must be clear evidence that the defendants have incriminating documents or things in their possession and a real possibility must exist that they may destroy the evidence.[171]

Given that a search order is most often granted in secret and without the defendant appearing or being represented, it was apparent that procedural safeguards were needed. These safeguards include: the need for the claimant to give a cross-undertaking in damages; time for the defendant to consider the order and seek independent legal advice; time for the defendant to seek a discharge of the order; the claimant's solicitor and an independent solicitor to accompany the search team; records to be kept of all mate-

---

[170] The rules for England and Wales can be found in Part 25 of the Civil Procedure Rules. In Scotland similar procedures exist under the Administration of Justice (Scotland) Act 1972, s 1 (search order) and an arrestment to found jurisdiction under the Civil Jurisdiction and Judgments Act 1982, Sch 8.

[171] *Anton Piller KG v Manufacturing Process Ltd* [1976] Ch 55 (CA), Ormrod LJ.

rial removed from the premises; and a date on which to report back to the court to facilitate claims for compensation to be made by the defendant.[172]

22.100 A freezing order may also be granted without the defendant being heard. If granted, the court orders that the assets of the defendant remain within the jurisdiction and that they may not be disposed of. As with a search order, there are safeguards to ensure that the procedure is fair to the defendant.[173] Thus, the claimant must show a good arguable case; reason to believe that the assets may be removed; give a cross-undertaking in damages; serve notice of the order on the defendant and any third party who may be affected by the order; and undertake to indemnify third parties against costs, expenses, and fees incurred in complying with the order.

 Exercise

Give examples of those types of infringements of intellectual property you think would justify the grant of a freezing and/or search order.

Self-help

22.101 An interesting measure, found in copyright legislation, permits copyright owners to seize infringing copies of protected works from market stalls and car boot sales (a similar measure exists in relation to illicit recordings).[174] A copyright owner is not, however, allowed to seize infringing goods from premises where the infringer has a permanent place of business. If an infringing copy of a work is found for sale or hire and it is one that would entitle the copyright owner to apply for an order for delivery up, then he may detain the copies, or authorise others to do so on his behalf. Certain conditions are attached to the procedure.[175] These are that:

- a notice of the time and place of the proposed seizure must be given to a local police station;[176]

- nothing may be seized that is in the possession, custody, or control of a person operating from a permanent or regular place of business;

- no force may be used;[177]

- at the time when anything is seized a notice must be left in the prescribed terms at the place where the infringing copy is seized.[178]

22.102 In practical terms, a copyright owner may not have the courage to seize infringing copies of works from the stalls of market traders. In those circumstances he may feel it necessary to authorise another to do so on his behalf, such as trading standards officers or FACT, the Federation Against Copyright Theft.

---

[172] Civil Procedure Rules Practice Direction 25A.
[173] *Z v A* [1982] 1 All ER 556; *CBS v Lambert* [1983] FSR 127.   [174] CDPA 1988, s 196.   [175] CDPA 1988, s 100.
[176] CDPA 1988, s 100(2).   [177] CDPA 1988, s 100(3).
[178] CDPA 1988, s 100(4). Copyright and Rights in Performances (Notice of Seizure) Order 1989 (SI 1989/1006).

> **Web links**
>
> Have a look at the FACT website at **http://www.fact-uk.org.uk**. Why was this organisation set up and who does it represent? Note also FAST (the Federation against Software Theft) at **http://www. fastiis.org/** and the Alliance Against IP Theft **http://www.allianceagainstiptheft.co.uk/**. Can you find any other similar organisations?

Survey evidence

22.103   In preparing a case concerning passing off or registered trade marks, survey evidence may be used to show, inter alia, that the public has been deceived by the misrepresentation, that the trade mark has become distinctive through use for registration purposes, or that the public is likely to be confused by the use of a sign that is similar to an already registered mark. Dealing with the question of distinctiveness for trade marks, the ECJ in *Windsurfing Chiemsee*[179] said that 'Community law does not prevent the competent authority, where it has particular difficulty in that connection, from having recourse, under the conditions laid down by its own national law, to an opinion poll as guidance for its judgement'.[180]

22.104   However, care needs to be taken over preparation of survey evidence. A number of guidelines were laid down in *Imperial Group v Philip Morris*,[181] a case in which passing off was alleged:

- The selection of interviewees must include a relevant cross-section of the public.

- The survey must be of a size to produce a statistically relevant result.

- Full details must be disclosed of the number of surveys carried out, how they were conducted, and the number of persons involved.

- The totality of all answers given to all surveys must be disclosed along with the exact answers given to the questions, the instructions given to the interviewers as to how to carry out the survey, and any computer coding instructions where the answers are coded for computer input.

- The questions themselves must not be leading nor should they lead the person answering into a field of speculation he would never have embarked upon had the question not been put.

22.105   There have been a number of cases in which survey evidence has failed to establish what it set out to do. For instance, in *GMG Radio Holdings v Tokyo Project Ltd*[182] the survey evidence did establish that interviewees recognised similarities between the claimant's get up and that of the defendant's products, but not that it was the right kind of association to establish passing off.[183] In *esure Insurance Ltd v Direct Line Insurance plc*[184] the Court of Appeal said that there was much to be said for the practice initiated by the

---

[179] Case C-108/97 *Windsurfing Chiemsee Produktions-und Vertriebs GmbH v Boots-und Segelzubehor Walter Huber* [2000] Ch 523, [2000] 2 WLR 205.   [180] *Windsurfing*, para 53.
[181] [1984] RPC 293.   [182] [2006] FSR 15.
[183] Eg also *Mothercare (UK) Ltd v Penguin Books* [1988] RPC 113 where the evidence did not establish that the term was being used 'in a trade mark sense'; *Quorn Hunt's Application v Opposition of Marlow Foods Ltd* [2005] ETMR 11 TMR where the attempt to use survey evidence to show that the reputation of the registered mark 'Quorn' would be damaged by the registration of 'Quorn Hunt' might have shown that interviewees made an association between the marks but could not have achieved the desired result—to show that the registered mark would be tarnished.   [184] [2008] EWCA Civ 842.

late Pumfrey J[185] where the parties sought the direction of the court as to the scope or methodology of any proposed consumer survey.[186]

 Exercise

How might you frame a question to be used in a survey which would elicit responses designed to show that the reputation of a mark would be damaged if a second were to be registered?

22.106   The introduction of expert evidence has also caused some difficulties in IP cases. In an application by esure for leave to appeal against a decision of the High Court, Arden LJ commented on the use of experts to determine consumer confusion.

> given that the critical issue of confusion of any kind is to be assessed from the viewpoint of the average consumer, it is difficult to see what is gained from the evidence of an expert as to his own opinion where the tribunal is in a position to form its own view … I note that in *The European Ltd v. The Economist Newspaper Ltd* [1998] FSR 283 at 290–291 … considered that the evidence of trade witnesses who gave their opinion of the likelihood of confusion was 'almost entirely inadmissible….'[187]

Remedies

Interim injunctions (England and Wales) and interdicts (Scotland)

22.107   In intellectual property disputes it is often of vital importance to the aggrieved party to have a case heard as quickly as possible with the aim to have the allegedly infringing act halted before full trial. Thus, many civil intellectual property actions are applications for interim relief.[188] However, care needs to be taken prior to granting interim orders such as an interim injunction or interim interdict, as, if granted, it can determine the outcome of the case if it does not proceed to full trial. A defendant, prohibited from carrying out a particular act, may choose an alternative business strategy rather than wait for a number of years for a full hearing of the case. For instance, if a dispute is over whether a substantial part of a work has been reproduced (copyright) or a sign is confusingly similar to a registered mark, then the defendant may decide to cease dealing in the goods that allegedly infringe the existing rights. Further, the grant of such an order may be enough to close down a business if there are insufficient resources to defend the action. For these reasons the courts have developed guidelines to be applied in cases where interim relief is sought.[189]

22.108   The leading case on interim injunctions in England and Wales is *American Cyanamid Co v Ethicon Ltd*.[190] The House of Lords enunciated a number of factors to be taken into account when deciding whether an interim injunction should be granted the steps of which are represented in Diagram 22.1.

---

[185] *O2 Ltd v Hutchison 3G Ltd* [2005] ETMR 61, and subsequently followed by Rimer J in *UK Channel Management Ltd v E! Entertainment Television Inc* [2008] FSR 5. See also *Interflora Inc v Marks & Spencer plc* [2012] EWHC 1722 (Ch) (under appeal); *A&E Television Networks LLC v Discovery Communications Europe Ltd* [2011] EWHC 1038 (Ch); *Specsavers International Healthcare Ltd v Asda Ltd* [2010] EWHC 1497 (Pat).
[186] Para 63.   [187] Para 62.
[188] On guidelines as to cross-undertakings and compensation of loss, *Lilly Icos LLC and another, Pfizer Enterprises SARL and others, Merck & Co Inc and others, AstraZeneca AB and others v 8PM Chemists Ltd, Vinesh Aggarwal, RDA Kollektif Sirketi* [2009] EWHC 1905 (Ch), 2009 WL 2392200; for a discussion on fairness and the grant of interim relief, see *Riemann and Co v Linco Care Ltd* [2007] EWHC 3466 (Ch); for circumstances in which an injunction will not be granted *Landor & Hawa International Ltd v Azure Designs Ltd* [2007] FSR 9.
[189] For a case in which an injunction was conditioned on a cross–undertaking, see *Wake Forest University Health Sciences v Smith & Newphew plc* [2009] EWHC 45 (Pat), [2009] FSR 11.   [190] [1975] AC 396.

Diagram 22.1 *American Cyanamid Co v Ethicon Ltd*

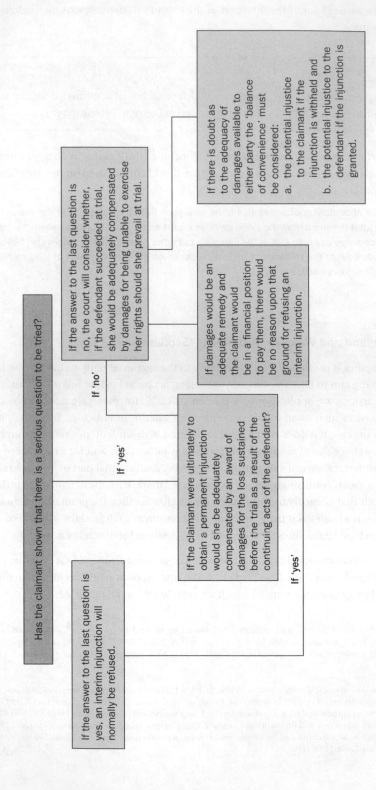

Has the claimant shown that there is a serious question to be tried?

If 'no'

If 'yes'

If the answer to the last question is yes, an interim injunction will normally be refused.

If the answer to the last question is no, the court will consider whether, if the defendant succeeded at trial, she would be adequately compensated by damages for being unable to exercise her rights should she prevail at trial.

If the claimant were ultimately to obtain a permanent injunction would she be adequately compensated by an award of damages for the loss sustained before the trial as a result of the continuing acts of the defendant?

If 'yes'

If damages would be an adequate remedy and the claimant would be in a financial position to pay them, there would be no reason upon that ground for refusing an interim injunction.

If there is doubt as to the adequacy of damages available to either party the 'balance of convenience' must be considered:
a. the potential injustice to the claimant if the injunction is withheld and
b. the potential injustice to the defendant if the injunction is granted.

General Comment:

The course to be taken is that which would involve the least risk of ultimate injustice, having regard to the actual and potential rights and liabilities of the parties on both sides.

22.109   In *Series 5 Software Ltd v Clarke*[191] Laddie J reformulated the principles stressing the importance of assessing the relative strengths of each of the parties' cases. That, however, did not require a mini trial on the facts. The case has been much cited, but is yet to be affirmed by a higher court.[192]

22.110   In Scotland the courts have had regard to the relative strength of the cases put forward by the parties at interlocutory stage as one of the factors that go to make up the balance of convenience for many years.

> Whether the likelihood of success should be regarded as one of the elements of the balance of convenience or as a separate matter seems to me an academic question of no real importance, but my inclination is in favour of the former alternative. It seems to make good sense; if the pursuer or petitioner appears very likely to succeed at the end of the day, it will tend to be convenient to grant interim interdict and thus prevent the defender or respondent from infringing his rights, but if the defender or respondent appears very likely to succeed at the end of the day it will tend to be convenient to refuse interim interdict because an interim interdict would probably only delay the exercise of the defender's legal activities.[193]

Freedom of expression, privacy, and interim relief

22.111   Of particular note in applications for interim relief are developments on the interaction between freedom of expression and privacy. Section 12(3) of the Human Rights Act 1998 provides that no relief should be granted that restrains publication prior to trial where such relief might affect the exercise of the right to freedom of expression as enshrined in the European Convention on Human Rights unless the applicant is *likely* to establish that publication should not be allowed.

22.112   There has been much discussion as to the correct interpretation of the word 'likely' in this context. It was suggested in *Imutran Ltd v Uncaged Campaigns Ltd*[194] that it implies a higher test than enunciated in *American Cyanamid*; that there should be a real prospect of success rather than success on a balance of probabilities. Subsequently, in *Cream Holdings Ltd v Banerjee*[195] the House of Lords confirmed that approach but left leeway for a court to do away with that higher standard where the circumstances make it necessary. The court emphasised that section 12(3) of the Human Rights Act 1998 made the 'likelihood of success' at trial an essential element in considering whether to make an interim order.[196]

22.113   The interaction between section 12(3) of the Human Rights Act 1998 and an application to have an interim injunction lifted has been considered by the Court of Appeal in *Douglas v Hello!*[197] For full details of this case see Chapter 19. The High Court initially granted an order restraining the publication by *Hello!* of a number of photographs taken at the wedding of Catherine Zeta-Jones and Michael Douglas allegedly in breach of obligations of confidentiality and a 'right of privacy'.

---

[191] *Series 5 Software Ltd v Clarke* [1996] 1 All ER 853, [1996], FSR 273.

[192] Eg *Guardian Media Group plc v Associated Newspapers Ltd* 2000 WL 331035, para 18; *Gadget Shop Ltd v Bug Com Ltd* [2001] CP Rep 13 (Ch D); *Berry Birch & Noble Financial Planning Ltd v Berwick and others* 2005 WL 1991635; *Quick Draw LLP v Global Live Events LLP* [2012] EWHC 233 (Ch); *Ate My Heart Inc v Mind Candy Ltd* [2011] EWHC 2741 (Ch); *Cephalon Inc v Orchid Europe Ltd* [2010] EWHC 2945 (Pat).

[193] *NWL Ltd v Woods* [1979] 3 All ER 614 at 628. See also *Boehringer Ingelheim Pharma GmbH & Co KG v Munro Wholesale Medical Supplies Ltd* 2004 SC 468, [2004] ETMR 66; *Schuh Ltd v Shhh ... Ltd* [2011] CSOH 123.

[194] [2002] FSR 2.   [195] [2004] UKHL 44, [2004] 3 WLR 918, para 20.

[196] *Miss World Ltd v Channel 4 Television Corporation* [2007] EWHC 982 (Pat). It was 'likely' for the purposes of HRA 1998, s 12(3) that the claimant would succeed in showing that the proposed broadcast of a programme called 'Mr Miss World' would infringe the registered trade mark 'Miss World' in terms of TMA 1994, ss 10(1) and 10(2). *Response Handling v BBC* [2007] CSOH 102 information on bank account details had been obtained in breach of confidence by an employee of the BBC, the court was not satisfied that the pursuers were more likely than not to succeed at proof to restrain publication of the resultant television programme. See also *Red Dot Technologies Ltd v Apollo Fire Detectors Ltd* [2007] EWHC 1166 (Ch). *Boehringer Ingelheim Ltd v VetPlus Ltd* [2007] EWCA Civ 583: the general threshold under HRA 1998, s 12(3) that a claimant will probably succeed at trial applies also to trade mark infringement in comparative advertising cases. *Unilever plc v Griffin* [2010] EWHC 899 (Ch), [2010] FSR 33.

[197] [2001] 2 All ER 289, [2001] QB 967.

The order was subsequently lifted by the Court of Appeal which considered that preventing *Hello!* magazine from publishing the pictures before a full trial could, potentially, lead to incalculable damages, whereas the damage that *OK!* magazine might suffer was capable of calculation.[198]

However, this result was subsequently criticised in the next round of the case when it went to the Court of Appeal. Here the court thought there was no public interest (as opposed to public curiosity) grounds that justified lifting the interlocutory injunction.[199] Insufficient consideration had been given by the lower court to the likely level of damages which the Douglases would recover if an interlocutory injunction was refused and publication of the unauthorised photographs infringed their rights.[200]

On the question as to whether the Douglases would be *likely* to succeed at trial, the Court of Appeal took particular note of the reasoning in *Campbell v MGN*[201] in the House of Lords, and *von Hannover v Germany*[202] in the European Court of Human Rights, both of which were handed down after the interlocutory injunction in *Douglas v Hello!* had been lifted. The appeal court considered that the 'likelihood of success' threshold had been satisfied by the Douglases who appeared to have 'a virtually unanswerable case for contending that publication of the unauthorised photographs would infringe their privacy'.[203] Only by granting an interlocutory injunction could the Douglases rights have been protected. By contrast, the financial interests of *Hello!* could have been satisfied by an undertaking by the Douglases to pay damages should they not be successful at trial.[204]

22.114   The courts are clearly alive to the tensions that arise at the stage of requesting interim relief in cases concerning both freedom of expression and privacy. After the comments on the harm done to the Douglases in allowing publication in *Hello!* courts may be more willing to grant interim relief where it is clear that there would be no satisfactory remedy should publication go ahead.[205]

 Exercise

The case of *Douglas v Hello!* was a particularly challenging one for the courts to deal with. The substantive law on breach of confidence has been developing apace in recent years, making it difficult to decide when it might be appropriate to grant an interim order. Do you think that the Court of Appeal was correct in its assessment of where the balance between freedom of expression and confidentiality lay when considering the grant of an interim injunction? Would the same arguments apply in copyright infringement cases? Consider *Ashdown v Telegraph Group Ltd* [2001] 2 All ER 370 (see para 5.47).

---

[198] For the High Court decision on the merits, see [2003] EWHC 786 (Ch) and for the appeal (No 3) [2005] EWCA Civ 595.
[199] (No 3) [2005] EWCA Civ 595, para 254.   [200] (No 3) [2005] EWCA Civ 595, para 255.
[201] [2004] UKHL 22, [2004] 2 AC 457, [2004] 2 WLR 1232, [2004] 2 All ER 995.
[202] *Von Hannover v Germany* (App No 59320/00) [2004] EMLR 21, (2005) 40 EHRR 16.
[203] (No 3) [2005] EWCA Civ 595, para 253.   [204] (No 3) [2005] EWCA Civ 595, para 259.
[205] Eg *Ms Elizabeth Jagger v John Darling and others* [2005] EWHC 683 (Ch). Note also HRA 1998, s 12(4)(b) which provides:
The court must have particular regard to the importance of the Convention right to freedom of expression and, where the proceedings relate to material which the respondent claims, or which appears to the court, to be journalistic, literary or artistic material (or to conduct connected with such material), to (a) the extent to which (i) the material has, or is about to, become available to the public; or (ii) it is, or would be, in the public interest for the material to be published; (b) any relevant privacy code.
   Guidance was given in interpreting this subsection by Woolf CJ in *A v B plc* [2002] EWCA Civ 337, para 11. In *Browne v Associated Newspapers Ltd* [2007] EWHC 202 (QB) various categories of information reviewed in coming to the decision that, considering the factors under HRA 1998, s 12(3) an injunction prohibiting the publication of information in the press would remain in force but to a limited degree.

22.115   The years following the *Douglas* case witnessed an exponential increase in the number of applications for interim relief in privacy cases. Many of these concerned the private lives of celebrities.[206] In early 2011 public opinion was roused against these measures—termed by many 'gagging orders'. The concern was that the balance had been tipped too far against freedom of expression and too far in favour of the private lives of celebrities. In the face of high anxiety expressed in Parliament, by the press, and by leading politicians, the Master of the Rolls led a group to investigate the matter. In their report, it was noted that there was a difference between two types of injunctions being granted. One was a so-called 'super-injunction'. This is 'an interim injunction which restrains a person from: (i) publishing information which concerns the applicant and is said to be confidential or private; and (ii) publicising or informing others of the existence of the order and the proceedings.'[207] This type of injunction was granted only very rarely, and always for a fixed, and short, period of time.[208] The second type of injunction, an 'anonymised injunction' is 'an interim injunction which restrains a person from publishing information which concerns the applicant and is said to be confidential or private where the names of either or both of the parties to the proceedings are not stated.'[209] It is the latter type of injunction that was granted in the majority of the celebrity cases. Practice Guidance for the courts was issued as a result of the investigation which sets out clear guidelines for when such injunctions should be granted.[210]

Exercise

Read the Report of the Committee on Super-Injunctions: 'Super-Injunctions, Anonymised Injunctions and Open Justice'. What do you think of the conclusions and recommendations that they arrived at? Does this represent a fair balance between the various stakeholder interests?

22.116   There are, however, times when the information may be so widely available that court would feel the grant of an interim order to be inappropriate. In *Max Mosley v News Group Newspapers Ltd*[211] the High Court had to decide whether to grant an interim injunction prohibiting further publication of videos of Mosley engaged in sexual activity with prostitutes. While the court had little difficulty in deciding Mosley would prevail at trial, preventing further publication at the interim stage was judged to be unlikely to make any practical difference because it was so widely available it was, in essence, 'in the public domain'.[212] Allied to that was the argument that it would be inappropriate to restrain one organisation from publishing material when it was open to other media outlets including competitors to publish the same information.[213] As a result, 'the granting of an order against this Respondent at the present juncture would merely be a futile gesture'.[214]

---

[206] Cases included *ABC Ltd v Y* [2010] EWHC 3176 (Ch), [2011] 4 All ER 113; *Ambrosiadou v Coward* [2011] EWCA Civ 409, [2011] EMLR 21; *AMM v HXW* [2010] EWHC 2457 (QB); *ASG v GSA* [2009] EWCA Civ 1574; *Browne v Associated Newspapers Ltd* [2007] EWCA Civ 295, [2008] QB 103, [2007] EMLR20; *G v Wikimedia Foundation Inc* [2009] EWHC 3148 (QB), [2010] EMLR 14; *Goldsmith v BCD* [2011] EWHC 674 (QB), (2011) 108(14) LSG 20; *Gray v UVW* [2010] EWHC 2367 (QB); *JIH v News Group Newspapers Ltd* [2011] EWCA Civ 42, [2011] 2 All ER 324, [2011] EMLR 15,

[207] Report of the Committee on Super-Injunctions: Super-Injunctions, Anonymised Injunctions and Open Justice, May 2011, p iv.

[208] *Ntuli v Donald* [2010] EWCA Civ 1276. *DFT v TFD* [2010] EWHC 2335 (QB). There had been two earlier cases which had raised concerns: *RJW & SJW v The Guardian Newspaper & Person or Persons Unknown* (Claim no HQ09) and *Terry v Persons Unknown* [2010] 1 FCR 659.   [209] Note 207.

[210] Practice Guidance: Interim Disclosure Orders, 1 August 2011 [2012] EMLR 5. Subsequent cases have included: *AMP v Persons Unknown* [2011] EWHC 3454 (TCC); *Spelman v Express Newspapers* [2012] EWHC 239 (QB); *KGM v News Group Newspapers* [2011] EWCA Civ 808; *Gray v News Group Newspapers Ltd* [2012] EWCA Civ 48; *Giggs v News Group Newspapers* [2012] EWHC 431 (QB). *Contostavlos v Mendahum* [2012] EWHC 850 (QB).

[211] *Max Mosley v News Group Newspapers Ltd* [2008] EWHC 687 (QB).   [212] *Max Mosley*, para 33.

[213] Op cit, para 35. Citing *Attorney-General v Times Newspapers Ltd* [2001] 1 WLR 885 at 895–896.

[214] Op cit, para 36. Mosley subsequently took his case to the European Court of Human Rights seeking a right to a pre-publication notification. He lost. *Mosley v United Kingdom* [2011] ECHR 774. On information being widely accessible and so refusing the grant of an interim injunction, see *BBC v HarperCollins Publishers Ltd* [2010] EWHC 2424 (Ch) (Stig).

Injunctions and interdicts

22.117   A final injunction or interdict may be granted to a claimant who proves his case at trial unless the claimant does not come with clean hands, the right is nearing its end, or repetition is unlikely. The scope of
an injunction in intellectual property cases has been the subject of some debate. (For a discussion on
the territorial scope of an injunction (cross-border injunctions) see paras 23.46ff.) An injunction is normally worded so as to prevent repetition of the infringement in issue. However, there are times when an
injunction might prevent activities which do not relate to the infringement in question, and which may
prevent other lawful activities. In *Coflexip v Stolt Comex Seaway*[215] concerning infringement of a patent,
Laddie J suggested that the objective of an injunction should be to:

- protect the claimant from a continuation of the infringement of its rights by the threatened activities
  of the defendant; and

- be fair to the defendant.

The reason given in *Coflexip* for the grant of an injunction narrow in scope was because the grant of a
broad injunction might result in restraining a defendant from doing things he had not threatened to
do, may never have thought of doing, or may be incapable of doing.[216] This was, however, overturned by
Aldous J in the Court of Appeal who agreed that, while an injunction should set out with clarity what
may not be done, such a test would be met by issuing the standard form of injunction.

22.118   More recently, in *Specsavers v Asda Stores Ltd*[217] the Court of Appeal acknowledged that while the normal
form of injunction will be sufficient in most cases, there will be times, in order to be fair to the defendant, that a qualified injunction may be required. In so doing, the Court of Appeal considered the following case:

■ *Sun Microsystems Inc v Amtec Computer Corporation Ltd* [2006] EWHC 62 (Ch)

This concerned the sale of Sun computers in the EEA by Amtec—computers which had not been put
on the market in the EEA with the consent of Sun. Sun thus took action against Amtec alleging trade
mark infringement.[218] Before selling computers in the EEA, Amtec had been to some lengths to ensure
the goods they resold had been lawfully placed on the market. They used only a reputable supplier and
included a term in their contract with that supplier stipulating that supplies should be of EU origin.
The court accepted that a broad injunction, prohibiting Amtec dealing in Sun products, would have
the practical effect of closing their legitimate business, a solution which would not be proportionate to
protect Sun's business. Further, it was impossible for Amtec to know that the Sun products that it dealt
with had been put on the market with consent unless Sun provided information on the products. Thus,
a qualified injunction would be granted which would allow Amtec to deal in Sun products if:

- Amtec informed Sun by writing or by email of the serial numbers of products they were going to sell
  together with a description of the product indicating whether it was new or second-hand;

- Sun had not responded within a defined period (between 7 to 14 days) indicating that its records
  showed to its satisfaction that the product had not been put on the market in the EEA by it or with
  its consent; provided that

---

[215] [1999] FSR 473.

[216] This has been followed in other cases concerning copyright, *Microsoft Corporation v Plato Technology Ltd* [1999] FSR 834, and
computer software, *Nutrinova Nutrition Specialties & Food Ingredients GmbH v Scanchem UK Ltd (No 2)* [2001] FSR 43. H Hurdle, 'What
should be the scope of a permanent injunction in UK patent infringement actions? An update' (2000) (Nov) Patent World 1.

[217] [2012] EWCA Civ 494.   [218] See also para 20.62.

- Amtec did not know or believe that the product had not been put on the market in the EEA by, or with the consent of, Sun.[219]

It is interesting to note that this type of limited injunction requires Sun and Amtec to work together to identify potentially infringing goods. Whether more limited injunctions of this type are granted will depend on the facts of individual cases.

Exercise

Can you think of cases other than those dealing with parallel imports in which the scope of an injunction should be narrow? Do you think such limited injunctions are fair to both claimant and defendant?

Delivery up

22.119 A court may order delivery up or destruction of infringing articles.[220] The purpose of such an order is to ensure that the infringing goods do not enter circulation. Where a person has committed a secondary infringement of copyright, trade mark, performers' rights, and unregistered design right, in other words the infringement has been committed in the course of a business, then the court may order delivery up to the right owner pending a further order for destruction or forfeiture.[221]

Damages

22.120 The most common form of remedy available in intellectual property cases is that of damages. The purpose of an award of damages is (in common with other actions in tort and delict) to put the claimant back in the position he would have been had the infringement not occurred.

22.121 It may not be possible to obtain an award of damages against an 'innocent infringer'. In cases of copyright, UK unregistered design right, and rights in performances, damages will not be awarded in an infringement action where, at the time of the infringement, the defendant did not know, and had no reason to believe, that a right subsisted in the work to which the action relates.[222] In the case of patents and UK registered designs, damages will not be awarded where the defendant proves that at the date of infringement they were not aware and had no reasonable grounds for supposing that the patent existed or the design was registered.[223] No innocent infringement defence exists to an infringement of registered or unregistered Community design right.[224] The fact that an article is accompanied by the words 'registered' or 'patented' does not thereby mean that the defendant has knowledge. However, that does not apply if the number of the registration is included. Therefore, the owner of a patent or registered design would be well advised to include the words 'registered' or 'patented' and the relevant number. For trade marks and passing off it would appear that damages can be awarded against an

---

[219] Op cit, note 174, para 46.　　[220] Patents Act 1977, s 61(1)(b); TMA 1994, s 16; Registered Designs Act 1949, s 24C.

[221] TMA 1994, s 16, CDPA 1988, ss 99, 108, 195, 199, 204, 230, 231.

[222] CDPA 1988, ss 97(1), 191J, 233(1). Under the 2004 Directive on the Enforcement of Intellectual Property Rights (EC Directive 2004/48) damages are mandatorily to be recoverable where there is knowing infringement.

[223] Patents Act 1977, s 62(1); Registered Designs Act 1949, s 24B. Amendments have been proposed to the Registered Designs Act that would allow for recovery of an account of profits from an innocent infringer but not damages which if implemented is likely to be in 2013.

[224] Council Regulation 6/2002 on registered and unregistered Community designs. EC Directive of 2004 on the Enforcement of Intellectual Property Rights, Art 13. Community Design Regulations 2005 as amended by the Intellectual Property Enforcement Regulations 2006. *J Choo (Jersey) Ltd v Towerstone Ltd and others* [2008] EWHC 346 (Ch).

innocent infringer as there is no distinction between the remedies available for innocent and intentional infringement.[225]

 Question

In what circumstances do you think that a person who infringes a right could successfully claim to be an 'innocent infringer'?

What, if any, liability would an individual face if the word 'registered' or 'patented' was used in connection with articles that were not registered or patented? (See also para 14.107.)

Additional damages

22.122 Additional damages may be awarded by a court in an action for infringement of copyright,[226] rights in performances,[227] and unregistered design right.[228] The court is required to have regard to all the circumstances, and in particular to the flagrancy of the infringement[229] and any benefit which may accrue to the defendant by reason of the infringement.[230] Additional damages are in addition to an award of 'normal' damages[231] and so a claimant can only elect for additional damages if normal damages are claimed.[232] This means that it is not possible to claim additional damages with an account of profits (for which see later), where the claimant has to elect either an account of profits or damages. Neither are additional damages available where ordinary damages are not granted, for instance in cases of innocent infringement.

22.123 The nature of the award of additional damages was considered at some length by Pumfrey J in the following case.

■ *Nottinghamshire Healthcare NHS Trust v News Group Newspapers Ltd* [2002] EWHC 409 (Ch)[233]

The case concerned the infringement of copyright in a photograph of a patient at Rampton Hospital published by the *Sun* newspaper. Copyright in the photograph belonged to the NHS Trust. While the measure of damages was to be calculated on the basis of infringement of copyright, the fact that the photograph was confidential, being part of a patient's medical records, does appear to have had a bearing on the decision. It was clear that the court wished to award additional damages taking into account the 'flagrancy of the infringement'.[234] But what did this phrase mean and what should the award of additional damages reflect? Should damages be exemplary in that an award would be intended both to compensate the claimant for the loss, and to teach the defendant that infringement does not pay? Or should they rather be aggravated, which would compensate the claimant for the loss, but would also take into account the injury to the claimant's feelings of pride and dignity, humiliation, distress, insult, or pain?[235] After much deliberation the court decided that an award of additional damages should not be punitive or exemplary in nature, pointing to the difficulties that would occur if this was not the case particularly

---

[225] L Bently and B Sherman, *Intellectual Property Law* (2nd edn, 2004) p 1024.

[226] CDPA 1988, s 97(2). An infringement of copyright committed in breach of an injunction restraining such infringement could found an award of additional damages. *Kabushi Kaisha Sony Computer Ent Inc v Owen* [2002] EWHC 45 (Ch). Also *PPL v Reader* [2005] EWHC 416 (Ch). [227] CDPA 1988, s 191J.

[228] CDPA 1988, s 229(3).

[229] Flagrancy can include sales in breach of a court order: *Sony Computer Entertainment v Owen* [2002] EWHC 45 (Ch).

[230] CDPA 1988, s 97(2). [231] *Ravenscroft v Herbert* [1980] RPC 193.

[232] *Redrow Homes Ltd v Bett Brothers plc* [1999] 1 AC 197, [1998] 1 All ER 385, [1998] FSR 345.

[233] See also *Experience Hendrix LLC v Times Newspapers Ltd* [2010] EWHC 1986 (Ch). [234] CDPA 1988, s 97(2)(a).

[235] *Nottinghamshire Healthcare NHS Trust v News Group Newspapers Ltd* [2002] EWHC 409 (Ch), para 33.

where an infringer was sued by successive claimants each seeking punishment for their respective interests. The example was given of a counterfeiter who had produced numerous CDs.[236] Pumphrey J did, however, consider that the section permitted an aggravation of an award of damages 'on a basis far wider than the factors admitted as aggravation at common law'.[237] In particular, it permitted an element of restitution. In the event £450 was awarded as the fee that would have been negotiated between a willing copyright owner and the newspaper and, having regard to the flagrancy and the need to do justice in the case, the total damages were set at £10,000.[238]

In the words of the judge: 'If this [sum of £10,000] exceeds the sum appropriate under section 97(2) having regard to the benefit to the Defendant, then no further infringements of this kind will take place. If further infringements consisting of the publishing of stolen photographs from medical records do take place, it will show the advantage to the newspaper still exceeds the award of damages'.[239]

 Question

Do you think that this finding will deter newspapers in the future from publishing information without consent that is confidential and protected by copyright?

Account of profits

22.124   An account of profits is available for infringement of most IPRs.[240] The remedy is based on the principle that the infringer has carried out the infringing act on behalf of the right owner. The owner is therefore entitled to the profits made from the infringement and, by extension, the infringer is deprived of unfair or unjustified profits.[241] Once liability is established, the owner can opt for either damages or an account of profits but not both.[242] The net profits, after deducting the profit attributable to the infringer's efforts, is the measure of damages that is awarded.[243]

EU Enforcement Directive

22.125   In response to the rising levels of counterfeiting and piracy (see paras 22.147) a European Directive on the Enforcement of Intellectual Property Rights was agreed in 2004.[244] The purpose of the Directive, which contains measures and procedures concerning civil sanctions and remedies, is to create a level playing field for right holders while acting as a deterrent to those engaged in counterfeiting and piracy. The focus of the measure is on infringements carried out for commercial purposes or those which cause significant harm to the right holder. The Directive which required implementation into member state legislation by the end of April 2006 covers the following IP areas:

- copyright;
- rights related to copyright;
- *sui generis* right of a database maker;
- rights of the creator of the topographies of a semiconductor product;

---

[236] *Nottinghamshire Healthcare*, para 51.   [237] *Nottinghamshire Healthcare*.   [238] *Nottinghamshire Healthcare*, para 60.

[239] *Nottinghamshire Healthcare*. See also *PPL v Reader* [2005] EWHC 416 (Ch).

[240] CDPA 1988, s 96; Patents Act 1977, s 61; TMA1994, s 14.

[241] *Bayer Cropscience KK v Charles River Laboratories Preclinical Services Edinburgh Ltd* [2010] CSOH 158.

[242] *Mulcaire v Phillips* [2012] UKSC 28.   [243] *Delfe v Delamotte* (1857) 3 K & J 581.

[244] Directive 2004/48/EC of the European Parliament and of the Council of 29 April 2004 on the enforcement of intellectual property rights (Enforcement Directive).

- trade mark rights;
- design rights;
- patent rights, including rights derived from supplementary protection certificates;
- geographical indications;
- utility model rights;
- plant variety rights;
- trade names, insofar as these are protected as exclusive property rights in the national law concerned.[245]

22.126   The substantive provisions of the Directive are drawn from a variety of national legislations of member states of the EU. For example, Article 5 provides that in addition to individual right holders, representatives of right holders such as trade association and rights management bodies should be entitled to sue for infringement of a right. This is said to be based on Article 98 of the Belgian Consumer Protection Law 1991, and Article IL-331-1(2) of the French Intellectual Property Code. On this point it should be noted that in England[246] the High Court has concluded that various claimants were allowed to bring a claim on behalf of other members of the music industry as well as themselves; in other words, in a representative capacity.

22.127   Turning back to the Directive, the provisions on seizure[247] and evidence[248] take inspiration from the search (Anton Piller) order in the UK and the saisie-contrefaçon system in France and Belgium. These procedures require that evidence found in the control of the opposing party be produced, and provide for the seizure of banking, financial, and commercial documents subject to guarantees being lodged should the action be unfounded at the end of the day.

22.128   Other Articles in the Directive require that judicial authorities be given the power to order information to be disclosed as to the origin of the infringing goods and services and distribution mechanisms, and personal details of producers, distributors, suppliers, wholesalers, and retailers.[249] Interlocutory injunctions should be available,[250] as well as orders requiring the recall and destruction of infringing goods. In addition, the Directive sets out a formula for calculating damages to be awarded to injured parties. This can either be a fixed payment equal to double the amount of royalties or fees which would have been due if the infringer had requested authorisation, or damages which correspond to the losses suffered by the right holder, including loss of earnings. In this the Directive suggests that factors such as 'moral prejudice' caused to the right holder could be taken into account.[251]

22.129   During gestation the Directive was the subject of much criticism—both from those who said that its provisions did not go far enough, and from those who argued that it went too far. At one time the draft was significantly broader than the text as finally agreed, and seemingly went beyond infringements of IPRs carried out on a commercial scale to be relevant to individual acts of infringement, such as downloading music files from the Internet. After criticism, the Directive was amended to its current form.

---

[245] Statement by the Commission concerning Article 2 of Directive 2004/48/EC of the European Parliament and of the Council on the enforcement of intellectual property rights (2005/295/EC) (13 April 2005). Both Sweden and Germany were found to have failed to transpose Directive 2004/48/EC on the enforcement of intellectual property rights into domestic law within the prescribed period (Cases C-395/07 and C-341/07).
[246] *Independiente Ltd and others v Music Trading On-Line (HK) Ltd* [2003] EWHC 470 (Ch).   [247] Enforcement Directive, Art 9.
[248] Enforcement Directive, Art 7.   [249] Enforcement Directive, Art 8.   [250] Enforcement Directive, Art 9.
[251] Enforcement Directive, Art 13. For the UK Government's view that it has largely implemented these obligations, see para 22.141.

22.130   Following both formal and informal consultations (most notable were concerns that there should be a balance between the legitimate interests of right holders and the public interest) the Directive was implemented in the UK in regulations that came into force on 6 April 2006.[252] Of particular note is regulation 3 which sets out the grounds on which damages should be assessed and includes an obligation to take into account the knowledge (actual or reasonable grounds for) of the defendant, and that the damages should be appropriate to the actual prejudice suffered taking into account the negative economic consequences the claimant has suffered. This may include unfair profits made by the defendant and the moral prejudice caused to the claimant. Alternatively damages may be awarded on the basis of what the claimant would have received as a fee or licence (note the discussion in para 22.125).

22.131   Regulation 4 introduced a new type of court order into Scotland enabling a pursuer (claimant) to ask the court to require the defendant to disclose information about distribution networks of goods or services which infringe IPRs. As always, this is subject to a number of checks and balances in particular that a court may only grant such an order where it is considered just and proportionate. If granted, the order can be the subject of such conditions as the court deems fit.[253] This type of order is already available in the English courts.[254]

22.132   Beyond that, the Regulations make a number of amendments to other primary and subordinate measures including the Patents Act 1977, the CDPA 1988, the Registered Designs Act 1949, and the Community Designs Regulations 2005, relating to such matters as orders for the disposal of infringing articles and orders for delivery up.[255] The Directive is increasingly cited in domestic cases as its impact, albeit limited, is felt in practice.[256]

 Question

The Directive and implementing regulations refer to taking into account the 'moral prejudice' caused to the claimant when assessing damages. What moral prejudice do you think might be relevant under this heading and for whom might it be applicable?

22.133   One of the pressing issues to face courts in interpretation of the Directive has been in relation to the grant of injunctions against Internet service providers (ISPs) within the meaning of Article 11 of the Directive which states:

Article 11

Injunctions

Member States shall ensure that, where a judicial decision is taken finding an infringement of an intellectual property right, the judicial authorities may issue against the infringer an injunction aimed at prohibiting the continuation of the infringement. Where provided for by national law, non-compliance with an injunction shall, where appropriate, be subject to a recurring penalty payment, with a view to ensuring compliance. Member States shall

---

[252] Intellectual Property (Enforcement, etc) Regulations 2006 (SI 2006/1028) (Enforcement Regulations) and the related Community Trade Mark Regulations 2006 (SI 2006/1027).

[253] Enforcement Regulations, reg 4(3).

[254] *Norwich Pharmacal v Customs and Excise Commissioners* [1974] AC 133.

[255] For a discussion on the laws of England and Wales and the Directive, see K Huniar, 'The Enforcement Directive: its effects on UK law' [2006] EIPR 92.

[256] Eg *Vestergaard Frandsen S/A (MVF3 APS) v Bestnet Europe Ltd* [2011] EWCA Civ 424 on the matter of proportionality; *Virgin Atlantic Airways Ltd v Premium Aircraft Interiors Group* [2009] EWCA Civ 1513.

also ensure that rightholders are in a position to apply for an injunction against intermediaries whose services are used by a third party to infringe an intellectual property right, without prejudice to Article 8(3) of Directive 2001/29/EC.

22.134   The matter is complicated by the provisions of the E-Commerce Directive[257] and of the InfoSoc Directive[258] both of which have their own provisions on liability of intermediaries. Two cases have been referred to the Court of Justice concerning ISPs and to which this provision has relevance (see also the discussion at para 16.54: *L'Oréal v eBay*[259] and *Scarlet v SABAM*.[260] In *L'Oreal* the Court held that under Article 11 national courts should be able to require the operator of an online marketplace to take measures to stop and prevent the recurrence of infringements of IPRs by users;[261] In *Sabam*, however, an injunction which required filtering systems to be installed to monitor user communications which had no time limit would result in serious infringement of the freedom of the ISP to conduct business and thus contrary to Article 3(1) of the Directive which requires remedies to be fair and equitable, not unnecessarily complicated or expensive, nor entail unreasonable time limits or delays.

22.135   A very different sort of order was granted by the court in *Samsung Electronics (UK) Ltd v Apple Inc.*[262] Apple had accused Samsung of infringing its registered Community design rights in its hand-held computers. Ultimately there was found to be no infringement. But in the meantime Apple had obtained an interim order prohibiting the sale of the computers by Samsung. A German court had also granted a European-wide injunction in favour of Apple. These had received huge publicity. The result was that the sale of Samsung computers dropped sharply. The High Court therefore ordered Apple to publicise the judgment on its website in Europe for a period of six months[263] and then, in the Court of Appeal, to provide a link to the notice for one month.[264] Noting that there was no legislative basis in the Enforcement Directive for such an order, the court nonetheless stated that it had equitable jurisdiction to require that course of action. The court noted that the decision was in keeping with the policy underpinning Article 15 of the Enforcement Directive which states:

Publication of judicial decisions

Member States shall ensure that, in legal proceedings instituted for infringement of an intellectual property right, the judicial authorities may order, at the request of the applicant and at the expense of the infringer, appropriate measures for the dissemination of the information concerning the decision, including displaying the decision and publishing it in full or in part. Member States may provide for other additional publicity measures which are appropriate to the particular circumstances, including prominent advertising.

In the instant case there was a purpose served by requiring a public statement that a product alleged by a right holder to infringe those rights did not in fact infringe them. The test was whether there was a real need to dispel commercial uncertainty.[265]

22.136   The Enforcement Directive was, in 2010, the subject of a report by the Commission followed by a consultation.[266] For those who sought changes to the Directive the key issues identified as in need of further

---

[257] Directive 2000/31 on certain legal aspects of information society services, in particular electronic commerce, in the internal market.

[258] Directive 2001/29 on the harmonisation of certain aspects of copyright and related rights in the information society.

[259] Case C-324/09.   [260] C-70/10.   [261] *L'Oreal*, paras 139–144.

[262] [2012] EWHC 2049 (Pat); aff'd on appeal [2012] EWCA Civ 1339; and re-inforced in response to the challenge that Apple had altered the wording of the notice [2012] EWCA Civ 1430.   [263] [2012] EWHC 2049 (Pat).

[264] [2012] EWCA Civ 1339.   [265] [2012] EWCA Civ 1339.

[266] Commission Report on the application of Directive 2004/48/EC of the European Parliament and the Council of 29 April 2004 on the Enforcement of Intellectual Property Rights (COM/2010/779 final) together with Commission Staff Working Paper (SEC(2010)1589). Both are synthesised in a report published in July 2011.

input included: clarification of the rules for intermediaries; stricter rules for file sharing; and the need for a level playing field for digital content. Those opposed to further amendments cited the lack of relevant data; an increase in legal uncertainty; the dearth of licit content; and safeguarding the freedom (and free exchange) of information.

 Exercise

Read the Commission Report and the Commission Staff Working Paper focusing on those sections on intermediary liability. How do you think that the rules should be balanced to take into account all stakeholder interests?

Key points on remedies

- Both interim and final injunctions (interdicts) are available in IP infringement actions

- Delivery up and damages are both available as remedies

- Damages are not available against innocent infringers (except possibly for trade marks, passing off, registered and unregistered Community design right)

- Additional damages are available for copyright, rights in performances, and unregistered design right

- ISP liability and the scope of injunctions which may be granted in respect of user infringement of IPRs are currently the subject of difference and debate throughout member states of the EU with the Court of Justice being called upon to adjudicate on the scope of the Enforcement Directive as it applies in this area

Alternative dispute resolution

22.137   Taking intellectual property disputes to court can be time-consuming and expensive, factors that may have contributed towards the increasing interest shown in recent years in alternative forms of dispute resolution. The most notable amongst these is the procedure that has been put into place for domain name disputes. Further information on this can be found in Chapter 16.

22.138   But it is not only domain name disputes that are referred to alternative dispute resolution. The number of organisations offering mediation and arbitration services in the sphere of intellectual property disputes have been increasing over the past years. WIPO has an Arbitration and Mediation Center which was established in 1994. Apparently it took several years after establishment for disputes to be referred to the Center, but it would appear that it is now increasing in popularity. As of 2012, over 280 mediation and arbitration disputes had been referred to the Center's service.

22.139   The UK–IPO launched an intellectual property mediation service in early 2006 partly in response to the Woolf Report, 'Access to Justice' which identified the need for mechanisms to promote the speedy and cheap resolution of disputes.

> ### Web links
>
> Details of the WIPO Arbitration and Mediation Center can be found at **http://www.wipo.int/ amc/en/index.html**. Details of the UK–IPO mediation service can be found at **http://www.ipo. gov.uk/types/patent/p-dispute/p-mediation.htm**.

Criminal enforcement

22.140   In the UK a number of criminal sanctions exist in the fields of copyright, performers' rights, and trade mark infringement. The offences relate to those circumstances where the infringer makes for sale, hire, or otherwise deals in the course of a business with infringing materials in the following circumstances, each of which is predicated on knowledge or reason to believe by the infringer (in contrast to civil actions where liability is strict).

Copyright

22.141   Making for sale, hire, or otherwise dealing with in the course of a business:

- copies of works that have been made without the authorisation of the copyright owner;[267]
- articles that are specifically designed or adapted for making infringing copies of copyright material;[268]
- communications of a work to the public;[269]
- performances of a work in public;[270]
- unauthorised decoders;[271]
- devices, products, or components which are primarily designed, produced, or adapted for the purpose of enabling or facilitation the circumvention of effective technological measures.[272]

In addition, criminal sanctions are also placed on those who distribute infringing articles otherwise than in the course of a business to such an extent as to *affect prejudicially* the owner of the copyright in the following circumstances:

- distribution of an article which is, and which the infringer knows or has reason to believe, infringes copyright in a work;
- communication of the work to the public;[273]
- distribution of any device, product, or component designed, produced, or adapted for the purpose of enabling or facilitating the circumvention of effective technological measures;[274]
- promotion or advertisement of a service the purpose of which is to enable or facilitate the circumvention of effective technological measures.[275]

[267] CDPA 1988, s 107(1).   [268] CDPA 1988, s 107(2).
[269] CDPA 1988, s 107(2A). *ITV v TV Catch Up* [2010] EWHC 3063 (Ch)   [270] CDPA 1988, s 107(4).
[271] Defined as 'Devices or other apparatus, including software, that allow people to access encrypted transmissions without paying the normal fee for their reception': CDPA 1988, s 297A. Case C-429/08 *Murphy v Media Protection Services* [2008] EWHC 1666 (Admin); see para 20.69 for a discussion on the free movement elements of the case.   [272] CDPA 1988, s 296ZB(1)(d).
[273] CDPA 1988, s 107(2A).   [274] CDPA 1988, s 296ZB(1)(d).   [275] CDPA 1988, s 296ZB(2).

Exercise

What do you think of the inclusion of criminal sanctions being used against those who do not infringe in the course of a business, but do infringe to the extent that the interests of the owner are prejudicially affected? What do you think the test 'affect prejudicially' means? What do you think of the inclusion of criminal sanctions against those who distribute devices which could circumvent technological protection measures? Does it make any difference that copyright need not be infringed for the sanction to attach?

22.142   Offences can be committed not just by individuals but also by corporate entities. In *Thames Hudson Ltd v Design and Artists Copyright Society Ltd*[276] a criminal action[277] was brought against the directors of Thames Hudson Ltd by the Design and Artists Copyright Society (DACS). The matter concerned the publication and distribution of a book which contained an infringing copy of a painting. The case was allowed to proceed at the same time as civil action was being taken. The criminal court suggested that the magistrate might, if the civil proceedings were found to be carried out with due diligence, use discretion to adjourn the final disposal of the criminal aspects of the case pending the decision in the Chancery Division.

Performers' rights

22.143   In relation to infringement of performers' rights, the following criminal sanctions exist:

- where copies of recordings of performances have been made without the authorisation of the performer(s) or a person having recording rights in the performance, that is, illicit or bootleg recordings;[278]

- where a performer's making available right is infringed.[279]

Trade marks

22.144   Under the Trade Marks Act 1994 criminal sanctions are available where:

- a trade mark has been applied without the consent of the owner to goods, on packaging, or on labels (ie counterfeit goods);

- articles are specifically designed or adapted for making unauthorised copies of a trade mark for use on such goods and other material.[280]

22.145   An interesting question concerning criminal liability fell to be decided by the House of Lords in *R v Johnstone*.[281] (See also para 15.12.) Johnstone had been making and disseminating CDs containing copies of bootleg recordings containing the name of the performer which had been registered as a trade mark. Johnstone was charged under section 92(1) of the Trade Marks Act 1994 for falsely applying and using a trade mark. It was argued that, to be liable, civil infringement had first to be established which was not so in the instant case as the performers' names had not been used as indications of origin[282] but merely to identify the artists. The House of Lords found this argument to be correct: as a matter of principle if a name of an artist was used exclusively as an indication of the name of the performer in

---

[276] [1995] FSR 153.   [277] Pursuant to CDPA 1988, ss 107 and 110.   [278] CDPA 1988, s 198(1).

[279] CDPA 1988, s 198(1A).   [280] TMA 1994, s 92.

[281] [2003] UKHL 28, [2003] 3 All ER 884, [2003] 2 Cr App Rep 493, [2004] Crim LR 244. See also *R v Malik* [2011] EWCA Crim 1107.

[282] TMA 1994, s 11(2)(b).

connection with the performance, this was merely descriptive and not an indication of the trade origin. Johnstone was therefore not guilty of this offence.

A different defence was raised in *R v Boulter (Gary)*.[283] The applicant was charged with selling counterfeit and pirated music CDs bearing the logos of EMI and other recording companies. He raised the defence that the CDs that bore the trade marks were of such poor quality that no one would think that its trade origin was that of the trade mark owners. In other words, there would be no confusion. The Court of Appeal ruled that no confusion was needed to be guilty of the offence in section 92 because the issue was identity, and not similarity, of the marks. Regardless of how badly the marks were copied, they were identical to those registered to the recording companies, and used on identical goods. A counterfeiter could not avoid criminal liability by claiming that the goods are 'genuine fakes'.[284]

Copyright, etc and Trade Marks (Offences and Enforcement) Act 2002

22.146 In 2002, the Copyright, etc and Trade Marks (Offences and Enforcement) Act 2002[285] amended the criminal provisions relating to copyright, rights in performances, fraudulent reception of conditional access transmissions by use of unauthorised decoders, and trade marks. The purpose of this Act was to rationalise the criminal procedures in these areas. It did so by:

- providing for maximum penalties for certain offences: the new maximum penalty for offences for conviction on indictment for copyright cases is an unlimited fine and/or up to ten years in prison, and on summary conviction a fine (up to the statutory maximum) and/or up to six months in prison (previously only a fine could be imposed);[286]

- rationalising police search and seizure powers relating to copyright and trade mark offences;[287]

- making provision for court orders on forfeiture of illegal material that may have been seized during investigation of copyright and trade mark offences.[288]

The 2002 Act made no changes to the scope of criminal offences.

Counterfeiting and piracy

22.147 Counterfeiting and piracy have been the subject of a number of European initiatives to harmonise the rules as within member states of the EU. In particular, procedures relating to border control of the movement of goods infringing IPRs have been strengthened and sanctions available within member states bolstered.[289]

---

[283] [2008] EWCA Crim 2375, [2009] ETMR 6.

[284] *R v Boulter*, para 9. For a discussion on whether a person charged with trade mark infringement believed on objectively reasonable grounds that the goods he was selling were genuine, see *Essex Trading Standards v Wallati Singh* [2009] EWHC 520 (Admin), 2009 WL 392234. In this case the High Court ruled that the respondent was not able to discharge the burden under TMA 1994, s 92(5).

[285] Copyright, etc and Trade Marks (Offences and Enforcement) Act 2002 (Commencement) Order 2002 (SI 2002/2749).

[286] CDPA 1988, ss 107(4), 198(5), 297A(2), 297A(2).   [287] CDPA 1988, ss 109, 200, 297B, 297A; TMA 1994, s 92A.

[288] TMA 1994, ss 97 and 98 allowing forfeiture of infringing goods, are inserted into the CDPA 1988 in respect of the offences in ss 107(1) and (2), 198(1), and 297A and offences under the Trade Descriptions Act 1968 and those involving dishonesty or deception. Section 97 of the TMA 1994 relates to forfeiture in England, Wales, and Northern Ireland and s 98 is a modified version relating to forfeiture in Scotland.

[289] Case C-132/07 *Beecham Group plc, SmithKline Beecham plc, Glaxo Group Ltd, Stafford-Miller Ltd, GlaxoSmithKline Consumer Healthcare NV and GlaxoSmithKline Consumer Healthcare BV v Andacon NV* for questions concerning powers of customs officers under Regulation (EC) No 1891/04 and Regulation (EC) No 1383/03.

22.148   The movement of goods infringing IPRs across borders has long troubled right holders. In recent years there appears to have been a significant increase in this activity, certainly into Europe. The Commission publishes statistics annually showing the number of detentions of articles made at the borders of the EU of goods suspected of infringing IPRs. In 2011, there were more than 91,000 detention cases, an increase of 15 per cent compared to 2010. The number of articles seized was 114,772,812 with a value of €1,272,354,795. Twenty-four per cent were medicines; packaging materials 21 per cent; cigarettes 18 per cent; and clothing 4 per cent.[290]

 Exercise

It can sometimes be very difficult to distinguish between a genuine article and a fake. Go to eBay and type in Mulberry handbag (or the name of any other designer goods you would like). Which are the genuine articles?

22.149   In July 2004 a European Regulation was brought into force concerning action to be taken by customs officials with respect to goods suspected of infringing certain IPRs and measures to be taken against goods found to infringe such rights.[291] It replaced a Regulation promulgated in 1994 which in turn replaced a Regulation of 1986[292] dealing with the same subject matter. In the 2004 Regulation counterfeit goods are defined as:

goods or trade mark symbols or packaging presented separately, bearing without authorisation a trademark identical to another trademark validly registered, or which cannot be distinguished in its essential aspects and which thereby infringes the trademark-holder's rights.

And pirated goods as:

goods that are or contain copies made without the consent of the holder of a copyright or related right or design right.

22.150   The Regulation is broad in scope and covers:

- patents;
- supplementary protection certificates;
- designs and models;
- copyright and related rights;
- trade marks;[293]
- designations of origin;
- new plant varieties;

---

[290]   *Report on EU Customs Enforcement of Intellectual Property Rights: Enforcement at the Border—2011* (ISBN: 9789279253621).

[291]   Council Regulation (EC) No 1383/2003 of 22 July 2003 concerning customs action against goods suspected of infringing certain intellectual property rights and measures to be taken against goods found to have infringed such rights came into force. Referred to by CDPA 1988, s 111(3B); TMA 1994, s 89(3). See also Commission Regulation 1891/2004 of 21.10.2004 laying down provisions for the implementation of this Council Regulation. Case C-93/08 *SIA Schenker v Valsts ieņe-mumu dienests.*

[292]   Council Regulation (EEC) No 3842/86 of 1 December 1986 laying down measures to prohibit the release for free circulation of counterfeit goods.

[293]   Case C-302/08 *Zino Davidoff SA v Bundesfinanzdirektion Südos* in which the ECJ ruled that the Regulation also covers international trade marks. The ECJ explained that, following the assimilation of internationally registered trade marks into Community trade marks pursuant to Art 146 of Council Regulation (EC) No 40/94 as amended by Council Regulation (EC) No 1992/2003, Art 5(4) of the Regulation allows 'the holder of an international registered trade mark to secure action by the customs authorities of one or more other Member State, besides that of the Member State in which it is lodged, just like the proprietor of a Community trade mark'.

- geographical indications;

- any mould or matrix designed or adapted for the manufacture of goods infringing an IPR.

The purpose of the Regulation is to facilitate the seizure and destruction of infringing goods (according to the law of the member state in which the goods are found) with the intention of preventing them from entering circulation in the EU. The Regulation sets out the procedure by which notice should be given to the relevant customs authorities and the action to be taken thereafter; although for difficulties that arose in the UK where Commissioners of HM Revenue & Customs (HMRC) refused to continue to detain a consignment of allegedly counterfeit mobile phones and accessories bearing the Nokia trade mark because they had not been placed on the market, see para 20.60 and Joined Cases C-446/09 (Philips) and C-495/09 (Nokia). Under the Regulation measures may also be taken to deprive the persons concerned of the economic benefits of the transaction.[294]

22.151   In May 2011 the Commission proposed a new Regulation dealing with counterfeiting and piracy. Three particular aspects are proposed. These are to: expand the range of IPR infringements covered; adjust procedures in order to reduce administrative burdens and costs; and ensure high-quality information is provided to customs to enable better risk management; and include measures better to ensure that the interests of legitimate traders are protected.[295]

22.152   National governments have also been busy in developing responses to the increased incidence of counterfeiting and piracy. Not only do trading standards officers have some responsibility for the enforcement of legislation in this area, but in addition, the UK Government established an IP Crime Group which launched a new intellectual property crime strategy in 2011 setting out how the UK–IPO will continue to enforce IP crime domestically.[296]

> ## Web link
>
> If you look at the IPO website at **http://www.ipo.gov.uk/ipenforce/ipenforce-crime.htm** you will find documents relating to the IP Crime Strategy, the 2011 Report, along with a number of documents concerning the activities of the Office and other organisations involved in measures aimed at tackling piracy and counterfeiting.

22.153   A network of organisations, such as FAST, the British Software Alliance, and FACT, monitor markets and alert the relevant regulatory authorities to incidents of counterfeiting and piracy. Counterfeiting and piracy were subjects also discussed at the G-8 meeting held at Gleneagles in Scotland in 2005. The ministers issued a document pledging to work together to draw up a plan to reduce the incidence of these activities over the coming years.[297] In 2006 the EU and the United States agreed to work together to develop approaches to defeat the rising tide of counterfeit and pirated goods coming from China and Russia, to be followed by Latin America and the Middle East.[298]

---

[294] Council Regulation (EC) No 1383/2003, Art 17(1)(b). Domestic procedures relating to copyright and trade marks are also available but are narrower than those to be found under the Regulation. CDPA 1988, ss 111, 112; TMA 1994, s 89.

[295] The proposal can be found at http://ec.europa.eu/taxation_customs/customs/customs_controls/counterfeit_piracy/legislation/index_en.htm. In 2012 OHIM was tasked with a variety of responsibilities relating to enforcement of IP rights including assembling a group of public and private sector stakeholders to form a European Observatory. See Regulation (EU) No 386/2012.

[296] http://www.ipo.gov.uk/ipenforce/ipenforce-crime/ipenforce-role.htm.

[297] At Gleneagles in July 2005 the G-8 statement 'Reducing IPR Piracy and Counterfeiting through more effective enforcement' was issued.

[298] 'US and EU Pledge to take action over fake Goods', *Financial Times*, 18 June 2006. See SABIP Report (Number EC001), 'IP Enforcement in the UK and Beyond: A Literature Review', 18 May 2009.

22.154   This may have heralded the start of the negotiations for a proposed new international treaty designed to combat counterfeiting. In 2007 the European Commission stated that it intended to seek a mandate from member states to negotiate a new Anti Counterfeiting Trade Agreement (ACTA) with major trading partners, including the United States, Japan, Korea, Mexico, and New Zealand.[299] Three particular avenues would be pursued:

- building international cooperation leading to harmonised standards and better communication between authorities;

- establishing common enforcement practices to promote strong intellectual property protection in coordination with right holders and trading partners; and

- creating a strong modern legal framework which reflects the changing nature of intellectual property theft in the global economy, including the rise of easy-to-copy digital storage media and the increasing danger of health threats from counterfeit food and pharmaceutical drugs.

ACTA proved to be highly controversial[300] not only because of the view that it was negotiated in secret but also because of the concern many held over the breadth of its provisions and effect on such rights as freedom of expression and privacy. In July 2012 the European Parliament voted to reject ACTA.[301] Whether the initiative will continue without EU involvement remains to be seen.

Exercise

The definitions of counterfeiting and piracy have changed and would appear to have expanded in scope over the years. See how many different definitions you can find used in both European and UK instruments. What do you think of the use of the term 'piracy' in connection with individuals who download music files from the Internet?

EU proposals on criminal enforcement

22.155   In June 2005 the Commission promulgated a proposal for a further Directive, this time aimed at criminal sanctions and remedies along with a proposal for a council Framework Decision to strengthen the criminal law framework to combat intellectual property offences.[302] This proposal, couched in language referring to obligations under TRIPS and Article 17(2) of the Charter of Fundamental Rights (which states that 'Intellectual property shall be protected') would extend criminal sanctions to all intentional infringements of an intellectual property right carried out on a commercial scale, as well as for attempting, aiding or abetting, and inciting such offences. The proposal for a Framework Decision set a threshold for criminal penalties of at least four years' imprisonment if the offence involved a criminal organisation or if it jeopardised public health and safety. The fine had to be at least €100,000–€300,000 for cases involving criminal organisations or posing a risk to public health and safety, although member states could apply tougher penalties.

22.156   The proposal was withdrawn after uncertainty as to the competence of the EC to legislate in the arena of criminal sanctions. That they did was (arguably) affirmed by the ECJ in *Commission v Council*[303] where

---

[299]   See IP/07/1573.

[300]   ACTA triggered a great deal of anxious blogging. See http://ec.europa.eu/trade/tackling-unfair-trade/acta/. Also Electronic Frontier Foundation's opinion on ACTA at http://www.eff.org/issues/acta. See also 'Fact Sheet: Anti-Counterfeiting Trade Agreement' at http://ec.europa.eu/trade/issues/sectoral/intell_property/fs231007_en.htm. But see M Blakeney, 'Trade mark survey: ACTA gives hope to trade mark owners' [2009] IPQ 1–6.

[301]   http://www.bbc.co.uk/news/technology-18704192.   [302]   2005/0127(COD), 2005/0128(CNS).

[303]   Case C 176/03 *Commission v Council*.

it was held that provisions of criminal law required for the effective implementation of Community law (in the instant case, criminal sanctions for environmental issues) fell under the EC Treaty.[304] The draft Directive was re-issued in amended form and adopted in April 2007 by the European Parliament. Concerns remain as to the scope of the measure and of the competence of the Commission to harmonise criminal sanctions.[305] The proposal apparently remains under discussion.

22.157   While there may be sympathy for the fight against organised crime and its relationship to counterfeiting and piracy, a general anxiety is that, as it stands, the draft Directive could reach far beyond this domain most notably by reference to the rather vague standards of 'attempting, aiding, abetting and inciting' infringements. What is notable are the grounds on which the proposal is justified. As with the original proposal, TRIPS is referred to. However, that Agreement only requires criminal sanctions to be applied in the area of wilful trademark counterfeiting or copyright piracy on a commercial scale.[306] This measure, by contrast, would apply across the IP domains. Reference to the Charter of Fundamental Rights remains, cited as evidencing the obligation to protect intellectual property and thus justify the proposal: human rights standards have most often in the past been used as arguments for limiting the exercise of IPRs rather than providing a justification for tougher enforcement measures.

22.158   Should the proposal proceed, the anxiety must be as to whether the result will represent a balance as between the legitimate concerns of right holders and those who fear for public health and the economy, whilst providing safeguards for non-commercial infringers and the general public interest.

> **Web link**
>
> The amended draft Directive COM(2006) 168 final can be found at **http://eur-lex.europa.eu/ LexUriServ/site/en/com/2006/com2006_0168en01.pdf**. Read the draft. What do you think of the proposals and the basis on which they have been justified?

22.159   Although civil, criminal, and border procedures and remedies are independent they are designed to work together in an integrated system. From border measures through to the receipt of an award of damages or a criminal prosecution, a right owner should be able to call upon appropriate procedures to vindicate a claim and receive a remedy for an infringement of a right.

> **Exercise 1**
>
> You are the owner of the copyright in a film. You have heard that DVDs featuring the film and copied without your consent or authorisation have been made in an East European country, not part of the EU. Some of these DVDs have been found in a market stall in Glasgow, others in retail shops in the Scottish Borders. You have heard that a further consignment is due to arrive at Rosyth within the next two weeks bound for a country outwith the EU. What do you do?

---

[304] For comment, see P Treacy and A Wray, 'IP crimes: the prospect for EU-wide criminal sanctions—a long road ahead?' [2006] EIPR 1.

[305] See House of Lords European Union Committee 11th Report of Session 2006–07: The Criminal Law Competence of the EC, follow-up Report, 13 March 2007.   [306] TRIPS, Art 61.

Exercise 2

You are the legal counsel for Legal and General. When on a trip to Myanmar you notice these T-shirts for sale on a stall by the side of the road. What do you do?

Figure 22.1 Gegal & Leneral

TRIPS

22.160   On enforcement matters, TRIPS is important for two reasons.

- TRIPS calls for effective enforcement measures to be available at the domestic level to allow action to be taken by intellectual property owners where rights are infringed. This includes the availability of certain remedies which should be considered a deterrent to further infringement.

- TRIPS provides a mechanism (through the WTO) whereby disputes between member states may be settled. This is particularly so where one country alleges that another is not adhering to its obligations to incorporate the minimum standards of intellectual property protection and enforcement mechanisms into domestic law as laid down in the Agreement.

Effective enforcement measures

22.161   TRIPS is the first international treaty in the IP sector to place obligations on member states relating to the enforcement of IPRs. Three areas of enforcement activity are laid down in the Agreement: civil and administrative procedures including remedies,[307] border measures,[308] and criminal procedures.[309]

22.162   Member states are to make available to right holders civil judicial procedures concerning the enforcement of any IPR including rules relating to representation,[310] evidence,[311] and the availability of injunctions and damages.[312] Border measures must be available to enable a right holder to prevent the importation

---

[307] TRIPS, Part III, s 2. [308] TRIPS, Part III, s 4. [309] TRIPS, Part III, s 5.
[310] TRIPS, Art 42. [311] TRIPS, Art 43. [312] TRIPS, Arts 44 and 45.

of counterfeit trade mark and pirated copyright goods.[313] Criminal procedures and penalties must be applied in cases of wilful trademark counterfeiting or copyright piracy on a commercial scale.[314]

22.163   Four principles underlie each type of enforcement measure. These are that the action should be effective,[315] procedures should be fair and equitable,[316] decisions should be reasoned,[317] and there should be the opportunity to seek judicial review.[318] In addition, the measures should be applied in a manner that avoids creating barriers to legitimate trade and which provide safeguards against their abuse.[319]

22.164   The UK meets all the requirements imposed by TRIPS, and indeed some aspects of domestic enforcement procedures and remedies go beyond those to be found in that Agreement.

 Exercise

Look at TRIPS and compare the procedures laid down in that Agreement with the provisions in the EU Enforcement Directive. Which, if any, of those measures in the Directive go beyond what is required by TRIPS?

22.165   However, not all states which are members of TRIPS have been, or are, in compliance with the obligations to be found in that Agreement, including those on enforcement and remedies. This highlights the second, and important, aspect of TRIPS. If a member does not comply with its obligations, then a complaint may be taken to the Dispute Settlement Body (DSB) established by the WTO Agreement. Representatives of every WTO member sit on the DSB which was created to deal with disputes arising under the WTO Agreements. This it does in accordance with the provisions of the Dispute Settlement Understanding (DSU). Member states or trading groups recognised by the WTO may bring an action before a WTO Dispute Settlement Panel if they believe that another country or trading group has failed to meet its obligations under TRIPS. If a country or group is found not to have complied with TRIPS, trade sanctions can be imposed.[320] This mechanism has been used in a number of intellectual property cases both where member states have not incorporated minimum standards on enforcement and remedies into their domestic law, as well as in cases concerning alleged failures to implement the correct substantive level of intellectual property protection.

22.166   On enforcement and remedies, the United States has brought complaints against, inter alia, Denmark[321] and Sweden[322] arguing that their domestic laws did not provide for provisional measures in civil proceedings as required by TRIPS. Both the actions settled when a mutually agreed solution was found. A case that went to a full panel hearing concerning the enforcement measures was taken by the United States against China alleging that China had not fulfilled a number of obligations in implementing the enforcement measures to be found in TRIPs into domestic law.[323] In a lengthy report, the Panel found that China failed to conform to its obligations in a limited number of ways concerning border measures and its failure to grant certain works protection by copyright.[324] The complexity of the dispute combined with the lack of clarity in the findings of the Panel has led commentators to conclude that

---

[313] TRIPS, Art 51.   [314] TRIPS, Art 61.   [315] TRIPS, Art 41.   [316] TRIPS, Art 41.2.   [317] TRIPS, Art 41.3.
[318] TRIPS, Art 41.4.   [319] See generally TRIPS, Arts 41, 42, 43, 48.
[320] The WTO Agreement provides that 'Each Member shall ensure the conformity of its laws, regulations and administrative procedures with its obligations as provided in the annexed Agreements' (Art XVI:4).   [321] US DS83.
[322] US DS86.
[323] Panel Report, China—Measures Affecting the Protection and Enforcement of Intellectual Property Rights, WT/DS362/R (26 January 2009).
[324] For a list of the documents, see http://www.wto.org/english/tratop_e/dispu_e/cases_e/ds362_e.htm.

the enforcement provisions lack the necessary precision and strength to cope with infringement on a global scale.[325]

22.167   Other complaints concerning the failure of member states' domestic substantive law to reflect obligations imposed by the Agreement have been heard by the full WTO Panel. The first in the copyright field was based on a complaint against the United States brought by the EC concerning section 110(5)(B) of the US Copyright Act.[326] This section exempts eating, drinking, and retail establishments of a certain size from liability for the public performance of music played from radio and television. It was alleged that this section was incompatible with obligations under both the Berne Convention and TRIPS.[327] In a lengthy decision the Panel analysed the compatibility of section 110(5)(B) with the three-step test to be found in both of those treaties.[328] On the first step of the test, the Panel found that section 110(5)(B) was not limited to certain special cases: it had been estimated that 70 per cent of eating establishments, 73 per cent of drinking establishments, and 45 per cent of retail establishments fell under the exemption. On the second part of the test the Panel found that section 110(5)(B) conflicted with a normal exploitation of a work. This was based on the principle that exempted uses may not compete with actual or potential means of economic exploitation: there would be a conflict between an exemption and normal exploitation if the exemption interfered with the ways in which a right holder would 'normally extract economic value' from a particular use of a work. On the third part of the test, the Panel found that the legitimate interests of the right holder were prejudiced saying that prejudice becomes unreasonable when an exception causes, or has the potential to cause, an unreasonable loss of income to the authors; that actual and potential prejudice to the right holder should be taken into account; and that in analysing unreasonable prejudice the legitimate interests of copyright holders at large should be taken into account and not only the interests of right holders of the WTO member that initiated the complaint. In conclusion, the Panel Report found that section 110(5)(B) was indeed incompatible with obligations to be found in TRIPS and recommended that the DSB request the United States to amend its legislation.[329]

22.168   Patent disputes have also been heard by the Panel. The EU challenged various aspects of Canadian patent law including the provision that would have meant that it was not an infringement of a patent to make a patented product during the life of the patent for the purpose of stockpiling it for sale after the patent expired. The Panel found this to be a violation of Canada's obligations under TRIPS saying that manufacture for commercial sale is a commercial activity and that the character of that activity is not altered by mere delay of the commercial reward. Thus, and in practical terms, the enforcement of the right to exclude others from 'making' and 'using' a patented product during the patent term will necessarily give all patent owners a short period of extended exclusivity after the patent expires. Therefore the stockpiling provision in the Canadian patent law was in breach of TRIPS and the Panel concluded that Canada should be required to amend its law to remove this provision.[330]

22.169   Many of the complaints settle prior to being heard by the Panel. For instance, a complaint was made by the United States against Ireland alleging that Irish legislation did not conform with, inter alia,

---

[325] KP Yu, 'The TRIPS Enforcement Dispute (September 13, 2010)' (2011) 89 Nebraska LR 1046–1131; Drake University Law School Research Paper No 11-16, available at SSRN at http://ssrn.com/abstract=1676558.

[326] As amended by the US Fairness in Music Licensing Act 1988.

[327] Arts 11*bis*(1)(iii) and 11(1)(ii) of the Berne Convention concerning rights of public performance and communication to the public incorporated into TRIPS by virtue of Art 9(1) and with the three-step test in TRIPS, Art 13.

[328] For a discussion of the three-step test, see Chapter 5.

[329] For the subsequent action, see R Owens, 'TRIPS and the Fairness in Music arbitration: the repercussions' [2003] EIPR 49. In an action against China DS362 the Panel found that China needed to amend certain of its laws relating to copyright and customs measures so as to conform with obligations under TRIPs.   [330] WT/DS1114/13.

obligations concerning rental rights for producers of phonograms.[331] The request for the establishment of the Panel was withdrawn after agreement was reached that Ireland would amend its copyright laws.

22.170   To 2012, 31 complaints had been brought before the DSB concerning TRIPS. It is difficult to know at this stage whether this number is likely to increase as states recognise the power of making a complaint in obtaining compliance with obligations under the WTO, or whether the fact that the procedure is available—and indeed will be used—will encourage members voluntarily to ensure that their domestic legislation is in line with obligations in TRIPS.

22.171   A different strategy concerning IPRs is being used by some states. Where a state had been found to be in violation of its obligations under TRIPs the Arbitrator may impose sanctions in an unrelated field. So when the United States was found in violation of its WTO obligations in respect of gambling and betting services, the Arbitrator found that Antigua may request authorisation from the DSB, to suspend the obligations under the TRIPS Agreement in the areas of copyright and related rights; trade marks; industrial designs; patents and undisclosed information at a level not exceeding US$21 million annually.[332]

Web link

The WTO webpages can be difficult to navigate until you find your way around. Go to the home page and see if you can find information about disputes that have arisen concerning TRIPS. If in difficulty look at **http://www.wto.org/english/tratop_e/dispu_e/dispu_agreements_index_e. htm?id=A26# selected_agreement.**
In the list of headings you will find Intellectual Property (TRIPs). Go to these pages and browse though the documents. Revisit the pages at regular intervals to keep abreast of developments.

 ## Exercise

Would you recommend establishing a procedure akin to that available for disputes arising under TRIPS to hear complaints made under other international treaties such as the Berne Convention? If so, why? If not, why not?

Key points on TRIPS and enforcement

- TRIPS places obligations on member states to implement into their national laws certain minimum standards concerning remedies and sanctions for infringement of IPRs (as well as substantive provisions)

---

[331] WT DS82/3, WT/DS115/3, IP/D/8/Add.1, IP/D/12/Add.1.
[332] See WT/DS285/ARB. United States—Measures Affecting the Cross-Border Supply of Gambling and Betting Services. Recourse to Arbitration by the United States under Article 22.6 of the DSU. Decision by the Arbitrator. The holding has prompted a great deal of discussion. See, eg, I Wohl, 'The United States–Antigua Online Gambling Dispute', Journal of International Commerce and Economics, Web version July 2009, available at http://www.usitc.gov/publications/332/journals/online_gambling_dispute.pdf. See also DS267 United States—Subsidies on Upland Cotton in which Brazil may 'suspend' certain US IP rights.

- TRIPS provides a mechanism (through the WTO) whereby disputes between member states as to their adherence or otherwise to obligations laid down in TRIPS may be raised and settled. TRIPS is the only international treaty to contain such an enforcement mechanism

Future developments

22.172   As will have been seen from this chapter, in common with all areas of IP, policy tensions are evident in this domain. New modes of exploitation are challenging the existing framework both in terms exploitation and enforcement. In civil matters the key concern is to ensure that the interests of the IP owner are sufficiently but not over protected at the expense of innovation. In criminal matters the articulated strategy is to combat counterfeiting and piracy not only because of its links with organised crime, but also because of the anxiety over consumer welfare. This has resulted in the enactment of a number of recent measures in the field of enforcement as discussed in the text, as well as further proposals to strengthen the regime. Although many initiatives emanate at international level and in Europe, both the Gowers Review of Intellectual Property and the Hargreaves Report made several recommendations in the field of enforcement including. For the Gowers Review these included the introduction of matching penalties for online and physical copyright infringement and reviewing the award of damages to ensure that an effective and dissuasive system exists for civil IP cases.[333] Sadly, it seemed that the impetus to implement all of the proposed reforms stalled. For the Hargreaves Report things seem to be progressing faster and the UK–IPO website contains a number of pieces of research and further reports that have investigated and analysed the subject. Full details can be found at **http://www.ipo.gov.uk/types/hargreaves.htm**. Of particular note is the work that has been done on the Digital Copyright Exchange, on exceptions and limitations for people with disabilities, and on parody.

 Exercise

Go to the UK–IPO website and read the various reports and papers concerned with implementing aspects of the Hargreaves Report. Which do you think will contribute the most to 'modernising' the copyright regime for the digital era and why?

Further reading

Books

S Anderman et al (eds), *The Interface between Intellectual Property Rights and Competition Policy* (2007)

L Bently, J Davis, and J Ginsburg (eds), *Copyright and Piracy: An Interdisciplinary Critique* (2010)

I Stamatoudi (ed), *Copyright Enforcement and the Internet* (2010)

O Vrins and M Scheider (eds), *Enforcement of Intellectual Property Rights through Border Measures—Law and Practice in the EU* (2006)

[333] Gowers Review of Intellectual Property, December 2006.

Reports

C Correa, *Intellectual Property and Competition Law: Exploration of Some Issues of Relevance to Developing Countries, ICTSD IPRs and Sustainable Development Programme* (2007), Issue Paper No 21, International Centre for Trade and Sustainable Development, Geneva, Switzerland

Articles

'Statement of the Max Planck Institute for Intellectual Property, Competition and Tax Law on the Proposal for a Directive of the European Parliament and of the Council on criminal measures aimed at ensuring the enforcement of intellectual property rights' (2006) 37(8) IIC 970–977

A Andreangeli, 'Interoperability as an "essential facility" in the *Microsoft* case—encouraging competition or stifling innovation?' (2009) ELRev 584

L Blakeney and M Blakeney, 'Counterfeiting and piracy—removing the Incentives through confiscation' [2008] EIPR 348

M Blakeney, 'International proposals for the criminal enforcement of intellectual property rights: international concern with counterfeiting and piracy' [2009] IPQ 1

V Bomhard, H O'Neill, and A Paz, 'Licences in OHIM practice' (2007) 2(11) JIPLP 756

E Bonadio, 'Remedies and sanctions for the infringement of intellectual property rights under EC law' (2008) 30(8) EIPR 320–327

O Brand, 'The dawn of compulsory patent licensing' [2007] 2 IPQ 216–235

P Chaudhry, 'Managing intellectual property rights: government tactics to curtail counterfeit trade' (2006) 17(4) EBL Rev 939–958

Q Cregan, 'Roving injunctions and John Doe orders against unidentifiable defendants in IP infringement proceedings' (2011) 6(9) JIPLP 623

WJ Davey, 'The WTO Dispute Settlement System: the first ten years' (2005) 8 JIEL 17A

I Davies and T Scourfield, 'Threats: is the current regime still justified?' (2007) 29(7) EIPR 259–265

GB Dinwoodie, 'International intellectual property litigation: a vehicle for resurgent comparativist thought?' (2001) 49 American Journal of Comparative Law 429

S Dusollier, 'Technology as an imperative for regulating copyright: from the public exploitation to the private use of the work' (2005) 27(6) EIPR 201–204

D Ehrlich, 'Trade mark warranties in M & A transactions' (2008) 3(8) JIPLP 501

M Elsmore, 'Trade mark coexistence agreements: what is all the (lack of) fuss about?' (2008) 5(1) SCRIPTed 7, available at http://www.law.ed.ac.uk/ahrc/script-ed/vol5-1/elsmore.asp

A Endeshaw, 'Free trade agreements as surrogates for TRIPs-Plus' (2006) 28(7) EIPR 374–380

G Evans, 'University patent licensing for the research and development of pharmaceuticals in developing countries' [2009] 3 IPQ 311–344

J Farchy, 'Are free licences suitable for cultural works?' [2009] EIPR 255

A Gagliardi, 'Trade mark assignments under EC law' [1998] EIPR 371

B Godart, 'IP crime: the new face of organized crime—from IP theft to IP crime' (2010) 5(5) JIPLP 378

G Grassie, 'The Scottish courts—the tartan alternative for resolving IP disputes?' (2004) 33(7) CIPAJ 406–408

G Grassie and R Buchan, 'Title and interest to sue in trade mark infringement proceedings' (2011) 6(7) JIPLP 450

R Halford-Harrison, 'Creation and enforcement of rights in digitized versions of public domain artworks' (2011) 6(8) JIPLP 542

K Huniar, 'The Enforcement Directive—its effects on UK law' (2006) 28(2) EIPR 92–99

S Hutchinson, 'In transition …when should in transit goods be seized for IP infringement in the EU?' (2010) 32(12) EIPR 614

MT Landova, 'Public policy exception to recognition and enforcement of judgments in cases of copyright infringement' [2009] IIC 642

S Lane, 'Goodwill hunting: assignments and licenses in gross after *Scandecor*' [1999] 2 IPQ 264–279

S Lawrance, '*Attheraces v British Horseracing Board*: what price abuse of dominance?' (2007) 2(9) JIPLP 605

V Lowe, 'The law of unintended consequences—a perspective on the draft Directive on criminal measures to enforce intellectual property rights' (2006) 163 Criminal Lawyer 3–5

D Matthews, 'The Lisbon Treaty, trade agreements and the enforcement of intellectual property rights' [2010] EIPR 104

D Meale and J Smith, 'Enforcing a trade mark when nobody's confused: where the law stands after *L'Oréal and Intel*' (2010) 5(2) JIPLP 96

G Mengistie, 'Intellectual property as a tool for development: the Ethiopian Fine Coffee designations and trade marking and licensing experience' (2010) Int TLR 1

M Mercedes Frabboni, 'Old monopolies versus new technologies—the CISAC decision in context' (2009) 20(3) EntLR 77

TT Nguyen, 'Competition rules in the TRIPS Agreement—the CFI's ruling in *Microsoft v. Commission* and implications for developing countries' (2008) 39 IIC 558

A Niedermann, 'Surveys as evidence in proceedings before OHIM' (2006) 37(3) IIC 260–276

R Owens, 'TRIPs and the Fairness in Music arbitration: the repercussions' (2003) 25(2) EIPR 49–54

L Pechan and M Schneider, 'Carriers and trade mark infringements: should carriers care?' (2010) 5(5) JIPLP 350

E Reid, 'No sex please, we're European: *Mosley v News Group Newspapers Ltd*' (2009) Edinburgh LR 116

T Riis, 'Collecting societies, competition, and the Services Directive' (2011) 6(7) JIPLP 482

E Smith, 'The bowl with the bitter taste' (2007) 2(8) JIPLP 510

C Stothers, 'Copyright and the EC Treaty: music, films and football' (2009) 31(5) EIPR 272–282

P Sugden, 'How long is a piece of string? The meaning of "commercial scale" in copyright piracy' (2009) 31(4) EIPR 202–212

P Treacy and A Wray, 'IP crimes: the prospect for EU-wide criminal sanctions—a long road ahead?' (2006) 28(1) EIPR 1–4

Yu-Lin Tsai, 'Compulsory licenses for access to medicines, expropriation and investor-state arbitration under bilateral investment agreements—are there issues beyond the TRIPS Agreement?' (2009) 40(2) IIC 152–173

B Ubertazzi, 'Licence agreements relating to IP rights and the EC Regulation on jurisdiction' (2009) 40(8) IIC 912–939

G Urbanchuk, and J Tumbridge, 'Patent damages: the European landscape' (2008) 3(9) JIPLP 576

J van Hezewijk, 'Montex and Rolex—irreconcilable differences? A call for a better definition of counterfeit goods' (2008) 39 IIC 775

NJ Wilkoff, 'A wake up call for UK law on trade mark licensing' (1998) 20(10) EIPR 386–390

KP Yu, 'The TRIPS enforcement dispute (September 13, 2010)' (2011) 89 Nebraska LR 1046–1131; Drake University Law School Research Paper No 11-16, available at SSRN at http://ssrn.com/abstract=1676558

23

Intellectual property and international private law

Introduction

23.1 As has been suggested throughout this work, although intellectual property law is territorial, the expansion of commerce means that various goods and services (the whole or some element of which may be protected by IP) can be traded in numerous different countries throughout the world. With this increase in international exchange where there are many opportunities for infringement it becomes increasingly difficult to apply the principle of territoriality which forms the basis of intellectual property law. If a music file protected by copyright, and owned by a recording company in the United States, is 'shared' by users in many different countries using peer-to-peer (P2P) software, who can be sued and where can they be sued? What law would apply to determine the matter? Would a judgment given in one country be recognised in another? When a trade mark is used in a website, that is the same as or similar to a trade mark registered by a separate entity in another country, would the second trade mark be infringed by its mere accessibility in a website? Can one country issue an order that would affect a registered right, such as a patent, in another (a cross-border injunction)?

23.2 Of these issues, those concerning copyright and trade marks have become particularly pressing due to the expansion of the Internet. For copyright, the dissemination of perfect copies of creative works across the net, out of the control of the right holders, has stretched the capabilities of the territorially based law. Similarly, the conflicting rights that may arise when trade mark owners of identical or similar registered marks in different territories use their respective marks within websites have given rise to some difficulties, as have the use of Adwords in search engines, all of which are likely to increase with the further expansion of e-commerce. Patents, too, have had their share of transnational problems, although to date this has not been as a result of Internet use. Rather, the cases have mainly concerned joining defendants in infringement cases and cross-border injunctions; where one court issues an injunction that can affect a patent in another.

Scope and overview of chapter

23.3 The purpose of this chapter is to discuss the development and application of the rules of international private law as they affect cross-border infringements of intellectual property rights in England and

Scotland and Europe. The focus will be on copyright, trade marks, and cross-border patent litigation. It is not the intention to discuss the rules in depth, but to explain those which are applicable to infringement and to highlight a number of Court of Justice and UK cases that have applied the rules in intellectual property cases.

23.4

Learning objectives

By the end of this chapter you should be able to describe and explain:

- jurisdiction and choice of law rules that apply where IP disputes arise: (1) where the defendant is domiciled in the EU; (2) where the defendant is furth of the EU; and (3) where the wrong occurs in the EU;

- why UK courts have been unwilling to hear a dispute concerning an infringement of intellectual property rights that occurred abroad, and what legislative changes have occurred to alter that approach;

- how the rules on international private law apply to cross-border intellectual property infringements and the attendant difficulties in applying those rules in an era of globalisation and digital dissemination.

23.5   The rest of the chapter looks like this:

- International private law (23.6–23.19)
- Developments in the EU (23.20–23.62)
- Contemporary developments (23.63–23.73)

International private law

23.6   The object of international private law (IPL) is to ensure, as far as possible, that disputes involving a foreign element are adjudicated by the court best placed to do justice to both parties, and that the appropriate law is applied to the dispute.

The rules of IPL thus determine:

- which court should hear a dispute (jurisdiction);
- which law governs the dispute (choice of law);
- what should be done to recognise and enforce a judgment.

It is important to note that although one court may have jurisdiction to hear a dispute, this does not mean that the law of that forum must necessarily be applied to the matter in hand.

 Question

Do any of the cases considered in other chapters of this book concern cross-border infringement of intellectual property rights? If so, which ones?

The legal frameworks

23.7 Where the defendant is domiciled in the EU and the matter concerns a civil or commercial matter, the rules in Europe on jurisdiction and recognition and enforcement of judgments are to be found in the Brussels Regulation which came into force on 1 March 2002[1] and which replaced the Brussels Convention.[2] The rules on contractual liability are in Rome I Regulation[3] which came into force on 17 December 2009 and applies to contracts entered into after that date. This replaced the 1980 Rome Convention on the law applicable to contractual obligations (a Hague Conference measure) which was implemented into UK law by the Contracts (Applicable Law) Act 1990. These rules will remain relevant to contracts entered into before 17 December 2009. The rules on non-contractual liability are in Rome II Regulation which came into effect from 11 January 2009.[4] These rules governing choice of law for non-contractual liability in the UK replaced those in the Law Reform (Miscellaneous Provisions) Act 1995 which remains relevant to contracts entered into before 11 January 2009. The Rome II Regulation now applies to all torts/delicts arising in the EU regardless of whether any of the parties is connected with a member state[5] except where specifically excluded. For these purposes the exclusions include non-contractual obligations arising out of violations of privacy and rights relating to personality, including defamation.[6] The second set of rules concerns those cases where the wrong occurs abroad furth of the EU. Here, in England, the English rules on justiciability and conflicts of law apply.

Historical development of the rules in the UK

23.8 Unlike some other areas of the law (eg family law or succession), there has been a reluctance by courts in one jurisdiction to hear a case concerning an infringement of intellectual property which took place in another jurisdiction. This stems in part from the development of the international treaties on intellectual property law, in particular the Paris[7] and Berne Conventions.[8] It will be recalled that there are two main principles underlying these conventions. The first is of national treatment where, as a general rule, a signatory state is obliged to offer protection to nationals of other signatory states in accordance to the protection afforded to its own nationals.[9] The second requirement is for signatory states to provide, in domestic law, certain substantive minimum levels of intellectual property protection. For example, signatories to the Berne Convention are required to afford owners of copyright a minimum term of protection of 50 years *post mortem auctoris* (pma)[10]—although many offer considerably more.[11] The international conventions do not, however, directly address or affect the question of IPL.

23.9 This has meant that, for example, when a copyright infringement dispute arose in one state party to the Berne Convention (State X) that concerned an author who hailed from another signatory state (State Y),

---

[1] The Brussels Regulation on jurisdiction and the recognition and enforcement of judgments in civil and commercial matters Council Regulation (EC) No 44/2001 of 22 December 2000.

[2] The Brussels Convention on Jurisdiction and the Enforcement of Judgements in Civil and Commercial Matters 72/454, 1972 OJ L299, p 32.

[3] Regulation (EC) No 593/2008 of the European Parliament and of the Council of on the law applicable to contractual obligations.

[4] Regulation (EC) No 864/2007 of the European Parliament and of the Council of 11 July 2007 on the law applicable to non-contractual obligations.

[5] Art 3. [6] Art 2(g). [7] Paris Convention for the Protection of Industrial Property 1883.

[8] Berne Convention for the Protection of Literary and Artistic Works 1886.

[9] Paris Convention, Art 2; Berne Convention, Art 5. [10] Berne Convention, Art 7.

[11] See Chapter 3 (copyright term).

on hearing the case the court in State X would apply and interpret national law. Intellectual property rights thus remained territorial. Where a case did arise before a court which concerned a foreign intellectual property right, the courts were reluctant to intervene.

23.10   In the UK, these concerns were reflected in rules which made it particularly difficult for an English or Scottish court to hear a case concerning an infringement of a foreign intellectual property right. The first was the public policy rule concerning jurisdiction. It was enunciated in *British South Africa Co v Companhia de Moçambique*[12] (the *Moçambique* rule). This rule classified torts (delicts) occurring in foreign lands as local in the sense that they had a particular connection with the territory on which they occurred. This in turn meant that it was appropriate for any action in relation to this tort to be heard in the local forum, that is, the place where the wrong occurred. So where an infringement of a patent occurred in one of the states in Australia, that was the appropriate forum in which the dispute should be heard.[13]

23.11   The second rule concerned a choice of law rule. The main choice of law approach in intellectual property *infringement* actions is determined by the territorial nature of intellectual property rights. Neither the Paris Convention nor TRIPS provides any detailed guidance in matters of trade mark or patent law. As noted, these Conventions are premised on principles of national treatment and territoriality of laws. This notion of territoriality has been seen as the basis for the application of the law of the place where protection is claimed.[14] This has caused few problems for registered rights. Whether an infringement has occurred will be judged in accordance with the law of the place where the right is registered. That law will also govern the extent of the infringement. More discussion has arisen with copyright and other unregistered rights such as passing off.

23.12   In relation to copyright, the Berne Convention contains a measure that some commentators have argued is a choice of law provision. Article 5(2) provides that:

> the extent of protection, as well as the means of redress afforded to the author to protect his rights, shall be governed exclusively by the laws of the country where protection is claimed.

23.13   What is meant by the phrase '*the country where protection is claimed*'? Some have argued that it should be interpreted as the law of the forum, as that is where the claimant seeks protection. Others argue it is rather to be interpreted as the country 'for which' protection is claimed against infringing acts occurring there. Most commentators now agree that the second interpretation is the one to be preferred[15] and, indeed, it is the interpretation that is consistent with the accepted notion that there is no such thing as international copyright law, but rather a collection of local laws.[16] For infringement cases, therefore, the law to be applied is the law of the place of the infringement.

---

[12] [1893] AC 602.

[13] *British South Africa Co v Companhia de Moçambique*. Note also *Satyam Computer Services Ltd v Upaid Systems Ltd* [2008] EWHC 31 (Ch), para 95 where the court, in discussing the *Moçambique* rule, did not think that it supported a wider proposition that the English courts should not make inquiry into the validity of a foreign patent or similar foreign intellectual property rights.

[14] J Fawcett and P Torremans, *Intellectual Property and Private International Law* (1998), 477–478.

[15] J Ginsburg, 'Private international law aspects of the protection of works and objects of related rights transmitted through digital networks', available on the WIPO website as Paper GCPIC/2 (30 November 1998), 35.

[16] Case C-28/04 *Tod's SpA and Tod's France SARL v Heyraud SA*. A question arose over shoes protected in Italy as designs. Could protection under the law of copyright be claimed in France? The ECJ said that: 'Article 12 EC, which lays down the general principle of non-discrimination on grounds of nationality, must be interpreted as meaning that the right of an author to claim in a Member State the copyright protection afforded by the law of that State may not be subject to a distinguishing criterion based on the country of origin of the work'. Thus, the rights enforceable by claimants in one country cannot be withheld from claimants from another.

23.14 For unregistered rights there has been a tendency to apply domestic UK law to two situations:

- where a wrong which takes effect or is likely to take effect abroad is threatened or committed in the UK;[17]
- where a wrong is threatened or committed abroad and the effect of the wrong or threatened wrong is felt in the UK.[18]

23.15 Pursuing a tort or delict in the English or Scottish courts where that tort occurred in a territory abroad has been an almost impossible task thanks to the double actionability rule.[19] This stipulated that the tort which occurred abroad should be classified as a tort in both the country where it occurred *and* in England or Scotland under English or Scots law. In effect, this meant that the laws of two different territories had to be applied to determine whether the infringement in question was unlawful. An exception to this rule was introduced in 1995 in *Red Sea Insurance v Bouygues*[20] which provided that where an issue between the parties had its most significant relationship with an occurrence in another country, then the law of that country should be applied to it. These rules nonetheless meant that the English and Scottish courts refused to entertain actions concerning foreign intellectual property rights.

23.16 Two useful and often cited examples from the UK can be given.

■ *Def Lepp Music v Stuart-Brown* [1986] RPC 273

In this case, the claimants, Deff Lepp, brought an action against a number of defendants for what they argued was an infringement of their copyright in the form of a tape recording that had been pirated, copied, and thereafter sold on under the control of entities located in Luxembourg and the Netherlands. Leave to serve the defendants outside the jurisdiction had been obtained. The defendants then applied to have the order set aside arguing that acts carried out by them outside the UK could not constitute infringements of UK copyright in the tape recording. Browne-Wilkinson V-C agreed saying: 'It is therefore clear that copyright under the English Act is strictly defined in terms of territory. The intangible right which is copyright is merely a right to do certain acts exclusively in the United Kingdom: only acts done in the United Kingdom constitute infringement, either direct or indirect of such right'.[21] Further, 'In my judgment, therefore, a successful action cannot be brought in England for alleged infringement of United Kingdom copyright by acts done outside the United Kingdom'.[22]

■ *Tyburn Productions Ltd v Conan Doyle* [1991] Ch 75, [1990] 1 All ER 909, [1990] 3 WLR 167, [1990] RPC 185

In the second and later case, the claimant was an English company which wished to distribute a television film featuring 'Sherlock Holmes' in the United States. Tyburn Productions were concerned that the defendant, who was the only surviving relative of Conan Doyle, author of the Sherlock Holmes books, would repeat previous assertions that she had the copyright in these characters. Tyburn thus applied to the English court for a declaration that the defendant had no rights under copyright, unfair competition, or trade marks of the United States to entitle her to prevent the distribution. Tyburn also sought an injunction preventing her from so doing. Having reviewed a number of previous authorities including *British South Africa Co v Companhia de Moçambique*,[23] *Boys v Chaplin*,[24] and *Def Lepp Music v Stuart-Brown*[25] Vinelott J concluded:

---

[17] *John Walker & Sons Ltd v Henry Ost & Co* [1970] 2 All ER 106.
[18] *Mecklermedia Corp v DC Congress GmbH* [1998] Ch 40, [1997] FSR 627. *Plentyoffish Media Inc v Plenty More LLP* [2011] EWHC 2568 (Ch). Merely having a business reputation in the UK was not sufficient to support a finding of goodwill in a trading name; actual customers were required.
[19] *Phillips v Eyre* (1870) LR 6 QB 1; *Boys v Chaplin* [1971] AC 356.
[20] [1995] AC 190.   [21] *Red Sea Insurance*, 275.   [22] *Red Sea Insurance*, 277.   [23] [1893] AC 602.
[24] [1969] 2 All ER 1085, [1971] AC 356, [1969] 3 WLR 322 (HL).   [25] [1986] RPC 273.

In my judgment therefore the question whether Lady Bromet is entitled to copyright under the law of the United States of America or of any of the states of the United States of America is not justiciable in the English courts.[26]

Points to note:

- Had an injunction been granted it would have had cross-border effect. In other words, it would (if recognised) have taken effect in another territory. In *Tyburn*, there was no evidence that if the validity of the rights claimed were justiciable in the English courts, the decision of the English courts would be treated as binding on any of the US states.

- The recognition by the English court that had it accepted jurisdiction, it would not be domestic law which applied to the question under consideration: 'which raises complex issues which may require a survey by the English courts with the assistance of experts of the laws of each of the states of the United States of America'.[27]

23.17   The choice of law rule in the UK law changed with the introduction of the Private International Law (Miscellaneous Provisions) Act 1995 which governed questions of choice of law in tort and delict. The Act abolished the double actionability rule[28] (except for defamation cases[29]) and provided that the applicable law is the law of the country in which the events constituting the tort or delict in question occur.[30] Where elements of those events occurred in different countries, the applicable law under the general rule was the law of the country in which the most significant element or elements of those events occurred.[31] For infringement actions the focus was on deciding which events constitute the tort, and applying the law of that country in the proceedings.[32]

Developments

23.18   In 2011 the Supreme Court ruled that the law had changed to the extent that there was now no bar to hearing a case for infringement of a foreign intellectual property in the English courts where there is no question in relation to validity of title. This was in a case concerning infringement of intellectual property rights furth of the EU, namely in the United States.

■ *Lucasfilm v Ainsworth* [2011] UKSC 39, [2012] 1 AC 208, [2011] 3 WLR 487

This case related to ownership of IP rights in the helmets worn by the Imperial Stormtroopers in the *Star Wars* films. Mr Ainsworth, who made these for Lucasfilm, subsequently sold some in the United States. He was sued in California where Lucasfilm won a judgment for US\$20 million. Lucasfilm then sued Mr Ainsworth in the UK for infringement of copyright in the helmets. While the Supreme Court found that no copyright existed in the helmets because they were not sculptures within the meaning of the Copyright, Designs and Patents Act 1988 (CDPA 1988), the question arose over the

---

[26] *Def Lepp.*   [27] *Def Lepp.*

[28] Private International Law (Miscellaneous Provisions) Act 1995, s 10.

[29] Private International Law (Miscellaneous Provisions) Act 1995, s 13.

[30] Private International Law (Miscellaneous Provisions) Act 1995, s 11(1).

[31] Private International Law (Miscellaneous Provisions) Act 1995, s 11(1).

[32] It was possible to displace the general rule under the Private International Law (Miscellaneous Provisions) Act 1995, s 12. It has, however, been argued that this section should not apply to infringements of intellectual property. If it did it 'would mean that there would be two IP rights competing in one country which appears contrary to the principle of national treatment upon which the IP Conventions and legislation are based ...' (WR Cornish in AV Dicey and JHC Morris, *Private International Law*, 4th Supplement (2004), 231; Supplementary Memorandum in HL Paper 36 (1995), 62 Annex by WR Cornish at 64).

justiciability of a claim in England for infringement of copyright in a foreign country (the United States). Overturning the Court of Appeal, the Supreme Court found that such a claim was justiciable as long as the court had *in personam* jurisdiction. In coming to this conclusion the court found that the *Moçambique* rule had been largely eroded, *Tyburn Productions* wrongly decided, and that there is no public policy rule that would militate against justiciability of copyright disputes in these circumstances.

The *Moçambique* rule will still be relevant where proceedings for infringement of rights in foreign land are 'principally concerned with a question of the title, or the right to possession, of that property'[33] and can thus apply to patents where questions of validity are involved—but not to copyright.[34]

The Supreme Court noted the EU framework: that the trend is towards enforcement of foreign intellectual property rights, remarking that Article 22(4) of the Brussels Regulation only assigns exclusive jurisdiction in cases concerned with registration or validity of rights.

On matters of choice of law, the Supreme Court noted that the rule in *Phillips v Eyre* was first eroded by case law in *Boys v Chaplin*[35] and in *Red Sea Insurance Co Ltd v Bouygues SA*[36] to the effect that the first limb of the rule in *Phillips v Eyre* could be displaced so that an issue might be governed by the law of the country which with respect to that issue had the most significant relationship with the occurrence and with the parties (applied in *Pearce v Ove Arup Partnership Ltd*[37]); and then abolished by statute in the Private International Law (Miscellaneous Provisions) Act 1995 which governs questions of choice of law in tort and delict. The Act abolished the double actionability rule[38] (except for defamation cases[39]) and provides that the applicable law is the law of the country in which the events constituting the tort or delict in question occur.[40] Where elements of those events occur in different countries, the applicable law under the general rule is to be the law of the country in which the most significant element or elements of those events occurred.[41]

23.19   The Supreme Court has thus confirmed that foreign IP rights may be litigated in the English courts except where matters of registration and validity are concerned—those questions will remain with the courts in the territory where the rights are granted. This, as will be seen from the previous discussion, is a complete change to the common law rules. It remains to be seen the extent to which litigants will avail themselves of the opportunities presented, decisions which depend on a host of commercial factors facing potential litigants at the point of deciding where to sue in any particular dispute.

 Exercise

Read *Lucasfilm v Ainsworth* [2011] UKSC 39, [2012] 1 AC 208, [2011] 3 WLR 487. Explain why you think the Supreme Court came to the conclusion that it did. Do you think that it is the right conclusion? (Compare the judgment of the Court of Appeal.[42]) What do you think the implications will be for IP litigation in the English courts?

---

[33] Para 105.   [34] Para 106.   [35] [1971] AC 356.   [36] [1995] 1 AC 190.   [37] [2000] Ch 403.
[38] Private International Law (Miscellaneous Provisions) Act 1995, s 10.
[39] Private International Law (Miscellaneous Provisions) Act 1995, s 13.
[40] Private International Law (Miscellaneous Provisions) Act 1995, s 11(1).
[41] Private International Law (Miscellaneous Provisions) Act 1995, s 11(1). Note that this has changed to the rules in Rome II for delicts/torts arising within the EU after January 2009.   [42] [2009] EWCA Civ 1328.

> ## Key point on historical development of the rules
>
> - English and Scottish courts were reluctant to hear disputes concerning infringement of an IP right in a foreign country in the absence of a specific direction to do so. The law has changed with the judgment by the Supreme Court in *Lucasfilm*, and English courts will now hear cases concerning the infringement of a foreign IP right where the matter does not concern matters of registration or validity.

Developments in the EU

23.20   As indicated previously, the law in the EU has now changed with the enactment of the Brussels Regulation concerning jurisdiction and enforcement of judgments and the Rome I and II Regulations concerning choice of law in contractual obligations and non-contractual liability respectively.

Jurisdiction

The Brussels Regulation

23.21   Matters governing jurisdiction and recognition of judgments in the EU fall under the Brussels Regulation which came into force on 1 March 2002.[43] This Regulation replaced the Brussels Convention.[44] However, as the majority of the cases that have been decided to date were concerned with facts that occurred and the law that was in force prior to the Brussels Regulation, the judgments generally refer to the older measure, as well as to the Lugano Convention which is a parallel Convention to the Brussels Convention but extending to EFTA states.[45] The wording of the Brussels Regulation is almost identical to that of the Brussels and Lugano Conventions, save for a few minor variations. In the following discussion, the wording of the Regulation will be referred to. Where there are important differences in the wording these will be highlighted.[46]

23.22   The original reason for harmonisation in this area was to ensure that judgments would be recognised and enforced throughout the EU. In order to facilitate this goal, the rules on jurisdiction were also aligned.

> ## Web link
>
> For information on and a link to the text of the Brussels Regulation see **http://europa.eu/ legislation_summaries/justice_freedom_security/judicial_cooperation_in_civil_matters/ l33054_en.htm.**
> Read in particular Articles 2, 5, 6, and 22.

---

[43] The Brussels Regulation on jurisdiction and the recognition and enforcement of judgments in civil and commercial matters Council Regulation (EC) No 44/2001 of 22 December 2000.

[44] The Brussels Convention on Jurisdiction and the Enforcement of Judgements in Civil and Commercial Matters 72/454, 1972 OJ L299, p 32.

[45] The Lugano Convention on Jurisdiction and Enforcement of Judgements in Civil and Commercial Matters Convention 88/592, 1988 OJ L319, p 9.

[46] The rules have been enacted in the UK in the Civil Jurisdiction and Judgments Act 1982 as amended to reflect the Brussels Regulation. The Civil Jurisdiction and Judgments Act 1982, Sch 1 contains rules for the UK; Sch 4 which only applies when Sch 1 rules

Scope of the Regulation

23.23   If the defendant is domiciled in the EU, and the dispute concerns a civil or commercial matter,[47] then the Brussels Regulation will apply to determine jurisdiction. The Regulation does not apply to defendants domiciled outwith the EU, where the domestic rules of the forum continue to apply.[48] The location of the claimant is irrelevant. Therefore the Brussels Regulation will apply if the claimant is outside the EU but the defendant within. No national rules providing for additional bases of jurisdiction can be applied against the defendant.

Article 2

23.24   The basic rule in the Regulation is that the defendant should be sued in the state in which he is domiciled.

> Subject to this Regulation, persons domiciled in a Member State shall, whatever their nationality, be sued in the courts of that Member State.[49]

Article 5(1)

23.25   Article 5(1)(a) of the Regulation provides that in matters relating to contracts, a person domiciled in a member states may be sued 'in the courts of the place of performance of the obligation in question'.

23.26   There has been some case law on the meaning of the place of the performance of the obligation in relation to intellectual property. *Falco v Weller-Lindhorst* concerned the issue of 'whether a contract under which the owner of an intellectual property right grants its contractual partner the right to use that right in return for remuneration is a contract for the provision of services'.[50] The European Court of Justice (ECJ) ruled that this type of contract is not a contract for services under the Regulation, and that reference must be made to the ECJ case law relating to Article 5(1) of the Brussels Convention in order to determine which court has jurisdiction. The Court explained that the concept of service implies the carrying out of a particular activity in return for remuneration. However, in the case of a licence to exploit intellectual property rights in particular member states, 'the owner of an intellectual property right does not perform any service in granting a right to use that property and undertakes merely to permit the licensee to exploit that right freely'.[51] In *JS Swan v Kall Kwik*,[52] a company based in Scotland sued an English franchising company for breach of a franchise agreement before a court in Scotland. Citing the principles laid down by the ECJ in relation to the Brussels Regulation, the Scottish court ruled that it had

---

do not; and Scottish rules on jurisdiction, Sch 8, which only applies when neither Sch 1 nor Sch 4 applies. On the applicability of cases decided under the Convention to interpretation of the Regulation, see Case C-616/10 *Solvay SA v Honeywell Fluorine Products Europe BV, Honeywell Belgium NV and Honeywell Europe NV*, para 42: insofar as Regulation No 44/2001 now replaces, in the relations between member states, the Brussels Convention, the interpretation provided by the Court in respect of the provisions of that Convention is also valid for those of that Regulation whenever the provisions of those Community instruments may be regarded as equivalent.

[47]   Civil or commercial matters include the enforcement of a judgment requiring the payment of a fine resulting from the infringement of an intellectual property right—in this case the infringement of a patent. Case C-406/09 *Realchemie Nederland BV v Bayer CropScience AG*.

[48]   Brussels Regulation, Art 4. For a case examining whether jurisdiction could be claimed in the English courts in relation to a matter concerning ownership of copyright in Australia, see *R Griggs Group Ltd and others v Evans and others* [2005] Ch 153, [2004] EWHC 1088 (Ch), [2005] 2 WLR 513.

[49]   Case C-281/02 *Owusu* established that where Art 2 confers personal jurisdiction in a court of a member state by reason of the defendant's domicile in that state, the court cannot refuse to hear the case because there is a more appropriate forum abroad.

[50]   Case C-533/07 [2009] ECDR 14.

[51]   *Falco*, para 31. B Ubertazzi, 'Licence agreements relating to IP rights and the EC Regulation on Jurisdiction' (2009) 40(8) IIC 912–939.

[52]   [2009] CSOH 99, 2009 WL 1949468.

no jurisdiction to hear the case because the franchise agreement did not explicitly state that the obligations should be performed exclusively in Scotland, and certain obligations that could be performed in Scotland were merely implied in their agreement. The court also said that following the ECJ's interpretations of the Regulation, Article 5 grounds for jurisdiction should be interpreted restrictively so as not to derogate the general rule that the defender must be sued in its domicile.

Article 5(3)

23.27   Under the title 'Special Jurisdiction', Article 5(3) of the Regulation provides that a defendant domiciled in a contracting state may be sued in another contracting state:

> in matters relating to tort, delict or quasi-delict, in the courts for the place where the harmful event occurred or may occur.

23.28   A number of issues have arisen in relation to this Article. In *Kalfelis v Schröder*[53] the ECJ said that the expression 'matters relating to tort, delict or quasi-delict' has an autonomous meaning; covering all actions which seek to hold a defendant liable and which are not related to a 'contract' within the meaning of Article 5(1) of the Regulation. As the measure is an exception to the general rule in Article 2 of the Regulation, a court only has jurisdiction over an action *insofar as* it is based on tort.[54]

23.29   As can be seen from the wording, Article 5(3) directs the claimant to the courts, or the place where the harmful event occurred or may occur. In *Shevill and others v Presse Alliance*[55] the ECJ held that action could be brought in the courts which gave rise to the harmful event, or in the court where the harm is felt. If the defendant was sued in the place giving rise to the damage (here the place of the publisher of the defamatory material) that forum is competent to award damages for the full harm.[56] If the defendant is sued in the courts of the place where the harm is felt (the place where the defamatory publication was received and where the claimant was injured) these courts are limited to only awarding damages for injury sustained within their own borders.[57]

23.30   *Shevill* concerned hard copy publication of defamatory material. Since then the Court of Justice has been asked to rule on questions of jurisdiction concerning the publication of defamatory material and the infringement of trade marks both involving the Internet. In both cases, recognising the challenges posed by potential multi-jurisdictional damage, the Court of Justice has modified the *Shevill* rule.

■ Joined Cases C-509/09 and C-161/10 *eDate Advertising GmbH v X* and *Martinez v MGN Ltd*

This case concerned alleged infringement of personality rights (defamation) by means of content placed on the Internet. The Court dealt with questions of jurisdiction under Article 5(3) of the Regulation, namely how the term 'the place where the harmful event occurred or may occur' is to be interpreted.

---

[53] [1988] ECR 5565.

[54] Referred to by the court in *Mackie T/A 197 Aerial Photography v Askew* 2009 SLT (Sh Ct) 146, para 31.

[55] [1995] 2 WLR 499.

[56] The wording of the equivalent provision in the Brussels Convention (and the wording in the Lugano Convention) referred to the place where the harmful event occurred. In *Verein fur Konsumenteninformation v Henkel* [2003] ILPr 1 ECJ (6th Chamber) the ECJ said that 'The courts for the place where the harmful event occurred are usually the most appropriate for deciding the case, in particular on the grounds of proximity and ease of taking evidence. These considerations are equally relevant whether the dispute concerns compensation for damage which has already occurred or relates to an action seeking to prevent the occurrence of damage' (para 46). The Brussels Regulation, Art 5(3) refers to 'the place where the harmful event occurred or may occur'. Thus, the question should not arise under the Regulation.

[57] The courts have allowed a plaintiff to sue for injury to feelings within a jurisdiction in a case of aggravated damages where the aggravating conduct occurred outside of the jurisdiction: *Clarke v Bain* [2008] EWHC 2636 (QB), 2008 WL 4963094.

The Court noted its ruling in *Shevill* but held that, given the ubiquity of information available on the Internet, the rule should be amended in such cases to allow a claim to be brought for all of the damage in the EU either in the place where the publisher is established or in the place where the claimant has the centre of her interests. She may also bring a case before the courts of each member state for the damage in that territory.

23.31　On the new limb of the rule, allowing the claimant to sue for all of the damage where she has the centre of her interests, the Court noted that these may be the courts where the person has their habitual residence, but need not be. Other factors could be relevant, such as the pursuit of a professional activity.[58]

■ Case C-523/10 *Wintersteiger AG v Products 4U Sondermaschinenbau GmbH*

Products4U registered 'Wintersteiger' as a keyword with google.de. Wintersteiger in Austria claimed infringement of their registered trade mark, Wintersteiger, in Austria. On the question of jurisdiction under Article 5(3) of the Brussels Regulation, the Court of Justice ruled that the place where the damage occurred is the state in which the trade mark is registered, and the place which gives rise to the damage is the member state of the place of establishment of the advertiser.

On this latter point, and in justifying the ruling that jurisdiction should be in the state where the advertiser is established, the Court reasoned that it should be the activities of the advertiser of the process that would end up with the display of the advertisement that should be regarded as the event which gave rise to the infringement, and not the display of the advertisement itself.[59] The Court noted also that it had already decided in the context of keyword advertising that it is the advertiser who chooses a keyword who uses it in the course of trade—and not the provider of the service.[60]

23.32　There are thus two sub-rules that the Court of Justice has developed to date that vary the general jurisdiction rule in *Shevill*.[61] While it could be argued that the development of extra grounds of jurisdiction leads to less, not greater predictability, the Court has recognised that the Internet raises specific problems in relation to the infringement of IP rights. Viewed in this light it could be argued that the rulings represent logical, and limited, advances to the grounds on which jurisdiction may be grounded.

 Question

What do you think of the rulings in *eDate* and *Wintersteiger*? What other circumstances involving the Internet and infringements of IP rights might necessitate further sub-rules being developed?

23.33　Further questions concerning infringement of an IP right in different member states have been referred to the CJEU.

In Case C-173/11 *Football Dataco Ltd, The Scottish Premier League Ltd, The Scottish Football League, PA Sport UK Ltd v Sportradar GmbH and Sportradar AG* the Court of Justice was asked where the infringing act for the purposes of the act of re-utilisation in the Database Directive took place. In the instant case did it take place in Austria, where Sportradar had its servers (the place of emission); or in England,

---

[58] Para 49.　　[59] Para 34.

[60] See also Cases C-236/08 to 238/08 *Google France and Google*, paras 52 and 58 for questions relating to where a trade mark is used for the purposes of infringement. Use in the course of trade is a key question in deciding whether there has been infringement of a trade mark.

[61] Note the approach taken by the English courts in *Mecklermedia Corp v DC Congress GmbH* [1998] Ch 40, [1997] FSR 627; *1-800 Flowers Inc v Phonenames Ltd* [2000] ETMR 369, [2000] FSR 697; *Euromarket Designs Inc v Peters* [2001] FSR 20 (Ch D) in deciding where jurisdiction should lie when a trade mark is accessible within a website. Questions of use are dealt with in paras 15.4ff and 16.33ff.

where the users received the sporting data (the place of reception)? The question was important because Sportradar was trying to avoid the jurisdiction of the English courts with regard to the content of the database and alleged infringement of the re-utilisation right under the Database Directive. At the time of writing, Advocate General Cruz Villalon has suggested that acts of infringement take place at both the place of emission and of reception of the data. If the Court of Justice follows this Opinion, jurisdiction can be claimed both in the courts of Austria and of England.

In Case C-170/12 *M. X v Kdg Mediatech AG* the French Cour de cassation has asked whether Article 5(3) means that in a case concerning online infringement of copyright a claimant can (1) bring an action in any member state where the site can be viewed—and claim damages for that jurisdiction; or (2) does the content of the website need to be targeted at the jurisdiction; and (3) does it make any difference if the infringing content is in a physical medium?

23.34   Other cases that have raised questions in relation to where acts infringing IP rights have taken place echo those asked in *Football Dataco*; and questions concerning when websites selling hard copy goods are targeted at specific jurisdictions, are discussed later (see para 23.59). These are relevant for both matters of jurisdiction and of the law to be applied to a dispute.

 Question

How do you think the Court of Justice will respond to the questions posed in Case C-170/12 *M. X v Kdg Mediatech AG*? How should the Court of Justice respond?

23.35   The trend in the Court of Justice seems to be to increase the bases of jurisdiction in IP cases, giving claimants a choice of where to bring an action for all of the damage. There are, however, it would seem limitations where jurisdiction is based on a tort with economic consequences and whether a claimant would be enabled to sue in a home forum for consequential damage.

23.36   Some guidance on what might amount to consequential damage was given in *Marinari v Lloyds Bank plc*[62] where an Italian domiciled claimant was arrested and had promissory notes sequestrated at the instance of the Manchester Branch of Lloyds Bank. The claimant sued in Italy for the exchange value of the notes and the damage to his reputation which he alleged he had suffered in Italy. The question for the ECJ was: 'In applying the jurisdiction rule laid down in Article 5(3) of the Brussels Convention … is the expression "place where the harmful event occurred" to be taken to mean only the place in which physical harm was caused to persons or things, or also the place in which the damage to the plaintiff's assets occurred?' The ECJ held that the Article should not be construed so extensively 'as to encompass any place where the adverse consequences of an event that has already caused actual damage elsewhere can be felt'. Further it could not be construed 'as including the place where, as in the present case, the victim claims to have suffered financial damage consequential on initial damage arising and suffered by him in another contracting state'. Thus the actual answer to the question was that Article 5(3) should be interpreted 'as *not* referring to the place where the victim claims to have suffered financial loss consequential on initial damage arising and suffered by him in another contracting state' (emphasis added).[63] Thus, a claimant is limited in the number of jurisdictions in which she can seek to bring an action based on the occurrence of the harmful event. For intellectual property cases this may mean that a claimant could not

---

[62] [1996] QB 217.

[63] In an action arising furth of the countries party to the Brussels Regulation the High Court has ruled that it was wrong to strike out libel actions filed by a resident of England against publishers based in the United States as an abuse of process on the ground that the extent of publication within England was very small: *Mardas v New York Times* [2008] EWHC 3135 (QB), [2009] EMLR 8.

claim jurisdiction on the grounds of, say, loss of profits flowing from an infringement of copyright or the database right in a different territory.[64]

Article 6(1)

23.37   In Article 6(1), also under the title 'Special Jurisdiction', the Regulation provides that:

> A person domiciled in a Contracting State may also be sued: (1) where he is one of a number of defendants, in the courts for the place where any one of them is domiciled, provided that the claims are so closely connected that it is expedient to hear and determine them together to avoid the risk of irreconcilable judgments resulting from separate proceedings.

This Article thus permits joint defendants to be sued in one go at the place where one of them is domiciled.[65] However, for this Article to be relevant, there has to be a sufficient connection between the defendants because to do otherwise might mean that irreconcilable judgments were handed down. As emphasised by the ECJ in *Kalfelis v Schröder*,[66] there must 'exist between the various actions brought by the same plaintiff against different defendants a connection of such a kind that it is expedient to determine the actions together in order to avoid the risk of irreconcilable judgments resulting from separate proceedings'.[67]

23.38   It should also be noted that the Article brings further complexity into questions of jurisdiction in that it gives scope for forum shopping in intellectual property cases. This was recognised in *Research in Motion UK Ltd v Visto Corporation*:[68]

> Intellectual property also adds three further complications. Firstly there is a range of potential defendants extending from the source of the allegedly infringing goods (manufacturer or importer) right down to the ultimate users. Each will generally infringe and the right holder can elect whom to sue. One crude way to achieve forum selection is to sue a consumer or dealer domiciled in the country of the IP holder's choice (jurisdiction conferred by Art. 2.1) and then to join in his supplier—the ultimate EU manufacturer or importer into the EU if the product comes from outside. Jurisdiction for this is conferred by Art. 6. Thus there is considerable scope for forum shopping—the very thing the scheme of the Regulation is basically intended to avoid.[69]

 Exercise

'Formally the appeal [in Research in Motion] is now only about costs, but it involves much more than that. The case is yet another illustrating the unsatisfactory state of the current arrangements for deciding European wide patent disputes. Too often one finds parties litigating as much about where and when disputes should be heard and decided as about the real underlying dispute'.[70] Critically comment on this statement.

---

[64]   See also Case C-220/88 *Dumez France v Hessische Landesbank* [1990] ECR I-49; *Mazur Media Ltd and another v Mazur Media GmbH* [2004] EWHC 1566 (Ch), [2005] 1 Lloyd's Rep 41, [2005] 1 BCLC 305, [2004] BPIR 1253. A claimant could not rely on Art 5(3) where the alleged loss flowed from an assignation of copyright but not the title to master recordings which could have been exploited in England among other countries. The damage in England was found to be indirect: 'I consider that for the purposes of Art 5(3) damage flowing from inability to exploit the copyright as a result of not having physical possession of the masters would be, for the purposes of Art 5(3), the kind of financial loss which the decision in *Marinari v Lloyds Bank plc (Zubadi Trading Co intervening)* [1995] ECR I-2719 rules out' (para 52). See also *Crucial Music Corp (formerly Onemusic Corp) v Klondyke Management AG (formerly Point Classics AG)* [2008] Bus LR 327.
[65]   Case C-98/06 *Freeport* [2007] ECR I-8319. The special rule in Art 6(1), because it derogates from the principle stated in Art 2 of Regulation No 44/2001 that jurisdiction be based on the defendant's domicile, must be strictly interpreted and cannot be given an interpretation going beyond the cases expressly envisaged by that Regulation (para 35).
[66]   [1988] ECR 5565.   [67]   *Kalfelis*, 5584.   [68]   *Research in Motion UK Ltd v Visto Corporation* [2008] EWCA Civ 153.
[69]   *Research in Motion*, para 6.   [70]   [2008] EWCA Civ 153, para 3.

23.39   Dutch courts have been quite active in joining defendants under Article 6(1). Dutch courts have applied Article 6(1) to join not only a Dutch company, but also the foreign parent company and affiliated companies in the same proceedings for infringement of the Dutch patent and patents granted in other territories, each of which had been granted under the same European Patent Convention (EPC) application.[71]

23.40   However, there are potential injustices arising from this practice. If defendants are joined under Article 6(1) in cases where they merely infringe the same European patent by selling the same product, not only does the claimant have opportunities for forum shopping leaving the defendant uncertain as to which court they may be required to appear before, but also the potential defendants may not know of each other's activities, and thus their risk of being joined under Article 6(1).

23.41   Perhaps aware of these concerns, the Dutch courts took a step back from what may have seemed to some as expansive jurisdiction under this Article. The Dutch Court of Appeal ruled in 1998 that Article 6(1) does not permit a Dutch infringer (for infringement of the Dutch patent) and a foreign infringer (for the infringement of the foreign patents belonging to the European bundle) to be sued as joint defendants. One exception, however, was accepted. Foreign defendants could be joined with Dutch defendants under Article 6(1) if the foreign defendants belong to the same group of companies and the European headquarters of that group of companies is located on the territory of the court.[72] This approach has been named the *'spider in the web'* theory; the defendants can be sued as joint defendants if they form a web among themselves. The action has to be brought before a court located in the centre of the web.[73]

23.42   The ECJ has now ruled on this question in the following case.

■ Case C-539/03 *Roche Nederland BV v Frederick Primus, Milton Goldenberg*

Primus brought an action in the Netherlands against Roche Nederland BV and eight other companies in the Roche group established in other countries. Primus claimed that the companies had infringed their European patent by placing on the market goods in the countries where they were established. The Roche group companies which were not established in the Netherlands contested the jurisdiction of the Dutch court arguing that there was no infringement of the patent in question and that it was invalid. The following questions were referred to the ECJ:

(1) Is there a connection, as required for the application of Article 6(1) of the Brussels Convention, between a patent infringement action brought by a holder of a European patent against a defendant having its registered office in the State of the court in which the proceedings are brought, on the one hand, and against various defendants having their registered offices in Contracting States other than that of the State of the court in which the proceedings are brought, on the other hand, who, according to the patent holder, are infringing that patent in one or more other Contracting States?

(2) If the answer to Question 1 is not or not unreservedly in the affirmative, in what circumstances is such a connection deemed to exist, and is it relevant in this context whether, for example,

   – the defendants form part of one and the same group of companies?
   – the defendants are acting together on the basis of a common policy, and if so is the place from which that policy originates relevant?
   – the alleged infringing acts of the various defendants are the same or virtually the same?

---

[71] Op cit, note Hoge Raad 24 november 1989, *Focus Veilin v Lincoln Electric*, p 16.

[72] *Expandable Grafts Partnership v Boston Scientific et al*, Court of Appeal The Hague, 23 April 1998 [1998] EIPR N-132.

[73] *Boston Scientific BV and others v Cordis Corporation* [2000] ENPR 87 Hof (Den Haag): 'In the view of the Court ... only the court of the domicile of the key defendant has jurisdiction ... [it] thus avoids the result that several fora have jurisdiction and this reduces the possibilities of forum shopping' (at 95). For an article discussing the spider in the web theory and related cases, see P De Jong, 'The Belgian torpedo: from self propelled armament to jaded sandwich' (2005) 27(2) *EIPR* 75–81. Note also that the English High

The ECJ said that the national court was asking whether Article 6(1) of the Brussels Convention must be interpreted as meaning that it is to apply to European patent infringement proceedings involving a number of companies established in various contracting states in respect of acts committed in one or more of those states and, in particular, where those companies, which belong to the same group, have acted in an identical or similar manner in accordance with a common policy elaborated by one of them.[74]

The ECJ pointed to the decision *Kalfelis*[75] where it had been held that for Article 6(1) of the Brussels Convention to apply there must exist, between the various actions brought by the same plaintiff against different defendants, 'a connection of such a kind that it is expedient to determine the actions together in order to avoid the risk of irreconcilable judgments resulting from separate proceedings'.

The ECJ noted the EPC which lays down common rules on the grant of European patents which are adjudicated according to national laws.[76] From this the court concluded that any diverging decisions could not, therefore, be treated as contradictory.[77]

> In those circumstances, even if the broadest interpretation of 'irreconcilable' judgments, in the sense of contradictory, were accepted as the criterion for the existence of the connection required for the application of Article 6(1) of the Brussels Convention, it is clear that such a connection could not be established between actions for infringement of the same European patent where each action was brought against a company established in a different Contracting State in respect of acts which it had committed in that State.[78]

Even where the defendant companies had acted in an identical or similar manner in accordance with a common policy thus the factual situation may be the same, the legal situation would not and therefore there would be no risk of contradictory decisions.[79] In other words, as there was no risk of irreconcilable judgments, so the defendants could not be joined. The decision has been the subject of criticism because of the fragmentation of litigation that can result from the ruling.[80]

23.43 The Court of Justice has had an opportunity to develop and refine its jurisprudence on Article 6(1) in another case concerning patents.

■ Case C-616/10 *Solvay SA v Honeywell Fluorine Products Europe BV, Honeywell Belgium NV and Honeywell Europe NV*

In this case companies based in different member states were accused of infringing European patents in different member states as well as in the same member state. The Court of Justice reaffirmed its ruling in *Roche* stating that the same legal bases cannot be inferred where infringement proceedings are brought in different courts in different member states in relation to a European patent granted in each state and the case is brought against defendants domiciled in those states in respect of acts committed in that territory. A European patent is governed by the national law of each contracting state for which it has been granted as per the Munich Convention.

However, where defendants are separately accused of committing the same infringement with respect to the same product and the infringements are committed in the same member state so that they affect

---

Court has issued a Community-wide injunction in respect of CTMs. See *Kabushiki Kaisha Sony Computer Entertainment and another v Electricbirdland Ltd* 2005 WL 1942171, [2005] EWHC 2296 (Ch). See now *Wintersteiger*, para 23.31.

[74] *Boston Scientific*, para 18.   [75] Case 189/87 *Kalfelis* [1988] ECR 5565.   [76] Case C-539/03, paras 29 and 30.
[77] *Roche Nederland*, para 32.   [78] *Roche Nederland*, para 33.   [79] *Roche Nederland*, para 35.
[80] A number of authors have been critical of the position. The European Max-Planck Group on Conflict of Laws in Intellectual Property (CLIP), *Intellectual Property and the Reform of Private International Law: Sparks from a Difficult Relationship*, IPRax (2007), No 4, p 284; H Muir Watt, 'Article 6' in U Magnus and P Mankowski (eds), *Brussels I Regulation* (2nd edn, 2012), 313; M Noorgård, 'A spider without a web? Multiple defendants in IP litigation' in S Leible and A Ohly (eds), *Intellectual Property and Private International Law* (2009), 211; C Gonzalez Beilfuss, 'Is there any web for the spider? Jurisdiction over co-defendants after *Roche Nederland*' in A Nuyts (ed), *International Litigation in Intellectual Property and Information Technology* (2008), 79.

the same national part of the European patent, then it is for the national court to determine if there is a risk of irreconcilable judgments if those claims are determined separately. As explained by the Advocate General: 'The two courts would each have to examine the alleged infringements in the light of the different national legislation governing the various "national parts of the European patent" alleged to have been infringed by applying the lex loci protectionis principle'.[81] They would, for instance, be called upon to assess according to the same Finnish law the infringement of the Finnish part of the European patent by the three defendants in the main proceedings by the marketing of an identical infringing product in Finland.'[82]

So here the Court of Justice has developed a more nuanced approach with the result that there are going to be circumstances in which defendants can be joined under Article 6(1): where the infringement is the same infringement of the same patent and the infringement occurs in the same member state.

 Question

Are there any intellectual property rights for which it might be appropriate to join defendants under Article 6(1)? Consider, for example, *Kabushiki Kaisha Sony Computer Entertainment and another v Electricbirdland Ltd* 2005 WL 1942171, [2005] EWHC 2296 (Ch).

23.44   On the question of whether it may be appropriate to join defendants in other IP cases, the ECJ has considered this question in a copyright case.

■ **Case C-145/10 *Eva-Maria Painer v Standard Verlags GmbH and others***

This case concerned photographs taken by a freelance photographer, Natascha Kampusch, of Eva-Maria who was abducted in Austria in 1998 and escaped in 2006. When Eva-Maria escaped, the photographs, some of which were altered to show her looking older, were reproduced by various newspapers in Austria and Germany. On matters of jurisdiction, the question arose as to whether all defendants could be joined in Austria under Article 6(1) of the Brussels Regulation where the infringements of copyright were substantially similar but were brought on national legal grounds which varied according the member state concerned.

The ECJ noted that it was not apparent from the wording of Article 6(1) that the conditions for its application include a requirement that the actions brought against different defendants should have identical legal bases (para 76). For judgments to be regarded as irreconcilable within the meaning of Article 6(1), a divergence must arise in the same situation of fact and law (para 79). In assessing whether there is a connection between different claims—in other words a risk of irreconcilable judgments if those claims were determined separately—the identical legal bases of the actions brought is only one relevant factor among others but not an indispensable requirement for the application of the Article (para 80). It is for the referring court to assess whether there is a connection between the claims: in other words, whether there is a risk of irreconcilable judgments if those claims were determined separately.

23.45   The ECJ seemed keen that the referring court consider the legal bases to be sufficiently similar to found jurisdiction where the national laws 'as in the main proceedings ... on which the actions against the various defendants are based are ... substantially identical (para 82).[83] In addition, in assessing whether

---

[81] Para 25.   [82] Para 31.   [83] Para 82.

there is a connection between the parts of the claims it was relevant to consider whether the defendants did or did not act independently (para 83).[84]

Cross-border injunctions

23.46   As will have become apparent from the previous discussion, one of the problems with Article 6(1) is that if the claimant is successful, it can result in the court granting a cross-border injunction. In other words, an injunction issued by a court in one territory that has effect in another as regards the patent infringement. English courts have had difficulty with this concept[85] although now, following the Court of Justice rulings, there will be times, albeit limited, that such injunctions will be issued as a result of jurisdiction being based on Article 6(1). The matter of cross-border injunctions also arises in relation to the unitary EU IP rights—notably the Community trade mark (CTM) and the Community design right. In relation to the CTM, member states are to designate certain national courts as Community courts for the purposes of hearing infringements that arise concerning a CTM. The cross-border effect of a ruling issued by the French court was raised before the Court of Justice:

■ **Case C-235/09 *DHL Express France v Chronopost SA***

The case concerned the interpretation of the Community Trade Mark Regulation (CTMR) as amended[86] and raised the question as to whether an injunction granted by a Community trade mark court in respect of a Community trade mark had effect throughout the territory of the EU. Chronopost, a courier company, owned a French and CTM registration for 'Webshipping'. DHL used various permutations of the words 'Web Shipping' for an Internet-based mail management service. Chronopost sued DHL in France. The French Cour de cassation asked the ECJ a number of questions including whether 'Article 98 CTMR be interpreted as meaning that the prohibition issued by a CTM Court has effect as a matter of law throughout the entire area of the [European Union]?' The ECJ responded by ruling that 'Article 98(1) CTMR must be interpreted as meaning that the scope of the prohibition against further infringement or threatened infringement of a CTM, issued by a CTM Court whose jurisdiction is based on Articles 93(1) to (4) and 94(1) of that regulation, extends, as a rule, to the entire area of the EU.'

23.47   Given that a CTM is designed to have effect throughout the entire area of the EU, this would seem a relatively straightforward decision. However, the reference by the ECJ to 'as a rule' in its judgment has caused further questions to arise in relation to when there might be an exception to the rule. In the course of judgment, the ECJ referred to the case brought by the claimant and whether this might have been limited to a particular territory; to the functions of a trade mark and the need for one or more of the functions to be affected by the activities of the defendant for liability for infringement to arise, an example of which might be linguistic differences between member states.[87] In both cases it would seem that an injunction might be limited to certain territories of the EU. The difficulty lies in the need to look into the laws of each territory to determine if an infringement has occurred; a procedure that would put the enforcement of a CTM beyond all but the deepest pockets.[88]

---

[84] For cases in the English courts, see *Alfa Laval Tumba AB v Separator Spares International Ltd* [2012] EWHC 1155 (Ch); *Pearce v Ove Arup* [2000] Ch 403, [2000] 3 WLR 332, [1999] 1 All ER 769, [1999] FSR 525; IBS Technologies (PVT) Ltd v APM Technologies SA and another [2003] All ER (D) 105: on Art 5(3) of the Lugano Convention.

[85] The English courts have had some difficulty with the practice of granting of cross-border injunctions. In the High Court Aldous J said that 'it would not be right for this Court to grant an injunction which had effect outside the United Kingdom' [1995] FSR 325 at 338.

[86] Council Regulation 40/94; see Chapter 14.   [87] Case C-235/09, para 48.

[88] Note *AS Watson (Health and Beauty Continental Europe) BV and others v The Boots Company plc and others* [2011] EWPCC 26 in which the claimants filed an action for infringement of a CTM against the defendants. The case was remitted from the Patents Court to the High Court because of the complexity that would arise in determining infringement of a CTM in 14 of the member states of the EU.

Question

Read Case C-235/09 *DHL Express France v Chronopost SA*. What do you consider might be some of the difficulties that arise with the judgment? How should the interests of the claimant and defendant be balanced against the need to ensure that the rights conferred by a CTM do not extend beyond their proper boundaries?

Article 22(4) (Article 16(4) of the Brussels Convention)

23.48   In Article 22(4) under the heading 'Exclusive jurisdiction' the Regulation provides:

> The following courts shall have exclusive jurisdiction regardless of domicile:
>
> … 4. in proceedings concerned with the registration or validity of patents, trade marks, designs, or other similar rights required to be deposited or registered, the courts of the Member State in which the deposit or registration has been applied for, has taken place or is under the terms of a Community instrument or an international convention deemed to have taken place.

23.49   Article 22(4) reflects the understanding that the *validity* of registered intellectual property rights can only be challenged in the state for which the right is registered. It is generally accepted that a state has autonomy over the grant of a property right, and only the state in which the property right exists should have the competence to adjudicate on its validity. Any judgment rendered by a court outwith that territory will have both private law implications in that it will affect the individual litigants and the property of one of those litigants, and public interest ramifications which have, in a patent action, been described thus:

> Although patent actions appear on their face to be disputes between two parties, in reality they also concern the public. A finding of infringement is a finding that a monopoly granted by the state is to be enforced. The result is invariably that the public have to pay higher prices than if the monopoly did not exist. If that be the proper result, then that result should, I believe, come about from a decision of a court situated in the state where the public have to pay the higher prices.[89]

23.50   The exclusive jurisdiction granted to national courts in cases concerning the registration and validity of a registered right has prompted some litigants to engage in forum shopping exercises. If a defendant is faced with infringement proceedings one tactic may be to call into question the validity of the right. Thus, jurisdictional competence is shifted to the state where the right has been registered.

23.51   This is illustrated by the case of *Coin Controls v Suzo International*[90] where the English Patent Court was requested to enforce British, German, and Spanish patents that had all originated from the same European Patent, against defendants domiciled in England, Germany, and Spain. Jurisdiction had been based on Article 6(1) of the Brussels Convention. The court struck out the pleadings insofar as they applied to the foreign patents. In so doing, the court said that if the conditions of Article 6(1) applied, the court had jurisdiction to deal with infringement of the German and Spanish patents. However, once the validity of the patents had been challenged, the provisions of Article 16(4) of the Brussels Convention (now Art 22(4) of the Brussels Regulation) came into play.

> The court cannot decline jurisdiction on the basis of mere suspicions as to what defence may be run. But once the defendant raises validity the court must hand the proceedings over to the courts having exclusive jurisdiction

---

[89] *Plastus Kreativ AB v Minnesota Mining and Manufacturing Co* [1995] RPC 438 at 447.   [90] [1997] 3 All ER 45.

over that issue ... infringement and validity of an intellectual property right ... are so closely interrelated that they should be treated for jurisdictional purposes as one and the same issue.[91]

The problem with this rule is that a defendant can easily block any infringement action based on foreign patent by raising a defence of invalidity.[92]

23.52   The matter has now been considered by the ECJ in the following case.

■ Case C-4/03 *Gat, Gesellschaft für Antriobstechnik mbH & Co KG v Luk Lamellen und Kupplungsbau Beteiligungs KG*

The case concerned patents in a number of countries including France for parts of motor vehicles. The case was brought by the applicant before a German court in Dusseldorf seeking a declaration that the defendant did not have any claims arising from the French patents. It was claimed that the French patents were invalid due to a prior sale of the allegedly infringing parts. On appeal the question was raised as to whether the German courts had jurisdiction on the basis of Article 16(4) (now Art 22(4) of the Regulation). Proceedings were stayed to refer a question to the ECJ as to whether Article 16(4) was to be interpreted as meaning that the exclusive jurisdiction conferred by that provision only applies if proceedings are brought to declare a patent invalid, or whether the Article was also relevant where a plea is made that a patent is invalid but in the course of infringement proceedings.[93]

The ECJ, in a relatively short judgment, said the Article must be construed in accordance with the objective it pursues: that is, that the rules seek to ensure that jurisdiction rests with courts closely linked to the proceedings in fact and law.[94] Article 16(4) means that the exclusive jurisdiction rule it lays down concerns all proceedings 'whatever the form of proceedings in which the issue of a patent's validity is raised, be it by way of an action or a plea in objection, at the time the case is brought or at a later stage in the proceedings'.[95] So even if validity is an incidental issue, exclusive jurisdiction is conferred on the courts of the place where the patent is registered. As with *Roche*, the effect is that litigation is fragmented which could result in claimants needing to bring cases in a number of different jurisdictions. The temptation for defendants will be to raise counterclaims that validity is an issue in order to split cases.

23.53   The Court of Justice has developed a refinement of the rule where provisional measures are in issue.

■ Case C-616/10 *Solvay SA v Honeywell Fluorine Products Europe BV, Honeywell Belgium NV and Honeywell Europe NV*

The ECJ ruled that Article 22(4) does not affect the application of Article 31 of the Regulation. Article 31 provides that application may be made to the courts of a member state for such provisional, including protective, measures as may be available under the law of that state, even if, under this Regulation, the courts of another member state have jurisdiction as to the substance of the matter

The Court considered that there is no risk of conflicting decisions (the objective of Art 22(4) is to avoid these) where the provisional decision taken by a court before which the interim proceedings have been

---

[91] *Coin Controls*, 60–61.
[92] See *Fort Dodge v Akzo* [1998] FSR 222 which was referred to the ECJ but settled prior to being heard.
[93] OJ C 55, 08.03.2003, p 14. GAT Judgments Convention/Enforcement of judgments.
[94] *Gat v Luk*, para 21.
[95] *Gat v Luk*, para 25. See also *Research in Motion UK Ltd v Visto Corporation* [2008] EWCA Civ 153.

brought will not prejudice the decision to be taken by the court having jurisdiction over the substance under Article 22(4).

Courts will thus be able to grant cross-border injunctions in cases concerning provisional measures.[96]

Review of Brussels Regulation

23.54   There have been moves to review the Brussels Regulation. The European Commission released a Green Paper on the Review of Council Regulation (EC) No 44/2001.[97] This was supplemented by the Commission's Report on the application of Council Regulation (EC) No 44/2001 on jurisdiction and the recognition and enforcement of judgments in civil and commercial matters.[98] Generally the reports find that the working of the Regulation is highly satisfactory and has facilitated cross-border litigation. Some suggestions are made for reform including the operation of the Regulation in a broader international context and its operation in connection with intellectual property cases in particular.

Key points on the Brussels Regulation

- The Regulation applies where the dispute concerns a civil or commercial matter
- Jurisdiction is in the state:
  - where the defendant is domiciled
  - where the harmful event occurred
  - where the defendant is one of a number of defendants
- Where the question concerns the registration or validity of the right then the courts of the place where registration takes place have exclusive jurisdiction

---

Choice of law for non-contractual obligations: Rome II Regulation

23.55   As noted previously, the double actionability rule in England and Scotland made deciding a case based on infringement of a foreign IP right in domestic courts almost impossible. This rule was changed in the Law Reform (Miscellaneous Provisions) Act 1995 which in turn was replaced by Regulation (EC) No 864/2007 of the European Parliament and of the Council of 11 July 2007 on the law applicable to non-contractual obligations, known as Rome II, and which came into effect from 11 January 2009. The common law rules (as now interpreted by the Supreme Court) will apply where the facts arise prior to the coming into force of the 1995 Act which itself will be superseded by Rome II for facts arising after 11 January 2009. Rome II deals with all torts/delicts arising in the EU regardless of whether any of the parties is connected with a member state[99] except where specifically excluded. For these purposes, the exclusions include non-contractual obligations arising out of violations of privacy and rights relating to personality, including defamation.[100]

---

[96] For an English court decision on whether there should be a stay of proceedings when questions of irreconcilable judgements was raised in a trade mark case, see *Kitfix Swallow Group Ltd v Great Gizmos Ltd* [2007] EWHC 2668 (Ch).

[97] Commission (EC), 'Green Paper on the Review of the Council Regulation (EC) No 44 on jurisdiction and the recognition and enforcement of judgments in civil and commercial matters', COM(2009) 175 final, 21 April 2009. See the references in fn 80.

[98] COM(2009) 174, 21 April 2009.   [99] Art 3.

[100] Art 2(g). The Committee on Legal Affairs has proposed an amendment to Rome II that would include a choice of law clause for infringements of personality rights (defamation) on the internet. Draft Report with recommendations to the Commission on the

Recital 26 of Rome II states:

> Regarding infringements of intellectual property rights, the universally acknowledged principle of the lex loci protectionis should be preserved. For the purposes of this Regulation, the term 'intellectual property rights' should be interpreted as meaning, for instance, copyright, related rights, the sui generis right for the protection of databases and industrial property rights.

Article 6 deals with unfair competition[101] and Article 8 with intellectual property rights.

Article 6 provides (where relevant):

> 1. The law applicable to a non-contractual obligation arising out of an act of unfair competition shall be the law of the country where competitive relations or the collective interests of consumers are, or are likely to be, affected.
>
> 2. Where an act of unfair competition affects exclusively the interests of a specific competitor, Article 4 shall apply.
>
> 3. The law applicable under this Article may not be derogated from by an agreement pursuant to Article 14.

Article 4 (the general provision) provides:

> 1. Unless otherwise provided for in this Regulation, the law applicable to a non-contractual obligation arising out of a tort/delict shall be the law of the country in which the damage occurs irrespective of the country in which the event giving rise to the damage occurred and irrespective of the country or countries in which the indirect consequences of that event occur.
>
> 2. However, where the person claimed to be liable and the person sustaining damage both have their habitual residence in the same country at the time when the damage occurs, the law of that country shall apply.
>
> 3. Where it is clear from all the circumstances of the case that the tort/delict is manifestly more closely connected with a country other than that indicated in paragraphs 1 or 2, the law of that other country shall apply. A manifestly closer connection with another country might be based in particular on a preexisting relationship between the parties, such as a contract, that is closely connected with the tort/delict in question.

Article 8 on infringement of intellectual property rights provides:

> 1. The law applicable to a non-contractual obligation arising from an infringement of an intellectual property right shall be the law of the country for which protection is claimed.
>
> 2. In the case of a non-contractual obligation arising from an infringement of a unitary Community intellectual property right, the law applicable shall, for any question that is not governed by the relevant Community instrument, be the law of the country in which the act of infringement was committed.
>
> 3. The law applicable under this Article may not be derogated from by an agreement pursuant to Article 14.

23.56   While it seems that this measure may codify the current law, there will be many questions that arise over interpretation of phrases such as the country 'for which protection is claimed' and 'the country in which the infringement is committed', among others. At the time of writing, the Supreme Court In *Lucasfilm* had noted the intent behind the Regulation—that infringements of intellectual property rights occurring abroad can be litigated at home; the High Court had ruled that a breach of confidential information did not amount to an infringement of an intellectual property right within the meaning of Article 8;[102]

---

amendment of Regulation (EC) No 864/2007 on the law applicable to non-contractual obligations (Rome II) (2009/2170(INI)), Committee on Legal Affairs Rapporteur: Diana Wallis (Initiative—Rule 42 of the Rules of Procedure).

[101] For cogent criticism of these provisions as they apply to unfair competition, see C Wadlow, *The Law of Unfair Competition: Passing Off by Misrepresentation* (2011), paras 10.076 et seq.

[102] *Force India Formula One Team Ltd v 1 Malaysia Racing Team and others* [2012] EWHC 616 (Ch).

and the Advocate General had referred to Rome II in *Criminal proceedings against Titus Donner*[103] opining that Article 8(3) meant that the law to be applied was the *lex loci protectionis* and it was not open to the parties to change that by contract.

23.57   Prior to the coming into force of Rome II, a number of cases were heard which considered matters including the conditions that give rise to the infringement of the IP right and where that takes place—facts that will be relevant to determine the law to be applied.

23.58   The case of *Football Dataco Ltd v Sportradar GmbH*[104] has been discussed previously (para 23.33). It will be recalled that the ECJ had been asked to determine where the infringing act of re-utilisation of the contents of a database took place. Here both the place of emission and the place of reception were found to infringe the right. So the laws of these two places will be applied within the jurisdiction in which each occurred.

23.59   Other cases heard by the ECJ have dealt with hard copy works and considered whether acts that take place outside the territory where rights are protected, but which are aimed at a particular territory, fell within the provisions of the law in that 'receiving' territory.[105] In relation to trade marks, it was argued in *L'Oreal*[106] that the offer of goods for sale originating outwith the EEA but accessible within the territory via an online marketplace amounted to an infringement of its CTMs. The ECJ held that it was for the national court to determine whether such an offer for sale or advertisement was targeted at consumers within the EU. Where the goods were targeted at consumers within a particular territory the trade mark owner could enjoin that activity within the relevant provisions of the trade mark Directive or Regulation. In a case concerning copyright, *Stichting de Thuiskopie*,[107] the question was whether compensation due for private copying could be avoided when selling blank media in Germany to the Netherlands under an arrangement where it was the individual who imported the goods and the national legislation provided for the payment of compensation by the manufacturer or importer. The ECJ held that it was for the private individual who made the reproductions to pay the compensation in these circumstances. In addition, and where it seemed unlikely to be possible to obtain fair compensation from the user, then national law had to be interpreted in such a way as to ensure compensation was obtained from the person acting on a commercial basis irrespective of the fact that the commercial operator was based in a different member state. This would seem to open the possibility for cross-border actions against commercial entities based in other member states—with all the attendant challenges of identification of those liable. In *Criminal proceedings against Titus Donner*[108] the ECJ was called on to rule on the place of distribution to the public in relation to a sale of works protected by copyright—which in the instant case was the place where delivery takes place.

23.60   On a different but related note, a question arose concerning the interaction between laws of succession and the artists' resale right.

■ Case C-518/08 *Fundación Gala-Salvador Dalí, Visual Entidad de Gestión de Artistas Plásticos (VEGAP) v Société des auteurs dans les arts graphiques et plastiques (ADAGP)*

Salvador Dalí died on 23 January 1989 in Spain. He left five heirs. In his will made in 1982 he had appointed the Spanish state as sole legatee of his intellectual property rights which are administered by the Fundación Gala-Salvador Dalí, a foundation established by Dali under Spanish law in 1983.

---

[103] Case C5/11.   [104] Case C-173/11.
[105] See the UK *Mecklermedia Corp v DC Congress GmbH* [1998] Ch 40, [1997] FSR 627, note 18.
[106] Case C-324/09 *L'Oreal and others v eBay and others*.
[107] C-462/09. See also Case C-467/08 *Padawan*.   [108] Case C-5/11.

Article L. 123-7 of the French Intellectual Property Code, which was not amended by the transposition of Directive 2001/84: provides: 'After the death of the author, the resale right referred to in Article L. 122-8 shall pass to the author's heirs and in usufruct—provided for in Article L. 123-6—to his or her spouse, to the exclusion of any legatees and successors in title, for the remainder of the year of the author's death and the next 70 years thereafter.'

Thus under Spanish law the rights belong to the Foundation. Under French law they belong to the five heirs. Was France permitted to restrict the persons entitled to French resale rights to heirs only?

The ECJ held that the Directive on the artists' resale right does not preclude a national law, which reserves the benefit of the resale right to the artist's heirs only, to the exclusion of testamentary legatees. It also stated that it is a matter for the French court to take into account the relevant rules of conflict of laws relating to the transfer on succession of the resale right.

 Question 1

How do you think the national court should answer the question in the *Dali* case? If copyright measures such as the artists' Resale Right Directive are to be considered mandatory, overriding provisions for the purposes of international private law, what might the consequences be as regards national regimes for the entitlement to intellectual property rights after death?

Question 2

How do you think the courts will interpret the choice of law provisions in Rome II?

Key points on choice of law

- The double actionability rule has been abolished
- The rules on non-contractual liability are now governed by the Rome II Regulation except for cases concerning personality rights (defamation)

Choice of law for contractual obligations: Rome I Regulation

23.61   Work has been ongoing over the years to update the rules on the law applicable to contractual obligations. The 1980 Rome Convention on the law applicable to contractual obligations (a Hague Conference measure) was implemented into UK law by the Contracts (Applicable Law) Act 1990. This was updated and replaced by Regulation (EC) No 593/2008 of the European Parliament and of the Council of on the law applicable to contractual obligations, also called Rome I. This came into force in December 2009. It applies to relations between parties to contracts which involve intellectual property. The main thrust is that of freedom of choice: parties are free to choose the law governing their contract[109] subject to a number of provisos including overriding mandatory provisions.[110]

---

[109] Art 2.   [110] Art 9.

Recognition and enforcement of judgments

23.62 As indicated previously, one of the main reasons for the introduction of the Brussels Convention and now the Brussels Regulation was to streamline the procedure for the recognition and enforcement of a judgment granted by one member state, but which would take effect in another. It was, in other words, to encourage the free flow of judgments. Recognition of a judgment of a court in another member state requires no special formality. Under the Regulation, the first stage of the enforcement procedure in the state in which enforcement is sought is virtually automatic. Under Article 33 of the Regulation, '[a] judgment given in a Member State shall be recognised in the other Member States without any special procedure being required'. A member state can, however, refuse to recognise a judgment given by another member state (Art 34) if 'such recognition is manifestly contrary to public policy in the Member State in which recognition is sought'.[111] However, a foreign judgment may not, under any circumstances, be reviewed as to its substance.[112]

Contemporary developments

23.63 There has been increasing discussion in recent years as to the problems posed by the ubiquitous nature of the Internet, the territorial nature of intellectual property rights, and the rules of international private law. The rules on jurisdiction, choice of law, and recognition and enforcement of judgments have been discussed previously. That discussion focused on the European approach with particular reference to the case law that has arisen from the Court of Justice. As has been seen, different rules apply in England when the issue concerns a matter outwith the Brussels Regulation and Rome Regulations, and other jurisdictions, furth of Europe, operate their own rules concerning international private law matters. The result, on an international scale, is a complex maze of rules, the operation of which can result in conflicting solutions to international private law questions concerning infringement of intellectual property rights. In an attempt to deal with these conflicts, proposals have been made to try to rationalise, on an international level, international private law rules particularly in relation to copyright and trade mark infringement cases.

The Hague Conference on Private International Law and the Convention on Choice of Court Agreements

23.64 For a number of years the Hague Conference on Private International Law has been working on the text of a convention that would harmonise jurisdiction and enforcement of judgments for commercial matters. However, the proposals have proved controversial, not least in the area of intellectual property. From ambitious beginnings in 1996: 'to include in the Agenda of the Nineteenth Session the question of jurisdiction, and recognition and enforcement of foreign judgments in civil and commercial matters'[113] the Convention, as finally agreed on 30 June 2005, concerns only agreed exclusive choice of court clauses[114] in civil or commercial matters and the enforcement of judgments.[115] The measures on intellectual property proved to be consistently difficult to negotiate. Questions arose as to whether intellectual property should be included at all and, if so, whether questions as to the validity of registered rights should be excluded.

---

[111] Brussels Regulation, Art 34(1).   [112] Brussels Regulation, Art 36.
[113] Eighteenth Session of the Hague Conference on Private International Law, Part B No 1.
[114] Hague Convention, Art 3.   [115] Hague Convention, Art 1.

On intellectual property matters the Convention does not apply to:

- the validity of intellectual property rights other than copyright and related rights;[116]
- infringement of intellectual property rights other than copyright and related rights, except where infringement proceedings are brought for breach of a contract between the parties relating to such rights, or could have been brought for breach of that contract;[117]
- the validity of entries in public registers.[118]

But Article 2.3 goes on to state that notwithstanding what is said in Article 2 if an excluded matter arises 'merely as a preliminary question and not as an object of the proceedings' in particular if it arises by way of defence, then proceedings are not excluded from the Convention 'if that matter is not an object of the proceedings'.

The European Council issued Council Decision 2009/397/EC signing, on behalf of the European Community, the Convention. The Convention is not yet in force (May 2013).

Web link

Details about the Hague Conference on Private International Law including the text of the Convention discussed previously can be found at **http://www.hcch.net/index_en.php.**

 Question

What sort of issues might arise in connection with the 'validity of copyright and related rights'? What sort of preliminary questions in relation to patents and trade marks might arise that could be covered under the Convention? What sort of argument in relation to patents or trade marks might be raised by way of defence that could be covered under the Convention?

Copyright reform proposals

23.65   Specific proposals that are directed towards the international arena have been made in relation to copyright. The purpose behind many of the suggestions is to streamline choices in relation to forum and of the law to be applied where many infringements occur as a result of the dissemination of a protected work over the Internet. In other words, the aim of the rules is to designate one applicable forum that would be competent to hear an action for infringement for all the subsequent loss, and one law that would be applicable to an infringement action. It is accepted that many different reproductions and therefore infringements occur of a work protected by copyright if it is digitised, uploaded on to a server, and further made available over the Internet. Under current rules, it may not be possible to consolidate claims for infringement in one place. The location and identity of the defendant may be unknown. The harm resulting from an initial act of digitisation and uploading an infringing work on to a server (which may itself be located in a copyright haven) is likely to be felt in many different fora.

---

[116] Hague Convention, Art 2n.   [117] Hague Convention, Art 2o.   [118] Hague Convention, Art 2p.

Which court, out of many possible options, should have jurisdiction to hear the case, and for what harm? Where, for the applicable law, is the place of the infringement? Is it where the initial infringing copy was made? Where it was uploaded on to a server? Downloaded onto a user's computer? Further communicated between individual surfers? Under present laws, and reflecting the territorial nature of copyright, not only may many different courts have jurisdiction to hear a case on the harm arising from the one initial act of infringement, but in addition many different laws may apply to the various infringements that occur.

23.66   Those states subject to the EU regime in the Brussels and Rome Regulations in particular now have a reference point for deciding many of these questions, some of which have been litigated and answers sought from the Court of Justice, albeit many questions remain. Many proposals have been made over the years to designate one single forum competent to hear an action for all the harm that arises. These range from choosing the courts located at the domicile of the defendant, to the courts in the place of the uplink (the server), to 'a court other than that of the place of emission which would be recognised to be competent to make good the full prejudice suffered at world wide level.' Such a tribunal would be the one 'having the closest link with the prejudice, with a presumption in favour of the court where the victim has his place of residence or principal establishment'.[119] The location of the server has been rejected by the Court of Justice in a trade mark case as an appropriate anchor for jurisdiction questions based largely on the arbitrary results that could arise given the ease with which servers can be located almost anywhere in the world.[120]

23.67   In the quest to apply a single law to all the infringements occurring over the Internet as a result of the unauthorised communication of a work, suggestions range from applying the law of the place where the author is domiciled;[121] the law of the country that affords the greatest protection among all countries having access to the network disseminating the infringing materials; and to the law of the place where the server is situated[122] subject to the application of a number of sub-rules intended to ensure that the minimum standards mandated by Berne (and TRIPS) and the WIPO Copyright Treaty are part of the law applied to the problem.[123]

23.68   Proposals have been made in this area by two US academics, Professors Dreyfuss[124] and Ginsburg.[125] Their work focuses on jurisdiction and enforcement of judgments in intellectual property disputes. They have suggested that these areas should be the subject of a discrete convention (with the possible exception of patents). The authors prepared a draft treaty that would be open to signature only by countries that have joined the World Trade Organization (WTO) and which are obliged to fully implement the TRIPS Agreement. The thrust of the proposal, first presented at a WIPO meeting in 2001,[126] is to enable a single forum to hear a case for harm that arises in a number of different jurisdictions as a result of multiple infringements. The Dreyfuss and Ginsburg proposals on jurisdiction, choice of law, and the

---

[119] Internet el les reseaux numeriques, Rapport du Conseil d'Etat prec Note 50, p 151, 1988, quoted in A Lucas, 'Aspects de Droit International Privé de la Protection d'Oeuvres et d'Objets de Droits Connexes Transmis par Réseaux Numériques Mondiaux', WIPO paper, November 1998. Available as GCPIC/1 paper on the WIPO website.

[120] Cases C-236/08 to 238/08 *Google France and Google*.

[121] F Dessemontet, 'Internet, la propriete intellectuelle et le droit international prive' in F Boele-Woelki and C Kessedjan (eds), *Which Court Decides? Which Law Applies?* (1998): 'finally infringement of intellectual property rights—of the author or his successors in title, for example—happens in a specific place: that of the economic harm' (at 47).

[122] Other commentators argue for a solution which finds its origins in the Satellite Directive: Ginsburg, note 15, 42.

[123] Ginsburg, note 15, 42; P Torremans, 'Private international law aspects of Internet–IP disputes' in L Edwards and C Waelde (eds), *Law and the Internet: A Framework for Electronic Commerce* (2000).

[124] New York University.   [125] Columbia University.

[126] R Dreyfuss and J Ginsburg, 'Draft Convention on Jurisdiction and Recognition of Judgments', available as paper WIPO/PIL/01/7 on the WIPO website.

enforcement of judgments abroad in international IP were presented to and approved by the American Law Institute in May 2007.[127] They were referred to with approval by the UK Supreme Court in *Lucasfilm v Ainsworth*.[128]

 Exercise

Do you think that a single law should be applied in multi-territorial copyright infringement disputes? If yes, which law should apply and why? How does this mesh with the proposals for a multi-territorial licensing system for online music distribution? (See para 22.42.)

Trade mark reform proposals

23.69   As indicated previously, discussions for reform of the rules of international private law in the copyright realm have largely focused on proposals where the difficulties associated with infringements on an international scale can be streamlined by designating one forum competent to hear all the harm, and one law to be applied to the infringements.

23.70   Reform proposals in the trade mark arena have a different focus. Instead of seeking consolidation, there is greater concern to find ways in which competing rights can coexist when used in connection with the Internet (see para 16.29ff). This difference in approach stems from the different nature of the rights. Copyright is an unregistered right. Because many states are bound together by virtue of the obligations undertaken in the Berne Convention and TRIPS, a copyright owner in one country will equally be the owner of copyright in the same work in another country as long as that country is also a signatory to the Berne Convention and/or TRIPS. By contrast, registered trade mark and unregistered rights are limited to the territory in which they are registered or used (subject to a mark being famous or well known). Therefore the concern has been to allow competing and equally legitimate rights to coexist on the Internet.

23.71   Central questions focus on those instances when a mark is used on the Internet: does the fact that it is accessible almost anywhere in the world mean that it is used everywhere in the world for the purposes of infringement? As has been seen, the Court of Justice is developing jurisprudence on use for trade mark infringement purposes in relation to search engine Adword advertising, and on at least some of the thorny problems concerning use of trade marks within websites when these are accessible in the territories of different member states. These tend to be nuanced responses to particular facts. Many more cases are likely to be litigated, each case developing our understanding of this area while also raising further questions.

WIPO proposals for use (see para 16.40ff)

23.72   the WIPO Standing Committee on the law of Trademarks, Industrial Designs and Geographical Indications has worked on proposals to harmonise national approaches to questions of 'use' of marks

---

[127] http://www.ali.org/doc/2007_intellectualproperty.pdf.
[128] 2011] UKSC 39, [2012] 1 AC 208, [2011] 3 WLR 487, para 93. M Landova, 'Public policy exception to recognition and enforcement of judgments in cases of copyright infringement' (2009) 40(6) *IIC* 642–665.

on the Internet.[129] The purpose was first to reduce the number of likely conflicts through restricting what may qualify as 'use' of a mark on the Internet and, secondly, to provide a mechanism for mediating conflicts that do occur.

On the question of *use* WIPO suggested:

> There seems to be a general understanding that the mere appearance of a sign or a mark on the Internet is not sufficient to establish a connection between that sign or mark and a given territory. Many comments suggest that a relationship between a sign used on the Internet and a given territory is only established through commercial use of that sign in respect of that territory or, as it was expressed in one comment, whether the sign used on the Internet has 'commercial effect' in a territory.

The report went on to outline a number of factors which could contribute to a finding of use. These included servicing of customers in the particular territory or country; entering into other commercially motivated relationships with persons in the particular territory or country; and actual visits to the website for which or on which the sign is used from persons in the particular territory or country.[130]

 Question

Compare WIPO's proposals on use with the court decisions in this area. What are the similarities and what the differences in approach? How will this area develop?

23.73   More recently, and in the light of the many cases around the world which have considered the use of trade marks on the Internet in a variety of forms and using a different methods and strategies, WIPO has asked whether further action should be taken at international level to address these issues.[131]

 Exercise

Read the WIPO Report on Trade Marks and the Internet. What do you believe will be the most pressing issues that arise in this area over the next decade?

---

[129] WIPO Standing Committee on the Law of Trademarks, Industrial Designs and Geographical Indications, Second Session, Second Part, Geneva, 7–12 June 1999, Study Concerning the Use of Trade Marks on the Internet, SCT/2/9 Prov.

[130] WIPO, note 129, Summary at 14.

[131] WIPO Standing Committee on the Law of Trademarks, Industrial Designs and Geographical Indications Twenty-Fourth Session, Geneva, 1–4 November 2010, Trademarks and the Internet, SCP/24/4.

Further reading

Books

For general information about international private law

P North and J Fawcett, *Cheshire and North's Private International Law* (13th edn, 1999)

For information about international private law and intellectual property

J Fawcett and P Torremans, *Intellectual Property and Private International Law* (2nd edn, 2012)

C Wadlow, *The Law of Unfair Competition: Passing Off by Misrepresentation* (2011)

C Wadlow, *Enforcement of Intellectual Property in European and International Law* (1998)

Articles

For a series of online articles

See generally 'WIPO Forum on Private International Law and Intellectual Property', Geneva, 30 and 31 January 2001

GW Austin, 'Private International Law and Intellectual Property Rights—A Common Law Overview'. Paper WIPO/PIL/01/5

F Blumer, 'Patent Law and International Private Law on Both Sides of the Atlantic'. Paper WIPO/PIL/01/3

GB Dinwoodie, 'Private International Aspects of the Protection of Trademarks'. Paper WIPO/PIL/01/4

RC Dreyfuss and JC Ginsburg, 'Draft Convention on Jurisdiction and Recognition of Judgments in Intellectual Property Matters'. Paper WIPO/PIL/01/7

JC Ginsburg, 'Private International Law Aspects of the Protection of Works and Objects of Related Rights Transmitted Through Digital Networks (2000 Update)'. Paper WIPO/PIL/01/2

A Lucas, 'Private International Law Aspects of the Protection of Works and of the Subject Matter of Related Rights Transmitted Over Digital Networks'. Paper WIPO/PIL/01/1

Others

G Austin, 'The concept of "justiciability" in foreign copyright infringement cases' (2009) 40(4) IIC 393–412

S Bariatti (ed), 'Litigating intellectual property rights disputes cross-border: EU Regulations, ALI Principles, CLIP Project' (Cedam, 2010)

A Dickinson, 'The Rome II Regulation: the law applicable to non-contractual obligations' (2009) IJL & IT

MAC Dizon, 'The symbiotic relationship between global contracts and the international IP regime' (2009) 4(8) JIPLP 559–565

P Johnson, 'ECJ plucks the spider from the web' (2006) 1(11) JIPLP 689–690

P Joseph, 'The rise and fall of cross-border jurisdiction and remedies in IP disputes' (2006) 1(13) JIPLP 850–857

J-J Kuipers, 'Determining jurisdiction in international licence agreements: *Falco Privatstiftung v Weller-Lindhorst* (C-533/07)' (2010) 32(12) EIPR 659–663

A Kur, 'A farewell to cross-border injunctions? The ECJ decisions *GAT v LuK* and *Roche Nederland v Primus and Goldenberg*' (2006) 37(7) IIC 844–855

M Landova, 'Public policy exception to recognition and enforcement of judgments in cases of copyright infringement' (2009) 40(6) IIC 642–665

P Morris, 'Pirates of the internet, at intellectual property's end with torrents and challenges for choice of law' (2009) 17(3) IJL & IT 282–303

S Neumann, 'Intellectual property rights infringements in European private international law: meeting the requirements of territoriality and private international law' (2011) 7(3) Journal of Private International Law 583–600

P Torremans, 'Star Wars rids us of subject matter jurisdiction: the Supreme Court does not like Kafka wither when it comes to copyright' (2011) 33(12) EIPR 813–817

P Torremans, 'Exclusive jurisdiction and cross-border IP (patent) infringement: suggestions for amendment of the Brussels I Regulation' [2007] EIPR 195

B Ubertazzi, 'Licence agreements relating to IP rights and the EC Regulation on Jurisdiction' (2009) 40(8) IIC 912–939

C Wadlow, 'Bugs, spies and paparazzi: jurisdiction over actions for breach of confidence in private international law' [2008] EIPR 269

C Wadlow, 'Trade secrets and the Rome II Regulation on the law applicable to non-contractual obligations' [2008] EIPR 309

A

Abridgements 4.40
Abuse of dominant position (Art 102 TFEU)
  Commission v Microsoft
    21.57–21.64
  dominant position 21.46–21.47
  ECJ case law 21.48
  essential facilities
    doctrine 21.65
  Eurodefences 21.70–21.77
  licensing 21.66–21.69
  meaning and scope 21.43–21.45
  policy tensions within
    intellectual property 1.34
  refusal to supply 21.49–21.56
  role in development of IP
    rights 1.61–1.63
Account of profits
  general principles 22.124
  principal remedy 1.44
Accretion 1.46
Acknowledgement of authorship
  criticisms or reviews 5.31
  current events reporting 5.34
  performers' rights 6.35
Adaptation of works
  computer programs and
    databases 4.67
  infringement by
    reproduction 4.31
  meaning and scope 4.66
Adelphi Charter 7.5, 10.10
Advertising
  comparative advertising
    EU law 15.126–15.127
    jeopardising of function of
      mark 15.129–15.132
    passing off 17.54
    relationship between UK and
      EU law 15.128
    statutory provisions 15.125
    trade mark defence
      15.122–15.124
  free movement of goods 20.47
  function of trade marks 13.14
  protection from passing
    off 17.34
Aesthetic creations 11.19
**Agreements between undertakings
  (Art 101 TFEU)**
  consequences of breach
    21.41–21.42

ECJ case law 21.23–21.28
Eurodefences 21.70–21.77
excluded restrictions
  21.38–21.40
exemptions
  block exemptions 21.33
  new regime 21.30–21.32
  technology transfer
    agreements 21.34–21.36
general principles and
  objectives 21.20–21.21
hardcore restrictions 21.37
horizontal agreements 21.18
licensing agreements 21.22,
  22.62–22.66
policy tensions within
  intellectual property 1.34
role in development of IP
  rights 1.61–1.63
severability of clauses 21.29
vertical agreements 21.19
Agricultural products
  cancellation 16.87–16.89
  registration as DO or GI 16.77
  registration procedures
    16.82–16.83
  required specifications
    16.78–16.79
  scope of protection
    16.84–16.86
Alternative dispute resolution
  benefits of breach of
    confidence 22.137
  domain names
    British courts 16.13–16.22
    ICANN UDRP 16.23–16.27
  PDOs, PGIs and trade
    marks 16.89–16.91
  scope 22.138
  UK-IPO mediation
    service 22.139
  WTO administration of
    GATT 10.42
Animal breeds 16.77
Anonymous works
  duration of protection 3.53
  first ownership of
    copyright 3.23
Anton Piller orders 22.98–22.99
Appearance (designs) 8.23–8.27
  registered designs 8.23–8.27
  Community unregistered
    designs 9.95

Appellations of origin *see*
    Geographical indications
Applicable law
  contemporary issues 23.63
  EU law
    overview 23.7
    Rome I Regulation 23.61
    Rome II Regulation
      23.55–23.60
  historical development of UK
    rules 23.8–23.17
  reform proposals
    copyright 23.65–23.68
    ongoing work of Hague
      Conference 23.64
  UK Supreme Court ruling
    in 2011 23.18–23.19
Application procedures *see*
    Registration procedures
Architecture 2.69, 2.82
Archives *see* **Libraries and
    archives**
Artistic craftsmanship 2.69,
    2.83–2.86
Artistic works
  adaptation 4.66
  author's resale rights 3.44–3.46
  copying 4.41
  defined 2.69
  duration of protection 3.50
  exclusions from
    patentability 11.19
  first ownership of copyright
    employers 3.25
    statutory presumption 3.6
  fixation 2.33
  indication of method and not
    quality 2.81
  meaning and scope
    architecture 2.82
    artistic craftsmanship
      2.83–2.86
    collages 2.80
    diagrams, maps, charts and
      plans 2.74
    drawings 2.73
    engravings 2.78–2.79
    films 2.87–2.89
    graphic works 2.71
    paintings 2.72
    photographs 2.75
    sculptures 2.76–2.77
    statutory provisions 2.70

Artistic works (*cont.*)
  moral right of privacy 3.48
  paternity rights 3.35
  protected subject matter 2.22
  public communication rights
    EU law 4.60
    meaning and scope 4.61–4.65
  public performances
    audience requirements 4.57
    broadcasts 4.59
    defined 4.53
    'direct representations or
      performances' 4.54–4.56
    performing for one's own
      benefit 4.58
  statutory provisions 2.70
Assignment
  licensing compared 22.10–22.11
  registration 22.7
  transfer of ownership 22.5
Auction sites 16.54–16.56
Audio-visual performances 6.37
Author works
  artistic works
    defined 2.69
    duration of protection 3.50
    fixation 2.33
    meaning and scope 2.71–2.81,
      2.71–2.89
    paternity rights 3.35–3.38
    protected subject matter 2.22
    statutory provisions 2.70
  author's moral rights
    right of integrity 3.39–3.43
  categorisation 2.49
  dramatic works
    adaptation 4.31
    duration of protection 3.50
    meaning and scope 2.66–2.67
    paternity rights 3.35
    protected subject matter 2.22
  duration of protection 3.50
  first ownership of copyright
    employers 3.25
    statutory presumption 3.6
  literary works
    adaptation 4.31
    defined 2.51
    duration of protection 3.50
    meaning and scope 2.52–2.63,
      2.52–2.65
    paternity rights 3.35
    subject matter 2.22
  media works
    distinguished 2.47–2.48
  moral right of privacy 3.48
  musical works
    adaptation 4.31

  derivative works 2.42
  duration of protection 3.50
  meaning and scope 2.68
  paternity rights 3.35
  protected subject matter
    2.42
  paternity rights 3.35
  taxonomy 2.50
**Authorisation of copyright
  infringements**
  cases where authorisation has
    taken place 4.70
  internet file-sharing 4.72–4.74
  meaning and scope 4.68–4.69
  notices and statements as
    defences 4.71
  'safe harbours' 4.75
Authorship
  see also **Ownership**
  acknowledgement of authorship
    criticisms or reviews 5.31
    current events reporting 5.34
    performers' rights 6.35
  alternative approaches to
    copyright protection 2.19
  author and media works
    distinguished 2.48
  joint authorship
    first ownership of
      copyright 3.7–3.14
    media works 3.21

B

Biotechnology
  harmonisation and
    approximation of EU
    law 1.54
  licensing 10.55–10.58
  moral issues arising 1.25
  patentability
    contemporary issues 12.3
    EU Directive 12.47–12.53
    excessively broad
      patents 12.38–12.42
    exclusions from
      patentability 11.16–11.17
    future concerns over
      implementation of EU
      Directive 12.63–12.70
    human embryology
      12.54–12.60
    industrial applicability
      (patents) 12.34–12.37
    inventions and discoveries
      distinguished 12.18–12.23
    inventive steps 12.30–12.33
    key questions about gene
      sequencing 12.8–12.9

    monopoly concerns
      12.71–12.76
    morality 12.43–12.46
    novelty 12.24–12.29
    synthetic biology 12.61–12.62
  product-by-process
    claims 11.98–11.99
  underlying techniques
    common technology used in
      the industry 12.12
    DNA sequencing 12.13
    general points of
      interest 12.14–12.17
    importance 12.10
    manipulation of living
      organisms 12.11
Blurring 15.97–15.99
Bolar exemptions 11.231
Branding
  current controversy 13.17–13.18
  inter brand competition 21.17
  intra brand competition 21.16
Breach of confidence
  see also **Privacy**
  ambit 1.13
  basis of claim 18.7–18.8
  challenges for business
    18.72–18.73
  codification of law 18.87
  defences
    prior knowledge 18.61
    public interest 18.56–18.60
    requirement for complainant
      to have 'clean hands' 18.60
    springboard doctrine
      18.62–18.63
  elements of action 18.15
  examples in practice 18.14
  'grace period' for patents 11.85
  impact of HRA 1998
    balance between Arts 8
      and 10 19.19–19.25
    key development 19.11
    overview 19.9–19.10
    pictures and images
      19.17–19.18
  important differences for
    IP 18.9–18.10
  international conventions and
    treaties 18.11
  know-how and confidentiality
    agreements 18.74–18.76
  legal nature of claim 18.12–18.13
  overview 18.5–18.6
  parties to action
    defendants 18.66–18.67
    standing to make
      claim 18.64–18.65

policy issues 18.68
protection for patents
    pending 11.85
relationship with other
    regulatory
    restrictions 18.77–18.86
relevant conduct
    detriment 18.50
    intention 18.51
    regulatory and statutory
        obligations 18.53–18.54
    relevance to obligation
        of confidentiality
        18.48–18.49
    risk of use and
        disclosure 18.52
requirement for obligation of
    confidentiality
    duration of obligation
        18.31–18.33
    employees 18.34–18.40
    indirect recipients
        18.44–18.47
    marriage 18.43
    need to identify scope of
        obligation 18.30
    overview 18.28–18.29
    professional
        relationships 18.41
    regulatory and statutory
        obligations 18.42
scope of protection 18.69–18.71
types of protected information
    government
        information 18.26
    importance of identifying
        relevant
        information 18.27
    information not in public
        domain 18.18–18.25
    overview 18.17
Broadcasts
copying 4.41
duration of protection 3.60
first ownership of
    copyright 3.19
meaning and scope
    internet transmissions 2.94
    repeats 2.95
    satellite broadcasting
        2.92–2.93
    teletext 2.94
    television and radio 2.91
originality 2.46
permitted acts 5.45
protected subject matter 2.22
public communication rights
    EU law 4.60

meaning and scope 4.61–4.65
public performances 4.59
Bundling of software 21.64
Business methods
exclusions from
    patentability 11.26–11.32
software-related
    inventions 12.111–12.124
Business names
protection from passing
    off 17.28
trade mark
    infringements 15.19–15.22

C
Cell culture technology 12.12
Certification marks
    14.106–14.108
Charts
as artistic works 2.74
statutory provisions 2.70
Choice of law rules *see* **Applicable
    law**
Circuit diagrams 2.64
copyright 2.64
UK unregistered design
    right 9.30–9.31
Co-ownership
joint authorship of copyright
    material
    duration of protection 3.54
    first ownership of
        copyright 3.7–3.14
    media works 3.21
patents 11.153–11.155
Collaborative works
collective works
    distinguished 3.15
joint authorship 3.7–3.14
Collages
as artistic works 2.80
statutory provisions 2.70
Collective licensing
impact of digitalisation
    22.43–22.44
overview 22.23–22.25
role of collecting societies
    in EU 22.29–22.42
    in UK 22.26–22.28
Collective marks 14.106–14.108
Collective works 3.15
Colours
designs (UK registered and
    Community designs) 8.16,
    8.23
graphic representations
    14.14–14.16

policy considerations 14.43
product marks and
    colours 14.75–14.76
trade mark registration 14.8
Common law protection
alternative approaches to
    copyright protection 2.18
breach of confidence
    ambit 1.13
    basis of claim 18.7–18.8
    challenges for
        business 18.72–18.73
    codification of law 18.87
    defences 18.55–18.63
    elements of action 18.15
    examples in practice 18.14
    important differences for
        IP 18.9–18.10
    international conventions
        and treaties 18.11
    know-how and
        confidentiality
        agreements 18.74–18.76
    legal nature of claim
        18.12–18.13
    overview 18.5–18.6
    parties to action 18.64–18.67
    policy issues 18.68
    relationship with other
        regulatory
        restrictions 18.77–18.86
    relevant conduct 18.48–18.54
    requirement for obligation of
        confidentiality 18.28–18.47
    scope of protection
        18.69–18.71
    types of protected
        information 18.16–18.27
contemporary issues
    conclusions 19.58
    merchandising 19.26–19.47
    overview 19.1–19.3
    practical examples 19.6
    privacy 19.7–19.25
passing off
    ambit 1.12
    basis of action 17.5–17.6
    'cyber-squatting' 17.62–17.68
    damage 17.57–17.60
    defences 17.61
    goodwill
        requirements 17.13–17.34
    international
        background 17.7–17.8
    meaning and scope 17.9–17.11
    misrepresentation
        requirements 17.35–17.56
    overview 17.4

Common law protection (*cont.*)
    requirement for business
        context 17.12
    unfair competition
        17.69–17.72
    protection prior to
        registration 1.42–1.43
'Commonplace' designs 9.53–9.58
    see also **Originality, UK
        unregistered design right**
Community designs
    see also **Designs, Registered
        designs**
    registration 8.98–8.105
**Community unregistered
    designs**
    commencement and
        duration 9.97–9.99
    designs to which Community
        UDR applies 9.95–9.96
    exclusive rights 9.101–9.102
    overview 9.94
    ownership 9.100
Community law *see* **EU law**
Community trade marks
    advantages 13.43–13.46
    assignment 22.6
    collective marks 14.106
    interaction with other registered
        trade marks 13.43–13.46
    main features 13.37–13.38
    overview 13.36
    registration procedure
        13.39–13.42
Companies
    name infringements
        15.19–15.22
    shared goodwill 17.20
Comparative advertising
    EU law 15.126–15.127
    jeopardising of function of
        mark 15.129–15.132
    passing off 17.54
    relationship between UK and
        EU law 15.128
    statutory provisions 15.125
    trade mark defence
        15.122–15.124
Compensation *see* **Damages and
    compensation**
Competition law
    see also **Unfair competition**
    abuse of dominant position
        (Art 102 TFEU)
        Commission v Microsoft
            21.57–21.64
        dominant position
            21.46–21.47

ECJ case law 21.48
essential facilities
    doctrine 21.65
Eurodefences 21.70–21.77
licensing 21.66–21.69
meaning and scope
    21.43–21.45
refusal to supply 21.49–21.56
agreements between
    undertakings (Art 101
    TFEU)
    consequences of
        breach 21.41–21.42
    ECJ case law 21.23–21.28
    Eurodefences 21.70–21.77
    excluded restrictions
        21.38–21.40
    exemptions 21.30–21.36
    general principles and
        objectives 21.20–21.21
    hardcore restrictions 21.37
    horizontal agreements 21.18
    licensing agreements 21.22
    severability of clauses 21.29
    vertical agreements 21.19
central focus 21.10
inter brand competition 21.17
intra brand competition 21.16
licensing of trade marks
    22.62–22.66
need for balance 1.27
overview 21.1
policy tensions within
    intellectual property 1.34
relevant markets 21.13–21.15
role in development of IP rights
    Arts 101 and 102 TFEU
        1.61–1.63
    driver for change 1.51–1.52
tension with IP rights 21.11
theoretical perspectives
    21.6–21.7
'workable competition'
    21.8–21.9
Compilations *see* **Tables and
    compilations**
Complex products 8.73–8.78
Component parts *see* **Complex
    products, Spare parts**
Compulsory licensing
    copyright 22.19–22.22
    patents
        access to medicines
            10.48–10.53
        legal provisions 22.50–22.53
        underlying rationale 11.148
    policy tensions within
        intellectual property 1.35

trade marks 22.61
Computer programs
    see also **Internet; Software-
        related inventions**
    abuse of dominant position
        (Art 102 TFEU)
        21.57–21.64
    adaptation 4.67
    copying 4.34–4.36
    duration of protection 3.52
    exclusion of moral rights
        paternity rights 3.38
        right of integrity 3.42
    exclusion from patentability
        continuing importance of Art
            52(2) 12.132
        evolution of liberal
            interpretation of
            EPC 12.131
        general provisions
            11.33–11.40
        IBM/Computer program
            case 12.133–12.140
        importance 12.79
        meaning and scope
            12.82–12.88
        rationale 12.80–12.81
    first ownership of
        copyright 3.22
    as literary works 2.54, 2.58
    permitted acts 5.44
    protected subject matter 2.22
    software-related inventions
        distinguished 12.78
    technical protection
        measures 5.53
    temporary copies 5.18
Confidentiality *see* **Breach of
    confidence**
Confusion *see* **Likelihood of
    confusion**
Consent
    free movement of goods
        absence of consent
            20.31–20.32
        batches of goods 20.51
        burden of proof 20.60–20.63
        differing levels of protection
            in member states
            20.22–20.29
        effect of consent by rights
            holder 20.16–20.21
        goods in transit 20.57–20.59
        goods 'put on the
            market' 20.55–20.56
        implied consent 20.52–20.54
        licensing 20.30
        pharmaceuticals 20.28–20.29

trade mark registration 14.112
Contemporary issues
applicable law 23.63
common law protection
conclusions 19.58
merchandising 19.26–19.47
overview 19.1–19.3
practical examples 19.6
privacy 19.7–19.25
continuing attempts to strike a
balance 1.36
copyright
authors' and neighbouring
rights distinguished
7.19–7.23
duration of protection
7.43–7.47
file-sharing 7.51–7.53
fixation 7.24
impact of internet 7.7–7.11
key developments 7.6
moral rights 7.38–7.42
overview 7.1–7.4
ownership 7.33–7.37
permitted acts 7.54–7.60
reproduction 7.48–7.50
rights management
information systems
7.61–7.63
technical protection
measures 7.61–7.63
underlying purpose of
copyright 7.12–7.17
exploitation of IP rights
public sector
information 22.77–22.84
sui generis rights 22.68–22.76
international
exhaustion 20.63–20.65
jurisdiction 23.63
patents
biotechnology 12.3
EU reforms 10.70–10.76
national reforms 10.77–10.88
software related
inventions 12.4
WIPO's ongoing programme
of harmonisation 10.69
recognition of foreign
judgements 23.63
trade marks
backlash from
consumers 13.17–13.18
criticisms of extended
functions 13.19–13.21
domain names 16.2–16.27
geographical
indications 16.57–16.94

use of marks on
internet 16.28–16.56
'Content scramble system'
CCS 5.51
Contractual provisions
copyright
contemporary issues 7.16
exclusion of fair
dealings 5.59–5.62
cross-border infringements
Brussels Regulation 23.21
Rome I Regulation 23.61
database exploitation
22.72–22.76
exclusive recording
contracts 6.30
Contributory infringement 4.73
Conventions *see* **International**
Conventions and treaties
Copying *see* **Reproduction**
Copyright
see also Sui generis **rights;**
Performers' rights
assignment 22.6–22.7
author works
artistic works 2.69–2.89
categorisation 2.49
literary works 2.51–2.65
media works
distinguished 2.47–2.48
taxonomy 2.50
authorisation of infringements
cases where authorisation has
taken place 4.70
internet file-sharing 4.72–4.74
meaning and scope 4.68–4.69
notices and statements as
defences 4.71
'safe harbours' 4.75
author's moral rights
Berne Convention 3.31
commercial publishing 3.43
contemporary issues
7.38–7.42
EU law 3.32
false attribution 3.47
key characteristics 3.34
paternity rights 3.35–3.38
resale rights 3.44–3.46
UK law 3.33
contemporary issues
authors' and neighbouring
rights distinguished
7.19–7.23
duration of protection
7.43–7.47
ever-expanding scope of
activities 7.5

file-sharing 7.51–7.53
fixation 7.24
impact of internet 7.7–7.11
key developments 7.5, 7.6
moral rights 7.38–7.42
originality 7.25–7.30
overview 7.1–7.4
ownership 7.33–7.37
permitted acts 7.54–7.60
reproduction 7.48–7.50
rights management
information systems
7.61–7.63
technical protection
measures 7.61–7.63
underlying purpose of
copyright 7.12–7.17
criminal sanctions
22.141–22.142, 22.146
duration of protection
anonymous works 3.53
author works 3.50
broadcasts 3.60
computer programs 3.52
contemporary issues
7.43–7.47
Crown copyright 3.55–3.56
films 3.58
general rules 3.49
joint authorship 3.54
moral rights 3.51
Parliamentary copyright
3.57
pseudonymous works 3.53
published editions 3.61
sound recordings 3.59
early developments in
international law 1.65
economic rights
directly or indirectly doing
restricted act 4.21–4.22
EU law 4.8–4.9
international
background 4.4–4.7
primary restricted acts
4.10–4.11
secondary
infringements 4.12
taking whole or substantial
part 4.15–4.20
fair dealing
contracting out 5.59–5.62
criticism or review 5.29–5.32
current events
reporting 5.33–5.35
fairness 5.36
overview 5.19
private study 5.24–5.28

Copyright (*cont.*)
research for non-commercial
purposes 5.21–5.23
'three-step test' 5.20
first ownership
anonymous works 3.23
broadcasts 3.19
collective works 3.15
computer programs 3.22
Crown copyright 3.25–3.29
employers 3.25–3.29
films 3.17
general rules 3.5
joint authorship 3.7–3.14,
3.21
Parliamentary
copyright 3.30
pseudonymous works 3.24
published editions 3.20
sound recordings 3.18
statutory presumption for
author works 3.6
transferees distinguished 3.4
free movement of
services 20.70–20.72
general limitations and
exceptions
human rights 5.49
public interest 5.47
spare parts 5.48
harmonisation and
approximation of EU
law 1.54
history and development
Berne Convention 1886
2.8–2.9
Copyright Acts 1911–88
2.10–2.11
early history 2.4–2.7
EU law 2.15–2.16
modern treaties and
conventions 2.12–2.14
infringement by issuing public
copies without authority
cross-border
infringements 4.45
'public' defined 4.47
publication
distinguished 4.46
transient copies 4.48
infringement by public
communication
EU law 4.60
meaning and scope 4.61–4.65
infringement by public
lending 4.49–4.52
infringement by public
performances

audience requirements 4.57
broadcasts 4.59
defined 4.53
'direct representations or
performances' 4.54–4.56
performing for one's own
benefit 4.58
infringement by reproduction
abridgements 4.40
adaptation
distinguished 4.31
admittedly derivative
work 4.37–4.38
basic requirements 4.24
broadcasts 4.41
computer programs 4.34–4.36
contemporary issues
7.48–7.50
films 4.41
ideas and impressions
4.32–4.33
knowledge of original
work 4.30
need to show causal
connection between two
works 4.27–4.29
parodies 4.39
published editions 4.42
similarity of two works 4.25
sound recordings 4.41
typographical
arrangements 4.42
works similar but not
same 4.26
interaction with UK registered
and Community
designs 8.122–8.126
interaction with UK
unregistered design
rights 9.81–9.93
international law
Berne Convention 1886
2.4–2.7
modern treaties and
conventions 2.12–2.14
justifications for protection
economic role of
copyright 2.18–2.21
response to early
printing 2.17
licensing
collective licensing
22.23–22.48
compulsory licensing
22.19–22.22
contemporary issues 7.5
equitable
remuneration 22.18

restraint of trade
doctrine 22.13–22.15
UK contract practices 22.12
undue influence 22.16–22.17
media works
author works
distinguished 2.47–2.48
meaning and scope 2.90–2.96
national laws
Copyright Acts 1911–88
2.10–2.11
early history 2.4–2.7
fixation requirements 2.31
originality
broadcasts 2.46
contemporary issues
7.25–7.30
derivative works 2.41–2.43
EU and UK approaches to
'intellectual creation'
distinguished 2.39–2.40
independent but similar
works 2.44
judicial definition 2.35
no requirement of quality or
merit 2.36
policy tensions within
intellectual property 1.38
skill, labour and
judgment 2.37–2.38
sound recordings 2.45
sound recordings, films and
published editions 2.45
statutory provisions 2.34
permitted acts
broadcasts 5.45
computer programs 5.44
contemporary issues
7.54–7.60
disabled persons 5.41
educational
establishments 5.37–5.38
EU law 5.9–5.11
fair dealings 5.19–5.36
incidental inclusion 5.43
international
background 5.8
libraries and archives
5.39–5.40
musical works 5.46
overview 5.1–5.3
overview of exceptions 5.14
public administration 5.42
public domain 5.4–5.7
temporary copies 5.13–5.18
policy tensions within
intellectual property
originality 1.38

registration 1.40
strength of protection 1.39
primary infringements
adaptation of works 4.66–4.67
copying 4.24–4.42
issuing public copies without
authority 4.43–4.48
public communication
rights 4.60–4.65
public lending 4.49–4.52
public performances
4.53–4.59
secondary infringements
distinguished 4.76
principal treaties and
conventions 1.72
public interest limitations
5.47
reform proposals 23.65–23.68
rights management information
systems
contemporary issues
7.61–7.63
EU controls 5.63–5.66
general approach 5.55
standing to sue 5.56
technical protection
measures 5.52
unauthorised reception of
transmissions 5.57
secondary infringements
categorisation 4.76–4.77
importance 4.78
primary infringements
distinguished 4.76
Sections 51 and 52 CDPA
1988 9.81–9.93
self-help 22.101–22.102
spare parts 5.48
subject matter
CDPA 1988 2.22
contemporary issues 7.15
fixation requirements
2.30–2.33
multiple copyrights in one
work 2.23
need for expression of work
over and above
ideas 2.24–2.28
need for work of relevant
kind 2.29
originality 2.34–2.46
survey evidence 22.103–22.106
symbol 1.45
technical protection measures
computer programs 5.53
contemporary issues
7.61–7.63

'content scramble system'
CCS 5.51
EU controls 5.63–5.66
other copyright works 5.54
overview 5.50
public domain 5.58
rights management
information systems 5.52
UK statutory rights 1.8, 1.43
Counterfeiting and piracy
criminal sanctions
22.155–22.159
EU initiatives 22.147
European Regulation
22.149–22.151
increased infringement 22.148
proposals for international
treaty 22.154
UK response 22.152–22.153
Creative Commons
contract provisions 7.14
establishment 7.5
moral rights 7.40
online licensing 22.46–22.47
recognition of copyright
value 7.10
Criminal sanctions
copyright 22.141–22.142,
22.146
performers' rights 22.143
trade marks 22.144–22.146
Criticism or review
meaning and scope 5.29
multiple copies 5.30
need for sufficient
acknowledgement 5.31
public availability of work 5.32
Cross-border infringements
applicable law
contemporary issues 23.63
copyright reform
proposals 23.65–23.68
historical development of UK
rules 23.7
overview of EU law 23.7
Rome I Regulation 23.61
Rome II Regulation
23.55–23.60
UK choice of law rules
23.8–23.17
UK Supreme Court ruling
in 2011 23.18–23.19
counterfeiting and piracy
criminal sanctions
22.155–22.159
EU initiatives 22.147
European
Regulation 22.149–22.151

increased
infringement 22.148
proposals for international
treaty 22.154
UK response 22.152–22.153
issuing public copies without
authority 4.45
jurisdiction
Brussels Regulation
23.21–23.54
contemporary issues 23.63
copyright reform
proposals 23.65–23.68
historical development of UK
rules 23.8–23.17
ongoing work of Hague
Conference 23.64
overview of EU law 23.7
UK Supreme Court ruling in
2011 23.18–23.19
passing off 17.47
recognition of foreign
judgements
Brussels Regulation 23.21
contemporary issues 23.63
ongoing work of Hague
Conference 23.64
overview of rules 23.7
procedure 23.62
reform proposals
copyright 23.65–23.68
ongoing work of Hague
Conference 23.64
trade marks 23.69–23.73
use of marks on internet
auction sites 16.54–16.56
keyword advertising
16.42–16.53
overview 16.28
permitted disclaimers
16.38–16.39
territoriality 16.29–16.32
user infringements
16.33–16.37
WIPO strategy 16.40–16.41
Crown
copyright
duration of protection
3.55–3.56
ownership 3.29
limitation on patent
rights 11.149
protected emblems 14.100
Culture
conflict with human
rights 10.19
contemporary issues for
copyright 7.12

Culture (*cont.*)
    distinctiveness of marks 14.66
    impact of post-modernism 7.19
Current events reporting
    acknowledgement of
        authorship 5.34
    examples from case law 5.35
    overview 5.33
Customary signs
    properties irrelevant 14.47
    statutory provisions 14.30
'Cyber-squatting' 17.62–17.68

D

Damage
    breach of confidence 18.50
    passing off
        dilution of name 17.59
        to goodwill 17.57–17.58
        prospective damage
            sufficient 17.60
Damages and compensation
    additional damages
        22.122–22.123
    employee inventions
        11.165–11.170
    general principles
        22.120–22.121
    principal remedy 1.44
Databases
    adaptation 4.67
    copying 4.34–4.36
    exploitation strategies
        application of competition
            law 22.68–22.69
        contractual
            provisions 22.72–22.76
        overview 22.67
        tariffs 22.70
        technological protection
            measures 22.71
    as literary works
        computer programs 2.58
        copyright in constituent
            elements 2.59–2.63
        EU law 2.56
        UK law 2.57
    protected subject matter 2.22
    sui generis rights
        contemporary issues 7.31–7.32
        criteria for protection 6.5–6.9
        duration of protection 6.11
        EU law 6.4
        first ownership 6.10
        infringements 6.12–6.16
        key example 1.17
        permitted acts 6.17–6.20
    temporary copies 5.18

Deceptive marks
    absolute grounds for refusing
        registration 14.98–14.99
    revocation 14.121–14.122
Declarations
    design rights 8.106–8.110
    non-infringement 11.204,
        22.96–22.97
Defences
    abuse of dominant position (Art
        102 TFEU) 21.70–21.77
    agreements between
        undertakings (Art 101
        TFEU) 21.70–21.77
    breach of confidence
        prior knowledge 18.61
        public interest 18.56–18.60
        requirement for complainant
            to have 'clean hands' 18.60
        springboard doctrine
            18.62–18.63
    copyright infringements 4.71
    passing off 17.61
    patent infringements
        Bolar exemptions 11.231
        experimental
            purposes 11.221–11.227
        farmers' privileges
            11.228–11.230
        private and non-commercial
            acts 11.220
        statutory provisions 11.219
    trade mark infringements
        accessories and spare
            parts 15.117–15.121
        comparative
            advertising 15.122–15.132
        honest practices
            15.107–15.108
        importance 15.105
        indications as to
            characteristics of
            products 15.112–15.116
        own name defence
            15.109–15.111
        statutory provisions 15.106
    UK registered and Community
        designs 8.117–8.119
Delivery up
    general principles 22.119
    principal remedy 1.44
Deposit libraries 5.40
Derivative works
    common source material
        4.37–4.38
    general copyright 2.41–2.43
Derogatory treatment *see* **Right
    of integrity**

Designs
    see also **Community designs,
        Registered designs, UK
        unregistered design right**
    Community designs
        Community registered
            designs 8.12–8.13
        Community unregistered
            designs 8.12–8.13,
            9.94–9.102
        EU role in development of
            rights
            EU Directive and
                Regulation 8.11–8.14
            harmonisation and
                approximation of EU
                law 1.54
            institution of Community
                rights 1.55–1.57
            policy tensions within
                intellectual property 1.35
            principal treaties and
                conventions 1.72, 8.4–8.9,
                9.4–9.8
    registered designs (UK and
        Community registered
        designs)
        appearance 8.23–8.27
        Community registration
            process 8.98–8.103
        complex products 8.73–8.78
        component parts 8.73–8.78
        dealing in Community
            designs 8.104–8.105
        dealing in UK registered
            designs 8.97
        definition of 'design'
            8.16–8.27
        declarations of
            invalidity 8.106–8.110
        defences 8.117–8.119
        designs 'available to the
            public' 8.50–8.61
        duration of rights
            8.120–8.121
        EU Directive and
            Regulation 8.11–8.14
        exclusions:
            functionality 8.62–8.68
        exclusions: 'must-fit'
            8.69–8.71
        exclusions: public policy and
            morality 8.72
        exclusive rights 8.111–8.116
        individual character
            8.32–8.49
        informed user 8.37–8.40
        infringement 8.111–8.116

interaction with other IP
    rights 8.122–8.126
international
    background 8.4–8.9
novelty 8.28, 8.29–8.31
overall impression 8.32–8.49,
    8.111
overview 8.1–8.3
product 8.18–8.22
repair clause 8.84, 8.88–8.89
spare parts 8.79–8.89
UK history 8.10
UK registration process
    8.91–8.96
symbol 1.45
UK statutory provisions 1.9, 1.43
unjustified threats of
    action 22.94–22.95
UK unregistered design right
    absence of exceptions 9.79
    article 9.22–9.24
    assessing UK UDR 9.80
    commencement 9.61
    commonplace 9.53–9.58
    definition of 'design'
        9.14–9.33
    design document 9.19
    duration of protection
        9.59–9.67
    exclusions: methods or
        principles of
        construction 9.36–9.37
    exclusions: surface
        decoration 9.34–9.35
    exclusions: 'must-fit'
        9.38–9.49
    exclusions: 'must-
        match' 9.38–9.40,
        9.50–9.52
    exclusive right 9.71–9.78
    infringement 9.71–9.78
    interaction with
        copyright 9.81–9.93
    international context 9.4–9.8
    licences of right 9.62–9.67
    originality 9.53–9.58
    overview 9.1–9.3
    ownership 9.68–9.70
    qualification 9.6–9.8
    reciprocity 9.6–9.8
    Sections 51 and 52
        CDPA 1988 9.81–9.93
    shape and
        configuration 9.29–9.33
    'trimming' 9.27
    UK background 9.9–9.13
Designation of origin (DOs) see
    Geographical indications

Diagrams
    as artistic works 2.74
    circuit diagrams 2.64
        copyright 2.64
        UK unregistered design
            right 9.30–9.31
    statutory provisions 2.70
Digital works
    see also Computer programs;
        Internet
    contemporary issues 7.5, 7.14
    impact on territoriality 23.1–23.2
    online licensing
        collective licensing
            22.43–22.44
        individual schemes
            22.45–22.48
Dilution of name
    passing off 17.59
    protection of trade marks with
        reputation 15.88
Disabled persons
    copyright exceptions and
        limitations 5.41
    future developments 22.172
Discoveries
    biotechnology 12.18–12.23
    excluded from
        patentability 11.15–11.18
Discoveries, scientific theories
    and mathematical
    methods 11.15–11.18
Dispute resolution see
    Alternative dispute
    resolution
Distinctiveness
    see also Similarity
    absolute grounds for refusing
        registration 14.30–14.31
    capacity to distinguish
        goods 14.32–14.33
    device marks 14.92
    effect of marks used for
        particular purpose 14.78
    expanding case law 14.68
    foreign words 14.66–14.67
    general considerations
        14.44–14.47
    geographical extent 14.71–14.74
    loss of distinctiveness 14.79
    names
        geographical names 14.65
        personal names 14.55
    numerals 14.64
    part of mark 14.77
    policy considerations 14.43
    product marks and
        colours 14.75–14.76

signatures 19.30
slogans 14.62
statutory provisions 14.7
symbols 14.63
three-dimensional marks
    importance of consumer
        perception 14.48, 14.54
    key question as to departure
        from norm 14.49–14.53
through use 14.69–14.70
underlying rationale 14.34–14.42
word combinations 14.56–14.61
DNA technology 12.12–12.13
Domain names
    defined 16.4–16.6
    dispute resolution
        British courts 16.12–16.27,
            16.13–16.22
        ICANN UDRP 16.12–16.27,
            16.23–16.27
        overview 16.12
    overview 16.2–16.3
    ownership disputes 16.9–16.11
    registration as trade mark
        16.7–16.8
Dominance see Abuse of
    dominant position (Art
    102 TFEU)
Dramatic works
    see also Performers' rights
    adaptation 4.31, 4.66
    duration of protection 3.50
    exclusions from
        patentability 11.19
    first ownership of copyright
        employers 3.25
        statutory presumption 3.6
    meaning and scope 2.66–2.67
    paternity rights 3.35
    protected subject matter 2.22
    public communication rights
        EU law 4.60
        meaning and scope 4.61–4.65
    public performances
        audience requirements 4.57
        broadcasts 4.59
        defined 4.53
        'direct representations or
            performances' 4.54–4.56
        performing for one's own
            benefit 4.58
Drawings
    meaning and scope 2.73
    statutory provisions 2.70
Duration of protection
    Community unregistered
        designs 9.97–9.99
    copyright

Duration of protection (*cont.*)
anonymous works 3.53
author works 3.50
broadcasts 3.60
computer programs 3.52
contemporary issues
7.43–7.47
Crown copyright 3.55–3.56
films 3.58
general rules 3.49
joint authorship 3.54
moral rights 3.51
Parliamentary copyright 3.57
pseudonymous works 3.53
published editions 3.61
sound recordings 3.59
patents 11.141–11.146
performers' rights 6.32–6.33
registered designs (UK and
Community registered
designs) 8.120–8.121
sui generis database rights 6.11
summary of common
themes 1.44
UK unregistered design right
commencement 9.61
general rules 9.59–9.60
licences of right during last
five years 9.62–9.67

E

Economic rights
copyright protection
author's resale rights
3.44–3.46
contemporary issues 7.12,
7.16
directly or indirectly doing
restricted act 4.21–4.22
economic role of
copyright 2.18–2.21
EU law 4.8–4.9
international
background 4.4–4.7
primary restricted acts
4.10–4.11
secondary
infringements 4.12
taking whole or substantial
part 4.15–4.20
justifications for IP law
competition issues 1.26
need for balance 1.27
trade marks
key policy issues 13.7–13.8
Educational establishments
fair dealings for private
study 5.25

permitted copying 5.37–5.38
sui generis database rights 6.19
'Effective competition' 21.8–21.9
Emblems 14.100
Embryology
future concerns over
implementation of EU
Directive 12.67–12.69
patentability 12.54–12.60
Employers
Community designs 8.100, 9.95
first ownership of copyright
author works 3.25
contemporary issues 7.33–7.35
Crown copyright 3.29
presumption against 3.28
works made in the course of
employment 3.27
obligation of confidentiality
to 18.34–18.40
ownership of patents
compensation 11.165–11.170
general rules 11.156–11.164
statutory provisions
11.156–11.157
UK registered designs 8.92
UK unregistered design
rights 9.68–9.69
Emulation 1.46
Endorsement and sponsorship
false endorsements 19.49–19.51
merchandising
distinguished 19.48
sponsorship agreements
19.52–19.54
Enforcement and remedies
see also **Alternative dispute
resolution**
account of profits
general principles 22.124
principal remedy 1.44
counterfeiting and piracy
criminal sanctions
22.155–22.159
EU initiatives 22.147
European
Regulation 22.149–22.151
increased
infringement 22.148
proposals for international
treaty 22.154
UK response 22.152–22.153
criminal sanctions
copyright 22.141–22.142,
22.146
performers' rights 22.143
trade marks 22.144–22.146
cross-border infringements

Brussels Regulation
23.21–23.54
contemporary issues 23.63
copyright reform
proposals 23.65–23.68
historical development of UK
rules 23.8–23.17
ongoing work of Hague
Conference 23.64
overview of EU law 23.7
Rome I Regulation 23.61
Rome II Regulation
23.55–23.60
UK Supreme Court ruling
in 2011 23.18–23.19
damages and compensation
additional damages
22.122–22.123
employee inventions
11.165–11.170
general principles
22.120–22.121
principal remedy 1.44
delivery up 22.119
general principles 22.119
principal remedy 1.44
EU law 22.125–22.136
final injunctions 22.117–22.118
freezing injunctions 22.100,
22.98
future developments 22.172
interim injunctions
EU law 22.133
general principles
22.107–22.110
interaction between freedom
of expression and
privacy 22.111–22.116
overview 22.85–22.89
principal forms 1.44
principal remedies 1.44
role of TRIPS 22.160–22.171
search orders 22.98–22.99
self-help 22.101–22.102
suspected infringements
threats of action 22.90
unjustified threats of
action 22.91–22.97
Engravings
as artistic works 2.78–2.79
statutory provisions 2.70
Equitable remuneration
6.40–6.41, 22.18
EU law
abuse of dominant position
(Art 102 TFEU)
Commission v Microsoft
21.57–21.64

dominant position
21.46–21.47
ECJ case law 21.48
essential facilities
doctrine 21.65
Eurodefences 21.70–21.77
licensing 21.66–21.69
meaning and scope
21.43–21.45
policy tensions within
intellectual property 1.34
refusal to supply 21.49–21.56
role in development of IP
rights 1.61–1.63
agreements between
undertakings (Art 101
TFEU)
block exemptions 21.33
consequences of
breach 21.41–21.42
ECJ case law 21.23–21.28
Eurodefences 21.70–21.77
excluded restrictions
21.38–21.40
general principles and
objectives 21.20–21.21
hardcore restrictions 21.37
horizontal agreements
21.18
licensing agreements 21.22
licensing of trade
marks 22.62–22.66
new exemptions
regime 21.30–21.32
policy tensions within
intellectual property 1.34
role in development of IP
rights 1.61–1.63
severability of clauses 21.29
technology transfer
agreements 21.34–21.36
vertical agreements 21.19
applicable law
overview 23.7
Rome I Regulation 23.61
Rome II Regulation
23.55–23.60
author's moral rights 3.32
Community trade marks
advantages 13.43–13.46
main features 13.37–13.38
overview 13.36
registration
procedure 13.39–13.42
comparative
advertising 15.126–15.127
copyright
author's resale rights 3.44

control of TPMs and
RMIs 5.63–5.66
databases as literary
works 2.56
economic rights 4.8–4.9
history and
development 2.15–2.16
originality 2.39–2.40
permitted acts 5.9–5.11
public communication
rights 4.60
'safe harbours' 4.75
counterfeiting and piracy
criminal sanctions
22.155–22.159
EU initiatives 22.147
European
Regulation 22.149–22.151
designs 8.11–8.14
enforcement and
remedies 22.125–22.136
free movement of goods
batches of goods 20.51
burden of proof 20.60–20.63
case law development
20.11–20.32
conflict with IP rights
20.5–20.6
diverse policy
arguments 20.7–20.10
goods in transit 20.57–20.59
goods 'put on the
market' 20.55–20.56
implied consent 20.52–20.54
international
exhaustion 20.48–20.50
opposition to further dealing
by trade mark
proprietor 20.33–20.46
overview 19.28–19.42
rationale for system of
international
exhaustion 20.63–20.65
tensions created by
TFEU 20.4
use of marks in
advertising 20.47
free movement of services
copyright 20.70–20.72
evolving law 20.66–20.69
geographical indications
agricultural products and
foodstuffs 16.77–16.89
alleged breaches of
TRIPS 16.92–16.93
animal breeds 16.77
dispute resolution 16.89–16.91
generic names 16.74–16.76

homonymous names 16.77
preparation of
foodstuffs 16.80–16.81
protected DOs and
GIs 16.70–16.71
protection of traditional
names 16.72–16.73
Regulation 510/2006
16.68–16.69
jurisdiction
Brussels Regulation
23.21–23.54
overview 23.7
orphan works 7.36
patents
attempts to create unitary
right 10.29–10.34
Biotechnology
Directive 12.47–12.53
EPO reforms 10.27–10.28
'Europeanisation' and 20th
century reforms
10.22–10.26
exceptions to
patentability 10.63–10.64
exclusions from
patentability 11.5
future concerns over
implementation of
Directive 12.63–12.70
human embryology
12.54–12.60
interpretation of
claims 11.188
interpretation of
exclusions 12.20
obviousness 11.135–11.137
structure of European Patent
Office 10.23
performers' rights 6.24
role in development of IP rights
competition law 1.61–1.63
concerns over single
market 1.51–1.52
free movement of
goods 1.58–1.59
harmonisation and
approximation of
laws 1.53–1.54
institution of Community
rights 1.55–1.57
international
exhaustion 1.60
software-related inventions
business methods
12.111–12.124
development of EPO
jurisprudence 12.89–12.91

EU law (*cont.*)
  developments from 1998/9 to
    present 12.131–12.140
  policy matters 12.141
  reform priority for EU
    Commission
    12.150–12.158
  relationship between
    technical character and
    technical effect
    12.92–12.93
  statutory provisions 12.77
  textual processing
    12.107–12.110
  three-stage approach
    12.94–12.106
  UK-IPO Guidelines
    12.125–12.130
  sui generis database rights
    introduction of new
      rights 6.4
    permitted acts 6.18
European Patent Organisation
  aims of EPC 2000 10.75–10.76
  functions 10.27–10.28
Evidence
  free movement of goods
    20.60–20.63
  freezing injunctions 22.98
  search orders 22.98
  survey evidence 22.103–22.106
Exceptions *see* **Permitted acts**
Exploitation of IP rights
  assignment
    differing requirements for for
      each IPR 22.6
    licensing compared
      22.10–22.11
    registration 22.7
    transfer of ownership 22.5
  compulsory licensing
    patents 11.148
    policy tensions within
      intellectual property 1.35
  contemporary issues
    public sector
      information 22.77–22.84
    sui generis rights 22.68–22.76
  licences of right, UK
    unregistered design
    right 9.62–9.67
  licensing
    abuse of dominant position
      (Art 102 TFEU)
      21.66–21.69
    agreements between
      undertakings (Art 101
      TFEU) 21.22

assignment compared
  22.10–22.11
biotechnology
  patents 12.71–12.76
copyright 7.5, 22.12–22.48
free movement of
  goods 20.30
overview 22.8–22.9
patents 22.49–22.58
trade marks 22.59–22.66
policy tensions within
  intellectual property 1.35
Extended functions
  criticisms of principle 13.19
  relative grounds for refusing
    registration 15.102–15.104

F

Fair dealing (copyright)
  alternative approaches to
    copyright protection 2.20
  contracting out 5.59–5.62
  criticisms or reviews
    acknowledgement of
      authorship 5.31
    meaning and scope 5.29
    multiple copies 5.30
    public availability of
      work 5.32
  current events reporting
    acknowledgement of
      authorship 5.34
    examples from case law 5.35
    overview 5.33
  fairness 5.36
  human rights limitations 5.49
  overview 5.19
  private study
    defined 5.24
    educational
      establishments 5.25
    typographical
      arrangements 5.26
    websites 5.27–5.28
  research for non-commercial
    purposes
    meaning of 'research'
      5.21–5.23
    non-commercial
      purposes 5.22
    typographical
      arrangements 5.23
  'three-step test' 5.20
False attribution 3.33, 3.47
False endorsements
  19.49–19.51
Farmers' privileges
  11.228–11.230

File-sharing
  contemporary issues 7.5, 7.11,
    7.51–7.53
  unauthorised file-sharing
    4.72–4.74
Films
  as artistic works 2.87–2.89
  copying 4.41
  duration of protection 3.58
  first ownership of
    copyright 3.17
  fixation 2.32
  moral right of privacy 3.48
  originality 2.45
  paternity rights 3.35
  protected subject matter 2.22
  public communication rights
    EU law 4.60
    meaning and scope 4.61–4.65
  statutory provisions 2.70
Fixation
  contemporary issues 7.24
  copyright requirements
    2.30–2.33
  performers' rights 6.29
Foodstuffs
  cancellation 16.87–16.89
  registration as DO or GI 16.77
  registration procedures
    16.82–16.83
  required specifications
    16.78–16.79
  scope of protection
    16.84–16.86
Foreign judgements *see*
  **Recognition of foreign
  judgements**
Foreign words 14.66–14.67
Franchises 17.21
Fraud
  see also **Misrepresentation**
  contemporary issues 7.5
  'cyber-squatting' 17.62–17.68
  trade mark registration
    applications made in bad
      faith 14.101–14.105
    deceptive marks 14.98–14.99
    statutory provisions 14.95
Free movement of goods
  20.57–20.59
  batches of goods 20.51
  burden of proof 20.60–20.63
  case law development
    absence of consent
      20.31–20.32
    differing levels of protection
      in member states
      20.22–20.29

effect of consent by rights holder 20.16–20.21
existence and exercise of IP rights distinguished 20.12–20.15
licensing 20.30
pharmaceuticals 20.28–20.29
terminology 20.11
conflict with IP rights 20.5–20.6
diverse policy arguments exhaustion rule 20.7
governmental differences 20.9
importance of price differentials 20.8
theoretical and political underpinnings 20.10
EU role in development of IP rights 1.58–1.59
goods in transit 20.57–20.59
goods 'put on the market' 20.55–20.56
implied consent 20.52–20.54
international exhaustion 20.48–20.50
opposition to further dealing by trade mark proprietor Directive 2008/95/ CE 20.33–20.46
repackaging and parallel imports of pharmaceuticals 20.34–20.46
overview 20.3
rationale for system of international exhaustion 20.63–20.65
tensions created by TFEU 20.4
use of marks in advertising 20.47

Free movement of services
copyright 20.70–20.72
evolving law 20.66–20.69

Freedom of expression
basis for breach of confidence claims 18.8
copyright exceptions 5.49
impact of HRA 1998 on UK law balance between Arts 8 and 10 19.19–19.25
overview 19.9–19.10
interim injunctions 22.111–22.116

Freezing injunctions 22.98, 22.100

Functional designs
UK registered and Community designs 8.62–8.68

UK unregistered design right 9.15

G
Games 11.24–11.25
Generic words and names
prohibited registration of geographical indications 16.74–16.76
revocation of trade marks 14.123–14.124
Genetics *see* **Biotechnology**
Geographical indications
background 16.57–16.58
distinctiveness 14.65
EU regime
agricultural products and foodstuffs 16.77–16.89
alleged breaches of TRIPS 16.92–16.93
dispute resolution 16.89–16.91
generic names 16.74–16.76
preparation of foodstuffs 16.80–16.81
protected DOs and GIs 16.70–16.71
protection of traditional names 16.72–16.73
Regulation 510/2006 16.68–16.69
international protection 16.63–16.67
principal treaties and conventions 1.72
protection from passing off 17.26
reform proposals 16.94
terminology 16.61–16.62
traditional function of trade marks 13.9–13.11
Gestures 14.8
Get-up 17.32–17.33
Goodwill
basis of action for passing off 17.5–17.6
damage to 17.57–17.58
false endorsements 19.49–19.51
foreign goodwill 17.15–17.16
product goodwill 17.19
protectable devices
advertising themes and techniques 17.34
business names 17.28
get-up 17.32–17.33
letters and numbers 17.29–17.30

names 17.26
overview 17.22
titles 17.27
words 17.23–17.25
regional or local goodwill 17.18
role of customers 17.13–17.14
shared goodwill
companies 17.20
franchises 17.21
Governing law *see* **Applicable law**
Gowers Review
copyright
'fair use' 7.57
filing of complaints 7.63
focus on exceptions 7.54
general recommendations 7.59
general remit 7.1
orphan works 7.37
sound recordings 3.59
subsequent UK–IPO consultation 7.60
enforcement recommendations 22.172
patents 10.80–10.86
biotechnology 12.8
general recommendations 11.39
infringement proceedings 11.173
model licence templates 11.148
research exemption 11.226
publication of report 1.36
Graphic representations
colours 14.14–14.16
smells 14.12–14.13
sounds 14.17–14.19
statutory provisions 14.7
taste marks 14.20
underlying rationale 14.21–14.22
Graphic works
meaning and scope 2.71
statutory provisions 2.70

H
Hargreaves Review
copyright
contracting out 7.61
failure of the framework to adapt 7.60
'fair use' 7.57
focus on exceptions 7.54
general recommendations 7.59
orphan works 7.37, 22.21
publication of report 7.1

Hargreaves Review (*cont.*)
enforcement
recommendations 22.172
patents 10.81–10.88
computer programs 12.82
publication of report 1.36
History and development of IP law
copyright
Berne Convention 1886
2.8–2.9
Copyright Acts 1911–88
2.10–2.11
early history 2.4–2.7
economic rights 4.4–4.7
EU law 2.15–2.16
modern treaties and
conventions 2.12–2.14
early developments in
international law
1.64–1.68
patents
early history 10.4–10.11
international
developments 10.12–10.13
performers' rights 6.21–6.23
registered designs (UK and
Community registered
designs)
EU Directive and
Regulation 8.11–8.14
international
background 8.4–8.9
UK history 8.10
UK choice of law rules
23.8–23.17
unregistered designs
(Community and UK
unregistered designs)
EU Directive and
Regulation 8.11–8.14
international context 9.4–9.8
UK background 9.9–9.13
Homonymous names 16.77
Honest practices 15.107–15.108
Horizontal agreements 21.18
Human embryology
future concerns over
implementation of EU
Directive 12.67–12.69
patentability 12.54–12.60
Human rights
breach of confidence
basis of claim 18.8
creation of new cause of
action 18.6
copyright exceptions 5.49
impact on IP law 1.73

impact on privacy
balance between Arts 8
and 10 19.19–19.25
key development 19.11
overview 19.9–19.10
pictures and images
19.17–19.18
'reasonable expectation of
privacy' 19.12–19.16
interim injunctions
22.111–22.116
opening of dialogue about IP
rights 10.20
relevance to patents 10.19–10.20
Hybridoma technology 12.12

I

ICANN
approval of domain names 16.5
dispute resolution
procedures 16.23–16.27
Image rights
conclusions 19.58
confidentiality
agreements 19.55–19.57
merchandising 19.31–19.42
sponsorship agreements
19.52–19.54
In silico **techniques** 12.12
**Incidental inclusion of copyright
material** 5.43
Individual character
Community unregistered
designs 9.95
designs already publicly
available 8.50–8.61
informed user 8.37–8.40
registered designs 8.32–8.49
Industrial applicability (patents)
biotechnology 12.34–12.37
criteria for patentability
11.138–11.140
Information
continuous expansion of state
of art 11.83
exclusions from
patentability 11.41–11.48
key element of intellectual
property protection 1.20
property rights 18.65, 19.56,
19.58
rights management information
systems
contemporary issues 7.5,
7.61–7.63
EU controls 5.63–5.66
general approach 5.55
standing to sue 5.56

technical protection
measures 5.52
unauthorised reception of
transmissions 5.57
Informed user 8.37–8.40
Infringements
see also **Cross-border
infringements**
Community designs 9.95,
9.101–9.102
copyright
directly or indirectly doing
restricted act 4.21–4.22
general principles 4.13–4.22
issuing public copies without
authority 4.45–4.48
primary restricted acts
4.10–4.11
reproduction 4.23–4.44
restricted lending and
rental 4.49–4.52
secondary
infringements 4.12
taking whole or substantial
part 4.15–4.20
patents
indirect infringement
11.185–11.186
interpretation of
claims 11.187–11.204
meaning and scope
11.175–11.184
overview 11.171–11.174
statutory provisions 11.175
registered designs (UK and
Community registered
designs) 8.111–8.116
sui generis database rights
extraction and utilisation
of substantial parts
6.13–6.14
overview 6.12
repeated extraction and
utilisation of insubstantial
parts 6.15–6.16
suspected infringements
threats of action 22.90
unjustified threats
22.91–22.97
trade marks
case law 15.7–15.18
company and business
names 15.19–15.22
defences 15.105–15.132
earlier marks with
reputation 15.68–15.100
extended functions
15.102–15.104

identical goods or services
already registered
15.24–15.32
likelihood of confusion
15.33–15.37, 15.57–15.67
marks and signs compared
in different contexts
15.38–15.40
similar goods and
services 15.49–15.56
similar marks 15.41–15.48
statutory provisions
15.4–15.6
UK unregistered design
right 9.71–9.78
Initial ownership *see* **First
ownership**
Injunctions (interdicts)
final injunctions 22.117–22.118
freezing injunctions 22.98,
22.100
interim injunctions
EU law 22.133
general principles
22.107–22.110
interaction between freedom
of expression and
privacy 22.111–22.116
principal remedy 1.44
Innovation
see also **Novelty**
benefit of compulsory
licensing 1.35
benefits of breach of
confidence 18.71
benefits of early patent
system 10.6
competition theory 21.11, 21.6
contractual controls 22.72
dangers of passing off 17.71
establishment of Creative
Commons 7.5
exclusion of functional designs
from registered design
protection 8.62
experimental purposes
defence 11.226
free movement of goods 20.10
human rights dialogue 10.20
need for new IP rights
10.87–10.88
overuse of competition
law 21.67
policy relationship with trade
secrets 18.72–18.73,
18.68
reconciliation of public and
private interests 1.30

restraint of moral interests 1.23
trade mark justifications 13.23
UK–IPO approach 12.130
WHO interest in the issue 10.56
Integrated circuits 1.72
Integrity *see* **Right of integrity**
Intellectual property
common expressions and
symbols 1.45
competing policies
protection of private interests
through property 1.29
reconciliation of public and
private interests 1.30–1.41
cyclical pattern of production
and protection 1.31
development
accretion and emulation
distinguished 1.46
development through national
laws
international mutual
recognition 1.49
jurisdictional restraints 1.48
overview of national and
international
influences 1.47
tensions created by judicial
reticence 1.50
EU role in development of IP
rights
competition law 1.61–1.63
concerns over single
market 1.51–1.52
free movement of
goods 1.58–1.59
harmonisation and
approximation of
laws 1.53–1.54
institution of Community
rights 1.55–1.57
international
exhaustion 1.60
human rights influences 1.73
international obligations
early developments 1.64–1.68
principal treaties and
conventions 1.72
TRIPS Agreement 1994
1.69–1.71
justifications
economic interests 1.26–1.27
moral interests 1.22–1.23
social interests 1.24–1.25
meaning and scope
'novel products of human
intellectual
endeavour' 1.19

protection of
information 1.20
relevant interests 1.21
protection prior to
registration 1.42–1.43
statutory rights
copyright 1.8
designs 1.9
patents 1.7
trade marks 1.10
summary of common
themes 1.44
Inter brand competition 21.17
Interdicts *see* **Injunctions
(interdicts)**
Interim injunctions
EU law 22.133
general principles 22.107–22.110
interaction between freedom of
expression and
privacy 22.111–22.116
**International conventions and
treaties**
author's moral rights 3.31
breach of confidence 18.11
copyright
Berne Convention 1886
2.4–2.7
economic rights 4.4–4.7
modern treaties and
conventions 2.12–2.14
permitted acts 5.8
counterfeiting and
piracy 22.154
geographical indications
16.63–16.67
importance of TRIPS for
enforcement 22.160–22.171
influence on development of IP
rights
mutual recognition
agreements 1.49
overview of national and
international
influences 1.47
passing off 17.7–17.8
patents
continuing negotiations
and responses to TRIPS
10.46–10.56
early history 10.12–10.13
impact of Doha
Declaration 10.61–10.67
role of WIPO 10.35–10.41
TRIPS Agreement 1994
10.42–10.45
WHO strategy to develop
Global Plan 10.57–10.60

International conventions and treaties (*cont.*)

WIPO's ongoing programme of harmonisation 10.69

registered designs 8.4–8.9

role in development of IP rights

early developments 1.64–1.68

role in development of IP rights 1.72

TRIPS Agreement 1994 1.69–1.71

trade marks

WIPO 13.48–13.58

WTO 13.59

unregistered design rights 9.4–9.8

International exhaustion

contemporary issues 20.63–20.65

free movement of goods 20.48–20.50

free movement of services

copyright 20.70–20.72

evolving law 20.66–20.69

policy arguments 20.09

role in development of IP rights 1.60

Internet

see also **Computer programmes**

broadcasting by 2.94

consequential reform proposals

copyright 23.65–23.68

ongoing work of Hague Conference 23.64

trade marks 23.69–23.73

copying of computer programs and databases 4.34–4.36

'cyber-squatting' 17.62–17.68

domain names

defined 16.4–16.6

dispute resolution 16.12–16.27

overview 16.2–16.3

ownership disputes 16.9–16.11

registration as trade mark 16.7–16.8

file-sharing

contemporary issues 7.5, 7.11, 7.51–7.53

unauthorised file-sharing 4.72–4.74

'no derogation from grant' principle 5.48

online licensing

collective licensing 22.43–22.44

individual schemes 22.45–22.48

private study 5.27–5.28

temporary copies by ISPs 5.15–5.17

use of trade marks

auction sites 16.54–16.56

keyword advertising 16.42–16.53

overview 16.28

permitted disclaimers 16.38–16.39

territoriality 16.29–16.32

user infringements 16.33–16.37

WIPO strategy 16.40–16.41

Intra brand competition 21.16

Inventions *see* **Patents**

Inventive step

biotechnology 12.30–12.33

meaning and scope 11.109–11.111

persons skilled in the art 11.117–11.119

state of the art 11.112–11.116

test for obviousness 11.120–11.133

Inverse passing off 17.50

Investment 13.15

Issuing public copies without authority

cross-border infringements 4.45

general principles 4.43–4.44

'public' defined 4.47

publication distinguished 4.46

transient copies 4.48

J

Joint authorship

duration of protection 3.54

first ownership of copyright 3.7–3.14

media works 3.21

Judgment *see* **Skill, labour and judgment**

Jurisdiction

contemporary issues 23.63

EU law

Brussels Regulation 23.21–23.54

overview 23.7

historical development of UK rules 23.8–23.17

reform proposals

copyright 23.65–23.68

ongoing work of Hague Conference 23.64

UK Supreme Court ruling in 2011 23.18–23.19

Justifications for IP law

copyright protection

contemporary issues 7.12–7.17

economic role of copyright 2.18–2.21

response to early printing 2.17

economic interests

competition issues 1.26

need for balance 1.27

moral interests

protection of personal interests 1.22

protection of time, labour and expenditure 1.23

patents 10.14–10.21

social interests

advantages and disadvantages 1.24

moral issues arising 1.25

trade marks 13.8, 13.23

K

Key words

as literary works 2.52–2.53

subject matter of copyright 2.24

use of marks on internet for advertising 16.42–16.53

L

Labour *see* **Skill, labour and judgment**

Lending *see* **Public lending**

Libraries and archives

authorisation of infringement 4.68

deposit libraries 5.40

Public Lending Right scheme 5.39

restricted lending 4.49–4.52

transient reproduction 4.36

Licensing

see also **Consent**

abuse of dominant position (Art 102 TFEU) 21.66–21.69

agreements between undertakings (Art 101 TFEU) 21.22

assignment compared 22.10–22.11

biotechnology patents 12.71–12.76

copyright

collective licensing 22.23–22.48

compulsory licensing
22.19–22.22
contemporary issues 7.5
equitable
remuneration 22.18
restraint of trade
doctrine 22.13–22.15
UK contract practices 22.12
undue influence 22.16–22.17
free movement of goods 20.30
overview 22.8–22.9
patents
compulsory licensing
22.50–22.53
overview 22.49
trade marks
competition law 22.62–22.64
compulsory licensing 22.61
overview 22.59–22.60
unregistered design right
licences of right 9.62–9.67
Likelihood of confusion
passing off
basis of claim 17.40–17.43
requirement for 'common field
of activity' 17.44–17.46
trade marks
link with likelihood of
association 15.61–15.67
overview 13.22
perception of relevant
consumers 15.57–15.58
relative ground for refusing
registration 15.33–15.37
relevant time 15.59–15.60
Literary works
see also **Performers' rights**
adaptation 4.31, 4.66
defined 2.51
duration of protection 3.50
exclusions from
patentability 11.19
first ownership of copyright
employers 3.25
statutory presumption 3.6
meaning and scope
circuit diagrams 2.64
computer programs 2.54
databases 2.56–2.63
single words and
phrases 2.52–2.53
tables and compilations 2.55
originality 2.45
paternity rights 3.35
public communication rights
EU law 4.60
meaning and scope 4.61–4.65
public performances

audience requirements 4.57
broadcasts 4.59
defined 4.53
'direct representations or
performances' 4.54–4.56
performing for one's own
benefit 4.58
subject matter 2.22

M

Maps
as artistic works 2.74
statutory provisions 2.70
Mareva injunctions 22.98,
22.100
Markets 21.13–21.15
Mathematical methods
11.15–11.18
Media works
author works
distinguished 2.47–2.48
broadcasts
duration of protection 3.60
first ownership of
copyright 3.19
meaning and scope 2.91–2.95
originality 2.46
protected subject matter 2.22
duration of protection
broadcasts 3.60
films 3.58
published editions 3.61
sound recordings 3.59
films
as artistic works 2.87–2.89
duration of protection 3.58
first ownership of
copyright 3.17
fixation 2.32
originality 2.45
protected subject matter 2.22
statutory provisions 2.70
first ownership of copyright
broadcasts 3.19
films 3.17
published editions 3.20
sound recordings 3.18
meaning and scope
broadcasts 2.91–2.95
published editions 2.96
sound recordings 2.90
public communication rights
EU law 4.60
meaning and scope 4.61–4.65
published editions
duration of protection 3.61
first ownership of
copyright 3.20

meaning and scope 2.96
originality 2.45
sound recordings
duration of protection 3.59
first ownership of
copyright 3.18
fixation 2.32
meaning and scope 2.90
originality 2.45
protected subject matter 2.22
Medical treatments
Bolar exemptions 11.231
diagnostic methods 11.73–11.76
exceptions to
patentability 10.63–10.64
implements and
apparatus 11.77
'new use' patents 11.102–11.108
surgery 11.69–11.72
therapy treatments 10.65–10.68
Mental acts 11.21–11.23
Merchandising
see also **Endorsement and
sponsorship**
endorsement
distinguished 19.48
meaning and scope 19.26–19.47
passing off 19.43–19.47
trade marks 19.28–19.42
**Methods and principles of
construction** 9.36–9.37
Misrepresentation
basis of action for passing
off 17.5–17.6
comparative advertising 17.54
deception in foreign
markets 17.47
extended passing off 17.56
general rules 17.35–17.39
inverse passing off 17.50
membership of professional
associations 17.55
quality misrepresentations
17.51–17.53
substitution selling 17.49
third party assistance 17.48
Misuse of private information
creation of new cause of
action 18.6
key development 19.11
Monopoly power
biotechnology patents 12.9,
12.71–12.76
focus of competition law 21.10
general nature of IP rights 20.6
market powers 21.44
rationale behind patents
11.207

Monopoly power *(cont.)*
  registration of celebrity
      names 19.31
  relevant markets 21.13
  theory of competition 21.7
  trade marks
      key policy issues 13.5
      other IP rights
          compared 13.23–13.25
  unfair threats to
      competition 21.3
Moral rights
  Berne Convention 3.31
  commercial publishing 3.43
  contemporary issues 7.38–7.42
  duration of protection 3.51
  EU law 3.32
  false attribution 3.47
  justifications for IP law
      1.22–1.23
      protection of personal
          interests 1.22
      protection of time, labour
          and expenditure 1.23
  key characteristics
      overview 3.34
  paternity rights
      excluded works 3.38
      meaning and scope 3.35
      need for 'assertion' 3.36
      public exhibitions 3.37
  performers' rights
      audio-visual
          performances 6.37
      avoidance of derogatory
          treatment 6.36
      overview 6.34
      right to be identified 6.35
  privacy in photographs and
      films 3.48
  resale rights 3.44–3.46
  right of integrity
      avoidance of derogatory
          treatment 3.39
      excluded works 3.42
      meaning and scope
          3.40–3.41
  UK law 3.33
Morality
  biotechnology patents
      EU case law 12.45–12.46
      key issue 12.43
      TRIPS Agreement 1994
          12.44
  exceptions to patentability
      10.45, 11.5–11.62
  excluded designs 8.72, 8.96,
      8.103

general concerns over IP
    rights 1.25
Musical works
see also **Performers' rights**
  adaptation 4.31, 4.66
  derivative works 2.42
  duration of protection 3.50
  exclusions from
      patentability 11.19
  exclusive recording
      contracts 6.30
  first ownership of copyright
      employers 3.25
      statutory presumption 3.6
  meaning and scope 2.68
  paternity rights 3.35
  permitted acts 5.46
  protected subject matter 2.22
  public communication rights
      EU law 4.60
      meaning and scope 4.61–4.65
  public performances
      audience requirements 4.57
      broadcasts 4.59
      defined 4.53
      'direct representations or
          performances' 4.54–4.56
      performing for one's own
          benefit 4.58
'Must fit' design exclusions
  Community unregistered
      designs 9.95
  registered designs (UK and
      Community registered
      designs) 8.69–8.71
  UK unregistered designs
      9.38–9.49
'Must match' design exclusions
see also **Repair clause**
  Community unregistered
      designs 8.88, 9.95
  registered designs (UK and
      Community registered
      designs) 8.81–8.89
  UK unregistered designs
      9.38–9.42, 9.50–9.52

N

Names
  business names
      protection from passing
          off 17.28
      trade mark infringements
          15.19–15.22
  geographical names
      distinctiveness 14.65
      protection from passing
          off 17.26

merchandising rights
    19.31–19.42
personal names
    distinctiveness 14.55
    own name defence 15.9–15.11
    protection from passing
        off 17.26
    trade mark registration 14.8
sponsorship agreements
    19.52–19.54
National laws
see also **EU law; United States
copyright**
  adaptation 4.66
  artistic works 2.70
  authorisation of
      infringements 4.68
  author's moral rights 3.33
  Copyright Acts 1911–88
      2.10–2.11
  databases as literary
      works 2.57
  dramatic works 2.67
  early history 2.4–2.7
  fair dealings 5.19
  fixation requirements 2.31
  originality 2.34
  public communication
      rights 4.60
  public performances 4.53
influence on development of IP
    rights
  international mutual
      recognition 1.49
  jurisdictional restraints 1.48
  overview of national and
      international
      influences 1.47
  tensions created by judicial
      reticence 1.50
patents
  application procedure 10.94
  contemporary issues
      10.77–10.88
  criteria for
      patentability 11.78
  employee rights
      11.156–11.157
  exceptions to
      patentability 11.49
  exclusions from
      patentability 11.6
  infringements 11.175, 11.185
  inventive steps 11.110
  obviousness 11.135–11.137
  state of the art 11.81
performers' rights 6.31,
    6.38–6.39

registered designs 8.10
software-related inventions
    statutory provisions 12.77
    UK jurisprudence
        12.142–12.149
trade marks
    absolute grounds for refusing
        registration 14.28
    comparative
        advertising 15.125
    defences 15.106
    domain name
        disputes 16.13–16.22
    identical goods or services
        already registered 15.24
    infringements 15.4–15.6
    protection of trade marks with
        reputation 15.68–15.75
    public policy and
        morality 14.95
    registration procedure
        13.31–13.35
    relative grounds for refusing
        registration 14.109–14.110
    statutory provisions 14.7
UK statutory rights
    copyright 1.8
    core features 1.43
    designs 1.9
    patents 1.7
    trade marks 1.10
UK unregistered design rights
    background 9.9–9.13
National treatment of
    foreigners 1.66
'No derogation from grant'
    principle 5.48
Non-commercial dealings
    fair dealings (copyright)
        5.21–5.23
    patents 11.220
    sui generis database rights 6.18
Non-obviousness *see* **Inventive**
    steps; Obviousness
'Notional skilled reader' 11.87
Novelty
    see also **Originality**
    designs (UK registered and
        Community designs)
    Community unregistered
        designs 9.95
    designs already publicly
        available 8.50–8.61
    registered designs 8.28–8.31
key element of intellectual
    property protection 1.19
patents
    biotechnology 12.24–12.29

criteria for
    patentability 11.79–11.96
exclusions from state of the
    art 11.101
'medical use' patents
    11.102–11.108
origins of system 10.06
product-by-process
    claims 11.98–11.99
selection patents 11.100
policy tensions within
    intellectual property 1.38
Numbers 14.8
Numerals 14.64

O

Obviousness
    EPO and UK approaches
        compared 11.135–11.137
    four step test 11.120–11.133
    inventive steps 11.110
    reform proposals 11.134
Opposition
    patents 10.25
    trade marks 13.63–13.64
Origin marks *see* **Geographical**
    indications
Originality
    see also **Novelty**
    copyright
        broadcasts 2.46
        contemporary issues
            7.25–7.30
        derivative works 2.41–2.43
        EU and UK approaches to
            'intellectual creation'
            distinguished 2.39–2.40
        independent but similar
            works 2.44
        judicial definition 2.35
        no requirement of quality or
            merit 2.36
        policy tensions within
            intellectual property 1.38
        skill, labour and
            judgment 2.37–2.38
        sound recordings 2.45
        sound recordings, films and
            published editions 2.45
        statutory provisions 2.34
    UK unregistered design
        right 9.53–9.58
    see also **Commonplace designs**
Orphan works
    compulsory licensing 22.20
    contemporary issues 7.5,
        7.36–7.37
    informal initiatives 22.22

WIPO discussions 22.21
'Outstanding benefits'
    11.165–11.170
Own name defence 15.109–15.111
Ownership
    see also **Authorship**
    Community designs 8.100, 9.95
    domain names 16.9–16.11
    first ownership of copyright
        anonymous works 3.23
        broadcasts 3.19
        collective works 3.15
        compilations 3.16
        computer programs 3.22
        contemporary issues
            7.33–7.37
        Crown copyright 3.25–3.29
        employers 3.25–3.29
        films 3.17
        general rules 3.5
        joint authorship 3.7–3.14,
            3.21
        Parliamentary
            copyright 3.30
        pseudonymous works 3.24
        published editions 3.20
        sound recordings 3.18
        statutory presumption for
            author works 3.6
        transferees distinguished 3.4
    patents
        co-owners 11.153–11.155
        employers 11.156–11.170
        inventors 11.150–11.152
    sui generis database rights 6.10
    UK registered designs 8.92–8.93
    UK unregistered design
        right 9.68–9.69

P

Paintings
    derivative works 2.42
    meaning and scope 2.72
    statutory provisions 2.70
Parallel imports
    burden of proof 20.60–20.63
    case law development
        absence of consent
            20.31–20.32
        differing levels of protection
            in member states
            20.22–20.29
        effect of consent by rights
            holder 20.16–20.21
        existence and exercise of IP
            rights
            distinguished 20.12–20.15
        licensing 20.30

Parallel imports (*cont.*)
  pharmaceuticals 20.28–20.29
  terminology 20.11
  EU role in development of IP
    rights 1.59
  necessity test 20.39–20.41
  notice to trade market
    proprietor 20.45
  pharmaceuticals 20.35
  policy arguments 20.8
Parliamentary copyright
  duration of protection 3.57
  ownership 3.30
Parodies
  future developments 22.172
  infringement by
    reproduction 4.39
Passing off
  ambit 1.12
  basis of action 17.5–17.6
  'cyber-squatting' 17.62–17.68
  damage
    dilution of name 17.59
    to goodwill 17.57–17.58
    prospective damage
      sufficient 17.60
  defences 17.61
  false endorsements 19.51
  goodwill requirements
    foreign goodwill 17.15–17.16
    product goodwill 17.19
    protectable devices
      17.22–17.34
    regional or local
      goodwill 17.18
    role of customers 17.13–17.14
    shared goodwill 17.20–17.21
  international background
    17.7–17.8
  likelihood of confusion
    basis of claim 17.40–17.43
    requirement for 'common
      filed of activity'
      17.44–17.46
  meaning and scope 17.9–17.11
  merchandising rights
    19.43–19.47
  misrepresentation
    requirements
    comparative
      advertising 17.54
    deception in foreign
      markets 17.47
    extended passing off 17.56
    general rules 17.35–17.39
    inverse passing off 17.50
    membership of professional
      associations 17.55

    quality misrepresentations
      17.51–17.53
    substitution selling 17.49
    third party assistance 17.48
  overview 17.4
  passing off
    likelihood of
      confusion 17.40–17.46
  requirement for business
    context 17.12
  survey evidence 22.103–22.106
  unfair competition 17.69–17.72
Patents
see also **Free movement of goods**
  application procedure
    10.104–10.113
    drafting claims 10.89–10.103
    examination process
      10.114–10.116
    importance 10.89–10.103
    persons entitled to
      apply 10.117–10.120
    WIPO attempts to streamline
      process 10.36–10.41
  assignment 22.6
  biotechnology
    contemporary issues 12.3
    EU Directive 12.47–12.53
    excessively broad
      patents 12.38–12.42
    future concerns over
      implementation of EU
      Directive 12.63–12.70
    human embryology
      12.54–12.60
    industrial applicability
      (patents) 12.34–12.37
    inventions and discoveries
      distinguished 12.18–12.23
    inventive step 12.30–12.33
    key questions about gene
      sequencing 12.8–12.9
    monopoly concerns
      12.71–12.76
    morality 12.43–12.46
    novelty 12.24–12.29
    synthetic biology 12.61–12.62
  common expressions and
    symbols 1.45
  computer programs
    contemporary issues 12.3
    developments from 1998/9 to
      present 12.131–12.140
    exclusion from
      patentability 12.79–12.88
  contemporary issues
    biotechnology 12.3
    EU reforms 10.70–10.76

    national reforms 10.77–10.88
    software-related
      inventions 12.4
    WIPO's ongoing programme
      of harmonisation 10.69
  criteria for patentability
    11.134
    biotechnology 12.34–12.37
    industrial applicability
      11.138–11.140
    inventive steps 11.109–11.137
    novelty 11.79–11.108
    obviousness 11.120–11.137
    reform proposals 11.134
    statutory provisions 11.78
  defences
    Bolar exemptions 11.231
    experimental
      purposes 11.221–11.227
    farmers' privileges
      11.228–11.230
    private and non-commercial
      acts 11.220
    statutory provisions 11.219
  duration of protection
    11.141–11.146
  early developments in
    international law 1.65
  early history 10.4–10.11
  EU law
    attempts to create unitary
      right 10.29–10.34
    contemporary issues
      10.70–10.76
    EPO reforms 10.27–10.28
    'Europeanisation' and 20th
      century reforms
      10.22–10.26
    structure of European Patent
      Office 10.23
  excluded and excepted subject
    matter
    aesthetic creations 11.19
    application
      procedure 10.104–10.113
    business methods
      11.26–11.32
    computer programs
      11.33–11.40
    discoveries, scientific theories
      and mathematical
      methods 11.15–11.18
    games 11.24–11.25
    information 11.41–11.48
    medical treatments
      10.63–10.77
    mental acts 11.21–11.23
    overview 11.5–11.14

harmonisation and
approximation of EU
law 1.54
infringements
indirect infringement
11.185–11.186
interpretation of
claims 11.187–11.204
meaning and scope
11.175–11.184
overview 11.171–11.174
statutory provisions 11.175
international developments
continuing negotiations and
responses to TRIPS
10.46–10.56
early history 10.12–10.13
impact of Doha
Declaration 10.61–10.67
role of WIPO 10.35–10.41
TRIPS Agreement 1994
10.42–10.45
WHO strategy to develop
Global Plan 10.57–10.60
WIPO's ongoing programme
of harmonisation 10.69
interpretation of claims
declarations of non-
infringement 11.204
general principles
11.187–11.203
inventive steps
biotechnology 12.30–12.33
meaning and scope
11.109–11.111
persons skilled in the
art 11.117–11.119
state of the art 11.112–11.116
test for obviousness
11.120–11.133
licensing
compulsory licensing
22.50–22.53
genetic inventions
10.55–10.58
overview 22.49
limitation on rights
11.147–11.149
novelty
biotechnology 12.24–12.29
criteria for
patentability 11.79–11.96
exclusions from state of the
art 11.101
'medical use' patents
11.102–11.108
origins of system 10.06
product-by-process
claims 11.98–11.99

selection patents 11.100
overlap with trade
marks 13.27–13.28
overview 11.1–11.4
ownership
co-owners 11.153–11.155
employers 11.156–11.170
inventors 11.150–11.152
policy tensions within
intellectual property
exploitation 1.35
patentability 1.37
registration 1.40
strength of protection 1.39
post-grant amendments 10.121
principal treaties and
conventions 1.72
rationale for protection
10.14–10.21
revocation 11.205–11.218
software-related inventions
computer programs
distinguished 12.78
developments from 1998/9
to present 12.131–12.140
EPO jurisprudence
12.89–12.130
policy matters 12.141
reform priority for EU
Commission
12.150–12.158
statutory provisions 12.77
UK jurisprudence
12.142–12.149
UK statutory rights 1.7, 1.43
unjustified threats of
action 22.93
Paternity rights
commercial publishing 3.43
excluded works 3.38
meaning and scope 3.35
need for 'assertion' 3.36
public exhibitions 3.37
Performers' rights
categorisation 6.26
criminal sanctions 22.143
duration of protection
6.32–6.33
EU reforms 6.24
exclusive recording
contracts 6.30
harmonisation and
approximation of EU
law 1.54
history and development
6.21–6.23
live performances 6.26
meaning and scope 6.25
moral rights

audio-visual
performances 6.37
avoidance of derogatory
treatment 6.36
overview 6.34
right to be identified 6.35
non-property rights 6.29
permitted acts 6.31
principal treaties and
conventions 1.72
property rights 6.27–6.28
remuneration
right to equitable
remuneration 6.40–6.41
royalties 6.42
symbol 1.45
UK approach 6.38–6.39
Permitted acts
copyright
broadcasts 5.45
computer programs 5.44
contemporary issues 7.54–7.60
disabled persons 5.41
educational
establishments 5.37–5.38
EU law 5.9–5.11
fair dealings 5.19–5.36
incidental inclusion 5.43
libraries and archives
5.39–5.40
musical works 5.46
overview 5.1–5.3
overview of exceptions 5.14
public administration 5.42
public domain 5.4–5.7
temporary copies 5.13–5.18
performers' rights 6.31
sui generis database rights
educational
establishments 6.19
EU law 6.17
non-commercial
research 6.18
Personal names
distinctiveness 14.55
own name defence 15.9–15.11
protection from passing
off 17.26
trade mark registration 14.8
Personal privacy *see* **Privacy**
Personality rights
conclusions
passing off 19.43–19.47
trade marks 19.28–19.42
**Persons skilled in the art
(patent applications)**
biotechnology 12.30–12.33
test for obviousness
11.117–11.119

Pharmaceuticals
consent 20.28–20.29
opposition to further dealing by
trade mark proprietor
artificial market
partitioning 20.38
minimum
intervention 20.43–20.44
necessity test 20.39–20.41
notice by parallel
importer 20.45
overview 20.34–20.37
repackaging 20.46
Photographs
as artistic works 2.75
breach of confidence 18.23–18.24
confidentiality
agreements 19.55–19.57
derivative works 2.42
false endorsements 19.49–19.51
merchandising rights 19.28
misuse of private
information 19.17–19.18
moral right of privacy 3.48
statutory provisions 2.70
Plans
as artistic works 2.74
statutory provisions 2.70
Plant varieties
cancellation 16.87–16.89
key example of *sui generis*
rights 1.16
principal treaties and
conventions 1.72
registration as DO or GI 16.77
registration procedures
16.82–16.83
required specifications
16.78–16.79
scope of protection 16.84–16.86
Policy issues
free movement of goods
exhaustion rule 20.7
governmental
differences 20.9
importance of price
differentials 20.8
theoretical and political
underpinnings 20.10
public policy limitations
biotechnology patents 12.73
breach of confidence 18.26,
18.56–18.60
copyright 5.47
patents 11.147–11.149
registered designs 8.72
trade mark registration
14.95–14.99

software-related
inventions 12.141
tensions within intellectual
property
protection of private interests
through property 1.29
reconciliation of public and
private interests 1.30–1.41
trade marks
monopoly power 13.5
proliferation of signs 13.4
trade secrets 18.68, 18.72–18.73
Premium system 10.9–10.10
Primary copyright infringements
adaptation of works
computer programs and
databases 4.67
meaning and scope 4.66
copying 4.24–4.42
general principles 4.10–4.11
issuing public copies without
authority
general principles 4.43–4.44
'public' defined 4.47
publication
distinguished 4.46
territoriality 4.45
transient copies 4.48
public communication rights
EU law 4.60
meaning and scope 4.61–4.65
public performances
audience requirements 4.57
broadcasts 4.59
defined 4.53
'direct representations or
performances' 4.54–4.56
performing for one's own
benefit 4.58
reproduction
abridgements 4.40
adaptation
distinguished 4.31
admittedly derivative
work 4.37–4.38
basic requirements 4.24
broadcasts 4.41
computer programs 4.34–4.36
contemporary issues 7.48–7.50
films 4.41
ideas and impressions
4.32–4.33
knowledge of original
work 4.30
need to show causal
connection between two
works 4.27–4.29
parodies 4.39

published editions 4.42
similarity of two works 4.25
sound recordings 4.41
typographical
arrangements 4.42
works similar but not
same 4.26
restricted lending and
rental 4.49–4.52
secondary infringements
distinguished 4.76
Priority
patents
first-to-file and first-to-invent
distinguished 10.18
importance 10.92
registered designs 8.5, 8.50
trade marks
earlier trade marks and
rights 14.111
interaction between various
systems 13.61–13.62
Privacy
see also **Breach of confidence**
author's moral rights 3.33
conclusions 19.58
false endorsements 19.51
impact of HRA 1998
balance between Arts 8
and 10 19.19–19.25
key development 19.11
overview 19.9–19.10
pictures and images
19.17–19.18
'reasonable expectation of
privacy' 19.12–19.16
interim injunctions
22.111–22.116
law prior to HRA 1998 19.7–19.8
photographs and films 3.48
Private study
defined 5.24
educational
establishments 5.25
typographical
arrangements 5.26
websites 5.27–5.28
Private use *see* **Non-commercial
dealings**
Procedure *see* **Registration
procedure**
**Product (UK registered and
Community designs)**
8.18–8.22, 9.95
Product-by-process claims
11.98–11.99, 12.25
'Product of nature'
doctrine 12.19

Property rights
balance between public
and private interests
1.35
implications for IP law 1.19
paradox arising 1.33
performers' rights 6.27–6.28
protection of information
19.56, 19.58, 18.65
restrictions imposed by
TFEU 10.30
reverter clauses 22.11
reward theory 1.31
state autonomy 23.49
Pseudonymous works
duration of protection 3.53
first ownership of
copyright 3.24
Public administration 5.42
Public communication rights
EU law 4.60
meaning and scope 4.61–4.65
Public domain
see also **State of the art**
breach of confidence
springboard doctrine
18.62–18.63
types of protected
information 18.18–18.25
contemporary issues 7.12
copyright exceptions in
general 5.4–5.7
novelty 11.80–11.82
registered designs 8.50–8.61
technical protection
measures 5.58
Public interest *see* **Public policy**
limitations
Public lending
performers' rights 6.28
Public Lending Right
scheme 5.39
restricted acts 4.49–4.52
Public morality
biotechnology patents
EU case law 12.45–12.46
key issue 12.43
synthetic biology 12.61
TRIPS Agreement 1994
12.44
exceptions to
patentability 10.45,
11.5–11.62
general concerns over IP
rights 1.25
registered designs 8.72
trade mark registration
14.95–14.99

Public performances
audience requirements 4.57
broadcasts 4.59
defined 4.53
'direct representations or
performances' 4.54–4.56
performers' rights
live performances 6.26
non-property rights 6.29
performing for one's own
benefit 4.58
Public policy limitations
biotechnology patents 12.73
breach of confidence 18.26,
18.56–18.60
copyright 5.47
patents 11.147–11.149
registered designs 8.72
trade mark registration
14.95–14.99
Public sector information
exploitation of
documents 22.77–22.84
Open Government
Licence 18.80
Published editions
copying 4.42
duration of protection 3.61
first ownership of
copyright 3.20
as media works 2.96
originality 2.45

R
Radio *see* **Broadcasts**
Rationales *see* **Justifications for**
IP law
Recognition of foreign
judgements
Brussels Regulation 23.21
contemporary issues 23.63
overview of rules 23.7
procedure 23.62
reform proposals
ongoing work of Hague
Conference 23.64
Recombinant DNA
technology 12.12
Reform proposals *see*
Contemporary issues
Refusal to supply 21.49–21.56
Registered designs
see also **Community designs,**
Designs
appearance 8.23–8.27
assignment 22.7
Community registration
process 8.98–8.103

complex products 8.73–8.78
component parts 8.73–8.78
dealing in Community
designs 8.104–8.105
dealing in UK registered
designs 8.97
definition of 'design' 8.16–8.27
declarations of
invalidity 8.106–8.110
defences 8.117–8.119
designs 'available to the
public' 8.50–8.61
duration of rights 8.120–8.121
EU Directive and
Regulation 8.11–8.14
exclusions: functionality
8.62–8.68
exclusions: 'must-fit' 8.69–8.71
exclusions: public policy and
morality 8.72
exclusive rights 8.111–8.116
individual character 8.32–8.49
informed user 8.37–8.40
infringement 8.111–8.116
interaction with other IP
rights 8.122–8.126
international background
8.4–8.9
novelty 8.28, 8.29–8.31
overall impression 8.32–8.49,
8.111
overview 8.1–8.3
product 8.18–8.22
spare parts 8.79–8.89
repair clause 8.84, 8.88–8.89
UK history 8.10
UK registration process
8.91–8.96
Registered trade marks
interaction between various
systems 13.61–13.62
overlap with patents 13.27–13.28
overview 13.22
Registration procedures
assignments 22.7
common law protection prior to
registration 1.42–1.43
Community registered
designs 8.98–8.105
patents
creation of gate-keeping
device 10.11
drafting claims 10.89–10.103
examination process
10.114–10.116
importance 10.89–10.103
persons entitled to
apply 10.117–10.120

Registration procedures (*cont.*)
  WIPO attempts to streamline
    process 10.36–10.41
  policy tensions within intellectual
    property 1.40–1.41
  summary of common
    themes 1.44
  trade marks
    absolute grounds for refusing
      registration 14.28–14.108
    Community trade
      marks 13.39–13.42
    domain names 16.7–16.8
    overview 13.22
    relative grounds for refusing
      registration 15.23–15.104
    UK trade marks 13.31–13.35
  UK registered designs 8.90–8.97
Relevant markets 21.13–21.15
Rentals *see* **Public lending**
Repair clause (UK registered
  and Community
  designs) 8.84, 8.88–8.89
  see also **Spare parts**
Repeats 2.95
Reproduction
  abridgements 4.40
  adaptation distinguished 4.31
  admittedly derivative
    work 4.37–4.38
  basic requirements 4.24
  broadcasts 4.41
  computer programs 4.34–4.36
  contemporary issues 7.48–7.50
  films 4.41
  ideas and impressions 4.32–4.33
  knowledge of original
    work 4.30
  need to show causal connection
    between two works
    4.27–4.29
  parodies 4.39
  performers' rights 6.28
  published editions 4.42
  similarity of two works 4.25
  sound recordings 4.41
  temporary copies
    databases and computer
      programs 5.18
    internet service
      providers 5.15–5.17
    overview 5.13
    transient and incidental
      copies 5.14
  typographical
    arrangements 4.42
  unregistered design rights 9.78
  works similar but not same 4.26

Reputation
  overview 13.22
  protection of trade marks with
    reputation
    avoidance of unfair
      advantage 15.80–15.87
    blurring 15.97–15.99
    dilution of reputation
      15.88
    need for link between sign
      and mark 15.77–15.79
    reputation within UK 15.76
    statutory provisions
      15.68–15.75
    tarnishment 15.89–15.96
    use without due
      cause 15.100–15.101
Resale rights 3.44–3.46
Research and development
  defence to patent infringement
    11.221–11.227
  fair dealings (copyright)
    meaning of 'research'
      5.21–5.23
    non-commercial
      purposes 5.22
    typographical
      arrangements 5.23
  harmonisation and
    approximation of EU
    law 1.54
  horizontal agreements 21.18
  justifications for IP law 1.23
  sui generis database rights 6.18
Restraint of trade doctrine
  22.16, 22.13–22.15
Reverse engineering 4.22
Review *see* **Criticism or review**
Revocation
  cancellation of PGI 16.87–16.89
  patents 11.205–11.218
  trade marks
    generic words 14.123–14.124
    misleading marks
      14.121–14.122
    for non-use 14.114–14.120
Reward theory
  free movement of goods 20.10
  patents 10.16
  reconciliation of public
    and private interests
    1.31–1.32
Right of integrity
  avoidance of derogatory
    treatment 3.39
  commercial publishing 3.43
  excluded works 3.42
  meaning and scope 3.40–3.41

Rights management information
  systems
  contemporary issues 7.5,
    7.61–7.63
  EU controls 5.63–5.66
  general approach 5.55
  standing to sue 5.56
  technical protection
    measures 5.52
  unauthorised reception of
    transmissions 5.57
Royalties
  author's resale rights 3.44–3.46
  performers' rights
    additional benefits 6.42
    right to equitable
      remuneration 6.40–6.41
  rates table 3.44
'Rule of reason' 21.26

S
'Safe harbours' 4.75
Satellite broadcasting 2.92–2.93
Scientific theories 11.15–11.18
Sculptures
  as artistic works 2.76–2.77
  statutory provisions 2.70
Search orders 22.98–22.99
Secondary copyright
  infringements
  categorisation 4.76–4.77
  general principles 4.12
  importance 4.78
  primary infringements
    distinguished 4.76
Sections 51 and 52 CDPA
  1988 9.81–9.93
Selection patents 11.100
Self-help 22.101–22.102
Semiconductor topography
  key example of *sui generis*
    rights 1.15
  symbol 1.45
Services
  free movement of services
    copyright 20.70–20.72
    evolving law 20.66–20.69
  trade marks
    ancillary retail
      services 14.24–14.26
    registration 14.23
    relative grounds for refusing
      registration 15.24–15.56
Shapes
  absolute grounds for refusing
    registration
    device marks 14.92
    general rules 14.80–14.91

shapes giving 'substantial value' to goods 14.93–14.94
policy considerations 14.43
three-dimensional marks
 importance of consumer perception 14.48, 14.54
 key question as to departure from norm 14.49–14.53
 trade mark registration 14.8
Shape and configuration (UK UDR) 9.29–9.33
'Sieckmann seven' 14.12
Signatures 19.29–19.30
Signs
 device marks 14.92
 marks and signs compared in different contexts 15.38–15.40
 meaning and scope 14.8–14.10
 statutory provisions 14.7
Similarity
 see also **Distinctiveness**
 copying
  basic requirements 4.24
  need to show causal connection between two works 4.27–4.29
  original copyright 2.44
  similarity of two works 4.25
  works similar but not same 4.26
 registrable goods and services
  complementarity 15.56
  general principles 15.49–15.55
 registrable marks
  marks with dominant element 15.45–15.46
  marks with specific meaning 15.47–15.48
  visual, phonetic or conceptual similarity 15.41
  weak marks and those with descriptive elements 15.42–15.44
Single market
 agreements between undertakings (Art 101 TFEU) 21.21
 free movement of goods
  conflict with IP rights 20.5–20.6
  tensions created by TFEU 20.4
 role in development of IP rights
  driver for change 1.51–1.52

free movement of goods 1.59
 international exhaustion 1.60
Skill, labour and judgment
 artistic craftsmanship 2.69, 2.83–2.86
 copyright requirements 2.37–2.38
 parodies 4.39
 persons skilled in the art (patent applications)
  biotechnology 12.30–12.33
  test for obviousness 11.117–11.119
Slogans 14.62
Smells 14.12, 14.13
Social interests
 advantages and disadvantages 1.24
 moral issues arising 1.25
Software-related inventions
 see also **Computer programmes**
 business methods 12.111–12.124
 computer programs distinguished 12.78
 contemporary issues 12.3
 development of EPO jurisprudence 12.89–12.91
 developments from 1998/9 to present
  continuing importance of Art 52(2) 12.132
  evolution of liberal interpretation of EPC 12.131
  IBM/Computer program case 12.133–12.140
 policy matters 12.141
 reform priority for EU Commission 12.150–12.158
 relationship between technical character and technical effect 12.92–12.93
 statutory provisions 12.77
 textual processing 12.107–12.110
 three-stage approach 12.94–12.106
 UK-IPO Guidelines 12.125–12.130
 UK jurisprudence 12.142–12.149
Sound recordings
 contemporary issues 7.5
 copying 4.41
 duration of protection 3.59
 first ownership of copyright 3.18

fixation 2.32
 meaning and scope 2.90
 originality 2.45
 protected subject matter 2.22
 public communication rights
  EU law 4.60
  meaning and scope 4.61–4.65
Sounds
 graphic representations 14.17–14.19
 trade mark registration 14.8
Spare parts
 copyright limitations 5.48
 registered designs (UK and Community designs) 8.79–8.89
 see also **Complex products, Component parts**
 trade mark defence 15.117–15.121
'Spin-off' databases 6.8
Sponsorship *see* **Endorsement and sponsorship**
Springboard doctrine 18.62–18.63
Standing to make claim
 breach of confidence 18.64–18.65
 rights management information systems 5.56
State of the art
 anticipated applications and inventions 11.84
 continuous expansion 11.83
 exclusions from 11.101
 inventive step 11.112–11.116
 statutory provisions 11.81
Statutory rights
 copyright 1.8
 core features 1.43
 designs 1.9
 patents 1.7
 trade marks 1.10
Subject matter
 copyright
  CDPA 1988 2.22
  contemporary issues 7.15
  fixation requirements 2.30–2.33
  multiple copyrights in one work 2.23
  need for expression of work over and above Ideas 2.24–2.28
  need for work of relevant kind 2.29
  originality 2.34–2.46
 exclusions and exceptions from patentability

Subject matter (*cont.*)
  aesthetic creations 11.19
  application
    procedure 10.104–10.113
  business methods
    11.26–11.32
  computer programs
    11.33–11.40
  discoveries, scientific theories
    and mathematical
    methods 11.15–11.18
  games 11.24–11.25
  information 11.41–11.48
  medical treatments
    10.63–10.77
  mental acts 11.21–11.23
  overview 11.5–11.14
Substitution selling 17.49
Sui generis **rights**
  contemporary issues 7.31–7.32
  criteria for protection
    databases defined 6.5
    'obtaining, verifying or
      presenting' content 6.6
    'spin-off' databases 6.8
    substantial investment 6.7
  duration of protection 6.11
  EU law 6.4
  exploitation strategies
    application of competition
      law 22.68–22.69
    contractual
      provisions 22.72–22.76
    overview 22.67
    tariffs 22.70
    technological protection
      measures 22.71
  first ownership 6.10
  infringements
    extraction and utilisation of
      substantial parts 6.13–6.14
    overview 6.12
    repeated extraction and
      utilisation of insubstantial
      parts 6.15–6.16
  key examples
    database rights 1.17
    plant breeders' rights 1.16
    semiconductor
      topography 1.15
  permitted acts
    educational
      establishments 6.19
    EU law 6.17
    non-commercial
      research 6.18
Surface decoration 9.34–9.35
Surgery 11.69–11.72

Survey evidence 22.103–22.106
Suspected infringements
  freezing injunctions 22.98,
    22.100
  search orders 22.98–22.99
  threats of action 22.90
  unjustified threats of action
    design rights 22.94–22.95
    other IP rights 22.96
    patents 22.93
    reform proposals 22.97
    trade marks 22.91–22.92
Symbols
  distinctiveness 14.63
  IP claims 1.45
Synthetic biology 12.61–12.62

T

Tables and compilations
  first ownership of
    copyright 3.16
  as literary works 2.55
Tarnishment 15.89–15.96
Taste marks 14.20
Technical protection measures
  computer programs 5.53
  contemporary issues 7.61–7.63
  'content scramble system'
    CCS 5.51
  database exploitation 22.71
  EU controls 5.63–5.66
  other copyright works 5.54
  overview 5.50
  public domain 5.58
  rights management information
    systems 5.52
**Technology transfer
  agreements** 21.34–21.36
Teletexts 2.87, 2.94
Television *see* **Broadcasts**
Temporary copies
  databases and computer
    programs 5.18
  internet service providers
    5.15–5.17
  overview 5.13
  transient and incidental
    copies 5.14
Term *see* **Duration**
Territoriality
  impact of digitalisation
    23.1–23.2
  patents 10.89
  trade marks
    Community trade
      marks 13.31
    relationship with other IP
      rights 13.26

  use of marks on internet
    16.29–16.32
Textual processing 12.107–12.1
Theoretical perspectives
  competition theory 21.6–21.7,
    21.11
  free movement of goods 20.10
  monopoly power 21.7
  reward theory
    free movement of
      goods 20.10
    patents 10.16
    reconciliation of public and
      private interests 1.31–1.32
  'workable competition' 21.8–21.9
Therapy treatments 10.65–10.68
Threats of action
  general principles 22.90
  unjustified threats of action
    design rights 22.94–22.95
    other IP rights 22.96
    patents 22.93
    reform proposals 22.97
    trade marks 22.91–22.92
Three-dimensional marks
  importance of consumer
    perception 14.48, 14.54
  key question as to departure
    from norm 14.49–14.53
Time-shifting 5.45
Tissue culture technology 12.12
Titles 17.27
Trade marks
  see also **Free movement of
    goods**
  absolute grounds for refusing
    registration
    applications made in bad
      faith 14.101–14.105
    certain shapes 14.80–14.91
    collective and certification
      marks 14.106–14.108
    non-distinctive
      marks 14.30–14.79
    protected marks and
      emblems 14.100
    public policy and
      morality 14.95–14.99
    statutory provisions 14.28
  assignment 22.6–22.7
  Community trade marks
    advantages 13.43–13.46
    assignment 22.6
    interaction with other
      registered trade
      marks 13.43–13.46
    main features 13.37–13.38
    overview 13.36

registration procedure
    13.39–13.42
contemporary issues
    domain names 16.2–16.27
    geographical
        indications 16.57–16.94
    use of marks on
        internet 16.28–16.56
counterfeiting and piracy
    criminal sanctions
        22.155–22.159
    EU initiatives 22.147
    European
        Regulation 22.149–22.151
    increased
        infringement 22.148
    proposals for international
        treaty 22.154
    UK response 22.152–22.153
criminal sanctions
    22.144–22.146
current trends
    backlash from consumers
        13.17–13.18
    criticisms of extended
        functions 13.19–13.21
defined
    EU and national law
        compared 14.4–14.6
    graphic representations
        14.11–14.22
    service trade marks
        14.23–14.26
    signs 14.8–14.10
    statutory provisions 14.7
distinctiveness
    absolute grounds for refusing
        registration 14.30–14.31
    capacity to distinguish
        goods 14.32–14.33
    device marks 14.92
    effect of marks used for
        particular purpose 14.78
    expanding case law 14.68
    foreign words 14.66–14.67
    general considerations
        14.44–14.47
    geographical extent
        14.71–14.74
    geographical names 14.65
    loss of distinctiveness 14.79
    names 14.55
    numerals 14.64
    part of mark 14.77
    product marks and
        colours 14.75–14.76
    slogans 14.62
    statutory provisions 14.7

symbols 14.63
three-dimensional
    marks 14.48–14.54
through use 14.69–14.70
underlying rationale
    14.34–14.42
word combinations
    14.56–14.61
domain names
    defined 16.4–16.6
    dispute resolution 16.12–16.27
    overview 16.2–16.3
    ownership disputes 16.9–16.11
    registration as trade
        mark 16.7–16.8
EU role in development of IP
    rights
    harmonisation and
        approximation of EU
        law 1.54
    institution of Community
        rights 1.55–1.57
free movement of goods 20.47
functions
    advertising 13.14
    communicative
        functions 13.16
    identifying origin of
        goods 13.9–13.11
    investment 13.15
    mark of quality 13.12–13.13
geographical indications
    background 16.57–16.58
    EU regime 16.68–16.93
    international
        protection 16.63–16.67
    reform proposals 16.94
    terminology 16.61–16.62
identical goods or services
    already registered
    identity and scope of goods
        and services 15.31–15.32
    meaning and scope of
        identity of marks
        15.25–15.30
    statutory provisions 15.24
infringements
    case law 15.7–15.18
    company and business
        names 15.19–15.22
    defences 15.105–15.132
    earlier marks with
        reputation 15.68–15.100
    extended functions
        15.102–15.104
    identical goods or services
        already registered
        15.24–15.32

likelihood of confusion
    15.33–15.37, 15.57–15.67
marks and signs compared
    in different contexts
    15.38–15.40
similar goods and
    services 15.49–15.56
similar marks 15.41–15.48
statutory provisions 15.4–15.6
international conventions and
    treaties
    WIPO 13.48–13.58
    WTO 13.59
licensing
    competition law 22.62–22.66
    compulsory licensing 22.61
    overview 22.59–22.60
merchandising rights
    19.28–19.42
opposition 13.63–13.64
opposition to further dealing
    by proprietor (free
    movement)
    Directive 2008/95/
        CE 20.33–20.46
    repackaging and parallel
        imports of
        pharmaceuticals
        20.34–20.46
overview 13.22
policy issues
    economic pressures
        13.7–13.8
    monopoly power 13.5
    proliferation of signs 13.4
    use 13.6
policy tensions within
    intellectual property 1.40
principal treaties and
    conventions 1.72
reform proposals 23.69–23.73
regulatory framework
    Community trade
        marks 13.36–13.46
    conclusions 13.65
    interaction between various
        systems 13.60–13.62
    international conventions
        and treaties 13.47–13.59
    overview 13.29
    UK trade marks 13.30–13.35
relationship with other IP rights
    comparisons of monopoly
        power 13.23–13.25
    overlap with patents
        13.27–13.28
relative grounds for refusing
    registration

Trade marks (*cont.*)
   consent to registration 14.112
   earlier marks with
      reputation 15.68–15.100
   earlier trade marks and
      rights 14.111
   extended functions
      15.102–15.104
   identical goods or services
      already registered
      15.24–15.32
   likelihood of
      confusion 15.33–15.37,
      15.57–15.67
   marks and signs compared
      in different
      contexts 15.38–15.40
   similar goods and
      services 15.49–15.56
   similar marks 15.41–15.48
   statutory provisions
      14.109–14.110
   specification
      requirements 14.27
   symbol 1.45
   UK statutory rights 1.10, 1.43
   unjustified threats of
      action 22.91–22.92
   use of marks on internet
      auction sites 16.54–16.56
      keyword advertising
         16.42–16.53
      overview 16.28
      permitted disclaimers
         16.38–16.39
      territoriality 16.29–16.32
      user infringements
         16.33–16.37
      WIPO strategy 16.40–16.41
   user provisions
      overview 14.113
      revocation for non-
         use 14.114–14.120
      revocation of generic
         words 14.123–14.124
      revocation of misleading
         marks 14.121–14.122
   WIPO proposals for
      harmonisation of national
      approaches to use
      23.69–23.73
Transient copies
   issuing public copies without
      authority 4.48
   reproduction 4.36
Treaties and conventions *see*
      International Conventions
      and treaties
Tying and bundling 21.64

Typographical arrangements
   copying 4.42
   fair dealings
      private study 5.26
      research for non-commercial
         purposes 5.23
   protected subject matter 2.22

U
Undue influence 22.16–22.17
Unfair competition
   see also **Competition law**
   basis of IP law 1.65–1.66
   Designs Directive 8.122
   passing off 17.69–17.72
United States
   antitrust provisions
      Commission v Microsoft
         21.57–21.64
      'rule of reason' 21.26
   applicable law 23.16, 23.1
   approaches to counterfeit
      and pirated goods
      22.153–22.154
   copyright
      acceptance of Berne
         Convention 2.9
      computer programs
         4.34, 2.54
      contributory
         infringement 4.73
      duration of protection 7.43
      fair dealings 5.59
      influences for change 7.5
      originality 7.26
      parodies 7.59
      'safe harbours' 4.75
      technical protection
         measures 7.62
      time-shifting 5.46
   Creative Commons 22.46
   enforcement and
      remedies 22.166–22.171
   false endorsements 19.49
   justiciability of claims 23.18
   moral rights 3.40
   motivation for the
      implementation of
      TRIPS 1.71
   patents
      anti-competitive
         effects 10.88
      biotechnological
         inventions 12.48
      business methods 12.112
      categories of patentable
         invention 11.12, 12.43
      data-processing
         systems 12.121–12.123

      experimental purposes
         defence 11.225
      first-to-invent
         procedure 10.118
      genetically engineered
         products 12.33
      'grace periods' 11.85
      industrial application
         12.34–12.37
      licensing 12.73
      'manner of new
         manufacture'. 10.7
      reaction to South African
         patent changes 10.47
      response to Doha 10.65
      software patents 11.39
      synthetic biology 12.62
      test for infringement 11.194
      treaty obligations 10.37
   topography 1.15
   trade marks
      accessibility 16.33
      computer programs 16.37
      opposition to Reg 2081/92
         16.92
      treaty obligations 16.67
Unjustified threats of action
   design rights 22.94–22.95
   other IP rights 22.96
   patents 22.93
   reform proposals 22.97
   trade marks 22.91–22.92
UK unregistered design right
   see also **Designs**
   absence of exceptions 9.79
   assessing UK UDR 9.80
   article 9.22–9.24
   commencement 9.61
   commonplace 9.53–9.58
   definition of 'design' 9.14–9.33
   design document 9.19
   duration of protection 9.59–9.67
   exclusions: surface
      decoration 9.34–9.35
   exclusions: methods or
      principles of
      construction 9.36–9.37
   exclusions: 'must-fit' 9.38–9.49
   exclusions: 'must-match'
      9.38–9.40, 9.50–9.52
   exclusive right 9.71–9.78
   infringement 9.71–9.78
   interaction with
      copyright 9.81–9.93
   international context 9.4–9.8
   licences of right 9.62–9.67
   originality 9.53–9.58
   overview 9.1–9.3
   ownership 9.68–9.70

qualification 9.6–9.8
reciprocity 9.6–9.8
Sections 51 and 52 CDPA 1988
    9.81–9.93
shape and configuration
    9.29–9.33
'trimming' 9.27
UK background 9.9–9.13
Use
'medical use' patents
    11.102–11.108
trade mark infringements
    case law 15.7–15.18
    company and business
        names 15.19–15.22
    statutory provisions
        15.4–15.6
trade marks
    distinctiveness
        through 14.69–14.70
    effect of marks used for
        particular purpose 14.78
    key policy issues 13.6
    overview 14.113
    revocation for non-
        use 14.114–14.120
    revocation of generic
        words 14.123–14.124
    revocation of misleading
        marks 14.121–14.122
    use of marks on
        internet 16.33–16.37
    WIPO proposals for
        harmonisation of national
        approaches 23.69–23.73

V

Vertical agreements 21.19

W

Words
distinctiveness

foreign words 14.66–14.67
word combinations
    14.56–14.61
keyword advertising on
    internet 16.42–16.53
keyword copyright 2.24
protection from passing
    off 17.23–17.25
revocation of generic
    words 14.123–14.124
trade mark registration 14.8
Work
need for expression of work over
    and above ideas
    leading cases 2.24–2.28
    'stand-alone'
        expressions 2.24
need for work of relevant
    kind 2.29
'Workable competition' 21.8–21.9
**World Health Organization
    (WHO)**
Commission on Intellectual
    Property Rights 10.56
hurdles for developing and
    least-developed
    countries 10.55
strategy to develop Global
    Plan 10.57
**World Intellectual Property
    Organization (WIPO)**
administration of treaties 1.68
classification of trade
    marks 13.22
conference to discuss audio-
    visual performances 6.37
copyright
    central deposit of
        applications 8.6
    contemporary issues 7.1
patents
    administration of treaties 10.35

definition of computer
    program 12.82
establishment of
    development agenda 10.69
Intergovernmental
    Committee 10.64–10.67
ongoing programme of
    harmonisation 10.69
report on worldwide
    activity 10.14
streamlining of application
    process 10.36–10.41
trade mark treaties and
    conventions
    Madrid Agreement and
        Protocol 13.53
    Nice International
        Arrangement 13.22, 13.58
    Paris Convention 1883
        13.48–13.52
    Singapore Treaty 13.55–13.57
    Trade Mark Law Treaty
        13.54
trade marks
    harmonisation of national
        approaches to use
        23.69–23.73
    use of marks on
        internet 16.40–16.41
World Trade Organization
comments on three-step
    copyright test 5.8
patents
    administration of GATT 10.42
    compulsory licensing
        22.50–22.53
    Public Health Declaration
        10.48–10.54
trade marks
    general responsibilities 13.59
    national treatment of
        GIs 16.92–16.93